C0-ADH-615

Poets
American and British

Poets
American and British

Ian Scott-Kilvert
(for the British Council)

George Stade
Leonard Unger
A. Walton Litz
Editors in Chief

VOLUME 2

CHARLES SCRIBNER'S SONS
An Imprint of Macmillan Library Reference
NEW YORK

Charles Scribner's Sons
An imprint of Macmillan Library Reference
1633 Broadway
New York, NY 10019

Library of Congress Cataloging-in-Publication Data

Poets : American and British / Ian Scott-Kilvert . . . [et al.], editors in chief.
p. cm.
Includes bibliographical references and index.
ISBN 0-684-80605-3 (set : alk. paper). — ISBN 0-684-80607-X (v. 1 : alk. paper)
1. American poetry—Bio-bibliography—Dictionaries. 2. English poetry—Bio-bibliography—Dictionaries. 3. American poetry—Dictionaries. 4. English poetry—Dictionaries. I. Scott-Kilvert, Ian.
PS308.P64 1998
821.009'03—dc21 98-36811
CIP

3 5 7 9 11 13 15 17 19 20 18 16 14 12 10 8 6 4 2

PRINTED IN THE UNITED STATES OF AMERICA

The paper used in this publication meets the minimum requirements of American National Standard for Information Sciences—Permanence of Paper for Printed Library Materials. ANSI Z39.48-1992.

A. E. HOUSMAN

(1859–1936)

IAN SCOTT-KILVERT

INTRODUCTION

CAMBRIDGE HAS SEEN many strange sights, remarked Housman when he bade farewell to University College, London, to become Kennedy Professor of Latin. "So the University which once saw Wordsworth drunk and once saw Porson sober will see a better scholar than Wordsworth, and a better poet than Porson, betwixt and between." The two names at first sight might appear only to emphasize how impassable a gulf is fixed between the achievements of poet and scholar at the level of genius. There have been, of course, other scholarly poets in English literature. Milton, Gray, Landor, Arnold, FitzGerald, and Bridges were not only erudite men; their lives were molded by a certain precision of mind and detachment from worldly affairs that mark the scholar, and the character of their poetry reflects these qualities. But their learning was wide rather than deep, and their scholarship scarcely more than an adjunct to their poetic gifts.

Housman, on the other hand, aspired to the life of learning as early as a man can discover such an aptitude in himself. He is one of the very few English scholars to attain a European stature and the only one who is also a poet of consequence. If we can isolate a single element common to both fields, it is surely that Housman was a master of words of a very rare order. His scholarship is seldom concerned with general ideas or literary judgments: its special achievement is to concentrate his unrivaled knowledge of the classical tongues and his poetic sensibility upon the narrow front of textual criticism. His talk arrested the few who were privileged to hear it by the extraordinary aptness and penetration of the phrases he could command, when his interest overcame his reserve. His verse was deliberately limited to a few themes, which are among the most universal and timeworn in poetic currency; what strikes home immediately is the compelling power of the language, the quality of something inevitably and rightly said.

But Housman was also one of those who are born to mystify their fellows by their attitude to the human condition. In this sense he has been compared to Jonathan Swift and to T. E. Lawrence, as men gifted far above the common lot, who show themselves at once contemptuous of the admiration of others, eager for fame on their own terms, and strangely indifferent to the gift of life itself. Both in his scholarship and in his view of human relationships, Housman was a perfectionist, tormented by any falling short of his ideal, and it is the vehemence of this protest that distinctively tunes and tautens his poetry. In it the satirist, the man moved by horror and scorn and indignation, is constantly at the elbow of the love poet, and his suffering seems to spring not so much from any particular circumstance as from the very nature of human association. If Housman's life provokes a curiosity extending beyond his work, a curiosity that exceeds anything we want to know concerning most modern poets, it is not a matter of unearthing clues to his emotional experience. It is because his achievement, charged as it is with the sense of something missed and desired, raises questions that human nature is never tired of exploring, the question, for example, of what prevents such a man from rising to his full height, and of the use that men make of great gifts.

EARLY LIFE

Alfred Edward Housman was born on 26 March 1859, the eldest of seven children, near Bromsgrove in Worcestershire, where his father practiced as an attorney. His mother's family was connected with the Drakes of Devon, and the Drakes's motto, *Aquila non capit muscas* (The eagle does not catch flies), could hardly have been better chosen to epitomize Housman's attitude to the world. Shropshire was never his home, nor did he at any period spend much time there. But the Shropshire hills had formed the western horizon of his childhood, and they imprinted themselves upon his memory as an imaginary world beyond the setting sun and the frontiers of everyday life. For the very reason that he did not know the county too intimately, it could later supply him with a rustic mythology and the music of place names, which served to evoke both memory and fantasy.

Housman was educated at Bromsgrove School and won a scholarship to St. John's College, Oxford. Here his true bent began to show itself, though at first with disastrous results. He was already devoted to exact and specialized study, and he could not bring himself to absorb the Greats curriculum,[1] with its widely spread interests.

One lecture from the celebrated Benjamin Jowett was enough to make him abandon the course in disgust at the professor's disregard for minutiae. Having obtained a first-class grade in the preliminary examination for Litterae Humaniores (Moderations), he may well have found the temptation irresistible to anticipate his degree and embark upon the work of a qualified scholar. At any rate when he sat for his finals his preparations proved quite inadequate, he could return only scrappy answers to some of the papers, and the examiners had no choice but to exclude him from an honors degree.

Housman's debacle at Oxford was a crucial episode in his career and resulted in the enforced relegation of his cherished classical studies to his spare time and an exile of eleven years before he could regain a position in academic life. It also offers some important clues to the austere personality he later developed, that of a man early disillusioned with the human lot, a controversialist who gave no quarter, a figure reserved and sardonic even to his closest friends, yet also capable of unexpected impulses of generosity and compassion.

Housman's biographer George L. Watson has argued persuasively that this academic disaster and its aftermath coincided and was linked with other critical stresses that had been developing for some time. Housman had been devoted to his mother, who had died on his twelfth birthday, and had become acutely conscious of the increasing incapacity of his father (who had failed in his chosen profession of attorney) to play his part as head of the family, and hence of his own responsibilities as the eldest of seven children. The crisis in his personal life centered on his fellow undergraduate and lifelong friend, Moses Jackson. This was a friendship of opposites, Jackson being a strongly extravert "all-rounder," who rowed for Oxford and took a first-class degree in science; he was a frank and steadfast friend, but one incapable of sharing the kind of emotional intimacy that the poet's nature sought. The differences that separated them are aptly summed up in these posthumously published verses:

Because I liked you better
Than suits a man to say,
It irked you, and I promised
To throw the thought away.
(*More Poems*, XXXI)

1. The honors school of Litterae Humaniores, which involved the study of Greek and Roman literature, history, and philosophy.

Whether this frustrated attachment contributed to the disastrous examination result can only be a matter for conjecture. But certainly Housman must have seen clearly the distress that his failure had brought upon his stricken family, and from this moment the desire to retrieve it became a consuming ambition.

After setting aside such money as he could spare for his family, Housman decided to leave home, take the civil service examination, and settle in London. Through the help of Jackson, with whom he now felt able to resume his friendship on a more pragmatic basis, he obtained a post in the patent office and moved into rooms he shared with Jackson and the latter's younger brother, Adalbert. The patent office was not an exacting employer, and Housman's main energies could now be devoted to his classical reading at the British Museum, where he proceeded to lay the foundations of his scholarship. Thus in the years when most men form their most lasting ties, his naturally reserved and solitary disposition was set in a still more inhibiting mold. According to his closest friends, his coldness of manner was imposed upon a nature that secretly craved affection, but the natural consequence was to secure his independence rather than his happiness.

Gradually his classical work began to bear fruit and his contributions to learned journals to attract attention. Finally the Chair of Latin at University College, London, fell vacant. Housman applied and was now able to support his candidature with seventeen testimonials from British, American, and German scholars. He did not fail to include the phrase, "In 1881 I failed to obtain Honours in the final School of Litterae Humaniores." Fortunately, the electors were unmoved, and in 1892 he took up the professorship he was to hold for nineteen years until his election to the Kennedy Chair of Latin at Cambridge.

CLASSICAL SCHOLARSHIP

Housman's appointment to Cambridge gave him the leisure and the higher standard of teaching that his gifts required for their full development. During these years he became recognized as the most eminent Latinist of the century and his name was ranked with Richard Porson's as the greatest of English scholars after Richard Bentley. Still, the nature of Housman's achievement is sufficiently remote from the interests of the general reader to require some explanation.

In the present age of mass education the public has come to expect that the distinguished scholar should, to some extent, act as a popularizer in his own field. He should not, it is held, address himself exclusively to his fellow experts. He should also communicate something of his enjoyment of his studies or pass judgment on them as literature, or relate them to the spirit or the preoccupations of his own times. The work of Gilbert Murray or C. M. Bowra might be taken as representative of this kind of scholarship. Housman's genius was of a different order. It belongs to the older, more austere tradition of scholarship, where it is assumed that the reader can supply his own appreciation and needs only to be furnished with the best possible text. The scholar, for his part, never ventures an aesthetic or moral judgment and limits himself strictly to the role of editor and to the perennial task of detecting and removing errors in the surviving manuscripts. Ideally, this work can absorb an almost unlimited measure of intellectual power, linguistic skill, and poetic sensibility: how far the results may justify the expense of so much talent is another question.

Housman upheld this point of view in his introductory lecture delivered to the combined faculties of University College in 1892. It is an eloquent address, warmer in sentiment, less waspish than his later prose, but its conclusions will fall strangely upon modern ears. The study of the arts and the sciences, he tells us, is often defended by unreal arguments. Science is not necessarily the most serviceable kind of knowledge and its true aim is not to be judged by utilitarian standards. On the other hand, the humanities are praised for their power to transform our inner natures. But in practice only a tiny fraction of the human race can profit from them and they can do so "without that minute and accurate study of the classical tongues which affords Latin professors their only excuse for existence." The only genuine justification for any of these studies, he concludes, is that in their different ways they satisfy man's desire for knowledge, and this innate human appetite is part of man's duty to himself.

The reader is left to conclude that any department of knowledge is of equal value with any other. Housman evidently assumes that the classics will continue to be read, but he does not find it necessary to explain how a work becomes or remains a classic, or why, if a severe philological discipline is the sole raison d'être for professors, it would not be equally valuable for them to study the poetry of the Mayas or the Tibetans.

This, at any rate, was the narrow frame from which Housman's own work never departed. It is true, of course, that the textual expert is often ill-equipped for making literary judgments and, if a warning had been necessary, Housman always had before him the fearful precedent of Bentley's edition of *Paradise Lost* (1732).[2] But in fact Housman was keenly aware of the frontier between textual and appreciative criticism, and the intellectual pride that appears so consistently throughout his classical writings made him a relentless judge of his performance as a literary critic. He wrote explicitly on this point when he declined an invitation to deliver the Clark Lectures on English literature:

> I do regard myself as a connoisseur: I think I can tell good from bad in literature. But literary criticism, referring opinions to principles and setting them forth so as to command assent, is a high and rare accomplishment and quite beyond me. . . . And not only have I no talent for producing the genuine article, but no taste or inclination for producing a substitute. . . .

Since he thus disqualified himself from discussing poetry, his classical writings are of distinctly specialized interest. The most important are the prefaces to his editions of Juvenal, Lucan, and Manilius, in which he sets out his editorial principles; a series of articles on the manuscripts of Propertius; and a paper given in 1921 to the Classical Association and ironically entitled "The Application of Thought to Textual Criticism." Besides these, he published well over a hundred articles in learned journals, notably on the Greek tragedians and on Propertius, Horace, Ovid, and Martial. Most of these papers consist of discussions of isolated textual problems. They are fragmentary reading in themselves, but to read even a few consecutively is a revelation of the intellectual discipline through which Housman developed his gifts. They display the immense range of his knowledge of the classical tongues and of the history of words, his vigilance in detecting corruption, his dexterity and insight in proposing remedies, and, above all, his unrivaled accuracy and patience, which can only have been acquired by a supreme effort of control over a brain so swift in reaching its conclusions.

While he was at the patent office, Housman published as much on Greek as on Latin poetry; after his appointment to University College he virtually ceased to write on Greek. His explanation was that he found he "could not attain to excellence in both" languages. This definition of excellence was all his own, for he certainly possessed more Greek than many professed Hellenists. What he demanded, as the bare essentials, was a complete mastery of grammar and of metrical and verbal usage, a comprehensive knowledge of manuscript history, and, beyond this, the capacity to absorb, year after year, a mass of minute detail bearing directly or indirectly on the chosen field. Judged by these standards, and remembering the far greater complexity of the Greek language and its literature, it becomes easier to understand his decision; and it must be re-

2. Bentley put forward the idea that Milton had employed both an amanuensis and an editor, who were held to be responsible for the clerical errors, alterations, and interpolations that Bentley professed to have found in the text.

membered that for Housman's particular talents Latin poetry offered the more tempting prospects. For his choice of the authors he was to edit was influenced more by the ambition to build himself a monument in scholarship than by his personal literary taste.

Housman's approach to editorial problems is sketched in the paper on textual criticism already mentioned, probably the most brilliant outline of the subject that has yet been written in English. Textual criticism, he insists, is by no means a professional mystery, as it is sometimes represented, but a matter of reason and common sense. But he is equally emphatic that it is not an exact science, and nothing angered him more than the so-called scientific approach to manuscript problems, which attempted to solve by a system of rules difficulties that required an independent and flexible judgment:

> A textual critic . . . is not at all like Newton investigating the motions of the planets: he is much more like a dog hunting for fleas. If a dog hunted for fleas on mathematical principles, basing his researches on statistics of area and population, he would never catch a flea except by accident. They require to be treated as individuals; and every problem which presents itself to the textual critic must be regarded as possibly unique. ("On the Application of Thought to Textual Criticism," *Selected Prose,* pp. 132–133)

The simile is characteristic. Housman was fond of testing academic generalizations by translating them into some homely and sensuous analogy, because, as he put it, the human senses have had a much longer history than the human intellect and are far less easy to deceive. Another target he singled out was the then fashionable dogma of the supreme authority of the oldest manuscript. According to this theory, the editor, having selected the earliest, is then bound to defend all its readings, unless they are hopelessly corrupt. Housman attacked it unmercifully, and he was among the first to understand, obvious though the truth may seem today, that such a doctrine was bound to become the standby of the laziest and least competent scholars.

When we come to his own editions, many lovers of the classics have found it inexplicable that a man who cared so passionately for poetry could choose for the main object of his life's work an author so little rewarding as Manilius. Lucan, we are told, was selected for him, while Juvenal is a poet entirely worthy of his gifts, whose influence on the tone of Housman's own poetry has perhaps never been fully appreciated. But Manilius, who composed a treatise on astronomy and astrology in the first century A.D., is an author whose poetic merit is less than second-rate and whose scientific value is almost nonexistent, who presents in fact the minimum of interest from any point of view but the professional scholar's. On the other hand, as Andrew Gow tells us, Housman saw in Manilius' text a better prospect "of approaching finality in the solution of the problems presented." He was an ambitious scholar, and it was no coincidence that he chose a poet previously edited by Julius Caesar Scaliger, whose Manilian commentary had been one of the most dazzling achievements of Renaissance scholarship, and by Bentley, the greatest of Housman's predecessors in England. From this point of view, he was taking up a challenge that could extend his powers to the full. This will not prevent many readers from regarding his choice as wayward and eccentric, especially since it involved the sacrifice of a commentary on Propertius, on whose text Housman had done much preliminary work and for whose poetry he cared far more.

Still, it would be wrong to suppose that Housman's poetic sensibility was shut out from his classical work. He possessed a talent excessively rare among scholars, an instinctive familiarity with the way in which poets handle words, and he succeeded in extending this so as to think poetically in the dead languages. In this way he was able to restore or to purify many lines of poetry and to perceive the deeper meaning of phrases obscured for centuries by the errors of scribes and scholiasts. Such a gift, controlled as Housman controlled it, is surely the quality that distinguishes the great from the merely competent textual critic and that guided Housman to many of his most brilliant emendations. Edmund Wilson has noted as a typical example a passage from Juvenal, where in place of the generally accepted reading, *Perditus ac vilis sacci mercator olentis* (The reckless merchant [on a stormy voyage] whose life is cheap [to himself], with his odorous bag of saffron), whose sense, if any, is obscure and labored, Housman by a small change suggests an immediately striking satirical image: *Perditus ac similis sacci mercator olentis* (The reckless merchant . . . turns as yellow as his odorous bag of saffron).

This power of responding to and recreating classical poetry found another outlet in his rare translations. Latin verse, which served as so admired a model to the Augustans, had seldom been translated by the romantics or by their Victorian successors; nor, with the exception of Landor, had it notably influenced their style. Housman's best translation is of the seventh ode of Horace's fourth book, in which his own idiom and diction, conspicuously Saxon though they are, seem perfectly matched to the original:

> The snows are fled away, leaves on the
> shaws
> And grasses in the mead renew their birth,
> The river to the river-bed withdraws,
> And altered is the fashion of the earth. . . .
>
> But oh, whate'er the sky-led seasons mar,
> Moon upon moon rebuilds it with her beams:
> Come *we* where Tullus and where Ancus
> are,
> And good Aeneas, we are dust and dreams. . . .
> (*More Poems,* V, "Diffugere Nives")

Housman has preserved the peculiarly Roman gift for expressing poetic commonplaces in monumental style, but his verses, while remarkably exact in their rendering, evoke a different kind of response, biblical in their vocabulary and romantic in the melody of their rhymed quatrains. The Latin speaks with a poignancy unusual in Horace, and Housman's language carries an emotional tension rarely achieved in Augustan translations.

Housman's eminence is inseparable from the moral passion that infused his studies. He possessed to a very high degree the scholar's willingness to sacrifice the present to the future; nothing could have proved this more forcibly than his career at Oxford. He put so much more into scholarship than is commonly understood by the term, making it an ideal that absorbed many of the loyalties and emotions that most men reserve for the world outside. "The faintest of human passions," he once wrote, "is the love of truth": for himself he could genuinely claim the contrary.

In consequence, his high ideal left little room for moderation. For several generations past, the elucidation of the classics had been treated as a subject deserving a calm, urbane, and tolerant approach. Housman did not see the matter in this light. He considered accuracy not a virtue but a duty. He regarded careless or lazy work as an insufferable affront to the dignity of learning, and he could seldom restrain his anger at what seemed to him the organized sloth and complacency of average scholarship. When an editor assigned to Propertius a metrically faulty line, he commented: "This is the mood in which Tereus ravished Philomela: concupiscence concentrated on its object and indifferent to all beside."And he kept a notebook in which shafts of this kind were stored up to be launched at the first deserving recipient. The layman coming fresh to his writings might feel that he was back in the age of pamphleteering, aptly described by Lytton Strachey, when "erudition was gigantic, controversies frenzied, careers punctuated by brutal triumphs, wild temerities and dreadful mortifications."

Housman was as certain of the importance of his work as he was of the rightness of his opinions, and he writes of the operations of scholars in the language of a historian surveying a line of princes:

> [Palmer's] talent, like that of Heinsius, resided in felicity of instinct: it did not proceed,

> like Madvig's, from the perfection of intellectual power. Now the class which includes Heinsius includes also Gilbert Wakefield; and Palmer's rank in the class is nearer to Wakefield than to Heinsius. His inspiration was fitful, and when it failed him he lacked the mental force and rightness which should have filled its place. His was a nimble but not a steady wit: it could ill sustain the labour of severe and continuous thinking; so he habitually shunned that labour. . . . He had much natural elegance of taste, but it was often nullified by caprice and wilfulness, so that hardly Merkel himself has proposed uncouther emendations. . . . ("Palmer's 'Heroides' of Ovid," *Selected Prose,* p. 91)

Though he refrains from passing judgment on the classical poets, he likes to sit as a Rhadamanthus of the world of learning, issuing elaborately qualified verdicts upon dead or living scholars:

> Say what you will, he [Jacob] has contributed to the *Astronomica* . . . a body of corrections not only considerable in number but often of the most arresting ingenuity and penetration. Yet the virtues of his work are quenched and smothered by the multitude and monstrosity of his vices. . . . Not only had Jacob no sense for grammar, no sense for coherency, no sense for sense, but being himself possessed by a passion for the clumsy and the hispid he imputed this disgusting taste to all the authors whom he edited; and Manilius, the one Latin poet who excels even Ovid in verbal point and smartness, is accordingly constrained to write the sort of poetry' which might have been composed by Nebuchadnezzar when he was driven from men and did eat grass as oxen. ("Prefaces," Manilius I, *Selected Prose,* p. 33)

Housman's supremacy within the limits he set for himself is beyond dispute. The depth of his learning and his capacity to focus it upon minute details, the force of his intellect and the scrupulous honesty with which he applied it (a virtue for which the great Bentley was not conspicuous)—these qualities place him in the front rank of scholars.

Concerning the ultimate value of his approach to the classics, there is less agreement. Scholarship, after all, is not an end in itself; it presupposes an original literature worth preserving, and its tasks may vary greatly from one age to another. A scholar such as Petrarch seeks above all to make discoveries, to stimulate and to fertilize, and at such a moment in history it may be more valuable to kindle enthusiasm than to enforce accuracy. In Bentley's day, the first requirement was a sustained and methodical criticism, to set in order the immense classical inheritance brought to light by the three preceding centuries. In our own age, we are faced with an ominous breakdown in communication between the expert and the layman. The latter is apt to feel that the classics have no relevance for the contemporary world, while the former disdains to make that relevance felt. In such times it is arguable that the greatest need is for scholars to check the fragmentation of our culture, to concentrate upon interpretation and skilled translation as much as on specialized research. Yet to assert this, to speak of "what the age demands," is to speak of lesser men. One might argue that had Housman lived in an earlier century his talents would have produced a richer harvest. But it is idle to regret that a scholar of his caliber, who set himself the highest standards and satisfied them, did not develop differently. At any rate, in the preface to his last volume of Manilius, published very near the end of his life, the question is faced in as uncompromising a fashion as we might expect: "Perhaps there will be no long posterity for learning: but the reader whose good opinion I desire and have done my utmost to secure is the next Bentley or Scaliger who may chance to occupy himself with Manilius."

FAME AND HONORS

It would be misleading to leave the impression that Housman spent his life in unrelieved seclusion. His early years in London were no doubt a painful and lonely experience. But later his growing fame and the duties of academic life imposed more social demands and enriched his circle of acquaintance. At University College he showed himself a formidable debater and impromptu speaker. He wrote light verse, which includes his "Fragment of a Greek Tragedy"—a brilliant parody of the Greek tragic idiom that is unique in English—and a number of excellent nonsense rhymes. Although he was notoriously averse to small talk, he took pleasure in conversation that challenged his interests, and at Cambridge he was at his best in the intimate society of a dining club. He became a renowned connoisseur of wine and his letters speak of travels in Italy, Turkey, and France.

It was in fact the contrast between all that life appeared to offer him, including fame, security, and congenial work, and what he was prepared to make of its rewards that perplexed all who knew him. With scarcely any exceptions Housman kept his friends at arm's length, and his distrust of his fellow men's judgment was not relaxed even when they desired to honor him. "You should be welcome to praise me if you did not praise one another," he once wrote, and this was evidently the motive that inclined him to refuse the doctorates and degrees that many universities offered him. The final honor he declined was the Order of Merit, on the ground that it was not always given to those who deserved it, and in particular that it was already held by an author for whose work Housman felt an extreme distaste. In his letter to the king's secretary, Housman, after respectfully declining the proposed award, went on to quote the words of Admiral William Cornwallis on a similar occasion: "I am, unhappily, of a turn of mind that would make my receiving that honour the most unpleasant thing imaginable."

POETRY AND CRITICISM

When *A Shropshire Lad* first appeared in 1896, it had been rejected by several publishers, among them Macmillan on the advice of John Morley, and it was finally issued at the poet's own expense. At first it was slow to attract attention, but after the Boer War, and indeed for the first quarter of the present century, its reputation grew immensely. It appealed to the sophisticated no less than to a far larger public, for whom the greater part of contemporary verse was a closed book. By the time that *Last Poems* was published in 1922, Housman probably commanded, with the exception of Rudyard Kipling, a wider audience than any contemporary poet in our language. Indeed, on the strength of *A Shropshire Lad* alone, Sir Walter Alexander Raleigh had already referred to him as the greatest living English poet.

Such success did not take Housman unawares, but neither did it alter a mode of life in which his poetry remained a submerged activity. He scarcely ever published in periodicals, and he consistently refused to allow *A Shropshire Lad* to appear in anthologies. He neither wrote about the poetry of others nor expounded his own creative processes, and even in his correspondence, to judge by what his brother has published, poetry is scarcely ever seriously discussed. His one public pronouncement on these subjects, *The Name and Nature of Poetry* (1933), was delivered almost at the end of his life, and then not without severe misgiving before and self-reproach after the event.

Because of this reticence it was generally believed that he had suppressed or destroyed a large number of poems, and it is not surprising that the legend should have grown up of the great scholar sternly disciplining his lyrical gifts and rejecting all but the most perfectly finished products of his muse. In reality, it seems clear that the creative impulse visited him only at rare intervals, and now that all his verses are in print, we may be equally surprised at the inferiority of some of the poems he published and the excellence of others he held back.

During his lifetime, Housman's poetic career presented as much of an enigma as his personal history, and his own actions served to deepen the mystery. The quality of the verse that he consented to publish was unusually consistent both in its merits and its limitations, so that until his unpublished poems were issued posthumously, it was extremely difficult to trace any pattern of development in his work.

The poet himself stated that most of *A Shropshire Lad* was composed during a period "of continuous excitement in the early months of 1895," and that the whole book had been finished at full stretch over eighteen months. Recently, however, the remains of Housman's verse notebooks have been completely and minutely scrutinized by American scholars, and their findings tell a different story. According to his friend Dr. Percy Withers, Housman first set himself seriously to write poetry soon after he had settled in London, his preparation consisting less in practicing versification than in an intensive study of his chosen models, mainly the Border Ballads, the songs of Shakespeare, and the lyrics of Heinrich Heine. For four or five years progress was painfully slow, but the notebooks suggest that his inspiration had begun to move freely as far back as 1890. The first five months of 1895 thus represent the climax of his creative power during which twenty-three of the sixty-three *Shropshire Lad* lyrics were drafted or finished; 1895, in fact, was his *annus mirabilis,* for in its later months were written not only the remaining third of *A Shropshire Lad* but drafts of some half-dozen pieces which later appear in *Last Poems,* and a still larger number good enough to be preserved for the posthumous *More Poems* (1936). There followed a prolonged aftermath of six years, during which fewer and fewer new poems were begun, and after 1902 the creative flow dwindled to a trickle until, apparently under the excitement of preparing *Last Poems,* it returned briefly in 1922.

Grant Richards, Housman's publisher after 1897, quoted him as saying early in their association, "I am not a poet by trade. I am a professor of Latin." Behind this statement one may read something other than modesty—namely, a disinclination to commit himself to the spiritual and material hazards of a career dedicated to poetry. His creative period had flung him, we are told, into an intense emotional disturbance whose recurrence he dreaded, and after it he may well have felt that poetry for him must be an accomplishment, not a vocation, a gift to be used as circumstances might allow, not a continually dominating presence with power to shape his life according to the changing stresses of experience.

The chronology of his poetry, so far as it can be established, confirms the impression that his style was formed early and that his verses at sixty or later display almost exactly the same qualities, marvelously unimpaired and yet undeveloped, as those he wrote as a young man. There are differences in tone and in his attitude to his material, but it is difficult to fasten upon any single composition as a landmark in his development, particularly since a number of the poems that appeared after *A Shropshire Lad* contain revisions carried out at widely separate periods. Reading the posthumously published poems, one often comes upon identical epithets or turns of phrase echoed with equally striking effects in a different context, and in this sense his poetry resembles a single perpetual "work in progress."

At present Housman's verse is passing through a necessary critical revaluation; 1922 saw the appearance both of *Last Poems* and of *The Waste Land,* and the year might serve, crudely, to mark an end and a beginning in English poetry, with Housman's work standing on the far side of the rift in poetic idiom that the modern movement has produced. For the very reason that Housman presents none of the difficulties of later poets, his work has suffered from uncritical admiration and all too frequent imitation, and when a poetic revolution takes place, the penalty for contemporary popularity of this kind is apt to be overpaid.

Housman began to write at a time when the romantic tradition, as inherited by the major Victorian poets, had all but exhausted its resources, and he felt strongly how stale the current poetic jargon had become in the hands of writers such as Andrew Lang and Arthur O'Shaughnessy.[3] Yet in the light of what was to come, his own approach might be called backward looking. He did not feel the need for fresh patterns of verbal association nor for changes in poetic structure: in later life he never became sympathetic to experiments in free verse nor to the abandonment of rhyme, and he regarded Bridges's praise of Hopkins' poetry, cautious though that was, as no more than a personal foible.

Today it is easier to recognize the traces in his work of the spirit of the 1890's; in particular the fastidiousness of expression—was there ever a period in which men trimmed and pared their writing so assiduously?—the choice of minor poetic forms and the note of weary disillusionment, the view of life as something to be endured:

> When shall this slough of sense be cast,
> This dust of thoughts be laid at last,
> The man of flesh and soul be slain
> And the man of bone remain?
> "The Immortal Part,"
> *A Shropshire Lad,* XLIII)

And it is noticeable that the five-line rhyming stanza of "Bredon Hill" and other lyrics was a favorite meter of Ernest Dowson's.

Housman himself, however, remained severely aloof from the poetic coteries that flourished in London at this time. He was older than Lionel Johnson, Dowson, and most of the members of the Rhymers' Club, and in any case the leanings of this group toward ritualism combined with a Bohemian life on the Parisian model must have been thoroughly antipathetic to his temperament. Many years afterward, replying to an editor who sought permission to include him in an anthology of the period, Housman wrote that it would be as technically correct and as essentially inappropriate to reprint his poems in such a collection as to include Lot in a book on the cities of the plain.

3. See *The Name and Nature of Poetry* (London, 1933), p. 23.

Certainly what most impressed the early readers of *A Shropshire Lad* was its *unlikeness* to the prevailing idiom. Here apparently was a poet who could voice the familiar passions of humanity with a strange, death-dealing sweetness in sharp contrast to the current urban poetry of languor and exotic sensibility. The contrast is striking enough, yet the simplicity is deceptive. The primitive ballad meters, which Housman revived, are employed for a poetry not of action but of introspection. The diction is natural at some moments, artificial at others, a curious yet assured blend of the archaic and the colloquial. In Housman's hands these were genuine achievements, but they were also poetic ventures that none but he could execute—a mile farther, says William Butler Yeats of *A Shropshire Lad,* and all had been marsh.

In his early style there are echoes of the shorter poems of Bridges and of the martial measures of Kipling and William Ernest Henley, and an affinity, which cannot have been conscious, to the rustic lyrics of Thomas Hardy. Housman's poem "The Sage to the Young Man" is remarkably reminiscent of Bridges's "O Youth whose hope is high," but one has only to see the two side by side to feel the far stronger impact of the former. It is this power to communicate direct and personal emotion, through a language that lodges instantly in the brain, that distinguishes Housman from all the poets of this period.

The comparison with Hardy is more illuminating. Housman also, it might appear, sought his inspiration in a part of England that still pursued the traditions of country life, uncontaminated by the Industrial Revolution. Like Hardy, too, he had been led by the scientific materialism of the age to form a deeply pessimistic view of human destiny, judging it to be ruled by forces absolutely indifferent to moral values. But Housman's gift for exquisite description of nature has obscured the difference between his poetry and that of a genuinely rural writer such as Hardy or John Clare. Housman was not a countryman, nor did he enjoy talking or mingling with rustics. It is easily forgotten that he spent the years between twenty-three and fifty-two almost continuously in London, and that the scenes of *A Shropshire Lad* were the product of his inward eye as he walked on Hampstead Heath. His friends have noted that he was indifferent to country landscape, though he was peculiarly sensitive to the shape and characteristics of trees. When he writes of them in a poem such as "The orchards half the way," the force and beauty of his language serve not so much to describe as to intensify them as dramatic symbols of a particular state of emotion.

Thus, at first glance, *A Shropshire Lad* is written in the character of a country youth uprooted from his surroundings and exiled to a hostile metropolis where he clings to his memories of a simpler life. But it is soon clear that "Shropshire" is not a native heath with a solid existence such as Hardy's Wessex. It is rather a personification of the writer's memories, dreams, and affections. In order to make his emotions articulate, Housman apparently needed an imaginary setting and a central character who could at once be himself and not himself.

This need to construct a personal world of the imagination, perhaps as a defense against the overwhelming inhumanity of city life, seems to have been shared by other poets of the same period. The gaslit and theatrical Bohemia of Arthur Symons and Dowson, the engine room of Kipling, the world of childhood and the supernatural of Walter de la Mare are sufficiently diverse instances of the same process. Housman found his mythology in the local tragedies of rustic life, the ballads of the country youths whose sweethearts die young or desert them, who are hanged in Shrewsbury jail for crimes of passion, or who commit suicide or take the queen's shilling[4] to march away and fall on fields forgotten. In such episodes he could express his indignation at the injustice of human destiny, and he did so by infusing into the pastoral convention a new note of irony. Pastoral poetry traditionally makes its appeal by invoking a countryside where youth seems eternal, and the calm and simplicity of nature are praised by contrast with the feverish corruption of a great capital. Housman's Shropshire is a blighted Arcadia, in which the poet is constantly reminded of the limitations of mortality. Here the beauty of the countryside only intensifies the pain of his experience, since Nature, he feels, is utterly indifferent to the emotions she arouses in him. Love, which alone might redeem our lives, does no more than beguile us with hope; then it proves to be unrequited or is cut short by a harsh fate:

His folly has not fellow
  Beneath the blue of day
That gives to man or woman
  His heart and soul away.
      (XIV)

The brave and the true gain nothing from their virtue, and indeed they are best out of a world that will never reward their qualities:

Be still, be still, my soul; it is but for a
  season:
Let us endure an hour and see injustice
  done.
      (LVIII)

Apart from this commerce with the outer world, Shropshire represents a more inward experience. The Shropshire hills, as we have seen, formed the western boundary of Housman's childhood, and the memory of them suggests to him a lost state of innocence and happiness. At its simplest, this feeling is communicated in the poems that lament his separation from the countryside:

Oh tarnish late on Wenlock Edge,
Gold that I never see;
Lie long, high snowdrifts in the hedge
That will not shower on me.
  (XXXIX)

It is pursued less overtly in a group of poems that seem to gather up the various

4. A recruit was paid the bounty of one shilling when he signed on. This practice continued until 1879.

themes of the book and to form its keystone; Housman lights upon the exact metaphor for this state of mind when he discovers, with a sharp thrust of irony, that the very recollection of the countryside serves no longer to invigorate but only to torment:

Into my heart an air that kills
From yon far country blows;
What are those blue remembered hills,
What spires, what farms are those?

That is the land of lost content,
I see it shining plain,
The happy highways where I went
And cannot come again.
(XL)

Last Poems represents the gleanings of several harvests. Most of its poems date from the *Shropshire Lad* period and its immediate aftermath, while a few others are associated with the Edwardian decade and World War I. In 1920 Housman decided to set in order the work of twenty-five years, and the effort of revising and completing his drafts set him writing again. Some of these late lyrics—"Eight o'clock," for example—are an astonishing echo of his youthful style; others, such as "Tell me not here, it needs not saying," inspired by his declared farewell to poetry, touch a note of elegiac tenderness richer than anything he had written before. Compared to *A Shropshire Lad,* the book appears uneven in quality; it contains some of Housman's tritest pieces, such as "Grenadier" or "Lancer," and it leaves an impression of less sustained power. Yet the style is more completely Housman's own, and the language at its best still more inevitable, so that the reader at times is scarcely conscious of description, so completely are the words identified with the mood and scene they create:

When the eye of day is shut,
And the stars deny their beams,
And about the forest hut
Blows the roaring wood of dreams,

From deep clay, from desert rock,
From the sunk sands of the main,
Come not at my door to knock,
Hearts that loved me not again.
(XXXIII)

Here also one meets for the first time several poems on astronomical subjects. Such imagery intensified Housman's sense of the power and indifference of the surrounding universe and of man's insignificance upon his turning planet. In "Revolution" the poet watches the alternations of day and night with the eye of a celestial mechanic:

See, in mid heaven the sun is mounted; hark,
The belfries tingle to the noonday chime.
'Tis silent, and the subterranean dark
Has crossed the nadir, and begins to climb.
(XXXVI)

Cold and disciplined, these are among the most faultless of Housman's poems, approaching unexpectedly close to the territory of wit, which he professed to abhor in poetry. There are echoes of them in a successor whose work bears other traces of Housman's influence, W. H. Auden.

Laurence Housman, as literary executor, was authorized to print all the finished poems that he considered not inferior to the average of those already published, and, thanks to his editorial tact, another seventy-two poems have been preserved. This collection defines the full range of Housman's verse and, since his earlier poems often take their effect in hit-or-miss fashion, it illustrates more clearly, by means of other similar attempts, the nature of his successes and failures. The full range, of course, is still a very narrow one. Housman is a repetitive writer and he was clearly right to publish only a selection of his poetry to avoid diluting its effect. *More Poems* and the "Additional Poems" (eighteen poems that have not been published separately but are included in his *Collected Poems*) consist of pieces that either could not be fitted into his thematic arrangement or that he felt echoed what he had already published. Yet both categories contain lyrics that can stand beside his finest work. It is difficult to understand why he could not find room for such truly classical pieces as "Crossing alone the nighted ferry" or the beautiful poem on Hero and Leander, "Tarry delight, so seldom met." Others, such as the "Easter Hymn" or his farewell to Venice, provoke regret that his themes are normally so restricted. Those poems devoted to battlefields and soldiers' graves, on the other hand, almost suggest a parody of his manner. Certainly the instinct to suppress these was sound, but it is impossible not to be struck by the unsureness with which Housman writes of this subject.

War is one of the dominant themes in his poetry, and the life of physical action clearly held a special excitement for him, no less strong because it was so remote from his own. In his early poems he takes pride in the martial virtues as a part of his rural heritage, and they are linked too with his feeling that youth is the supreme testing time of life. In *A Shropshire Lad,* written in an era of apparently endless peace and security, war is merely a heroic fantasy, a rumble that falls thrillingly upon the ears of rustic lovers but never approaches nearer than the frontiers of empire:

On the idle hill of summer,
Sleepy with the flow of streams,
Far I hear the steady drummer
Drumming like a noise in dreams.
(XXXV)

Last Poems, besides several excessively literary pieces on the same theme, contains others directly inspired by the Boer War and World War I. For these he chose a formal, epigrammatic style reminiscent of the classic military epitaphs of Simonides, though the tone is quite distinct:

For pay and medals, name and rank,
Things that he has not found,
He hove the Cross to heaven and sank
The pole-star underground.
("Astronomy," XVII)

So Housman wrote of his younger brother killed in South Africa, and this note of irony is sounded still more decisively in the famous "Epitaph on an Army of Mercenaries":

Their shoulders held the sky suspended;
They stood, and earth's foundations stay;
What God abandoned, these defended,
And saved the sum of things for pay.
(XXXVII)

A Greek poet could use understatement in this context because it epitomized the Spartan code, which was the Hellenic military ideal, but the homage that Simonides wishes to communicate is quite unreserved. It is difficult for a modern poet to praise war so unequivocally. Hardy, in his Boer War poem "Drummer Hodge," is moved above all by the pathos of the ignorant country boy who never knew the meaning of the broad Karoo and the southern stars. Housman, not wishing to pay a conventional tribute, strengthens his effect by stressing the element for which all can agree the sacrifice was *not* made. War, or the trade of man, as he calls it, remained for him a subject that, at worst, demanded a certain decorum of treatment: it never presented itself, as it did to other poets, as a target for satire, yet his irony still preserves the edge of his poem, after more explicit denunciations have lost much of theirs.

Housman is often praised as a "classical" writer, but this verdict needs a good deal of qualification. He is a poet who borrows freely, though with distinction, and his style is more strongly influenced by the language of the Old Testament and of Shakespeare than by the Greek or Latin poets. The classical element, in fact, is more apparent in the outward form than in the spirit of his verse. His poems often suggest the effect of a vase painting, of a clear-cut design dexterously executed within narrow limits, and the strictness of his versification, his inversions of word order, and his skill in placing his isolated, significant epithets all strengthen this impression. Certainly classical history and mythology often enrich his imagery and provide a core for his poems. "The Oracles," for example, follows closely Herodotus' description of the Spartan sang-froid before Thermopylae, and its seven-foot lines echo the rough hexameters in which the Delphic Oracle uttered its prophecies. And the epigram on the Boer War,

Here dead lie we because we did not choose
To live and shame the land from which we
sprung.
Life, to be sure, is nothing much to lose;
But young men think it is, and we were
young.
(*More Poems,* XXXVI)

has a possible ancestor in the epitaph attributed to Simonides on the Athenian dead at Chalcis:

A gift desired, for youth is sweet
And youth we gave, nor turned away,
Though sharp the tide of battle beat,
That darkened all our day.

Where Housman parts company from the classical spirit is in the emotional appeal of many of his poems. Though he rejects any belief in an afterlife, at the same time he rails against the very conditions of human existence. The classical poets, though they may warn us to count no man happy until he is dead, have nonetheless come to terms with the mortal state: suffering is not for them to be softened into a yearning for death, nor do they undervalue the gift of life itself:

The joys I have possessed, in spite of fate,
are mine.
Not Heaven itself upon the past has power;
But what has been, has been, and I have had
my hour.
(Dryden trans., Horace, *Odes* III. 29.8)

John Dryden's verses are an utterance of the classical spirit; in Housman, on the contrary, we find that aspiration constantly outruns fulfillment. There are exceptions, but these, significantly, are mostly found among those poems that he did not publish. His poetry in fact occupies an ambiguous position between two worlds of feeling; this lends them a special poignancy but also leaves them peculiarly exposed to the dangers of false or facile sentiment.

Housman works always to a simple and distinctly conceived idea of the form a poem should take. His verse is almost brutally explicit and quite contradicts the ideal of pure poetry that he upholds in *The Name and Nature of Poetry,* perhaps because he did not possess the gift of sustained melody. His poetry often came to him in snatches, the gaps having to be filled in by conscious effort, and to write in this way he needed a regular metrical framework. He has been censured for the monotony of his versification, and there is force in this criticism, for he lacks the metrical subtlety of Yeats or de la Mare. His meters are primitive and his pauses heavy, at times even mechanical. But they are appropriate for the particular tones that he wished to render, for most of his lyrics are tinged with an element of the dramatic or the rhetorical. The four-line rhymed stanza, with the lines alternating between eight and six beats, is pressed so strongly into this service that it comes to represent the typical mood and cadence of a Housman poem, in which the note of challenge is sounded in the longer line and subsides in negation in the shorter:

June suns, you cannot store them
To warm the winter's cold,
The lad that hopes for heaven
Shall fill his mouth with mould.
(*More Poems,* XXII)

The characteristic effects are those of paradox, sudden poignancy, unexpected irony, and to achieve these, the ear needs to be led on by a smooth versification to the epithet or rhyme that is the point of stress. For this purpose too he employs a closely knit syntax in which nouns and verbs carry the main weight of his images:

Or beeches strip in storms for winter
And stain the wind with leaves.
(*Last Poems,* XL)

Their effect is often reinforced by alliteration, which creates a peculiar harmony and interdependence of sound and sense. He uses epithets sparingly, but when he does they are often inspired inventions: such phrases as "light-leaved spring," "felon-quarried stone," "the bluebells of the listless plain" perfectly combine a decorative with an emotional value in their context. His brother has pointed out how frequently Housman's capacity for self-criticism improved his poetry; how, for example, in the poem "Be still, my soul," the alternatives—vex, plague, tear, wrench, rend, wring, break, and pierce—were all rejected before the line took its final shape: "All thoughts to *rive* the heart are here, and all are vain."

The lecture on *The Name and Nature of Poetry* provoked, partly for fortuitous reasons, a considerable stir when it was delivered. Housman's personal distinction and the fact that this was his first and only venture into literary criticism had aroused high expectations. The poetic values that it defends, which Housman had long held, might be described as an extension of the position established by Matthew Arnold, and this part of the lecture, uttered twenty or even ten years earlier, would hardly have excited much comment. But by 1933 the shift in critical opinion, which had received such an impetus from Eliot, was already well under way, so that Housman's words were naturally interpreted as something of a counterattack in defense of the romantic conception of poetry. Looking back, however, and particularly in view of his avowed difficulty in writing the lecture, it seems unlikely that he was consciously entering upon controversy. In any case it is important to remember that this is a lecture, not a treatise, and that its virtues are those which belong to a formal public utterance of limited length. It is superbly phrased, it possesses wit, provocative emphasis, and felicity of quotation. It gives the verdict of a great classical scholar upon the English neoclassical poets, and it modifies Arnold's superficial and evasive estimate of Dryden and Alexander Pope. But it is not a fully developed critical position. Housman once more disclaims the office of critic, and what he offers, far from being a twentieth-century Poetics, is no more than a statement of what poetry meant to him.

He is more confident that he can feel poetry than that he can define it. He offers, in passing, various tentative definitions, none of which can be pressed very closely—"poetry seems to me more physical than intellectual," "meaning is of the intellect, poetry is not." But he is categorical in laying down what is *not* poetry, and here his taste excludes metaphysical poetry and the bulk of the verse produced between Milton's *Samson Agonistes* (1671) and William Wordsworth and Samuel Taylor Coleridge's *Lyrical Ballads* (1798). The most poetical of all writers for him is William Blake who, he says, gives us poetry "adulterated with so little meaning that nothing except poetic emotion is perceived and matters."

In saying this, Housman places himself with those critics who identify the poetic process with communication rather than with expression. He is also tacitly following the modern tendency to pass over architectonic qualities in poetry and to regard the lyric as somehow intrinsically more poetical than dramatic or narrative poetry. This point of view, he freely admits, is influenced by his own experience of composition. His description of how his own poetry came to be produced is the best-known part of the lecture, and his normal reticence gives what he had to say on this subject an authority all the more commanding. But it is plain that the process he describes could apply only to the composition of lyrics and not to the major literary forms, in which construction, balance, and sustained creative energy have an important part to play.

In the end, the only infallible criterion that Housman admits is the instinctive reaction that poetry produced upon his physical and nervous system. This verdict is startling, coming from a scholar whom one would suppose to be steeped in the teaching of Plato, Aristotle, and Horace on the moral basis of poetry; on the other hand, Housman had given warning that he regarded true literary criticism as the rarest of gifts, and any other kind as possessing no more authority than personal taste. It is not very profitable, in short, to analyze his lecture in detail. A poet often works by intuitions that he cannot explain any more satisfactorily than anyone else, and *The Name and Nature of Poetry* is best read as a statement not of critical doctrine but of a poet's instincts.

When a decisive change takes place in poetic taste, such as has been experienced in the last sixty years, not only a poet's virtues and vices, but even his aims and much that he has taken for granted, come to be differently regarded. Few writers of so slender an output can have satisfied so fully—for a time even molded—the poetic ideals of their generation as did Housman; in the event, he has suffered the fate of a minor poet thrust by popularity into the role of a major one, in that his verse has been acclaimed as much for its message as for its strictly poetic excellence, and its imperfections overlooked. In judging his work today, it is surely an advantage that our sensibility has turned to a different, more complex ideal of poetic art and that the shortcomings of Housman's pessimistic philosophy have become more apparent.

Housman's original inspiration sprang from the emotions of youth, the period when untried ideals and untutored desires at their strongest first encounter a hostile or indifferent world. At his best, he can voice these passions with an extraordinary force, with a sensuous yet cold fury—"fire and ice within me fight"—in which feeling, language, and meter are completely fused. But at this stage of emotional development he stops short. The rest of his experience is measured by the same standards, and indeed much of the emotion of his later poetry springs precisely from this vehement refusal to come to terms with life's demands and disillusionments. His choice is to reject the cup, to condemn the human situation proudly and without compromise. He would not have conceded, as Yeats could do:

I am content to live it all again
And yet again, if it be life to pitch
Into the frog-spawn of a blind man's ditch. . . .

These limitations in Housman's outlook and choice of material are familiar enough. There remain his superb powers of expression, the capacity to write verses of great poetry, if not to be a great poet. In his prose and verse alike, Housman is limited to the short flight and the minor form; but for the strength and purity of his expression, he can take his place in the company of the acknowledged masters of the English tongue. In an age of constant confusion and debasement of speech he has stood forth as one of the true heirs of the language, in whom its latent riches, the passionate simplicity of Anglo-Saxon, the splendor and eloquence of Latin, have once more found a voice. At his best he possesses the indefinable poetic faculty of conferring on words a new life, so that one turns eagerly to any new Housman fragment not so much for a fresh poetic experience as for some sudden felicity of language. Much was sacrificed for these ideals, but he possesses them securely; the command of words and the proud integrity with which he practiced it are his greatest gifts.

Selected Bibliography

BIBLIOGRAPHY

Carter, J.,and J. Sparrow, *A. E. Housman:An Annotated Handlist,* (London, 1952), annotations contain important biographical material.

COLLECTED AND SELECTED WORKS

Collected Poems, (London, 1939), repr. in the Cape paperback series (1967); *Collected Poems,* (London, 1956), in the "Penguin Poets" series; J. Carter, ed., *Selected Prose,* (London, 1961), contains lectures mentioned below, several of Housman's most important papers on classical subjects, including critical prefaces to his eds. of Manilius and Juvenal "On the Application of Thought to Textual Criticism," and selection of reviews, letters to the press, and other occasional writings; F. C. Horwood, ed., *Poetry and Prose: A Selection,* (London, 1971).

SEPARATE WORKS

Introductory Lecture, University College, London (London, 1892; privately repr., 1933; repr., 1937); *A Shropshire Lad,* (London, 1896), verse; *Last Poems,* (London, 1922); Platt, A., *Nine Essays,* (London, 1927), contains important preface by Housman; *The Name and Nature of Poetry,* (London, 1933), the 1933 Leslie Stephen Lecture; *More Poems,* (London, 1936); *The Confines of Criticism,* (London, 1969), complete text of Housman's Cambridge Inaugural Lecture, 1911, with notes by J. Carter; J. Diggle and F. R. D. Goodyear, eds., *The Classical Papers of A. E. Housman,* 3 vols. (London, 1972).

CLASSICAL TEXTS

M. Manilii: Astronomicon, 5 vols. (London, 1903–1930), repr. in 1 vol. (1932); *D. Ivnii Ivvenalis: Satvrae,* (London, 1905) 2nd ed., corrected (1931); *M. Annaei Lucani: Bell Civilis Libri Decem,* (Oxford, 1926) 2nd ed., corrected (1927).

LETTERS

T. B. Haber, ed., *Thirty Letters to Witter Bynner,* (New York, 1957); H. Maas, ed., *The Letters of A. E. Housman,* (London, 1971).

BIOGRAPHICAL AND CRITICAL STUDIES

Garrod, H. W., *The Profession of Poetry,* (London, 1929), includes lecture on Housman as poet and scholar; Gow, A. S. F., *A. E. Housman,* (London, 1936), sketch with definitive handlist of Housman's contributions to classical scholarship, and other prose papers; *"The Bromsgrovian": Housman Memorial Supplement,* (London, 1936), this supplement to Housman's old school magazine contains reminiscences and appreciations by his brother, his sister, and other hands, published in book form (New York, 1937); Housman, L., *A. E. H.: Some Poems, Some Letters and a Personal Memoir,* (London, 1937), includes quotations from Housman's letters and notebooks and 18 additional poems never published separately but contained in *Collected Poems;* Wilson, E., *The Triple Thinkers,* (London, 1938), contains essay on Housman's scholarship; Chambers, R. W., *Man's Unconquerable Mind,* (London, 1939), contains sketch of Housman's career at University College, London; Garrod, H. W., "Housman: 1939," in *Essays and Studies,* XXV (London, 1939); Withers, P., *A Buried Life,* (London, 1940); Richards, G., *Housman: 1897–1936,* (London, 1941), biographical study by Housman's first publisher, includes appendix by G. B. Fletcher analyzing classical influences in Housman's poetry; Connolly, C., *The Condemned Playground,* (London, 1945), contains article on Housman and the subsequent controversial letters in response, repr. from the New Statesman; Haber, T. B., *The Manuscript Poems of A. E. Housman,* (London, 1955), publishes for the first time a large number of fragments and lines from Housman's MS notebooks (previously excluded from publication by Laurence Housman under the terms of his brother's will) in the Library of Congress; also discusses chronology of the poems; Watson, G. L., *A. E. Housman: A Divided Life,* (London, 1957); Marlow, N., *A. E. Housman: Scholar and Poet,* (London, 1958), sensitive study of biographical rather than critical interest; Haber, T. B., *A. E. Housman,* (New York, 1967); C. Ricks, ed., *A. E. Housman: A Collection of Critical Essays,* (London, 1969), in the Twentieth Century Views Series; Leggett, B. J., *Housman's Land of Lost Content: A Critical Study of A Shropshire Lad,* (Lincoln, Nebr., 1970); Leggett, B. J., *The Poetic Art of A. E. Housman,* (Lincoln, Nebr., 1978); Graves, R. P., *A. E. Housman. The Scholar Poet,* (London, 1979).

Langston Hughes
(1902–1967)

ARNOLD RAMPERSAD

In March 1966, about a year before his death, Langston Hughes flew from his home in New York City to Africa, to the city of Dakar in Senegal, to attend the widely heralded First World Festival of Negro Arts. As a leader of the large United States delegation, but more so as an individual in his own right, Hughes stood out among the more than two thousand visitors who had come from all over the world to celebrate the international appeal and influence of black culture. Known at home as the "poet laureate of the Negro race" and as the dean of African American writers, in this international setting he was honored for the worldwide impact of his lifetime of writing about the lives and cultures of his fellow blacks. Langston Hughes was both respected and immensely popular. While the poet-president of Senegal, Léopold Sédar Senghor, who had organized the festival, singled him out for his historic contribution to the development of black poetry and the concept of negritude, the *New York Times* also reported of Hughes that "young writers from all over Africa followed him about the city and haunted his hotel the way American youngsters dog favorite baseball players."

This honoring on an international scale in Africa followed on the heels of national honors at home that testified to the stature Hughes had achieved by the end of his life. In 1961 the National Institute of Arts and Letters had elected him a member, and in 1960 the National Association for the Advancement of Colored People (NAACP), then probably at the height of its prestige because of the civil rights movement, had awarded him its annual Spingarn Medal for his contribution to the lives of black Americans. These honors were the result not only of diligent efforts but also of a striking identification on his part. From virtually the start of his career Hughes had forged a special bond with black readers in the United States and abroad through his conspicuous love of his people, which he demonstrated not simply by creating attractive portraits but also by saturating his art in the most significant popular expressive forms within the community, as well as in the struggles, sorrows, victories, and joys in the day-to-day lives of ordinary black people.

James Langston Hughes was born on 1 February 1902, in Joplin, Missouri, but grew up mainly in Lawrence, Kansas, in the home of his maternal grandmother, Mary Langston. Hughes and his mother, Carrie Langston Hughes, moved to Lawrence after his ambitious father, James Nathaniel Hughes, frustrated by racism in his determination to be a lawyer in Oklahoma, left his family behind and emigrated to Mexico. From his grandmother Hughes learned constantly about the need to struggle on behalf of the ideals of social justice and African American progress. A radical abolitionist in her youth, she had lost her first husband, Lewis Sheridan Leary, when he was shot and killed as a member of John Brown's band in its doomed assault at Harper's Ferry. Her second husband, Charles Langston (Hughes's grandfather), had himself taken part in a celebrated abolitionist action, the Oberlin-Wellington rescue, on behalf of a fugitive slave; and Charles's brother, John Mercer Langston, also an ardent abolitionist, had become one of the most famous black Americans of the nineteenth century as a lawyer, an educator, a diplomat, and a United States congressman from Virginia in the 1890s.

In spite of this colorful and prestigious background, Hughes passed his boyhood in poverty, as his mother searched for jobs to support her son and her mother. The frequent absences of his mother and the increasing withdrawal of his aging grandmother combined to make him a troubled child, according to his own account, "unhappy for a long time, and very lonesome." He was rescued from sadness by his discovery of books: "Then it was that books began to happen to me, and I began to believe in nothing but books and the wonderful world in books—where if people suffered, they suffered in beautiful language. His love of reading, then of writing, was first fostered by both his grandmother and his mother, who herself wrote verse and acted, and even hoped for a career on the stage.

As he later recalled, Hughes wrote his first poem after he left Lawrence for Lincoln, Illinois, where he spent a year with his mother between 1915 and 1916. But his main apprenticeship as a writer came in high school in Cleveland, Ohio, where he lived from 1916 to 1920. In the monthly school magazine he published short stories that showed an early concern with questions of social justice, though not with racism. His poetry in the magazine, at first undistinguished, revealed at one crucial point the decisive influence of Walt Whitman and then of Carl Sandburg, the Illinois poet of radical democracy—and free verse—whom Hughes remembered as my "guiding star." Under this influence, as well as that of Paul Laurence Dunbar and W. E. B. Du Bois from earlier in his life, he matured quickly. Within a year of graduating from high school, Hughes had composed memorable poems in what would later be regarded as his authentic voice: "The Negro Speaks of Rivers," in which he quietly extolled the historic beauty and dignity of the African peoples; "Mother to Son," composed entirely in dialect but free of the stereotypes of low comedy or extreme pathos that had come to mar most black dialect verse; and "When Sue Wears Red," which ecstatically praises the beauty of a black woman and links her honorably and dramatically to Africa.

These poems were Hughes's first major literary response to the racism and segregation he had personally encountered, but more so to the plight of blacks in less fortunate circumstances than he had experienced as a young black in the Midwest. In addition to the tales of slavery and freedom told to him by his grandmother, he also knew from her and other blacks about the complex network of segregation, whether de jure or de facto, that marred the lives of blacks particularly in the South but also virtually across the country, and about the reign of terror through lynchings to which southern blacks were subjected. He himself had first experienced segregation and racist insult as a small child in Lawrence. However, Cleveland had proved a relatively benign place for his adolescent years, and he had actually flourished at Central High under conscientious teachers and with students, many of them the children of European immigrants, who in his senior year elected him class poet and editor of the annual.

Between his departure from high school in 1920 and the appearance of his first book in 1926, Hughes led an almost compulsively varied life. A disastrous year with his father in Mexico, when he finally faced the fact that "I hated my father" for his harshness and materialism, was followed by a disappointing year (1921–1922) at Columbia University, which Hughes found cold and hostile. He then descended into a succession of humble jobs, including delivery boy for a florist in Manhattan and worker on a vegetable farm on Staten Island (also in New York City). A desire to go to sea led to several months as a messman on ships anchored in the Hudson River, then to steamer voyages to Africa that allowed him to visit ports on the west coast of Africa from Senegal in the north to Angola in the south. Next came a similar job on a ship in Europe, where, after jumping ship, he passed several months in Paris as a dishwasher in a nightclub that featured black American entertainers.

Hughes returned to the United States near the end of 1924, then passed the following year in Washington, D.C., where his mother was living. Again he worked at lowly jobs—in a laundry and in restaurant kitchens, for example. During all this time of travel and work in the early 1920s, however, he had been diligently publishing poems—at first mainly in the *Crisis,* edited for the NAACP by W. E. B. Du Bois; then in Charles Johnson's *Opportunity,* sponsored by the Urban League; and in a widening circle of journals. Thus he had returned from Paris relatively well known to black lovers of poetry. In 1925 he finally made the decisive contacts that led to the publication by Alfred A. Knopf, in January 1926, of his first volume of verse, *The Weak Blues.*

From his first publication of verse in the *Crisis,* Hughes had reflected his admiration for Sandburg and Whitman by experimenting with free verse as opposed to committing himself conservatively to rhyme. Even when he employed rhyme in his verse, as he often did, Hughes composed with relative casualness—unlike other major black poets of the age, such as Countee Cullen and Claude McKay, with their highly wrought stanzas. He seemed to prefer, as Whitman and Sandburg had preferred, to write lines that captured the cadences of common American speech, with his ear always especially attuned to the variety of black American language. This last aspect was only a token of his emotional and aesthetic involvement in black American culture, which he increasingly saw as his prime source of inspiration, even as he regarded black Americans ("Loud laughers in the hands of Fate— / My People") as his only indispensable audience.

Early poems captured some of the sights and sounds of ecstatic black church worship ("Glory! Hallelujah!"), but Hughes's greatest technical accomplishment as a poet was in his fusing of the rhythms of blues and jazz with traditional poetry. This technique, which he employed his entire life, surfaced in his art around 1923 with the landmark poem "The Weary Blues," in which the persona recalls hearing a blues singer and piano player ("Sweet Blues! / Coming from a black man's soul") performing in what most likely is a speakeasy in Harlem. The persona recalls the plaintive verse intoned by the singer ("Ain't got nobody in all this world, / Ain't got nobody but ma self") but finally surrenders to the mystery and magic of the blues singer's art. In the process, Hughes had taken an indigenous African American art form, perhaps the most vivid and commanding of all, and preserved its authenticity even as he formally enshrined it in the midst of a poem in traditional European form.

"The Weary Blues," a work virtually unprecedented in American poetry in its blending of black and white rhythms and forms, won Hughes the first prize for poetry in May 1925 in the epochal literary contest sponsored by *Opportunity* magazine, which marked the first high point of the Harlem Renaissance. The work also confirmed his leadership, along with Countee Cullen, of all the younger poets of the burgeoning movement. For Hughes, it was only the first step in his poetical tribute to blues and jazz. By the time of his second volume of verse, *Fine Clothes to the Jew* (1927), he was writing blues poems without either apology or framing devices taken from the traditional world of poetry. He was also delving into the basic subject matters of the blues—love and raw sexuality, deep sorrow and sudden violence, poverty and heartbreak. These subjects, treated with sympathy for the poor and dispossessed, and without false piety, made him easily the most controversial black poet of his time.

The previous year (1926), with his essay "The Negro Artist and the Racial Mountain" in the *Nation,* he had composed the manifesto of the younger artists who were determined to assert racial pride and racial truth in the face of either black or white censure or criticism:

> We younger Negro artists . . . intend to express our individual dark-skinned selves without fear or shame. If white people are pleased we are glad. If they are not, it doesn't matter. We know we are beautiful. And ugly too. The tom-tom cries and the tom-tom laughs. If colored people are pleased we are glad. If they are not, their displeasure doesn't matter either. We build our temples for tomorrow, strong as we know how, and we stand on top of the mountain, free within ourselves. (*The Nation* 122:694 [June 1926])

Now, with *Fine Clothes to the Jew,* he faced a volcano of criticism from black reviewers. Never before had a black poet so clearly exposed these aspects of black culture to the white world, and the middle-class black critics responded to the volume with outrage. Langston Hughes was a "SEWER DWELLER," blared one headline; to another journal, he was the "poet 'low-rate' of Harlem"; yet another called the book "about 100 pages of trash" that reeked of "the gutter and the sewer." But Hughes refused to retract a line. Most blacks were of the lower class, he asserted; "even I myself, belong to that class." In any event, "I have a right to portray any side of Negro life I wish to."

In 1926, seeking a greater degree of stability in his life, Hughes joined the almost all-black student body at Lincoln University in Pennsylvania, from which he graduated in 1929. About this time another, more private involvement proved to be at least as important. In 1927 he began to benefit from the patronage of the remarkable Mrs. Charlotte Mason, or "Godmother," an older white woman whose generosity to black writers and artists included support for Zora Neale Hurston and Alain Locke, among others. A firm believer in parapsychology and in the spiritual power of the darker races contrasted to the materialism of Europe, Mrs. Mason applied her powerful, highly volatile temperament to the task of guiding Hughes in his career. Alternately pampered and stimulated by her, and driven by her relentless editing, he somewhat unwillingly wrote his first novel, *Not Without Laughter* (1930). This often lyrical, charming, and moving story of a black Midwestern boyhood reflects only slightly the actual details of Hughes's past. However, this story of an old black mother, her three grown daughters, her son-in-law, and her grandson Sandy as they struggle for survival and even respectability against racism, poverty, and natural disaster is both a graphic portrait of a broad aspect of the black American world and a projection of Hughes's own desire as a child for a loving family, especially a father and a mother to shower him with the love he had craved and missed.

Hughes's sudden and highly dramatic expulsion by Mrs. Mason—for reasons still altogether unclear—virtually upended his life early in 1930. Deeply hurt but chronically unable to vent anger, he fell ill. His sickness was compounded when Zora Neale Hurston—with whom he had written *Mule Bone,* a folk comedy set in the deep South, while both were under Mrs. Mason's patronage—claimed the play as her sole property and denounced him as a liar. With four hundred dollars from the Harmon Prize for literature in 1930, he fled to Cuba and Haiti. He did not return until he had passed several weeks living almost aimlessly on the north coast of Haiti, near the famed citadel begun by Jean-Jacques Dessalines and completed by Henri Christophe, the most imposing symbol of black ambition and determination in the Western Hemisphere. During this time, however, Hughes clearly brooded on the major choices he had made in his life, and came to decisions about changes for the future.

Returning to the United States, which had started its downward slide into the Great Depression, Hughes moved swiftly toward the far Left. He published anti—imperialist essays and poems in *New Masses* and elsewhere, and made ready to work closely with the Communist John Reed Club of New York. Then, aided by a Rosenwald Fund grant, he headed south to begin a yearlong tour bringing his poetry to the people. Reading mainly in black churches and school halls for modest fees, and selling books, pamphlets, and posters from the back of a Ford driven by a friend, he moved steadily through the South before heading west. He stirred vicious controversy and risked his life at least twice: by making a rare appearance at the all-white University of North Carolina in Chapel Hill and by involving himself in the Scottsboro Boys controversy, first by visiting the town where the condemned black youths had been captured and accused of the rape of two white women, then by visiting some of the accused on death row in an Alabama prison.

By this point Hughes had given up blues and lyric poetry for militantly radical socialist utterance, such as *Scottsboro Limited* (1931), a verse play about the Scottsboro case. His radicalism reached its zenith following his reading tour, which took him as far as Oregon and Washington, when he joined a band of twenty-two young blacks recruited in the United States for a film on American race relations to be made in the Soviet Union. In June 1932, Hughes arrived in Moscow, but the poorly planned film project soon collapsed in a mire of controversy. Warmly received as a writer, he decided to spend a year in the Soviet Union. He traveled in the Central Asian republics with fellow writers, including the young journalist Arthur Koestler. In a small book published in Moscow, *A Negro Looks at Soviet Central Asia* (1934), he contrasted the humane Soviet treatment of its ethnic minorities with the horrors of American segregation.

While in the Soviet Union, Hughes wrote and published the most radical verse of his life, including "Good Morning Revolution," "Coumbia" (a sensational attack on American imperialism), and his single most controversial work, "Goodbye Christ," in which the speaker caps his or her rough dismissal of various well-known evangelists of dubious integrity with the dismissal of Christ in favor of "Marx Communist Lenin Peasant Stalin Worker ME—." This poem was published in the German-based radical magazine *Negro Worker,* apparently without Hughes's knowledge or permission. However, he did not repudiate it on its appearance, as he would later do.

In August 1933, Hughes returned to the United States via China and Japan. Noël Sullivan, a liberal patron of the arts whom he had met in San Francisco during his tour the previous year, then arranged to support Hughes's writing of a series of short stories for a year at Sullivan's cottage in the wealthy resort village of Carmel, on the Monterey Peninsula. Neither patronage nor friendship prevented Hughes from showing his new cynicism about race relations in America in the stories penned in Carmel, which formed the heart of his important collection *The Ways of White Folks* (1934). In stories such as "These Blues I'm Playing" and "Slave on the Block," he attacked the insincerity and confusion of many whites in their dealings with blacks. Other stories pilloried racism in various forms, at times with such harsh psychological realism that the collection in some ways sounded a note of unprecedented bitterness in African American fiction. It also established Hughes with the leading magazines as a writer of fiction, a major consideration given his determination to live solely by his writing.

At the end of his Carmel year, late in 1934, the death of his father, whom he had not seen since 1921, took Hughes to Mexico. His hopes for a legacy were soon dashed, but he remained in Mexico for several months. His major work there was an act of typical generosity and cosmopolitanism—the translation of several short stories written by progressive young Mexicans, for possible publication in the United States. Unfortunately, nothing came of this project; American editors were uninterested in such material. Almost penniless, Hughes returned in 1935 to the United States to join his mother, who was then living in Oberlin, Ohio, where her parents had passed some of their youthful abolitionist days before the Civil War.

Almost at once his career took a sudden turn with the news that his *Mulatto: A Play of the Deep South,* about miscegenation and written in 1930, was about to open on Broadway. In *Mulatto,* Hughes drew to some extent on his family history, in that his grandfather Charles Langston had been the somewhat rebellious son of a white Virginia planter and a slave, Lucy Langston, with whom the planter had lived as if in marriage, even bequeathing most of his property to his children upon his death. In the play, a mulatto son of a similar "marriage" demands recognition by his father. When Colonel Norwood refuses, he inaugurates an action that ends with his death at the hands of his son, who is soon on the brink of being lynched even as his grieving mother goes mad. Thus Hughes dramatized the tragedy of American race relations as epitomized in the segregated South, with its denial of the humanity of blacks and their essential part in the nation, and the disaster awaiting the republic as a result of that denial.

With certain sensational changes in Hughes's text and with a series of ingenious publicity ploys, the white producer of *Mulatto* kept the play alive in spite of harsh reviews that questioned Hughes's skill as a playwright. *Mulatto* remained on Broadway longer than any other play by a black playwright until Lorraine Hansberry's *A Raisin in the Sun* (with its title from a Hughes poem) more than a generation later. In the next few years, working closely with the Karamu Theater in Cleveland, Hughes tried to repeat the success of *Mulatto.* First came the farce *Little Ham* (1936), set mainly in a shoeshine parlor, with its diminutive bootblack hero, Hamlet Hitchcock Jones, and his many women friends and admirers and his passion for playing the "numbers." In 1936, Karamu staged the premiere of *Troubled Island* (later retitled *Emperor of Haiti*), Hughes's drama of the Haitian revolution, with its emphasis on the failure of Jean-Jacques Dessalines to sustain the national spirit that had won independence from France. Not long afterward, the Cleveland group staged Hughes's *Joy to My Soul,* a broad comedy about a rich but dim young man come from Texas to Harlem in search of a bride. Still later in the 1930s Karamu staged the melodrama *Front Porch,* about a striving black family living uneasily in a mainly white neighborhood, and a daughter who is forced into an abortion that kills her.

None of these Karamu plays resulted in a commercial or a major critical success. Among Hughes's other plays in the 1930s, the brief *Soul Gone Home* is a provokingly macabre comedy about a dead young man who "comes alive" to scold his heartless mother as she prepares to go out on the town. *Don't You Want to Be Free?* was written by Hughes for his radical Harlem Suitcase Theater, which he founded in 1938 after returning from several months in besieged Madrid as a war correspondent for a black newspaper. This radical play, which combines several of Hughes's poems with the music of the blues and a loose story line that ends in a rousing call for class unity and for revolution, ran for over one hundred performances in Harlem. The year 1938 also marked the appearance of Hughes's only collection of radical socialist poetry, *A New Song,* with an introduction by the radical writer Mike Gold. It was published by the leftist International Workers Order, which was also behind the Harlem Suitcase Theater.

None of these plays made Hughes much money. In fact, most made him virtually nothing, so that throughout the 1930s he lived close to poverty. In 1939 he accepted with alacrity the chance to work as a writer in Hollywood with the black actor and singer Clarence Muse on *Way Down South,* a movie intended as a vehicle for the popular boy singer Bobby Breen. To Hughes's chagrin, the movie, set on a plantation in the days of slavery, was denounced in progressive circles when it opened later that year. He soon had another setback of at least equal consequence. A major book luncheon at a hotel in Pasadena, California, at which his freshly published autobiography, *The Big Sea* (1940), was to be featured, was canceled following picketing by an evangelical group who accused Hughes of atheism and communism. At the heart of their objections was his 1932 poem "Goodbye Christ." Hughes then repudiated the poem as an aberration of his youth, and ended his decade-long identification as a radical socialist.

The Big Sea, written before this repudiation, shows clearly that Hughes was already well prepared to make the shift; the volume makes virtually no mention of socialism. Penned in the clear, simple, unpretentious prose characteristic of Hughes, the book unfolds in a succession of brief, episodic chapters narrated in an often droll manner. However, this approach does not entirely conceal some of his more serious purposes and concerns, notably his anger at his parents and his unhappy childhood. In a disarming manner, Hughes portrayed his father as a Satan-like figure who tries to tempt the young black poet with an offer of untold riches in Mexico if only Hughes will surrender his soul—that is, give up blacks and poetry for profit. Hughes also tells frankly of his disaster with his patron, "Godmother," his inability to vent his anger, and his resulting serious illness. At the center of the text is a smiling, even-tempered young black hero who gracefully endures the vicissitudes of life, including those heaped specially on blacks, without ever falling into bitterness or despair. *The Big Sea* is also invaluable in that it provides a firsthand account, never surpassed, of the main personalities and events of the Harlem Renaissance.

With the entry of the United States into World War II, Hughes completed his withdrawal from the Left. His next volume of verse, *Shakespeare in Harlem* (1942), took him back, as he put it, to "Nature, Negroes, and love." The volume is dominated by the blues, which he had neglected as a writer throughout the preceding decade. Near the end of 1942, he started another line of work that would sustain him for the rest of his life. He accepted an invitation to write a column, "Here to Yonder," for the black weekly *Chicago Defender*. The column was conventional until early 1943, when Hughes related a conversation he had had in a bar with a man he called only "My Simple Minded Friend." This friend, barely literate but highly opinionated and possessed of a powerful, sometimes even bizarre, racial pride, eventually was identified as Jesse B. Semple, or "Simple"; the rather stuffy narrator was identified early on as Langston Hughes but was later called "Boyd." First intended as a ploy by Hughes to bolster support for the war effort among blacks, many of whom felt a sense of kinship with the nonwhite Japanese in the war, Simple quickly grew into by far the most popular aspect of the column and one of the more original comic creations in American journalism. The column lasted for more than twenty years, and was edited and adapted by Hughes into five books of Simple sketches, including *Simple Speaks His Mind* (1951), *Simple Takes a Wife* (1953), and *The Best of Simple* (1961). A musical play, *Simply Heavenly*, opened successfully off Broadway in 1957.

In retreating from the far Left around 1940, Hughes shifted his considerable energy back in the direction of matters pertaining to segregation and civil rights for blacks—the direction, in a sense, from which he had started. His decision to write for the *Chicago Defender* was of a piece with this shift, as was his collection of propagandistic verse, *Jim Crow's Last Stand* (1943). On the other hand, he saw this new emphasis in his work as consistent with a broad view of American and world culture. The centrist magazine *Common Ground*, edited by M. Margaret Anderson for the Common Council for American Unity, published more of his poems in this decade than did any other journal.

These gestures toward a more centrist position coalesced at some point with Hughes's desire, as he grew older, to enjoy at last a measure of financial security. Thus in the early 1940s he wrote dozens of songs both in support of the war effort and in vain hope of a commercial hit. His songwriting at last paid off in 1947, with the Broadway premiere of the musical play *Street Scene*, a fusion of opera and Broadway on which Hughes had worked as lyricist with the composer Kurt Weill and the dramatist Elmer Rice. Weill and Rice had turned to Hughes, they explained, because of the simple lyricism, as opposed to slickness, of his verse. *Street Scene* closed after only five months on Broadway, but it had been hailed as a milestone in American musical theater and opera. It also netted Hughes enough money to buy a house of his own at last, in the heart of Harlem at 20 East 127th Street, where he lived for the rest of his life.

The year 1947 also saw the appearance of Hughes's only volume of poetry entirely without racial reference, *Fields of Wonder.* Some critics emphasized the beauty of his verse, others its apparent lack of purpose and originality. Two years later, Hughes's next volume of verse, *One-Way Ticket* (1949), returned him squarely to the black urban world and its rich cast of characters; the work included a suite devoted to one of Hughes's most brilliant creations, Alberta K. Johnson—"Madam to You." In between these two volumes, he had begun work on yet another volume of verse. The richly symbolic and emotional event of finally having his own home appeared to inspire, just after he moved in, his finest volume in many years, *Montage of a Dream Deferred* (1951). This collection of poems, which Hughes offered as really one long poem about Harlem, reflected his keen sense not only of the tremendous pressures of northern urban life on black migrants from the South but also of the spectacular way in which the jazz musicians maturing around the end of World War II responded to those pressures in the new "bebop" jazz. His book-length poem, Hughes wrote, "is marked by conflicting changes, sudden nuances, sharp and impudent interjections, broken rhythms, and passages . . . punctuated by the riffs, runs, breaks, and disc-tortions of the music of a community in transition." At least one of the poems, "Harlem" ("What happens to a dream deferred?"), joined the long list of his poems known widely and cherished among blacks for their special insight into the African American condition.

As the decade of the 1940s closed and the cold war intensified, Hughes found himself increasingly under fire from organized right-wing forces for poems and essays written years before, and in particular for "Goodbye Christ." In vain he protested that he had never been a member of the Communist party and was no longer sympathetic to the far Left. The effort to censure him reached its climax in March 1953, when a subpoena brought him before Senator Joseph McCarthy's investigating committee concerned with Communist subversion in the United States. In contrast to other writers called, Hughes generally cooperated with McCarthy although he had little respect for him and his aims. He agreed that the presence of some of his books in official American libraries overseas was odd, given his politics at the time they were written (he did not identify any particular book), and he again repudiated "Good-bye Christ." Although Hughes was criticized by elements on the Left for appeasing McCarthy, he spared himself the fate of black leaders such as Paul Robeson and W. E. B. Du Bois, and preserved his special relationship with black institutions and his special place in the black community.

Although attacks from the right wing never ceased completely, Hughes was now free to exploit his considerable talents and his distinguished record as a writer. His output, always steady, became voluminous as he accepted contract after contract for a variety of books, plays, and musical projects. In addition to his five Simple collections, he published two new collections of short stories, *Laughing to Keep from Crying* (1952) and *Something in Common* (1963), as well as an amusing little novel of somewhat dubious origin, *Tambourines to Glory* (1958), which had started as a gospel musical play before Hughes converted it into fiction. *The Sweet Flypaper of Life* (1955), a small volume comprising a brief but spiced urban narrative inspired by Roy DeCarava's accompanying photographs of Harlem, was hailed as an extraordinarily fine marriage of image and text.

Hughes's main work in poetry after *Montage of a Dream Deferred* came almost a decade later with the publication of *Ask Your Mama* (1961). The genesis of this poem in twelve parts was his agitated response to a riot by young whites in 1960 in Newport, Rhode Island, after they were shut out of a session of the Newport Jazz Festival, of which Hughes had for some years been an officer. Based on the "dozens," the game of ritual insult played in black American culture especially by young men, *Ask Your Mama* is freighted with musical references and annotations; indeed, the main text demands accompaniment by jazz and blues music, which offsets the fragmented and at times almost incoherent modernist language of Hughes's poetic lines. Like the riot over black jazz that inspired it, the poem ominously anticipated the explosive pressures on American society that would surface soon in the 1960s. Nevertheless, the volume was generally either ignored or ridiculed by literary critics, who evinced no interest in responding to the challenges posed by its allusions and innovations.

Another important aspect of Hughes's career was his writing for children. In 1932, he and Arna Bontemps had published their affecting children's tale *Popo and Fifina,* set in Haiti and drawing on Hughes's visit to the country in 1931. Well received by the critics, the book also sold well over several years. His *The First Book of Negroes* (1952), which offered information about blacks to young children, began a constant effort on Hughes's part to write for this market. In part, this was a commercial decision; in larger part, however, the effort reflected his sincere love of young people and his concern for their education. Other "First" books (in a series from the publisher Franklin Watts) included *The First Book of Rhythms* (1954) and *The First Book of Jazz* (1957), as well as others on the West Indies (1956) and on Africa (1960). The book on jazz drew particular praise from reviewers in the field. For a somewhat older youth audience, he emphasized history in volumes that included *Famous American Negroes* (1954) and *Famous Negro Music Makers* (1955).

Sometimes with historic results, Hughes also kept busy as editor and anthologist. His 1949 anthology with Arna Bontemps, *The Poetry of the Negro 1746–1949,* included work by Caribbean writers as well as "tributary" verse on blacks by white writers. As the first such book since James Weldon Johnson's revised edition of *The Book of American Negro Poetry* in 1931, the anthology brought an entire generation of poets before the general public for the first time. Hughes's alertness to the new forces in black literature, and his unstinting desire to assist younger writers, resulted in other anthologies such as *New Negro Poets USA* (1964), with a foreword by Gwendolyn Brooks, and *The Best Short Stories by Negro Writers* (1967), which included the first story published by Alice Walker.

A major effort in collaboration with Milton Meltzer, who provided most of the pictures, resulted in *A Pictorial History of the Negro in America* (1956), the first volume of its kind to be published in the United States. The two men collaborated again on *Black Magic: A Pictorial History of the Negro in American Entertainment* (1967). Hughes edited a sampling of his own work in *The Langston Hughes Reader* (1958) and again in *Selected Poems* (1959). The latter volume is notable not least of all for its strenuous exclusion of the poet's socialist verse.

From early in his life, Hughes had a powerful sense of internationalism, which his traveling reinforced. Reasonably fluent in French and Spanish, he translated or helped to translate four books. The first was Federico García Lorca's *Gypsy Ballads* (1951), most of which Hughes translated while living in Madrid in 1937. Poems by Nicolas Guillien, *Cuba libre* (1948), capped his long friendship with Cuba's national poet. On Hughes's visit to Havana in 1930, Guillén had been decisively influenced by the American's work on the blues. His first book of poems, *Motivos de son,* was a landmark in Cuban writing because of its radical employment of African-based popular music and dance. *Selected Poems of Gabriela Mistral* (1957) was the first American book-length translation of the Chilean-born Nobel Prize winner. The novel *Masters of the Dew,* by Jacques Roumain, perhaps Haiti's finest writer of this century, was translated by Hughes and the scholar Mercer Cook of Howard University. Hughes had first met Roumain in Haiti in 1931, and had shared many of his radical socialist sympathies for the poor of that country.

With the exception of the poems by Gabriela Mistral, where critics questioned

Hughes's appropriateness as a translator of a woman's poetry and his decision not to translate certain poems he found too complex, his translations were well received. Two anthologies of African writing, *An African Treasury: Articles, Essays, Stories, Poems by Black Africans* (1960) and *Poems from Black Africa, Ethiopia, and Other Countries* (1963), introduced the writings of a wide range of Africans to readers in North America. Many of the writers who later achieved major international success, including Wole Soyinka, Amos Tutuola, and Chinua Achebe, were represented in these anthologies, which benefited from Hughes's various visits to Africa in the 1950s and 1960s. At least two other anthologies are worth noting: *The Book of Negro Folklore* (1958), compiled with Arna Bontemps and the first comprehensive collection ever published on the subject; and *Book of Negro Humor* (1966), also largely unprecedented.

Fight for Freedom (1962), commissioned by the NAACP, was a lively and well-researched history of the organization. (As a radical, Hughes had opposed the NAACP, especially in its struggles with Communists over the Scottsboro case, but he supported it staunchly in the later stages of his life.) His major prose effort of the 1950s and 1960s, however, was unquestionably his second volume of autobiography, *I Wonder as I Wander* (1956). Here Hughes traced his life from 1931, where *The Big Sea* ended, to 1938, as he prepared to leave Europe, over which war clouds were gathering, after his grim experience of the Spanish Civil War. The volume reflects a coming to terms with the Left, in that much of the book is devoted to a detailed account of Hughes's year in the Soviet Union. Although many of the inconveniences and weaknesses of the Soviet system are pointed out, the book is entirely free of the anti-Soviet hysteria of the cold war. *I Wonder as I Wander* retains the genial tone and episodic structure of *The Big Sea* but is even less revealing of Hughes's inner life. On the other hand, it is a larger, denser narrative, highly satisfying as an account of one segment of an American life of almost unique variety.

In all this prodigious output, perhaps the most significant aspect of Hughes's career in his last twenty years was his work for the stage, starting with *Street Scene* in 1947 and his opera with the black composer William Grant Still, *Troubled Island,* in 1949. For the classical composer Jan Meyerowitz, a refugee from Germany who had immigrated to the United States at the end of the war, he wrote several librettos and related texts. Probably their most successful collaboration was the opera *The Barrier,* based on Hughes's 1935 Broadway play *Mulatto.* To excellent critical reviews, *The Barrier* had its premiere at Columbia University in 1950. Later, however, it failed miserably on Broadway. But Hughes's main interest was in the commercial theater. His first fruitful attempt in this area after *Street Scene* led him to collaborate with the Harlem composer David Martin in their production *Simply Heavenly,* which opened to steady interest and applause off-Broadway in 1957. This jaunty Harlem comedy, susceptible to being played as farce and even burlesque in spite of its author's intentions, drew heavily on the Simple newspaper columns.

In this collaboration, as with Meyerowitz, Hughes deferred in musical matters to the composer. Even before the premiere of *Simply Heavenly,* however, he was at work on another play that would find him making more inventive use of black music. Fascinated by the rise of black gospel music, itself a fusion of the hymn and the blues, he decided to address it in the theater as he had addressed the blues and jazz in his verse. The first result was *Tambourines to Glory,* set in the colorful world of the black storefront evangelical church. With much of its music written by Harlem composer Jobe Huntley, *Tambourines to Glory* marked the first use of gospel music on the theatrical stage. Unfortunately, the broadly comic aspects of the show, with its burlesque of religion, offended many critics, included blacks, and it fared poorly when it reached Broadway late in 1963.

From this point, Hughes ceased collaborating with composers but delved more experimentally into the fusion of gospel and the stage. The resulting productions often featured spare but stunning narrative lines married to effulgent music drawn from the burgeoning gospel tradition. Among these were *Black Nativity* (1961; a black gospel counterpart, perhaps, to Gian Carlo Menotti's internationally popular opera *Amahl and the Night Visitors*), which seldom failed to arouse audiences; *Jericho-Jim Crow* (1964), on the civil rights movement, which earned Hughes the most celebratory reviews of any of his stage ventures in his life; and *The Prodigal Son* (1965), which also garnered fine reviews.

Hughes was hard at work on various literary projects—including the posthumously published collection of verse *The Panther and the Lash* (1967), which focuses on the civil rights movement and the nascent black power movement—virtually until his death in a New York hospital on 22 May 1967.

The sheer quantity and the variety of his written work inevitably have led some critics to question whether Hughes sacrificed his integrity and his talent as an artist for a more functional vision of himself as a man of letters. Hughes himself seemed to have few such misgivings, although he often joked about the multiplicity of his commitments and jobs, and ruefully called himself, more than once, a "literary sharecropper." In the end and to the end, nevertheless, he was proud to have been the first black American, as far as he knew, to live solely by his writings. He had established and maintained his career at great personal sacrifice. He was proud that his career had been tied closely to the African American community, and he was even proud that the height of his fame found him living securely in the middle of a typical black neighborhood in Harlem—and not in a suburb or, above all, in exile.

From the start, Hughes's art was responsive to the needs and emotions of the black world even as he held to an inclusive view of America and the whole world. In his artistic experimentations, he increasingly looked to blacks, especially black musicians, for direction and inspiration. Much of his work, even his broad comedies, celebrates the dignity and humanity of black culture. In turn, while many other major black writers looked elsewhere for approval and endorsement, Hughes basked in the high regard of his primary audience, which was black.

His poetry, with its original jazz and blues influence and its prominent demotic element, almost certainly is the most influential written by any black in this century. Certain of his pieces, such as "The Negro Speaks of Rivers, "Mother to Son," and "Harlem," are virtual anthems of black America. He strove hard in the theater, and while his success was mixed, his record of productivity and innovation establishes him as one of the main voices of the black American stage. His "Simple" is probably the most memorable figure to emerge from black journalism. "The Negro Artist and the Racial Mountain" is timeless as a statement of the young black artist's constant dilemma, caught between the contending forces of black and white culture, and caught between class divisions within his or her own racial group. Arguably, Langston Hughes was black America's most original poet. Certainly he was black America's most representative writer and a significant figure in world literature in the twentieth century.

Selected Bibliography

PRIMARY WORKS

POETRY

The Weary Blues, (New York: Knopf, 1926).
Fine Clothes to the Jew, (New York: Knopf, 1927).
Montage of a Dream Deferred, (New York: Henry Holt, 1951).
Selected Poems, (New York: Knopf, 1959).
Ask Your Mama: Twelve Moods for Jazz, (New York: Knopf, 1961).

FICTION

Not Without Laughter, (New York: Knopf, 1930).
The Ways of White Folks, (New York: Knopf, 1934).

AUTOBIOGRAPHY

The Big Sea: An Autobiography, (New York: Knopf, 1940).

I Wonder as I Wander: An Autobiographical Journey, (New York: Rinehart, 1956).

JOURNALISM

The Best of Simple, (New York: Hill and Wang, 1961).

DRAMA

Five Plays of Langston Hughes, Edited by Webster Smalley (Bloomington: Indiana University Press, 1963).

ANTHOLOGIES

The Langston Hughes Reader, (New York: George Braziller, 1958).

Good Morning Revolution: Uncollected Social Protest Writings by Langston Hughes, Edited by Faith Berry. (Westport, Conn.: Lawrence Hill, 1973).

SECONDARY WORKS

BIOGRAPHICAL AND CRITICAL STUDIES

Barksdale, Richard, *Langston Hughes: The Poet and His Critics,* (Chicago: American Library Association, 1977).

Berry, Faith, *Langston Hughes: Before and Beyond Harlem,* (Westport, Conn.: Lawrence Hill, 1983).

Emanuel, James, A., *Langston Hughes,* (New York: Twayne, 1967).

Jemie, Onwuchekwa, *Langston Hughes: An Introduction to Poetry,* (New York: Columbia University Press, 1976).

Mullen, Edward J, *Langston Hughes in the Hispanic World and Haiti,* (Hamden, Conn.: Archon Books, 1977).

O'Daniel, Therman., ed., *Langston Hughes, Black Genius: A Critical Evaluation,* (New York: William Morrow, 1971).

Rampersad, Arnold, *The Life of Langston Hughes,* vol. 1, *1902–1941: I, Too, Sing America.* Vol. 2, 1941–67: *I Dream a World* (New York: Oxford University Press, 1986–1988).

Tracy, Steven C., *Langston Hughes & The Blues,* (Urbana: University of Illinois Press, 1988).

BIBLIOGRAPHIES

Dickinson, Donald C., *A Bio-Bibliography of Langston Hughes: 1902–1967,* 2nd ed., rev. (Hamden, Conn.: Archon Books, 1972).

Miller, R. Baxter, *Langston Hughes and Gwendolyn Brooks: A Reference Guide,* (Boston: G. K. Hall, 1978).

TED HUGHES
(b. 1930)

KEITH SAGAR

I

EDWARD JAMES HUGHES was born in Mytholmroyd, west Yorkshire, on 17 August 1930 in an end terrace house backing onto the canal. Beyond the canal was the main trunk road connecting the Yorkshire woolen towns and the Lancashire cotton towns, with its constant rumble of heavy lorries. Beyond that the railway. Then, rising almost sheer from the valley and seeming to fill half the sky, Scout Rock:

> This was the *memento mundi* over my birth: my spiritual midwife at the time and my godfather ever since—or one of my godfathers. From my first day, it watched. If it couldn't see me direct, a towering gloom over my pram, it watched me through a species of periscope: that is, by infiltrating the very light of my room with its particular shadow. ("The Rock")

It seemed to seal off everything to the south. Since to the north the land rose almost as steeply from immediately in front of the house up to the high bleak moors, "the narrow valley, with its flooring of cricket pitch, meadows, bowling greens, streets, railways and mills, seemed damp, dark and dissatisfied" and felt like a trap. Mount Zion chapel literally stooped over his cradle:

> Above the kitchen window, that uplifted
> mass was a deadfall—
> Darkening the sun of every day
> Right to the eleventh hour.

Later he was dragged there every Sunday in an atmosphere of terror:

> The convicting holy eyes, the convulsed
> Moses mouthings.
> Men in their prison-yard, at attention,
> Exercising their cowed, shaven souls
> Lips stretching saliva, eyes fixed like the
> eyes
> Of cockerels hung by legs,
> As the bottomless cry
> Beat itself numb again against Wesley's
> foundation stone.
> "Mount Zion"

The purpose of the place seemed to be simply to eradicate the joy of life, even if that meant eradicating life itself. Once the place was thrown into a state of battle-fury by a cricket singing from a crack in the wall:

> Long after I'd been smothered in bed
> I heard them
> Riving at the religious stonework
> With screwdrivers and chisels.

Now the cracks are widening and the only singing heard in many of the chapels is the singing of crickets.

What the boys preferred to do with their Sundays was to dig, Sunday after Sunday, with iron levers, even while the bells summoned them elsewhere, for the Ancient Briton, supposed, according to local folklore, to lie under a half-ton rock:

> We needed that waft from the cave
> The dawn dew-chilling of emergence,

The hunting grounds untouched all around
us.
"The Ancient Briton Lay Under His Rock"

That rock could not be shifted, nor what it hid, the buried life of England, the repressed needs of the human psyche, eradicated.

In the short story "Sunday," the boy has to endure a stifling, scrubbed Sunday morning, the churchgoing slopes spotless and harmless, forbidden grass in the Memorial Gardens, even the pavements "untouchably proper." The men wear "tight blue pin-stripe suits" and the boy his "detestable blue blazer." Sitting in chapel, the situation of greatest constraint he knows, he lets his imagination be taken over by the image of a wolf that "urged itself with all its strength through a land empty of everything but trees and snow." This wolf, the ghost of the last wolf killed in Britain, appears again and again in Hughes:

These feet, deprived,
Disdaining all that are caged, or storied, or
pictured,
Through and throughout the true world
search
For their vanished head, for the world

Vanished with the head, the teeth, the quick
eyes.
"February"

The wolf is that in the boy which refuses to be constrained, tamed, disciplined; like those Vikings ("the snow's stupefied anvils") who spent themselves in "beforehand revenge"

For the grueling relapse and prolongueur of
their blood
Into the iron arteries of Calvin.
"The Warriors of the North"

The boy lives for the afternoon, when his father has promised to take him to Top Wharf Pub to see for the first time Billy Red kill rats in his teeth like a terrier. The Cretans sacrificed a living bull to Dionysus by tearing it with their teeth. Billy Red degrades this archaic religious act, communion with the god by eating the god, to a Sunday afternoon secular entertainment for a bored denatured public in exchange for a free pint. But the boy is not yet denatured. The thought of that savagery, that unthinkable closeness of the human and the animal, reduces everything else in his consciousness to unreality. The story is autobiographical. There really was a Billy Red.

Animals were of tremendous importance to Hughes from the beginning, living representatives of another world, "the true world," "the world under the world." Yet the only relation that seemed possible between town boys and the surrounding wildlife was to catch and kill. The lesson was being driven home that animals were, by nature, victims. It was the natural order of things that any creature outside the ordered world of men should be killed. And if a human being chose to step outside that ordered world, he became fair game. The lesson was reinforced by a story his brother told him "of the tramp sleeping up there in the bracken, who stirred at an unlucky moment and was shot dead for a fox by an alert farmer and sent rolling down the slope" ("The Rock").

The life we have already killed off and got under, which now marauds destructively in the underworld of the unconscious, is the wolf. The life now making its last stand in remote fastnesses is adder and otter. The life we keep trying to kill, but which somehow survives, is stoat (see "Strawberry Hill") and fox. The landscape itself is a huge animal that seems to let itself be tamed. The network of walls is "harness on the long moors." But now these Pennine hills are breaking loose again, slowly shaking the mills, chapels, and houses to pieces as in a great sieve. That landscape was Hughes's inheritance. It gave him his earliest metaphors, which later gave him his distinctive way of looking at the world and of thinking about himself, and anchored his consciousness in the permanent realities. The geography of his childhood world became his map of heaven and hell; the interplay of the elements in that place gave him his sense of the creating and destroying powers of the world; the local animals became his theriomorphic archetypes. That landscape was imprinted on his soul and, in a sense, all his poems are about it—not only those poems like *Remains of Elmet,* where the magical transformation from description to metaphor to myth takes place before our eyes. Hughes ends that early essay "The Rock" (1963) with these words: "From there the return home was a descent into the pit, and after each visit I must have returned less and less of myself to the valley. This was where the division of body and soul, for me, began."

It was a great advantage to Hughes to have been born not in a city, where he might have allowed himself to be shut up in the little box of the exclusively human—

The country, to townies,
Is hardly more than nice,
A window-box, pretty
When the afternoon's empty;
When a visitor waits,
The window shuts.
(Kingsley Amis, "Here Is Where")

—nor in the country, where he might have become just another "nature" poet, but on the very frontier where the two were engaged in a "fight to the death." He suffered in childhood the crisis of our civilization in a very pure form. The experience forced him into a fiercely dualistic attitude to life that released the amazing energies of his first three books: *The Hawk in the Rain, Lupercal,* and *Wodwo.* The subsequent books have been a gradual healing of that split. From that deep early dualism Hughes has moved painfully but surely toward "a proper knowledge of the sacred wholeness of Nature, and a proper alignment of our behaviour within her laws."

When Hughes was seven, the family moved to Mexborough in south Yorkshire, where, like D. H. Lawrence before him in a similar area, he was obliged to lead a double life, one with the town boys, sons of miners and railwaymen, the other in his bolt-hole—a nearby farm or a private estate with woods and lakes. Mexborough Grammar School fostered his interest in poetry, and he was already writing it at fifteen, his favorite topics Zulus and the Wild West. In 1948 he won an Open Exhibition in English to Pembroke College, Cambridge, but before taking it up he did two years of national service as a ground wireless mechanic in the R.A.F. on an isolated three-man radio station in east Yorkshire, where he had "nothing to do but read and re-read Shakespeare and watch the grass grow." Reading English at Cambridge proved sterile, and Hughes changed to anthropology and archaeology. Cambridge gave him time to read a great deal, especially the ballads and Old English, and to learn by heart the *Collected Poems* of W. B. Yeats.

After graduating in 1954, Hughes worked briefly as a rose gardener, night watchman in a steel factory, zoo attendant, schoolteacher, and reader for J. Arthur Rank. In June 1956 he married Sylvia Plath, whom he met at Cambridge. From the spring of 1957 until the end of 1959 they lived in the United States. In 1957 Hughes's first book of poems, *The Hawk in the Rain,* was published.

II

"The Hawk in the Rain" stands appropriately at the threshold of the book, for it announces the major themes—man in relation to the animals, the earth, the weather, time and mortality—and expresses them with characteristic energy and hyperbole. The narrator feels like a "last-moment counting morsel in the earth's mouth" as he fights against mud (which sucks "with the habit of the dogged grave") for survival and identity,

. . . but the hawk

Effortlessly at height hangs his still eye.
His wings hold all creation in a weightless quiet
Steady as a hallucination in the streaming air.

The sea-drowner, any man buffeted and dying, must fix his eyes upon something stable, some "master-fulcrum of violence"—pole-star or hawk's eye. The hawk himself will, ultimately, fall and "mix his heart's blood with the mire of the land," but "in his own time," with acquiescence.

And is it possible for a man, without madness, to draw that stability, assurance, into himself; to come to terms with a world of horrors and miracles hardly to be told apart? When Charles Tomlinson reviewed an anthology of new verse, *New Lines,* in 1957, he said of the poets represented there: "They show a singular want of vital awareness of the continuum outside themselves, of the mystery embodied over against them in the created universe." That vital awareness is perhaps the outstanding characteristic of Hughes's work, which was not represented in *New Lines.*

The mystery takes many forms. There is no ignoring it when it takes the form of a gale:

> The tent of the hills drummed and strained
> its guyrope,
>
> The fields quivering, the skyline a grimace,
> At any second to bang and vanish with a
> flap:
> The wind flung a magpie away and a black-
> Back gull bent like an iron bar slowly. The
> house
>
> Rang like some fine green goblet in the note
> That any second would shatter it. Now deep
> In chairs, in front of the great fire, we grip
> Our hearts and cannot entertain book,
> thought,
>
> Or each other. We watch the fire blazing,
> And feel the roots of the house move, but
> sit on,
> Seeing the window tremble to come in,
> Hearing the stones cry out under the
> horizons.
> "Wind"

The window is the delicate membrane that separates us from the "wandering elementals" outside and within. The breaking of that membrane would be the end of books, thought, civilized human relationships, would be madness or miracle. To be at one with these forces, to answer unto death or life their terrible imperatives, is to be madman or martyr or genius, more or less than human. For the rest of us there are "moments of purity and crisis" that call in question the reality of our more ordinary lives.

Most of the time we can ignore the inaudible battle-shouts and death cries that are everywhere around us. But horrors not only nudge the root of the water lily. The largest horror continually presses against us. For that horror is simply the truth that kills everybody:

> The truth of a man is the doomed man in him or his dead body. . . . The murderous skeleton in the body of a girl, the dead men being eaten by dogs on the moonlit desert, the dead man behind the mirror, these items of circumstantial evidence are steadily out-arguing all his high spirits and hopefulness. (Introduction to the *Selected Poems of Keith Douglas,* 1964)

In "Six Young Men" Hughes adds his own evidence, a photograph of six young men on a Sunday jaunt, each as alive as any man you can confront "and shake by the hand, see hale, hear speak loud." Yet they all died within six months and forty years ago. One's own vivid life, for all its bulk and weight, is equally flimsy. The poet is no more alive than they were, than, here in this photograph, they still are, as, by a bilberried bank, a thick tree, a black wall "which are there yet and not changed," they listen to the waterfall that roars yet in that valley.

Some of Hughes's earlier poems are marred by overstatement, a forcing of rhetoric and imagery. We hardly ever find, in contrast to most of his contemporaries, any deficiency of force and sinew. There are occasionally echoes of other poets: of Yeats and Lawrence; of Gerard Manley Hopkins—"freer, firmer world found"; of Dylan Thomas—"the sargasso of a single sandgrain"; of T. S. Eliot at his worst (as in the choruses of *Murder in the Cathedral*):

. . . with eel and hyena and vulture,
With creepy-crawly and the root,
With the sea-worm, entering its birthright.
"Mayday in Holderness"

Such echoes are striking precisely because of their rarity in relation to the occasions inviting them.

For the most part we find a language characterized by its faithfulness to the facts, the evidence of the senses, shaped by a strong inspiration into images that, like those of Henry Moore, seem to have been waiting for aeons within the living rock, the living language, and now, released, will stand for aeons and could not be otherwise. It is a language spiced with great relish for experience, even when that experience is unpleasant or horrifying. Most distinctively it is a language able to cope with the biggest things; it can generate energies equal to the great primary energies of the world. In "Pennines in April" it is the thrust of the Pennines rolling like a huge sea from Yorkshire into Lancashire:

Those barrellings of strength are heaving
slowly and heave
To your feet and surf upwards
In a still, fiery air, hauling the imagination,
Carrying the larks upward

In "October Dawn" it is the irresistible coming of winter:

First a skin, delicately here
Restraining a ripple from the air;

Soon plate and rivet on pond and brook;
Then tons of chain and massive lock

To hold rivers. Then, sound by sight
Will Mammoth and Sabre-tooth celebrate

Reunion while a fist of cold
Squeezes the fire at the core of the world,

Squeezes the fire at the core of the heart,
And now it is about to start.

The power here does not reside in the Mammoths and Sabre-tooths so much as in that ruthless march of monosyllables, that relentless rhythm. Hughes's language at its best has the same qualities to which he has himself testified in "the true ballads," where we find "words that live in the same dimension as life at its most severe, words that cannot be outflanked by experience" (the *Guardian,* 14 May 1965).

To release such linguistic resources, Hughes had to get out from under "the terrible, suffocating, maternal octopus of ancient English poetic tradition," which meant getting back beyond Chaucer. Every educated modern English poet finds his head swimming with iambic[1] rhythms. English prose is still predominantly trochaic, true to its Germanic origins, but in verse the courtly, alien iamb drove the trochee and spondee underground, after William Langland's last stand, into folk songs, ballads, nursery rhymes, and dialect verse. In Hughes the old rhythms surface again (twenty-seven of the twenty-eight two-syllable words in the "The Hawk in the Rain" are trochees), and we see what we had lost in weight, sinew, and urgency in all those centuries of artifice and gentility.

III

Lupercal followed in March 1960. In *The Hawk in the Rain* there had been a relatively simplistic dualism—vitality versus death, mind versus body, ancient versus modern, and so on. In *Lupercal* there is a much higher degree of artifice and complexity, with occasional lapses into versified opinions, as in Auden.

The speedy recognition of a great talent at work in *The Hawk in the Rain* and *Lupercal,* not only as promise but as achievement, was not an unmixed blessing. For Hughes was labeled Nature Poet or, more patronizingly, Animal Poet. The titles alone contained horses, hawks, crows, thrushes, doves, a jaguar, a macaw, a fox, a bull, a mouse, a pig, an

1. The iamb is a two-syllable verse foot (short-long) (e.g., forget); the trochee, a two-syllable verse foot (long-short) (e.g., music).

otter, a bullfrog, and a pike. The poems featured many other animals, most of them predatory. "Hughes is very fine, but what will he do when he runs out of animals?" was a comment that did not look as silly at the time as it does now. If we look a little more closely at these volumes, we see that the majority of the poems are not about animals; that many of the references to animals are metaphorical; and that even those poems which are about animals are usually also about human experiences, for which the animals serve as analogues.

In nearly all his poems Hughes strives to find metaphors for his own nature. And his own nature is of peculiar general interest not because it is unusual, but because it embodies in an unusually intense, stark form the most typical stresses and contradictions of human nature and of nature itself, as Shakespeare's did. The poems are bulletins from the battleground within.

In the early poems the metaphors Hughes found were so often animals because animals live out in such naked extremity the primary struggles, particularly that between vitality and death. They roar or bellow the evidence that men wrap in sophistry or turn a blind eye to. Their reality seems less questionable than ours. The "attent sleek thrushes on the lawn" are terrifying not for their ravening of writhing things, but for the too streamlined efficiency with which they pursue their unwavering purpose—the efficiency of a bullet (whose one path is direct through the bones of the living). Hughes stands in awe of animals. Their efficiency is too horribly automatic, like the shark's mouth

> That hungers down the blood-smell even to
> a leak of its own
> Side and devouring of itself.
> "Thrushes"

What a man does neither defines nor deifies him, nor can he, unless he is that hardly human thing, a genius, crash straight through doubts, obstructions, temptations, sin, guilt, and despair:

> how loud and above what
> Furious spaces of fire do the distracting
> devils
> Orgy and hosannah, under what wilderness
> Of black silent waters weep.
> "Thrushes"

Beyond the little area lit by his consciousness, his desk lamp, is a vast darkness peopled by demons. The distracting devils that sin, praise, or despair are those suppressed powers within any man which will not let him be satisfied with the heroisms he invents at his desk, nor with any enclosed self-worshiping activity. A man totally given over to those powers, genius or hero, is a madman or an automaton. A man totally cut off from them denies, trivializes, or perverts the life that is in him, drops out of the divine circuit from which alone come the energies to destroy or create.

The gulf between man and animal is also the gulf between civilized man and his animal self, which is also his angelic or demonic self—the only self capable of recognizing a divinity in the darkness and being at one with it. It is the doom of all animals to live according to one categorical imperative. Man's doom is different: the doom of consciousness and choice, the burden precisely of not knowing what to do, of perpetually questioning a deaf-and-dumb world and peering into the darkness for a sign.

IV

After *Lupercal* was published, Ted Hughes and his wife returned to England. Their children, Frieda and Nicholas, were born in 1960 and 1962. Hughes and Plath entered upon a phase of intensely productive creative partnership until their separation in 1962. At least a third of the poems in *Recklings* and in *Wodwo* were written then; so were the stories and the play in *Wodwo* and other stories and plays (the BBC broadcast "The House of Aries" in 1960, "Difficulties of a Bridegroom" in 1962, and "Dogs" in 1963), and it was at this time that Hughes began to write regularly for children and to review regularly in the *New Statesman* and the *Listener.*

Hughes's first three books of verse for children seem to me undistinguished (though he added some better poems to later editions of *Meet My Folks!,* 1961). *How the Whale Became* (1963), Hughes's first prose work for children, is another matter. The stories are, in a sense, very traditional, taking their place in the tradition that runs from Aesop's *Fables* to Rudyard Kipling's *Just So Stories.* But they are also thoroughly original and could only have been written by a poet. The prose is simple but distinguished. The stories are witty but grounded, despite the free inventiveness, in reality—this owl cleans the blood from his beak. Some of them are moving—this elephant saves all the creatures of the forest, then disappears quietly into the depths. "We would make him our king," they say, "if we could get him to wear a crown." And some are imagined at the same depth as the adult poems—this bee has been made out of diamond-dust moistened by a demon's tears: "The sadness of the demon's tears was always in him. It was part of him. It was what flowed in his veins." The bee must steep himself in beauty and gather all its sweetness until it oozes from him to counteract that paralyzing sadness.

The Iron Man (1968) is another fine story, or rather three stories. In the first, the iron man falls over a cliff and is smashed to pieces on the rocks below. The parts laboriously put themselves together again, and the iron man, lacking only an ear stolen by gulls, walks into the sea. The story is vivid and eerie. It has the absolute authenticity of the inexplicable. *The Return of the Iron Man* is more conventional and straightforward. People try to kill him because he is eating all their machines. He is unkillable. Then they realize that they can use him to get rid of all the scrap metal and old cars.

The third story has the iron man no longer a threat to the human world, but its champion in single combat against a terrible space-monster the size of Australia. (This is not bedtime reading.) The monster is a star-spirit drawn down by "the battling shouts and the war-cries of the earth" to join in. The iron man lies on a grid over a great fire until he becomes white hot, then challenges the monster to do the equivalent by lying on the sun. Twice they compete and suffer and survive. At the third challenge, the scorched monster gives in, flies back into space and sings "a strange soft music that seemed to fill the whole of space, a deep weird singing, like millions of voices singing together," and this music brings peace to the world. The theme has much in common with Hughes's latest work. The iron man is the hero of myth who voluntarily undergoes the most terrible trials, agonies, purification, and, having given everything, miraculously redeems the world.

Even finer than his stories are Hughes's verse plays, written for radio, but ideal for school and children's theater productions. They will soon become classics of the repertory. They are mainly reworkings of myths and folktales. In each of them Hughes has something urgent to say, and the verse, at its best, is as good as anything he has done for adults:

> Once more we grew blisters inside our
>   boots,
> Stumbling over the wastelands of this
>   world.
> We came to the mountains, the blue tepees
>   of the gods.
> I am a simple man, I believe in gods.
> We climbed, where wild goats leaned out
> Over gulfs full of the whisper of torrents
> And gunfire of landslides. We climbed
> Where eagles slid from us and hung out
> Over a five-mile drop into the forest.
> We climbed. We climbed till our brains
>   altered
> And we could see mountains upside-down
> On top of the mountains.
>   (*The Tiger's Bones*)

The Tiger's Bones is a satire on the modern scientific mentality. The Master can build a telescope to look death in the face, factories and mental hospitals and crematoria, but he cannot make the dead live or create grass. When he does at last learn to bring to life a dead tiger with a hypodermic, the tiger eats him. In *Beauty and the Beast,* another play in *The Coming of the Kings* (1971), Hughes brings out, with no heavy-handedness, the psychological implications already there in the original story.

But the best of these plays is not in *The Coming of the Kings.* It is a play called *Orpheus,* broadcast in January 1971. The music Orpheus plays, pop music, is an expression of his happiness in the love of Eurydice. He ignores the warning voice telling him that every song must be paid for. Eurydice dies and he can no longer play. He goes to the underworld after her and there begins to play another kind of music (Hughes suggests Handel, Bach, Vivaldi, or earlier composers) that expresses his love of life, but also his recognition of death. He returns with the soul of Eurydice and refuses to play ever again the music of life and happiness only, which accumulates so many debts to reality. As the play ends, he plays his new music:

> The trees did not dance. But the trees listened.
> The music was not the music of dancing
> But of growing and withering
> Of the root in the earth and the leaf in the light,
> The music of birth and of death.
> And the stones did not dance. But the stones listened.
> The music was not the music of happiness
> But of everlasting, and the wearing away of the hills,
> The music of the stillness of stones,
> Of stones under frost, and stones under rain, and stones in the sun,
> The music of the sea-bed drinking at the stones of the hills.
> The music of the floating weight of the earth.
> And the bears in their forest-holes
> Heard the music of bears in their forest-holes
> The music of bones in the starlight
> The music of many a valley trodden by bears,
> The music of bears listening on the earth for bears.
> And the deer on the high hills heard the crying of wolves
> And the salmon in the deep pools heard the whisper of the snows
> And the traveller on the road
> Heard the music of love coming and love going
> And love lost forever,
> The music of birth and of death.
> The music of the earth, swaddled in heaven, kissed by its cloud and watched by its ray.
> And the ears that heard it were also of leaf and of stone.
> The faces that listened were flesh of cliff and of river.
> The hands that played it were fingers of snakes and a tangle of flowers.

This is for children at an age when they need to know what maturity means and what tragedy means, and it is not only for children.

Season Songs (1975) has so much to offer to adult readers that I shall deal with it later as a book for all ages. *Poetry in the Making* (1967) is the best book I know about the writing (and reading) of poetry in schools. It is about poetry as a natural and common activity; about the fun, but also the seriousness, the centrality, of this activity: "not 'How to write' but 'How to try to say what you really mean'—which is part of the search for self-knowledge and perhaps, in one form or another, grace." Writing poetry is not merely self-expression. The poem has a life of its own and a wisdom of its own that we must learn. To write a poem is to capture a wild animal (as in Hughes's first animal poem, "The Thought-Fox"):

> The special kind of excitement, the slightly mesmerized and quite involuntary concentration with which you make out the stirrings of a new poem in your mind, then the outline, the mass and colour and clean final form of it, the unique living reality of it in the midst of the general lifelessness, all that is too familiar to mistake. This is hunting and the poem is a new species of creature, a new specimen of the life outside your own.

The poem is also seen as a series of events, or a lens, or a raid on the inarticulate; and the best way to release the single spirit that must move through the parts is by "headlong, concentrated improvisation," "an all-out flowing exertion"—against the clock. One's only reservation is that Hughes has nothing whatever to say about technique; the poetry he wishes to encourage is purely inspirational. Perhaps it is not worth bothering with any other sort. But is there not something to be done with the inspired verse afterwards? We see the dangers in Hughes's own practice in *The Earth Owl* (1963). However, what was wanted was a book that would help teachers to present the imagination of a pupil with opportunities, not restraints, with confidence and a natural motive for writing, so that "something of our common genius will begin to put a word in." His brief was to aim at ten- to fourteen-year-olds. In fact the upper age limit could be extended indefinitely, at least to the undergraduate level, and the book constitutes an invaluable commentary on Hughes's own method.

V

With the separation from Sylvia Plath in 1962 and her suicide the following year, Ted Hughes seems to have entered a fallow, if not sterile, period of two or three years during which he published only a handful of poems. Then, in a rush, came *Recklings* and *The Burning of the Brothel* in 1966 and *Wodwo* and *Scapegoats and Rabies* in 1967.

A note at the beginning of *Wodwo* tells us that the poems, stories, and play are to be read as constituting "a single adventure." It is perhaps easier to recognize the unifying theme by looking first at the stories and the play.

The earliest story in *Wodwo,* "The Rain Horse," is an exercise in the Lawrence manner, taking the opening from "A Modern Lover" and the encounter with the horse from *The Rainbow.* Nevertheless it is distinctively Hughes and shares its structure with two of the other stories, "Sunday" and "The Harvesting." First there is the evocation of a highly realistic scene, vivid and immediate. Then, into this reality erupts another, the nightmare, the reality of the nonhuman world beyond houses and Sundays and pinstripe suits and consciousness and time, a reality of crisis and instinct and violence in which the human protagonist is diminished and defenseless. He panics as though the monstrous horned God had revealed himself. In "Sunday" the screeching of the rats has the same effect as in the poem "Song of the Rat," "supplanting every human brain inside its skull with a rat body that knots and unknots." In "The Harvesting" the human mind is supplanted by sunstroke and enters the mind of a hunted hare in extremity. In "The Wound," the mind of a soldier has been supplanted by a bullet. As he staggers nine miles through thick mud, nightmarish horrors enter the hole in his head. In "Snow" the protagonist's mind has been supplanted from all he is and knows by God-knows-what disaster. And in each case the horror is more vivid and more real that the reality it supplants.

The man in "The Rain Horse" insists on bringing his rational intelligence to bear, trying to account for the horse's malice, predict its movements and outwit it, while the horse obviously inhabits a reality not subject to such reasoning: "Its whinnying snort and the spattering whack of its hooves seemed to be actually inside his head." He is running from and fighting against something he carries within him, from which he can escape only by damaging his heart and cutting out an important part of his brain. In a sense he has already done that, and this is what provokes these powers to such malevolence against him. He is tame. He has taken it for granted that horses are tame, either working or making their contribution to the picturesque landscape. This landscape refuses to gratify him by being picturesque. It is a part of his own life that he has denied which rears against him.

In "Snow" we have an even clearer case of a man attempting to interpret rationally a world for which there can be no rational explanation. His thinking proceeds with rigorous logic grounded in the merest hypotheses. He is dead or mad, certainly doomed. He deduces his own existence from his consciousness. He thinks of himself as commendably openminded, but, with Cartesian failure of nerve, his doubts stop there, at an article of faith he can no more dispense with than he can dispense with his absurd chair. The rest of his universe is made up entirely of evidence to the contrary.

Most of the poems are also about the risk of exposure to the other. When a man takes that risk,

> A leaf's otherness,
> Te whaled monstered sea-bottom, eagled
> peaks
> And stars that hang over hurtling
> endlessness,
> With manslaughtering shocks
> Are let in on his sense:
> So many a one has dared to be struck dead
> Peeping through his fingers at the world's
> ends,
> Or at an ant's head.
> "Egg-Head"

The risk is of losing the unreal stability of prudence and complacency, of losing self-assurance and sanity under the shock, of yielding up one's humanity to the staring angels, the huge and beautiful powers of the world, who, at night, become giant ghost crabs:

> All night, around us or through us,
> They stalk each other, they fasten on to
> each other,
> They mount each other, they tear each
> other to pieces,
> They utterly exhaust each other.
> They are the powers of this world.. . .
> They are God's only toys.
> "Ghost-Crabs"

And the man who takes these risks, what will he be like? What will he do? In earlier poems Hughes had offered us heroes who are "huge chested braggarts," "their chariot wheels tumbling the necks of screams," "restuffing their deaf fame with fresh sacks-full of heads." More often now the Hughes hero is the humble Man Seeking Experience, the poet who looks at the world without arrogance, recognizes it as neither bad variant nor tryout, but what we are stuck with, sees the absence of clear signs and certainties (except for the mass of evidence of his own fragility), sees dangers and horrors, beauties and miracles in the way (though not the difference between them), and then, alert in all his faculties, moves forward to confront the world.

In *Sir Gawain and the Green Knight,*[2] the hero in his journey through the Wirral fights with, among other creatures of that remote region, wodwos. Etymologically the word simply means "wooddwellers." The notes to the poem give "trolls." The *Oxford English Dictionary* gives "wild men of the woods." This uncertainty of status—man or beast or monster or goblin—is precisely what attracted Hughes. In "Wodwo," the speaker is a wodwo finding himself at large in a world inhabited by other creatures whose relation to himself he does not in the least understand, without roots ("dropped out of nothing casually"), not knowing why his nose leads him to water or his hands pick bark off a rotten stump, not knowing who he is or what he is doing there, supposing himself to be the exact center of "all this" and seeking to discover the circumference of himself. "Very queer," he concludes, "but I'll go on looking."

Hughes is a wodwo in all his poems, asking these same questions of the world in which he finds himself, looking at that world and its creatures to discover where he ends and the other begins, and what relation exists between "the endless without-world of the other" and the "other" within—"the pitch dark where the animal runs." If he can come to terms with the facts of life and the fact of death, he will become the still center within the violence. He can know "the redeemed life of joy" in normal daily experience, when,

2. An anonymous fourteenth-century poem much admired by Hughes.

with an unspectacular access of grace, the elements of a scene (human, animal, domestic, rural, cosmic) suddenly cohere and reveal a plenitude. Hughes, with supreme delicacy of utterance, captures it:

> A cool small evening shrunk to a dog bark
> and the clank of a bucket—
> And you listening.
> A spider's web, tense for the dew's touch.
> A pail lifted, still and brimming—mirror
> To tempt a first star to a tremor.
>
> Cows are going home in the lane there,
> looping the hedges with their warm
> wreaths of breath—
> A dark river of blood, many boulders,
> Balancing unspilled milk.
>
> "Moon!" You cry suddenly, "Moon! Moon!"
>
> The moon has stepped back like an artist
> gazing amazed at a work
> That points at him amazed.
> "Full Moon and Little Frieda"

The fragility and transience of that moment celebrated in "Full Moon and Little Frieda" is more evident in the original version of the poem (published in the *Atlantic Monthly,* December 1963), which has several additional lines and ends:

> Any minute a bat will fly out of a cat's ear.

The eeriness of that line calls in question the boulderlike solidity of the cows and the reality of the familiar sights and sounds—dog bark and clank of bucket. Nor is the poem at all typical of *Wodwo* as a whole.

It now seems in retrospect that it ought to have been possible, from *Wodwo,* to predict the way Hughes was going. There was the uncompromisingly bleak vision of poems like "Pibroch," the savage humor of "The Warriors of the North"; there were poems inhabiting the no-man's-land between the human and the animal ("Wodwo") and between the natural and the supernatural ("Ghost Crabs"). Hughes showed in *Wodwo* that he had learned from Wilfred Owen and Keith Douglas how to present the evidence, from Emily Dickinson how to lighten its oppressiveness with a gnomic wit, and from Vasco Popa, a Yugoslav poet, how to evade the limitations of realism by the creation of miniature myths out of (in Popa's case) two bones or a quartz pebble:

> It is in this favourite device of his, the little fable of visionary anecdote, that we see most clearly his shift from literary surrealism to the far older and deeper thing, the surrealism of folklore. . . . Folktale surrealism . . . is always urgently connected with the business of trying to manage practical difficulties so great that they have forced the sufferer temporarily out of the dimension of coherent reality into that depth of imagination where understanding has its roots and stores its X-rays. (Introduction to *Selected Poems* of Popa, 1969)

What he had learned from Sylvia Plath is material for an essay in itself, but certainly his ability to anatomize pain under a fierce white light. He taught her to open herself fully to whatever powers might choose to speak through her.

Several poems in *Wodwo* clearly announce the coming of Hughes's later archetypal figure, Crow. Wodwo asks:

> . . . Why do I find
> this frog so interesting as I inspect its most
> secret
> interior and make it my own?
> "Wodwo"

Crow

> . . . plucked grass-heads and gazed into them
> Waiting for first instructions.
> He studied a stone from the stream.
> He found a dead mole and slowly he took it
> apart
> Then stared at the gobbets, feeling helpless.
> He walked, he walked
> Letting the translucent starry spaces
> Blow in his ear cluelessly.
> "Crow Hears Fate Knock on the Door"

In "Logos," "Reveille," and "Theology" all the main characters of *Crow* (1970) except Crow himself are assembled: God, Adam, Eve, and the Serpent. And all the conditions for his annunciation, the conviction that this cannot be the world God sought to create, perhaps not even the world he did create ("this is the dark intestine"), that there must be something outside God, prior to him, unimpressionable, inimical to his purposes, perhaps itself the creator of God or a precondition of his existence, or his necessary incarnation:

> Creation convulses in nightmare. And
> awaking
> Suddenly tastes the nightmare moving
> Still in its mouth
> And spits it kicking out, with a swinish
> cry—
> which is God's first cry.
>
> . . .
>
> God is a good fellow, but His mother's
> against Him.
> "Logos"

The nightmare may be the mother of God. It is certainly the mother of Crow.

VI

In 1957 Ted Hughes met the American sculptor, engraver, and publisher Leonard Baskin. Baskin is obsessed by crows, which he engraves with disturbingly anthropoid characteristics. A later invitation from Baskin to Hughes to write a few little poems to accompany his engravings was the cause of the first Crow poems. Up to 1963 Hughes had never written about crows, though he was familiar with the prominent and rather grim part they play in so much of the world's folklore.

Why did Hughes choose a crow as his protagonist? The prevalence of ravens and crows in folklore derives largely from the real bird's characteristics. The crow is the most intelligent of birds, the most widely distributed (being common on every continent), and the most omnivorous ("no carrion will kill a crow"). They are, of course, black all over, solitary, almost indestructible, and the largest and least musical of songbirds. It is to be expected that the songs of the crow will be harsh and grating. He kills a little himself, and, as carrion eater, is dependent on the killing of others and first on the scene at many disasters.

Eskimo legend tells that in the beginning the raven was the only creature and the world was, like him, black. Then came the owl, and the world became white like him, with the whiteness of unending snow. Hughes's mythology of Crow is deeply rooted in such legends. The whole myth is to be told as an epic folktale in prose, with songs by and about Crow interspersed.

> God, having created the world, has a recurring nightmare. A huge hand comes from deep space, takes him by the throat, half-throttles him, drags him through space, ploughs the earth with him then throws him back into heaven in a cold sweat. Meanwhile man sits at the gates of heaven waiting for God to grant him an audience. He has come to ask God to take life back. God is furious and sends him packing. The nightmare appears to be independent of the creation, and God cannot understand it. The nightmare is full of mockery of the creation, especially of man. God challenges the nightmare to do better. This is just what the nightmare has been waiting for. It plunges down into matter and creates Crow. God tests Crow by putting him through a series of trials and ordeals which sometimes result in Crow being dismembered, transformed or obliterated, but Crow survives them all, little changed. Meanwhile Crow interferes in God's activities, sometimes trying to learn or help, sometimes in mischief, sometimes in open rebellion. It is, perhaps, his ambition to become a man, but he never quite makes it. (K. Sagar, *The Art of Ted Hughes,* 1975, p. 106)

His efforts to understand the world in which he finds himself bring him into contact with the products of human culture, with religion and literature and science, all of which seem to him to have got it all wrong, according to what he has seen of the world, so he rearranges the traditional elements in a way which seems to him more in accordance with the facts, in "Apple Tragedy" and "Song for a Phallus," for example. Also he tries his hand at original composition with notes for some little plays, always with the same two characters.

He becomes curious about his own nature and purpose, and wonders who could have created him. He finds himself embarked on a quest for this creator. His adventures bring him into contact with various women and female monsters. Because they are ugly, often horrific, he fights them, or evades them, or in some way mismanages the situation, not realizing that each time he is meeting his own mother, his intended bride. He comes to a river. Beside it sits a gigantic horrible female, an ogress, who will not let him cross unless he carries her on his back. As they cross, she gets heavier and heavier, driving Crow into the river-bed until the water is up to his mouth. Then she asks him a question to which he must sing the right answer, quickly. The questions recapitulate the various mistaken encounters he has had with her in the past; that is, they are all, in some sense, questions about love. He knows little about it, and desperately tries the principle of permutation, singing every answer he can think of until one satisfies her, and her weight decreases again. This happens seven times before they reach the other side. "Lovesong" is one of Crow's answers to the question: "Who paid most, him or her?." "The Lovepet" is an answer to the question: "Was it an animal? Was it a bird? Was it an insect? Was it a fish?" The right answer to the question: "Who gives most, him or her?" is the lovely poem "Bride and groom lie hidden for three days," also in *Cave Birds.* (K. Sagar, rev. ed., 1978, p. 235)

Much misinterpretation of *Crow* has resulted from the failure of critics to read the jacket note, which explains that *Crow* contains only a selection of poems from the earlier part of this epic, the part that deals largely with Crow's mistakes and failures and dismemberments; but he is on the way toward an eventual successful outcome of his quest—his reconstitution and marriage in the Happy Land.

What first strikes the reader of *Crow* is the sheer rhetorical force and vitality. There are many different kinds of poems here. The language and poetic technique are more varied than before. In the best poems there is no striving for local effects; they are direct and spare, colloquial. The verse is less regular, more mimetic. And there is much more use of the oldest poetic devices—repetitions and refrains, parallelism, catalogs and catechisms, incantations and invocations. These devices are so powerful in Hughes's hands that they have scared many reviewers into defensive postures. They accuse Hughes of using these facile devices as a substitute for a fully controlled, rational ordering. It is the rational ordering that would be facile in comparison with the discipline needed to free the imagination from its constraints. Hughes employs these devices precisely to avoid a fully controlled, rational ordering, to free his imagination, stimulate it to come up from the depths and yield its secrets. Some of the finest poems in *Crow* are inexplicable, visionary, magical, but carry their own unquestionable authenticity, like some of the inexplicable poems or passages in Yeats and Eliot; and like them they will take root in us and work upon us unseen.

Hughes's symbols have no allegorical meanings and are not literary. Insofar as they have antecedents, they are in totemism, folklore, and the archetypes of Jungian psychology. They do not "mean" anything; they embody something, and perhaps magically invoke the powers they make manifest. Although inexplicable, they are more objective and more potent than symbolism that is invented for the purpose or drawn from some literary tradition. Some of Hughes's images are invented, but without a knowledge of anthropology and folklore as extensive as his own, it is impossible to say which. They are all drawn from the same depths of consciousness and racial experience. The myth controls the energies they release.

Crow has something of the wodwo in him—an embryonic conscience. He asks bigger questions than the wodwo and has all the evidence spread before him. That evidence seems to demonstrate conclusively that the world is uninhabitable by humans, habitable by Crow only because he is less than human, without spiritual aspiration, without a sense of sin, and specialized for survival.

What Hughes is seeking to communicate, centrally, is a vision of the wrongness of things, of humanity seeking to survive and live meaningfully in conditions for which it is patently unfitted. The survival is of the fittest to survive, of those who are able and willing to accept these conditions, since they are permanent, ingrained, part of the very fiber of the material world. But is survival on these terms worth the price? And is the material world the only world? Is it even real? In one of the earliest poems, "A Kill," the birth of Crow (or every man) is described as a death, or at least a loss of consciousness, life as a "dream flash." The title of the previous poem, "Examination at the Womb Door," indicates that Hughes wanted to keep open in these poems the possibility that the Buddhists may be right in believing that life is an illusion and the only worthy purpose in it is to learn to recognize it as such, to make oneself spiritually independent of it and thereby acquire the discipline that, after death, will close the womb-door and avoid further incarnation in a world that belongs entirely to death.

In some of the poems Crow is simply a witness of "the hallucination of the horror":

He saw this shoe, with no sole, rain-sodden,
Lying on a moor.
And there was this garbage can, bottom
  rusted away,
A playing place for the wind, in a waste of
  puddles.

There was this coat, in the dark cupboard,
  in the silent room, in the silent house.
There was this face, smoking its cigarette
  between the dusk window and the fire's
  embers.

Near the face, this hand, motionless.

Near the hand, this cup.

Crow blinked. He blinked. Nothing faded.

He stared at the evidence.

I choose to quote this poem, "Crow Alights," rather than several others in which Crow also stares at evidence, as an example of what Hughes can do with understatement. Here is no blood, violence, melodrama. Yet the evidence is just as conclusive, and perhaps more moving in its simplicity.

Sometimes Crow experiences the first stirrings of compassion:

He grasped he was on earth.
          He knew he grasped
Something fleeting
Of the sea's ogreish outcry and convulsion.
He knew he was the wrong listener
  unwanted
To understand or help—

His utmost gaping of brain in his tiny skull
Was just enough to wonder, about the sea,

What could be hurting so much?
  "Crow on the Beach"

He finds himself an unwilling participant in the horror:

Crow thought "Alas
Alas ought I
To stop eating
And try to become the light?"

But his eye saw a grub. And his head,
  trapsprung, stabbed.
  "Crow Tyrannosaurus"

Crow is Everyman who will not acknowledge that everything he most hates and fears—the Black Beast—is within himself. Crow's world is unredeemable. God made the Redeemer as a defeatist act of submission to Crow:

When God went off in despair
Crow stropped his beak and started in on
  the two thieves.
  "Crow's Song of Himself"

Christianity, for Hughes, is "just another provisional myth of man's relationship with the creator." Its inadequacies, as such, give rise to much of the comedy of *Crow,* where the God of Genesis figures as something of a well-meaning booby. "Apple Tragedy," for example, is also apple farce. Hughes here interprets the connection between the apple and original sin as cider, invented by God, drunk by Adam, Eve, and the serpent, and responsible for all their subsequent transgression. In "A Childish Prank," God, having created Adam and Eve, is beaten by the problem of how to invest them with any kind of purpose or stimulate them to any activity. In a Talmudic version of the creation, God, having made man and woman of the clay of the earth, tries for hundreds of years to lure into these inert bodies the free souls that fly through space. But the souls value their liberty and will be neither cajoled nor tricked into bodies. Crow steps in and invents sexuality, which has kept the race in perpetual motion ever since. An even more serious intervention occurs in "Crow Blacker than Ever":

> When God, disgusted with man,
> Turned towards heaven,
> And man, disgusted with God,
> Turned towards Eve,
> Things looked like falling apart.
>
> But Crow   Crow
> Crow nailed them together,
> Nailing Heaven and earth together-
>
> So man cried, but with God's voice.
> And God bled, but with man's blood.
>
> Then heaven and earth creaked at the joint
> Which became gangrenous and stank—
> A horror beyond redemption.

Here is an example of the ease with which Hughes can move from comedy to deepest seriousness, of how Crow's wildly improbable escapades can dramatize the biggest theological issues. The incongruity is already there in the gap between the world as it is and the world as a loving God must have intended it. What has this earth to do with that heaven, that men must strain to become light and God be nailed to a cross in a vain attempt to teach man to pronounce the word "love"?

One of the earliest essays on Hughes was called "The Violence of Ted Hughes"; many subsequent ones would have used the same title had it not been preempted. It has become axiomatic that Hughes is violent, both in style and subject matter, that violence is his stock in trade, that he admires violence. If any critic had stopped to ask seriously *why* Hughes writes obsessively about violence, especially in *Crow,* he would have had to recognize that Hughes does so because he lacks the thick skin, the layer of insulation or complacency, which enables most of us to ignore it, just as we turn a blind eye to such other uncomfortable and not quite respectable (certainly uncivilized) realities as birth and death. Hughes does not *invent* the violence in his poems, any more than he invents the newspaper headlines that we try not to register as we search for the arts and sports pages. Crow registers everything, puts himself to school to reality. He sees that a "mishmash of scripture and physics" has resulted in recurring wars that have come to be accepted as inevitable, normal:

> And when the smoke cleared it became
>   clear
> This had happened too often before
> And was going to happen too often in future
> And happened too easily
> Bones were too like lath and twigs
> Blood was too like water
> Cries were too like silence
> The most terrible grimaces too like
>   footprints in mud
> And shooting somebody through the midriff
> Was too like striking a match
> Too like potting a snooker ball
> Too like tearing up a bill
> Blasting the whole world to bits
> Was too like slamming a door
> Too like dropping in a chair
> Exhausted with rage
> Too like being blown to bits yourself
> Which happened too easily

> With too like no consequences.
> "Crow's Account of the Battle"

The issue of *Newsweek* in which *Crow* was reviewed carried on the front cover a photograph of Lieutenant Calley and the bodies of a few of his victims. Inside, a Gallup poll showed that 50 percent of those questioned thought that such incidents were common. Seventy-nine percent disapproved of the verdict against Calley, 20 percent because they thought that what had happened at My Lai was not a crime. Even Crow, the hard-bitten trap-sprung survivor, cannot evade the response of outrage or compassion; he is not yet that civilized.

Ted Hughes, as a poet, is very like the man in "Criminal Ballad." He is automatically tuned in to the suffering to which the rest of us are automatically deafened and blinded, because it is happening somewhere else and to someone else:

> And when he walked in his garden and saw his children
> Bouncing among the dogs and balls
> He could not hear their silly songs and the barking
> For machine guns
> And a screaming and laughing in the cell
> Which had got tangled in the air with his hearing
> And he could not turn towards the house
> Because the woman of complete pain rolling in flame
> Was calling to him all the time
> From the empty goldfish pond

Not at all by choice, he comprehends all the suffering of the universe, animal and human, as his own. It is the burden of the tragic artist. Hughes is not open to the charge of morbidity, for there is always the desperate hope that "having come so far, and against such odds," something might yet be won from the struggle.

Hughes is interested in reform and palliation like any other thinking and feeling person, and this interest occasionally enters his poetry, but it is not at the heart of it. For Hughes cannot take quite seriously any attitude to experience that takes for granted the continuance of our civilization with very much its present structure and values, the continuance of the race, or even the reality of the physical universe. To assume these things is to ignore or willfully misread the evidence.

> Popa, and several other writers one can think of, have in a way cut their losses and cut the whole hopelessness of that civilization off, have somehow managed to invest their hopes in something deeper than what you lose if civilization disappears completely, and in a way it's obviously a pervasive and deep feeling that civilization has now disappeared completely. If it's still here, it's still here by grace of pure inertia and chance, and if the whole thing has essentially vanished, one had better have one's spirit invested in something that Will not vanish. And this is a shifting of your foundation to completely new Holy Ground, a new divinity, one that won't be under the rubble when the churches collapse. (*London Magazine,* January 1971)

Crow is part of Hughes's heroic search, on behalf of us all, for that Holy Ground.

Hughes published *Crow* in this incomplete form because he could not finish his epic, could see no way forward for Crow. He thought he had perhaps exhausted the possibilities of Crow; but Crow kept popping up, and a few years later, Hughes was able to return to *Crow* and continue it. It still remains to be completed.

VII

In 1971 Hughes accompanied Peter Brook and his International Centre for Theater Research to Iran for the Fifth Shiraz Festival. There he wrote *Orghast,* which is the name both of the play and of the invented language in which it is written. *Orghast* was based on several myths and folk tales, but at the center was the story of Prometheus. At the same time Hughes wrote a sequence of little poems about Prometheus, in English, twenty-one of which were collected in *Prometheus on His Crag* (1973) and revised in *Moortown* (1979).

Prometheus is immortal but shares with man the ability to suffer pain. As punishment for stealing fire from heaven to give to men (thus launching them on the path toward a godless technological civilization), Zeus has Prometheus nailed to a rock at the world's edge. Every day a vulture comes out of the sun to feed on his liver, which grows again overnight. Most of the poems are internal monologues in which Prometheus tries to get beyond his pain and anger to an understanding of his situation, of the god who has condemned him to it, of the vulture, and of his fellow-sufferer Io, a maiden turned by Zeus into a heifer perpetually pursued by a hornet. Prometheus' punishment is that he cannot move; Io's that she cannot rest.

Prometheus is not like the Contender in *Crow,* rigidly committed to a senseless trial of strength he can never win. He retains through all his agony a faith that there is some key, some secret, which would enable him to understand the situation and thereby come to terms with it. This faith develops through daily refinements of suffering and is focused on the vulture:

> It knew what it was doing
>
> It went on doing it
> Swallowing not only his liver
> But managing also to digest its guilt
>
> And hang itself again just under the sun
> Like a heavenly weighing scales
> Balancing the gift of life
>
> And the cost of the gift
> Without a tremor—
> As if both were nothing.
> (poem 10)

Prometheus, the prototype of the human condition, also hangs weighing the cost, but for a long time he can find nothing to set against its weight, the weight of the whole earth, but a butterfly in a dream. The first real clue comes, in poem 18, from a lizard

> Listening near the ear of Prometheus,
> Whispering—at his each in-rip of breath,
> Even as the vulture buried its head—
>
> "Lucky, you are so lucky to be human!"

All Prometheus has that the lizard has not is consciousness, which gives him the possibility of understanding the situation, and thereby converting the pain into the payment, redeeming mankind not by mere cunning and prescience but by the deepest knowledge that can be won only from suffering. In poem 20 Hughes permutes all the possible meanings of the vulture:

> Prometheus on His Crag
>
> Pondered the vulture. Was this bird
> His unborn half-self, some hyena
> Afterbirth, some lump of his mother?
>
> Or Was it his condemned human ballast—
> His dying and his death, torn daily
> From his immortality?
>
> Or his blowtorch godhead
> Puncturing those horrendous holes
> In his human limits?
>
> Was it his prophetic familiar?
> The Knowledge, pebble-eyed,
> Of the fates to be suffered in his image?
>
> Was it the flapping, tattered hole—
> The nothing door
> Of his entry, draughting through him?
>
> Or was it atomic law—
> Was Life his transgression?
> Was he the punished criminal aberration?
>
> Was it the fire he had stolen?
> Nowhere to go and now his pet,
> And only him to feed on?
>
> Or the supernatural spirit itself
> That he had stolen from,
> Now stealing from him the natural flesh?
>
> Or was it the earth's enlightenment—
> Was he an uninitiated infant
> Mutilated toward alignment?

Or was it his anti-self—
The him-shaped vacuum
In unbeing, pulling to empty him?

Or was it, after all, the Helper
Coming again to pick at the crucial knot
Of all his bonds . . . ?

Image after image after image. As the
 vulture
Circled

Circled.

Pain, the midwife at his rebirth, breaks for him the hard shell of his ego:

And the cloudy bird
Tearing the shell
Midwifes the upfalling crib of flames.

And Prometheus eases free.
He sways to his stature.
And balances. And treads

On the dusty peacock film where the world
 floats.

Hughes's version of the myth dramatizes the resolution in Prometheus of all the basic dualities of human nature—spirit and matter, male and female, beauty and horror. But it happens abruptly and mysteriously. There remain big gaps between the last four Prometheus poems which call for further examination, perhaps when Hughes himself is surer that he is out of the psychic limbo and the mouth-sealing numbness out of which these hard little poems had grown as pearls grow upon sandgrains in the flesh. That surer, fuller, and more distanced elaboration was to come in *Cave Birds.*

VIII

It was in 1974 that Hughes saw a set of twenty bird drawings by Baskin—marvelous vivid drawings of owls and eagles and many other birds, real and imaginary—that again fired his imagination. Interpreting them in his own way, he wove a story round them, cast them as characters in a sort of static mystery play. At first there was simply a poem for each drawing—poems unusually studied and formal for Hughes. Then he felt the need to add eight more poems, outside the bird drama but parallel to it, giving the same story in direct and human terms, and in a free and simple style. Baskin then did eight more drawings to go with these.

The protagonist is an innocent ("that is," says Hughes, "a guilty one"), an Everyman. He has certain features in common with Socrates, whom Hughes holds responsible for the disastrous course of Western civilization, the committer of the original sin: "The whole abstraction of Socrates' discourse must inevitably, given enough time and enough applied intelligence, result in machine gun"[3] But since he is also an ordinary man trying to live in the modern world, he appears simply normal, no more guilty than any of us. In the bird drama the protagonist is, at this stage, a cockerel—a subtler version of what would have been called, in a mystery play, Pride of Life. All is apparently well with him: at least he thinks so. Suddenly, without warning, he suffers a psychic split; his consciousness is invaded by spectral birds who are representatives of an otherworldly court where he is to be tried for some nameless but apparently capital crime. The action passes to the underworld, where the protagonist is tried and condemned to death. Swallowed by a raven, he emerges as a Crow, to a new adventure, new trials. He passes through various initiation ordeals, supervised by owls and eagles, culminating in a marriage (he is by now almost human) with an earthly woman, which is also his rebirth as a falcon. Several poems from *Cave Birds*, especially the latter part, will probably also find their way into the complete *Crow.*

It gradually emerges that the protagonist's crime has been to get into a wrong relation-

3. From a reading at Leeds University, 10 March 1979.

ship with the female. They are lost, dead, to each other. And since the female is not only wife and mother but also nature and psychic demon, this failure is both murderous and suicidal. No real living is possible until this damage has been repaired, but the remaking cannot begin until the criminal has been scoured of his Socratic rationality and egocentricity. The birds work on him like a team of alchemists, refining and refining, breaking down and reconstituting, until finally both he and his victim are able to take over and reconstitute each other in marriage:

> So, gasping with joy, with cries of
> wonderment
> Like two gods of mud
> Sprawling in the dirt, but with infinite care
> They bring each other to perfection.
> "Bride and Groom"

Never before had Hughes worked so closely with Baskin or any artist. The two are obviously very close in spirit, but their imaginations are not identical. As an artist Baskin is necessarily concerned with forms and surfaces and textures and the grotesque distortions to which they lend themselves. Hughes can do the verbal equivalent, and in some poems it is an appropriate thing for him to do, but it is not the way to the heart of his vision. That vision is revelatory not by distortion and construction but by far-seeing clarity and bare sensitivity, the qualities we find in most of the poems in *Cave Birds* that are outside the bird drama. Of the poems written to preexisting Baskin drawings only two, "The Knight" and "The Loyal Mother," seem to me to approach the quality of the others.

The themes of psychic split, guilt, suffering, ego-death, and rebirth are so important and central for Hughes, and certain elements (such as the use of marriage as a primary image of rebirth) so new and crucial for his development that, given the initial stimulus of the drawings, Hughes then needed all the freedom possible for his imagination to find its own framework without such exigencies as the need to write a poem to fit every Baskin drawing. In attempting to organize the Baskin drawings into a bird-drama that would enable him to follow the stages in the destruction and renewal of an essentially human protagonist, Hughes was surely attempting the impossible-like going for a four-minute mile in a three-legged race. It is amazing that he came so near to bringing it off. He has given us a dozen fine poems, two or three great ones, some of which will, I hope, reappear in a less constraining context. For all its unevenness, *Cave Birds* constitutes a stage Hughes had to go though to find a way forward for Crow (toward his marriage in the Happy Land on the other side of the river), and to be able to write the epilogue to *Gaudete.*

IX

Adam and the Sacred Nine (1979) is, in a sense, a sequel to *Cave Birds.* Adam lies inert in Eden. The other creatures expect great things of him, but he feels miserably helpless and exposed. His dreams—of technological achievements and immortality—are so madly incongruous with his bruised body "too little lifted from mud" that they merely bewilder him. He is visited by nine birds, each of which offers him an image of how to live. The Falcon could not be more different from his weeping and shivering self, with its unfaltering gunmetal feathers, mountain-diving and world-hurling wing-knuckles, bullet-brow, grasping talons, tooled bill. Then the Skylark, living and dying in the service of its crest, cresting the earth, trying to crest the sun, with bird-joy. Then the Wild Duck, getting up out of cold and dark and ooze, and spanking across water quacking Wake Wake to the world. Then comes the Swift, wholeheartedly hurling itself against and beyond the limits. Then the Wren, who lives only to be more and more Wren—Wren of Wrens! Then the Owl, who floats, the moving center of everything, holding the balance of life and death, heaven and earth. Then the Dove, the perpetual victim, but rainbow-breasted among thorns. Then the Crow comes to Adam and whispers in his ear a waking, reject-nothing truth. Finally comes the Phoenix, which offers itself up again and again and laughs in the blaze. Each bird has found what Adam lacks, its own distinctive mode of living fully within the given conditions. It is not for Adam to try to imitate any of them. He is defined precisely by his lack of wings. His business is with the earth. He stands, and it is the first meeting of the body of man with the body of the earth. The sole of Adam's foot is grateful to the rock, saying:

> I am no wing
> To tread emptiness.
> I was made
>
> For you.
> "The sole of a foot"

X

The development of Hughes's vision from the crucified Prometheus to the resurrected Adam spanned the years 1971 (also the year of his marriage to Carol Orchard) to 1976. Other work being done simultaneously also contributed to the remarkable access of hopefulness and affirmation. In 1968 Hughes had written *Five Autumn Songs for Children's Voices* for the Little Missenden Harvest Festival. On his return from Iran he set himself to write five poems for each of the other seasons, and these were published in 1974 as *Spring, Summer, Autumn, Winter.* A dozen more poems were added for *Season Songs* in 1975. While writing these poems Hughes was spending most of his time farming—cows and sheep—in partnership with his father-in-law, Jack Orchard. He had little time for anything else, but kept a rough verse diary of the more memorable events of the farming year, intending later to work these entries into poems. Jack Orchard died in 1976, the Moortown farm livestock was sold, and Hughes returned to the farming diary. But he found that anything he could do to the entries lost more than it gained, so he left them as they were and published them as *Moortown* in 1979. As with *Season Songs* it was Hughes's intention initially that these would be upbeat poems for children, but as the poems engaged his deeper concerns, the age of the "children" rose until he was writing for adults, but trying to stay within hearing of children.

Perhaps Hughes embarked on these poems as an attempt to cheer himself up after the limbo of *Prometheus on His Crag.* In the event, the renewed contact with the natural world, its births and deaths and failures and harvests—simply looking at things and recording them—proved so revitalizing, so revelatory, that it was to help to transform Hughes's entire vision, even the world of Crow, which had been, up to then, a world of fallen vision.

All the poems are sacramental, some of them visionary, but they remain rooted in common everyday realities. They are poems of observation, but such is Hughes's knowledge of and feel for natural processes that the observed details are selected and rendered effortlessly, in such a way that they reveal not appearances but inner workings and connections. After the isolation and paralysis of *Prometheus,* all is now color and variety, bustle and change, as the earth swings through its cycles on the poles of birth and death.

One would have thought that there was little new to say about the seasons. And indeed Hughes is only showing us what we see every year but take for granted. He writes like the only one of us who is really awake.

> The sun lies mild and still on the yard
> stones.
>
> The clue is a solitary daffodil—the first.
>
> And the whole air struggling in soft
> excitements
> Like a woman hurrying into her silks.
> Birds everywhere zipping and unzipping
> Changing their minds, in soft excitements,
> Warming their wings and trying their
> voices.
>
> The trees still spindle bare.

Beyond them, from the warmed blue hills
An exhilaration swirls upward, like a huge
 fish.

As under a waterfall, in the bustling pool.

Over the whole land
Spring thunders down in brilliant silence.
 "Spring Nature Notes"

Every April is our real birthday, when the world bombards us with gifts:

And the trees
Stagger, they stronger
Brace their boles and biceps under
The load of gift. And the hills float
Light as bubble-glass
On the smoke-blue evening
And rabbits are bobbing all over, and a
 thrush
Rings coolly in a far comer. A shiver of
 green
Strokes the darkening slope as the land
Begins her labour.

Season Songs tells us, and what amazing news it is, what it is like to be alive in this world, with five senses and normal feelings. They embody what Lawrence called "a man in his wholeness wholly attending." Hughes's earlier books record the hard struggle toward this wholeness. When it is achieved, life's charge flows freely again and can be communicated to others through poems. The agony of Prometheus is behind the apparently spontaneous and joyful balance of these poems and the humility of their thanksgiving. Perhaps the harvest poems illustrate this most fully. Here is one written too late for inclusion in *Season Songs*:

BARLEY

Barley grain is like seeds of gold.
When you turn a heap with a shovel it flows
With the heavy magic of wealth.
Every grain is a sleeping princess—
Her kingdom is still to come.
She sleeps with sealed lips.
Each grain is like a mouth sealed,
Or an eye sealed.
In each mouth the whole bible of barley.
In each eye, the whole sun of barley.
From each single-grain, given time,
You could feed the earth.

You treat them rough, dump them into the
 drill,
Church them up with a winter supply
Of fertiliser, and steer out onto the tilth
Trailing your wake of grains.

When the field's finished, fresh-damp,
Its stillness is no longer stillness.
The coverlet has been drawn tight again
But now over breathing and dreams.
And water is already bustling to sponge the
 newcomers.
And the soil, the ancient nurse,
Is assembling everything they will need.
And the angel of earth
Is flying through the field, kissing each one
 awake.
But it is a hard nursery.
Night and day all through winter huddling
 naked
They have to listen to the pitiless lessons
Of the freezing constellations
And the rain. If it were not for the sun
Who visits them daily, briefly,
To pray with them, they would lose hope
And give up. With him
They recite the Lord's prayer
And sing a psalm. And sometimes at night
When the moon haunts their field and
 stares down
Into their beds
They sing a psalm softly together
To keep up their courage.
Once their first leaf shivers, they sing less.
And start working. They cannot miss a day.
They have to get the whole thing right.
Employed by the earth, employed by the
 sky,
Employed by barley, to be barley.
And now they begin to show their family
 beauty.
They come charging over the field, under
 the wind,
like warriors,
"Terrible as an army with banners"
Barbaric and tireless, a battalion of
 Amazons.

That is how they win their kingdom.
Then they put gold, for their coronation.
Each one barbed and feathered, a lithe weapon,
Puts on the crown of her kingdom.
Then the whole fieldful of queens
Swirls in a dance
With their invisible partner, the wind,
Like a single dancer.

That is how barley inherits the kingdom of barley.

Season Songs is not at all sentimental or escapist. Death is ever-present. A fledgling swift suffers "the inevitable balsa death." Foxes and stags are hunted to death. A pheasant hangs from a hook with its head in a bag. A cranefly is going through with its slow death—the poet a watching giant who "knows she cannot be helped in any way." But death, for all the deep compassion it evokes, does not cancel vitality.

Any honest record of farming, especially of livestock rearing, is bound to be a record largely of disasters, and the proportion of deaths in *Moortown* is even greater than in *Season Songs*. Some, such as "February 17th," where Hughes describes in detail his decapitation of a half-born dead lamb, are likely to sicken the sensitive. But if we do not exact a full look at the worst, we falsify the whole and devalue the best. When a three-year-old nephew persistently asks, of a lamb killed by ravens, "Did it cry?" Hughes answers at last, "Oh yes, it cried." Death must be confronted, taken seriously. A lamb suffering from a disgusting and incurable disease must be shot:

I shot the lamb.
I shot him while he was looking the other way.
I shot him between the ears.

He lay down.
His machinery adjusted itself
And his blood escaped, without loyalty.

But the lamb life in my care
Left him where he lay, and stood up in front of me
Asking to be banished,
Asking for permission to be extinct.
For permission to wait, at least,

Inside my head
In the radioactive space
From which the meteorite had removed his body.
"Orf"

Such endings make doubly precious the survivals:

. . . We leave her
To her ancestors, who should have prepared her

For worse than this. The smell of the mown hay
Mixed by moonlight with driftings of honeysuckle
And dog roses and foxgloves, and all
The warmed spices of earth
In the safe casket of stars and velvet

Did bring her to morning. And now she will live.
"Little Red Twin"

XI

We have all seen the newspaper headlines: "VICAR'S SECRET HAREM." "ORGIES IN THE VESTRY." "HUSBANDS HOUND VICAR FROM VILLAGE." Something works beneath the surface of a typically genteel English village, with its retired army officers, commuting businessmen, squire, farmers, poachers, doctor, publican, and priest, which erupts in this sensational way surprisingly frequently, to the great joy of the journalists. In 1964 Ted Hughes wrote a film scenario on such a theme, never used. From his attempt to understand the psychology of minister, women, and husbands, he found himself with a potent myth on his hands, which he later developed in the form of a long narrative poem, *Gaudete*.

Gaudete (1977), an amazing and unique work, is in three parts. In the Prologue an Anglican minister, Nicholas Lumb, is abducted by the powers of the spirit world in order to carry out an act of healing there. This part of the story takes place in a nightmarish landscape where everything is savage, potent, and pregnant, but little is clear. Lumb's task seems to be to heal the terribly scarred face of the goddess of that world, an injury for which man is somehow responsible. It is the ravaged face of the earth itself, a patchwork of the remains of all the living creatures mangled by men, the torn hearts of all the women denied, bullied, and exploited by men. His task is also to help her with a difficult birth. She must be reborn of him before he can be reborn of her. It is his own rebirth at which he must play the roles of midwife and mother. Meanwhile, a duplicate of himself, painfully created out of a live oak and given his memory and sense of himself, is sent to replace him. But the changeling cannot escape his own essential nature as a fertility spirit, a wood-demon. He comes from a world where nature is all, into a world of cars, fashions, interior decoration, elaborate social codes, rigid unspoken rules, Women's Institute meetings with cucumber sandwiches, a world where the sterile bodies of the women are owned by husbands whose only interest in nature is that it provides them with something to kill. Here he is obliged to preach and practice a religion he has been inadequately briefed in and misinterprets, woodenly, by the values of the other world. His spiritual orientation lost, he looks vainly for something in this profane world he can recognize as sacred, from which he can take his bearings. He stares at an image of the goddess he serves, "an archaic stone carving," a Sheela-na-gig:[4]

> Her square-cut, primitive fingers, beneath
>   her buttocks
> Are pulling herself wide open—
> An entrance, an exit.
> An arched target centre
> A mystery offering
> Into which Lumb is lowering his drowse.
>   (105–110)

He sees all the women of his parish as incarnations of that goddess. At first his effort is probably to haul up through that opening other spirits to renew the race. This he easily translates into a Christian framework by claiming that he is to father a second savior. What woman is to him, his only perceived hope of getting back into a meaningful, that is sacred, world, he is to the women of his parish, whose lives have become so desacralized that they are all too receptive to the offer of sacred sex, and the promise that one of them is to be the mother of a god. Later, when he is doomed, he wants to get back through that trapdoor into his own underworld, or, as an oak makes most mast when it fears death (as during severe drought), tries to broadcast his seed before his inevitable cancellation. But he is only crucifying himself. His frantic priapic sexuality, far from healing or renewing, or even providing an escape route, simply draws him into a fatal tangle of destructive passions leading finally to two suicides, two murders, and a conflagration.

The long central narrative section of *Gaudete* is about this changeling's last day, when the powers who created him abandon him to the murderous husbands, who hunt him down, then burn him together with his high priestess and his intended bride, in a parody of a Beltane bonfire.

In the Epilogue the real Lumb returns to this world, in the west of Ireland, transformed by his traumatic experiences in the underworld. There is no narrative of those experiences (though a few of them leak through into the consciousness of the changeling). Instead we are given forty-five short, beautiful, eerie lyrics that Lumb has written during or shortly after his exile, many of them prayers to the unnamed goddess of both worlds.

Many readers will already find themselves inclined to sneer. Spirits? Men made of oaks? Goddesses? Even the religious among us are

4. For a description and illustration of the Sheela-na-gig, see John Sharkey, *Celtic Mysteries* (London, 1975).

conditioned to respond to these things as belonging, in the contemporary world, only to the context of horror films. But myths that are ever true myths cannot die, for it is part of their definition that they exist outside time, making intelligible the permanent realities. They can, of course, become inoperative, not because they have died but because we have died to them, after thousands of years of denial of the basic realities in the name of all the isms—rationalism, idealism, puritanism, humanism, materialism, dualism, asceticism. We need the haruspex more than the Etruscans did, to look into the depths of nature, come to understand its innermost workings, and show us what the implications of these realities are for human life.

No one can really invent new myths. It is a matter of selecting and recombining under high imaginative pressure from the mass of mythic material that we have forgotten, or relegated to ancient history at the conscious level, but which lies in suspended animation in the unconscious waiting to be reactivated. There are several shamanistic myths in which the shaman is called upon to exercise his powers of healing upon the goddess herself in the other world. In one the Lady of the Seals is infested about the head with parasites that represent all the aborted children and needlessly slaughtered animals on earth. There are all the Scottish and Irish folktales and ballads of men abducted to the fairy world to marry or heal the fairy queen, and of changelings; all the resurrection myths collected by J. G. Frazer, especially those of Attis, Adonis, and Actaeon; all the myths of the moon goddess of creation and destruction gathered by Robert Graves in *The White Goddess.* There are all the Herakles and Dionysus myths; the *Bacchae,* though there Euripides put his thumb in the balance in favor of Dionysus, by draining his rites of all phallic and orgiastic content (all that is merely in the diseased imagination of Pentheus); and all the Grail legends, especially *Parsifal.*

Hughes has read very widely and makes full use of his reading, but not, like Eliot in *The Waste Land,* in the form of quotations and allusions; everything has to be recycled through his imagination to emerge fused, charged, authenticated. Charged, that is, not with a few thousand volts of Hughes's patented "verbal energy," as though that were something that could be switched on at will, but with the deepest contemporary human relevance and a deep, all-embracing compassion. His myth in *Gaudete* has a quality distinctive of all genuine myths, that it can be interpreted equally well as applying to a supernatural cosmos of spirits and powers, for those who can believe literally in such things, to the natural world, or to the psychic world. It is at its richest if we can apprehend its relevance to all three at once; when it forces us to realize the crassness of such distinctions. And the power of Hughes's writing ensures that this is so. *Gaudete* is Hughes's most deeply and overtly religious book. What he is attempting, as a matter of the utmost and immediate practical necessity, as a matter of life and death, is the recovery of the lost sense of the sacredness of nature—not, of course, the sentimental nature of traditional English nature poetry, but the savage, elemental, demonic (as well as incredibly lovely and tender and fresh) nature all his books go to define. Sacredness has nothing to do with metaphysics. "Sacred means simply "real." That is, to see something as real, in all its fullness of being, is to recognize it as a hierophany, a manifestation of the sacred.

Hughes's method, in *Gaudete,* is to take the sacred, in the form of the flora and fauna of the world and the elemental powers beneath it, and the profane, in the form of our normal surface life, and to jam them into each other. They are, of course, never separate. The underworld pushes up into this world with every grass blade, explodes into it with every hatched egg, licks and flickers like green fire everywhere round the sterile houses. Every window is also

> . . . a door on to the furnace of the bright
> world
>
> The chill bustle
> Of the blossom-rocking afternoon

> The gusty lights of purplish silver,
> brightenings, sudden darkenings
> Teeming with wings and cries
> Under toppling heaven.
> (103–108)

The fullness of being of everything in the natural world continually invades the human world as if it were a vacuum, so that the reality of one of the husbands is almost extinguished by the mere lilac scents that waft into his room:

> He leans at the door, emptied, merely his
> shape,
> Like a moth pinned to a board,
> While the nectars of the white lilac
> And the purple and dark magenta lilac
> Press through the rooms.
> (84–88)

Human life is largely a series of devices to keep nature at bay. Nature is farmed, gardened, photographed, looked at through binoculars or the telescopic sights of a high-velocity rifle. What undermines this safe coziness from within is sex. The girls and young women of the village are walking incitements to devilry. And the older women, with the changeling, are flung

> With more life than they can contain
> Like young dogs
> Unable to squirm free from their torturing
> infinite dogginess.
> (91–93)

He is impregnating the women with a reality too immense for their girdled bodies and etiolated selves:

> She is gripped by the weird pathos of biochemistry, the hot silken frailties, the giant, gristled power, the archaic sea-fruit inside her, which her girdle bites into, which begins to make her suit too tight. She feels the finality of it all, and the nearness and greatness of death. Sea-burned, sandy cartilage, draughty stars, gull-cries from beyond the world's edge.

The human world is a waste land, a world of "polished modernity, the positioned furniture, in ultra colour, . . . like the demortalised organs of a body"; of "stuffed wild life," cactus windowsills, hall chimes, souvenir ashtrays. It cannot possibly accommodate a fertility spirit. It cannot even accommodate its domestic animals (a faithful retriever savages its master, who is savaging his wife; a cat becomes a demon and seduces his mistress) or real art (a Beethoven sonata havocs the house like a vandalizing demon). The village is a trap for the wood-demon as well as for its inmates. His powers, compromised by the straitjacket of his temporary human identity, cannot prevent him from being profaned, reduced to the helpless plaything of frustrated and jealous women and the victim of perverted and jealous men.

Meanwhile, the real Lumb, jammed into the world of the dead and unborn, his mind assailed by nightmarish horrors, cannot cope with all that. But he can and does survive, and brings back with him a tentative raw wisdom. His poems are the songs of a man who has come through, but only just. *Gaudete* means Rejoice! It is the only word on a gravestone. The resurrected Lumb brings back with him the capacity to rejoice even in that which appalls him, and the capacity to perform small miracles, like drawing an otter from the loch by whistling on the back of his hand. The miracle of summoning the sacred, which the changeling Lumb had so laboriously failed to perform for his parishioners, is now effortlessly performed by the real Lumb and magically communicates itself, through the innocence of three small girls, to an ascetic priest, an anchorite who is fired by the thought of what God had whistled up out of the waters of chaos:

> And as he spoke the priest was suddenly carried away by his words. His thoughts flew up into a great fiery space, and who knows what spark had jumped on to him from the flushed faces of the three girls? He seemed to be flying into an endless, blazing sunrise, and he described the first coming of Creation, as it rose

> from the abyss, an infinite creature of miracles, made of miracles and teeming miracles. And he went on, describing this creature, giving it more and more dazzlingly-shining eyes, and more and more glorious limbs, and heaping it with greater and more extraordinary beauties, till his heart was pounding and he was pacing the room talking about God himself, and the tears pouring from his eyes fell shattering and glittering down the front of his cassock. (epilogue, 165–175)

The priest then copies out the poems from the notebook Lumb has left with the girls. Here one will have to stand for all:

> The grass-blade is not without
> The loyalty that never was beheld.
>
> And the blackbird
> Sleeking from common anything and worm-
> dirt
> Balances a precarious banner
> Gold on black, terror and exultation.
>
> The grim badger with armorial mask
> Biting spade-steel, teeth and jaw-strake
> shattered,
> Draws that final shuddering battle cry
> Out of its backbone.
>
> Me too,
> Let me be one of your warriors.
>
> Let your home
> Be my home. Your people
> My people.
> (epilogue, 176–190)

These are poems to be possessed by. Each is like a fine bloody thread being pulled through our hearts.

The main narrative of *Gaudete* is based on the image of the split-the split psyche, the split between man and woman, man and nature, the sacred and the profane. The epilogue poems strain for atonement; the mind and body of a man precariously balanced on a fine taut wire of images above the chasm. They are the furthest any modern writer has gone toward the recovery of the sane and the sacred without forfeiting the real.

XII

Hughes's progress from the 1950's to the 1980's can be described using William Blake's "fourfold vision" as a paradigm. *The Hawk in the Rain* is about man imprisoned in single, fallen vision as in his own body, looking out through the window of his eye at the surrounding energies, the "wandering elementals," making no effort to come to terms with them, as though that were inconceivable, but cowering, hiding, peeping through his fingers, gripping his own heart, running for dear life; or with ridiculous arrogance and complacency posturing as a god in a universe that dwarfs him. In *Lupercal* the energies are released and confronted, but they are seen as nightmarish and destructive, so that it seems only a saint or genius or madman can live with them. This stage, "twofold vision," the release of the energies and the search for strategies to control them, continues through *Wodwo* and *Crow.* What is enacted here is a "descent into destruction," an ego-death, a journey to the source and back, which is followed in *Prometheus on His Crag, Cave Birds, Gaudete,* and *Adam and the Sacred Nine* by the painful process of reintegration in terms of a recovered innocence ("threefold vision") on the far side of experience. This brings with it a cleansing of the doors of perception, so that what had formerly been seen as ugly or horrific in nature is now seen as beautiful and holy. This atonement is "fourfold vision." It is apparent everywhere in Hughes's most recent work, most notably in the salmon poems in *River* (1983).

As in the farming poems, Hughes never takes his eye from the object. Never for a moment does the salmon cease to be a real salmon and become a counter for something else. Yet Hughes's vision reveals, without ever saying so, that the salmon is our prototype, its life cycle a paradigm of nature's purposes and of the religious life.

In "Salmon Eggs" the mating salmon are "emptying themselves for each other." This selfless giving, generosity, openness is a form of dedication or worship, as is the acquiescence of the October salmon in his slow death:

> All this, too, is stitched into the torn
> richness,
> The epic poise
> That holds him so steady in his wounds, so
> loyal to his doom, so patient
> In the machinery of heaven.
> "October Salmon"

The dying salmon is the defeated, torn, and sacrificed hero, about to become a god.

Blake asks:

> How do you know but ev'ry Bird that cuts
> the airy way,
> Is an immense world of delight, clos'd by
> your senses five?
> (*The Marriage of Heaven and Hell*)

What Blake means, surely, is that everything contains within itself the clue to the mystery, the principle of the whole, and being continuous with the whole (which cannot be seen in its immensity) witnesses to the whole and makes it accessible to vision. The mystery is "the redeemed life of joy." It is a mystery because there is no mechanistic or rational explanation for the transformation of suffering (and everything that cries out for redemption) into joy. The language of poetry can reenact it. Joy, as Blake or Hughes understands it, has little to do with happiness—a relatively trivial, uncreative state, a distraction, temptation, backwater from the true way through tragic experience. It is the grace of atonement, the exaltation of being used by the goddess for her sacred purposes, "her insatiable quest."

The language of all these river poems is a rich weave of interrelationships. A poem may be ostensibly about a single creature, but that creature is defined by its relations with other creatures, with weather and season and landscape. Since "all things draw to the river," it is therefore the language of atonement. The life of the salmon is the life of the living waters, sea and river, which is the life of earth and sky, which is our only life. Each poem is a microcosm. The salmon is part of a flow that "will not let up for a minute." The river is itself an archetypal image for life in time, process, the one-way helpless journey toward death. But a river is by no means a one-way wastage:

> Something else is going on in the river
>
> More vital than death—death here seems a
> superficiality
> Of small scaly limbs, parasitical. More grave
> than life
> Whose reflex jaws and famished crystals
> Seem incidental
> To this telling—these toilings of plasm—
> The melt of mouthing silence, the charge of
> light
> Dumb with immensity.
> The river goes on
> Sliding through its place, undergoing itself
> In its wheel.
> "Salmon Eggs"

And here the poem approaches the mystery. For the wheel, karma, the "cycles of recurrence," had formerly been for Hughes, as for most religions, images of horror or absurdity, needing to be transcended. Now it seems that the horror was a product of defective vision, the split psyche, the spiritual blindness caused by dualism, the hubristic desire to improve on the given life, to redeem nature. In the words of Lawrence's risen Christ (in *The Escaped Cock*): "From what, and to what, could this infinite whirl be saved?"

Since logical analysis is the language of single vision, one would expect the language of fourfold vision to be paradoxical synthesis. The very title of Blake's finest work, *The Marriage of Heaven and Hell*, declares that this is so. "Salmon Eggs" moves through a series of oxymorons—"burst crypts," "time-riven altar," "harrowing, crowned," "raptures and rendings"; appropriating on the way all the claims of the Christian mystery of transcendence—"crypt," "altar," "liturgy," "tidings," "Sanctus," "mass," "font"; claiming them all for the wheel itself, "the round of unending water," and the salmon egg that is its "blessed issue," toward the river's simple annunciation: "*Only birth matters.*"

For this poem to work as a spiritually fertilizing experience, it is necessary to believe that these words express a truth uttered by the river, and not a theory uttered by Hughes. And that is unlikely to happen unless we have accompanied him imaginatively through the four stages of his arduous quest, through all the horrors, sufferings, and deaths that his earlier poems enact.

What saved Hughes in those worst years in the 1960's from despair and world denial and a Beckettian absurdism was a Blake-like tenacity, against all the odds, in holding firm to the conviction that the human spirit, with its desire for existence, is "the only precious thing, and designed in accord with the whole universe. Designed, indeed, by the whole universe," and that the universe knows what it is about: "The infinite terrible circumstances that seem to destroy man's importance, appear as the very terms of his importance. Man is the face, arms, legs etc. grown over the infinite, terrible All." These words were written by Hughes in 1966 in his introduction to Popa's poems. When he came to rewrite this essay in 1977, he attributed to the Eastern European poets something of the vision to which he had himself come in the interim:

> At bottom, their vision, like Beckett's, is of the struggle of animal cells and of the torments of spirit in a world reduced to that vision, but theirs contains far more elements than his. It contains all the substance and feeling of ordinary life. And one can argue that it is a step or two beyond his in imaginative truth, in that whatever terrible things happen in their work happen within a containing passion—Job-like—for the elemental final beauty of the created world.

Hughes could not have written that final phrase in the 1960's. Then he would have regarded beauty with suspicion, as something likely to blind man to the essential elemental starkness and awesomeness of the world. As his vision matured, beauty forced its way in again, and to the center, not as something cozy and pretty and picturesque, but as a radiance testifying to miracle.

The poem in which Hughes most fully receives and expresses that radiance is the poem with which he has chosen to end his *Selected Poems* (1982), "That Morning." In 1980 Hughes and his son, Nicholas, spent some weeks salmon-fishing in Alaska. The place and its creatures demanded a sacramental response. The sheer profusion of salmon was like a sign and a blessing:

> Solemn to stand there in the pollen light
> Waist-deep in wild salmon swaying massed
> As from the hand of God. There the body
>
> Separated, golden and imperishable,
> From its doubting thought—the spirit-
> beacon
> Lit by the power of the salmon
>
> That came on, came on, and kept on coming
> . . .
> So we stood, alive in the river of light
> Among the creatures of light, creatures of
> light.

The conclusion of Hughes's *Selected Poems* is the same as the conclusion of *The Marriage of Heaven and Hell*: "For everything that lives is Holy."

In December 1984, Hughes was appointed Poet Laureate. He is the first great poet to fill the post this century. His first poem in office, "Rain Charm for the Duchy," is an affirmation of the potency and sacredness of rain. Both the appointment and the poem were received mockingly by the Philistine press and grudgingly by the critical establishment. The most generous tribute came from the Irish poet Seamus Heaney, who saw that in that poem Hughes was reaffirming "a sacerdotal function for the poet in the realm."

Selected Bibliography

BIBLIOGRAPHY

Sagar, K. and Tabor, S., *Ted Hughes: A Bibliography 1946–1980,* (London, 1983).

TED HUGHES

SELECTED POEMS

Gunn, Thom and Hughes, Ted, *Selected Poems,* (London, 1962); *Selected Poems, 1957–1967,* (London, 1972; New York, 1973); *Selected Poems, 1957–1981,* (London, 1982) pub. in U.S. as *New Selected Poems,* (New York, 1982).

SEPARATE WORKS

The Hawk in the Rain, (New York-London, 1957), verse; *Lupercal,* (New York-London, 1960), verse; *Meet My Folks!* (London, 1961; (New York, 1973), verse for children; *The Earth Owl and Other Moon People,* (London, 1963), verse for children; *How the Whale Became,* (London, 1963; New York, 1964), stories for children; *Nessie, the Mannerless Monster,* (London, 1963), reiss. as *Nessie the Monster* (New York, 1974), story in verse for children; *The Burning of the Brothel,* (London, 1966), verse, lim. ed.; *Recklings,* (London, 1966), verse, lim. ed.; *Scapegoats and Rabies,* (London, 1967), verse, lim. ed.; *Wodwo,* (New York-London, 1967), verse, stories, and a play; *Poetry in the Making,* (London, 1967), pub. in the U.S. as *Poetry Is,* (New York, 1970), radio talks for children; *The Iron Man,* (London, 1968), pub. in U.S. as *The Iron Giant,* (New York, 1968), story for children; *Seneca's Oedipus,* (London, 1969; New York, 1972), play; *Crow,* (London, 1970; New York, 1971), verse; *The Comings of the Kings,* (London, 1971), plays for children; *Crow Wakes,* (London, 1971), verse, lim. ed.; *Poems: Fainlight, Hughes, Sillitoe,* (London, 1971), verse, lim. ed.; *Eat Crow,* (London, 1971), play for radio, lim. ed.; *The Tiger's Bones,* (New York, 1974), plays for children, contains *Orpheus* in addition to the plays in *The Coming of the Kings; Season Songs,* (New York, 1975; London, 1976), verse, reiss. with several new poems, (London, 1986); *Moon-Whales,* (New York, 1976) verse for children; *Gaudete,* (New York-London, 1977), verse; *Moon-Bells,* (London, 1978), verse for children; *Orts,* (London, 1978), verse, lim. ed.; *Cave Birds,* (London, 1978; New York, 1979), verse; *Remains of Elmet,* (New York-London, 1979), verse; *Moortown,* (London, 1979; New York, 1980), verse; *Under the North Start,* (New York-London, 1981), verse; *A Primer of Birds,* (London, 1981), verse, lim. ed.; *River,* (London, 1983; New York, 1984), verse; *What Is the Truth?,* (New York-London, 1984), story with poems for children; *Ffangs the Vampire Bat and the Kiss of Truth,* (London, 1986), story for children.

INTRODUCTIONS

Selected Poems of Keith Douglas, (London, 1964; New York, 1965); *A Choice of Emily Dickinson's Verse,* (London, 1968); *Vasco Popa: Selected Poems,* (London, 1969), rev. for *Collected Poems* (Manchester, 1978); *Children as Writers 2,* (London, 1975); *Selected Poems of Janos Pilinszky,* (Manchester, 1976); Amichai, Yehuda, *Amen,* (New York, 1977; Oxford, 1978); Sagar, Keith, *The Reef,* (Ilkley, England, 1980); A. Fern and J. O'Sullivan, eds., *The Complete Prints of Leonard Baskin,* (New York, 1984).

ESSAYS

"The Genius of Issac Bashevis Singer," (*New York Review of Books,* April 22, 1965); "The Environmental Revolution," *Your Environment* 3 (Summer 1970); "Myth and Education," *Children's Literature in Education* 1 (1970); "Myth and Education," in G. Fox et al., eds. *Writers, Critics and Children,* (London, 1976), a completely different essay; "Sylvia Plath," (*Critical Quarterly,* Summer 1971); "Orghast: Talking Without Words," (*Vogue,* December 1971); "A Reply to My Critics," *Books & Issues* 1 (181); "Sylvia Plath and Her Journals," (*Grand Street,* Spring 1982).

INTERVIEWS AND AUTOBIOGRAPHICAL PIECES

"Context," *London Magazine* (February 1962); "The Rock," *Writers on Themselves,* (London, 1964); "Desk Poet," (*Guardian,* March 23, 1965); "Ted Hughes' 'Crow,'" (*Listener,* July 30 1970); "Ted Hughes and 'Crow,'" (*London Magazine,* January 1971); "Orghast," (*Times Literary Supplement,* October 1, 1971); "The Persepolis Follies of 1971," (*Performance,* December 1971).

CRITICAL STUDIES

Thurley, G., *The Ironic Harvest,* (London, 1974); Sagar, K., *The Art of Ted Hughes,* (Cambridge, 1975), rev. and ext. (1978), contains a full bibliography; A. Bold, Thom Gunn and Ted Hughes, (Edinburgh, 1976); Uroff, M. D., *Sylvia Plath and Ted Hughes,* (Urbana, Ill., 1979); Faas, E., *Ted Hughes: The Unaccommodated Universe,* (Santa Barbara, Calif., 1980), with selected critical writings by Hughes and two interviews; Hirschberg, S., *Myth in the Poetry of Ted Hughes,* (Dublin, 1981); Gifford, T. and Roberts, N., *TedHughes: A Critical Study,* (London, 1981); K. Sagar, ed. *The Achievement of Ted Hughes,* (Manchester, 1983) a collection of sixteen critical essays, with thirty uncollected or unpublished poems by Hughes; West, T., *Ted Hughes,* (London, 1985).

RECORDINGS

The Poet Speaks 5, (Argo PLP 1085), Hughes reading nine poems from *Wodwo; Jupiter Anthology of 20th Century English Poetry 3* (JUR OOA8), Hughes reading "The Hawk in the Rain" and "Hawk Roosting"; *Listening and Writing* (BBC RESR 19M), Hughes reading two talks "Capturing Animals" and "Learning to Think"; *Crow* (Claddagh CCT 9–10), Hughes reading all but three of his *Crow* poems; *The Poetry and Voice of Ted Hughes,* (Caedmon TC 1535), Hughes reading "The Thought-Fox," "The Jaguar," "Wind," "Six Young Men," "Mayday on Holderness," "The Retired Colonel," "View of a Pig," "Sunstroke," "Pike," "An Otter," "Hawk Roosting," "Icecrust and Snowflake," "Sheep 1," "His Legs Ran About," "Bride and Groom" and twelve poems from the epilogue of *Gaudete; Ted Hughes and R. S. Thomas Read and Discuss Selections of Their Own Poems* (Norwich Tapes, 1978) Hughes reading and discussing six poems from *Moortown; Selections from "Crow" and "Wodwo" Read by the Poet Ted Hughes* (Caedmon TC 1628); *Ted Hughes and Paul Muldoon* (A Faber Poetry Cassette), Hughes reading and introducing "Whiteness," "Go Fishing," and "An October Salmon" from *River,* "Life Is Trying To Be Life," "Ravens," and "February 17th" from *Moortown,* "Bridge and Groom," from *Cave Birds,* "Do Not Pick Up the Telephone," from *Selected Poems 1957–1981,* "Emily Bronte" and "When Men Got to the Summit" from *Remains of Elmet,* and "Apple Dumps," from *Season Songs.*

RANDALL JARRELL
(1914–1965)

M. L. ROSENTHAL

ALTHOUGH RANDALL JARRELL wrote a very witty novel and a good deal of lively criticism as well, his most enduring interest as a writer lies in his poems. Between the appearance of an early group in the New Directions anthology *Five Young American Poets* in 1940 and his death at fifty-one in 1965, he prepared seven books of verse. Their usually melancholy titles suggest the desolation with which he constantly contended and which seems to have won out in the breakdown he finally suffered.

To review very briefly the curve of this psychological struggle as it manifests itself in the succeeding volumes: The first book, *Blood for a Stranger* (1942), reveals amid its many echoes of Auden and others certain underlying motifs of loss and confused focus. The next volumes, *Little Friend, Little Friend* (1945) and *Losses* (1948), take their main strength from a number of elegiac war poems. In these poems Jarrell was often able, because of their concreteness and directness, to objectify the motifs that had knotted up so much of his previous work. Also, he learned a good deal about immediacy from such poets of World War I as Siegfried Sassoon and Wilfred Owen. A period of broadening perspectives followed, marked by the appearance in 1951 of *The Seven-League Crutches,* in 1954 of the novel *Pictures from an Institution,* and in 1955 of *Selected Poems.* This last-named volume, containing only two new pieces, was the result of careful reconsideration and, often, revision of past work.

It was not until 1960, actually, that Jarrell published his first book of new poems since *The Seven-League Crutches.* But in the decade and a half after the war he had had a varied experience. He had been literary editor of the *Nation,* poetry consultant at the Library of Congress, visiting lecturer in American colleges and abroad, and, with occasional interruptions, a professor in the Woman's College of the University of North Carolina. He had established himself as one of a small, elite group of poets, protégés originally of Allen Tate and John Crowe Ransom. But Jarrell's outward successes did not anesthetize him against his painful need to gain inward clarification, which finally led him to write the autobiographical poems of *The Woman at the Washington Zoo* (1960) and *The Lost World* (1965).

In a sense, Jarrell tried to make a European of himself, to change over from a bright young American southerner to a sort of German-Austrian-Jewish refugee of the spirit. His interest in Rilke, in the German *Märchen,* and in the neglected European heritage of Americans seems in part an effort to repossess for himself a nourishment denied him in his childhood. Yet this effort, by a process analogous with that described in Keats's "Nightingale" ode, eventually "tolled him back to his sole self."

The word *fey,* meaning both *intensely excited or gay* and *doomed,* is perhaps too grim for Jarrell's poetic personality. Yet it is useful when we think of that side of him which is at once high-spiritedly brilliant and superciliously overinsistent, engaging yet irritating, and which assorts so ill with his capacity for gentleness and for an almost sentimental love of the quieter and more pedestrian virtues—and with the absorption of his imagination by bleakness and horror. The impact on others of this complex of qualities comes through strikingly in the collection of affectionate essays and reminiscences, *Randall Jarrell, 1914–1965,* that appeared in 1967 as a memorial volume. An unusually valuable piece in this excellent collection is "A Group of Two," written by his widow. It is a lovingly drawn portrait of a baffling man: his varied enthusiasms, his childlike ebullience and depressions, his sparkling if somewhat shrill spirit. Mrs. Jarrell is straightforward but protective. She never spells out the nature of his psychic disturbance or the exact circumstances of his death while walking on a highway. She does nevertheless suggest that he carried about with him throughout his life the burden of childhood insecurity, both psychological and financial. His parents were divorced, and for a while he lived happily with his paternal grandparents and great-grandmother, working-class people, in Hollywood, California, before his reluctant return to his mother in Nashville, Tennessee. The gifted, volatile child never "grew up" entirely. The intensity, the traumatic moments, and the accumulated guilt and resentment behind these experiences were never resolved.

He returns to the Hollywood period a number of times in his poetry, most notably in the title sequence of *The Lost World.* The confusion and displacement of that period are crucial, though many of their implications are suppressed. "Mama" and "Pop" in Jarrell's poems are the *grandparents,* while his mother is "Anna." The sense of universal sadness, betrayed vulnerability, and emptiness at the center of the self in Jarrell's work is rooted in these childhood events and relationships, and doubtless helps account for this strong attraction to European literature of tragic consciousness.

In his poems there is at times a false current of sentimental condescension toward his subjects, especially when they are female. But more often another current carries us toward a realization of the ineradicable innocence and pity of the common life in all its alienating reality. This current did not really show itself, as a directive element in Jarrell's art, until the war poems of his second volume. In the first, *Blood for a Stranger,* some of his major themes were visible but neither voice nor tone was yet quite his own. One hears a sort of Auden-static everywhere, with other voices cutting in every so often. In the most accomplished poem of the book, "The Skaters," the voice seems a duet of Hart Crane and Edwin Muir:

> I stood among my sheep
> As silent as my staff;
> Up the sea's massy floor
> I saw the skaters pass.
>
> Long like the wind, as light
> I flowed upon their track
> Until at evening's edge
> I marked their breathless flocks.
>
> I sped among them then
> Like light along its lands—
> Love wreathed their lips, and speed
> Stiffened their tissue limbs. . . .

Half vision, half nightmare, the poem closes in on a note of lost personal focus. The speaker discerns in the stars the image of "one obsessing face," with which he comes into a precarious sympathy or relationship while caught up in the swirling skaters' movement that controls the curve of the poem. But finally, abandoned and abandoning, he is whirled into "the abyss":

> But the iron's dazzling ring, the roar
> Of the starred ice black below
> Whirl our dazed and headlong strides
> Through the whirling night into
>
> The abyss where my dead limbs forget
> The cold mouth's dumb assent;
> The skaters like swallows flicker
> Around us in the long descent.

These motifs of coldness and distance, and of a fantasy realm that is only a heightening of desolate reality, persist throughout Jarrell's career. It is hard not to see "The Skaters" as a suicidal projection of the symbolic search for the irretrievably lost mother:

> The million faces flecked
> Upon my flickering gaze
> Bent to me in the stars
> Of one obsessing face . . .

A hopeless distance, a bewildering cosmos. Another poem in the volume, "The Bad Music," is addressed to "Anna" and uses the same pattern of symbolic imagery as "The Skaters" without reaching the glitteringly impersonal final set of that poem. Here the speaker sits by a window watching students as they return home from caroling. They carry candles that "wink out and on and out, like mixed-up stars," and

> I sit here like a mixed-up star:
> Where can I shine? What use is it to shine?
> I say; and see, all the miles north inside my
> head,
> You looking down across the city, puzzling.
> . . .
> High over the millions who breathe and
> wait and sparkle . . .

"The Bad Music" makes almost embarrassingly explicit the buried reference, which is not the literal meaning, of "The Skaters." In its first stanza, the speaker blurts out his accusation of abandonment to Anna:

> The breast opening for me, the breaths
> gasped
> From the mouth pressed helplessly against
> my wrist
> Were lies you too believed; but what you
> wanted
> And possessed was, really, nothing but
> yourself:
> A joy private as a grave, the song of death.
> . . .

Poetically, what is interesting in the relation of the two poems is the similarity of their *process.* Each starts in a state of passive melancholy and moves into active despair. Under surface differences of tone and theme, they share a configuration of feeling and imagery. The "mixed-up star" symbolism in both poems projects the speaker's relation to the elusive object of his love. Faces appear as part of a subjective constellation in which confusion reigns, and it is all but impossible to sort out lover from beloved (son from mother) or either one from the shifting mass of other people or, indeed, from the whole objective universe. The pattern of movement is characteristic of Jarrell: a static initial state of sadness; then a phase of confusion that lets deeper depression flood into the poem; and then a final bitter thrust. We see it working in the famous five-line war poem "The Death of the Ball Turret Gunner":

> From my mother's sleep I fell into the State,
> And I hunched in its belly till my wet fur
> froze.
> Six miles from earth, loosed from its dream
> of life,
> I woke to black flak and the nightmare
> fighters.
> When I died they washed me out of the
> turret with a hose.

This poem is "impersonal." The speaker is not the poet himself but a dramatic character, a soldier who has been killed in the war. Yet the ironic womb imagery recalls the earlier mother theme, as of course the word *mother* itself does. We begin with the abstract yet unhappy assertion in the first line, an assertion that the young man received into the military world from the dreaming family world of childhood has hardly had time to emerge from fetal unconsciousness before he is in a new womb, that of war. Attention shifts in the next line to the chill, metallic character of that new womb. Suddenly then, the next two lines transport us to the gunner's moment of "waking" into nightmarish vision, at the moment his plane is hit by flak in the sky. The image is fetal; a note by Jarrell in *Selected Poems* stresses the fact that, "hunched upside-down in his little sphere," the gunner "looked like the foetus in the womb." The scene itself here is close to the confused cosmos of the two poems already discussed. Life is seen as only a "dream," whereas death is the reality into which the protagonist is born. In the harshly distorted womb images of this poem, we have once again the motif of love betrayed.

What Jarrell forces on our imaginations through his grotesque symbolism is the obscenity of war, its total subversion of human values. In highly compressed form, he has summoned up his subconscious preoccupations and the dynamics of poetic association they generate to make a poem that gets outside his own skin. The conversion process was not simple, though the result is emphatically clear in its narrative movement and in its succession of tones and intensities. Instead of the anapests that launch the first two lines, a suddenly lurching hovering-accent gets the third line off to a wobbling start that helps shake the poem open to let in wider ranges of felt meaning. (Effects of confusion and ambiguity, in rhythmic shifts as in the literal suggestions of language, often have this function in poems.) The brutal nastiness of the closing line refocuses the poem sharply, yet the final effect is not abrupt. The line is in hexameter, longer by a foot than any of the preceding lines. It has the impact of a final "proof" of war's nature as a mockery of all that is life-giving.

It is easy to see how such a poem was prefigured in *Blood for a Stranger*. If we think of that book as comprising a definite unit of sensibility, we shall perceive it as, in large part, a complaint against loss of the world of childhood. (Jarrell specialized in psychology as an undergraduate at Vanderbilt University and was, in his omnivorous way, a reader of Freud; he is very likely to have "psychoanalyzed" himself to some degree at least.) The unresolved discontents of childhood are certainly present, but the real complaint is against separation, against initiation into adulthood, against the loss of an insufficiently discovered and savored life of innocence. "What we leave," mourns the opening poem ("On the Railway Platform"), "we leave forever." Another poem, "90 North," makes explicit the contrast between the secure childhood where

> At home, in my flannel gown, like a bear to
> its floe,
> I clambered to bed,

and the present, "meaningless" moment where

> all lines, all winds
> End in the whirlpool I at last discover.

True enough, a bear climbing onto its floe is not the most secure of beasts; but the nightmares of childhood, in Jarrell's poem, do end in "rest" and a "warm world" of dependable certainties where "I reached my North and it had meaning." Of the poems in *Blood for a Stranger* specifically about childhood and separation, the most poignant is "A Story," a monologue by a boy sent away to school. It has none of the portentous phrasing that mars "90 North" and other poems of this volume. Its thoughts are always appropriate to the speaker. "I liked home better, I don't like these boys" is more to the point than the generalizations in "90 North" about "wisdom" and "pain."

Not to linger overlong with this first book, it has other, though related, points of interest besides this central one of the child soul's vulnerability. In "Children Selecting Books in a Library," for instance, Jarrell meditates charmingly, if slightly pedantically, on the value of reading fairy tales. Another piece, "The Cow Wandering in the Bare Field," has been praised by Allen Tate, who remembers seeing it when Jarrell, then a freshman at Vanderbilt, was seventeen. Its beginning at least is slightly reminiscent of Hart Crane's "Black Tambourine," the details at once starkly literal and accusatory:

> The cow wandering in the bare field,
> Her chain dangling, aimless,—
> The Negro sitting in the ashes,
> Staring, humming to the cat . . .

Jarrell rarely again tried this kind of distanced yet incisive presentation. Indeed, he loses track of it later on in this very poem; he was after a faint modulation toward a theme of social protest, perhaps, and he did think of himself as a "radical" in his youth. But that side of him is seen in poems strongly indebted to Auden and Spender, with such titles as "The Machine-Gun," "The Refugees," "A Poem for Someone Killed in Spain," and "For an Emigrant." Part I of the last-named poem, with its final stanza greatly altered, was salvaged for the *Selected Poems* and retitled there as "To the New World." It was interesting as showing special sympathy for the victims of the Nazis and for its insight into the life of exiles:

> Free—to be homeless, to be friendless, to be
> nameless,
> To stammer the hard words in the foreign
> night . . .

"For an Emigrant" shows, also, Jarrell's early realization that, ultimately, the refugee condition is universal; the balm of America is only a salve.

> You escaped from nothing; the westering
> soul
> Finds Europe waiting for it over every sea. . . .

"For an Emigrant," despite its political clichés and its sermonizing, meant something for Jarrell's future development. Much of it has to do with the effect of anti-Semitism and fascism on a *child's* life in Europe, and it attempts to assimilate the political lessons of the thirties in such a way as to bring the poet's childhood-obsession into a wider, more adult context of awareness. The poem anticipates, as well, Jarrell's later tendency to assume a European consciousness and graft it onto his American personality—a tendency for which Pound and Eliot had doubtless provided models. Jarrell, however, differed from them by playing the role of an exile in his own land, if far more modestly than they and with a lesser genius though a real, and kindred, sense of cultural mission.

Jarrell served in the Army Air Force between 1942 and 1946. "In the first months of the War," Robert Lowell writes in an "appreciation" appended to the 1966 paperback edition of *The Lost World,* "Jarrell became a pilot. He was rather old for a beginner, and soon 'washed out,' and spent the remaining war years as an aviation instructor. Even earlier, he had an expert's knowledge. . . . Nine-tenths of his war poems are air force poems, and are about planes and their personnel, the flyers, crews, and mechanics who attended them. No other imaginative writer had his precise knowledge of aviation, or knew so well how to draw inspiration from this knowledge." His mind was similar to Hardy's and to Owen's in its fusion of informed objectivity with a compassion as close to sentimentality as intelligence and taste would allow. Of course, the world of which he wrote was very far from Hardy's, and he lacked Owen's combat experience. But in his war poetry he was like Hardy in bringing to bear on it his whole, extraordinarily literate intelligence—an intelligence of the kind that feels imaginative literature as the distillation of considered experience, the usable treasure of a contemplative mind. And he was like Owen in the way the pressure of his empathy with the pilots he knew made him envision their war experience in a vivid, accurate manner unmatched by most of his writing having to do with civilian life. The poetry of their condition lay for him, as for Owen, "in the Pity." For both poets this is a sort of passionately apprehended disproportion between the young soldiers' ultimate innocence and the terror they both suffer and inflict. It is realized not in sentiment but in action.

Jarrell's war poems are found mainly in his *Little Friend, Little Friend* and *Losses* volumes, which came directly out of the war years, and there are a few more in *The Seven-League Crutches.* His vision of the soldier as betrayed child is clearly epitomized in "The Death of the Ball Turret Gunner," a poem strategically placed at the end of *Little Friend, Little Friend.* As with most American and British poets of the second world war, the ultimate implied attitude is an ambiguous, or at any rate a tentative, one. The shock, horror, and questioning that mark the poetry of the first world war were the discovery of a generation, a discovery crystallized on the run, in the midst of death—the discovery that war *was* the trenches, the barbed wire, the humanly pointless slaughter while, in Owen's words, "God seems not to care." Jarrell and his contemporaries had been teethed on that earlier work; for them it was the definition of war experience. All later war poetry is in an important sense informed by the World War I "tradition." However, there are at least two significant differences for Jarrell's generation. First, they felt a far greater initial detachment from official rhetoric and from the assumptions of the social system. And second, though there was a good deal of old-fashioned combat in the later war, the over-all organization and the far greater importance of the air forces and long-range technology and communication made the involvement of most soldier-poets far less immediate than before.

These differences may be overstressed, but I am trying to suggest that the poetry of Jarrell's generation feels the impact of war with a double awareness. It is still in touch with the original shock of World War I, but is further away from the almost tribal sense of participation in a ritual gone wrong. Herbert Read's poem "To a Conscript of 1940" is a bridge between the two positions in time. The ghost of a soldier of 1914–18 speaks to the poet, a survivor who now faces the new war situation:

> We think we gave in vain. The world was not renewed.
> There was hope in the homestead and anger in the streets
> But the old world was restored and we returned
> To the dreary field and workshop, and the immemorial feud
>
> Of rich and poor. Our victory was our defeat.
> Power was retained where power had been misused
> And youth was left to sweep away
> The ashes that the first had strewn beneath our feet.
>
> But one thing we learned: there is no glory in the deed
> Until the soldier wears a badge of tarnish'd braid;
> There are heroes who have heard the rally and have seen
> The glitter of a garland round their head.
>
> Theirs is the hollow victory. They are deceived.
> But you, my brother and my ghost, if you can go
> Knowing that there is no reward, no certain use
> In all your sacrifice, then honour is reprieved.
>
> To fight without hope is to fight with grace,
> The self reconstructed, the false heart repaired. . . .

Basically, this is the position—acceptance of the war (presumably because of the policies and aggression of the Nazi government) but without any chivalric or apocalyptic illusions. The history of the between-wars governments was too well known; certain Marxian and pacifist conceptions, admittedly contradictory, had irrevocably entered Western sensibility; and the fact that military victory would not solve the great social problems of the age was widely understood. Jarrell's way of encompassing all this was, on the whole, to adopt an existential approach. Here were men—*child*-men, really—in circumstances beyond their control or even their comprehension. It was not existential*ist*—neither a revolutionary perspective, nor a challenge to men to be as fully and heroically human as possible in the circumstances of limited choice open to them, is implied. Jarrell's emphasis is on the saving innocence of those whom these circumstances have after all made, as he says in "Eighth Air Force" (*Losses*), "murderers." That is a bitter word, yet Jarrell uses it a bit lightly and ironically. Because the young

American airmen also run the risk of death, as he himself does not, he compares them with Christ. The comparison has some validity. Whitman, in "A Sight in Camp in the Daybreak Gray and Dim," had used it for the soldier as *victim;* and even when the soldier is constrained to kill he is in some sense still a victim. Pressed too hard, though, the argument is obviously forced and sentimental. Could one have put the case otherwise about young German soldiers in the same situation? Hardly. And if not, must not one say also that the most hardened killer is ultimately an innocent victim, a Christ crucified on the cross of his particular fate? But Jarrell did not follow the logic through:

> The other murderers troop in yawning;
> Three of them play Pitch, one sleeps, and
> one
> Lies counting missions, lies there sweating
> Till even his heart beats: One; One; One.
> *O murderers!* . . . Still, this is how it's done:
>
> This is a war . . . But since these play, before
> they die,
> Like puppies with their puppy; since, a man,
> I did as these have done, but did not die—
> I will content the people as I can
> And give up these to them: Behold the man!
>
> I have suffered, in a dream, because of him,
> Many things; for this last saviour, man,
> I have lied as I lie now. But what is lying?
> Men wash their hands, in blood, as best
> they can:
> I find no fault in this just man.

In these lines Jarrell makes explicit the prevailing social assumption about war: that men cannot be held responsible for what history compels them to do, especially when they are on the "just" side of the struggle. But he tries, too, to make a subtly paradoxical argument to get past the objections to this assumption, and his style turns to putty in the process because the thought is too contrived. The reality of the situation requires the most relentless intellectual toughness and unwillingness to be an apologist for war mentality. Otherwise, the paradoxical fact that one can, in a sense, be good and innocent while behaving murderously becomes merely another sophistical argument for further mass murder. Jarrell himself recognizes this problem by his play on the word *lie,* but self-irony does not always purge a speaker of the error he confesses by it. Indeed, Jarrell's note on this poem, given in his introduction to *Selected Poems,* has no self-irony at all: " 'Eighth Air Force' is a poem about the air force which bombed the Continent from England. The man who lies counting missions has one to go before being sent home. The phrases from the Gospels compare such criminals and scapegoats as these with that earlier criminal and scapegoat about whom the Gospels were written."

The limitation in Jarrell's war poetry is not, however, political or intellectual. It is a matter of energy. He focuses on the literal data of war—their irreversible actuality, and the pity of the human predicament implicit in that actuality. The poems stop short of anger, of programs, of anything that would constitute a challenge to soldiers or to their commanders or to the statesmen who make policy. Letting the facts of war experience speak for themselves, Jarrell sank all his real poetic imagination into primary acts of empathy; ordinarily he resisted any obvious political rhetoric. In "Eighth Air Force" we have a rare instance of his swinging out of his usual orbit to deal with the moral issues of mass bombing. His failure to handle the problem poetically lay in inadequate resources of emotional complexity and intellectual power.

But within the narrower limits of its engagement, Jarrell's war poetry is often superb. In poems like "A Front," "A Pilot from the Carrier," "Pilots, Man Your Planes," and "The Dead Wingman"—the last of these a dream poem, but one that presents the essence of a familiar situation: a pilot searching for a sign of a shot-down wingman—the poet's entire effort is to project the sense of men and machines in action, from the viewpoint of a participant. In all the poems just named, Jarrell has a double aim. First, he wishes to get the technical and atmospheric details in coherent order (a bombing plane whose radio has gone bad, so that the pilot cannot be diverted from a closed landing field to another still open and therefore crashes; a plane that has been hit and is burning, from which the pilot parachutes; a carrier under attack from a Japanese torpedo plane; the situation of the airman hunting for a lost comrade). And second, he desires to make the perspective that of a living, suffering man. "A Pilot from the Carrier" and "A Front" are in the same volume, *Little Friend, Little Friend,* as "The Death of the Ball Turret Gunner." They carry a kindred birth-death motif, though less explicitly. The pilot in the plane from the carrier, "strapped at the center of his blazing wheel," tears himself loose from that womb of death and is reborn via parachute

> In the sunlight of the upper sky—
> And falls, a quiet bundle in the sky,
> The miles to warmth, to air, to waking:
> To the great flowering of his life. . . .

The pilot in "A Front" cannot be wrenched free in time, and perishes. In *Losses,* the men on the carrier in "Pilots, Man Your Planes" are sleeping "hunched in the punk of Death" until awakened into their own literal deaths unless they escape in time. The pilot in "The Dead Wingman" searches in his dream over that same amniotic sea into which so many figures of "Pilots, Man Your Planes" have disappeared, but he never finds the dreadful evidence of the birth into death that he seems to need for deep inward confirmation of his own reality:

> The plane circles stubbornly: the eyes
> distending
> With hatred and misery and longing, stare
> Over the blackening Ocean for a corpse. . . .

I have not really meant to labor this womb referent, which appears and disappears, usually very fleetingly, in Jarrell's shifting float of associations His creation of an ambience of confused details, a dream of total self-loss, before a final note of profound sadness is equally important in all the poems I have just mentioned. What gives them more authority than the poems of *Blood for a Stranger* is not only the precision within the confusion, but also the definiteness of the military setting within which the lost, childlike psyche of Jarrell's soldiers (with the poet's standing in for them, as it were) speaks its pain. Several times in the two "war" books the persons spoken for are women or children. The title of *Little Friend, Little Friend,* which evokes just the childlike psyche to which I have referred, is taken from a phrase used in the book's opening poem, "2nd Air Force." Here, as Jarrell's note tells us, a "woman visiting her son remembers what she has read on the front page of her newspaper the week before, a conversation between a bomber, in flames over Germany, and one of the fighters protecting it: 'Then I heard the bomber call me in: "Little Friend, Little Friend, I got two engines on fire. Can you see me, Little Friend?" I said, "I'm crossing right over you. Let's go home."'

The woman of this poem might just as well have been the mother of the ball turret gunner in the closing poem. Her son—this is the whole burden of the poem—has indeed fallen from her womb into that of the state. The barren and dangerous world of the air base appears amid "buses and weariness and loss," with its "sand roads, tar-paper barracks," and "bubbling asphalt of the runways." A specific womb image dramatizes what has happened to her transplanted son: "The head withdraws into its hatch (a boy's)." This alien world—"The years meant *this?*"—is her and our bleak introduction to what the war means for the soldiers as Jarrell understands them. Between "2nd Air Force" and "The Death of the Ball Turret Gunner," then, the volume makes its journey through a wasteland of deadly machinery and pathetic soldiers who "pass like beasts, unquestioning," through their new life where "the bombers answer everything."

Both *Little Friend, Little Friend* and *Losses* contain many closeups and vignettes of soldiers: men being classified, a soldier whose leg has been amputated, prisoners, a soldier being visited in the hospital by his wife and baby, men being discharged from service, a field hospital. Politically and historically, the war may have been unavoidable, but for Jarrell this is more an existential than a moral reality. Despite his recognition of the monstrousness of the Nazis in "A Camp in the Prussian Forest" (*Losses*)—

> Here men were drunk like water, burnt like
> wood.
> The fat of good
> And evil, the breast's star of hope
> Were rendered into soap—

it is the pointlessness and cruelty of the war that emerges as the poet's repeated insight. Each soldier, as the mother sees in "2nd Air Force," is "heavy with someone else's death" and a "cold carrier" of "someone else's victory." The poem "Losses," in the earlier book but clearly the source of the later one's title, utters a complaint on behalf of all the young *and* of their victims. Although its speaker does not explore the moral dilemma involved, he does raise an ultimate question:

> In bombers named for girls, we burned
> The cities we had learned about in school—
> Till our lives wore out; our bodies lay
> among
> The people we had killed and never seen.
> When we lasted long enough they gave us
> medals;
> When we died they said, "Our casualties
> were low."
> They said, "Here are the maps"; we burned
> the cities.
>
> It was not dying—no, not ever dying;
> But the night I died I dreamed that I was
> dead,
> And the cities said to me: "Why are you
> dying?
> We are satisfied, if you are; but why did
> I die?"

It is interesting that World War II produced no great poem at once absolutely ruthless in its fidelity to the realities of human experience in the war and encompassing in its understanding of all their complex contradictions: particularly, the crushing choice seemingly thrust on the most advanced spirits between pure pacifism and accepting the need to destroy the Nazi power. The rhetorical questions at the end of "Losses"—slightly confused because of the ambiguous use of the word "I" in the closing line—suggest the epic psychological exploration needed, but not furnished, to give body to their meaning. At a pragmatic and popular level the questions were certainly answerable by reference to recent history. The answers were both moral and practical, involving the fate of nations and of ethnic groups as well as of political and economic systems. The contradiction lay, as Malraux perceived in an only slightly different context, the Spanish Civil War, in the fact that the methods of war compel imitation of the enemy and indeed outstripping him in his own methods. It is indeed possible to present the voice of an innocent and ignorant soldier asking "Why?" Yet even the boys Jarrell wrote about had more of a sense, however inarticulately they might express themselves, of "why" than he quite gives them credit for. As for the poet himself, a number of the pieces show the usual intellectual's grasp of the economic and historical aspects of modern war. Of the American poets who emerged immediately after the war, only Robert Lowell was keyed to the demands of the materials, but on the other hand he had neither the literal experience nor the inclination to work on *the* war poem. Perhaps Pound and Eliot, by their keen location of the inner contradictions of Western culture, had rendered a large effort of this sort redundant for later poets.

That Jarrell wanted to suggest large historical and mythological considerations is clear from "The Wide Prospect," which comes just before "The Death of the Ball Turret Gunner" at the end of *Little Friend, Little Friend,* and from the two poems that close *Losses:* "In the Ward: The Sacred Wood" and "Orestes at Tauris." The influence of Marx via Auden is obvious in the opening stanza of "The Wide Prospect":

> Who could have figured, when the harnesses improved
> And men pumped kobolds from the coal's young seams
> There to the west, on Asia's unrewarding cape—
> The interest on that first raw capital?
> The hegemony only the corpses have escaped?

The poem ends, after a determinedly sustained exposition along these lines, with an imagery of ritual sacrifice that links Marxian, Freudian, and myth-and-ritual-oriented motifs:

> the man-eaters die
> Under the cross of their long-eaten Kin.
>
> All die for all. And the planes rise from the years . . .
>
> When men see men once more the food of Man
> And their bare lives His last commodity.

The poems at the end of *Losses* are superior in being free of the long, expository sections, with a forced liveliness of imagery but without driving energy, of "The Wide Prospect." "Orestes at Tauris," the closing poem, was according to Jarrell an early composition written before any of the poems from *Blood for a Stranger* included in the *Selected Poems.* Very different in character from anything else in the war books, it shows Orestes arriving in Tauris after being pursued relentlessly by the Furies, under compulsion, "in expiation for his crime, to bring back to Greece that image of Artemis to which the Tauri sacrificed the strangers cast up on their shores" (Jarrell's note in *Losses*). This long, partially surrealist narrative poem imagines the sacrificial beheading of Orestes by his sister Iphigenia, now a priestess, instead of their triumphant escape. Jarrell's recasting of the myth, in a well-sustained unrhymed pattern of four- and five-stress lines that focuses on the succession of impressions, states of feeling, and sensations that Orestes experiences, makes for an effect of terror amidst psychological confusion and barbaric splendors. The condition of Orestes and Iphigenia at the end then becomes a perfect mythic embodiment of Jarrell's vision of war as the sacrifice of driven innocents for the sake of a savage, mindless determinism inherent in our natures:

> The people, silent, watching with grave faces
> Their priestess, who stands there
> Holding out her hands, staring at her hands
> With her brother's blood drenching her hands.

"In the Ward: The Sacred Wood," which precedes "Orestes at Tauris," is perhaps Jarrell's most determined effort to give mythic dimensions to his theme of the sacrificed innocent in war. His own description of the poem, in his introduction to *Selected Poems,* goes: "The wounded man has cut trees from paper, and made for himself a sacred wood; with these, the bed-clothes, the nurse, the doctor, he works his own way through the Garden of Eden, the dove and its olive-leaf, the years in the wilderness, the burning bush, the wars of God and the rebel angels, the birth and death and resurrection of Christ." This account, and the style of the poem, somewhat recall the symbolic distortions of thought and syntax of Lowell's early poems—

> Is the nurse damned who looked on my nakedness?
> The sheets stretch like the wilderness
> Up which my fingers wander, the sick tribes,
> To a match's flare, a rain or bush of fire. . . .

But Jarrell's movement does not rip free into Lowell's frenzied piling up of associations and allusions. In this poem, however, he surpasses Lowell in one important respect though he does not achieve that state of passionate intensity of speech which makes the whole language an electric field of highly charged, crackling movements of realization. At each point along the way, as the wounded soldier ponders the symbolic analogies with

Christ implicit in his condition, he nevertheless at the same time maintains a basic simplicity and a distance from the mental game he is playing. Unlike "Eighth Air Force," this poem does not press an identity between the dying soldier and Christ. The dominant tone is one of a real man, without hope, letting go though aware of a dream of divinity incarnate—a tone corresponding to the progress of negative heroism in Read's "To a Conscript of 1940." Negation is accepted quietly; this is one of Jarrell's most touching and thoughtful poems:

And beneath the coverlet
My limbs are swaddled in their sleep, and
  shade
Flows from the cave beyond the olives, falls
Into the garden where no messenger
Comes to gesture, "Go"—to whisper, "He is
  gone."

The trees rise to me from the world
That made me, I call to the grove
That stretches inch on inch without one
  God:
"I have unmade you, now; but I must die."

Earlier, in discussing "The Death of the Ball Turret Gunner," I ventured a description of the characteristic structural dynamics of Jarrell's poems as involving a static initial state of sadness, then a phase of confusion that lets deeper depression flood into the poem, and then a final bitter thrust. Most lyric-contemplative poetry since the early Romantics has, in fact, a comparable structure. That is, an initial state of unease or depressed feeling is followed by the introduction of complicating matter for contemplation: any of a number of contexts of awareness that enlarge and, very likely, confuse the original perspective. The final "resolution" of the poem is a reorientation of the speaker's initial attitude in the light of the intervening complication. It may take the form of acceptance or reconciliation though at the same time what is being "affirmed" is defeat of a sort—what we might call "depressive transcendence." Needless to add that shifts of style, rhythm, intensity, and level of diction are as important as the literal statements.

Without forcing the point, we can say that Jarrell's whole poetic career follows a similar pattern of movement. After the early poems of childhood desolation, the speaking psyche confronts three bodies of material external to itself: war experience, the world of myth and folk legend (to which are added, often, the associations of music, painting, and literature), and individual human suffering. In the final phase of his career, the poet objectifies himself, in relation to his childhood life, as one of the sufferers over whom his attention has hovered with such empathy. That is, he has brought back his earliest preoccupations into the center of his work, but in a focus altered by the discipline through which he has passed and the knowledge he has accumulated. He has learned to isolate the pity of the irrecoverable and, therefore, of the irredeemable in existence and is free to present sharp, concrete memories and to play with them in a number of ways.

In *Losses,* we see the three bodies of "external" material (war, myth and legend, and suffering individual people) already present. War is, of course, the overwhelming major subject. But there are other myth-involved poems besides the two we have already examined, among them "The Märchen" and "The Child of Courts"; Jarrell's fascination with the German *Märchen* (folk tales, in this case those of the brothers Grimm) is at this point related to the historical fatalism induced by his response to the war. The dreams and terrors of primitive life foreshadowed those of the modern age with its discovery of the limitations of man's hopes and prospects:

Listening, listening; it is never still.
This is the forest: long ago the lives
Edged armed into its tides (the axes were its
  stone
Lashed with the skins of dwellers to its
  boughs);
We felled our islands there, at last, with iron.
The sunlight fell to them, according to our
  wish,

And we believed, till nightfall, in that wish;
And we believed, till nightfall, in our lives.

These are the open, and on the whole the best, lines of "The Märchen," a somewhat preciously proliferative poem which nevertheless shows Jarrell's characteristic wit, ingenuity, and sympathy with the common lot. He had learned, in his war poems, how to write with economy, but there is no economy in this poem of over a hundred lines of moderately roughened blank verse. Jarrell luxuriates in the way the Märchen bring folk motifs and folk wisdom, simple and often comic materials related to the life of peasants, together with the symbolic and archetypal motifs of religious or mythical tradition: Christ and the old gods, Hell, "the Scapegoat," "Paradise," and "the Cross, the Ark, the Tree." The perspective he introduces has to do with primitive man's desire, never fulfilled but never forgotten or relinquished either, even in our time, to make reality conform to his wish. Herein, for Jarrell, lies the inescapable pathos of the human condition, of which the vulnerable innocence of children is the most obvious embodiment. The *Märchen* show that it is not so much our inability to make wishes come true as the paltriness of the wishes themselves that is defeating. In Romantic tradition generally, it is the disparity between desire and reality, between subjective and objective "truths," with which the poet is obsessed—ultimately, the pity that we cannot stamp our own images on nature. In Jarrell there is a curious turn of emphasis: the inadequacy of imagination, driven as it is already by conditions imposed on it by nature, is the heart of the problem—

Poor Hänsel, once too powerless
To shelter your own children from the cold
Or quiet their bellies with the thinnest
gruel,
It was not power that you lacked, but
wishes.
Had you not learned—have we not learned,
from tales
Neither of beasts nor kingdoms nor their
Lord,
But of our own hearts, the realm of death—
Neither to rule nor die? to change! to
change!

"The Child of Courts" (reprinted in *Selected Poems* as "The Prince") presents the ambivalent night-terror of a child who fears that the ghost of a buried man has come up out of the grave toward him but who then is disappointed: "I start to weep because—because there are no ghosts." The poem at first ambiguously suggests a prison atmosphere. But the child calls out "Mother?"—in an equally ambiguous context, however—and thus there is a suggestion not so much of a prison as of a castle or palace in which there is intrigue and insecurity. One thinks of young Prince Edward after Henry's death, a thought mildly encouraged by the two titles. The situation of this brief and simple poem suggests, at one and the same time, the well-known situations of Edward and other English princes, the grisly circumstances of certain folk legends, and the excited imagination of any sensitive child at certain times.

After the door shuts, and the footsteps die,
I call out, "Mother?" No one answers.
I chafe my numb feet with my quaking
hands
And hunch beneath the covers, in my curled
Red ball of darkness; but the floor creaks,
someone stirs
In the other darkness—and the hairs all rise
Along my neck, I whisper: "It is he!"

Many years after *Losses,* in his 1965 volume *The Lost World,* Jarrell published "A Hunt in the Black Forest," which begins exactly as "The Child of Courts" does, except for a shift to the third person that heralds a new, or at least a redirected, point of view toward the same situation:

After the door shuts and the footsteps die,
He calls out: "Mother?"

The speaker now, however, is not the child but an omniscient narrator. The circumstances, like the title, suggest the world of the

Märchen, projected in a Freudian nightmare fantasy. A king, out hunting, comes to a hut in the forest where a deaf-mute feeds him a stew that poisons him while a red dwarf watches through the window. At the end of this poem, whose every stage is brilliantly and dramatically clear and sinister, there is a blending of supernatural and psychologically pointed details that brings us all the way over from the climax of the king's death to the further, greater climax of the child's sensibility underlying the entire story.

> Then a bubbled, gobbling sound begins,
> The sound of the pot laughing on the fire.
> —The pot, overturned among the ashes,
> Is cold as death.
>
> Something is scratching, panting. A little
> voice
> Says, "Let *me*! Let *me*!" The mute
> Puts his arms around the dwarf and raises
> him.
>
> The pane is clouded with their soft slow
> breaths,
> The mute's arms tire; but they gaze on
> and on,
> Like children watching something wrong.
> Their blurred faces, caught up in one wish,
> Are blurred into one face: a child's set face.

The mute, the dwarf, and the child thus share horrified, guilty fascination; they are three facets of innocence, despite their involvement in a primal tragic scene. It would not be difficult to "interpret" the story as one in which the child (into whose face the other faces blend at the very end of the poem) is both the victim—the stew that the king, his father, ate—and the killer who destroys his father through the very act of being devoured by him. If we put "The Child of Courts" and "A Hunt in the Black Forest" side by side and consider each a gloss on the other, it becomes clear that the addition of the third-person narrator enabled Jarrell to fill out the symbolic context of the original poem's conception. But he added to it the distanced understanding of an adult voice presenting the unresolved anguish of one kind of disturbed childhood. "A Hunt in the Black Forest" brings both its psychological and its archetypal motives directly to bear on the tale it has been telling by a final refocusing of elements present in the story from the start. It represents, as do the more literally autobiographical poems of the final volume, an achieved objectification of the speaking self and an achieved clarity as well. Thought is presented experientially, with sharply sketched action and description that leave room for shadows, depths, and implied complexities.

One poem in *Losses,* "Lady Bates," especially foreshadows Jarrell's turn, after the war period, to poems centered on suffering individual persons, often women. The Lady Bates of the title is, says Jarrell in his notes to *Selected Poems,* "a little Negro girl whose Christian name is *Lady.*" The child has died, and the poem is addressed to her as an epitome of everything helpless and betrayed in human existence. Viewed unsympathetically, the poem is an example of sophisticated sentimentality, a humanitarian southerner's attempt to speak to his knowledge of the hurt done to Negroes in a language appropriate to both. "Lady Bates," significantly, comes first in *Losses,* the only poem quite of its kind in this book, preceding all the war pieces. A certain oversimplification of the meaning of ordinary people's lives, comparable to what we have seen in the war poems, comes through in "Lady Bates" despite its genuinely touching aspects. The worst of Jarrell is concentrated into parts of this poem that mercilessly expose both his condescension and the presumptuousness of his spokesmanship for the girl:

> Poor black trash,
> The wind has blown you away forever
> By mistake; and they sent the wind to the
> chain-gang
> And it worked in the governor's kitchen, a
> trusty for life;
> And it was all written in the Book of Life;
> Day and Night met in the twilight by your
> tomb

And shot craps for you; and Day said,
pointing to your soul,
"This *bad* young colored lady,"
And Night said, "Poor little nigger girl."

"Lady Bates," with its weaknesses, continues Jarrell's development toward the objectification of the speaking self that I have suggested is the chief triumph of *The Lost World.* Like the many soldiers who are his subjects in the war volumes, the little black girl in this poem serves two functions in this development. First and most obviously, she is one of the many figures in his poems whose reality he seeks to repossess as persons outside himself. Secondly, though, she and the other figures are the beneficiaries (or victims) of an empathy that enables him to project onto them certain basic features of the child psyche familiar in his earlier poems—its confusion, innocence, and betrayal by life. It would be accurate to say that each of these figures is at once himself or herself *and* Randall Jarrell; not, of course, Jarrell the wit, translator of Rilke, and edgily competitive poet, but the essential Jarrell whose sensibility defines itself in his poems in the way we have been tracing.

This essential sensibility enters many of the speaking voices in Jarrell's next volume, *The Seven-League Crutches.* In fact, reading through this volume, one is pierced by the realization of how completely possessed by it his writing is and what a chilling desolateness he coped with. It is not only the specific *child* minds he presents that make the realization so forcible, though indeed this volume gives us several such characterizations to add to "Lady Bates." The one closest to "Lady Bates" in tone is "The Truth," in which, Jarrell explains in *Selected Poems,* "the little boy who speaks . . . has had his father, his sister, and his dog killed in one of the early fire-raids on London, and has been taken to the country, to a sort of mental institution for children." This poem has none of the cultural overlay of "Lady Bates," the treacherous sense of "understanding" the black child's world that cuts across Jarrell's finer sense of her as one abandoned by life in her own idiosyncratic way. "The Truth" is stripped down to the essential anguish and bewilderment:

When I was four my father went to
Scotland.
They *said* he went to Scotland.

When I woke up I think I thought that I was
dreaming—
I was so little then that I thought dreams
Are in the room with you, like the cinema.
That's why you don't dream when it's still
light—

They pull the shades down when it is, so
you can sleep.
I thought that then, but that's not right.
Really it's in your head.

And it was light then—light at night. . . .

And yet, as with the play of thought in "Lady Bates," one can well ask of this poem whether the anguish and bewilderment are really the little boy's or Jarrell's. All that charming talk about a child's notion of what dreams are is really in Jarrell's grown-up voice, reminiscing about his own memories. Naturally, these thoughts about dreams being like the cinema might occur to any child, and my only point is that Jarrell is using this kind of situation, so close to his own constant preoccupation, as a suitable instrument on which to play. He is a virtuoso of pity, and the form his virtuosity takes is to work his own voice into his materials so as to bring out their intrinsic pathos and his active insight simultaneously.

In "The Black Swan," a poem about another child, this fusion of sensibilities works superbly. The preface to *Selected Poems* tells us that this poem was "said, long ago, by a girl whose sister is buried under the white stones of the green churchyard." "The Black Swan" and a number of other poems in *The Seven-League Crutches* mark a considerable advance in the artistic isolation and redirection of Jarrell's deepest motifs. The loneliness, the sense of a chaotic universe, and the lost focus of identity (expressed as a shared or confused identity) of his best later work are all present at the very start of "The Black Swan":

> When the swans turned my sister into a swan
> I would go to the lake, at night, from milking:
> The sun would look out through the reeds like a swan,
> A swan's red beak; and the beak would open
> And inside there was darkness, the stars and the moon. . . .

This beginning, a decisive act of empathic imagination, opens up a world of associations to the end of recovering the stab of primal pathos. The swan images proliferate, and the mad or nightmare-ridden speaker becomes a swan herself as, out of the realm of heartless nature and death, her sister responds to her call. This poem alone would make it clear that Jarrell's poetic control had grown enormously by 1951. He could now deal purely and forcefully with psychological and mythic or archetypal materials and could write his own thoughts directly without overintellectualizing and without superciliousness. "The Orient Express" opens *The Seven-League Crutches* on a note of unpretentious intimacy that combines his ever-present child-mindedness with his adult intelligence:

> One looks from the train
> Almost as one looked as a child. In the sunlight
> What I see still seems to me plain,
> I am safe; but at evening
> As the lands darken, a questioning
> Precariousness comes over everything. . . .

All of Jarrell is there, as simply apparent as possible. But the form itself has a new sort of interest when compared to much of Jarrell's earlier work. The ease and grace of movement, the sustained clarity of speech, and the engaging, concrete thoughtfulness keep the reader listening and moving along with the speaker. The lines of this passage, as in the poem as a whole, tend toward a three-stress unit but often —here in the two opening lines—depart from it. Rhyming effects (an exact rhyme in lines one and three, the echoing of *-ing* in lines four, five, and six, the repetitions of "look" and "one," and the sequence of the monosyllabic verbs "look" and "looked" and "see" and "seems" and "comes") are introduced lightly yet saturate the sound structure as in the even richer "The Black Swan." One finds a similar felicity and immediacy in the two poems that close the book, "The Venetian Blind" and "Seele im Raum"—poems which both recall—the former in its literal theme and the latter in its title—a poem of Rilke's. "The Venetian Blind" does indeed present its protagonist as a "Seele im Raum" or "soul in space."

> He is lost in himself forever.
>
> And the Angel he makes from the sunlight
> Says in mocking tenderness:
>
> "Poor stateless one, wert thou the world?"
> . . .
>
> The bars of the sunlight fall to his face.
>
> And yet something calls, as it has called:
> "But where am *I*? But where am *I*?"

Rilke's "Seele im Raum," written in 1917, has as its literal subject the condition of a soul torn from its body and suddenly become pure potentiality in a realm of pure being. The soul feels stripped of comforts, exposed, and tremulously fearful in its ignorance of its own destiny. Jarrell's "Seele im Raum" has in part the same theme, but the central situation of his poem is that of a woman who once had the grotesque illusion that an eland was present wherever she was. The woman's pathetic obsession would be hilariously absurd were it not, as her monologue shows, symptomatic of her sense of being a lost self despite the fact that she was a wife and mother. Her period of madness is now over; but in an important way she misses the eland, which was so tangibly and oppressively present to her and yet was the only thing that was hers alone: her soul's embodiment of its own misery.

Today, in a German dictionary, I saw *elend*
And the heart in my breast turned over, it
was—

It was a word one translates wretched. . . .

—It was worse than impossible, it was a
joke.

And yet when it was, I *was*—
Even to think that I once thought
That I could see it is to feel the sweat
Like needles at my hair-roots, I am blind

—It was not even a joke, not even a joke.

Yet how can I believe it? Or believe that I
Owned it, a husband, children? Is my voice
the voice
Of that skin of being—of what owns, is
owned
In honor or dishonor, that is borne and
bears—

Or of that raw thing, the being inside it
That has neither a wife, a husband, nor a
child
But goes at last as naked from this world
As it was born into it—

And the eland comes and grazes on its
grave. . . .

The passage I have just quoted takes us from the punning proof that the eland had been for the speaker a projection of her soul's *elend* condition, its misery, to the bitter sense she has now of all that she has lost and then, finally, to that sense of being stripped of a human past and utterly out in space of which Rilke writes. Jarrell's absorption in Rilke was one of his great passions; it must have been of tremendous importance to him in the progress of his art that I have described. He immersed himself in the greater poet, whose themes were so close to his own. The sensibilities of children and of women dominate the attention of both poets. Both are in search of points of directive contact with chaotic reality—both are "souls in space." Both, incidentally, had noncombatant military service involving a certain disillusionment, and there were temperamental affinities as well (as in their mixture of endearing traits with ruthless critical attitudes).

Rilke's essential influence on Jarrell seems to have been to encourage him to widen his poetic thought and to reach for a more concentrated and evocative imagery, a more personal and vital poetic speech and rhythmic movement, and a style both natural to him and in touch with European cultural tradition. It is interesting that *The Seven-League Crutches* begins with a section called "Europe"—poems with European settings to which Jarrell attaches his American awareness. The displacement of context enables him to convert old sets of thought into deepened historical and philosophical musings. Looking out from the Orient Express, he can see that the whole world (not just his own empirical life) is unassimilable to the soul in space and yet has its own aesthetic magnetism we cannot avoid:

It is like any other work of art.
It is and never can be changed.
Behind everything there is always
The unknown unwanted life.

One could conceivably make the same observation looking from an American train, but just that kind of consideration is involved in the implied comparison. It is just the sensed history behind the fields, people, houses, and villages that makes the feeling of an essential changelessness of existence such a powerful one. In "A Game at Salzburg," the same principle is at work. Jarrell's explanation in *Selected Poems* shows how much he relishes the knowledgeableness behind the poem, the kind of Europeanized wit its subject enables him to cultivate: "I put into 'A Game at Salzburg' a little game that Germans and Austrians play with very young children. The child says to the grown-up, *Here I am,* and the grown-up answers, *There you are;* the children use the same little rising tune, and the grown-ups the same resolving, conclusive one. It seemed to me that if there could be a conversation between the world and God, this would be it." And so, in the poem, the whole style is delightfully relaxed until the very end. The poet (during the year in which he was a participant in the Salzburg Seminar in American Civilization) is seen passing lazy, happy days amid the innumerable tokens not only of an old civilization but also of the recent war. One notices with some surprise and interest that his juxtapositions of a modern American intelligence like his own with all these surrounding signs and symbols, under circumstances at once so congenial and so poignantly and volatilely suggestive, have led him into a tone and rhythm that must have influenced Robert Lowell's style in *Life Studies*:

> A little ragged girl, our ball-boy;
> A partner—ex-Afrika-Korps—
> In khaki shorts, P. W. illegible.
> (He said: "To have been a prisoner of war
> In Colorado iss a *privilege.*")
> The evergreens, concessions, carrousels,
> And D. P. camp at Franz Joseph Park;
> A gray-green river, evergreen-dark hills.
> Last, a long way off in the sky,
> Snow-mountains.

These are the social and political and historical realities, all within the unchanged ancient landscape. When, later on, the poet finds himself playing the little game of *Hier bin i'—Da bist du,* with a three-year-old, there is an inevitably ironic echo from that opening scene. Reality is intractably itself, and the fact is softly underlined in the persistence of a language and a ritual even in a tiny girl "licking sherbet from a wooden spoon" as she engages the poet in the game. Later still, he moves "past Maria Theresa's sleigh" and the statues, mostly broken, in the garden where "the nymphs look down with the faces of Negroes." The two worlds suddenly related in this image are one world after all, as is the prewar world that became the one at war and then the post-war one. At the end, Jarrell's old, persistent insight is thrust into the foreground, but the voice adopted is a European one recalling the "dreamy" American to the imponderable:

> In anguish, in expectant acceptance
> The world whispers: *Hier bin i'.*

We cannot pursue all the examples of Jarrell's "Europeanization" in *The Seven-League Crutches.* One further instance is the translation of Corbière's "Le Poète contumace." Corbière's tough-mindedness and scathing but funny self-characterizations show up the sentimental limits of Jarrell's own work. Nevertheless, Jarrell admired Corbière and aspired to his kind of mentality.

Jarrell's one novel, *Pictures from an Institution,* bears extended analysis because so much that was important to him is packed into it, and also because it is an extremely clever work of satire as well as a humanely intelligent book. It is set in a progressive women's college not altogether unlike Sarah Lawrence College, and its pictures of the academic and personal life of all concerned remain extremely amusing. I shall discuss it only very briefly, in relation to Jarrell's poetic development. It represents, I think, a completion of his attempt to assimilate his own frame of thought to that of cultivated and sensitive Europeans. The novel is written in the first person, from the viewpoint of a poet who has been teaching at Benton College for a number of years. The real hero, though, is an Austrian-Jewish composer named Gottfried Rosenbaum through whose eyes the provincialism, complacency, and emptiness of much of American education is made, somewhat lovingly, clear, while certain genuine American strengths and potentialities are seen as goods after all. Dr. Rosenbaum's mind is razor-keen, though he does not ordinarily use it to slash people. That role is taken by a visiting novelist, Gertrude Johnson, whose analytical savagery has no kindness in it and who is often malignantly inventive in her sizing up of people, all grist for her novels. She is going to do a novel about the college, and it will be merciless—presumably far more so than *Pictures from an Institution* itself. Yet this necessary comparison gives one to think. Gertrude, as it were, discharges the hostile and supercilious side of Jarrell's critical intelligence, while Gottfried represents a more genial ideal. John Crowe Ransom, in his contribution to *Randall Jarrell, 1914–1965,* notes the indications that Gertrude undergoes something like a "conversion" to a more humane attitude in the course of the novel, and I would suggest that the improvement of Gertrude is something in the nature of a purgation for Jarrell himself. The "I" of the novel, the poet who is ready to leave the limited campus scene at the end of the year, has been close to both Gertrude and Gottfried. Gottfried, with his elderly Russian wife who shares his cultivation and his sense of tragic history, will remain after the writers have left. With them will stay the talented and loyal Constance Morgan, who in her life embodies the best of American openness and possibility as Gottfried and Irene embody the living tradition of European art with which we must remain in vital touch. Constance, an orphan, is thus one of four figures who represent ideals or characteristics of Jarrell himself. The book reaches a certain serenity and insight into the best qualities of each of the characters, despite the fun at the expense of most of them along the way.

What an injustice I have done to this novel, with its marvelously amusing passages that Jarrell wrote in an ecstasy of acerbic release. It is his most balanced work, done not long after his marriage to Mary von Schrader in 1952, and it helped him gain a precarious personal balance. It was also a self-deceptive balance, a standoff between barely repressed total revulsion and sentimental voting for the triumph, in any one person, of decency over stupidity and mean-spirited worldliness. A variety of sexual repression is involved as well. In the novel, as in Jarrell's poetry, sexuality in itself seems hardly present as a factor in his own thought and emotions or in those of his characters. His attitude toward women is a little like his attitude toward unhappy children and a little like Sophocles' toward "the Mothers": awe, mystification, and, sometimes, a cozy sympathy with a bitter edge nevertheless. The sense of a life ridden by despair that comes through in his last two books of poems is linked with that bitter sympathy. The balanced feeling of control of the mid-1950's dissolves into something harsher, more convincing finally, and at its best more brilliant.

The three poems that open the 1960 volume, *The Woman at the Washington Zoo,* are rather precise examples of Jarrell's feeling for women. He thinks about them a great deal, and passionately, but in the ways I have suggested. The title poem is one of a number written from the point of view of a woman, usually aging, who feels that, as she says, "The world goes by my cage and never sees me." (Jarrell discusses the composition of this poem brilliantly in one of his essays in *A Sad Heart at the Supermarket,* 1962.) The poem begins with a tone of quiet desperation and in a sometimes banal cadence of a sort occasionally cultivated by Eliot, but rises to a hysterical pitch at the end—an accusation against fate and an appeal to be transformed. The woman's outcry is directed toward a vulture, both real and symbolic. She wants to be devoured and transformed, and her language suggests that the bird of prey to which her protest and prayer are addressed embodies the male principle:

> Vulture,
> When you come for the white rat that the
> foxes left,
> Take off the red helmet of your head, the
> black
> Wings that have shadowed me, and step to
> me as man:
> The wild brother at whose feet the white
> wolves fawn,
> To whose hand of power the great lioness
> Stalks, purring. . . .
> You know what I was,
> You see what I am: change me, change me!

It is the first time in his poems that Jarrell speaks so fiercely through a woman's voice. In the next poem, "Cinderella," he does so again, but here, for once, female toughness—and even hardness—of spirit comes through. Both Cinderella and her fairy godmother are presented as coolly anti-male. Cinderella, on her very wedding day, under the "pulsating marble" of her wedding lace, "wished it all a widow's coal-black weeds." Later she became "a sullen wife and a reluctant mother." The godmother is sophisticated into an archetypal "God's Mother" who comes into her own whenever her son is away. At these times she invites Cinderella into the "gold-gauzed door" of her Heaven that exists only in the flames of the male-created Hell, and they gossip comfortably apart from male ideas, ideals, and laws. This poem is far more effective than the long, rather involved, and precious one that follows: "The End of the Rainbow." In this latter poem, about a woman "old enough to be invisible," Jarrell's proliferating details carry a certain pathos but, even more, suggest the poet's extraordinary identification with his protagonist.

After these opening poems of human sensibility gratingly out of phase come the four most striking pieces of the book—poems that, together with those in the title sequence of *The Lost World,* complete Jarrell's work by closing in on intimate realities of his own actual life and memory. Again we have an interesting parallel to Lowell, for both poets were moving into their confessional period at the same time. Lowell's *Life Studies* had appeared the year before, an enormous gathering of concentrated neurotic energy centered on his childhood and the personalities of his parents as somehow symptomatic of America's and the world's malaise. Although Jarrell's confessional poems are less ambitious formally and symbolically than Lowell's, they are in many ways closer to the anomie and the disturbances that mark the common life in our day.

Jarrell is in his own way as much an exotic as Lowell. The strains of his boyhood are as atypical as those of the privileged Bostonian, and the adult lives of both men have been atypical too. But often in these poems he summons up the world of plain-living, laboring souls and the hardships and pleasures of ordinary life. The confusing images of his beloved grandmother wringing a chicken's neck and of the already dead bird still running about in circles recur, for instance, in a number of the poems. Each is an image of the brutal nature of existence and cannot be separated out from the meaning of love. Millions of ordinary folk know the experience described in "A Street off Sunset" (in *The Lost World*):

> Mama comes out and takes in the clothes
> from the clothesline. She looks with
> righteous love
> At all of us, her spare face half a girl's.
> She enters a chicken coop, and the hens
> shove
> And flap and squawk, in fear; the whole
> block whirls
> Into the farthest corner. She chooses one,
> Comes out, and wrings its neck. The body
> hurls
> Itself out—lunging, reeling, it begins to run
> Away from Something, to fly away from
> Something
> In great flopping circles. Mama stands like a
> nun
> In the center of each awful, anguished ring.
> The thudding and scrambling go on, go on—
> then they fade,
> I open my eyes, it's over . . . Could such a
> thing
> Happen to anything? It could to a rabbit, I'm
> afraid;
> It could to . . .

The details here are as plain, and as hideous, as, say, those in John Clare's "Badger." Where Jarrell differs from a true *naïf,* though, is in his superimposed notes of observation, themselves simple in tone but implying mediative and informed intelligence: "righteous love" (a note of psychological insight, for the woman's look is a gesture both of self-encouragement and of apology and self-justification); "away from Something" (a note to underline the presence of universal terror); "like a nun" (again, the note of reaffirmed innocence, which is yet "the center of each awful, anguished ring"); and at last the deliberate pointing up of the child's reactions. The easily colloquial iambic pentameter lines run on quite naturally; one hardly notices the alternating rhymes that help rock the movement into hysteria—that is, into the child's momentarily traumatized hypnosis by the impossible thing that is happening. Jarrell uses this pattern throughout the "Lost World" sequence. It makes for a slightly relaxed, anecdotal tone that drags boringly at times but provides a frame at others for effects such as this one. This weakness, in itself, is a reflection of Jarrell's desire to keep his form open to common speech and common psychology—something he much admired in Robert Frost's work.

Returning to *The Woman in the Washington Zoo* and the four poems there that I have noted, we can see that "In Those Days" and "The Elementary Scene" are both exceedingly simple in form. "In Those Days" consists of four quatrains with the simplest of rhyme schemes, *abcb,* and is in a basic iambic tetrameter with much variation for naturalness and dramatic immediacy. It reads, except for the deliberate avoidance of smoothness of meter, like an afterbeat from Heine, particularly in the last stanza:

> How poor and miserable we were,
> How seldom together!
> And yet after so long one thinks:
> In those days everything was better.

Almost doggerel—but this ending shrugs off a painful nostalgia for a past love, the whole adolescent atmosphere of which has been evoked, with all its bittersweet frustration and sense of wintry isolation of the two young people, in the preceding stanzas. The poem strikes a new personal key for Jarrell, and serves as an overture to the further exploration of the speaker's lost past. Then come "The Elementary Scene" and "Windows," still quite simple in their diction and the scenes they envision: the first a rural elementary school at Hallowe'en, the second the home of dead elders who once loved and cherished the speaker. Jarrell's ability to suggest, with utmost economy, a milieu at once provincial and inarticulate and yet full of unmet challenge—the reality of an irretrievable folk past that might have led to a far different life for the speaker, less to be regretted, perhaps—is his greatest strength.

> The thin grass by the girls' door,
> Trodden on, straggling, yellow and rotten,
> And the gaunt field with its one tied cow . . .

—the lines recall his very early "The Cow Wandering in the Bare Field" and the curious persistence of images demanding clarification again and again during a poet's lifetime. The self-reproach at the end of "The Elementary Scene"—"I, I, the future that mends everything"—is the final evidence that this is one of his purest poems, a poem of unearned but heavily felt depression, in which the speaker takes upon himself the guilt of time's passing. So also in "Windows," it is the unbearable irrevocability of the past that the speaker lives with and endures (in this respect a true heir to Frost and E. A. Robinson). The beloved dead, imagined alive in their time, are compared in their vivid presence to "dead actors, on a rainy afternoon," who "move in a darkened livingroom" on a television screen.

> *These* actors, surely, have known nothing of
> today,
> That time of troubles and of me. . . .
> They move along in peace. . . . If only I were
> they!
> Could act out, in longing, the impossibility
> That haunts me like happiness!

Sentimentality is held at a distance in this poem by the sheer force of illusion: the construction of a moment of the recaptured past so keenly present to the speaker's desire that it goes beyond imagination—

> It blurs, and there is drawn across my face
> As my eyes close, a hand's slow fire-warmed
> flesh.
>
> It moves so slowly that it does not move.

The poem "Aging," which follows, does not have the fine sensuous conviction of "Windows" and does lapse into sentimentality. When, in the "Lost World" sequence and in "Remembering the Lost World," literal memory again picks up these motifs, the intensity and concentration are sacrificed for the anecdotal colloquialism we have seen. These are poems banking on total rather than on selected recall and striving to hold their recovered, or reimagined, reality intact against the poisonous fact of elapsed time. Theirs is an opposite method, allowing room for something like a novelistic play of mind over bizarre contradictions of a child's life in Hollywood, a life at once disciplined by good gray work and indulged by an almost sensually remembered aunt and her friends, one of whom owned the MGM lion. It is a bath of charming, touching, and heartbreaking memory in the new open mode that Jarrell had discovered. The new mode seems to have freed him from a vision too sharp to be endured, and to have taken him over the line of belief in the present reality of the past. "Thinking of the Lost World" ends:

> LOST—NOTHING. STRAYED FROM NOWHERE.
> NO REWARD.
> I hold in my own hands, in happiness,
> Nothing: the nothing for which there's no
> reward.

"I felt at first," writes John Crowe Ransom in the essay I quoted from earlier, "that this was a tragic ending. But I have studied it till I give up that notion. The NOTHING is the fiction, the transformation; to which both boy and man are given. That World is not Lost because it never existed; but it is as precious now as ever. I have come to think that Randall was announcing the beginning of his 'second childhood.' There is nothing wrong about that, to the best of my knowledge." Perhaps, but what Mr. Ransom is describing is the letdown, or failure of nerve, in the face of the issues (which Jarrell nevertheless did to a certain important extent face) that often takes the form of a paradoxically melancholy complacency in writers just below the energy level of genius. Jarrell himself approaches the issue wryly in the quoted lines, and also in the self-ironically named poem "Hope," which takes us into the poet's grown-up life with all its gaiety, fears, and gallant playing of roles. It is almost as though he had given the tragic its due in "The Elementary Scene," "Windows," and the very dark-spirited Rilke translations of *The Woman at the Washington Zoo* and then turned his back on the discipline of greatness.

But this would be too harsh a judgment. At fifty-one, Jarrell was still expanding his range of technique and of personal sympathies. He might well have reversed his direction once more and made another fresh start as he had done in the war poems and again in *The Seven-League Crutches* and the last books. With all the intelligence and openness to varied literary influences reflected in his criticism and his translations during the two postwar decades, he was surely capable of a great deal of further development despite a deep formal conservatism. Our poetry—and it is Jarrell's *poetry* almost exclusively that we have been concerned with—is today struggling in a new way with the question of the role of an active, many-sided intellectuality in essential poetic structure. Jarrell might conceivably have contributed something of interest to this exploration. Meanwhile, he remains a force among us as a poet of defeat and loneliness who nevertheless does not allow himself to become less spirited. He is like that ex-P.W. in his poem "A Game at Salzburg" who says, "To have been a prisoner of war in Colorado is a *privilege.*"

Selected Bibliography

WORKS OF RANDALL JARRELL

NOTE: The quotations in the foregoing text are all taken from the original volumes rather than from the revised versions in *Selected Poems* and in *The Complete Poems.*

POETRY

"The Rage for the Lost Penny," in *Five Young American Poets* (Norfolk, Conn.: New Directions, 1940).

Blood for a Stranger, (New York: Harcourt, Brace, 1942).
Little Friend, Little Friend, (New York: Dial, 1945).
Losses, (New York: Harcourt, Brace, 1948).
The Seven-League Crutches, (New York: Harcourt, Brace, 1951).
Selected Poems, 1st ed. (New York: Knopf, 1955); 2nd ed., including *The Woman at the Washington Zoo* (New York: Atheneum, 1964).
The Woman at the Washington Zoo, (New York: Atheneum, 1960).
The Lost World, (New York: Macmillan, 1965). Paperback reprint with Robert Lowell's essay "Randall Jarrell, 1914–1965: An Appreciation," appended (New York: Collier, 1966).
The Complete Poems, (New York: Farrar, Straus and Giroux, 1969). Includes *Selected Poems,* poems omitted from *Selected Poems,* and sections of "Uncollected Poems (1934–1965)" and "Unpublished Poems (1935–1965)."

NOVEL

Pictures from an Institution, a Comedy, (New York: Knopf, 1954).

CRITICISM

Poetry and the Age, (New York: Knopf, 1953).
A Sad Heart at the Supermarket, (New York: Atheneum, 1962).
The Third Book of Criticism, (New York: Farrar, Straus and Giroux, 1965).

BIBLIOGRAPHIES

Adams, Charles M., *Randall Jarrell: A Bibliography,* (Chapel Hill: University of North Carolina Press, 1958). A supplement to this bibliography appears in *Analects* (1: 49–56, Spring 1961).
Gillikin, Dure J., A Check-List of Criticism on Randall Jarrel, 1941–1970 with an Introduction and a List of His Major Works," *Bulletin of the New York Public Library* (74: 176–94 , April 1971).
Kisslinger, Margaret V., "A Bibliography of Randall Jarrell," *Bulletin of Bibliography* (24: 243–47, May–August 1966).
Shaprio, Karl, *Randall Jarrell,* (Washington, D.C.: Library of Congress, 1967). Includes a bibliography of primary works and a list of Jarrell materials in the collections of the Library of Congress: manuscripts, phonodiscs, magnetic tapes, and motion pictures as well as books and uncollected poems and prose.

CRITICAL AND BIOGRAPHICAL STUDIES

Fein, Richard, "Major American Poetry of World War II," Unpublished dissertation New York University (1960).
Lowell Robert, Peter Taylor, and Robert Penn Warren, eds.*Randall Jarrell, 1914–1965,* (New York: Farrar, Straus and Giroux, 1967). Essays by Hannah Arendt, John Berryman, Elizabeth Bishop, Philip Booth, Cleanth Brooks, James Dickey, Denis Donoghue, Leslie A. Fiedler, Robert Fitzgerald, R. W. Flint, Alfred Kazin, Stanley Kunitz, Robert Lowell, William Meredith, Marianne Moore, Robert Phelps, Sister M. Bernetta Quinn, John Crowe Ransom, Adrienne Rich, Delmore Schwartz, Maurice Sendak, Karl Shapiro, Allen Tate, Eleanor Ross Taylor, Peter Taylor, P. L. Travers, Robert Watson, and Mrs. Randall Jarrell. Pages xi–xii list all of Jarrell's books, including editions in preparation, as of the volume's date of publication.
Mazzaro, Jerome, "Between Two Worlds: The Post-Modernism of Randall Jarrell," (*Salmagundi,* Fall 1971) 93–113; Rideout, Walter B., *Poems in Progress,* " 'To Change! to Change!'," edited by Edward Hungerford (Evanston, Ill.: Northwestern University Press, 1967).
Rosenthal, M. L., *The Modern Poets: A Critical Introduction,* (New York: Oxford University Press, 1960).

Robinson Jeffers

(1887–1962)

R. W. BUTTERFIELD

"And west of the west / I have lived," wrote Robinson Jeffers in the epilogue to his first volume of poems. In an otherwise unremarkable book they are the most significant words, simply because at an early age and at the beginning of his literary career they point directly to where he was to make his lifelong home, body and soul. For "west of the west" was where a few years later, stone by laborious stone, he would start to build his Tor House, with its Hawk's Tower, at Carmel in California on the continent's western coast. And "west of the west" was his spirit's familiar country, as though in the wake of an immense procession winding over several thousand years he was the last frontiersman, the ultimate westerner.

> I am building a thick stone pillar upon this shore, the very turn of the world, the long migration's
> End; the sun goes on but we have come up to an end,
> We have climbed at length to a height, to an end, this end: shall we go down again to Mother Asia?
> Some of us will go down, some will abide, but we sought
> More than to return to a mother.

At the end of that long migration across space and through time, he seemed to stand at a precise spot, balked by the ocean, on the edge of a concluded plane, at "the very turn of the world," just before the plane reveals itself to be a revolving globe that goes down again to Asia. "Bred west of Caucasus," he seemed to stand west of a west that never quite touched east, as the Western world's final man.

Perhaps appropriately, since going west is part of the classical western experience, his childhood was spent not in California but in and around Pittsburgh, where his father, a minister, was professor of Old Testament literature at the Western Theological Seminary, and where he was born on January 10, 1887. His paternal grandfather had emigrated in 1810 from County Monaghan in Ireland, but on his mother's side he was descended from much earlier American settlers, including the McCords from Scotland; the Robinsons, who had arrived in 1730 from Ulster; and the Tuttles, who had come over as long ago as 1635 and in New Haven acquired land on which Yale University was eventually built. Seventeenth-century New England, Scottish, Northern Irish, his ancestry was deeply, vigorously Protestant; and though Jeffers was to discard Christianity and to find in its elevation of man above the rest of creation a root cause of latter-day disjunction, his mind and sensibility remained in important respects irrevocably Protestant. These ancestors were outwardly of little interest to him, but some sort of affinity for them he clearly did feel, because on his rare journeys to the British Isles, it was to Scotland and especially to Ulster, lands of his forefathers, that he was drawn, rather than to England's "soft alien twilight / Worn and weak with too much humanity."

There was considerable disparity between the ages of Jeffers' parents. His father was nearly fifty at the time of his son's birth, and his mother only twenty-seven. The couple were evidently dissimilar in temperament also, for he was something of a recluse, whereas she was remembered by her daughter-in-law as being "fond of society and very gay." However, the marriage seems to have been by and large a happy one, although clearly the difference in age and personality provided models for those several occasions in Jeffers' narrative poems when lively young women are wedded, shackled, to men either much older than themselves or much more dour. "What right has a wild old man in the useless beauty of a young wife?" asks the poet on behalf of a character in "The Coast-Range Christ," able to recall from his own childhood a woman still in her thirties married to a man past sixty.

Nevertheless, of the two it was the impress of the father that was, if not the more profound, at any rate the more visible, upon the mature Jeffers. It was his father's memory that was cherished in poems, his death that was mourned, his ghost that returned in them, and his presence that Jeffers so often silently or audibly invoked. "Father, / Forgive me. I dishonored and wasted all your hopes of me, one by one; yet I loved you well." His father's most enduring gift was the laying of the foundations of a wide, traditional learning, based on an intimate knowledge of the Bible and of literature in Greek, which he began to learn at the age of five. In this cultivated and comfortable, if rather austere, home Jeffers was an only child until the age of seven, when a brother was born. Having few companions, he passed his time in books, in daydreams, and in watchful observation of the natural world. The habit of solitariness was implanted in him early.

Between 1899 and 1902 Jeffers traveled extensively with his family in Europe, attending schools in Leipzig, Lausanne, and Geneva, and adding to his biblical and classical grounding a proficiency in French and German. In 1903 the family made their western exodus to Pasadena, and Jeffers, now sixteen, entered nearby Occidental College. He studied literature, graduated with the B.A. in 1905, and took up further study at the University of Southern California, switching to medicine in 1907, and to forestry at the University of Washington in 1910. The influence of his medical training persists in the physiological imagery and descriptions that permeate his poetry; while his studies of forestry served him daily throughout his life, as he tended the hundreds of trees that he planted around his house.

If Jeffers as a student was changeable, there was at least one constant in his life. This was his love for Una Call Kuster, two years his senior and the wife of a Los Angeles lawyer, whom he first met in 1905. Eight years of confusion, emotional storm and struggle, and parental disapproval followed for them until 1913, when Una was divorced, quite unacrimoniously. The couple were married on August 2 of that year. What had been of paramount importance to Jeffers was that their union should receive the blessing of both his parents, which it finally did a few months before their wedding.

Jeffers had been publishing poems in magazines since 1903, and in 1912 his first volume, *Flagons and Apples*, appeared, financed by himself. Writing poetry was evidently his vocation, and literature was Una's passion, so the couple's first intention, like that of such contemporaries as Robert Frost, Ezra Pound, Hilda Doolittle, and T. S. Eliot, was to go and live in England. Jeffers even confided to a friend that "probably a good deal of our future life will be spent in England or on the continent." But it was not to be. Una became pregnant; they remained in America; she gave birth in May 1914 to a daughter, who lived only one day. As Europe tumbled toward war, the Jeffers made their way up the coast to Carmel, where amid hills and trees and by the ocean they knew that they had come to their "inevitable place" that the poet was to make "Jeffers country." They were to live here for the rest of their lives, with simple tastes and modest expectations, on the basis of a modicum of inherited money, supplemented later by his literary earnings.

In December 1914, Jeffers had to endure the grief of a second death, less poignant, but more deeply disquieting to him, that of his father at the age of seventy-six. Over the next year or so his life was commemorated and his death mourned in a sonnet, "To His Father," in a lengthy elegy, "The Year of Mourning," and by an autobiographical persona in the large dramatic poem, "The Alpine Christ." Jeffers was writing poetry regularly now, descriptive and occasional pieces, odes, and especially narrative poems, which were still conventional in form and meter but which in their often startling content increasingly foreshadowed his later work. His second volume, *Californians,* was published in 1916, and in November of that year twin sons were born.

The next few months were the most critical and emotionally tumultuous of Jeffers' life. In his father, however much he had disagreed with him over mores and metaphysics, he had lost an anchor; and his consequent mental waywardness became the more pronounced as the civilization, in the name of whose highest established values, originally classical and Christian, his father had spoken, barbarized and destroyed itself on the battlefields of Europe. Now in April 1917 the United States entered the war, and Jeffers underwent an intense period of anguish over whether, when, and in what capacity he should commit himself to this Armageddon. The marriage was severely strained, doubtless also by whatever circumstances inspired such luscious and passionate writing as there is in "Fauna" and "Mal Paso Bridge." But this time of trial passed, the marriage survived, and the war ended; and when in 1919 they bought land on Carmel Point, Jeffers began to heal his spirit and regulate his heart by building a permanent home, on "foundations of sea-worn granite," with "my fingers" that "had the art to make stone love stone," a steady activity that occupied him many years.

During this time of crisis and resolution Jeffers' poetry, especially its diction and measure, changed character beyond recognition. Around 1917 and 1918 this change took shapes that were obviously experimental, under the pressure of heightened emotion and events; later, with a greater sense of assurance and the effect of an achieved form, it was under the calming, stabilizing influence of stonemasonry. By about 1921, the year of his mother's death, Jeffers had finally discovered the mature voice with which he was to speak, sometimes varying the pitch, but scarcely ever the accent or phrasing, for the remainder of his life.

Coincident with this discovery, the Jefferses' lives began to take on an apparently contented, habitual, and virtually unchanging pattern. "I am as attached to this rock," he announced, "as if I were a feudal serf with an iron collar." As the boys grew older, the family did a certain amount of traveling, particularly to Una's beloved Ireland and to New Mexico, home of Mabel Dodge Luhan and Frieda Lawrence. But "to stay at home," Jeffers considered, "is more interesting"; and for the most part he did stay at home. Between 1918 and 1929, for instance, he never once visited San Francisco, little more than a hundred miles away. He spent his days nurturing his plantation; collecting and transporting boulders for the continuous building of his house; walking the hills and shores with Una and watching the birds and animals; broadly educating his sons; entertaining a few, treasured friends; and, of course, writing poetry.

Behind this outwardly tranquil life, the furies were penned in his poetry. "Imagine victims," he wrote, "Lest your own flesh be chosen the agonist . . . Burn sacrifices once a year to magic / Horror away from the house." So, about once a year, starting in 1924 with *Tamar and Other Poems,* he "imagined victims," "burned sacrifices," and published a new volume, generally consisting of one or two agonizing, burning, horror-filled narrative or dramatic poems, supplemented by twenty or so shorter meditative, descriptive, or prophetic poems composed during the same period.

These volumes brought Jeffers a wide readership for a poet and a wider reputation, with enthusiasts as ardent as those who celebrated Walt Whitman. The apogee of this fame was probably reached somewhere around the early 1930's. But just as Whitman, though almost sanctified by some, was reviled by others, so also was Jeffers. For traditional moralists and rationalists, eventually for the New Criticism, Yvor Winters led the way most effectively, with a systematic demolition in 1930; while among populists and Marxists, Jeffers gradually damned himself by his historical "defeatism" and lofty impartiality. By the end of the 1930's the careless, utterly inaccurate imputation to him of incipient fascist sympathies was heard more than once. Having been famous, Jeffers became first notorious and then neglected, "a poet without critics."

Jeffers, however, was apparently unaffected either by zealous admirers or by scornful adversaries. What did affect him, though, violently disrupting his detached, even tenor of mind, as it had done over twenty years previously, was the United States' entry into another world war, the coming of which he had long predicted. Intensely isolationist, outragedly pacifist, intimating in one suppressed poem that he was every bit as capable of patriotically motivated treason as Ezra Pound, he railed against American and Allied leadership in a volume of poems, *The Double Axe,* published after the war, from whose prevailing sentiments his publishers felt bound to dissociate themselves in a prefatory note.

Nevertheless, through waxing and waning renown, the character of the Jefferses' daily life scarcely changed. The sons took careers in forestry and accountancy, and presented their parents with a succession of grandchildren. Jeffers and his wife were usually to be found at Carmel, traveling only to the eastern United States on a reading tour in 1941 and to Ireland again in 1948. Then in January 1949 Una fell ill, to linger, declining, until on September 1, 1950, she died. They had been together in their Carmel quietness for thirty-six years. He had loved her devotedly, more dependently than is disclosed in the poetry. Uneasy in company, he had become habituated to sheltering behind her. A forceful, possessive, protective woman, she had been an immeasurable source of strength to him. He worked deep into his sorrow for her in the narrative poem "Hungerfield":

> September again. The gray grass, the gray
> sea,
> The ink-black trees with white-bellied
> night-herons in them,
> Brawling on the boughs at dusk, barking
> like dogs—
> And the awful loss. It is a year. She has died:
> and I
> Have lived for a long year on soft rotten
> emotions,
> Vain longing and drunken pity, grief and
> gray ashes— . . .

His epitaph for her concludes the poem, the words of one who, believing in no personal immortality, conjures a pantheistic reunion out of barely tolerable agony.

> Here is the poem, dearest; you will never
> read it nor hear it. You were more
> beautiful
> Than a hawk flying; you were faithful and a
> lion heart like this rough hero
> Hungerfield. But the ashes have fallen
> And the flame has gone up; nothing human
> remains. You are earth and air; you are in
> the beauty of the ocean
> And the great streaming triumphs of
> sundown; you are alive and well in the
> tender young grass rejoicing
> When soft rain falls all night, and little rosy-
> fleeced clouds float on the dawn.
> —I shall be with you presently.

But it was not to be "presently." He outlived her by more than eleven years, lonely but not alone, since one of his sons and his young family had come to live at Tor House. While taking delight in his grandchildren, he returned to those "quiet and solitary ways" that had long been essential to him. In his last few years, as his bodily strength faded slowly, he wrote only short poems, some of his finest, celebrating the universe, the physical and natural worlds, from atom to galaxy; inveighing against the social world; and musing on suicide, but emphatically rejecting it, as he had always done. He died at home on January 20, 1962, ten days past his seventy-fifth birthday.

What a reader must find most noticeable about the young Jeffers is his exceptional precocity at the age of sixteen but his lack of development over the next decade. Like his similarly forward contemporary, Ezra Pound, he began, unsurprisingly, by echoing a variety of late Victorian poets, among them Dante Gabriel Rossetti, who accorded him a "passionate springtime" of appreciative "intoxication"; William Butler Yeats in his Celtic-twilight period; and the hearty Henry John Newbolt. In "Man's Pride" he rings a note of airy didacticism that probably owed something to Percy Bysshe Shelley:

> What is man that he should be proud?
>   And what is the race of men
>   That they should think high things?
> Behold, the deep cries aloud,
>   The high mountains answer again,
>   The swift wind stops and sings. . . .

Sounded there already is his conviction of human insignificance alongside natural grandeur; and elsewhere a later characteristic, imaginative vantage point is prefigured in the youthful romantic's preference for a sublime pulpit, "A Hill-Top View," from which to measure man.

In contrast with that of Pound, however, who over the next half dozen years was more than anybody else to alter the shape and scope of poetry in English, Jeffers' writing evolved by scarcely an irregular foot. In 1912, when Pound was articulating the principles of imagism and of modernist poetics in general, Jeffers produced in *Flagons and Apples* a volume, consisting chiefly of love poems, that abounded in conventional fin-de-siècle sentiments and postures, that was dyed in the bittersweet, lacklove world-weariness of a speaker either "mad and drunken" or "blind and deaf and broken," and awash with alliterative liquids and an imagery of old wine and crimson partings, wailing winds and soulless stars.

The poetry is no worse than that in many contemporaneous volumes; it is usually competent, and there are effective moments. But it is wholly, uninterruptedly derivative; and there are no intimations of what is to come. Jeffers' love for Una at this time was substantial enough, but not these literary loves of *Flagons and Apples,* the Helens, Canidia, Nyssa, Aileen-of-the-Woods, and a "pretty waitress."

When his second book appeared four years later, Jeffers had been living for some time in his "inevitable place" at Carmel. As the title, *Californians,* suggests, he at least now knew that he was not a compatriot of Rossetti's: all the eleven story-poems have Californian settings, and the "Invocation" is addressed to the lodestar of the westward historical process. The verse forms are still traditional, in particular blank verse and ottava rima, but the lines, being basically pentameter, are longer and weightier than those in *Flagons and Apples.* He is stretching toward the spaciousness of line and the gravity of pace that are to be the hallmarks of his mature poetry. The influences and affinities are more proper to him, too: chiefly John Milton, William Wordsworth, Shelley, Ralph Waldo Emerson, and Edwin Arlington Robinson, an essentially Protestant (or nonconforming) succession. Wordsworth's importance for the young Jeffers stands out precisely by the intensity with which the poet is castigated for his apostasy in becoming "apologist for kings and priest and lies."

If Jeffers has not yet found his style here, he has found several of his subjects. True to his romantic and transcendentalist heritage, toward which the names of Wordsworth and Emerson must have directed us, all good in *Californians* resides in the natural world or in the simpler forms of rural life, and in the isolated, integrated self rather than in the group or mass. Alone amid nature, a descendant of Wordsworth's leech gatherer, Stephen Brown, in the poem of that name, has become "self-stationed, self-upheld as the all-beholding sky," an exemplary figure. Conversely, the city only withers, crushes, corrupts, "rotting" its prisoners away. Lindsay, alone again "At Lindsay's Cabin," has saved himself from that "life / Alien to men though all composed of men, / Unfriendly, menacing, fearfully alive"; whereas "The Old Farmer," retiring in poor health to live with his son in the city, breaks his homesick heart there and commits suicide. Peter Graham, narrator of "Maldrove," bewailing a "cankered world" in this "dreadfully degenerate age," and dreaming of "lovely and glorious sons, / Successors of these little and verminous ones," is a more extreme creation, drawn from that late nineteenth-century world in which the language of degeneration and regeneration became current. Graham may not speak for Jeffers, but this is the kind of large distaste that was to point him toward his "Inhumanism," the terms of which are already at hand, in the question asked rhetorically in "A Westward Beach":

> Can man wash off humanity
> And wed the unmarriageable sea?

There are also in these poems specific narrative prefigurations, notably in "The Three Avilas," with its tale of incest and double sibling murder, the tangled stuff of so many stories to come, and in this case also, seemingly, in part a device for exhuming his own earlier guilt about the original character of his relationship with Una.

Jeffers writes in this volume not only as a resident of California, but also as, imaginatively, the latest of history's westward travelers. The final coast may have been reached, but the questions remain and tantalize. "What farther west? What wanderings more sublime?" "When Alaska is peopled, will Venus lack ploughland? / I have dreamed that our children may even ascend to the stars."

Although he wandered and ascended no further himself, Jeffers was deeply imbued with a frontier mentality, and in some respects his lifework may be seen as a continuous attempt to find new ways, now that no more territory lies ahead, of putting the East, population, society, and history, behind him. Such a cast of mind must assume, in simplified outlines, that only man is ugly and that only nature or land sparsely settled is beautiful. Jeffers was always acutely responsive toward the beautiful, and indeed it is expressly the beauty of nature that first enchants him and in which value inheres.

Californians concludes with an "Ode on Human Destinies," which itself concludes as an ode to beauty, although in this instance a beauty less natural than ideal:

> I, driven ahead on undiscovered ways
> Yet predetermined, do not fail to see,
> Over the fog and dust of dream and deed,
> The holy spirit, Beauty, beckoning me.

Jeffers did not publish any more poetry in book form for another eight years, but that long period of silent struggle, painful transformation, and eventual poetic self-revelation has been brilliantly reconstituted by Jeffers' lifelong devotee and self-styled disciple, the poet William Everson (Brother Antoninus). As a consequence of Everson's painstaking literary detective work, two books now exist that represent Jeffers at this interim time of most radical change. *The Alpine Christ and Other Poems* contains poems not collected elsewhere and adjudged by Everson to have been composed mainly in 1916. *Brides of the South Wind: Poems 1917–1922* also consists of uncollected poems and fragments but in addition contains poems that were to appear in the 1924 publication of *Tamar and Other Poems.*

"The Alpine Christ," despite its many missing pages and sections, is an immense dramatic poem, indebted in part to Shelley's *Prometheus Unbound* and in part, Everson is surely right to propose, to Thomas Hardy's *The Dynasts.* It is composed predominantly in blank verse, with passages of prose and colloquial dialogue, and with choruses reminiscent of measures as different as those of Algernon Charles Swinburne's "Hymn to Man" and Emerson's "Merlin." It is the poem of a man grieving the death of a father and, more to the point here, the death of a father's religion and culture; and it is the poem of a man horror-stricken to the marrow after long, solemn, if distant,contemplation of the European war. It is no less than a total statement about the spiritual and psychological condition of the Western world after two years of carnage—a statement anguished, though not despairing, of heroically proportioned fatalism. (In 1916, it might be remembered, Mark Twain's determinist tour de force, *The Mysterious Stranger,* was posthumously published, final word from that post-Christian fatalist literary generation of Ambrose Bierce, Stephen Crane, Frank Norris, and in England of Hardy.)

In the world of "The Alpine Christ," God is dead. Only impersonal Fate rules in Eternity. Power presides, not purpose, least of all justice. The sole value that can be given to life is in terms of human love, preached here by the holy simpleton, Manuel; but this love, in its very conception and being, is inseparable from grief and agony. "The Alpine Christ" is the unachieved work of an unformed poet, whose vision is running far ahead of his poetic and dramatic capabilities. But it is also the work of a man of rare seriousness and largeness of imagination, which for all its incompleteness is a valuable relic of the war years.

The war continues to cast its shadow over many of the poems gathered by Everson for *Brides of the South Wind;* for instance, over "The Coast-Range Christ," which Jeffers liked well enough to retain for publication in *Tamar.* This is a narrative poem in rhyming couplets, whose protagonist, David Carrow, a conscientious objector and visionary Christian idealist, is erotically drawn to a married woman called Peace. He fights down her temptation, but she, scorned, has it rumored about that he has forcibly abused her, so that he is hunted out and killed for a coward and a rapist by his outraged father. Carrow is evidently a mask for Jeffers, likewise tormented at this time by problems of conscience and desire, both challenging his father's ghost and seeking chastisement from it.

The armistice and its immediate aftermath are treated in "God's Peace in November," a sonnet sequence aching with the consciousness of insoluble contradictions, between those celebrating victory and those still suffering, between rich and poor, between God and man, between public and private, and between the terrible knowledge possessed by Europe and the ignorance of California, where "we have not suffered enough / To understand."

Finally, in "The Beginning of Decadence," like Pound in *Hugh Selwyn Mauberley* and *The Cantos* although less vehemently, Jeffers gives vent to his retrospective fury against jingo poets and battle-hungry churchmen, against massacre-minded war leaders, against profiteers and liars and postwar avengers.

But war is not the chief subject of the book. That subject is Jeffers' discovery, simultaneous and intertwined, of psychological integrity and a unique poetic speaking voice. Having experienced at length his own vulnerability, his suffering sensitivity, he was slowly learning, especially while building his house, how to stiffen his backbone and strengthen his breastwork "with ribs of rock round a hot soft heart." And within that lesson he was also learning, belatedly but definitively, how to speak in accents of his own ("To the Stone-Cutters"):

> Stone-cutters fighting time with marble,
>   you foredefeated
> Challengers of oblivion. . . .

and, in "Continent's End":

> At the equinox when the earth was veiled in
>   a late rain, wreathed with wet poppies,
>   waiting spring,
> The ocean swelled for a storm and beat its
>   boundary, the ground-swell shook the
>   beds of granite.

Here at last are the sounds of authentic Jeffers.

The style, which served him for a lifetime, was forged over a period of about three years. Until the age of thirty, in virtually all the poems of *Californians,* Jeffers had employed regular meter and rhyme. The first release was from rhyme; and it was as a release that Jeffers explicitly felt it. During his turmoil in 1917, when war and sex together shattered his ethical composure, rhyme was one of the shapes of authority that in defiant, exhilarated, nihilistic abandon he pledged himself to cast off ("Mal Paso Bridge"):

> Therefore I swore to drink wine while I could,
> Love where I pleased, and feed my eyes
> With Santa Lucien sea-beauty, and moreover
> To shear the rhyme-tassels from verse.

He went back to being a constant husband and to drinking wine in moderation; but apart from its intermittent, reassuring usage over the next year or so and its later appearance in occasional loose-limbed sonnets, rhyme had disappeared for good from his verse.

The device of alliteration, however, was retained permanently, to be employed with decreasing conspicuousness and increasing subtlety. When used to excess or harnessed for a few strides to an anapestic canter, it is obvious that Swinburne has been the tutor; but often it has a regulating function in the manner of Old English poetry, which Jeffers admired. These lines from "The Beginning and the End" will show the persistent role and the various musical parts that alliteration (and indeed assonance) play in his verse:

> Meanwhile they had invented
>
> Chlorophyll and ate sunlight, cradled in peace
> On the warm waves, but certain assassins among them
> Discovered that it was easier to eat flesh
>
> Than feed on lean air and sunlight: thence the animals,
>
> Greedy mouths and guts, life robbing life,
>
> Grew from the plants. . . .

Shearing the rhyme from his poetry, and also the unrhymed pentameter on the grounds that blank verse had been exhausted by earlier masters, Jeffers arrived by another route at the open ground that Pound and William Carlos Williams had cleared for themselves a few years earlier. As his characteristic poetry emerged, it was often taken to be either a free verse broadly in the tradition of Whitman's *Leaves of Grass* or a prose-poetry deriving from the Authorized Version of the Bible.

Certainly, Jeffers owed much to both books. With Whitman he felt what has been called "a profound fellowship," despite their obvious great differences, some of which at least can be explained in terms of the two generations of fearful history that separated them. However, as far as form is concerned, what the poets share does not go much beyond the sheer, capacious length and adaptability of line; although this is enough to align Jeffers more closely with Whitman than with any other American antecedent.

In the case of the Bible, as the son of his father, Jeffers could not help but be saturated in the Holy Book, so that every so often one may hear an echo of the verbal texture of the Song of Solomon or a rhetorical reminiscence of Ecclesiastes or the Book of Job. But as with *Leaves of Grass,* one staple element of Jeffers' verse is missing from the poetry of the translated Bible. And that is, for all Jeffers' absolute break with the world of rhyme and traditional meter, a notion of rhythmic regularity, of predictability, of prior aural design.

As Jeffers confessed in 1930 to Arthur Klein, a student of his work: "People talked about my 'free verse' and I never protested, but now I am quite touched to hear that someone has at last discovered the metrical intention in it." He goes on in the same letter to mention Coleridge's regularity of accent rather than syllable in "Christabel," Old English accentual verse, and, briefly, quantity.

In principle therefore (if only in principle), or in gesture or intention, Jeffers' verse is governed by a rhythmic norm, which consists of a regular number of accents to the line or pair of lines, a stress prosody that is derived from such examples as those just cited. Within the lines the weight is also distributed according to quantity, as in the classical poetry familiar to Jeffers from childhood and, in the case of

Greek, translated by him throughout his life, and as in some of the experiments of Swinburne, a more celebrated and flamboyant classical scholar, so many aspects of whose poetry (alliteration, phrasing, prosody) were incorporated more or less audibly into Jeffers' mature style.

However, the primary influences on Jeffers' poetry are not literary but natural. Living within the sound of the ocean and within sight of the mountains, planting his long-lived trees, handling, transporting, and positioning his granite boulders, Jeffers in his few remarks about poetry and poetics always refers to the qualities of the natural world—to "tidal regularity" or "tidal recurrence," to "perpetual renewal"—and, for the subject matter, to the "essential element" of "permanence."

What he was after was a natural condition, neither freedom nor strict rule, but the broadly timed recurrences and variable regularity of nature. If William Carlos Williams, seeking a freedom from the old that would nevertheless be a "new order" to satisfy an inner need, discovered for himself the regularity of the variable foot, perhaps one may say that Jeffers for similar reasons discovered for himself the regularity of the variable line. His fullest statement is this:

> I want it rhythmic and not rhymed, moulded more closely to the subject than older English poetry is, but as formed as alcaics if that were possible too. The event is of course a compromise but I like to avoid arbitrary form and capricious lack or disruption of form. My feeling is for the number of beats to the line. There is a quantitative element too in which the unstressed syllables have part. The rhythm comes from many sources—physics, biology, beat of blood, the tidal environments of life, desire for singing emphasis that prose does not have.

"Morro Bay," from a late volume, *Hungerfield and Other Poems,* is chosen almost at random for its shortness, so that it may be printed in full to demonstrate in its typicality the simple aural constituents of Jeffers' poetry. These are alliteration, constant but irregular; and a stress pattern, regular but not fixed, here over five pairs of lines, the first line of the pair (of five or six stresses) being visually longer than the second (of basically four stresses), but since it contains many syllables of short quantity, lighter and swifter.

> Beautiful years when she was by me and we visited
> Every rock and creek of the coast—
> She gave life from her eyes. Now the bay is brown-stagnant
> With rotting weed, and the stranded fish-boats
> Reek in the sun; but still the great rock hangs like a thundercloud
> Over the stale mist and still sea.
> They say that it swarms with rattlesnakes—right—the stored lightnings
> In the stone cloud. Guard it well, vipers.
> That Norman rockhead Mont St. Michel may have been as beautiful as this one
> Once, long ago, before it was built on.

This natural, elemental rhythm was a fit vessel to carry the burden of his poetry—or its message, let us unabashedly call it—since he indeed was a man with a message, a preacher's lesson, even if he purported not to be much concerned whether anyone listened to it. The main clause of this message was that man had drastically abused, distorted, or wholly emptied out his relationship with nature, that he had lost touch with the primary elements of life, and that he had extravagantly overvalued the importance of his place in the cosmos and the natural order of things, all with catastrophic consequences for himself: that this was a universal human condition but especially was it true of the Western world, that is to say, the entire Judeo-Christian pale, and even more particularly was it true, perhaps with the character of a terminal disease, of modern, industrial, secular, or materialistic society. In some shape or other this was either the meditative focus or narrative spring of nearly all that he wrote over his forty years of mature life as a poet, in some fifteen narrative poems set around Carmel, in a half dozen dramatic poems based upon Greek, biblical, or Germanic legend, and in about two hundred and fifty shorter poems.

Jeffers' first premise is not an intellectual proposition but a sensory commonplace: that the universe is beautiful, beautiful because it is beautiful, beautiful to behold as a spectacle, the eyes raised to the stars, beautiful to contemplate in its composition, the mind dwelling upon the cell and the atom. There can be few poets, and certainly there are no other modern poets, who employ the words "beauty" and "beautiful" as often as Jeffers does; and he does so without embarrassment, apology, or fanciful elaboration. He does not ask us to ponder the nature of the beautiful but merely seeks to remind us, since we are continuously forgetful, that it is always there, beside, before, and around us.

Beauty may appear in many forms; in earlier years, during aviation's romantic youth, to this high priest of antimechanism it could come even in mechanical guise. In poems from his 1925 volume, it is in "the navy's new-bought Zeppelin going by in the twilight, / Far out seaward;" or in the "bitter earnestness" of the deep-sea fishermen returning to harbor, the engines of their boats throbbing through the fog, "following the cliff for guidance" as they go about "their business among the equally / Earnest elements of nature." Beauty may be "intense and terrible" with "great seas jagging the west and on the granite / Blanching" in "Gale in April"; or it may be come upon, not in energetic, elemental drama, but in quiet meditation upon "the beauty of things," the "one beauty," the rhythm of the wheel "of life as of death and of light as of darkness."

Half a lifetime later, having come through the worst of his grief over Una's death, he knows once again that "to feel / Greatly, and understand greatly, and express greatly, the natural / Beauty, is the sole business of poetry," for "it is only a little planet / But how beautiful it is." It is altogether appropriate, therefore, that the last words of his last volume invite us to expect and enjoy, while watching the activities of the natural world, "not mercy, not mind, not goodness, but the beauty of God."

God, the final word in Jeffers' works. For Jeffers, God may be either immanent or transcendent, to be perceived within the world, or to be sought within the self. The immanent predominates: the universe is all-beautiful, a radiant manifestation of God, who is all, the all that is God. The eyes should merely have to see to believe, the lungs should merely have to breathe to inhale God's spirit.

In "The Answer" we are told, simply, that "Integrity is wholeness, the greatest beauty is / Organic wholeness, the wholeness of life and things, the divine beauty of the Universe." In the long poem "The Inhumanist," the old man, who is the figure in Jeffers' poetry most nearly approaching a guru or fount of wisdom, rejoices in "the stars, the winds and the people: one energy, / One existence, one music, one organism, one life, one God."

The American transcendentalist heritage is clearly visible here: the links with Emerson, whom he had read so thoroughly as a young man and who was also introduced to the perfect whole by his sense of beauty; and with Whitman, who heard and beheld God in every object and saw something of him each hour of the twenty-four. It is often a virtual pantheism, with God not only "the whole splendor of things and the sacred stars, but also the cruelty and greed, the treacheries / And vileness, insanities and filth and anguish." Above all, God and his beauty, the beauty that is God, are experienced in natural and elemental power, whether in the stallion, the hawk, and the eagle, or in the vast eons-long beating of the universal heart and in cosmic "faceless violence, the root of all things."

That is Jeffers, the visionary pantheist, looking out on the physical world that had always seemed to him, he told a correspondent, "immeasurably more real" than the soul. But he could own to another, more inward conception of God, one closer to that of his Protestant forebears, a transcendent or at least an exclusive God, to be awaited in the patient, mystic air of the "soul's desert" at those times when, outside, the dust storms of human fury, most likely of war, obscured the "astonishing beauty of things."

But however meditative and mystically inclined, Jeffers did not travel in spirit across the Pacific to the faiths of the Orient, like so many fellow-Californian poets, especially of the succeeding generation. He might express a considerable regard for Buddhism and Oriental religions, for their quietism and cyclical view of existence, and he might scorn the "anthropoid God" of "decaying Christianity." But he was always at the farthest point of the West rather than at the beginnings of the East. Differing from an Asian contemplative in his poem "Credo," he finds "in my blood / Bred west of Caucasus a harder mysticism." The "harder mysticism" is a philosophical materialism that attributes a prior reality to matter before mind, to the world before the soul, to the light in "the beauty of things, not men."

This materialism within an essentially religious temperament is testimony, first, simply to Jeffers' exceptional, respectful sensitivity toward the objective, tactile, physical world, his poetic comprehension of the thingness of things; and second, to the effect upon him at an impressionable age of nineteenth-century positivist modes of thought. The American literary generation immediately senior to him, whether influenced directly by science (for instance by Charles Darwin and his popularizers) or by literary-theoretical mediators like Émile Zola, must have seemed predominantly atheist and materialist, or at least cynically commonsensical: the aging Mark Twain, Stephen Crane (another minister's son), Frank Norris, Ambrose Bierce and Jack London (local lights in California), and Edgar Lee Masters (who became a personal friend).

In such an intellectual atmosphere, as he rebelled against his father's faith and undertook medical studies that required a scientific attitude and curiosity, the foundations of a lifelong materialism were laid, never to be thoroughly broken up and demolished. Thus, although Jeffers may rightly if, loosely, be described as a quietist, and then again as a pantheist, he must also be recognized as a firm materialist, convinced alike of the primacy of matter and of personal mortality—a "hard, mystical" materialist, to use his own terms of self-description.

Jeffers' is a poetic materialism that for closest analogy sends us back as far as two thousand years to one of the few figures he openly acknowledges in his poetry and to whom he pays tribute: the Roman poet Lucretius, author of the great expository poem, the epic of a joyous materialism, *De rerum natura.* Jeffers adapted Lucretius' title for his celebration of the earth and the galaxy, "De Rerum Virtute"; he gave Lucretius and Plato the heroic parts in one of his poems on historical decline, "Prescription of Painful Ends"; he deferred to Lucretius in his own powerful poem on natural origins and destiny, "The Beginning and the End"; and in general he seemed to watch and muse upon the world's aimless frenzy from a similarly cool, elevated position, "the little stone-girdled platform" of his Hawk's Tower, Lucretius' "quiet citadel, stoutly fortified by the teaching of the wise." Apart from the few English and American poets previously mentioned, the only other figure who ever came near to being as influential upon him was Friedrich Nietzsche, whose hostility to Christianity was another spur to his rebellion in those early years and whose dictum, "The poets lie too much," he was fond of repeating.

It was this sense of the marvelous "divinity" of the physical universe that Jeffers felt to be so drastically missing from the mind of modern, Western man. The basis for any sort of sanity, any sort of integrity, must be reverence for the cosmos, in which man is such a tiny item, when viewed from amid the salutary dimensions of Carmel Point, against the background of ocean and redwood forest, beside the time spans of mountains and planets. (A tiny item, maybe, but part of that divine whole, so that, of course, "even / The poor doll humanity has a place under heaven.") Thus, the best life that can be lived by man is one that leaves as much space as possible for silent wonder at natural processes and their invisibly slow evolution, for quiet amazement at the immense splendor and all the diminutive miracles.

It should be a life lived in a simple relation to nature, such as can be found most readily in the pastoral stage of human development and in the less technologically advanced forms of cultivation. It can perhaps be discerned in an earlier American ideal, in Michel de Crèvecoeur's American farmer, surviving in California in a few inaccessible valleys at the end of unpaved roads. "The Coast-Road" presents a picture of such life and what threatens it in the 1930's:

> I too
> Believe that the life of men who ride horses, herders of cattle on the mountain pasture, plowers of remote
> Rock-narrowed farms in poverty and freedom, is a good life. At the far end of those loops of road
> Is what will come and destroy it, a rich and vulgar and bewildered civilization dying at the core.

And the picture, repainted for his last volume, is virtually unaltered:

> What's the best life for a man? To ride in the wind. To ride horses and herd cattle
> In solitary places above the ocean on the beautiful mountain, and come home hungry in the evening
> And eat and sleep. . . .
> I will have shepherds for my philosophers,
> Tall dreary men lying on the hills all night
> Watching the stars, let their dogs watch the sheep.

But these are disappearing ways of life, or nostalgic myths and timeless idylls, as Jeffers knew only too well. The dominant theme in human history, certainly in Western history, has been quite different. It has been a history not of man's accommodation with nature, but of his separation from it, subjection of the earth, exploitation of its gifts, and self-appointment as lord of creation. In his lifelong treatment of man's relationship with nature, Jeffers writes both within and against the Judeo-Christian heritage. He can be said to be within it insofar as he subscribes to an idiosyncratic, naturalistic version of the doctrine of original sin and of the fall, and insofar as his work continuously illustrates the consequences of that sin and the manifestations of the fall in so many facets of human behavior. He is against it, radically, insofar as he would regard that heritage, and even more so its secular succession of whatever political emphasis, as being from its very beginnings a direct expression of that original sin, in its initial presupposition of man's privileged or central place in the universe.

The sin, to put it in the most broadly traditional terms, is the sin of pride, man's arrogant promotion of himself above the level accorded him by God. And if God is identified with the cosmos, then the original sin occurred at that mythic moment when man first felt himself to be singled out as distinct from the rest of creation and superior to it, with the earth a stage for the drama of his energies and the heavens an auditorium concentrated on a God, formed in man's own image, whose attention is fixed upon the inner and outer life of his own proudest creation.

For Jeffers, then, the loss of paradise coincided with the development of an isolating self-consciousness. (In "Margrave" he even plays with the fancy of the far, speeding stars of an expanding universe "fleeing the contagion / Of consciousness that infects this corner of space.") In terms of biological evolution, this moment, he intimates in "Original Sin," must be as original as the appearance of the species *Homo sapiens.* In consequence, the human race's few heroes include those whose scientific discoveries have had the effect of eroding man's self-importance and returning him toward his rightful place in the scheme of things. Thus, the old man of "The Inhumanist" wonders to whom he should dedicate the cairn of stones he has erected:

> "To whom this monument: Jesus or Caesar or Mother Eve?
> "No," he said, "to Copernicus: Nicky Kupernick: who first pushed man

Out of his insane self-importance and the
world's navel, and taught him his place."
"And the next one to Darwin."

Because of this "insane self-importance" and the breaking of the umbilical connection with nature, "life's norm is lost" and "monsters possess the world," toying with atomic power. Twenty years before the invention of nuclear weapons, in a poem entitled simply and comprehensively "Science," Jeffers already envisages the potentiality of total destruction, as nature is reassembled into ever more terrifying new energies:

Man, introverted man, having crossed
In passage and but a little with the nature of
things this latter century
Has begot giants; but being taken up
Like a maniac with self-love and inward
conflicts cannot manage his hybrids.
Being used to deal with edgeless dreams,
Now he's bred knives on nature turns them
also inward: they have thirsty points
though.
His mind forebodes his own destruction; . . .

And Aphrodite concludes in the dramatic poem "The Cretan Woman," composed in the early 1950's against a background of nuclear bomb testing, the Korean War, and accelerating domestic prosperity:

In future days men will become so powerful
That they seem to control the heavens and
the earth,
They seem to understand the stars and all
science—
Let them beware. Something is lurking
hidden.
There is always a knife in the flowers.
There is always a lion just beyond the
firelight.

But of course the threat of doom appears in the shape not only of physical destruction but also of the spiritual reduction that follows upon the heedless abuse of nature by a too clever, too prolific race. So, decades before the word "ecology" ventured far from the textbooks and before lip service to conservationist sentiments became conventional piety, Jeffers in "The Broken Balance" was

Mourning the broken balance, the hopeless
prostration of the earth
Under men's hands and their minds,
The beautiful places killed like rabbits to
make a city,
The spreading fungus, the slime-threads
And spores; my own coast's obscene
future. . . .

Jeffers saw megalomania and introversion as the major, pervasive psychological expressions of this "broken balance," the species dangerously self-aggrandized and hopelessly self-centered. As he explained to James Rorty in connection with one of his narrative poems:

> There is no health for the individual whose attention is taken up with his own mind and processes; equally there is no health for the society that is always introverted on its own members, as ours becomes more and more. . . . All past cultures have died of introversion at last, and so will this one, but the individual can be free of the net, in his mind. . . .

So the narratives and dramas, with their sexual heat, scorching jealousies, incestuous couplings, family murders and massacres, homestead holocausts, and crazed, towering ambitions, enact for us time and again individual catastrophes that are microcosms of the conclusive disaster overhanging our whole megalomaniac, introverted civilization.

Nearly all these poems are flawed in some quite conspicuous respect; frequently they spill into melodrama, macabre or ludicrous, and into monstrous horror shows; and one or two are undoubtedly failures as vital poetry, coherent psychology, or credible stories. It is certain that Jeffers' finest art is to be found either in his short poems or in sections of these longer poems that are in effect detachable, self-contained lyrics. Nevertheless, like few other modern writings, for powerful, extended stretches the best of these poems have something of the gravity, the awesomeness, and the grandeur of ancient tragedy. They are charged with Jeffers' dread-filled, brooding knowledge of the seriousness of his imagination's task ("Imagination, the traitor of the mind, has taken my solitude and slain it."); and they are freighted with his sense of enormity in the breaking of taboo, in the bursting of conventional limits, in the upturning of nature, and in the excavation of the psyche's depths. As he wrote in "Apology for Bad Dreams":

> It is not good to forget over what gulfs the spirit
> Of the beauty of humanity, the petal of a lost flower blown seaward by the night-wind, floats to its quietness.

There is in Jeffers a primordial quality, at the very least an exceedingly old-fashioned quality, that touched him on several occasions with the original imagination of tragedy.

"Tamar," the first of these narratives, was written in 1922 and derived from the story in the second Book of Samuel, where one of King David's sons, Amnon, rapes his sister, Tamar, and is later killed on the orders of his brother, Absalom. In this poem, as in several others, Jeffers makes incest central to his story, in part because within the world of the family it is the most intense, shocking form of the conflict between natural energy and customary morality, but, especially and programmatically, in his own explanation, because it is the appropriate symbol for the introverted character of the whole race. However, in contrast with the biblical Tamar, a passive victim distracted with shame, Tamar Cauldwell is the forceful, flamboyant, driving spirit behind the action of Jeffers' poem. She lives in the isolated family home, overlooking the ocean, with her widowed father, David, a Bible-reading farmer, her brother, Lee, her mother's sister, Stella, and another aunt, the idiot Jinny. The setting is specific and realistic (California at the time of World War I), but the story has an essentially mythic quality, with Tamar often as much elemental as human, a personified natural force upturning conventional morality, as when she seduces her brother in the cold mountain pool:

> Was it the wild rock coast
> Of her breeding, and the reckless wind
> In the beaten trees and the gaunt booming crashes
> Of breakers under the rocks, or rather the amplitude
> And wing-subduing immense earth-ending water
> That moves all the west taught her this freedom?

Tamar and Lee become lovers, until she finds herself with child by him. To cover herself, she takes another lover, Will Andrews, with a distaste that she did not feel for her brother, for now "the house is broken / And any thief can enter it."

But this incest is not the family's first. From her Aunt Stella, who sees visions and hears voices, she discovers that the same license had been taken more than forty years previously by her father and his long-dead sister, Helen. The House of Cauldwell is rotten to the core from the root. In this putrid atmosphere, Tamar's desire turns to loathing, of men, of life, and of the source of life, with "all the world growing hateful, both her lovers / Hateful, but the intolerably masculine sun hatefullest of all."

She dreams of the oblivion of the present human race and the beginning of a new race out of the union of her father and herself; and, to atone for the sins of her ancestors who had slaughtered the Indians or driven them from their lands, she is symbolically enjoyed in an orgy by the ghosts of a vanished tribe. She comes to wield over the hopelessly corrupted house ever greater destructive power, taunting her father, racked by his lustful body and Christian guilt, and the two young rivals for her bewildering affections. At length she maneuvers all the men into her bedroom and drives Lee and Will into a violent, maddened fight in which Will is stabbed to death. Aunt

Jinny, unconscious agent of purification, sets fire to the house; and with Tamar in nihilistic delight clinging to Lee against his escape and with the father calling upon the pity of Christ, the house collapses to its infernal doom, consuming all the inhabitants. A people turned inward upon itself has suffered an ultimate punishment for its self-absorption. The human blot has been erased; the things of nature reassert their permanence.

> Grass grows where the flame flowered;
> A hollowed lawn strewn with a few black
> stones
> And the brick of broken chimneys; all about
> there
> The old trees, some of them scarred with
> fire, endure the sea wind.

"Tamar" is an impressive and memorable poem, but a puzzling one, because of the author's ambivalent feelings about Tamar herself, who is simultaneously an emblem of exhilarating freedom and a vehicle of the utmost impurity. Jeffers himself recognized this confusion of purpose, when in retrospect he admitted to the poem's "tendency to romanticize unmoral freedom."

"Roan Stallion," composed about three years later, is a more compact poem and possessed of a greater symbolic clarity. Again the central and exciting figure is a woman, of Scottish, Spanish, and Indian ancestry, whose name, California, immediately designates her as the quintessence of the West, "erect and strong as a new tower." The mother of an infant daughter, Christine, she is married to Johnny, a farmer of sorts but chiefly a drunken gambler, "burnt-out . . . twisted . . . shriveled with bad living." He represents contemporary humanity at its most diminished and degraded, slothful, greedy, physically debauched, spiritually null. In contrast, California is characterized by her love and care for her child, by her sense of obligation, by her pertinacity and quiet courage, and by her religious imagination and faith.

Johnny and the humanity he typifies having nothing to offer her, she begins to look away from the human for a God "not in man's shape" to awaken and stretch her ready spirit.

> Humanity is the
> start of the race; I say
> Humanity is the mould to break away from,
> the crust to break through, the coal to
> break into fire,
> The atom to be split.

The nonhuman shape in which this deity appears to her is that of Johnny's magnificent stallion, the embodiment of everything of which its master is a negation—beauty, power, nobility, cleanliness, aspiration.

One night under a brilliant moon California steals out of the house and down to the corral, leaps onto the horse, and in a simulacrum of resplendent sexual union rides this "savage and exultant strength of the world" to the mountain top. Dismounting "here on the calvary" with "nothing conscious / But the possible God and the cropped grass," she prostrates herself before this natural divinity.

After such communion, there can be no going back to suffering Johnny's abject humanity. The following night when, lurching and stumbling, he pursues her out of the house with his dog, she lures him into the corral, where the dog frets and snaps at the mighty stallion. Slipping out of the corral, she runs back to the house, fetches a rifle, shoots the dog, and watches from a distance in the moonlight, curious and detached, as the horse tramples Johnny to death. "Then California moved by some obscure human fidelity / Lifted the rifle." She shoots the stallion and "turned then on her little daughter the mask of a woman / Who has killed God." There will be no more degradation; there will be the dignity of loving and raising her child amid natural surroundings; but there will be no more exaltation. At the last California has chosen humanity. The God, beautiful, powerful, elemental, but amoral and unhuman, she has killed.

The announcement of a truth that is free of any human relation is also the end of "The Tower Beyond Tragedy," which was published in the same volume as "Roan Stallion." This dramatic poem is Jeffers' version of the *Oresteia* and the *Electra* plays. In character it owes most to Aeschylus, and the events of the story loosely follow those of the *Agamemnon* and the *Choephori*. However, Jeffers' final purpose is to release Orestes from history and human concerns rather than, as in the *Eumenides,* to have him return to Argos and participation in its affairs, after judgment and the lifting of the curse. For Jeffers' Orestes, history is hopeless, and the curse is to be human. His Cassandra foresees a cyclical future of ever swifter rises to ever wider power and ever greater catastrophe. She curses in succession Athens, Rome, Spain, France, and England, yet there is still

> A mightier to be cursed and a higher for malediction
> When America has eaten Europe and takes tribute of Asia, when the ends of the world grow aware of each other
> And are dogs in one kennel, they will tear
> The master of the hunt with the mouths of the pack: new fallings, new risings, O winged one
> No end of the fallings and risings?

That future, perpetually gestating another Trojan war, another Vietnam, is what Orestes, in ancient Greece, in modern California, would cast off. And his sister's offer of her body to him, to entice him to reenter history, take up power, and rule in his father's place, is again, as in "Tamar," a small, single instance of the total racial inversion. It is all a huge imbroglio in which Orestes sees men writhe

> like a full draught of fishes, all matted
> In the one mesh; when they look backward they see only a man standing at the beginning,
> Or forward, a man at the end; or if upward, men in the shining bitter sky striding and feasting,
> Whom you call Gods. . . .
> It is all turned inward, all your desires incestuous, the woman the serpent, the man the rose-red cavern,
> Both human, worship forever. . . .

Bearing a message of salvation by detachment from the world, he takes to anonymity and the high, wild country, as one "Who had climbed the tower beyond time, consciously, and cast humanity, entered the earlier fountain."

Jeffers' next narrative poem, *The Women at Point Sur,* published in 1927, was his longest and the only one to occupy a volume by itself. Like Tamar Cauldwell, the poem's protagonist, the Reverend Dr. Barclay, is a demonic hero, source of chaos and destruction at the same time that he is often the voice of sentiments that Jeffers elsewhere approves. However, Jeffers claimed shortly after the poem's publication that this was exactly his cautionary intention, to point out the dangers of the idea of "breaking out of humanity" being "misinterpreted in the mind of a fool or a lunatic." So Barclay's inhumanism does not release him from the burden of human involvement and turn him outward toward nature and God, but throws him inward on destructive sexuality, nihilism, self-deification, and the totalitarian domination of others. He is Jeffers' most Faustian creation, which is also to say most Ahab-like in his attempted refusal of human limits and pride in having "voyaged outside the maps, these waters not charted," to "break through to" the "power behind the appearances." His exuberant self-reliance must furthermore be ironically reminiscent of Emerson: "Nothing you can do is wicked. I have seen God. He is there in the hill, he is here in your body."

The preacher is very much a casualty of the war, in which he has lost in turn his son, his Christian faith, and his moral compass. Abandoning his church and his congregation ("I have nothing for you"), he wanders down the coast in search of more complete and pliant disciples, and finds lodging at a farmhouse. Here he begins to strip from himself the layers of traditional, Christian restraint, in the main by ever more extravagant sexual acts. First, he buys sex from the farm's Indian servant girl; then he encourages a lesbian relationship between two of the other girls there; and finally he rapes his daughter, April, who has come looking for him.

Gradually, this fiery revivalist is transformed into a diabolic messiah, exerting a lethal influence upon those he has gathered around him, in a manner that must bring to mind certain other horrifying evil geniuses of more recent years, also emanating, significantly, from California. One of his entourage murders her infant daughter to save her the pain of life and to atone for the "crime" of conceiving her; Barclay's daughter, "without brakes, without rudder" since her father's rape of her, kills herself in front of him to feel at the last "one thing done wisely / In the vast insanity of things." Ever more nihilistic ("I preserve nothing") and ever more megalomaniac ("believing himself God"), delirious with salvationist mission ("I'll save the beasts, too"), the crazed minister makes his way alone into the hills, where at the entrance to a deserted mine he collapses, dying but still self-exalting ("I am inexhaustible"), bequeathing a legacy of madness and despair.

Although *The Women at Point Sur* is not entirely successful as a narrative, it does present a disturbing, compelling study of revivalist excess and mesmeric, apocalyptic leadership, lunatic or evil forms that have cast such shadows over the forefront or corners of later history.

"Cawdor," published the following year, has less overt didactic purpose than the previous long poems. It is a tale of sexual rejection and revenge, of accidental killing and fearful self-punishment, set in California in 1909. The title, of course, sends us to *Macbeth,* but for little more common property than blood and atmospherics; it may also bring to our notice how often Jeffers' main characters have names with Scottish associations (Cauldwell, Barclay, Cawdor, and later Thurso, Fraser, Bothwell, and Ferguson), presumably to suggest from the first instant an ambience of repressed, explosive, puritanical passion.

In "Cawdor," Martial, an old farmer, just now blinded in a fire from a bursting oil drum, is led down the valley by his daughter, Fera, to Cawdor's farm, where he stays for the brief remainder of his ill-fortuned, maimed life. Cawdor, a brooding widower with three grown children, takes pride in the hard, tough life he has led and in the violent, populist hatred he feels for "the fooled and rotten faces of rich and successful men. / And the sons they have." After Martial's death, he marries Fera, who is as wild-natured as her name, a being from an earlier time easily at home in a bloody, freshly flayed puma skin. She falls for Cawdor's elder son, Hood, and having been resisted by him, tells Cawdor that he has raped her. Cawdor pursues his son up the mountain, where after a brief struggle Hood falls to his death over a precipice. There remains for Fera first to attempt suicide and then, after teasing her husband with further lies and fantasies, to reveal the truth to him of his son's innocence. Tempted to strangle her but then turning upon himself, Cawdor, his horror and remorse overflowing, gouges out his own eyes, those offending eyes that had first desired Fera—a modern Oedipus on a farm in California.

Those are the principal events of the story; but there is yet to be mentioned the finest passage in the poem, several pages of Jeffers' greatest poetry, in which he wrote of the death by revolver shot of a caged eagle, its spirit soaring away from its body and from the physical earth in ever wider circles of space and time. Like the roan stallion, like the many hawks in his shorter poems, the eagle is the symbol of a strength, a purity, a nobility, a wisdom, and a farseeing vision beyond the scope of shortsighted, entangled, enervated humanity. Higher still and higher, it looks further still and wider upon the alternations of pride and pain, of life and death, of the yearning to be born and the yearning to be quiet, until its visionary spirit enters and encloses itself in peace at the zenith. It is a sustained piece of sublime writing.

Jeffers' Jesus, the subject of his next dramatic poem, "Dear Judas" (1929), has more than a little in common with the megalomaniac, power-hungry Barclay of *The Women at Point Sur.* This poem, the form of which was influenced by the Japanese No plays, is a treatment of the later stages of the gospel story, in particular of Judas' betrayal of Jesus. It opens with the flat statement of a materialist premise: "They have all died and their souls are extinguished."

Jesus is not metaphysical; indeed, the mainspring of his psychology is his obsession with his physical parentage. It is the shame of his probable bastardy that has driven him to discover God to be his father and to make his mark upon the world with a supposedly supernatural authority. He burns with a truly revolutionary ardor to transform the world and rule the future. His zeal, though, is purificatory and uplifting rather than humanitarian; it is inspired by his mystic confidence in his own lofty, magnificent spirit. As with Barclay, it is of Ahab stretching after the mystery of the white whale that we are reminded, as Jesus proclaims the "lightnings," "pinnacles," and "towers" of his soul and its "immeasurable height above men." "All greatness is a wrestling with time."

Recognizing that he will not be able to establish his revolutionary kingdom during his lifetime, Jesus invents heaven and hell as devices of reward and terror with which to implement his sway over the future. He goes to his death exulting in his unprecedented domination of human history.

> I go a stranger passage to a greater dominion
> More tyrannous, more terrible, more true,
>   than Caesar or any subduer of the earth
>   before him has dared to dream of . . . no
>   man shall live.
> As if *I* had not lived.

In contrast with this Jesus who is all energy and leaping spirit, Judas is introspective, moral, and ethical, a decent, worried, concerned, liberal humanist. Aching with pity and bowed beneath the world's suffering ("the moaning of men and beasts torments me . . . others' joy is not mine, / Only their pain"), he has sought in Jesus a reformist leader who would make living a little kinder and sweeter for all. But as Jesus' dream goes wild and mad, his modest hope turns to a nightmare vision of Roman suppression, with "all the roadside masted with moaning crucifixion." Sensitive and anguished, he betrays Jesus "to get the firebrand locked up, to save the city," expecting, in his softheaded benevolence, that Jesus will go to the lunatic's cell rather than the rebel's cross. He leaves the drama, pathetic, well-intentioned, self-loathing, to hang himself; in his ears ring Lazarus' terrible last words upon this good neighbor's involvement with the overreaching superman who was Jesus:

> you enter his kingdom with him, as the
>   hawk's lice with the hawk
> Climb the blue towers of the sky under the
>   down of the feathers.

"Dear Judas" was coupled in its volume with "The Loving Shepherdess," a study, commented Jeffers, of "nearly pure" love, in contrast with the misdirected affections and passions of the gospel figures. It is the least eventful and the most tender of Jeffers' poems, and of lighter weight than others, although it has not wanted for admirers. Clare Walker, the shepherdess, with her little flock of sheep wanders the Californian coast along much the same paths as Barclay (who is mentioned in the poem, as are Tamar and Cawdor, all inhabitants of this Jeffers country); but, unlike Barclay's, her spirit is formed not of the will to power but of love, and her vision is a selfless one of peace and delight for all created things. Rather than being a child of the Protestant fundamentalism in which most of Jeffers' characters have been molded, she has about her a quality of the Franciscan or even, loosely, of the Hindu, in her refusal to restrain love or to interfere with the processes of nature, even at the certain cost of her own life.

Six years later, in 1935, Jeffers again made Christianity the central issue of a dramatic poem. This was in "At the Birth of an Age," which was derived from Germanic legend and set at the time of Europe's change from a heroic, pagan culture to the Christian one. Writing of the birth of this Christian age within sight of its end (of its faith, he considered, although not of its secularized ethics), Jeffers could charge his poem with an ominous historical significance that more than compensates for the dramatic weaknesses. For the poem is structurally broken-backed: its first part is a dramatic reenactment of the deaths of Nordic heroes, dying by their honor and their dishonor, by their courage and their treachery; and the second part is a series of spiritual and philosophical tableaux, revealing some of the components of the culture that will supersede this paganism. These include the Greek Prometheus, the Norse Hanged God, and Christ.

Masked simply as The Young Man, Christ speaks here not as the exhilarated megalomaniac of "Dear Judas," but as a disillusioned, self-confessed, false prophet, who has clamped upon mankind a "ridiculous delusion" of personal immortality in a further world. Self-tormenting ("If Judas for a single betrayal hanged himself, / What for me, that betrayed the world?"), he prays that he himself and his myth of divinity be forgotten and that only his message of human love and brotherhood be remembered. Predictably, Jeffers does not end on such an uncharacteristic note, and the most compelling and conclusive poetry is given to the Hanged God, whose privilege it is to speak the language of exalted, inhumanist indifference:

> I am also the outer nothing and the
> wandering infinite night. These are my
> mercy and my goodness, these
> My peace.

However extravagant and horrifying the incidents of their plots may be, Jeffers' narratives from the 1930's are all predominantly realistic in conception and characterization rather than mythic. The principal poems are "Thurso's Landing" (1932), "Give Your Heart to the Hawks" (1933), "Solstice" (1935), and "Such Counsels You Gave to Me" (1937). They are all tales of unrelieved disaster and destruction: in "Thurso's Landing" of infidelities, two suicides, an accidental crippling, and a mercy killing; in "Give Your Heart to the Hawks" of infidelity, fratricide, subsequent corrosive guilt, and two further suicides; in "Solstice" of a mother's murder of her children to keep them from their father and her flight into the mountains; in "Such Counsels You Gave to Me" of a son's patricide and attempted incestuous seduction by his mother.

In each poem the strongest personality is a woman: Helen Thurso, Fayne Fraser, Madrone Bothwell, and Mrs. Howren. And each of these women is the lively but unfulfilled and discontented wife of a dour or coarsened husband. It is the wilder, more instinctual female energy that directs the turn of events. The men, further from nature, are governed by stubborn will and the pride of possession (Reave Thurso); by whiskey and the inward torture of a Puritan conscience (Lance Fraser); by the values of the city and mechanical progress (Bothwell); by an anti-imaginative materialism (Howren); and by intellectual ambition (his son Howard).

Between sexual desire and traditional morality, between independent self and conformist society, between nature and culture, the people of these stories, of this coast and country, are bruised, cracked, and crushed. There are, it is true, positive attributes to be distinguished amid the welter of catastrophes: such qualities as courage and endurance, responsiveness to the natural world, self-reliance, and a preparedness to face the music, however discordant. And there are moments of awe (humanity's "terrible shining" against "the dark magnificence of things" in "Thurso's Landing") and of melodramatic elevation (Madrone Bothwell's barbaric "fierce unsubdued core" that is translated into the storm-wracked heights of the Rocky Mountains in "Solstice"). But the prevailing sense is of man's contemptible insignificance, of the unimportance of his self-induced suffering, and of the inconsequence and superfluity of his life.

The emphasis in these poems falls on the pettiness and ugliness of humanity rather than on the inhuman beauty and the natural divinity that Jeffers tells us elsewhere it is the poet's business to praise and in so doing restore man to his right, small, contented place. Without such constructive purpose, with few such rhapsodic notes, with little of the mythic or transcendent dimensions, these realistic narratives risk too much becoming mere dismal catalogs, newssheets of crime and cruelty, fury and folly.

These furies and follies Jeffers saw gathering over many years toward their inevitable conclusion in a second world war. Virtually all that he wrote at this time sounded with the approach of war, so that in the prefatory note to *Be Angry at the Sun* (1941) he felt bound to lament his "obsession with contemporary history."

This volume opens with "Mara," another tale of infidelity, marital hatred, and suicide, set as usual in California, but now in a world enlarged by radio to include the voice of Hitler, "wailing" like "a lost child." The situation is familiar. A heavyhearted protagonist, Bruce Ferguson, is married to a lively, spirited wife, Fawn, who is having an affair with Bruce's more vigorous younger brother, Allen; while upstairs in the same house their father lies painfully dying, despised by their misused and embittered mother. However, what differentiates Ferguson from most of the previous characters in the realistic narratives is that his pain is primarily philosophical. His thoughts and dreams run on the coming of war and its attendant horrors, on historical decline and the collapse of values ("Nobody knows the difference between right and wrong. / So the wolves will come back to Europe"), and on the crippled weakness of good in the world and the brute strength of evil. "I guess you think too much, honey," says a girl in a bar. And weighed down with thinking, he hangs himself, so as not to feel "two thousand years of instruction sag underfoot / Like a rotted floor," and "the great retreat from truth and the moral confusions / Deeper confounded." He dies a victim of mind and pessimism, leaving to his wife and brother the gift to pursue their affair in "freedom and happiness."

Also in this volume is "The Bowl of Blood," a masque that features Hitler, who comes anonymously as The Leader to seek counsel from a medium. Jeffers' attitude toward Hitler here as elsewhere is a most ambivalent one, deriving from the poem's basic contention, which is that Hitler is no more than anyone else a master of history but its creature: "Listen: the man does not have power, / Power has the man." "Whoever thinks this man is more wicked / Than other men knows not himself." Hitler's original patriotic motives were unambiguously commendable ("Blood and soil are poetry, you can fight for them"), but now, having put on power and taken to himself a cast of disciples, like Jeffers' Barclay and Jesus before him, he is caught on the public stage and destined to "play out the tragedy," the requisite descent into "Exhaustion and shabby horrors and squalid slavery, / The Russian theme."

It is an utterly fatalistic view of history, working itself out here in Europe. Hence, while always fearfully assuming the likelihood of America's eventual involvement, Jeffers was politically an absolute isolationist, at this time of American history when isolationism had ready political meaning. For, history was "what our people came over / From stifled Europe to escape."

That last statement of unqualified, separatist Americanism, in the tradition of Emerson, Thoreau, and Whitman, was made by Hoult Gore in Jeffers' most shocking and sensational poem, "The Love and the Hate," which forms the first part of *The Double Axe*, published in 1948 with his publisher's disclaimer. The volume consists almost exclusively of poems inspired either by the war or by the still vaster theme of the collapse of the Christian era.

In "The Love and the Hate," written in 1944, the young soldier, Hoult Gore, having died in battle on a Pacific island, returns home not just as a ghost, but as a stinking, slimy, putrefying corpse. Licensed by his personal fate to speak on behalf of the slaughtered, he is the uninhibited mouthpiece of all Jeffers' horror of war, mutilation, and violent death, and all his irrepressible hatred of those who, for whatever cause, send others out to die. Through Hoult, who before his final decomposition, in this witches' broth of a story, shoots his father for supporting the war, Jeffers gives voice to sentiments of quite amazing ferocity:

> I wish that every man who approved this
> war,
> In which we had no right, reason nor
> justice,
> Were crawling there in the fire's way with
> his back broken, . . .

Three years after this unrestrained howl of rage and vicarious pain, Jeffers attached to the poem—for relief, for balance, for transcendence—a second part entitled "The Inhumanist." This latter poem is less a narrative than a treasury of wisdom, a new book of proverbs, a seasonal round of fifty-two sections that ends with the beginning of a fresh dawn, after the utter dead end of "The Love and the Hate." The only common element is the Gore estate, which is now the home of the main character, who is called simply "the old man." After Hoult Gore's obliterating nihilism, he purifies a cursed spot with the most extended articulation of "inhumanism" that Jeffers ever composed. From mass society and mass politics, from secular humanism and from anthropocentric religion, even from the human race, the old man is unequivocally disaffected. "But still remains the endless inhuman beauty of things . . . and there is endurance, endurance, death's nobler cousin. Endurance." He counsels stoicism and self-adjustment on the personal level, with space enough between fellow men to permit steady contemplation of the whole, marvelous, sentient, natural divinity ("nothing is not alive"), the quiet adoration of which restores and redeems man. Precisely:

> Moderate kindness
> Is oil on a crying wheel: use it. Mutual help
> Is necessary: use it when it is necessary.
> And as to love: make love when need drives.
> And as to love: love God. He is rock, earth
> and water, and the beasts and stars; and
> the night that contains them.
> And as to love: whoever loves or hates man
> is fooled in a mirror.

Of his remaining longer works two were adaptations from Euripides, the Greek tragedian who lived in a time of deep-seated cultural change most like Jeffers' own. In his *Medea* (1946), the title figure, after only slight modification of her Euripidean character, takes her fit place in Jeffers country among his other wild, passionate women confronting the less instinctive world of men. (She had indeed been reincarnated previously in "Solstice" as Madrone Bothwell.) Jeffers' language thrills to her barbaric, elemental, "dark" nature, as it is thrown in deathly conflict with Jason's convenient, opportunistic, "better-lighted" reason. She begins with the wish that "from that blue sky the white wolf of lightning / Would leap, and burst my skull and brain." She goes out, revenged, inaccessible to pity, beyond humanity: "Now I go forth / Under the cold eyes of the weakness-despising stars:—not me they scorn."

The second adaptation was of *Hippolytus,* published in 1954 under the title "The Cretan Woman." The most conspicuous aspect of this poem is Jeffers' attribution to Hippolytus of an explicitly homosexual formation, which finds expression in his fastidiousness, his clean-limbed, athletic camaraderie with Alcyon and Andros, and in his fatal inability to respond to Phaedra. Over the tragedy Aphrodite presides and disposes, delivering in the closing lines a homily on hubris that seems pertinent less to the particular drama it concludes than generally to the technological civilization of the twentieth century.

In the same volume with "The Cretan Woman" is "Hungerfield," a short narrative written a year or so after Una's death, the finest passages of which are addressed to her memory. The poem had first and last a therapeutic function for Jeffers, for its subject is the coming to terms with the death of loved ones, with the pain of their dying, and with the fact of their deaths. Hawl Hungerfield's failure to do so, his refusal to let his mother die and be dead, starts a plague of death that does not complete its course until it has devoured all the animals around his farm, his brother, his wife and children, and himself. While Jeffers resigns himself:

> It is no good. Una has died, and I
> Am left waiting for death.

He waited many years and learned, doubtless with the help of "Hungerfield," how to renew purpose in his daily living and rediscover "the beauty of God."

Such beauty was a common one, the beauty that is all around us, of which we are a part; but perhaps it was a rare God, emanating from the peculiar intensity of Jeffers' response to that beauty. He responded simply and powerfully at a time when complication and subtlety were the prevailing poetic modes. It is in part owing to this direct accessibility of speech that he has been found to be "the most sui generis" of modern American poets, the most "his own man." Indeed, as a poet, he does seem to stand apart from his generation, and the literary contemporaries he calls to mind are quite miscellaneous.

In the case of the claustrophobic, doomed, self-destroying families of his narrative poems, there is surely a correspondence with Eugene O'Neill, and with William Faulkner, who would seem to have read "Tamar" closely. But neither of his major connections is American. First there is Yeats, fellow dweller in a stone tower in the west of a country, similarly patrician in temper and declamatory in style, albeit in more traditional meters, and likewise haunted by images of disastrous change. And second, there is D. H. Lawrence, for a posthumous volume of whose poems Jeffers wrote an introduction, and whose widow the Jeffers family came to know and visit. Both Lawrence and Jeffers were rebellious scions of Protestant fervor and the puritan conscience; both were resounding, vatic voices improvising on the free-verse line of Whitman; and both were in pursuit of sources of power and light beneath and beyond the human.

O'Neill, Faulkner, Yeats, and Lawrence make a most various company. But if a single category is sought in which Jeffers may be properly situated, it must be a geographical one. He is very much a western American, a Californian poet, to be read as an elder poetic kinsman of Kenneth Rexroth (for all that writer's surprisingly heated antipathy to Jeffers), and of such diverse but distinctively western poets as William Everson, Gary Snyder, Charles Bukowski, and Jack Spicer, all of whom have acknowledged, briefly or at length, Jeffers' extraordinary achievement.

Indeed, it is impossible to imagine Jeffers living and writing anywhere except in the west of the American continent, perhaps even anywhere except in a house within sight and sound of the Pacific Ocean. For he is in every respect and in all assumptions a westerner, an heir of the frontiersman of myth, a direct descendant of the westward-looking literary romantics. Behind him stand Emerson and Whitman, travelers in mind and gesture, and Henry David Thoreau, frontiersman by analogy in *Walden.* And larger still out of a further past looms James Fenimore Cooper's exemplary hero, Natty Bumppo, for whom also God disclosed himself in natural beauty, albeit in more Christian, less pantheist shape; for whom also the good life consisted of living as closely as possible in accord with nature, taking from it only what was essential in the way of food and clothing for survival; and for whom also the greatest threat to the good life (of society as well as of the individual) lay in the heedless, exploitative misuse of the natural world by a proliferating, densely packed population.

In a late poem, "Passenger Pigeons," Jeffers considers the possibility of man's self-extinction despite his present billions, just as in his death-dealing arrogance he had previously annihilated the countless numbers of the passenger pigeon. By a nice, absolutely appropriate irony, this is the species that is subjected to wholesale, black-farcical massacre, to Natty's contemptuous disgust, in the first book of the Leatherstocking Series, nearly a century and a half before, in the early years of American westward and industrial expansion. Cooper saw ahead with such alarming clarity; and it was further along the same line of sight that Jeffers gazed.

Thus, a redeemer, in the poem of that title, has to redeem a history of indiscriminate rapacity, mechanized utilitarianism, extirpation, and genocide—the history of a people who

> . . . have done what never was done before.
> Not as a people takes a land to love it and
>   be fed,
> A little, according to need and love, and
>   again a little; sparing the country tribes,
>   mixing
> Their blood with theirs, their minds with all
>   the rocks and rivers, their flesh with the
>   soil: no, without hunger
> Wasting the world and your own labor,
>   without love possessing, not even your
>   hands to the dirt but plows
> Like blades of knives: heartless machines;
>   houses of steel: using and despising the
>   patient earth . . .
> Oh, as a rich man eats a forest for profit
>   and a field for vanity, so you came west
>   and raped
> The continent and brushed its people to
>   death. Without need, the weak
>   skirmishing hunters, and without mercy.

So, removing himself as far as possible from that continuous process of history, Jeffers found himself a place where, with hands to the dirt, he planted his trees in the patient earth and slowly built his house, not of steel, but of stone. It was a life's work, a life's dedication; but in any time span longer than the individual's, merely a moment's holding action. History (which is "what our ancestors came over / From stifled Europe to escape") advances, a progress that may be delayed but not deflected:

> We have built the great cities; now
> There is no escape. We have gathered vast
>   populations incapable of free survival,
>   insulated
> From the strong earth, each person in
>   himself helpless, on all dependent. The
>   circle is closed, and the net
> Is being hauled in.

There was no further to go. Centuries, millennia even, of westward yearning and outreaching were coming to an end. The globe's circle was closed. It was the moment that Whitman had awesomely imagined years before, projecting himself in space and time until, in "Facing West from California's Shores," "Long having wander'd since, round the earth having wander'd / Now I face home again." What then, he had wondered, what then?—and indeed he had left his poem on a question: "But where is what I started for so long ago? / And why is it yet unfound?" In that same cast of westward mind, Jeffers spent most of his life "facing west from California's shores," with no further western land before him but with the end of the West, he felt, piling up and darkening the sky behind him, as he looked outward, away from humanity.

This circular shape of westward movement around the globe was repeated for Jeffers in the shapes he discerned of the many cycles of culture. The cycles, smaller and larger, intersected one another-Judaic, Greco-Roman, Nordic—and were all contained within the vaster cycle of Western history. During his lifetime, he believed, the Christian cycle had turned, with its weight of at least fifteen centuries, heavily downward. Rising swiftly to meet its fall, to cut its descending path with terrifying, clashing possibilities, was the age of the machine:

> The first of these curves passing
>   its noon and the second orient
> All in one's little lifetime make it seem
>   pivotal.
> Truly the time is marked by insane
>   splendors and agonies.
> But watch when the two curves cross:
>   you children
> Not far away down the hawk's-nightmare
>   future: you will see monsters.

As with cultures, so with nations. In the case of his own country, Jeffers saw its history in terms of an ever steeper decline from a high point, probably in the early years of independence, as a republic of austere, self-reliant libertarians, to its present condition of a sprawling, luxury-loving, parasitic, bureaucratized empire. From his "ideally, aristocratic and re-publican" position, as Una characterized his politics, he addressed a number of public poems over the years to the American nation. Already in the early 1920's he felt that a "perishing republic" was "heavily thickening to empire"; by the 1940's "Now, thoroughly compromised, we aim at world rule, like Assyria, Rome, Britain, Germany, to inherit those hordes of guilt and doom."

No, he saw little hope for the world, if by the world is meant the world of power politics and historical tendency. That story was just the one about original sin, the tale of hubris writ large, larger, and ever more destructive. As a result of his political pessimism, he has often, although much less frequently of late, been misinterpreted as nihilistic or life-denying or despairing. Such judgments are very far from the truth.

Of course, Jeffers knew that to be alive was to suffer, that pain was intrinsic to life: "The poets who sing of life without remembering its agony / Are fools and liars." But he also knew for himself that to be alive was not, very much not, to be in despair, nor, save when personal sorrow or public catastrophe prompts it, to be unhappy. As he politely replied to Dorothy Thompson in 1938: "You speak of the present isolation and spiritual despair; and I must confess that I value the isolation and don't feel the despair." He valued the isolation because it enabled him to concentrate his rapt attention upon the enormous beauty of the world; and he didn't feel the despair because, with the "bad dreams" exorcised in his stories, as he explained early on in his "Apology for Bad Dreams," from contemplation of the world's beauty his spirit drew a constant serenity.

In fact, Jeffers should be seen as finally and essentially a religious poet. His was a great, solemn, watchful, meditative spirit, concerned, as he wrote, "with permanent things and the permanent aspects of life." It is in such a spiritual context that he may be associated with the Greek tragedians and with the Old Testament prophets. He has that kind of weight, that kind of seriousness, that kind of salutary fierceness. He is a major poet, uncomfortable, disturbing, savage at times, yet inspiriting and enhancing. We neglect him at the peril of our own seriousness.

Selected Bibliography

WORKS OF ROBINSON JEFFERS

POEMS

Flagons and Apples, (Los Angeles: Grafton, 1912).

Californians, (New York: Macmillan, 1916).

Tamar and Other Poems, (New York: Peter G. Boyle, 1924).

Roan Stallion, Tamar, and Other Poems, (New York: Boni and Liveright, 1925).

The Women at Point Sur, (New York: Boni and Liveright, 1927).

Cawdor and Other Poems, (New York: Liveright, 1928).

Dear Judas and Other Poems, (New York: Liveright, 1929).

Descent to the Dead, (New York: Random House, 1931).

Thurso's Landing and Other Poems, (New York: Liveright, 1932).

Give Your Heart to the Hawks and Other Poems, (New York: Random House, 1933).

Solstice and Other Poems, (New York: Random House, 1935).

Such Counsels You Gave to Me and Other Poems, (New York: Random House, 1937).

The Selected Poetry of Robinson Jeffers, (New York: Random House, 1938).

Be Angry at the Sun, (New York: Random House, 1941).

Medea, (New York: Random House, 1946).

The Double Axe and Other Poems, (New York: Random House, 1948).

Poetry, Gongorism and a Thousand Years, (Los Angeles: Ward Ritchie, 1949).

Hungerfield and Other Poems, (New York: Random House, 1954).

The Beginning and the End and Other Poems, (New York: Random House, 1963).

Selected Poems, (New York: Vintage, 1965).

Not Man Apart, edited by David Ross Brower (San Francisco: Sierra Club, 1965).

Jeffers Country, (San Francisco: Scrimshaw Press, 1971).

The Alpine Christ and Other Poems, with commentary and notes by William Everson (Monterey, Calif.: Cayucos Books, 1974).

Brides of the South Wind: Poems 1917–1922, with commentary and notes by William Everson (Monterey, Calif.: Cayucos Books, 1974).

The Double Axe and Other Poems, Including Eleven Suppressed Poems, (New York: Liveright, 1977).

ROBINSON JEFFERS

LETTERS

The Selected Letters of Robinson Jeffers, 1897–1962, edited by Ann N. Ridgeway (Baltimore: Johns Hopkins, 1968).

BIBLIOGRAPHIES

Alberts, Sydney S., *A Bibliography of the Works of Robinson Jeffers,* (New York: Random House, 1933).

Nolte, William H., *The Merrill Checklist of Robinson Jeffers,* (Columbus, Ohio: Charles E. Merrill, 1970).

Tate, Allen, *Sixty American Poets, 1896–1944,* rev. ed. (Washington, D.C.: Library of Congress, 1954).

Vardamis, Alex A., *The Critical Reputation of Robinson Jeffers,* (Hamden, Conn.: Archon, 1972).

BIOGRAPHICAL AND CRITICAL STUDIES

Alexander, John R., "Conflict in the Narrative Poetry of Robinson Jeffers," (*Sewanee Review* 80: 85–99, January–March 1972).

Bennett, Melba Berry, *The Stone Mason of Tor House: The Life and Work of Robinson Jeffers,* (Los Angeles: Ward Ritchie, 1966).

Boyers, Robert, "A Sovereign Voice," (*Sewanee Review* 77: 487–507, Summer 1969).

Brophy, Robert J., *Robinson Jeffers: Myth, Ritual and Symbol in His Narrative Poems,* (Cleveland: Case Western Reserve University Press, 1973).

Carpenter, Frederic I., "The Values of Robinson Jeffers," (*American Literature* 11: 353–66, January 1940).

Carpenter, Frederic I., *Robinson Jeffers,* (New York: Twayne, 1962).

Coffin, Arthur B., *Robinson Jeffers: Poet of Inhumanism,* (Madison: University of Wisconsin Press, 1971).

Cunningham, Cornelius C., "The Rhythm of Robinson Jeffers' Poetry as Revealed by Oral Reading," (*Quarterly Journal of Speech* 32: 351–57, October 1946).

Demott, Robert, "Robinson Jeffers's 'Tamar'." *The Twenties,* edited by Warren G. French (Deland, Fla.: Everett, Edwards, 1975).

Dickey, James, "First and Last Things," (*Poetry* 103: 320–21, February 1964).

Everson, William, *Robinson Jeffers: Fragments of an Older Fury,* (Berkeley, Calif.: Oyez, 1968).

Everson, William, "Archetype West". In *Regional Perspectives: An Examination of America's Literary Heritage,* edited by J. G. Burke (Chicago: American Library Association, 1973).

Flint, Frank S., "Verse Chronicle," (*Criterion* 11: 276–81, January 1932).

Gregory, Horace, *The Dying Gladiators,* (New York: Grove Press, 1961).

Highet, Gilbert, *People, Places, and Books,* (New York: Oxford University Press, 1953).

Kunitz, Stanley J., "Day Is a Poem," (*Poetry* 59: 148–54, December 1941).

Lutyens, David B., *The Creative Encounter,* (London: Secker and Warburg, 1960).

Monjian, Mercedes C., *Robinson Jeffers: A Study in Inhumanism,* (Pittsburgh: University of Pittsburgh Press, 1958).

Nolte, William H., "Robinson Jeffers as Didactic Poet," (*Virginia Quarterly Review* 42: 257–71, Spring 1966).

Powell, Lawrence Clark, *Robinson Jeffers: The Man and His Work,* (Pasadena, Calif.: San Pasqual Press, 1940).

Robinson Jeffers Newsletter, (Los Angeles: Robinson Jeffers Committee, Occidental College, 1962–).

Scott, R. I., "Robinson Jeffers's Tragedies as Rediscoveries of the World," (*Bulletin of Rocky Mountain Modern Language Association* 29: 147–65, 1975).

Shebl, James M., *In This Wild Water: The Suppressed Poems of Robinson Jeffers,* (Pasadena, Calif.: Ward Ritchie, 1976).

Squires, James Radcliffe, *The Loyalties of Robinson Jefferson,* (Ann Arbor: University of Michigan Press, 1956).

Waggoner, Hyatt M., *The Heelof Elohim: Science and Values in Modern American Poetry,* (Norman: University of Oklahoma Press, 1950).

White, Kenneth, *The Coast Opposite Humanity,* (Llanfynydd, Carmarthen: Unicorn Bookshop, 1975).

Wilder, Amos N., *Theology and Modern Literature,* (Cambridge: Harvard University Press, 1958).

Winters, A. Yvor, "Robinson Jeffers," (*Poetry* 35: 279–86, February 1930).

JOHN KEATS

(1795–1821)

MIRIAM ALLOTT

INTRODUCTION

JOHN KEATS WAS born in London on 31 October 1795 and died of tuberculosis in Rome, where he had been sent for recovery, on 23 February 1821, having been unable to write any poetry during the last fourteen months of his life because of his illness. His brief poetic career falls roughly into four stages: 1816–1817, when he wrote most of the thirty-three poems in his first collection; 1817, when he was chiefly engaged in writing *Endymion*; 1818, a year bringing crucial personal experiences that deeply affected his imagination and that closed with his first attempts at *Hyperion*; and 1819, when he wrote his major poems. The precipitating events of 1818 included his parting with his brother George, who emigrated to America that June; the loss of his other brother, Tom, who died of tuberculosis in December, aged nineteen; his first sight, during his summer walking tour with his friend Charles Brown, of the dramatic mountain scenery in the Lake District and Scotland; and his introduction in the autumn to Fanny Brawne, the girl he loved and whom he was unable to marry, first because they lacked means and later because he was too ill.

Keats had little longer in which to discover his individual poetic voice and learn something of his craft than many students need to study for a first arts degree in a British university; but he lived to see published his two collections, *Poems* (1817) and *Lamia, Isabella, The Eve of St. Agnes, and Other Poems* (1820), and, in the interval between these, his lengthy *Endymion: A Poetic Romance* (1818). Much of the rest of his work, including a selection of his remarkable letters, appeared posthumously in two small volumes published in 1848 by Richard Monckton Milnes as *Life, Letters and Literary Remains of John Keats.* Milnes added to these in 1856 by printing for the first time *The Fall of Hyperion,* a reworking of the earlier, unfinished *Hyperion.*

The total output is not large and its quality is uneven; but it became a seminal influence for other poets in the nineteenth century, remains widely familiar today, even if only by hearsay, and receives from modern scholars the serious critical attention given to major writers. It is the product of a young talent wholly dedicated to its poetic calling and to poetry as a supreme expression of the beautiful, approaching perfection only with the writer's approach to maturity. This was a state reached, as Keats saw it, by growing away from unreflecting delight in external nature and into a wise understanding of the harsher realities of existence and the annihilation of self-regarding impulses through empathic identification with others. This he called "negative capability" and associated it above all with the Shakespearean creative imagination. He did not reach it in his own poetry, though the quick human intelligence and breadth of feeling in his letters make us think that with time he might have done so.

But Keats constantly sought to further the dual development of his poetic and his personal selves by working hard at his craft, experimenting with different genres and metrical structures, submitting himself to various literary influences, and searching for a balance between what he called "sensations"—responsiveness to the concrete particulars of life—and "thoughts"—the exercise of his powers of intellect and understanding, and the nourishing of them by wide reading and varied personal experience.

If we look in turn at Keats's first collection of verse, his narrative poems, his major odes, his final effort to forge a new kind of poetic statement by reworking his abortive "epic," *Hyperion,* into a highly personal "vision," and certain passages in his letters, we can distinguish, at least in outline, the movements of this self-discipline and something of the quality of the work it helped to produce. Critical judgments of Keats have sometimes been drawn out of true, partly because the human appeal of an existence haunted by poverty and fatal disease, which nonetheless finds compensation in the activity of a vivid creative intelligence, can distract attention from the work to the life (the tendency is still common in some modern studies of the Brontë sisters). In the case of Keats it encouraged the legendary image of a chlorotic youth too sensitive to withstand hardship and done to death by hostile reviewers. Readers fastened on passages that suggested exclusively the poet of luxurious "sensations" and exquisite longing for death, a habit that encouraged a simplistic view of romanticism in general and of Keats's romanticism in particular. It became easy to isolate his confession in the "Ode to a Nightingale":

> . . . many a time
> I have been half in love with easeful Death,
> Called him soft names in many a musèd rhyme,
> To take into the air my quiet breath,
> Now more than ever seems it rich to die,
> To cease upon the midnight with no pain,[1]
> (st. 6, 1–6)

to overlook his recognition that death, after all, means insentience:

> Still wouldst thou sing, and I have ears in vain—
> To thy high requiem become a sod.
> (st. 6, 9–10)

and with this to ignore the entire movement of thought and feeling that at first carries the poet from "The weariness, the fever and the fret" into an ideal world of beauty and permanence, and finally returns him to what is actual and inescapable.

This curve of feeling shapes, in some degree, all Keats's major poetry. It is connected with that side of his creative temper where a flexible intelligence seeks to penetrate feeling with the vitality that certain Victorian readers anticipated modern criticism in recognizing. An arresting instance is William Howitt's remark, in a book published in 1847, that Keats's poetry was "a vivid orgasm of the intellect." David Masson, in his long article of November 1860 for *Macmillan's* magazine (he was then its editor), saw as outstanding in Keats "the universality of his sensuousness," but found the true sign of poetic greatness in the evidence, even in early poems, "of that power of reflective and constructive intellect by which alone so abundant a wealth of the sensual element could have been ruled and shaped into artistic literary forms."

This "potentiality" adds to our difficulties. In longer-lived and more prolific writers we can follow the individual imagination developing in accordance with its own laws of growth and movement. In Keats we catch little more than a glimpse of these laws and of how they might have come to order and direct his work. Had he lived, he would probably have suppressed or destroyed a great many early poems and, judging by certain comments in his letters, perhaps even some of those we most admire. As it is, we have to understand a talent that made many false starts; produced hundreds of journeyman lines; took time to shake off the insipidities of various unfortunate adoptive styles (espe-

1. Quotations from the poems are from M. Allott, ed., *The Poems of John Keats* (London, 1970).

cially the current neo-Elizabethanisms most damagingly influential in Leigh Hunt); and produced only a handful of fully achieved poems. Among these are "The Eve of St. Agnes" and the major odes of 1819; one or two unfinished works that, paradoxically, convey a sense of fine poetic accomplishment, notably the first *Hyperion* and (on a different scale) "The Eve of St. Mark"; and a few passages elsewhere—outstandingly the description of Moneta in *The Fall of Hyperion*—that hint at the approach of a new poetic maturity.

But we must remember that except for poets of the very first rank, and perhaps even here too, there is in the canon a relatively small area in which the shadow falling between conception and execution is dispelled by a high noon of creative intensity. Keats had his own feelings about the not fully achieved work of art as early as March 1817, when, at the age of twenty-one, he wrote a sonnet on first seeing the Elgin Marbles, the celebrated sculptures from the Parthenon brought to England by Thomas Bruce, seventh earl of Elgin, and bought for the nation in 1816, when they were housed in the British Museum. "I never cease to wonder at all that incarnate delight," he once said, when he was discovered gazing at them with his customary intentness.

My spirit is too weak—mortality
  Weighs heavily upon me like unwilling
    sleep,
(1–2)

he begins, expressing in the sonnet his baffled consciousness of his own artistic inadequacy, his longing to overcome it and the "dim-conceivèd glories of the brain," which "Bring round the heart an indescribable feud." "These wonders," broken but still withstanding the erosions of time, irradiate the imagination with gleams of something greater than either he or they, in their present form, can convey. They mysteriously mingle

. . . Grecian grandeur with the rude
Wasting of old Time, with a billowy main,
  A sun, a shadow of a magnitude.
(12–14)

The architect Charles Robert Cockerell, contemplating Michelangelo's unfinished tondo of the Holy Family in 1823, found it "striking in its unfinished state . . . the subject seems growing from the marble and emerging into life . . . you trace and watch its birth from the sculptor's mind. . . ." A similar sense of emergent power distinguishes the "shadow of a magnitude" in Keats's unfinished *Hyperions* and the individual intelligence struggling to realize itself in the 1819 odes and the vivacious letters. We cannot scrutinize here what is "classical" and what "romantic," but Keats's writings remind us that incompleteness is a characteristic of one kind of romantic art. The aesthetic experience offered suggests "nature naturing," *natura naturans,* rather than "nature natured," *natura naturata,* which affords another kind of experience, one that we might be forgiven for identifying with what is "classical."

EARLY YEARS AND POEMS

The prelude to Keats's poetic career runs from his birth in 1795—Thomas Carlyle was born that year, which should remind us that Keats would have been a man in his forties at the time of the Oxford movement, the last flare-up of Chartism, and Matthew Arnold's first volume of poems—to 1815, when he entered Guy's Hospital as a medical student; he had left the Clarke School at Enfield in 1811 to be apprenticed to Thomas Hammond, a surgeon and apothecary of Edmonton.

The events of a writer's life sometimes seem in retrospect to be designed exclusively for the needs of his creative imagination. Certainly Keats's early years suggest a necessary "set." On one side is the schoolboy, small in height—Keats was always rueful about his want of inches—and sensitive to hurt, who yet was robust, affectionate, and mettlesome; there are stories of his squaring up to boys who bullied his brothers and his routing of a butcher's boy who was cruel to a cat. On the other side are the experiences that constantly tested these qualities: fatal family illnesses, deaths, separations, material losses.

Keats's father, the head ostler at a local inn, died in an accident in 1804; his mother, for whom he felt deeply, remarried shortly after being widowed, and six years later died of tuberculosis, which also killed his brother Tom in 1818. His grandmother, who since 1804 had cared for the three brothers and their young sister, Fanny (the recipient of some of Keats's gayest and most tender letters), died in 1814. By this time Keats was away at Hammond's, and George—Tom accompanied him later—was taken on as a clerk by Richard Abbey, one of the two guardians appointed for the young family. Their latest loss brought more financial hardship because Abbey seemingly was slow to hand over money placed in trust for them. At this stage, though, he did keep on George and Tom, take Fanny into his home, and continue in the belief that he had secured a good professional opening for his eldest ward.

Keats's true calling announced itself in 1814, at the end of his eighteenth year, when, fired by *The Faerie Queene* and "enamoured of its stanza," he composed his first known poem, "Imitation of Spenser"; the calling was confirmed on 3 March 1817, when C. & J. Ollier published his *Poems* and set the seal on his abandonment of medicine for poetry. In intervals of walking the wards at Guy's Hospital, attending lectures, and passing, in July 1816, his qualifying examinations at Apothecary's Hall, he wrote most of the thirty-three poems in the collection. They reflect little of his student life except the loneliness and oppression he felt on leaving the Edmonton countryside to live in lodgings in the crowded capital.

> O Solitude, if I must with thee dwell,
> Let it not be among the jumbled heap
> Of murky buildings, . . .
> (1–3)

he writes in "To Solitude" (1815), picturing the wooded places

> . . . where the deer's swift leap
> Startles the wild bee from the foxglove bell.
> (7–8)

These two lines, with their Wordsworthian ring, are the best in this youthful piece, but it is momentous as his first published work. Its appearance in Leigh Hunt's *Examiner* for 5 May 1816 signaled his entry into the literary world.

Hunt, whom Keats admired not only for his verses but also for his liberal idealism and his admirable periodical (it served Keats as a kind of Open University), had been a hero since school days. The 1817 volume is suffused with his influence, and opens with a dedicatory sonnet rejoicing that though "Glory and loveliness have passed away," the author can feel

> . . . a free,
> A leafy luxury, seeing I could please
> With these poor offerings a man like thee.
> (12–14)

The first of the three sections of the *Poems* consists of eleven pieces, usually saluting in Hunt's sugary style the "Spenserian" delights of chivalric love and a natural world filled with "leafy luxury," white-handed nymphs, and "bowery" glades designed for poetic reverie. Two pieces, "Specimen of an Induction to a Poem" and "Calidore," inspired by Hunt's tripping style in *The Story of Rimini* (1816), are Keats's abortive first attempts at narrative poetry.

Of the three verse epistles in pentameter couplets in the second section, "To My Brother George" and "To Charles Cowden Clarke," composed in August and September 1816, show an advance on the earlier and more flowery "To George Felton Mathew," addressed to a poetaster associate of still more youthful days. (Clarke was the estimable schoolmaster and friend who fostered Keats's early enthusiasm for poetry and introduced his poems to the Hunt circle.) They emulate Hunt's informal verse letters recently published in the *Examiner* but, as elsewhere in the volume, are distinguished by the intermittent accents of an individual voice struggling for expression.

> With shattered boat, oar snapped, and canvas rent,
> I slowly sail, scarce knowing my intent,
> (17–18)

says Keats despondently in the epistle to Clarke, but his manner gathers buoyancy as he recalls the poetry that his friend taught him:

> The grand, the sweet, the terse, the free, the fine;
> What swelled with pathos, and what right divine;
> Spenserian vowels that elope with ease,
> And float along like birds o'er summer seas. . . .
> (54–57)

In the third section Keats grouped seventeen Petrarchan sonnets, mostly celebrating recent literary friendships and artistic enthusiasms. Among them are "On Seeing the Elgin Marbles," "Great Spirits Now on Earth Are Sojourning . . . ," which praises Hunt, William Wordsworth, and the painter Benjamin Haydon, and "On First Looking into Chapman's Homer," unquestionably the finest performance of this early period. He closed the volume with his reflective, confessional "Sleep and Poetry," running to some 400 lines in pentameter couplets and linked with "I Stood Tip-toe," written in the same meter and printed in the first section. Unequal in quality and awkward in meeting the simultaneous demands of sense, syntax, and rhyme, these nevertheless foreshadow later achievements. "I Stood Tip-toe" is a first gesture toward *Endymion.* Foremost among nature's "luxuries" that quicken poetic inspiration is the moon:

> O Maker of sweet poets, dear delight
> Of this fair world. . . .
> (116–117)

It was "a poet, sure a lover too" who, from his post on Mount Latmus,

> Wept that such beauty should be desolate.
> So in fine wrath some golden sounds he won
> And gave meek Cynthia her Endymion.
> (202–204)

Touched by Wordsworth's account of Diana, Apollo, and other rural deities in book IV of *The Excursion,* which was a profoundly influential work for the second generation of romantic poets, Keats too finds that myths originate in imaginative response to the beauties of nature, and "I Stood Tiptoe" singles out the haunting legends of Eros and Psyche (141–150), Pan and Syrinx (157–162), and Narcissus and Echo (163–180). The theme recurs in "Sleep and Poetry," which brings together for the first time central ideas concerning the interdependence of sleep, reverie, and poetic creativity; the vitalizing of the natural world through classical myth; and individual progress from what Keats later termed, in a letter of 3 May 1818 to John Hamilton Reynolds, the "Chamber of Maiden-Thought" to the darker world of "Misery and Heartbreak, Pain, Sickness and oppression." "Byron says, 'Knowledge is Sorrow,'" reflects Keats in the same letter, "and I go on to say that 'Sorrow is Wisdom.'"

The influence of Wordsworth's "Tintern Abbey," working on his own views about personal development, mitigates to some degree the debilitating prettinesses of Keats's poetic language.

> Oh, for ten years, that I may overwhelm
> Myself in poesy . . .
> (96–97)

he writes in "Sleep and Poetry," looking for the time when simple delight in "the realm . . . of Flora and old Pan" will yield to

> . . . a nobler life
> Where I may find the agonies, the strife
> Of human hearts—
> (123–125)

Keats conjures up an image of the creative imagination, partly inspired by the portrayal in certain of Nicolas Poussin's paintings of a chariot driven across the sky by Apollo, who was always an immensely potent figure for him. A charioteer descends to earth and communes with nature, but then focuses on the "shapes of delight, of mystery, and fear" embodied in the procession of men and women now passing before him. The conception is sufficiently striking, but ultimately eludes his poetic reach. At this stage of his career, the distance between Keats's available resources and his high sense of poetic vocation began to narrow when he freed his language from its fustian clutter by concentrating on "the object as in itself it is": in "To Charles Cowden Clarke" the moon seen among clouds,

As though she were reclining in a bed
Of bean blossoms, in heaven freshly shed,
(95–96)

the uneven sound of Clarke's parting footsteps at night, sometimes resonant on the "gravelly" path, sometimes muffled as he stepped on the grass verge; or the attaching particularity found in his sonnet "To My Brothers,"

Small, busy flames play through the fresh-laid coals,
And their faint cracklings o'er our silence creep,
(1–2)

and felt again in his description of setting out at night after the warm gathering at Hunt's Hampstead cottage:

Keen, fitful gusts are whispering here and there,
Among the bushes, half leafless and dry;
The stars look very cold about the sky,
And I have many miles on foot to fare.
("Keen, Fitful Gusts," 1–4)

The clarity and immediacy usually peter out too soon; but the promise of poetic vigor is sustained in the Chapman sonnet, where the creative imagination as a "golden" realm filled with "wonders" generates the poem's unifying imagery of exploration and discovery and, for once (it was long before this happened again), the poem's structure and style are consistent with the movement of thought and feeling. Keats wrote it rapidly one October night in 1816, after he and Clarke had spent many hours poring excitedly for the first time over George Chapman's translation of Homer. (Homer had been familiar to them hitherto only in Alexander Pope's version, which never afforded Keats the keen delight he found, for instance, in his favorite line from Chapman on Odysseus shipwrecked: "The sea had soaked his heart through. . . .") In another sonnet of the period, "How Many Bards," Keats records the "thronging" in his mind of recollections from his favorite poets, which "make pleasing music" like the mingling of evening sounds—birdsong, "the whispering of the leaves," "the voice of waters"—as they lose their individual identity in the distance.

This sonnet vividly describes the working of Keats's densely associative literary memory, and the Chapman sonnet is a rare early illustration of his successful "alchemizing" of these recollections into his own idiom. It draws on wide literary memories, many of them probably half-conscious, some gathered from contemporary authors (Wordsworth included) and most of them echoed from his schoolroom reading: the most influential were accounts, in William Robertson's *History of . . . America,* of Balboa, Cortez, and the discovery of gold in the New World, and, in a schoolbook on astronomy, of the first sighting by William Herschel of the planet Uranus in 1781. The individual instances in the sestet of man's encounters with dazzling new experience and knowledge reinforce the fine opening breadth of the octave. Leigh Hunt celebrated the "prematurely masculine" vein in this "noble sonnet," which closed "with so energetic a calmness and which completely announced the new poet taking possession."

NARRATIVE POEMS

With his first volume of poems in print, Keats devoted the rest of 1817 to *Endymion,* the

"Poetic Romance" that was to be "a test, a trial of my Powers of Imagination and chiefly of my invention by which I must make 4,000 lines out of one bare circumstance," the "circumstance" being the legend that the moon goddess—known variously in classical myth as Diana, Phoebe, and Cynthia—fell in love with the shepherd Endymion as he lay asleep on the mountain heights of Caria.

For his first major literary enterprise Keats obeyed the narrative impulse that prompted his fragmentary Huntian-Spenserian tales in 1816 and led him, in 1819 to compose "The Eve of St. Agnes," "La Belle Dame Sans Merci," and the more ambitious and uneven "Lamia." But, as A. C. Bradley saw in his *Oxford Lectures on Poetry* (1909), the "long poem" in the romantic period, adding its weight to a progressive breakdown of genres, contains lyrical, confessional, and reflective elements as well as a narrative interest. Keats usually relates a love story that expresses personal ideas and feelings rather more urgently than it arouses interest in "what happens next" to the lovelorn characters. *Endymion* uninhibitedly dramatizes his current aspirations for the supreme experience of an ideal passion. Later (as with William Butler Yeats, who met Maud Gonne after celebrating the legendary Niamh in *The Wanderings of Oisin*) his relationship with what he called in "Lamia" a "real woman" gave his work a new emotional charge.

"The Eve of St. Agnes" was written in January–February 1819, a few weeks after Keats's first "understanding" with Fanny Brawne on Christmas Day, and celebrates the warmth of a requited passion but, characteristically, cannot forget its attendant hazards or its vulnerability to time. His young brother had just died, and love and death are inextricably bound together in his imagination. In "La Belle Dame Sans Merci" and "Lamia," written, respectively, on 21 April and between about 28 June and 5 September in the same year, where the destructiveness of passion is expressed as keenly as its delight, the emotion is still more ambivalent and the presence of death yet more haunting. The earlier "Isabella, or the Pot of Basil," on the other hand, written during March–April 1818, before the most overwhelming personal experiences of that year, is in spite of its authorial interpolations the least "personal" of these love stories. It led Keats a step or two along a road not taken elsewhere in his poetic life.

All these poems are consciously exploratory in their diverse techniques and source materials. *Endymion* continues in the pentameter couplets used for its precursor, "I Stood Tip-toe"; but Keats also handles ottava rima for his Italian "Isabella," Spenserians for "The Eve of St. Agnes," ballad-style quatrains for "La Belle Dame Sans Merci," octosyllabic couplets freely interspersed with seven-syllable lines for the fragmentary "The Eve of St. Mark," and Drydenesque couplets for "Lamia." The first and last draw on classical, the rest on medieval, sources. The latter suited Keats's liking for rich pictorial effects and, as it turned out, provided themes that allowed him to balance the inner and the outer, so that the work could be quickened by personal feeling without falling into disabling subjectivity.

Endymion, with more flats than elevations in its four long books, which here we can only glance at in passing, is for many readers a monument of misdirected effort. But its general style is an improvement on *Poems* (1817), reflecting (as in the fine April 1817 sonnet "On the Sea") the first effects of Keats's simultaneous disenchantment with Hunt and renewed passion for Shakespeare, whom he now saw as his "Presider." Some passages, especially the "Hymn to Pan" in book I, which is his first major ode (the "Ode to Sorrow" in book IV is less distinguished), look forward to the work of 1819. New ground is broken in his use of a narrative medium to express current ideas about human experience, while his poetic creativity is stimulated afresh by his "thronging" literary recollections, now chiefly from George Sand's translation of *Ovid* and classical reference books "devoured" (as Clarke put it) at school; allusions to Endymion and the moon in the Elizabethans, particularly Shakespeare, Edmund Spenser, and Michael Drayton; and details of magical journeys from *The Arabian Nights* and colorful modern verse narratives including Walter Savage Landor's *Gebir* (1798) and Robert Southey's two lengthy poems, *Thalaba the Destroyer* (1801) and *The Curse of Kehama* (1810).

Endymion's journeys—he seeks the shining amorous girl of his dream vision on the earth (book I), beneath it (book II), under the sea (book III), and in the air (book IV)—rework the stages of individual development outlined in "Sleep and Poetry." From his carefree existence among his native woods and hills, he passes into melancholy obsession with the difference between the ideal and the actual, and is finally admitted to unshadowed bliss only after learning selfless identification with the pain of others. Since love appears in this poem as the supreme good, its frustration is the type of all pain. Endymion's succoring of Glaucus and the drowned lovers in book III, and his sacrifice of his "dream" for the lovelorn Indian maid in book IV, ensure the transformation of this dusky girl into his fair divinity (in context this has a startling and somewhat perfunctory effect that suggests the author's growing fatigue), who summons him to share with her "an immortality of passion."

The poem follows too many side winds of inspiration to qualify as a sustained allegory, as it is sometimes mistakenly described; but the ordering of the story implies—perhaps as an answer to Shelley's gloomy "Alastor" (1816)—that the ideal is indeed attainable, provided one first enters into and accepts the bliss and bale of everyday life. This suggestion is strengthened by the famous "pleasure-thermometer" passage in *Endymion*, book I (777–842), tracing the gradations of human happiness, which rise from delight in nature and art to the human ties of friendship and, supremely, physical love. The driving force throughout is man's longing for "fellowship with essence," by which he will ultimately

> . . . shine
> Full alchemized, and free of space. . . .
> (I. 779–780)

The mystery of an ultimate knowledge, felt but not realizable in words, is conveyed in the "Hymn to Pan," where the god of universal nature is invoked as the "unimaginable lodge / For solitary thinkings" that

> . . . dodge
> Conception to the very bourne of heaven.
> . . .
> (I. 294–295)

The lines anticipate the "silent form" in the "Ode on a Grecian Urn" that teases the poet

> . . . out of thought
> As doth eternity. . . .
> (44–45)

Keats's fine preface shows that he judged the immaturity of *Endymion,* which is very noticeable in its boyishly succulent love scenes, more penetratingly than its many unfriendly reviewers in the Tory periodicals, who disliked Keats on principle as a member of the "Cockney" school associated with Leigh Hunt. He found similar weaknesses in "Isabella"—what I should call were I a reviewer 'A weak-sided poem' —and in "The Eve of St. Agnes," only "not so glaring," but thought "Lamia" was stronger and had more "fire."

His readers generally take a different view: "Isabella" is flawed but represents an advance from adolescence to adulthood;[2] "The Eve of St. Agnes" imaginatively blends with its sumptuous Elizabethan opulence individual feeling for what has "no joy, nor love, nor light"; while "Lamia," with some highly accomplished versification to its credit, uneasily mingles virtuoso pictorial effects, intense feeling, and would-be sophisticated satire, a mode in which Keats was never at home—as the quasi-Byronic "The Cap and Bells," also of late 1819, unhappily demonstrates at some length.

2. See F. W. Bateson, *English Poetry* (London, 1950), p. 222 *n.*

It can be argued that Keats's need to assimilate the experiences of 1818 and 1819 worked as much against as for his success in narrative poetry. "Isabella," which hints at the possibility of a different kind of achievement, was written before George's departure, Tom's death, and the arrival in his life of Fanny Brawne. It was undertaken in obedience to a "public" impulse—the suggestion in William Hazlitt's February 1818 lecture, "On Dryden and Pope," that modern translations of Giovanni Boccaccio's tales, "as that of Isabella," might win a popular success. It is less poised than its successor, "The Eve of St. Agnes," and matches *Endymion* in its lush love scenes and awkward attempts at naturalistic dialogue. "Those lips, O slippery blisses," says Keats in *Endymion*; and Lorenzo's lips "poesy" with Isabella's "in dewy rhyme." "Goodbye! I'll soon be back" is one of several bathetic touches in the lovers' conversation; and the rodomontade in the stanzas castigating Isabella's brothers, who kill Lorenzo because he is too poor, is out of keeping with the fine plangency in the rest of the tale.

Yet Keats's modern fellow poet Edward Thomas praised the ottava rima stanzas, with their "adagio" effect, for making "Isabella," appropriately, "a very still poem" and for accommodating, better than his early couplets, Keats's "choiceness of detail." Thomas could have added that this detail is more purposefully employed to focus both the events in the narrative and the feelings they generate. The dead Lorenzo, appearing to Isabella in a dream, mourns his lost love and the small, touching sounds of life in the world she inhabits. The chestnut leaves and "prickly nuts" fall onto his grave, a "sheep-fold bleat" reaches him from beyond the river, he hears "the glossy bees at noon . . . fieldward pass"; but

> . . . those sounds grow strange to me,
> And thou art distant in humanity.
> (st. 39, 311–312)

The "immortality of passion" sought in *Endymion* yields to another order of feeling:

> Thy beauty grows upon me, and I feel
> A greater love through all my essence steal.
> (st. 40, 319–320)

A year later, in "The Eve of St. Agnes," Keats's growing concentration on "the object as in itself it is" seems for most of the story to be at the service of a less universalizing vision. But the hostile setting, which includes Madeline's family, who play Capulet to Porphyro's Montague, the bleak winter and rising storm, and the chill of age and death stiffening the figures of the Beadsman and old Angela, provide an oblique commentary on the stolen night in Madeline's room, where Keats introduces the richest "luxuries" yet, exquisitely indulging the senses with music, delicacies from "silken Samarkand to cedared Lebanon," and a love effortlessly consummated in a dream in which the actual and the ideal "melt" deliciously into one another. This interplay of warmth and cold, color and paleness, love and death, constitutes the "criticism of life" in the poem—this time, it seems (since Madeline escapes with Porphyro to his home "over the southern moors"), with a measured optimism about reaching a longed-for good here and now. But the oppositions suggest a more restless preoccupation with the difference between ideal and actual experience than one might have expected after the touching quietude briefly achieved in "Isabella."

Technically, Keats is no less at home with Spenserian stanzas than with ottava rima, commanding in them the peculiarly rich pictorial details that enliven his improvisation on the "popular superstition" that a girl who goes fasting to bed on St. Agnes' Eve will see her future husband in a dream. The medieval coloring, which is more lavish than in "The Eve of St. Mark," the unfinished poem that William Morris saw as a main inspiration behind the Pre-Raphaelite movement, paradoxically owes much to contemporary rather than earlier writers, especially Sir Walter Scott's *The Lay of the Last Minstrel* (1805), Ann Radcliffe's "Gothick" tales, and Samuel Taylor Coleridge's "Christabel" (1816). It owes something, too, to Keats's recent visits to Chichester Cathedral and the newly established chapel at Stansted. Of course the family feud and the role of Madeline's aged attendant Angela come straight from *Romeo and Juliet,* one of the many plays densely marked in his copy of Shakespeare (now at the Keats House in Hampstead).

It is impossible to represent adequately here the textural richness nourished by these currents of literary and personal experience, but the following is an instance of the contrasts between warmth and encompassing cold that make the poem something more than a pretty piece of medievalism inspired by wishful erotic fantasy. The Beadsman, "meagre, barefoot, wan," opens the poem, returning after prayer along "the chapel aisle":

> The sculptured dead, on each side, seemed
> to freeze,
> Imprisoned in black, purgatorial rails . . .
> (st. 2, 14–15)

And his death ends it:

> The Beadsman, after thousand aves told,
> For aye unsought for slept among his ashes
> cold.
> (st. 42, 377–378)

In the interval are the events in Madeline's room, which open with the hidden Porphyro secretly watching her say her prayers and prepare for bed, a description much worked over in the manuscript (the self-criticism revealed by Keats's habits of revision is a subject on its own). The final version, with its suggestions of warmth, youth, and physical immediacy, marvelously counterpoints the aged Beadsman's solitary devotions and his approaching death:

> Full on this casement shone the wintry
> moon,
> And threw warm gules on Madeline's fair
> breast
> As down she knelt for heaven's grace and
> boon;
> Rose-bloom fell on her hands, together
> pressed,
> And on her silver cross soft amethyst,
> And on her hair a glory, like a saint.
> She seemed a splendid angel, newly dressed,
> Save wings, for Heaven. Porphyro grew
> faint;
> She knelt, so pure a thing, so free from
> mortal taint.
>
> Anon his heart revives; her vespers done,
> Of all its wreathèd pearls her hair she frees;
> Unclasps her warmèd jewels one by one;
> Loosens her fragrant bodice; by degrees
> Her rich attire creeps rustling to her knees.
> Half-hidden, like a mermaid in sea-weed,
> Pensive awhile she dreams awake, and sees,
> In fancy, fair St Agnes in her bed,
> But dares not look behind, or all the charm
> is fled.
> (st. 25–26, 217–234)

As I have said elsewhere, in "La Belle Dame Sans Merci," written on 21 April 1819, and "Lamia," written in September of the same year, when Keats had left London to "wean" himself from his passion for Fanny Brawne, so that he could try to make his way with his writing:

> The moderate "wishful" optimism of "The Eve of St. Agnes" is rejected for something much more uncompromising. The "knight-at-arms" awakens "on the cold hillside," and Lycius is destroyed. The lady encountered "in the meads," and the "maiden bright" whom Lycius finds "a young bird's flutter from a wood," both turn out to be fatal enchantresses who spell disaster for their victims and are themselves somehow doomed.[3]

Formally, though, there is no similarity between the two narratives. The earlier, perhaps Keats's most magical and self-sufficient poem, is very short; and its austere ballad stanza, forbidding the indulgence of luxuriant detail, relies on compression and spare figurative imagery for emotional effect. The density of imaginative experience that helped to

3. " 'Isabella,' 'The Eve of St. Agnes' and 'Lamia,' " in K. Muir, ed., *John Keats: A Reassessment* (London, 1958; repr., 1969), p. 56.

bring this deceptively simple little poem into being makes it barely easier to comment upon in a short space than *Endymion.* But it can be said at once that, in contrast with Keats's earlier narratives, where love is a kind of dream that quickens and delights every sense and is constantly threatened by the hard realities of the ordinary world, the enchantment is now itself a threat, and from the beginning carries the seeds of its own destruction. The poem opens, like "The Eve of St. Agnes," with winter images that affect us the more because the absences recall what once existed in a happier season:

> The sedge has withered from the lake,
> And no birds sing!
> (st. 1, 3–4)

The "lady" and her enchantment are identified with "winter" even more than with "summer," for her thrallèd knights have caught from her an everlasting cold:

> I saw their starved lips in the gloam
> With horrid warning gapèd wide,
> And I awoke, and found me here
> On the cold hill side.
> (st. 11, 41–44)

The echoes in the poem arrive most resonantly, perhaps, from Spenser and Chatterton; but the resemblance to the traditional ballad of True Thomas the Rhymer, victim of another enchantress, makes it almost certain that Keats's preoccupation with the destructiveness of love and the inevitability of death is closely associated with fears for his own poetic destiny. His treatment of the three central characters in the much longer "Lamia" and his general uncertainty of direction in that poem suggest his continued concern with an increasingly unsettling dilemma.

Keats based his new story on an anecdote in Robert Burton's *Anatomy of Melancholy.* Lycius, a student of philosophy and "twenty-five years of age," is beguiled by a beautiful woman who leads him to her house in Corinth with promises of music, song, feasting, and eternal love—the pattern of the Keatsian enchanted dream. They live blissfully until Lycius insists on a public wedding; thereupon the philosopher Apollonius appears among the guests, recognizes the lady as an enchantress, "a serpent, a lamia," and all about her "like Tantalus's gold . . . no substance but mere illusions."

In the source she vanishes "in an instant," together with her house and everything in it. In the poem the destiny of both lovers is tragic. Lamia has the power "to unperplex bliss from its neighbour pain" (which the "dreamer" certainly cannot do, according to the argument in *The Fall of Hyperion,* where he "vexes mankind"), and is herself the victim as well as the caster of spells. And when she is destroyed, Lycius is destroyed too.

> And Lycius' arms were empty of delight,
> As were his limbs of life, from that same
> night.
> . . .
> . . . no pulse, or breath they found,
> And, in its marriage robe, the heavy body
> wound.
> (II. 307–308; 310–311)

Here, then, is the problem posed in the 1819 odes. Where does the "truth" lie? In ideal experience or everyday reality? At the far end of the spectrum from the "dream" is "cold Philosophy," though this is not to be confused with the "wisdom" that Keats elsewhere sees nourished by imaginative response to life and art. Matthew Arnold felt that the romantic poets "did not know enough." This was Keats's worry, too. But to "know enough" might mean exercising processes of ratiocination and abstract thought inimical to the poetic imagination. Keats had seen in 1817 and early in 1818 that "a gradual ripening of the intellectual powers" was essential "for the purposes of great productions," and had felt that the way lay through "application, study and thought"; at the same time he had always found it difficult to see "how any thing can be known for truth by consequitive reasoning." Hence his vivid simile "The Imagination may be compared to Adam's dream—he awoke and found it truth" and his call "O for a Life of Sensations rather than of Thoughts."

Torn between Apollonius' "consequitive reasoning" and the quickening "sensations" of Lamia's enchanted dream, he produced a poem interesting to dissect thematically but compelling imaginative assent only in relatively few phrases and passages. To set against his awkward shifts of tone and his stylistic gaucheries, especially his attempted worldly manner in describing "a real woman" as "a treat" and love as always short-lived,

> Love in a hut, with water and a crust,
> Is—Love, forgive us!—cinders, ashes, dust,
> (II. 1–2)

are Hermes seen as "the star of Lethe"; Lamia described first in her brilliantly marked "gordian shape . . . rainbow sided, touched with miseries" and later in her quasi-Miltonic transmogrification, "convulsed with scarlet pain" as she assumes her human form; the ritualistic and inventive construction of her magic palace; and, expanded from a few hints in Burton, the portrait of Corinth:

> And all her populous streets and temples lewd,
> Muttered, like tempest in the distance brewed,
> . . .
> Men, women, rich and poor, in the cool hours
> Shuffled their sandals o'er the pavement white,
> Companioned or alone; while many a light
> Flared, here and there, from wealthy festivals . . .
> (I. 352–353; 355–358)

The latter makes a first-rate companion piece for the cool and charming account of Bertha's quiet cathedral town in the tantalizingly fragmentary "The Eve of St. Mark":

> The city streets were clean and fair
> From wholesome drench of April rains,
> And, on the western window panes,
> The chilly sunset faintly told
> Of unmatured green valleys cold,
> Of the green thorny bloomless hedge,
> Of rivers new with spring-tide sedge,
> Of primroses by sheltered rills,
> And daisies on the aguish hills.
> Twice holy was the Sabbath-bell;
> The silent streets were crowded well
> With staid and pious companies,
> Warm from their fireside orat'ries,
> And moving with demurest air
> To even-song and vesper prayer.
> Each archèd porch, and entry low
> Was filled with patient folk and slow,
> With whispers hush and shuffling feet,
> While played the organ loud and sweet.
> (4–22)

THE 1819 ODES

Certain anxieties underlying "Lamia" became explicit in lines that Keats wrote for Fanny Brawne on their reunion in October 1819. He mourns his lost liberty and the tyranny of a love that impedes his "winged" Muse, in earlier days

> . . . ever ready . . . to take her course
> Whither I bent her force,
> Unintellectual, yet divine to me.
>
> Divine, I say! What sea-bird o'er the sea
> Is a philosopher the while he goes
> Winging along where the great water throes?
> ("To Fanny," 12–17)

But in the interval since "The Eve of St. Agnes" Keats had written his famous odes, which could not be what they are without their "intellectual" components and the interpenetration in them of feeling and thought. With Wordsworth's "Ode: Intimations of Immortality," John Milton's "On the Morning of Christ's Nativity," and Coleridge's "Dejection," these are probably the best-known odes in English, and they have generated a quantity of critical and scholarly discussion so vast that it is impossible now to compute its scale. Yet Keats singled out the weakest, "Ode on Indolence," as the poem he most enjoyed writing in 1819, and pushed the manuscript of the "Ode to a Nightingale" behind some books (whence it was rescued by Charles Brown). Although he copied out or mentioned most of his recent poems in his journal-letters to his brother George in America, only the "Ode to Psyche" and "To Autumn" received comment.

The circumstance adds to the mysteriousness of Keats's achievement in these poems. They display a sudden advance in his mastery of poetic skills and in his use of them to explore, more concentratedly than in the narratives and with a stronger gnomic effect, the relationship between human suffering, the ideal in art and individual aspiration, and the role of the poet, whose representations of the beautiful and enduring "tease us out of thought" because we cannot be sure whether they constitute a vision of truth or a wishful dream. At the heart of the odes is the necessity to accept suffering and the transience of youth, beauty, and love, and to do so without destroying imaginative order and harmony.

Earlier, in the "Epistle to John Hamilton Reynolds," written during March 1818, Keats had wished that "dreams" of poets and painters could take their coloring "From something of material sublime" rather than from gloomy inner conflict and, longing for wisdom, had grieved that he was too untutored to "philosophize" without despondency:

> . . . It is a flaw
> In happiness to see beyond our bourn—
> It forces us in summer skies to mourn;
> It spoils the singing of the nightingale.
> (82–85)

A year later, in "Ode to a Nightingale," the singing is not "spoilt"; rather, its intense delight sharpens the poet's pain in the everyday world,

> Where youth grows pale, and spectre-thin, and dies,
> Where but to think is to be full of sorrow,
> (26–27)

but that still compels a movement of necessary assent. The mental and emotional processes that prepared the way for these poems were reinforced by a bold series of technical experiments. Keats's youthful odes—"Ode to Apollo" is an instance—gesture toward English Pindarics, but his metrical structure in 1819 is entirely new. He evolved his characteristic stanza from long practice with existing sonnet forms. As we have seen, he had a brilliant early success with the Petrarchan kind. He turned after January 1818 to the Shakespearean, which inspired "When I Have Fears" and the "Bright Star!" sonnet, two of his memorable poems on the Shakespearean themes of love, poetic ambition, and the passage of time.

But in April 1819 he set about discovering "a better sonnet stanza than we have," the Petrarchan having too many "pouncing rhymes" and the Shakespearean being "too elegiac—and the couplet at the end . . . has seldom a pleasing effect." His experiments—they include the unrhymed sonnet "If by Dull Rhymes Our English Must Be Chained . . ." and the understandably often anthologized "To Sleep"—seem not to have satisfied him. Yet they led to his ode stanza's combination of a "Shakespearean" quatrain and a "Petrarchan" sestet and to the form that gave him both discipline and flexibility in a manner removed from the neatly tripping seven-syllable trochaic couplets he had used for his "Fancy" and "Bards of Passion . . ." in the previous December. He gives a hint of his future development, though, in his attractive fragment of an "Ode to May" written earlier that year.

Keats acknowledged his renewed concern with craftsmanship when he copied out the "Ode to Psyche" on 30 April 1819 in a journal-letter, claiming that it was "the first and only [poem] with which I have taken even moderate pains—I have for the most part dash'd off my lines in a hurry—this I have done leisurely—I think it reads more richly for it." This is a matter of debate among readers, though it seems true to say that just as "To Autumn" is more complex than the direct statement of reconciliation and acceptance it is often taken to be, so the undertones in Keats's celebration of Psyche make it more interesting than "a pretty piece of Paganism" (Wordsworth's ill-fitting description of the "Hymn to Pan").

Keats, we know from his letter, understood that Psyche meant the soul. Elsewhere in the same letter he images the world as "the vale of soul-making," and its "pains and troubles" as "necessary to school an intelligence and make it a soul." He must have fastened on the resemblance between Psyche's quest for Eros and Endymion's quest for the goddess in his own story, since both are "schooled" by "pains and troubles" before reaching "an immortality of passion." It is Psyche thus translated whom Keats celebrates, picturing her in his first stanza asleep beside Eros in the lush grass and disappointingly—but unsurprisingly, if we accept the association—reverting to the artificial style of *Endymion* ("soft-conchèd ear," "tender eye-dawn of aurorean love"). Yet it is difficult not to detect in his later stanzas—which recall that she came "too late" to "Olympus' faded hierarchy," and so missed "the happy pieties," the "antique vows," and "the fond believing lyre"—mingled tones of regret for the vanished "simple worship of a day" (the phrase is from the "Ode to May") and belief that to the "fond worshippers" Psyche's destiny would mean less than to the hard-pressed poet of a darker age.

All the same, Keats's "pains" serve his themes less than the pictorial effects and the quasi-liturgical incantatory rhythms and repetitions, sometimes echoing Milton's "On the Morning of Christ's Nativity," which he strove to create from his studiedly loose Pindaric form with its irregular verse paragraphs and varying length of line. In the densely worked last stanza, which describes the "fane" to be built for Psyche in some "untrodden region of my mind," the emphasis finally shifts from "the pale-mouth'd prophet dreaming" and returns to an individual idiom, especially in the lines (deeply admired by John Ruskin) about the "dark-clustering pines" that fledge "the wild-ridged mountains"; the conception of "the wreath'd trellis of a working brain," which combines with medical recollections Keats's habitual sense of the "labyrinthine" and "Daedalian" nature of the creative imagination; and the closing reference to the window open at night "To let the warm love in," an allusion to Eros now openly visiting Psyche and perhaps also, as at least one critic has thought, to his feelings about Fanny Brawne. She was living at this time next door to him in Hampstead, and he would have been able to see her lighted window at night.

In his next two odes, both of May 1819, Keats "schools" his intelligence by posing against the "worlds of pains and sorrows" an object suggesting the possibility of permanence: in the first the nightingale's song, unchanged from age to age and identified with the beauty of the natural world; in the second an ancient Greek urn, fresh as when the artist made it, and on its frieze depicted a world of unchanging youth, love, and "happy piety." His interrogation determines a poetic structure based on the flight from everyday reality and the return to it; but the "Ode on a Grecian Urn," because it is more ostensibly a "dialogue of the mind with itself" about the ambiguous relationship between ideal and actual experience—taken up from its predecessor's final line, "Fled is that music. Do I wake or sleep?"—possesses wider tonal range with less textural richness. (Keats printed it after the "Ode to a Nightingale" in his 1820 volume, perhaps as an intended reply.)

The new ten-line stanza serves these diverse effects well, though Keats afterward dropped the short eighth line in the "Ode to a Nightingale," which was possibly meant to accord with the lyrical movement of the bird's song. The melodic pattern of onomatopoeic effects, worked at with "pains" in the Psyche ode largely for its own sake, now enacts successive states of feeling: "drowsy numbness" (a state often prefacing Keats's moods of creativity) induced by excessive pleasure in the bird's song; longing to escape with the singer from "the weariness, the fever and the fret" into the flower-scented woods; delight in his own lullingly rich evocation of them; and back, through thoughts of death, to the solitary self, grieving at the term set to human happiness and puzzled about the validity of the reverie. Death, at first seemingly a "luxury," becomes a repellent finality from which only the bird can escape to comfort with its "self-same song" generations of suffering men and women, "emperor and clown" alike, and also "perhaps," in an unforgettable image of loss and exile,

> . . . the sad heart of Ruth, when, sick for home,
> She stood in tears amid the alien corn.
> (st. 7, 66–67)

The celebrated stanza imagining the woods on an early summer night transmutes with the familiar Keatsian alchemy passages about summer sweetness, renewal, and growth remembered from other poets (particularly Coleridge's "To a Nightingale" of 1798 and Shakespeare's "I Know a Bank Whereon the Wild Thyme Grows") into an individual celebration of nature's "luxuries" now entangled with thoughts of death. It is in an "embalmèd" darkness that the poet guesses "each sweet" and summons in his session of silent thought the "white hawthorn and the pastoral eglantine," the "fast-fading violets," and

> . . . mid-May's eldest child,
> The coming musk-rose, full of dewy wine,
> The murmurous haunt of flies on summer eves.
> (st. 5, 48–50)

This ode questions the validity of the poet's "fancy" and not the quality of the song that inspires it, but Keats's urn arouses feelings the ambivalence of which affects the tone of his celebration, as the effort is made alternately to subdue and to define uncertainty. The movement is between contrasts of activity and stillness, warmth and cold, permanence and transience, with the sestet in each of the five stanzas countering or expanding upon the quatrain, which may itself set forward puzzling contrarieties. The opening quatrain defines the "still" perfection of this Attic objet d'art, but the humanizing terms—"unravished bride of quietness," "foster-child," "sylvan historian"—direct attention to a paradoxical union of age and youth, the human and the artificial, while the breathless questions of the sestet—

> What men or gods are these? What maidens loth?
> What mad pursuit? What struggle to escape?
> (st. 1, 8–9)

—clearly no longer suggest stillness. In the sestet of the second stanza, the figures are neither vital nor reposed, but imprisoned:

> Fair youth beneath the trees, thou canst not leave
> Thy song, nor ever can those trees be bare.
> (st. 2, 15–16)

The ostensibly comforting lines

> She cannot fade, though thou hast not thy bliss,
> For ever wilt thou love and she be fair!
> (st. 2, 19–20)

recall the antithetical real world in the nightingale ode,

> Where Beauty cannot keep her lustrous eyes,
> Or new love pine at them beyond to-morrow,
> (st. 3, 29–30)

and lead into the plaintive invocation, "More happy, happy love" (the epithet is equally insistent in the two earlier odes), which conveys the total absence of happiness in the poet himself. Simultaneously the urn becomes remote:

> All breathing human passion far above,
> That leaves a heart high-sorrowful and cloyed.
> (st. 3, 28–29)

The entire stanza risks a damaging self-indulgence, from which Keats rescues himself by the brilliant innovation in his subsequent sestet, which turns from the urn to the "actual" world from which its figures came, a "little town" where empty streets

> . . . for evermore
> Will silent be; and not a soul to tell
> Why thou art desolate can e'er return,
> (st. 4, 38–40)

a conception alien to the creator of the urn but typical of the poet, who—this time obliquely—leads us back through the terms "empty" and "desolate" to his "sole self." From this he modulates into his attempted final summary, where the urn at first becomes no more than an "Attic shape" covered with "marble"—not "warm" or "panting"—figures. Yet his first delight still lingers with his new "reflective" position, and the entire complex that teases "us out of thought/As doth eternity" finds its only possible expressive outlet in the paradox "Cold pastoral."

This may be seen as the true imaginative climax of the poem. The sestet, with its too-much-discussed closing lines,[4] represents Keats's final effort to subdue his doubts about the urn. He had opened *Endymion* with the line "A thing of beauty is a joy for ever," a conception reintroduced with the urn, again humanized, as "a friend to man" that will console future generations "in midst of other woe/Than ours" with the one message it can offer. Its statement—

> "Beauty is truth, truth beauty"—that is all
> Ye know on earth, and all ye need to know
> (st. 5, 49–50)

—may be right or wrong. Keats does not say. It is the offering of the urn, and his decision to close with it brings a moment of repose.

There is a correspondence with these themes and ideas in the "Ode on Melancholy," where the references to spring and early summer in the second of its three stanzas suggest that it too was written in May. The poem is perhaps the most concentrated expression of Keats's belief in the necessary relationship between joy and sorrow.

> Welcome joy and welcome sorrow,
> Lethe's weed and Hermes' feather;
> Come today and come tomorrow,
> I do love you both together!

are the opening lines of his "little song" written in October 1818. Earlier he had described his "pleasure-thermometer" in *Endymion*, book I, as "a first step" to his central theme, "the playing of different Natures with Joy and Sorrow," and had linked his "Ode to Sorrow" in book IV with his "favourite Speculation" set out in a letter of 22 November 1817 to his friend Benjamin Bailey: "I am certain of nothing but of the holiness of the Heart's affections and the truth of Imagination—What the Imagination seizes as beauty must be truth . . . our Passions . . . are all in their sublime, creative of essential Beauty."

Keats's youthful ode is attributed to the forlorn Indian maid. The burden of her song is

> Come then, Sorrow!
> Sweetest Sorrow!
> Like an own babe I nurse thee on my breast.
> I thought to leave thee
> And deceive thee,
> But now of all the world I love thee best
> (IV. 279–284)

It foreshadows the "Ode on Melancholy" in connecting melancholy with the perception of beauty and its transience. But it has nothing of the later poem's richness or economy. To repeat an earlier summary of mine, Keats's "argument" now runs "Melancholy is not to be found among thoughts of oblivion (stanza 1); it descends suddenly and is linked with beauty and its transience (stanza 2); it is associated with beauty, joy, pleasure and delight and is felt only by those who can experience

4. For a summary of the principal arguments, see M. Allott, ed., *The Poems of John Keats*, pp. 537–538.

these intensely (stanza 3)."[5] The three stanzas possess an imaginative consistency and must have "come clear" after Keats had canceled the false start of his original first stanza with its macabre and violent imagery:

> Though you should build a bark of dead
> men's bones,
> And rear a phantom gibbet for a mast,
> Stitch creeds together for a sail, with groans
> To fill it out, blood-stainèd and aghast. . . .
> (1–4)

The climax then is that one would still fail

> To find the Melancholy—whether she
> Dreameth in any isle of Lethe dull. . . .
> (9–10)

The finished poem picks up this allusion in its opening lines,

> No, no, go not to Lethe, neither twist
> Wolf's-bane, tight-rooted, for its poisonous
> wine;

and thereafter unfolds images and ideas that are integral to Keats's self-communings of May 1819. He speaks of the death moth as a "mournful Psyche": the former has markings that resemble a human skull, and Psyche—the soul, as we know—was frequently represented as a butterfly. He rejects the drugged relief of oblivion—"shade to shade will come too drowsily/And drown the wakeful anguish of the soul. . . ."—because, as he finds in the nightingale ode, awareness, even if it is awareness of pain, is better than insentience; and, what is more, the "wakeful anguish" fosters imaginative creativity just as the "weeping cloud" of an April shower "fosters the droop-headed flowers all." He senses the close kinship of intense pleasure and intense pain: "aching Pleasure nigh,/Turning to poison while the bee-mouth sips. . . ."

And, finally, from this keen sensitivity to suffering and change, Keats seeks to evolve a statement the imaginative order of which provides its own stay against impermanence. More explicit than elsewhere, and on another level from his young eroticism in *Endymion*, is his use, noticeable in the closing stanza, of sexual imagery as a paradigm for the inextricable relationship between joy and sorrow:

> Aye, in the very temple of Delight
> Veiled Melancholy has her sovran shrine.
> (25–26)

As Douglas Bush said,[6] the ensuing lines,

> Though seen of none save him whose
> strenuous tongue
> Can burst Joy's grape against his palate fine;
>
> His soul shall taste the sadness of her
> might,
> And be among her cloudy trophies hung,
> (27–30)

indicate a recollection of *Troilus and Cressida*, marked by Keats in his copy of Shakespeare:

> . . . what will it be
> When that the wat'ry palates taste indeed
> Love's thrice-repurèd nectar? Death, I fear
> me;
> Sounding destruction; or some joy too fine,
> Too subtle-potent, tun'd too sharp in
> sweetness,
> For the capacity of my ruder powers. . . .
> (III. ii. 19–24)

The parallel strengthens the felt presence of sexual elements in the stanza. Moreover, the curve of feeling, familiar from the structure of the other odes and also found in other poems, which takes the poet from languor to intense sensation and out of this to another, sadder, and more anticlimactic state of being, corresponds to the pattern of Keats's moods of poetic creativity.

It is the "languor" alone that Keats celebrates in his "Ode on Indolence." The poem, not surprisingly, lacks the confident order of

5. See M. Allott, ed., p. 358.

6. *John Keats: His Life and Writings* (London, 1966), p. 147.

the other odes, which were written in obedience to a more urgent creative impulse. Keats, it seems, found difficulty even in deciding on the final arrangement of the individual stanzas, which differs in the various manuscripts. Understandably he omitted the ode from his 1820 collection, though he wrote to Sarah Jeffrey on 9 June, "You will judge of my 1819 temper when I tell you that the thing I have most enjoyed this year has been writing an ode to Indolence." Whatever its weaknesses, its first inception represented a stage in the process leading to the "Ode on a Grecian Urn." On 19 March Keats had written in a journal-letter: "This morning I am in a sort of temper indolent and supremely careless. . . . Neither Poetry, nor Ambition, nor Love have any alertness of countenance as they pass by me; they seem rather like three figures on a greek vase—a Man and two women. . . . This is the only happiness. . . ."

Keats must have begun the poem some time after rereading this passage before sending the letter off in May (its closing entry is 3 May); there are throughout references to summer warmth, and the adoption of his special ode stanza suggests that it followed the "Ode to a Nightingale" and the "Ode on a Grecian Urn." The theme runs alongside certain ideas belonging to the "half" of Wordsworth that Keats said he greatly admired (the other "half" he connected with Wordsworth's "egotistical sublime"—at the opposite pole to Shakespearean "negative capability"—and with the "palpable design,' of his explicit didacticism).

Keats's earlier unrhymed sonnet, "What the Thrush Said" (of February 1818), restates in his own terms the Wordsworthian theme of "wise passiveness," especially as this is expressed in "The Tables Turned" (1798):

> Books! 'tis a dull and endless strife:
> Come, hear the woodland linnet,
> (9–10)

and

> . . . how blithe the throstle sings!
> He, too, is no mean preacher:
> Come forth into the life of things,
> Let Nature be your Teacher.
> (13–16)

Keats's thrush sings:

> Oh, fret not after knowledge—I have none,
> And yet my song comes native with the warmth.
> Oh, fret not after knowledge—I have none,
> And yet the evening listens. . . .
> (9–12)

His "Ode on Indolence" is less serene. It captures fleetingly the mood of deep passivity in the summer heat,

> . . . Ripe was the drowsy hour;
> The blissful cloud of summer indolence
> Benumbed my eyes; my pulse grew less and less;
> Pain had no sting, and pleasure's wreath no flower
> (15–18)

and turns away from the imaginatively quickening delight aroused by the display of energetic feeling celebrated in the "Ode on Melancholy":

> . . . glut thy sorrow on a morning rose,
> Or on the rainbow of the salt sand-wave,
> Or on the wealth of globèd peonies;
> Or if thy mistress some rich anger shows,
> Imprison her soft hand, and let her rave,
> And feed deep, deep upon her peerless eyes.
> (st. 2, 15–20)

As the "three figures" in "Indolence" pass again before him (one guesses that some time has elapsed between the writing of one part of the poem and another),

> . . . like figures on a marble urn,
> When shifted round to see the other side
> (st. 1, 5–6)

he remains, it seems, unmoved:

> The morn was clouded, but no shower fell,
> Though in her lids hung the sweet tears of May;

> The open casement pressed a new-
> leaved vine,
> Let in the budding warmth and throstle's
> lay;
>
> . . .
>
> So, ye three Ghosts, adieu! Ye cannot raise
> My head cool-bedded in the flowery grass.
> (st. 5–6, 45–48; 51–52)

A belying want of ease nevertheless weakens the rest of the closing stanza, which falls into the irritable manner that often accompanies Keats's attempts at satirical humor:

> For I would not be dieted with praise,
> A pet-lamb in a sentimental farce!
> (st. 6, 53–54)

Other instances of stylistic clumsiness affect Keats's discourse about his three visitants—

> Oh, why did ye not melt, and leave my
> sense
> Unhaunted quite of all but—nothingness?
> (st. 2, 19–20)

—and it becomes increasingly plain that a certain bravado mars his "wise passiveness":

> . . . to follow them I burned
> And ached for wings because I knew the
> three;
> The first was a fair maid, and Love her name;
> The second was Ambition, pale of cheek,
> And ever watchful with fatiguèd eye;
> The last, whom I love more, the more of
> blame
> Is heaped upon her, maiden most unmeek,
> I knew to be my demon Poesy.
> (st. 3, 23–30)

Like the other odes, this one draws on, even if it cannot organize as they do, the feelings generated by Keats's major concerns in 1819. It assembles what are, in effect, a series of direct personal statements, and so sheds some light on important fluctuations of feeling in his "1819 temper." Its pretensions to detachment present a remarkable contrast with his movement in "To Autumn" toward an unprecedentedly calm acceptance of "the object as in itself it is." He wrote this ode at Winchester about 19 September, when he had not yet returned to London and to Fanny Brawne, and was enjoying a brief mood of quietude and self-containment. "I 'kepen in solitarinesse,' " he said peacefully, quoting his own "imitation of the authors in Chaucer's time" from "The Eve of St. Mark." The weather was mild and tranquilizing. He wrote to Reynolds on 21 September:

> How beautiful the season is now. How fine the air. A temperate sharpness about it. Really, without joking, chaste weather—Dian skies—I never lik'd stubble-fields so much as now—Aye better than the chilly green of the Spring. Somehow a stubble-plain looks warm—This struck me so much in my sunday's walk that I composed upon it.

There is no flight from and return to actuality, as in the spring odes. "Where are the songs of Spring" he asks. "Aye, where are they?" And answers, "Think not of them, thou has thy music too." He replaces the images of renewal and growth drawn on for the "Ode to a Nightingale" with images of fullness and completion, for it seems now that "ripeness is all." Autumn is in league with the sun,

> To bend with apples the mossed cottage-
> trees,
> And fill all fruit with ripeness to the core;
> To swell the gourd, and plump the hazel
> shells
> With a sweet kernel; to set budding more,
> And still more, later flowers for the bees.
> (st. 1, 5–9)

But the poem depends for its unusual poise on exactly that sense of process and the movements of time that accompanied the evocation of summer in "Ode to a Nightingale" and that is found in all Keats's major poetry. The difference lies in the manner in which it is brought under command. Keats had reached a moment of stillness at the close of his debate about the Grecian urn by reproducing, with a strong desire to suspend disbelief, what he took to be its individual message of consolation and reassurance. In this poem he celebrates the period of time that lies between high summer and the onset of winter, as Collins in his "Ode to Evening" celebrates the period that lies between day and night. For both poets, the subject subsumes ideas of process and change, while saluting a point of repose within that process.

In Keats the balanced, but still contrary, aspects of his chosen time are felt from the beginning, for this is a season of "mists" as well as "mellow fruitfulness," and throughout the poem words that suggest fullness also convey heaviness and the hint of decay. Summer has "o'erbrimmed" the "clammy cells" of the bees. Autumn, personified in the second stanza, watches "the last oozings" of the cider press and, in the guise of a reaper, "Spares the next swath and all its twined flowers," so that one senses, along with munificence, the ineluctable destructiveness of the scythe (for if Autumn is a reaper, so is Time). The third stanza has the line "in a wailful choir the small gnats mourn" of which the touchingly vivid visual and auditory effect owes much to the thought that the gnats are lamenting the shortness of their life and the lateness of the season. As Arnold Davenport put it, "The music of Autumn which ends the poem is a music of living and dying, of staying and departure, of summer-winter."[7]

The success of the poem lies in its equipollent balancing of the contraries. The passage

> And sometimes like a gleaner thou dost
> keep
> Steady thy laden head across a brook . . .
> (19–20)

forms part of Keats's address to Autumn at the end of the second stanza; and the subject, with the subtle metrical movement of the lines, could be taken as a figure for his own poetic control. F. R. Leavis admired the lines because "In the step from the rimeword 'keep', across . . . the pause enforced by the line-division to 'Steady', the balancing movement of the gleaner is enacted." Douglas Bush, also testifying to the metrical and structural skills of the poem, has spoken of the ordered deploying through the three stanzas of Keats's sense responses to the ripeness and fulfillment of the season: "In the first stanza the sense of fullness and heaviness is given through mainly tactile images; in the second they are mainly visual . . . in the last the images are chiefly auditory." It should be added that in this, the last and for many readers the finest, of his 1819 odes, Keats worked further on his own metrical innovations, adding an extra line to his ten-line stanza. This gave him still ampler room to "load every rift with ore" at the same time that it imposed an additional discipline in its demand for another rhyming line.

For all this, I do not think we can say that "To Autumn" represents a decisive new turn in Keats's artistic development. Rather, it seems to enact through its subject and style just such a moment of pause and equilibrium in his "1819 temper" as the tranquilizing season he celebrates may introduce into the cycle of the natural year. For a hint of the direction his genius might have taken, we need to look at the successive stages of his work on *Hyperion.*

THE TWO HYPERIONS

These incomplete poems belong to a different and weightier order of achievement than the rest of Keats's poetry. If we take into account their germination, planning, composition, and reconstruction, they can be said to span his entire poetic career, from his "Ode to Apollo" in February 1815 to his final reworkings in December 1819, after which he wrote little more poetry of any significance. His first recorded references in 1817 are associated with Endymion, who is united with the goddess of the moon, sister to Apollo, the god of

7. "A Note on 'To Autumn,'" in K. Muir, ed., *John Keats: A Reassessment*, p. 98.

the sun, of healing, and, above all, of music and poetry. "Thy lute-voiced brother will I sing ere long," Keats tells his hero (*Endymion,* IV.774); and he refers in his 1818 preface to "the beautiful mythology of Greece," which he wished "to try once more, before I bid it farewell." The projected poem had its title by 23 January 1818, when Keats advised Haydon, who wanted to use a passage from *Endymion* to illustrate a frontispiece, "Wait for . . . *Hyperion* . . . the nature of *Hyperion* will lead me to treat it in a more naked and grecian Manner . . . the march of passion and endeavour will be undeviating . . . Apollo in *Hyperion* being a foreseeing god will shape his actions like one."

Keats began composition in the autumn, but the juxtaposing of the two names shows that his subject matter was already established as the defeat of the Titans by the new race of Olympian gods, with the old and the new gods of the sun as the figures centrally opposed. The law of progress affirmed by Oceanus in the poem,

> . . . 'tis the eternal law
> That first in beauty should be first in might
> (II. 228–229)

and the identification of "beauty" with wisdom and knowledge through suffering, by which Apollo is transfigured and immortalized, continue the arguments about individual development explored in "Sleep and Poetry" and in Keats's letter to Reynolds of 3 May 1818. This presents life as a "Mansion of Many Apartments" beginning with "the infant or thoughtless Chamber" and going on to the "Chamber of Maiden-Thought" which at first is filled with "pleasant wonders" but is "gradually darken'd" as we come to understand "the heart and nature of Man" and the world as a place filled with "Misery and Heartbreak, Pain, Sickness and oppression. . . ." "Knowledge enormous makes a God of me," says Apollo in the presence of Mnemosyne, who has deserted the Titans for his sake,

> . . . agonies
> Creations and destroyings, all at once,
> Pour into the wide hollows of my brain,
> And deify me, as if some blithe wine
> Or bright elixir peerless I had drunk,
> And so become immortal. . . .
> (III. 115–120)

Keats abandoned the first version of the poem at this climax in April 1819, and went on to write his shorter narratives, his experimental sonnets, and the spring odes. His reconstruction, *The Fall of Hyperion,* at which he worked intermittently from July to September, and seemingly again from November to December, stops short at the entry of Apollo's predecessor Hyperion. Of the various reasons offered as an explanation for this second abandonment of the poem, the most important are connected with Keats's attempt to reconstruct it as a vision in which the defeat of the Titans is related by the priestess Moneta, an august reincarnation of Mnemosyne.

The theme of suffering and its effect on the poetic imagination receives a stronger personal emphasis, with the poet assuming Apollo's role as he drinks the magical "elixir" that induces his vision. It is central to the debate in the first canto, which turns on the general question of the poet's value to humanity and the particular question of Keats's poetic achievement. He is admitted to Moneta's shrine as one of those

> . . . to whom the miseries of the world
> Are misery, and will not let them rest,
> (I. 148–149)

but her stern lesson is that this is not enough:

> . . . "Art thou not of the dreamer tribe?
> The poet and the dreamer are distinct,
> Diverse, sheer opposite, antipodes.
> The one pours out a balm upon the world,
> The other vexes it." . . .
> (I. 198–202)

The poet "pours . . . balm" on suffering because of his knowledge and wisdom; the dreamer "vexes" it, adding to it by dwelling on "miseries" without suggesting how to face them. On 21 September Keats told Reynolds that he had given up the poem because "there were too many Miltonic inversions in it—Miltonic verse cannot be written but in an artful or rather artist's humour. I wish to give myself up to other sensations. English ought to be kept up." The same letter records his composition of "To Autumn," his association of Chatterton with the season, and his admiration of him as "the purest writer in the English language."

But clearly there was also the problem of sustaining his exploratory personal statement at the same time as Moneta's "seer's" vision of the past. Above all, there was the intractable fact that in his revised first canto—which takes its direction from the climactic third canto of the original *Hyperion*—Keats had already given vivid dramatic expression to his central themes.

The evolution and expression of these themes in the two versions reflects Keats's imaginative development from the youthful celebrant of "poesy" in "Sleep and Poetry," who yearned to

> . . . die a death
> Of luxury and my young spirit follow
> The morning sunbeams to the great Apollo
> Like a fresh sacrifice . . .
> (58–61)

to the poet acquainted with the "sharp anguish" of death who in *The Fall of Hyperion* records, in his vision of Moneta's unveiled face, the mystery and dignity of suffering:

> . . . Then saw I a wan face,
> Not pined by human sorrows, but bright-blanched
> By an immortal sickness which kills not.
> It works a constant change, which happy death
> Can put no end to; deathwards progressing
> To no death was that visage; it had passed
> The lily and the snow; and beyond these
> I must not think now, though I saw that face.
> (I. 256–263)

There are no Miltonic inversions in this blank verse, nor is it ostensibly the work of an "epic" poet, though in 1817 the writing of an epical poem probably would have appeared to be a natural sequel to the long trial run of *Endymion,* which had given Keats practice in sustaining a narrative through which to dramatize ideas important to him. Further, in 1817 he had added to his renewed familiarity with Shakespeare by beginning to read Milton seriously for the first time. "Shakespeare and the paradise Lost every day become greater wonders," he wrote to Benjamin Bailey on 14 August 1819, adding in a letter of 24 August to Reynolds, in a similar context, "The more I know what my diligence may in time probably effect, the more does my heart distend with Pride and Obstinacy."

The following month Keats changed his mind—"I have but lately stood upon my guard against Milton. Life to him would be death to me"—and asked Reynolds to "pick out some lines from *Hyperion* and put a mark X to the false beauty proceeding from art, and one || to the true voice of feeling." That his instinct was true as usual to his current poetic needs is apparent from his handling of the new material in *The Fall of Hyperion,* but his former ardor accounts for strength as well as weakness. His Miltonic constructions are certainly intrusive—"thunder . . . rumbles reluctant"; "came slope upon the threshold of the west"; "gold clouds metropolitan"; "Regal his shape majestic." Yet Keats's "stationing" of his figures owes much to the grouping that he praised in a marginal note to *Paradise Lost,* VII. 420–424: "Milton . . . pursues his imagination to the utmost . . . in no instance . . . more exemplified than in his *stationing* or *statury.* He is not content with simple description, he must station. . . ." His own finest instance provides the first *Hyperion* with its impressive opening:

> Deep in the shady sadness of a vale
> Far sunken from the healthy breath of morn,
> Far from the fiery noon, and eve's one star,
> Sat grey-haired Saturn, quiet as a stone,
> Still as the silence round about his lair . . .
> (I. 1–5)

Keats's disposition of the other fallen Titans, situated amid cavernous rocks and "the solid roar/Of thunderous waterfalls and torrents hoarse" in attitudes of anger, grief, and despair, aims, though not with consistent success, for a similar effect, and their ensuing debate obviously derives from the "Stygian council" in Milton's Pandemonium. But inspiration is not imitation, and Keats's poem takes its own course. As always in his work, it is nourished by a wide range of literary and personal experiences. Some of the "Miltonic" grandeur is in fact owed to his enthusiastic response to the scenery in the Lakes and Scotland during his summer walking tour. He wrote then a number of slight poems and many lengthy, vivid letters, among them a description for Tom of Fingal's Cave, which he called "this cathedral of the sea"— suppose the Giants who rebelled against Jove had taken a whole Mass of black Columns and bound them together like bundles of matches—and then with immense Axes had made a cavern in the body of these columns"—and which he remembered later in his "stationing" of Saturn and Thea in *Hyperion*:

> . . . these two were postured motionless,
> Like natural sculpture in cathedral cavern.
> (I. 85–86)

Keats's reading on the tour was confined to the 1814 edition of Dante's *Divine Comedy,* which added its own contribution to the solemnity of the first *Hyperion* and was instrumental in shaping the second, for it stimulated Keats's eager study during the following summer of the original Italian—especially, to judge by the cadences and echoes in *The Fall of Hyperion,* the *Purgatorio,* which certainly affected his own purgatorial "vision" and gave his portrayal of Moneta some of the flavor of the mingled awe and benignity surrounding Dante's Beatrice.

The "shaping force" at work upon these diverse elements is still unequal to a sustained flight, and is at its most disappointing in the handling of the pivotal theme. The Titans are beings of power and identity; their successors, the Olympians, whose qualities are epitomized in Apollo, have no identity and represent Keats's idea of the poetical character as he expressed it in a letter to Richard Woodhouse of 27 October 1818:

> . . . the poetical Character . . . that sort distinguished from the wordsworthian or egotistical sublime . . . is not itself—it has no self. . . . A Poet is the most unpoetical of any thing in existence; because he has no Identity—he is continually . . . filling some other Body.

He had written to Benjamin Bailey the previous November: "Men of Genius are great as certain ethereal Chemicals operating on the Mass of neutral intellect . . . they have not any individuality, any determined Character. I would call the top and head of those who have a proper self Men of Power."

Keats knew from his classical reading that although Hyperion preceded Apollo as god of the sun, he was endowed with no power over music and poetry. In the first *Hyperion,* although he makes his Titan less consistently magnificent than the gorgeous palace he inhabits (it takes some hints from Wordsworth's cloud palace in *The Excursion,* II. 839–840, and the halls of Eblis in William Beckford's *Vathek*), he succeeds nevertheless in making him unmistakably a "Man of Power."

> He entered, but he entered full of wrath;
> His flaming robes streamed out beyond his
> heels,
> And gave a roar . . .
> . . .
> . . . On he flared,
> From stately nave to nave, from vault to
> vault . . .
> (I. 213–215; 217–218)

His self-centered rage is the expression of his threatened "identity":

> ". . . Why
> Is my eternal essence thus distraught
> To see and behold these horrors new?
> Saturn is fallen, am I too to fall?

> Am I to leave this haven of my rest,
> This cradle of my glory . . ."
> (I. 231–236)

This invests the figure with at least sufficiently appropriate poetic force; but on the entry of Apollo in canto III, Keats reverts disastrously to the fruity manner of his *Endymion.* Apollo, deified by "knowledge enormous" of the suffering of the world and supposedly endowed with the imaginative power dependent on such knowledge, remains an effeminate figure who "weeps and wonders somewhat too fondly," as Leigh Hunt said in 1820, though Hunt also thought that "His powers gather nobly on him as he proceeds." The "nobility" belongs, in truth, only to the few lines, quoted earlier, that record the accession of his visionary insight. The poem closes with a semierotic description:

> Soon wild commotions shook him, and
> made flush
> All the immortal fairness of his limbs,
> . . .
> . . . So young Apollo anguished;
> His very hair, his golden tresses famed,
> Kept undulation round his eager neck.
> (III. 124–125; 130–132)

Mnemosyne the while holds up her arms "as one who prophesied," and

> . . . At length
> Apollo shrieked—and lo! from all his limbs
> Celestial . . .
> (III. 134–136)

And there it ends, with the poet seemingly (and understandably) stumped and the entire war of the Titans against the Olympians yet to record. A year later Keats had transformed this material into the intensely imaginative personal statement of the first canto of *The Fall of Hyperion.*

If we try to hold the two versions together in our mind as one poem, it is apparent at once that they represent two totally different kinds of poetic impulse. Keats's themes and his creative temper could never have lent themselves fully to expression through an epic conflict in the high Miltonic style, for which he had tried in his first version. He makes, it is true, a valiant, and far from unsuccessful, effort to dramatize his ideas about suffering and creativity in his Titans, especially when he differentiates between the grief of the fallen Saturn and Thea, whom sorrow has made "more beautiful than Beauty's self"; the rage of "huge Enceladus," whose words boom among his fellows

> . . . like sullen waves
> In the half-glutted hollows of reef-rocks,
> (II. 305–306)

and the different kinds of pain felt by the stoical Oceanus, who understands the law by which he must perish, and the simpler Clymene, who alone has heard the song of Apollo, felt the "living death" of its melody, and knows what it is to be

> . . . sick
> Of joy and grief at once. . . .
> (II. 288–289)

But Keats's recasting of the material for *The Fall of Hyperion,* whatever the rights and wrongs of moving from a more "objective" to a more "subjective" kind of writing, is entirely consistent with two strong impulses seen at work in his poetry from the beginning. There is the confessional impulse, which found early expression in "Sleep and Poetry," and there is the impulse toward a more oblique expression of important personal themes that shapes in some degree all the narrative poems and the major odes.

Looked at in this way, *The Fall of Hyperion,* with its mixture of earnestness about the importance of the poet's "public" role, its jealous feeling nevertheless for the poet's individual voice, and its projection of personal themes through a fictional situation, not only is seen to build on these impulses but also offers an early example of the tendency toward the fictionalized spiritual autobiography so common in Victorian prose and poetry.

Carlyle, as we said, was born in the same year as Keats, and his *Sartor Resartus* is often regarded as the first major example of the Victorian habit of disguising as a fiction the history of pressing inner conflict. Other examples, dealing especially with the role of the creative writer in his struggle to penetrate the romantic dream, run from Tennyson's "The Lady of Shalott" to Matthew Arnold's *Empedocles on Etna.* It could be said that all these have an early precursor in *The Fall of Hyperion,* and that Keats's "vision" hints at a potential development of the youthful romantic poet into a writer who might have been a particularly eminent Victorian.

THE LETTERS

At about the time of his last attempts to rework *Hyperion,* Keats wrote to his publisher John Taylor, on 17 November 1819:

> I have come to a determination not to publish any thing I have now ready written; but for all that to publish a Poem before long and that I hope to make a fine one. As the marvellous is the most enticing and the surest guarantee of harmonious numbers I have been endeavouring to persuade myself to untether Fancy and let her manage for herself—I and myself cannot agree about this at all. Wonders are no wonders to me. I am more at home amongst Men and Women. I would rather read Chaucer than Ariosto—The little dramatic skill I may as yet have however badly it might show in a Drama would I think be sufficient for a Poem—I wish to diffuse the colouring of St Agnes Eve throughout a Poem in which Character and Sentiment would be the figures to such drapery—Two or three such Poems, if God should spare me, written in the course of the next six years, would be a famous *gradus ad Parnassum altissimum* . . . they would nerve me up to the writing of a few fine Plays—my greatest ambition when I do feel ambitious.[8]

This is one of the last major statements about his poetic intentions in Keats's letters, and it demonstrates the shrewdness of his self-knowledge and the consistency of his debate with himself about his poetry since at least late 1816. Behind his wide range of poetic experimentalism in the unchanging impulse to overcome his native longing for an ideal "romantic" world, in order to reach a Shakespearean understanding and acceptance of the world as it is. In June 1819, a few months before his letter to Taylor, he had distinguished Matteo Boiardo from Shakespeare as "a noble Poet of Romance; not a miserable and mighty Poet of the human Heart." His gifts, at the stage we see them, and particularly in his narratives where he tries to present the passions of "Men and Women," are plainly not in keeping with his ambitions. We find Keats less the "Poet of the human Heart" that he wished to be than the poet of the "wonders" he wanted to grow away from. It is hardly surprising that his one play, the melodramatic *Otho the Great,* written in collaboration with Charles Brown and worked on in the months when he was composing "Lamia" and revising *Hyperion,* is not "fine" at all, nor that the quality of the fragmentary *King Stephen* of the same period, which also was designed as a vehicle for his admired Edmund Kean, rests exclusively on its few but by no means unimpressive passages of quasi-Shakespearean blank verse.

As a writer of prose, on the other hand, Keats is often several jumps ahead of his poetic practice. His letters are perhaps the most vivacious expression of lively and unpretending intelligence in English literary history (there is no eye to posterity in them). They mirror from day to day, and sometimes from hour to hour, the rapid movements of his thinking and feeling, his excited gaiety in observing the world around him, and his remarkably knowledgeable, sensitive, and unselfregarding feeling for other people. Few

8. Quotations from the letters are from H. E. Rollins, ed., *The Keats Circle: Letters and Papers and More Letters and Poems of the Keats Circle* (Cambridge, Mass., 1965).

literary figures—few people anywhere—have won so much affection and respect from their associates. Many of his circle—prominently Charles Brown, John Hamilton Reynolds, and Richard Woodhouse—are known to posterity primarily because of his correspondence with them and their own care in preserving copies of his letters and poems (this is one reason there is such a wealth of Keatsian manuscript material in existence). Characteristically, once his brother George had left for America with his wife Georgiana in June 1818, Keats took pains to write long, affectionate, newsy journal-letters, recording daily happenings and copying out with comments many of his recent poems.

Thus his letters provide a magnificent gloss on his poetry; they also help to explain why he has been so fortunate in his modern biographers, who since 1958 have been able to consult them in Hyder Rollins' superb annotated edition. They form, in effect, an integral part of his creative life, and should be required reading for anyone interested in literature, particularly poetry, the poetic process, and the nature of poetic sensibility. If there is immaturity in their volatile expression and flexibility,[9] there is also unusual self-knowledge.

Keats had no doubts about his ultimate goal, only about how to reach it, and recognized that in exploring possibilities he would swing between opposite poles and "take but three steps from feathers to iron." He used this sharp image on 13 March 1818 to Benjamin Bailey, after copying his sonnet "The Human Seasons," which foreshadows the balanced mood, but not the imaginative poise, of "To Autumn." The relaxed, informal prose of his accompanying remarks, with their darting parentheses and sudden flashes of insight, enacts the ebb and flow of his "speculations." "I shall never be a reasoner because I do not care to be in the right," he declares, and persuades his reader through the suggestiveness rather than the logic of his improvisations on the theme that "Every mental pursuit takes its reality and worth from the ardour of the pursuer—being in itself a nothing." There are

> Things real—such as existences of Sun Moon & Stars and passages of Shakespeare—Things semireal such as Love, the Clouds &c which require a greeting of the Spirit to make them wholly exist—and Nothings which are made Great and dignified by an ardent pursuit. . . .

Even "poetry itself," in his "very sceptical" moods, may appear "a mere Jack a lantern to amuse anyone who may be struck with its brilliance."

This letter clearly represents a stage in the continued communings by Keats with himself and his friends that carried him from his ideas about "negative capability" at the end of 1817 to his definition in October 1818 of the "poetical character" and his poignant affirmation of his dramatic ambitions in November 1819. As he walked away from a Christmas pantomime in December 1817, he was caught up in "a disquisition with [Charles] Dilke" and "several things dovetailed in my mind":

> at once it struck me, what quality went to form a Man of Achievement, especially in Literature, & which Shakespeare possessed so enormously—I mean *Negative Capability*, that is when man is capable of being in uncertainties, Mysteries, doubts, without any irritable reaching after fact & reason.

A day or two earlier, while admiring a painting by Benjamin West, Keats had missed in it "the excellence of every Art," which lies "in its intensity, capable of making all disagreeables evaporate, from being in close relationship with Beauty and Truth—examine 'King Lear' and you will find this examplified [*sic*] throughout." He closes his "negative capability" passage with the reflection that he is saying no more than that "with a great poet the sense of Beauty overcomes every other consideration."

A year later his description of "the poetical character" once more emphasizes his openness of response and refusal to tie himself to

9. And also, one should add, in their engagingly idiosyncratic spelling and punctuation.

unexamined axiomatic systems ("Axioms in philosophy are not axioms until they are proved on our pulses," Keats explains in a May 1818 letter to John Reynolds). He is not concerned, he says to Woodhouse in October 1818, with "the wordsworthian or egotistical sublime . . . a thing *per se*," for which he felt mingled admiration and distaste. "We hate poetry that has a palpable design upon us," he said in February 1818 when thinking of Wordsworth's "bullying" didacticism. "Poetry should be great and unobtrusive." Yet he was deeply indebted to this elder statesman among contemporary poets, and in the previous month had praised *The Excursion* as one of the few artistic achievements "to rejoice at in this Age." The "poetical character" with which Keats identifies himself in a letter to Woodhouse of 27 October 1818

> . . . has no self—it is every thing and nothing—It has no character—it enjoys light and shade; it lives in gusto, be it foul or fair, high or low, rich or poor, mean or elevated—It has as much delight in conceiving an Iago as an Imogen. What shocks the virtuous philosop[h]er, delights the camelion Poet. . . . A Poet is the most unpoetical of any thing in existence; because he has no Identity—he is continually . . . filling some other Body.

The ability to re-create his own experience of "filling some other Body" is at best fitful in Keats's poems, but the experience itself is constantly displayed in his letters. He is aware of it in his letter to Bailey of 22 November 1817 when he speaks of being "annihilated" when in a room full of other "identities," of being "pressed" upon by the identity of Tom or his sister Fanny; and "if a Sparrow come before my Window I take part in its existence and pick about the Gravel." He responds instinctively to the individual temper of his correspondents. Bailey, the friend who studied theology and took orders, prompted his discussion in this November letter, quoted earlier, about the relative value of "consequitive reasoning" and "sensations" as a means of penetrating truth, and led him on to his celebrated reflections about a possible afterlife, where perhaps "we shall enjoy ourselves . . . by having what we called happiness on Earth repeated in a finer tone."

Keats's letters to Reynolds, including the verse epistle written in March 1818 to cheer him when ill, are stimulated by his responsiveness to this close friend's own interests in writing poetry, and read like continuations of their conversations together. His analysis of life as a "Mansion of Many Apartments" (3 May 1818) is designed to draw Reynolds into its reassuring arguments about the uncertainties of youthful years:

> We see not the ballance of good and evil. We are in a Mist—We are now in that state—We feel the "burden of the Mystery", To this point was Wordsworth come . . . when he wrote "Tintern Abbey" and . . . his Genius is explorative of those dark Passages. Now if we live, and go on thinking, we too shall explore them. . . .

It was Reynolds, as we saw, whom he asked to distinguish the Miltonisms from "the true voice of feeling" in *Hyperion*.

To John Taylor, his publisher, and Richard Woodhouse, the lawyer who faithfully transcribed numerous letters and poems, and sometimes acted as an intermediary with his publishers, Keats writes, so to speak, more "publicly" and informatively about his artistic progress, setting out for Taylor on 27 February 1818, as a kind of apologia, "axioms" about poetry that he thinks *Endymion* has not met ("Poetry should surprise by a fine excess. . . . Its touches of beauty should never be half way. . . . if Poetry comes not as naturally as the leaves to a tree it had better not come at all. . . ."). He adapts himself quite differently to the Reynolds sisters, whom he quizzes inventively while staying with Bailey at Oxford in September 1817: ". . . here am I among Colleges, Halls, Stalls . . . but you are by the sea . . . argal you bathe—you walk—you say how beautiful—find out resemblances between waves and Camels—rocks and dancing Masters—fireshovels and telescopes—Dolphins and Madonas. . . ."

He writes for his brothers vigorously raffish Regency jokes about his dancing and drinking parties in late 1817 and early 1818, when he was released from his dogged labors on *Endymion* and for a short time could indulge his pleasure in company and his liking for claret; cracks awful puns for them and for Charles Brown, who was waggish in this way and encouraged such jokes (not very happily for his poetry) when Keats was walking with him in Scotland and living with him at Hampstead after Tom's death; and he invents amusing fantasies to entertain his young sister Fanny. For his brothers, again, he particularizes the magnificences of the waterfalls, the changing colors of slate and stone, and the mixed exhilaration and discomfort of climbing the vast heights of Ailsa Craig and Ben Nevis during his walking tour with Brown.

This quickness of sensibility made it impossible for Keats to respond to experience or to compose poetry tranquilly. The word "fever" recurs in his accounts of his active creative moods, which were usually preceded and followed by the "indolence" that he celebrates in his 1819 ode ("Thou art . . . a fever of thyself" is Moneta's scathing reproach in *The Fall of Hyperion*). It appears in another context when finally, in late 1819, he begins to speak, circuitously, about his current feeling for women. A beautiful woman, he tells George and Georgiana Keats, can haunt him "as a tune of Mozart's might do," and if she distracts him from poetry, "that is a fever."

About his feelings for Fanny Brawne he was deeply reticent to everyone except her. His letters to her worried Matthew Arnold, who thought them effeminate (this was the later, settled Arnold, who long ago had made his own troubled accommodations about his feelings for Marguerite). But in the context of everything we know about Keats, these love letters, with the generosity of their total emotional commitment, are exactly what we should expect from him. They are at first passionate, tender, and amusingly inventive. Later, when he was torn apart first by fears for his imaginative freedom and afterward by his appalling despair at having been separated from her through illness and the tragically ill-advised journey to Italy, they become the most ravaging of any personal letters to have appeared in print.

We see everywhere in all these extraordinarily attaching human documents the play of a particular kind of creative sensibility that vitalizes everything it contemplates, and does so by the peculiar immediacy with which it simultaneously senses and reflects upon the objects of its experience. Long before T. S. Eliot's remarks about the "dissociation of sensibility," Arthur Hallam, the subject of Tennyson's *In Memoriam* and himself a young poet (he died at twenty-two), saluted in a brilliant article of 1831 the interplay of "sensation" and "thought" in certain modern poets, notably Keats and Shelley. "The tenderness of Keats," he says, "cannot sustain a lofty flight" and, like Shelley, he is a poet "of sensation." Yet "so vivid was the delight attending the simple exertions of eye and ear, that it became mingled more and more with their trains of active thought, and tended to absorb their whole being in the energy of sense." Had he lived long enough to read more of Keats's letters in Milnes's 1848 edition of the *Life, Letters and Literary Remains,* and also *The Fall of Hyperion* when it appeared a few years later, Hallam would probably have emphasized even more strongly the "reflective" components contributing to that "energy of sense" in Keats. Eliot saw "traces of a struggle towards unification of sensibility" in the second *Hyperion*. We could add that there is evidence of such a struggle from the beginning, and that Keats in his letters provides a conscious and continuous commentary upon it.

Selected Bibliography

BIBLIOGRAPHY

Detailed bibliographical information can also be found in the appropriate volumes of the *New Cambridge Bibliography of English Literature* and the *Oxford History of English Literature.* See also the *Keats-Shelley Journal,* which carries annual bibliographies.;

Catalogue of a Loan Exhibition Commemorating the Anniversary of the Death of John Keats (1821–1921) Held at the Public Library, Boston, February 21–March 14, 1921 (Boston, 1921); G. C. Williamson, ed. *The John Keats Memorial Volume,* (London, 1921) contains T. J. Wise, "A Bibliography of the Writings of John Keats"; T. J. Wise, comp. *The Ashley Library: A Catalogue of Printed Books, Manuscripts and Letters,* (London, 1928), printed for private circulation, contains a description of books and MSS by or relating to Keats; MacGillivray, J. R., *Keats: A Bibliography and Reference Guide, with an Essay on Keats' Reputation,* (Toronto, 1949); D. B. Green and E. G. Wilson, eds. *Keats, Shelley, Byron, Hunt and Their Circles: Bibliographies from the Keats-Shelley Journal, July 1, 1950–June 30, 1962* (Lincoln, Nebr., 1964).

COLLECTED EDITIONS

The Poetical Works of Coleridge, Shelley and Keats, (Paris, 1829), the Galignani ed.; *The Poetical Works,* (London, 1840), in Smith's Standard Library, the first English collected ed.; *The Poetical Works,* London (1854) with a memoir by R. M. Milnes (Lord Houghton), the first illustrated ed., with 120 designs by G. Scharf; W. M. Rossetti, ed. *The Poetical Works,* (London, 1872), with critical memoir by Rossetti; Lord Houghton, ed. *The Poetical Works,* (London, 1876), the Aldine ed.; *The Poetical Works and Other Writings,* H. B. Forman, ed. 4 vols. (London, 1883), vols. III and IV contain Keats's letters; G. Thorn-Drury, ed. *The Poems,* 2 vols. (London, 1896), with intro. by R. Bridges; H. E. Scudder, ed. *The Complete Poetical Works and Letters,* (Boston-New York, 1899), the Cambridge ed.; H. B. Forman, ed. *The Complete Works,* 5 vols. (Glasgow, 1900–1901) brings the eds. of 1883 and 1889 up to date with new material and biographical notes; E. de Selincourt, ed. *The Poems,* (London, 1905, rev. eds. 1907, 1926), with intro. and notes; H. B. Forman, ed. *The Poetical Works,* (London, 1906) also in H. W. Garrod, ed. London (1956) with intro. and textual notes; J. M. Murry, ed. *Poems and Verses of John Keats,* (London, 1930, rev. ed. 1949) arranged in chronological order; *Poetical Works,* H. W. Garrod, ed. London (1939, rev. ed. 1958) the Oxford variorum ed.; M. Allott, ed. *The Poems of John Keats,* (London, 1970, repr. with revs., London-New York 1972, rev. paperback ed. 1973) the first complete, chronological, annotated ed.; J. Barnard, ed. *John Keats: The Complete Poems,* (London, 1973) useful, inexpensive annotated ed., with poems in chronological order.

SELECTED WORKS

R. Monckton Milnes, ed. *Life, Letters and Literary Remains of John Keats,* 2 vols. (London, 1848), prints many poems and letters for the first time, including the tragedy *Otho the Great*; *The Eve of St. Agnes, and Other Poems* (Boston, 1876) in the Vest-Pocket series of standard and popular authors; *Odes and Sonnets,* (Philadelphia, 1888) with illustrations by W. H. Low; *Selections from Keats,* (London, 1889) with preface by J. R. Tutin, includes all the poems from the 1820 vol. and a selection from that of 1817; *The Odes of Keats,* (Oxford, 1897), facs. ed. (Tokyo, 1965) with notes and analyses and a memoir by A. C. Downer; H. B. Forman, ed. *Endymion and the Longer Poems,* (London, 1897); H. Ellershaw, ed. *Poetry and Prose,* (Oxford, 1922) with essays by C. Lamb, L. Hunt, R. Bridges, and others; C. W. Thomas, ed. *Poems. With Selections from His Letters and from Criticism,* (London, 1932), includes criticism by E. de Selincourt, R. Bridges, and A. C. Bradley; J. A. Walsh, ed. *Selected Letters and Poems,* (London, 1954); E. C. Blunden, ed. *Selected Poems,* (London, 1955); R. Gittings, ed. *Selected Poems and Letters of John Keats,* (London, 1967).

SEPARATE WORKS

Poems, (London, 1817), facs. ed. in Noel Douglas Replicas series (London, 1927); *Endymion: A Poetic Romance,* (London, 1818), type-facs. ed. with intro. and notes by E. C. Notcutt (London, 1927), also in T. Saito, ed. (London, 1931), with notes; *Lamia, Isabella, The Eve of St. Agnes, and Other Poems,* (London, 1820, facs. ed. 1970); "La Belle Dame Sans Merci," *Indicator,* (May 10, 1820) signed "Caviare"; R. M. Milnes, ed. *Another Version of Keats's "Hyperion",* (London, 1857 [?]) repr. of Milnes's contribution to *Miscellanies of the Philobiblion Society* 3 (1856–1857) the basic text of *The Fall of Hyperion: A Dream* until the discovery of the Woodhouse transcript in 1904; *Hyperion. A Facsimile of Keats's Autograph Manuscript with a Transliteration of the Manuscript of The Fall of Hyperion: A Dream,* (London, 1905) with intro. and notes by E. de Selincourt; R. Gittings, ed. *The Odes of Keats and Their Earliest Known Manuscripts,* (London, 1970), with intro. and notes by Gittings.

Students should also consult the *Examiner,* the *Indicator, Annals of the Fine Arts, Blackwood's* magazine, and other periodicals of Keats's day.

LETTERS

Letters to Fanny Brawne, 1819–1820, (London, 1878) with intro. and notes by H. B. Forman; J. G. Speed, ed. *Letters,* (New York, 1883); S. Colvin, ed. *Letters to His Family and Friends,* (London, 1891), excludes letters to Fanny Brawne; H. B. Forman, ed. *Letters,* (London, 1895), contains every letter of Keats's known at the time; T. Watts-Dunton, G. Williamson, and H. B. Forman, eds. *The Keats Letters, Papers and Other Relics Forming the Dilke Bequest,* (London, 1914); H. B. Forman, ed. *Letters,* 2 vols. (London, 1931, 2nd ed. 1935, 3rd ed. 1947), the ed. of 1935 adds 10 letters; H. E.

Rollins, ed. *The Keats Circle: Letters and Papers, 1816–78,* 2 vols. (Cambridge, Mass., 1948); H. E. Rollins, ed. *More Letters and Poems of the Keats Circle,* (Cambridge, Mass., 1955), new ed. entitled *The Keats Circle: Letters and Papers and More Letters and Poems of the Keats Circle* (Cambridge, Mass., 1965), contains the 1948 and 1955 eds. in 2 vols.; H. E. Rollins, ed. *The Letters of John Keats, 1814–1821,* (London, 1958) the definitive ed.; R. Gittings, ed. *Letters of John Keats,* (London, 1970), replaces F. Page's selection in the World's Classics. See also under COLLECTED EDITIONS, SELECTED WORKS, and BIOGRAPHICAL AND CRITICAL STUDIES.

BIOGRAPHICAL AND CRITICAL STUDIES

Shelley, P. B., *Adonais: An Elegy on the Death of John Keats,* (London, 1821); Hunt, L., *Lord Byron and Some of His Contemporaries,* (London, 1828), contains an account of Keats with criticism of his poetry, also in J. E. Morpurgo, ed. (London, 1949); Hallam, A., "On Some of the Characteristics of Modern Poetry," in *Englishman's* magazine 1 (August 1831), 616–621, discusses Tennyson, with arresting analysis of Keats as his forerunner, repr. in G. Matthews, ed., *The Critical Heritage* (London, 1971); S. C. Hall, ed. *The Book of Gems, III,* (London, 1838), contains comment on Keats by L. Hunt; Hunt, L., *Imagination and Fancy,* (London, 1844), also in E. Gosse, ed. (London, 1907); Medwin, T., *The Life of Percy Bysshe Shelley,* 2 vols. (London, 1847), contains comment on Keats, based on information from L. Hunt, Fanny Brawne, and Shelley; R. M. Milnes, ed. *Life, Letters and Literary Remains of John Keats,* 2 vols. (London, 1848) (reviewed by A. de Vere in *Edinburgh Review* 90, (October 1849), 388–433 in a perceptive essay comparing Keats, Shelley, and Tennyson; review repr. in G. Matthews, ed. *The Critical Heritage,* (London, 1971); Dallas, E. S., *Poetics: An Essay on Poetry,* (London, 1852); T. Taylor, ed. *Life of B. R. Haydon from His Autobiography and Journals,* 3 vols. (London, 1853). Masson, D., "The Life and Poetry of Keats," in *Macmillan's* magazine 3, (November 1860), 1–16, an important essay anticipating some aspects of modern criticism of Keats, repr. in G. Matthews, ed., *The Critical Heritage* (London, 1971); Arnold, M., *On the Study of Celtic Literature,* (London, 1867) ch. 4 refers to Keats's "natural magic"; see also Arnold's essay "Maurice de Guérin," in his *Essays in Criticism* (London, 1865); J. R. Lowell, ed. *My Study Windows,* (London, 1871) in Low's American Copyright Series of American Authors; Dilke, Sir C. W., *The Papers of a Critic,* 2 vols. (London, 1875), the memoir contains letters from Keats and other material; Clarke, C. C., and Clarke, M. C., *Recollections of Writers,* (London, 1878); Owen, F. M., *John Keats: A Study,* (London, 1880); T. H. Ward, ed. *The English Poets: Selections,* (London, 1880) with general intro. by M. Arnold, vol. IV contains an essay on Keats by Arnold that was repr. in his *Essays in Criticism,* 2nd ser. (London, 1887); Colvin, S., *Keats,* (London, 1889, new ed., 1889), in the English Men of Letters series; Rossetti, W. M., *Life of John Keats,* (London, 1887), contains a bibliography by J. P. Anderson; Sharp, W., *The Life and Letters of Joseph Severn,* (London, 1892); Bridges, R., *John Keats: A Critical Essay,* (London, 1895) privately printed, also in the Muses' Library (London, 1896) repub. in Bridges' *Collected Essays,* IV (London, 1929).

The Bookman, Keats double number (October 1906) contains original material relating to Keats; Bradley, A. C., *Oxford Lectures on Poetry,* (London, 1909), contains essay "The Letters of Keats," followed by a comparison of Keats's *Endymion* and Shelley's "Alastor," repr. with intro. by M. R. Ridley (London, 1965); Wolff, L., *John Keats: Sa vie et son oeuvre, 1795–1821,* (Paris, 1910); Thomas, E., *Keats,* (London, 1916); D. L. Baldwin, ed. *A Concordance to the Poems of John Keats,* (Washington, D.C., 1917); Colvin, S., *John Keats: His Life and Poetry, His Friends, Critics and After-Fame,* (London, 1917, rev. ed. 1925); Keats House Committee *John Keats Memorial Volume,* (Hampstead, 1921); Fausset, H. I'A., *Keats: A Study in Development,* (London, 1922); Lowell, A., *John Keats,* 2 vols. (Boston, 1925); Murry, J. M., *Keats and Shakespeare: A Study of Keats's Poetic Life from 1816 to 1820,* (London, 1925); Garrod, H. W., *Keats,* (London, 1926); Blunden, E., *Leigh Hunt's Examiner Examined,* (London, 1928); G. L. Marsh, ed. *John Hamilton Reynolds, Poetry and Prose,* (London, 1928), with intro. and notes by Marsh; Spurgeon, C., *Keats's Shakespeare: A Descriptive Study,* (London, 1928), based on Keats's markings and marginalia in his copies of Shakespeare; Saito, T., *Keats's View of Poetry,* (London, 1929); Wolff, L., *Keats,* (Paris, 1929).

Murry, J. M., *Studies in Keats,* (London, 1930), rev. and enl. as *Studies in Keats, New and Old* (London, 1939) as *The Mystery of Keats* (London, 1949) and as *Keats* (London, 1955); Ridley, M. R., *Keats' Craftsmanship: A Study in Poetic Development,* (Oxford, 1933); *Keats House and Museum: An Historical and Descriptive Guide,* (London, 1934, new ed. 1966, 7th ed., 1974); Blunden, E., *Keats's Publisher: A Memoir of John Taylor,* (London, 1936); Finney, C. L., *The Evolution of Keats's Poetry,* 2 vols. (Cambridge, Mass., 1936); Saito, T., *John Keats,* (Tokyo, 1936); Brown, C. A., *Life of John Keats,* (Oxford, 1937) D. H. Bodurtha and W. B. Pope, eds., with intro. and notes, the first publication of reminiscences by Keats's friend Charles Brown; Hewlett, D., *Adonais: A Life of John Keats,* (London, 1937), rev. and enl. as *A Life of John Keats* (London, 1949, 3rd rev. ed. 1970); White, W. H., *Keats as Doctor and Patient,* (London, 1938).

Blunden, E., *Romantic Poetry and the Fine Arts,* (London, 1942), Warton Lecture on English Poetry for

1942, first printed in *Proceedings of the British Academy* 28 (1942) 101–118; Ford, G. H., *Keats and the Victorians: A Study of His Influence and Rise to Fame, 1821–1895,* (London, 1944); Bate, W. J., *The Stylistic Development of Keats,* (New York, 1945); Fogle, R. H., *The Imagery of Keats and Shelley: A Comparative Study,* (Chapel Hill, N.C., 1949); Trilling, L., *TheOpposing Self: Nine Essays in Criticism,* (New York, 1950), contains "The Poet as Hero: Keats in His Letters"; Ford, N. F., *The Prefigurative Imagination of Keats: A Study of the Beauty-Truth Identification and Its Implications,* (Stanford, Calif., 1951); Richardson, J., *Fanny Brawne: A Biography,* (London, 1952); Gittings, R., *John Keats: The Living Year, 21 September, 1818 to 21 September, 1819,* (London, 1954); Gittings, R., *The Mask of Keats: A Study of Problems,* (London, 1956); Pettet, E. C., *On the Poetry of Keats,* (Cambridge, 1957) includes an extended analysis of *Endymion*; K. Muir, ed. *John Keats: A Reassessment,* (London, 1958, repr. 1969) essays by Muir, K. Allott, M. Allott, A. Davenport, R. T. Davies, J. Grundy, and others; Perkins, D., *The Quest for Permanence: The Symbolism of Wordsworth, Shelley and Keats,* (Cambridge, Mass., 1959).

Bayley, J., *Keats and Reality,* (London, 1962), lively British Academy lecture; Bate, W. J., *John Keats,* (Cambridge, Mass., 1963), highly distinguished and indispensable critical biography; Richardson, J., *The Everlasting Spell: A Study of Keats and His Friends,* (London, 1963); Ward, A., *John Keats: The Making of a Poet,* (London, 1963), biographical study, making suggestive use of the poems to illuminate Keats's character and temperament; W. J. Bate, ed. *Keats: A Collection of Critical Essays,* (Englewood Cliffs, N.J., 1964), in Twentieth Century Views series; Gittings, R., *The Keats Inheritance,* (London, 1964) on the question of the Keats family's financial position; Evert, W. H., *Aesthetic and Myth in the Poetry of Keats,* (Princeton, N.J., 1965); Bush, D., *John Keats: His Life and Writings,* (London, 1966), admirably succinct and informative intro. for the Masters of World Literature series; Jack, I., *Keats and the Mirror of Art,* (London, 1967), an examination of Keats's cultural milieu, especially the influence of painters and art critics on his poetic development; J. O'Neill, ed. *Critics on Keats,* (London, 1967), extracts from important critical works, arranged in chronological order of Keats's writings; Gittings, R., *John Keats,* (London, 1968), impressively detailed biographical study; J. Stillinger, ed. *Twentieth Century Interpretations of Keats's Odes: A Collection of Critical Essays,* (Englewood Cliffs, N.J., 1968), includes essays by M. H. Abrams, K. Allott, W. J. Bate, C. Brooks, D. Perkins, R. P. Warren, and others; Jones, J., *John Keats's Dream of Truth,* (London, 1969) on Keats and "Romantic feeling."

Patterson, C. I., *The Daemonic in the Poetry of John Keats,* (London, 1970), argues that the "daemonic" in Keats is a nonmalicious, pre-Christian, Greek conception, and is in conflict with his personal feeling for the actual world; Dickstein, M., *Keats and His Poetry: A Study in Development,* (Chicago, 1971), explores the contrarieties in and the development of Keats's imagination through close reading of the texts, especially *Endymion,* the odes, *The Fall of Hyperion,* and some minor poems; Hilton, T., *Keats and His World,* (London, 1971), useful pictorial biography; G. Matthews, ed. *Keats: The Critical Heritage,* (London, 1971), invaluable collection of early nineteenth-century and Victorian commentaries on Keats; Stillinger, J., *The Hoodwinking of Madeline and Other Essays on Keats's Poems,* (Urbana, Ill., 1971), offers an individual view of Keats's "realism"; Redpath, T., *The Young Romantics and Critical Opinion, 1807–1824,* (London, 1973); Sperry, S. M., *Keats the Poet,* (Princeton, N.J., 1973), discusses the connection between "sensation" and "thought" in Keats; Ricks, C., *Keats and Embarrassment,* (Oxford, 1974), vivacious essay on evidence in Keats's poems and letters of his sensitivity to and intelligence about embarrassment; Stillinger, J., *The Texts of Keats's Poems,* (Cambridge, Mass., 1974), offers a detailed analysis of textual problems in Keats and suggests principles for establishing a standard text; reviewed by M. Allott in *Times Literary Supplement* (December 12, 1975).

Periodicals containing valuable regular contributions about Keats include *Keats-Shelley Journal,* (1952–) and *Bulletin of the Keats-Shelley Memorial* vol. I, (1910), vol. II, Sir R. Rodd and H. N. Gray, eds. (1913, repub. 1962), vol. III (etc.), D. Hewlett, ed. (1950–).

Galway Kinnell
(b. 1927)

CELESTE GOODRIDGE

. . . we are not really at home in
our interpreted world. . . .
(Rilke, *The Duino Elegies*,
"The First Elegy")

. . . But listen to the voice of the wind
and the ceaseless message that forms itself
out of silence.
(Rilke, *The Duino Elegies*,
"The First Elegy")

POET, NOVELIST, TRANSLATOR, and occasional poet–critic and writer of children's literature, Galway Kinnell has been called "a kind of evangelist of the physical world," "dishearteningly prolix," "a shamanist, rather than a historicist, of the imagination," and a poet whose "risks are so great, his very lapses seem preferable to the limited successes of many other poets." He has published nine volumes of poetry: *What a Kingdom It Was* (1960), *Flower Herding on Mount Monadnock* (1964), *Body Rags* (1968), *First Poems 1946–1954* (1971), *The Book of Nightmares* (1971), *The Avenue Bearing the Initial of Christ into the New World: Poems 1946–64* (1974), *Mortal Acts, Mortal Words* (1980), *Selected Poems* (1982), and *The Past* (1985)

He has also, like many of his contemporaries, translated the work of artists who captured his imagination. "When you translate a poet," Kinnell remarked in a 1971 interview with Mary Jane Fortunato, "you invite or dare that poet to influence you." Kinnell's translations include René Hardy's novel *Bitter Victory* (1956), *The Poems of François Villon* (1965, and a second version in 1977), Yves Bonnefoy's *On the Motion and Immobility of Douve* (1968), and Yvan Goll's *Lackawanna Elegy* (1970). In addition, he has published one novel, *Black Light* (1966); a selection of interviews, *Walking Down the Stairs* (1978); and a children's book, *How the Alligator Missed Breakfast* (1982

Applauded as one of the most vibrant voices in contemporary American poetry, Kinnell has received major recognition for his work: the Pulitzer Prize (1983) for his *Selected Poems*, an award from the National Institute of Arts and Letters (1962), two Guggenheim Fellowships (1961–1962, 1974–1975), Fulbright teaching appointments, two Rockefeller Foundation grants (1962–1963, 1968), the Brandeis Creative Arts Award (1969), the Shelley Prize of the Poetry Society of America (1974), the Medal of Merit from the National Institute of Arts and Letters (1975), the Harold L. Landon Translation Prize (1979), the American Book Award (shared with Charles Wright, 1983), and a MacArthur Foundation grant (1984). While Kinnell's awards and honors might suggest that he has relied on the safety and security of the academy, his numerous temporary academic appointments, extensive traveling, and political activities suggest otherwise.

Kinnell received his first tenured position in 1985, when he became the Samuel F. B. Morse Professor of Arts and Science at New York University. Before that, he held temporary appointments in the United States, in Europe, and in Australia. He also had been politically active, particularly during the 1960's, when he took part in anti-Vietnam War poetry readings, and in the 1980's, when he became involved in the antinuclear movement. In addition, he was president of P.E.N. during 1983–1984.

Some of Kinnell's poems refer to his political activities; "The Last River," for example, which appeared in *Body Rags* (1968), chronicles the time he spent in Louisiana in 1963, working in the voter registration campaign for the Congress of Racial Equality, and the week he was jailed there for his activities. It also points up Kinnell's increasing need to personalize his politics, to transcend the historical moment:

> Through the crisscross
> of bars at the tiny window
> I could see the swallows
> that were darting in the last light,
> late-flying creatures that surpass us in plain
> view . . .
> bits of blurred flesh . . .
> wavy lines . . .
>
> Nothing's there now but a few stars
> brightening
> under the ice-winds of the emptiness . . .
>
> Isn't it strange
> that all love, all granting of respect,
> has no face for its passing expressions but
> yours,
> Death?

Kinnell's meditation in jail does not ground him in the particular moment; instead, he focuses on how such moments are necessarily absorbed by the emptiness around us. The shadow of our mortality is ever present. This posture looks forward to *The Book of Nightmares* and *Mortal Acts, Mortal Words.*

Given Kinnell's prolific canon, made up of some exquisitely compressed short lyrics and some long poems that revitalize the use of rhythm, the short line, and the sentence, it is striking how little his concerns and preoccupations have changed over the decades. Reading through his poems, we encounter, albeit in different poetic forms, the same issues: the poet in a state of exile, "the comfort of darkness," "the sadness of joy," emptiness and silence as a plenitude, the purification afforded by flames, ruins, and ashes, song as redemptive, the inextricable relationship between eros and loss, the search for "the sublime" in an American landscape, a Stevensian celebration of "death [as] the mother of beauty," and a loving attentiveness to, as Kinnell notes, "the things and creatures that share the earth with us."

Thus, the question we are tempted, even compelled, to ask of most artists' work—"Does the aesthetic and poetic vision change and evolve over time?"—must be abandoned. As Lee Zimmerman points out, "Like Yeats, his early master, Kinnell spends his career working the same set of insights, but, predicated on changing experience, these are refashioned at every point." It is the continual refashioning of self, then, in a changing constellation of new and unexpected experiences that we must attend to in Kinnell's work.

Though only occasionally linked with James Merrill, Kinnell shares Merrill's early poetic preoccupation with the "need to make some kind of house / Out of the life lived, out of the love spent" ("An Urban Convalescence"). But, unlike Merrill, Kinnell starts from the premise that he is in a state of exile, "seeking home" but seldom finding such a resting place. For Kinnell the journey, composed of crossings and transitions, is everything. "And yet I can rejoice / that everything changes, that / we go from life / into life" ("Lost Loves"). It is these changes that his poetic project maps and that this essay will trace.

Born in Providence, Rhode Island, on February 1, 1927 (the same year as James Wright, John Ashbery, and W. S. Merwin), Galway Kinnell was the youngest of four children. Both of his parents were immigrants: his mother, from Ireland, and his father, a carpenter and teacher of woodworking, from Scotland. In "The Sadness of Brothers" (in *Mortal Acts, Mortal Words*), Kinnell remembers them, highlighting their differences:

> . . . the serene-seeming,
> sea-going gait
> which took him down Oswald Street in dark
> of each morning
> and up Oswald Street in dark of each
> night . . .
> this small, well-wandered Scotsman
> who appears now in memory's memory,
> in light of last days, jiggling
> his knees as he used to do—*get*
> *out of here,* I knew
> they were telling him, *get out of here,*
> *Scotty*—
> control he couldn't control
> thwarting his desires down
> into knees which could only jiggle
> the one bit of advice least useful
> to this man who had dragged himself to the
> earth's ends
> so he could end up
> in the ravaged ending-earth
> of Pawtucket, Rhode Island; where the Irish
> wife willed
> the bourgeois illusion all of us dreamed
> we lived, even he, who disgorged
> divine capitalist law
> out of his starved craw
> that we might succeed though he had failed
> at every enterprise but war . . .

His father, "who had dragged himself to the earth's ends," is an outcast from life's feast, while his mother, more wedded to her dreams, "willed the bourgeois illusion all of us dreamed / we lived."

In a 1990 interview published in *New York Woman,* Kinnell described his childhood to Lois Smith Brady as "almost unbearably lonely." As a child his reading and desire to write gave him access to a private world of his own. He alludes to this in a 1971 interview with A. Poulin, Jr., and Stan Sanvel Rubin:

> As for the impulses that set me writing, I remember I lived a kind of double life: my "public" life with everyone I knew—brother, sisters, parents, friends, and so on—and my secret life with the poems I would read late at night. I found my most intimate feelings were shared in those poems more fully than in the relationships I had in the world.

In 1932 the family moved to Pawtucket, Rhode Island, where Kinnell attended public schools until his senior year of high school, when he was awarded a scholarship to Wilbraham Academy in Massachusetts. In this setting he was encouraged to write and probably was steered toward Princeton, which he entered, along with W. S. Merwin, in 1944. When asked by Wayne Dodd and Stanley Plumly in a 1972 interview if he and Merwin had written poems while at Princeton and shared them with one another, Kinnell replied:

> Yes, we showed each other poems—though mine, by comparison, were crude. Even at nineteen Merwin was writing poems of extraordinary skill and grace. His sense of the richness of English, his ear for its music, were then, and remain now even in his leaner poems, superior to anyone's.

During his junior year Kinnell studied with Charles Bell, who took his early efforts quite seriously; that summer he went to Black Mountain College, where Bell was lecturing. Bell fondly recalls one of their first encounters:

> In the winter of 1946–47, when I was teaching at Princeton University, a dark-shocked student, looking more like a prize fighter than a literary man, showed me a poem, maybe his first. I remember it as a Wordsworthian sonnet, not what the avant-garde of Princeton, Blackmur or Berryman, would have taken to—old diction, no modern flair. But the last couplet had a romantic fierceness that amazed me. The man who had done that could go beyond any poetic limits to be assigned. I was reckless enough to tell him so.

At Merwin's insistence, Kinnell began reading Yeats. He frequently alludes to the significance of this influence; for instance, we know from the interview with Dodd and Plumly that Yeats influenced Kinnell's structuring of poems:

> In my early twenties I thought Yeats was not only the greatest of all poets, but also in a

> manner of speaking, poetry itself. In everything I wrote I tried to reproduce his voice. If my poems didn't sound like Yeats, I thought they weren't poetry. . . . Yeats became a more useful mentor when I began to see his limitations, I think my interest in the poem made of sections, of elements that don't come together until the end, probably derives from Yeats, from poems like "Among Schoolchildren." I've always loved how all the materials of that poem come back woven together and transformed.

This remark looks forward to a poem like "Freedom, New Hampshire," which appeared in *What a Kingdom It Was.* The poem is an elegy to Kinnell's older brother, Derry, who died in a car crash when Kinnell was thirty. The poem's first sections, which include memories of their time together on a farm in New Hampshire, contain images of death—"We came to visit the cow / Dying of fever," and "We found a cowskull once; we thought it was / From one of the asses in the Bible . . ."—as well as their vision of birth, a vision that pays homage to the darkness from which we come and to which we return:

> That night passing Towle's Barn
> We saw lights. Towle had lassoed a calf
> By its hind legs, and he tugged against the grip
> Of the darkness. The cow stood by chewing millet.
> Derry and I took hold, too, and hauled.
> It was sopping with darkness when it came free.

In the last section, Kinnell moves from the past to a present that acknowledges and makes audible "the abruptly decaying sounds" around us. While he recognizes that at the moment of death "only flesh dies, and spirit flowers without stop," he also realizes that his brother's death, and everyone's, encompasses a certain finality: "When he is dead the grass / Heals what he suffered, but he remains dead, / And the few who loved him know this until they die." The pathos of this impersonal generalization is mitigated a bit by the more personal and particular recognition that only Kinnell, and "the few who loved" Derry, can preserve his memory. As Zimmerman maintains: "Later in his career, Kinnell comes closer to James Merrill's complex but comforting proposition that 'nothing either lasts or ends,' but here his sense of temporariness is fierce. . . ."

After graduating from Princeton in 1948, Kinnell attended the University of Rochester, where he received an M.A. in English in 1949. This was the end of his formal education. After two years as an instructor at Alfred University, Kinnell moved to Chicago, where, between 1951 and 1954, he supervised the liberal arts program at the downtown campus of the University of Chicago.

Kinnell's *First Poems 1946–1954,* those composed at Princeton and during the early 1950's, address "the comfort of darkness" and its relationship to "the feast" of life. In "The Feast," (1954), for example, Kinnell anticipates his 1971 essay "The Poetics of the Physical World," in which, following Rainer Maria Rilke, Wallace Stevens, and Elizabeth Bishop, he makes a virtue of Stevens' assertion in "Peter Quince at the Clavier": "The body dies; the body's beauty lives. / So evenings die, in their green going." "That we last only for a time," Kinnell asserts, ". . . that we know this, radiates a thrilling, tragic light on all our loves, all our relationships, even on those moments when the world, through its poetry, becomes almost capable of spurning time and death." In "The Feast," Kinnell also flirts with the possibility of "spurning time and death":

> The sand turns cold—or the body warms.
> If love had not smiled we would never grieve.
> But on every earthly place its turning crown
> Flashes and fades. We will feast on love again
> In the purple light, and rise again and leave
> Our two shapes dying in each other's arms.

Most of Kinnell's early poems display their indebtedness to his precursors, particularly

Yeats, Robert Frost, William Carlos Williams, and Theodore Roethke; the more compelling influences of Walt Whitman and Rainer Maria Rilke come later. In a 1977 *Partisan Review* piece, Alan Helms finds *First Poems 1946–1954* "most remarkable for the unassimilated debts Kinnell incurs"; he also points out that "in *What a Kingdom It Was* (1960) Kinnell pays off some of his debts; [while] in *Flower Herding on Mount Monadnock* (1964) he's in the black, writing his own good poetry, especially in Part II of that book."

Certain poems in *What a Kingdom It Was* are memorable for what they portend in Kinnell's canon: "First Song," with its realization that song can lead to a "fall" into "darkness and into the sadness of joy"; "Freedom, New Hampshire," Kinnell's elegy to his brother, which anticipates "Another Night in the Ruins," in which the poet imagines a world where there is no phoenix but, rather, "the cow / of nothingness, mooing / down the bones"; and "The Supper After the Last," which announces that it is desirable to give up the "Lech for transcendence" in favor of "Intricate and simple things / As you are, created / In the image of nothing." *What a Kingdom It Was* is significant, however, because of the long poem that comprises Part IV: "The Avenue Bearing the Initial of Christ into the New World."

This poem, which many of Kinnell's critics feel is only partially successful, grew out of his experience of living on Avenue C on the Lower East Side of New York from 1957 to 1959. The thirty-year-old Kinnell was one of several poets who took up residence in this neighborhood during the 1950's. According to Lois Smith Brady, "Denise Levertov lived in his building; Allen Ginsberg lived within walking distance; Robert Bly used to come over in the afternoons." In this same interview Kinnell comments on the relationship between this setting and his poetic project, and on Whitman's influence. He began reading Whitman seriously while teaching at the University of Grenoble in 1956–1957, just before he moved to Avenue C.

> In those days the Lower East Side was a terribly vivid and active exotic world. I had just discovered Whitman, who wandered around New York with his notebook, looking into butcher shops and blacksmith shops and taking notes, so I did the same. Gradually, I realized I wanted to write a little hymn to this part of the world, and that turned out to be "The Avenue Bearing the Initial of Christ into the New World."

An interview with Ken McCullough in 1976 sheds additional light on Kinnell's project. In it he points out an important distinction between his vision and Whitman's: "Much of Whitman's poetry is devoted to celebrating ordinary sights and sounds and in this respect the 'Avenue C' poem probably does follow Whitman. But in my poem, time and progress appear as enemies, as they never do in Whitman." Despite this important difference in focus, it is clear that Whitman had a profound influence on the form of Kinnell's poem. Thirty years after the poem was written, in the introduction to *The Essential Whitman* (1987), Kinnell described the change that took place in his poetry when he discovered Whitman: "Under Whitman's spell I stopped writing in rhyme and meter and in rectangular stanzas and turned to long-lined, loosely cadenced verse; and at once I felt immensely liberated."

Morris Dickstein claims that Kinnell's "little hymn" to Avenue C "is less a poem than a vast poetic notebook that enabled [him]—by a discipline of attention to the world around him—to slough off the artificialities and tired literary devices of the old style." Paul Mariani also maintains that Kinnell's subject allowed him to abandon "earlier formalist techniques" and

> to pursue new rhetorical models, to see what he could do, for example, with the Whitmanian catalogue, the language of the image, and—unlike Whitman but very much like Villon—with the suppression of a poetic self in favor of allowing the mirror world on the other side of the poet's window to reveal

something of the interiority of the human condition.

We can also see Kinnell's kinship with Villon when he identifies with the marginal individual—the transgressor, who might at any time be banished from society. This identification emerges in Kinnell's vision of "the wiped-out lives—punks, lushes, / Panhandlers, pushers, rum-soaks . . ." on Avenue C.

Even though the influence of Whitman's catalogs, speech rhythms, and readiness to make observations lurks behind Kinnell's aesthetic and form in the poem, the voice is Kinnell's, perhaps for the first time. It is Kinnell's close observation of the life and energies surrounding these "wiped-out lives" that vitalizes the poem. Section 6, for example, focuses on "the pushcart market, on Sunday," where vegetables display a subterranean energy, giving us a vision of how all life comes into the light from darkness:

> A crate of lemons discharges light like a
> battery.
> Icicle-shaped carrots that through black soil
> Wove away lie like flames in the sun.
> Onions with their shirts ripped seek
> sunlight
> On green skins. The sun beats
> On beets dirty as boulders in cowfields,
> On turnips pinched and gibbous
> From budging rocks. . . .

And in section 11 Kinnell describes the fishmarket with its "Fishes [which] do not die exactly, it is more / That they go out of themselves. . . ." He allows us to see the fish in their otherness; they are laid out to be sold, but he banishes the consumer by taking us in after hours.

> The fishmarket closed, the fishes gone into
> flesh.
> The smelts draped on each other, fat with
> roe,
> The marble cod hacked into chunks on the
> counter,
> Butterfishes mouths still open, still trying
> to eat,
> Porgies with receding jaws hinged apart
> In a grimace of dejection, as if like cows
> They had died under the sledgehammer,
> perches
> In grass-green armor, spotted squeteagues
> In the melting ice meek-faced and croaking
> no more,
>
> . . .
>
> . . . two-tone flounders
> After the long contortion of pushing both
> eyes
> To the brown side that they might look up,
> Brown side down, like a mass laying-on of
> hands,
> Or the oath-taking of an army.

Kinnell's metaphors at the end of this section remind us of his own poetic enterprise in the poem. His observations, like Whitman's in "Song of Myself," become a kind of faith healing—"a mass laying-on of hands." Perhaps Kinnell wishes to heal himself: seeing with the inclusiveness of Whitman and cataloging the images around him become means toward redemption, means of temporarily forgetting the historical moment and those "enemies": "time and progress."

But it takes a leap of faith to see such a project as politically viable at this time in our history. As Cary Nelson perceptively points out:

> Kinnell's verbal motives require not deftly managed synecdoche but a sense of broad inclusiveness established through accumulated detail. So long as the details are American, the method is patently Whitmanesque, and by now culturally approved and politically safe. Yet our history has soured us for such projects. . . . We can now *see* with Whitman's eyes; the vast poem of America founders all about us. Visually, we can cross the continent in a minute. If the trip takes longer, the poem of community succumbs to the obvious visual evidence of violence and greed.

In *Flower Herding on Mount Monadnock,* Kinnell asks us to make still another leap of faith by beginning with "The River That Is East." We might expect him in this poem, which focuses on the East River rather than the Mississippi, to write off the American dream; instead, Kinnell finds a way, reminiscent of Nick Carraway's vision at the end of Fitzgerald's *The Great Gatsby,* to reinscribe its potency even in the face of the wonderless river "Which drags the things we love, / Processions of debris like floating lamps, / Towards the radiance in which they go out?"

The first section pays homage to the movement of things on the river: the clanging buoys, the tugs, the carfloat, and the "white-winged gulls which shriek / And flap from the water. . . ." Traveling along this working river, we see its shores and the Williamsburg Bridge 'That hangs facedown from its strings / Over which the Jamaica Local crawls."

In section 2 Kinnell moves from this concrete and particular perspective, shifting our attention to a boy sitting by the river and trying to conjure up some romance of his own. The poet wonders if the young boy can be linked to others in American literature who had their unrealized, though no less potent, dreams. In this context Kinnell offers a meditation on the male twentieth-century American romance tradition of questing. Orson Welles, F. Scott Fitzgerald, Ernest Hemingway, Thomas Wolfe, and Theodore Dreiser define this tradition. Taking us out of the present moment of section 1, Kinnell, a diehard romantic, looks back at these cultural "heroes":

> On his deathbed
> Kane remembered the abrupt, missed Grail
> Called Rosebud, Gatsby must have thought back
> On his days digging clams in Little Girl Bay
> In Minnesota, Nick fished in dreamy Michigan,
> Gant had his memories, Griffiths, those
> Who went baying after the immaterial
> And whiffed its strange dazzle in a blonde
> In a canary convertible, who died
> Thinking of the Huck Finns of themselves
> On the old afternoons, themselves like this boy. . . .

Section 3 focuses on "a man," rather than "a boy," who "has long since stopped wishing his heart were full / Or his life dear to him." Yet despite this disavowal, he still thinks, when he sees "the dirty water," of the possibility of some transcendent moment: "If I were a gull I would be one with white wings, / I would fly out over the water, explode, and / Be beautiful snow hitting the dirty water." This conditional conjecture prepares us for the Nick Carraway-like sentiments in section 4:

> And thou, River of Tomorrow, flowing . . .
> We stand on the shore, which is mist beneath us,
> And regard the onflowing river. Sometimes
> It seems the river stops and the shore
> Flows into the past. Nevertheless, its leaked promises
> Hopping in the bloodstream, we strain for the future,
> Sometimes even glimpse it, a vague, scummed thing
> We dare not recognize, and peer again
> At the cabled shroud out of which it came,
> We who have no roots but the shifts of our pain,
> No flowering but our own strange lives.

What begins as a critique of why this "River of Tomorrow" is inseparable from "the past" of "leaked promises" turns into a reaffirmation of the Emersonian mythology of "self-reliance"; Emerson's mythology celebrates the possibility of knowing "No flowering but [one's] own strange [life]" and of denying historical contingencies: knowing "no roots but the shifts of [one's] pain." This particular type of "self-fashioning" obviously serves to take us back to Kinnell's allusions to Kane, Gatsby, Nick Adams, Eugene Gant, and Clyde Griffiths in section 2. Most important, it signals Kinnell's increasing concern with being true to "the shifts of [his own] pain" and the "flowering [of his] own strange [life]." Without being confessional in the sense that Merrill and Robert Lowell are, Kinnell turns again and again in his poems to the shape and texture of his life, to the trajectories of the journeys he has taken and will take.

When he moves from the cityscapes in Part I of *Flower Herding on Mount Monadnock* to the rural landscapes of Part II, Kinnell's relationship to the life he is living begins to change as he confronts his own mortality. Charles Molesworth points this out when he maintains that "it is only when Kinnell escapes the city for the country that the possibilities of mortality become positive rather than negative." This impulse is played out in Kinnell's embrace of the darkness and in his Rilkean realization that "we are not really at home in / our interpreted world. . . ." Some lines from "Middle of the Way," a poem about an actual journey through a particular landscape, whose signs cannot be deciphered, illustrate the point: "I love the earth, and always/In its darknesses I am a stranger"; "All I see is we float out / Into the emptiness, among the great stars, / On this little vessel without lights"; "But I know I live half alive in the world, / I know half my life belongs to the wild darkness."

The final poem of the collection, "Flower Herding on Mount Monadnock," is striking in its evocation of Rilke's knowledge of "Things, / which live by perishing . . ." (*The Duino Elegies,* "The Ninth Elegy"). The poet realizes as he looks at this flower that "Its drift is to be nothing." Dropping out of sight in the final endstopped lines of the poem, Kinnell gives the flower its autonomy, allowing its finitude a visibility and prominence: "The appeal to heaven breaks off. / The petals begin to fall, in selfforgiveness. / It is a flower. On this mountainside it is dying." This relinquishing of the poetic I, but not the poetic eye, is an unfamiliar posture in Kinnell's canon up to this point. More often, he is like Frost's speaker at the beginning of "The Most of It," who "thought he kept the universe alone." Kinnell's desire, like his precursor's, is to have "original response" from his surroundings rather than "copy speech" in return for his efforts to connect to the things of this world.

In 1965, the year Kinnell's translation of Villon was published, he took part in an anti-Vietnam War reading at Town Hall in New York City. During the 1960's Kinnell was an active presence at such readings. "Vapor Trail Reflected in the Frog Pond," which appeared in *Body Rags,* captures his virulent antiwar, and by extension anti-American, feelings at this time. In the poem, which some critics have described as a parody of Whitman's "I Hear America Singing," Kinnell listens to the "varied carols" America *now* sings; he hears the dissonance of

> crack of deputies' rifles practicing their aim
>   on stray dogs at night,
> sput of cattleprod,
> TV groaning at the smells of the human
>   body,
> curses of the soldier as he poisons, burns,
>   grinds, and stabs
> the rice of the world,
> with open mouth, crying strong, hysterical
>   curses.

Kinnell mirrors the dissonance of the "singing" in his seemingly arbitrary line lengths and in his convoluted syntax. While we might expect to see the soldier's tortured body language—"open mouth, crying strong, hysterical curses"—before his violent actions, Kinnell disorients us by delaying the description.

In 1965 Kinnell married Inés Delgado de Torres. A year later their daughter, Maud, was born and his novel, *Black Light,* was published. *Black Light,* which Kinnell describes as "closer to a fable than to a novel," grew out of the year he spent in Iran (1959) as a lecturer for six months at the University of Tehran and then as a journalist for an English-language edition of a Tehran newspaper. While working for the newspaper, he traveled around the country, "sometimes with friends who knew Iran very well, more often alone. . . ."

Black Light anticipates *Body Rags,* his third volume of poetry, in dealing with how exile can be empowering. The protagonist, a carpet mender named Jamshid, commits a murder; the circumstances surrounding this action lack a fundamental meaning or logic. We are asked instead to focus on the consequences of this action: Jamshid is forced to leave his village, to wander somewhat aimlessly, and to redefine his relations with others and his past. Paradoxically, he can begin to reconstruct his history only in the moment that he appears most cut off from it. By giving up the possibility of repairing or restoring the rug on which he has been working so that it will be whole again, he can begin to know the painful fragments—a vision of the dissonances—that constitute his life:

> He had spent all those years in Meshed weaving closed the gaps, as if he had thought that if you perfected a surface what it was laid upon no longer had to be reckoned with. Now that he had broken through the surface, it seemed he had no choice anymore but to die into the essential foulness of things.

It is no coincidence that two of the poets Kinnell translated—Villon (1965) and Yvan Goll (1970)—also experienced the feeling of being exiled and explored the implications of this state in their work. Villon, who was repeatedly arrested (for street fights and thefts), was finally banished from Paris for ten years. When asked in an interview with Mary Jane Fortunato about his translations of Villon, Kinnell maintained that "When you translate a poet, you invite or dare that poet to influence you. In my case I think one can see Bonnefoy in *Flower Herding* and possibly shades of Villon in *Body Rags.*"

Although Kinnell's interest in Goll's work looks forward to his own poetic vision in *The Book of Nightmares,* it also may be seen as integral to his aesthetic in *Body Rags,* where, like Goll, Kinnell moves steadily toward a recognition of "the permanence of his [own] solitude." Goll, whose French poems captivated Kinnell, left France during World War II and resided in New York City until after the war. In his preface to his translation of the *Lackawanna Elegy,* Kinnell links Goll's creative project to his state of feeling exiled: "The permanence of his solitude was the terrible discovery of his exile: knowing finally that he belonged nowhere. Out of this solitude he wrote this masterpiece, the grave and beautiful poems of the *Lackawanna Elegy.*"

Body Rags, Kinnell's third volume of poems, appeared in 1968, the year his son, Finn Fergus, was born. It moves away from the somewhat pastoral forays of *Flower Herding on Mount Monadnock* toward "the cold, savage thumpings of a heart" ("Going Home by Last Night") that knows the cost of spending "Another Night in the Ruins." As Richard Howard points out, " . . .life for Galway Kinnell [in *Body Rags*] becomes a matter of sacred vestiges, remnants, husks." In a state of perpetual exile—"terrified, seeking home, / and among flowers / I have come to myself empty" ("The Porcupine")—Kinnell tries to see what still remains, what is not lost, what can be recovered from the ruins. In "The Fossils," for example, his survey of prehistoric plant and animal life leads him to affirm: "Over the least fossil / day breaks in gold, frankincense, and myrrh." Kinnell learns in *Body Rags* what Frost's ovenbird "frames in all but words": "what to make of a diminished thing."

Body Rags is probably best known for Kinnell's concluding poems, "The Porcupine" and "The Bear." Many critics have pointed to the poet's need to identify with these animals. The identification is particularly acute in "The Bear": The poet eats a bear "turd sopped in blood," then climbs inside the dead bear's carcass:

> I hack
> a ravine in his thigh, and eat and drink,
> and tear him down his whole length
> and open him and climb in
> and close him up after me, against the wind,
> and sleep.

At this point in the poem, the poet's existence is likened to the bear's; like the bear he lumbers "flatfooted / over the tundra, / stabbed twice from within." And as he absorbs the "illdigested bear blood" and "the ordinary, wretched odor of bear," he is recalled, momentarily, to the possibility of hearing "a song / or screech, until I think I must rise up / and dance." But this poet's/bear's dance only enables him to wander, wonder, and question, knowing only the certainty of hunger and loneliness.

> And one
> hairy-soiled trudge stuck out before me,

the next groaned out,
the next,
the next,
the rest of my days I spend
wandering: wondering
what, anyway,
was that sticky infusion, that rank flavor of
blood, that
poetry, by which I lived?

The poet's dance and song have been replaced by "that rank flavor of blood." Associated with the pain of being wounded and hunted, poetry, or the project of writing—finding what will suffice—becomes that "sticky infusion," pulled out of his guts. This dream / descent prepares us for the nourishing nightmares in *The Book of Nightmares.*

Many of the best poems in *Body Rags,* particularly the short lyrics, focus on those moments in which the speaker gains knowledge that allows him to reimagine both his existence and his poetic project. In "Another Night in the Ruins" the poet remembers his brother, Derry, who "used to tell [him]":

"What good is the day?
On some hill of despair
the bonfire
you kindle can light the great sky—
though it's true, of course, to make it burn
you have to throw yourself in . . ."

By the end of the poem Kinnell finds a way to embrace these words, but first he must confront "the eaves of [his] ruins." He must know "the cow / of nothingness, mooing / down the bones" and the rooster who "thrashes in the snow / for a grain. Finds / it. Rips / it into / flames." Kinnell must become the rooster who "Flaps. Crows. / Flames/ bursting out of his brow" before he can give up the image of the phoenix:

How many nights must it take
one such as me to learn
that we aren't, after all, made
from that bird which flies out of its ashes,
that for a man
as he goes up in flames, his one work
is
to open himself, to *be*
the flames?

Richard Howard provides a useful frame for Kinnell's purification rite:

> The poetry of Galway Kinnell . . . is an Ordeal by Fire. It is fire which he invokes to set forth his plight, to enact his ordeal, and to restore himself to reality. It is fire—in its constant transformations, its endless resurrection—which *is* reality, for Kinnell as for Heraclitus. . . . The agony of that knowledge—the knowledge or at least the conviction that all must be consumed in order to be reborn, must be reduced to ash in order to be redeemed—gives Galway Kinnell's poetry its astonishing resonance. . . .

The notion of purification is reconfigured in different terms in "Lost Loves," in which Kinnell likens his existence, in the face of both "ashes of old volcanoes" and his body's "deathward flesh in the sun," to "the tadpole, his time come, tumbling toward the / slime."

In *Body Rags,* Kinnell repeatedly looks for ways of living without the phoenix. In "How Many Nights," for example, he finds peace in "the frozen world" from an unlikely source:

How many nights
have I lain in terror,
O Creator Spirit, Maker of night and day,

only to walk out
the next morning over the frozen world
hearing under the creaking of snow
faint, peaceful breaths . . .
snake,
bear, earthworm, ant . . .

and above me
a wild crow crying *'yaw yaw yaw'*
from a branch nothing cried from ever in
my life.

When asked about the crow in a 1969 interview with William Heyen and Gregory Fitz

Gerald, Kinnell responded with a poem that provides an interpretation of the last two lines of "How Many Nights":

> I know the line about that crow is puzzling. In fact, when the poem was first published, some friends telephoned me, to ask whether I'd thought of the crow as benign or as an unwelcome presence. I wrote this bit of verse to explicate those last lines. It's called "The Mind."
>
> Suppose it's true
> that from the beginning, a bird has been
>   perched
> in the silence of each branch.
>
> It is this to have lived—
> that when night comes, every one of them
> will have sung, or be singing.
>
> I was thinking of those diagrams—I still don't know if they are of the nervous system or of the blood vessels—that show the brain in the shape of a tree. At moments of full consciousness all the birds would be singing. Whether or not the crow's cry is beautiful mattered less to me than that this hitherto mute region comes into consciousness.

Kinnell might have settled for the "faint, peaceful breaths" of the hibernating creatures under the snow. Instead, in a moment reminiscent of Stevens' speaker in "Autumn Refrain," who hears "some skreaking and skrittering residuum" of grackles now gone, Kinnell looks up at a single wild crow, who cries "from a branch nothing cried from ever in my life." Like Stevens, Kinnell will never hear the nightingale. But, unlike Stevens, Kinnell finds nothing "desolate" in the sound of his wild crow. This crow does not change "the frozen world," but it does begin to affect Kinnell's inner landscape. The crow restores him, in a way that the "Creator-Spirit" cannot, to a part of his existence. This unexpected restoration is a kind of grace.

Kinnell's next volume of poetry, *The Book of Nightmares* (1971), is less concerned with such moments of earth-born grace. If possible, Kinnell's journey is still darker and more probing of those "mute region[s]" of the self/soul. The most ambitious and most successful of Kinnell's work to date, the poem took four years to write. "A lot of that time," Kinnell notes in a 1972 interview with James J. McKenzie, "I worked on it day after day." When asked about the genesis of the poem, Kinnell replied:

> I began it as a single ten-part sequence. I had been rather immersed in the *Duino Elegies.* In the Ninth Elegy, Rilke says, in effect, "Don't try to tell the angels about the glory of your feelings, or how splendid your soul is; they know all about that. Tell them something they'd be more interested in, something that you know better than they, tell them about the things of the world." So it came to me to write a poem called "The Things." Like the *Elegies* it would be a poem without plot, yet with a close relationship among the parts, and a development from beginning to end. . . . The poem has moved far from its original intention to be about things and now probably does try to tell the angels about the glory of my feelings!

In this long poem modeled upon Rilke's *Duino Elegies,* made up of ten sections of seven parts each, Kinnell confronts death's "two aspects—the extinction, which we fear, and the flowing away into the universe, which we desire. . . ." The epigraph from Rilke, which appears underneath the dedication to Kinnell's children, Maud and Fergus, further illuminates his emphasis on death in the poem:

>   But this, though: death,
> the whole of death,—even before life's
>   begun,
> to hold it also gently, and be good:
> this is beyond description!

In the 1972 interview with Dodd and Plumly, Kinnell provides a useful commentary on the relationship between the epigraph and the dedication, one that serves to illuminate the poem's concerns as a whole:

This passage appears after the dedication to Maud and Fergus. From one point of view, the book is nothing but an effort to face death and live with death. Children have all that effort in their future. They have glimpses of death through fatigue, sleep, cuts and bruises, warnings, etc., and also through their memory of the nonexistence they so recently came from. They seem to understand death surprisingly clearly. But now time passes slowly for them. It hardly exists. They live with death almost as animals do. This natural trust in life's rhythms, infantile as it is, provides the model for the trust they may struggle to learn later on. *The Book of Nightmares* is my own effort to find the trust again. I invoke Maud and Fergus not merely to instruct them, but also to get help from them.

In the first section of the poem, "Under the Maud Moon," Kinnell's description of the birth process as a cutting of Maud's "tie to the darkness" magnificently captures how close children are to death—to the memory of "the nonexistence they so recently came from."

> . . . And as they cut
>
> her tie to the darkness
> she dies
> a moment, turns blue as a coal,
> the limbs shaking
> as the memories rush out of them. . . .

At the end of this section Kinnell looks toward a future that no longer includes his protective presence and hopes that his book of nightmares, drawing "from everything that dies," will comfort his daughter, who thus far is more familiar with the darkness from which she came:

> And in the days
> when you find yourself orphaned,
> emptied
> of all wind-singing, of light,
> the pieces of cursed bread on your tongue,
>
> may there come back to you
> a voice
> spectral, calling you
> *sister*!
> from everything that dies.
>
> And then
> you shall open
> this book, even if it is the book of
> nightmares.

Kinnell also draws inspiration from Maud in section VII—"Little Sleep's-Head Sprouting Hair in the Moonlight"—when he makes a list of things he might do to protect her from the finality of death that he embraces.

> I would blow the flame out of your silver
> cup,
> I would suck the rot from your fingernail,
> I would brush your sprouting hair of the
> dying light,
> I would scrape the rust off your ivory bones,
> I would help death escape through the little
> ribs of your body,
> I would alchemize the ashes of your cradle
> back into wood,
> I would let nothing of you go, ever. . . .

Later in the same section he encourages Maud to see the relationship between "enduring love" and "the still undanced cadence of vanishing." When she is most sure of the permanence of love, she will "learn to reach deeper / into the sorrows / to come. . . ."

If Kinnell is instructing Maud, and later Fergus, he is also preparing himself for "the mercy of darkness" and "the sorrows / to come." In section II, "The Hen Flower," he thinks in a moment of almost mystical union:

> . . .—if only
> we could let go
> like her, throw ourselves
> on the mercy of darkness, like the hen,
>
> tuck our head
> under a wing, hold ourselves still
> a few moments, as she
> falls out into her little trance in the
> witchgrass,
> or turn over
> and be stroked with a finger
> . . .

. . . until the fatted thing
woozes off, head
thrown back
on the chopping block, longing only
to die.

In a 1976 interview with Margaret Edwards, Kinnell comments on his "fascination with hens." Explaining that his family had "had a henhouse" when he was growing up, he remarked:

> Though not very personable, hens have an unusual psychic dimension, due, I like to think, to the suppression of their capacity to fly. When you hold their heads under their wings they slump into a strange coma. You might think they think it is the night, except that they do the same thing if you turn them on their backs and stroke their throats.

In "The Hen Flower" Kinnell seems to identify with "the suppression of their capacity to fly": "—and unable / to fly, / land waiting, therefore, / for the sweet, eventual blaze in the genes, / that one day, according to gospel, shall carry [them] back / into pink skies. . . ." He also waits for a future in which he might "let go." Yet the only certainty he has for now is that "these feathers freed from their wings forever / are afraid."

In section III, "The Shoes of Wandering," Kinnell wonders if our wandering "is the last trace in us / of wings?" He returns to the hen who cannot fly:

And is it
the hen's nightmare, or her secret dream,
to scratch the ground forever
eating the minutes out of the grains of sand?

Kinnell desires the certainty of "the great wanderers, who lighted / their steps by the lamp / of pure hunger and pure thirst," but must settle instead for "the Crone's" words:

You live
under the Sign
of the Bear, who flounders through chaos
in his starry blubber:
poor fool,
poor forked branch
of applewood, you will feel all your bones
break
over the holy waters you will never drink.

In the final section of the poem, "Lastness," Kinnell makes his peace with his journey toward his own death. In the first section, he had lit "a small fire in the rain." This fire is now "somewhere behind me":

Somewhere behind me
a small fire goes on flaring in the rain, in
the desolate ashes.
No matter, now, whom it was built for,
it keeps its flames,
it warms
everyone who might wander into its
radiance,
a tree, a lost animal, the stones,

because in the dying world it was set
burning.

As in section I, Kinnell is still the black bear sitting alone; this time, however, the image leads him to imagine his own death:

. . . a death-creature
watches from the fringe of the trees,
finally he understands
I am no longer here, he himself
from the fringe of the trees watches
a black bear
get up, eat a few flowers, trudge away,
all his fur glistening
in the rain.

This image of the bear frames Maud's birth in section I; in "Lastness" it frames Fergus' birth. The mother and maternal nurturing are curiously absent in both sections of the poem. Kinnell puts the spotlight on himself as father and receiver of life.

When he [Fergus] came wholly forth
I took him up in my hands and bent
over and smelled
the black, glistening fur
of his head, as empty space

must have bent
over the newborn planet
and smelled the grasslands and the ferns.

We next see the poet "walking toward the cliff. . . ." From this vantage point he calls out to "the stone," which "calls back, its voice hunting among the rubble / for my ears." Conjuring up his echo / presence leads him to imagine his death / absence—a world "where the voice calling from stone / no longer answers, / turns into stone, and nothing comes back." Kinnell finds himself back in "the old shoes / flowed over by rainbows of hen-oil," "the whole foot trying / to dissolve into the future." And he asks an old question: "Is it true / the earth is all there is, and the earth does not last?" The answer is implicit in the end-stopped lines, which strive for a sense of closure in a poem that usually denies such a possibility: "Stop. / Stop here. / Living brings you to death, there is no other road." As Robert Langbaum perceptively points out: "Stated so baldly, these seem rather banal observations." The lines are certainly anticlimactic, if not banal, at this point in the poem, though the case could be made that they are the unsaid chant underlying each section of the poem.

Finally the poem celebrates the poet's struggle to make the "earthward gesture" while still trying to be "the sky-diver"—to be the hen who has forgotten what it might mean to fly:

This poem
if we shall call it that,
or concert of one
divided among himself,
this earthward gesture
of the sky-diver, the worms
on his back still spinning forth
and already gnawing away
the silks of his loves, who could have saved
 him,
this free floating of one
opening his arms into the attitude
of flight, as he obeys the necessity and
 falls. . . .

If the poem had ended here, it might seem like the last poem Kinnell would need to write; it ends, however, with some rather flip advice for his son.

On the body,
On the blued flesh, when it is
laid out, see if you can find
the one flea which is laughing.

The stark image of the "blued flesh" is muted, or undermined, by the image of one flea laughing. We might, more appropriately, have been given an image of the ghastly "flesh-fly," "starved for the soul," from Kinnell's poem "The Fly," which appeared in *Body Rags.*

Kinnell's next volume of poetry, *Mortal Acts, Mortal Words,* did not appear until 1980. In 1977 his revised version of *The Poems of François Villon* was published. In 1979 he received the Harold L. Landon Translation Prize. In the fall of 1978 he held a Fulbright lectureship in France at the University of Nice. That same year, *Walking Down the Stairs: Selections from Interviews* was published, providing his readers with new insights into his aesthetic. In 1979 Kinnell was a visiting writer in Sydney, Australia, at MacQuarie University. He spent the next two years teaching in Hawaii; in 1980, the year *Mortal Acts* was published, Kinnell returned to New York briefly to visit James Wright, who was dying of lung cancer. Anne Wright describes their last meeting:

> Galway came straight from the airport to the hospital. As soon as he saw James he leaned over his bed and hugged him, tubes and all. James couldn't talk but he wrote notes to Galway on a yellow-lined pad. During that visit James was alert, a little bit stronger, well aware his friend was there.
>
> Galway returned in March. When he came to the hospital I had a photocopy of James's manuscript, *This Journey,* for him. Galway had always gone over manuscripts with James and, sick as he was, James urged me to have his latest one ready for Galway.

In "A Winter Daybreak at Vence," the poem Kinnell suggested should complete *This Jour-*

ney, Wright remembers the time he and Anne spent with the Kinnells in southern France:

> I turn, and somehow
> Impossibly hovering in the air over
> everything,
> The Mediterranean, nearer to the moon
> Than this mountain is,
> Shines. A voice clearly
> Tells me to snap out of it. Galway
> Mutters out of the house and up the stone
> stairs
> To start the motor. The moon and the stars
> Suddenly flicker out, and the whole
> mountain
> Appears, pale as a shell.

In *Mortal Acts,* Kinnell turns away from the dark nightmares of *The Book of Nightmares* and *Body Rags* toward "the singing / of mortal lives, waves of spent existence" ("There Are Things I Tell to No One"). He renews his belief that song can heal: "for those who can groan / to sing, / for those who can sing to heal themselves" ("The Still Time"). He explores, as he had in previous volumes, the inexorable relationship between eros and loss, as the following lines from "The Apple" illustrate:

> No one easily
> survives love; neither the love
> one has, nor the love
> one has not; each breaks down
> in the red smoke blown up
> of the day when all love will have gone on.

Kinnell has not traveled very far from the sentiment expressed in his early poem "The Feast": "If love had not smiled we would never grieve." Nevertheless, there is a kind of faith, absent from his early poems, that he can make the journey "from night / into day, from transcending union always forward into difficult day" ("Flying Home").

Mortal Acts includes some delightfully self-contained lyrics, particularly in Part II, where we find "Daybreak," "The Gray Heron," and "Blackberry Eating." These poems celebrate in uncomplicated ways the things and creatures of the earth. In "Daybreak," Kinnell likens "dozens of starfishes" to "enormous, imperfect stars." As the starfishes sink into the mud, they become invisible, like "the true stars at daybreak." Kinnell sustains his simile without reaching after anything grander than his analogy. In "The Gray Heron" he watches a heron that moves out of sight; he then encounters a three-foot-long lizard whose head reminds him of "a fieldstone with an eye / in it." Still watching, he suddenly realizes he is being watched. The shift in perspective is highlighted by the final lines, in which the possibility emerges that in being watched, he may change shape or evolve into some other form of life: the lizard "was watching me / to see if I would go / or change into something else." And in "Blackberry Eating" finding language to describe the blackberries is as sensuous as the process of devouring the berries:

> lifting the stalks to my mouth, the ripest
> berries
> fall almost unbidden to my tongue,
> as words sometimes do, certain peculiar
> words
> like *strengths* or
> *squinched,*
> many-lettered, one-syllabled lumps,
> which I squeeze, squinch open, and splurge
> well
> in the silent, startled, icy, black language
> of blackberry-eating in late September.

For Kinnell grace comes in moments like this when he finds "certain peculiar words" with which to embrace the things of this world.

Mortal Acts is the most autobiographical of Kinnell's works. In "Wait," Kinnell asserts that "the need / for the new love *is* faithfulness to the old." He might have said that going forward requires turning back to the past, to remembering, to reconstructing, to making new stories out of the old. "Distrust everything if you have to. / But trust the hours. Haven't they / carried you everywhere, up to now?" "Time," as Zimmerman points out, is a "palpable presence" in this volume: "Kinnell's efforts 'to reach a new place' in his poetry . . . repeatedly lead, in *Mortal Acts,* to the old places, to the subject and substance of memory."

Perhaps in homage to the final section of *The Book of Nightmares, Mortal Acts* begins appropriately with a poem about Fergus' need "to get out of the shadow" "of this father"; such a perspective leads naturally to his "fall" toward "the blued flesh." Sitting on a branch of a white pine, Fergus sees Bruce Pond in the distance for the first time; "its oldness" and "its old place in the valley" make him feel "heavier suddenly / in his bones / the way fledglings do just before they fly." At this point the branch cracks, Fergus falls, and the poet hears his cry "as though he [Fergus] were attacked." "His face went gray, his eyes fluttered closed a frightening moment. . . ." The pond initiates Fergus into a world where things and people are "gone." Kinnell may also be drawing on the Celtic myth of Fergus, who, in Yeats's poem "Fergus and the Druid," wants to abandon his kingdom for "the dreaming wisdom that is" the Druid's. In this sense Fergus' fall in Kinnell's poem may be a movement away from the possibilities afforded by poetic language or by dreaming.

Kinnell's need to witness his son's fall, reminiscent of his need to attend to people, particularly family members, who are gone, requires a different vision of how the past impinges on the present than that found in *The Book of Nightmares.* Kinnell in a sense gives up "the dreaming wisdom" of his previous volume.

In Part III of *Mortal Acts,* Kinnell writes about his family, finding a language to stress both the connections he feels with them and those he missed. In "52 Oswald Street," he announces that life is "unrepeatable." He also positions himself in the family as one of three "who have survived the lives / and deaths in the old house / on Oswald Street. . . ." Placing himself in the family configuration, rather than beside it, he hopes to find a language to talk about "bodies of mother and father / and three children, and a fourth, / sleeping, quite long ago."

Kinnell's brother, Derry, who appears in Kinnell's poems "Freedom, New Hampshire" and "Another Night in the Ruins," is the initial focus of "The Sadness of Brothers," the first poem in Part III of *Mortal Acts.* In Part 1 of the poem, Kinnell starts from the premise that he can no longer call Derry up from the depths of memory:

> He comes to me like a mouth
> speaking from under several inches of water.
> I can no longer understand what he is
> saying.
> He has become one
> who never belonged among us, someone
> it is useless to think about or remember.

Then suddenly, "this morning," "twenty-one years too late," he begins to recover his brother; the recovery is about repositioning himself in relation to his brother. He imagines an exchange with his brother and finds that the reaching backward to him is a way of reaching forward:

> But this morning, I don't know why,
> twenty-one years too late,
> I imagine him back: his beauty
> of feature wastreled down
> to chin and wattles, his eyes
> ratty, liver-lighted, he stands
> at the door, and we face each other, each of
> us
> suddenly knowing the lost brother.

In Part 2, Kinnell alludes to his brother's dream of being a pilot—a dream he held "until pilot training, 1943, / when original fear / washed out / all the flyingness in him. . . ." Unmoored from himself, Derry wanders:

> a man who only wandered
> from then on; on roads
> which ended twelve years later
> in Wyoming, when he raced his big car
> through the desert night, under
> the Dipper
> or Great Windshield Wiper
> which, turning, squeegee-ed existence every
> where,

even in Wyoming, of its damaged dream
life. . . .

Derry's wandering gives Kinnell access, in Part 3 of the poem, to their father, who also was "well-wandered." A connection between brothers leads to a web of familial connections and divisions.

Finally, in Part 5 Kinnell returns to his brother, imagining an embrace between them now—in the present:

We embrace in the doorway,
in the frailty of large,
fifty-odd-year-old bodies
of brothers only one of whom has imagined
those we love, who go away,
among them this brother . . ..

Conjuring up his brother here, in the present, allows the poet to return to "the memory that came to me this day / of a man twenty-one years strange to me." But this gap is not divisive; rather, it is binding: "we hold each other, friends to reality, / knowing the ordinary sadness of brothers." The adjective "ordinary" is important; for Kinnell "ordinary sadness" is a luxury because it is "commonplace" and "normal" and occurs in the daylight of today. In contrast, at the beginning of the poem his sadness was subterranean, hard to see, and thus his brother was "one / who never belonged among us."

In "The Last Hiding Places of Snow," Kinnell attempts to recover some "ordinary sadness" about not being with his mother when she died. "I was not at her bedside / that final day, I did not grant her ancient, / huge-knuckled hand / its last wish. . . ." Calling up her love—"its light / like sunlight"—Kinnell feels his mother has empowered him to "wander anywhere, / among any foulnesses, any contagions." Yet what follows is a curiously disturbing and threatening image of his mother as a devourer/destroyer:

My mother did not want me to be born;
afterwards, all her life, she needed me to
return.
When this more-than-love flowed toward
me, it brought darkness;
she wanted me as burial earth wants—to
heap itself gently upon but also to
annihilate—
and I knew, whenever I felt longings to go
back,
that is what wanting to die is. That is why

dread lives in me,
dread which comes when what gives life
beckons toward death,
dread which throws through me
waves
of utter strangeness, which wash the entire
world empty.

This passage in the poem might remind us of Maud's birth—her cutting of "the tie to darkness"—in *The Book of Nightmares,* though Kinnell does not in that instance invoke the presence of her mother as an active agent in the birth process. Here, in contrast, the image of Kinnell's "tie to the darkness" is swallowed up by the image of his mother, who rapaciously wills his return to the womb, an image more than a little offensive. As Lorrie Goldensohn points out:

In this stance, Kinnell is not Antaeus, deriving strength from a reaffirmation of the ground of earth which is his being. While the lines depend on a basic identification of woman as earthmother, they also follow the traditional misogynist conflation of womb/tomb, where the chthonic female is not muse; but instead the fixedly mortal part: the dread mother who in giving life beckons toward death.

Kinnell avoids confronting his own missed past connection with his mother by focusing instead on a future link he might have with his own children:

I would know myself lucky if my own
children
could be at my deathbed, to take
my hand in theirs and with theirs
to bless me back into the world as I leave,
with smoothness pressed into roughness. . . .

By imagining this bond with his own children, he can look back again—this time with a renewed sense of his complicated relation to his mother:

> in an imaginary daybreak, I see her,
> and for that moment I am still her son
> and I am in the holy land
> and twice in the holy land, remembered
> within her, and remembered in the memory
> her old body slowly executes into the earth.

These lines are as close as Kinnell can come to expressing "ordinary sadness" about his mother, a sadness safely placed in the burial ground and consumed by the earth.

Kinnell's *Selected Poems* (1982) contains a generous selection of pieces from all six of his previous collections, spanning his career from 1946 to 1980, when *Mortal Acts, Mortal Words* appeared. *Selected Poems* gives us insights into Kinnell's evolution as a poet; while some of his early derivative poems seem haunted by the influences of Yeats, Roethke, or Frost, the poems from *Body Rags* and *The Book of Nightmares* pay homage to the influences of Villon, Whitman, and Rilke in ways that heighten Kinnell's distinctive and individual poetic voice. Gathering these poems together takes a certain courage and conviction about one's project over time. As Liz Rosenberg notes in a review of *Selected Poems*: "These early poems indicate influences that a poet is later smart enough to hide, or outgrow." Kinnell chooses to show his readers something about the process of outgrowing these influences.

The year *Selected Poems* appeared, Kinnell published a children's book, *How the Alligator Missed Breakfast.* Nancy Tuten maintains that while the book "was written to entertain children, it reflects themes common to Kinnell's other works. For example, when the animal characters . . . endeavor to be something they are not, by nature, meant to be, Kinnell alludes to his disgust with twentieth-century technological man's false sense of dominion over nature."

In 1982 Kinnell helped organize an antinuclear reading, "Poets Against the End of the World," at Town Hall in New York City. His poem "The Fundamental Project of Technology," which appeared in *The Past* (1985), probably dates from this time. Beginning with a reference to the bombing of Hiroshima and Nagasaki in 1945—"A flash! A white flash sparkled!"—Kinnell takes us inside the Nagasaki museum:

> Under glass: glass dishes which changed
> in color; pieces of transformed beer bottles;
> a household iron; bundles of wire become
>   solid
> lumps of iron; a pair of pliers; a ring of
>   skullbone
> fused to the inside of a helmet; a pair of
>   eyeglasses
> taken off the eyes of an eyewitness, without
>   glass,
> which vanished, when a white flash
>   sparkled.

But such a repository for the visible signs of destruction is no safeguard against future annihilation. Each stanza ends with an image of "a white flash," as if the dropping of the atomic bomb is bound to be repeated. And the poem itself ends on an apocalyptic note; archives, museums, and guardians of "history" are a thing of the past: "no one lives / to look back and say, a flash, a white flash sparkled."

In 1985 Kinnell and his wife, Inés, divorced and Kinnell took a permanent position on the faculty of New York University. In a 1990 interview with Lois Smith Brady, Kinnell mused that "Marriage is like throwing yourself out of an airplane. . . . There's something irrevocable about it. You just sail on forever. You can't say let's stop, as you can in most things. Even after you get divorced, it's irrevocable."

The Past (1985), a collection of new poems written between 1980 and 1985, is a disappointment. There is a falling off of energy, an exhaustion and weariness; old concerns seem old. For the first time Kinnell does not find a way formally or thematically to energize the familiar insights of previous poems. "The

Road Between Here and There," for example, employs a Whitmanesque catalog to arrive at some links between "here"—this place—and the past events in the landscape. The place has not changed—a slightly romantic posture in the late twentieth century—but the poet has. There is something self-indulgent and monotonous about the list of past activities and the prosaic, endstopped lines:

> Here I abandoned the car because of a clonk
> in the motor and hitchhiked (which in
> those days in Vermont meant walking the
> whole way with a limp) all the way to a
> garage where I passed the afternoon with
> exloggers who had stopped by to oil the
> joints of their artificial limbs.

As in previous work, Kinnell looks back at himself and his family in two of the poems, but "The Man Splitting Wood in the Daybreak" and "The Frog Pond" are not in any sense autobiographical. They are not about Kinnell's desire to recover a story—untold or told—about his connection to his wife or his children. Rather, in both poems, place is the anchor. In "The Frog Pond," for example, Kinnell describes his particular relation to the pond: "In those first years I came down / often to the frog pond." Then "the frog pond became the beaver pond"; "A few years after I got here, the beavers came." When the family is introduced—"the four / of us would oar, pole, and bale out"—the poet becomes a man sitting on the bank who watches the four people in the boat. The family becomes every family: "the man seems happy, / the two children laugh and splash, / a slight shadow crosses the woman's face." Suddenly, we shift from the past to a future in which Kinnell imagines himself alone—though he is still "the man"—without his children and with "true love broken." The only constant here is his memory of the pond:

> The man who lies propped up
> on an elbow, scribbling in a notebook
> or loafing and thinking, will be older
> and will remember this place held a pond
> once,
> writhing with leeches and overflown
> by the straight blue bodies of dragonflies,
> and will think of smallest children
> grown up and of true love broken
> and will sit up abruptly and swat
> the hard-biting deer fly on his head,
> crushing it into his hair, as he has done
> before.

Although Kinnell seems to be saying, "So you see, / to reach the past is easy. A snap" ("The Past"), the past is most accessible in the moments when Kinnell lives at a distance from himself. This signals a departure from his earlier poems. In "The Past" Kinnell wants to be in "the ordinary day the ordinary world / providentially provides" ("The Waking"), but he seems to have lost his way.

Looking back at *Mortal Acts, Mortal Words* and *The Past,* we see a poet who has moved away from the emotional expenditures, the lyric grace, and the search for a mythology that we find in *Body Rags* and *The Book of Nightmares.* Nevertheless, Kinnell continues to be a poet whose vision and risks matter. As his new poems appear, they will be read with care; his ear and eye will be measured against both his past accomplishments and his future writings. Few contemporary American poets are guaranteed this attention, for, as Harold Bloom maintains, Kinnell is "a poet who cannot be dismissed, because he seems destined still to accomplish the auguries of his grand beginnings."

Selected Bibliography

WORKS OF GALWAY KINNELL

POETRY

What a Kingdom It Was, (Boston: Houghton Mifflin, 1960).

Flower Herding on Mount Monadnock, (Boston: Houghton Mifflin, 1964).

Body Rags, (Boston: Houghton Mifflin, 1968).

First Poems 1946–1954, (Mt. Horeb, Wis.: Perishable Press, 1970).

The Book of Nightmares, (Boston: Houghton Mifflin, 1971).

The Avenue Bearing the Initial of Christ into the New World: Poems 1946–1964, (Boston: Houghton Mifflin, 1974).

Mortal Acts, Mortal Words, (Boston: Houghton Mifflin, 1980).

Selected Poems, Boston (Houghton Mifflin) (1982).

The Past, (Boston: Houghton Mifflin, 1985).

TRANSLATIONS

Bitter Victory, by Rene Hardy (Garden City, N.Y.: Doubleday, 1956) Novel.

The Poems of François Villon, (New York: New American Library, 1965) Rev. ed. (Boston: Houghton Mifflin, 1977).

On the Motion and Immobility of Douve, by Yves Bonnefoy (Athens: Ohio University Press, 1968). Poems.

Lackawanna Elegy, by Yvan Goll. (Fremont, Mich.: Sumac, 1970). Poems

PROSE

"Only Meaning Is Truly Interesting," *Beloit Poetry Journal* 4: 1–3, (Fall 1953).

Black Light, (Boston: Houghton Mifflin, 1966) Rev. ed. (San Francisco: North Point, 1980) Novel;

"The Poetics of the Physical World," (*Iowa Review* 2: 113–126, Summer 1971).

"Poetry, Personality, and Death," (*Field* no. 4: 56–77, Spring 1971).

"Whitman's Indicative Words," (*American Poetry Review* 2: 9–11, March/April 1973).

Walking Down the Stairs: Selections from Interviews, (Ann Arbor: University of Michigan Press, 1978).All of the interviews quoted in this essay are collected in this volume.

How the Alligator Missed Breakfast, (Boston: Houghton Mifflin, 1982). Children's book.

Introduction to *The Essential Whitman,* (New York: Ecco, 1987).

BIBLIOGRAPHY

Galway Kinnell: A Bibliography and Index of His Published Works and Criticism of Them, (Potsdam, N.Y.: State University College, 1968).

BIOGRAPHICAL AND CRITICAL STUDIES

Altieri, Charles, *Self and Sensibility in Contemporary American Poetry,* (New York: Cambridge University Press, 1984).

Bell, Charles G., "Galway Kinnell," *Contemporary Poets* 3rd ed., edited by James Vinson (New York: St. Martin's, 1980) 835–837.

Bloom, Harold, "Straight Forth out of Self: *Mortal Acts, Mortal Words,*" (*New York Times Book Review,* June 22 1980) p. 13

Brady, Lois Smith, "Poet About Town," (*New York Woman,* April 1990) 98–100

Davie, Donald, "Slogging for the Absolute," (*Parnassus* 3: 9–22, Fall/Winter 1974).

Dickey, James, *Babel to Byzantium: Poets and Poetry Now,* (New York: Farrar, Straus & Giroux, 1961, 1968; New York: Ecco, 1981).

Dickstein, Morris, "Intact and Triumphant," (*New York Times Book Review,* September 19 1982) 12, 33 Review of *Selected Poems;*

Gallagher, Tess, "The Poem as a Reservoir for Grief," *American Poetry Review* 13: 7–11, (July/August 1984).

Goldensohn, Lorrie, "Approaching Home Ground: Galway Kinnell's *Mortal Acts, Mortal Words.*" (*Massachusetts Review* 25: 303–321, (Summer 1984).

Guimond, James, *Seeing and Healing: The Poetry of Galway Kinnell,* (Port Washington, N.Y.: Associated Faculty Press, 1986).

Hall, Donald, "A Luminous Receptiveness," (*Nation* 213: 377–378, October 18 1971) Review of *The Book of Nightmares*

Hall, Donald, "Text as Test: Notes on and Around Carruth and Kinnell," (*American Poetry Review* 12:27–32, November/December 1983).

Helms, Alan, "Two Poets," (*Partisan Review* 44, no. 2: 284–293, 1977). Review of *The Avenue Bearing the Initials of Christ* and *Book of Nightmares* pp. 288–293.

Howard, Richard, *Alone with America: Essays on the Art of Poetry Since 1950,* (New York: Atheneum, 1969).

Howard, Richard, "Changes," *Partisan Review* 38: 484–490, (Winter 1971–1972).

Langbaum, Robert, "Galway Kinnell's *The Book of Nightmares,*" *American Poetry Review* 8: 30–31, (March/April 1979).

Mariani, Paul, "Kinnell's Legacy On 'The Avenue Bearing the Initial of Christ into the New World.' In " *On the Poetry of Galway Kinnell: The Wages of Dying* Edited by Howard Nelson (Ann Arbor: University of Michigan Press, 1987).

Molesworth, Charles, *The Fierce Embrace: A Study of Contemporary American Poetry,* (Columbia: University of Missouri Press, 1979).

Nelson, Cary, *Our Last First Poets: Vision and History in Contemporary American Poetry,* (Urbana: University of Illinois Press, 1981).

Nelson, Howard, ed. (*On the Poetry of Galway Kinnell: The Wages of Dying,* (Ann Arbor: University of Michigan Press, 1987).

Perloff, Marjorie, "Poetry Chronicle: 1970–71," *Contemporary Literature* 14: 97–131, (Winter 1973) Review of *Nightmares* pp. 123–125.

Ricks, Christopher, "In the Direct Line of Whitman the Indirect Line of Eliot," (*New York Times Book Review,* January 12 1975) p. 2.

Rosenberg, Liz, "A Poet with the Flame of Greatness," (*Philadelphia Inquirer,* February 13 1983) p. R-06 Review of *Selected Poems.*

Tuten, Nancy Lewis, "Galway Kinnell," *Dictionary of Literary Biography Yearbook 1987* pp. 257–264 (Detroit, Mich.: Gale Research, 1987).

Weston, Susan B., "Kinnell's *Walking Down the Stairs,*" *Iowa Review* 10, no. 1: 95–98, (1979).

Williamson, Alan, *Introspection and Contemporary Poetry,* (Cambridge, Mass.: Harvard University Press, 1984).

Wright, Anne, "Sitting on Top of the Sunlight," In *On the Poetry of Galway Kinnell: The Wages of Dying.* Edited by Howard Nelson (Ann Arbor: University of Michigan Press, 1987).

Yenser, Stephen, "Recent Poetry: Five Poets," *Yale Review* 70: 105–128, Autumn (1980) Review of *Mortal Acts, Mortal Words, pp.* 123–128.

Zimmerman, Lee. *Intricate and Simple Things: The Poetry of Galway Kinnell.* Urbana: University of Illinois Press, 1987.

MAXINE KUMIN
(b. 1925)

STEVEN A. NARDI

BECAUSE OF HER preference for traditional verse forms and New England settings, Maxine Kumin is frequently compared with Robert Frost. Attempts to label her a "transcendentalist," in the tradition of Thoreau and Emerson, also have been advanced. Although she has never declined the characterization, and has even called the comparison with Frost a "high compliment," there is much in her poetry that must be accounted for by comparing her with her more apparently "confessional" contemporaries—Robert Lowell, Anne Sexton, Sylvia Plath—rather than stressing a simple allegiance to New England predecessors. Alicia Ostriker situates Kumin midway between the contrasting styles of Elizabeth Bishop on the one hand, and Anne Sexton and Sylvia Plath on the other. Like Bishop, Kumin spends much energy on detail. Like Sexton and Plath, however, she writes poetry that frequently appeals and refers to the personal. Likewise, her adherence to traditional literary forms is not simply an attempt to position herself within the traditions of the past. In Kumin's view, this allegiance to form is poetically liberating, allowing her to work with the more personal material of the confessional poets. Asked by Martha Meek if she uses any particular forms for more intimate material, Kumin replied, "I generally choose something complex and difficult. The tougher the form the easier it is for me to handle the poem, because the form gives permission to be very gut-honest about feelings." Kumin was born into a middle-class world that destined women for home and family life. Against the expectations of her times, she blossomed into a novelist and a Pulitzer Prize—winning poet. As a result of her background, although she often remains within a New England tradition of poetry about nature, she presses against the limitations of that tradition, and introduces into it new themes and perspectives particular to her experience.

For much of her best work, Kumin has exploited the genre of elegy. She told Karla Hammond that she believes "very strongly that poetry is essentially elegiac in its nature, and that all poems are in one sense or another elegies." "Love poems, particularly," she told Hammond, "are elegies, because if we were not informed with a sense of dying we wouldn't be moved to write love poems." Although some of her best poetry takes the loss of family, friends, and the natural world as its subject, Kumin has never been strictly a poet of pessimism. Her work holds to an ironic style, and answers the difficulty and pain of the world with the quiet humor and strength of the born survivor too frequently to be dismissed as a poetry solely about loss. Kumin told Shelley Armitage, "I like to combine grotesqueness and humor. I think they go together. They are very subtle and unexpected, and they keep colliding. That's the saving thing. To be able at least to smile, if not laugh. It's a way of putting up with the world. A way of enduring. Certainly not controlling it, but a way of saving yourself."

Born Maxine Winokur in the Germantown section of Philadelphia, on June 6, 1925, Kumin was the youngest of the four children of Doll Simon and Peter Winokur, and the only daughter. She hiked and explored the wooded areas around her parents' suburban home. Recollecting these preadolescent days in an interview with Jo-Ann Mapson, she remembered them as "simple and pleasurable." At age eleven she spent a summer on a dairy farm, and later worked as a camp counselor. In contrast to this idyllic childhood, Kumin's adolescence was difficult and stormy. She told Mapson, "I now think looking back on those otherwise gloomy years that the expectation of July–August in the Berkshires of Massachusetts saved my soul."

After graduating from Radcliffe with an A.B. in 1946, Kumin returned to take an M.A. in history and literature in 1948. She was exposed there to existentialism, and read W. H. Auden, Stephen Spender, Louis MacNeice, and Randall Jarrell. In 1946, she married Victor Kumin, an engineering consultant. Over the next few years they had three children. In retrospect, she would see the time as one of unfocused dissatisfaction. She later described herself and her friend Anne Sexton, as they were when they met in 1957, as "two shy housewives, a pair of closet poets." Poetry became for Kumin an outlet for energy that eluded the confines of the life expected of the postwar American woman—to get a college degree, get married, raise a family. She told Martha Meek, "I came to poetry as a way of saving myself because I was so wretchedly discontented, and I felt so guilty about being discontented. It just wasn't enough to be a housewife and a mother."

By 1953 Kumin had begun publishing what she would later call "comic" or "light" verse in the glossy magazines, and making money at it. "I made a pact with myself," she told Elaine Showalter, "that if I didn't sell anything by the time this child [her third] was born, I would chuck all my creative discontents. And in about my eighth month I started really landing with little four-liners, there, here and everywhere. *Saturday Evening Post* and *Cosmopolitan,* and so on." The avenues for women's poetry, however, were few. In *To Make a Prairie,* she recounts an anecdote that must have been typical of the times: an editor of a national magazine responded to her submission by sending his regrets that he couldn't publish anything of hers for six months or so because the magazine had published a woman poet the previous month.

It was against this background that in 1957 Kumin decided to take a poetry workshop at the Boston Center for Adult Education. This was to be a major turning point in the life and career of the poet. The professor, John Holmes, was a figure in the Boston literary circles of the time, reviewing and writing books of poetry and serving as the president of the New England Poetry Club. He was friends with many of the leading poets of the day and a devoted teacher. When Kumin entered Holmes's class, with what she later would call "great fear and trembling," she began the trajectory that would make her one of the leading poets of the day. The workshop would go on for three years. Holmes's influence was crucial in advancing Kumin's career. He secured her a job teaching composition at Tufts University and helped get her work published. Through the workshop and John Holmes, Kumin met fellow poets and prominent figures in contemporary poetry. Among these were George Starbuck, to whom she would later send manuscripts for comment; the poet and scholar Theodore Weiss; and, most important, Anne Sexton, with whom Kumin rapidly became what she would call after Sexton's death "intimate friends and professional allies." While Sexton would later complain bitterly about John Holmes, Kumin has expressed a high opinion of him. She later said of that group, "We were all writing frantically in response to each other. It was wonderful and terrible all at once. It was a very yeasty and exciting time." John Holmes's best poems, Kumin told Martha Meek, were those he wrote in the company of the workshop. At Sexton's funeral, Kumin chose to recall the days of the workshop, and the eagerness with which the budding poets "prayed that our poems would rise to the top of the pile under

Professor Holmes's fingers as he alternately fussed with his pipe and shuffled pages."

At first the friendship between Kumin and Sexton must have seemed unlikely. In later descriptions of their first meetings, Sexton appears as the well-dressed sophisticate, and Kumin as something of the dowdy housewife. In a conversation with both poets recorded by Elaine Showalter in 1974, Sexton recalls Kumin's appearance as "the most frump of the frumps," and Kumin recalls Sexton as "a little flower child . . . the ex-fashion model." Because Kumin had recently lost a friend to suicide, she was initially "put off by Sexton's self-dramatizing references to the mental hospital." Nevertheless, their relationship grew increasingly close and productive. According to Kumin's account of it, their telephone conversations became so frequent that each installed a second phone line in order to speak privately and at leisure.

The strain of being a housewife as well as a poet is very evident in these early years of their relationship. Sexton recounts being on the telephone, at the time of the Holmes workshop, and having to quiet her children so that she could hear Kumin read her poems. Because the children were so small, the poets could not leave them alone; therefore they relied upon the telephone to revise poems together. Kumin describes it in *To Make a Prairie:*

> I confess we sometimes connected with a phone call and kept that line linked for hours at a stretch, interrupting poem-talk to stir the spaghetti sauce, switch the laundry, or try out a new image on the typewriter; we whistled into the receiver for each other when we were ready to resume.

What is perhaps most striking about that passage is the casual integration of the daily routine of the housewife with the work of poetry. Kumin's easy movement between laundry, meal, and typewriter is telling of the pressures that her role as a wife and homemaker imposed. Lacking the framework of the women's movement, both women later described a guilty sense that their close friendship and habit of writing were wrong. They felt the need to keep poetry a secret.

The literary products of Kumin and Sexton's friendship, nevertheless, were immediate and outstanding. A great many of the poems that Sexton was writing in Holmes's workshop appeared in her first book, *To Bedlam and Part Way Back* (1960). Kumin's first book, *Halfway,* appeared in 1961. The reviewers made clear that the idea of a woman poet was still a little odd. The *Saturday Review* called her style "womanly" in its attention to detail, and the *Christian Science Monitor* found it necessary to remind its readers that the term "poetess" had fallen out of use with the Victorians.

Although Kumin has asserted that she has developed much from this first volume, and it has been, perhaps, the least well received of her volumes, much of her later development is prefigured in it. Many of the themes that Kumin would make her own appear in *Halfway:* loss and the fear of loss, cultural identity, religion, and the importance of dreams. An elegy, "One Dead Friend," prefigures many of the poems of mourning that she wrote later in the 1960s and 1970s: poems mourning the death of her father, brother, and friends. Likewise, in the poem "Nightmare," which begins as if comforting a terrified child, the line "I hold my heartbeat on my lap and cannot comfort her" reveals the body to be physically permeable to terror. In treating the response of the body as if it were something separate and detachable, "Nightmare" offers a taste of much more developed poems, such as "Apostrophe to a Dead Friend" and "Body and Soul: A Meditation," that dwell on the split between body and mind. Poems such as "Nightmare," "The Journey: For Jane at Thirteen," and "Poem for my Son" begin the persistent theme of her "tribal poems," which address Kumin's geographical and personal roots, and her sense of their overwhelming importance.

Only her father's disapproval of bathing suits prevented Kumin from becoming an Olympic or professional swimmer. Perhaps because of this early frustration of an ambition, swimming in her poems is frequently a metaphor for poetic achievement. Susan Ludvigson points out that the sestina "High Dive: A Variant" uses the metaphor of the diver to explore the poet's persistent challenge: "to perfect technical skills through diligent study and practice, and then to take chances—to attempt more than one can be sure of accomplishing, no matter how high the price of failure." Likewise, her most unconventional experiment with form is the poem "400-Meter Free Style," in which the lines imitate the swimmer's back-and-forth motion. The volume as a whole is strong evidence of Kumin's early mastery of conventional technique rather than of an experimental temperament. She skillfully uses rhyme and half rhyme as well as traditional meters.

Kumin's second book, *The Privilege* (1965), came armed with evidence of her increasing technical facility. This facility, however, is carefully tied to the developing themes and preoccupations of her poetry. These poems often meditate on poetry as a dialogue with the past. There is a new emphasis in *The Privilege* on Kumin's roots and her painful childhood experiences with anti-Semitism. Particularly in the elegies for her father, "Lately, at Night" and "The Pawnbroker," the impact of the past on the present is a central concern. In interviews, Kumin has stressed the importance that she attributes to background and heritage. She told Karla Hammond, "I feel I have a strong sense of tribe and ancestor, an ancestor worship or desire to find out about my roots." The attempt is not purely to develop a personal history, but "the hope that the poem draws on some sort of unconscious, collective, archetypal thing so that myth and experience will cohere." She seems to be attempting to develop a relationship to the past from which she can draw support and strength. It is to this sense of heritage that the title seems to refer; the past gives something to the present, or the present takes something from the past.

Poems in *The Privilege* address not only Kumin's religious heritage but also the internal disquiet that it caused her. Her early life was that of a religious outsider. She grew up next to a convent in a predominantly Protestant suburb. Despite being a Jew, Kumin went to the convent school because it was convenient. "To a child who is looking for absolutes," she wrote, "these two [Christian and Jewish] opposing views of the world are terribly confusing." This early need to situate herself in a religious context would become an important theme in Kumin's poetry. The poem "Mother Rosarine" praises one of the nuns whom she remembered from childhood. God, however, would gradually become less absolute and identified more often with poetry. Echoing advice a young priest gave her friend Anne Sexton, Kumin told Martha Meek in 1975, "Words are the only 'holy' for me. Any God that exists for me is in the typewriter keys." She seems to mean that it is language, rather than a divine existence, that creates form and order.

In "Sisyphus" a young girl's reaction to anti-Semitism is explored through her relationship, part fear and part awe, to a legless man given to roadside preaching. She accepts her conscription out of a sense of duty to God, and perhaps shame, to wheel the man about town. For her kindness, the man calls her a "perfect Christian child." The end-stopped and rhythmically regular lines of the second-to-last-couplet throw her reaction into stark relief against the rest of the poem, which is enjambed and relaxed:

> One day I said I was a Jew.
> I wished I had. I wanted to.
>
> The basket man is gone; the stone
> I push uphill is all my own.

In the final couplet "gone" and "stone" are a visual, but not an aural, rhyme. The unsure nature of the rhyme emphasizes the unsure nature of the claim that the "going" of the past still holds upon the present. In place of the "gone" basket man, the poet now pushes a "stone" totally "her own." It is as if the "going" has been transformed into the "stone."

The impact of the passing of the past is to create a burden in the present, a burden of which the poet is in sole possession. A profound gap separates the world of the dead legless beggar from the world of the grown-up poet, but it is this gap that makes the child's silence about her religion the weight of the event, because it cannot be changed or affected. It remains whole and inaccessible to rectification. The little girl of "Sisyphus" mourns the gap between what she wanted to say and what she could not say. She must live instead with her silence. In later elegies it is made clear that figures from the past remain to haunt the present and insist on a joint possession of the past, but the little girl in "Sisyphus" is left alone, bearing a burden of which she must accept complete possession—"my own."

Another poem, "The Pawnbroker," presents the poet's relationship to the past as a debt that must be fulfilled. In Kumin's "tribal poems," acknowledging a "debt" becomes a means of claiming a cultural heritage. This poem is one of two elegies for Kumin's father in *The Privilege*. This particular one she called "the hardest poem I ever wrote." What is striking about the poem is the insistence that the poet's relationship with the dead father is one of economic exchange. The father is the poet's "creditor" and "appraiser." She writes:

> I was the bearer he paid up on demand
> with one small pearl of selfhood.
>   Portionless,
> I am oystering still to earn it.

The metaphors are, of course, appropriate to the father's occupation. They are used to imagine the poet's relationship with the dead. The poet, calling herself the "bearer," has received "one small pearl of selfhood" for whatever it is that she has pawned. The problem then becomes how to "pay off" the debt, evening the score and assuaging grief. Figured as an economic exchange, the past can be bought off. The poet, then, is "oystering still to earn" back "the pearl of selfhood," something without price. Yet "portionless" indicates that there has been no inheritance from the father, and there is no way to pay off the debt. This is, then, the significance of the metaphor of pawning. The debt that cannot be paid to the banker becomes a debt that the banker comes back to collect; a debt owed to the pawnbroker, however, becomes the permanent loss of the item pawned.

Later in the poem the poet and her brothers drink a bottle of Scotch to alleviate the pain of "easing down the ways" their father has "ruled off the balance sheet." The process of mourning is figured as the process of pawning, in which after thirty days, "giver and lender, no longer in hock to himself. / ruled off the balance sheet." Likewise, the poet concedes her debt and forfeits what was originally pawned to the past. In actual pawning, what is left to the debtor is the ticket, a valueless reminder of what could not be salvaged from debt. As in "Sisyphus," the loss in the past results in an ambiguous figure of loss in the present. In "Sisyphus," it is the stone that symbolizes a failure that cannot be rectified. In "The Pawnbroker," it is the ticket, representing a debt that is forfeited. Owing everything, but unable to pay it, the poet instead calls it even and accepts this exchange. This relationship to the past will change over the course of Kumin's career as she explores the potential and healing power of poetry. Here the "I" is stabilized by the past. Memory does not erode the poet's sense of self but instead reinforces it. These poems view the past as irrecoverable and respond to it with the need to make sense of it, even though they lack access to its truth.

Although Kumin is best known as a poet, she also has produced a substantial body of prose fiction that has received critical acclaim. In addition, alone and with Sexton, she has written many children's books. In interviews, Kumin has stated that she considers herself equally a fiction writer and a poet. They are, however, quite distinct enterprises to her. In contrast to poetry, which is about the unconscious and the symbolic events of dreams, and so "closer to the wellspring," "fiction is more a matter of invention and manipulation. There's much less shaping paradoxically, in being a poet than there is in being a writer of novels." In 1965, the year that *The Privilege* was published, Kumin's first novel, *Through Dooms of Love,* appeared. The story works over much the same ground as the tribal poems. Set in 1939, it is based on the conflict between a Bolshevik daughter and her pawnbroker father. The *New York Times* review of *Through Dooms of Love* praised its "lyric intensity" and the "luminous brilliance" with which Kumin defines her characters.

Kumin's next novel, *The Passions of Uxport* (1968), is a revealing account of her emerging relationship with Anne Sexton. Despite Sexton's strenuous denial that she is represented by the character Sukey, Kumin affirms that the novel is based on the early years of their relationship. Diane Middlebrook claims that Sexton even had an enthusiastic hand in writing whole speeches. The story concerns two suburban housewives: Sukey, who has a death wish, and Hallie, who has a psychosomatic pain in her stomach. While flirting with sentimentality (the novel begins with a mare named Cassandra failing to conceive and ends with her success), the book is most interesting for being about the bond between women. Elaine Showalter comments, "There are very few relationships in books that are like it [Hallie and Sukey's]. Women are generally supposed to destroy each other." Because of this new theme, book reviewers expressed much uncertainty as to what to make of *The Passions of Uxport.* Many of the reviews seem puzzled by the central drama concerning such ordinary characters as housewives, and even offended by the suggestion that the problems of suburbia might be worth noting. In the *New York Times Book Review,* Mary Carter compares the novel to a television drama, dismissing it as "two housewives' neuroses." Carter seems vexed that "the anguish seems so arbitrary, risen not from a universal, but a private source, willful, insulated and resistant." Her response to the novel, while admiring of the style, is a rather prim dislike for the characters, and she closes by sneering that Sukey does not seem to find her children sufficient. The *Yale Review* protests that the psychoanalyst is not handled with sufficient depth and sympathy, and finally describes the problems of the Sexton character as being rooted in the sexual loss of her husband.

Questions of growing up Jewish in a Christian culture return powerfully in Kumin's next volume of poetry, *The Nightmare Factory* (1970). Kumin seems to have shed any reluctance to embrace this portion of her heritage. The same debt to the past that was present in the previous collection is apparent in her address to another ancestor, but now is gratefully acknowledged: "Welcome ancestor, Rosenburg, The Tailor, / I choose to be a lifetime in your debt." The third section of the book is titled "Tribal Poems," and it focuses on family members. The fourth section is a series of love poems, some of which detail an apparently fictional adulterous love affair. These, however, seem less convincing than her more affirmative love poems. This may reflect Kumin's uneasiness with the conventions of the confessional mode.

Written to exorcise a series of bad dreams about her father, who had just died, "The Nightmare Factory" was a way of surviving something "inchoate and very painful." "I then had this fantasy," Kumin told Martha Meek, "that there is some distant Detroit-of-the-Soul where all bad dreams are created and that out of the warehouse of goods we are assigned certain recurrent nightmares. . . . One must descend into the abyss and dream the nightmare of one's choice and dream it through to the very end." Raising the unconscious into the conscious is, therefore, a major concern of the poem: "I have a lot of reverence for what goes on at the dream level in the unconscious—those symbolic events," Kumin told Martha Meek. "I have a tremendous reverence for raising it up into language, which I think is what it's all about." She uses dreams as a way of addressing an unbearable truth. Some things are manageable only through dreams, she seems to imply. But those unmanageable truths are not just personal; they reach back into the general historical experience:

night after night in
the bowels of good citizens
nazis and cossacks ride
klansmen and judases.

Another poem, "The Presence," is also a meditation on absent things. As "The Nightmare Factory" attempts to imagine the unimaginable unconscious, so "The Presence" attempts to penetrate the veil of otherness that separates nature from the mind. In its concentration on traces rather than substance, the poem is more reminiscent of "The Wood-Pile" by Robert Frost. In that poem the speaker encounters a pile of firewood in a place in the forest that seems to be no place:

The view was all in lines . . .
Too much alike to mark a name or place by
So as to say for certain I was here
Or somewhere else.

Where the woodpile lies, seems to resist man. No one's footprints appear in the snow around the woodpile; the "hard snow" seems to repel prints from the poet's shoes. Nature itself seems to have absorbed that person and his work. It is the work of poetry to recover the lost story. Like the mysterious "someone" in Frost's poem, the "presence" in Kumin's poem is understood only as a "something." Its reality and importance are insisted on, even though they are evident only from traces left behind—marks left in the snow.

Something went crabwise
across the snow this morning.
Something went hard and slow
over our hayfield.

Kumin, like Frost, does not accept the otherness and inaccessibility of the "something" that has passed out of sight. In the lines that follow, it is the role of the imagination to reconstruct, as a detective does, that "something's" identity, what that presence could have been. She considers first absurd yet familiarized anthropomorphic images, a "raccoon / lugging a knapsack," or a "porcupine / carrying a tennis racket." Whatever it was, however, she imagines at last that it must have been linked to the natural process of killing and eating. Her last suggestion is a scene believably out of nature: a red fox dragging its prey back to its lair. The traces, though, are already in the process of becoming renewed:

those bones are seeds now
pure as baby teeth
lined up in the burrow.

The last lines insist that even the devoured carcass, in the very act of its consumption, has become a "seed," a potential to become something new. The transformation of the bones to seeds is not done literally, as one might imagine the merely naturalistic observation might have been. Bones are what is not eaten, what is left behind as the residue of the animal. Rather, the bones are seeds for the imagination, which can build from residue, as the entire scene is built up from mere markings on the snow.

Despite her insistence on the distinct identity of whatever it was that has passed, the poet retains a critical role in nature. The poem does not end with the imagined scene enacted below ground, where it remains out of the reach of the human, but with the reintroduction of the observing "I" into the landscape. The poet, too, drifts over the landscape, relying on mediation from the remains of the animal that went into making her snowshoes:

I cross on snowshoes
cunningly woven from
the skin and sinews of
something else that went before.

Her passage over the snow, then, is similar to the imagination's reconstitution of the unseen animal, and the chewed-up bones. From something left behind, the remains of something natural, she has gained the power to interact with nature. Again something dead is the means for gaining an insight or passage. Ludvigson sees the poem as demonstrating the "irresponsible dominance" of man over the natural world. She allies it with "The Vealers" in protesting humanity's misuse of the natural. Perhaps because the poem is in the first person, however, Kumin does not seem to allow so much distance between herself and the subject of the poem. Instead, she seems invested in this as a necessary sacrifice. This attitude is one of profound respect for the otherness of nature, of allowing that nature has an autonomous existence. Kumin is allowed to approach nature only through the traces of what once was. In another poem, "Country House," she imagines the world without humans. The house of the title is a space where things run riot, "the walls break into conversation," "Two clocks tick themselves witless." Unstructured by time, this is a place that is incomprehensible to normal experience. It might, however, be accessible to poetry.

Although these later sections of the book, and particularly the title poem, are decidedly dark, the book is on balance an affirmation. The first part, "Pasture Poems," is much more typical Kumin nature poetry. It contains the first of a series of "Henry Manley" poems that serve as a precursor to the more famous "hermit" poems in her Pulitzer Prize—winning volume, *Up Country*. These poems are not entirely distinct from the poems in the later sections, sharing the theme of pressing against the isolation of the mind. "Hello, Hello Henry" is a poem about communication and the difficulty of communication. While Kumin's older neighbor, "shy as a girl come calling," walks two miles to ask her to telephone him once in a while, the poet misses her own telephone call made to her home in Boston. Neither the telephone nor a face-to-face meeting seems adequate communication. The poem ends by again attempting to talk: "Hello, hello Henry? Is that you?" It is not clear, however, that even the poem is received. We are not sure that Manley has answered. Making that connection is vitally important for Kumin. Henry Manley is a figure of mortality and aging, but most important, he is one who is alone. As Alicia Ostriker wrote in the *New York Times,* "If she [Kumin] had her way, no loved (or hated) human or animal would die unremembered."

Up Country won the Pulitzer Prize in 1973. The volume takes the New England countryside as its heart, strongly recalling Frost and Thoreau. The poems are not transcendental, however, in that Kumin does not imply that mankind should or can merge with nature. Joyce Carol Oates acknowledges Kumin's debt to her New England predecessors, "though in my opinion Kumin's poetry gives us a sharp-edged, unflinching and occasionally nightmarish subjectivity exasperatingly absent in Thoreau." That subjectivity, embodied in the eight "hermit" poems that begin the volume, is asserted in the face of a life in which "nothing is sure." Oates claims that Kumin's more powerful restatement of the transcendental experience is that it is rooted firmly in experience, "however private or eccentric."

Despite its apparent orientation toward nature poetry, Kumin has acknowledged the impact of Anne Sexton on *Up Country*. Sexton actually named it (as Kumin named Sexton's *Transformations*). Barbara Swan, who illustrated several volumes for Sexton, contributed drawings. Sexton's input was vital in the final wording of the last stanza of "The Hermit Meets the Skunk." Kumin told Diana Hume George:

> When I wrote "The Hermit Meets the Skunk," I probably rewrote that final stanza thirty times, because I couldn't decide on the order of those final things. And so of course I showed them to Annie, and she said immediately, the mother bed, the ripe taste of carrion, the green kiss. That was the order. I just absolutely trusted her instincts in a situation like that.

In an interview after Sexton's death, Kumin acknowledged that Sexton could at times function as a type of poetic "id." She considered that her "directness, openness" and her "ability to confront feelings" were a "natural outcome" of the development of her relationship with Sexton.

The figure of the hermit, Kumin has acknowledged, is a close stand-in for herself. In their interview, Kumin agreed with Meek that the family, the tribe, is the last unit of society that can be "balanced between order and disorder." She denied that the hermit repudiates modern life; rather, he is just a "cop-out." Kumin noted that the writer's profession is by nature solitary. "You lock yourself up to do your job," she told Meek. It is this extreme sense of privacy and isolation that serves as a revision of Thoreau and the idea of the visionary. Ludvigson notes that, confronted with mounting unknowns, Kumin's hermit responds by seeming to go on as he ever has. The poems end with a return to the ordinariness of everyday life in "The Hermit Picks Berries":

> The hermit whistles as he picks.
> Later he will put on his shirt
> and walk to town for some cream.

What is gained from nature is a matter-of-fact acceptance of the close relationship that humanity has with nature.

Other poems are in the form of extended observations of things in nature, as in "Stones," where Kumin surprises us with rocks.

> Eyeless and unsurprised they behave
> in the manner of stones: swallow turnips,
> heave graves
>
> rise up openmouthed into walls and from time
> to time imitate oysters or mushrooms.

The priority of description in this poem recalls the importance that things in themselves hold for Kumin. The stones are not seen as doing anything special; it is the power of the poet's imagination in seeing them that is extraordinary. The power of description makes the poem. Nature's surface here is impenetrable to seeing, permeable only to the imagination.

The autonomy of things has been very important for Kumin's poetics. In *House, Bridge, Fountain, Gate* (1975), she catalogs her usual subjects with a detailed accuracy but a refusal to elaborate. The title of the book derives from the importance of naming. Kumin found the title in Louis Simpson's memoirs, *North of Jamaica:* "Poetry is a mixture of thoughts and objects," he wrote, "it is as though things are trying to express themselves through us. It may be, as a poet had said, we are here only to say house, bridge, fountain, gate." She placed this sentence in the book as an epigraph. In her interview with Meek, Kumin stressed the importance of the naming and particularization of things: "I think that the one thing that's been consistently true about my poetry is this determination to get at that authenticity of detail."

In the *New York Times Book Review,* Helen Vendler complained that *House, Bridge, Fountain, Gate* suffers from a "disease of similes." As examples, she gives "naked as almonds," kisses like "polka dots," and a visit "as important as summer." While there may be some truth to this charge, there are also counterexamples of similes that seem especially apt and startlingly fresh: Ludvigson mentions "Grandmother's corset / spread out like a filleted fish." It might be best, however, to remember that simile and metaphor go hand in hand with the project of naming. To produce a simile is to find a new name that surprises the reader by revealing a side of the thing that is ordinarily forgotten or missed. Robert Frost often uses similes in this way. In "The Silken Tent," for instance, he constructs a sonnet by exploring at length the possibilities in a single unlikely simile—comparing a women to a tent. Just as a tent balloons in the breeze as if it were ready to fly, yet remains firmly staked to the earth, so the woman in Frost's poem looks resolutely heavenward with "sureness of soul," yet is bound to the earth by "silken ties of love and thought." The unlikely simile precisely captures a tension in the woman's personality.

A woman is not usually thought of as being like a tent. Frost's surprising simile invites the reader to look at the familiar with new eyes. Likewise, Kumin's poem "Heaven as Anus" uses the simile in the title to make the reader rethink his or her presuppositions about both "heaven" and "anus." Kumin described this to Karla Hammond as an "anti-war, anti-behaviormodification poem"; she uses the process of renaming to disturb our commonsense notions of good and bad, heaven and earth. After graphically describing the torture of animals in Defense Department tests, Kumin asks,

> And what is this to the godhead,
> these squeals, whines, writhings,
> unexpected jumps,
> whose children burn alive, booby-trap the dead,
> lop ears and testicles, core and disembowel?

The answer may be that God does not care, and that realization may make possible the shocking simile of the title, a yoking together of the idea of a holy place with the anus. The poem, however, goes further. It insists on raising up the idea of excrement even as it deflates the idea of heaven.

> It all ends at the hole. No words may enter
> the house of excrement. We will meet there
> as the sphincter of the good Lord opens wide
> and He takes us all inside.

Heaven and anus meet in the impossibility of appeal and the limit of knowing. There is no knowledge of what lies ahead, no passing through in the same form. Indeed, even the passage into heaven is equated with a sense of the reversal of the usual bodily functions. In "The Excrement Poem," Kumin writes, "I honor shit for saying: We go on." Body and soul are inseparable here. Sybil Estes writes, "Kumin, unlike Bradstreet or Dickinson, cannot imagine soul or Spirit apart from body or matter. . . . For her, the body gives evidence that Spirit is."

The Retrieval System (1978), Kumin's next volume, is dedicated to her daughters. Alicia Ostriker said that "no poet writes more richly and more subtly of mother-daughter relations." Perhaps this dedication's emphasis on inheritance and renewal was a reaction to the profound impact of a tragedy outside of the family. Anne Sexton committed suicide in October 1974, just before the publication of *House, Bridge, Fountain, Gate.* Since that book was already at the press, it includes no poems that address her suicide. It is not until *The Retrieval System* that Sexton's death is faced at length. The incompleteness of Sexton's goodbye is the subject of "Splitting Wood at Six Above"; Kumin addresses her friend: "See you tomorrow, you said. / You lied." The two friends had met the day before the suicide to review galleys for Sexton's upcoming book. Kumin recalls that Sexton gave no warning of the decision she apparently had made: "when she was ready to kill herself," Kumin recalls, "she kept it a deep dark secret." Sexton's death seems to have precipitated a crisis in Kumin's poetic career as well as her personal life. At a Women's Writer's Conference in 1979, Kumin informed a public audience that she was very concerned that she could not write after Sexton died, that she had lost a vital link to her art. For a writer who had previously written elegies on deaths in the family, Sexton's death touched a deeper nerve, one that rendered the project of elegy difficult. Sexton's death was a challenge to poetry that previous deaths had not been.

Sybil Estess admires "Splitting Wood at Six Above" as one of Kumin's saddest poems about Sexton. She argues that "the underlying thematic question of the poem, however, is what happens to the 'soul' of something after death." Although Kumin seems to settle with herself that Sexton has safely reached "the other side," the poem focuses on what still bothers her, the "sound of your [Sexton's] going." The poem, it seems, has been sparked by the sound of the ax into the wood, which Kumin associates with the sound of the soul leaving the body:

> It is the sound
> of your going I drive
> into heartwood.

What is disconcerting is the sense that the poet is driving the sound itself into the wood, rather than simply producing it. Although she is responsible for repeating the very sound that torments her, that sound seems dissociated from the actions presumably producing it. Naming of the wood with a body part, repeated again in the next lines, where the split wood lies "face up," identifies Sexton with nature in a particularly gruesome way. Further, metrically, the poem carries the chopping sound associated with Sexton's "going." Estess points out that "the chopping rhythm of the poem suggests the hard, flint-like reality of being split apart"; forty-three lines end with a stressed monosyllable, and many of the disyllabic line endings are spondaic, both syllables stressed equally. Far from being gone, Sexton's spirit is imbued in nature and everything surrounding the poet. Yet Kumin derives no comfort from her friend's presence. It seems, rather, to be threatening.

Kumin's inability to dispel her sense of guilt or anger at Sexton's death might be, in part, linked to her unwillingness to attach an easy explanation to the suicide. In an interview with Diana Hume George, coeditor of Sexton's *Selected Poems,* Kumin declined the invitation to frame Sexton's suicide in political and philosophical terms. Sexton's suicide, Kumin insisted, was not a "protest against mortality," as George suggested, but a reaction to the overwhelming "sense of total hopelessness" that overcame her. While feminism might have offered a valuable support system, Kumin told George, it would not have addressed the critical problem, which was medical: "If she had stayed on Thorazine, in my opinion she would be alive today." Sexton's death, in other words, served no cause, responded to no politics.

In two essays, one printed in the collection *Aging and Gender in Literature,* the other in *Original Essays on the Poetry of Anne Sexton,* Diana Hume George has produced some of the more interesting academic writing on Kumin, focusing most usefully on the elegies for Sexton. According to George, Sexton's death was a turning point in Kumin's career. In *Original Essays,* she argues that "since Sexton's death, Kumin has become Sexton's successor, her inheritor, the voice that speaks both of and for Sexton now that Sexton is silent." The implication is that Kumin, after Sexton's death, developed very Sexton-like qualities in her poetry. The two poets, according to George, are inextricably linked, differentiated only by minor characteristics and the "choice" each made, one to live and one to die. This argument rests on the difference between Kumin's poetry of mourning before and after Sexton's suicide. In *Aging and Gender,* George argues that "although many of these poems [on the deaths of "her uncles, her brother, her animals, her Anne"] were written before Anne Sexton's death, that death seems to have allowed her to do sustained instead of intermittent mourning." She points out that in the elegies Sexton joins Kumin in "every activity of daily life." The conversations between them are always picked up as if they were constantly ongoing. All of Kumin's elegies to Sexton could have been written at the same time; there seems to be no progression of the style or mourning. For George, that "sustained mourning" is what allows Kumin to step into Sexton's shoes. George admits that, of Kumin's work, she vastly prefers the poetry written after the suicide, which she calls Kumin's "mature period," to that written before.

It is true that after Sexton's death, Kumin's poetry takes a radically different attitude toward the dead. In a 1917 essay, "Mourning and Melancholia," Sigmund Freud distinguishes between mourning, which is the normal healing process of grief, and melancholia, a pathological state of interminable sorrow that defies cure. It has been suggested by Peter Sacks, in *The English Elegy: Studies in the Genre from Spenser to Yeats* (1985), that elegy plays a role in the normal process of mourning. Sacks argues that an elegy, by working through the loss of its object, assists the poet in overcoming sorrow and proceeding with life. Kumin's elegies for Sexton, however, do not seem to follow this model. Instead of providing a healing counterweight to Sexton's death, they appear to be bound to a repetition of the loss. In "Itinerary of an Obsession" Kumin addresses her dead friend, "here you come / leaping out of the coffin again." Instead of the enabling relationship that she had ascribed to the dead animals that made up her snowshoes, and the power of the dead and absent relatives in her tribal poetry, Sexton as a dead friend becomes a persistent shade, refusing to stay safely buried. Another critic, Jahan Ramazani, suggests in *Poetry of Mourning: The Modern Elegy from Hardy to Heaney* (1994) that this type of poem, an elegy of melancholy rather than of mourning, is a distinctly twentieth-century phenomenon.

In its structure, Kumin's next book, *Our Ground Time Here Will Be Brief* (1982), revises her previous view of the past. *Our Ground Time* includes both new poems and a selection of the best poems from her previous six volumes. Unconventionally, the poems are ordered from most recent to earliest. Reading backward seems to demand that the older poems be read in the light of the newer ones. With this odd configuration of the volume, Kumin seems to insist on the priority of the present in understanding the past, rather than the more apparent need to have the past in order to understand the present, which was the theme of "The Pawnbroker" and "Sisyphus." Priority is given to the most recent work, as if it were the most relevant. In *The Privilege* and *The Nightmare Factory,* the past enters the present in symbols of its loss. In *The Retrieval System* and *Our Ground Time Here Will Be Brief,* the past enters the present still living, and impossible to escape.

Of the series of stunning elegies for Sexton included in *Our Ground Time,* perhaps the most affecting is "Apostrophe to a Dead Friend." As the subtitle "(On Being Interviewed by Her Biographer)" makes clear, this poem comes out of an experience of testimony: the retelling of the friendship between the two poets to Sexton's biographer, Diane Wood Middlebrook. The first lines of the poem divide the voice of the poet from her body and her "gender":

> Little by little my gender drifts away
> leaving the bones of this person
> whose shoe size was your size.

Referring to her body as "this person" objectifies it. Further, because the speaker refers to her body as if it were a corpse—"bones"—and puts her own shoe size in the past tense, her body seems to become the object mourned. In the last stanza the confusion of time suggests that the dead Sexton is more present than the live body that belongs to the poet's voice.

> Soon I will be sixty.
> How it was with you now
> hardly more vivid than how
> it is without you, I carry
> the sheer weight of the telling
> like a large infant, on one hip.
> I who am remaindered in the conspiracy
> doom, doom on my lips.

Although the syntax is difficult, it seems that the "How it was" in the past is more vivid than the "how it is" in the present. The line "How it was with you now" has the effect of making "was" seem as if it were "now." Confusing the past with the present, the living with the dead, the poet reverses the neat process of inheritance from the dead formed in her earlier poetry. Carried in place of an infant, "telling" takes the place of inheritance. But this metaphor does not equate the telling with the infant, as one might expect; the metaphor only describes in what way the telling is carried. Telling, then, is only carried like an infant; it does not have the infant's power of continuing a lineage and producing descendants. In place of reproduction, the poem allows only a continual telling. Unlike her earlier poems, which contemplated a relationship with the past that was productive, in this poem Kumin asserts a relationship to the past that produces nothing but a repetition of the difference between "how it was" and "how it is." It produces only a repetition of loss.

Many of the themes that Kumin develops in the elegies to Sexton are echoed throughout these two volumes in poems that otherwise seem to having nothing to do with Sexton's death. In "Henry Manley, Living Alone, Keeps Time," from *The Retrieval System,* Kumin returns to Manley, who has, in the meanwhile, aged and, "los[ing] words when the light fades," stands in danger of losing his grip on language. As Ludvigson notes, in Manley's awkward attempts to remember the words *"window, wristwatch, cup, knife"* we hear a faded echo of the confidence in the power of naming that provided the title for Kumin's *House, Bridge, Fountain, Gate*. Manley's difficulty with language suggests the difficulty that Kumin's poetry has encountered in assimilating loss. Another poem, "Henry Manley Looks Back," in *Our Ground Time Here Will Be Brief,* explores the failure of memory as a compensation for loss. Convalescing in bed with a broken hip, "Henry loves / his new life as the sage of yesteryear," but, face to face with the collapse of his home that results from his absence, Manley can only muse "*You can't look back*." He is no longer able to accept stories about the past as compensation for what is gone.

In "Body and Soul: A Meditation," also in *The Retrieval System,* the soul is disassociated from the body in much the same way as it is in the elegy for Sexton, "Apostrophe to a Dead Friend." Like the division between gender, voice, and body in that elegy, in this poem there is a division between soul, body, and voice. In an optimistic tone, Estess interprets "Body and Soul: A Meditation" to mean that the "soul, or Spirit, both exists and survives the body's destruction." The poem, however, undermines such an optimistic reading. Nowhere apparent in the body, the soul arrives stealthily in a simile:

> Still unlocated, drifting,
> my airmail half-ounce soul
> shows up from time to time
> like those old-fashioned
> doctors who used to cheer
> their patients in girls' boarding schools
> with midnight bedside visits.

While the soul may continue to exist, and while it returns to the body, it does so in the guise of the deeply suspicious figure of the doctor. An "old-fashioned" doctor who is prone to "midnight bedside visits" may be a figure of nostalgia, but he may also be a rapist or child molester. A few lines later the relationship between the soul and the body is explicitly sexualized, when soul and "we [body and voice] touch tongue." In these lines, the power of the soul over the body seems threatening. Their reunion may be joyful, but it is just as likely to be a moment of trauma.

Kumin's next book, *The Long Approach* (1985), takes up where *Our Ground Time Here* left off, with the question of the poet's responsibility to the world. Both titles refer to air travel, but whereas *Our Ground Time* implies the brevity and transitoriness of life, *The Long Approach* refers to a careful, and permanent, setting down. Printed last in the volume, the title poem departs from the rural setting in favor of a highway scene, and then an imagined plane ride. The "long approach," we find out, is the soft landing that a horse needs when it is transported by plane. A horse is loaded facing the tail of the plane so that it can brace its feet during takeoff. At landing, however, the horse is on its own, relying on luck and the pilot's willingness to set down with an easy "long approach." Here, at the very end of the volume, Kumin reveals to us what she has been doing. The poems together provide Kumin with a soft landing from the crisis of Sexton's death and a reentrance into her long-running theme of the plight of nature and humanity in a world that increasingly wishes to deny both.

In structure, this book moves through three sections, from private to public to the farm. The first section is a collection of detailed remembrances and vignettes in family poems addressed, once more, to Kumin's father, mother, and ancestors. At the heart of "The Chain," a pair of braids discovered coiled in a hatbox brings the poet to imagine having her mother's memories. The poem warns us, however, that recovering the past is not simply a personal affair. This is a "nation losing its memory," dedicated to "turning / its battle grounds into parking lots." Other poems in the volume dwell on the risks inherent in remembering. In "Introducing the Fathers," a pair of dead fathers, Kumin's and a friend's, are likened to a pair of hot air balloons: "Macy daddies ready for the big parade." While conversing, they become something like a pair of grotesque dandies, "matching net worths, winning big at blackjack," and "rising toward the Big Crash." "Big Crash" refers, of course, to the Great Depression, but it also implies that there is a point when memory itself becomes dangerous, as an overfilled hot air balloon might explode.

The next section is devoted to public poems, concerned with Kumin's Judaism and the burden of history. In details of a trip to Israel, and musings on politics, Kumin attempts to situate herself in history. Critics have complained that the politics, especially the meditations on the atomic bomb, are predictable. Wendy Lesser, in the *Washington Post Book World,* complains that the "poems on 'issues' . . . founder on their opinion making." Nevertheless, Kumin's efforts to site her distinctive voice inside this historical frame are frequently unique and gripping. History, and the poet's relationship to it, have always been in the background of her poetry—in "The Nightmare Factory," for instance. In this volume, history seems to be the impact of the unpredictable and unimaginable—terrorism, nuclear war, the holocaust—on the individual. For Kumin, the past and public resurface only by colliding sharply with the present and personal. In "In the Absence of Bliss," subtitled "Museum of the Diaspora, Tel Aviv," she writes,

> We walk away from twenty-two
> graphic centuries of kill-the-Jew
> and hail, of all things, a Mercedes
> taxi,

which is all the more surprising for including a couplet. In these lines, the past gains its power by disrupting the way that things are seen in the present. Unless seen in the light of history, a Mercedes taxi is just another car. These poems, however they raise difficult questions, refuse to resort to easy answers. Kumin recognizes that the urge to self-immolation is deep inside the practice of religion, and not limited to the crimes of historical figures. Her attempt to ground speculation on a "higher moral plane" is necessarily a failure, one that ends on the same note as "In the Absence of Bliss" ends: with "No answers. Only questions."

The third section of *The Long Approach* is titled "On the Farm." In the context of the book, however, these poems come to query the possibility of a simple pastoral retreat out of the world, in the mode of the hermit. The first poem of this last section opens with an apology "for all the snow falling in / this poem so early in the season." It proceeds to weave an elaborate metaphor around the snow, never surrendering the primary reference to the weather but refusing to lose sight of larger issues. This is an "elegiac snow," a "biographical snow," weather that is to be endured. The snow, in cutting off the outside world, may stifle the sounds of the bombs and cries of the previous section, but it does not eliminate them. In "In the Upper Pastures," a title that might imply the promise of a route toward the transcendental, Kumin asks, "Is this a pastoral?" Her answer is that despite the wealth of pastoral detail, the animal skins and smells, there is no cause for comfort: "Each of us whimpers his way through the forest alone." What the poem can do is preserve a small space, not unlike a pasture, "out of the weather." A "small thing," to be sure, yet one that at least provides a minimum of shelter.

Kumin's volumes, *Nurture* (1989) and *Looking for Luck* (1992), return to pastoral scenes similar to those of *Up Country*. This has left her vulnerable to criticisms, such as that of Lisa Zeidner, that "[Kumin] seems so at peace with herself and the world, so downright nice, that it is hard to imagine what tension or turbulence keeps her writing. In *Looking for Luck,* as in past collections, she sets herself the daunting task of documenting ordinary happiness. Whole poems concern not bliss but contentment." This criticism, however, is far from self-evident. One might recall the found poem, "You Are in Bear Country," that opens *The Long Approach*. Kumin breaks into poetic lines with a public service pamphlet warning the camper of the danger from grizzly bears. What appears to be pastoral poetry, she implies, might well reveal itself to be bear country.

Carol Muske argues that the poems in *Nurture* are better seen as an ongoing writing of elegies for nature: "These poems are exhaustive in their sorrow: they are predominantly short, brutal, elegies for the natural world. She recites, in bitter, gripping litanies, the roster of extinct life-forms, along with those about to be extinct, and casts a cynical eye on humankind, the 'unaware' species responsible for the destruction of the living world." Remarking on the terse, understated couplets, Muske says, "The overall effect is one of anguished enumeration—as if the poet stood on the deck of a sinking Noah's ark, counting again each animal we are losing." Nowhere is the disconnection between Kumin's complacent image and the hard-edged elegiac tone of much of her poetry as apparent as in the cover of *Nurture,* a fawn nesting in a grassy bower. Kumin complained at the publisher's decision to market the book in this fashion. She told Jo-Ann Mapson, "They stuck me with that terrible Bambi cover that looks like it ought to be on the front of a feminine hygiene product."

In the title poem of *Nurture,* Kumin issues a challenge to the critical cynicism that accuses her of "an overabundance of maternal genes." The poem goes on to insist on the value of this "fault." Kumin imagines a wild child brought to her home, mute and uncomprehending, for her to care for. This is not, however, merely a case of an overprotective mother. As Muske points out, instead of merely trying to appropriate the wild child and "smother the wild creature with love," Kumin wishes to "find a way to talk to wildness." In *House, Bridge, Fountain, Gate,* Kumin insisted on the importance of naming things. Here the process of naming lies in its ability not merely to bond members of society together but also to insist on a place in the social for what seems to be outside of its protection. The wild child is recovered through language, through the language that

> we two, same and not-same,
> might have constructed from sign,
> scratch, grimace, grunt, vowel:
>
> Laughter our first noun, and our long verb,
> howl.

Kumin's project of extending language to the speechless extends as well to natural things. In "Sleeping with Animals," the poet insists that we are bound by languages that are available to us merely as a result of being loving creatures. Watching and touching her horse as it sleeps, Kumin writes,

> What we say to each other in the cold black
> of April, conveyed in a wordless yet perfect
> language of touch and tremor, connects
> us most surely to the wet cave we all
> once burst from gasping, naked or furred,
> into our separate species.

We are bound to animals by a sense of common existence that is as sure and palpable as language, should we choose to acknowledge it. Other poems also associate the possession of a voice with the ability to resist extinction. In "Bringing Back the Trumpeter Swan," for example, the cost of bringing back the "klaxon"-voiced trumpeter swan in the nest of the mute swan is the "eggs of the mute." This poem, and others, recall Marianne Moore's "He 'Digesteth Harde Yron,'" in which the ostrich is deemed heroic for his resistance to being made into a symbol. Like Moore's ostrich, Kumin's animals insist on their separate and autonomous existence, and thus the real importance of their deaths.

The prologue of *Looking for Luck* begins with a prayerlike statement of belief in the power of transformation:

> I believe in magic. I believe in the rights of
> animals to leap out of our skins
> as recorded in the Kiowa legend:
> *Directly there was a boy where the bear*
> *had been.*

The border between human and animal, the world and poetry, viewed as permeable, is at the heart of this book. It is no coincidence that Kumin chooses as an epigraph a line from Howard Nemerov appealing to a flight of swallows to know that "poems are not / The point. Finding again the world, / That is the point." In this spirit, she gives the title *"Ars Poetica:* A Found Poem" to a monologue in which a trainer gains the trust of a foal. The first part of the title, *"Ars Poetica,"* uses the process of approaching a wild animal as a metaphor for the process by which a poem is realized. Never called a "foal," but only "him," the foal holds the place of the perfectly realized poem. Although in a note at the back of the book Kumin reveals that this is indeed a "found poem," drawn from the words of a horse trainer, the subtitle "found poem" also refers to the horse itself, discovered beautiful and whole in nature. As in *Nurture,* communicating with nature and finding a poem are the same process.

Using nature, however, bears risks. Kumin's poem "Taking the Lambs to Market" acknowledges that the use of nature is destructive, however much our own desires may be gratified. In "The Presence" Kumin willingly paid the price for a privileged view of nature—the body of an animal destroyed to make her snowshoes; in "Taking the Lambs to Market" she insists on acknowledging that this is a necessary hypocrisy. Even Keats, she tells us, after imagining a type of unity with a sparrow, sat down to a dinner of mutton. The "naming" that has played such an important role in her poetry is here used to tell her butcher exactly what cuts of meat she wants. In this poem the butcher stands for one who, "no matter how much we deplore his profession," "deserves our praise." Perhaps he merits praise precisely because, as a "decent man who blurs the line of sight / between our conscience and our appetite," the butcher makes clear to us our own complicity in the destruction of what we admire.

In the epilogue poem to this volume, "The Rendezvous," Kumin returns to the figure of the bear. The first four sentences do not have verbs or subjects. They are assertions of "how," as if the poem is a paraphrase of another story. We are told first "how" the bear's trail through the forest is; then "how," "according to the legend," a woman confronted by a bear should remove her clothes, as bears are capable of feeling shame and will run away from the sight of a naked woman; "how" the poet herself meets a bear and then removes her clothes. Instead of fleeing, however, the bear reciprocates by removing his fur, "which he casts to the ground / for a rug." Their actions serve to break down the differences between them. The bear begins acting human; the poet, naked, might be viewed as becoming more animal-like. The volume closes by repeating "how":

> How
> can he run away, unfurred?
> How can I, without any clothes?
>
> How we prepare a new legend.

Looking for Luck ends with an affirmation that even if this new story of man and nature intermingled cannot yet be told, and perhaps can never be told, at least the warning against pastoral that appeared in "You Are in Bear Country" has been circumvented. Although the poet admits that she is "wet with fear," she has come to confront nature once more.

Selected Bibliography

WORKS OF MAXINE KUMIN

FICTION

Through Dooms of Love. New York: Harper & Row, 1965.

The Passions of Uxport. New York: Harper & Row, 1968.

The Abduction. New York: Harper & Row, 1971.

The Designated Heir. New York: Viking, 1974.

SHORT STORIES

Why Can't We Live Together like Civilized Human Beings? New York: Viking, 1982.

Women, Animals, and Vegetables: Essays and Stories. New York: Norton, 1994.

ESSAYS

To Make a Prairie: Essays on Poets, Poetry, and Country Living. Ann Arbor: University of Michigan Press, 1979.
In Deep: Country Essays. New York: Viking, 1987.

POETRY

Halfway. New York: Harper & Row, 1961.
The Privilege. New York: Harper & Row, 1965.
The Nightmare Factory. New York: Harper & Row, 1970.
Up Country: Poems of New England. New York: Harper & Row, 1972.
House, Bridge, Fountain, Gate. New York: Viking, 1975.
The Retrieval System. New York: Viking, 1978.
Our Ground Time Here Will Be Brief. New York: Viking, 1982.
Closing the Ring. Bucknell University Fine Editions, Series in Contemporary Poetry. Edited by John Wheatcroft. Lewisburg, Pa.: Press of Appletree Valley/Bucknell University, 1984.
The Long Approach. New York: Viking, 1985.
Nurture. New York: Viking, 1989.
Looking for Luck. New York: Norton, 1992.

CHILDREN'S BOOKS.

Sebastian and the Dragon. New York: Putnam's 1960.
Follow the Fall. New York: Putnam's, 1961.
Spring Things. New York: Putnam's, 1961.
A Summer Story. New York: Putnam's, 1961.
A Winter Friend. New York: Putnam's, 1961.
No One Writes a Letter to the Snail. New York: Putnam's 1962.
Archibald, the Traveling Poodle. New York: Putnam's, 1963.
Eggs of Things. New York: Putnam's, 1963. Written with Anne Sexton.
The Beach before Breakfast. New York: Putnam's, 1964.
More Eggs of Things. New York: Putnam's, 1964. Written with Anne Sexton.
Speedy Digs Downside Up. New York: Putnam's, 1964.
Paul Bunyan. New York: Putnam's, 1966.
Faraway Farm. New York: Norton, 1967.
The Wonderful Babies of 1809 and Other Years. New York: Putnam's, 1968.
When Grandmother Was Young. New York: Putnam's, 1969.
When Mother Was Young. New York: Putnam's, 1970.
Joey and the Birthday Present. New York: McGraw-Hill, 1971. Written with Anne Sexton.
When Great-Grandmother Was Young. New York: Putnam's, 1971.
The Wizard's Tears. New York: McGraw-Hill, 1975. Written with Anne Sexton.
What Color Is Caesar? New York: McGraw-Hill, 1978.
The Microscope. New York: Harper & Row, 1984.

AUDIOCASSETTE

Progress Report. Washington, D.C.: Watershed Tapes, 1977.

BIOGRAPHICAL AND CRITICAL STUDIES

Beaver, Harold. "Refuge in the Library, on the Farm, and in Memories." *New York Times Book Review,* March 2, 1986, pp. 14–15.
Booth, Philip. "Poet, not Poetess." *Christian Science Monitor,* August 9, 1961, p. 9.
———. "Maxine Kumin's Survival." *American Poetry Review,* 7: 18–19 (November–December 1978).
Carter, Mary. "Hallie and Sukey's Hangups." *New York Times Book Review,* May 5, 1968, p. 37.
DuPlessis, Rachel Blau. "Individual Writers: Maxine Kumin in Deep." *Journal of Modern Literature,* 15, nos. 2–3: 366–367 (1988).
Estess, Sybil P. "Past Halfway: *The Retrieval System,* by Maxine Kumin." *Iowa Review,* 10: 99–109 (Fall 1979).
Gearhart, Jean B. "Courage to Survive—Maxine Kumin." *Pembroke Magazine,* no. 20: 272–275 (1988).
George, Diana Hume. "Itinerary of an Obsession: Maxine Kumin's Poems to Anne Sexton." In *Original Essays on the Poetry of Anne Sexton.* Edited by Frances Bixler. Conway: University of Central Arkansas Press, 1988. Pp. 243–266.
———. "'Keeping Our Working Distance': Maxine Kumin's Poetry of Loss and Survival." In *Aging and Gender in Literature: Studies in Creativity.* Edited by Anne M. Wyatt-Brown and Janice Rossen. University Press of Virginia, 1993. Pp. 314–338.
Gordon, David J. "New Books in Review." *Yale Review,* 58: 119–121 (Autumn 1968).
Lesser, Wendy. "Poetic Sense and Sensibility." *Washington Post Book World,* February 2, 1986, p. 11.
Ludvigson, Susan. "Maxine Kumin." In *Dictionary of Literary Biography.* Vol. 5, *American Poets since World War II,* pt. 1. Edited by D. J. Greiner. Detroit: Gale Research, 1980. Pp. 416–423.
Middlebrook, Diane Wood. *Anne Sexton: A Biography.* Boston: Houghton Mifflin, 1991.
Miller, David. "Out Far and In Deep." *Sewanee Review,* 96, no. 4: 684–687 (1988).
Muske, Carol. "Go Be a King in a Field of Weeds." *New York Times Book Review,* November 5, 1989, pp. 32–33.
Oates, Joyce Carol. "One for Life, One for Death." *New York Times Book Review,* November 19, 1972, pp. 7, 14.
Ostriker, Alicia. "Memory and Attachment." *New York Times Book Review,* August 8, 1982, pp. 10, 22.

Park, Clara Claiborne. "Mature Fruits." *The Nation,* July 24–30, 1982, pp. 89–90.

Raver, Anne. "The Storyteller in the Garden." *New York Times Book Review,* August 28, 1994, p. 12.

Slater, J. Joseph. "All's Well in the Garden of Verse." *Saturday Review,* May 6, 1961, pp. 29–30.

Vendler, Helen. "False Poets and Real Poets." *New York Times Book Review,* September 7, 1975, pp. 6–8, 10.

Vertreace, Martha M. "Secrets Left to Tell: Creativity and Continuity in the Mother/Daughter Dyad." In *Mother Puzzles: Daughters and Mothers in Contemporary American Literature.* Edited by Mickey Pearlman. Westport, Conn.: Greenwood, 1989. Pp. 77–89.

Webster, Harvey Curtis. "Six Poets." *Poetry,* 133, no. 4: 227–234 (1979).

Zeidner, Lisa. "Empty Beds, Nests, and Cities." *New York Times Book Review,* March 21, 1993, p. 14.

INTERVIEWS

Armitage, Shelley. "An Interview with Maxine Kumin." *Paintbrush,* 7–8, nos. 13–16: 48–57 (1981).

George, Diana Hume. "Kumin on Kumin and Sexton: An Interview." *Poesis,* 6, no. 2: 1–18 (1985).

Hammond, Karla. "An Interview with Maxine Kumin." *Western Humanities Review,* 33, no. 1: 1–15 (1979).

Mapson, Jo-Ann. "An Interview with Maxine Kumin." *High Plains Literary Review,* 7, no. 2: 68–86 (1992).

Meek, Martha George. "An Interview with Maxine Kumin." *Massachusetts Review,* 16, no. 1: 317–327 (1975).

Showalter, Elaine, and Carol Smith. "A Nurturing Relationship: A Conversation with Anne Sexton and Maxine Kumin." *Women's Studies,* 4, no. 1: 115–135 (1976).

~

DENISE LEVERTOV
(1923–1997)

WILLIAM DORESKI

DENISE LEVERTOV HAS earned praise for her mastery of free verse and other nonmetrical forms, and for her urgent and powerful attempt through her poetry to conflate private and public languages in the grave, calm texture of myth. Though she has been described as more interested in the psychology of the poet than in the resulting poem, most of her admirers consider her commitment to craft and preoccupation with language to be the heart of her poetics. For her, perception is inseparable from the act of making poetry. In *The Poet in the World* (1973), she argues that

> the poet does not see and then begin to search for words to say what he sees: he begins to see and at once begins to say or to sing, and *only in the action of verbalization does he see further.* His language is not more dependent on his vision than his vision is upon his language.

This organic view of the creative process so closely links the psychology of perception with the impulse to make a poem—arguing, in fact, that for a poet, making a poem *is* perception—that they become inseparable. This view also reflects her conviction that the form and the content of a poem must coincide as fully as possible.

Levertov's understanding and articulation of her own poetic has given her a deservedly high reputation as a critic. Her poetry, while sometimes receiving mixed reviews, has earned her a reputation as one of the finest contemporary American poets and almost certainly the best of those committed to the formal ideas of William Carlos Williams and Charles Olson. Kenneth Rexroth in 1961 called her "incomparably the best poet of what is getting to be known as the new avant garde," and in 1970 said, "She . . . resembles Mallarme or Pierre Reverdy, except that she is easily understood." Her work has developed and varied its focus over the five decades of her career, notably providing some of the most controversial public poetry of our time, but her characteristic techniques and concerns give it a consistency and tone peculiarly her own.

Most important is Levertov's aesthetic requirement that the poem form a coherent, cohesive whole, rejecting or reinterpreting the fragmentation and loose association of the poetry of her mentors, William Carlos Williams and Charles Olson. James F. Mersmann points out that "Levertov tries to give her poems the shape and pattern she discovers outside the poem." Perhaps because of this poetic animism, this desire to imitate in the poem the form of its subject, she focuses entirely on the short poem, or on brief sequences of short lyrics, and avoids the larger-scale enterprise of Williams' *Paterson,* Ezra Pound's *The Cantos,* or Olson's *The* Maximus *Poems.* But rather than limiting her subject matter, her aesthetic program makes available a wide range of content.

The search for poetry of an inner harmony, a harmony of form and content that by 1965 Levertov would call "organic poetry," coincides with her desire for a poetic that would be flexible enough to admit both polemical responses to political and social concerns and the larger abstractions that the imagism of the modernist period generally prohibited. The formal cohesion of the poem, derived from the cohesion of individual perception, makes available any subject of genuine interest to the perceiving mind of the poet. "Organic poetry," she writes in her 1965 essay "Some Notes on Organic Form" "is a *method of apperception,* i.e., of recognizing what we perceive, and is based on an intuition of an order, a form beyond forms, in which forms partake, and of which man's creative works are analogies, resemblances, natural allegories."

Only under the pressure of realized poetic form can these varied perceptions fully cohere and harmonize. Her recognition that poetic form and language tend to allegorize natural imagery has directed Levertov toward myth: not, until recent years, toward the inclusive, narrative mythology of the Bible and the classical period, but rather to a sense of the power of language to transcend the banalities of actuality and to embody, in some small degree, an otherwise elusive ideal or ineffable sense of the presence of spiritual mystery. To Levertov the primary task of the language of poetry is to give voice to the potential myth of natural landscape and the quotidian by asserting the strangeness, the otherness, of the familiar, as in "Matins" (*The Jacob's Ladder*): "The cow's breath / not forgotten in the mist, in the / words." She describes that process of language-discovery, one that actively engages the reader in the making of myth, in "To the Reader," the brief *ars poetica* that opens her 1961 volume, *The Jacob's Ladder*:

As you read, a white bear leisurely
pees, dyeing the snow
saffron,

and as you read, many gods
lie among lianas: eyes of obsidian
are watching the generations of leaves,

and as you read
the sea is turning its dark pages,
turning
its dark pages.

What is happening in this little poem? What sort of questions does it respond to, given that Levertov (in *The Poet in the World*) argues that "what the poet is called upon to clarify is not answers but the existence and nature of questions?" Its most obvious response is to the question, "What happens when we read?" Rather than a direct answer the poem offers a group of mysterious images and directs us toward the source of myth and the process of making it out of nature. The white bear that "leisurely / pees" may seem a slightly satiric figure of the writer, who inscribes the white absence (the blank page) with the effluvia of the mind. But it is also a fairy-tale figure rendered in actual terms, a mysterious white animal (white animals are usually magical) that functions with physiological verisimilitude. This illustrates what Richard Pevear has identified in a review of *Footprints* in the *Hudson Review* (1973) as "a natural piety that tends toward animism," and suggests that for the poet the natural world is not entirely objective but in some way is caught up with our inner lives.

Linking the half-concealed life in nature with the inner world of the self is a primal task for the writer. The critic Northrop Frye has identified this project as the "final cause" of art. But this poem gives the reader the responsibility of making that link, equating reading with the greater temporal process of vegetative succession ("generations of leaves") and the evolution of order out of chaos, turning the pages of the book as the sea turns its dark pages. The shape of the poem, an unfolding that turns, finally, on the word "turning," mimes with mostly enjambed free-verse lines the larger act of turning pages.

The figure of the reader, according to Levertov's 1968 lecture "origins of a Poem" (in *The Poet in the World*), is half of a dialogue of the artist with herself. She approvingly quotes Ernst Barlach, a German playwright and sculptor, who argues that "Every art needs two—one who makes it, and one who needs it," then extends the argument by postulating a reader within one's self. This reader will respond "with the innocence you bring to a poem by someone unknown to you." Thus the reader-self is a critical buffer between the poet-maker and the unknown, anonymous reader out there somewhere. "To the Reader" then addresses both the self, carrying on that inner colloquy Levertov finds at the heart of many of her poems, and the traditional reader.

Levertov's poetics of organic order and natural piety inform even her stridently antiwar poems of the late 1960's and early 1970's. This poetic may derive in part not only from the early influence of Herbert Read and the other British neo-Romantics popular in her youth and from the objectivism learned from Robert Duncan, Robert Creeley, and Charles Olson, but also from her complex family background. Doris Earnshaw argues that as "granddaughter on her father's side of a Russian Hasidic Jew and on her mother's of a Welsh mystic," Levertov "was fitted by birth and political destiny to voice the terrors and pleasures of the twentieth century." Because Levertov so often derives her poems from the immediate or the past events of her life, her biography can usefully inform responses to her poetry.

Levertov's father was a Russian Jew who had immigrated to England and become an Anglican minister. Denise Levertov was born there on October 24, 1923, and grew up in suburban Ilford, Essex. (Sources conflict over whether her city of birth was actually London or Ilford.) Her father, who spelled his name Levertoff, descended from the founder of Habad Hasidism. Some of the characteristics of this sect seem to survive in Levertov's poetry, since she describes it as embodying both "a very great strain of asceticism" and "a recognition and joy in the physical world" (quoted in Wagner, *Denise Levertov: In Her Own Province*). This seems to describe perfectly a great deal of her own work, though it also suggests that Levertov has chosen to understand this sect on her own terms. Her mother was Welsh and, like Levertov's father, was descended from a religious figure, the preacher-tailor Angel Jones of Mold. Though Levertov's poetry, even her later overtly Christian work, is more pantheistic than conventionally religious in the Judeo-Christian tradition, it is infused with this strongly religious family background.

Levertov did not receive a good deal of formal education (she attended neither grammar school nor a university), but her schooling at home was thoroughly literary. Her mother introduced her to the work of the great Victorian writers, particularly Tennyson, of whom she later said, "I had him practically stuck under my armpit for several years of my childhood" (quoted in Wagner, *In Her Own Province*). Through reading at home, through the formal study of ballet, and through exposure to the refugees, artists, and eccentrics her father befriended, she came early in life to believe in the importance of art and its place in her own life.

As Levertov recounts in the introduction to her *Collected Earlier Poems,* at the age of twelve she sent some poems to T. S. Eliot, who responded some months later with a lengthy letter "full of advice." She then recalls that at sixteen she met Herbert Read, whose ideas on art and culture are a major influence on her poetry to the present day. By the time she was nineteen her work was appearing in journals such as *Poetry Quarterly, Outposts,* and *Voices.* During the war Levertov served as a civilian nurse in St. Luke's Hospital in Fitzroy Square, London. There she wrote most of the poems in her first book, *The Double Image,* published in 1946 by the Cresset Press. To achieve this publication, Levertov by her own account walked naively into the office (mistakenly entering through the stockroom) and handed her "ill-typed manuscript" to an editor. Though doubtful, the editor passed the manuscript on to John Hayward, the director of the press, who decided to publish it.

Critics have usually described the poems in *The Double Image* as characteristic of the neo-Romantic mood of British poetry at the time. However, the best poems already display a tendency to defamiliarize the domestic and natural world and emphasize the essentially private way the individual is forced to confront otherness. The second half of "Christmas 1944" illustrates the mixture of

Georgian imagery and startling and effective personification ("a dark excited tree," "hearing hatred crackle in the coal") that defines her work of the 1940's:

> A painted bird or boat above the fire,
> a fire in the hearth, a candle in the dark,
> a dark excited tree, fresh from the forest,
> are all that stands between us and the wind.
> The wind has many tales to tell of sea and
>   city,
> a plague on many houses, fear knocking on
>   the doors;
> how venom trickles from the open mouth of
>   death,
> and trees are white with rage of alien battles.
> Who can be happy while the wind recounts
> its long sagas of sorrow? Though we are safe
> in a flickering circle of winter festival
> we dare not laugh; or if we laugh, we lie,
> hearing hatred crackle in the coal,
> the voice of reason, the voice of love.

The free verse is almost as measured as blank verse, and the orderly, fluent syntax and manifest faith in natural epiphany characterize her work at this time. The faith in epiphany is Wordsworthian and will remain with her through a long, productive career, so that even late work like "The day longs for the evening" from *Breathing the Water* (1987) can ask of an almost wholly personified landscape "What is that promised evening?" and find the illumination of faith in natural occurrence.

The poems of *The Double Image* embody a recurring sense of loss, which in the context of Levertov's natural piety requires the ritualizing of death. To defer the bottomless mystery of death, Levertov in "To Death" addresses it directly and offers its personified form the honors due a god. But the poem also invites death to play a role, to be an image rather than an actuality, a sign instead of a referent. "Enter with riches. Let your image wear / brocade of fantasy, and bear your part / with all the actor's art and arrogance." If death does this (that is, if it accepts the role of image and actor) it "will receive, deserve due ritual," and the speaker will be able to address this fictional version of death as "eloquent, just, and mighty one"—praise that otherwise, except for the last modifier, actual death hardly deserves. This Romantic personification of death typifies the early Levertov's withdrawal from the modernist urban imagery of Eliot and Auden and the avoidance of the horrors of the just-concluded war. Later, although retaining the concern with mythmaking, the devices of personification and apostrophe, the natural piety and idealism, Levertov would move sharply in the other direction, embracing the mundane horror of modern war in a language that if anything was too nakedly eager to confront its subject matter. But in doing so she demonstrated how flexible an instrument her early poetic was, and proved that her commitment to an expressive, Romantic aesthetic by no means limited her range.

Levertov first appeared in an American publication in 1949 in Kenneth Rexroth's anthology *New British Poetry.* By then she had married Mitchell Goodman, an American soldier, novelist, and poet, had moved to New York City, and had produced a son, Nikolai. Sometime during her first few years in New York, Levertov began to read William Carlos Williams, whose influence transformed her poetry and gave her a new idiom that amalgamated her early romanticism with a more hard-edged language of immediate perception. Her interest in two other younger poets confirmed her sense of the importance of Williams. Robert Creeley, who published her work in *Black Mountain Review* and *Origin,* and Robert Duncan became her friends in the early 1950's. Both poets taught at Black Mountain College, under the direction of Charles Olson, and through them Levertov became known as a "Black Mountain" poet. But her poetry cannot be assigned to any school, and while she admires Duncan and Creeley she has always considered her work distinct from theirs. Williams is the common denominator. Though the full effect of exposure to Williams appeared gradually, by 1957 when her second book, *Here and Now,* appeared, the shift from her rich but somewhat Georgian early poetry was complete.

This second book and the third, *Overland to the Islands* (1958), have interesting and overlapping histories. They are so linked that Levertov now thinks they should have appeared as a single volume. Weldon Kees, Levertov reports, had solicited a collection of her work for a small press he planned to start with a friend. Unfortunately for Levertov and American poetry, Kees shortly thereafter leapt from the Golden Gate Bridge. The following year, Lawrence Ferlinghetti, who had obtained the manuscript material in Kees's possession, offered to publish a book, and after sifting through available poems produced *Here and Now.* The following year, Jonathan Williams published *Overland to the Islands,* which according to Levertov consisted of the "rejects" from the earlier volume, and a few more recent poems. In her introduction to *Collected Earlier Poems* Levertov comments that "poems that should really have been in a single book together because of their interrelationships were arbitrarily divided between *Here and Now* and *Overland to the Islands."* Further, Robert Duncan suggested that both books suffered from a lack of clear ordering. Levertov points out that "to *compose* a book is preferable to randomly gathering one."

Whatever the problems with the ordering of these books, the individual poems display a firmness of imagery, a clarity of language, and the first signs of Levertov's mastery of the "variable foot" of Williams, which would become central to her theory of rhythm and the organic unity of her poetic. In an interview with Walter Sutton (in *Poet in the World*), Levertov describes the source of the variable foot as "a sense of pulse, a pulse in behind the words, a pulse that is actually sort of tapped out by a drum in the poem." She considers this form distinct from free verse, believing that verse requires a regularity, and rejects the "breath-spaced" line as well on the grounds that it attempts to imitate speech, while the poem should reflect an "inner voice" that may not be reproducible in speech. This "inner voice," she argues, "is not necessarily identical with [the poet's] literal speaking voice, nor is his inner vocabulary identical with that which he uses in conversation." By rejecting an easy identification of poetry with speech Levertov distinguishes herself from the less thoughtful imitators of Williams and retains the Romantic-expressive core of her poetic. Despite or perhaps because of her animism there can be no perfect clarity in the relationship between the natural world and the language in which she describes it. The clarity of her rhythms, however, would brilliantly outline that mystery and help give her poems a structural firmness that would more than make up for slack language and occasional vagaries of metaphor.

Levertov's early, pre-Williams poems have the virtues of conventional form as well as a flair for unexpected phrasing. Her primary weakness is an overreliance on symbolic convention and predictably poetic subject matter. By *Here and Now,* though, the example of Williams had begun to free her from conventions, both of form and content, and her poems open themselves to the domestic and commonplace, while embracing a paradoxical sense of both the otherness and the spiritual congeniality of the natural world—a paradox that by the period of *The Jacob's Ladder* would give her poems a rich mythic texture. The poems of *Here and Now* are sometimes too insistently joyful, their language often too decorative, but the grasp of Williams' rhythmic principles lends them a drive and energy that the poems of *The Double Image* lacked. "Jackson Square" illustrates the strengths and weakness of her mid-1950's idiom:

> Bravo! the brave sunshine.
> A triangle of green green contains
> the sleek and various pigeons
> the starving inventors and all
> who sit on benches in the morning,
> to sun tenacious hopes—indeed
> a gay morning for hope to feed on
> greedy as the green
>   and gray
>   and purple-preening birds . . .

The repetition of "green," the typographical insistence on the colors of the birds, the poem's tendency toward self-explication ("to sun tenacious hopes . . . a gay morning for hope") echo Williams' weaker mannerisms, but the adroit flexing of syntax against the loose but regular rhythms imposed by the line-breaks shows how well Levertov has grasped his rhythmic principles.

If the language of *Here and Now* sometimes is too ornately pictorial, *Overland to the Islands,* although supposedly made up of rejects from the previous book, often displays a more concentrated focus on the everyday world, less tendency to rhapsodize. The most interesting poems focus on domestic concerns in a fresh, colloquial voice, as in "The Dogwood":

> The sink is full of dishes. Oh well.
> Ten o'clock, there's no
> hot water.
> The kitchen floor is unswept, the broom
> has been shedding straws. Oh well.

This poem illustrates another lesson well learned from Williams: the clearly defined, colloquial speaking voice gives a necessary life to things not by imposing abstractions upon them but by acknowledging them for what they are. Williams learned this from his early reading of Keats, so it is a lesson perfectly compatible with Levertov's Romantic faith in the sufficiency of the world.

Levertov's next book would be her first by a major publisher. Rexroth, she believes, brought her work to the attention of James Laughlin, and in 1960 New Directions published *With Eyes at the Back of Our Heads.* The title directs the reader to Levertov's concern with indirection, with finding what one wants by avoiding looking directly for it, and her belief that what we see with the physical eye is less essential than what we see with the mind's eye, the unconscious back-of-the-head eye directed by a mind alert to myth. This is the topic of her title poem:

> With eyes at the back of our heads
> we see a mountain
> not obstructed with woods but laced
> here and there with feathery groves.

Unlike real mountains, which tend to be obstructed with woods, this one, the sheer bulk of the mythic world available to the imagination, with its "feathery groves" is the background against which we can construct more personal fantasies. The personal fantasy of this poem revolves about a house, perhaps a facade, that is both shelter and garment. Architect and knitter, two functionaries of the imagination combine their talents to render the house accessible so that we may pass through it and reach the mountain beyond:

> When the doors widen
> when the sleeves admit us
> the way to the mountain will be clear,
> the mountain we see with
> eyes at the back of our heads, mountain
> green, mountain
> cut of limestone, echoing
> with hidden rivers, mountain
> of short grass and subtle shadows.

The imagination, here embodied in the arts of knitting and architecture, bridges the gap between the mind and the exterior world. The house, though only a facade—something that like a sweater we "wear" to define ourselves better—gives admittance to the natural world beyond. Both the created and the natural world in this poem are products of imagination, but art, not their mutual source in the mind, links them. The pleasure Levertov takes in the poetic function, the power of joining self and nature in the common medium of mythic language, shapes this book and gives it an affirmative tone distinct from the ironic, cool, witty, or learned tones of contemporaries such as Creeley, Lowell, Rich, or Olson.

"To the Snake" most clearly points to the source of that joy, the pleasure in working through natural symbol to produce a synthesis between the self and the world. By hanging the green snake around her throat the poet assumes the power of the goddess (the subject of another poem in this volume). She also takes a risk—snakes tempt, lie, and bite—but the poet is willing to assume the full weight of the symbol, and by avoiding the illusion that myth is necessarily either positive or negative she experiences a richer sense of its place in the world:

> Green Snake—I swore to my companions
> that certainly
> you were harmless! But truly
> I had no certainty, and no hope, only
> desiring to hold you, for that joy,
> which left
> a long wake of pleasure, as the leaves moved
> and you faded into the pattern
> of grass and shadow, and I returned
> smiling and haunted, to a dark morning.

This implied definition of the poet's task, to assume the mantle of myth and risk losing one's self in the larger patterns of the natural world, would be refined in *The Jacob's Ladder* (1961), in which Levertov turned to the problem of the proper language of poetry. The first poem (after the poem "To the Reader"), "A Common Ground," sites the poet's work in the "common ground" of agriculture, which is "here and there gritty with pebbles / yet elsewhere 'fine and mellow— / uncommon fine for ploughing.' " The poem's second section turns to the issue of the place of both poetry and nature in the contemporary world of New York's Central Park where "the girls / laugh at the sun, men / in business suits awkwardly / recline" and poetry occupies a secretive, almost subversive role: "Poems stirred / into paper coffee-cups, eaten / with petals on rye in the / sun. . . ." The third section turns to the question of language: "Not 'common speech' / a dead level / but the uncommon speech of paradise," she argues, "a language / excelling itself to be itself."

This book refines that language through the dictates of a more sophisticated and compelling sense of rhythm. "Six Variations" catalogs some of the rhythmic possibilities available to the organic poem with its unified field of imagery. One kind of rhythm (in the third variation) is onomatopoeic in origin:

> Shulp, shulp, the dog
> as it laps up
> water
> makes intelligent
> music . . .

Another section (fourth variation) in the manner of Alexander Pope manipulates vowels to slow the line in imitation of its subject:

> when your answers
> come
> slowly, dragging
> their feet

But the title poem reminds us that poetry isn't entirely a matter of craft. "The Jacob's Ladder" argues that the humility of the religious supplicant is also a necessary aspect of poetry (its visionary aspect) and argues that whatever the poem envisions it experiences as real:

> A stairway of sharp
> angles, solidly built
> one sees that the angels must spring
> down from one step to the next, giving a
> little lilt of the wings:
>
> and a man climbing
> must scrape his knees, and bring
> the grip of his hands into play. The cut
> stone
> consoles his groping feet. Wings brush past
> him.
> The poem ascends.

This poem demonstrates how Levertov's neo-Romantic tendencies have given way to a more vividly mystic aspiration, perhaps derived in part from the work of Robert Duncan and surely linked to the Hasidic tradition of her early years. The idiom of William Carlos Williams, though, helps ground this mysticism in a feeling for actuality. Rather than ecstatic revelation, these poems make ritual encounters with concrete particulars of nature the basis of the relationship between the speaker and the subjects of the poems. Though vague spirit-figures prowl on the fringes, the source of mystery seems to lie in the human ability to bond through imagination the self and the exterior world.

This sense of mystery as something rooted in us haunts Levertov's work to the present. The failure to realize or to respect this essential link with otherness disappoints or even enrages her. The difficulty in effectively directing her frustration with the narrow, unimaginative, inhumane vision of establishment politics is one of the causes of the aesthetic failures of some of her Vietnam War-era poems. She sometimes forgets her own injunction (in *Poet in the World*) that "Insofar as poetry has a social function it is to awaken sleepers by other means than shock." But even in those difficult times her poetry, as we will see, retains its organic ideals of form and rhythm, its faith in individual vision, and its trust in nature as the source of metaphorical and spiritual significance.

The Jacob's Ladder and the two books that followed confirmed Levertov as a distinct, unique, and powerful voice in American poetry. In reviewing *The Jacob's Ladder,* James Wright called her "one of the best living poets in America," and other reviewers, if not always so effusive, accorded her the respect due an important writer. *O Taste and See* (1964) is a more sensuous book, with more imagery of the body, sex, childbirth, and marriage. But the domesticity of the subject matter does not exclude the mystic vision central to *The Jacob's Ladder.* "Eros at Temple Stream" typifies the language of bodily pleasure that permeates this book, and it also demonstrates how these poems work toward transcendence through, not despite, the body and the other material things of this world:

> The river in its abundance
> many-voiced
> all about us as we stood
> on a warm rock to wash
>
> slowly
> smoothing in long
>   sliding strokes
> our soapy hands along each other's
> slippery cool bodies

The poem retains this sensuous materiality but introduces a visionary note as the hands become flames and the entire body becomes "sleek and / on fire." Linking flesh to fire is a way of asserting the immortality of the spirit as something derived from the vitality of the body itself. As nature inspirits language in Levertov's world, so the body now inspirits the soul and will continue doing so through her future work.

In 1965, the year after the publication of *O Taste and See,* Levertov's important essay "Some Notes on Organic Form" appeared in *Poetry* magazine. This is her clearest and most prescriptive comment on her art and has been reprinted several times, most influentially in Stephen Berg and Robert Mezey's anthology *Naked Poetry* (1969). Her description of the poetic process is so concrete and so aptly applies to her own work that it is hard to remember that for other poets the writing experience may be quite different: "I think it's like this: First there must be an experience, a sequence or constellation of perceptions of sufficient interest, felt by the poet intensely enough to demand of him their equivalence in words: he is *brought to speech.*"

Like Wordsworth, she places the origin of poetry in individual experience and gives less importance to the larger, cultural experience that like language itself makes poetry possible. Arguing from the amalgamation (a "constellation") of perceptions, as Eliot does for the metaphysical poets, she makes the poem entirely a product of sense perception and emotion. Though not completely original, her assertion that organic poetry is self-formative, that instead of refusing form it creates a fresh form with every effort, had great appeal and influenced many other poets, particularly those coming to maturity in the 1960's.

By 1965 the Vietnam War was a dominant political and moral issue in American life. Levertov became one of the most outspoken opponents of the war, which contravened her belief in the centrality of nature and the imagination. The war violated nature and betrayed the imagination, denied the spirit and degraded the body. One of her best books, *The Sorrow Dance* (1967), describes in eight carefully arranged sections her growing commitment to political action. The transition from celebration of the natural world of love to poems of social protest was triggered in part by the terrible spectacle of Vietnam (which in many of the poems of *The Sorrow Dance* is represented by the depiction of peace- and nature-loving Buddhists assuming activist roles) and partly by the death of her sister Olga, who had been more committed to political activism than Levertov herself was at this point.

The elegiac sequence entitled "The Olga Poems" is one of Levertov's strongest poems. Levertov depicts her closeness to her sister in the language of nature, as if Olga in death had entered the very being of the world:

> Now as if smoke or sweetness were blown
> my way
> I inhale a sense of her livingness in that
> instant,
> feeling, dreaming, hoping, knowing boredom
> and zest like anyone
> else—
>
> a young girl in the garden, the same
> alchemical square
> I grew in.

Yet perhaps because she was so attuned to nature, Olga was willing to oppose its inertia and stasis and consequently set herself to impossible tasks:

> . . . To change,
> to change the course of the river! What rage
> for order
> disordered her pilgrimage—so that for years
> at a time
>
> she would hide among strangers, waiting
> to rearrange all mysteries in a new light.

Levertov had begun to realize that praising nature is not enough to shape adequate human ideals. Because the natural order of things does not necessarily correspond to the most desirable human order, one must sometimes "change the course of the river" and place one's self in opposition to impossible forces. Olga would become her model for such opposition, but so would the Buddhists of Southeast Asia and the young people of America who in the late 1960's looked to nature, farming, communal living, and the utter rejection of war as they attempted to make new metaphors for the human community.

By 1967 Buddhist protestors in Vietnam had demonstrated the necessity, the beauty, and the consequences of such opposition. In "The Altars in the Street" Levertov acknowledges their heroism in terms that pit nature against the city, the innocence of natural religion against the spiritual corruption of repressive violence.

> Children begin at green dawn nimbly to
> build topheavy altars, overweighted with
> prayers
> . . .
> . . . by noon
> the whole city in all its corruption,
>
> all its shed blood the monsoon cannot wash
> away,
> has become a temple,
> fragile, insolent, absolute.

The next to last section of *The Sorrow Dance,* which includes "The Altars in the Street," is called "Life At War" and contains a poem prophetically entitled "Didactic Poem." The title indicates the direction that much of Levertov's work would take during the next few years.

The poems Levertov wrote in the late 1960's reflected her own involvement in protest and the sacrifices she and her husband made on behalf of the peace movement. She traveled to Hanoi, participated in peace rallies as a featured speaker, and joined with Robert Bly, Galway Kinnell, and other poets in organizing readings against the war. Mitchell Goodman's involvement was even deeper, and eventually he was tried with Benjamin Spock on charges of conspiracy to incite resistance to the draft. The poems concurrent with these activities often are journalistic, fragmentary, apparently disordered.

Most of the reviewers of *Relearning the Alphabet* (1970) and *To Stay Alive* (1971) objected to her rhetoric of protest, finding it an inflexible use of language that discouraged the play of imagery that informed her best work, though some of those reviewers were also sympathetic to the aesthetic as well as the moral necessity behind these poems. Marie Borroff, writing in the *Yale Review,* commented of Levertov that "the time-honored impulse to celebrate, to wonder, to sing is basic in her, and this impulse is, literally, disturbed by the knowledge that an unassimilable evil exists which must be hated and which must be fought on the level of action." Most reviewers seemed aware of and sympathetic to the pressure Levertov felt from what she took to be the forces of evil, the war and its supporters and profiteers.

But the resultant poetry discouraged even many of Levertov's previous supporters. Marjorie Perloff's review of *To Stay Alive* typifies the negative reaction to both the strong rhetorical stance and the dubious formal characteristics of the poems of this period: "Her anti-Vietnam War poems, written in casual diary form, sound rather like a versified *New York Review of Books*—the same righteous indignation, the same uncompromising moral zeal and self-important tone. It is difficult to believe that the poet who, as one of the most promising heirs of William Carlos Williams, wrote 'The world is / not with us enough / O taste and see,' should now resort to the flat abstractions, the facile polemics, and the careless rhythms of *To Stay Alive.*"

To Stay Alive opens by reprinting "The Olga Poems," and the high quality of those elegies contrasts starkly with the rambling, inefficient journal-poems gathered under the title "Staying Alive":

> Chuck Matthei
> travels the country
>   a harbinger.
> (He's 20. His golden beard was pulled and
>   clipped
>   by a Wyoming sheriff, but no doubt
>   has grown
>   again
> though he can't grow knocked-out teeth.
> He wears sneakers even in winter,
> to avoid animal-hide; etc.)

One might feel that the journal-world signified by "etc." could continue indefinitely. But worse than the rambling and seemingly disorganized, decidedly inorganic quality of the verse is the trite sentiment that crops up in place of the crisp epiphanies that empowered her earlier poems:

>   But Chuck has found in it
> a message for all who resist war,
>   disdain to kill,
>   try to equate
>   'human' with 'humane.'

In recent years, however, more scholarly approaches to these poems have partly rehabilitated them. Richard Jackson finds that their journal aesthetic constitutes an interesting problem in the way a text manipulates its subject matter and temporal framework. Nancy J. Sisko finds merit even in the disorderliness of many of the poems, arguing that "when Levertov accurately records her own struggle she in turn mirrors the struggle of others like her during that era." And Bonnie Costello comments that "*Relearning the Alphabet* was Levertov's most successful effort of identification [empathy with victims], for it showed how history had turned the very tools of the poet—language and imagination—into cruel weapons of distortion." With distance these poems have acquired some of the charm history confers on the artifact, but also they seem more clearly now to reveal beneath the sometimes shrill rhetoric Levertov's respect for life as the subtext of her rage.

Footprints, her 1972 volume, returned to her old concerns, but many of the poems seem exhausted and unraveled. Levertov's faith in organic form no longer engenders tightly knit poems like those in *The Jacob's Ladder* and *O Taste and See.* Instead, a looser kind of association and tone of elegiac uncertainty mark the poems of her next few books. "A Place to Live" exemplifies both the style and the ethos of her changed voice:

> Honeydew seeds: on impulse
> strewn in a pot of earth. Now,

(the green vines) wandering
down over the pot's edges:

certainly no room here to lay
the egg of a big, pale,
green-fleshed melon.
                    Wondering

where the hell to go.

Where indeed? Levertov's antiwar poems opened up new possibilities, looser structures, more journalistic ideas of form, but she had not yet found a way to link her evolving formal ideas to her earlier concern with myth-making and vision.

In *The Freeing of the Dust* (1975) the thematic concern with Vietnam continues with poems about her visit to North Vietnam in 1972, about a trip to Moscow, and about lost, misdirected, or failed personal relationships. In North Vietnam she visited the Bach Mai Hospital and was moved to write poems like "Weeping Woman" as well as the important essay "Glimpses of Vietnamese Life" in *The Poet in the World* (1973). Meanwhile, at home in America, her marriage was dissolving, and the book that resulted, by conflating essentially private grief with a public outrage over Vietnamese war casualties, seems unwittingly to equate these markedly distinct sources of pain.

Though Levertov carefully divided *The Freeing of the Dust* into nine well-considered sections to give it a clearly autobiographical shape that would help justify the inclusion of such different kinds of poems, the impression remains of a poet still somewhat at odds with herself. More journal-like poems ("Conversation in Moscow," "Modes of Being") alternate with poignant though sometimes bathetic brief lyrics of suffering and loss. Strong antiwar poems such as "The Pilots," which attempts to deal with her complex feelings about the participants in the war (and is frank about her sense of moral and class superiority to these American prisoners of war), stand beside poems that lapse into the preachy abstractions of *To Stay Alive.* The best poems in this book, however, such as "Room," call for a renewal of the poetry and aesthetic of celebration. Harry Marten's comment that "the lyrics in *The Freeing of the Dust* . . . represent an expansion of Levertov's range of experience" is correct, but the match between her essentially mystical, visionary sensibility and public and political subject matter remains an uneasy one.

Life in the Forest (1978) is a book of healthy metaphorical vision, of poems in which most personal emotions find objective correlatives, though its more historical or public poems still display a flaccid, sometimes sentimental rhetonc. In its best poems and this is a book with many fine poems—the dominant sense is of private experience opening into metaphor, and through that language process, of emotion finding correlation in the natural world. Instead of the abstraction into which the weaker poems in *The Freeing of the Dust* lapsed, here imagery shapes the argument of the poems. Partly this is the result of rejecting some aspects of the autobiographical voice as she had established it. In her introduction, Levertov says she wanted to "try to avoid overuse of the autobiographical, the dominant first-person singular of so much of the American poetry—good and bad—of recent years." Many of the poems are, in fact, written in the first person, and many use highly personal subject matter, but her statement may be an indirect way of acknowledging her desire to escape the tendency to moralize and draw abstract conclusions.

As Bonnie Costello argues in a long review, "When Levertov makes myth serve humanity—that idol of prophets and politicians—it is sluggish in its duties. She is a dreamer at heart, and her best moments are stolen, solitary ones, glimpses of a landscape at one A.M. when 'humanity' has long since gone to bed." Her public myths tend toward the polemic, her private ones achieve the luminosity of real vision. For this reason, moralizing for Levertov may be the most anti-autobiographical of acts. If she came to recognize this it would explain why most of *Life in the Forest* breaks so cleanly with the weaker work of her recent past. Also in her introduction, Levertov points to her poems that imitate the manner of Italian poet Cesare Pavese. His poems are actually much like many of those in Levertov's early volumes, so it is not surprising that her discovery of his work prompted a renewal of her own strongest mode. Though *Life in the Forest* uses a variety of voices and strategies, and includes discursive long-lined poems, brief intense imagistic lyrics, and some looser journal-like poems, she brings to all of this variety a greater sureness, a keener sense of language and the poetic line, and most important, a greater faith in imagery and metaphor than her poetry had displayed since *The Sorrow Dance.*

Levertov has often worked with poets whose sensibilities are compatible with her own and whose work in some way points toward her current thematic or structural concerns. The strategy of drawing upon translations to complement and illuminate her own work began with her important, separately published translation of Eugene Guillevic's *Selected Poems* (1969). Guillevic's loosely strung, vaguely political sequence "Interrogation" points toward the journal-poems Levertov would write in protest of the war, while Rilke's mystic vision became in a later work a model for her growing inwardness, her attempts to reconcile the visionary spirit with the limitations and pleasures of the flesh. "Variations on a Theme by Rilke," derived from a poem in his *Book of the Hours,* is one of a pair of translations that frame *Breathing the Water* (1987). Part two of this poem makes explicit Levertov's resignation to contextual human limitations:

> There will never be that stillness.
> Within the pulse of flesh,
> in the dust of being, where we trudge,
>   turning our hungry gaze this way and that,
> the wings of the morning
> brush through our blood
> as cloud-shadows brush the land.
> What we desire travels with us.
> We must breathe time as fishes breathe
>   water.
>   God's flight circles us.

But resignation to mortality is not the only mood in Levertov's recent work. A renewed sense of harmony between self and nature, language and feeling, pervades her four books of the 1980's. As her invocation of Rilke suggests, to a great extent this is due to a renewal of her religious and mystical sensibility. Her six-part sequence, "Mass for the Day of St. Thomas Didymus," from *Candles in Babylon* (1982), most fully represents this new awakening to the mysterious otherness of the world. It is utterly frank in acknowledging her inability to link the known to the unknowable and her new inclination to refuse the didacticism and arrogant tone of the poetry of the war years:

> We live in terror
> of what we do not know,
> in terror of not knowing,
> of the limitless, through which freefalling
> forever, our dread
> sinks and sinks,
>   or
>   of the violent closure of it all.

But the poem takes its consolation where Levertov first found it, in a pantheistic but now increasingly Christian sense of the order of nature:

> The name of the spirit is written
> in woodgrain, windripple, crystal,
> in crystals of snow, in petal, leaf,
> moss and moon, fossil and feather . . .

This nature is similar to us in sensibility, so that our attempt to impose order through the word (an attempt she would soon repudiate) bears at least some analogy to the larger order of things:

> blood, bone, song, silence,
> very word of
> very word.
>
> flesh and
> vision.

This renewed sense of contact with visionary mystery, and further, an enlarged sense of privilege in sensing or touching such cosmic matters, informs the best poems of *Candles in Babylon, Oblique Prayers* (1984), *Breathing the Water,* and *A Door in the Hive* (1989). One of the dominant notes in these books is submission to natural order, which is not an entirely new idea but one that would be more insistently presented after her profession of Christianity in the early 1980's. This new submissiveness does not represent a repudiation of her rage at the perversion of natural and social order represented by war, but another, more oblique way of approaching the same problem. The rage remains, with its attendant problems of rhetoric and didacticism, as "El Salvador: Requiem and Invocation" in *A Door in the Hive* demonstrates. But the political note no longer dominates. Nor does the raised voice of the revolutionary calling for overt action. Instead the most compelling voice of her recent work argues that the important task is to submit to nature and learn from it, learn not to attempt to force or reshape it to our will (to "interpret" it). This is illustrated by "The Absentee" (from *Breathing the Water*):

> Uninterpreted, the days
> are falling.
>
> The spring wind
> is shaking and shaking the trees.
>
> A nest of eggs,
> a nest of deaths.
>
> Falling
> abandoned.
>
> The palms rattle, the eucalypts
> shed bark and blossom. Uninterpreted.

If we heed this call for the acceptance of death and a meditative refusal of the intellect's urge to imposed order, what will we gain? The answer, unsurprisingly, is faith. Levertov in "A Poet's View" (1984) describes her own coming to faith as "not inevitable" but nearly so, a function of her very existence as a poet, a person dependent on the imagination.

> It must therefore be by the exercise of that faculty [the imagination] that one moves toward faith, and possibly by its failure that one rejects it as delusion. Poems present their testimony as circumstantial evidences, not as closing arguments. Where Wallace Stevens says, "God and the imagination are one," I would say that the imagination, which synergizes intellect, emotion and instinct, is the perceptive organ through which it is possible, though not inevitable, to experience God.

Through the imagination one may experience God and so come to faith. But that faith, though hard earned, is difficult to maintain against the human will to entropy and the relentless numbing routine of the ordinary. And as "The Love of Morning," in Levertov's *A Door in the Hive,* warns us, it is easy to accept God's love on mornings of birdsong when "sunlight's gossamer lifts in its net / the weight of all that is solid," but harder to realize "on gray mornings" when "all incident . . . is hard to love again" and "we resent a summons / that disregards our sloth, and this / calls us, calls us." This is the test.

But Christianity may be a resting place for the imagination, not a stimulus. That God should call us to the love of things when in exhaustion and depression we find little love in ourselves is neither a fresh nor unnoticed problem, and some of these late poems, instead of reaching for the sudden epiphany of a well-turned image, settle for rehashing familiar Christian themes. In such poems the imagery, like "sunlight's gossamer," lacks the vitality of the unexpected yet telling phrase.

On the other hand, poems like "Flying High," "Ikon: The Harrowing of Hell," "Midnight Gladness," and "Praise of a Palmtree," all from *A Door in the Hive,* demonstrate that Levertov remains capable of writing in language of rich ambiguity and producing poems in which rhythmic harmony and sensuous imagery generate convincing visions of the spiritual endowment of the world of things. "Midnight Gladness" exemplifies this unity of vision and imagery with its quiet but dramatic enactment of the act of perception:

The pleated lampshade, slightly askew,
dust a silverish muting of the lamp's fake
  brass.
My sock-monkey on the pillow, tail and
  limbs asprawl,
weary after a day of watching sunlight
      prowl the house like a wolf.
Gleams of water in my bedside glass.
Miraculous water, so peacefully
waiting to be consumed.

Though in the sixth decade of her career she has become a professed Christian, Levertov in her most alert poetic mode fixes her gaze not on the abstract ideal of paradise but on the things of this world and the embodied spirit that moves them—a spirit that like the transcendentalist world-soul is analogous to our own. Her myth-making now assumes distinctly biblical overtones, but the organic sense of the oneness of language and perception still endows her work with a feeling of wholeness and completion. Public and academic regard for her poetry remains high. A steady flow of scholarly articles testifies to a continuing interest in and respect for her work, and through her readings and teaching she still exerts considerable influence on younger poets. In her most recent books her poems remain clear and satisfying, their aesthetic and rhythmic integrity perfectly in tune with her evolving spiritual vision and admirably principled life.

Selected Bibliography

WORKS OF DENISE LEVERTOV

POETRY

The Double Image, (London: Cresset, 1946).
Here and Now, (San Francisco: City Lights, 1957).
Overland to the Islands, (Highlands, North Carolina: Jargon, 1958).
With Eyes at the Back of Our Heads, (New York: New Directions, 1960).
The Jacob's Ladder, (New York: New Directions, 1961).
O Taste and See, (New York: New Directions, 1964).
The Sorrow Dance, (New York: New Directions, 1967).
Relearning the Alphabet, (New York: New Directions, 1970).
To Stay Alive, (New York: New Directions, 1971).
Footprints, (New York: New Directions, 1972).
The Freeing of the Dust, (New York: New Directions, 1975).
Life in the Forest, (New York: New Directions, 1978).
Collected Earlier Poems 1940–1960, (New York: New Directions, 1979).
Candles in Babylon, (New York: New Directions, 1982).
Poems 1960–1967, (New York: New Directions, 1983).
Oblique Prayers, (New York: New Directions, 1984).
Poems 1968–1972, (New York: New Directions, 1987).
Breathing the Water, (New York: New Directions, 1987).
A Door in the Hive, (New York: New Directions, 1989).

PROSE

The Poet in the World, (New York: New Directions, 1973). Includes her 1965 essay "Some Notes on Organic Form."
Light Up the Cave, (New York: New Directions, 1981).

TRANSLATIONS

In Praise of Krishna: Songs from the Bengali, Translated by Edward C. Dimock, Jr. and Denise Levertov (Garden City, N.Y.: Anchor Books, 1967).
Selected Poems, by Guillevic, Eugene. With an introduction by Denise Levertov (New York: New Directions, 1969).
Black Iris, by Jean Joubert (Port Townshend, Wa.: Copper Canyon Press, 1988).

UNCOLLECTED PROSE

Untitled statement, *The New American Poetry,* edited by Donald M. Allan (New York: Grove Press, 1960) 411–412.
"Foreword," *Where Silence Reigns: Selected Prose by Rainer Maria Rilke,* translated by G. Craig Houston (New York: New Directions, 1978) iv–vi.
"The Ideas in the Things," *Ezra Pound and William Carlos Williams: The University of Pennsylvania Conference Papers,* edited by Daniel Hoffman (Philadelphia: University of Pennsylvania Press, 1983) 313–342.
"Remembering Kenneth Rexroth," *American Poetry Review* 12, no. 1: 18–19 (January–February 1983).
"A Poet's View," *Religion and Intellectual Life* 1: 46–53 (Summer 1984).
"On William's Triadic Line: or How to Dance on Variable Feet," *Ironwood* 12: 95–102 (Fall 1984).
"Horses with Wings," *What Is a Poet?* edited by Hank Lazer (Tuscaloosa: University of Alabama Press, 1987) 124–134.

INTERVIEWS

Atchity, Kenneth John, "An Interview with Denise Levertov," (*San Francisco Review of Books,* March 1979) 5–8.

Estes, Sybill. Interview with Denise Levertov. In *American Poetry Observed: Poets on Their Work,* edited by Joel Bellamy (Urbana: University of Illinois, 1984) 255–267.

Hallisey, Joan, " 'Invocations of Humanity,' Denise Levertov's Poetry of Emotion and Belief," (*Sojourners,* February 1986) 32–36.

Ossman, David, ed. "Denise Levertov," *The Sullen Art* (New York: Corinth, 1963) 73–76.

Packard, Vance, "Craft Interview with Denise Levertov," *The Craft of Poetry* (New York: Doubleday, 1974) 79–100.

Reid, Ian, " 'Everyman's Land': Ian Reid Interviews Denise Levertov," *Southern Review* (Australia) 5: 231–236 (1972).

Smith, Lorrie, "An Interview with Denise Levertov," *Michigan Quarterly Review* 24, no. 4: 596–604 (1985).

Sutton, Walter, "A Conversation with Denise Levertov," *Minnesota Review* 5: 322–338 (December 1965).

ARCHIVES AND BIBLIOGRAPHIES

Lockwood Memorial Library Poetry Collection, State University of New York at Buffalo, Buffalo, N.Y. Microfilms of Levertov's worksheets.

Sakelliou-Schultz, Liana, *Denise Levertov: An Annotated Primary and Secondary Bibliography,* (New York: Garland, 1988).

Wilson, Robert A., *A Bibliography of Denise Levertov,* (New York: Phoenix Book Shop, 1972).

Yale University Library, American Literature Collection, New Haven, Conn. Letters from Levertov to William Carlos Williams.

BIOGRAPHICAL AND CRITICAL STUDIES

Altieri, Charles, "Denise Levertov and the Limits of the Aesthetics of Praise," *Enlarging the Temple: New Directions in American Poetry During the 1960s* (Lewisburg, Pa.: Bucknell University Press, 1979) 225–244.

Borroff, Marie, "New Books in Review," *Yale Review* 62, no. 1: 81–83 (Autumn 1972).

Breslin, James E. B., *From Modern to Contemporary: American Poetry, 1945–1965,* (Chicago: University of Chicago Press, 1984).

Carruth, Hayden, "What 'Organic' Means," *Sagetrieb* 4, no. 1: 145–146 (Spring 1985).

Costello, Bonnie, " 'Flooded with Otherness.'," *Parnassus* 8, no. 1: 198–212 (Fall/Winter 1979).

Dargan, Joan, "Poetic and Political Consciousness in Denise Levertov and Carolyn Forche," *CEA Critic* 48, no. 3: 58–67 (1986).

Earnshaw, Doris, Review of Levertov's *Collected Earlier Poems 1940–1960. World Literature Today* 55, no. 1: 109–110 (Winter 1981).

Elder, John, *Imagining the Earth: Poetry and the Vision of Nature,* (Urbana: University of Illinois Press, 1985).

Felstiner, John, "Poetry and Political Experience: Denise Levertov," *Coming to Light: American Women Poets in the Twentieth Century,* edited by Diane Wood Middlebrook and Marilyn Yalom (Ann Arbor: University of Michigan Press, 1985) 138–144.

Gilbert, Sandra M., "Revolutionary Love: Denise Levertov and the Poetics of Politics," *Parnassus* 12–13, nos. 2–1: 335–351 (Spring–Winter 1985).

Glitzen, Julian, "From Reverence to Attention: The Poetry of Denise Levertov," *Midwest Quarterly* 16: 325–341 (1975).

Hallisey, Jane, "Denise Levertov's 'Illustrious Ancestors': The Hassidic Influence," *Melus* 9, no 4: 5–11 (Winter II 1982).

Hallisey, Jane, "Denise Levertov '. . . Forever a Stranger and a Pilgrim'," *Centennial Review* 30, no. 2: 281–291 (Spring 1986).

Harris, Victoria, "The Incorporative Consciousness: Levertov's Journey from Discretion to Unity," *Exploration* 4, no. 1: 33–48 (December 1976).

Jackson, Richard, "A Common Time: The Poetry of Denise Levertov," *Sagetrieb* 5, no. 2: 5–46 (Fall 1986).

Juhasz, Suzanne, *Naked and Fiery Forms: Modern American Poetry by Women: A New Tradition,* (New York: Harper's, 1976).

Lacey, Paul A., "The Poetry of Political Anguish," *Sagetrieb* 4, no. 1: 61–71 (Spring 1985).

Marten, Harry, "Exploring the Human Community: The Poetry of Denise Levertov and Muriel Rukeyser," *Sagetrieb* 3, no. 3: 51–61 (Winter 1984).

Marten, Harry, *Understanding Denise Levertov,* (Columbia: University of South Carolina Press, 1988).

Mersmann, James F., "Denise Levertov: Piercing In," *Out of the Vietnam Vortex: A Study of Poets and Poetry Against the War* (Lawrence, Kans.: University Press of Kansas, 1974) 77–112.

Middleton, Peter, *Revelation and Revolution in the Poetry of Denise Levertov,* (London: Binnacle, 1981).

Mills, Ralph J., Jr., *Contemporary American Poetry,* (New York: Random House, 1965) 176–196.

Mills, Ralph J., Jr., *Cry of the Human: Essays on Contemporary American Poetry,* (Urbana: University of Illinois Press, 1975).

Ostriker, Alicia Suskin, *Stealing the Language: The Emergence of Women's Poetry in America,* (Boston: Beacon Press, 1986).

Perloff, Marjorie, "Poetry Chronicle: 1970–71," *Contemporary Literature* 14, no. 1: 97–131 (Winter 1973).

Pope, Deborah, "Homespun and Crazy Feathers: The Split-Self in the Poems of Denise Levertov," *A Separate Vision: Isolation in Contemporary Women's Poetry* (Baton Rouge: Louisiana State University Press, 1984) 84–115.

Rexroth, Kenneth, "Denise Levertov," *Assays* (New York: New Directions, 1961) 231–235.

Rexroth, Kenneth, "Poetry in the Sixties," *With Eye and Ear* (New York: Herder & Herder, 1970) 69–77.

Sisko, Nancy, "*To Stay Alive:* Levertov's Search for a Revolutionary Poetry," *Sagetrieb* 5, no. 2: 47–60 (Fall 1986).

Smith, Lorrie, "Songs of Experience: Denise Levertov's Political Poetry," *Contemporary Literature* 27, no. 2: 213–232 (Summer 1986).

Surman, Diana, "Inside and Outside in the Poetry of Denise Levertov," *Critical Quarterly* 22, no. 1: 57–70 (Spring 1980).

Wagner, Linda Welshimer, *Denise Levertov,* (New York: Twayne, 1967).

Wagner, Linda Welshimer, "Levertov and Rich: The Later Poems," *South Carolina Review* 11, no. 2: 18–27 (Spring 1979).

Wagner, Linda Welshimer, ed., *Denise Levertov: In Her Own Province.* With an introduction by Wagner (New York: New Directions, 1979).

Wright, James, "Gravity and Incantation," *The Minnesota Review* 2: 424–427 (Spring 1962).

Younkins, Ronald, "Denise Levertov and the Hasidic Tradition," *Descant* 19, no. 1: 40–48 (Fall 1974).

HENRY WADSWORTH LONGFELLOW

(1807–1882)

EDWARD L. HIRSH

THE SPAN OF Henry Wadsworth Longfellow's life, from 1807 to 1882, arched over the transforming years between two American worlds. The New England of his birth was agricultural and mercantile in its economy, anchored to seaports, rivers, and farms, provincial but refined in its culture, engaged in reconciling inherited, semi-aristocratic values with the ideals of a circumscribed but dynamic republicanism; the New England of his death was shaped by post-Civil War industrialism, with its noisy railroads, smoky cities and grim mill towns, emerging class conflicts, and crumbling pieties. Of the nature of this transformation, and its real import, Longfellow was, like most of his contemporaries, only partly and at moments aware. To the issues and occurrences susceptible of judgment by his clear, unexamined moral principles or his somewhat vague but deeply religious convictions, he responded vigorously—to the "shabby" Mexican war, the antislavery movement, and the human misery caused by financial panics. The range of his interests, however, is clearer in his diaries, journals, and letters than in his poetry. Although his poetry is more frequently topical than is sometimes realized, its relation to the age's history is usually indirect: with some exceptions, events and causes served as catalysts rather than as subject matter or primary topics of the verse. Before many contemporary developments, Longfellow could only confess his bewilderment. Always affective and associative rather than analytic and theoretic in his response to life, he could sense the reality of profound change, and its menace, but he could not criticize it. His characteristic answer was the tireless reassertion of the values cherished by the stable society of his early maturity or drawn from his own love of traditional Western culture and the experiences of his childhood and youth.

Born at Portland, Maine, on February 27, 1807, Henry was the second of eight children, descended from Wadsworths and Longfellows who had already established their families' provincial importance. His mother, Zilpah, shared his literary interests and inspired him with her own religiously motivated idealism, including a lifelong hatred of war and violence. His father, Stephen, a public-spirited lawyer, a trustee of Bowdoin College, and briefly congressman from Maine, was an efficient adviser to his son, and later provided him with financial aid as well as encouragement at the beginning of his career. Hardly second to happiness at home was the joy provided by life in a coastal city. The nearby woods and the northward sweep of primeval forest beyond them; the color and bustle of the harbor; above all, the restless Atlantic with its changing moods—these were to haunt Longfellow's imagination throughout his life and to give much of his poetry its dominant imagery. In his almost obsessive recall of time and happiness past, Arcadia lay in childhood and its geography was that of the New England coastline. His most intense poetic exercise in personal recollection is "My Lost Youth," whose familiar third stanza echoes the tone of the whole.

I remember the black wharves and the slips,
And the sea-tides tossing free;
And Spanish sailors with bearded lips,
And the beauty and mystery of the ships,
And the magic of the sea.
And the voice of that wayward song
Is singing and saying still:
"A boy's will is the wind's will,
And the thoughts of youth are long, long
thoughts."

In 1821, Longfellow was admitted to Bowdoin College, at Brunswick, Maine, although he did not take up residence there until his sophomore year. Inadequate as the young college was in several respects, its curriculum, modeled on Harvard's, prescribed substantial study of the classical languages, mathematics, Scripture, and the branches of philosophy, as well as briefer study of natural science. Longfellow, well prepared by Portland Academy and by his own extensive reading, readily mastered the required subjects and also took the then rare opportunity to receive part-time instruction in French. As important as his work in course was the informal education he received, especially through his membership in the Peucinian, a literary society with a well-stocked library. The reading and critical discussion of papers at its meetings sharpened Longfellow's growing desire for a literary career. This bias may have been further encouraged by a faculty member, Thomas Coggswell Upham, who came to Bowdoin in 1824 with a missionary zeal for the creation of a native American literature. So well did Longfellow profit from the combined influences of his collegiate years that his academic promise came to the attention of the trustees. In 1825 the new graduate was offered a just-established professorship in modern languages, with the stipulation of a period of European study—at his own expense—as preparation for the position. The offer was quickly accepted, and on May 15, 1826, Longfellow sailed from New York.

The three years in France, Spain, Italy, and Germany were touched with enchantment as Longfellow's romantic imagination responded to a past still visible in monuments and customs, and to the storied associations which were, the associationist critics maintained, the source of poetic beauty. Longfellow also laid down solid intellectual foundations, especially in Romance languages and literature, but the new task he envisaged from his steadily American perspective was essentially artistic: to help create a great national literature not by radical novelty, as the so-called "Young American" writers urged, but by transmitting to America a rich European heritage for incorporation into its own culture. His pursuit of this goal through essays, lectures, translations, and adaptations from foreign literature exacted a price: if it did not cause, it certainly intensified the bookish tendency of Longfellow's writings. It also resulted, however, in an important contribution to the increasingly important relationship between American and European literature.

Assuming his professional duties in September 1829, Longfellow discovered that he had virtually to establish a new area of studies and to provide its very materials; between 1830 and 1832 he edited or translated six texts in French, Spanish, and Italian. His labors were rewarded: his competence in basic instruction, skill as a lecturer, and courtesy to students quickly made him an influential teacher. Further, he was making a professional reputation. His translations—the book-length *Coplas de Don Jorge Manrique* appeared in 1833—attested his linguistic proficiency, in Spanish particularly; he was also publishing essays on southern European languages and literature that demonstrated scholarship. Longfellow's attention in these years was focused primarily on academic achievement; the writing of original poetry, begun before he entered Bowdoin and continued during his college days, had almost ceased after 1825, and his literary ambitions now found outlet in prose sketches of his travels interspersed with tales in the manner of Washington Irving. After an abortive beginning in serial form, the completed account was published in 1833–34 as *Outre-Mer: A Pilgrimage beyond the Sea.*

There were also nonprofessional reasons for satisfaction. After a short courtship, Longfellow was married in 1831 to Mary Storer Potter, a delicately attractive girl interested in mathematics and poetry, who made a self-effacing but effective helpmate. Yet, for all his success, Longfellow found Brunswick distressingly provincial after Europe, and energetically sought a larger public stage. This he attained in 1834, when the distinguished George Ticknor, Smith Professor of Modern Languages at Harvard College, designated Longfellow as his successor. Once more preparatory study abroad, this time in Germanic languages, seemed wise, and the Longfellows left for Europe in April 1835.

The pattern of Longfellow's life was decisively changed by the second European journey. The linguistic goals were accomplished: Longfellow added Dutch, Danish, Icelandic, Swedish, and some Finnish to his store of languages, acquired a thorough knowledge of German romantic literature, and began his life-long reading in Goethe. It was not intellectual achievement, however, that made the period crucial, but the violent emotional experience originating in his wife's death. Mary's health had always been uncertain; now she was pregnant, and the rigors of a Scandinavian trip exhausted her. Back in Holland, she suffered a miscarriage; infection subsequently developed, and on November 29 she died. Soon after sending her body home for burial, Longfellow received news of the death of his closest friend. Suddenly, it seemed to him, life had taken on the unreality, the transiency, of a dream. Courageously, at times hectic ally, he pushed on with his work, haunted by loneliness and often acutely depressed.

In the spring of 1836, his spirits slightly improved, Longfellow visited the Tyrol. In July, at Interlaken, he encountered the wealthy Bostonian Nathan Appleton and his family, and with the beautiful, talented, and sensitive young Frances Appleton he fell promptly, passionately in love. In August he had to leave for America, his love unreturned; thus began an extended courtship, long unpromising and broken off by Fanny after publication of the too-autobiographical *Hyperion* in 1839. A chance meeting four years later begot a reconciliation, and on April 17, 1843, Longfellow received a note from Fanny that set him walking at top speed from Cambridge to Boston through a transfigured day, and into one of the happiest marriages on record.

The seven-year wait, however, was not spent in palely loitering. Occupying rented quarters in Brattle Street's dignified Craigie House, now maintained as a Longfellow museum, Longfellow performed with distinction his duties as Smith Professor. Although he came to detest departmental business and the drilling in fundamentals, and conducted a continuous, low-keyed quarrel with Harvard's then-conservative administrative policies, he took real delight, as did his listeners, in the delivery of his scrupulously prepared lectures. He not only gave the expected instruction in the history of European languages, but also opened to his students the world of modern German literature, of Jean Paul Richter, Schiller, and, above all, Goethe. His teaching of *Faust,* indeed, was the first such offering in an American college.

More important to his own future, he also resumed writing, the European experience having reawakened the long-dormant creative impulse. In 1839, in addition to the prose *Hyperion,* there appeared *Voices of the Night,* his first collection of poems, some of which, including the sensationally popular "A Psalm of Life," had been previously printed in magazines. *Ballads and Other Poems* followed in 1841; *Poems on Slavery,* written during his return from a brief third European trip, in 1842; and a poetic drama, *The Spanish Student,* in book form, in 1843. The renewed conflict between academic and literary ambitions was increasingly resolved in favor of the latter, until it was settled in 1854 by the cessation of teaching.

Longfellow's success was already making him a public figure, a role for which he was well suited. Striking in appearance, elegant, even dandified in dress, urbane and mildly witty, endowed with innate courtesy and a peculiarly masculine sweetness of temper, he made the very model of a New England gentleman-author, and his genuine talent for friendship rapidly wove a web of lasting relationships that embraced the obscure and the famous alike. When he and Fanny were married on July 13, 1843, his father-in-law's gift was Craigie House itself, and the young Longfellows soon gave it a wide reputation as a center of cultivated hospitality.

The years from 1843 to 1860 were Longfellow's most fruitful. Besides editing and contributing to three collections of verse, he wrote many of his best shorter poems, gathered in *The Belfry of Bruges and Other Poems* (1846) and *The Seaside and the Fireside* (1850), as well as "Paul Revere" and "The Saga of King Olaf," to be used later in *Tales of a Wayside Inn*; a novel, *Kavanagh* (1849); and his most successful long poems: *Evangeline* (1847), *The Golden Legend* (1851), *The Song of Hiawatha* (1855), and *The Courtship of Miles Standish* (1858). Many of the volumes sold in numbers and with a speed unprecedented in American publishing history.

Public acclaim mounted yearly in Europe as in America, while distinguished guests and unimportant strangers descended endlessly upon Craigie House and seriously hindered Longfellow's work. Moreover, his domestic happiness was nearly complete, shadowed only by the death of one of the six children born to the Longfellows. The single source of continuous anxiety was the national scene. Longfellow observed the sharpening prewar tensions closely and with growing concern, until the opening of hostilities left him torn between his abhorrence of slavery and his hatred of war, and dejected by public disaster.

To national tragedy was soon added personal. On July 9, 1861, Longfellow was resting on a couch in his study while, in an adjoining room, his still romantically loved wife was sealing locks of their daughters' hair in packets: a scene so Victorian as to seem a period piece. Then a spark or a drop of hot wax ignited Fanny's flimsy summer dress. Ablaze and in agony she ran to Longfellow, whose efforts to beat out the flames left him critically burned. During the night Fanny died and, while she was being buried, Longfellow lay helpless in bed, his life feared for, his sanity at first despaired of by his friends and himself. Physically he made a thorough recovery, although the circumstances of Fanny's death had a grotesque consequence; the scars on Longfellow's face made further shaving impossible, and thus was created the placid bearded image that was destined to gaze from the walls of a thousand future classrooms. Psychic recovery came more slowly, and the inner wounds never completely healed. The journals for the following months he later destroyed, but evidence of his near-despair survives in communications with his friends.

To this shattering experience Longfellow directly refers only once in all his later poetry, although knowledge of it is necessary to a full understanding of several poems, including the six sonnets prefixed to his translation of Dante, and the tone of his lyrics is pervasively affected by it. The sole direct reference is a sonnet written in 1879, when Longfellow came upon a picture of a mountain in whose ravines lay a cross-shaped deposit of snow, and found there the image of his unrelenting pain.

In the long, sleepless watches of the night,
  A gentle face—the face of one long
    dead—
  Looks at me from the wall, where round
    its head
  The night-lamp casts a halo of pale light.
Here in this room she died; and soul more
    white
  Never through martyrdom of fire was led
  To its repose; nor can in books be read
  The legend of a life more benedight.
There is a mountain in the distant West
  That, sun-defying, in its deep ravines
  Displays a cross of snow upon its side.
Such is the cross I wear upon my breast
These eighteen years, through all the
    changing scenes
And seasons, changeless since the day she
    died.

"The Cross of Snow" was published posthumously; like another sonnet, the "Mezzo

Cammin" of 1842, it seemed to Longfellow too personal for print.

Initially forcing himself to resume writing as an escape from grief, Longfellow was soon engaged in some of his most ambitious undertakings. The three series of narrative poems constituting *Tales of a Wayside Inn* were published in 1863, 1872, and 1874 respectively; the translation of the whole of the *Divina Commedia* occupied the years from 1865 to 1867; the *New England Tragedies* appeared in 1868 and *The Divine Tragedy* in 1871, two works that were linked with *The Golden Legend* by prologue, interludes, and epilogue to make up the complete *Christus* in 1872. From 1876 to 1879 Longfellow acted as editor, in practice as editor-in-chief, of the thirty-one volumes of *Poems of Places,* which included several of his own contributions. Meantime, a but slightly diminished flow of shorter poems, including the fine sonnets, continued, filling most of six volumes: *Flower-de-Luce* (1867); *Three Books of Song* (1872); *Aftermath* (1873); *The Masque of Pandora and Other Poems* (1875); *Kéramos and Other Poems* (1878); and *Ultima Thule* (1880).

These last years were for Longfellow the years of apotheosis. The distinctions between the poet and the venerable figure of Craigie House were lost in a chorus of affectionate acclaim, in which the dissenting voices of the younger generation were drowned out. The last European journey in 1868–69 was an almost royal progress, with honorary degrees conferred by the universities of Oxford and Cambridge, to the cheers of the undergraduates, and with a reception by Queen Victoria. From the Continent, Victor Hugo saluted Longfellow as a man who brought honor to America, and at home the schoolchildren of Cambridge presented him with an armchair made from the wood of the original spreading chestnut tree. In American eyes, he was clearly the uncrowned poet laureate, and he played his part to the end. On March 12, 1882, he finished ten six-line stanzas of "The Bells of San Blas," typically celebrating with nostalgia a past of picturesque devotion when "the priest was lord of the land." On March 15, he also typically added a single-stanza counterstatement:

> O Bells of San Blas, in vain
> Ye call back the Past again!
> The Past is deaf to your prayer;
> Out of the shadows of night
> The world rolls into light;
> It is daybreak everywhere.

He had reassured himself and his readers for the last time. Nine days later, after a very brief illness, he was dead at the age of seventy-five, and the spontaneous mourning was international. Enough uncollected poems remained to provide *In the Harbor* (1882), and, in 1883, the impressive fragment of his projected poetic drama, *Michael Angelo,* was separately published. With this his art had reached its period, a fact emphasized by the substantially complete and massive edition of his works in 1886. In its eleven volumes the results of sixty-two literarily active years were assembled for the judgment of posterity.

Longfellow's prose works are, with one exception, of minor importance. *Outre-Mer* contains vivid descriptions of Western Europe in the 1820's, and reflects Longfellow's romantic sensibility in a charming manner, but its studied picturesqueness palls, and it remains inferior to the *Sketch Book* that it too obviously imitates. Longfellow's various essays and articles, important in their day, are now chiefly of historical and biographical interest. Their knowledge has been superseded, and their critical methods and point of view seem outmoded, although they still yield some appreciative insights. The one novel, *Kavanagh,* lacks the technical and imaginative unity necessary to success. Its moderately realistic representation of life in a rural New England community deserves the praise Emerson gave it, and there are some amusingly lively scenes satiric of old-line Calvinism and of the patriotic literary theory that assumed the future greatness of American poetry as a consequence of the greatness of American scenery. The love story, however, is flat and sentimentalized, and the characters are insubstantial, save for the sensitive but ineffectual Mr. Churchill, apparently Longfellow's wry portrait of an aspect of himself. *Kavanagh's* most serious interest perhaps lies in its reflection of the religious and cultural changes beginning to transform New England life, but this, too, suffers from the novel's episodic construction. Only in *Hyperion: A Romance* did Longfellow succeed in extended prose fiction.

Hyperion, the most autobiographical of all Longfellow's works, describes under a thin veil of fiction the personal crisis of 1835–36; by Longfellow's own account, its writing was a therapy by which he worked his way from morbidity to health. The spiritual journey, a frequent theme in his works, is imaged here in a romanticized account of the second European trip. Paul Flemming, the hero, despairing over the loss of his "dear friend," retraces Longfellow's expeditions and experiences; at Interlaken he meets and falls in love with Mary Ashburton (Frances Appleton) and is rejected by her. Finally, restored to mental health, he self-reliantly faces the future alone—a stance that his creator and original was unable to adopt. So immediately identifiable were the persons and events of *Hyperion* that "all Boston" was soon happily gossiping and being scolded by Longfellow for its narrow-minded censoriousness. Only as passing years dimmed the topical interest could *Hyperion* be read as an imaginative representation of a not simply personal but generic ally youthful and romantic odyssey.

Into *Hyperion* Longfellow poured the accumulations of three years. Traveler's notes, long descriptions, general reflections, anecdotes and tales, extended literary and philosophic commentaries, topics from his Harvard lectures, translations from German literature—all are crowded in, often with little explicit connection, and are set in a romantic-plush style certain to try the patience of post-romantic readers. Longfellow was then under the spell of Jean Paul Richter, whose style, in apparent chaos, mingled the serious, comic, sublime, and grotesque; it delighted in abruptly changing moods, materials, and manners, in archaic phrasing, flamboyant figurative expression, and rhapsody. In varying degree, these qualities are also in *Hyperion,* so that the first impression is of confusion and cloying whimsicality. Beneath the patchwork, however, lies a real unity of emotion and experience.

The symbolism of the central journey is developed in simple, traditional imagery. Beginning on a dark, cold, mist-shrouded December morning in the Rhine valley, the action moves, for the climactic scenes of Book IV, up into the Swiss mountains in full summer, with the sun high and strong. The past is figured throughout by darkness and the grave, and is extended to include not only Flemming's personal past but the historical past whose monuments surround him in Europe; similarly, the present is a brightness into which not only he but mankind must enter. As Flemming's enthrallment began at a grave, so deliverance comes in St. Gilgen's churchyard among the tombs. The liberating formula he finds, as Longfellow actually found it, on a tablet affixed to a tomb: "Look not mournfully into the Past. It comes not back again. Wisely improve the Present. It is thine. Go forth to meet the shadowy Future without fear, and with a manly heart."

The immediate result of this directive Flemming calls almost miraculous, but later he asks, "Can such a simple result spring only from the long and intricate process of experience?" The process of a single experience is precisely what unifies, however loosely, the widely disparate materials of *Hyperion* and revivifies its traditional imagery by providing a freshly individual context. Embodying a conflict that runs throughout Longfellow's life and poetry and displaying at length the recurrent terms and images of that conflict, as well as of its outcome, *Hyperion* forms the literary substratum of a large part of Longfellow's later work.

Outre-Mer and *Hyperion* played a significant part in making Europe's thought and art available to the American public; so, too, did Longfellow's translations of poetry, which occupy a substantial place in his canon and were produced with varying frequency throughout his career. To translation Longfellow was drawn by his personal, sometimes indiscriminate delight in European literature, as well as by the literary and linguistic challenge of the task itself and the pedagogical usefulness of the results. Spanish, Italian, and German literature furnished the most numerous originals, but there are also translations from French, Danish, Swedish, Anglo-Saxon, and Latin poetry, and even three renditions, by way of extant prose translations, of Eastern poems. The originals are qualitatively a hodgepodge of everything from sentimental trivia to Dante's *Divina Commedia.*

Accepting Goethe's belief that the translator should adopt the author's situation, mode of speaking, and peculiarities, Longfellow scrupulously attempted to minimize the unavoidable sacrifices of translation and to move as close to literal correspondence as other considerations permitted. His earlier translations take measured liberties, such as the use of "equivalent stanzas in rendering the *Coplas de Don Jorge Manrique*; his later translations are austerely restrictive. The great test was the translation of the *Divina Commedia.* After pondering the insurmountable difficulties of Dante's *terza rima*, Longfellow decided to abandon the rhyming so that he could preserve the tercet structure and achieve literal precision. The justification of this decision is the translation itself, which, in spite of unevenness and deficiencies, reflects something of the linguistic economy and rhythmic severity of the original. Although Longfellow's rendition does not attain the semi-independent poetic value of great verse translations, it remains one of the most faithful and effective Englishings of Dante.

On the value of translation to the practicing poet, Longfellow was of divided mind. Judging from his own experience, he insisted that successful translation evidenced real creative power, and that the act of translating served as stimulus to the poet's own thought and feeling; but he also refers to the attendant dangers. Translation is, in his own words, "like running a ploughshare through the soil of one's mind; a thousand germs of thought spring up (excuse this agricultural figure), which otherwise might have lain and rotted in the ground—still it sometimes seems to me like an excuse for being lazy,—like leaning on another man's shoulder." For Longfellow, whose art was highly responsive to external suggestion, translation probably did start ideas, and it undoubtedly contributed to his notable skill in versification. Nevertheless, his preoccupation with translation, even during a period of life normally crucial in the development of independence, may indeed have encouraged a habit of leaning on other men's shoulders that partly explains the limited originality of his own subsequent poetry.

Longfellow's first published poem, "The Battle of Lovell's Pond," derivatively celebrating a skirmish whose importance was monumentally local, appeared in the *Portland Gazette* for November 17, 1820, over the signature "Henry." Between this and the final "Bells of San Blas" stand well over five hundred poems whose variety makes generalization pause. Ranging from such brief, pure song as "Stars of the Summer Night" to the composite *Christus,* which occupies one hundred and sixty double-columned pages in the Cambridge Edition, the poetry includes not only "ode and elegy and sonnet" in abundance, but hortatory, meditative, and imagistic lyrics; poetic dramas; and many kinds of narrative from popular ballad to epic-tinged idyll, of widely varying length and manner. The gamut of quality is almost as extended, the good poems being sometimes obscured by the disproportionately large number of bad or indifferent ones. Some lines of development can be chronologically traced, especially for the long poems, but these, with rare exception, mark tonal and emphatic changes, or shifts in predominant verse forms or genres, rather than fundamental alterations in Longfellow's major ideas or attitudes, which, although modified with time, persist in recognizable form from *Voices of the Night* to the end.

The essential characteristics, even the qualitative variance, of Longfellow's poetry are related to his humanistic although unsystematized views on art. Art, he held, is the revelation of man, and of nature only "through man." His abandonment of nature description, Longfellow explained, meant not that he loved nature less, but man more. This basically traditional attitude receives a distinctively nineteenth-century coloring from Longfellow's understanding of artistic usefulness in terms of "elevation." Poetry, he argued in his 1832 "Defence of Poetry," is an instrument for improving the condition of society and advancing the great purpose of human happiness; in America's democratic society, this implied an endorsement of literature's growing concern with the literate common man. So Longfellow's Michael Angelo, in the drama bearing his name, defines art as

> "All that embellishes and sweetens life,
> And lifts it from the level of low cares
> Into the purer atmosphere of beauty;
> The faith in the Ideal . . ."

Thus poetry, even at the risk of losing itself in the "low cares," will serve to charm, to strengthen, and to teach—a formula in which many critics and poets concurred: Walt Whitman, praising Longfellow as an unrecognized master in the treatment of common occurrences, declared his evocation of the poetic quality of everyday things to be truly representative of the spirit of democracy.

That a useful muse might become too housewifely Longfellow was aware. The nature and the problems of the artistic process make a recurrent theme in his poetry, especially from the two poems "Prometheus" and "Epimetheus" of 1854 to the poems of the 1870's, *The Masque of Pandora,* "Kéramos," and *Michael Angelo,* and the problem most reflective of his own experience was that of the frustrating distance between the exaltation of original inspiration and the flatness of final achievement. Longfellow knew that the highest inspiration is Promethean, and he suspected that great art comes only from the continual isolation and the total commitment of struggling with the gods—the art of a Shakespeare or Dante, before whose accomplishment he openly confessed his own inadequacy. Yet, like many of his contemporaries, he half-feared this heroic posture as a humanly perilous one, a cutting-off of the artist from humanity's common lot, from the world of Pandora's opened box and Epimetheus' humanitarian compassion. How the initial lofty vision could without betrayal and without obscurity be made accessible and instructive to a wide audience was the puzzle. Finding no solution, Longfellow accepted without undue repining the Epimethean role of poetic concern with daily sorrows and hopes, but he was haunted by the figure of Prometheus, symbol of the daring act of imagination essential to the birth of all poetry, even that which apparently ended up in slippers at the fireside.

The major ideas underlying Longfellow's poetry are characteristically expressed in a conventional nineteenth-century terminology that invites partial misreading, partly because of subsequent changes in meaning, especially in connotation, and partly because important terms are often so inclusive as to seem indeterminate. Longfellow's constant appeal to the heart is frequently understood as the consequence of a vague, sentimental notion that the gentler emotions could resolve problems and order life, to the near-exclusion of thought. His usage, however, like that of his contemporaries, reflects an older and wider meaning of *heart.* The word refers not only to the emotions, but also to will and intuitive reason. The heart is the source of insight as well as of joy or grief; it embraces the moral sensibility that accepts or rejects truth and that acts as conscience in its unstudied response to generally self-evident laws. When Longfellow writes,

> "It is the heart, and not the brain,
> That to the highest doth attain . . ."

his use of "heart" is close to that of the Pauline formula, in the phraseology of the Authorized Version, "with the heart man believeth to righteousness." The heart, therefore, may stand for all of man's immaterial nature, save his discursive reason, which is often signified by "brain." Moreover, in his simple division of man into body and soul, Longfellow assigned all thoughts, all feelings, all desires to the soul, not the body, which is only the instrument. "It is the soul," he insisted, "that feels, enjoys, suffers. . . ." Thus the affections themselves are spiritual, and, directed to good ends, can properly be called "holy."

Longfellow's frame of ultimate reference is formed by his religious convictions. When he established in 1824 the first Unitarian society at Bowdoin, he was not simply revolting against the "consociation of 'old sanctities,' " as he once called the college's conservatively Congregationalist clergy, but affirming the strong personal faith that pervaded his life and writings. Like his father, Longfellow in general accepted the teaching of William Ellery Channing: that man is fundamentally good, endowed by God with reason, conscience, and an intuitive awareness of the divine; and that Christianity, the purest faith known to man, is progressing toward a full realization of its ideals in a universal church of the future. The core of man's religion is a self-sacrificial love issuing in noble actions and sentiments, and in humanitarian concern for human welfare. Not by creeds, whether Athanasian or Calvinistic, but by deeds is man judged, and his faith made effective.

For so optimistic a belief, the chief problem is that of sin and evil, and the greatest imaginative failure of Longfellow's poetry is its inability to probe life's dark or sordid aspects. The causes of failure were partly temperamental. A natural fastidiousness led Longfellow to recoil from the physical and spiritual ugliness that caused him actual pain. Although he was personally subject to periods of neurotic depression with moments of panic, he regarded these visitations as transient phenomena that raised no intellectual question about man's nature or destiny. What experience failed to provide, faith could not supply. Especially in his long poems, Longfellow represents or alludes to the malicious, fanatic, and selfish behavior men are capable of, but he suggests no deeper cause than a defect incidental to man's present condition, reformable although not yet reformed. The chief weakness of *The Golden Legend* is therefore the characterization of Satan, who, although cast as a fallen angel, is in action only a badly behaved, treacherous superman, neither terrifying nor awe-inspiring, and almost cursorily dismissed. Somehow—and Longfellow is never deeply curious about "how's"—everything will come out all right. So, at least, his reasoning assured him. Yet his attraction to Dante, the pessimistic feeling that tinges *Christus,* and the powerful vision of final nullity in *Michael Angelo* all suggest a sensibility whose perceptions are often at variance with the formulating ideas.

Indeed, the simply held ideas by which Longfellow attempted to order experience are frequently unable to contain the strong current of feeling that is a distinctive quality of his romantic sensibility. Although he was sharply critical of what he considered the excesses and absurdities of romanticism, his own poetry is saturated with a romantic sense of life's fragility. The crumbling ruins, encroaching darkness, and vivid but fleeting visions are not fashionable accessories, but the authentic images of Longfellow's deepest emotion, as his journals testify. That human life is a dream in which the apparent solidities of time and place dissolve into insubstantial forms is a nearly obsessive theme. To Longfellow, the most powerful flow of time and consciousness is backward, from present to past, from actuality to dream, and into the magic night of communion and reminiscence that gives access to the remembered past. However tempered in expression by his almost classical restraint and social poise, the dominant mood of Longfellow's poetry is a melancholy not unlike that of Washington Irving, compounded of nostalgia, the sadness of personal loss, and the painful awareness of transcience and mortality. If there is truth in the comment that Longfellow did not face the primary facts of life and nature, one reason may be his feeling that "facts" are neither primary nor solid, but the phenomena of a dream. So pervasive is dream or reverie in

Longfellow's imagination that his most effective lyric or meditative poems are likely to be built on dreamlike associations, and the felicitous "legend style," as he called it, of some of his longer works depends upon an atmosphere of dreamy distance.

When physical surfaces lose their bounds and firmness, the natural world is easily invaded by the circumambient world of spirit. From the early "Footsteps of Angels" to the late "Helen of Tyre," Longfellow's poetry is recurrently haunted by phantoms, as the planes of nature and spirit, always thought by Longfellow to be exactly correspondent, seem to converge at a visionary point somewhere between reality and unreality. Longfellow's belief in the interaction of the invisible world and the world of sense led him actually to experiment with spiritualism a few times. In practice, he found spiritualism unconvincing and unedifying, but he never lost the sense of continuity between this world and another, between the living and the dead, that makes the pervasive mysteriousness of many poems so memorable.

To withdraw into the haunted night, to surrender to nostalgia and reverie, was Longfellow's natural inclination, intensified by his domestic catastrophes and, in his later years, by loneliness. His beliefs and character, however, prohibited such a retreat: the voices of night must be answered by the voices of day, or by aspiration the dreaming night must be made holy with stars. To assert present reality and the possibility of meaningful action in it becomes the necessary countermovement against the pull of the past; it is the thrust of health against incipient morbidity. On the side of reality are religious faith, human love, and the achievements and obligations of civilization; these are the foundations of hope and inescapable duty. Thus the longing for imaginative flight is characteristically confronted by a resolute will: this was the fundamental conflict in Longfellow's experience and, mirrored in his art, provides the only continuous tension in a poetry whose structure and language have little of that quality.

The conflict is often described rather than presented, and the resolution stated rather than achieved. Even in such simple poems, however, there is occasionally a conviction successfully communicated that seems unaccountably to be an increment from the underlying experience itself. In the once overacclaimed, now overabused "A Psalm of Life," the conflict exists chiefly as a background for the celebration of triumphant resolve, directly expressed. That this hortatory poem should have a witnessed effect denied to countless other exhortations may be due to a residual force not earned, according to the modern prescription, through the strategy of the poem itself, but subtly transmitted to it as a tone from the prior struggle and its resolution that was indeed earned, since "A Psalm of Life" springs from the same experience that produced *Hyperion.* In Longfellow's more complex didactic poems the countering assertion of hope or purpose is not always poetically successful; at times it is imposed, or inadequate to the strength of the preceding melancholy. But in the best poems it is sufficiently implied in the foregoing situation or images to be a valid climax.

The major ideas of Longfellow are clearly reflected in his poetry considered as a whole; he repeatedly makes explicit reference to them, and indulges in overt teaching based upon them. His poetry, nevertheless, is not a poetry of ideas: certainly it is not philosophic or genuinely reflective, if "reflective" implies extended analysis of experience and systematic deliberation upon it. Except occasionally and on some few subjects, notably art, Longfellow's poems are primarily meditative; they express intuitions of experience, whether personal or literary, their thought usually arising immediately from feeling and remaining closely attached to it, or interwoven with it. Habitually, there is little progressive development of idea or attitude: a poem's underlying experience is made concrete in a described object, situation, or story—an image whose significance is presented sometimes as almost a short allegorization, more often as a correspondence or connotation on another plane.

Since the image, from whatever source it is drawn and however simple or complex it may be, not only determines the tone of the whole poem but is also the essential figure of the experience, Longfellow's meditative poetry is, on the whole, fundamentally metaphoric, although in many poems the lack of compression, the extended statement, and the failure to renew conventional images all dissipate metaphor's possible intensity.

Some of Longfellow's important images by their complexity, recurrence, and stability become true symbols, at times restricted or extensively modified by particular contexts, but possessing a sufficiently persistent significance throughout the poetry to express Longfellow's imaginative apprehension of life. A few symbols are based on artifacts or on artistic creation—bells, walled forts or castles, music—but most are drawn from nature. Largely traditional, they are sometimes casually used as cultural hand-me-downs; more often, however, their significance has clearly been rediscovered at a deep level of experience. The most pervasive symbols are archetypal: the darkness of haunted night, oblivion, and the past, whose chill is the coldness of the grave; the warm light of reality, of vital energy, and, for Longfellow, of love, concentrated in the sun; water, whose flow is the motion of feeling, spirit, and time, and whose fluidity Longfellow attributes also to sky, air, and light; the stars of divine or spiritual order and, more personally, of aspiration.

Above all others are the symbols drawn from Longfellow's memory of youthful experience; his landscape of the human situation and of individual inner life is that of the Maine coastline: the sea, the nearby forest, and the narrow habitable strip between. This last, the scene of rational and civilized life, additionally provides a symbol of precarious security, the home centered in the hearth, whose warmth is the focus of human relationships and a protection against the storms without: although Longfellow's fireside scene is likely to be sentimentalized, it occasionally reflects in muted fashion the ancient image of man huddled by his saving fire. The forest, boundless and majestic, frequently wailing in the wind, embodies a primitive life somewhat ominous for civilized man. The sea is Longfellow's deepest and most inclusive symbol; no contemporary writer save Melville was more profoundly or constantly responsive to it. In Longfellow's poetry, the sea is the restless mystery of existence, and its unfathomable source; it is the energy of unconfined and subconscious life, and of liberty. In its effects, it is also paradoxical, merciful and merciless, purifying yet dangerous, at once death-giving and life-giving.

In spite of the importance of images and symbols, however, the typical movement of a poem by Longfellow is toward a formulated decision; that is, however complex the underlying feelings or situation, any tension or conflict, or any balance of opposites, is resolved by a choice amongst the possibilities or by a limiting statement of specific significance. Since the poems ordinarily do not fully present whatever struggle or turbulence there may have been in the originating experience, but only selected, usually subdued aspects of it, the resolution often appears easy or oversimplified. In the best poems, however, the concluding statement is at once a natural consequence of an imaginative prior development and an explication sufficiently complex to embrace all the possibilities.

The lyric and meditative poems, and several of the shorter narratives, are characteristically, although not exclusively, developed in distinguishable stages, moving from image to analogy or statement, or from image to analogy to statement; much more rarely, from statement to image. In a large number of the poems, the image is fully presented in one or more initial stanzas of verse paragraphs and its moral or spiritual significance set forth in the following ones, frequently with an exact correspondence in the lengths of presentation and of statement, a balance well exemplified in "Seaweed" and "The Beleaguered City." Alternatively, the statement may be a comparatively brief conclusion, or even a counterstatement of denial, revulsion, or change of direction, as in "The Bells of San Blas," rather than a climax to what has preceded it. In many poems, the movement between image and comparison or statement is continuously back and forth, the image being presented in steps, each of which is accompanied by an immediate reflection upon it. The poems that do not move by clearly defined stages may conveniently be designated as one-stage. Classification by stages, however, can be only approximate: an indicated spiritual significance, for example, may cling so closely to an image, as it does in "Sandalphon," that it seems simply to be an overtone of it.

In the one-stage poems, the presentation may be hortatory, descriptive, or narrative; it either produces a direct, uncomplicated, often emotional effect or clearly implies a further meaning without openly indicating or stating it. Into this category fall most of the short narratives and also many of the poems most appealing to modern taste, the quasi-imagistic poems that present a concentrated image with expanding overtones: "Chrysaor," "The Bells of Lynn," "Aftermath," "The Tide Rises, the Tide Falls" are representative of this group, and "The Ropewalk" is similar in its reliance on suggestion, although it employs a series of images, central and associated, rather than one image alone. A few two-stage poems are also primarily imagistic in effect, some of them, like "The Warning," developing their analogy closely in terms of the original image, others, like "Snowflakes," using their analogy actually to reinforce the image. However stimulating Longfellow's imagistic poems may be, they are nonetheless too small in number to be typical of his poetry.

The three-stage poems usually consist of initial image, analogy, and explicit statement, with attention more or less evenly distributed among them, a method that is obvious in the three stanzas of the feeble "Rainy Day," whose initial lines run "The day is cold, and dark, and dreary . . . My life is cold, and dark, and dreary . . . Be still, sad heart! and cease repining . . ." For some reason, the three-stage poems include many of Longfellow's bad and indifferent pieces; on the other hand, they also include some of the more completely satisfying meditative verses, such as "Palingenesis" and a sensitively wrought ode, "The Building of the Ship," whose oratorically eloquent, hortatory last stanza begins with the familiar "Thou, too, sail on, O Ship of State!" and makes an illogical but emotionally appropriate and powerful new application of the poem's structural analogy between the construction and launching of a ship and the progress of romantic love climaxed in marriage.

The largest number of Longfellow's shorter poems, including the sonnets and such important compositions as the brief "In the Churchyard at Cambridge" and "Jugurtha" and the lengthier "Fire of Driftwood," "My Lost Youth," and "Morituri Salutamus," are two-stage; if his imagination found any method especially congenial, it is this one, so that his notable achievement in sonnet form is not surprising.

The early two- or three-stage poems usually end in explicit declaration; after the mid-1840's there is increasing reliance on a final metaphor or symbol, as in "Autumn Within":

> It is autumn; not without,
> But within me is the cold.
> Youth and spring are all about;
> It is I that have grown old.
>
> Birds are darting through the air,
> Singing, building without rest;
> Life is stirring everywhere,
> Save within my lonely breast.
>
> There is silence: the dead leaves
> Fall and rustle and are still;
> Beats no flail upon the sheaves,
> Comes no murmur from the mill.

The poem is too short to be widely representative, but it bears the Longfellow impress: the quatrains observe a 2–2 rhetorical division; the lines are four-stress, in falling rhythm; the accommodations of stress and pause to meaning are minor but careful; the language is simple and the word order nearly normal, save for the deliberate departure in the concluding lines; there is a touch of showy pathos in the eighth line; the images are traditional, and, especially in the last two lines, rather "poetic" or literary. The fundamental comparison of inner states and outer seasons allows easy further comparison between seasons and thus inner states, and so moves into the suggestive final revelation of age's fruitlessness in a favorite image: the cessation of sound. In so short a poem, the procedure is abbreviated but clear. The initial image is quickly introduced in three words; its spiritual significance is explicitly stated at once; the comparison is somewhat tenuously explored, and the conclusion intensifies the comparison by shifting the images associated with autumn to the signified spiritual state. Like so many of Longfellow's good if obviously minor poems, this has a personal feeling that manages, even if barely, to come through the conventional scenery; it also has something of Longfellow's typical facility, attended, as often, by the bad and good angels of glibness and grace.

Like much nineteenth-century poetry, Longfellow's seems in retrospect leisurely, even too relaxed. The slow development of ideas, the elaboration of details, the multiplication of parallels, the explication of the already-evident are practices that destroy some of his poems and in varying combinations and degrees characterize most of them. The language, too, bears the stamp of its time in its tendency to expansive statement, its often predictable vocabulary and phraseology, and its fondness for literary diction. Like the sporadic addiction to poetically picturesque subject matter, these qualities are alien to sophisticated modern taste, although whether or to what extent they are necessarily faults is a problem of literary theory and the absoluteness of critical standards. Historically considered, the kind of poetry Longfellow wrote lay within a poetic tradition that with various adaptations served the larger part of a century, and was imaginatively satisfying to the romantic-Victorian sensibility. Within the age's literary conventions, Longfellow used language skillfully and sensitively. At its best, his language is simple and economical, natural in movement, emotionally exact in its use of words and phrases, and restrained in statement. Furthermore, Longfellow's handling of language is largely responsible for his achievement of an impressive tonal range from the formality of semi-epic narrative to the humor-seasoned easiness of the discourse of polite society. He makes the traditional poetic language, with often minimal alteration, express distinctively his own insights and feelings.

As a poet more evocative than creative of experience, Longfellow employs language with a notable awareness of the way in which it becomes charged with meaning from the inescapable situations of human life. Frequently he depends not upon connotations or overtones developed within the context of a poem, but upon a resonance provided immediately by general experience itself and renewed in the poem by allusions to the appropriate common events or situations, or by brief descriptions of them. This habit demands from the reader a supply of significance from his private store and a willingness to accept suggestive reference rather than precise control in the poem—a concession not demanded by great poetry, and by some critics austerely refused to any. It is, however, a concession habitually made to occasional poems, whose otherwise vague or flabby language may acquire exactness from setting and event. When, in "Morituri Salutamus," Longfellow recalls his audience from thoughts of friends dead and buried to

> . . . these scenes frequented by our feet
> When we were young, and life was fresh and sweet,

the last line is not vaguely sentimental, but, like the poem's title, genuinely moving because emotionally appropriate and provided with definable meaning by the situation: an aging poet addressing the dwindled number of college classmates at certainly their last reunion, held fifty years after graduation.

Like other aspects of his poetry, Longfellow's prosody is remarkable for resourcefulness and variety within traditional limits. His uncommon talent in versification and his absorption in its technical problems led to no prosodic revolution; indeed, a dangerous facility, combined with a taste for euphony, brings his verse at moments close to that of the typical Victorian "sweet singer." Within accepted bounds, however, Longfellow's versatility in rhythmical, metrical, and rhyming patterns and his constant experimentation, directed toward the creation of a unique effect for each poem, reveal a technical mastery rarely approached in American poetry. Although his prosodic variety is most obvious in the surprisingly various patterns of his stanzaic verse, it is perhaps more subtly displayed in meeting the resistance of a set form like the sonnet, where, employing the Italian pattern and almost invariably observing a strict octet-sestet division, Longfellow achieves striking rhythmic differences by ingenious handling of metrical substitution, run-on and end-stopped lines, and caesuras. In freer forms, his skill is no less evident: the extremely uneven blank verse of *The Divine Tragedy* has reflective passages in which comparative rhythmic freedom works with approximately normal word order to produce lines that sometimes collapse into prose but that occasionally attain a thoroughly natural movement barely but unmistakably tightened into poetry, as in the course of the soliloquy by Manahem the Essenian in the third part of the "First Passover":

> The things that have been and shall be no
>   more,
> The things that are, and that hereafter shall
>   be,
> The things that might have been, and yet
>   were not,
> The fading twilight of great joys departed,
> The daybreak of great truths as yet unrisen,
> The intuition and the expectation
> Of something, which, when come, is not the
>   same,
> But only like its forecast in men's dreams,
> The longing, the delay, and the delight,
> Sweeter for the delay; youth, hope, love,
>   death,
> And disappointment which is also death,
> All these make up the sum of human life;
> A dream within a dream, a wind at night
> Howling across the desert in despair,
> Seeking for something lost it cannot find.

The technical virtuosity of Longfellow's art is manifested in several accomplishments: the successful maintenance of falling rhythm in spite of English poetry's strong tendency to rising rhythm; the dexterous control of varied rhythm and free rhyming by an organization based on parallelism, balance, and alliteration; and the giving of widely varied movement to such uncomplicated verse forms as the quatrain. Even so straightforward a narrative as "Paul Revere" shows a meticulous attention to technical detail that partly accounts for the rather complex effect of an apparently simple poem. As a rule, the closer the examination of Longfellow's verse technique, the greater is the appreciation of a diversity that can succeed in the subdued four-line stanzas of his meditative poetry, in the stately hexameters of *Evangeline,* and in the jaunty tetrameter couplets of "The Rhyme of Sir Christopher."

The shorter poems of Longfellow enjoyed a contemporary popularity, in England and other countries as well as in America, that has rarely been rivaled, yet it was not these poems but his long ones on which his reputation chiefly rested, especially the long narratives: *Evangeline, Hiawatha, The Courtship of Miles Standish,* and *Tales of a Wayside Inn.* More recently the major narrative poems have been relegated to the classroom, often at a rather elementary level, in acknowledgment of Longfellow's ability to tell a story in them, and with the implication that he does no more. The nineteenth century knew better: when *Evangeline* was published in 1847, one English reviewer hailed it as "the first genuine Castalian fount which has burst from the soil of America!" In spite of his fanciful image, the critic was properly celebrating what was in fact the first important sustained poem by an American and was endorsing the general acclaim that made Evangeline herself a symbol of the Acadian "cause."

Like all of Longfellow's major poems, *Evangeline* was, in modern academic jargon, "well researched," and one result of Longfellow's reading was to make the poem in part a richly descriptive tour of expanses of western and southern America. The story itself, however, is an altogether simple one, whose essentials were first given to Longfellow by Hawthorne: in the dispersal of the French Acadians in 1755, two lovers, Evangeline and Gabriel, are separated, and for weary years Evangeline attempts to trace Gabriel through the settlements and wilds of the American colonies; finally, aging and losing earthly hope, she becomes a Sister of Mercy in a Philadelphia hospital, where, during a plague, the dying Gabriel is brought and the lovers are reunited just before his death. Gabriel early recedes into the background as the sought rather than seeker, and the focus of the whole poem is upon Evangeline, giving the temperamentally chivalric Longfellow full scope for the development of an idealized, simple woman of absolute fidelity, the kind of heroine most congenial to his imagination. In a realistically represented milieu Evangeline would seem too etherealized, but the deliberately legendary treatment of the story and the touch of dreamlike remoteness in the setting create an idyllic effect appropriate to the characterization. Moreover, the idealization of the heroine is closely related to the poem's meaning: Evangeline is increasingly spiritualized by the patiently endured sufferings of her nearly endless journey until she finally emerges as a saintly figure.

The journey of Evangeline and the whole story in which she moves are raised to semiheroic proportions by Longfellow's mythologizing of his materials. Acadia is also Arcadia; the simple lives of the peasants, viewed under a summer sun, recall the Golden Age and Eden, and the murmuring pines and hemlocks color the scene with childhood innocence recalled. With expulsion and separation, a mythic pattern specifically Christian develops: the pious Evangeline is the exiled wayfarer making her dedicated journey through the world to her final renunciation of it and her entering upon the more purely spiritual pilgrimage of return to the true Arcadia of Heaven, where alone reunion can be lasting. When the two lovers at one dramatic point miss each other by the narrowest of margins, it is, as one critic has said, like the touch of God's hand reserving Evangeline for another marriage. Despite the slowness and occasional thinness of the narration, the pattern of *Evangeline* gives the poem substance and dignity.

In creating the hexameter lines of *Evangeline* Longfellow sensibly treated the problem of English hexameter as a practical one, and paid little heed to the theoretic objections that have enlivened criticism since the Renaissance. Encouraged by Goethe's example and by the experiments of Southey and Coleridge, he solved the immediate problems by using a basically dactylic line with a trochaic close and free trochaic substitution; the minimally necessary spondees he obtained by juxtaposing monosyllabic words and by coaxing the second syllable of trochees into an approximation of spondees. The resultant hexameters give *Evangeline* a slow processional movement; the longer line admits lavish introduction of concrete detail through additional modifying words, and has a pleasantly lingering effect appropriate to idyllic tone, as Longfellow apparently realized, since extended use of hexameters occurs chiefly in his idylls—*Evangeline, The Courtship of Miles Standish,* and "Elizabeth" in *Tales of a Wayside Inn.*

The Courtship of Miles Standish, although published eleven years later, resembles *Evangeline* in measure, in use of a legendary-historical foundation, and in pastoral coloring. The *Courtship,* however, has a vein of humor that leaves readers suspended between sentiment and amusement. The story has long since passed into folklore: how John Alden loved Priscilla Mullins but, out of friendship, wooed her in Captain Miles Standish's behalf, and how, with a false report of Standish's death, John and Priscilla married, with the captain returning just in time to assent. It is not the tale but the telling that has distinction. Longfellow moves through variations of tone with impressive assurance, from satirical humor to romance tinged with sentimentality, through sobriety and comedy alternatively.

The success of the *Courtship* lies principally in its humorous juxtaposition of two extravagant attitudes, each described in appropriate language and imagery, with each other and with common sense. One attitude is embodied in Captain Miles Standish, the hot-tempered commander of a twelve-man army, a swaggerer, a valiant man, and a student of the wars of the Hebrews, *Caesar's Commentaries,* and an artillery guide "designed for belligerent Christians"; on the other side is John Alden, sincere, hard-working, overscrupulous, compelled to disguise pleasure as duty before he can enjoy it, and fearful lest his preference of love over friendship may be "worshipping Astaroth blindly, and impious idols of Baal." At the center is commonsensical Priscilla, quiet, loving, amused at her suitors' posturings, and busy at the spinning wheel emblematic of settled life with its civilizing domesticity.

The marriage of John and Priscilla, however humorous its preliminaries, is nevertheless, in the barely surviving Plymouth colony that is the setting, an affirmation of faith in America's future and a promise of its fruitfulness. Thus the almost lush description of the climactic bridal day is without serious incongruity set forth in images of religious ritual and of fertility, as the sun issues forth like a high priest, with the sea a laver at his feet, and Priscilla rides on a snow-white bull to her wedding while golden sunlight gleams on bunches of purple grapes. Longfellow again introduces the imagery of Eden and expulsion as he describes the land of privation and hardship lying before John and Priscilla, and adds,

> But to their eyes transfigured, it seemed as
> the Garden of Eden,
> Filled with the presence of God, whose
> voice was the sound of the ocean.

The final balance of sometimes broad humor, romantic sentiment, and gravity is a tonal achievement of no small order.

With *Hiawatha* Longfellow made his chief contribution to nineteenth-century American literature's search for a usable national past, whose necessity to the creation of a native culture was assumed from the analogy of European cultural history. America's antiquity, however, was Indian and primitively tribal, and therefore both racially and culturally alien. The pieties of nationalism nonetheless demanded that the gap between the two worlds be bridged; countless authors valiantly responded, and, with a few notable exceptions, artistically perished in the attempt. To Longfellow the whole effort seemed misdirected, since America's cultural past was essentially European, although he had been long interested in Indian lore and history, and was acquainted with such authorities on Indian life as Heckewelder and Schoolcraft. Typically, he found his own formula for relating the Indian past to the American present in a European national poem, the Finnish *Kalevala,* which suggested the use of legends linked together by the central figure of a culture hero, the creations of myth and folklore being, for the cultivated imagination, more viable than the grubby data of actual primitive living. In American terms, the Indians' passage from savagery to a low level of civilization could be treated as preparatory to the climactic arrival of high civilization represented by the white man, and poetry could thus create the continuity that history had failed to provide. One result of this plan is the weakest moment in *Hiawatha,* when the hero unreservedly recommends to his people the religion and culture of the white man, represented by the Jesuit missionaries: the abrupt transition from a legendary world to that of fictionalized history in unconvincing, as it was probably certain to be, in spite of its theoretical justification as a means of relating Indian and white civilization, the chief desideratum of the age.

Like the creators of the Noble Redman, Longfellow adapted his Indians to contemporary tastes and interests. His hero is a bowdlerized version of a mythic Algonkian chief, and Hiawatha's romance with Minnehaha is conducted by the rules of sentimental fiction. The idealization, however, is largely intended by Longfellow, as a part of the deliberately legendary atmosphere of the narration. Criticisms based on realistic assumptions, whether Emerson's mild blame or Schoolcraft's praise, were, in Longfellow's eyes, fundamentally irrelevant: Hiawatha was, he stated, a kind of "American Prometheus," and the poem was "an Indian Edda," a recognizably poetic romance, based on ancient myths and traditions and thus to be read as an attractively colorful reflection not of Indian actuality, but of primitive imagination.

The language and versification of *Hiawatha* were designed as part of its legendary effect. The trochaic tetrameter meter, suggested by the *Kalevala* and by earlier Indian romances, has an accentuation sufficiently strong to invite easy exaggeration into singsong, an invitation readily accepted by most modern readers. In so long a poem, the conspicuous rhythm, the constant use of parallelism and repetition, the profusion of exotic Indian names, and the simple personifications all finally threaten monotony and make parody irresistible. Critical objections to *Hiawatha*'s verse can be countered only by treating the verse, according to Longfellow's intention, as a part of the primitive machinery. Thus regarded, the verse loses its apparent eccentricity and contributes a suitable effect of chant and of quaintness to the legendary atmosphere Longfellow sought to create. Unfortunately, it also heightens the sense of artifice pervasive in *Hiawatha* and perhaps inseparable from a pseudo-primitive genre.

Present-day concern with myth, legend, and folklore gives *Hiawatha* a more serious interest than it possessed in the recent past, even if the modern reader usually prefers to take his myth neat or as revitalized in current forms. The episodes of *Hiawatha* are based upon now familiar mythic patterns. Hiawatha himself, begotten by the West Wind upon the daughter of moon-descended Nokomis, is a demigod aligning himself with humanity. He teaches his people how to plant and cultivate maize, and begins to instruct them in the arts of civilization, the skills of fishing and agriculture, and the art of picture-writing. With the help of his few close companions and of the helpful animals of folklore, he slays the spirit of evil, the serpent-guarded Magician, and Pau-Puk-Keewis, the champion of the old, anarchic savagery, and finally departs for the Islands of the Blessed. From one standpoint, *Hiawatha* is a set of picturesque variations on mythic themes, and its recapitulation of a whole mythic pattern gives it in its entirety an imaginative strength greater than its incidental faults would apparently support. Its major weakness as a whole arises primarily from its literarily calculated primitivism: the sophistication of its simplicity makes it too manifestly a tour de force.

Longfellow's last major narrative work, *Tales of a Wayside Inn,* was published in three installments over an eleven-year period. The design of the work, a collection of stories in a unifying framework, recalls the *Canterbury Tales,* but Longfellow's self-confessed inability to rival Chaucer makes the Chaucerian work properly a point of reference rather than of comparison. In Longfellow's *Tales,* the stories are clearly primary, the framework a support. The setting is the Red-Horse Inn (now the reconstructed Wayside Inn) in Sudbury, Massachusetts, a hostelry well known to Longfellow and his friends. The narrators, designated by profession, avocation, nationality, or race, are all based upon actual acquaintances of Longfellow's: the Poet was Theophilus Parsons, a translator of Dante; the Musician was the Norwegian violinist Ole Bull; the Sicilian was Luigi Monti, an instructor in Harvard's modern languages department. Their individual characteristics are generalized into more or less typical ones, but there can be no satirical representation or socially or dramatically significant quarreling: the narrators form a friendly and homogeneous group. What is possible in the framework is realized—an animated running discussion of topics suggested by the tales and of points of view expressed by the tellers. In flexible tetrameter couplets, Longfellow takes the discussion from aesthetics to religion, and achieves an effect of individually colored discourse sufficient to support the tales and often interesting in itself.

Individually considered, the tales vary greatly in nature, interest, and quality. A few, like "Lady Wentworth" and "Azrael," dwindle into anecdote, and ofliers, like "The Ballad of Carmilhan," are principally evocative of mood or of that ghostly atmosphere that Longfellow could always effectively create. Most of the stories, however, are marked by Longfellow's real narrative talent: the ability to make well-selected, continuously progressing events and vividly, if broadly, drawn characters deliver in a climactic scene some comment upon an aspect of life or a typical movement of human feeling. The accomplishment of the *Tales,* however, lies less in particular stories, as good as several of them are, than in the variety of the gathered narratives. Contrasting with each other in scene, tone, and poetic structure, and held together by the framework, the stories in juxtaposition suggest the inclusive range possible to the simple, immemorial activity of storytelling, and the way in which even traditional tales may reflect attitudes and feelings of the narrators. Many kinds of effects are embraced, from the grimness of "Torquemada" to the broad fabliau humor of "The Monk of Casal-Maggiore" or the vividness of "The Saga of King Olaf," one of the most vigorous of all Longfellow's poems, with its balladlike but well-developed dramatization of the mingled zeal and barbarism of the first Viking champions and enemies of Christianity. Moreover, a few of the tales, like "Emma and Eginhard" and "The Falcon of Ser Federigo," reflect a more realistic and tolerant assessment of human behavior than Longfellow's poetry commonly displays. The reputation of the *Tales* is unavoidably linked to the fortunes of narrative poetry, especially of straightforward narrative; within that limited area, the *Tales* occupies a place of considerable honor.

The major irony of Longfellow's literary career was the commitment of his hopes for distinctive major achievement to the form in which he was most consistently unsuccessful, the poetic drama. From 1849 to 1872 he intermittently labored over what he regarded as "his loftier song in sublimer strain," as his greatest work, "the equivalent expression for the trouble and wrath of life, for its sorrow and mystery." The completed *Christus: A Mystery* consists of three parts comprising four poetic dramas, all so manifestly closet dramas that they could be properly described as dramatically organized poems. The first part is *The Divine Tragedy,* the last to be published; the second part is *The Golden Legend,* the first published; the third part, *The New England Tragedies,* consists of two dramas, *John Endicott* and *Giles Corey of the Salem Farms.* The three parts are linked by interludes and the whole *Christus* is provided with an "Introitus" and "Finale." No other works of Longfellow's had such intended scope or received such dedicated attention; and none were so disappointing in result. The twenty-odd years spent in composition, the lapse of time between publication of the parts, and the fact that each part is also a substantially self-contained work explain why the *Christus* seems partly to be an assemblage; indeed, it is surprising that the whole does achieve a loose unity which makes it more than the sum of its parts.

Longfellow's general failure in dramatic form is understandable. His talent was narrative and lyrically meditative, and he could not refrain from reliance on narration and exposition, even to the destruction of dramatic effect. The sequence and relationship of episodes and actions is basically determined, especially in the last two parts of the *Christus,* by narrative not dramatic logic and development. It is thus unfortunate that from 1849 on he increasingly looked to drama as the vehicle of his most important ideas. It is his least pretentious dramatic work, the early *Spanish Student,* that is in many respects the most successfully realized; in spite of its lack of intellectual significance, it is a colorful, pleasant comedy of intrigue, technically more proficient than the later poetic dramas. Two minor dramatic works, *Judas Maccabeus* and *The Masque of Pandora,* have interesting themes but are extremely weak in execution. Only the partly completed *Michael Angelo,* closely related to Longfellow's own life and work, and containing in a few passages some of his strongest poetry, shows an apparently emerging mastery of dramatic form in the 1870's.

The fundamental obstacle to the *Christus'* success, however, is not simply a flawed dramatic technique, but an internal conflict in the work between its ostensible intention and its meaning. Originally planned as a dramatizing of the progress of Christianity, the *Christus* loosely employs the theological virtues of faith, hope, and charity as the basis of organization, *The Divine Tragedy* expressing hope through its representation of Christ's life and mission, the *Golden Legend* depicting faith in its full medieval flowering, and the *New England Tragedies* pointing to the religious freedom of the age of charity or love. The optimism of the design is realized in some scenes and is recurrently asserted as a proposition, but it is not borne out in the *Christus'* development and accumulated feeling, which are finally somber and even pessimistic in their tendency. Longfellow's emotional recoil from several aspects of the contemporary religious scene apparently caused him to lose much of his professed hope for the future and left its mark especially on the first and third parts, the latest composed, of the *Christus.* If the last part inculcates love and tolerance at all, it does so only by exhibiting the horrors of bigotry, and the relentless power of intolerance is in fact the dominant force; in *John Endicott* a series of special providences, occurring near the conclusion, indicate divine displeasure with persecution, but the Quakers are saved only by an intervening royal mandate of that unlikely *deus ex machina,* Charles II; in the final, still grimmer *Giles Corey,* where the maliciously accused though innocent Corey is put to death by pressing, this climactic scene is followed by a hasty, excessively short speech by Cotton Mather predicting that never again will such things happen, a judgment perhaps validated by history, but certainly not by the action or tone of the drama. Furthermore, the interlude preparing for the *New England Tragedies* is a soliloquy by Martin Luther that alternates between an announcement of spiritual freedom recovered from religious tyranny and a condemnation of humanism reflecting the sectarianism and hatred most repellent to Longfellow: it is an unpromising introduction to the latest stage of an assertedly progressive historical movement.

That the *New England Tragedies* made a darkened climax Longfellow was probably aware. He originally planned a third, more confident concluding play based on the simple, pious life of Pennsylvania's Moravian sisterhood. This, however, he never wrote, and its abandonment may be explained by the actual state of his sentiments and especially by the developing mood of the *Christus* itself. The opening "Introitus" finds in the sadness of pre-Christian ages the sign of a coming Redeemer, but the "Finale" is not a celebration of redemption achieved; rather, it is a melancholy review of the Christian centuries, concluding that "the evil doth not cease." The survey is not despairing, but its limited hope is proclaimed in spite of rather than out of Christian history, and hope's realization seems indefinitely postponed: meanwhile

> Poor, sad Humanity
> Through all the dust and heat
> Turns back with bleeding feet,
> By the weary road it came. . . .

So the tracing of the human condition comes nearly full circle back to the "Introitus," and is saved from cyclical completion only by Longfellow's characteristic emphasis upon the persistence of the ideal and the possibility of individual Christian action.

Perhaps the most successful part of *Christus* is the *Golden Legend,* which, in spite of an elementary plot, an unmedievally melancholy hero, and a sentimentalized heroine, effectively profits from Longfellow's knowledge of the Middle Ages. Although the deepest intellectual and spiritual life of the medieval world is not mirrored here, the varied contrasts and conflicts of the medieval surface, as well as the immediately underlying crosscurrents, are colorfully represented through skillfully shifted scenes presented in a freely handled answerable verse. An acid portrayal of Goliardic friars is set against a simple, reverentially composed nativity play, and the satiric presentations of wrangling scholastics and of a sensational preacher are placed in a sympathetically imagined background of ringing bells and chanting pilgrims. So picturesquely drawn are the diverse actions of a world where "the will is feeble and passion strong," but where everything is seen in a transcendent light, that the effect is of a pageant arranged by religious and historical feeling, almost rich enough to conceal the weaknesses of the dramatic core.

The Divine Tragedy, composed in three "Passovers" or acts, with an "Introitus" and an epilogue, is based, often closely, on the Biblical account of Christ's life. The faults are many and obvious, ranging from insubstantial scenes to timidity in handling the text of the Bible, but in centering the action upon the effects of divine love and human response to it, Longfellow achieves some genuine thematic and dramatic development. Each "Passover" concentrates upon one aspect of Christus' expanding mission: upon the casting out of demons, which is the ejection of irrationality and fear; the curing of blindness, which is the dispelling of ignorance; and sacrifice, the perilous commitment of love. Recurrent themes and images, and frequent cross references, make the action less episodic than it at first appears to be, and an interpretative chorus is provided by Manahem the Essenian. Above all, a basic unity is found in Longfellow's preoccupation with that most persistent and personal of his themes, the problem of dream and reality. The fear expressed throughout *The Divine Tragedy* is that life is a delusive dream within a dream, and Christus the visionary of an unreal kingdom. The act of faith thus becomes primarily an assertion of reality, its validity being finally confirmed by the appearance of the risen Christus. Yet the haunting fear is too powerfully expressed to be completely dissolved even by an apparently victorious conclusion.

The study of Longfellow's poetic reputation is perhaps more relevant to the history of criticism than to the evaluation of his art. His most literate contemporaries delivered varying decisions, some finding the poetry seriously deficient, others praising it without reservation, most setting a very high value on the best poems while pointing out the weakness of others. It was popular acclaim, hailing the man as much as the poet, that elevated Longfellow to a position no sober critical judgment could sanction. With the emergence of modern literature and the literary wars it evoked, the defenders of the new order found it necessary and not unpleasant to counter the hostility of presumably Victorian attitudes by attacking Victorian ideals and achievements. In America, Longfellow, in his popular canonization, offered himself as the surest target for an assault on the nineteenth century; at the nadir, one influential critic advanced the proposition that Longfellow's poetry has no iota of the poetic character. Later, however, as the early twentieth-century revolution itself receded into the past, it became possible for Longfellow to share in the general revaluation of Victorian literature. To this more objective examination, dating especially from Odell Shepard's reserved but often acute essay prefixed to his selective edition of Longfellow's poems, many studies have contributed, including such full-length ones as Lawrance Thompson's reassessment of the young Longfellow's experience, Edward Wagenknecht's two important and sympathetic interpretations of Longfellow as person and author, Newton Arvin's uniquely valuable analysis of the poetry as a whole, and Cecil Williams' placing of Longfellow in the American literary tradition. From this continuing reconsideration has come a clear view of the many limitations of Longfellow's talent, but also a new respect for his accomplishment within them.

Selected Bibliography

WORKS OF HENRY WADSWORTH LONGFELLOW

Coplas de Don Jorge Manrique, Translated from the Spanish . . . (Boston: Allen and Ticknor, 1833).

Outre-Mer: A Pilgrimage beyond the Sea, 2 vols. (Boston Hilliard, Gray Vol. I; Lilly, Wait Vol. II 1833–34).

Hyperion: A Romance, 2 vols. (New York: S. Colman, 1839).

Voices of the Night, (Cambridge, Mass.: J. Owen, 1939).

Ballads and Other Poems, (Cambridge, Mass.: J. Owen, 1841).

Poems on Slavery, (Cambridge, Mass.: J. Owen, 1842).

The Spanish Student, A Play in Three Acts (Cambridge, Mass.: J. Owen, 1843).

The Poets and Poetry of Europe, with Introductions and Biographical Notices by Henry Wadsworth Longfellow (Philadelphia: Carey and Hart, 1845).

The Belfry of Bruges and Other Poems, (Cambridge, Mass.: J. Owen, 1846).

Evangeline, a Tale of Acadie, (Boston: Ticknor, 1847).

Kavanagh, a Tale, (Boston: Ticknor, Reed, and Fields, 1849).

The Seaside and the Fireside, (Boston: Ticknor, Reed, and Fields, 1850).

The Golden Legend, (Boston: Ticknor, Reed, and Fields, 1851).

The Song of Hiawatha, (Boston: Ticknor and Fields, 1855).

Drift Wood, A Collection of Essays (Boston: Ticknor and Fields, 1857).

The Courtship of Miles Standish and Other Poems, (Boston: Ticknor and Fields, 1858).

Tales of a Wayside Inn, (Boston: Ticknor and Fields, 1863).

The Divine Comedy of Alighieri, Translated by Henry Wadsworth Longfellow. 3 vols. (Boston: Ticknor and Fields, 1865–67).

Flower-de-Luce, (Boston: Ticknor and Fields, 1867).

The New England Tragedies, (Boston: Ticknor and Fields, 1868) Privately printed (1867).

The Divine Tragedy, (Boston: Osgood, 1871).

Christus: A Mystery, 3 vols. (Boston: Osgood, 1872).

Three Books of Song, (Boston: Osgood, 1872).

Aftermath, (Boston: Osgood, 1873).

The Hanging of the Crane, (Boston: Mifflin, 1874).

The Masque of Pandora and Other Poems, (Boston: Osgood, 1875).

Kéramos and Other Poems, (Boston: Houghton, Osgood, 1878).

Ultima Thule, (Boston: Houghton Mifflin, 1880).

In the Harbor, (Boston: Houghton Mifflin, 1882).

Michael Angelo, (London: Houghton Mifflin, 1883).

SELECTED AND COLLECTED EDITIONS

Complete Works, edited by Horace E. Scudder, Riverside Edition. 11 vols. (Boston: Houghton Mifflin, 1886) Reprinted in Standard Library Edition, with *Life* by Samuel Longfellow and illustrations. 14 vols. (Boston: Houghton Mifflin, 1891) Reprinted also in Craigie Edition, with illustrations. 11 vols. (Boston: Houghton Mifflin, 1904).

Complete Poetical Works, edited by Horace E. Scudder Cambridge Edition (Boston: Houghton Mifflin, 1893) Reprinted in Household Edition, with illustrations (Boston: Houghton Mifflin, 1902).

Longfellow's Boyhood Poems, edited by George T. Little (Saratoga Springs, N.Y.: Ray W. Pettengill, 1925).

Henry Wadsworth Longfellow: Representative Selections, edited by Odell Shepard. American Writers Series (New York: American Book, 1934).

Kavanagh, a Tale, edited by Jean Downey. Masterworks of Literature Series (New Haven, Conn.: College and University Press, 1965).

LETTERS

Letters of Henry Wadsworth Longfellow, edited by Andrew Hilen. Vol. I (1814–36) Vol. II (1837–43) other volumes in progress (New York: Oxford University Press, 1966–).

BIBLIOGRAPHIES

Dana, H. W. L., "Henry Wadsworth Longfellow," in Vol. II of the *Cambridge History of American Literature* 4 vols. (New York: G. P. Putnam's Sons, 1917).

Livingston, Luther S., *A Bibliography of the First Editions in Book Form of the Writings of Henry Wadsworth Longfellow,* (New York: Privately printed, 1908).

CRITICAL AND BIOGRAPHICAL STUDIES

Arms, George T., "Longfellow," *The Fields Were Green* (Stanford, Calif.: Stanford University Press, 1948).

Arvin, Newton, *Longfellow: His Life and Work,* (Boston: Little, Brown, 1963).

Austin, George L., *Henry Wadsworth Longfellow: His Life, His Works, His Friendships,* (Boston: Lee and Shepard, 1883).

Gorman, Herbert, *A Victorian American, Henry Wadsworth Longfellow,* (New York: Doran, 1926).

Hatfield, James T., *New Light on Longfellow, with Special Reference to His Relations with Germany,* (Boston: Houghton Mifflin, 1933).

Hawthorne, Manning, and Dana Henry, *The Origin and Development of Longfellow's "Evangeline,"* Dana, Henry, (Portland, Maine: Anthoensen Press, 1947).

Higginson, Thomas W., *Henry Wadsworth Longfellow,* American Men of Letters Series (Boston: Houghton Mifflin, 1902).

Hilen, Andrew, *Longfellow and Scandinavia,* (New Haven, Conn.: Yale University Press, 1947).

Johnson, Carl L., *Professor Longfellow of Harvard,* (Eugene: University of Oregon Press, 1944).

Jones, Howard M., "Longfellow," *American Writers on American Literature* edited by John Macy (New York: Liveright, 1931).

Longfellow, Samuel, *Life of Henry Wadsworth Longfellow,* 2 vols. (Boston: Ticknor, 1886).

Longfellow, Samuel, *Final Memorials of Henry Wadsworth Longfellow,* (Boston: Ticknor, 1887).

Martin, Ernest, *L'Evangeline de Longfellow et la suite merveilleuse d'un poème,* (Paris: Librairie Hachette, 1936).

More, Paul Elmer, "The Centenary of Longfellow," *Shelburne Essays, Fifth Series* (Boston: Houghton Mifflin, 1908).

Morin, Paul, *Les Sources de l'oeuvre de Henry Wadsworth Longfellow,* (Paris: Emile Larose, 1913).

O'Neil, Rev. Joseph E., S.J. "Poet of the Feeling Heart," *American Classics Reconsidered* edited by Rev. Harold C. Gardiner, S.J. (New York: Scribners, 1958).

Scudder, Horace E., "Longfellow and His Art," *Men and Books* (Boston: Houghton Mifflin, 1887).

Thompson, Lawrance, *Young Longfellow, 1807–1843,* (New York: Macmillan, 1938).

Van Schaick, John, Jr., *The Characters in "Tales of a Wayside Inn,"* (Boston: Universalist Publishing House, 1939).

Wagenknecht, Edward, *Longfellow: A Full-Length Portrait,* (New York: Longmans, Green, 1955).

Wagenknecht, Edward, *Mrs. Longfellow: Selected Letters and Journals of Fanny Appleton,* (New York: Longmans, Green, 1956).

Wagenknecht, Edward, *Henry Wadsworth Longfellow: Portrait of an American Humanist,* (New York: Oxford University Press, 1966).

Whitman, Iris, *Longfellow and Spain,* (New York: Instituto de las Españas en los Estados Unidos, 1927).

Williams, Cecil B., *Henry Wadsworth Longfellow,* (New York: Twayne, 1964).

Williams, Stanley T., "Longfellow," in Vol. II of *The Spanish Background of American Literature,* 2 vols. (New Haven, Conn.: Yale University Press, 1955).

ROBERT LOWELL

(1917–1977)

JAY MARTIN

"FOR ALL THE horrors of this age, and for all the attractions of others . . . I'd rather be alive now than at any other time I know of. This age is mine, and I want very much to be a part of it," Robert Lowell remarked in 1965. Though deeply, irredeemably, involved in the present, Lowell characteristically approaches the present through the perspective of the past. This is hardly surprising. Born on March 1, 1917, into a family whose history was mingled with New England's, Lowell was personally obliged to acknowledge the importance of his lineage and forced to recognize the influence on him of what he inherited. The first woman to step off the *Mayflower* was one of Lowell's ancestors; another was twice elected governor of Plymouth. The earliest Lowell in America, Percival, became a merchant in Massachusetts in 1639. John Lowell served in the provincial and federal congresses and founded Boston's first United States Bank. Other distinguished Lowells included the builder of the Lowell cotton mills, the founders of the Lowell Institute and the Lowell Observatory, and two poets, James Russell Lowell and Amy Lowell. Rebels against tradition, yet forebears of traditions, the Lowells were energetic, curious, and inventive—but also conservative; individualistic—but also formal and ceremonious.

In Robert Lowell these paradoxes would be sharpened into a poetry equally remarkable for a sense of the apocalyptic present and a knowledge of past history, for force and control, for richness and restraint. Under the pressure of such a system of contraries, Lowell's poetic manner has changed drastically during the last thirty years. His earliest verse was characterized by a tone of baroque exaltation —for instance, in "The Drunken Fisherman" (1944):

> Wallowing in this bloody sty,
> I cast for fish that pleased my eye
> (Truly Jehovah's bow suspends
> No pots of gold to weight its ends);
> Only the blood-mouthed rainbow trout
> Rose to my bait. They flopped about
> My canvas creel until the moth
> Corrupted its unstable cloth.
>
> A calendar to the the day;
> A handkerchief to wave away
> The gnats; a couch unstuffed with storm
> Pouching a bottle in one arm;
> A whiskey bottle full of worms;
> And bedroom slacks: are these fit terms
> To mete the worm whose molten rage
> Boils in the belly of old age?

By the sixties, Lowell's poetry had experienced many modifications. No longer oratorical and less pointedly symbolic, it might be dramatic—as in "The Drinker" (1964):

> The man is killing time—there's nothing
>   else.
> No help now from the fifth of Bourbon
> chucked helter-skelter into the river,
> even its cork sucked under.
>
> Stubbed before-breakfast cigarettes
> burn bull's-eyes on the bedside table;
> a plastic tumbler of alka seltzer
> champagnes in the bathroom.

No help from his body, the whale's
warm-hearted blubber, foundering down
leagues of ocean, gasping whiteness.
The barbed hooks fester. The lines snap
tight.

Or intensely personal, even confessional—as in "Fourth of July in Maine" (1967):

We watch the logs fall. Fire once gone,
we're done for: we escape the sun,
rising and setting, a red coal,
until it cinders like the soul.
Great ash and sun of freedom, give
us this day the warmth to live,
and face the household fire. We turn
our backs, and feel the whiskey burn.

Despite such striking external shifts, all of Lowell's work exhibits the same preoccupations. His basic subject has always been the fate of selfhood in time, and his basic method the examination of the convergence in man of past history and present circumstance. Much that seems contradictory in Lowell's development becomes clear when we understand that he imaginatively projects a system of tensions and contrasts which is designed to express both his will to believe and his capacity for doubt, his necessary reverence toward man or God as well as his inevitable irreverence toward the universe. Like the skeptical satirists of the Renaissance or the encyclopedists of the seventeenth and eighteenth centuries—Montaigne, Burton, Rabelais, Diderot—Lowell is essentially an ironist, interested in enigma rather than in certitude, in awareness more than in knowledge. The critic of Lowell, then, must trace out the stages and varieties of his development in order to show the unity of his work and describe the nature of his achievement.

Robert Lowell's youth was characterized, he has said, by "the anarchy of my adolescent war on my parents." His mother "did not have the self-assurance for wide human experience; she needed to feel liked, admired, surrounded by the approved and familiar." As for his father, "By the time he graduated from Annapolis. . . . he had reached, perhaps, his final mental possibilities. He was deep—not with profundity, but with the dumb depth of one who trusted in statistics and was dubious of personal experience." For the "morose and solitary" young Robert, "hurting others was as necessary as breathing." Since he was uncertain of his own identity he concluded that his heritage was not precisely the one he wanted and that he would need to reshape it if he were ever to accept it.

It was in poetry that he sought principles upon which to base an education, and to define himself and his vocation. Around the age of seventeen he wrote a metrical epic about the Crusades which he showed to Robert Frost. ("You have no compression," Frost said.) Richard Eberhart, who was then on the faculty of Lowell's prep school, St. Mark's, remembers that Lowell brought him about sixty poems, "shyly placing [them] on my desk when I was not there." These included "Madonna," Lowell's first published poem ("Celestial were her robes: / Her hands were made divine; / But the Virgin's face was silvery bright / Like the holy light: Which from God's throne / Is said to shine"), "Jericho," "New England," "Death," "Easter, an Ode," "Jonah," and "Phocion." Written in difficult Latin forms, these poems mixed Catholic with Puritan materials ("When Cotton Mather wrestled with the fiends from Hell"), bewailed the conflict between the poet and society ("Most wretched men / Are cradled into poetry by wrong"), and emphasized mystical awareness ("A sight of something after death / Bright Angels dropping from the sky"). Eberhart remembers that "a heavy driving force and surd of prose which would bind the lyric flow in strict forms" were already evident in them.

At Harvard between 1935 and 1937, Lowell attempted to find "new life in his art" and shed "his other life." He rebelled against the pedantry of the Harvard English Department and scorned the *Advocate*—which refused to print his violent poems. He put Leonardo and Rembrandt prints on his walls and Beethoven on his phonograph, and collected "soiled metrical treatises . . . full of glorious things: rising rhythm, falling rhythm, feet with Greek names." Aided by these, he "rolled out Spenserian stanzas on Job and Jonah surrounded by recently seen Nantucket scenery. Everything I did was grand, ungrammatical and had a timeless, hackneyed quality." In 1937 his discovery of William Carlos Williams' work unsettled his convictions about the necessity for exotic meters, intricate style, and elaborate diction and left him still longing for guidance, while rebelling against the negative identities which America, his parents, Harvard, and Boston tradition threatened to impose upon him.

At this crucial moment he defined himself through another series of writers. On the strength of a casual invitation from Ford Madox Ford, he drove to Monteagle, Tennessee, to visit him at the house of Allen Tate and Caroline Gordon. Ford had not yet arrived. But Tate immediately offered himself as friend, magisterial teacher, and literary father —exactly what Lowell was seeking. "Stately yet boheinian, leisurely yet dedicated," Tate learnedly maneuvered Lowell through the English, Greek, and Latin classics, while "blasting" most "slipshod" modern poets. His unequivocal declaration that "a good poem had nothing to do with exalted feelings" convinced Lowell that a poem "was simply a piece of craftsmanship, an intelligible or cognitive object," and that he might master its techniques. After completing the Harvard term, Lowell returned to Monteagle. With "keen, idealistic, adolescent heedlessness," he camped for three months on Tate's lawn and sweated out a series of "grimly unromantic poems—organized, hard and classical as a cabinet."

That fall, with Tate's encouragement, Lowell transferred to Kenyon College, where John Crowe Ransom set the self-consciously Aristotelian, anti-Romantic, ceremonious, and politically orthodox intellectual tone. Lowell was to be permanently affected by the influences exerted on him at this time—Ransom's New Critical emphasis on wit and paradox, Tate's "attempt to make poetry much more formal . . . to write in meters but to make the meters look hard and make them hard to write," contemplative religious literature, Hart Crane, the classics, and criticism like William Empson's *Seven Types of Ambiguity.* Attempting to synthesize all these, he found each poem he wrote "was more difficult than the one before, and had more ambiguities." To make matters more difficult, Lowell was experiencing a spiritual crisis which ended in his rejection of the secularistic accommodations of his Protestant heritage and his conversion to Catholicism. His personal crisis resounded in his poems. Though regarding them as "forbidding and clotted," Ransom accepted two Lowell poems for *Kenyon Review* in 1939.

During the year following his *summa cum laude* graduation from Kenyon in 1940, Lowell and his new wife, Jean Stafford, lived with the Tates. While their wives hummed along on fiction, the two poets studied, talked, and wrote slowly; Lowell completed only a handful of poems in this year. Still, the creative energies released by Lowell's education, conversion, marriage, and poetic apprenticeship finally took form in a slim first volume, *Land of Unlikeness* (1944).

Strengthened by what Tate called "a memory of the spiritual dignity of man," Lowell writes in this book as an avowed Christian, with T. S. Eliot and G. M. Hopkins as his conscious models. Reviewing Eliot's *Four Quartets* in 1943, he argued that "*union with God* is somewhere in sight in all poetry." A 1944 "Note" on Hopkins shows Lowell interested in the way Hopkins' "unique personality and holiness" flowered in poetry. Certainly, much of the turbulence of Lowell's early poetry comes from his conscious struggle to approach Christian perfection. "According to Catholic theology," he wrote, "perfection demands a *substantial transformation* which is called first 'sanctifying' grace and then beatitude, it involves the co-working of grace and free will." His effort to order his language and perfect his verse was analogous (as he saw it) to the discipline of contemplation, the achieved aesthetic experience of a poem analogous to spiritual illumination. But Lowell's way with poetry would be neither Hopkins' nor Eliot's. In the American romantic tradition, he not only merged poetry with religion but equated both with culture, and thus attempted to be oratorical and satirical, exalted and apocalyptic, visionary and prophetic, idealistic and pessimistic, hortatory and violent. Yearning for a civilization in which men bear a likeness to God, he finds in the modern world only St. Augustine's *regio dissimilitudinis*—capitalism, war, secularized consciousness.

Lowell had learned much from his soiled metrical treatises-most of all from Bridges' *Study of Milton's Prosody.* His poetic techniques in *Land of Unlikeness* are carefully calculated to convey strain and tension. "There is not," R. P. Blackmur commented, "a loving metre in the book." The use of thud-meter with sporadic substitution and hard, short run-over lines, often with strong caesuras immediately preceding the final stress, clogs the rhythms and hints at an agonized consciousness, able only to stab itself into language. Short, heavily stressed lines and jangling rhymes shatter the harmony, as if mellifluousness were a disease which threatened to infect him. Strained verbs call attention to the harshness of being. Repetition is the basis of his style: repeated symbols (instead of narrative development), serious puns, frequent allusions, parallelism, formal recurrence, lack of transitions, and repeated assonantal and alliterative sound devices all suggest astonished concentration on the same matter, taken up from different aspects. In losing his perception of his eternal soul's likeness to God, man is lost in time. "The Park Street Cemetery" begins the volume; "Leviathan," an apocalyptic poem of the future, ends it. Between them is a senseless present. Secular man cannot see that he is the "ruined farmer" Cain, that the Charles River is the Acheron, that war renews Christ's crucifixion, that King Philip's severed head is John the Baptist's, that the Puritans are Dracos. Such equivalences, literally understood, were basic to Lowell's imaginative conviction that history is reiteration. They necessarily kept his poems from developing: there are no climaxes in them, only the momentary shutting down of vision.

"The Boston Nativity" typifies Lowell's effects and themes. A child stillborn on Christmas Eve parallels Christ, whose redemption of man is also abortive since men at the "spun world's hub" celebrate a secular Christmas, forgetting their likeness to God and their kinship to Christ. "Progress can't pay / For burial," the poet admonishes this Christ/child.

> Child, the Mayflower rots
> In your poor bred-out stock. Brave mould,
> here all
> The Mathers, Eliots and Endicots
> Brew their own gall. . . .

He concludes by symbolizing in this child the apocalyptic anti-Christ whose nativity—World War II—signalizes the consummation of this civilization: "Soon the Leviathan / Will spout American."

"The Park Street Cemetery," "On the Eve of the Immaculate Conception, 1942," and "Christ for Sale" are similar. There may be hope, the poets suggests in the last—"Us still our Savior's mangled mouth may kiss / Although beauticians plaster us with mud"—but only for the kiss of death, the boon of extinction. The true analogue for these poems is not mystic contemplation, but the desperation of Tashtego's last in *Moby Dick*—spiking the sky-hawk to the mast and so taking down a form of divinity with the damned *Pequod.* Lowell is fully aware of its many echoes in his concluding "Leviathan":

> Great Commonwealth, roll onward, roll
> On blood, and when the ocean monsters
> fling
> Out the satanic sting,
> Or like an octopus constrict my soul,
> Go down with colors flying for the King.

Although Lowell retained ten poems from *Land of Unlikeness* for *Lord Weary's Castle* (1946), he dropped the outraged, Christian poems that Tate pointed to as the core of *Land of Unlikeness,* and kept only those which could be rewritten with dramatic and elegiac points of view. *Lord Weary's Castle* studies the dulled consciousness of modern man, weary of morality and responsibility, indifferent to crime, numb to punishment, ungrateful and purposeless. Like the Lord Wearie of the ballad, man has neglected the payment due Lambkin, Christ, the architect of his salvation. The prophet of conscience, who had taken the epigraph for *Land of Unlikeness* from St. Bernard's sermon on the Song of Songs, shifted to the poet of consciousness, who found in a traditional ballad and a humanistic use of Christian myth vehicles to express the new concerns of his imagination.

These are best indicated by Lowell's revisions of the earlier "Christmas Eve in the Time of War: A Capitalist Meditates by a Civil War Monument." "Tonight," the capitalist bitterly remarks in the original version, "the venery of capital / Hangs the bare Christ-child on a tree of gold"; hysterical, he cries "for Santa Claus and Hamilton / To break the price-controller's strangle-hold." At the conclusion, the avenging Christ answers his bawling:

> "I bring no peace, I bring the sword," Christ
> said,
> "My nakedness was fingered and defiled."
> But woe unto the rich that are with child.

Thoroughly rewritten, reduced from five to three stanzas, and retitled "Christmas Eve under Hooker's Statue," *the Lord Weary's Castle* version dramatizes man's historic infidelity to himself in war and usury. An anonymous speaker compares the Civil War to his own disillusion; both his nation and he have been stung by knowledge. He is answered not by an apocalyptic Christ, but by Herman Melville—and not the Melville of *Moby Dick,* but of *Battle-Pieces,* a book ruled by conciliation and forgiveness. Thus Lowell hints at a stage beyond vengeance, a promise of reconciliation.

> "All wars are boyish," Herman Melville
> said;
> But we are old, our fields are running wild:
> Till Christ again turn wanderer and child.

Awakened to the dramatic possibilities of restoration, Lowell can end his poems climactically instead of catastrophically. Irony had resulted from his earlier method of contrasting doubt and faith, affirmation and rejection, synthesis and disintegration: now their interaction results in drama.

The first poem in *Lord Weary's Castle,* "The Exile's Return," announces and defines the principles of this shift. At the end of *Land of Unlikeness* Lowell had pointed to the consequences of man's disobedience: "When Israel turned from God's wise fellowship, / He sent us Canaan or Exile." But the exile has returned. He can, Lowell suggests in Shelleyan imagery of the seasons, have spring, a return from exile, by enduring the winter of his death. Lord Weary's destroyed castle—specifically the broken buildings and "torn-up tilestones" of occupied Germany—might be rebuilt. But man is still "unseasoned," unchanged. Lowell's symbol for contemporary man in "The Exile's Return" is Thomas Mann's Tonio Kröger, torn between nineteenth-century serenity and twentieth-century Armageddon. Thus, the poet, pointing hesitantly toward a revivification of European Christianity ("already lily-stands / Burgeon the risen Rhineland, and a rough / Cathedral lifts its eye"), considers man's renewal unlikely. "*Voi ch'entrate,* and your life is in your hands," he ambiguously concludes.

"The Exile's Return" is Lowell's inscription to the hell of his volume. Subsequent poems poise man in the Purgatorio of his indecision. "The year / The nineteen-hundred forty-fifth of grace," he writes in the second poem ("The Holy Innocents"), "Lumbers with losses up the clinkered hill / Of our purgation." "Colloquy in Black Rock," which follows, dramatizes the dialects of indecision central to the first two poems. In its first and second sestets, locating the poem in an industrial section of Bridgeport, Connecticut, Lowell parallels the technological "jackhammer" hell of machine-society to the frenzied human heart beating jackhammer-like toward death, breaking down into elemental "Black Mud." But the quatrain connecting these sestets, alluding to "the martyre Stephen, who was stoned to death," reminds the reader that Lowell took his epigraph for *Lord Weary's Castle* from the Secret of the Mass for St. Stephen, the first martyr for his faith. The second quatrain develops this theme: even though Stephen "was broken down to blood," his heart was the "House of our Savior" and his death a "ransom," salvation. Resolved to mud, man might escape the mire of flesh; then, mud "Flies from his hunching wings and beak—my heart, / The blue kingfisher dives on you in fire." Although this final image recalls the "dove descending" of *Little Gidding* and Hopkins' "The Windhover," it provides a violent, and successful, epiphany. By developing ordered moral connections between the Black Rock of civilization (hell), the Black Mud of death (purgatory), and the blue kingfisher-Christ (salvation), Lowell created an image of salvation as powerful as his images of destruction. The poem which investigates their connections coheres and develops.

Asked to comment on his poetry, Lowell said he was "essentially in agreement" with Randall Jarrell's review of *Lord Weary's Castle.* Lowell's poems, Jarrell argued, "understand the world as a sort of conflict of opposites": there is "the cake of custom," the realm of inertia, complacence, and necessity, everything that blinds or binds: "the Old Law, imperialism, militarism, capitalism, Calvinism, Authority, the Father, the 'proper Bostonians,' the rich . . ."; against this grinds "everything that is free or open, that grows or is willing to change." Lowell's earliest poems moved toward the closed world—from unfulfilled possibility to the necessity of apocalypse. Now he moves them from necessity toward intimations of liberation.

The major poem of the second mode is "The Quaker Graveyard in Nantucket." New England's whaling industry, based on the greedy exploitation of nature; Ahab's arrogant vengeance in *Moby Dick*; modern war, resulting in the death at sea of Lowell's cousin Warren Winslow; and modern politics, Hobbes's Leviathan, the state, are all analogues of each other. Constricting human possibility, all hint at the way that modern men prey on each other and point to the "promised end" described in *King Lear* as the result of violations of the cosmic order.

Sections I to V of the poem are generally pervaded by images of the closed world, all that is wrecked and destroyed—Winslow himself, the shipwreck described in Thoreau's *Cape Cod,* the doomed *Pequod,* and, at last, secular America. But in this poem Lowell works from the apocalyptic to the elegiac tradition—the obvious model for his prosody, themes, and organization coming from Milton's "Lycidas." Like Milton, Lowell asserts that disaster can be averted and the moral order restored through Christ. The apocalyptic analogies are balanced by a redemptive series: the design of Creation announced in Genesis; Quaker traditions of pacifism; the traditional symbolization of Christ as a whale, "IS, the whited monster"; Father Mapple's warnings in *Moby Dick* about the neglect of gospel duty; St. Matthew's claim (12:40) that Jonah's imprisonment in the whale's belly for three days prophesied Christ's resurrection; the Jewish mystical tradition that (as summarized in Jessie L. Weston's *From Ritual to Romance*), "at the end of the world, Messias will catch the great Fish Leviathan, and divide its flesh as food among the faithful"; and, at last, the Virgin's shrine at Walsingham, destroyed in the Reformation and recently restored. By section VI, these suggest a cosmic arc of liberation, the promised end of salvation—for Winslow and "the world [that] shall come to Walsingham" to contemplate the Unknowable "expressionless / Face" standing above the world of profane action. At first associated with the closed world, Winslow is finally identified with the liberating re-creation. Lowell's last line, "The Lord survives the rainbow of His will," alludes to God's covenant with Noah after the flood wiped away a corrupt world, as well as to Shelley's famous conclusion to "Adonais." Like Keats, trampled to fragments in life, Winslow is transfigured in the image of the rainbow, the "dome of many-colored glass" of a renewed genesis and covenant with man. The self—of Winslow or of the poet who meditates on his death—is defined by its absorption into suprapersonal structures of behavior and belief.

Elsewhere in the volume Lowell employs the opposite method—defining the ego by its separation from coherent spiritual guides. In poems of this mode, he mixes psychological, naturalistic, and clinical with phantasmagoric images and perspectives. "I lean heavily to the rational, but am devoted to surrealism," he has said. The utterly rational man, he implies, can be described only by surrealist techniques; the self locked in itself is nightmarish, and makes surrealism "a natural way to write our fictions."

The major poem of this mode is "Between the Porch and the Altar." Its contemporary hero "thinks the past / Is settled. It is honest to hold fast / Merely to what one sees with one's own eyes." For past affirmations of social, political, or religious communities, he has only "awed contempt." Separated from these, he has only a lost self talking and dreaming itself into existence, and he must conclude: "Never to have lived is best." The final section of the poem is his death fantasy. At a Boston nightclub called "The Altar" he and his mistress watch an ice-skating floor show. Driving home, he dreams he has an automobile accident near a church where his funeral mass is being performed. Self-contained, his existence has had no meaning except the numbed agony of self-consciousness; his birth and death are one wheel of fire—"The bier and baby-carriage where I burn."

Yet, submerged in his unconscious reflections, dreams, and memories are suprapersonal archetypes by which the hero might have been more than a Meredith and enter ancient passion even through modern love. The title of the poem is derived from Joel 2:17, the epistle read in the Mass on Ash Wednesday, and hints at the whole of sacred history between genesis (the Porch) and apocalypse (the Altar). The fall of Adam is re-created in the speaker's failure. Images of idols, serpents, and dragons writhe in his mind from Ezekiel and Revelation. Even his dream that he has raced "through seven red-lights" is a phantasmagoric oveflow of his suppressed guilt over committing the seven deadly sins. Unable to acknowledge these beliefs, which torment him into guilty nightmare, the speaker is tragic, his poem a drama of consciousness.

The major modes of *Lord Weary's Castle* are (1) the definition of the individual through suprapersonal structures and (2) the dramatization of the self's terrifying alienation from these through the divorce of observation from feeling and of sensibility from culture. "In Memory of Arthur Winslow" combines these modes. In a well-defined theological tradition of New England writing—Mrs. Stowe's *The Minister's Wooing* is an earlier example—this poem, a meditation on Winslow's death outside the religious community, raises basic questions concerning the relation between belief and salvation. Winslow, section I suggests, is conducted "Beyond Charles River to the Acheron" and hell (a greater Boston) by "longshoreman Charon," damned because he had no faith. He contrasts to earlier New England's "Pilgrim Makers," in whose lives politics were united with belief in God's Holy Will for his people in America. In the family cemetery where Winslow is buried (section II), the tombstones of the early settlers "are yellow," "sunken landmarks," echoing unheeded "what our fathers preached." Their faith had made the Pilgrims "point their wooden steeples lest the Word be dumb"; now, dwarfed pines (instead of steeples), "the first selectman of Dunbarton," a "preacher's mouthings," and a dying sun symbolize the dwarfed civilization (the "shell of our stark culture") of which Winslow has been a part. He "must have hankered for our family's craft," Lowell writes in III. But lacking his ancestors' sense of permanency, he has not attached himself to anything permanent. His modern "craft" substitutes capitalistic for communitarian accomplishments and allows him to lose in Boston real-estate speculations the gold hosed out from Colorado.

In section IV, "A Prayer for My Grandfather to Our Lady," the poet defines his own permanent attachments. He will not unsay his judgments of the "painted idols" adored by his grandfather, but he musters the faith to pray for him: "Mother, run to the chalice, and bring back / Blood on your finger-tips for Lazarus who was poor." His prayer is a collage of his two modes. Imitating the stanzaic form of Matthew Arnold's "The Scholar Gypsy" and recalling the "sea of faith" in "Dover Beach," Lowell symbolizes in Winslow the closed world, "Beached / On . . . dry flats of fishy real estate," sterile even at the edge of the sea. But the poet is in the sea striking for shore. Denouncing modern degradation, he yet achieves a dramatic ecstasy of awareness; and mediating between the closed and open worlds, he speaks for himself.

Lord Weary's Castle brought Lowell, barely thirty, a Pulitzer Prize, praise from T. S. Eliot, Conrad Aiken, William Carlos Williams, and George Santayana, and appointment as the consultant in poetry at the Library of Congress. His third volume, *The Mills of the Kavanaughs* (1951), showed further development of his technical range. Having explored Puritan and Catholic Christian humanism in his first two books, he now gave up orthodox affiliation with any church and proceeded to use Western civilization and his personal crisis as material for his poetry. This new work showed the increasing influence of Ransom rather than Tate; of narrative poets like Chaucer, Dryden, Milton, Browning, Hardy, E. A. Robinson, and Conrad Aiken rather than of the metaphysicals or Hart Crane; and of prose writers like Henry Adams, James, Tolstoi, Chekhov, and Faulkner. Earlier, Lowell's language had been characterized by its tension, a straining to push to and beyond the capacities of language. In *The Mills of the Kavanaughs* he moved toward the language of urbanity, where the strain exists in the sensibility and consists in the attempt to conceal the strain which periodically leaps through the conversational surface. Lowell reined his tendency toward generalization and accusation and developed single-mindedly his talent for complex plots, conversational ease, and vivid characters. While his verse shows a marked decrease in religious fervor it correspondingly increases in sensuous observation, interest in sexual passion, preoccupation with individual yearning and frustration, and emphasis on particularized character.

Love and morality are the central themes of *The Mills of the Kavanaughs.* The speaker of each of the seven poems has experienced a crisis of belief which arises from his involvement with morality and love. In "Falling Asleep over the Aeneid" an old man dreams that at the funeral of Pallas he is Aeneas. He remembers that years before, his aunt called him away from reading the *Aeneid*—"'Boy, it's late. / Vergil must keep the Sabbath'"—to prepare for his Uncle Charles's funeral, attended by "Phillips Brooks and Grant," the cultural and military heroes of the American Civil War. The *Aeneid* and the Civil War merged in the boy's mind and affected his life. Now the old man, missing church for Vergil and using his uncle's sword for a crutch, comes to understand the meaning of his uncle's death as a heroic aspect of American history by redreaming it through the perspective of the Roman epic of man and nation. Though Lowell's technique is borrowed from *Sweeney Agonistes,* his old man achieves stature denied to Sweeney by asserting the power of memory over habit and of perspective over the present. Though outwardly pathetic, the old man himself is a hero in emphasizing, like Vergil, the enduring powers of morality and love and celebrating them imaginatively.

Lowell's longest consecutive poem, "The Mills of the Kavanaughs" brings cultural memory together with psychological analysis through the mode of drama. Based on the principles of mythic literature that Eliot defined in reviewing *Ulysses,* the poem manipulates "a continuous parallel between contemporaneity and antiquity," as "a way of controlling, or ordering, of giving a shape and significance to the intense panorama of fertility and anarchy which is contemporary history." Anne Kavanaugh, suddenly faced with a crisis of memory and self, plays solitaire with the Douay Bible as her partner and "dummy" opponent. But, irresistibly, she finds her analogue not so much in Christian myth as in

Ovid's account of Persephone in *Metamorphosis*, V. Four-parted, in imitation of Persephone's circle of seasons, her reverie details her life in relation to her husband's. Beginning in spring, when she meets Harry (stanzas 1–7), and continuing through the summer of their courtship (8–15), the autumn of marriage (16–22), and the winter of Harry's manic depression and suspicion (23–38), her recollections join myth and fact in daydreams and nightmares. Harry, the Demeter-Pluto to her Persephone, turns "whatever brought one gladness to the grave."

As characters in his poems find secular stability through suprapersonal forms of belief, myth, or meditation, so perhaps Lowell himself turned to drama as a way of achieving poetic objectivity and personal stability during the breakup of his first marriage. His crisis of self prompted him to portray people at critical moments. That he did not yet dare express personal emotions directly, but concealed them in myth and dramatic monologue, prompted W. C. Williams to complain that he preferred "a poet of broader range of feeling" than that shown in *The Mills of the Kavanaughs.*

Still, this volume points directly to Lowell's development in his subsequent work, in which three strains predominate: (1) imitations, disconnected from the mythic method, however "repoeticized" (as in *Imitations,* 1961, and *The Voyage and Other Versions of Poems by Baudelaire,* 1968); (2) drama, associated either with the mode of imitation (as in *Phaedra,* 1961, and *Prometheus Bound,* 1969) or with Lowell's efforts to dramatize the history of culture (as in *The Old Glory,* 1965); and (3) poems exploring the central character of the poet himself (as in *Life Studies,* 1959, *For the Union Dead,* 1964, and *Near the Ocean,* 1967).

An important influence on *The Mills of the Kavanaughs* was Chaucer, whom Lowell called "our one English poet to tell stories in a clear, distinguished, witty, absorbing style." For Lowell, Chaucer provided not only an example of narrative clarity; Chaucer's contemporaries called him the "great translatour" in recognition of the skill with which he freely rendered foreign tales into English poetry. Already interested in translation, Lowell in the fifties began seriously to write what he would call "imitations," repoetizations of European authors. This work was not published until 1961, however. In the fall of 1949 Lowell went with his second wife, Elizabeth Hardwick, to teach at the Writer's Workshop of the University of Iowa and promptly announced a course called "Five Poets in Translation" (Rimbaud, Baudelaire, Valéry, Rilke, Horace), soon adding others to these (Foscolo, Leopardi, Vigny, Musset, Verlaine, Mallarmé, Gautier, and Hugo). Inevitably led to study the heritage of these poets, he next offered a "Greek Poetry Workshop" in Homer (his favorite poet) and Pindar. His critical method, as recalled by one of his Iowa undergraduates, is illuminating. After reading a poem in the original and loosely translating it, he proceeded to commentary: "He would describe a phrase in terms of another phrase, another poet, a group of people, a feeling, a myth, a novel, a philosophy, a country. . . . He would compare and contrast, describe." Such teaching, followed by three years' residence in Europe, led to Lowell's imitations. Imitation became his way of discovering himself in poetic tradition. But he also regarded the act of translation as an act of culture-the retrieval or the preservation of a heritage of sense and sensibility, for the sake of contemporary life. He said that because "no [earlier] translator [had] had the gifts or the luck to bring Racine into our culture," he attempted to translate *Phèdre,* a play adapted by Racine from Euripides' *Hippolytus.* By doing so, he hoped, some of the concerns shared by classical and enlightenment culture would be made available to modern men. He also claims contemporary relevance for his rendering of *Prometheus Bound*: "I think my own concerns and worries and those of the time seep in." As Americans have often learned their Americanism abroad, Lowell sharpened his American vision through classical and European poetry. Williams had warned Lowell not to remain in Europe. His imitations brought him back by showing him how best to possess Europe as an American.

Lowell rewrote, shortened, lengthened, or otherwise altered others' poems with Jamesian boldness, as if revising his own earlier work according to his mature perspective, designing *Imitations* to be read as a sequence of original poems. Finding "something equivalent to the fire and finish of [the] originals" involved, Lowell remarked, "considerable rewriting." Stressing the unity of his selections by rendering all in the same style, he also ordered them in a continuous sequence which breaks chronology in order to repeat and interweave themes. Not at all an eclectic collection of European poems, *Imitations* resembles many modern long poems based on the principle of "Song of Myself" in developing through a sequence of insights, investigations, images, and observations.

In *Imitations* a single mode of the imagination predominates: the poet confronts and understands himself through engagement with all that is not-the-self—others' selves, as in "For Anna Akmatova"; historical objects, as in "A Roman Sarcophagus"; other poets, as in the Gautier elegies; myth, as in "Helen." But the self confronts itself chiefly through what Lowell calls the "mania" in man and physical nature. The first poem is Lowell's description (from Homer) of the killing of Lykaon by Achilles. "Sing for me, Muse," he begins, "the mania of Achilles." Rich in the imagination of atrocity, the speech of Achilles is indeed mamc. In his last poem (Rilke's "Pigeons," dedicated to Hannah Arendt, who has written of the manias of modern man) Lowell reminds us of the persistence in modern times of the ancient Achillean way, closing the volume with an image of mania's eternal return:

> Over non-existence arches the all-being—
> thence the ball thrown almost out of bounds
> stings the hand with the momentum of its
> drop—
> body and gravity,
> miraculously multiplied by its mania to
> return.

A meditation on historical circularity, then, *Imitations* begins with Achilles' manic joy in irrationality and violence and shows man repeating his madness. The Trojan War provides Lowell's main symbols—in the first and last poems, in Sappho ("Helen forgot her husband and dear children"), Villon ("Helen has paid this debt—no one who dies dies well"), Heine ("That fellow in Homer's book was quite right"), Valéry (the poem "Helen"), and Pasternak ("Summer . . . hears the god's Homeric laughter"). Troy, of course, merely represents man's ever-present mania for violence.

But equally strong and as omnipresent is man's impulse toward boredom. Indeed, though violence and ennui seem to be opposites, they are really, Lowell suggests, but the two faces of the single mania of the human condition, the alternating poles between which human activity runs. Sappho ("to have lived is better than to live!") and Montale ("even your ennui is a whirlwind") both hint at this relatedness, directly treated in Lowell's imitation of Baudelaire's "To the Reader": "Among the vermin, jackals, panthers, lice, / gorillas and tarantulas" driving man, his central impulse, Lowell writes, "makes no gestures, never beats its breast, / yet it would murder for a moment's rest, / and willingly annihilate the earth. / It's BOREDOM." Atrocity and ennui, the manias which Lowell orchestrates in his sequence, combine at the book's center in Rimbaud's "The Poet at Seven": "What he liked best were dark things: / . . . dizziness, mania, revulsions, pity!" Other recurrent themes, concerning the melancholy state of existence, old age and death, and endeavor and frustration, provide a dark background for these even darker main themes.

Certainly, what Lowell called "the dark . . . against the grain" stands out in *Imitations*; but blind mania is not the unabated concern of the book. In *Prometheus Bound* his hero declares that "Zeus has consented to let [man] live, miserable, dying, though equal to the gods in thought." This distinction between a blank, unremitting universe and man's consciousness runs through *Imitations*. The artist's confrontation of human atrocity in himself and others, and the self-consciousness which, in consequence, he may turn ito art as a heritage for others—this alone prevents history from being merely a sequence of manias. The light against the grain in Lowell's series is the growth of sensibility. Lowell constructs a myth by using other poets and their poems as characters and themes; those he imitates as well as the contemporaries to whom he dedicates his imitations—Williams, Eliot, William Meredith, and Stanley Kunitz—are characters in this cultural myth. His poems are testaments of the consciousness which artists have achieved in the "troubled depths" of atrocity and indifference.

His imitations, Lowell said, were guided by his sense of "what my authors might have done if they were writing their poems now and in America." *The Old Glory,* his dramatic trilogy, is a forceful restoration, on native grounds, of Hawthorne and Melville, who perceived in the 1850's the development of national dilemmas which have culminated disastrously in the present. The mania for authority pervading American culture connects the separate plays of *The Old Glory.* Ideals are inevitably compromised by becoming institutionalized; their triumphs include the promise of their defeats; fearing, yet wishing, their own destruction, men hold power through oppression, even while knowing that this must bring their downfall. In Lowell's first play, *Endecott and the Red Cross,* two versions of authority collide through Blackstone and Morton. Blackstone argues for a hierarchical world in which "Our kingdom is a pyramid, / Charles Stuart stands at the top. Below him, / his subjects descend uniformly and harmoniously / down to the lowest farmer." "That's your theory," replies Morton, who represents the commercial values of the merchant class. "I have mine for this country. / Lords and college men are needed in England. I'm needed here." Holding the power to establish either Blackstone's political or Morton's commercial authoritarianism on American soil, Endecott, the governor of Puritan Salem, inclines toward both; wavering, feeling himself a "suit of empty armor," and knowing that he must betray one part of himself whatever he does, he determines to establish Puritan Theocracy—the authority of God—and to expunge both Blackstone and Morton.

The result is foreseeable. By the Revolutionary period, when *My Kinsman, Major Molineux* takes place, Puritanism has become decadent through power and Blackstone's and Morton's authoritarianisms are once again in conflict. Molineux, representative of the King, a later Blackstone, has gained power; but he is once again opposed by the commercial spirit of Morton, represented by the democratic Man in Periwig, who cries: "I have / authority, authority!" When political power leads to oppression, democratic commercialism seems to promise freedom. Molineux is ousted and his kinsman, Robin, the central figure in the play, remains in the commercial town of Boston. "It's strange / to be here on our own—and free," he says. But already sensing the impermanence of freedom, he also asks uneasily: "Where will it take us to?" Inevitably, as *Benito Cereno* shows, in democracy different forms of authority and oppression are instituted. Convinced that in his "icy dignity" a captain is the opposite of a slave, Captain Amasa Delano loves hierarchy of all kinds and re-creates Blackstone's pyramidal world on his ship. "*A good master deserves good servants*!" he declares. His name, he thinks, has "some saving / Italian or Spanish virtue in it"; he tells his mate: "We need inferiors, Perkins, / more manners, more docility, no one has an inferior mind in America."

Delano is a later Endecott whose democracy is compromised by his power. Lowell wrote *Benito Cereno,* he said, "to show my horror of slavery and violence." Though Delano can kill Babu, the trilogy shows that the exercise of power is the doom of authority. "The future is with us," the slave cries before he is killed; and Delano answers, as he shoots, "This is your future." Their future—our own time—is different from what either could envision, yet both are right: Endecott, the revelers of Merry Mount, Robin, his brother, the citizens of Boston, Delano, Perkins, and Babu are all innocents spun about by their involvement in history. "America's is the Ahab story of having to murder evil: and you may murder all the good with it if it gets desperate enough to struggle," Lowell has written. "God help me," Delano moans, "nothing's solid." What is solid, *The Old Glory* shows, is the mania for power in history and the inevitability of its corruption through the "occult connection" between idealism and violence.

Lowell's poetic and dramatic imitations constituted only one of the developments in his work in the fifties and sixties. For a time after completing *The Mills of the Kavanaughs,* Lowell seemed unable to write original poems—his imagination seemed clogged. Dissatisfied with his "distant, symbol-ridden, and willfully difficult" manner, he felt that all his work had the same "stiff, humorless and even impenetrable surface." A number of factors were important in the unbinding of his imagination. His imitations freed him from too narrow a concentration on America by prodding him to discover in his own voice the equivalent to the voices of earlier, non-American poets. Settling in Boston in 1954 with a view toward rediscovering some roots, he made a start on a prose autobiography. He became interested in psychoanalysis, particularly in Freud. Now, "Freud seemed the only religious teacher" to him. He began giving poetry readings, and "more and more [he says] I found that I was simplifying my poems. If I had a Latin quotation I'd translate it into English. If adding a couple of syllables in a line made it clearer I'd add them." His readings loosened his tight, difficult forms; and his interest in autobiography and self encouraged respect for prose ("less cut off from life than poetry is") and diminished his interest in highly rhetorical poetry. In short, he became interested in the discovery, the invention, and the definition of his self; and he attempted to incorporate into his work the contemporary forms, myths, and metaphors which describe the individual imagination.

The result was *Life Studies,* published in 1959. Believing that personal experience alone guarantees truth, many modern poets have written autobiography. But Lowell's confessional poetry derives less from alienation than from an understanding of the destiny of personality in culture. Terrorization of individual man, he knows, has been continuous in the history of society; but culture sometimes nourishes the best achievements of the self. Involved in both, he renders the interconnected realities of personality and culture without simplifying or distorting either. Modernizing Thoreau through Freud, Lowell writes letters from the distant land of self to kindred selves. Even his most painfully personal poems have public dimensions and (as confessions) imply a listener—the analytic faculty of the poet's imagination overhearing the secrets of his personality. The New Englander and the Viennese Jew are Lowell's distant kindred, and their sharply different cultures the mixed audience he assumes.

Lowell gave *Life Studies* coherence through carefully structuring his book into four parts. In the first poem, "Beyond the Alps," he describes his meditations during a train trip from Rome to Paris; concluding that he will leave "the City of God where it belongs" to take up citizenship in the City of Man, he announces the point of view from which the volume is organized. Through commentary on economics, politics, and militarism, the next three poems in Part One explore the societal context for human activity outside the City of God. The remaining three parts investigate the consolations given to the sensibility willingly exiled in the City of Man. Human responsiveness—to humor and guilt, memory and remorse, consciousness and conscience—in short, receptivity to experience, still remains. "91 Revere Street," an autobiographical prose fragment, shows Lowell in the process of revivifying his own responsiveness by remembering its origins in his youth. Reviving Henry James's concept of autobiography in *A Small Boy and Others,* he first gives an account of the solitary "small boy," then of the "others" through whom he further defines himself and grows to manhood. He implies that a childhood constituted as his was led him to the discovery of artistic sensibility and made it inevitable that he become a poet. Appropriately, then, "91 Revere Street" is followed by four poems exploring varieties of aesthetic impulses. "Ford Madox Ford," "For George Santayana," "To Delmore Schwartz," and "Words for Hart Crane" suggestively parallel the first four poems of the volume and explore what satisfaction art opens to men having to do without faith though "divorced" from the "whale-fat" of corrupted social life. These form a dramatic interlude equipping the man of experience with intimations about how to make experience meaningful, a substitute for the lost life of the City of God, through art.

The synthesis of experience and art is tested in the fifteen confessional poems of Part Four, "Life Studies." Section I of this part, consisting of eleven poems, continues the reminiscential materials of "91 Revere Street." But now the poems imply connections between the poet in the present and his accounts of his past. This is obvious by the ninth poem, "During Fever," when Lowell refers to his own child, his "daughter in fever." In the next two poems, "Waking in the Blue" and "Home after Three Months Away," Lowell defines his present dilemmas as the result of his heritage and writes about himself, "frizzled, stale and small." In contrast to his first three volumes, where experience grates against the perception of it, in *Life Studies* Lowell is unwilling and unable to locate value through the absolutes of the City of God and accepts the City of Man as the single context for the content of human experience.

This shift of context is stressed in "My Last Afternoon with Uncle Devereux Winslow," a poem designed to remind the reader of "In Memory of Arthur Winslow." Both are four-parted; and, as the earlier poem is followed in *Land of Unlikeness* by a coda ("Winter in Dunbarton"), "My Last Afternoon" precedes "Dunbarton," an account of the burial place of Devereux Winslow. As before, Lowell hints at the vacuity, spiritual hollowness, and pretensions of his ancestors. But he also adopts the perspective of the Jamesian small boy, to whom "Nowhere was anywhere after a summer / at my Grandfather's farm"; the boy's puzzled and sympathetic point of view prevails. Certainly, as F. W. Dupee wrote of *Life Studies,* "The book abounds in second-class Lowells, in mothers who were unequal to their pretensions when alive and to their black and gold coffins when dead"; but the poems as critically observe the boy, "who had chronic asthma, chronic truculence, and got himself expelled from the public gardens. Lowell's often merciless anatomy of his parents is matched by his merciless account of himself." Like his Victorian ancestors, whom he can now accept with their unmitigable faults, the poet is on a journey-toward the acceptance of his own faults, and so of himself as their inheritor. Thus in *Life Studies* there is no gritting between the poet and his experience. Both are criticized, understood, and accepted from the same perspective.

"My Last Afternoon" epitomizes Lowell's synthesis of material experience with art, its images paralleling the four basic elements with kinds of art. Section I combines images of earth ("One of my hands was cool on a pile/ of black earth, the other warm / on a pile of lime") and the fertility of the earth ("oranges, lemons, mint, and peppermints") with images of literature ("A pastel-pale Huckleberry Finn"). Section II develops this order by naming water ("Distorting drops of water") and expanding the plastic imagery of section I in references to sculpture: the boy speaks of the "Olympian poise of my models" and sees himself as a "stuffed toucan." Moving upward in the elements in section III, he looks "Up in the air," and also portrays his Great Aunt Sarah and the "soundless" music which he practices on a dummy piano. Deepening his perception of the connections between nature and art in this section, he summarizes his earlier images —of earthly fertility and literature ("troublesome snacks and Tauchnitz classics"), of water ("by the lakeview window," "a thirsty eye"), of statuary ("naked Greek statues draped with purple") and the bird ("risen like the phoenix").

All these are focused on section IV, as, combining nature with art, the poet prepares to face the otherwise meaningless early death of Devereux Winslow. While the fourth element of fire ("a barrage of smoke-clouds") is hinted at, and another form of art, posters and photographs, is introduced, the important movement of the imagery in section IV is its aesthetic synthesis of the boy's metaphoric experience; he has achieved perspectives whereby to view death as an aspect of natural and artistic order. His heightened sense of the connections between experience and art allows the poet to become simultaneous with his own childhood and assert "I wasn't a child at all." The child who experienced the death and the adult artist are united. At the end of the poem, he returns to the earth, meaningful in terms of the whole ordered cycle of creation.

> He was dying of the incurable Hodgkin's
> disease. . . .
> My hands were warm, then cool, on the
> piles of earth and lime,
> a black pile and a white pile. . . .
> Come winter,
> Uncle Devereux would blend to one color.

The four poems in the second section of "Life Studies" unify the volume by closely paralleling the four which began it. Since secularism, economics, politics, militarism, and insanity—public and private madness—have assumed personal meaning through the revelations and identifications of the intervening poems, the poet renders them through his own experiences, rather than those of Marie de Médicis, President Eisenhower, or a mad Negro soldier. Having delineated experience through symbols external to his own experience, Lowell made himself his central symbol and so passed (as he remarked of "Skunk Hour") "way beyond symbols into reality." "I want the reader of my poems to say, this is true," he declared in an interview. "I want him to believe he is getting the *real* Robert Lowell."

The authentic Lowell dominates "Skunk Hour," where he writes of the crisis of self which led to the mental derangements and hospitalization dramatized earlier in *Life Studies.* Here he investigates the principles by which the ill mind moves—tentatively, and through art—back to health. Hinting in his title at the formalized Chinese calendar, Lowell suggests that he too will have his hour of truth—new awareness. Stanzas 1–4 center on the paradoxical association of role-playing with death: in the aged "hermit/heiress"; in the gaily dressed summer millionaire who has either died or become bankrupt; and in the Maine landscape, whose ruddy autumn barely conceals the white death of approaching winter. Masks have less and less efficacy to hide the dead hollows beneath them. The portrait of the decorator in stanza 4 outrightly names him "our fairy"; and though he laments that "there is no money in his work, / he'd rather marry," the feminine rhyme (fairy/marry) strikes through the mask. Human corruption—through solitude, fraudulence, and trivialization—is vividly portrayed in this first half of the poem. The second half focuses on the poet, himself implicated in the masquerading "ill-spirit" he observes in others. How can he avoid the corruption that he sees? And if he responds intensely to it, how can he preserve himself from despondency and madness, the derangements in his heritage?

"We poets in our youth begin in sadness; / thereof in the end come despondency and madness," Lowell had given Delmore Schwartz to say in Part Three of *Life Studies.* Schwartz cannot be a Wordsworth to Lowell's Coleridge; though "resolution" and "independence" might preserve him at the end of "Skunk Hour," Lowell is obliged to write odes to dejection before lyrics of affirmation. He defines his emotional crisis, then, by references to a variety of familiar passages describing spiritual disaster: St. John of the Cross's Dark Night of the Soul ("One dark night"), Christ's crucifixion ("the hill's skull"), Lear's confusion on the heath ("My mind's not right"), and Satan's self-condemnation at the prospect of Eden in Book IV of *Paradise Lost* ("I myself am hell; / nobody's here"). His sense of tradition does not save him—it simply gives him a way of understanding (and so for a moment controlling) his personal crisis, an aspect of the general human madness.

That the leap which his mind takes toward restoration occurs in the sole run-on stanza conveys vividly the mental rush necessary to revivify the disordered mind before self-disgust extinguishes it. The available image ("only skunks") which he almost hopelessly seizes upon for support turns out to possess extraordinary power as a symbol for naturalness, passion ("eyes' red fire"), fertility, and persistence—human qualities which the poet must revive in himself. Not the literature of disaster, but the primitive nature religion of the racial unconscious provides his symbols—the column and the pail, the "wedge-head" and the "cup"—reminders (from *The Golden Bough*) of continuing fertility. "Skunk Hour," in short, describes a poet who has moved from contemplation of the hermit-mother "in her dotage" to the skunk-mother in her prime, from a decadent human world to individual revitalization. Lowell began *Life Studies* by pointing to the journey he would take. In "Skunk Hour" he is still traveling. He has gone beyond Paris, the City of Man, to himself, in Maine. Often set adrift, and through the shipwreck of his absolutes made "frizzled, stale and small," he ascends in this last poem "the hill's skull' for one more crucifixion. But by finding in the mother skunk a way to express the possibility of vitality, he stands at the end "on top / of our back steps." The steps of his own house are all the Alps or Golgotha he will have; for he has shown through the volume that the City of Man—of society and of self—will suffice. Now, like the skunk, he "will not scare." Instead, as in a symposium Lowell said of his composition of this poem, he survives his "strange journey . . . clinging to spars, enough floating matter to save [him], though faithless."

After the completion of *Life Studies* Lowell felt emptied of self, uninterested in individuality. "Something not to be said again was said," he wrote to M. L. Rosenthal. "I feel drained, and know nothing except that the next outpouring will have to be unimaginably different—an altered style, more impersonal matter, a new main artery of emphasis and inspiration." At the Boston Arts Festival in 1960, Lowell remarked: "When I finished *Life Studies* I was left hanging on a question mark. . . . I don't know whether it is a death rope or a lifeline." It remained for him to join the modes of *Imitations* and *Life Studies* by investigating simultaneously the sense that self makes out of the history it hoards and the culture that draws back the self which would be lost through fleeing it. The possibilities of this synthesis provide the "new main artery of emphasis and inspiration" of *For the Union Dead* and *Near the Ocean.*

In *For the Union Dead* old poems are revived, previous themes are reinvigorated, the vatic utterance of his earliest manner and the confessional tone of his most recent are recalled. It is not so much a coming to grips with a new poetry as a completion of all that was implied in the earlier. The parallels with previous volumes are innumerable: "Water" recalls "The Quaker Graveyard" and "The North Sea Undertaker's Complaint," and (in its scene and situation) "Skunk Hour." "The Old Flame" rewrites the marriage sequence of *The Mills of the Kavanaughs* in personal terms, and recalls such *Life Studies* poems as "Man and Wife" and " 'To Speak of Woe That Is in Marriage.' " "Memories of West Street and Lepke" ("These are the tranquillized *Fifties,* / and I am forty") is updated by "Middle Age" ("At forty-five, / what next, what next?"). "Grandparents" of *Life Studies* ("They're all gone into a world of light") is generalized both in "The Scream" and in "Those before Us." "The Public Garden," "Beyond the Alps," and "Epigram" are revisions of poems which appeared first in *The Mills of the Kavanaughs, Life Studies,* and *Imitations.* "The Drinker" secularizes "The Drunken Fisherman." "Salem," which presented the half-unconscious meditations of an old seaman concerning the past glory and present decay of the port, had alluded to the "Custom House" section of *The Scarlet Letter*; in "Hawthorne" Lowell treats his source directly. As a description of Hawthorne himself he goes on to incorporate into the poem Hawthorne's portrait of Septimius Felton and to gloss it with his own comment on the imaginative mode he shares with Hawthorne, who, he says, broods on "the true / and insignificant." In "Jonathan Edwards in Western Massachusetts" and "Fall 1961" he repeats the same process, openly recalling two earlier poems, "Mr. Edwards and the Spider" and "After the Surprising Conversions." Most strikingly recollective is "Soft Wood," another in the series of Winslow elegies. Its opening metaphor ("Sometimes I have supposed seals / must live as long as the Scholar Gypsy") alludes directly to the stanzaic form of "In Memory of Arthur Winslow." But like other recent work, the new poem relies on ironic balances and self-identification with tragedy. "Soft Wood" is perhaps Lowell's first poem in which the chief values are the mixed, but triumphant, human values of weakness, "a wincing of the will," a bending to the wind "forever," mortality and compromise, sensitivity, and endurance.

The Americans about whom Lowell writes in the title poem gave up everything to serve the state. Resembling poems like Tate's "Ode to the Confederate Dead" and James Russell Lowell's "Ode Recited at the Harvard Commemoration," "For the Union Dead" elegizes the war dead through a succession of apparently unrelated "views"—the Old South Boston Aquarium, the construction of a garage under Boston Common, Augustus Saint-Gaudens' memorial relief of Colonel Robert Gould Shaw leading his black regiment, and an advertisement in a store window. Each becomes an apocalyptic analogue of the other, each a monstrous emblem of man's self-destructiveness. The central image of the poem derives from Albany's remark in *King Lear*: "It will come. / Humanity must perforce prey on itself, / Like monsters of the deep." The aquarium is closed and its fish tanks are dry; breathing is cut off, life suffocated. The steam shovels digging the garage resemble monstrous metal fish, yellow dinosaurs; and the fence around the construction site is a cage hardly protecting the city from these rough apocalyptic beasts. The shaking Boston Statehouse is encircled by girders, and the Shaw monument is unceremoniously "propped by a plank splint against the garage's earthquake." Compounding catastrophic signs, on Boylston Street, "a commercial photograph / shows Hiroshima boiling / over a Mosler Safe." The state demands servility; no longer confined to the aquarium, its underworld is loosed upon the world: "Everywhere, / giant finned cars nose forward like fish; / a savage servility / slides by on grease." *For the Union Dead* seems destined to conclude as *Lord Weary's Castle* did, with the poet declaring himself "a red arrow on this graph / of Revelations," pointing a livid finger to the day of wrath, when man consumes himself through the inhumanity of the Leviathan state he has created to protect and nourish him.

But *Life Studies* had made a difference; even while terror accumulates about the emblems of final darkness, the poet's memory is not extinguished by the apocalypse of the state. He is in touch with the energy of true primitivity: "I often sigh still / for the dark downward and vegetating kingdom / of the fish and reptile." And he can restore, if not the Shaw monument, the more important recollection of what energies for human rights might still be symbolized by Shaw "and his bell-cheeked Negro infantry." Shaw can be a "compass-needle" pointing to a kind of human integrity which the state might extinguish, but whose importance it cannot alter. The millennial "ditch is nearer"; yet Shaw, who "waits / for the blessed break" of the political bubble which drifts from the mouth of Leviathan, points to an alternative mode of political life. Enduring in the aquarium of memory, Shaw's monument reminds the poet of a life of service; his decision "to choose life and die" freed his life from the state. The poet, similarly, though hedged by apocalypse, can assert his own "blessed break" with the state through a poetic career. This poem concludes a volume which summarizes that career by refocusing and revising the themes and emblems of his earlier work.

In *Near the Ocean* Lowell emphasizes invention over memory and makes striking combinations and juxtapositions of his central themes—the horrors and attractions of antiquity, of Western civilization, of nineteenth-century New England, and of his own age. Between Rome and America Lowell makes deft connections; both have the same imperial urge for dissipation and extinction. The sea extending from Europe to America is the ocean of his title, America is as near the ocean as Rome, and the Roman disease of power has washed over the American land. Juvenal's Romans know the terrors of night, where "each shadow hides a knife or spear"; while Lowell interrupts his night thoughts in "Central Park" to observe of the present: "We beg delinquents for our life. / Behind each bush, perhaps a knife." Lowell's Romans are characterized (by way of Horace, Juvenal, Dante, and Gongora) as vain, envious, greedy, and lustful; their power is the fountain of their disgrace, their possessions the wellsprings of their unhappiness; their military triumphs the reason for their defeat; their desires reservoirs for the numbing of desire. From their greatness issues the chief horror—the insignificance of glory, the triumph of the quotidian: "what was firm has fled. What once / was fugitive maintains its permanence."

The same is true of the America described in "Waking Early Sunday Morning." Its subject is the degradation of the Pilgrim hopes for a Promised Land, and its form, consisting of eight-line stanzas of octosyllabic couplets, is that of a typical New England hymn. The poet stirs just before dawn; possessed by a sublime dream of freedom, he imagines himself a chinook salmon breaking loose from the sea to clear a waterfall—an Adamic man. But the dawn brings "blackout," domestic data that keep his mind from maintaining this imaginative intensity: the objects that possess his waking imagination are "serene in their neutrality." Lowell's reference to Wallace Stevens' "Sunday Morning" is self-deprecative; and fragments recalling romantic intensities available imaginatively to Wordsworth, Masefield, Whitman, and Homer mock the poet's inability to humanize nature or to naturalize the mind.

His meditation (stanzas 6–7) on the dream of the "City on a Hill" in America—as expressed in Puritanism ("they sing of peace, and preach despair") and in Transcendentalism ("Better dressed and stacking birch")—is interrupted by a recollection of Baudelaire's poem of despair "Anywhere Out of This World." Obliteration of the spirit is the only release in this post-Baudelairean world. Instead of going to church, then, the poet explores the woodshed of his imagination for "its dregs and dreck."

The "dregs and dreck" of the Puritan dream were revivified in America through the Federalist dream of the democratic republic. In stanzas 9–13 the poet extends his meditation to the contemporary consequences of that dream; recalling the decay of Israel and Rome into militarism, he finds in America as well only "Hammering military splendor, / top-heavy Goliath in full armor," restlessness, excess, self-deception, and "ghost-written rhetoric." Again, he cries: "anywhere, but somewhere else." The Adamic dream of the individual, the Promised Land of America, and the dream of democracy have all been betrayed. Lowell's final stanza is a hymn whose theme is the poet's inability to sustain or create new hymns:

> Pity the planet, all joy gone
> from this sweet volcanic cone;
> peace to our children when they fall
> in small war on the heels of small
> war—until the end of time
> to police the earth, a ghost
> orbiting forever lost
> in our monotonous sublime.

What remains for the poet who has been made aware of the degradation of his democratic dogmas is his continuing ability to perceive (even to pity) the planet, to discover individual objects worth observing and naming, and to give them permanence through memory, and so preserve the self by its attachment to itself through things. The permanence of mind is the subject of "Fourth of July in Maine," another elegy on Harriet Winslow, where Lowell makes his cousin an emblem of the "genius" of memory. Although all the transcendental dreams—of personal freedom (she is "ten years paralyzed"), of religion ("not trusting in the afterlife"), and of politics (she dies in Washington, D.C.)—escaped her, she avoided the disasters which accompany them; she has the permanence of memory, of the transient, of the gentle. From writing poems in which his ancestors are emblems of all that is wrong with the past, Lowell found in her an emblem of what may be right about the future, and took Harriet Winslow as the genius for his own child, "mistress of / your tireless sedentary love."

In 1943 Lowell, "a fire-breathing Catholic C.O.," had been sentenced to a year and a day for refusing to serve in World War II. After attempting to enlist earlier, he contended that now the Allies were fighting as ruthlessly as their opponents. In a published letter to President Roosevelt he reminded the President that he was "an American, whose family traditions, like your own, have always found their fulfillment in maintaining, through responsible participation in both civil and military services, our country's freedom and honor." From 1943 to the present, Lowell has been concerned with the relations between politics, society, and the individual. Active in civil-rights and antiwar protests, he refused an invitation from President Johnson in 1965 to appear at a White House arts festival, since "every serious artist knows that he cannot enjoy public celebration without making subtle public commitments." Somewhat later, introducing Soviet poet Andrei Voznesensky to a large Town Hall audience, he said: "This is indiscreet, but both our countries, I think, have really terrible governments. But we do the best we can with them."

Lowell's continuing concern with the relations between politics, society, and individual conscience is the subject of *Notebook 1967–68* (1969), a volume designed, he says, "as one poem, jagged in pattern." Its "plot" consists of the daily accumulations of memory, as chance events, which might drive the poet out of himself, instead bring his submerged thoughts, half-thoughts, and unanswered puzzles into sharp focus and allow him, through meditation on them, to reach the partial answers and tentative solutions possible on that day. "Famished for human chances," he will not turn away from the daily dates of his culture—but he is also faithful to himself and asserts of events only what he can truly know or feel of and through them. As a man participating in culture, he experiences its daily flux; as a poet so participating, he derives from the experience of culture and self the tentative, but objective, perception of value upon which a civilization can be based or an individual preserved. Through poetic form he saves the unsavable.

Notebook 1967–68 is unified through the development, restatement, and repetition of several themes and concerns: (1) growing, a theme embodied particularly in poems on Lowell's daughter, Harriet; (2) the relation between the past—what one grows from—and the present that one daily grows into (this theme leads Lowell to reflect on his childhood); (3) the contexts of growing: history (of Lowell's ancestors, of America, and of Europe), politics, and consciousness; (4) concern with the poet's personal history; (5) achievement of an uneasy, but joyful, acceptance of the dark side of history, politics, and modern life, so that even the apocalyptic poem "Dies Irae" can be subtitled "A Hope" (he ultimately asserts in "Mexico," 5: "I am learning to live in history"); (6) a willing involvement of himself with the tragedies of family, society, other persons, and self. What defenses are there against age and change and death, Lowell asks early in his poem (in "Long Summer," 11)—"Who can help us from our nothing to the all, / we aging downstream faster than a scepter can check?" His own right to involvement, hardwon in the book, provides the answer.

These themes develop within the general framework of the moving seasons. The poem begins in midsummer with "Harriet" and Lowell's reflection on growing. But the autumnal, Indian summer mood soon enters. Saying "we asked to linger on past fall in

Eden," he moves from the innocence of growing to the state, "past fall," of experiencing other, adult concerns. Poems on "Aunt Sarah" and "My Grandfather," autumnal Victorians, and those, like "Munich, 1938" and "October and November," on modern degradation dominate this season's meditations. He recalls his own youth in "Harvard" and "In the Forties." The coming of winter inevitably leads him to pursue the theme of his growing to his present situation—as writer ("Writers"), as teacher ("Blizzard in Cambridge"), and as traveler ("Lines from Israel"). "Infirmity," he can at last declare (in "Mexico," 10) is "a food the flesh must swallow,/ feeding our minds."

April and the approach of spring turns his mind to "shining remembrance"—of Harriet ("Words of a Young Girl"), who continues to grow, of women friends ("Mania"), and of historical personages whose power was more benevolent than others introduced earlier—Roland, Bishop Berkeley, and F. O. Matthiessen. Exhausted by winter, he finds a kind of rebirth in April and places his "New Year's Eve 1968" at this point, as the poem moves, through difficulty, upward. He affirms this restoration by revising, in the direction of acceptance, two poems from *For the Union Dead,* "Night-Sweat" and "Caligula," and one from *Near the Ocean,* "For Theodore Roethke: 1908–1963." Because he has experienced authentically the pain emphasized earlier, he can forcefully reject nihilism ("The Nihilist as Hero").

"Circles" introduces the expected return to summer. Several poems on Harriet and Lowell's wife appear as he moves toward passionate involvement with other people: his wife and child, his "family chronicle" ("Sound Mind, Sound Body"), and politics ("The Races"). Lowell has insisted, "It is harder to be a good man than a good poet." Understanding life as the supreme art, even in poems on writers (like Tate and Berryman) Lowell emphasizes their personal struggles. He has grown through art to life: instead of the book of a century ("Growth"), he writes the notebook of a year. "Summer" comes at last to complete the circle—of the seasons, and of his changing mind. To express the new birth of energy which he has experienced, he writes of his possible reincarnations—as a seal ("If we must live again, not us; we might / go into seals") and again as a poet ("Some other August, / the easy seal might say, 'I could not sleep / last night; suddenly I could write my name' ").

Affirming such imaginative energies, he can write a series of codas—"Close the Book," "Half a Century Gone," and "Obit"—ending in a vision of his personal death and his fierce continuance in eternal return, through involvement in life.

> I'm for and with myself in my otherness,
> in the eternal return of earth's fairer
> children,
> the lily, the rose, the sun on dusk and brick,
> the loved, the lover, and their fear of life,
> their unconquered flux, insensate oneness,
> their painful "it was . . ."
> After loving you so much, can I forget
> you for eternity, and have no other choice?

His passionate involvement in what continues, continues him.

Notebook 1967–68 illustrates Lowell's refusal to repeat himself, his insistence on development. "Somehow [I] never wrote something to go back to," he writes in "Reading Myself." He has moved with his culture. Like earlier New England poets, he first developed his sensibility in opposition; but unlike them, he has been forced by the rapid changes in American life repeatedly to reconstitute his principles of opposition, and thus always to define freshly his relation to his fellows. He has developed three basic directions for his work: a critique of public action and attitude in America; a critique of the state of the individual ego; and a sense of the historical, religious, mythological, and literary contexts which provide perspectives whereby to understand the possibilities of public or private life at any time. As his society has shifted during the last twenty-five years, Lowell has emphasized various combinations of these.

During the mid-forties, while Americans were confident, Lowell's poetry boiled with apocalyptic despair and condemnation of the diseases which infected Americans. During the late forties and early fifties, the era of the "silent generation," Lowell's poetry was rhetorical and extravagant. While Americans wished to consolidate minor triumphs, Lowell's verse suggested that success of an ordinary kind was impossible and undesirable.

By the late fifties, disillusioned with war and international involvements, Americans sought various escapes from self-consciousness and the powerhouse of history. In *Life Studies* and *Imitations* Lowell faced himself and America's European heritage directly. Increasingly, in the sixties, a sense of alienation and collective disaster darkened the American mind. Lowell well described the attitude: "We're burning, we're decaying, we're in mid-century. . . . Genocide has stunned us; we have a curious dread it will be repeated." Americans had arrived at his earlier despair. But in *The Old Glory, Prometheus Bound,* and *For the Union Dead* Lowell was emphasizing the continuities of culture and the inevitable involvement of the private self with public concerns.

While Americans in the late sixties began stressing immediate social reform without correcting the roots of social ills, Lowell stressed the values of contemplation, a quiet faith amid public clamor, and intelligence in *Near the Ocean* and *Notebook 1967–68.* Even justice, he showed, can become a dogma and murder itself. "We must bend, not break," he says. Where Americans have understood new moral incoherence, he has seen new moral possibilities. He has defined the four major contemporary problems as "how to join equality to excellence, how to join liberty to justice, how to avoid destroying or being destroyed by nuclear power, and how to complete the emancipation of the slaves." As a radical he has identified these, as a conservative declared them "almost insoluble"; as a liberal he has worked to solve them and written poems describing a state of widened consciousness which might encourage solutions; and as a traditionalist, he has identified similar dilemmas in Roman history and nineteenth-century America, in the careers of Plutarch's heroes and Abraham Lincoln. He has kept his mind flexible and contradictory, allowing the half-truths of any position to support and absorb its opposite. An account of his career is a history of how he has allowed his contradictions to seep into his poetry as the society to which he is responding changes.

His work, in short, has been a mirror to his culture, supplying society with elements for advance. He has criticized the poets of his generation whose "writings seem divorced from culture." Culture, he came to see, provides the necessary background for art: neither, without the other, can endure. Constantly updating old poems for inclusion in new volumes, he moves with culture and refuses to let society catch up with him. "One side of me," he has said, "is a conventional liberal, concerned with causes, agitated about peace and justice and equality. . . . My other side is deeply conservative, wanting to get at the roots of things, wanting to slow down the whole modern progress of mechanization and dehumanization, knowing that liberalism can be a form of death too." He has been able to combine these tendencies intricately and to employ his imaginative powers to locate and express permanent aspects of mind which his civilization has temporarily forgotten or rejected. "One feels," he said in criticism of Wallace Stevens, ". . . that a man is able to be an imagination and the imagination able to be disinterested and urbane only because it is supported by industrial slaves. Perhaps if there are platonists, there must always be slaves." Lowell has refused to be a Platonist, an imagination, and has insisted on being a man of imagination. Serving and leading his culture by opening, through his work, the lines along which it might evolve, he has built a career like those of Jonson, Dryden, Goethe, Howells, and James. His power as a poet derives from his understanding that, like these writers, he can be a man of letters only insofar as he can remain a man among men.

Selected Bibliography

WORKS OF ROBERT LOWELL

POETRY

Land of Unlikeness, (Cummington, Mass.: Cummington Press, 1944).

Lord Weary's Castle, (New York: Harcourt, Brace, 1946).

The Mills of the Kavanaughs, (New York: Harcourt, Brace, 1951).

Life Studies, (New York: Farrar, Straus and Cudahy, 1959).

Imitations, (New York: Farrar, Straus and Cudahy, 1961).

For the Union Dead, (New York: Farrar, Straus and Giroux, 1964).

Near the Ocean, (New York: Farrar, Straus and Giroux, 1967).

The Voyage and Other Versions of Poems by Baudelaire, (New York: Farrar, Straus and Giroux, 1968).

Notebook 1967–68, (New York: Farrar, Straus and Giroux, 1969); second printing, revised 1969.

PLAYS

Phaedra, in *Phaedra and Figaro,* translated by Robert Lowell and Jacques Barzun (New York: Farrar, Straus and Cudahy, 1961).

The Old Glory, (New York: Farrar, Straus and Giroux, 1965); revised edition 1968.

Prometheus Bound, (New York: Farrar, Straus and Giroux, 1969).

PROSE

"Four Quartets," *Sewanee Review,* 51: 432–35 (1943).

"A Note," *Kenyon Review,* on Hopkins 6: 583–86 (1944).

"The Verses of Thomas Merton," *Commonwealth,* 42: 240–42 (1945).

"Imagination and Reality," *Nation,* 164: 400–02 (1947).

"Thomas, Bishop, and Williams," *Sewanee Review,* 55: 493–503 (1947).

"Paterson II," *Nation,* 166: 692–94 (1948).

"John Ransom's Conversation," *Sewanee Review,* 56: 374–77 (1948).

"Prose Genius in Verse," *Kenyon Review,* 15: 619–25 (1953).

"Visiting the Tates," *Sewanee Review,* 67: 557–59 (1959).

"I. A. Richards as a Poet," *Enounter,* 14: 77–78 (February 1960).

"Yvor Winters: A Tribute," *Poetry,* 98: 40–42 (April 1961).

"William Carlos Williams," *Hudson Review,* 14: 530–36 (1961–62).

"Randall Jarrell," *Randall Jarrell, 1914–1965,* edited by Robert Lowell, Peter Taylor, and Robert Penn Warren (New York: Farrar, Straus and Giroux, 1967).

CRITICAL STUDIES

Alvarez, A., *Encounter,* "A Talk with Robert Lowell," 24: 39–43 (February 1965).

Cambon, Glauco, *The Inclusive Flame: Studies in American Poetry,* "Robert Lowell: History as Eschatology," (Bloomington: Indiana University Press, 1963).

Eberhart, Richard, *Sewanee Review,* "Four Poets," 60: 327–31 (1947).

Ehrenpreis, Irvin, *American Poetry,* "The Age of Lowell," (New York: St. Martin's Press, 1965).

Hochman, Baruch, "Robert Lowell's *The Old Glory,*" *Tulane Drama Review,* 11: 127–38 (Summer 1967).

Kunitz, Stanley, *New York Times Book Review,* "Talk with Robert Lowell," (October 4, 1964) pp. 34–36, 38–39.

Martz, William J., *The Achievement of Robert Lowell,* (Glenview, Ill: Scott, Foresman, 1966).

Mazzaro, Jerome, *The Poetic Themes of Robert Lowell,* (Ann Arbor: University of Michigan Press, 1965).

Mills, Ralph J., Jr., *Contemporary American Poetry,* (Randon House, 1965).

Parkinson, Thomas, ed., *Robert Lowell: A Collection of Critical Essays,* (Englewood Cliffs, N.J.: Prentice-Hall, 1968).

Perloff, Marjorie, "Death by Water: The Winslow Elegies of Robert Lowell," *ELH,* 34: 116–40 (1967).

Ricks, Christopher, "The Three Lives of Robert Lowell," 69: 496–97 (March 26, 1965).

Rosenthal, M. L., *The New Poets: American and British Poetry since World War II,* (New York: Oxford University Press, 1967).

Seidel, Frederick, "An Interview," *The Paris Review Interviews, Second Series,* edited by Malcolm Cowley (New York: Viking Press, 1963).

Staples, H. B., *Robert Lowell,* (New York: Farrar, Straus and Cudahy, 1962).

Waggoner, Hyatt H., *American Poets from the Puritans to the Present,* (Boston: Houghton Mifflin, 1968).

Wilbur, Richard, and others, *The Contemporary Poet as Artist and Critic,* "On Robert Lowell's 'Skunk Hour,' " edited by Anthony Ostroff (Boston and Toronto: Little, Brown, 1964).

Woodson, Thomas, "Robert Lowell's 'Hawthorne,' Yvor Winters and the American Literary Tradition," *American Quarterly,* 19: 575–82 (1967).

CLAUDE McKAY

(1890–1948)

WAYNE F. COOPER

FROM THE PERSPECTIVE of literary history, Claude McKay's reputation as a pioneer in the development of twentieth-century African American literature seems secure. His literary influence was felt far and wide, in the West Indies and in Jamaica, his native island, as well as in the United States and Africa. Poets as diverse as J. J. Rabearivelo from Madagascar, Aimé Césaire from Martinique, Léopold Sedar Senghor from Senegal, and Langston Hughes in the United States all at one time or another expressed their debt to McKay. In the post–World War I United States his verses inspired a whole generation of "New Negro" writers associated with the Harlem Renaissance of the 1920s. His poetry broke the constraints of Victorian respectability and drew without reserve from his deepest feelings as an African American man.

In his fiction McKay affirms the self-sufficiency of black folk cultures. African American basic values, he believed, derived from their own experiences, cultural traditions, and racial heritage more than from a Western tradition that had historically tried to exclude black experiences. Western progress, McKay argued, continued to endanger black life and black culture. To him, industrialization, urbanization, and bureaucratization, whether managed by the Left or the Right, was killing the souls of Western men and women by cutting them off from their ancient relationship to the natural world. African American culture, McKay believed, deeply rooted as it was in rural folkways, many of which derived from Africa, not only had resisted the oppressive exploitation of slavery and racial segregation but still stood in opposition to the soul-destroying tendencies of modern life. Like all pastoralists, McKay believed that those who led an agricultural life and followed the rhythms of the seasons, as most African Americans did prior to World War I, were more closely attuned to nature's ways than urban dwellers in the industrial West. In his novels and short stories, McKay affirmed black culture at its most elemental level by celebrating the lives of its most marginal members in the urban ghettos of the northern United States and in the small, isolated mountain villages of his native Jamaica. In the 1930s, his novels inspired the founders of the French West African and West Indian Negritude movements. Those in the United States, such as the critics George Kent and Addison Gayle, as well as others, who defend the idea of black cultural autonomy acknowledge McKay's importance as a forerunner to their own ideas.

McKay made his odyssey from Jamaica through the United States, the Soviet Union, Western Europe, and North Africa decades before other West Indian expatriate intellectuals and literary artists more familiar to modern readers, among them C. L. R. James, Frantz Fanon, Derek Walcott, and V. S. Naipaul. McKay was, in a sense, doubly an expatriate. After leaving Jamaica, he made the United States his second home, and then he joined the American expatriate caravan in France during the 1920s, thereby preceding, once again, better-known African Americans, such as Richard Wright and James Baldwin. Even before Paul Robeson was lionized in the Soviet Union, McKay had received similar treatment there in 1922 and 1923. Because he had experienced his radical political phase a full decade or more before most African American writers and intellectuals who came of age in the 1920s or 1930s, McKay's anti-Communist stance as a member of the Federal Writers' Project in New York in the 1930s placed him sharply at odds politically with many of his fellow writers and with critics.

Among all the writers associated with the Harlem Renaissance, McKay remains the most controversial. During his lifetime, he was a man whose personality and works provoked strong, conflicting reactions. To some he seemed an opportunist who, blown by shifting ideological winds, merely wrote whatever was acceptable to the reading public, largely white in his day. In 1937, the then Marxist critic and poet Melvin Tolson called McKay a black Ulysses who never found his way home; in the same year Alain Locke dismissed him as "the playboy of the Negro Renaissance" and its aging enfant terrible who had by 1937 "repudiated all possible loyalties." Although he had his detractors, he also had steadfast defenders, among them such varied figures as James Weldon Johnson, Max Eastman, and John Dewey.

Since his death, critics have been as divided about McKay's achievements as his contemporaries were during his lifetime. A few have insisted that McKay's poetry and prose were pioneering works of genius. A French Catholic, Jean Wagner, and a black nationalist critic, George Kent, have both given high praise to McKay, though for diametrically opposed reasons. To Wagner, McKay's poetry exhibits a universality of appeal that elevated his work above "folklorists" like Langston Hughes and Sterling Brown. Kent, by contrast, finds McKay's work important because it prepared the way for a self-consciously independent black literature. For Kent, McKay displayed "a positive *niggerhood*, . . . a naturalness of being to be maintained in the face of the most complex patterns of western culture."

Others, however, have dismissed his poetry, his fiction, or both as dated, uneven in quality, and generally lacking in artistic merit. To such critics, he was at best a transitional figure of passing historical importance. At worst, they have endorsed his enemies' contentions that his career was fatally flawed by ideological contradictions, opportunism, and a general failure of vision. Harold Cruse claims McKay peddled Communist nostrums, S. P. Fullenwider accuses him of pandering to white tastes, and Nathan Huggins argues that he generally lacked artistic merit. Still others, such as Robert Bone, Stephen Bronz, and James R. Giles, have sought more balanced assessments of McKay, concluding that although he had a significant impact as a literary figure, his own artistic achievements in poetry, the novel, and the short story were limited.

Anyone whose work has been so variously judged over so many years deserves careful attention. McKay's life mirrored in complex ways important aspects of the African American experience in the first half of the twentieth century. The anger, alienation, and rebellion he expressed in his poetry and the search for community he attempted in his fiction reflected not only his own life stages from youth to maturity but also the efforts of African Americans to triumph over the adversities that beset them. He was also deeply involved with the larger society, its social and political movements, and its literary trends. As an editor of the *Liberator* in New York City and the *Workers' Dreadnought* in London after World War I, and as a committed but critical international socialist and opponent of Western imperialism during the interwar years, McKay consistently presented a black viewpoint where one was otherwise seldom heard. Clearly, his importance as a pioneering African American writer lay not only in his specific artistic accomplishments, but also and more broadly in his ability to project African American concerns through his art and career upon the broadest possible stage and to claim for African Americans a voice and a role in the unfolding drama of world history and literature.

At the same time, McKay's work itself, so closely related to his life at every stage, deserves closer scrutiny. Underneath its apparent failures and contradictions, one can discern in his poetry, fiction, and essays a consistency of vision that in the end defines the man and artist as a writer of genuine achievement. McKay defined the problem he so forthrightly faced in his life and art when he wrote in *A Long Way from Home* (1937) of the differences that separated him from white American expatriates in Paris during the 1920s:

> Color consciousness was the fundamental of my restlessness. And it was something with which my fellow-expatriates could sympathize but which they could not altogether understand. For they were not black like me. Not being black and unable to see deep into the profundity of blackness, some even thought that I might have preferred to be white like them. They couldn't imagine that I had no desire merely to exchange my black problem for their white problem. For all their knowledge and sophistication, they couldn't understand the instinctive and animal and purely physical pride of a black person resolute in being himself and yet living a simple civilized life like themselves. Because their education in their white world had trained them to see a person of color either as an inferior or as an exotic. (p. 245)

The key words in this passage—"a black person resolute in being himself and yet living a simple civilized life like themselves"—indicate the dilemma that, as W. E. B. Du Bois had pointed out long before, lay at the heart of the black man's struggle in America. To resolve this problem, McKay insisted throughout all his work that blacks, as one identifiable race and many distinct ethnic groups, must insist upon their right to be themselves, fully and without reservation, and also to be participants in the world's larger community, both as individuals and as a group. But first, McKay insisted, African Americans had to recognize and embrace their own communal life as the foundation of their existence—as McKay himself did in his own life and art.

McKay was born on 15 September 1890 on the family farm, Sunny Ville, located in the mountainous center of upper Clarendon Parish in Jamaica. His parents, part of the independent black peasantry that had emerged there after emancipation in the 1830s, successfully educated all their children. The eldest, U'Theo, became a planter, businessman, and civic leader well known throughout Jamaica. In McKay's childhood, U'Theo was just beginning his career as a schoolteacher. In fact, between the ages of seven and fourteen, Claude lived with and received almost all his primary education from U'Theo in various schools around Montego Bay and in Clarendon Parish. A graduate of Mico Teachers College in Kingston, U'Theo was a free thinking agnostic and rationalist who communicated his intellectual independence to his youngest brother.

At the time, Jamaica was a poor but proud backwater colony of Great Britain. Its heyday as a producer of great wealth in the sugar trade had long passed, but Britain had remained to cast upon her impoverished black subjects the reflected glories of great empire. For the youthful McKay, to be a part of the British Empire seemed adventurous and romantic. As he observed ruefully in his late memoir, *My Green Hills of Jamaica* (1979), "the direction of our schooling was of course English, and it was so successful we really believed we were little black Britons."

As a descendant of black African slaves, however, McKay also had a different heritage to which he early laid claim. In a poem, first published in the Kingston *Daily Gleaner* in 1912, "Gordon to the Oppressed Natives," he identified with Jamaica's history of slave rebellions and more specifically with the post-slavery Morant Bay Rebellion of 1865, which had led to substantial governmental reforms in Jamaica. The complex heritage of McKay's Jamaica—British and African, free peasant and imperial colony—was reflected in his Jamaican dialect poetry. Out of this heritage emerged his lifelong literary themes. These themes are largely pastoral—the innocence and joys of childhood, the superiority of black rural community values over the degradations of the alien, white-dominated city. These pastoral themes clashed in the dialect poetry with a striking realism in his treatment of the economic limitations of black peasantry and their social frustrations under British colonial rule. His dialect poetry expresses the spirit of protest and the complete identification with the sufferings of his race that figure prominently in his later American verse.

The poems collected in *Songs of Jamaica* and *Constab Ballads* (both published in 1912) were written between 1910 and 1912. During at least six months of that period, McKay served on the island constabulary and heard many complaints from the island's black peasants about the difficulties of earning a living in and around Kingston. Their complaints were also directed against black policemen, such as himself, whom the black Jamaican peasantry, as they moved between country and city, identified as tools of the ruling British. Thus, in "A Midnight Woman to the Bobby" (in *Songs of Jamaica*), a Jamaican woman taunts a "constab" who has questioned her motive for being on the street so late at night, by reminding him that until he donned the uniform of the constabulary, he, like many he now accosts, had been a half-starved, ill-clad country fellow: "You lef' you district, big an' coarse, / An' come join buccra Police Force."

The best poems in McKay's *Songs of Jamaica* and *Constab Ballads* are dramatic monologues like "A Midnight Woman" and "The Apple-Woman's Complaint" or vivid descriptions of the poor in town or country such as "Two-an'-Six," "Pay-Day," "Knutsford Park Races," and "Papine Corner." In these early volumes, though sentimentally drawn to England and compelled by a naive allegiance to anti-Christian, pro-evolutionary rationalism, McKay emphatically states his basic loyalty to the Jamaican peasantry, "My people, my people, me owna black skin" (in *Constab Ballads*). He pledges to them a return to the countryside of his happy childhood and renounces the temptations of the city. Although, in fact, he soon left Jamaica and never went home again, he carried with him a deep loyalty to rural black folk and a mythic memory of childhood innocence in a self-sufficient black peasant community. This pastoral vision nurtured his creative energies for the rest of his life.

After the publication of his dialect poems in 1912, McKay was persuaded by Walter Jekyll that he could not earn his living as a poet. He consequently decided that he would return to the countryside only as a trained agronomist, and left Jamaica to study at Booker T. Washington's Tuskegee Institute in Alabama. McKay's education in the United States was largely financed by Walter Jekyll, an English "gentleman" resident in Jamaica, who had befriended McKay and tutored him in European literatures and languages. An admirer of the Jamaican peasantry, Jekyll had encouraged the young poet to write Jamaican dialect poems and had found a publisher for them. He also guided the inexperienced young author through the publishing process, supplied both volumes with a glossary and footnotes, and wrote a preface to *Songs of Jamaica.* An ex-minister who had left the Church of England to become an exponent of free thought and social Darwinism, Jekyll himself wrote several books on a variety of topics, such as *The Art of Singing* (1884), *The Bible Untrustworthy* (1904), *The Wisdom of Schopenhauer* (1911), and *Jamaica Song and Story* (1907), a classic collection of Jamaican songs and folklore.

McKay arrived at Tuskegee in the early fall of 1912 but stayed only a few weeks before transferring to Kansas State University in Manhattan, Kansas. Tuskegee had disappointed him. He hated its discipline and rules, and its student body and curriculum fell below his academic expectations. He remained at Kansas State for two years before deciding he had had enough of agronomy and college. His next move was in 1914, to New York City. There he married his Jamaican sweetheart,

Eulalie Emelda Lewars. With money from Jekyll, McKay opened a small West Indian restaurant. Neither his business nor his marriage lasted long. The dynamism and variety of the city, both day and night, combined with the variety and vitality of its growing black community, distracted McKay from both business and marriage. His restaurant went bankrupt, and Eulalie, pregnant and dissatisfied with her husband's inattentiveness, returned to her family in Jamaica to have their baby. Although not divorced, the McKays never lived together again. A daughter was born of their brief union; McKay never met her, but she eventually maintained a long correspondence with him. A portion of his irregular and often meager earnings went to her support in Jamaica.

McKay's sexual preferences proved highly unorthodox and clashed at every point with conventional notions of marriage. He believed in free love, he was bisexual, and he had affairs with whomever attracted him, man or woman. In New York, perhaps for the first time, he was able to give free reign to his homosexual inclinations, which he had previously implied in his dialect poetry (see "Bennie's Departure," in *Constab Ballads*).

Freed of marriage and the responsibility of business, McKay took a series of menial jobs and resumed his writing career. From 1914 until 1919, he worked and wrote poetry in his spare moments. In his new verses he moved away from dialect poetry and wrote short, rhymed lyrics, many of them sonnets, about his Jamaican childhood, love, and aspects of the racial conflict in America. Stylistically, they were modeled upon the Elizabethan and Romantic models most admired by Jamaicans, but in them McKay infused his own passions and concerns for racial justice.

McKay's renewed literary efforts began at a fertile time and in a fertile place. In the United States, the assault against Victorian gentility was already well under way, and New York would soon be its center. McKay avidly read the city's newspapers and literary magazines. He also familiarized himself with the radical political movements and journals of the day. His first New York publication was in *Seven Arts,* which published the poems "The Harlem Dancer" and "Invocation" in October 1917. *Pearson's Magazine* included four of his poems—"The Conqueror," "Harlem Shadows," "Is it Worthwhile," and "To the White Fiends"—in its September 1918 issue. And in its July 1919 issue Max Eastman's *Liberator* published two pages featuring his sonnets and other lyrics that included "If We Must Die," McKay's defiant call for blacks to fight back against white mobs that were attacking blacks that summer. The post-war period in the United States saw violent white reactions against blacks eager to share the fruits of democracy. "If We Must Die" brought McKay immediate fame among African Americans, and he became a regular contributor to the *Liberator,* then America's foremost journal of radical art and literature.

Late in 1919 McKay accepted an offer of free passage to England from an admirer; from the late fall of 1919 through 1920, he lived in London and wrote articles and poems for Sylvia Pankhurst's Communist weekly, the *Workers' Dreadnought.* Under his own name and the pseudonyms Eli Edwards and Hugh Hope (the pseudonyms used to keep his employer from knowing he was a writer), McKay wrote revolutionary poetry and political articles in which he clearly defined his belief that those involved in international communism and colonial movements for national independence were natural allies against European and American imperial domination. British and American Communists, he said, must accept the colored peoples of the world as equals and assist in the demise of European imperialism abroad if they desired revolution at home. He stated that he was supporting Marcus Garvey's international black nationalist movement because "for subject peoples, at least, nationalism is the open door to communism."

McKay's sojourn in London coincided with the efforts of Pankhurst's group and other radical socialists in England to form the British Communist Party. As a participant in Pankhurst's faction, McKay gained valuable experience as a radical journalist and observed closely the strengths and shortcomings of Communists in Great Britain. Although he trusted Pankhurst because she championed blacks and supported the Irish and other colonial independence movements, from the start, McKay adopted a generally critical stance toward most Communists. For them to succeed, he believed they had to accept blacks as absolute equals, just as the Industrial Workers of the World (IWW) had done earlier in the United States.

Although deeply involved politically with Pankhurst's *Workers' Dreadnought,* McKay went elsewhere to publish his poetry. For it, he sought out C. K. Ogden, the editor of the prestigious *Cambridge Magazine.* In the summer 1920 issue Ogden published twenty-three of McKay's nonpolitical lyrics. Ogden ranked McKay with Siegfried Sassoon and Rupert Brooke as the young poets of the World War I generation he most admired. He persuaded the London publisher Grant Richards to print McKay's verse in a slender volume entitled *Spring in New Hampshire and Other Poems* (1920). Ogden even called upon his friend and fellow critic I. A. Richards to write a short introduction to the volume.

Shortly after *Spring In New Hampshire* appeared in the fall of 1920, Pankhurst and some of her associates were jailed for printing articles that violated Great Britain's wartime Defence of the Realm Act. The articles dealt with disaffection in the Royal Navy. They had been written by a young British sailor whom McKay had befriended and encouraged. McKay destroyed the original articles and letters by the sailor and made sure that when agents from Scotland Yard visited his room, they found only poems. With Pankhurst's arrest, however, her associates split into quarreling factions and McKay decided to return to the United States. Early in 1921 he was back in New York, where he spent 1921 and most of 1922 as an associate editor of the *Liberator.* For a while in 1922, after its chief editor, Max Eastman, had left the *Liberator,* McKay coedited the magazine with Michael Gold, the author of the semiautobiographical novel *Jews Without Money* (1930).

In his earlier sojourn in New York, between 1914 and 1919, McKay had been politically closest to Hubert Harrison, Harlem's foremost pre-war socialist and IWW organizer. He had also met or corresponded with A. Phillip Randolph and Chandler Owen, editors of the *Messenger,* a black socialist monthly based in Harlem. In addition, there were a few other West Indian socialists in Harlem at this time whose ideas concerning the connections between the Bolshevik Revolution, European imperialism, and colonial independence movements influenced McKay's political thought. Besides Harrison, a Virgin Islands native, these included W. A. Domingo and Cyril Briggs both fellow Jamaicans. When Marcus Garvey's Universal Negro Improvement Association and African Communities League (UNIA) emerged as a mass movement after World War I, all these men, including McKay, tried to assist it in various ways, but Garvey proved unamenable to their socialist thought. By the time of McKay's return in 1921, Harrison had become an independent lecturer, while Briggs was directing his own semisecret African Blood Brotherhood (founded in 1919), which would shortly merge with the Communist party. McKay himself wrote an article critical of Garvey's unrealistic attitudes and goals, "Garvey as a Negro Moses," for the *Liberator* (5:8–9 [April 1922]).

Aside from Max Eastman, McKay's most valuable literary benefactor was Joel Spingarn, a distinguished professor of literature at Columbia University. Spingarn was also an important official of the National Association for the Advancement of Colored People, already the nation's leading black civil rights organization, with headquarters in New York City. Through Spingarn's influence, McKay had published his first verses in the United States in 1917. After his return from London, McKay resumed his contact with Springarn, who was also instrumental in getting Harcourt, Brace to accept his next volume of poetry, *Harlem Shadows,* an enlarged version of *Spring in New Hampshire,* in 1922.

McKay's heart lay, however, with *Liberator* and its predecessor, *Masses,* which had been suppressed during World War I. The artists and writers of *Masses* and *Liberator* were free-spirited, innovative, and yet politically committed to remaking society along socialist lines. He could join them without giving up any of his concerns as a black man. When offered the chance by Max Eastman to help edit the publication in 1921, he had accepted the challenge without any hesitation. He loved the camaraderie of its editors and contributors, the bohemian life of Greenwich Village, and the sense of achievement he felt with the appearance of each issue. He developed a lasting friendship with Max Eastman, the magazine's guiding spirit, whose attachment to conventionally romantic verse forms he shared. He also became friends with significant American artists who contributed to the magazine and many other notable writers and personalities of the period. He had a good time, a stimulating and rewarding time. But through it all, he remained committed to revolutionary change. He joined Briggs's African Blood Brotherhood and no doubt influenced its wholesale commitment to the recently emerged American Communist party. At the same time, he continued his criticism of white Communists and urged upon them the importance of international socialism of blacks and colonials.

While engaged in all these activities, he continued to write sonnets and remained committed to his literary career, a career that he in no way regarded as subservient or secondary to his career as a political journalist. On the Left in post-World War I America, political ideologies had not yet hardened to the point where artistic freedom and left-wing politics had become incompatible. In fact, McKay and others like him believed their allegiance to radical politics was simply an extension of their artistic concerns. In 1922, *Harlem Shadows,* McKay's fourth book of poetry, appeared. It was an enlarged version of *Spring in New Hampshire,* from which McKay's most militant racial protest poems and political verse had been omitted. He had grown ashamed of these omissions, and *Harlem Shadows,* with its inclusion of "If We Must Die" and other protest poems, pleased him immensely. Critics, especially black critics such as James Weldon Johnson and Walter White, received *Harlem Shadows* enthusiastically, and McKay found himself praised as a leading voice among the newer black poets.

Although he patterned his poetry upon the Elizabethan and Romantic models that had become the clichés of Victorian England, McKay, after 1914, slowly elaborated his own vision of the past and present condition of himself and his race. The persona who emerges from these World War I verses is a Romantic, a pastoral poet who worships beauty and truth but is mired, like his race generally, in a society that has attempted to deny him not only fundamental social and political rights, but the basic fullness of life itself. In McKay's American poetry he depicts blacks still struggling upward from slavery, which in Orlando Patterson's illuminating definition was a kind of social, if not literal, death (*Slavery as Social Death,* 1982). McKay's protest sonnets written between 1914 and 1922 are in fact impassioned descriptions of the liminal state blacks found themselves in for generations after Emancipation, caught between the old social death that was slavery and the new suppressed status of freedmen still powerfully linked to their slave forebears. In the poem "In Bondage" (in *Spring in New Hampshire*), McKay writes:

> Somewhere I would be singing, far away.
> . . .
> But I am bound with you in your mean
>   graves,
> O black men, simple slaves of ruthless
>   slaves.

And again in "Outcast" (in *Harlem Shadows*), echoing John Keats's "Ode on a Grecian Urn" (1819), McKay laments the loss of his ancestral African culture and his assumption of Western ideals, for in the process,

Some vital thing has gone out of my heart,
And I must walk the way of life a ghost
Among the sons of earth, a thing apart;
For I was born, far from my native clime,
Under the white man's menace, out of time.

In "Mulatto" (first published in *Bookman*; [September 1925], later included in Wagner's *Les poètes nègres*), another key sonnet for understanding the roots of McKay's alienation, anger, and rebellion in its American context, the poet literalizes his dilemma of double heritage by assuming the persona of a mulatto. The "mulatto" of the poem should also be interpreted as a symbol of the cultural and social condition of all American blacks for whom slavery in the New World meant the acquisition of and participation in a culture that continued to reject them as equals. In creating black slavery, the white culture of America also fathered the black American's striving for social equality and full recognition of his rights as a part of the "American family." Without such recognition there can be no resolution of racial conflict in America, because without it American blacks can never cease to hate those who, in effect, deny them the fullness of life, which in human terms includes the certainty of belonging to a body politic that recognizes your kinship and includes you in its legitimate social life. In "Mulatto," McKay concludes

Because I am my cruel father's child,
My love of justice stirs me up to hate,
A warring Ishmaelite, unreconciled,
When falls the hour I shall not hesitate
Into my father's heart to plunge the knife
To gain the utmost freedom that is life.

The late Jean Wagner was the first critic to analyze the unusually penetrating and courageous frankness of McKay's discussion of black hatred of white injustices. In a late untitled sonnet found in his unpublished "Cycle Manuscript" at Yale, McKay exclaimed that "I stripped down harshly to the naked core / of hatred based on the essential wrong!" In "The White House" (in the *Liberator* [May 1922], later included in *Selected Poems*), he makes clear that it is "the potent poison" of white hate, the harsh exclusiveness of white society, that has aroused his own anger, which is at times almost uncontrollable—so white hot, so incandescent that "The pavement slabs burn loose beneath my feet, / A chafing savage, down the decent street." To balance such rage he must at "every hour" find "wisdom . . . To hold me to the letter of your law!" To those who protested that McKay expressed too much bitterness in his work, he replied:

> The spirituals and the blues were not created out of sweet deceit. There is as much sublimated bitterness in them as there is humility, pathos and bewilderment. And if the Negro is a little bitter, the white man should be the last person in the world to accuse him of bitterness. For the feeling of bitterness is a natural part of the black man's birthright as the feeling of superiority is of the white man's. It matters not so much that one has had an experience of bitterness, but rather how one has developed out of it. To ask the Negro to render up his bitterness is asking him to part with his soul. For out of his bitterness he has bloomed and created his spirituals and blues and conserved his racial attributes—his humor and ripe laughter and particular rhythm of life. (*Passion of Claude McKay,* pp. 134–135)

In reviewing *Harlem Shadows,* Robert Littel of the *New Republic* pointed out that McKay's "hospitality to echoes of poetry he has read" too often "obscured a direct sense of life and made rarer those lines of singular intensity" that revealed his "naked force of character" (12 July 1922, p. 196). Such criticism perhaps obscures another truth. McKay often used such echoes in fresh and often ironical ways to illuminate directly and intensely aspects of the psychology of the oppressed vis-à-vis his oppressors. By articulating so forcefully and directly not only naked hatred but also much subtler psychological effects that slavery had upon black slaves and white slave owners alike, McKay communicated in his sonnets aspects of American race relations that succeeding generations of scholars and writers still have trouble grasping or confronting. The objective of McKay's quest as a poet was wholeness, as a man and as a member of a racial group long denied the opportunity to be truly free to develop their full potential. Only as a child in Jamaica had he known the psychological freedom and unity with his community that he sought as an adult, and some of the best-realized verses in *Harlem Shadows* are those in which he evokes his pastoral vision of Jamaica: in "Flame-Heart," "My Mother," "Adolescence," and "The Tropics in New York."

Harlem Shadows received generally good reviews, but once again, he moved on shortly after the book appeared. In June 1922, McKay resigned from the *Liberator.* For the rest of the summer, he planned a trip to Moscow to attend the Fourth Congress of the Third International in November. Although nominally a Communist party member, he was not active enough in party affairs to be chosen an official delegate. Unable to raise enough funds through the special sale of *Harlem Shadows*—friends and admirers were asked to buy signed copies at a premium price—McKay in the late summer of 1922 sailed as a stoker on a merchant ship as far as England. From there he journeyed to Berlin and obtained a visa to the Soviet Union.

He arrived there in time to participate in the Fourth Congress as a special delegate-observer, despite the objections of the American party delegates, who wished to see him expelled. He ended up criticizing them severely because, he alleged, they still harbored common prejudices against blacks and did not understand the critical position of black laborers in America. His color, good looks, and happy smile won over the Moscow crowds, and the Moscow leadership subsequently sent him on a six-month tour of Moscow, Leningrad, and their environs. Through it all, however, he insisted he was primarily a poet, not a politician, and though he thoroughly enjoyed the wooing, he left the Soviet Union determined to resume an independent literary career. He had grown disillusioned with his British and American comrades, and he had begun to suspect that the dominance of the Soviet national party in the Third International meant the subservience of other national revolutionary movements to the Soviet Union's national interest. While there, McKay had written for Soviet newspapers and journals a series of articles and short stories on the racial situation in the United States, which were collected into two pamphlet-sized books. One was an analysis of the black situation in the United States, *Negry v Amerike (The Negroes in America,* 1923); the other was a slim volume of short stories entitled *Sudom lincha (Trial by Lynching,* 1925).

After leaving the Soviet Union in the spring of 1923, McKay lived and worked in Western Europe and North Africa until 1934. While abroad McKay turned to fiction. From 1923 until 1927, he struggled in France and Spain to produce a marketable novel. With the financial and artistic assistance of many friends, he managed to survive several illnesses—including syphilis, grippe, and high blood pressure—and to persevere in his apprenticeship in fiction. Louise Bryant, the widow of John Reed, persuaded him to engage William Aspenwall Bradley, the leading American literary agent in Paris, as his representative. Bradley secured him a contract with Harper & Brothers that called for three novels and a collection of short stories. McKay responded by producing his first published novel, *Home to Harlem,* in 1928. It appeared in New York at the height of white publishing interest in blacks, received good publicity, and for a while made the local best-seller lists. It presented a story of marginal, working-class black migrants and their stark scrabble for love and a living in Harlem. Black readers were divided in their opinion of *Home to Harlem.* Some thought McKay was merely pandering in it to white enjoyment of black stereotypes. Others defended McKay's story of the hedonistic, instinctually positive hero, Jake Brown, as simply a healthy assertion of the black man's basic strength and vitality. Since his departure in 1922, a new generation of African American writers had emerged to give substance in literature to Alain Locke's assertion in "The New Negro" that a "New Negro" had come forth whose "mind" had "slipped from under the tyranny of social intimidation and [was] shaking off the psychology of imitation and implied inferiority." In the process, many had begun to assert emphatically the positive aspects of black folk life in country and city. Langston Hughes was one such writer, and he in particular welcomed Claude McKay's contribution from afar. Hughes insisted in a letter to McKay that *Home to Harlem* was "undoubtedly . . . the finest thing 'we've' done yet." Not everyone in the black intellectual community agreed with him. McKay's characters were rough, hard-drinking, and hard-living. In their everyday pursuits, many skated a thin line between legality and illegality. To W. E. B. Du Bois and many other reviewers, a novel in praise of such characters was simply reprehensible.

McKay wrote *Home to Harlem* in the tradition of the picaresque. Jake Brown is an idealized folk type, a black man who during World War I deserts his army labor unit in Brest, goes to London, and exists there as a stevedore for a few months. Well after the war, he ships as a stoker on a merchant ship back to New York and Harlem, where he has a series of loves and adventures while working as a cook on the Pennsylvania Railroad. Through Jake's movement from episode to episode, McKay reveals aspects of black working-class existence as he himself experienced it as a solitary male in New York City between 1914 and 1919.

There are no children in *Home to Harlem,* no married couples, no ministers, and few professionals of any sort, with the exception of Ray, the Haitian intellectual who, as Jake's fellow worker on the railroad, forms a friendship with him. Ray acts as McKay's thinly disguised alter ego who comments periodically upon Jake and the conditions in which he lives. To Ray, Jake is a natural man who lives for the moment, happily meeting the daily challenges of an unfair world with natural wit, humor, courage, and intelligence. He cannot be beaten down but rolls like an unsinkable ship across America's stormy ocean of racial strife and oppression. Jake is McKay's triumphant primitive. He is only the best of a good lot in *Home to Harlem.* Those with whom he mingles share his essential virtues in lesser degrees. The gambler and loan shark, Billy Biasse; Jake's inept rival in love, Zeddy; and the pathetic but self-reliant Gin-head Suzy—all are lovingly portrayed by McKay. In sharp contrast, only Ray—literate, lonely, and confused—suffers from self-doubt and self-consciousness. *Home to Harlem* was a deliberate insult to respectability, black and white, and a glorification of the staying power of the poor, the ignorant, and the dispossessed.

McKay continued his assault on black respectability in his second novel, *Banjo: A Story Without a Plot* (1929), in which he shifts and expands his locale to include a new, international set of black characters, a group of beached seamen, adrift in that fleshpot of international commerce, Marseilles's *vieux port* (or the Ditch, as McKay's characters call it). Once again, his hero is an archetypal black primitive, Lincoln Agrippa Daily, or "Banjo," as he is called because of his mastery of that stereo typically black instrument. Around Banjo there gather several West Indian and black American seamen, who like him are temporarily without a ship and living by their wits in the Ditch. They form a band and play for handouts and meals. In Marseilles are Africans from various French colonies, as well as a few black students from the French West Indies. Even more than Jake, Banjo is adrift upon the alien sea of Western civilization and enjoying it. As McKay remarks, he and those like him refuse to "disappear under the serried crush of trampling white feet." They are a puzzle and a mystery, a challenge, like a "red rag to the mighty-bellowing, all-trampling civilized bull." In Marseilles, Banjo meets Ray, the Haitian intellectual from *Home to Harlem,* who, like McKay, has fled the United States to become an expatriate writer in France. Together Ray and Banjo encounter Jake, who has become a seaman in order to support a wife and child.

This international mélange of uprooted black men drinks, sings, dances, fights, and philanders its way through the Ditch, all the while discussing every possible aspect of the problems faced by blacks in Africa, the Caribbean, and the United States. McKay's fundamental position is expressed through his archetypal "natural" man, Banjo, and his own fictional alter ego, Ray. Banjo lives the role, while Ray explains how blacks survive in a hostile white society that seeks to hold them literally in a ditch. McKay argues in both *Home to Harlem* and *Banjo* that blacks are a people in closer proximity to the soil, and hence to nature, than industrialized, urbanized, white Europeans. They are more natural, more spontaneous, less driven by greed, less hampered by sexual inhibitions and other neurotic complexes. And they possess, too, rich racial attributes of humor, rhythm, courage, and physical and psychological resiliency, out of which they fashioned for themselves New World cultures strong enough to see them through slavery. Whether consciously or unconsciously (and one suspects a bit of both), McKay was seizing upon traditional stereotypes and using them as positive images of black racial differentiation. Blacks emerged from slavery with rich legacies of music, stories, humor, and history. These attributes and legacies, McKay insisted, were not embodied in racial leaders and black social climbers, but in the common people and especially in the best of the common folk who, like Jake or Banjo, could fashion satisfying lives for themselves because they knew their own strengths, related to each other and their neighbors as fellow humans, and preserved a self respect nothing could destroy.

McKay believed black leaders everywhere had to build upon this already existing folk community. Only with nurturing roots deep sunk in their own experiences, values, and culture could blacks expand and develop economically, politically, and socially. In this regard, blacks, he believed, and especially African Americans, were no different from other ethnic groups. Like the Jews, the Italians, the Poles, and many others, they must become conscious of their inalienable rights as a group to act together for their own self-advancement. Thus, in *Banjo* Ray angrily advises a French West Indian student not to try to become a black Frenchman but to build from his island culture an identity he already has but refuses to acknowledge as legitimate and self-sufficient in its own right. Ray goes on to explain that if the student wishes to emulate whites, he should turn to the promoters of "the Irish cultural and social movement," to the Russian writers who espoused the cause of the peasants before the Russian Revolution, and to Gandhi's movement in India. He should also learn some of the languages of Africa and its cultures instead of feeling embarrassed and ashamed of them and the poor African laborers of the Marseilles dock.

Banjo was McKay's last picaresque novel. *Gingertown* (1932), a collection of short stories, represented an effort to break new ground stylistically and thematically. Some of the Harlem stories in *Gingertown* told of characters very like those found in his novels, but in his Jamaican stories his whole tone changed to a lush pastoral mode that he sustained in his last novel, *Banana Bottom,* which appeared the next year. This novel, McKay's most mature and artistically successful prose effort, was his attempt to find his way back home, to reintegrate himself imaginatively with the black community of his youth. McKay became eager to write about the Jamaica of his childhood after he settled in Tangier, Morocco, in 1930. For seven years he had lived the precarious life of the expatriate writer in Paris, Nice, Marseilles, and various other cities in France and Spain. He was forty in 1930 and felt the need to settle somewhere and establish a more stable existence. He needed a retreat, and he found it in Tangier. Morocco's French colonial existence during the interwar years, with its blend of ethnic groups and strong West African influences, reminded him of Jamaica. Now middle-aged and shaken, physically and emotionally, from all his experiences, he retreated imaginatively to Jamaica to record the community of his dreams, a black community strong upon its own foundations.

In *Banana Bottom,* the artistic soul who returns to Jamaica after years of education in England is a woman, Bita Plant. She is raped as a young girl by an insane mulatto fiddler of genius called Crazy-Bow; afterward she is sent to England by sympathetic but misguided missionaries for a "proper" education. When she returns, they envision for her a marriage to a native minister. Together, the young couple might carry on the civilizing mission they themselves had dedicated their lives to achieving. None of this happens. Bita finds the ministerial student stuffy and boring. She is happy to rediscover for herself the quiet pleasures of her parents' rural life, the excitement of country dances, and the temporarily beguiling enticements of a seductive but feckless local Romeo called Hopping Dick. The ministerial student is caught in flagrante delicto with a nanny goat. The white missionary and Bita's father, a deacon in the church, drown while attempting to ford a flood-swollen stream as they return from a distant church meeting. For consolation Bita turns to Jubba, a black orphan boy of the hill country, raised by her parents in her absence, who has grown into a quiet, self-assured peasant farmer. He assumes control of the family farm after the death of Bita's father.

As Bita's story unfolds, McKay re-creates in rich, loving, and humorous detail the distant Jamaican hill country and the stable peasant culture of his youth. In *Banjo,* he writes that Ray's efforts as an expatriate "to be educated black and his instinctive self was something of a big job to put over." In *Banana Bottom,* he accomplishes this task for himself by returning to the pastoral innocence of youth and by choosing as his main character a woman who could do what the character Ray in *Home to Harlem* and *Banjo* could never do: reconcile through marriage her educated self with her peasant origins in a black community that had created for itself a way of life free from white missionary efforts to mold it wholly in Western patterns of morality and behavior.

In reality, of course, matters were more complicated, both for himself and for Jamaica. Though *Banana Bottom* received fair reviews, it appeared in 1933 at the height of the Depression and sales were dismal. *Gingertown* had also sold poorly. McKay found himself suddenly isolated, penniless, and without any prospects in Tangier. With assistance from friends, he managed to return to New York City early in 1934. For the remainder of the decade he struggled hard to continue his literary career and to regain the limited financial success that had briefly been his after *Home to Harlem* and *Banjo.* Despite periods of utter poverty, between 1934 and 1940, he managed to produce a memoir, *A Long Way from Home* (1937) and a study, *Harlem, Negro Metropolis* (1940). Both volumes had only modest sales and received mixed reviews. To support himself, McKay appealed to foundations and wrote numerous articles on Harlem's labor scene and grass-roots social movements for a variety of newspapers and magazines. He also worked for the New York Federal Writers Project (FWP). The FWP both saved him financially and enabled him to collect the large body of information about Harlem folk life and movements that he used in his articles and in *Harlem, Negro Metropolis.*

The FWP also involved him deeply in the political disputes in which it had been mired from its inception. McKay had returned from Europe disillusioned with the course of the Bolshevik Revolution and disinclined to join its Trotskyist opposition or any other political movement. As early as 1925, he had predicted the course of Stalinist tyranny and had written Eastman of his disgust with revolutionary parties in the other countries that were willing to follow obediently Moscow's ideological line. He had turned to fiction and ceased political agitation. Once back in Harlem, however, he began to argue that African Americans should not join the American Communist party, nor should they ally themselves with it. He considered the party a tool of Soviet foreign policy. Blacks had enough trouble, he pointed out, without identifying themselves with alien national interests and goals. He also opposed the underhanded tactics used by the Communist party in the FWP to silence its critics, and he warned American writers that Stalinist policies in literature had led to the death of all free expression in the Soviet Union.

At the same time, McKay remained basically a socialist and a black populist, a free spirit who severely criticized the established black leadership in America. Group improvement, and not integration and the acquisition of legal rights alone, should be the immediate goal of African American leadership, he insisted. Black communities such as Harlem, he believed, remained essentially leaderless because African Americans, alone among all ethnic groups, hated and rejected their communities because they identified them with white-imposed segregation. Segregation was a policy, McKay believed, that should be abolished.

But in the meantime, he emphasized, African Americans had to embrace their communities, recognize the legitimate aspirations of their grass-roots labor and religious movements, and build upon the yearnings of their own people for a better life and a real community with labor, business, and social institutions capable of cleansing "the Augean stables" in which they lived. After all, McKay reasoned with admirable prescience, the acquisition of equal civil rights and the abolition of all legal segregation would not mean the disappearance of "the Negro" as an ethnic group in America. African Americans must not wait but must act decisively to build for themselves within their own communities the infrastructure of civic, business, labor, and social institutions common to every community in America. Otherwise, unable to integrate as a whole into American life, they would remain a permanently backward, crime-ridden, and unhealthy sore upon the American body politic. African American leaders, McKay passionately declared, must cease to evade their community responsibilities by using white racism as a permanent excuse for all black ills. The black masses were eager for improvement but lacked the leadership they needed.

McKay's harsh critique won him few friends. A. Phillip Randolph encouraged him; Zora Neale Hurston admired his frankness; and James Weldon Johnson never deserted him. But McKay was viewed by most black leaders as a harping outsider. Nevertheless, his criticism poured forth in the pages of the *New Leader*, the *Nation*, the New York *Amsterdam News*, the *Jewish Frontier*, and other journals.

Finally, however, illness, poverty, and isolation led McKay to enter the Roman Catholic church. In 1944 he moved to Chicago, joined the church, and worked, between bouts of illness, for Bishop Bernard J. Sheil's Catholic Youth Organization until his death in 1948. McKay's conversion surprised most of his friends because he had been an agnostic all his life. However, he was ill, he had found no place within international socialism he could accept, and he likewise had found no security within the African American community or in the United States generally. He needed solace and a cessation of spiritual strife. He sought them in the church and in memory. McKay had envisioned for the black community, as he envisioned for himself, psychological and spiritual freedom to be themselves. Only then could they be proud black citizens of their country and the world. He had found such freedom only in the Jamaican hill country of his youth, and in the last months of his life, it was there he returned by composing a final memoir of his youth, *My Green Hills of Jamaica*.

Selected Bibliography

PRIMARY WORKS

NOVELS

Home to Harlem, (New York: Harper & Brothers, 1928).
Banjo: A Story Without a Plot, (New York: Harper & Brothers, 1929).
Banana Bottom, (New York: Harper & Brother, 1933).

CLAUDE McKAY

POETRY

Constab Ballads, (London: Watts & Co., 1912).

Songs from Jamaica, (London: Augener, 1912) Six dialect poems set to music by Walter Jekyll.

Songs of Jamaica, (Kingstown, Jamaica: Aston W. Gardner, 1912).

Spring in New Hampshire and Other Poems, (London: Grant Richards, 1920).

Harlem Shadows, (New York: Harcourt, Brace, 1922).

SHORT STORIES

Sudom lincha, (Moscow: Ogonek, 1925). Translated as *Trial by Lynching: Stories About Negro Life in North America,* by Robert J. Winter. Edited by Alan L. McLeod Mysore, India (1979).

Gingertown, (New York: Harper & Brothers, 1932).

MEMOIRS

A Long Way from Home, (New York: Lee Furnam, 1937).

My Green Hills of Jamaica and Five Jamaican Short Stories, Edited by Mervyn Morris (Kingstown and Port of Spain, Jamaica: Heinemann Educational Books, 1979).

OTHER WORKS

Negry v Amerike, Translated into Russian by P. Okhrimenko (Moscow: Gosudarstvennoe, 1923). Translated as *The Negroes in America,* by Robert J. Winter. Edited by Alan L. McLeod. (Port Washington, N.Y.: Kennikat Press, 1979).

Harlem: Negro Metropolis, (New York: E. P. Dutton, 1940).

COLLECTED WORKS

Selected Poems of Claude McKay, (New York: Bookman Associates, 1953).

The Dialect Poems of Claude McKay, Vol. 1, *Songs of Jamaica* Vol. 2 *Constab Ballads.* (Freeport, N.Y.: Books for Libraries, 1972).

The Passion of Claude McKay: Selected Poetry and Prose, 1912–1948, Edited by Wayne F. Cooper. (New York: Schocken Books, 1973).

MANUSCRIPTS AND PAPERS

The Claude McKay Papers are in the James Weldon Johnson Collection of Negro Literature and Art, American Literature Collection, Beinecke Rare Book and Manuscript Library, Yale University.

SECONDARY WORKS

BIOGRAPHICAL AND CRITICAL STUDIES

Barksdale, Richard K., "Symbolism and Irony in McKay's *Home to Harlem,*" *CLA Journal:* 15: 338–344 (March 1972).

Bone, Robert, *The Negro Novel in America,* Rev. ed. (New Haven: Yale University Press, 1965).

———. *Down Home: A History of Afro-American Short Fiction from its Beginnings to the End of the Harlem Renaissance.* (New York: G. P. Putnam's Sons, 1975).

Bronz, Stephen, *Roots of Negro Racial Consciousness: The 1920s, Three Harlem Renaissance Authors,* (New York: Libra, 1964).

Brown, Lloyd W., *West Indian Poetry,* (New York: Twayne, 1978).

Cartey, Wilfred, "Four Shadows of Harlem," *Negro Digest:* 18: 22–25, 83–92, (August 1969).

Collier, Eugenia, "The Four-Way Dilemma of Claude McKay," *CLA Journal:* 15: 345–353 (March 1972).

Conroy, Sister M. James, "The Vagabond Motif in the Writings of Claude McKay," *Negro American Literature Forum:* 5: 15–23 (Spring 1971).

Cooper, Wayne F., *Claude McKay: Rebel Sojourner in the Harlem Renaissance, a Biography,* (Baton Rouge: Louisiana State University Press, 1987).

Cruse, Harold, *The Crisis of the Negro Intellectual: From Its Origin to the Present Day,* (New York: William Morrow, 1967).

Dorris, Ronald, "Claude McKay's *Home to Harlem*: A Social Commentary," *McNeese Review:* 29: 53–62 (1982–1983).

Dover, Cedric, "These Things We Shared: An Appendix," *Phylon:* 14, no. 2: 145–146 (1953).

Drayton, Arthur, "McKay's Human Pity: A Note on His Protest Poetry," *Black Orpheus:* no. 17: 39–48 (1965).

Elimimian, Issac I., "Theme and Technique in Claude McKay's Poetry," *CLA Journal:* 25: 203–211 (December 1981).

Fullinwider, S. P., *The Mind and Mood of Black America: 20th Century Thought,* (Homewood, Ill.: Dorsey, 1969).

Gayle, Addison, *Claude McKay, the Black Poet at War,* (Detroit: Broadside Press, 1972).

Giles, James R., *Claude McKay,* (Boston: Twayne, 1976).

Greenberg, Robert M., "Idealism and Realism in the Fiction of Claude McKay," *CLA Journal:* 24: 237–261 (March 1981).

Huggins, Nathan, *Harlem Renaissance,* (New York: Oxford University Press, 1971).

Kaye, Jacqueline, "Claude McKay's *Bango,*" *Présence africaine:* 73: 165–169 (1970).

Kent, George, *Blackness and the Adventure of Western Culture,* (Chicago: Third World Press, 1972).

Kesteloot, Lilyan, *Black Writers in French: A Literary History of Negritude,* Translated by Ellen Conroy Kennedy. (Philadelphia: Temple University Press, 1974).

LeSeur, Geta J., "Claude McKay's Romanticism," *CLA Journal:* 32: 296–308 (March 1989).

Lewis, Rubert, and Lewis, Maureen, "Claude McKay's Jamaica," *Caribbean Quarterly:* 13, nos. 2–3: 38–53 (1977).

Lively, Adam, "Continuity and Radicalism in American Black Nationalist Thought, 1914–1929," *Journal of American Studies:* 18: 207–235 (August 1984).

Locke, Alain, "Spiritual Truant," (*New Challenge* 2: 81, 83–84, Fall 1937) Review of *A Long Way from Home.*

McLeod, A. L., "Claude McKay, Alain Locke, and the Harlem Renaissance," *Literary Half-Yearly* 27: 65–75 (July 1986).

Morris, Mervyn, "Contending Values: The Prose Fiction of Claude McKay," *Jamaica Journal:* 9, nos. 2–3: 36–42, 52 (1975).

Priebe, Richard, "The Search for Community in the Novels of Claude McKay," *Studies in Black Literature* 3: 22–30 (Summer 1972).

Ramchand, Kenneth, *The West Indian Novel and Its Background,* (New York: Barnes and Noble, 1970).

Smith, Gary, "The Black Protest Sonnet," *American Poetry:* 2: 2–12 (Fall 1984).

Smith, Robert P., Jr., "Rereading *Banjo*: Claude McKay and the French Connection," *CLA Journal* 30: 46–58 (September 1986).

Stoff, Michael B., "Claude McKay and the Cult of the Primitive," In *The Harlem Renaissance Remembered: Essays* Edited by Arna Bontemps. (New York: Dodd, Mead, 1972). Pp. 126–146.

Tolson, Melvin B., "Caviar and Cabbage: Claude McKay, a Black Ulysses," Undated clipping (1937) in Claude McKay Clippings Folder, Trevor-Arnett Library, Atlanta University. Review of *A Long Way from Home.*

———. "Claude McKay's Art," *Poetry:* 83: 287–290 (1954). Review of *Selected Poems.*

Wagner, Jean, *Black Poets of the United States: From Paul Laurence Dunbar to Langston Hughes,* Translated by Kenneth Douglas. (Urbana: University of Illinois Press, 1973).

Archibald MacLeish

(1892–1982)

GROVER SMITH

As a poet and man of letters, Archibald MacLeish has illuminated the most serious problems which the twentieth-century literary artist must face, and at the same time has shown how they may be solved. This is not to say that in his work MacLeish himself has completely solved them; but his achievement has been so generally adequate that his poetry seems likely to survive the present antipoetic age and become an inspiration to happier times. The problems are, of course, derived from that famous romantic alienation from the environment almost two centuries ago, a disorder now apparently aggravated out of all cure in an era of mass culture. They consist, on the one hand, in the poet's ethical need to maintain the traditional concern with craftsmanship and, on the other hand, in his equally great desire to communicate with the public—a desire which also is a need. Few successful poets of the present day manage without compromising the one or the other of these endeavors. To sacrifice craftsmanship is to submit to the tyranny of common values, produced by the demotic passion for *equality*; to sacrifice communication, though imaginably in the cause of *quality*, invites, and often with full justice, the charge of snobbishness. In the case of MacLeish, the love of craftsmanship is not snobbish and the sympathy for the contemporary world is genuine. His poetry has avoided the animosity toward ordinary conditions of modern life which is shown, for example, in some of T. S. Eliot's work. At the same time it—or the best of it—is a poetry of ideas as well as emotions.

MacLeish was born in Glencoe, Illinois, on May 7, 1892. A good private secondary school, Hotchkiss, prepared him for Yale. At the university he was in most ways a thoroughly typical young man of his station (well-to-do middle class) and generation: he has spoken of how much more important it was, to him at Yale, that he played football than that he was enrolled in such and such academic courses. Yet he was elected to Phi Beta Kappa without, presumably, any enormous efforts as a student—a fact suggesting the appropriate commentary. Being graduated in 1915, and already planning to be married, he went to Harvard for the study of law. His marriage, to Ada Hitchcock, took place the following year. In 1917 he enlisted and served with the American army in France, where he attained the rank of captain. His brother Kenneth was killed in the war. MacLeish returned to Harvard and took the law degree in 1919; he stayed there as a teacher of government for a year, but from 1920 to 1923 practiced law in Boston.

He was already a published poet (and at Yale winner of a prize for poetry), and he continued to write, though without a strong sense of accomplishment. It was nevertheless for the sake of his poetry that he gave up his law office and took his wife and young children to Paris. He hoped, by devoting himself solely to poetry, to be able eventually to make it his vocation and means of support. He lived abroad for nearly six years and there matured as a poet. Those years have been called his expatriate period. Ernest Hemingway, John

Dos Passos, F. Scott Fitzgerald, and the already long-uprooted Ezra Pound were among the wandering Americans whom MacLeish knew in Paris. Hemingway, who stayed with the MacLeishes for an extended time, remained one of his closest friends for the next decade. Pound, clearly, was on principle an expatriate; but as applied to himself and the others this term is distasteful to MacLeish, who is certainly correct about it: "expatriate" had better be reserved as a name for those who exiled themselves irrevocably.

MacLeish never had any intention of remaining in Paris for the rest of his life. In 1928 he came back to the United States, a recognized poet at last. Here he was to make his permanent home, although he traveled from time to time, for example to Mexico, where he gathered material for a poem about the expedition of Cortez (*Conquistador*). In the early years of the New Deal he diverted his energies into lucrative journalism, and for the magazine *Fortune* he wrote carefully researched articles on current social problems (see the bibliography following). He composed a stage play in verse, *Panic,* and a series of verse plays for radio—these latter a notable contribution to a new genre already beginning to thrive in Britain but undeveloped in the United States.

Not only his journalistic but also his poetic and especially his dramatic writings in the 1930's manifested the extroverted temperament which equipped MacLeish for the role of "communicator," or public spokesman. This was no new attribute: his poems of the 1920's and earlier could only have come from a man of this type, but in technique they resembled works of introspective writers, symbolists and impressionists, who were very different from MacLeish. In the 1940's he proved perhaps all too well extroverted, in the sense that his public duties left him less time for poetry. As curator of the Nieman journalism collection at Harvard (1938) and as a sympathizer with the Roosevelt administration he became a "target" for presidential appointment to the post of librarian of Congress, in which capacity he served from 1939 to 1944. In 1941–42 he was also director of the Office of Facts and Figures, a wartime information agency of the government; in 1942–43 he worked as assistant director of the Office of War Information, a fullscale propaganda bureau. In 1944–45 he was assistant secretary of state. In 1945 and 1946 he led official American participation in establishing UNESCO and starting its programs. It is clear that MacLeish was not only highly extroverted but also patriotic—something not at all surprising: In World War I he had served with honor. Never truly expatriated, because neither an alienated intellectual nor an aesthete nor a communist, he had lived abroad as a poet in the 1920's when France was less expensive than America and Paris was the capital of the arts. In the 1930's he joined with millions in America who acclaimed Franklin D. Roosevelt first for economic reforms and then for the courage to arm against Hitler. And in the decade that followed, he stood among those who believed that the best hope for future peace lay in international cooperation through the United Nations. If MacLeish can be said to have had a mission as distinguished from a vocation, it has been to integrate the role of poet with that of public man.

Substantially MacLeish's poetic output of the 1940's was limited to the collection *Actfive and Other Poems.* Apart from radio plays, the bulk of his publications in the decade was made up of prose pieces. The best of these, articles dating from the years after Hitler came to power in Germany, appeared in the 1941 volume *A Time to Speak.* In a companion volume of 1943, *A Time to Act,* was published a selection of wartime addresses. The latter are comparatively high-keyed and have now far less interest than the articles, which argued MacLeish's political convictions as these were sharpened in the context of current history. His beliefs, like many other people's in America during those years, underwent two phases: the one of response to the economic ideologies debated generally in the 1930's, the other of response to the Italians' and Germans' strategies of conquest. Since MacLeish has consistently opposed Marxism, and even though he was then a New Dealer with affinities for the native revolutionary tradition as celebrated, for example, by Carl Sandburg, his response in the first phase took a civil-libertarian rather than a socialistic character. It thus was, as in retrospect it appears, irrelevant in fact to the main social issues of the period, when an altered balance of economic power was being brought about between capital and government. His response in the second phase, beginning about the time of the Spanish Civil War, was antifascist and, because libertarian, anti-Marxist still; in 1937 he could use the phrase "common front" in referring to enemies of the fascists, but he rejected the popular-front frenzy and stood ready with a half-Jeffersonian, half-populist definition of American national principles as the United States prepared for war (*The American Cause,* 1941). This time his response was clearly in the spirit of the moment. His wartime and post-war-reconstruction papers, the later ones geared to "peaceful coexistence" as against the cold war, may be found in *Freedom Is the Right to Choose* (1951). He was skeptical of the Truman Doctrine but favored the Marshall Plan.

Withdrawn from government posts, MacLeish enjoyed a long academic career at Harvard as the Boylston professor of rhetoric and oratory from 1949 to 1962, and after a short interval served for four years (1963–67) as Simpson lecturer at Amherst College. His almost twenty years of teaching turned out to be one of the richest periods for his art, especially as a playwright. He has published four more verse plays, one of which, *J.B.,* gained the Pulitzer Prize for drama in 1959 (MacLeish had already won two Pulitzer prizes for poetry—one in 1933 for *Conquistador* and one in 1953 for *Collected Poems 1917–1952*); several volumes of literary criticism and incidental social commentary; and two additional volumes of poems, *Songs for Eve* and *The Wild Old Wicked Man, and Other Poems.*

When MacLeish assembled his *Collected Poems 1917–1952,* he conformed to usual practice in suppressing most of the early work; but as one examines the early poems they are seen to relate, in various and sometimes contradictory ways, to his mature verse. The first volumes, *Songs for a Summer's Day* (1915) and *Tower of Ivory* (1917), display a lively interest in verse forms as such. The former contains sonnets only; but the latter includes, as well, a number of stanzaic exercises and one precocious dramatic piece, "Our Lady of Troy" (which, despite a Swinburnean promise in its title, is akin rhetorically to Jonson's humor plays). The sonnets in *Tower of Ivory* show the inevitable debt to Shakespeare; some of them, the best indeed, could only have derived from the "soldier" sonnets of Rupert Brooke. What is more significant, they imply a taste and probably a need for strict formal boundaries within which to manipulate tone, music, imagery, and argument. A few Keatsian couplets (in "A Library of Law"), examples of ballad measure (notably in "A Sampler"), some regular quatrains (as in "Escape"), a ballade (so entitled), paired sonnets ("Certain Poets"), a Petrarchan sonnet but with two octaves ("Baccalaureate"), and miscellaneous lyrical stanzas fill out this group. The themes are amatory and visionary, mainly in the Aesthetic tradition: there is some superficial paganism, sometimes yoked with Christian symbols, and a great deal of hedonism and a rather Yeatsian preoccupation with an enchanted realm of dream. Antiscientific or at least antipragmatic sentiments, characteristically late-Victorian, come out in the dream poems "Jason" and "Realities." A time-worn motif of mutability devouring Time, and Death the inexorable recurs abundantly. Yet, even with their intellectual representations, most of these poems seem to achieve more through music than through argument. Often the sound is more *interesting* than the sense. Imagery appears not to be handled deliberately or for the sake of symbolic possibilities, but to be mainly decorative. (At the same time a few emblematic images strike the attention, as in MacLeish's sonnet "The Altar," which uses a metaphysical conceit. Here certain carved garlands, intended as symbols of beauty in general, are discovered to have accidentally shaped the letters spelling a particular woman's name. Various baroque analogues may have influenced the poem.)

In his *Dialogues* with Mark Van Doren (1962; published 1964), MacLeish remarked that when he began writing verse he "took off from Swinburne." That, certainly, was Swinburne as musician only: Swinburne the sensualist was no model in any of MacLeish's early poetry. The decorous "Realities" is as Swinburnean as you please; in fact, it is quite good, though of low intensity—Swinburne sober. After a few years' fascination with such music, MacLeish reacted against it. It seems that his reaction was a vehement one: his later poetry has, if anything, avoided musicality and has often been downright unmusical. At any rate sense and argument reasserted themselves strongly; an intricate, even devious, rhetoric began to dominate. For a time the sonnet retained his favor, as in the title piece of the volume *The Happy Marriage, and Other Poems* (1924). That long poem (a sort of non-tragical *Modern Love*) is made up partly of sonnets and partly of other regular forms, and the verbal effects produced with these are very skillful. Two sections of "The Happy Marriage" in rhyming couplets (beginning respectively "The humid air precipitates" and "Beside her in the dark the chime") have survived into *Collected Poems,* where they may remind the reader that MacLeish's next important model, after Swinburne, was Eliot. The first of these lyrics was indebted to Eliot in his "Sweeney" period, the second to his "Portrait of a Lady." Both employ symbolistic imagery in a quasi-dramatic context of emotional confrontation—as Eliot's poems had done.

Between 1917 and 1924 MacLeish's style acquired the features of its maturity—conscious symbolism; witty, almost metaphysical strategies of argument; compressed and intense implications—all of these owing much, though quite certainly not everything, to Eliot's example. MacLeish was usually able to resist the Eliot rhythms. His cadences were to have great diversity and to echo many predecessors. His voice, moreover, did not have much in common with the self-conscious orotundity of Eliot's middle period (it bad something in common with the Prufrockian tones), and he seldom undertook vocal productions such as dramatic monologues. Indeed, a lasting mark of MacLeish's work has been the weakness of the persona. At times the diction is remote from speech; at other times it may be close to speech but bare of individuality, diffuse, as though spoken by a chorus. For this reason, despite his partial debt to Eliot, MacLeish belongs not only outside of the Browning-Tennyson traditions of monologue but also outside of the American schools which have stemmed from those, the diverse movements represented by E. A. Robinson and Vachel Lindsay, by Frost and the early Pound. Like stream-of-consciousness fiction, which owes a great deal to it, the dramatic monologue indulges introspection in the safety of a disguise. (Perhaps in fiction, as in the poetry of Yeats, freedom rather than safety is in request—the *complexification* rather than the *disengagement* of the writer.) MacLeish's poetry, for the most part, is not introspective, and this is why indeed no persona is wanted. According to its own purposes, its diminution of the persona is a strength: by this means it turns the reader away from the endless labyrinths of subjective illusion and irony, the "echoing vault" of the poetic self, and invites him to contemplate the phenomenal world. It does not vocalize that self: it can and often does fabricate a kind of disembodied speech, or speech whose origin need not be known. It aspires to be, and sometimes becomes, a poetry of spectacle—not always, but especially when, as in the near masterpiece "Einstein" (1926), it is wholly under the control of an intellectual concept. Then the images arrange themselves as objective counterparts of the progress of an idea—Eliot's "objective correlative" intellectualized.

MacLeish in the 1920's increasingly took pains with the formal structure of his poetry. Only through form could the swelling rhetoric be channeled. After the 1924 volume, the sonnet was neglected for a while, but it was not discarded even in *Streets in the Moon* (1926), where free verse of a highly regulated type alternates with blank verse and stanzaic patterns. Blank verse, with a few rhyming lyric passages, was used also for his symbolistic poem *The Pot of Earth* (1925) and his closet drama *Nobodaddy* (1926).

The theme and scope of *Nobodaddy*, referred to by MacLeish as a "poem," are indicated in his preface, which adds that the "emotional experiences" treated there are "not unlike" those dealt with in *The Pot of Earth*, written after it but published before. *Nobodaddy* takes its title from Blake's derisory name for the scriptural God of prohibitions. It adapts the Adam-and-Eve, Cain-and-Abel story to dramatize what MacLeish calls "the condition of self-consciousness in an indifferent universe"; it is a poetic essay, of course, not Biblical commentary. In it, Adam has emerged into humanity, into consciousness of himself as a being distinct from the rest of creation. In this condition he has two choices, a fact which disquiets him and in itself presumably inclines him to the choice he makes. He can either stand in awe of nature ("the Gardener"), accepting the inferiority implicit in obedience to a system he does not understand, or else assert his will to become a god—that is, a rational being superior to nature. Urged by the Voice of his will (metaphorically the Serpent) and by Eve, who does not fear what she has never experienced, natural harshness, Adam eats the forbidden fruit and thus alienates himself by act as well as by will. The consequence is misery: his daring to break the bond of obedience brings down upon his head a flood of superstitious terrors. The Gardener, far from changing into an Avenger, seems to have vanished; but, frantic with guilt, Adam flees the garden, and he and Eve seek the desert. It remains for their sons, Abel and Cain, to complete the drama by, in effect, modernizing the situation. Abel, representative of Adam fallen and burdened with guilt, attempts a mystical reconciliation with the supposed Avenger. Longing to return to the garden, to ignorance and servitude, he invents a relationship with an invented god: religion is born. By blood sacrifice he strives to atone. His brother, Cain, realist and rationalist, and similar to Adam as he was when he heard the Voice of his humanity exhorting him to free himself, asserts human values and the will to power. Abel grovels before the voice of thunder and tries to pull Cain down to his knees in humility. Cain, already godlike in mind, kills him.

It is not clear why Adam is so constituted that he cannot profit from his fall, but because he cannot his son Abel cannot either. It is left for Cain to vindicate reason against superstition; that he has to do so by murder is ironic, to say the least. At any rate none of the four characters comprehends the meaning of these actions. It is for the reader to understand in terms, primarily, of acceptance and rejection. So long as man believed himself to be simply part of nature, he lived in a paradise. Death was there already, the biological cycle had begun, but man had not yet taken it personally—it was still objective. When man became self-conscious, his acceptance of nature changed into resistance, and with its normal machinery of death it seemed a threat to him. Not only was he utterly different from nature, but it was also indifferent to him—though physically he remained within it. He had imagination; nature was all process. The "Gardener" of *Nobodaddy* is merely the principle of life viewed as sympathetic harmony. When this view disappears, and reason replaces it with the stark vision of process, the Gardener gives way to the enemy, the unsympathetic. Physical nature converted into the antagonist of man's will is a desert, a region which will not behave as man desires. The harmony of prelapsarian Eden was that of man's acquiescent ignorance; the disharmony of the natural world, to fallen man, is that of its uncontrollability. His selfhood defies nature and battles with it but at the last must sink defeated. Abel's attempt to return symbolically to the unfallen state takes the form of a conscious imitation of nature's unconscious cruelty; he grafts human motives upon the indifferent. Abel's sacrifice of a ram is wrong because consciousness cannot atone with unconsciousness. Nature's own profuse bloodletting sets no store by covenants and bargaining; apart from man's imagination such "deals" are meaningless. If human ideals estrange man from nature, and if, nevertheless, with the justice of indifference, nature punishes every act not in harmony with its laws, then man is automatically unhappy.

The idea that human feelings meet nothing like themselves, no sympathetic responses, in nature, and that nature governs the life of the body as if the desires of the mind did not occur, is present in *The Pot of Earth.* But the theme of this poem is the bitterness and pity of those desires so subjected to the Gardener's indifference. Here is the case of the toad beneath the harrow. The poem was published three years after *The Waste Land* of Eliot. The two works are of roughly the same length. They have much similarity, in technique and symbolism alike. In certain notable ways they are dissimilar. *The Waste Land* is a first-person monologue to which are subordinated various genre adaptations. *The Pot of Earth* is mainly a third-person narrative, though with some first-person stream-of-consciousness effects. Stylistically *The Waste Land* is by far the more experimental and radical. Both poems, however, draw upon Sir James Frazer's work *The Golden Bough* for vegetation symbolism which, mythologically and ceremonially, represents the death and resurrection of a fertility god (e.g., Adonis) as a type of the seasonal decay and revival of nature. Both also, in applying this symbolism within a modern context of life, emphasize not the victory of life over death, but the reverse of this. On the other hand, they again differ most significantly in what they apply such symbolism to. *The Waste Land,* exploring a gnostic and "spiritualized" sense of death and rebirth, uses a special myth (the Grail legend) concerning an *arrest* of fertility, whose equivalent in the poem is the male protagonist's state of emotional aridity and despair. *The Pot of Earth* applies the vegetation symbolism to its female protagonist's organic functions: the biological cycle takes place in her, as if in a plant springing up, flowering, being fertilized, bearing fruit, and dying. Or, more exactly, the girl or woman herself can be regarded as such a "pot of earth," or Garden of Adonis described by Frazer in the passage which MacLeish prefixed to his poem as a general epigraph. For, like those shallow-rooted plants forced into brief and hectic life under the Syrian sun, only to wither and to be thrown into the sea as symbols of the god bewailed by his sectaries, she leads a transient existence, devoid of any lasting meaning except the biological one. The resurrection of the fertility god means new life for nature, not for the individual. At the conclusion of *The Pot of Earth,* the woman has borne a child and has died; a chestnut tree is in flower; but she rots in the earth. Here the Adonis myth becomes the vehicle for a realization of the inextricability of life and death. MacLeish's second epigraph to the poem (later transferred to Part I) is the "god kissing carrion" passage from *Hamlet*; and Part III is called "The Carrion Spring." In *Hamlet* "carrion" is the prince's coarse designation for Ophelia: evidently the woman in *The Pot of Earth* has a sacrificial role like that to which the Ophelia personage is doomed in *The Waste Land.* But she has been sacrificed by the indifference of nature, not the brutality of man.

The 1925 text of *The Pot of Earth,* several pages longer than the text printed in *Poems, 1924–1933* (1933) and thereafter, adopts the *Waste Land* technique of making the past and present interpenetrate, so that the modern woman's life cycle is depicted in timeless fusion with that of a primitive world: its incidents are abruptly juxtaposed to details from the Adonis ritual. But the three principal passages in which this effect is created have been omitted from the later printings, leaving the poem free of the startling "intertemporal" counterpoint typical of Eliot, and with a contemporary texture purely. Yet, beneath this, continual allusions to the Adonis ritual remain to suggest a theme of unending recurrence. Perhaps recapitulation, rather than recurrence, is the universalizing motif in *The Pot of Earth* (as, for example, it is in Joyce's *Finnegans Wake*): this woman is eternal woman, and eternal woman typifies reproductive nature, whose dream is her life. She, life the Garden of Adonis in antiquity, blossoms as an emblem, a signature, of some omnipresent and all-involving archetype of cyclical life and death. Her anonymity is as profound as that of Tiresias, the *Waste Land* persona; but whereas he is obscured by Eliot's pretentious legerdemain with literary cross references, she has a constant, though shadowy, identity.

There seems to be a philosophical difference between *The Pot of Earth* and *The Waste Land* in the ways they pose their protagonists against the world. Eliot's poem is very much in a "psychological" tradition; that is, starting from an Idealist's assumption that the individual point of view is of paramount importance because it uniquely focuses knowledge of externals, *The Waste Land* attains form by offering a view from a single point, or through a single narrow peephole. It recalls Bergsonian and stream-of-consciousness fiction. MacLeish's poem seems to start from a Realist's assumption that there is nothing special in point of view as such; that the law of things is common to all. It depicts a *typical* relation of the natural to the human, indeed choosing to examine the fate of someone quite average. Whatever the resemblance of MacLeish's techniques to those of subjectivists and symbolists, his *fond* was otherwise. His poem, like Eliot's, uses Aesthetic and symbolist procedures to assist naturalistic statement, but his is closer to a philosophical naturalism which assumes the total subjection of man to time and chance.

There was much of the eighteenth-century rationalist in the MacLeish of the 1920's and in his political character later; much, also, of the scientific observer of life. He had made an almost complete break with his antiscientific and aesthetical beginnings as a poet. He now accepted the scientists' description of reality—only boggling at its falsification of experience. The external world he confronted was the one described by the astronomers, by the biologists, and above all by the mathematical physicists of his own day. Whereas Eliot and Pound and Yeats were ancients, MacLeish was a modern. One may believe that Einstein's space-time-energy continuum receives, in the work of MacLeish, its most important poetic treatment to date—a treatment not through casual allusion for contemporary color, but through exact intellectual integration with the subject matter of felt life. A thematic carry-over takes place from *The Pot of Earth* to later poems—the conflict between personal hopes and natural law, developed first, perhaps a little less pessimistically, in *Nobodaddy.*

The volume *Streets in the Moon* scrutinizes the state of man the conscious animal in the disheartening universe of curved space and irreversible entropy. In his "Prologue" to this collection, MacLeish salutes a hypothetical "crew of Columbus" who are westward bound but, as in nightmare, toward a "surf that breaks upon Nothing"; and he comments, concerning this apparent fate of the whole human race,

> Oh, I have the sense of infinity—
> But the world, sailors, is round.
> They say there is no end to it.

The paradox of infinite aspirations confined in a world closed and therefore without "end" to aspire beyond is a leading theme of *Streets in the Moon.* The title of the book suggests the double vision: "streets" a symbol of the here and now of consciousness, the "moon" a symbol (defined partly by the counter-romantic use to which Jules Laforgue put it in his poetry) of a myth degraded by science. The volume concludes with the wry humor of "The End of the World," in which a temporal "end" to the circus of life reveals the nothingness above man's head. The poems in between, several of them conspicuously indebted to Laforgue ("Nocturne," "Selene Afterwards," "Hearts' and Flowers' "), to Eliot, or to Pound, and one of them most notably ("Einstein") written in a symbolic manner recalling Mallarmé's "L'Après-midi d'un faune" (but in a rather Miltonic strain!), deal variously with the mystery of existence, with the problem of time (symbolized by the sun, among other things), with death, with love and other relations, and with human character. A few are imagistic; others are elegiac, anecdotal, or narrative and Browningesque. One of the finest poems in this fine collection is the three-part "Signature for Tempo," a meditation on the relativity of time and movement:

> Think that this world against the wind of
> time
> Perpetually falls the way a hawk
> Falls at the wind's edge but is motionless;

on fourth-dimensional extension:

> How shall we bury all
> These time-shaped people,
> In graves that have no more
> Than three dimensions?

(though why not, one could retort, since in fact the graves have the same number of dimensions as the people); and on death as the point in time where all are united:

> Whom time goes over wave by wave, do I lie
> Drowned in a crumble of surf at the sea's
> edge?—
>
> And wonder now what ancient bones are
> these
> That flake on sifting flake
> Out of deep time have shelved this narrow
> ledge
> Where the waves break.

"The Too-Late Born," rhetorically very brilliant, is most meaningful in the context of the time poems (its later title, "The Silent Slain," constricts its meaning); it, too, is about the community of the dead. The death of Roland at Roncesvalles has been made archetypal: the "silent slain" could belong to any army, and the fact that "we" survive them is an accident of time—an ironic one, for in due time we shall loin them in the universal graveyard of the earth. Themes of mortality are further explored in "No Lamp Has Ever Shown Us Where to Look," "Interrogate the Stones," and "Le Secret humain," in terms of speculations on the "answer" that death is supposed to have in reserve for man, an answer that may simply annihilate the questioner. "Raree Show" asks whether the question is within the mind, but ends with a new question, "Where?" "L'An trentiesme de mon Eage" (its title taken from a line by François Villon which was a favorite of Pound's, and which was used by Eliot in an epigraph and by Pound in "Hugh Selwyn Mauberley") is somewhat in the mood of Eliot's "Gerontion." Through a multiplicity of memories its speaker has arrived at his present place; he then asks, "And by what way shall I go back?" One could answer that there is no need of going back, for "place" is temporal as well as spatial, and what belongs to time contains its past. The poem, having reviewed the past, has already returned to it, through art. But this reply would be satisfactory only to a Bergsonian. In any realistic analysis the question is unanswerable, though MacLeish was to continue asking it in later poems.

One of the most often cited anthology pieces from *Streets in the Moon* is the paradoxical and enigmatic "Ars Poetica." In spite of its Horatian title, which seems to imply simply a verse essay in legislative criticism, a poem about the art of poetry, its true workings are otherwise. It does not frame an address to poets generally, much less to their critics; it is no essay in criticism. Nor yet does it introspectively comment, like Eliot's poem "La Figlia che Piange," on the poet's relation to his own creative process. Perhaps some readers, remembering chiefly the distichs "A poem should be equal to: / Not true" and "A poem should not mean / But be," have interpreted what "Ars Poetica" *says* (that a poem should be like an object beheld in stasis, not like a message or a paradigm) as what it is *for.* If so, they have taken it for a critical essay and have violated its supposed counsel. The central paradox of "Ars Poetica" is that it makes sense only when the reader accepts its sense as a function of form. It then survives as the aesthetic object it approves—with the proviso that the approval must be held as an utterance in *vacuo*, a silence.

> A poem should be palpable and mute
> As a globed fruit,
>
> . . .
>
> A poem should be wordless
> As the flight of birds.

The real subject of "Ars Poetica" is itself, by a sort of narcissism of the written word as "pure poetry"; this poem exhibits aestheticism circling round, as it were, and returning like the equator upon the round earth. The result contrives a stasis indeed, free or nearly free of time's rotation. The moon of the second part, MacLeish's recurrent symbol of the imaginative world ideally transcending the naturalist's inner and outer landscapes, drifts as poetic subjectivity defying its antithesis, the solar clock. "Ars Poetica," somewhat Yeatsian like various other short poems in the volume, looks also Keatsian: the whole poem speaks with a voice which, like that of the Grecian urn when it equates beauty and truth, belongs to a realm of ideality and is relevant only to that. Such a realm, proper to poetry, conflicts with nature; MacLeish's long poem "Einstein" reviews the naturalistic conception that man, at last, cannot quite escape the prison of his time-bound flesh. That, too, is a Keatsian thought.

"Einstein" in theme recalls *Nobodaddy*; the resemblance proves useful in the unraveling of its complexities. Not only is the subject difficult (like most subjects) unless one already understands it, but also the rhetoric lumbers in obscurity. Nevertheless the poem operates compellingly upon the emotions, and it ought to be one of the best-known philosophical poems of the period. The Einstein of the title is modern intellectual man, scientist, represented microcosmically as a sort of Leopold Bloom, atomic and entire (*ein Stein*, perhaps—a stone, or at least a pebble!), who has inherited the problem and the mission of MacLeish's Cain, the mission of rationality. The Einsteinian universe is rationality triumphant, as indeed it is the triumph of the modern spirit. The poem (a narrative showing the process of "going back," by reason, to a condition which seems to repeal Adam's alienation from nature and to reunite his posterity with the primal creator—i.e., in effect deifying man) reveals the way back by recapitulating the way forward, from any infancy to full consciousness. First there is Einstein, man secure in his body-sense and self-contained. Then, his awareness of sense impressions. Then, his mental abstraction of these into a coherent world—

> A world in reason which is in himself
> And has his own dimensions.

Then, his discovery of his ignorance and impotence in the world's vastness and mystery. Then, his attempt to gain mystical identification with this mystery by sensory and aesthetic contemplation, and most through music,

> When he a moment occupies
> The hollow of himself and like an air
> Pervades all other.

Then (in a passage to which Eliot, who seems to owe several points to this poem, suggests a reply in the closing lines of "Burnt Norton"), his realization that there is no longer a "word" which can translate beauty into thought and thus into himself (the word described as known to the Virgin of Chartres but as now become "three round letters" in a carving was presumably the "AVE" which hailed, in effect, the Incarnation). Then, upon his rejection of mysterious access and Abel's quest, his intellectual formulation of Albert Einstein's theories. And finally, the godlike subduing of nature to himself, so that the physical universe is comprehended in his consciousness, which itself becomes all.

Only one stage remains, and this is denied him. His own flesh cannot melt into his thought: he keeps "Something inviolate. A living something." These phrases return him to the state which was his at the beginning of the poem, where, at minimal definition, the "something inviolate" is the fact "that / His father was an ape." The original Adam, sprung from nature and subject to it, by it condemned to die, persists despite this victory. Those critics are surely wrong who see "Einstein" as anti-scientific; rather, the poem, like *Nobodaddy,* affirms the necessary destiny of man to subdue everything to his knowledge—everything but the stubborn, atavistic ape within, which *must* refuse to yield. The anecdotal poem "The Tea Party" says all that need be said about man's sense of his primitivism; "Einstein" says something further, that the animal residuum is man's very life. The tragic fate awaiting this life has already been revealed in *The Pot of Earth.* "Einstein" is not tragic; it is not even precisely critical. It is an intellectual celebration of an intellectual triumph, attended by a voice bidding the *triumphator* remember that he is dust.

MacLeish's tragic sense of the buried life, exposed in the impersonal symbolism of *The Pot of Earth,* is deeply sounded in *The Hamlet of A. MacLeish* (1928). An observation by MacLeish more than a decade later, in his essay "Poetry and the Public World," was made to introduce a kind of renunciation of this poem or at least of the attitudes it expresses: "The Hamlet of Shakespeare was the acceptance of a difficult age and the demonstration of the place, in that age, of poetry. The Hamlet of Laforgue, and after him of Eliot and after him of the contemporary generation, is the rejection of a difficult age and a contemptuous comment upon the hope of poetry to deal with it. . . . [N]ot until contemporary poetry writes the Hamlet of Laforgue and Eliot out of its veins, will poetry occupy, and reduce to the order of recognition, the public-private world in which we live." *The Hamlet of A. MacLeish* is in the tradition of Jules Laforgue's "Hamlet" and of Eliot's Prufrockian and wastelandish poems; and it focuses, certainly, upon the sufferings of the sensitive man, not upon the problems of the age in its "public" bearings. From the point of view of 1939, after a decade of experiment with "public" themes and at a moment of intense uneasiness about the future of civilization, MacLeish saw his *Hamlet* as too negative, as too much lacking in what the same essay called "acceptance" and "belief." Yet it was probably just as well that he aimed his criticism expressly against Laforgue and Eliot and only lumped his *Hamlet* implicitly with theirs; for really there is a difference in kind between their pessimism and his own in that poem. Quite simply, their pessimism is social, whereas his is cosmic. What Laforgue and Eliot (in his early poetry) found fault with was the special uncongeniality of life for the special personae in their poetry. What MacLeish complains of in his *Hamlet* is the injustice of the universe. Surely a poem which says that life is a fraud is hardly to be criticized for not telling us how to live optimistically.

In "Einstein" there are marginal notes with the double purpose of punctuating the stages of consciousness and locating these in the mind of one individual. In *The Hamlet* such notes have a different purpose: they key the psychological action to Shakespeare's *Hamlet,* from which (being quotations, stage directions, or episode descriptions) they are taken. MacLeish's poems can be thought of as analogous to a transparent overlay which, when superimposed on the map or chart to whose details it is keyed, provides new information or modifies the old. In this case the so-called overlay is fully a map in its own right. It is divided into fourteen sections, corresponding to as many scenes of the Shakespeare play. What it maps with these is the world of consciousness belonging to its protagonist, the modern Hamlet; and this world, like that of the play, shows temporal movement or more properly historical movement, for it is a world common to mankind, whom this Hamlet represents. (As with *The Pot of Earth,* some resemblance to *Finnegans Wake* may be seen.) And if Hamlet is mankind, it would appear that the Ghost is the mysterious father-god of creation, the unknown Nobodaddy, maybe to be known in, or as, Death; Hamlet's mother is the Earth; and the Claudius figure, symbolized in the opening section as both Hyperion (the sun) *and* a satyr, is the tyrant enemy, Time. The characters in this cast do not emerge allegorically, as in a morality play, but symbolistically. That is, as addressed by Hamlet they are persons, but as described and further characterized they become actions, narratives, even landscapes; and the actions take the place of drama. The poem is not dramatic except in that sense in which a speaking voice implies a dramatic situation; nor is that implication a vivid one, Hamlet being mainly a stage-managing consciousness, like Tiresias in *The Waste Land.* The protagonist's mood and temper, conforming to the "nighted color/choler" of Shakespeare's Hamlet, do, however, determine the tone of anguish throughout the poem.

Two of the episodes or symbolic actions of MacLeish's *Hamlet* are particularly bold and memorable. Part III, corresponding to Horatio's description of the Ghost (*Hamlet,* I, ii), is presented in terms of that portion of a Grail romance (the Bleheris version, freely adapted) which contains the adventure of the Chapel Perilous and the adventure of the Grail Castle, including the disclosure of the Grail talismans. The point of this (and of Part IV, answering to the appearance of the Ghost to the prince) is the inscrutability of the death mystery, from whose silence there can be no appeal and into whose secret there can be no initiation—such as the initiation supposed by Jessie L. Weston, in her book *From Ritual to Romance,* to have given rise to the Grail legends. A theme is here restated from *Streets in the Moon.* Part IX, corresponding to the play within the play, the play of the mousetrap, has a subject recalling St. J. Perse's "migration" poem *Anabase,* namely the movements of peoples and tribes into new lands, the rise and fall of cultures, the cycle of civilization. And the point of this, in relation to the Shakespearean scene, is that, as the memorial of human aspirations, the whole earth is a bloodstained chronicle of the guilt of nature and Time. These episodes of the poem have the profoundest import because they establish the necessity of the cosmic pessimism which is the mainspring of its tragic movement. They furthermore universalize the rage and grief of the protagonist, inviting all mankind to take part in execrating the conditions of life.

The gloom pervading *The Hamlet of A. MacLeish* is left behind in the next collection, *New Found Land: Fourteen Poems* (1930). Here the over-all tone is one of acceptance—not the unreflecting acceptance urged but resisted in the closing part of the earlier poem, but something urbanely detached. There is a return to the meditativeness of an even earlier period, in poems about memory and time; along with this there is an advance toward a new theme of affirmation, for which a tone of optimism comes into being. Such poems as "'Not Marble Nor the Gilded Monuments,'" "Return," "Tourist Death," and "You, Andrew Marvell" are retrospective in two senses: they look back to the years and places of MacLeish's sojourn abroad, and they recall his obsessive concern, in those circumstances, with the erosion of life by time. "You, Andrew Marvell" has been anthologized too often, but it is as nearly perfect a poem as MacLeish has ever written. Yet it is only one of a group (Part IV of his *Hamlet* belongs with these) in which he again used the "cinema" technique of passing across the mind's eye a succession of places and faces, each an objective repository of some emotional association for him. The subject of "You, Andrew Marvell" is the poet's past as lodged in the places named, quite as much as it is the poet's present conceived as a moment in the light which is soon to be covered by the darkness inexorably rising in the east. The specific wit in his highly serious "metaphysical" handling of this subject depends not merely on a paradoxical view of diurnal motions (the night rises in the east) but on his present geographical position in relation to the regions reviewed in his mind. Being now presumably in the middle of the American continent, he, at noon, imagines the eastern world slipping into physical night just as, figuratively, it darkens by receding into his personal past.

The new, affirmative theme, though not fully realized in this poem or perhaps anywhere in the collection before the concluding piece, "American Letter," seems to grow out of a personal sense of the east-west imagery. At least "American Letter" defines the line of separation between the past, Europe and Asia, old lands of darkness, and the future, America the "new found land," by declaring that for the American born his life must unfold here: the Old World may enshrine a remembered joy, but the man of the New World is not fulfilled by it. And in "Salute" MacLeish hails the sun, dayspring and midday, as if to assert the preeminence of his symbol of the West. Indeed, he tends now to neglect the moon, which becomes a symbol no longer of that sought realm of myths and dreaming but of a world of stasis, sterility—something praised only in the almost hymnal "Immortal Autumn." His style tends toward greater impersonality as, following Perse, he cultivates dissociated concrete images of immense but vague significance. One very successful instance of this practice occurs in "Epistle to Be Left in the Earth," where its gnomic qualities suit the speaker's list of specific phenomena unreduced to abstract classification.

Conquistador (1932) is a long poem but not an epic, though of epic magnitude in theme, nor yet a chronicle, though based on an account of the Spanish rape of Mexico, *The True History of the Conquest of New Spain,* by Bernál Díaz del Castillo. Its interest derives neither from the portrayal of heroic character nor from adventurous narrative, but from its rendering of discrete episodes as experiences recollected by its narrator. It can hardly be termed panoramic; it is kaleidoscopic, a fantasia of emotions. Though not primarily a narrative at all but a series of tableaux with subjective coloring, it would perhaps remind one of Dante's *Divine Comedy* even if, typographically, its verse did not resemble *terza rima.* Like the *Divine Comedy* it presents a psychological, if not quite a spiritual, quest. This quest, outlined in fifteen books, has the usual temporal and spatial dimensions—temporal into the past buried within the speaker's self, spatial into the Mexican interior and the death of the Aztec culture. The hallmark of the poem, unfortunately, is an unrelieved sense of enormous confusion. In the memory of the speaker, the successive episodes are crowded with detail; and an effect of "nonlinear" construction is heightened by the frequent use of parataxis. That is, the language depends a good deal on coordinated statements, whether or not with conjunctions. That this device was intentional is evident from the special use of the colon as a divider; it is made to separate phrases of all kinds. The elements which are thus compounded stand in any order: logic seems not to be in question, since free association controls largely.

If the influence of St. J. Perse dominates the larger framework of the poem, affecting the shape of its "grand sweep," still another influence, that of the Ezra Pound of the *Cantos,* often prevails at close quarters. The arbitrary juxtaposition of "significant" details is Poundian. So, too, is one ingredient of MacLeish's subject matter, the use of Book XI of the *Odyssey* in the "Prologue," where Bernál Díaz is given a role like that of the Homeric Tiresias, summoned from the dead along with fellow ghosts to speak to the living. MacLeish drops this mythological device after the "Prologue," in favor of Díaz's book narrative; but the latter may be considered a realistic equivalent to ghostly speech. Though more in key with the Biblical rhapsodies of Perse than with the social grumblings of Pound, *Conquistador* lacks optimism. For one thing it is based on one of the bloodiest and most barbarous exploits in history, one which destroys the empire it conquers and which ends in a retreat. Furthermore it is set forth by a spokesman for the dead and disillusioned, himself aware, in his very book, that death hangs over him. At the last he longs for the impossible resurrection of youthful hope.

> O day that brings the earth back bring again
>
> That well-swept town those towers and that
>   island. . . .

In general this poem, far from acclaiming the origin of the New World as the harbinger of American civilization, is negative as well as confessional. Díaz, like MacLeish's Hamlet, is a wastelander, and what he longs for is a lost innocence that in fact was never real at all: certainly it did not dwell in the Aztec priestly slaughterhouse or in the hearts of the Spanish butchers either. In the poem it only tantalizes like a gilded dream of El Dorado.

Whatever its defects—and its failures, for if it succeeds it does so as a sequence of vibrant short poems, not as a big poem—*Conquistador* brings MacLeish back definitely to American scenes. *Frescoes for Mr. Rockefeller's City* (1933) restores the affirmative tone. What is affirmed now is the American dream—the wholesome one—not as an abstraction but in its embodiment by the American land and the pioneer past. The first of the six poems, "Landscape as a Nude," revives an allegorical convention (like *Finnegans Wake,* by the way) to romanticize the land as a voluptuous woman. "Wildwest" and "Burying Ground by the Ties" pay tribute to defeated energies of a past era, to Crazy Horse and to the laborers dead after laying the tracks of the Union Pacific; and at the same time these poems satirize the millionaire railroaders, as does the opening section of the fifth poem, "Empire Builders." The longer, second section of the latter invokes for its contrast the unviolated wilderness explored by Lewis and Clark on their expedition to the Northwest—the description being treated as an "underpainting" beneath a supposed series of panels beautifying the robber barons Harriman, Vanderbilt, Morgan, and Mellon, and for anticlimactic good measure the advertising executive Bruce Barton. The fourth poem, "Oil Painting of the Artist as the Artist," lampoons the anti-American expatriate snob—the T. S. Eliot type, who

> . . . thinks of himself as an exile from all this,
> As an émigré from his own time into history
>
> (History being an empty house without owners
> A practical man may get in by the privy stones . . .)

A final poem, "Background with Revolutionaries," makes a point with regard to the controversy (current at the time MacLeish was writing but now almost forgotten) surrounding the Diego Rivera murals for Radio City in New York. Rivera had depicted Lenin among his inspirational figures; Nelson Rockefeller had demurred; and the painting was expunged, to the accompaniment of howls from the Left, amusingly reinforced with the aesthetic plea that art is sacred beyond politics. MacLeish's point in the concluding poem was that Lenin is irrelevant to the spirit of America, which lives in the communion of land with people; a further point, which involves one's reading the fifth poem, optionally, as a code to the other four, can be that Lenin in his irrelevance is somehow analogous to J. P. Morgan.

There are not only ideological but also functional problems in the *Frescoes.* Ideologically it is dubious whether MacLeish quite conveyed the absurdity of Leninism with his selected profiles of ignorant, neurotic, or simply enthusiastic believers in it; a suggestion emerges from "Background with Revolutionaries" that the fault with these communists may lie in their intellectual pretensions, which do not suit the nonintellectual mystique urged in the poem. And by the same token, earlier in the series, that mystique has been manipulated in order to pillory the railroad magnates, who were not "men of the people" and who ravaged the land for their money-making. Crazy Horse was admirable, apparently, and the virgin wilderness was good and so were the track gangs; but beyond this mystique of the primitive and the peasant the *Frescoes* offered little to a people who owed their power to the railroads and who, in distinction of achievement, had long since outdone the spike-drivers. Obviously the *Frescoes* laud a homegrown radicalism; they reject Leninism as sophisticated (and foreign); but they ignore the complex life of a modern people. Calling themselves frescoes and claiming a pictorial function, they fail to cover, as it were, the wall. They say almost nothing about what Americans do, or why.

Given pictorial form, they would pose as great an irrelevance—to Mr. Rockefeller's or anyone's city—as Diego Rivera with his intrusive Lenin.

MacLeish's next volume, *Poems 1924–1933,* not only reprinted the best of his work up to 1933 but also arranged it in nonchronological order. This order could form the subject of a separate study: it seems to indicate many of the relations which MacLeish intended to hold in balance between separate poems. The volume begins with the *Hamlet* and ends with *Conquistador,* the long poems most antithetical to each other as "private" and "public" documents. Scattered through it are previously uncollected pieces; at least six of these rank among the finest of his middle period, namely "The Night Dream," "Broken Promise," "Before March," "Epistle to Léon-Paul Fargue," "Invocation to the Social Muse," and "Lines for an Interment." A sardonic note recalling a few of the poems in *Streets in the Moon* comes up occasionally; of these six, "Invocation to the Social Muse" is the poem most ruled by it. In "Lines for an Interment" a similar note heard before in "Memorial Rain" is intensified into a savage agony. Elsewhere the tone is dispassionate, conveyed through imagery and syntax of a crystal precision reminiscent, almost, of Dryden's noble renderings of Horace and worthy of Landor or Housman at their most painstaking. Of this character are "Before March" and a slighter poem, "Voyage."

> Heap we these coppered hulls
> With headed poppies
> And garlic longed-for by the eager dead . . .

Such effects are concentrated in the poems having great intimacy of theme and voice.

The short volume *Public Speech: Poems* (1936) is strong in social implication, like MacLeish's plays in the same decade; but for part of its length it is different in manner from the usual "public" poetry. It ends with a series of ten poems in various lyric forms, assembled under the general title "The Woman on the Stair"; this, more than anything else in the volume, harks back to an earlier period. One thinks especially of "The Happy Marriage," which also is a series of this type: "The Woman on the Stair," too, is made up of meditative descriptions which chart an emotional relationship. Why should this sequence have been inserted in a book whose very title points to MacLeish's new preoccupation with what poetry can deliver to the public concerning themselves? The answer is that the adjective *public* is not synonymous with *national* or with *political* or with *cultural* in a social scientist's sense; it connotes all that is common, all that touches everyman. Those of MacLeish's poems that treat of the individual in society, or of society in history, do seem public in a more "communal" sense than is possible to a lyric commemoration of love; but this subject, too, can be so treated that its private values become general meanings. Moreover, the first poem in the volume, "Pole Star," celebrates social love, the observance of charity for all, as a guiding principle in an age of misdirections; almost the whole collection is about human bonds of feeling. What *public* meant to MacLeish at this juncture seems to have been dual: in one aspect it came close to our present slack sense of *relevant*; in another it rather implied *impersonal* in something like Eliot's sense, that is, marked by avoidance of self-absorption. In "The Woman on the Stair," personal subject matter becomes archetypal.

"The Woman on the Stair" is really about the psychology of love. The Eros who rules here is the god of maturity; it would be instructive to set beside this another group of lyrics, also a sequence and also a chronicle of love's progress, but focusing on youthful love—Joyce's *Chamber Music.* There the intensities of feeling wear romantic disguises which in turn undergo transformations into fabrics of symbol. Here, viewed alike from the masculine and the feminine sides, are the great intensities—need, selfishness, shame, jealousy, fickleness, boredom—and time's deadly gift, detachment, all of them functions of a pragmatism that often governs human relations in the mask of the romantic spirit.

This sobering vision culminates in the remarkable closing poem, "The Release," a meditation on past time as stasis. What "The Woman on the Stair" projects as a "cinema" sequence, a passional affair involving two people only, becomes in projection a far-reaching commentary on behavior and motivation.

Not only "Pole Star," concerning love, but several other poems at the beginning of *Public Speech* meditate contemporary bearings for traditional wisdom. "Speech to Those Who Say Comrade" defines true as against specious brotherhood. "Speech to the Detractors" rebukes debunkers and petty journalists and acclaims the love of excellence, arguing that a people unwilling to honor its outstanding men is a self-degrading people. "Speech to a Crowd" exhorts men to be self-reliant, not to wait on leadership, not to *be* a crowd. These poems, along with a few in the middle of the volume, may be too inspirational to appeal to readers who are moved by the psychological shrewdness of "The Woman on the Stair." One poem, "The German Girls! The German Girls!" (its title to be understood as a sardonic toast?), takes the form of a quasi-choric exchange and is therefore dramatic in structure though not in form. It damns the militaristic spirit by cataloguing the coarse, brutal, and perverted types that abound among the Nazis. Propaganda though this is, the poem remains fresh because it is dramatic and also because it escapes "pulpit diction."

Two separately published poems on social themes, *Land of the Free—U.S.A.* (1938) and *America Was Promises* (1939), both with topical bearing, relate to diverse areas of concern. The first is hard to judge as poetry because, as published, it was tied to a series of eighty-eight contemporary photographs in order that (according to a note by MacLeish) it might illustrate *them.* The photographs were already collected before the poem was written. The letterpress still makes a poem, but is at some disadvantage in proximity to the pictures. The two arts combine to tell a horrifying before-and-after story of the pioneer settlers in a rich land who, after many generations, have sunk into poverty and squalor through disease, over-crowding, economic exploitation, soil deterioration, industrialization, and all the rest. The horror is conveyed mainly by the impact of the photographs as a set, which embraces many contrasts; but the most distressing, i.e., pathetic, are far beyond the power of the poem to annotate. The pictures are violent, shocking; the poem is "cool," relying on irony. Certainly the contrasts are intrinsic to the two modes: photography is presentational, ruminative poetry representational. The style is itself cool, in form a kind of collective monologue; but the pronoun "we" serves also to make the voice impersonal, as if the speaker were radiobroadcasting the report of a disaster. MacLeish's use of a "broadcast announcer" voice was frequent in the 1930's. Whether radio was responsible directly (other poets having experimented with the same device—Auden, for example, and Eliot in "Triumphal March"), the fact that MacLeish had written radio plays, in which such a voice was normally essential, suggests that the medium exerted some influence. One problem with having this voice accompany a photographic series is that, *ex hypothesi,* it belongs to a subject confronting human objects seen by the camera, yet it purports to speak in the character of those objects, and this without so much as adopting their dialect.

America Was Promises is indisputably the most eloquent of the "public" poems. It contrives an absolute alliance between theme and voice; actually the theme helps to flesh the voice so that it surmounts its usual anonymity and acquires the solidity of a persona. Who the persona is is unclear, but what he is is obvious, a prophet but contemporary, a liberator but traditionalist, a revolutionary but sage. The working question asked is "America was promises to whom?"—one answered in several ways, by Jefferson, by John Adams (philosopher of usury for Pound's *Cantos*), by Thomas Paine, and finally in the oracular formula *"The promises are theirs who take them."* The rest of the poem beseeches the vast community of America to believe that unless they "take the promises" others will; but there is something inconclusive about this, for a rhetoric capable of sounding a call to arms seems to have been expended on a plea for faith. References to nations made captive by the Falange, the Germans, or the Japanese might imply something like a war message (the year being 1939); on the other hand, the historical material is of the sort that, unlike MacLeish, a Marxist would have exploited seditiously. In its intellectual ambiguity *America Was Promises* had much in common with the philosophy of the national administration at that period. So seen, of course, the poem is milder than the rhetoric of its conclusion: it is simply urging people to remain loyal to New Deal doctrines at home and American policy abroad. Really it is much better as a poem than as a message: for once, MacLeish's adaptation of St. J. Perse's geographic evocations seems precisely right.

The long lapse before the appearance of *Actfive and Other Poems* (1948) would itself suffice to set this volume apart. But the double circumstance of the war and MacLeish's public service, along with the new personal vitality he seems to have experienced at this time, may account for its energies. In spirit this book is fully postwar, and it contains the perceptions of a man who had worked within government and who now had a far more exact idea of the gulf between political dreams and reality. It is the book of his second renaissance. A number of the poems, quite apart from the title piece, are of immense interest technically. They range from "Excavation of Troy," an amusing metaphysical exercise in the slow manipulation of imagery and simile (in the mind of a drowsing girl her lover of many nights gone is like Troy buried under many intervening "layers"), to "What Must," a quick medley of narrative, dialogue, and meditation (telling virtually in a cataract of rhymes the events of a brief love idyl). Several of the poems are ideological: thus "Brave New World," a ballad to Jefferson in his grave (in the tradition of Yeats's "To a Shade") taunts postwar America for its indifference to the plight of nations still unliberated.

The title piece, "Actfive," was the most significant poem by MacLeish since the publication of his *Hamlet.* It does what a major work by a developing poet has to do: it clarifies the meaning of his previous major works in relation to one another, and it subjects to new form the world which his art is trying now to deal with. This poem relates to *The Pot of Earth,* to "Einstein," and to *The Hamlet of A. MacLeish*; and though quite intelligible independently of those, it gains depth and complexity by the relation. The general title, with the ranting manner of Part I, "The Stage All Blood . . ." brings the *Hamlet* to mind; "Actfive" continues, in a manner of speaking, the actions of that nightmarish poem, advancing them beyond the circle of a single protagonist's mind and showing that they involve all men.

Part I proclaims the death of God, of Kingship, and of Man deified—the last murdered by tyrants; and it appeals for one who can become in their stead "the hero in the play," a hero to restore not only peace but Eternity, the principle of very reason. Implicitly both *The Pot of Earth* and, at some distance, *Nobodaddy* are drawn upon here, the one for the indifference of the Absolute, the other for, as well, the human alienation from it. In turn both are implicitly criticized: they have too palely depicted the stark loathsomeness of the death which proud man has inherited. Part II, "The Masque of Mummers," parades before the reader an absurd train of expressionistic figures, nonheroes yet "each the Hero of the Age"; it is an age whose inhabitants, stripped of privacy and individuality, cling together as in a public amphitheater and witness a charade of social lies—those of the Science Hero, of the Boyo of Industry, of the Revolutionary Hero with the Book, of the Great Man, of the Victim Hero or "pimp of death," of the Visitor or dreamer of millennium, of the State or utopia, of the I or egotist-introspectionist, of the lonely Crowd. Part III, "The Shape of Flesh and Bone," identifies the sought hero at last; it is flesh and bone, unidealized, existential man, instinctive, physical, able to define the meaning of his universe to himself—man the transitory but in spirit indomitable. Archetypes present themselves: "The blinded gunner at the ford," an image borrowed presumably from Hemingway's *For Whom the Bell Tolls*; a profile of Franklin D. Roosevelt, "The responsible man . . . / [who] dies in his chair . . . / The war won, the victory assured"; and other images, of an invalid and a hostage. These exemplify the unposturing, unselfish performance of duty,

> Some duty to be beautiful and brave
> Owed neither to the world nor to the grave
>
> . . .
>
> But only to the flesh the bone.

The closing lines reaffirm the unutterable loneliness of man in his universe of death, but, like "Einstein," leave him with his inviolate creaturehood. It is ironic that "Actfive" should so circuitously return to the point insisted upon in "Einstein"; for it steers by the opposite pole, assuming that man's lordly reason, far from having subdued nature to its understanding, has been dethroned utterly. Equally, the animal self here, which can still "endure and love," is all that preserves man from destruction; whereas in "Einstein" it is the only thing that debars him from godhead.

Collected Poems 1917–1952 incorporates a section of "New Poems" which might have made a book by themselves. They protract the *Actfive* renaissance (indeed it has lasted MacLeish into old age). Some half-dozen of them are modern "emblem" poems, being dominated by single images (often elaborated) with connotative value. Blake's "Ah! Sun-flower" is analogous; in MacLeish's "Thunderhead" the physics of lightning symbolizes an aspect of conjugal behavior; in; "Starved Lovers" chrysanthemums symbolize sensuality; in "The Linden Branch" a green bough is metaphorically a musical instrument playing silent music. The newness of this effect consists in the way whole poems are now built round it, as Emily Dickinson's or (using symbol rather than metaphor) Yeats's often are. Yeats, who was to become a major inspiration for MacLeish, must have influenced the style of the end poem of "New Poems," the meditation on metaphor "Hypocrite Auteur," which essentially offers a justification for the effect.

Songs for Eve (1954) really consists of two collections joined together: first the twenty-eight tight, riddling poems (corresponding to the days of the month?) called "Songs for Eve"; then "Twenty-One Poems" of miscellaneous kinds. Despite the general title of the initial set, some of its pieces are for Eve but others are for Adam, the Serpent, the Green Tree, Eve's children, and so on. Perhaps in some sense all indeed are "for" Eve, she being central in the mythic context. Like Yeats's Crazy Jane, Eve is carnal and vicariously creative—in short, Blakean. Through her, Adam is enabled to wake from animality into consciousness; with her, he falls upward "from earth to God," his soul growing as the awareness within his body, his children succeeding him as rebels and creators destined to rear, in place of the Green Tree of consciousness, the Dry Tree (the Cross) of godlike knowledge. The theme is that of *Nobodaddy* enriched with that of "Einstein." The twenty-eighth poem ends the sequence by lauding "man / That immortal order can"; and in like manner the last of the "Twenty-One Poems," entitled "Reasons for Music" and dedicated to Wallace Stevens, defines the poet's task as the imposition of form upon the fluid world (a theme of Stevens' own; MacLeish would ordinarily refer to the *discovery* of natural, intrinsic order, except probably in the aesthetic or the moral sphere). The fine keynote poem "The Infinite Reason" paraphrases "Songs for Eve" in effect by speaking of the human mission to read meaning in external reality.

> Our human part is to redeem the god
> Drowned in this time of space, this space
> That time encloses.

Clearly the leading theme of *Songs for Eve,* the whole book, is man's ordering function; the collection is closer to "Einstein" and the other space-time poems of *Streets in the Moon* than are the works in between. Here much is made of the origin of the human soul within space-time, particularly in "Reply to Mr. Wordsworth," where the proposition that the soul "cometh from afar" is refuted by an appeal to Einsteinian physics and—paradoxically—to the felt life of the emotions. The poems "Infiltration of the Universe," "The Wood Dove at Sandy Spring," "The Wave," "Captivity of the Fly," and "The Genius" are emblematic, and they happen also to compose a miniature bestiary. The volume pays tribute impartially to matters of intellect and of feeling; these compressed parables divide between them.

The Wild Old Wicked Man (1968) explores the whole scale of MacLeish's concerns, still optimistically. Old age and youth, time, domesticity, contemporary manners, love, death—these predominate. Introspection is not overworked, but two of the most arresting poems in the volume are "Autobiography," on childhood vision, and "Tyrant of Syracuse," on the subliminal self. In a memorable group of elegies, MacLeish bids farewell to Sandburg, Cummings, Hemingway, and Edwin Muir. The Hemingway poem, only eleven lines long, is one of numerous tributes paid by MacLeish to that onetime friend; it adapts Yeat's concept of "the dreaming back" for a skillful and moving analysis of the unity of the man Hemingway in his life and death. The Muir poem quotes "The Linden Branch," applying to a *green memory* the graceful conceit of the green bough as a musical staff with leaves for notes. Yeats furnished the title of the volume; and the title poem, placed at the end, closes on the theme of

> . . . the old man's triumph, to pursue
> impossibility—and take it, too,

which is a signature for MacLeish's poetry, restating the theme of Adam victorious, fallen upwards into a stasis of art and eternity.

As playwright, MacLeish began with closet drama, with *Nobodaddy* (not to forget the rhetorically lively dramatic poem "Our Lady of Troy" behind that). Though excellent as a trial of philosophical drama, such a work could not have taught him much; thus the strength of his first stage play, *Panic* (1935), is very impressive. For the dialogue, as he explains in a prefatory note, he chose a five-accent line in free (or sprung) rhythm; other passages, those of a choric nature allotted to various supplementary voices, he wrote in three-accent lines. The experiment was contemporary with Eliot's *Murder in the Cathedral*; and while MacLeish's verse shows less flexibility than Eliot's there, it is at least as stageworthy. The play is an admirable and curious hybrid. In sum, it is an Aristotelian tragedy with a special catastrophe, the withdrawal of the supporting characters' loyalty (the protagonist, a great man, suddenly ceases to be accepted as that); and this plot is superimposed on a proletarian drama conveyed by expressionistic techniques (anonymous voices of the poor and unemployed in a time of financial crisis). It is the unemployed who make the protagonist's fellow bankers lose confidence in him; and not what he does because of pride, but his vulnerability to the hatred of the mob because of who he is, precipitates the "panic" causing his downfall. The play remains solidly in the classic tradition; for the protagonist, the super-banker McGafferty (the play was first called "J. P. McGafferty"), possesses nobility of spirit and authentic powers of leadership: he really could avert his country's economic collapse if his colleagues would rally round him and pool their resources instead of defaulting. Their refusal to do so might support a "proletarian" interpretation, but in fact the whole botch happens because the proletariat prophesy that it will, when they invade his office and one of their number (a blind "Tiresias") pronounces his doom. "Proletarian" is converted into "psychological." The weakness in *Panic* consists in the unintegrated role of the feminine lead, McGafferty's mistress, Ione, who exercises only a reflector function of emphasizing his arrogance. Her role is crucial theatrically, but in structure the play suffers from it.

In his foreword to *The Fall of the City* (1937), MacLeish discussed the advantages of radio as a medium for verse drama. Looking back a third of a century, one must now regret bitterly the lost opportunities for this genre, which was killed when, in America, radio was killed by television. MacLeish's claims for radio verse were not exaggerated, but the moment was wrong and the remaining time too short. His own early contributions, notably this play and its successor *Air Raid* (1938), have, alas, chiefly a memorial importance. *The Fall of the City,* in which the radio announcer's unique function as described by MacLeish is essential, appears to follow expressionistic models. The Announcer, the Dead Woman, the Messenger, the Orator, as voices bring the most presentational style into the most presentational medium. The poetry has absolute immediacy: since it must express action, it hews to what happens, never deviating into mere lyricism. The techniques are of the simplest: the play employs the unity of (supposed) place, with everything taking place under the Announcer's eyes. *Air Raid* is at once more realistic in terms of radio drama, and more conventional—although less realistic in one sense, for it uses the "newsreel" technique of picking up scenes at which the Announcer is not present. And in this play the poetry ranges away from the main action, as the characters' feelings digress from their imminent danger, so that it has a more various texture. Both plays use a poetry of vivid images and plain colloquialism. In *The Fall of the City* the unit is a line of varying length in sprung rhythm; in *Air Raid* it is a line of five or, less commonly, fewer accents.

When, in the postwar television age, MacLeish returned to radio verse drama tentatively, it was with recognition of its anachroills tic status. He called *The Trojan Horse* (1952) a play for broadcasting or for reading without scenery (i.e., like Dylan Thomas' *Under Milk Wood*). It is a one-act piece with one moment of high drama, when Helen realizes that the wooden horse contains those who will destroy her happiness. Otherwise the speeches seem unduly level—a problem in the play for voices, which often thus depends on elocutionary artifice for sharp characterizations. The verse line is of three accents, except in formal speeches, where blank verse occurs. In place of an announcer, there is a brief prologue in which a "modern" voice calls upon an "ancient" voice (Homer) to explain the action; within the play there are a blind man (also Homer) and a girl, whose dialogue serves for choric commentary. This structure foreshadows *J.B.* The effect is of a kind of Chinese-boxes perspective. *This Music Crept by Me upon the Waters* (1953) has been staged as well as broadcast. It is conversational, with no fewer than ten characters filling the one act; they speak a three-accent verse a little like Eliot's in *The Cocktail Party,* but with less straddling from line to line and much tighter rhythm. The people are contemporary, the setting Caribbean, a Paradise island like Prospero's; the theme is the impossibility of a return to innocence and Eden, except for saints or primitives. Others, the romantics, sink into dreams but soon are recalled to reality; still others, the merely idle, are overwhelmed with boredom and drink. The play chides the rich and irresponsible who demand Eden without earning it.

J.B.: A Play in Verse (1958) and *Herakles* (1967) are respectively based on the book of Job and on the Greek hero myth; between them they represent man suffering and acting. J.B. is a King Lear who, divested of all illusions about a benevolent universe, is taught to endure and love, like the survivors in *Actfive.* Herakles is an Einstein mastering nature, a Cain seeking godhead, confronted finally by the limits of human power and made to see his mere humanity. *J.B.* is constructed as a play within a play, with a remote director-prompter as deity offstage. The God and Satan of the scriptural drama are here impersonated by actor-clowns, Zuss the circus balloon-vendor and Nickles the popcorn-seller, who first stage a play in the deserted circus tent and then become involved in it as chorus for J.B.'s tribulation. J.B. triumphs both over Zuss's humiliation of him and Nickles' temptation to hatred. Learning the truth about his god, he forgives him his injustice. With a love stronger than the unreasoning tyranny of heaven, he justifies that love by beginning to live again when his torment is finished.

Against this eloquent, superbly theatrical play, *Herakles* seems brittle; yet, fantasy though it is, it is founded on a sacred and profound myth. A modern scientist, Professor Hoadley, has received international recognition for his discoveries. Symbolically he is Herakles, his work for human knowledge and power analogous to the hero's labors. His wife corresponds to Herakles' wife, Megara. The analogy extends to the Hoadleys' son, effeminate and hostile, alienated by his father's profession; he represents the sons slaughtered by Herakles in his overweening frenzy after returning from the underwold. If, like Euripides' play (from which MacLeish drew hints), this action begins as a triumph in Act I, it continues as a fantasy of pathos. In Act II Mrs. Hoadley and Megara occupy the stage together, as their two worlds of history and myth interpenetrate and the myth is shown as eternal meaning: Herakles' homecoming and his reunion with the mother of his dead children, at once the repetition and archetype of Professor Hoadley's (the two parts are presumably doubled in production), become symbolic of the mere ruin of life to which the Promethean hero is condemned. He obeys the necessity of fighting evil and harnessing power for man's welfare, but he is destroyed by hatred and the unnatural burden of godhead.

Herakles and *J.B.* show Janus faces of the human struggle to neutralize the blind sentence of death passed upon mankind. Their two scales of poetry, exemplifying MacLeish's maturest talents, correspond to extremes of lyricism and tragic realism in speech.

The prose drama *Scratch* (1971), amplifying Stephen Vincent Benét's 1936 story "The Devil and Daniel Webster," creates a parable with ethical overtones of "Actfive" as well as the Blakean exaltation of Liberty over Law. The story, transformed by MacLeish, achieves a certain mythic dimension, not really because it deals with inveterate problems of American life, though it can indeed symbolize these as MacLeish's "Foreword" contends, but because its hero, Daniel Webster, thinks and acts as if, obedient to a categorical imperative, he embodied the meaning of civilization: he is a type of Prometheus. This strong drama involves a more complex system of implication than *J.B.* Its actual events reduce to a simple linear form. They begin with the leveling of charges against Webster by two accusers, a moral New Englander (Webster's friend Peterson) and the Devil himself (Scratch). They continue with Scratch's attempt to "foreclose" the soul of Jabez Stone, who has bartered it for seven years' good luck. They end with Jabez's legal defense by Webster before a ghostly judge and jury consisting of thirteen dead and damned enemies of American freedom. In the story by Benét, Webster is pure lawyer: he argues successfully on behalf of Jabez that the terrible forfeit must be ruled null and void because the Devil, as a foreign potentate, cannot exercise dominion over a freeborn American citizen. In MacLeish's version, a protagonist more like the historical Webster appears, who has to argue both Jabez's case and *his own*—the latter amounting, in fact, to the whole substance of the drama. The charges against Webster in *Scratch* concern his alleged expedient "sell-out" of Liberty to preserve the American Union, through his adoption of the Compromise of 1850; in accepting the Fugitive Slave Law, he seems a traitor to his fundamental axiom "Liberty and Union, now and forever, one and inseparable." When the jurymen bring in a verdict favorable to Jabez, they do so because touched by Webster's *argumentum ad hominem,* his appeal to their own sense of the "huge injustice" of man's life and death. In particular this appeal holds that every man, even such as the feckless Jabez, owns the Liberty to alleviate his poverty, his suffering, without being accountable to the strictness of the Law. Webster's argument itself is a sufficient reply to his accusers: it demonstrates his devotion to Liberty but does not undermine his resolution as a statesman. Accordingly the jury's verdict (like that of any audience) finds not only for Jabez but also for Webster as, in effect, a co-defendant; and in purely dramatic, theatrical terms the "case" against Webster ends simultaneously with the suit against Jabez Stone. In the forum of history, as Webster sadly acknowledges, the charges against him for accepting the Fugitive Slave Law remain unquashed. MacLeish, too, seems to believe that the historical Webster erred; but in *Scratch,* paradoxically, he arrays against his protagonist only two accusers, the Father of Lies and a New England Abolitionist.

Scratch is a lively drama and a moving one. Yet it had only a brief New York run in 1971. Perhaps, in the years between *J.B.* and *Scratch,* the strong, representative or mythic hero went out of fashion. Perhaps the improvident blasphemer Jabez Stone, if glorified as an antihero, would better have fitted the occasion. Perhaps *Scratch* is both too intellectual and too highly civilized (and patriotic) for the American theatre of the 1970's.

MacLeish from the beginning has held to a course of lonely exploration. His standards are classical and aristocratic. Once his friend Mark Van Doren, presented with an award for "services to poetry," responded with slow and deliberate emphasis that, as for himself, he had tried to serve only the *best* poetry. The remark could have been made by Archibald MacLeish with equally merited pride (the pride which knows the humility exacted by such service) and with equal truth. Part of his devotion has been accorded to craftsmanship. One can praise poets for this, not too much, certainly, but with too much exclusiveness. Often when one has praised it, in Frost or Stevens or Eliot, say, or in Rimbaud, it does not seem sufficient. This century still paddles in the backwash of Aestheticism; but there have been ages, before the subjectivist era, when poetry and the other arts pertained to the things of man—Cicero's *artes quae ad humanitatem pertinent*—and not just to one man's special quirk of vision, to express which he devises exquisite forms. Part of MacLeish's devotion has gone to the human state. Such concern is not poetry, but one is entitled to ask whether, without it, good poetry, let alone the best, can come into being. It must be set down that MacLeish, like the great poets—Yeats, for example—has striven to give form to what pertains not just to himself but to his fellow men.

Selected Bibliography

WORDS OF ARCHIBALD MacLEISH

POETRY

Songs for a Summer's Day (A Sonnet-Cycle), (New Haven, Conn.: Yale University Press, 1915).

Tower of Ivory, with a foreword by Lawrence Mason (New Haven, Conn.: Yale University Press, 1917).

The Happy Marriage, and Other Poems, (Boston and New York: Houghton Mifflin, 1924).

The Pot of Earth, (Boston and New York: Houghton Mifflin, 1925).

Streets in the Moon, (Boston and New York: Houghton Mifflin, 1926).

The Hamlet of A. MacLeish, (Boston and New York: Houghton Mifflin, 1928).

New Found Land: Fourteen Poems, (Boston and New York: Houghton Mifflin, 1930).

Conquistador, (Boston and New York: Houghton Mifflin, 1932).

Frescoes for Mr. Rockefeller's City, (New York: John Day, 1933).

Poems 1924–1933, (Boston and New York: Houghton Mifflin, 1933).

Public Speech: Poems, (New York: Farrar and Rinehart, 1936).

Land of the Free—U.S.A., (New York: Harcourt, Brace, 1938).

America Was Promises, (New York: Duell, Sloan and Pearce, 1939).

Actfive and Other Poems, (New York: Random House, 1948).

Collected Poems 1917–1952, (Boston: Houghton Mifflin, 1952).

Songs for Eve, (Boston: Houghton Mifflin, 1954).

The Wild Old Wicked Man, and Other Poems, (Boston: Houghton Mifflin, 1968).

The Human Season: Selected Poems, (Boston: Houghton Mifflin, 1972).

PLAYS

Nobodaddy: A Play, (Cambridge, Mass.: Dunster House, 1926).

Union Pacific—A Ballet, Produced 1934; published in *The Book of Ballets,* edited by Gerald Goode (New York: Crown, 1939).

Panic: A Play in Verse, (Boston and New York: Houghton Mifflin, 1935).

The Fall of the City: A Verse Play for Radio, (New York and Toronto: Farrar and Rinehart, 1937).

Air Raid: A Verse Play for Radio, (New York: Harcourt, Brace, 1938).

The States Talking, In *The Free Company Presents . . . A Collection of Plays about the Meaning of America* (New York: Dodd, Mead, 1941).

The American Story: Ten Broadcasts, (New York: Duell, Sloan and Pearce, 1944).

The Trojan Horse: A Play, (Boston: Houghton Mifflin, 1952).

This Music Crept by Me upon the Waters, (Cambridge, Mass.: Harvard University Press, 1953).

J.B.: A Play in Verse, (Boston: Houghton Mifflin, 1958).

Three Short Plays: The Secret of Freedom, Air Raid, The Fall of the City, (New York: Dramatists Play Service, 1961).

Herakles: A Play in Verse, (Boston: Houghton Mifflin, 1967).

Scratch, Suggested by Stephen Vincent Benét's short story "The Devil and Daniel Webster," (Boston: Houghton Mifflin, 1971).

PROSE

Housing America, by the Editors of *Fortune* (New York: Harcourt, Brace, 1932). Written by MacLeish.

Jews in America, by the Editors of *Fortune* (New York: Random House, 1936). Written by MacLeish.

Background of War, by the Editors of *Fortune* (New York: Knopf, 1937). Of the six articles in this collection, all but the third were written by MacLeish.

The Irresponsibles: A Declaration, (New York: Duell, Sloan and Pearce, 1941).

The American Cause, (New York: Duell, Sloan and Pearce, 1941).

A Time to Speak: The Selected Prose of Archibald MacLeish, (Boston: Houghton Mifflin, 1941).

American Opinion and the War, (Cambridge, Mass.: Harvard University Press, 1942).

A Time to Act: Selected Addresses, (Boston: Houghton Mifflin, 1943).

Poetry and Opinion; The Pisan Cantos of Ezra Pound: A Dialog on the Role of Poetry, (Urbana: University of Illinois Press, 1950).

Freedom Is the Right to Choose: An Inquiry into the Battle for the American Future, (Boston: Beacon Press, 1951).

Poetry and Experience, (Boston: Houghton Mifflin, 1961).

The Eleanor Roosevelt Story, (Boston: Houghton Mifflin, 1965).

A Continuing Journey, (Boston: Houghton Mifflin, 1968).

Champion of a Cause: Essays and Addresses on Librarianship, compiled and with an introduction by Eva M. Goldschmidt (Chicago: American Library Association, 1971).

AUTOBIOGRAPHY

The Dialogues of Archibald MacLeish and Mark Van Doren, edited by Warren V. Bush (New York: Dutton, 1964).

BIBLIOGRAPHY

Mizener, Arthur, *A Catalogue of the First Editions of Archibald MacLeish,* (New Haven, Conn.: Yale University Press, 1938).

CRITICISM

Falk, Signi Lenea, *Archibald MacLeish,* (New York: Twayne, 1965).

James Merrill
(1926–1995)

J. D. McCLATCHY

In 1939, when James Merrill was thirteen, his parents divorced. Because his father was a powerful financier, the co-founder of the famous brokerage house of Merrill, Lynch, and the man who had turned down President Roosevelt's request that he become secretary of the treasury, the divorce trial was front-page news, even in *The New York Times.* Its effect on the child was sad but not extraordinary—except insofar as it came to shape one of the most imaginative and esteemed poetic minds in American literature.

James Merrill was born in New York City on March 3, 1926, the son of Charles E. Merrill and his second wife, Hellen Ingram. His privileged childhood was passed in a city brownstone and a Long Island estate. "It strikes me now maybe," he told me in an interview (collected in *Recitative*) in 1982, "that during much of my childhood I found it difficult to *believe* in the way my parents lived. They seemed so utterly taken up with engagements, obligations, ceremonies. . . . The excitement, the emotional quickening *I* felt in those years came usually through animals or nature, or through the servants in the house—Colette knew all about that—whose lives seemed by contrast to make such perfect *sense.*" He was sent to St. Bernard's and Lawrenceville, and then enrolled at Amherst College, his father's alma mater. During college, he took a year off to serve in the Army, and graduated with the class of 1947, having written his undergraduate thesis on Proust. He taught at Bard College in 1948, and at various later times has taught briefly at Amherst, the University of Wisconsin, Washington University in St. Louis, and Yale University. Merrill was elected to the American Institute of Arts and Letters in 1971, and raised to the more exclusive Academy in 1989. He has been awarded honorary degrees from Amherst and Yale, and in 1986 was named Poet Laureate of Connecticut. In 1954, he moved with his companion David Jackson to Stonington, Connecticut, a picturesque seacoast village; they purchased a building on Water Street, restored its upper floors, and have lived there ever since. For two decades starting in 1964, Merrill and Jackson spent part of each year in Greece; since 1979 they have wintered in Key West. His different homes, and the displacements and discoveries of his travels, are the subject of many poems. But the domestic focus of his work has at its heart—in ways both overt and implicit, descriptive and symbolic—the wrenching upheaval of his adolescence: the divorce.

It would be absurd to reduce Merrill's genius to any formula. In fact, if any word describes his temperament, it is "mercurial." If any word describes the shape of his career, it is "surprising." Few readers would have anticipated that the author of Merrill's early books, with their exquisite, highly wrought lyrics, would have come to write *The Changing Light at Sandover* (1982), a gigantic and unnerving epic poem. But both those early lyrics and that late epic—along with the narratives and meditations of his middle period—resolve to a phrase used about Merrill's work by Mirabell, one of the characters in the poet's Ouija board trilogy. The strange voice wants to usurp Merrill's, but promises to return him to his "CHRONICLES OF LOVE & LOSS." There is no better description of Merrill's achievement than that, not least because it stresses the autobiographical and narrative thrust of Merrill's work, his sense of a life lived and understood over time, and also because it links this poet's two great themes, love and loss. Love is not fully itself until it is lost, until it becomes memory, becomes art.

Again and again, in small poems and large, Merrill returns to the greatest loss of love in his life—that occasioned by his parents' divorce. It is as if that split threw into stronger relief a personality split in the poet himself. Certainly his mind prefers doubled perspectives, prefers to be "of two minds" about all matters. And the elegant tensions in his work derive from characteristics we may as well call paternal and maternal. Merrill is as much his mother's boy as he is his father's son, as much the heir to Father Time as to Mother Nature. Mind and style, reason and sensation, idea and fact, America and Europe, Connecticut and Athens, German and French, verse and language, legend and realism—the list could be extended through nearly every impulse in the poems, which tingle with such opposition. But Merrill's ambition is not merely to display the two aspects of his personality, but to reconcile them, as the child's fantasy is to reconcile his warring parents. Merrill's own image for this is the Broken Home, and the truest energies of his work derive from his effort—and they extend from the delicacies of metaphor to the creation of an entire cosmological mythology—to unite or harmonize the sides of his life those opposing tendencies represent. Plato says that Love's child is the son of Need and Resource; just so, both the obsessions and inventions at the heart of Merrill's poetry must be attended to. The poet's homosexuality, which is at times his subject and always an influence on his work, may likewise be viewed as a kind of ambivalence, both a need and a resource. But this is to leap ahead. Little of this was apparent at the start of Merrill's career—or it is apparent only in retrospect. *His First Poems* (1951) were only jeweled examples of the period style; the poet had not yet found his distinctive voice.

On the back of *First Poem's* dust jacket, the publisher advertised recent books by three of its other authors: John Crowe Ransom, Elinor Wylie, and Wallace Stevens. In retrospect, it does not seem an accidental grouping; though not his most important models and certainly not his most enduring, each of these poets did have a crucial bearing on Merrill's early work. In the late 1940's Ransom was the courtly dean of the New Critics, who insisted that a poem represented an action, that its dramatic effects were extensions of its voice, that it unfolded its meanings not by way of discursive logic but by way of an expressive complex of images. The sort of poem that Ransom favored, indeed that was of the prevailing fashion in which Merrill was schooled, most nearly resembled the creative mind itself: sedulous, self-reflective, allusively cultured, having an aloof integrity and an evident, though not necessarily apparent, continuity between its manifold surfaces and its unconscious depths or motives.

What was clear from the start and has remained a hallmark of Merrill's career is the sensuous allure of his work's textures, the lapidary brilliance of its imagery, the fluent, refined eloquence of its tone—qualities that complement its thought-provoking designs. This is a side, a decorum of his poetry for whose source Merrill himself has pointed to Elinor Wylie, the first of his maternal muses and models. Rather than her sentimental temperament, it was the glazed perfection of her technique that attracted the young Merrill—the miniaturist' s adroit prosodic skill, the variety of her gleaming lyric forms. He may even have acquired from Wylie's many expert examples his own enthusiasm for the sonnet form, prominent in his work from his fledgling efforts to the virtuosic instances throughout the trilogy, entitled *The Changing Light at Sandover* (1982). Whatever his individual success with the form, his most interesting use of it is the sonnet sequences that make up longer single poems. Among them are several of his pivotal poems, "The Broken Home" and "Matinees" from *Nights and Days* (1966) and *The Fire Screen* (1969) respectively, and it is curious to note that Merrill returns to the sonnet when dealing with his own childhood, as if he associated the form with its ability both to release and control his autobiographical impulses.

The influence of Wallace Stevens is more difficult to summarize because it is more extensive and profound. Stevens endowed Merrill with the joint legacy of Emerson and the symbolists, along with a vocabulary by turns playful and severe, gaudy and abstract, by means of which a poem might seem both charged with thought and absolved from it. That vocabulary, and the exotic or painterly particulars it attended, gave shape to a world Merrill quickly found himself at home in, a world in which the distinction between idea and image is dissolved in metaphor. Without embarrassment or swagger, Stevens had made the creative acts of the imagination the central subject of art; and throughout his career Merrill, too, has turned to the formalities of art and the dreamy play of language, to the mind and the "theater of trope," as types of what George Santayana called "the primary tendencies of our nature and the ultimate possibilities of our soul."

The title *First Poems* is neither as straightforward nor as modest as it seems. In fact, the book was Merrill's third. The first, privately printed at his father's expense in 1942, was *Jim's Book*—fifteen poems, eight stories and sketches, an essay on Wylie, and two translations of Baudelaire. The work is remarkably precocious for an author just sixteen, displaying a felicity of diction and conceit. If his range is narrow, usually limited to the Great Themes, that is compensated for by a delicate and winning sophistication. Four years later his second book, *The Black Swan,* was privately published in Athens. Five of its twelve poems were reprinted a few years later in *First Poems,* and they are the first manifestation of Merrill's adult voice. There is here a fresh wit that gives a poem surprising depth, but his elaborately devised metrical schemes and the top-heavy momentum of glittering details tend to obscure the motives and meaning of the poems. Still, there is a confidence and polish and intelligence at work that are remarkable for a poet not yet out of college, and several features of the book anticipate Merrill's later interests. The contrast between the perceived and reflected worlds is one recurrent theme. And when the speaker of these poems is not invoking a beloved or lost lyrical "you," he usually addresses a child. It is a role Merrill will himself often assume later, and a figure that fascinates him all along. Here the child stands in for a number of possibilities: the innocent soul, the as-yet-unrealized or idealized self, an image of power, a type of the artist, and the agent of love itself, as Eros. *The Black Swan*'s attention is directed mainly at love and its aftermath: on the necessity and impossibility of love, and on the passage of love into memory and art. Clearly, Merrill chose, or had been chosen by, his principal themes from the beginning.

As a title, then, *First Poems* is a misleading description. But it was never meant to be merely that. Instead, it pays homage by way of allusion, an intentionally doubled echo of Rainer Maria Rilke's *Erste Gedichte* and Stéphane Mallarmé's *Premiers Poèmes.* Characteristically, Merrill is turning toward an older heritage and singling out both a French and a German affinity. Temperamentally, Merrill cannot be identified with either of his predecessors. His wry wit has forestalled the stark exaltation of Rilke's "Aufsingen"; his sociable irony and critical intelligence have kept him from assuming a role as ascetic, even as sacerdotal, as Mallarmé's.

The type of poem Merrill first wrote declares his marked preference for—to borrow a distinction from W. H. Auden—"mythological" rather than "occasional" poetry; that is, for poems whose overt subjects are universal and impersonal, and whose personal or historical occasions are latent. Of course, throughout his career, Merrill has been drawn to traditional or local myths, indeed, has been obsessed by certain of them; in his later work he has discovered or devised the archetypal dimensions of his past, and in the trilogy he has elaborated a grand mythology for the life of his mind and heart. But in the literal sense of Auden's term, a "mythological" poetry is a wise preference for the young poet especially, whose private feelings and ideas lack the significance that years of living will earn. The myths Merrill sought in Mallarmé and Rilke—the myth of The Word, and the myth of Experience, the one a transformation of the world into art, the other a transumption of art by the world—together constitute the economy of suffering and wisdom, of loss and transcendence that characterizes *First Poems.* Undoubtedly too Merrill was drawn to Rilke's powers of concentration on the immanent significance of unlikely humble details; it is a quality Merrill later picks out for praise in the work of Eugenio Montale and Elizabeth Bishop. And he learned from Mallarmé's array of exquisite images how to evoke rather than explain: things are known by their essences (as Merrill puts it later, an image is that dram of essence distilled from the flowering field of experience), but defined by their effects. It is evident, too, from the most ambitious of these *First Poems* that he had studied Mallarmé's art of blocking poems into episodes of tone and rhythm on the analogy of musical composition. And although it is more apparent later on—in the hermeticism of *Nights and Days* and *Braving the Elements* (1972), where the world becomes text—even in *First Poems* Merrill fashions a poetic language on the principle that words create rather than record their subject, that poems are suggestive networks of elliptical but complementary images.

Among the most appealing poems in the book are a series of emblematic meditations on the poet's lot: "The Black Swan," "The Parrot," "The Pelican," and "The Peacock." "Transfigured Bird" has the last word on the matter. The poem is a series of four fables, done in terza rima. In the first, a "child fond of natural things"—a literalist, one might call him—discovers "the eggshell of appearance," broken but glowing, pearly within and blue (the imagination's color) without. In the second section, an older child's microscope examines the fertile yolk's "point of blood," which hatches a "throbbing legend" in his mind. These two planes, the discernible and the unseen, the literal and imaginary, are brought together, sharply and unsettlingly, in the long third section with the introduction of Philippa, a "belle dame sans merci"; her beauty is a thoughtless, regressive power:

. . . I must begin
To tell her of this music in my touch:

Of God who like a little boy with a pin
Shall prick a hole in either end of the sky
And blow it clean away, the thing within,

Away, before it waste, or hatching fly
Out of his reach in noisy solitude,
Or kill him with the oracle of its eye;

Blow all away, the yolk with its X of blood,
The shelves of jewels away, this drowsing girl
At whose hand, away, the shapely animals fed;

Till the egg is void of all but pearl-on-pearl
Reflections and their gay meanderings;
Shall, tiring, burst the shell, let the fragments whirl.

"Transfigured Bird" argues that the world imagined is the ultimate good. That argument, however, is neither justified by much practical testimony nor proposed with any absolute conviction. In part, Merrill has not yet discovered the true scope of its exigencies and cost, and certainly not explored its often wrenching autobiographical entanglements. The majority of poems in this first book, by their very protocols, are designed to inhibit such discoveries. Still, the tensions tell. And the two best poems in this volume, "Variations: White Stag, Black Bear" (a poem dedicated to the poet's father) and "Variations: The air is sweetest that a thistle guards," succeed largely because Merrill loosens his metrical grip and allows himself more leeway to develop the implications of his subject. These are more restless and ambitious poems, and wander closer to psychic currents that churn beneath the surface of *First Poems.*

Eight years elapsed between *First Poems* and the publication of *The Country of a Thousand Years of Peace* (1959), the longest interval between any two of his collections. During that time, Merrill both traveled around the world (and introduced exotic observations into poems) and settled into Stonington, Connecticut, a small coastal village that prompted a more domestic focus in his poems. He had also written a novel and two plays, and this experience helped him toward a more fluent and inflected line, a more credible and versatile address. The poems in this volume translate the play of mind into the feints of a voice now talking to itself, now explaining to a sympathetic listener. Some of the energy and props of fiction support his new work as well. A superior narrative skill braces these poems; rhetorical questions, private jokes, lapses and leaps are combined into episodic, *knowing* accounts that rely on the quirks of character and events, instead of image and hypothesis, to catch up the poem's thematic intentions. There is a technical advance as well in *The Country of a Thousand Years of Peace,* more sparkle and salt, the mercurial play of mind that comes with technical control. There is a corresponding obliquity too; many of the poems are darkly inspired and unyielding. Not until *Water Street* (1962) do his poems show a clear-eyed understanding and ironic appreciation of themselves. But here he seems to hesitate before the new and surprising depths he has discovered.

Despite their alluring or even learned trappings, many poems in this book pursue what one of them calls "the inner adventure." "Fire Poem" is one. It takes up the conflict between passion and intelligence, between ardor and ashes, the song of once-burned innocence and twice-shy experience. At one point the fire itself speaks:

If as I am you know me bright and warm,
It is while matter bears, which I live by,
For very heart the furnace of its form:
By likeness and from likeness in my storm
Sheltered, can all things change and
changing be
The rare bird bedded at the heart of harm.

Merrill is writing here about the symbolic function of language to reclaim and transform phenomena, a point he also makes in "The Doodler," whose speaker idly sketches a world of figures on the page's white void.

The fullest version of this presiding theme is to be found in the several poems that deal with "glassen surfaces." In "The Octopus," for example, the "vision asleep in the eye's tight translucence" is compared to an octopus behind an aquarium's plate glass. In another poem, "Some Negatives: X. at the Chateau," the eye is replaced by a camera lens and its "images of images." On the other side of the looking glass, the life beneath the life is deeply ambivalent and disturbing, a sometimes threatening source of psychological and emotional engulfment. "In the Hall of Mirrors" takes up the problem of reproduction, and the mirror as the Edenic, silvery version of the self. But the book's best-known poem, "Mirror," is Merrill's fullest account of the dilemma. The poem is a dramatic monologue in the voice of a tall standing mirror, addressed to the wide-open window opposite. It can be read as a debate between the reflective mind and the perceiving eye, or between a perfected but stale art and natural, generational life. But the poem is too astute to deal exclusively with such standard contrasts. Instead, it is a brooding study of frustration and transfiguration. Instead of taking Merrill's preferred role of vulnerable child or artist, the mirror's disembodied voice is that of a surrogate parent, growing old "under an intensity / Of questioning looks." The question is "*how to live*"—how to come to life, as well as how rightly to live. Between its moralizing prologue and epilogue is a compressed, novelistic account of the mirror's "children," who stand before it with their secrets. As time slowly blisters away the mirror's backing—making it into a sort of window—it yields to a higher power, "a faceless will, / Echo of mine." The self accepts determinism *and* exaltation, experience *and* language. It is increasingly characteristic of Merrill's work, here as in later, more accomplished poems, to work not with a set of opposites but with a series of dissolves. The reader is invited to watch the poem's subject through a constantly shifting framework.

Some critics take *Water Street* to be Merrill's decisive collection, the first evidence of his mature style. That distinction more likely belongs to his next book, *Nights and Days,* but the best poems in *Water Street* brilliantly predict the subsequent shift. Like Marcel Proust, this book's presiding mentor, Merrill here seeks in childhood, in family or domestic scenes, the sources of his poetic strength. There is a new attention to motivation, the use of involuntary memories, a heightened awareness of the imperfection of the present and the transience of the past. *Water Street* is in some ways a slighter book than *The Country of a Thousand Years of Peace,* but its strongest work—"An Urban Convalescence," "A Tenancy," and "Scenes of Childhood"—have an autobiographical emphasis and circumstantial intimacy unlike anything he had written before. The best of his earlier style—its brio, its lavish textures and paradoxes—remains in *Water Street,* but the poet is now less content with intellectual conceits and more dependent on vivid phenomenal details. The poems tend to question their own assumptions, to revise their attitudes toward the very experience they recount. The effect, for all the opportunities it gives the poet to vary a poem's pace and to manipulate a reader's responses, is one of emotional honesty, an openness that belies the very artistry used to achieve it. This becomes a hallmark of Merrill's best work from here on, and his most affecting poems succeed not because of how they expose or suppress the facts of his life, but because they rely on an intellectual scrupulosity while searching out the truths of the heart.

"An Urban Convalescence" finds the poet out for a recuperative walk during which the city becomes an image of his own past:

> Out for a walk, after a week in bed,
> I find them tearing up part of my block
> And, chilled through, dazed and lonely, join
> the dozen
> In meek attitudes, watching a huge crane
> Fumble luxuriously in the filth of years.

The speaker broods on the uncaring ravages of time and of a discontented civilization. That theme with its attendant images of demolition and fragmentation, of convulsive change and wasting, is the theme of modern poetry itself. But Merrill next introduces a series of ghostly image—a building, an engraving, a woman in Paris—to explore how the world becomes internalized and spiritualized for us. The woman is the embodiment of an idealized city, a dreamy Paris of *temps perdu,* so unlike the clangorous brutality of New York. Merrill wants to test in this poem how private experience is shaped by myth, an impulse nowhere more apparent (and resolving) than in the last stanzas, where the underworld of memory yields a rueful wisdom, and the past shelters the present:

> . . . back into my imagination
> The city glides, like cities seen from the air,
> Mere smoke and sparkle to the passenger
> Having in mind another destination
>
> Which now is not that honey-slow descent
> Of the Champs-Elysées, her hand in his,
> But the dull need to make some kind of
> house
> Out of the life lived, out of the love spent.

"An Urban Convalescence" is not a poem of the Broken Home, whose theme is dispossession, but of the Missing Home, whose theme is self-possession. From "The House" in *First Poems* through "18 West 11th Street" in *Braving the Elements* to "The House in Athens" in *The Changing Light at Sandover,* this series of poems addresses the question of how art stabilizes the passage of time. Style, they tell us, is finally an instrument of discovery and freedom, of reconciliation.

Other poems in *Water Street* orbit these themes. "A Tenancy" is about the poet's occupancy of the house in Stonington. Again, a few casual details prompt a deepening recollection until the reverie emerges into a moralizing resolution. But it seems a more elliptical poem than "An Urban Convalescence." The poet strikes a Faustian deal with himself:

> That given a few years more
> (Seven or ten or, what seemed vast, fifteen)
> To spend in love, in a country not at war,
> I would give in return
> All I had. All? A little sun
> Rose in my throat. The lease was drawn.

That "little sun" is not a child, but a poem, an effective symbol both of the dawning of poetic song and also of the isolation and sacrifice demanded of that gift. The unborn child dominates another poem, "Childlessness," as well. "Scenes of Childhood," though, is superior for its keen understanding of its own disclosures and equivocations. The family romance is at its troubled heart. The poet and his mother are watching home movies of themselves thirty years before, introjected scenes that reveal to the poet past connections and his present relationships, a tiny oedipal melodrama enacted and witnessed by its protagonists.

> The man's
> Shadow afflicts us both.
> Her voice behind me says
> It might go slower.
> I work the dials, the film jams.
> Our headstrong old projector
> Glares at the scene which promptly
> Catches fire.

Other poems in *Water Street* seek to house the past and to identify the enclosing shelter of memory with poetry itself. "Scenes of Childhood" is a more private attempt to do the same thing, substituting heroic for domestic images. And the poem introduces a series of dilemmas Merrill confronts in later books with increasing confidence but persistent anxiety.

When *Nights and Days* was given the 1967 National Book Award, the judges (W. H. Auden, James Dickey, and Howard Nemerov) cited Merrill for "his scrupulous and uncompromising cultivation of the poetic art, evidenced in his refusal to settle for any easy or profitable stance; for his insistence on taking the kind of tough, poetic chances which make the difference between esthetic success or failure." Indeed the book displays a range and depth altogether new: and everywhere convincing. It is not a long book, there are only eighteen poems. Five of them remain among his very best. Two of them, "The Thousand and Second Night" and "From the Cupola," are long, demanding, even experimental poems that express the two sides of Merrill's temperament. The first of them is set in Istanbul and Athens, the old world, exotic, seductive, masculine, and at the same time threatening and bracing. The second poem is set in an imagined Connecticut, a world of women and weather, at once demanding, sympathetic, and authoritative.

Like "An Urban Convalescence," "The Thousand and Second Night" opens with an illness. It is "the creative malady" familiar from Proust—and here, in the poet's imagined diary entry, it is a kind of facial paralysis that sends him out into the city in search of a cure. What he finds are other versions of the self—each mosque's dome or hamam's marble cell is another "transcendental skull." This is a poem not so much about faces (though it deals with many sides of the notion of facade, of losing face, of masks and styles) as it is a poem about flesh. Or better, about the flesh and the spirit—an old philosophical bone, and abiding poetic theme. Merrill takes the story of the cruel Sultan and his story-telling slave Scheherazade to be a version of the relationship between flesh and spirit:

> And when the long adventure reached its end,
> I saw the Sultan in a glass, grown old,
> While she, his fair wife still, her tales all told,
> Smiled at him fondly. "O my dearest friend,"
>
> Said she, "and lord and master from the first,
> Release me now. Your servant would refresh
> Her soul in that cold fountain which the flesh

Knows not. Grant this, for I am faint with
thirst."

And he: "But it is I who am your slave.
Free me, I pray, to go in search of joys
Unembroidered by your high, soft voice,
Along that stony path the senses pave.

But this is the poem's end, by which time it is also apparent that the pair are types of the poet's own parents, set apart and reconciled within the poem's own myth. But this image is more dramatically pursued in a later poem, "Lost in Translation" (in *Divine Comedies* [1976]). In "The Thousand and Second Night," Merrill moves—in a brilliant series of maneuvers that vary prose, crisp quatrains, and free-verse rambles—through a lively meditation of the "mind-body problem." Which is master of the self? Which is the god in masquerade? Anecdotes about a meeting with a stranger in an Athens park, or fanning a stack of old pornographic postcards, or lecturing a class of undergraduates speed the poet through perspectives on the question. The poem's "long adventure," like the soul's in flesh, takes to the seas; structures he had previously looked to for shelter, here become a means of transport:

Voyages, I bless you for sore
Limbs and mouth kissed, face bronzed and
lined,
An earth held up, a text not wholly
undermined
By fluent passages of metaphor.

The poet's distrust here of his own powers bespeaks a desire present throughout *Nights and Days* and perhaps linked with Merrill's having bought a house in Athens, and living in a culture and language foreign to him. It is the desire for unmediated experience, prior to language, or beyond it. This same longing is at the heart of the book's other long, and exceptionally difficult, poem, "From the Cupola." The poem draws on another myth about storytelling, that of Psyche and Eros (as first told by Apuleius). Again, it is a story about a divorced couple, but Merrill's focus here is on the nature of desire. His Psyche is a young New England woman, who lives with her two sisters, Gertrude and Alice, all of them originally from the South. Details from Merrill's own life overlap with this imaginary (or projected) history, and the poet has said that the poem took its start from some mysterious letters he began receiving from an admiring reader. The poem, with its eerie incarnations and vatic messages, is the clearest foreshadowing of Merrill's Ouija board epic. "The history of our loves," Santayana once wrote, "is the record of our divine conversations, of our intercourse with heaven." Sexual ecstasy, like the literary sublime, is a metaphor for this sort of possession. It is also helpful to read this poem as a dialogue between the id (or Eros), ego (or Psyche), and superego (the poet himself, who intervenes in the course of things to address his heroine).

No poem in the book—and not many in his entire output—is so extreme, so entirely a landscape of phrases. Other poems in *Nights and Days* take up the same themes, but in more conventional ways. "Time" is one, a disquisition on the concept played out within a sequence of interconnected metaphors (a game of solitaire, mountain climbing, record spinning). Still easier to read, and more heartbreaking, is "Days of 1964" (the first of a series of "Days of" poems that thread through different books, all of them deriving from Constantine Cavafy's erotic poems of Alexandrian life with that formulaic title). The narrative is clear and compelling enough. The poet, enraptured by a new lover, one day finds his devoted housekeeper Kleo dressed and working as a whore. Shaken, he returns to his own lover, but questions now the role of illusion in love, only to have his question stopped by a kiss:

I had gone so long without loving,
I hardly knew what I was thinking.
Where I hid my face, your touch, quick,
merciful,
Blindfolded me. A god breathed from my
lips,
If that was illusion, I wanted it to last long;

> To dwell, for its daily pittance, with us there,
> Cleaning and watering, sighing with love or pain.

Again a version of the Psyche and Eros story, "Days of 1964" is a poem of consummate narrative skill, its characters and tone vivid, its reflections complex but lightly sketched, wise and surprising.

Nights and Days also includes one of Merrill's signature poems, "The Broken Home," a varied sequence of seven sonnets that tells directly the archetypal story that animates all of Merrill's work: "Father Time and Mother Earth, / A marriage on the rocks." One sonnet characterizes each; others comment on their stormy marriage; still others try to calculate the effect of their lives on the child-poet's own.

> I see those two hearts, I'm afraid,
> Still. Cool here in the graveyard of good and evil,
> They are even so to be honored and obeyed.

The process of affiliation—of making himself both "time's child" and "earth's no less"—is meant to function as "the unstiflement of the entire story." By making the pain of experience over into art, by distancing his real parents to myth, Merrill again makes a shelter out of the love spent.

The Fire Screen is one of Merrill's overlooked books. With a few exceptions, it seems his most occasional collection. But like the others, it shows him of two minds about matters. The long (156 stanzas) ballad that anchors the book, "The Summer People," though set in a fictional Maine seacoast town (called Caustic!), is based on village life in Merrill's Stonington. (He returns to the ballad form, and even more successfully, in "Days of 1935" in his next book, *Braving the Elements* [1972], and he may have been inspired to write these poems by the example of Elizabeth Bishop's ballad, "The Burglar of Babylon.") "Figures in a ballad," the poem comments, "Lend themselves to acts Passionate and simple." But that is precisely what Merrill does not do. He uses the "primitive" form to handle sophisticated subject matter—domestic tangles (including a suicide) among a group of six villagers that is part E. F. Benson, part Lady Murasaki.

If "The Summer People" is set in America, most of the book transpires in Greece. The self-conscious, virtuosic ballad is offset by poems that celebrate the life of the senses. "To My Greek," for instance, a witty tribute to both language and lovers, longs for

> Those depths the surfacer
> Lives, when he does, alone to sound and sound.
>
> The barest word be what I say in you.

"Sound" here means both to versify and to know. What Merrill wants is, as he has said, meaning relieved of sense. It is to sensuality he looks for that; there are tortured love poems in this volume—"An Abdication," "The Envoys," "Remora." But he also looks to the vitality of the unexamined life, in such poems as the dramatic monologue "Kostas Tympakianakis," or "Ouzo for Robin" (addressed to the poet's nephew Robin Magowan). The most exquisite of these poems is the short lyric "Another August." It is in three sections—the first in prose, the second in free verse, and the third, an envoi, a rhymed quatrain. The effect is musical, like a recitative, arioso, and cabaletta. The poem is Proustian, and takes as its text the old catch-phrase "One swallow doesn't make a summer," in order to explore how things change in order to remain the same. The poem opens with a return, to Greece, to "so much former strangeness" the "glaze of custom" by now has made home. The second section remembers a wrenching love affair, but then turns to the self, seeking to efface pain by memory:

> Open the shutters. Let variation
> abandon the swallows one by one.
> How many summer dusks were needed
> to make that single skimming form!
> The very firefly kindles to its type.

Here is each evening's lesson. First
the hour, the setting. Only then
the human being, his white shirtsleeve
chalked among treetrunks, round a waist,
or lifted in an entrance. Look for him.
Be him.

Having receded into nature, become an unfeeling "type," he can afford the envoi's farewell, spoken to the lover:

Whom you saw mannerless and dull of
heart,
Easy to fool, impossible to hurt,
I wore that fiction like a fine white shirt
And asked no favor but to play the part.

Playing a part, the whole sense that life is fiction in disguise, has fascinated Merrill throughout his career. The mythologies of the self dramatized by Proust or Sigmund Freud make sense of these poems, though they cannot be reduced to their formulas. Merrill's poems instinctively recognize the limited repertory of drives we are motivated by, and the roles our emotions assume. It is why the opera has always seemed to him, and been used by him as, a sure model of the inner life—melodramatic, intense, at times ridiculous, at times sublime. Two magical poems about the opera are center stage in *The Fire Screen.* "The Opera Company" concerns the goings-on in another house, especially the professional rivalry of two sopranos, whose voices now, on memory's scratchy old recording, "soar and mix, will not be told apart." Opera for Merrill is a feminine world, a stagy one of outsize "counterfeit emotions," and also of heartbreaking gestures of renunciation for love, and of self-sacrifice. "Matinees," a sequence of eight sonnets, is an enchanting poem about the way a young boy's morals are corrupted by opera—that is to say, brought to maturity by art. It is art that helps us to our emotions, both to have and understand them.

The point thereafter was to arrange for one's
Own chills and fever, passions and
betrayals,
Chiefly in order to make song of them.

He is led to these revelations in the poem not just by the performers, but by his mother and a society dowager, Mrs. Livingston, to whose opera box he was invited. There are other maternal muse figures in this book, among them Maria Mitsotáki, the subject of "Words for Maria," and later a central character in the *Sandover* trilogy. But the crucial poem in *The Fire Screen,* and the source of the book's title, is "Mornings in a New House." Like the earlier "Scenes of Childhood," the poem projects the psychic outlines of a mother-and-son relationship, at once operatic (with its overtones of Brünnhilde) and autobiographical. The screen here is no longer a movie screen, but the fire screen on which the poet's mother had stitched *her* mother's house. He stands there

. . . Still vaguely chilled,

Guessing how even then her eight
Years had foreknown him, nursed him, all,
Sewn his first dress, sung to him, let him
fall,
Howled when his face chipped like a plate.

This is what Freud would call a "dream screen," the projection of other, fearsome memories. What he most fears is what he seems to celebrate about the opera: the foreknown, the overdetermined. This fear is the subtext of *The Fire Screen*'s other strong poem, "The Friend of the Fourth Decade," another sonnet sequence, this time in couplets. The titular friend is, of course, the poet himself—though other friends are mentioned, along with their advice on how to manage one's boredom with life. One suggests soaking the messages off all his old postcards—the images remain, language is washed away. When the poet tries this with a card from his mother, it does not work:

Chances are it was
Some simple matter of what ink she used,

And yet her message remained legible,
The memories it stirred did not elude me.

I put my postcards back upon the shelf.
Certain things die only with oneself.

This sense Merrill cultivates of being the vessel of experience, of having been imprinted, is important to any understanding of his work. The most obvious instance of it is the Ouija board trilogy, in which the poet literally receives messages, and in which atoms and angels are identical. This kind of wise passivity resonates everywhere, and nowhere more mysteriously than in his most hermetic book, *Braving the Elements.* Rather than attempt any stylistic change, as other poets might (Robert Lowell, say, or James Wright), Merrill has always sought new experience in order to give his work both new material and direction. The landscape of the American Southwest and the ghostly presence of a new lover there loom in this book like the giant rock formations in Monument Valley—"the crazy shapes things take," as the poet puts it in his poem (a rather Frostian parable) about that place. Many of the poems in this collection are private, resolute, abstract, heraldic; they resist the intelligence almost successfully, as Wallace Stevens said. The natural history of America, above all a violent one, manifests itself in Merrill's references to the political terrorism of the 1960's. Loss dominates the book. These poems rise from the ashes; they recount experience "after the fire." Those fires are oedipal or passional, erotic or psychic, and from each the poet withdraws, most often into style itself, the screen of language.

The volume's dedicatory poem is "Log," a prayer that things be brought to light. The next poem is "After the Fire," and recounts a fire in the poet's house in Athens (as another poem in the book, "18 West 11th Street," concerns the bombing of the poet's childhood home). "After the Fire" indicates the start of a new book, of course, after *The Fire Screen* (other of Merrill's book titles are elemental), but the poem also revisits the scene and characters of an earlier poem, "Days of 1964." Merrill's poems do this continually, enacting his basic impulse to revise or reconstitute the past. Again we are introduced to Kleo the housemaid, and now to her aging mother and wastrel son, a sleazy character who, it turns out, during a tryst set fire to the poet's house. As Kleo is a type of the long-suffering mother, her son is a skewed version of the poet himself. Under the guise of a Chekhovian comedy, Merrill can once again explore his themes of love's enriching blindness and knowledge's merciless hindsight.

> The snuffed-out candle-ends grow tall and shine,
> Dead flames encircle us, which cannot harm,
> The table's spread, she croons, and I
> Am kneeling pressed to her old burning frame.

Other poems take up old, burned-out loves. "Strato in Plaster" and "Days of 1971" do so humorously; "Flèche d'Or" (the title is that of a train, but also a homonym for "flesh door") does so eerily. A current, diffident lover seems to have been the inspiration behind those poems set in the Southwest: "Under Libra: Weights and Measures," "In Nine Sleep Valley," and the first part of "Up and Down." These and other poems such as "The Black Mesa," where the landscape itself speaks, are as difficult a group of poems as Merrill has ever written, recessed and encoded. He drives his style hard here; its intensities and harmonies are thrilling, and not a little dizzying. The final poem in the book, "Syrinx," can stand in here for a hermeticism that suffuses the book. Syrinx was the nymph pursued by Pan, and turned by Zeus into reeds, from which Pan fashioned his pipe. In Merrill's extraordinary poem she is turned into other things as well, including a mathematical equation and the solfege scale ("Who puts his mouth to me / Draws out the scale of love and dread— / O ramify, sole antidote!"). Pan here is "the great god Pain," and his panpipes become a flute (Debussy's, no doubt, who wrote a solo with the same title)

> Whose silvery breath-tarnished tones
> No longer rivet bone and star in place
>
> Or keep from shriveling, leather round a stone,
> The sunbather's precocious apricot

Or stop the four winds racing overhead
Nought
Waste Eased
Sought

There are, of course, less demanding poems in the book. "Days of 1935," for example, is a bravura ballad about an imaginary kidnapping, another example, as well, of Merrill's circling the oedipal drama. A more direct, and rather more sentimental, version of it occurs in the second section of "Up and Down," called "The Emerald." The poet and his mother descend to her bank vault, where she presents him with a ring. "'Here, take it for—/ For when you marry.'" But, looking at the emerald, the poet thinks

Indeed this green room s mine, my very lift.
We are each other's; there will be no wife;
The little feet that patter here are metrical.

And he slips the ring onto her finger. "Wear it for me," the poet silently tells her, "Until—until the time comes. Our eyes meet. / The world beneath the world is brightening." "Dreams About Clothes" is likewise about an inheritance, and deals with the father (here disguised as a dry cleaner named Art). The poet's dream-plea is at once a boast about his preference for "the immaterial," and a confession of his doubts:

Tell me something, Art.
You know what it's like
Awake in your dry hell
Of volatile synthetic solvents.
Won't you help us brave the elements
Once more, of terror, anger, love?
Seeing there's no end to wear and tear
Upon the lawless heart,
Won't you as well forgive
Whoever settles for the immaterial?
Don't you care how we live?

The peace the poet tries to make here with his parents, with his past, is a tentative, wary one. But the project Merrill next, and unwittingly, embarks on, finally makes that peace by taking his past up into a grand mythology of memory, a high romance of reconciliation.

Divine Comedies, which was awarded the Pulitzer Prize in 1977, may be the single most resplendent of Merrill's individual collections. Its verse combines the conversational fluency of *The Fire Screen* with the oracular density of *Braving the Elements.* The major poems in the volume's first part bring to perfection his preference for the poem of middle length, between one hundred and three hundred lines, with an elegant maze of narrative, a metrical array, and daunting range of allusions. The four preeminent poems in this first part of *Divine Comedies*—"Lost in Translation," "Chimes for Yahya," "Yánnina," and "Verse for Urania"—are all reminiscences or reveries, their narratives shuttling between past event and present meditation. Their tone is one of autumnal resignation, rather like that of Shakespeare's late harmonic romances. (The publication of *Divine Comedies* coincided with the poet's fiftieth birthday.) Each of the poems involves some sort of trip, literal or figurative, so that their recurring plot is the voyage of self-discovery, during which the poet tours his own past, in settings local or exotic. "Chimes for Yahya" opens and closes in Merrill's Athens home, but opens out to and closes in on a recuperative stay in Esfahan, Iran, decades earlier, with a chieftain prince. The poem can be read as a mock nativity ode whose playful epiphany becomes an emblem of "the pain so long forgiven / It might as well be pleasure I rise in." The prince in this poem is a mild, beneficent counterpart to the tyrant Ali Pasha in "Yánnina," both of them types of the father. Screened by metaphors of dream, shadow play, and magician's tent, "Yánnina" reconstructs the shifting images of feminine and masculine, each split between the destructive and the seductive. That split informs the broken-home theme, which again is the setting for "Lost in Translation," likely destined to be Merrill's signature poem. The jigsaw puzzle which the young Merrill and his governess piece together—during a time when "A summer without parents is the puzzle Or should be"—is a tableau of yet another "Sheik with beard / And flashing sword hilt," attended by "a dark-eyed woman veiled in mauve." The child wonders

> . . . whom to serve
> And what his duties are, and where his feet,
>
> And if we'll find, as some before us did,
> That piece of Distance deep in which lies
> hid
> Your tiny apex sugary with sun,
> Eternal Triangle, Great Pyramid!

The way we translate life to art, art to life, as if they were each a language indifferently learned but unhesitatingly spoken, is the animating energy behind this brilliant, affecting work, which resolves itself in language—a scene of instruction in which Rilke puzzles out a translation of Paul Valéry's "Palme," sacrificing felicity for sense:

> But nothing's lost. Or else: all is translation
> And every bit of us is lost in it
> (Or found—I wander through the ruin of S
> Now and then, wondering at the
> peacefulness)
> And in that loss a self-effacing tree,
> Color of context, imperceptibly
> Rustling with its angel, turns the waste
> To shade and fiber, milk and memory.

The subject of "Lost in Translation," the poet's relationship to his own past, is slightly deflected in "Verse for Urania" but only in order to provide a still more penetrating and embracing meditation on time. The poem is addressed to the infant daughter of his Greek-born, too-Americanized tenants in Stonington on the occasion of her baptism. She is the poet's godchild, perhaps even a type of the Divine Child that Jung considered the most constant and potent symbol of the self in fullest potentiality, and thus a poignant reminder of one's unfulfilled desires. That this child's name is also that of the muse of astronomy and cosmological poetry allows the poet to roam to other details, both abstruse and homely. Since "the first myth was Measure," the very rhythms of life, like those of verse, "Prevail, it might be felt, at the expense / Of meaning, but as well create, survive it." All things pass—"Such is the test of time that all things pass"—only to return upon themselves, and Merrill would hold with Friedrich Nietzsche that he "who consents to his own return participates in the divinity of the world." That is what this poem finally celebrates. We *are* the time we pass through, in a measured design greater than either, as Merrill tells his godchild:

> It was late
>
> And early. I had seen you through shut eyes.
> Our bond was sacred, being secular:
> In time embedded, it in us, near, far,
> Flooding both levels with the same sunrise.

The second half of *Divine Comedies* is entirely taken up with "The Book of Ephraim," a poem of nearly one hundred pages, arranged into twenty-six abecedarian sections to match the letters of the Ouija board. For two decades, Merrill and his companion David Jackson had been sitting down to the Ouija board, enthralled by their conversations with the dead, and especially with their contact or medium, Ephraim, a Greek Jew, born in Asia Minor in A.D. 8, later a favorite of Tiberius on Capri, and killed by the imperial guard at age twenty-eight for having loved the monstrous Caligula. There are precedents among poets for this sort of spiritualism—one recalls Victor Hugo's sessions at the *table parlante* or Yeats's correspondence with his familiar spirit Leo Africanus—but it is a risky subject. Throughout, Merrill incorporates his own sceptical doubts, in order to forestall a reader's. Did Merrill himself "believe" in these voices—or not voices actually, but messages, spelled out letter by letter with a teacup's handle? At one point he is told (in the upper case that transcribes a message) "ALL THESE OUR CONVERSATIONS COME FROM MEMORY & WORD BANKS / TAPPD IN U." And to an interviewer Merrill once explained:

> Well, don't you think there comes a time when everyone, not just a poet, wants to get

> beyond the self? To reach, if you like, the "god" within you? The board, in however clumsy or absurd a way, allows for precisely that. Or if it's still yourself that you're drawing upon, then that self is much stranger and freer and more farseeing than the one you thought you knew.

Merrill was not aware, when he wrote "The Book of Ephraim," that it was only the first part of a much longer encounter with the spirit world, and that subsequent demands on his credulity and imagination (and on his reader's) would be much greater.

Merrill had hinted at his interest in the Ouija board before, in such early poems as "Voices from the Other World" (in *The Country of a Thousand Years of Peace*), perhaps "From the Cupola," in his short story "Driver" (1962), and most notably in a long episode in his 1957 novel *The Seraglio.* But in "The Book of Ephraim" we have the whole story. Its telling transpires over the course of a year (1974) which includes both the events of the composition itself and the odd coincidences of a novel, now lost, that Merrill had planned to write—as well as the revelations Merrill and Jackson entertained throughout the twenty years that they used the board. The story began in 1955, when "We had each other for communication / And all the rest. The stage was set for Ephraim." Slowly the formula of the Other World is divulged, a scheme not dissimilar to Orphic, Platonic, or Vedic analogues. This formula holds that, while alive, each of us is the representative of a patron beyond, who attends to us only when, after death, we are recycled into other lives—"the quick seamless change of body-stocking"—which recurs until we are sufficiently purged of life to begin the divine nine-stage ascent, where we assume the age "AT WHICH IT FIRST SEEMS CREDIBLE TO DIE" and, patrons now ourselves, rise in station through degrees of "PEACE FROM REPRESENTATION." None of this becomes dogmatic, as Ephraim tells them, "U ARE SO QUICK MES CHERS I FEEL WE HAVE / SKIPPING THE DULL CLASSROOM DONE IT ALL / AT THE SALON LEVEL." In fact, though his gossip about the greats, from Mozart to Montezuma, is always engagingly witty, Ephraim spells out his answers to guide his devotees toward an understanding of themselves, to prompt them in their parts on the world's stage. For Merrill and Jackson, their life with Ephraim (a psychiatrist in the poem terms it their *folie à deux*) parallels their life with each other—gradually domesticated in two villages (Stonington and Athens), on Grand Tours (for which long passages of the poem provide beautifully detailed views), undergoing the difficult dynamics of intimacy, disillusion, and endurance. Ephraim begins as tour guide, and eventually becomes friend and co-conspirator.

> We were not tough-
> Or literal-minded, or unduly patient
> With those who were. Hadn't—from books, from living—
> The profusion dawned on us, of "languages"
> Any one of which, to who could read it,
> Lit up the system it conceived?—bird-flight,
> Hallucinogen, chorale and horoscope:
> Each its own world, hypnotic, many-sided
> Facet of the universal gem.
> Ephraim's revelations—we had them
> For comfort, thrills and chills, "material."
> *He* didn't cavil. He was the revelation
> (Or if we had created him, then we were).
> The point—one twinkling point by now of thousands—
> Was never to forego, in favor of
> Plain dull proof, the marvelous nightly pudding.

Two references within the poem are important glosses on the significance of "belief." At one point, Merrill reminds us that

> Stevens imagined the imagination
> And God as one; the imagination, also
> As that which presses back, in parlous times,
> Against "the pressure of reality."

But Stevens actually posits the imaginer as God, which might encourage us to read the poem as an intricately displaced hymn of praise to the creative power—at an abstract level, of the imagination itself, and at an autobiographical level, of Merrill's own. The other reference draws us still closer to the poem's deeper purposes. Later in the poem Merrill echoes the earlier citation:

> Jung says—or if he doesn't, all but does—
> That God and the Unconscious are one.
> Hm.
> The lapse tides us over, hither, yon;
> Tide that laps us home away from home.

Among the many prospective patrons for this poem—Plato, Dante, Proust, Stevens, Auden—it is Carl Jung who presides, especially the later sage of *Answer to Job* and *Memories, Dreams, Reflections.* Again, Merrill has obscured his source's qualification, for Jung himself says that "strictly speaking, the God-image does not coincide with the unconscious as such, but with a special content of it, namely the archetype of the self." Jung thought of us all as "representatives" of the collective unconscious—what the ancients called the "sympathy of all things" and what Ephraim calls "the surround of the living"—personified in the anima-figure who communicates with consciousness through primordial images that reveal as much of life as has ever been lived or imagined. To that extent, each of us contains and transmits "another world"—the dead living in us. Lost paradises, said Proust, are the only true ones.

Compared with its two massive successors, *Mirabell: Books of Number* (1978) and *Scripts for the Pageant* (1980), "The Book of Ephraim" may be seen as merely a prelude. The sheer delight the poem affords is overbalanced by the sublime instructions of the two subsequent panels of *The Changing Light of Sandover,* which complete the trilogy. But its tone, its verse schemes, its cast of characters, make it the most immediately appealing of the three. The title of the volume, *Divine Comedies,* points to Dante, though the poem's tone often recalls the Pope of the *Dunciad,* the romantic exuberance of a Byron or Auden. The theme of "The Book of Ephraim," says Merrill at the start, is "the incarnation and withdrawal of / A god." The main prop or stage for this process is a Ouija board (its arc of letters a trope for language itself) and a mirror (a trope for the self). Out of such instruments of the imagination, Merrill has made a whole world that alludes to this one, like Plato's definition of time as "a moving image of eternity." No discussion of this poem, or of the entire trilogy, can do justice to its parquetry and prosody. At one point, Merrill compares the give-and-take between realism, ours and Theirs, to the texture of verse itself: the enlightened power of art's own second nature like "rod upon mild silver rod." Auden's *The Sea and the Mirror* comes to mind as a similar, though less ambitious (Merrill's trilogy, after all, comes to seventeen thousand lines), example of a long poem whose cumulative impact derives, in part, from its dramatic variety of styles and verse forms. Blank verse, odes, sonnets, terza rima, couplets, canzones—the trilogy is a virtual anthology of received and invented forms. Merrill's particular genius lies in his use of metrics and darting rhymes to explicate his elaborate syntax, of puns or enjambment to create an enriching lexical ambivalence. His timing, his poise, his instinct for allowing experience to discover itself in language are impeccable.

In a review of *Divine Comedies,* the critic Harold Bloom said (in a *New Republic* review) that "Ephraim" could not be overpraised, "as nothing since the greatest writers of our century equals it in daemonic force," and he predicted that the poetic results of Merrill's occult journey, "should they equal or go beyond 'The Book of Ephraim,' will make him the strangest, the most unnerving of all this country's poets." But few readers could have anticipated—the poet himself did not—what came next. Merrill's association with the occult intensified; unexpected encounters at the Ouija board followed the publication of "Ephraim"; new powers were both revealed to and granted the poet. At two-year intervals, further installments of his epic poem appeared. First came *Mirabell,* its subtitle, *Books of Number,* an indication of its format which, instead of the board's letters, takes its numerals to organize the poem's ten major divisions. The poem is twice as long as "Ephraim," and more than twice as complex. Numbers play a further role in its complications. Two new major characters are introduced: the shades of Auden and Maria Mitsotáki (a friend to Merrill and Jackson in Athens), a pair easily seen as a parental couple. The sessions at the Ouija board are hijacked by fourteen creatures, who appear to the dead as hideous batlike beings and are subsequently revealed to be subatomic particles. One of their number, whom we know as 741, replaces Ephraim as interlocutor, and conducts his listeners, living and dead (the five of them now engaged in what is called their "V WORK"), through a series of seminars on matters that range from creations previous to ours and the chemical composition of humankind, to the nature of the atom, the universe, the fall, the soul, heaven, hell, and earth. Explanations are dense, sometimes contradictory, always astonishing. As a cosmogony, Merrill's far outdoes Milton's and Dante's. He, or his informants, are intent to reveal nothing less than the "FORMULAS GOVERNING HUMAN LIFE." The book is an account of these formulas, and of the receiving and ordering of them by the poet during 1976. That is to say, the poem includes his reluctance, resistance, skepticism, and wonder, thereby making of otherworldly revelation a human drama. And when the discussion comes around to manners, there is a remarkable transformation: 741 turns into a peacock, and is given the name Mirabell by his human friends. There follows another set of lessons on the nature of life and the elements. (Each of the five main characters has assumed the attributes of an element: JM is air, DJ is nature, WHA is earth, MM is water, and 741 is fire.) To demonstrate there is "NO ACCIDENT," but that everything is part of God Biology's scheme, examples are brought forward of various relationships (cause to effect, for instance) and phenomena (DNA, say, or dreamwork). These lessons are as much masque as seminar, and instruction is mingled with villanelle or ode. The poem concludes with ten more revelations, their splendor rising as (in the Stonington house where this all takes place) a hurricane rages—until, at the very end, a strange new and powerful voice commands our attention, and clearly anticipates the next installment.

"Why should we fear to be crushed by savage elements," Emerson asked in his 1852 essay "Fate," "we who are made up of the same elements? Let us build to the Beautiful Necessity, which . . . educates . . . to the perception that there are no contingencies." Nature is Merrill's concern in *Mirabell,* as history was in "Ephraim," and mind will be in *Scripts.* And contingency is his text in *Mirabell,* as power is in "Ephraim," and sense is in *Scripts.* But it may be fairer to say that power drives all three poems. In a literary translation, we are talking about the poet's ascent to the sublime: his encounter with imaginative power at its most uncanny; in Emerson's phrase, "the deep power" that is the soul's own final, enormous claim. This power can be daemonic or divine; it may sometimes be internalized or idealized, and thereby involve the self's compensatory response to loss, as it does throughout Merrill's trilogy—his greatest effort to reconcile, to bring his parental forces back together again. The stillness of the *dictées,* the occult panoply and scared precincts, passages of dread, distortions of time and space, the solemnity of "GREAT ORIGINAL IDEAS"—these all give the trilogy a faintly gothic air, and provide critical moments when the poet is, as he says, imbued with otherness. At the very end of *Mirabell,* for example, after the refrains of doubt and fear, the life-and-death issues, the poem rises to an eerie quiet that modulates from suspense to surrender. There has been a daylong vigil for an angel. In the final minutes of that "hour when Hell shall render what it owes," the sun is about to set, and an emblematic gull rises over the waters.

> The message hardly needs decoding, so
> Sheer the text, so innocent and fleet
> These overlapping pandemonia:

Birdlife, leafplay, rockface, waterglow
Lending us their being, till the given
Moment comes to render what we owe.

The book might have ended here, its final word an echo of the word that had opened the poem ("Oh very well, then"), but it does not. The shapeliness of the poem is broken, and a new voice—a voice whose long, imperious lines we learn belong to the archangel Michael—commandeers the poem, replaces the voice of the poet with an "epic" voice totally other than Merrill's, and ends the book on an unprecedented high note of its own:

GOD IS THE ACCUMULATED, INTELLIGENCE IN CELLS SINCE THE DEATH
OF THE FIRST DISTANT CELL.
WE RESIDE IN THAT INTELLIGENCE

. . .

I AM MICHAEL
I HAVE ESTABLISHED YOUR ACQUAINTANCE & ACCEPT YOU

. . .

LOOK! LOOK INTO THE RED EYE OF YOUR GOD!

This is one of what Wordsworth named the "extraordinary calls" of the sublime. And it could be added that the Ouija board considered as a terrain—and it is by Merrill, who even maps it—is the most compelling trope for the sublime since the rugged mountain heights of Romantic landscape, an occult sublime having replaced a "natural" sublime.

This ascent to the upper case of higher meaning, this access to power, comes at a price: the sublimation of the self. At the end of *Mirabell,* Merrill first surrenders himself to the symbolic scene's sheer text, and then surrenders his voice, or poetic control. Such moments of obliteration and exaltation, of withdrawal and incarnation, are deeply ambivalent for this poet. They are both cultivated and resisted. Power terrifies and charges. Merrill's uneasiness helps shape the trilogy. Often the *telling* of the poem, both its plot and its style, depends on tones that counter the sublime, that evade or undermine it. The whole domestic side of the poem does so. When the poem's mythical undertones or divine injunctions elevate the planchette into a holier-than-thou grail, we are quickly reminded of two human hands on a dime-store teacup. Another of these inhibiting tones is the poem's psychological realism, its exhaustions, anxieties, or skepticism. And a third is the beautiful. In Merrill's case, this is synonymous with style itself, with his language's imagistic resistance to "some holy flash past words." His style is willing to try on anything that fits—allusive, witty, ironic, tender; rhetorically intricate and metrically ingenious; extremely composed and sociable—that is to say, always aware of itself addressing a subject, being attended to by an audience. The opposite, in other words, of the egotistical (or narcissistic) sublime; it is a style happier with sensuous detail than with abstract discourse or hieratic utterance.

Merrill can describe his own poem (as he does late in "Ephraim") as continually drawing him toward, *and* insulating him from, the absolute, or sublime mode. In a sense, then, Merrill's trilogy is of two minds about itself—the poet's and the poem's. When told of his affinities with the element of air in *Mirabell,* Merrill is further reminded that his true vocation is for

MIND & ABSTRACTION—THE REGION
OF STARRY THOUGHT COOLER THAN
SWIFTER THAN
LIGHTER THAN EARTH.

Yet throughout the trilogy he refuses, or wants to refuse, such a calling. His temperamental diffidence in "Ephraim" grows into a nagging reluctance in the face of the sublime task in *Mirabell,* until finally resistance itself becomes the subject of *Scripts for the Pageant*—indeed, its very format, YES & NO.

Those two responses, plus the ampersand that both separates and joins them, are the remaining characters on the homemade Ouija board Merrill had been using all along. They provided him with the basis for a final poem, an exploration of themes of acceptance ("Ouija," after all, is an amalgam of the French and German affirmatives), resistance, and ambivalence. *Scripts for the Pageant* is by far the longest of the trilogy's three parts, and the most resplendent. Its cast is larger, its ambitions ampler, its verse richer. The interlocutors now are the four archangels: Michael, the Angel of Light; Emmanuel, the Water Angel; Raphael, the Earth Angel; and their dark, menacing brother Gabriel, the Angel of Fire and Death. They are in service to the final parents in Merrill's evolving private mythology of the Broken Home—God Biology (known as God B) and his twin, Mother Nature, also known as Psyche and Chaos. The supporting cast includes the nine Muses, Akhnaton, Homer, Montezuma, Nefertiti, Plato, Jesus, Gautama, Mohammed, and Mercury, plus two more recently deceased friends of Merrill's, George Cotzias (a scientist) and Robert Morse (a dilettantish neighbor). And there are cameo appearances by the likes of Maria Callas, Robert Lowell, Gertrude Stein, and W. B. Yeats. Ephraim and Mirabell return, and are joined by a new creature, a unicorn named Unice. The poem, in other words, is dizzyingly crowded, and Merrill as stage manager maneuvers his cast with authority. Again, the thrust of the poem is one of initiation. A series of schoolroom seminars, and then a trial—sides taken, pleas entered and argued—argue the case for humankind, and seek to explain some of our most enduring, intractable ideas. The two main questions are put by Michael and Gabriel. Michael's is this riddling proposition: "THE MOST INNOCENT OF IDEAS IS THE IDEA THAT INNOCENCE IS DESTROYED BY IDEAS." Gabriel, in his turn, speaks for the "BLACK BEYOND BLACK," and announces: "MY THEME IS TIME, MY TEXT: / OF ALL DESTRUCTIVE IDEAS THE MOST DESTRUCTIVE IS THE IDEA OF DESTRUCTION." It is Merrill's task to "MAKE SENSE OF IT"—that is, both to understand the gnomic revelations and to embody them in images and meanings his readers can understand. At the very end, masks pulled off (so that we learn Ephraim all along was a disguise for Michael, and that Maria and Wystan have returned to earth as elements), there is a ceremony of farewell. A mirror is broken into a bowl of water.

> Giving up its whole
> Lifetime of images, the mirror utters
>
> A little treble shriek and rides the flood
> Or tinkling mini-waterfall through wet
> Blossoms to lie—and look, the sun has set—
> In splinters apt, from now on, to draw
> blood,
>
> Each with its scimitar or bird-beak shape
> Able, days hence, aglitter in the boughs
> Or face-down, black on soil beneath, to
> rouse
> From its deep swoon the undestroyed
> heartscape
>
> —Then silence. The champagne.
> And should elsewhere
> Broad wings revolve a horselike form into
> One Creature upward-shining brief as dew,
> Swifter than bubbles in wine, through
> evening air
>
> Up, far up, O whirling point of Light—:

In 1982, the three poems were combined into a single long work, now called *The Changing Light of Sandover.* This collected edition was awarded the National Book Critics Circle Prize for that year. To the existing long poems was added a thirty-page coda called "The Higher Keys," a poem that continues and (again) revises the revelations, adds five ceremonies of rebirth for one character, and concludes with an extraordinary section in which the characters all gather to hear the poet read aloud his now completed epic. That all this transpires in "the old ballroom of the Broken Home" is a tribute to the autobiographical impulses that underlie Merrill's vast poem. His effort all along has been less to explain than to reconcile—contending powers, conflicting views. Also in 1982, Merrill's publisher issued a collection of selected poems, *From the First Nine: Poems 1946–*

1976, so that it was possible to see, in the nine hundred pages of these two books, the thematic consistency and stylistic bravura of an entire career.

Since then, Merrill has published two more collections. *Late Settings* (1985) seems a little overshadowed by the trilogy. It gathers together a number of smaller poems Merrill had written before and during the trilogy's composition, and adds several longish poems to them; but much of the work is devoted to the same concerns the poet had been exploring over the Ouija board. Poems of reminiscence, such as "The School Play" and "Days of 1941 and '44," have an autumnal plangency. Other poems—"Trees Listening to Bach," "A Day on the Connecticut River," or "An Upset"—put on display his hard-edged, gem-bright flair for invention. The major poems in the book, however, are its three longer ones: "Clearing the Title," "Bronze," and "Santorini: Stopping the Leak." The first of these, taken up with the purchase of a house in Key West (as a sort of domestic and emotional exchange for the one in Athens), can be linked with earlier poems about tenancy, or entitlement. "Bronze," another voyage of discovery and recovery, was occasioned by a visit with a former lover to the great bronze statues at Riace, Italy, and ends with a look at a bronze head made of the poet himself as a child. Images of the self, hardening with age or in art, are given a more fluent context in "Santorini: Stopping the Leak." It is a poem that returns to Greece, and involves a disorder (a plantar wart, troublesome old memories) that leads the poet on through dreamy divagations and temporary solutions.

Awarded the prestigious Bobbitt Prize for Poetry by the Library of Congress in 1990, *The Inner Room* (1988) includes a small play (for puppets), and a prose memoir (with haiku) called "Prose for Departure." It deals in part with the death of a friend, the critic David Kalstone—the same friend memorialized in other poems in the book, "Investiture at Cecconi's" and "Farewell Performance." There is a sense in which the huge *Sandover* trilogy is an anti-elegy; the death of friends, like the waning of affections, is elided by the Ouija board trope: they are all reborn as voices, and the poetic medium itself overcomes any loss. "Farewell Performance" is a more realistic account of the poet's feelings. Written in sapphics, the poem opens with one of Merrill's favorite settings, a theater. We are at a ballet performance—one of Kalstone's favorite pastimes. The fairy-tale transformation of the straw of experience into the gold of art informs this first section, which begins with a truism to be tested:

> Art. It cures affliction. As lights go down and
> Maestro lifts his wand, the unfailing sea
> change starts within us. Limber alembics
> once more make of the common
>
> lot a pure brief gold. At the end our bravos
> call them back, sweat-soldered and leotarded,
> back, again back—anything not to face the
> fact that it's over.

The ghosts of these memories return to haunt another sort of ceremony. When the poet describes scattering his friend's ashes at sea, he notices "the gruel of selfhood / taking manlike shape for one last jeté on / ghostly-wait, ah!—point into darkness vanished." And when the poem returns at the end to its opening conceit, the tone has changed. The very distance at which art keeps us from the stark realities of loss is abruptly foreshortened, and the poem concludes on a rare, stricken note:

> Back they come. How you would have loved
>   it. We in
> turn have risen. Pity and terror done with,
> programs furled, lips parted, we jostle
>   forward
> eager to hail them,
>
> more, to join the troupe—will a friend
>   enroll us
> one fine day? Strange, though. For up close
>   their magic
> self-destructs. Pale, dripping, with downcast
>   eyes they've
> seen where it led you.

This sense of loss is offset elsewhere in the collection by poems of new love and travel. "A Room at the Heart of Things," for instance, and "Walks in Rome" lightly or mysteriously take up the burden of "actor and lover." Merrill's verse here demonstrates an easy mastery, but he continues to place new demands upon it, "Raw luster, rendering its human guise." "Morning Glory" and "Losing the Marbles" are further examples of Merrill's specialty, the diversified poem of middle length. The first has to do with renewal, the second with age. Though he mocks here his own decline ("Long work of knowing and hard play of wit Take their toll like any virus."), Merrill has all along been celebrating his losses, turning their leaden echo into poetic gold. One section of "Losing the Marble" offers us the sapphic fragments of a poem left out in the rain, and effaced by the storm. Two sections later, the poem is restored, surprisingly different from what we might have expected it to be. Its conclusion, though, comes as no surprise to the reader attentive to Merrill's abiding themes:

> Humbly our old poets knew to make
> wanderings into
> homecomings of a sort—harbor, palace,
> temple, all
> having been quarried out of those blue
> foothills
> no further off, these last clear autumn
> days, than infancy.

Selected Bibliography

WORKS OF JAMES MERRILL

POETRY

Jim's Book: A Collection of Poems and Short Stories, (New York: privately printed, 1942).
The Black Swan, (Athens: Icaros, 1946).
First Poems, (New York: Knopf, 1951).
The Country of a Thousand Years of Peace, (New York: Knopf, 1959); rev. ed. (New York: Atheneum, 1970).
Water Street, (New York: Atheneum, 1962).
Nights and Days, (New York: Atheneum, 1966).
The Fire Screen, (New York: Atheneum, 1969).
Braving the Elements, (New York: Atheneum, 1972).
The Yellow Pages, (Cambridge, Mass.: Temple Bar Bookshop, 1974).
Divine Comedies, (New York: Atheneum, 1976).
Mirabell: Books of Number, (New York: Atheneum, 1978).
Scripts for the Pageant, (New York: Atheneum, 1980).
The Changing Light at Sandover, (New York: Atheneum, 1982).
From the First Nine: Poems 1946–1976, (New York: Atheneum, 1982).
Late Settings: Poems, (New York: Atheneum, 1985).
The Inner Room, (New York: Knopf, 1988).

NOVELS

The Seraglio, (New York: Knopf, 1957).
The (Diblos) Notebook, (New York: Atheneum, 1965).

PLAYS

The Immortal Husband. In *Playbook: Five Plays for a New Theatre* (New York: New Directions, 1956) First produced in New York in 1955.
The Bait, In *Artists'Theatre: Four Plays,* Edited by Herbert Machiz (New York: Grove Press, 1960) First produced in New York in 1953.

PROSE

Recitative, edited and with an introduction by J. D. McClatchy (San Francisco: North Point Press, 1986) Essays, interviews, and short stories, including "Driver."

BIBLIOGRAPHIES

Hagstrom, Jack W. C., and Bixby, George, "James Merrill: A Bibliographical Checklist," *American Book Collector,* NS 4: 34–47 (November/December 1983).
Hall, Holly, *James Merrill, Poet,* (St. Louis, Mo.: Washington University, 1985) Catalog of exhibits drawn from the extensive collection of Merrill papers and manuscripts in the Modern Literature Collection of Washington University Libraries.

BIOGRAPHICAL AND CRITICAL STUDIES

Baird, James, "James Merrill's Sound of Feeling: Language and Music," *Southwest Review* 74: 361–377 (Summer 1989).
Bloom, Harold, ed. *James Merrill,* (New York: Chelsea House, 1985).
Gardner, Thomas, *Discovering Ourselves in Whitman: The Contemporary American Long Poem,* (Urbana: University of Illinois Press, 1989).
Howard, Richard, "James Merrill," *Alone with America* rev. ed. (New York: Atheneum, 1980).

Keller, Lynn, *Re-making It New: Contemporary American Poetry and the Modernist Tradition,* (Cambridge: Cambridge University Press, 1987).

Labrie, Ross, *James Merrill,* (Boston: Twayne, 1982).

———, "James Merrill at Home: An Interview," *Arizona Quarterly* 38: 19–36 (Spring 1982).

Lehman, David, and Charles Berger, eds,.*James Merrill: Essays in Criticism,* (Ithaca, N.Y.: Cornell University Press, 1983).

Materer, Timothy, "Death and Alchemical Transformation in James Merrill's *The Changing Light at Sandover." Contemporary Literature* 29: 82–104 (Spring 1988).

McManus, Kevin and Bruce Hainley, eds, James Merrill Special Issue, *Verse,* 5 (July 1988) Essays by George Bradley, Amy Clampitt, Alfred Corn, Richard A. Grusin, J. D. McClatchy, Robert Polito, and Stephen Sandy.

Moffett, Judith, *James Merrill: An Introduction to the Poetry,* (New York: Columbia University Press, 1984).

Perkins, David, "The Achievement of James Merrill," *A History of Modern Poetry: Modernism and After* (Cambridge, Mass.: Harvard University Press, 1987).

Sloss, Henry, "James Merrill's *The Book of Ephraim," Shenandoah* 27: 63–91 (Summer 1976) and 28: 83–110 (Fall 1976).

Spiegelman, Willard, "The Sacred Books of James Merrill," In *The Didactic Muse: Scenes of Instruction in Contemporary American Poetry* (Princeton, N.J.: Princeton University Press, 1989).

Vendler, Helen, "James Merrill," In *Part of Nature, Part of Us: Modern American Poets* (Cambridge, Mass.: Harvard University Press, 1980).

Vendler, Helen, "James Merrill," In *The Music of What Happens: Poems, Poets, Critics* (Cambridge, Mass.: Harvard University Press, 1988).

Yenser, Stephen, *The Consuming Myth: The Work of James Merrill,* (Cambridge, Mass.: Harvard University Press, 1987).

Zimmerman, Lee, "Against Apocalypse: Politics and James Merrill's *The Changing Light at Sandover." Contemporary Literature* 30: 370–386 (Fall 1989).

W. S. MERWIN
(b. 1927)

JIM KRAUS

ALTHOUGH W. S. MERWIN has written successfully in several genres, he has published more than twelve volumes of poetry, the first of which, *A Mask for Janus* (1952), was chosen for the Yale Younger Poets series. *The Carrier of Ladders* (1970), his seventh book of poetry, won the Pulitzer Prize in 1971. Merwin's poetry is rooted in both American history and American literary tradition, and in it his readers have discovered a profound expression of the post-World War II literary imagination. While readers have often written approvingly of Merwin's pessimism, they have also found satisfaction in the way he has advanced and modified the concerns of literary modernism by advancing the free-verse line while asserting a more personal, at times autobiographical, level of imagery. Like T. S. Eliot and Ezra Pound, he has spent a significant part of his life in Europe. As a translator, he has contributed much to the internationalization of literature by translating from several other traditions into English, counting among his favorite poets François Villon and Dante.

Besides his poetry, Merwin has written several books of prose, which are a mix of fable, parable, fairy tale, and autobiography, and several plays. He has also translated over eleven volumes, mostly from the French or Spanish. All told he has published well over thirty volumes. In addition, throughout his career he has regularly written nonfiction prose for leading American periodicals, including *The New Yorker* and *The Nation*.

He graduated from Princeton University in 1948, where, as a student, he became acquainted with R. P. Blackmur, his mentor, and John Berryman, who also taught there. During the same period, he visited Ezra Pound at St. Elizabeth's Hospital in Washington, D.C. Merwin was barely twenty at the time, and Pound advised him to translate. Afterward, Pound wrote Merwin postcards, saying in one, "Read seeds, not twigs" (in Hirsch, "W. S. Merwin XXXVIII"). While at Princeton, he also met Galway Kinnell and William Arrowsmith. Through most of his career, Merwin has stayed away from work in academic institutions, giving his attention to translation and the production of poetry and essays.

Merwin's best poetry is that which is driven by the combination of a desire for wisdom and a broad-based emotional force, both of which are at times historical and political in their scope. His poetry of the late 1960's and early 1970's, namely in *The Lice* (1967) and *The Carrier of Ladders*, responds to the horrors of the Vietnam War as well as to the historical and emotional assumptions about American culture that are rooted in the nineteenth century. Then, in the late 1980's, after Merwin had lived in Hawaii for more than ten years, a similar theme, embodied in a somewhat different tone, returns to his work as he bears witness to the destruction of Hawaii's native culture in *The Rain in the Trees* (1988). In much of his poetry, readers have found an elegiac sensibility tempered by a vision of what poet Richard Howard has called the "via negativa." Although pessimism is dominant in Merwin's tone, his poetry reveals a considerable capacity for wonder and a reverence for language that seeks to approach, even if it can never accurately render, the dark unknown.

Much can be made of Merwin's inverse relation to Walt Whitman, to the optimism of Whitman's "Song of Myself." Merwin has said that he simply does not like Whitman and has never been able to sustain an interest in him. It is clear that Merwin refers to the Whitman whose optimism correlates to progress and the idea that civilization in America, characterized by westward movement and by the consumption of wilderness, is destined to overcome and subdue the native. Merwin stands in firm opposition to Whitman's notions of American optimism and progress. He aligns himself instead with Henry David Thoreau, and in many ways the wilderness ethic embodied in Merwin's writing can be seen as paralleling Thoreau's. Both writers are grounded in the deep recognition of humankind's dependence on the natural world and in the importance of wilderness.

An early poem, "The Wilderness," from *Green with Beasts* (1956), illustrates a number of themes that form a consistent pattern throughout Merwin's career:

> Remoteness is its own secret. Not holiness,
> Though, nor the huge spirit miraculously
> avoiding
> The way's dissemblings, and undue
> distraction or drowning
> At the watercourses, has found us this
> place,
>
> But merely surviving all that is not here,
>
> Till the moment that looks up, almost by
> chance, and sees
> Perhaps hands, feet, but not ourselves; a few
> stunted juniper trees
> And the horizon's virginity. We are where
> we always were.
>
> The secret becomes no less itself for our
> presence
> In the midst of it; as the lizard's gold-eyed
> Mystery is no more lucid for being near.
> And famine is all about us, but not here;
> For from the very hunger to look, we feed
> Unawares, as at the beaks of ravens.

By defining wilderness as remote and secret, Merwin requires a reading that is concerned both with the physical part of nature, which is being consumed by human progress, and with the abstraction of the human mind, perceiving fragments of the present and hungering for a glimpse of the "secret." This view of wilderness as being neither "holy" nor "miraculous," in contrast to the philosophy claiming that God resides in the wilderness, renders a kind of counterexistence, capable, perhaps, of perceiving fragments—say, hands or feet—but not a totality of the type which would suggest God. If one could assert, as Whitman seems to, that self emerges as the summation of physical reality, Merwin might counter by asserting that at best one can perceive only fragments of physical reality, and that in hungering for totality, one is hungering for the revelation of self. It is this hunger which defines a sort of counterexistence. In a relative sense, our relationship to the counterexistence is static, for wherever we are, we are always surrounded by where we are not. Thus, absence for Merwin could be called the not-self, and it finds value to the extent that it is sought out, yet remains unknown. When Merwin points to "a few stunted juniper trees / And the horizon's virginity," he concludes that our relationship to this remote and secret counterexistence is essentially static—"We are where we always were." The counterexistence is neither diminished nor revealed; the self hungers for revelation, yet in its inevitable absence, Merwin seems to say, perceiving "famine . . . all about," the self feeds anyway, as if on hunger itself.

In the foreword to *Asian Figures,* his 1973 collection of translations of proverbs, aphorisms, and riddles from Korean, Burmese, Japanese, Philippine, Chinese, Malay, and Lao cultures, Merwin approaches the tenuous matter of defining poetry. Although he focuses primarily on those aspects of poetry that are exemplified by short, Asian literary forms, one can extract his notion of what poetry in general embodies: "an urge to finality of utterance . . . to be self-contained, to be whole . . . related to the irreversibility in the words that is a mark of poetry." Merwin has also said that poetry should center on a concern for the spoken idiom rather than the conventions of writing. This idea goes far in explaining the deemphasis of syntactic convention in Merwin's poetry. To be truly singular and irreducible, a poem may need to be marginally free from the traditions of grammar and punctuation; in this way it can be truer to the idiosyncrasies of spoken language.

William Stanley Merwin was born in New York City on September 30, 1927. Growing up he lived in Union City, New Jersey, and Scranton, Pennsylvania. Merwin recollects his childhood, which he has described as repressed, in *Unframed Originals: Recollections* (1982). His father, a Presbyterian minister, seems to be the subject of numerous poems written in an autobiographical tone, most notably in the first section of *Opening the Hand* (1983).

After completing an undergraduate degree in English at Princeton, Merwin did graduate work there in the department of modern languages. Over thirty years later, writing about Blackmur and his Princeton years, Merwin describes himself as having been "busy being Shelley . . . and a bit of Beethoven, in ill-fitting pieces of discarded army uniform" that had been given to him by his father, who was an army chaplain. Merwin knew he wanted to be a poet and was advised by Anne Fleck, the proprietor of the Parnassus Bookshop on Nassau Street in Princeton, to send some poems to Blackmur. Although Merwin never took a formal course from Blackmur, the two became friends. In a poem about Berryman included in *Opening the Hand,* the older poet advises Merwin,

> don't lose your arrogance yet
> . . .
> you can do that when you're older
> lose it too soon and you may merely replace
> it with vanity

About publishing, Berryman advised Merwin to cover his wall with rejection slips.

After one year at Princeton Graduate School, Merwin left America for Spain and Portugal, where he worked as a tutor: during this period he tutored Robert Graves's son in Majorca. By 1951, Merwin was living in London, writing radio scripts for the British Broadcasting Corporation, including *Rumpelstiltskin, Pageant of Cain Huckleberry Finn,* and *Robert the Devil.* The BBC also produced Merwin's translation of the anonymous fourteenth-century French drama *Robert the Devil,* as well as his translations of two plays by Lope de Vega. It is during this period that *A Mask for Janus* was published.

W. H. Auden wrote in the preface to *A Mask for Janus* that Merwin seems to present the reader with the "collapse of civilization." Yet, as Auden asserts, for Merwin "this collapse is not final" for "on the other side of disaster, there will be some kind of rebirth, though we cannot imagine its nature." Jarold Ramsey writes in "The Continuities of W. S. Merwin" that in *The Lice* Merwin's vision is one of the continuity of life, specifically of Merwin's own life as a poet and more broadly of humanity in general. In books that follow *The Lice,* this sense of continuity becomes more expansive and considerably less anthropocentric, as life is seen in more fundamentally biological terms. And while any vision of the collapse of civilization must be seen as essentially pessimistic, Merwin's rendering of this collapse becomes more generally life-affirming as his career progresses. Whereas in his early work the "other side of disaster" is most often characterized by considerable ambiguity, images of shadow, blackness, and silence, in *The Rain in the Trees* the poet focuses more on the continuity of life, even though such continuity may exclude human civilization.

Merwin offers his first glimpse of this in *A Mask for Janus,* where images of regeneration seem to emerge at the end of "Cancion y Glosa," with its emphasis on speech, breath, sight, and anonymity; an image of composing, "dry leaves in my hand," suggests that perhaps it is the regenerative process of the earth itself that closes the gaps between pain, desperation, hope, desire, pleasure, and regeneration. This process continues in "A Poem for Dorothy," suggesting the ambiguous peace of death, which contains the past. Remembering the past is an act of regeneration which Merwin associates closely with the fundamental pleasure of kissing.

> Sitting on stones we kiss to please
> Some stilled remembrance that shares our
> blood,
> And warmth whose shape and name were
> From ruin moving amends our peace.

In the earliest poems of his first book, Merwin establishes a clear relationship with another of his central themes—the nature of selfhood. In "Anabasis (I)" one finds the transformative self, shrouded in negation, always in proximity to elemental, physical nature. The poem reveals the self as tenuous, "estranged almost beyond response," yet clinging, through thought, dream, and memory, to time, to eternity. The "exhausted leaves" of poplars and beeches, perhaps emblems of selfhood surviving the transformations of time, might be burned, but would remain "unconsumed, / The flame perduring, the still / Smoke eternal in the mind." The self emerges as a shadow in a realm where both philosophical belief and religious faith are uncertain and unsatisfying. The aged man, "stroked always by / The vague extremities of sleep," is entangled in the physical and governed "by euphory and the leaves' dictions." Ironically, the self passes toward its grave "blessed, among the many mansions."

In "Anabasis (II)" Merwin asserts the theme of selfhood directly:

> We survived the selves that we
> remembered;
> We have dozed on gradual seas where slowly
> The hours changed on the silence, and a
> word,
> Falling, expired in the sufficient day.

Here Merwin explores the fullness of a questioning not-self, caught between dream and "the monstrous fixities of innocence." This is self-hood exiled from dreams of its own certainty; even though the dreams provide "rumors" of self-understanding, the self is like water that has "slipped from an escaping land / all night." Because the self vigorously seeks transformation, it plunges into the poet's metaphor, declaring, "we are tidal and obey." In this context, language itself is a small thing, failing to account adequately for experience in which finally "mind and body lose / The uncertain continent of a name.

Negation, in its relationship to melancholy, figures strongly in much of Merwin's early work. In his concern with the inability of language to reveal truth accurately, his tone is elegiac. In *A Mask for Janus,* this tone emerges obviously in "Ballad of John Cable and Three Gentlemen" and "Dictum: For a Masque of Deluge." In the latter, the narrator of the poem observes the beasts walking "beside their shadows"; rather than coming in pairs, they are observed as "wrought for singularity." As emblems of negation, shadows are the animals' "lean progeny." After the deluge, when the land reappears, the solitary man, unlike the habitué of Plato's cave, must recover speech out of its negation, silence; thus he "moves in an amazement of resurrection, / Solitary, impoverished, renewed." Yet whatever glimmer of hope this might provide is itself negated by "the gestures of time" and "a low portent of rain."

"Tower," the first poem in *The Dancing Bears* (1954), points toward both disillusionment and astonishment at the pain of separation; for example, the separation of head from body:

> I saw my body
> As a smooth alien
> On stones and water walking
> Headless, not noticing

Decapitation finally leads to ironic discovery: rather than leaves of birches or apple trees, the speaker of the poem sees green light while life's untruths are revealed in the song of the mindless magpie, mouthing the cliche, " 'Love, love, oh lover, / Oh King live forever.' " The conclusion of the poem suggests the poet's frustrations with worn-out beliefs, grounded in superstition or religion, regarding immortality. Ultimately it is the poet's careful observation of the natural world that leads him toward self-discovery. Out of this grows a fascination with mirrors and the color white, moonlight, and blindness as in "The Lady with the Heron":

> And my eyes thirst
> On the birdless air;
> Blindness I learned
> At the feet of the heron.

Yet it is a blindness teased with amazement and light, and finally, as in "When I Came from Colchis," a question:

> A stranger up from the sunned
> Sea of your eyes, lady,
> What fable should I tell them,
> That they should believe me?

Thus, in the early poems of the book, begins a major theme that dominates the remainder of the book—the transformative power of language to encompass "breath and knowledge" and the "grammar of return," shot through with "the long light of wonder," as in "You, Genoese Mariner." Merwin, here and in much of his writing during this part of his career, seems in awe of the discoveries that language can lead to, but at the same time he increasingly questions the fundamental truths which language has led to in the past. In "Fable" Merwin's language assumes an almost penitential tone while the narrator considers two heartless lovers. A somewhat questing tone is revealed in which the pilgrim prays "for" folly, as though the journey to wisdom could be navigated by witnessing the grievous weeping of heartless ghosts. In the end, the pilgrim seems to realize the futility of his quest:

> I am a sullen unseemly man—
> Pray now no more for folly—
> Who in the bleak and tolling hour
> Walk like a chime without a tower,
> Rending a story, and complain
> Heartless and foolishly.

The recognition that the quest for wisdom is futile seems to lead to self-discovery, in large part because the poet experiences pain. This pain may result from an unfulfilled quest or from losing something or someone once held close. In "The Passion" Merwin suggests that it is pain which characterizes the common, shared element of experience; the poem concludes by asserting that pain "consumes us by / Dividing infinitely" and suggesting that in the scriptural rendering of Christ's passion one might find eternal truth. Although Merwin here explores the redemptive aspects of spiritual pain, the nature of his allusions to Christianity changes dramatically as his poetic career progresses.

"East of the Sun and West of the Moon," Merwin's longest poem at over five hundred lines, follows five "songs" in *The Dancing Bears.* The songs seem to reach out toward hopefulness, but the smiles that might signify hope in "Song of Three Smiles" are rendered as the triumph of pain. In "East of the Sun and West of the Moon" Merwin retells a Norwegian folktale, exploring the self through a consideration of the nature of metaphor:

> What is a man
> That a man may recognize, unless the
> inhuman
> Sun and moon, wearing the masks of a man,
> Weave before him such a tale as he
> —Finding his own face in the strange
> story—
> Mistakes by metaphor and calls his own,
> Smiling, as on a familiar mystery?

Later, the moon reveals a white bear, who marries the youngest daughter of a peasant. At night the bear turns into a man who explains she must not see him in the light. After she lights a candle and is overcome with the man's beauty, she kisses him. When drops of tallow from her candle fall on him, he awakes and says that he must depart. She begins a quest for the palace that lies east of the sun and west of the moon, for it is there she will find the prince. When she finally arrives at the castle, she finds that the prince is betrothed to another. The prince then requires that his wife-to-be prove herself by washing the tallow stains out of a white shirt; the peasant's daughter accomplishes this and says, "How should I not, since all pallor is mine." In the final stanzas of the poem, the moon muses about her own existence, diffused as it is among thousands of mirrors. She recognizes that she is merely "a trick of light, and tropically." Because she is a trick, she finds her existence questionable: "unless I go in a mask / How shall I know myself among my faces?" Her magic, she declares, is metaphor, and she acknowledges that the story itself, though "an improvisation," defines the continuum of her own being. Finally, she sings out to the sun to save her from her mirrors, to turn into a white bear and marry her, for she is the daughter of a peasant. The moon's plea contains an air of futility, though. Although the reader could assume that after washing the prince's shirt, the peasant's daughter would marry the prince, the poem stops short of describing the union. For such a union would go against the central proposition of the poem. It is the futility of the moon's desire for the sun that provides the impetus for the turning of the world. The poem concludes by declaring the moon an ultimate trope, or final metaphor, who in her turning creates a world of images.

The closing sequence of the book, a group of three poems, each titled "Canso," extends the book's central theme, the transformational power of language, sounding occasionally like Eliot's *Four Quartets* ("The idiom of order is celebration, / An elegance to redeem the graceless years") and Wallace Stevens' *Notes Toward a Supreme Fiction* ("Fictive, among real familiars, or / Real but immortal among the figurative / But dying"). Containing a strong sense of the futility and painfulness of man's attempts to overcome desire, Merwin's vision here is considerably less hopeful than that in either of these works.

In *Green with Beasts* Merwin shifts in style—there are fewer mythographic poems, the poems are shorter, and in general a more lyric than narrative presentation of themes is demonstrated—yet his themes are much the same as in his first two books of poetry. Concern with nature, language, and self-identity seems to dominate much of the book. Many poems contain names of animals, as the title suggests. "Leviathan," possibly Merwin's most anthologized poem, is the first poem of the collection. The animals of the book are largely threatening and destructive, as Leviathan is chaos itself, like the sea in a storm before creation. The animals occupy a place that Merwin strives to locate in "The Wilderness"—a place that is remote and secret, even if one is near it. Yet it is also a place that is immediate and present, as well as a place that is shared with others. "Leviathan" has something of the quality of a riddle, though the riddle's answer is the poem's title. The images of death that dominate much of the first two books become in *Green with Beasts* images of the unknown, and the device that Merwin uses to approach this realm is the negative.

While much of Merwin's development suggests a movement from cool, abstract perception toward a warm and more concrete engagement of the natural world, a countermovement is just as notable, as the more direct description of the concrete, natural world leads to frustration with the failures of the abstract world. In his earlier work, one can easily see Merwin's identification of language with concrete experience, thus his early experiments with style and traditional poetic forms. In his later work, especially in *The Rain in the Trees,* one can clearly see a more direct engagement with the world of biological experience; that is, the specifics of trees and animals become more concrete. But as this happens, the poet's sense of the inadequacy of human language becomes more pronounced. This linguistic sensibility is described in "Learning a Dead Language," from *Green with Beasts.* The entire poem revolves around the act of learning a dead language, of remembering it by attempting to perceive "the whole grammar in all its accidence" and of ultimately finding "the passion that composed it." Thus, the imagery of the poem is exclusively abstract.

In Merwin's examination of "the other side of disaster" the poet makes a considerable point of describing the tenuousness of existence—partially portentous, partially elegiac—which is characterized by the imminence of disaster; it might be said that Merwin writes much about the side of disaster that is inherent in the human spirit. Although his is a poetry of life that is at times joyous, the poems' tendency toward the muting of desire emphasizes the premonitory and elegiac. Such an approach deemphasizes the present and the immediate perception of self and allows the poet to reach toward the future while grieving for the past. It might be added here that this approach also suggests how the self is aligned with the idea of the concrete moment of experience having a locus defined by the not-self of past and future. This at times prescient tone creates the impression that the poems are foretelling a disaster as inevitable as life itself.

This tone characterizes the entire sequence of sea poems that includes Part Three of *Green with Beasts* and the first twelve poems of *The Drunk in the Furnace* (1960). For example, in "Odysseus," from *The Drunk in the Furnace,* Merwin extends this sense of the inevitable in the figure of Odysseus, who finds himself in a constant state of departure because

> The knowledge of all that he betrayed
> grew till it was the same whether he stayed
> Or went. Therefore he went.

Images of a sea voyage seem to define much of the early part of the book; the mariner is always willing to confront the unknown.

In "The Iceberg," the second poem from *The Drunk in the Furnace,* the landscape of desolation, "the terror / That cannot be charted," finally dissolves into a prescience of apple trees. Although it does not dissolve, "Deception Island" is almost as illusory as an iceberg, "filled with silence," a landscape of the lonely imagination of the sea-weary sailor longing for a place to anchor. Characteristically expressed as negative potential, the landscape is "barren / Of all the vegetation of desire"; thus desire is posited as the immediate relative of absence and memory. In "The *Portland* Going Out" the conversion of absence and memory becomes premonitory, "beyond reckoning," when the narrator remembers the last time a doomed ship was seen before it disappeared in a winter storm:

> Yet we keep asking
> How it happened, how, and why Blanchard
> sailed,
> Miscalculating the storm's course. But what
> We cannot even find questions for
> Is how near we were: brushed by the same
> snow,
> Lifted by her wake as she passed. We could
> Have spoken, we swear, with anyone on her
> deck,
> And not had to raise our voices, if we
> Had known anything to say. And now
> In no time at all, she has put
> All of disaster between us: a gulf
> Beyond reckoning. It begins where we are.

The sequence of marine poems in which the two mentioned above are included begins in Part Three of *Green with Beasts.* Here the sea is seen as consuming, as in "The Fisherman," where those who "carry the ends of our hungers out to drop them / To wait swaying in a dark place we could never have chosen" are depicted. As it is inevitable that the sea consumes the fisherman, it is inevitable that the tone of the poem is elegiac in its evocation of transience (the laying of wreaths on the water) and permanence (the commemoration the poem becomes): "We lay wreaths on the sea when it has drowned them." Although most of Merwin's books contain sea poems of one type of another, beginning with "Anabasis I" and "Anabasis II," the first two poems of Merwin's first book, the sea in this later sequence is itself the subject, uncertain with fog and foreboding, yet, as in "The Shipwreck" full of "elemental violence" and a wisdom so intense that it is associated with death. It is the physical embodiment of wildness, yet in its chaos it is "without / Accident" and "in its rage" it is "without Error."

Following the sea poems, *The Drunk in the Furnace* can be divided into two parts. The first part, beginning with "The Highway" and ending with "The Gleaners," is considerably more concrete than poems in his earlier books. The last part of the book, beginning with "Pool Room in the Lions Club," represents a set of strong autobiographical poems. The book concludes with "The Drunk in the Furnace," which describes how a derelict artifact from the past, possibly part of an old still, can occasionally be rejuvenated. While the mysterious drunk bellows away in the junk heap, the "witless offspring" of the overly pious townspeople "flock like piped rats to its siren." The poet explains the irony of this regeneration in the last lines, as the children, "agape on the crumbling ridge," gather and "stand in a row and learn."

After marrying Dido Milroy, Merwin and his wife collaborated on the verse play *Darkling Child,* which was produced in London in 1956. While living in Boston, the Merwins became acquainted with Sylvia Plath and Ted Hughes. The Merwins returned to England, and in 1960, Plath and Hughes also moved, and the Merwins helped them find a place to live. Later Merwin loaned them the use of his study while he and Dido were at their farm near Lot, France. From 1961 to 1963, Merwin served as Poetry Editor of *The Nation.* Merwin's poetry, translations, reviews, and journalism were published with astonishing regularity in *The Nation,* as well as many other major and minor periodicals in America.

For Merwin's poetry, the decade of the 1960's was a time of great transformation. Richard Howard observes how the poetry that characterizes *The Moving Target* (1963), *The Lice,* and *The Carrier of Ladders* is foreshadowed by Merwin's earlier work as dramatist and translator. Merwin's dramas of this earlier period (*Darkling Child* and *Favor Island,* produced in Cambridge, Massachusetts, in 1957) and his translations (*Robert the Devil,* an anonymous fourteenth-century French play produced by the BBC in 1954; *Punishment Without Vengeance* and *The Dog in the Manger,* both by Lope de Vega, produced by the BBC in 1954; *The Poem of the Cid,* published in 1959, *The Satires of Persius,* published in 1961; and *Spanish Ballads,* published in 1961) indicate the character of Merwin's vision of human experience and of his metric. The "spooky stoicism," Howard says, of the "relaxed octosyllabics" of the verse epilogue of *Favor Island* is hardened by the emphasis put on the sea, "its never-ending finality, its irreversible otherness." According to Howard, finality and otherness characterize Merwin's work during this period and become the embodiment of "Merwin's capacity to moralize his surround, to win from the not-self an appropriate emblem of what the self intends."

In *The Moving Target,* Merwin's investigation of selfhood seems to operate on two somewhat contrary levels. First is the level of the isolated image, which is increasingly realistic, made up of animals; the natural world is revealed through sensory experience. Second is the level of the psyche, concerned in large part with memory and grief. The essential tension of the poems arises from the conflict between the two levels, which finds expression most often (as many of his earlier poems do) in somewhat of a Keatsian negative capability, as in "Recognition":

> I came home as a web to its spider,
> To teach the flies of my household
> Their songs. I walked
> In on the mirrors scarred as match-boxes,
> The gaze of the frames and the ticking
> In the beams. The shadows
> Had grown a lot and they clung
> To the skirts of the lamps.
> Nothing
> Remembered who I was.

Here is an active nothingness, a silence pregnant with unrealized memory; the poet registers a moment of recognition when the self is revealed momentarily, not as sensory experience, not as the spider itself, not as light, not as hope for the future, but as a premonition of the future projected onto the past: "Tomorrow / Marches on the old walls." The recognition coincides with the imminent arrival of memory, a "coat full of darkness."

By removing the future to the past and shrouding the result in darkness, Merwin emerges as one of this century's great poets of melancholy. It is, however, a melancholy considerably more removed from beauty and desire than that of Keats (although no less aimed at the truth of the imagination) and increasingly more apocalyptic than his own writing of the 1950's. Although explicit in the prose "Letter from Aldermaston" he wrote for *The Nation* about a nuclear disarmament protest march, the imagery of the poems, beginning with *The Moving Target,* increasingly reveals a grim prospect for human survival. In "The Crossroads of the World Etc." Merwin accomplishes a transformation of style, especially of diction and syntax, and the book as a whole finds its culmination in this poem. It is at this point in *The Moving Target* that the poet drops all punctuation, a practice that he continues to employ in his later books and that no doubt contributes to the frequent observation by critics that his work is enigmatic. Whether or not the practice is responsible for this criticism, it has become one of the chief identifiers of Merwin's poetic style. The bare appearance of the lines on the page suggests that a barren, perhaps desolate psychic landscape cannot be far removed. By removing the convention of punctuation, the poet reveals a landscape of woe, where syntactic repetition becomes the funeral march of time.

Commenting in 1969 about the nature of poetic form in "On Open Form" from the anthology *The New Naked Poetry: Recent American Poetry in Open Forms,* Merwin said it is "the setting down of a way of hearing how poetry happens in words. The words themselves do not make it. At the same time it is testimony of a way of hearing how life happens in time." Thus, in poems like "The Crossroads of the World Etc." time exists only in the dominion of memory, where "In the mirrors the star called Nothing / Cuts us off." Time is a desolate metropolis, being ruined as its inhabitant prepares an elegy for the future:

Ruin
My city
Oh wreck of the future out of which
The future rises
What is your name as we fall

Occasionally during his career, Merwin has put great emphasis on animals in his poetry, having planned to publish a bestiary some day. With the publication of *The Lice* in 1967, Merwin discloses his identification of animals with language, particularly insects, which take on the unlikely shape of hope. "The Animals" reflects a rare affirmation of hope in Merwin's entire corpus:

All these years behind windows
With blind crosses sweeping the tables

And myself tracking over empty ground
Animals I never saw

I with no voice

Remembering names to invent for them
Will any come back will one

Saying yes

Saying look carefully yes
We will meet again

It is, of course, a tentative affirmation, for one could deduce that since the animals have never been seen, it is unlikely that the poet will meet an actual animal, rather only its deceptive name.

This poem and others appearing late in *The Moving Target* and early in *The Lice* seem to correlate to the relationship between language and human emotion; language disguises emotion, attempting to freeze it in time, to objectify that which is entirely subjective. Although the language that Merwin evokes is tempted by personification, it finds its central force in its effort to bypass the portion of sensory experience associated with sight and transfer what energy, or meaning, one would find there to silence and the pregnant emptiness of listening. This is evident in "The Man Who Writes Ants" from *The Moving Target*:

Called

By what trumpet

He leaves my eyes he climbs my graves
I pass the names

He is not followed I am not following him
no

Today the day of the water
With ink for my remote purpose with my
pockets full of black
With no one in sight
I am walking in silence I am walking in
silence I am walking
In single file listening for a trumpet

Merwin's poetry in its entirety, but especially in *The Lice,* is part of a tradition of writing about the natural world that echoes back to Carolus Linnaeus, the eighteenth-century Swedish botanist who began systematizing the naming and classification of plants. Particularly during the post-Darwinian era it becomes plausible for the popular mind to conceive of humankind not as the highest form of life and the friendly steward of the life of the planet, but as the destroyer of life. Keenly aware of the part both Linnaeus and Charles Darwin played in shaping twentieth-century attitudes toward the natural world, Merwin shapes, especially from *The Lice* onward, a kind of misanthropy that becomes increasingly pervasive. By the time he writes *The Rain in the Trees,* he is able to assert that insects are wiser than humans.

In *The Lice* the naming of animals, along with the searching out of them, becomes a primary concern, a concern that in the Edenic tradition is closely associated with the origins of language. Merwin extends this tradition by attempting to remember "names to invent for them," by trying to recover a wisdom associated with the primal creativity of the garden. Yet such wisdom must inevitably confront disaster. In "The Hydra" the notion of naming is associated with death, as though human language, the naming of the natural world, is an attempt to keep that world from dying:

As the grass had its own language

Now I forget where the difference falls

One thing about the living sometimes a
piece of us
Can stop dying for a moment
But you the dead

Once you go into those names you go on
you never
Hesitate
You go on

Merwin suggests that wisdom is always receding, like a riddle with an irrational answer, that it is some sort of deity, outside of time and outside of language. If the poems of *The Lice* seem cryptic or enigmatic to some, it is because Merwin locates the poems in a realm where the words appear to have died. The poet's illusion here is that, although he cannot literally make the words vanish, he can present them in such ambiguous contexts that conventional notions of their meanings seem inappropriate. In "I Live Up Here," the poet adopts the tone of a displaced magician, a fugitive from conventional meaning and from life itself, leaning heavily on an irony that is built out of heightened cliches—"It's perfectly fair . . . I give what I can . . . It's worth it"—to parody a view of the world that is above politics and above the actual pain and suffering of the living:

Oh down there down there
Every time
The glass knights lie by their gloves of
blood

In the pans of the scales the helmets
Brim over with water
It's perfectly fair

Although this ironic tone runs through much of Merwin's work, a related irony—not condescending or aloof, but one thoroughly engaging the theme of the opposition of self and other—emerges in "My Brothers the Silent." The reader may identify stars, blackness, shepherds, and animals, specifically sheep, with the brothers. Including time and "the invisible," the family of possible associations to the brothers of the title is so far-reaching that it is best described as generalized other. Additionally, the two words, "brother" and "other," are linked by a degree of common spelling and meaning. It is because the speaker of the poem believes so much in words that he can claim an inheritance, although one that he cannot have:

What an uncharitable family
My brothers shepherds older than birth
What are you afraid of since I was born
I cannot touch the inheritance what is my
    age to you
I am not sure I would know what to ask for
I do not know what my hands are for
I do not know what my wars are deciding

It is an "uncharitable family" to which the speaker of the poem claims lineage. The brothers in this poem are emblems of the knowable unknown. Thus, the poem revolves around the ironic notion that while the self finds meaning by establishing relationship to the unknown, wisdom, a kind of inheritance, cannot actually be touched. Finally, in the degree to which it employs negative statement, the poem as a whole seems shot through with the general feelings of isolation and loneliness. Perhaps the poet says, ironically, that like unrequited love for a cold family, the pursuit of self-knowledge is a one-way affair.

In *The Carrier of Ladders,* Merwin continues to use animals as guides to the deepest levels of experience; at the same time one sees the reemergence of his early mythographic style in "The Judgment of Paris" and of a beautiful elegiac tone in "Psalm: Our Fathers." When he reviewed *The Carrier of Ladders,* Richard Howard commented on its intimacy, but claimed that it remains successfully impersonal. To appreciate the poems, according to Howard, is to proceed along the "via negativa," which is the way of the visionary, although a way characterized by negative perception of one's surroundings: in this manner, the self is defined by what the self is not.

If Whitman's project was to take in, to encompass history, to make it part of the self, Merwin's is precisely the opposite; however, in order to empty the self, as Ed Folsom explains in "I Have Been a Long Time in a Strange Country," one must first recognize the elements of history which make up the self. In Merwin's work these are autobiography and mythography. It is the mythographic in "The Judgment of Paris" through which the reader is able to witness that Paris is innocent of the historical consequences of his judgment; in turn, the reader is able to judge Paris.

The central sequence of poems in *The Carrier of Ladders* is one that Folsom has aptly called the American sequence, comparing it to Theodore Roethke's "North American Sequence," Hart Crane's *The Bridge,* Gary Snyder's *Turtle Island,* and William Carlos Williams' *In the American Grain.* The sequence begins with "The Approaches" and ends with "The Removal." In "The Approaches" Merwin begins his recovery of American history. He sets off for the promised land, knowing that there is fighting going on there and that the ruins are still warm. So used to writing about the ancient past, the poet suggests the relatively recent "removal" of Native Americans. The entire sequence emphasizes the tragedy of their treatment, underlined by the irony that as civilization marches west, the promised land is being destroyed:

no one to guide me
afraid
to the warm ruins
Canaan
where the fighting is

In terms of the evolution of Merwin's style, one of the most significant poems in the sequence is "Lackawanna." Here he merges recollection of his Pennsylvania boyhood with the developing theme of the sequence, the difficulty of finding one s self in the context of history. Identifying the river with the place the dead drift off to, and thus with history, the narrator remembers its blackness and as a child being "told to be afraid / obedient." Yet the child knows that the river is more than history; it is the truth about history, about the passing of the dead into the past:

you flowed from under
and through the night the dead drifted down
you
all the dead
what was found later no one
could recognize

From the autobiographical tone of "Lackawanna," the sequence moves forward into biography, with references to William Bartram, the eighteenth-century naturalist who wrote about the American wilderness, and John Wesley Powell, who with one arm led the geologic survey that mapped much of the western American wilderness in the late nineteenth century. It is a mark of Merwin's imagination to make much of absences, and so it is in "The Gardens of Zuñi" that Powell's missing arm "groped on / for the virgin land / and found where it had been." In "Homeland," Merwin transforms the western landscape itself into a curse on Andrew Jackson, the American president known for killing Native Americans:

The sky goes on living it goes
on living the sky
with all the barbed wire of the west
in its veins
and the sun goes down
driving a stake
through the black heart of Andrew Jackson

In "Presidents" Merwin writes one of his most vicious attacks on the forces that pushed the American frontier forward. Standing also as a good example of how the poet is able to turn a surrealistic tone to political ends (as is Pablo Neruda, many of whose poems Merwin translated), "Presidents" abandons logic in favor of dagger-sharp invective:

the president of lies quotes the voice
of God
as last counted
the president of loyalty recommends
blindness to the blind
oh oh
applause like the heels of the hanged
he walks on eyes
until they break

In "The Removal," which is dedicated "to the endless tribe," Merwin shifts to a more elegiac tone. Here the river takes on a lethean form, and the sense of loss extends to the "lost languages, so that the tongue itself "comes walking / shuffling like breath." Shadows and mourners go in on one side of the river, hoping to be healed; then on the other side "ribbons come out / invisible." Immediately following the American sequence, Merwin resumes an autobiographical tone, but it is not until much later in the book, in "The Thread," that the theme of history and the search for self emerges again. Here, the black thread is a song that covers the period of time's beginning to "beyond your dead." Along the way one encounters touchstones of physical identity, the soles of shoes "standing / out in the air you breathe" and "bodies / stacked before them like bottles / generation upon / generation."

To be sure, in this collection Merwin seems to eschew elegy, "The Removal" and several other poems notwithstanding, by locating one of the shortest poems in the English language, "Elegy," in the position next to last. Here is "Elegy" in its entirety: "Who would I show it to." In his exhaustive treatment of the poem's seven words, Robert Scholes in his essay "Reading Merwin Semiotically" (collected in *W. S. Merwin: Essays on the Poetry*) describes the poem as an anti-elegy. Because the preceding poem ends with "The darkness is cold / because the stars do not believe in each other," one can read "Elegy" as doubly ironic, as likely anti-elegiac as it is elegiac. So much of Merwin's writing plays on opposites, as though his works reflect one another, usually canceling one another out, pointing to a vision that is at least marginally solipsistic. If Merwin's work seems dark to many, perhaps it is because the alienated self—and for that matter the poem itself—often seems so rarefied that it stands alone at the center of a universe of its own making.

Nevertheless, like many of Merwin's books, *The Carrier of Ladders* ends with a small ray of hope, in that the poet is able to call out through history for a response. "In the Time of the Blossoms" reconciles, for a brief time, life with the forces of darkness:

Ash tree
sacred to her who sails in
from the one sea
all over you leaf skeletons
fine as sparrow bones
stream out motionless
on white heaven
staves of one
unbreathed music
Sing to me

Charles Altieri explains in "Situating Merwin's Poetry Since 1970" (collected in *W. S. Merwin: Essays on the Poetry*) that in such reconciliation "the fullness of life is never far from the realities of death and judgment." "In the Time of the Blossoms" returns to a myth-time out of which the poet wishes to invoke the "great language" that held the ash tree to be sacred and that is large enough to describe how closely "death participates even in the fullest moments of natural blossoming."

Merwin's next book, *Writings to an Unfinished Accompaniment* (1973), begins with a sequence of lyrics, some of which can be read as answers to the "Sing to me" of the closing poem of *The Carrier of Ladders.* "The Silence Before Harvest" contains the idealized sound suggested in "In the Time of Blossoms" by "staves of one / unbreathed music"; as a harvest poem, it, too, reaches back into myth-time, depicting sounds received from "somewhere else." It suggests that the reconciliation of opposites is possible—the sound arrives as light, while the hands that play the harp are dark:

The harps the harps
standing in fields
standing
and dark hands
playing
somewhere else the sound
sound
will arrive
light from a star

Charles Molesworth in "W. S. Merwin: Style, Vision, Influence," however, reading the opening sequence of the book as a "self-contained and self-glossing set of texts," has characterized Merwin's poetic as one "that inevitably turns one emotion into its opposite and then is left with only absence to celebrate." Molesworth finds, for example, in "Looking Back," reference to such an immense frame of time—from "before the first cell"—the poem "renders details insignificant and turns hope into something furtive and numbing." He points to "Words" and "The Unwritten," later in the book, as further examples of "an aesthetic dead end," citing "Words" as a version of Frost's "Fire and Ice." What Molesworth objects to is Merwin's movement toward unbounded generalization. In "Words," the "pain of the world finds words" that "sound like joy." And in "The Unwritten," the tension of "words that have never been written" crouching "inside this pencil" gives way to the supposition "that there's only one word / and it's all we need" and finally "every pencil in the world / is like this."

On the other hand, some critics, notably Cary Nelson and Ed Folsom, editors of the important collection *W. S.* Merwin*: Essays on the Poetry* (1987), suggest that readers not look at the books as self-contained units; rather, they should look at the larger movement of style and theme. For example, Nelson says, "All the poems from *The Moving Target* to *Writings to an Unfinished Accompaniment* may be read as though they were written simultaneously—in the winter of an eternal present." For many readers Merwin's poems seem to represent problems of interpretation because the poet maintains a considerable distance from conventional diction and syntax; however, in the broad view of his writings over several decades, he succeeds in establishing a poetic that is, as he described it in "On Open Form," "something that would be like an echo except that it is repeating no sound." The poem should communicate "something which always belonged to it: its sense and its conformation before it entered words."

While Merwin's next two books, *The Compass Flower* (1977) and *Finding the Islands* (1982), are in many ways the ones in which the poet comes closest to the aesthetic he admires in Thoreau, they are also the books in which he seems to elude many of his critics. Contrary to his earlier books, these replace the "rhetoric of absence" with a pastoralism that celebrates the presence of landscape. In this way, Merwin, like Thoreau, meticulously observes the quality of his day-to-day experience in the context of a profound participation in the life of the place in which he lives. When it appeared in his earlier work, Merwin's pastoralism was often qualified by a subtle misanthropy; however, in these books human companionship and an energetic eroticism mediate the pastoral, contributing to the tone of affirmation. Altieri explains that as Merwin moves away from the rhetoric of absence and the "taut surreal logic" that characterize his earlier work, his lyrics "become less moments of discovery than examples of a faith." In this way, Altieri says, they fail to provide a necessary level of dramatic immediacy.

It needs to be said, however, that through the late 1970's Merwin was becoming increasingly interested in Zen Buddhism and that Altieri's criticism is part of a common Western response to Zen-inspired art. To appreciate fully the intensity of observation that these delicate poems show, one must remember the tradition of Japanese haiku. Dating from the fifteenth century, *hokku,* as it was originally called, is a form made up of seventeen syllables that aims at the direct presentation of experience itself. In its early use, the form introduced a series of linked short poems. Although Merwin makes it clear in his 1984 interview with David L. Eliot that the short poems of *Finding the Islands* are not intended to be haiku, it seems evident that the poems represent the same sort of union of aesthetic and spiritual experience that the early haiku writers cultivated. Merwin's attraction to Zen may be related to something that is fundamental to his aesthetic: the rendering of an appropriate interaction with nature. This interaction is in some respects different from that defined by American romanticism, which sometimes failed to register objections to the nature-destroying capacities of industrialization.

Nonetheless, the ethic of utilitarian simplicity and harmony with the forces of nature that Thoreau describes is one that Merwin obviously emulates. A similar ethic can be found in the writings of Muso Soseki, the twelfth-century Zen teacher whose poetry Merwin has translated in collaboration with Soiku Shigematsu. In his introduction to that volume of translations, titled *Sun at Midnight* (1989), Merwin writes of Muso's accomplishments as a builder of gardens. In describing the garden at Tenryuji, which Muso planned, Merwin observes a combination of "a great sweep of landscape and a feeling of space with one of intimacy and simplicity." In all his teaching Muso emphasized a "vision of emptiness" that comes out of his ability to balance, as Merwin puts it, "convention and control, on the one hand, and spontaneity on the other."

In *Opening the Hand,* Merwin moves back toward the "rhetoric of absence" that characterizes so much of his work before *Compass Flower* and *Finding the Islands*; by restoring this source of tension in his poetry, Merwin makes an important contribution to his active examination of humankind's relationship to the natural world. This is especially true if *Opening the Hand* is seen in conjunction with *The Rain in the Trees,* the book that follows it. In addition, *Opening the Hand* introduces a technical device, the variable caesura, and it contains an important sequence of autobiographically oriented poems.

As Edward Brunner has pointed out in "*Opening the Hand*: The Variable Caesura and the Family Poems," Merwin's use of the device seems related to, yet distinct from, the caesura found in works that he has translated, specifically medieval Spanish and French poetry. Among Merwin's contemporaries, the caesura is also found in the work of James Dickey and Adrienne Rich, although, as Brunner points out, Dickey uses it to slow the line down and Rich uses it for punctuation. Instead, Merwin uses the open space of the caesura to create lines with patterns of hesitation. As Merwin himself has explained regarding the line generally in the interview "'Fact Has Two Faces,'" "it's making a continuity of movement and making a rhythm within a continuity. It's doing these two things at the same time." It is, in a sense, creating a line within a line, along with the feeling of ambiguity and at times contradiction.

In the first section of *Opening the Hand,* Merwin presents a set of poems centered for the most part on the theme of the father. This sequence is especially significant because it provides a commentary on the qualities of relationship between father and child that contribute to a sense of the poetic imagination, as in "A Pause by the Water":

> After the days of walking   alone in the
>   mountains
> between cities and after the nights   again
>   under dripping trees
> coming down I kept seeing   in my mind
>   the ocean
> though I knew it would not be   like
>   anything I imagined
>
> after hearing of the old man's   dying and
>   after the burial
> between rainy morning and rainy
>   evening   the start of a cold summer
> coming down the misted path alone   I
>   kept finding
> in my thought the ocean   though I told
>   myself
> step by step that it could never   be at all
>   like that

Thus, it is the child's sense of wonder at the interaction of his imaginings and the actual world outside that moves the poem forward. The caesura causes the reader to feel the hesitation and uncertainty that attend the child's movement toward the conclusion of the final line. In "The Houses," the father scolds his son when the child reports seeing two houses in the woods; even as he later sees similar houses, the son passes through a period of denying both the reality of his original sighting and his own imagination. However, all the while it seems inevitable that the son's vision will triumph, and "after the father / is dead the son sees the two houses." "The Houses" points to a theme that is central to all autobiography, the simultaneity of memory and experience. Later in the section, in "Talking," Merwin addresses the theme explicitly:

> Whatever I talk about is yesterday
> by the time I see anything it is gone
> the only way I can see today
> is as yesterday
>
> . . .
>
> I tell parts of a story
> that once occurred
> and I laugh with surprise at what
>   disappeared
> though I remember it so well

The middle section of *Opening the Hand* is decidedly focused on an urban landscape, although it occasionally comments on a deteriorating Hawaiian landscape, for example in "Questions to Tourists Stopped by a Pineapple Field." The contradiction between the urban and the rural, which this particular poem centers on, foreshadows the movement of the last section of the book in which poems like "The Palm" and "The Black Jewel" point to the major theme of *The Rain in the Trees.* Both poems describe a source of knowledge and truth that resides in nature; it is a knowledge of which humanity for the most part is oblivious.

Merwin's 1988 collection, *The Rain in the Trees,* uses plants and insects as its central metaphors. But the book is about language, especially the failure of language to transcend direct sensory experience. Early in the book, "West Wall" establishes a major motif, absence, in describing the disappearance of shadows and branches of a tree while leaves and apricots become more vivid. In the second stanza, the apricots themselves vanish as the experience of eating transforms them into taste, the taste of apricots then transforming into the taste of the sun:

> I might have stood in orchards forever
> without beholding the day in the apricots
> or knowing the ripeness of the lucid air
> or touching the apricots in your skin
> or tasting in your mouth the sun in the
> apricots.

This sense of transformation makes up an important part of Merwin's rhetoric of absence because the transformation results in leaving something behind. Consequently, this process often becomes elegy, and as such is the occasion for a celebration of the fundamental tension between hope and despair. Much of the poetry in *The Rain in the Trees* carries this elegiac sense. For example, "Night Above the Avenue" links "the point of birth" and "the point of death" in an abstract "somebody" surrounded "in pain and in hope." The poem suggests that everybody plays a part in some vast transformative dialectic that defines the terms of being. The first-person speaker of the poem, sounding a bit like Eliot's J. Alfred Prufrock, sits up late at night and becomes like an antenna receiving the paired messages that make up the news:

> and I have sat up late
> at the kitchen window
> knowing the news
> watching the paired red lights
> recede from under the windows down the
> avenue
> toward the tunnel under the river
> and the white lights from the park rushing
> toward us
> through the sirens and the music
> and I have wakened in a wind of messages

The early poems in the book operate with an autobiographical style characterized by a first-person speaker who at times is in dialogue with father and mother. In "Native Trees" and "Touching the Tree" the parental figures are agents of negation when they forget the names of trees and stop the speaker from entering the magical world of the tree. In other poems it is the urban world generally that is associated with negation and the destruction of nature, as in the sequence beginning with "Touching the Tree" and ending with "Shadow Passing." In some ways these poems recall the negativity of *The Lice* (of special note is the relation between "Shadow Passing" and "The Last One"), yet the later poems suggest occasional movements toward hope as the poems shift from an emphasis on urban landscape to rural, more pastoral settings. For example, in "Summer of '82" the speaker and a companion move away from the dirty streets of the city:

> and in the evening we alone
> took the streetcar to the rain forest
> followed the green ridge in the dusk
> got off to walk home through the ancient
> trees

Throughout the book trees become the enduring figures for that wisdom which the urban world either destroys or ignores. The poems represent a seeking out of this wisdom, while rain and wind become metaphors of the process that includes the acquiring of knowledge and the use of language. The poems occasionally call out to a muse that is in some ways omniscient, yet always close to language, to forgetfulness, and to primal origins. In "The Sound of Light" the speaker simultaneously hears the sounds of a pastoral world and forgets those of the urban world. In "Sight" the speaker personifies a one-cell organism, which is the first to perceive light and therefore the first to create sight. Then transforming into bird, goat, and fish, the first-person narrator of the poem finally becomes a generalized "I" seeking relationship with "you":

> I
> look at you
> in the first light of the morning
> for as long as I can

In later poems, the speaker seeks to displace time by emphasizing a longing for human companionship, as in "The Solstice":

at the thought of the months I reach for
your hand
it is not something
one is supposed
to say

we watch the bright birds in the morning
we hope for the quiet
daytime together
the year turns into air

In this and in poems like "Coming to the Morning," it is as if the speaker strives to give himself totally to otherness, so that creation itself is the result of listening and remembering: "and our ears / are formed of the sea as we listen."

The idea of listening also recalls Merwin's work as a translator of medieval poetry engaged in the remembering of language that much of modern culture has neglected. When Merwin writes "After the Alphabets," in which he is "trying to decipher the language of insects," he describes a paradigm for language that cuts through all abstraction, language that is not limited by time or grammar, and that points toward a grim human future, for after all, the insects "are the tongues of the future."

Much of the remainder of *The Rain in the Trees* moves as an elegy for a lost Hawaiian culture. "Strangers from the Horizon" establishes the point of view of Hawaiians meeting the first European ships. "Chord" parallels Keats's life with the removal of sandalwood forests in the Hawaiian Islands; as the trees are removed the Hawaiian language itself is lost. "Losing a Language" depicts the slow, almost imperceptible destruction of the native language:

when there is a voice at the door it is
foreign
everywhere instead of a name there is a lie
nobody has seen it happening
nobody remembers

In "Term" Merwin brings a similar sensibility to bear on a protest against the proposed closing of an old road to make way for a development. The developers, of course, are not Hawaiian, and Merwin remains pessimistic, as he had been much earlier when writing about the destruction of Native American culture in *The Carrier of Ladders*:

where the thorny
kiawe trees smelling
of honey
dance in their shadows along the sand

the road will die
and turn into money at last
as the developers
themselves hope to do

In the closing poems of the book Merwin writes as if he were seeing through the eyes of a botanist. He is searching for the ancient wisdom of the natural world by engaging in the recovery of that which is dying the fastest. In Merwin's poems the act of raising plants seems to cohere with the act of writing, as well as the acts of remembering the past and creating the future, as in "The Archaic Maker":

But here is ancient today
itself
the air the living air
the still water

In general terms W. S. Merwin's career can be divided into at least three periods. During the first period, delineated by his first four books, his interest in medieval poetry and in a certain rhetorical firmness emphasizes a search for selfhood. For much of this part of his career, Merwin lived in Europe, making a living by tutoring and translating, as well as writing radio scripts and book reviews. Although his tone never approached the confessional style characteristic of many poets of the period, Merwin began writing sequences of poems that are autobiographical.

With the publication of *The Moving Target* in 1963, Merwin broke with his earlier inclination toward formalism and began writing free verse characterized by the absence of all punctuation and the use of irregular meter. The generally negative sensibility of his earlier poetry continued to expand as the subjects of his poems shifted from mythographic to political. During this second period Merwin lived in New York City, on a farm near Lot, France, and in Mexico. He became more politically active, participating in protests against the Vietnam War and writing poems critical of that part of American culture associated with progress and the destruction of the primitive.

In a statement printed in *The New York Review of Books* following the announcement that he had been awarded the 1971 Pulitzer Prize for *The Carrier of Ladders*, Merwin said:

> I am too conscious of being an American to accept public congratulations with good grace, or to welcome it except as an occasion for expressing openly a shame which many Americans feel, day after day, helplessly and in silence.

He asked that the prize money be given to Alan Blanchard, a painter in Berkeley, California, who had been blinded by a police weapon, and to the Draft Resistance.

The third period of his career began roughly with the publication of *The Compass Flower* in 1977. As had been the case throughout his career, Merwin traveled throughout the United States giving poetry readings. By 1978, after several visits to Hawaii, he decided to live at Haiku on the island of Maui. During this period Merwin began to study Buddhism seriously, and *The Compass Flower* and *Finding the Islands* (1982) develop a more affirmative aesthetic, which seems related to his religious studies.

In the late 1980's and early 1990's Merwin increasingly withdrew from a life of travel, prefering instead to work at his home in Hawaii. Throughout the 1980's and into the 1990's, Merwin campaigned vigorously for the preservation of native Hawaiian flora and fauna. His poetry recovered some of the "rhetoric of absence" that had fueled his writing during the 1960's and early 1970's. The absence, as it had been in some poems of the earlier periods, is his own past, and this is reflected in the return to an autobiographical mode. However, the absence in these later poems is also associated with environmental degradation.

Selected Bibliography

WORKS OF W. S. MERWIN

POETRY

A Mask for Janus, (New Haven: Yale University Press, 1952).

The Dancing Bears, (New Haven: Yale University Press, 1954).

Green with Beasts, (New York: Knopf, 1956).

The Drunk in the Furnace, (New York: Macmillan, 1960).

The Moving Target, (New York: Atheneum, 1963).

The Lice, (New York: Atheneum, 1967).

The Carrier of Ladders, (New York: Atheneum, 1970).

Writings to an Unfinished Accompaniment, (New York: Atheneum, 1973).

The First Four Books of Poems, (New York: Atheneum, 1975) Collects *A Mask for Janus, The Dancing Bears, Green with Beasts,* and *The Drunk in the Furnace;*

The Compass Flower, (New York: Atheneum, 1977).

Finding the Islands, (San Francisco: North Point Press, 1982).

Opening the Hand, (New York: Atheneum, 1983).

The Rain in the Trees, (New York: Knopf, 1988).

Selected Poems, (New York: Atheneum, 1988).

PROSE

The Miner's Pale Children, (New York: Atheneum, 1970).

A New Right Arm, (Albuquerque, N. Mex.: Road Runner Press, 1970).

"On Being Awarded the Pulitzer Prize," *New York Review of Books* 16: 41 (June 3, 1971).

"On Open Form," *The New Naked. Poetry* Edited by Stephen Berg and Robert Mezey (Indianapolis: Bobbs-Merrill, 1976) pp. 276–278. Also in *Regions of Memory: Uncollected Prose, 1949–1982.* Edited by Ed Folsom and Cary Nelson (Urbana: University of Illinois Press, 1987) 298–300.

Houses and Travellers, (New York: Atheneum, 1977).
Unframed Originals: Recollections, (New York: Atheneum, 1982).
Regions of Memory: Uncollected Prose, 1949–1982. Edited by Ed Folsom and Cary Nelson (Urbana: University of Illinois Press, 1987).

DRAMA

Rumpelstiltskin, BBC television production (1951).
Pageant of Cain, BBC Third Programme (1952).
Huckleberry Finn, BBC television production (1953).
Darkling Child, Arts Theatre production, (London, England, 1956).
Favor Island, (Cambridge, Massachusetts: Poets' Theater production, 1957) BBC Third Programme (1958) Act I appears in *New World Writing* 12:154 (1957).
The Guilded West, (Coventry, England: Belgrade Theatre production, 1961).

TRANSLATED WORKS

Robert the Devil, BBC Third Programme (1954) (Iowa City, Iowa: Windhover Press, 1981).
Punishment Without Vengeance, [Lope de Vega] BBC production (1954).
The Dog in the Manger, [Lope de Vega] BBC production (1954).
The Poem of the Cid [El poema del mio Cid], (New York: Las Americas, 1959) (New York: New American Library, 1962, 1975).
The Satires of Persius, (Bloomington: Indiana University Press, 1961) (Port Washington, New York: Kennikat Press, 1973).
Spanish Ballads, (New York: Doubleday, 1961).
The Life of Lazarillo de Tormes: His Fortunes and Adversities, (New York: Doubleday, 1962).
The Song of Roland, in *Medieval Epics* (New York: Modern Library, 1963; Vintage 1970).
Yerma, [Federico Garci'a Lorca] Lincoln Center production (New York, 1966).
Selected Translations 1948–1968, (New York: Atheneum, 1969).
Twenty Love Poems and a Song of Despair, [Pablo Neruda] (London: Cape, 1969; New York: Grossman, 1969; Penguin, 1976).
Products of the Perfected Civilization: Selected Writings of Chamfort, [Sebastien-Roch-Nicholas Chamfort] (New York: Macmillan, 1969; San Francisco: North Point Press, 1984).
Voices, [Antonio Porchia] (Chicago: Follett, 1969).
Transparence of the World: Poems by Jean Follain, (New York: Atheneum, 1969).
Asian Figures, (New York: Atheneum, 1973) Proverbs, aphorisms, and riddles from various Asian cultures.
Osip Mandelstam: Selected Poems, (New York: Atheneum, 1974) Translated with Clarence Brown.
Sanskrit Love Poetry, (New York: Columbia University Press, 1977) Translated with J. Moussaieff Masson. Reprinted as *The Peacock's Egg: Love Poems from Ancient India* (San Francisco: North Point Press, 1981).
Vertical Poetry, [Robert Juarroz] (Santa Cruz, Calif.: Kayak, 1977).
Euripides: Iphigeneia at Aulis, (New York: Oxford University Press, 1978) Translated with George E. Dimock, Jr.
Selected Translations 1968–1978, (New York: Atheneum, 1979).
Four French Plays, (New York: Atheneum, 1985) Includes *Robert the Devil;* Alain-René Lesage's *The Rival of His Master* and *Turcaret* ḍ Pierre de Marivaux's *The False Confessions.*
From the Spanish Morning, (New York: Atheneum, 1985) Includes *Spanish Ballads;* Lope de Rueda's *Eufemia;* and *The Life of Lazarillo de Tormes.*
Soseki, Muso, *Sun at Midnight: Poems and Sermons,* (San Francisco: North Point Press, 1989) Translated with Soiku Shigematsu.

BIOGRAPHICAL AND CRITICAL STUDIES

Altieri, Charles, "Situating Merwin's Poetry Since 170," In *W. S. Merwin: Essays on the Poetry.* Edited by Cary Nelson and Ed Folsom (Urbana: University of Illinois Press, 1987) pp. 159–197.
Brunner, Edward, "*Opening the Hand*: The Variable Caesura and the Family Poems," In *W. S. Merwin: Essays on the Poetry.* Edited by Cary Nelson and Ed Folsom (Urbana: University of Illinois Press, 1987) pp. 276–295.
Christhilf, Mark, *W. S. Merwin the Mythmaker,* (Columbia: University of Missouri Press, 1986).
Clark, Tom, *The Great Naropa Poetry Wars,* (Santa Barbara, Calif.: Cadmus Editions, 1980).
Davis, Cheri, *W. S. Merwin,* (Boston: Twayne, 1981).
Folsom, Ed, " 'I Have Been a Long Time in a Strange Country': W. S. Merwin and America," In *W. S. Merwin: Essays on the Poetry* Edited by Cary Nelson and Ed Folsom (Urbana: University of Illinois Press, 1987) pp. 224–249.
Howard, Richard, "W. S. Merwin," *Alone with America* Enlarged edition (New York: Atheneum, 1980) pp. 412–449.
Molesworth, Charles, "W. S. Merwin: Style, Vision, Influence," In *W. S. Merwin: Essays on Poetry.* Edited by Cary Nelson ad Ed Folsom (Urbana: University of Illinois Press, 1987) pp. 145–158.
Nelson, Cary, "The Resources of Failure: W. S. Merwin's Deconstructive Career," *Boundary* 2: 573–598 (Winter 1977) Revisied version in *W. S. Merwin: Essays on the Poetry.* Edited by Carl Nelson and Ed Folsom (Urbana: University of Illinois Press, 1987).
Nelson, Cary, and Ed Folsom, eds., *W. S. Merwin: Essays on the Poetry,* (Urbana: University of Illinois Press, 1987) This volume contains an extensive bibliography of Merwin's collected and uncollected works

through 1985 and an excellent summary of the contents of the W. S. Merwin Archive at the University of Illinois at Urbana-Champaign.

Ramsey, Jarold, "The Continuities of W. S. Merwin: 'What Has Escaped Us We bring with Us'," *Massachusetts Review* 14:569–590 (1973) Also in *W. S. Merwin: Essays on the Poetry.* Edited by Cary Nelson and Ed Folsom (Urbana: University of Illinois Press, 1987).

Scholes, Robert, "Semiotics of the Poetic Text," *Semiotics and Interpretation* (New Haven: Yale University Press, 1982) pp. 37–56 Also in *W. S. Merwin: Essays on the Poetry.* Edited by Cary Nelson and Ed Folsom (Urbana: University of Illinois Press, 1987).

INTERVIEWS

"A Conversation with W. S. Merwin," *Audience* 4: 4–6 (1956).

Clifton, Michael, "W. S. Merwin: An Interview," *American Poetry Review* 12: 17–22 (July/August 1983).

Eliot, David L., "An Interview with W. S. Merwin," *Contemporary Literature* 29: 1–25 (Spring 1988) A 1984 interview.

Folsom, Ed, and Nelson, Cary, " 'Fact Has Two Faces': Interview," In W. S. Merwin, *Regions of Memory: Uncollected Prose.* Edited by Cary Nelson and Ed Folsom (Urbana: University of Illinois Press, 1987) pp. 320–361.

Gerber, Philip L., and Gemmett, Robert J., " 'Tireless Quest': A Conversation with W. S. Merwin," *English Record* 19: 9–18 (February 1969).

Hirsch, Edward, "The Art of Poetry XXXVIII: W.S. Merwin," *The Paris Review* 29: 56–81 (Spring 1987).

Jackson, Richard, "Unnaming the Myths," *Acts of Mind: Conversations with Contemporary Poets* (University of Alabama Press, 1983) pp. 48–52.

MacShane, Frank, "A Portrait of W. S. Merwin," *Shenandoah* 21: 3–14 (Winter 1970).

Myers, Jack, and Simms, Michael, "Possibilities of the Unknown: Conversations with W. S. Merwin," *Southwest Review* 68: 164–180 (Spring 1983).

Ossman, David, "W. S. Merwin," *The Sullen Art* (New York: Corinth Books, 1967) pp. 65–72.

Pettit, Michael, "W. S. Merwin: An Interview," *Black Warrior Review* 8: 7–20 (Spring 1982).

~

Metaphysical Poets

MARGARET WILLY

RICHARD CRASHAW
(ca. 1613–1649)

Poet and *Saint*! to thee alone are given
The two most sacred *Names* of *Earth* and
Heaven.

THUS, SEVEN YEARS after his friend's death, Abraham Cowley apostrophized Richard Crashaw. A writer in 1657 named Crashaw in the same breath as the "refined witts" of Francis Bacon, Sir Philip Sidney, Ben Jonson, John Donne, and William Shakespeare; and thirty years later another critic was acclaiming him as "the Darling of the Muses . . . charming the ear with a holy Rapture." During the next hundred years Crashaw's reputation suffered the inevitable decline. But the nineteenth century found Coleridge declaring: "Where he does combine richness of thought and diction nothing can excel." Lines 43–64 of Crashaw's "A Hymn to the Name and Honor of the Admirable Sainte Teresa" had, he added, been constantly with him while he was writing the second part of *Christabel,* "if indeed, by some subtle process of the mind they did not suggest the first thought of the whole poem." Today Crashaw has less general appeal than Donne and Herbert; although T. S. Eliot found him "sometimes more profound and less sectarian" than either Herbert or Henry Vaughan.

Born in London in 1612 or early in 1613, the poet was the only son of a then famous father, the Puritan preacher and controversialist William Crashaw. He was educated at the Charterhouse School, where he had a thorough grounding in the classical poets and in writing verse exercises in imitation of their style. To this, no doubt, he owed something of the ability attributed to him in the preface to his *Steps to the Temple*: of having, "under locke and key in readinesse, the richest treasures of the best Greeke and Latine Poets, some of which Authors hee had . . . at his command by heart."

In 1631 Crashaw went up to Pembroke College, Cambridge, and three years later took his degree; in the same year he published a volume of Latin epigrams on selected New Testament texts entitled *Epigrammatum Sacrorum Liber.* In 1635 he became a fellow of Peterhouse, then the center of Laudian High Churchmanship in Cambridge. For eight years Crashaw enjoyed the "little contentfull kingdom," as he called it, of his "beloved Patrimony in St. Peter." Although the date of his ordination is not known, he served, during this time, as curate in the adjoining church of Little St. Mary's. His earliest biographer refers in glowing terms to the eloquence of Crashaw's preaching there ("those thronged Sermons on each Sunday and Holiday, that ravished more like Poems . . . scattering not so much Sentences as Extasies"). None of these, unfortunately, has survived.

It was during his Cambridge years, too, that Crashaw became friendly with Nicholas Ferrar, founder of the Anglican community at Little Gidding, and he was a frequent visitor at the celebrated vigils there.

Like all his friends and colleagues, Crashaw was a staunch royalist; and two years after the outbreak of civil war he was ejected from his fellowship by the parliamentary commissioners. Thenceforth his biography is a history of rootlessness, frustration, and repeated disappointments. He was for a time in Holland, and later in Paris where, about 1646—according to the contemporary historian Anthony à Wood—Cowley found him, "being a meer Scholar and very shiftless . . . in a sorry condition." Crashaw had by now become converted to the Roman Catholic faith; and Henrietta Maria, exiled in Paris, addressed a dispatch to the pope recommending the poet and his edifying example (praise that is echoed by Cowley in his elegy: "His *Faith* perhaps in some nice Tenents might/Be wrong; his *Life,* I'm sure, was *in the right.*"). The queen's influence had little effect. Although Crashaw went at once to Rome, he was still there, waiting, over a year later, and suffering from poverty and ill health. He obtained, for a time, some employment in the service of Cardinal Palotto. But by 1649, shortly after his appointment to a post at the Cathedral of Loreto, Crashaw was dead (according to Cowley, of a fever) at the early age of thirty-seven.

Steps to the Temple. Sacred Poems, With Other Delights of the Muses had been published in London in 1646, followed by a new edition including a number of fresh pieces in 1648. With its substantial recasting of poems from the earlier volume, this second edition offers interesting evidence of Crashaw's habit of polishing, revising, and amplifying his work: often pruning stylistic extravagances (as, for example, some of the alterations made in the final versions of "Sainte Mary Magdalene, or The Weeper" and "A Hymne of the Nativity") in favor of more concrete expression. The additional poems show, too, that three wretched years of exile nevertheless yielded a good deal of creative activity. To the time between 1648 and Crashaw's death belong the "divine" poems that came out for the first time in 1652 in *Carmen Deo Nostro, Te Decet Hymnus, Sacred Poems,* published posthumously in Paris. This book consisted largely of poems that had appeared in their revised versions in 1648 or were first printed there.

The anonymous writer of the preface to *Steps to the Temple* (possibly Crashaw's friend and fellow poet Joseph Beaumont, a Peterhouse colleague who after the Restoration became master of the college) speaks of Crashaw as being "excellent in five Languages . . . *vid.* Hebrew, Greek, Latine, Italian, Spanish, the two last whereof hee had little helpe in, they were of his owne acquisition." Crashaw's reading in other languages played an important part in the development of his work. As already mentioned, he had been trained as a schoolboy in the artificial rhetoric of the Latin and Greek epigram; and as an undergraduate, much influenced by the style and spirit of Ovid, he continued these exercises. Many of Crashaw's essays in religious epigram show his gift for the striking phrase and achieve a concentrated intensity of poetic impact. This mastery of epigram reveals itself in his longer poems in the single telling line: as in "Immortall Hony for the Hive of Loves" ("Sospetto d'Herode"); "Candidates of Blissefull Light" ("To the Name of Jesus"); or in the final line of his poem on the Circumcision, "This knife may be the speares *Praeludium.*"

Still more potent in his evolution as a poet was Crashaw's self-acquired knowledge of Spanish and Italian. The life and work of St. Teresa of Avila, canonized in 1622, made a deep impression on his imagination. As he wrote of her:

> What soule soever in any Language can
> Speake heaven like hers, is my soules
> country-man.

Equally pervasive was the influence of the Neapolitan poet Marino. In Marino's relentless emphasis on literal detail and in the highly colored, flamboyant elements in his style, Crashaw found encouragement for a strain of sensationalism in his own temperament. To this Italian influence we owe much of Crashaw's habit of elaborating, for their own sake, merely decorative metaphors that neither advance the movement nor illuminate the inward truth of a poem. Some of his poetic lapses into banality and bad taste, exhibiting the worst excesses of the "metaphysical conceit" (see "The Weeper"), as well as his exercise of wit in arid surface ingenuities, derived largely from Marino.

The cult of the emblem, then so popular in England and on the Continent, also made a distinct contribution to the shaping of Crashaw's style. Originating in medieval fable and allegory, emblems were allusive, often highly ingenious drawings symbolizing some moral precept, with companion verses translating the picture into words. With that of the impresa or heroic symbol, which epitomized a character or life by means of a single abstract sign, the influence of the emblem is plain in Crashaw's pictorial representation of abstract ideas and in his constant blend of literal with figurative, of homely realistic image with symbolic sublime.

Crashaw's happiness in his "little contentfull kingdom" of Peterhouse shows that his was a nature well satisfied by a life of study and contemplation. The "soft silken Houres" envisaged with

> That not impossible shee
> That shall command my heart and mee;

in "Wishes to His (Supposed) Mistresse," never in fact became reality. Perhaps Crashaw's truer desire was expressed in his epigram "On Marriage":

> I would be married, but I'de have no Wife,
> I would be married to a single Life.

A college fellowship then imposed upon its holder the rule of celibacy; so when, sometime about 1645, Crashaw entered the Roman Catholic church, he merely exchanged one mode of monastic existence for another. Admiring the Lessian virtues of temperance and abstinence,[1] he had consciously chosen the contemplative way. Thomas Car says of him in his introductory verses to *Carmen Deo Nostro*,

> No care
> Had he of earthly trashe. What might suffice
> To fitt his soule to heavenly exercise,
> Sufficed him. . . .
> What he might eate or weare he tooke no thought.
> His needful foode he rather found than sought.

And yet as Joan Bennett points out in *Five Metaphysical Poets*, "The images of the ascetic Crashaw are far more predominantly sexual than those of Donne, who had known the pleasures of sensuality, or of Herbert, who never seems to have desired them." The needs of an enthusiastic and warmly emotional nature, disciplined by asceticism, found liberation both in the ritual of the church whose shelter Crashaw finally sought, and in poetic expression of his religious experience and belief; sometimes, in his poetry, betraying him into extravagance, a lush and cloying oversweetness. For him the sensuous is present in, and inextricable from, his conception of the most rarefied spiritual experience. The exalted mystical communion of the soul with God—of

> the divine embraces
> Of the deare spowse of spirits—

is communicated in terms of languorous physical sensation:

> Amorous Languishments, Luminous trances,
> Sights which are not seen with eyes,
> Spirituall and soule peircing glances.
> Whose pure and subtle lightning, flies
> Home to the heart, and setts the house on fire;
> And melts it downe in sweet desire. . . .
>
> . . . Delicious deaths, soft exhalations
> Of soule; deare, and divine annihilations.

1. Crashaw's commendatory poem "In Praise of Lessius His Rule of Health" had accompanied the 1634 Cambridge translation of Lessius' *Hygiasticon*.

A thousand unknowne rites
Of joyes, and rarifyed delights.
("On a Prayer Booke Sent to Mrs M. R.")

The poet goes on to invoke the joys of divine love, the experience of the soul who

shall discover,
What joy, what blisse,
How many heavens at once it is,
To have a God become her lover,

in symbols of the "pure inebriating pleasures" known to human sense.

Constantly Crashaw uses images of physical love—of "birth, milk and all the rest," as Gerard Manley Hopkins put it in a poem peculiarly reminiscent of Crashaw—to communicate his perceptions of its spiritual and divine counterpart. Mary Magdalene's eyes are "swolne wombes of sorrow"; the Easter sepulchre is "Natures new wombe, . . . faire Immortalities perfumed Nest"; while the day of Christ's name, coming to earth, is welcomed as the "Womb of Day" and exhorted to

Unfold thy fair Conceptions; And display
The Birth of our Bright Joyes.

There are, too, the many "nursing" images: "Two sister-Seas of Virgins Milke" in "A Hymne of the Nativity"; the infant martyrs' heaven, which will be "at the worst / Milke all the way"; or in "The Weeper," where heaven's bosom drinks the "gentle stream" of the Magdalene's tears:

Where th' milky rivers creep,
Thine floates above; & is the cream.

The nest, both as refuge sheltered by parental protection and the nourishing source of all love, is one of the most frequently recurring symbols in Crashaw's work.

From the same, sensuous source in his nature sprang Crashaw's characteristic—often, it must seem to us, morbid—preoccupation with experiences of physical agony in a religious context. His detailed, intensely literal attention to different aspects of Christ's body (as in the poem on the Circumcision and those on the Passion) owes much, of course, to Marino, and something to a European form of contemplative exercise that influenced other English religious verse of the time. Some of Crashaw's epigrams and lyrics on these subjects actually originate in lines by the Italian poet. Nevertheless, an obsessive compulsion to contemplate, even luxuriate in, bodily torment does seem to be an undoubted trait of Crashaw's poetic individuality. He speaks of Christ's torturers clothing him in the rich garment of his own blood, "Opening the purple wardrobe of thy side," and elsewhere declares that "Not a haire but payes his River / To this *Red Sea* of thy blood." In writing of the Christian martyrs Crashaw elaborates, almost voluptuously, the visual aspect of their sufferings. The weapons of their persecutors, he says,

. . . sett wide the Doores
For Thee: Fair, purple Doores, of love's
devising;
The Ruby windows which inrich't the EAST
Of Thy so oft repeated Rising.
Each wound of Theirs was Thy new Morning;
And reinthron'd thee in thy Rosy Nest . . .

The poem "On the Wounds of Our Crucified Lord," with its conjunction of bleeding flesh with erotic imagery, implicitly identifies and fuses the anguish of crucifixion with sensations of love:

O these wakefull wounds of thine!
Are they Mouthes? or are they eyes?
Be they Mouthes, or be they eyne,
Each bleeding part some one supplies.

Lo! a mouth, whose full-bloom'd lips
At too deare a rate are roses.
Lo! a blood-shot eye! that weepes
And many a cruell teare discloses . . .

This foot hath got a Mouth and lippes,
To pay the sweet summe of thy kisses . . .

Clearly the wounds of martyrdom symbolized for Crashaw the most complete and eloquent physical expression of spiritual love. As he says in one of his poems to St. Teresa:

For in love's field was never found
A nobler weapon than a WOUND.

Crashaw wrote three poems celebrating the life of this saint, and her martyrdom.[2] The first of them (which was praised by Coleridge), "A Hymn to the Name and Honor of the Admirable Sainte Teresa," with its superb opening lines:

Love, thou art Absolute sole lord
OF LIFE & DEATH,

is among Crashaw's finest and most fully realized poems. Here again we hear the note of pleasure in pain:

O how oft shalt thou complain
Of a sweet & subtle PAIN.
Of intolerable JOYES;
Of a DEATH, in which who dyes
Loves his death, and dyes again.
And would for ever so be slain.

It should be noted that the same idea, of an extremity of physical pain mounting to merge in spiritual bliss, occurs in the autobiographical *La Vida de la Santa Madre Teresa de Jesus,* an English translation of which appeared in 1642 and with which Crashaw was doubtless familiar.

The concluding invocation of his third St. Teresa poem, "The Flaming Heart Upon the Book and Picture of the Seraphicall Saint Teresa," rises to a height of lyrical rapture unsurpassed anywhere in Crashaw's work:

O thou undaunted daughter of desires!
By all thy dow'r of LIGHTS & FIRES;
By all the eagle in thee, all the dove;
By all thy lives & deaths of love;
By thy large draughts of intellectuall day,
And by thy thirsts of love more large than
they;
By all thy brim-fill'd Bowles of fierce desire
By thy last Morning's draught of liquid fire;
By the full kingdome of that finall kisse
That seiz'd thy parting Soul, & seal'd thee
his;
By all the heav'ns thou hast in him
(Fair sister of the SERAPHIM!)
By all of HIM we have in THEE;
Leave nothing of my SELF in me.
Let me so read thy life, that I
Unto all life of mine may dy.

Just as Crashaw seems to savor the pleasurable sensations of pain, he likewise invites and finds a similar sweetness in grief:

Welcome my Griefe, my Joy; how deare's
To me my Legacy of Teares!

or, in "The Weeper":

No where but here did ever meet
Sweetnesse so sad, sadnesse so sweet.

Even allowing for the special fascination tears held for the seventeenth-century metaphysical poet (see, among other poems, Donne's "A Valediction: Of Weeping," Andrew Marvell's "Eyes and Tears," and Thomas Vaughan's "The Stone"), their attraction for Crashaw appears peculiarly compelling. The very thought of them at once conjures for him a multitude of affinities, with stars, diamonds, pearls, watery blossoms, liquid jewels and rain showers, streams and milky rivers, seas and floods. He writes an epigram on the tears of Lazarus, exhorts them from Pilate, and devotes a well-known poem, "The Teare," to those of the Virgin; while in his lines "Upon the Death of a Gentleman" he declares:

Eyes are vocall, Teares have Tongues,
And there be words not made with lungs;
Sententious showers, ô let them fall,
Their cadence is Rhetoricall.

Tears are the central, sustaining image of "The Weeper," a poem strongly influenced by

2. In fact St. Teresa died a natural death.

Marino in subject, stanza form, and even specific phrases, although the intensity of religious emotion and of vision are Crashaw's own. Here the objects of contemplation, and starting point for elaborating the various ideas they suggest to him, are the weeping eyes of Mary Magdalene (". . . sister springs! / Parents of sylver-footed rills!"). The timelessness of her ever-falling tears, as well as the dignity and majesty of sorrow, are finely communicated in stanzas twenty-three ("Does the day-starre rise?") and twenty-six ("Not, so long she lived"). Among the exuberant fancies Crashaw's imagination calls up are that of a "brisk Cherub" sipping the Magdalene's tears, so that ". . . his song / Tasts of this Breakfast all day long"; and of a heavenly feast (with verbal echoes of Donne's "Twicknam Garden") at which

> Angels with crystall violls come
> And draw from these full eyes of thine
> Their master's Water: their own Wine.

But the lines most frequently quoted, in illustration of how precipitately the metaphysical conceit could plunge a poet into bathos, are Crashaw's description of Christ being

> . . . follow'd by two faithfull fountaines;
> Two walking baths; two weeping motions;
> Portable, & compendious oceans.

To the modern mind the whole visual suggestion is keenly ludicrous. Yet (as L. C. Martin points out in the commentary to his edition of Crashaw's poems) what seems to us the incongruity of mundane epithets like "portable" and "compendious" in such a context, and of the prosaically concrete "bath" metaphor, has in fact many parallels in both English and continental poetry of the time.

That element in his nature that sometimes led Crashaw into poetic excess was also the source of his greatest strength. The strong sensuous vein lends his work a special purity, warmth, and sweetness; a limpid flow of cadence whose music appeals to the ear as powerfully as its impressions of scent, light, and color entrance the other senses. Crashaw writes best when apparently with the most ease and simplicity, his utterance unclogged by lush imagery or artificial conceits. This can be seen in the extracts from his St. Teresa poems quoted above; in the melodious tenderness of the shepherds' "Hymne of the Nativity," full of such felicities as "Love's architecture is his own"; in the second stanza of "Easter Day":

> Of all the Gloryes Make Noone gay
> This is the Morne.
> This rocke buds forth the fountaine of the streames
> of Day.
> In joyes white Annals live this houre,
> When life was borne,
> No cloud scoule on his radiant lids, no tempest lowre,

or these from "Sospetto d'Herode":

> That the Great Angell-blinding light should shrinke
> His blaze, to shine in a poore Shepheards eye.
> That the unmeasur'd God so low should sinke,
> As Pris'ner in a few poore Rags to lye . . .
> . . . That a vile Manger his low Bed should prove,
> Who in a Throne of stars Thunders above.
>
> That hee whom the Sun serves, should faintly peepe
> Through clouds of Infant flesh: that hee the old
> Eternall Word should bee a Child, and weepe.
> That hee who made the fire, should feare the cold . . .

This poem, Crashaw's translation of the first canto of Marino's *La Strage degli Innocenti,* is far more striking in concreteness of imagery and atmospheric detail than its original. Here especially—in the mellifluous cadences, crowding personifications, and above all in the use of sensuous richness to communicate moral sentiment and spiritual meaning—Crashaw's debt to Spenser is plain. The pictorial and musical qualities of his verse may have owed something also to his natural talents for "Musicke, Drawing, Limning, Graving" mentioned in the preface to *Steps to the Temple.* (It is thought that at least two engravings in *Carmen Deo Nostro* are his own illustrations.) With his fragrant showers dropping "a delicious dew of spices," his perfumed and balmy air, his lambs in the "laughing meads" and sun-gilded fleece of grazing flocks, his April flowers and "pure streames of the springing day," Crashaw at his best has the vernal freshness, delicacy, and radiance of Botticelli.

HENRY VAUGHAN
(ca. 1622–1695)

Perhaps through Nicholas Ferrar at Little Gidding, Crashaw knew, and much admired, the work of George Herbert. He sent to a friend, as an aid to prayer, a copy of Herbert's poems, and probably derived from Herbert's *The Temple* the title for his own first volume; while the writer of the preface to *Steps to the Temple* declared that "Here's Herbert's second, but equall, who hath retriv'd Poetry of late."

In Henry Vaughan, Herbert found a still more devout disciple. Vaughan's preface to *Silex Scintillans* refers to "the blessed man, *Mr George Herbert,* whose holy *life* and *verse* gained many pious *Converts,* (of whom I am the least)." In all his work after the first volume, the influence of Herbert is pervasive not only in subject and spirit, but in many obvious echoes of Herbert's titles, meters, and phrases.[3] That Vaughan was no mere imitator of the man who was his acknowledged master in both his poetry and his religious life can be seen in the finest poems in *Silex Scintillans.* In this volume Herbert's influence, though nowhere stronger, has been assimilated and transmuted by Vaughan's individual way of seeing. At his best, he speaks with the distinctive voice of a poet in his own right: one whose apprehension of reality is different from Herbert's (especially in their respective attitudes to nature); who is more lyrical in the soaring of his religious exaltation or grief; and who, at the moments of his most intense spiritual vision, "sees *Invisibles*" with a quality of mystical rapture quite outside Herbert's scope.

Henry Vaughan and his younger twin, Thomas, were born in 1621 or early in 1622 at Newton St. Bridget, Brecknockshire, by the river Usk. Vaughan spent most of his life in Wales; and on all his books after the first he called himself by the title "Silurist," after the ancient tribe of Silures, who had once inhabited that southeastern district of his native country. The boys were educated locally by Matthew Herbert, rector of a neighboring parish. In 1638 they went up to Jesus College, Oxford. Henry left without taking his degree and was sent to London sometime in 1640, being, he says, "designed by my father for the study of the Law."

Like that of Crashaw, though neither so permanently nor so disastrously, Vaughan's career suffered through the outbreak of hostilities in 1642. According to him, "our late civil warres wholie frustrated" the plans for his legal future. Like most Welshmen, Vaughan was strongly royalist and seems for a time to have served with the king's forces. His "Elegie on the Death of Mr R. W. Slain in the Late Unfortunate Differences at Rowton Heath, Neer Chester, 1645," contains what reads like an eyewitness account of his friend's prowess in the battle. Another, humorous, poem "Upon a Cloke Lent Him by Mr J. Ridsley" also refers to Vaughan's own presence on the scene of the "differences" at Rowton Heath, and to the time ". . . this Jugling fate / Of Souldierie first seiz'd me!"

It is not known when Vaughan began to practice medicine; but in 1673 he wrote from Brecon telling his cousin Aubrey, the antiquary, that he had been a physician "for many years with good successe . . . & a repute big enough for a person of greater parts than my

3. These are far too numerous to cite here. Readers interested in tracing the similarities and borrowings should see the Notes to L. C. Martin, *The Works of Henry Vaughan* (2nd ed., 1957), especially those to *Silex Scintillans,* pp. 727–751.

selfe." He died in 1695, and was buried in his birthplace, where his grave in the churchyard may still be seen.

Vaughan's first book of poems was published the same year as Crashaw's *Steps to the Temple* appeared. *Poems, with the Tenth Satyre of Juvenal Englished* (1646) contains a number of love poems addressed to Amoret (sometimes identified with Vaughan's first wife, Catherine Wise). These are conventionally fashionable songs, of tears and sighs, a cruel fair one with "a Womans easie Faith," and a young man dying of love. Echoes, here, from Vaughan's contemporaries Habington and Randolph recur in his later secular volumes, with others from Cartwright and Owen Felltham's *Resolves.* Still more obvious is the borrowing from Donne, especially from "A Valediction: Forbidding Mourning." (Compare the fourth and fifth stanzas of that poem with the third and fourth of Vaughan's "To Amoret, of the Difference 'twixt Him, and Other Lovers, and What True Love Is," and also with the penultimate couplet of "To Amoret Gone from Him.")

Vaughan's second collection of secular verse, *Olor Iscanus,* followed in 1651. From the date of its dedication, only a year after the appearance of his first book, it seems that publication was postponed for some time and that much of what Vaughan originally intended to publish was withdrawn. The publisher's preface affirms that "The Author had long agoe condemn'd these Poems to Obscuritie." Vaughan's reticence, perhaps partly due to the political uncertainties of the later 1640's, possibly owed still more to the profound influence exerted on his whole habit of mind by his discovery of Herbert. This deepening seriousness led him, in his preface to *Silex Scintillans,* published the previous year, to deplore in vigorous terms his contemporaries' "inexcusable desertion of *pious sobriety*" in their taste for "*vicious verse,*" "*lascivious fictions,*" and "*idle books*" and to announce that he himself had "suppress [his] *greatest follies.*"

The title poem in *Olor Iscanus* celebrates the "*lov'd Arbours*" and "*green banks* and *streams*" of the Usk. The book contains verses to various friends, and in praise of the work of admired writers, including John Fletcher, William Cartwright, Sir William Davenant, and Katherine Philips, the "wittie fair one" known to her circle as "the matchless Orinda." There are verse translations from Ovid, Ausonius, Boethius, and the Polish poet Casimir, and some in prose from Plutarch and other writers. (Throughout the 1650's Vaughan published prose works such as *The Mount of Olives,* a manual of meditation and prayer free from the "fruitlesse curiosities of Schoole-Divinity"; or *Flores Solitudinis,* "collected in his Sicknesse and Retirement," which contained three translations and a biography of St. Paulinus of Nola.)

The third volume of Vaughan's secular poems, *Thalia Rediviva,* subtitled "The Passtimes and Diversions of a Countrey-Muse," was published in 1678 (although it contains work of much earlier date). Apart from further translations, and a group of not very remarkable love poems addressed to "Etesia," there are several religious pieces in the mood of *Silex Scintillans,* probably written after the second part of that collection appeared in 1655. Some of these, "Looking Back," "The Recovery," and the opening of "The World," depart from the eight- or ten-syllable couplets favored by Vaughan in his secular poems to share the greater metrical flexibility and variety of the work in *Silex Scintillans.* The last poem in *Thalia Rediviva,* entitled "Daphnis, an Elegiac Eclogue" between two shepherds, may have been written for the death of Vaughan's younger brother William in 1648, and afterward adapted for that of Thomas, his twin, in 1666.

According to their mutual friend Dr. Thomas Powell, Henry and Thomas Vaughan resembled each other as closely in spirit as in body. "Not only your *faces,*" he declared, "but your *wits* are *Twins.*" Certainly there are striking parallels between passages in the prose writings of Thomas Vaughan and such poems by his brother as "Regeneration," "Resurrection and Immortality," "Vanity of Spirit," "Corruption," and "Cock-crowing."

After his eviction from his living in 1650, Thomas Vaughan studied alchemy; and he is described by Anthony à Wood as "a great chymist, a noted son of the fire, an experimental philosopher." Under the name of Eugenius Philalethes, he published a number of alchemical and mystical treatises that owe much to Hermeticism, the occult philosophy that originated in the Greek texts attributed to Hermes Trismegistus. Hermetic traditions, both philosophical and scientific, exercised a powerful attraction for the seventeenth-century mind. The poetry of Donne, for example, and the prose of Sir Thomas Browne abound in Hermetic allusions to elixirs, tinctures, essences, influences, and signatures, and in *Religio Medici,* Browne defines death in alchemical terms. This Hermetic interest is plainly recognizable in the work of Henry Vaughan: not only in his translations of two treatises by Nollius, published as *Hermetical Physick* (1655) and *The Chymist's Key* (1657), expounding the medical aspects of Hermetic doctrine, but also in images and ideas found in the symbolism of "Vanity of Spirit," "Cock-crowing," "The Night," "The World," "The Constellation," and "Resurrection and Immortality." On the whole, however, the imagery in *Silex Scintillans* carries many more echoes both of Herbert, and of biblical language and allusion, than of Hermetic ideas. Essentially Vaughan's are Christian poems that Hermetic terms and notions sometimes furnished with analogies, both apt for his purpose and familiar to contemporary readers, to illustrate the apprehensions of spiritual reality he sought to communicate.[4]

What is the nature of the experience embodied by *Silex Scintillans*? Despite the all-pervading influence of Herbert, this is the work (first published in 1650 and, in a new edition with a second part added, in 1655) that assures Vaughan his secure and permanent place among English religious poets. In it two contrasting themes are clearly defined. One is that of a desolating sense of separation from God through man's sin, which fills the poet with self-disgust and despair; the other, joy in the Presence that animates and illumines all creation, itself visible proof of his power and love.

In his vein of distaste for human life, Vaughan sees earthly existence as a

> . . . sad captivity,
> This leaden state, which men miscal
> Being and life, but is dead thrall.
> ("The Ass")

The imprisoned spirit "truly hates to be detained on earth"; and in "Love-sick" Vaughan complains that

> These narrow skies . . .
> So barre me in, that I am still at warre,
> At constant warre with them.

All through Vaughan's work recurs the desire to escape, "winged and free," into the "true liberty" of heaven. And not only is man a prisoner on earth, he is an exile, banished from home and forever pining for it:

> He knows he hath a home, but scarce
> knows where,
> He sayes it is so far
> That he hath quite forgot how to go there.
> ("Man")

The poem "Corruption" relates how "He came (condemned,) hither," and

> . . . sigh'd for *Eden,* and would often say
> *Ah! what bright days were those*?

In a world variously referred to as "wilde woods," parching desert, and wilderness, the spirit yearns with nostalgia:

> O how I long to travell back
> And tread again that ancient track!
> ("The Retreate")

The nature of the place from which man is shut out is memorably epitomized in "Peace":

4. Ross Garner, in *Henry Vaughan: Experience and the Tradition* (1959), gives in chapter 3 a useful summary of the relative importance of Hermeticism in Vaughan's work.

My Soul, there is a Countrie
  Far beyond the stars . . .
If thou canst get but thither,
  There grows the flowre of peace,
The Rose that cannot wither,
Thy fortresse, and thy ease;

Much preoccupied with the cause of this exile from grace, Vaughan views with loathing "the mule, unruly man," whose body is a "quicken'd masse of sinne." Repeatedly the flesh is denounced in such terms as vile, foul, obscene: "impure, rebellious clay," "all filth, and spott." This uncleanness, which obscures the light and alienates man from God, evokes from Vaughan the impassioned cry:

O that I were all Soul! that thou
        Wouldst make each part
Of this poor, sinfull frame pure heart!
  ("Chearfulness")

But although in moods of world-weariness and self-disgust Vaughan aspired to an impossible ideal of "man all pure love, flesh a star," he did not share the Hermetic view of matter as intrinsically evil. Many poems make clear that, for him, the source of sin and separation lies not in the body itself but in the "dark Confusions" it houses, which "soyl thy Temple with a sinful rust" ("Dressing"). Vaughan blames the weakness and waywardness resulting from man's apostasy: his "black selfwil" and "sinfull ease," the peevish stubbornness, disobedience, and rebellion of his "hard, stonie heart."

Abundant proof that Vaughan did not despise material substance as such lies in his frank and lyrical delight in the universe. He saw the wonders of nature as bodying forth the goodness of God, whose "glory through the world dost drive," and all creation actively proclaim him:

        There's not a *Spring,*
Or *Leafe* but hath his *Morning-hymn;*
  Each *Bush*
And *Oak* doth know *I AM;*
  ("Rules and Lessons")

and, in "The Morning-watch":

        In what Rings,
And *Hymning Circulations* the quick world
    Awakes, and sings;
    The rising winds,
    And falling springs,
    Birds, beasts, all things
Adore him in their kinds.
    Thus all is hurl'd
In sacred *Hymnes,* and *Order,* The great
  Chime
And *Symphony* of nature.

That "All things here shew [man] heaven . . . and point him the way home" is, to Vaughan, their ultimate justification. Visible, finite beauty is a bridge to the invisible, infinite, and transcendent one it symbolizes. The "Heraldrie / Of stones, and speechless Earth" shows us our "true descent" ("Retirement"); the "weaker glories" of "some *gilded Cloud,* or *flowre*" intimate to the gazing child "Some shadows of eternity" ("The Retreate"). God's "wondrous Method" in creating the universe is, in short, the outward proof and pledge of his omnipresence:

Thou canst not misse his Praise; Each *tree,*
  herb, flowre
Are shadows of his *wisdome,* and his Pow'r.
  ("Rules and Lessons")

It is here that Vaughan differs most from Herbert, in whose work nature is little more than a convenient source of telling metaphor; whereas Vaughan's conception of it is central to his religious belief. In the plan of creation he perceived a marvelous unity of design, in which the ordering of natural phenomena was echoed and repeated in the patterns of man's spiritual processes. In all of it, as he says in "The Book," Vaughan "lov'd and sought [God's] face."

"No one else among Donne's followers," affirms Joan Bennett, "watched the earth, sky and water, the birds and flowers with the same emotion, nor with the same delicacy of observation." This loving precision of eye and felicity of phrase may be seen in Vaughan's descriptions of a spring path "*Primros'd,* and hung with shade," of snow that "*Candies* our Countries wooddy brow," or of the "purling Corn"; in a glimpse of dawn:

I see a Rose
Bud in the bright East, and disclose
The Pilgrim-Sunne . . .
("The Search")

or of stars that "nod and sleepe,/And through the dark aire spin a firie thread"; of "man [as] such a Marygold . . . That shuts, and hangs the head." One of Vaughan's favorite images for the soul is that of a flower or plant. "Surly winds," he says in "Regeneration," "Blasted my infant buds"; and, in "The Morning-watch":

with what flowres,
And shoots of glory, my soul breakes, and
buds!

"True hearts," Vaughan believed, "spread, and heave / Unto their God, as flow'rs do to the Sun." Sometimes they send out "Bright *shootes* of everlastingnesse" (this image of shoots recurs in several poems); but at others, shaken by the storms of sin, the spirit is a "sully'd flowre," a "sapless Blossom" thirsting for dew and, at worst, a "frail" or "thankless" weed.

E. K. Chambers has said, in his preface to *The Poems of Henry Vaughan, Silurist* (1896), that Vaughan "is very much the poet of fine lines and stanzas, of imaginative intervals"; that in a number of poems he begins well and tails off, or else "some very flinty ground yields a quite unanticipated spark." The truth of this has to be admitted. Many of Vaughan's poems of conventional religious sentiment are as commonplace as the average hymn, unlit by any memorable flash of poetic insight or language. Vaughan can be—as in "Church Service," "The Passion," "Tears," "Holy Scriptures," "The Relapse," or the jogtrot jingle of "Thou that know'st for whom I mourne"—disconcertingly trite and sententious, even banal. He has, compared with Herbert, little sense of form or the disciplines of verbal economy. But there are whole poems—"The Retreate," "The Morning-watch," "Peace," "Affliction," "Man," "They Are All Gone Into the World of Light!"—that do sustain a high poetic level; and for the isolated splendors, where (in Vaughan's own image) the flint does strike off sparks, how luminous some of these are.

I saw Eternity the other night
Like a great *Ring* of pure and endless light,
All calm, as it was bright,
And round beneath it, Time in hours, days,
years
Driv'n by the spheres
Like a vast shadow mov'd, in which the
world
And all her train were hurl'd;
("The World")

or

There is in God (some say)
A deep, but dazling darkness . . .
O for that night! where I in him
Might live invisible and dim.
("The Night")

or his apostrophe in "They Are All Gone Into the World of Light!":

Dear, beauteous death! the Jewel of the Just,
Shining nowhere, but in the dark;

and, from the same poem:

It glows and glitters in my cloudy brest
Like stars upon some gloomy grove . . .

All these lodge in the imagination with the unforgettable impact, the haunting inevitability, of pure poetry.

It will be noticed how many of these magical lines enshrine images of light. Present in many contexts, light glows through and permeates all Vaughan's work. His books are "Burning and shining Thoughts." Man before the fall was as "intimate with Heav'n, as light." The saints

Like Candles, shed
Their beams, and light
Us into Bed,

while the dead walk

in an Air of glory,
Whose light doth trample on my days.

Imploring "The beams, and brightness of thy face," the poet appeals to God to

brush me with thy light, that I
May shine unto a perfect day;

and aspires toward a state where he may

Rove in that mighty, and eternall light
Where no rude shade, or night
Shall dare approach us.

For Vaughan light is the primary symbol of spiritual illumination, of that clarity and purity of vision man possessed most fully when he "Shin'd in [his] Angell-infancy."

Two human conditions, Vaughan believed, enable the achievement of this illumination at its steadiest and most radiant. One (as already seen) is in man's attunement to natural beauty in constant awareness of its being divinely infused:

. . . *rural shades* are the sweet fense
Of piety and innocence . . .
If Eden be on Earth at all,
'Tis that, which we the *Country* call.
("Retirement")

The other state of being which, in Vaughan's view, is the habitation of angels and reflects the image of Eden is our early years of innocence: that

first, happy age;
An age without distast and warrs,

as he sees it in "Looking Back"; and, in "Childehood," as the

Dear, harmless age! the short, swift span,
Where weeping virtue parts with man.

Leaving infancy behind, man finds that, amid the world's insistent claims and clamor, sin has "Like Clouds ecclips'd [his] mind":

I find my selfe the lesse, the more I grow;
The world
Is full of voices; Man is call'd, and hurl'd
By each, he answers all.
("Distraction")

The most complete embodiment of Vaughan's belief in the sanctity of childhood experience is "The Retreate," a poem that has sometimes been regarded as one of the germinative influences on Wordsworth's *Ode on the Intimations of Immortality.* Although this is not established, the two poets certainly share the same nostalgic reverence for the vision of those years when, according to Wordsworth:

trailing clouds of glory do we come
From God, who is our home:
Heaven lies about us in our infancy!

and, in the words of Vaughan:

Happy those early dayes! when I
Shin'd in my Angell-infancy.
Before I understood this place
Appointed for my second race,
Or taught my soul to fancy ought
But a white, Celestiall thought,
When yet I had not walkt above
A mile, or two, from my first love,
And looking back (at that short space,)
Could see a glimpse of his bright-face;
When on some *gilded Cloud,* or *flowre*
My gazing soul would dwell an houre,
And in those weaker glories spy
Some shadows of eternity;
Before I taught my tongue to wound
My Conscience with a sinfull sound,
Or had the black art to dispence
A sev'rall sinne to ev'ry sence,
But felt through all this fleshly dresse
Bright shootes of everlastingnesse.

The phrase "first love," or "early love," recurs with peculiar poignancy in different poems—"Corruption," "The Constellation," "The Seed Growing Secretly"—for man's relation with God. In the same way the idea of angels, walking and talking as man's familiars, is one of Vaughan's favorite symbols—as in "Religion," "Corruption," "The Jews," "Childe-hood," and "Retirement"—to convey his conception of our lost Eden. A return to the state of mind, heart, and spirit known in childhood is, Vaughan believed, the way back to that original fullness of communion between man and his Creator:

> Some men a forward motion love,
> But I by backward steps would move,
> And when this dust falls to the urn
> In that state I came return.

THOMAS TRAHERNE
(ca. 1637–1674)

In 1895 two unsigned manuscript notebooks, one in prose, the other verse, were discovered on a London bookstall. First ascribed to Vaughan, because of certain resemblances to the style and spirit of his writing, they were finally established as the work of a contemporary, Thomas Traherne.

The original confusion of authorship was understandable. A strong vein of mysticism runs through the writing of both Vaughan and Traherne—one a Welshman, the other born in Herefordshire, near the Welsh border. There are similarities in vocabulary as well as in verse forms. But the most striking affinity lies in their common attitude toward childhood. Vaughan's thought in "The Retreate" is vividly paralleled by Traherne's writing, both in verse and prose, about early experience. Everything then, says Traherne, seemed to have "been made but to Day Morning," and was seen with the eyes of an angel or of the first man:

> Certainly Adam in Paradise had not more sweet and curious apprehensions of the World, than I when I was a child.
>
> I was Entertained like an Angel with the Works of GOD in their Splendour and Glory; I saw all in the Peace of Eden; Heaven and Earth did sing my Creators Praises and could not make more Melody to Adam, then to me.[5]

In the poem "Eden," Traherne recalls that

> Only what Adam in his first Estate,
> Did I behold . . .
>
> Those things which first his Eden did adorn,
> My Infancy
> Did crown.

For Traherne, as for Vaughan, "The first Impressions are Immortal all" ("Dumnesse"); the purity of infant intuitions provides the key to life's most fundamental realities, a mystery "which the Books of the Learned never unfold":

> Those Pure and Virgin Apprehensions I had from the Womb, and that Divine Light wherewith I was born are the Best unto this Day. . . . Verily they seem the Greatest Gifts His Wisdom could bestow, for without them all other Gifts had been Dead and Vain.[6]

We see Vaughan, in the poem "Childe-hood," aspiring to recapture the unique quality of that early vision:

> I cannot reach it; and my striving eye
> Dazles at it, as at eternity,

and apostrophizing the "age of mysteries":

> How do I study now, and scan
> Thee, more then ere I studyed man.

In the same way Traherne, throughout his adult life, regarded it as the first duty of a man to regain that wisdom, "unattainable by Book," that informs our childhood apprehensions of a world beyond the visible one. The felicity possible for all human beings could,

5. *Centuries of Meditations.*
6. *Centuries of Meditations.*

he believed, be achieved by deliberately and diligently cultivating the innocence of the "Infant-Ey," and "becom[ing] as it were a little Child again."[7]

The son of a shoemaker, Thomas Traherne was born about 1637, in Hereford. He was brought up by well-to-do relatives; and it was almost certainly through the provision of his uncle, Philip Traherne, a prosperous innkeeper and twice mayor of Hereford City, that Thomas, in his fifteenth year, went to Oxford—the first in a family of farmers and tradesmen to achieve the distinction of a university education. His zestful pursuit of his studies, which he describes in *Centuries of Meditations,* and his intellectual curiosity and eagerness to explore the individual mysteries and whole nature of the universe were typical of the spirit of his age.

Like Crashaw, Traherne made a deliberate choice of the "little contentfull kingdom" of celibacy and study. At the end of 1657, having resolved

> to Spend [all my Time] whatever it cost me, in Search of Happiness . . . [choosing] rather to live upon 10 pounds a yeer, and to go in Lether Clothes, and feed upon Bread and Water, so that I might have all my time clearly to my self . . . (*Third Century*: 46)

he went as rector to the parish of Credenhill, near Hereford. There, with intervals of absence at Oxford, Traherne lived the simple, but for him deeply satisfying, life of an obscure country parson. In 1667 he went to London as private chaplain to Sir Orlando Bridgeman, Charles II's lord keeper of the seal. He remained in Sir Orlando's service until his patron's death in 1674. But a few months later, at the same early age as Crashaw, Traherne himself died. Opening up far wider horizons to one who was, on his own admission, "a sociable Creature . . . a lover of company," and thereby enlarging and enriching his terms of reference, the last seven years were of immense benefit to the vitality of his work.

7. *Ibid.*

Traherne's writings cannot be placed in any certain order of composition. The only book to be published in his lifetime was *Roman Forgeries,* which appeared in 1673, anonymously, but with a bold dedication to Traherne's patron, by now disgraced and deprived of office. This was one more installment in the ceaseless religious controversy between the Anglican church and Rome; and its author accused "the Pope's sworn Adjutants" of forging early church records. Its interest today is slight, but it does reveal something of Traherne's formidable intellectual capacity—both the scope of his scholarship and the clarity and incisiveness of his argument.

Christian Ethicks, dispatched to the publisher immediately before Traherne's death, appeared the following year. It is a treatise on human conduct, a discussion of morality with a difference; for, unlike many contemporary writers on ethics, Traherne was little concerned with castigating vice, being "entirely taken up with the Worth and Beauty of Virtue." A protest against the materialism of Hobbes's *Leviathan* (1651), the book is an impassioned and eloquent exposition both of the reality of spiritual values and of Traherne's personal creed of joy—what he called "Christian epicureanism." Structurally *Christian Ethicks* is rambling and uncoordinated; but as a record of inner adventure and discovery, written out of the knowledge its author "gained in the nature of *Felicity* by many years earnest and diligent study," it is an impressive piece of spiritual autobiography.

In 1699 there appeared, again anonymously, the book of devotions with a cumbersome title (probably not the author's own), which is generally known simply as *Thanksgivings.* These are a series of prose poems in gratitude for such benefits as "The Glory of God's Works" and "The Wisdom of his Word," carrying echoes of the *Devotions* of Lancelot Andrewes and, in their rhythms and reiterations, of the Psalms. In the exuberant outpouring of synonymous phrases, the incantatory piling up of images in freely flowing, flexible lines, and their sense of soaring, triumphant vitality, these "rapturous tumbling catalogue[s] of delights and interests" (as Sir Arthur Quiller-Couch described them) convey the impression that the writer can scarcely contain his exultation: being "in danger of bursting, till we can communicate all to some fit and amiable recipient, and more delight in Communication than we did in the Reception."[8] A sense of urgent, impetuous motion is as characteristic of Traherne's writing as its quality of radiance diffused through images of light ("Pure Primitive Virgin Light," "burning Ardent fire," "Glorious Rayes," "Shining Beams"), for which he has a fondness almost equaling Vaughan's.

A Collection of Meditations and Devotions in Three Parts, which appeared in 1717, also apparently belongs to Traherne's Credenhill years. The first part, "Hexameron," or "Meditations on the Six Days of Creation," has the same energy and sense of the wonderful diversity of life that characterizes the "Thanksgivings." The second, "Meditations and Devotions upon the Life of Christ," contains many incidental passages of self-revelation: in particular, misgivings about personal faults and failures, fluctuations of mood and faith, and, above all, concerning that desolation of spiritual banishment the writer calls "the dark dismal Destitutions of all Light."

Traherne's poems were not published until the early twentieth century, the first volume in 1903, and a second—which had been prepared by his brother Philip, with assiduous and often disastrous "revisions," under the title *Poems of Felicity*—in 1910. Traherne employed the heroic couplet or, more frequently, the long, elaborately patterned, irregular stanza. His exaltation of childhood innocence, and perception of its kinship with the mystic's awareness of harmony and happiness, produced some of his best poems, such as "The Salutation," or the opening of "Wonder":

How like an Angel came I down!
    How Bright are all Things here!
When first among his Works I did appear
    O how their GLORY me did Crown!

8. *Christian Ethicks.*

The World resembled his ETERNITIE,
    In which my Soul did Walk;
And evry Thing that I did see

Did with me talk.

In "News" he describes those intimations of immortality that are the child's memories of the place whence he came, their now "Absent Bliss" beckoning him to its rediscovery.

But Traherne's poetry is, on the whole, far inferior in quality to his prose. There are the scattered felicities, as

I within did flow
With Seas of Life like Wine;
    ("Wonder")

or

Drown'd in their Customs, I became
A Stranger to the Shining Skies,
    Lost as a dying Flame.
    ("The Apostasy")

But too often the long, cumulative lists of attributes or blessings sprawl, as in the third and fourth stanzas of "Desire," into trite and repetitive diffuseness. Traherne as a poet lacked the discipline to prune superfluous verbiage, to cut out the meaningless, redundant phrase used merely to achieve a rhyme; the rhyming itself is frequently facile and expected enough to result in a jingle.

Traherne's strength as a writer of prose lay in his equal mastery of two styles, employed according to the subject and purpose of the work in hand. In *Christian Ethicks,* and the energetic argument of *Roman Forgeries,* he rejected what a Royal Society writer of 1644 had impatiently dismissed as the current "luxury and redundance of speech . . . amplification, digressions, and swellings of style," in favor of short sentences and plain, straightforward exposition. The personal note of frank and easy address to his reader, which is so engaging a feature of nearly all Traherne's prose work, derived largely from Abraham Cowley (borrowing in his turn from Montaigne).

These new trends in English prose were a reaction against pompous and bombastic "volubility of Tongue." But, when occasion demanded, Traherne could command all the dignity and sonorous splendor of the older manner, with its stately rhythms, reiterations, and antitheses. Indeed, it is through his successful blend of the vigorous simplicity of the new style and rhetorical grandeur of the old with a tone of friendly, familiar discourse that Traherne achieves so remarkable a range and richness of expression in *Centuries of Meditations.*

This book, which after the manuscript's chance discovery was published in 1908, places Traherne among the masters of English religious prose. Here, as nowhere else in his writing, he attained a harmonious fusion of form and content. To compare a passage from the *Centuries* with one from the *Thanksgivings* will at once show how his earlier stylistic exuberance has been disciplined by a new economy and restraint.

Centuries of Meditations was written, as a manual of instruction in the way of felicity, for a friend (almost certainly Mrs. Susanna Hopton of Kington, near Credenhill). This fact partly accounts for its note of intimacy and fullness of self-revelation. For his friend's spiritual guidance, Traherne filled the small leather notebook she had given him "with Profitable Wonders . . . Things Strange yet Common; Incredible, yet known; Most High, yet plain; infinitly Profitable, but not Esteemed" (*First Century*: 1 and 3). The manuscript consisted of four complete groups, and part of a fifth, of a hundred numbered prose sections. In these we find the inner history of their author's achievement of happiness: the most complete expression of his profound religious convictions and philosophy of dedicated joy. *Centuries of Meditations* is a testament of praise: those praises which, Traherne declared, are "the Marks and Symptoms of a Happy Life . . . the very End for which the World was created" (*Third Century*: 82).

Nowhere, perhaps, have the feel and flavor of childhood experience been more vividly recaptured. In his infancy, Traherne affirms in the second section of the *Third Century* (and also in the poem "Wonder"), he was oblivious of adult cares:

> I Knew not that there were any Sins, or Complaints, or Laws. I dreamed not of Poverties Contentions or Vices. All Tears and Quarrels, were hidden from mine Eys. Evry Thing was at Rest, Free, and Immortal. I Knew Nothing of Sickness or Death, or Exaction.

Later, "the first Light which shined in my Infancy in its Primitive and Innocent Clarity was totally ecclypsed." Yet before that inevitable loss, and the conflicts of adolescence so convincingly described in poems like "Dissatisfaction" and "Solitude" — despite, too, an early inclination "secretly to Expostulate with GOD for not giving me Riches" (*Third Century*: 14)—the picture of childhood felicity shines bright and unflawed. In the magic circle of the self-enclosed, yet limitless, world the child inhabits

> All appeared New, and Strange at the first, inexpressibly rare, and Delightfull, and Beautifull. I was a little Stranger which at my Enterance into the World was Saluted and Surrounded with innumerable Joys. (*Third Century*: 2)

It is not, of course, as mere straightforward autobiography that we should read Traherne's revelations of his childhood. The child's imaginative preoccupations, such as those of the poem "Shadows in the Water," or the speculations described in *Third Century*: 17 and 18, are intended always to symbolize the spirit's activity in a sphere beyond the everyday material one. "A man's life of any worth," said Keats, "is a continual allegory." It is as an allegory of the adventures of the spirit that Traherne's early life is to be interpreted; the *Centuries* and poems—like Shakespeare's works as envisaged in Keats's letter—are the comments on it.

The essence of Traherne's apprehension of the child's-eye view of the universe is concentrated in the famous third section of the *Third Century,* beginning:

> The Corn was Orient and Immortal Wheat, which never should be reaped, nor was ever sown. I thought it had stood from everlasting to everlasting. The Dust and Stones of the Street were as Precious as GOLD. The Gates were at first the End of the World, The Green Trees when I saw them first through one of the Gates Transported and Ravished me; their Sweetness and unusual Beauty made my Heart to leap, and almost mad with Extasie, they were such strange and Wonderfull Things.

In the subtle shadings of sentence pattern and gradations of rhythm, which so skillfully communicate the pulse of mounting exultation, this is one of the sublime passages of English prose. Once heard, its majestic, reverberating cadences continue to haunt the imagination and the inward ear.

Three main aspects of Traherne's attitude to life are expressed here. First, there is his exaltation of the child's ignorance of the "Dirty Devices of this World." Then there is the sense of wonder that springs directly from that innocence: the freshness and luminous intensity of vision that can transmute the common dust and stones of the street into a substance as precious as gold, turn the tumbling playmates into "moving Jewels," and cause the very trees to ravish the beholder's eyes and make his heart leap, "almost mad with Extasie." Thirdly, and perhaps most potently of all, we are conscious of release into a state of boundlessness: of the illimitable horizons, unconfined by either time or space, that Traherne is looking back to praise as the purest of his early joys. For him, then, "All Time was Eternity, and a Perpetual Sabbath" (*Third Century*: 2). It was no ordinary corn but immortal wheat that waved in the harvest fields; human life was still unshadowed by mortality ("I knew not that they were Born or should Die"). There was neither beginning nor end in this region where "Eternity was Manifest in the Light of the Day, and som thing infinit Behind evry thing appeared." It is in his communication of these world-without-end intimations that Traherne comes nearest to Blake, for whom also it was an "augury of innocence" to

> Hold Infinity in the palm of your hand
> And Eternity in an hour.

No child is ever actively conscious of being happy: indeed it is that very freedom from awareness of self, oblivious of the rarity of his state, that is a condition of the child's wonder and freshness of vision. Yet Traherne's pursuit of felicity, in *Centuries of Meditations,* depends largely on an enriching *consciousness* of happiness:

> You never Enjoy the World aright, till you so love the Beauty of Enjoying it, that you are Covetous and Earnest to Persuade others to Enjoy it. (*First Century*: 31)

Striving to recapture and perpetuate in maturity the timeless joys of infancy, Traherne the man was consciously practicing what, as a child, he had unconsciously possessed.

"Enjoy" and "enjoyment" are among the most frequently used words in *Centuries of Meditations.* It could be said that Traherne was one of the world's great "enjoyers"; and nowhere does this emerge more triumphantly than in the twenty-ninth and thirtieth sections of the First Century. These express the passionate conviction of a man who could never have been so joyous a servant of God if he had not first loved the earth's beauty to his fullest capacity as a human being:

> You never Enjoy the World aright, till the Sea it self floweth in your Veins, till you are Clothed with the Heavens, and Crowned with the Stars: and Perceiv your self to be the Sole Heir of the whole World: and more then so, becaus Men are in it who are evry one Sole Heirs, as well as you. Till you can Sing and Rejoyce and Delight in GOD, as Misers do in Gold, and Kings in Scepters, you never Enjoy the World.

> Till your Spirit filleth the Whole World, and the Stars are your Jewels, till you are as Familiar with the Ways of God in all Ages as with your Walk and Table . . . you never Enjoy the World.

And it was not only the immensities of sea, sky, and stars that were Traherne's objects of enjoyment and, therefore, of worship. We are reminded of Blake's grain of sand in the opening of the twenty-seventh section of the *First Century*:

> You never Enjoy the World aright, till you see how a Sand Exhibiteth the Wisdom and Power of God.

Nothing was too small or insignificant to minister to this man's delight and call forth his praise; from such familiar daily blessings as the "lovly lively air," the "Precious Jewel" of a waterdrop, and "evry Spire of Grass," to the diverse personalities of men and women, who are, he affirms in *Third Century*: 22, "when well understood a Principal Part of our True felicity." Traherne rejoiced in everything from the simple fulfillment of his material needs—bread, meat and drink, his clothes, fuel, and "Household stuff, Books, Utensils, Furniture"—to the intricate mechanism of the human body (*First Century*: 66) and the treasures of art.

If, in brief, Traherne's eyes were for the most part fixed on things beyond this earth, his feet were always firmly planted upon it. His appetite for enjoyment was wonderfully comprehensive. He saw the gift of human existence so constituted that man might taste both the sensuous pleasure of the animals and the spiritual ecstasy of the angels. To be satisfied as God is, he declares in the *First Century,* men must first want like gods: for "Infinit Want is the very Ground and Caus of infinit Treasure."

To despise and dismiss the divinely planned pattern of the earth seemed to Traherne a sin against man's potentialities for praise; an "abominable corruption" of his nature that denied that "heavenly Avarice" implanted in him as positive proof of his immortal soul and its destination. And so the universe became for him the "Book from Heaven" he had demanded in adolescence, a book in whose pages he constantly read the power and love of its Author. Traherne did, however, perceive the necessity for disciplining sensuous enjoyment through dedicating it. The senses could never, to him, be more than—in the metaphor of "News"—ambassadors bringing tidings from a foreign country that housed his true treasure. Men are spiritual, Traherne believed, according to the degree in which they esteem and enjoy their temporal gifts:

> Wine by its Moysture quencheth my Thirst, whether I consider it or no: but to see it flowing from his Lov who gav it unto Man Quencheth the Thirst even of the Holy Angels. To consider it, is to Drink it Spiritualy.

In that last sentence lies the core of Traherne's philosophy. To "consider," and in doing so, to praise: thus, for the contemplative man, could the everyday pleasures of sense be perpetually sanctified.

It was this capacity for enjoying the world on two planes, natural and transcendental—for extracting, here and now, the essence from temporal delight while simultaneously viewing it sub specie aeternitatis—that made Thomas Traherne "Felicity's perfect lover." For him indeed

> Life! Life [was] all: in its most full extent
> Stretcht out to all things, and with all
> Content!

ABRAHAM COWLEY (1618–1667)

Abraham Cowley has already been mentioned as a Cambridge friend and admirer of Crashaw. Six years his junior, he too was born in London, in 1618, the son of a wealthy stationer and bookseller, and was educated at

Westminster School. His early reading of Spenser's *Faerie Queene* inspired a precocious poetic talent, and between the ages of ten and twelve Cowley composed two epic romances. Both appeared in his *Poetical Blossomes,* published in 1633; and while he was still a schoolboy he also wrote a pastoral comedy, *Love's Riddle,* published in 1638 with a Latin comedy entitled *Naufragium Joculare,* two years after he had gone up to Trinity College, Cambridge. He took his degree in 1639 and was elected a fellow of his college the following year. His literary activities at Cambridge included a play called *The Guardian*—later published in 1650, then revised and reissued in 1663 under the title *Cutter of Coleman Street*—which was acted at the college before Prince Charles.

Cowley's fortunes, like those of Crashaw, were adversely affected by the Civil War. Because of his royalist sympathies, he too—with, as he says in a characteristic passage, his "heart wholly set upon Letters"—was "torn" from the university by "that violent Publick storm which would suffer nothing to stand where it did, but rooted up every Plant, even from the Princely Cedars to Me, the Hyssop." In 1643 he joined Charles I at Oxford; and in the following year he went to Paris as secretary to Lord Jermyn and cipher secretary to Queen Henrietta Maria, decoding the correspondence that passed between her and the king. He was also employed on various diplomatic missions. In his absence abroad there appeared in 1647, without his authority, a volume of love poems, *The Mistress,* which immediately earned him a high reputation.

During the next decade Cowley returned to England; and in 1655 he was arrested and imprisoned as a royalist spy. Though later released on bail, he thereafter was viewed suspiciously by both sides. The first verse of "Destinie" was interpreted by his own side as a reference to royalist mistakes, while a passage in the 1656 preface to his *Poems* seemed even more conciliatory in its submission to the Commonwealth. This undoubtedly contributed to Cowley's disappointment at the Restoration in his expectations of certain promised preferments for his services to the royalist cause. He was, however, restored to his Cambridge fellowship in 1661; and his patrons secured him a lease of lands that afforded a sufficient income and leisure at last to enjoy the kind of life he had always desired.

Cowley's later withdrawal from the political arena recalls the attitude during the Civil War of another eminent royalist gentleman of similar tastes and temperament: John Evelyn, to whom he dedicated his essay "The Garden." Like Evelyn's, it was probably dictated less by caution than the natural bent of his inclinations and studious, retiring nature. Even as a boy, he tells us in his engaging essay "Of My Self," he preferred solitude in the fields with a book to playing with his companions. In a poem published as early as 1647, "The Wish," he plainly perceived that "This busie world and I shall ne're agree"; and recoiling from "The *Crowd,* and *Buz,* and *Murmurings* / Of this great *Hive,* the *City,*" unequivocally voiced his modest ambition to be "The happy *Tenant*" of "a *small House,* and *large Garden*" in company with "a *few Friends,* and *many Books,* both true," and "A *Mistress* moderately fair." In "Destinie" he sees himself preordained not for public life but a secluded one, as a poet in the line of "all thy great *Forefathers* . . . from *Homer* down to *Ben*"; while in his 1656 preface he expressed still more uncompromisingly his wish "to forsake this world for ever, with all the *vanities* and *Vexations* of it, and to bury my self . . . in some obscure retreat." In England, before the Restoration, he had turned from politics to botany and lived in the country, collecting plants (and composing in Latin verse six books on herbs, flowers, and trees) as part of the medical studies for which in 1657 he received the degree of doctor of physic, at Oxford. After his final retirement he was able to devote his time to rural pursuits and to writing the *Essays in Verse and Prose,* reflective in the manner and spirit of Montaigne and colored by the thought of the ancients he so copiously quotes, which were posthumously published in the 1668 edition of his *Works.* Their style of "smooth and placid equability," as Samuel Johnson described it, and their very titles—"Of Greatness," "Of Obscurity," "The Dangers of an Honest Man in Much Company," "Of Solitude"—mirror the mind "courtly though retired, / . . . and finding rich amends / For a lost world in solitude and verse" later celebrated by William Cowper in *The Task.*

The reality did not quite match the imagined idyll, and Cowley ruefully admitted to "many little encumbrances and impediments" in his country life. "His Solitude from the very beginning," said his earliest editor and biographer, Thomas Sprat, "had never agreed so well with the constitution of his Body, as of his Mind"; and Cowley suffered much ill health before dying, in 1667, at Chertsey, in Surrey, at the age of forty-nine. Evelyn gives an eyewitness account of his funeral—"near one hundred coaches of noblemen and persons of quality following, among them all the wits of the town, divers bishops and clergymen"; and he was buried near Chaucer and Spenser in Westminster Abbey. Sprat paid tribute to his friend's "unaffected modesty. . . . always content with moderate things," to his "great integrity, and plainness of Manners"; and a contemporary obituary hailed him as a "great ornament of our nation, as well by the candour of his life as the excellency of his writings." Charles II himself, on receiving news of his death, was moved to declare *"That Mr. Cowley had not left a better Man behind him in England."*

Cowley was the most popular poet of his day: praised by Clarendon and revered by Dryden as an "authority . . . almost sacred to me," while Milton ranked him with Spenser and Shakespeare. The impact of his influence on his contemporaries, and later, may be traced in clear echoes of his images and cadences in poets as diverse as Milton, Marvell, Dryden, and Pope.

In the perspective of literary history it is not difficult to understand the reasons for what must today seem such extravagantly high esteem. Cowley was a writer of wide-ranging interests, active enterprise, and versatile accomplishment—and one, as Johnson says, "replete with learning." He epitomized the Restoration mind, at once elegant and inquiring, expressed the prevailing temper of his time, and satisfied its tastes. Coming at the end of the age of Donne, he could write in the still fashionable manner of metaphysical wit, while making none of the emotional and imaginative demands of his predecessors. This cooling of passion could only commend him to readers tired of the intensities and turmoil of the "rough and troubled" times, as he described them, earlier in the century. They welcomed his concept of poetry as (like God's creation of the world in *Davideis*) a *"Storehouse* of all *Proportions"*; of order, and a harmony "without *Discord* or *Confusion,"* imposed upon the "ungovern'd" chaos of contrarieties. The restraint of "Unruly *Phansie* with strong *Judgment"* commended in "The Muse," the "well-worded *dress"* of a poetry in which Reason must "the *Inferior Powers* controul," was equally congenial to the spirit of the succeeding Augustan Age, which it anticipated. Johnson found Cowley "undoubtedly the best" of the metaphysicals, and nearly thirty years after the poet's death Addison declared that he possessed "as much true wit as any Author that ever writ; and indeed all other Talents of an extraordinary Genius."

Moreover, Cowley shared a lively interest in science, the "new philosophy," with eminent contemporaries like Evelyn and Samuel Pepys. His name appeared with theirs (as, appropriately, Dr. Cowley) among the founder members of the Royal Society; and in 1661 he published a pamphlet entitled *A Proposition for the Advancement of Experimental Philosophy,* which set forth the aims of the institution that received its royal charter the following year. Sprat's *History of the Royal Society of London* in 1667 included an ode by Cowley (probably the last poem he wrote) in honor of these "few exalted Spirits" active in encouraging discovery in the natural sciences. Cowley had earlier seen his vocation in the "god-like *Poets* fertile *Mind"*; but here he values "The Riches which doe hoorded for [Man] lie / In Natures endless Treasurie," and "the plain Magick of true Reasons Light," above "painted Scenes, and Pageants of the Brain." His emphasis has shifted "From Words, which are but Pictures of the Thought . . . / To things, the Minds right Object," much as in his praise of Sir William Davenant's *Gondibert* he preferred the new world of "*Men* and *Manners*" to the former "fantastick *Fairy Land*" of heroic poetry. Impatiently dismissing the subtleties of the medieval Scholasticism—"all the cobwebs of the schoolmen's trade"—that had so richly nourished the imagination of Donne, he declared in his ode "To Mr. Hobs" that the "*Living Soul*" of philosophy "in the *School-mens* hands . . . perisht quite at last." It was to thinkers like Thomas Hobbes and to Bacon—hailed in "To the Royal Society" as the "mighty Man" who "like *Moses,* led us forth at last" into the light of knowledge from the wilderness of ignorance and superstition—that Cowley's "bright dry intellect" (as Grierson well describes it) was irresistibly attracted. In "To Mr. Hobs" he expresses unbounded admiration for this "great *Columbus* of the *Golden Lands* of *new Philosophies*"; and celebrates in another ode, "Upon Dr. Harvey," the achievement of the physician whose treatise on the circulation of the blood had been published in 1628. Cowley's images—of star and meteor, "multiplying" glass, his comparison of nature to the "springs and smallest wheels" of a "well-set clock," and many more—are likewise vividly expressive of his scientific enthusiasm.

Yet this topical appeal, which was responsible for his astonishing contemporary success, likewise accounted for the later, and no less striking, decline of Cowley's reputation. A century after his death his wit was no longer in fashion: Johnson was using its more "fantastic" flights to castigate the whole metaphysical school, and Cowper was lamenting its "erroneous taste." Still earlier Pope, another opponent of the metaphysicals' "glittering thoughts," demanded in his *Epistle to Augustus* (1737), "Who now reads Cowley?" The question has had a continuing relevance. In the nineteenth century, Coleridge contrasted Milton's "highly *imaginative*" mind with Cowley's "very *fanciful*" one, and his poetry was largely neglected; while in the modern revival of interest in Donne and his fellows, Cowley's work alone has seemed frigid and artificial.

Generally regarded as the last considerable poet in the metaphysical manner, he does indeed in this context exhibit what Eliot called "a kind of emotional drought, and a verbal ingenuity" that has "no great depth of feeling to work upon." The concept of wit expounded in Cowley's ode of that title is radically opposed to the fusion of feeling with thought described by Herbert Grierson as "passionate ratiocination," through which Donne and Marvell achieved such intensity and illumination of their imaginative insights. "Judgement begets the strength and structure," pronounced Hobbes, "and Fancy begets the ornaments of a Poem"; and Cowley, his disciple, echoes in both theory and practice this view of the conceit as a mere decorative embellishment rather than as a fundamental of poetic meaning.

This essential difference from his metaphysical predecessors is most apparent in Cowley's love poems. In itself the imagery is substantially similar: lovers' exchange of hearts, the broken heart, eyes and tears, sighs associated with winds, and so on. Cowley shared Donne's and Marvell's delight in metaphors of voyages to new worlds and in the resonance of exotic place names: Egypt as an analogy for the man parched by love ("Sleep"); travel in "uncivilis'd" countries of the heart, "Either by savages possest, / Or wild, and uninhabited," with lust in some as "the scorching dog-star," in others "Pride, the rugged Northern Bear" ("The Welcome"); or the "Vain weak-built isthmus" of man's life "o'erwhelm'd" by "the endless oceans" ("Life and Fame"). But there the resemblance ends. We have only to place the idea of the heart sighed out in the lover's breath, in the last line of Cowley's "The Concealment," beside Donne's similar closing conceit in "A Valediction: Of Weeping"; to contrast his expression of the feminine ideal opposed to its reality, in "Against Fruition," with Donne's in the first verses of "Aire and Angels" and "The Good-Morrow"; or to compare the alchemical images of the reconstituted heart, and of metal and alloy, in Cowley's "The Given Heart" with those used by Donne in "A Valediction: Forbidding Mourning" and "The Exstasie," to see how far and how fatally the pressure and urgency of passion have been drained from conceit. In "Platonic Love," presenting a reasoned consideration of the relative roles of body and soul, Cowley reduces the charged argument in "The Exstasie," with its magnificent culminating image of their complementary necessity, "Else a great Prince in prison lies," to flat prose statement:

When souls mix 'tis an happiness;
But not complete till bodies too combine,
And closely as our minds together join . . .
That souls do beauty know,
'Tis to the bodies help they owe . . .

Another characteristic difference in the treatment of a similar idea may be seen by comparing the cool classicism of Cowley's "The Spring" (one of his most gracefully accomplished love lyrics) with Donne's address to the countess of Bedford ("Madame, You have refin'd mee").

But more than anywhere we may detect the lowering of poetic and emotional temperature when three poems by Cowley are juxtaposed with Marvell's "To His Coy Mistress," whose opening "geographical" images echo those of Cowley's "The Account":

I have not yet my *Persian* told,
Nor yet my *Syrian* Loves enroll'd

nor the Indian, Arabian, African, and the rest. Cowley's illustration of the central conceit of his mistress as "Th' *Arithmetician* of my *Love*" provides still more striking parallels with Marvell:

An hundred Loves at *Athens* score,
At *Corinth* write an hundred more . . .
Write me at Lesbos ninety down,
Full ninety *Loves,* and half a One . . .
Three hundred more at *Rhodes* and *Crete* . . .

The figure is sustained with a humorous dexterity that pleases on its intended level. But this mood, persisting to the end of the poem, makes it a charming ingenuity and no more: on a different plane from Marvell, whose whimsical introduction is only a starting point for moving on into somber meditation on the themes of change, mortality, and dissolution. Again, the last verse of Cowley's "My Dyet" anticipates some of the initial conceits in Marvell's poem:

On' a *Sigh* of Pity I a year can live,
One *Tear* will keep me twenty 'at least,
Fifty a gentle *Look* will give;
An hundred years on one *kind word* I'll
feast:
A thousand more will added be,
If you an *Inclination* have for me;
And all beyond is vast *Eternity.*

Marvell's idea of time as relative to the lover's experience is also foreshadowed by Cowley in "Love and Life":

Now sure, within this twelve-month past,
I'have *lov'd* at least some twenty years or
more:
The account of *Love* runs much more fast
Than that, with which our *Life* does score
. . .

. . . the self same *Sun,*
At once does slow and swiftly run . . .

When *Soul* does to *my self* refer,
'Tis then my *Life,* and does but slowly move;
But when it does relate to her,
It swiftly flies, and then is *Love* . . .

Yet nowhere here has Cowley's thought finally "modified his sensibility" (as Eliot so memorably observed of Donne) to transcend the merely clever cerebral exercise of wit.

Nevertheless the impressive diversity of Cowley's literary achievement, from metaphysical ingenuity to Jonsonian classical elegance, commands respect. His spirit of enterprise made him a pioneer in both religious epic and the ode form. In days of slavishly literal translation, his ventures in this field earned Johnson's approval for having "freed translation from servility, and, instead of following his author at a distance, walked by his side." Johnson likewise admired Cowley's critical acumen, whose influence on Pope may be seen in passages in the *Essay on Criticism;* while his remarks in the preface to *Pindarique Odes* about viewing poets in the context of their time anticipate the "historical" attitude in later criticism. As a poet he ranged over love lyrics, elegies, and Latin verse; and his polished philosophical prose has continued to give pleasure through succeeding centuries.

The greater part of *Davideis,* a "*Heroical Poem* of the *Troubles of David,*" of which only four books were completed of a projected twelve, was, according to Sprat, written while Cowley was still an undergraduate, although it was not published until 1656. Little regarded in its day, this ambitious undertaking essayed, for the first time in English poetry, the composition of an original sacred epic rather than mere paraphrase of biblical narrative. Modestly disclaiming success for his "weak and imperfect attempt," Cowley expressed the hope that it might open "a way to the courage and industry of some other persons, who may be better able to perform it." This was fulfilled eleven years later, with the publication of Milton's epic handling of a scriptural theme in the classical manner, *Paradise Lost;* and also in having provided for Dryden an invaluable model and inspiration for the development of the heroic couplet.

Among Cowley's formal elegies, "On the Death of Sir Henry Wootton" dutifully eulogizes the knowledge and industry of a diplomat now "gone to *Heav'n* on his *Fourth Embassie.*" More personal in feeling, his ode "On the Death of Mr. William Hervey" mourns a Cambridge contemporary who died there in 1642. Although Johnson found "very little passion" in this elegy, it communicates with genuine poignancy a young man's grief for his "truest *Friend* on earth . . . / My sweet *Companion,* and my gentle *Peere,*" with whom he had walked in the fields sharing such talk of "deep *Philosophy, / Wit, Eloquence,* and *Poetry*":

> Henceforth, ye gentle *Trees,* for ever fade;
> Or your sad branches thicker joyn,
> And into darksome shades combine,
> *Dark* as the *Grave* wherein my *Friend* is laid.

"On the Death of Mr. Crashaw," with its self-contained couplets and alexandrines, is by contrast metrically less flexible and more rhetorical—but still a sincere and memorable tribute to a venerated fellow poet.

These elegies appeared in 1656 among Cowley's *Miscellanies,* which display a great variety of manner and mood. The "familiar and festive" vein approved by Johnson in *Anacreontiques* celebrates amorous and convivial delights ("Let me alive my pleasures have: / All are Stoics in the grave") in deft and graceful pieces like "The Swallow," "Drinking," and "The Epicure." Johnson also applauded as an "airy frolic of genius" the "gaiety of fancy" and "dance of words" in "The Chronicle," a lighthearted account of the virtues and "politick Arts" of a succession of imaginary mistresses. He did not extend such unqualified enthusiasm to the love poems in *The Mistress,* finding outrageously "far-fetched" such amorous conceits as that of a lover's heart which, tormented by his "stubborn" mistress, will "tear and blow up all within, / Like a grenado shot into a magazine." In his preface to the *Poems,* Cowley had observed "that *Poets* are scarce thought *Free-men* of their *Company,* without paying some duties, and obliging themselves to be true to Love"; and Johnson commented tartly upon this attitude of conventional "obligation to amorous ditties." The justice of this complaint that Cowley's mistress "has no power of seduction: 'she plays round the head, but reaches not the heart,' " her attributes producing "no correspondence of emotion," has already been acknowledged. In his witty lip service to love, that imagined "one dear *She*" of "The Wish" is nowhere more than a generalized abstraction envisaged by an ingenious but ultimately uninvolved spectator.

Yet Marvell's indebtedness to Cowley is plain: "To His Coy Mistress" did not appear until 1681, while "My Dyet" and "Love and Life" were published in *The Mistress* as early as 1647, and "The Account" included among the 1656 *Anacreontiques.* And in fact not only many of his contemporaries, but later poetic generations down to the great nineteenth-century romantics, owed much to Cowley's active, alert, and adventurous mind. The influence of the classical poets in whom he was from schooldays so deeply versed is pervasive throughout his work: from his books on plants in imitation of their style, and his meditative Horatian essays, to the *Anacreontiques* paraphrasing the manner of the Greek poet Anacreon. He aspired to literary immortality through emulation of the "mighty *Three,*" Aristotle, Cicero, and Vergil. But it was the triumphal and processional odes of Pindar that inspired Cowley's important legacy to posterity. Many of his addresses to persons—"To Mr. Hobs," "Ode upon Dr. Harvey," "To the Royal Society"—and to abstractions—"Of Liberty," "Destinie," "Hymn. To Light"—were written in Pindaric stanzas, irregularly rhymed and varying in both the length and number of their lines, to afford greater technical scope and freedom than the familiar formal pattern of such Horatian odes as Marvell's *Upon Cromwell's Return from Ireland.*

Two main classical models have served as inspiration for the English ode: the Greek poet Pindar (*ca.* 518–*ca.* 438 B.C.), who composed ceremonial songs in honor of the victorious athletes and their families in the annual national festivals; and the Roman poet Horace (65–8 B.C.), who wrote not to celebrate great occasions but in an altogether more intimate, thoughtful, and sometimes ironical vein. Pindar's festal poems were designed for performance by choir and orchestra, and this is reflected in the exuberant lyrical surge of their rhythms and irregular lengths of line, the darting, impulsive thought that often follows no logical sequence, and an intense imaginative energy infectiously communicating the excitement of communal rejoicing. Their sentence structure and verse patterns are governed by the pulse beat and breathing pauses in the music and dancing that accompanied them; so Cowley was right to insist, in his preface to *Pindarique Odes,* upon the importance of relating Pindar's work to the time and purpose for which it was written.

The great difference between Pindar and Horace is that between the public and the private poet. Horace wrote in carefully molded, precisely ordered stanzas usually of four lines, with few variations on this traditional form. This "calm, restrained, elegant, enlightened Epicurean," as Gilbert Highet describes him,[9] warned later poets of the dangers of trying to imitate or emulate what seemed to him the torrential, undisciplined power of his great predecessor. Highet admirably sums up the distinguishing characteristics of the two, and of their poetic successors:

> The Pindarics admire passion, daring, and extravagance. Horace's followers prefer reflection, moderation, economy. Pindaric odes follow no pre-established routine, but soar and dive and veer as the wind catches their wing. Horatian lyrics work on quiet, short, well-balanced systems. . . . Pindar loves the choir, the festival, and the many-footed dance. Horace is a solo singer, sitting in a pleasant room or quiet garden with his lyre.

Horace had been familiar to European readers in the Middle Ages, and in England his odes were taught and quoted in schools before poets began to imitate him. Mindful that the word *ode* means "song," Horatian writers in the Renaissance and baroque periods often set their odes to music, or attempted to reproduce the effect of music in the movement and harmony of the words; but any accompaniment was envisaged for the solo singer, or at most

9. In *The Classical Tradition: Greek and Roman Influences on Western Literature* (Oxford, 1949). See chapter 12 for a detailed and illuminating discussion of the respective influences of Pindar and Horace upon English poetry.

a small group, by contrast with the bold choric and orchestral sweep of Pindar. The odes of the Greek master were known in Europe only through Horace's qualified admiration, until they were printed at Venice in 1513. They were thus still something of a poetic novelty to the seventeenth-century reader when Milton wrote, in 1629, the first great Pindaric poem in English, his hymn "On the Morning of Christ's Nativity," shortly after he had bought a copy of Pindar (now in Harvard University Library); and Ben Jonson in the same year composed his "Ode on the Death of Sir H. Morison," a poem more characteristically Horatian in thought and tempo, but Pindaric in its verse patterns.

Cowley was in fact the first to direct the attention of English readers to the odes of Pindar, to offer any detailed and sympathetic scrutiny of his spirit and technique, and to attempt to translate his poetic principles into his own practice. It was a conscious and carefully considered innovation, which aimed not at slavish imitation but set out to recreate the manner in which Pindar might have written in contemporary English. Discussing his methods at length in the preface to his *Poems,* he expressed doubt that this unfamiliar form would be understood by many of his readers; for, as he said:

> The digressions are many, and sudden, and sometimes long. . . . The *Figures* are unusual and *bold,* even to *Temeritie,* and such as I durst not have to do withal in any other kind of *Poetry*: The *Numbers* are various and irregular, and sometimes (especially some of the long ones) seem harsh and uncouth, if the just measures and cadencies be not observed in the *Pronunciation.*

Anticipating Samuel Johnson's complaint of the "lax and lawless versification" licensed by the removal of traditional restraints, he concluded by affirming that "though the *Liberty* of them may incline a man to believe them easie to be composed, yet the undertaker will find it otherwise."

Cowley's enthusiasm for his model is given full rein in "The Praise of Pindar," written in imitation of the Second Ode of Horace: extolling—in Horace's own image—"The *Theban Swan*" and the "rich embroidered *Line*" of "his *Nimble, Artful, Vigorous* Song," with its

> impetuous *Dithyrambique Tide,*
> Which in no *Channel* deigns t'abide,
> Which neither *Banks* nor *Dikes* controul.

"The Resurrection," an ode that Cowley himself called "truly *Pindarical,* falling from one thing into another, after his *Enthusiastical manner,*" also characterizes the nature of the "*Pindarique Pegasus*":

> an unruly, and a *hard-Mouth'd Horse,*
> Fierce, and unbroken yet,
> Impatient of the *Spur* or *Bit.*
> Now *praunces* stately, and anon flies o're the place,
> Disdains the *servile Law* of any settled *pace,*
> *Conscious* and *proud* of his own *natural force*

which will fling "*Writer and Reader* too that *sits* not *sure.*" "The Muse" further elaborates, in the Pindaric manner, Cowley's characteristic ideas about the nature and function of poetry.

The widespread influence of Cowley's Pindaric odes was responsible for many pompously pretentious effusions for more than a century to come. Yet his was—in his own phrase—"no *unskilful Touch*"; and, as Sprat contended, the very irregularity of the form made "that kind of Poesie fit for all manner of subjects . . . the frequent alteration of the Rhythm and Feet, affects the mind with a more various delight, while it is soon apt to be tyr'd by the setled pace of any one constant measure." In Cowley's hands, he concluded, "this loose, and unconfin'd measure has all the Grace, and Harmony of the most confin'd." Addison too praised Cowley's felicitous adaptation of "the deep-mouth'd *Pindar*":

whom others in a labour'd strain,
And forc'd expression, imitate in vain.
Well-pleas'd in thee he soars with new
delight;

and even Johnson had to admit "great fertility of fancy," and that "no man but Cowley could have written" his Pindarics.

If for us today Cowley's Pindaric experiments are neither wholly successful as free imitations of their original, nor vividly memorable as poems, his pioneering exploitation of the flexible possibilities of a form comparatively new then in England proved a liberating force for generations of poets to come. Its impact may be traced from Dryden's "Alexander's Feast" and his great public odes, through Gray's "Progress of Poesy," to the powerful ebb and flow of alternating joy and regret evoked by the irregular verse forms of William Wordsworth's "Immortality" ode; and is to be detected even as late as Alfred Lord Tennyson's "Ode on the Death of the Duke of Wellington." Percy Bysshe Shelley was another of the great romantics notably indebted to the freedom of Pindaric improvisation in poems such as his "Ode to Naples," and even more clearly in the mounting, impetuous urgency of image and emotion in "Ode to the West Wind"; and Grierson points a parallel between lines 45–48 of Cowley's "Hymn. To Light" and the third stanza of Shelley's "Hymn of Apollo." John Keats, like William Collins, was more Horatian in mood, yet the contemplative solitude of his great odes generates an intensity that soars to Pindaric peaks of spiritual exaltation. In fact, small distinction between the two classical influences was made by many English nineteenth-century poets; and in their work the solitary serenity of Horace often blends effortlessly with the passionate imagination and transcendental visionary quality of the Greek poet made generally familiar by Cowley nearly two centuries earlier. Whatever his shortcomings when viewed as the last major representative of metaphysical poetry, in the sphere of the Pindaric ode Cowley did indeed, in his own words about Davenant, "leave bright *Tracks* for following Pens to take."

Selected Bibliography

RICHARD CRASHAW

BIBLIOGRAPHY

See L. C. Martin, ed., *The Poems, English, Latin and Greek*, and Wallerstin, R. C., *Crashaw: A Study in Style and Poetic Development*, below.

COLLECTED WORKS

A. B. Grosart, ed., *Complete Works*, 2 vols. (London, 1872–1873), with suppl. (1887–1888), in the Fuller Worthies' Library; A. R. Waller, ed., *Poems*, (Cambridge, 1904); J. R. Tutin, ed., *Poems*, (London, 1905); L. C. Martin, ed., *The Poems English, Latin and Greek*, (Oxford, 1927; 2nd ed., 1957), the definitive ed., with notes on the MSS and early eds.

SEPARATE WORKS

Epigrammatum Sacrorum Liber, (London, 1634); *Steps to the Temple. Sacred Poems, With Other Delights of the Muses*, (London, 1646), 2nd ed., 1648, added new pieces; *Carmen Deo Nostro, Te Decet Hymnus, Sacred Poems, Collected, Corrected, Augmented*, (Paris, 1652), reprinted with the 1646 ed. of *Steps to the Temple*, (1670); *Poemata et Epigrammata, Editio Secunda, Auctior et Emendatior*, (Cambridge, 1670).

SOME BIOGRAPHICAL AND CRITICAL STUDIES

Loudon, K. M., *Two Mystic Poets*, (London, 1922), treats Crashaw and Vaughan; Bennett, J., *Four Metaphysical Poets*, (Cambridge, 1934; rev. ed., 1953), treats Donne, Herbert, Vaughan, and Crashaw, 2nd rev. ed., titled *Five Metaphysical Poets*, (London, 1964), adds a chapter on Marvell; Wallerstein, R. C., *Crashaw: A Study in Style and Poetic Development*, (Madison, Wisc., 1935), includes full bibliography of Crashaw's sources and of work by Crashaw scholars; Warren, A., *Crashaw: A Study in Baroque Sensibility*, (Baton Rouge, 1939); Praz, M., *Crashaw*, (Brescia, 1946); Willey, B., *Crashaw*, (London, 1949), a perceptive and illuminating memorial lecture delivered at Peterhouse Cambridge; Williams, G. W., *Image and Symbol in the Sacred Poetry of Richard Crashaw*, (Columbia, S.C., 1963).

HENRY VAUGHAN

BIBLIOGRAPHY

For the early eds. see L. C. Martin, ed., *The Works*, below. The work of Vaughan scholars through the end of 1945 is listed in Marilla, E. L., *A Comprehensive Bibliography of Henry Vaughan* (University, Ala., 1948).

COLLECTED WORKS

The Sacred Poems and Private Ejaculations, (London, 1847), with a memoir by H. F. Lyte; A. B. Grosart, ed., *The Works in Verse and Prose Complete,* (London, 1870–1871), in the Fuller Worthies' Library; E. K. Chambers, ed., *The Poems of Henry Vaughan, Silurist,* 2 vols. (London, 1896); L. C. Martin, ed., *The Works,* (Oxford, 1914; rev. ed., 1957), the definitive ed.; E. L. Marilla, ed., *The Secular Poems,* (Cambridge, Mass., 1958); L. C. Martin, ed., *Poetry and Selected Prose of Henry Vaughan,* (London, 1963), Oxford Standard Authors ed., based on Oxford English Texts ed., *Poetry and Selected Prose of Henry Vaughan,* (London, 1957), above, contains all the poetry and *The Mount of Olives, Man in Darkness,* and *Primitive Holiness.*

SEPARATE WORKS

Poems, With the Tenth Satyre of Juvenal Englished, (London, 1646); *Silex Scintillans: Sacred Poems and Private Ejaculations,* (London, 1650), so-called "Second Edition," consisting of a reiss. of the first with a second "Book," 1655, and W. A. L. Bettany, ed., (London, 1905); *Olor Iscanus: Select Poems, and Translations,* (London, 1651; reiss., 1679); *The Mount of Olives: or Solitary Devotions . . . ,* (London, 1652); *Flores Solitudinis: Collected in His Sickness and Retirement,* (London, 1654), a translation of four Latin prose works; *Hermetical Physick . . . Englished,* (London, 1655), a translation of Nollius' *Systema Medicinae Hermeticae Generale,* (1613); *The Chymist's Key,* (London, 1657); *Thalia Rediviva,* (London, 1678).

SOME BIOGRAPHICAL AND CRITICAL STUDIES

Hodgson, G. E., *A Study in Illumination,* (London, 1914); Loudon, K. M., *Two Mystic Poets,* (London, 1922); Holmes, E., *Henry Vaughan and the Hermetic Philosophy,* (Oxford, 1932); Bennett, J., *Four Metaphysical Poets,* (Cambridge, 1934; rev. ed., 1953), and *Five Metaphysical Poets,* (London, 1964); Leishman, J. B., *The Metaphysical Poets,* (Oxford, 1934) treats Donne, Herbert, Vaughan, and Traherne; Martin, L. C., "Henry Vaughan and the Theme of Infancy," in *Seventeenth-Century Studies, presented to Sir Herbert Grierson,* (Oxford, 1938); Hutchinson, F. E., *Henry Vaughan: A Life and Interpretation,* (Oxford, 1947), the standard biography; Garner, R., *Henry Vaughan: Experience and the Tradition,* (Chicago, 1959); Pettet, E. C., *On Paradise and Light,* (London, 1961), a study of Vaughan's *Silex Scintillans;* Durr, R. A., *On the Mystical Poetry of Henry Vaughan,* (Harvard, 1963).

THOMAS TRAHERNE

BIBLIOGRAPHY

Wade, G. I., *Traherne: A Critical Biography,* (Princeton, 1944), contains a bibliography; "The Manuscripts of Traherne," *Bodleian Library Record III,* (1951).

COLLECTED WORKS

G. I. Wade, ed., *The Poetical Works,* (London, 1932); A. Quiller-Couch, ed., *Felicities of Thomas Traherne,* (London, 1934); H. M. Margoliouth, ed., *Thomas Traherne: Centuries, Poems and Thanksgivings,* 2 vols. (Oxford, 1958), the definitive ed.; A. Ridler, ed., *Thomas Traherne: Poems, Centuries, and Three Thanksgivings,* (London, 1966), Oxford Standard Authors ed., based on the Oxford English Texts ed., (London, 1958), above, a fresh collation of texts with manuscripts, includes all the poems *Centuries of Meditations* in entirety, three *Thanksgivings* and short extracts from *Christian Ethicks.*

SEPARATE WORKS

Roman Forgeries, By A Faithful Son of the Church of England, (London, 1673); *Christian Ethicks,* (London, 1675) contains eight of the eleven poems printed in the poet's lifetime; G. Hickes, ed., *A Serious and Pathetical Contemplation of the Mercies of God, In Several Most Devout and Sublime Thanksgivings for the Same,* (London, 1699), R. Daniells, ed., (Toronto, 1941); *A Collection of Meditations and Devotions in Three Parts,* (London, 1717); B. Dobell, ed., *The Poetical Works, Now First Published, From the Original Manuscripts,* (London, 1903); B. Dobell, ed., *Centuries of Meditations, Now First Printed from the Author's Manuscript,* (London, 1908; rev. ed., 1928); H. I. Bell, ed., *Poems of Felicity,* (London, 1910), text from the MS in the British Museum, contains thirty-nine poems not in the Dobell MSS in the Bodleian Library; J. R. Slater, ed., *Of Magnanimity and Chastity,* (New York, 1942).

BIOGRAPHICAL AND CRITICAL STUDIES

Leishman, J. B., *The Metaphysical Poets,* (Oxford, 1934); Needale, Q., *Traherne,* (Oxford, 1935); Wade, G. I., *Thomas Traherne,* (Princeton, 1944), contains the fullest biography and a detailed examination of the individual writings; Salter, K. W., *Thomas Traherne: Mystic and Poet,* (London, 1964).

ABRAHAM COWLEY

COLLECTED WORKS

T. Sprat, ed., *Works,* (London, 1668), with the earliest biography of Cowley, the 2nd part appeared in 1681, and the 2nd and 3rd parts together in 1689; A. B. Grosart, ed., *The Complete Works in Verse and Prose,* 2 vols. (London, 1881); J. R. Lumby, ed., *Prose Works,* (London, 1887), revision by A. Tilley, ed., (London, 1923); A. R. Waller, ed., *The English Writings,* 2 vols. (London, 1905–1906); A. B. Gough, ed., *Essays and Other Prose Writings,* (London, 1915); J. Sparrow, ed., *The Mistress with Other Select Poems,* (London, 1926); L. C. Martin, ed., *Poetry and Prose,* (Oxford, 1949), a representative selection, including Sprat's

Life and comments on the work by critics from Dryden to Grierson.

SEPARATE WORKS

Poetical Blossomes, (London, 1633; 2nd ed., 1636), second ed. includes *Sylva; Love's Riddle and Naufragium Joculare*, (London, 1638); *The Puritan and the Papist*, (London, 1643); *The Mistress*, (London, 1647), published without Cowley's authority during his absence from England; *The Guardian*, (London, 1650; rev. ed., 1663), revision entitled *Cutter of Coleman-Street; Poems*, (London, 1656), comprised *Miscellanies, The Mistress, Pindarique Odes*, and *Davideis*, Cowley's critical preface to this first authorized ed. of his mature poems is highly illuminating in its comments on his own work, his political attitude, and his views on poetry as a whole; *A Proposition for the Advancement of Experimental Philosophy and A Vision*, (London, 1661), the former a pamphlet to promote the institution of the Royal Society; *A. Couleii Plantarum Libri Duo*, (London, 1662); *Verses Lately Written upon Several Occasions*, (London, 1663); *A Poem on the Late Civil War*, (London, 1679).

SOME BIOGRAPHICAL AND CRITICAL STUDIES

Johnson, S., "Abraham Cowley," in *Lives of the Poets* (London, 1779), in World's Classics ed. and Everyman's Library ed., important for its typical Augustan view not only of Cowley but of the metaphysical school in general; Nethercot, A. H., *Abraham Cowley, the Muse's Hannibal*, (Oxford, 1931); Loiseau, J., *Abraham Cowley, sa vie,son oeuvre*, (Paris, 1931); Wallerstein, R., "Cowley as a Man of Letters," in *Transactions of the Wisconsin Academy of Sciences, Arts, and Letters*, 27 (1932); Leavis, F. R., "The Line of Wit," in *Revaluation*, (1936); Hinman, R. B., *Cowley's World of Order*, (Cambridge, Mass., 1960).

ANTHOLOGIES

H. J. C. Grierson, ed., *Metaphysical Lyrics and Poems of the Seventeenth Century*, (Oxford, 1921) with a prefatory essay that constitutes the best critical intro. to seventeenth-century metaphysical poetry; N. Ault, ed., *Seventeenth-Century Lyrics*, (London, 1925); H. J. C. Grierson and G. Bullough, eds., *The Oxford Book of Seventeenth-Century Verse*, (Oxford, 1934); H. Gardner, ed., *The Metaphysical Poets*, (London, 1957), contains an illuminating critical intro.; L. L. Martz, ed., *The Meditative Poems*, (New York, 1963).

GENERAL CRITICISM

Eliot, T. S., "The Metaphysical Poets," in the *Times Literary Supplement* (London, 1921), reprinted in *Selected Essays*, (1932); Leishman, J. B., *The Metaphysical Poets*, (Oxford, 1934); Bennett, J., *Four Metaphysical Poets*, (Cambridge, 1934; rev. ed., 1953), and *Five Metaphysical Poets* (London, 1964); White, H. C., *The Metaphysical Poets: A Study in Religious Experience*, (New York, 1936); Praz, M., *Studies in Seventeenth-Century Imagery*, (London, 1939); Bush, D., *English Literature in the Earlier Seventeenth Century*, (Oxford, 1945); Tuve, R., *Elizabethan and Metaphysical Imagery*, (Chicago, 1947); Freeman, R., *English Emblem books*, (London, 1948); Wallerstein, R. C., *Studies in Seventeenth-Century Poetic*, (Madison, Wisc., 1950); R. F. Jones, et al., *The Seventeenth Century*, (Stanford, 1951), studies in the history of English thought and literature from Bacon to Pope; Martz, L. L., *The Poetry of Meditation: A Study in English Religious Literature of the Seventeenth Century*, (New Haven, 1954); B. Ford, ed., *From Donne to Marvell*, (London, 1956), The Pelican Guide to English Literature, III; Alvarez, A., *The School of Done*, (London, 1961); Williamson, G., *Seventeenth-Century Contexts*, (London, 1961); Williamson, G., *The Proper Wit of Poetry*, (London, 1962); W. R. Keast, ed., *Seventeenth-Century English Poetry: Modern Essays in Criticism*, (New York, 1962); Hamilton, K. G., *The Two Harmonies: Poetry and Prose in the Seventeenth Century*, (London, 1963); Nevo, R., *The Dial of Virtue: A Study of Poems on the Affairs of State in the Seventeenth Century*, (Princeton, 1963); Martz, L. L., *The Paradise Within: Studies in Vaughan, Traherne and Milton*, (New Haven, 1964); Williamson, G., *Milton and Others*, (London, 1965).

SOCIAL AND LITERARY BACKGROUND

Grierson, H. J. C., *The First Half of the Seventeenth Century*, (London, 1906); Grierson, H. J. C., *Cross Currents in English Literature of the Seventeenth Century*, (London, 1929); Willey, B., *The Seventeenth-Century Background*, (London, 1934); Wedgwood, C. V., *Seventeenth-Century English Literature*, (London, 1950).

Edna St. Vincent Millay
(1892–1950)

DEBRA FRIED

> One wonders sometime what the critic of literature would do were he left entirely in the dark as to the age, sex, amorous proclivities and political affiliations of the writer whose work he is considering. Fortunately, he does not often find himself n this predicament. For the most part, he is in the enviable position of the graphologist who writes, "Send me a sample of your handwriting, and I will read your character," having just looked one up in *Who's Who,* skimmed through one's recently published autobiography, and had an hour or so's ever-so-interesting conversation with one's most garrulous friend.

THE ABOVE REMARKS in Millay's preface to her 1936 translation of Charles Baudelaire's *Flowers of Evil* might be taken as a warning against reading her poetry too exclusively in the context of her life. Poems, not poets, Millay insists, are the proper subject of our attention, for a great poem is almost self-authoring: "The poem is the thing. Is it interesting?—is it beautiful?—is it sublime? Then it was written by nobody. It exists by itself." A prodigious success, bursting into the literary world with a poem she wrote at nineteen, Millay never had a chance to be nobody.

Widely seen as an exemplar of the "new woman" of the 1920s, Millay remained in the public eye throughout most of a productive life. She acted onstage in her own plays. In 1923 she was the first woman to receive the Pulitzer Prize for poetry. Her marriage that year to businessman Eugen Boissevain gave her a partner supportive of her public career. She went on reading tours, made recordings and radio broadcasts, and gave frequent interviews. During an almost thirty-year span, her readers were treated to a regular succession of volumes of poetry, including the much-noticed debut *Renascence and Other Poems* (1917) and the light verse of *A Few Figs from Thistles* (1920), which contains many of the best-known of her poems. This was followed by *Second April* (1921); The *Harp-Weaver and Other Poems* (1923); *The Buck in the Snow* (1928); the sonnet sequence *Fatal Interview* (1931); *Wine from These Grapes* (1934); a verse drama that found its way to the stage, *Conversation at Midnight* (1937); *Huntsman, What Quarry?* (1939); and a series of collections of topical poems during the war years, including works written for radio broadcast.

Harper & Brothers, her publisher from 1923 onward, compiled collections of her sonnets (1941) and lyrics (1943). She published five plays between 1920 and 1932, including the libretto for Deems Taylor's opera *The King's Henchman* (1927), commissioned for the Metropolitan Opera and performed there and on tour with great success. (The published libretto enjoyed eighteen printings in its first year.) Her satirical prose sketches written for the magazines *Vanity Fair* and *Ainslee's* were collected as *Distressing Dialogues* (1924). Millay was often in the limelight for her political views and activities as well. She publicly protested the controversial Sacco-Vanzetti execution of 1927, and she was America's poetic mouthpiece during World War II. By then her poetic reputation had begun to ebb, partly on account of the roughness and haste of the advocacy poetry she churned out during the war, and her next book did not appear until the posthumous collection *Mine the Harvest* (1954). Her last decade, largely spent in relative isolation at Steepletop, near Austerlitz, New York, was marked by illness and stagnation. Millay was unable to write for two years following a nervous breakdown in 1944. Boissevain died in 1949, and the grieving poet plunged back into solitary work at Steepletop. She died there of heart failure on 19 October 1950.

For many years after her death, Millay seemed to have been dropped from serious critical consideration. She was and continues to be subject to the occupational hazards befalling the celebrity: public images of Millay have repeatedly distorted or eclipsed the light by which her poetry is read. As the poet Louise Bogan recognized in a 1939 essay on Millay, these hazards are particularly threatening to a woman poet: "It is a dangerous lot, that of the charming, romantic public poet, especially if it falls to a woman."

This dangerous lot fell to Millay early. From the start, readers paid more attention to her personal proclivities and affiliations than to her poetic ones. "Renascence," her first published poem (not counting juvenilia), appeared in *The Lyric Year,* an anthology of the "best verse" of 1912. Although it did not win first prize, it immediately won vocal defenders. Among "Renascence" enthusiasts were two young contributors to the volume, Arthur Davison Ficke and Witter Bynner, who felt sure that they could deduce the poet's identity from the poem. They praised it to the anthology's editor, Ferdinand Earle, as "a real vision, such as Coleridge might have seen," adding that Earle's biographical note about its author, one "E. St. Vincent Millay," must be a joke: "No sweet young thing of twenty ever ended a poem precisely where this one ends: it takes a brawny male of forty-five to do that." The "brawny male" wrote back to her admirers, averring that she was indeed a woman of twenty, but thanking them for their praise. If being told that she wrote like a man was a mixed blessing, it was also a short-lived one. When the author of "Renascence" was revealed to be a charming young woman not yet twenty-one, her poem began to garner accolades that cast its qualities in the feminine mode. The brawny male's Coleridgean vision became, in the words of one contemporary reviewer, the girl's "untutored simplicity accompanying an indefinable magic."

As Millay's life tends to upstage her work, her early work tends to upstage her later. From the start of her career she was a public figure, and she spent much of her creative life living up to, or living down, her youthful coup. "I'm so tired of hearing about Renascence," she confided in 1922. "I find it's as hard to live down an early triumph as an early indiscretion; if Renascence had been an illegitimate child people couldn't have flung it in my face any oftener" (*Letters,* 166). Readers expected her to continue in the visionary, exuberant manner of her first-born, and it was hard to keep herself from meeting their expectations. Yet popular acclaim buoyed her, and when in the late 1930s her acclaim dwindled, popular censure angered her. The censure was generally the censure of contrast, charging that the new Millay was not like the old—that is, young. The maturing writer watched with dismay as her early poetry, garnished in the public eye with her youthful legend, became a marketable item. She tried to veto selections for the 1950 *Oxford Book of American Verse,* protesting the tendency of the editors (headed by F. O. Matthiessen) "to include the poems which they think will have the most popular appeal," namely "simple and youthful poems." The advertising copywriter in Millay's 1937 play *Conversation at Midnight* may speak for her when he remarks: "'The Finest,' 'The Best,' 'The Purest'—what do they mean now?— / Something somebody wants to sell." To understand her poetic achievement, then—both its limits and its strengths—we must learn to tell the story of Millay's life not as the legend of, as John Ciardi dubbed her, "a figure of passionate living," but as the life of a poet.

She was born on 22 February 1892 in Rockland, Maine, first child of Cora Buzzelle Millay and Henry Tolman Millay, a school administrator. While pregnant with what both parents were convinced would be a son, Cora Millay learned that an injured brother was recovering in good hands at St. Vincent's Hospital, and she decided to name the boy Vincent. When her daughter was born, she retained "St. Vincent" as the middle name; in the family circle she was called "Vincent." Throughout her life she rechristened herself for different friends. Millay signed her letters variously "Bincent," "Eddyner," (or, in a joky pairing of archaic formality and slangy dialect, "Thine, Edner"), and, once, "Edna St. Vitus Millstone." Her husband sometimes called her "Vincie"; she was never, not even to the tax collector, "Mrs. Boissevain." Over the light, satirical prose she wrote in the twenties her byline was "Nancy Boyd." ("Bird" in Brooklynese? Vincent Sheean's 1951 memoir documents Millay's fascination and perhaps identification with birds.) Edna St. Vincent Millay's name of many names may have helped to foster the poet's proclivity for role-playing and speaking in a range of voices, and her sense that a mercurial variety is part of identity.

In 1900 Cora Millay divorced her husband, though Henry Millay remained on good terms with the family. A former singer, Cora Millay worked as a practical nurse to support her three daughters, Edna, Kathleen, and Norma. Millay grew up in a frugal but literate, closely-knit female household whose only luxuries were the necessities of good music and books. Her mother gave Millay her first music lessons. Under a professional teacher she then studied piano with serious ambition for three years, until about 1908. The Millay sisters made up songs and jingles for their own entertainment, a natural extension of their mother's encouragement in music and literature. In 1906 *St. Nicholas,* a children's magazine, printed Millay's poem "Forest Trees." By the time she was eighteen—and no longer eligible for membership in the St. Nicholas League for young writers—she had published six poems in the magazine. "The Land of Romance," which she wrote at fourteen, won the magazine's Gold Badge and was reprinted in *Current Literature* alongside the work of established adult poets. At seventeen she won the Cash Prize—*St. Nicholas's* highest accolade—for "Friends," a pair of witty monologues that shows an early sophistication about the play of power between the sexes. The *St. Nicholas* poems reveal Millay's early metrical skill.

After a few years of transient living with her mother's sisters in various Maine towns, in 1903 Mrs. Millay settled the family in Camden, Maine, on Penobscot Bay. In 1909 Millay graduated from Camden High School, where she wrote for the school newspaper, then lived at home, took odd jobs, and cared for her sisters while her mother's nursing took her out of town. In 1912 she went to Kingman, Maine, where her father was in failing health. There her mother sent her notice of the *Lyric Year* competition, which she had come across in a magazine, and urged her daughter to enter it, as she had earlier encouraged her to send poems to St. Nicholas. Millay finished a long visionary poem already in progress, sent it in with the title "Renaissance" (the editor Englished it to "Renascence," with her consent) and also submitted a blank-verse monologue, "Interim."

The famous poem begins with a survey of everything the speaker can see from where she stands. She can inventory the world ("three long mountains and a wood"; "three islands in a bay"), but not possess it. She sees only the limits of her world, "the things that bounded me." No sooner does she, in claustrophic terror, touch the sky at her finger's ends, palpable and too close for comfort, than "Infinity / Came down and settled over me." Crushing the speaker, almost grappling her in a wrestling hold, Infinity then grants her extraordinary powers of perception:

> Whispered to me a word whose sound
> Deafened the air for the worlds around,
> And brought unmuffled to my ears
> The gossiping of friendly spheres,
> The creaking of the tented sky,
> The ticking of Eternity.

How Infinity's whispered secret alters the speaker's perception shows in her language: from the simplicity of the poem's opening survey of countable mountains, wood, and sea—a crayon-like drawing of the world—and the childlike self-dares ("The sky was not so very tall"), the poem's voice is curiously transmuted into remade idioms ("worlds around" instead of the expected "miles around") as it handles immensities in short lines. Pressed down below the earth by the hand of Infinity, the speaker pleads for a rainstorm fierce enough to wash her grave away. It comes, releasing the poet into "A sense of glad awakening." Reborn, she can hear the grass "whispering" to her: in place of Infinity's enclosing whispered secret word, she finds the simple noise of wind through the grass. The poem ends with the speaker having learned a lesson: that "the sky" is "No higher than the soul is high":

> And he whose soul is flat—the sky
> Will cave in on him by and by.

The poem ends not with jubilation but admonition. The threat of a crushing power to be resisted only through a sufficiently vibrant imagination would recur in a number of forms in Millay's love poems and political verse.

In a 1912 letter to Ficke (the two became lifelong correspondents, and briefly lovers), Millay denied the influence of Coleridge's "The Rime of the Ancient Mariner" on "Renascence." She further declared to Ficke that "I never get anything from a book. I see things with my own eyes, just as if they were the first eyes that ever saw, and then I set about to tell, as best I can, just what I see." As Millay well knew, this is one of the most traditional claims a poet can make; indeed, it is almost a declaration of poetic vocation. The meter of "Renascence" is rhyming tetrameter couplets, and Millay's ear is plainly full of Andrew Marvell's "To His Coy Mistress," a poem she loved (compare the line "A grave is such a quiet place" with Marvell's "The grave's a fine and private place"). The brash directness of "Renascence" is built from its amalgam of Coleridgean outcries, Marvellean cadences, and observations of the Maine landscape. This is to say not that the poem is derivative, but that it is not an unlettered schoolgirl's spontaneous effusion. It is the work of a young writer who has read a great deal of poetry and absorbed it into her way of seeing with her own eyes. As she notes in a late poem, the astringent Maine landscape was in some degree a blankness the young poet peopled with figures from her reading; the apples in her Maine orchards were "Half Baldwin, half Hesperides."

"Interim," her other (and apparently her preferred) submission to *The Lyric Year*, is largely forgotten. But this pair of poems illustrates the two sides of her childhood that shaped the contours of her poetry. The first is growing up on the Maine coast. From "Renascence" on, regional images abound in Millay's poetry: the rugged shoreline, seabirds, the cold Atlantic's ebb and flow, local wildflowers. The second, exemplified by "Interim," is her wide reading of English poetry, chiefly Shakespeare, Milton, Wordsworth, Coleridge, Keats, Browning, and Tennyson.

More plainly bookish than "Renascence," "Interim" is a dramatic monologue in blank verse. The male speaker mourns the death of a woman by a survey of the things in the room she left behind: a book half-read, the diary he gave her. Coming across the ordinary words of her last diary entry, the speaker sees a new "dignity" in the simple phrase ("I picked the first sweet-pea today") because it was the last she wrote. His grief centers on the crushing power of the simplest words, and he marvels that he

> can make
> Of ten small words a rope to hang the
> world!
> "I had you and I have you now no more."

The poem might be read as a bitter parable about a struggle between male and female brands of writing. Killing off the little lady who jots notes about sweet-peas, ignorant of the weight her death will bestow on her simple words, Millay releases the male mourner to write in full knowledge of the import of words: his own. Concerns of Millay's own writing are distributed between the mourned woman and the mourning man. "Interim" reflects on the problem of how to reconcile a poetry built from the stockpile of homely, conventional images and largely devoted to traditional forms with the authority and power granted to men's voices in poetry. This would prove to be a particularly vexing issue for Millay, as she stuck to conventions amid the innovation and experimentation of the modern movement in poetry.

Cora Millay's encouragement of her daughter's gifts was crucially seconded by a number of women in education and the arts. At a gathering of Camden summer visitors in 1912, Millay sang and recited her poetry. Among the appreciative crowed was Caroline B. Dow, head of the YWCA National Training School in New York City. She proposed that if Millay applied for a scholarship, Dow would cover the rest of her college expenses. After a semester's preparatory work at Barnard College in New York City, where she was lionized by the literati, including the poet Sara Teasdale, and Jessie B. Rittenhouse, secretary of the newly inaugurated Poetry Society of America, in 1913 Millay, then twenty-one, entered Vassar College. While her studies focused on literature, creative writing, and languages (Latin, Greek, French, Italian, Spanish, and German), she also turned her attention to theater. She wrote and performed in college plays and pageants, inluding two pieces with medieval or fairy-tale settings—a blank-verse drama, *The Princess Marries the Page,* and *Two Slatterns and a King,* a brief "Moral Interlude" in four-beat couplets—and an unperformed prose play, *The Wall of Dominoes,* about a bohemian young woman's struggle to maintain her honor in the milieu of contemporary New York.

After graduation in 1917, Millay's interest in music and theater drew her back to New York. She joined the acting companies of two Greenwich Village theater groups, the Provincetown Players and the Playwrights' Theatre. She wrote and directed a morality play in blank verse, *Aria da Capo,* for the Provincetown Players; it opened on 5 December 1919. This play borrows elements of commedia dell'arte—a feature of other art plays of the period—for a serious indictment of human callousness and cruelty. Exchanges of banter between the harlequin figures Pierrot and Columbine bracket a tragic scene in which the shepherds Corydon and Thyrsis treacherously kill each other out of petty greed. Warmly received as an "antiwar" play, *Aria da Capo* typifies Millay's skill at blending literary modes, and using traditional figures to explore contemporary concerns. It also looks forward to the political commitment of her writing during World War II.

Millay's first book, *Renascence and Other Poems* (1917), includes "Interim" and another monologue, "The Suicide." The book introduces what would become Millay's two dominant modes: the short lyric and the sonnet. The brief poems, many in rhyming stanzas reminiscent of folk ballads, revisit some of the gamut of emotions of the title poem, but also raise some of the concerns about woman's power alluded to in "Interim." Constrasting sketches of women sit side by side in the volume. "Indifference" is spoken by a woman who tearfully surrenders to "Life" but can only wait passively for it. The next poem is "Witch-Wife," whose male speaker grudgingly acknowledges that although his beloved "resign[s]" herself to him, "she never will be all mine." Perhaps a thumbnail portrait of Millay herself, this untameable woman is said to have "learned her hands in a fairy-tale, / And her mouth on a valentine." Her connection to a mixture of old poetic genres is part of her power. Like most of Millay's succeeding collections, *Renascence* closes with a short grouping of sonnets. They demonstrate Millay's early dexterity with both the Petrarchan and Shakespearean patterns. But their formal dutifulness houses a rebellious voice that can break into a sonnet by denying received wisdom ("Time does not bring relief; you all have lied / Who told me time would ease me of my pain!") or rejecting time-worn comparisons

("Thou art not lovelier than lilacs,—no, / Nor honeysuckle"). In *Renascence's* final sonnet we hear a female version of the voice of "Bluebeard," insisting to a meddling lover on the sanctity of a room of her own. While biographers read "Bluebeard" as Millay's response to the radical editor and playwright Floyd Dell's interference in her life, the sonnet itself cautions against such an interpretation. Millay turns Bluebeard's locked room into a poet's private sanctuary, which "alone out of my life I kept / Unto myself, lest any know me quite." Millay's first book, while not yet revealing her full poetic power, illustrates what she could make in that locked room out of love poems and ballads, fairy tales and valentines.

The legend of Millay as bohemian gadabout grew in large part from *A Few Figs from Thistles* (1920), a gathering of lighter poems first brought out by Frank Shay, a Greenwich Village publisher, in his series of chapbooks called "Salvos." The book begins with the famous declaration "My candle burns at both ends." Some of the best-known poems from *Figs* are characterized by the flip bravura of a Dorothy Parker. A woman lightly boasts of her infidelity in "Thursday" and "To the Not Impossible Him," citing the time-worn language of love declarations only to undercut it:

> The fabric of my faithful love
>   No power shall dim or ravel
> Whilst I stay here,—but oh, my dear,
>   If I should ever travel!

Figs is a compendium of wayward female voices. It is as though the "Witch-Wife" of *Renascence* had been given a chance to speak in such poems as "The Singing-Woman from the Wood's Edge." Even in the poems spoken by more conventional women overpowered by love, the glum sagacity with which these women acknowledge their own time-worn predicament is itself a way of rising above it. The longing woman of "The Philosopher" knows the man is unworthy of her infatuation, too ordinary to earn the woman's endless pining. By ending her lament with an echo of *Othello,* she ranks her own love, however ill-placed and "witless," with the devotion of a tragic hero: "And what am I, that I should love / So wisely and so well?" The five Shakespearean sonnets gathered at the end of *Figs* advocate impulse and Jazz Age rebellion. A woman in love so defiantly declares her faithlessness that she transforms it from the traditionally bemoaned fickleness of women to a bitter concession to the way things are, for "Whether or not we find what we are seeking / Is idle, biologically speaking." Millay would continue to turn the sonnet into a vehicle in which we can hear a woman speaking "biologically," declaring her sexual desire outright, with no guarantees of fidelity. Maxwell Anderson praised the book's "almost flawless sensitiveness to phrase"; another reviewer dubbed the author of *Figs* "an urban pagan and a sophisticated dreamer."

Millay wrote the soberer poems collected in *Second April* at the same time she was writing *A Few Figs from Thistles.* The initial poem, "Spring," her first foray into free verse, sets the volume's tone of a more mature reflection on the exuberance of "Renascence." The ambitious "Ode to Silence," if a bit too full of breathless apostrophes to be entirely persuasive, nonetheless deserves more attention than it has received, for its exploration of the poet torn between the urgency of the "hungry noises" that demand to be written and the pull of Silence, Song's "other sister and my other soul." "Memorial to D. C.," for a Vassar classmate, presages the grace and formal variety of Millay's later elegies, such as the sonnet for Elinor Wylie in *Huntsman, What Quarry*? A longing for the Maine shoreline runs through such shorter poems as 'Inland," "Low-Tide," "Ebb," and "Exiled." The twelve love sonnets that close *Second April* combine the cynical voice of the worldly-wise new woman, who knows how shortlived lust can be mistaken for love, with the unabashed declarations of the poet, whose love is fueled by the passions that animated such legendary figures as Lilith, Lesbia, Lucrece, and Helen ("No rose that in a garden ever grew").

Second April appeared while Millay was traveling in Europe on assignment for the magazine *Vanity Fair.* The satirical sketches she wrote at this time, occasionally acerbic underneath their lightness, were later collected under the pseudonym Nancy Boyd in *Distressing Dialogues* (1924). They helped keep Millay financially afloat while she was working on a novel under contract with Horace Liveright. An "unmistakable allegory," it was to be called *Hardigut,* about a land "where people . . . do not eat in public, or discuss food except in inuendos [*sic*] and with ribald laughter" and "where the stomach is never mentioned, and if you have a stomach-ache, you tell people you have a head-ache or writer's cramp" (*Letters,* p. 167). She did not finish the novel. But Millay's invective against sexual hypocrisy and double standards was carried out in her poetry instead.

Her next volume, *The Harp-Weaver and Other Poems,* begins "My heart, being hungry, feeds on food / The fat of heart despise." The metaphor of sexual longing as hunger recurs in "Feast" and "Never May the Fruit Be Plucked." The title poem, which came out separately as a pamphlet earlier in 1923, is a ballad with fairytale elements, told in simple four- and six-line stanzas. The poem tells of a poor mother who weaves a kingly wardrobe for her son by playing on a golden harp. Leaving behind a toppling pile of garments, the mother is found frozen to death at the end of the poem. If the poem is a tribute to Cora Millay, as it is often read, it is a somewhat disturbing one, and raises difficult questions about the sacrifices women may be called upon to make in any sort of creation. Many of the best poems in Millay's succeeding volumes arouse similarly disquieting reflections about what it means to be a woman who writes poetry and what relation that poetry can or should have to her life. If Millay is to some degree the child who is royally dowered by a selfless, richly creative mother, she is also the desperate harp-weaver herself.

A less entrapping image of a creature weaving for dear life appears in "The Dragonfly":

> I wound myself in a white cocoon of
> singing,
> All day long in the brook's uneven bed,
> Measuring out my soul in a mucous thread.

The wording recalls Whitman's comparison of his soul to a spider that "launch'd forth filament . . . out of itself," but with a significant difference. Whitman's spider casts its "gossamer thread" in a vast world, till it catches somewhere to anchor the poet. Millay's dragonfly seems to be "walled in an iron house of silky singing," but it will arise winged and spangling, free of slime and shallows of the pond and "making a song of them." Weaving, in Millay's metaphor, is means of self-transformation, a prelude to metamorphosis, rather than a bridge spun out to connect the soul with its surroundings. The woman poet's challenge, the poem suggests, is to make her sacrifices to avoid entrapments, not to weave them herself. Whereas Whitman can send out his filament to connect himself with the world, Millay must be careful lest the very threads she sends out to the world make it impossible for her to rise above it and make poetry out of it. The woman speaker of "The Concert" refuses to allow her lover to attend a concert with her, lest we "make of music a filigree frame."

A number of Millay's poems suggest that the entire issue of what counts as an authentic anchoring of poetry in the world outside the poet may itself differ for men and women writers. The speaker of "An Ancient Gesture" in *Mine the Harvest,*" wiping her tears on her apron, reflects:

> This is an ancient gesture, authentic,
> antique,
> In the very best tradition, classic, Greek;
> Ulysses did this too.
> But only as a gesture,—a gesture which
> implied
> To the assembled throng that he was much
> too moved to speak.
> He learned it from Penelope . . .
> Penelope, who really cried.

Throughout her career, Millay had to consider whether gestures from "the very best tradition" authenticate a poet's experience or merely ventriloquize another's. To share classical sentiments can be ennobling, as it is for the literate, ardent woman of *Fatal Interview* (xxvi), who declares that "of all alive"

> I only, in such utter, ancient way
> Do suffer love; in me alone survive
> The unregenerate passions of a day
> When treacherous queens, with death upon the tread,
> Heedless and wilful, took their knights to bed.

But Millay's archaisms and use of traditional genres can make her poetry look oddly retrograde to our eyes. While the experiments of modernism were burgeoning around her, Millay was using the lexicon of Renaissance sonnets and folk balladry. Still, she is arguably closer to T. S. Eliot, Ezra Pound, and William Carlos Williams than we might initially suppose. Like them, Millay uses archaisms deliberately, to set off the contrast between older stabilities and the modern world. Other poets were using current slang and being sexually daring in their poems, but Millay is doing so in sonnets, thereby giving a peculiar textual twist to the contemporary language. The traditional form enhances the shock value of this influx of the raw, the urban, the everyday, and the commercial into the world of poetry. The foil of form allows revisions to be seen. Millay's sonnets may be "Shakespearean" or "Petrarchan," but such labels point to their formal schemes rather than their scope and inflections. Her sonnets partake of the loosening of the sonnet in the English Romantic period, in which she had read deeply and widely. Sounding the coda of each of her books, Millay's sonnets may also be taken together to make a mega-sequence that ties the individual volumes together. Many of Millay's best-known poems are sonnets, such as "What lips my lips have kissed, and where, and why" and "Love is not all: it is not meat nor drink." But Millay deprecated anthologists' "preference . . . to use only love sonnets" (*Letters,* 371). Her sonnets take up many topics, including even geometry ("Euclid alone has looked on Beauty bare").

Millay's major sonnet sequences are "Sonnets from an Ungrafted Tree" (the final section of *The Harp-Weaver*), *Fatal Interview* (1931), and "Epitaph for the Race of Man" (the final section of *Wine from These Grapes*). They illustrate the wide range of concerns she was able to treat in this form. "Sonnets from an Ungrafted Tree" is a sequence of seventeen sonnets, each with an elongated fourteenth line of seven feet. It tells the story of a woman who returns to an isolated New England village to nurse the dying husband she has left or divorced years before, and who is now little more to her than "a strange sleeper on a malignant bed." The emotional background of the story is implied rather than told, as the woman's daily tedium of caretaking mixes with reflections on her past. The sequence is largely devoted to an account of the simple tasks the woman performs: hastily gathering wood in a storm, building a reluctant fire, hiding in the cellar from a deliveryman and neighbors, scrubbing the kitchen. Gradually these tasks come to emblematize the emotional history of the marriage, until by the end, with the man's death, we can piece this unremarkable story together. Millay may have had her own parents' marriage in mind, combined with the period when she attended her dying father at his home. But there are no names in this story of "she" and "he." We learn of a misjudged marriage prompted chiefly by need and loneliness, the slow erosion of passion, the woman's increasing isolation and withdrawal from common fellowship, and the dull pain of her dutiful pity at the man's death. New readers of Millay could well begin with "Sonnets from an Ungrafted Tree," which gives a truer picture of Millay's work than does "Renascence," while rich with the New England color of the earlier poem. The fifty-two sonnets of *Fatal Interview* tell the story of a love affair from the woman's point of view. "Epitaph for Race of Man" narrates in eighteen sonnets the grim tale of the human race's self-destruction, "Being split along the vein by his own kind."

In 1938 Millay accompanied a submission to the magazine *Poetry* with a deprecating note, wishing she had sent poems "less early-Millay in character; poems more concerned with, apparently, things going on in the world outside myself today; poems more, if we may still use that old-fashioned word, 'modern' " (*Letters*, 302). With the advent of war in Europe, Millay's verse turned sharply toward the world outside. Critically regarded as "not poems, posters" and "tragic books from which the last vestige of gift has disappeared," volumes such as *Make Bright the Arrows* (1940) may have done their part for the war effort, but they did nothing to redeem Millay's literary reputation. Except for the posthumously published *Mine the Harvest* (1954), all of Millay's subsequent books were collected editions of earlier work.

Three issues deserve more general discussion: the status and dissemination of Millay's voice, literally and figuratively; the crafting of the individual poem and the arranging of poems into books; and the significance of Millay's status as a woman poet wielding such precise control of poetic form and meter.

Millay praised the author of a 1937 "essay in appreciation" of her work for his "almost infallible understanding of my poetry considered as speech." The responsive reader "knows not only what I am saying, but also under the impulsion of what sort of urge, what sort of temperamental and circumstantial exigency, I am saying it" (Yost, p. 3). Millay's theatrical and musical training shaped the public presentation of the poems as well as their composition. She not only gave many public readings of her work but also performed it over the radio and made recordings of it. This range of public performance of her poems should shape our response to what often seem the intensely private feelings that appear to prompt them, whether heated declarations of love or heart-stricken elegies. The novelist and critic Edmund Wilson, an early admirer of Millay and her work, noted in her reading aloud "her power of imposing herself on others through a medium that unburdened the emotions of solitude. The company hushed and listened as people do to music—her authority was always complete; but her voice, though dramatic, was lonely."

Millay's poetry was also read aloud by a range of voices not her own, in a number of different registers. Throughout her life, others sang her verses—from her sisters at home, to Vassar students singing the words of her Baccalaureate Hymn, to the Metropolitan Opera professionals singing her libretto to *The King's Henchman.* A number of her poems were commissioned for public reading on a particular occasion: Millay read "Invocation to the Muses" at Carnegie Hall for a 1941 ceremony of the National Institute of Arts and Letters. On other occasions, her work was read by voices made famous by Hollywood: Ronald Colman read her "Poem and Prayer for an Invading Army," written in advance for radio broadcast on D-Day (6 June 1944). Paul Muni was the reader for the short-wave broadcast of Millay's *The Murder of Lidice,* written at the behest of the Writers' War Board, in response to the 1942 Nazi massacre of civilians in the Czech village of Lidice.

The formal, declamatory nature of Millay's poetry, even at its most intimate, suggests that it is designed to unburden the emotions of solitude. Millay's work designedly recasts private emotion for public utterance. Elocutionary, eloquent, recitable, her poems are best understood as scripts for an impassioned but public voice, speaking *for* others as well as to them. In that sense they bear only a superficial resemblance to the more colloquial, embittered "confessional" poetry of such later poets as Sylvia Plath or Anne Sexton. Millay's are intimacies pitched for audibility, lyric confessions magnified through declaratory rhetoric into stage whispers, designed to be heard in the last row of the balcony. Or more accurately, they partake of the peculiarly twentieth-century intimacy of thoughts spoken into a microphone.

Millay's exposure as an accomplished reciter of her own poetry no doubt helped to spread the legend of the passionate woman whose emotions fed directly into her verse. Any questions about where this poetry came from seem to be fully answered in the figure of the redheaded woman with the beautiful voice. But Millay's public readings, like her poetry, raise vexing questions about what kind of authority a woman's voice may have in lyric poetry. Beautiful women with musical voices have a long history in lyric poetry—but as the subjects, not the authors. Women are traditionally the muses who inspire poetry, but no muse is expected to take pen to paper and do the writing herself. We can feel the tension of these issues even in such conventional compliments as Wilson's praise of Millay's "lovely and very long throat that gave her the look of a muse, and her reading of her poetry was thrilling" (Wilson, 749).

But the muse's-eye-view may be different. In an offhand verse self-portrait of 1920, Millay lists among her features "A long throat, / Which will someday / be strangled" (*Letters*, p. 99). As a woman cast in the incompatible double role of poet and poet's muse, Millay found her throat constricted. Seeing her poems as merely the biographical outpourings of womanly emotions is as inaccurate as seeing her as a muse. In 1948 Millay turned down a request by Harper and Brothers to issue a collection of love poems to be gathered from her published volumes. Her letter of refusal underscores the publisher's questionable motives: Harper's "proposal" that she compose a foreword confiding " 'when, where, and *under what compulsion'* (the italics are mine) these poems were written, leaves me strangely cold" (*Letters*, p. 348). A woman poet is not simply a woman to be wooed, Millay's protest implies, any more than her love poems are just diary entries that rhyme. It is difficult to reconcile the figure of the woman as muse to a world in which women are no longer (if they ever were) merely the passive inspirers of men's poetry. It is difficult also to reconcile the myth of the muse to the horrors of history in the twentieth century. Millay's 1942 "Invocation to the Muses" begins with a self-consciously orotund call for the "Great Muse of Song:

> . . . And thy vast throat builded for Harmony,
> For the strict monumental pure design,
> And the melodic line"

but soon turns to a remembrance of those "herded into prison camps," where, "Though the great voice be there, no sound from the dry throat across the thickened tongue / Comes forth."

Important as the sound of the poem to the ear was to Millay, she was also concerned with the look of the poem to the eye. The material design of her volumes, from binding to typography, interested her deeply. To write a book was to fashion a fine artifact. She reveled in the fact that *Renascence* was "printed on that beautiful, very rough, very torn-edgy paper. The paper that words were printed on was part of their personality, and Millay, cultivating a beautiful roughness, found herself at odds with "the smooth-browed, bridal-satin periodicals" that occasionally solicited her work (*Letters*, p. 303). Sheer legibility was a pleasure: she writes gratefully to her publisher that "the italics are the least alarming I ever saw."

She did not expect her readers to judge a book by its italics, of course. The crafting of her volumes goes much deeper. Most readers today encounter Millay in the two volumes Harper & Row keeps in print as her *Collected Lyrics* and *Collected Sonnets*. (There is also a slightly more inclusive single-volume *Collected Poems*.) But during her lifetime, readers would have watched the Millay canon grow in a series of relatively short volumes every five years or so. Today we may tend to think of her as the author of one or two thick books, but during her lifetime she was in the public eye as the producer of a series of thin ones.

Each volume was assembled with detailed care. Millay designed the succession of poems in individual volumes to suggest both continuity and growth in her poetic career. Designed shifts of mood, meter, and poetic genre characterize her books: their "torn-edgy" quality is balanced by the closure and poise of the poems. Nearly every collection concludes with a gathering of sonnets. One principle of arrangement was variety, as in her and George Dillon's translation of *Flowers of Evil*: "I've kept in mind the desirability of varying the meter from poem to poem whenever possible;

of having no two poems close together repeat each other in any important way" (*Letters,* 264). She had the same eye for variety in the groupings of poems she submitted for magazine publication, advising one editor to include "The Snow Storm" in a gathering of her verses, since "it is a lyric, and otherwise it seems to me there'll be a sort of top-heaviness of those long loose irregular lines that Edna Millay is that way about" (*Letters,* p. 305). In *Conversation at Midnight* she aimed for "differences in metrical style" throughout. Here the variety serves a playwright's purposes, but it points to a larger aim behind Millay's mixtures: there is a similar dramatist's touch for modulated changes in voice, tone, mood, and the ordering of the poems. The emotional modulations as one moves from poem to poem in the individual books is thus part of their crafted design. While individual lyrics can stand alone—and in anthologies frequently do—Millay's volumes benefit from being read in order, cover to cover. Her collections of short poems are not simply compilations, but sequences. In this sense they are cast in the mold of what is arguably her strongest genre: the sonnet sequence.

Similarly, Millay thought of her succeeding volumes of poetry as both echoing and revising previous ones. The title of *Wine from These Grapes* (1934) comes from a poem in *The Buck in the Snow* (1928), the first two lines of which appear as the later book's epigraph: "Wine from these grapes I shall be treading surely / Morning and noon and night until I die." As *Second April* declares a breach with the cheer of "Renascence," and the poet is still rethinking that early effort as late as "The Parsi Woman," from *Mine the Harvest.*

Even an abbreviated sketch of the structure of *Wine from These Grapes* will illustrate Millay's orchestrating of her books. There are five sections. The first deals with nature, the keynote poem focusing on nature's indifference to human grief ("The Return"). Then come two detailed vignettes of autumn landscapes ("October—An Etching" and "Autumn Daybreak"). In the next poem, clinging autumn foliage becomes a surrogate for the poet, refusing to accept change and death. The second section is a numbered sequence of six poems in memory of Cora Millay. The eulogy covers a wide range of metrical styles. There is the blunt staccato of "In the Grave No Flower":

> Here dock and tare.
> But there
> No flower.

And there are long lines that infuse adult grief into the rambling rhetoric of a child:

> To be grown up is to sit at the table with people who have died, who neither listen nor speak.

The fourth poem of this section employs the ballad stanza of iambic tetrameter rhyming *a b a b.* And there is a sonnet to close the section (as a sonnet sequence will close the whole book).

The third section consists of two poems treating death in reference to literary tradition (chivalric romance in "Aubade," Greek lyric in "Sappho Crosses the Dark River into Hades"), thus transcending private mourning. The elegiac strain continues in section IV, but in accord with the third section, mourned loss turns to the matter of poetry itself. This passage constitutes a varied elegy to the dip in the poet's own powers, like a falcon that refuses to soar ("On Thought in Harness"). In this section the autumnal landscape of the opening section returns as self-admonition: "When will you learn, my self, to be / A dying leaf on a living tree?" Section V is the sonnet sequence "Epitaph for the Race of Man" (which Millay had begun drafting as early as 1920). The sections are thus self-contained but also resonant with each other. Distributed throughout *Wine* are poems about a creature that takes flight ("The Fledgling," "The Fawn," "On Thought in Harness"). The "reassuring" graveyard glimpsed "From a Train Window" (section I) returns for scrutiny in the grim "Lines for a Grave-Stone" (section IV).

When we reach "Epitaph for the Race of Man," we have already seen a number of epitaphs, and the sequence's protest against war has been sounded earlier in the volume (the acid "Apostrophe to Man," "Conscientious Objector"). The overall trajectory of *Wine from these Grapes* thus is from particular to general: it turns from loss and ruin in the natural landscape, to mourning for an individual grief, through the widening perspective in Section IV, where individual losses figure those shared by the entire "detestable race." But the general retains its particularity: section IV closes with the image of a man on a lonely road at night, all but palpably confronting the specter of his own death, as "the draughty caverns of his breath / Grow visible." The title reflects the book's autumnal, elegaic one, its sense of mulling over the results of a late harvest. The epigraph tells us that it is in a sense her own poetic vintage that the poet is testing.

Millay was a painstaking vintner of her own work. Her career may be seen as a large-scale version of her writing habits. She makes a promise to enclose a new poem in a letter, but breaks it in the postscript, calling the poem "lousy. Perhaps I can delouse it, in which event I will send it" (*Letters,* p. 305). Preparing her books for the press was a similarly arduous series of tasks that Millay inventoried as "the business of cutting, cleaning, polishing; of documenting, of correlating; of fitting into place; the masonry of art." Arthur Ficke often helped her ready each book manuscript for Harper. The one exception to these work habits was the period of writing propagandistic verse. But the poet's self-perfecting habits were even harder to break than to maintain. Millay was concerned about ruining the reputation for poetic precision she had worked so hard to attain; a stickler, she hated even a syllable to be wrong in the poems she really cared about and wrote with full attention and discrimination.

Adept as she was at intricate formal schemes, Millay believed that an elemental part of crafting the poem preceded the handling of the materials. As much as any modernist, she makes no distinction between form and content:

> The shape of the poem is not an extraneous attribute of it: the poem could not conceivably have been written in any other form. When the image of the poem first rises before the suddenly quieted and intensely agitated person who is to write it, its shadowy bulk is already dimly outlined; it is rhymed or unrhymed; it is trimeter, tetrameter, or pentameter; it is free verse, a sonnet, an epic, an ode, a five-act play. To many poets, the physical character of their poem, its rhythm, its rhyme, its music, the way it looks on the page, is quite as important as the thing they wish to say.

In the poetry of late 1970s and 1980s a nascent "new formalism" is discernible; the return of meter and rhyme as options surely makes Millay's work look more timely. But Millay's reputation, and our ability to read her work instead of her life, may continue to rest on what we think her technical virtuosity amounts to. This idea of Millay tussling with her muse—or is the "shadowy bulk" an anti-muse?—may seem a bit far-fetched for a poet who turned out a variety of lyric genres with ease: ballads, folk songs, fairy tales, elegies, epitaphs, commemorative poems, blank verse, and tetrameter couplets, among others. But the tussle continues with dismissive estimates of this facility. Floyd Dell claimed that Millay "learned the molds first, into which she later poured her emotions while hot." Dell's comment has an epigrammatic flair that has made it a persistently quoted favorite of Millay's commentators. Dell may be simply borrowing Millay's lines from an early sonnet: "Into the golden vessel of great song / Let us pour all our passion." The sonnet advocates making poetry over making love. Songs of longing are a nobler result of desire than its consummation.

But Dell's remark begs important questions about the function of Millay's poetic form. Even molten-hot emotions cannot simply be poured into poetic molds, nor should we expect them to be. The emotions will, must, be themselves reshaped by the mold of lyric form, as the need for a rhyme may occasion a new idea or image in the process of writing a poem. Emotions may even be prompted by the molds themselves, a reversal that can be ennobling, raising an ordinary love to heroic heights, or artificial, in the manner of teenagers learning to kiss from the movies. Infusing her modern love with classical myth, the speaker of *Fatal Interview* feels an emotion grander than the unworthy beloved alone could prompt. Millay's love poetry often acknowledges that loving by someone else's book can be entrapping, especially for women. In the light of the recognition by feminists that seemingly timeless ideas or conditions of the human heart like "falling in love" are to a large degree constructed by societal norms, the use of traditional poetic conventions becomes something of a political issue. Millay's work raises the question of whether emotions identifiably exist outside of molds, conventions, and structures (poetic and social) imposed from without. Against Dell's formula, much of Millay's poetry acknowledges that, for better or worse, we often feel what poems have taught us to expect to feel. The point is not to costume Millay as a radical thinker ahead of her time. Although she was in some ways exactly that, we have also noted that being so much of her time was both a strength and the bane of her literary career. The point is rather to hold Millay's work up to the light of our time and see what has been heretofore hidden in shadow.

The poet on the verge of starting a poem, "suddenly quieted and intensely agitated," is like the listener to Beethoven savoring the moment of "the tranquil blossom on the tortured stem" ("On Hearing a Symphony of Beethoven"). The "shadowy bulk" of the nascent poem looms all but palpably for her: "I am possessed of a masterful and often a cruel imagination," she claimed. But the wording leaves open the question of who is in charge here. Is a poet so endowed possessed or possessor? Can such a cruelly overmastered poet be master? By Millay's report, she worked "not like a dog, not like a slave; dogs and slaves must be relieved and rested from time to time, otherwise they crack up; like a poet, let's say." Part of this labor is the arduous "masonry of art," but the greater part is the very impulse coercing the architect. Millay's poetry figures the relationship between the poet and her imagination through a range of recurrent metaphors: the imagination can be her prisoner or slave, or she its. To write a sonnet was to "put Chaos into fourteen lines," and tame it to

> the strict confines
> Of this sweet Order, where, in pious rape,
> I hold his essence and amorphous shape,
> Till he with Order mingles and combines.
> ("I Will Put Chaos into Fourteen
> Lines," from *Mine the Harvest*)

That Millay figures sonnet-writing as a prison rape points to the erotic side of this tussle with the imagination. When biographers tell us that Millay wrote poems when she was in love (and they dutifully tell us with whom), they obscure the fact that for Millay the writing of poetry itself has complex erotic connotations.

Our strongest impression of many Millay poems may be, as her first readers noted, that no one has "ended a poem precisely where this one ends." The closing couplets of her Shakespearean sonnets can be logical summations, flip dismissals, surprising reversals, punch lines, clichéd knots, or elegiac decrescendos. Her focus on skillful endings also reveals a connection between the freedom accorded the new woman and the restriction voluntarily taken on by a writer in old forms. Paradoxically Millay identifies the workings of the sonnet with the ethos of the bohemian life. The sonnet, freighted with restrictions, may seem utterly at odds with Millay's search for freedom. By titling a poem a sonnet, the poet signs a stringent metrical contract from which she cannot waver. But Millay makes this restrictiveness consistent with a philosophy of burning one's candle at both ends, of using one's life up completely. The sonnet can embody metrically, sonorously, and syntactically a kind of perfectly efficient hedonism, culminating in a closure with no residue. At the close of "Thou famished grave, I will not fill thee yet" from *Huntsman, What Quarry?* the poet defiantly tells Death how lives and poems are to be ended:

> I cannot starve thee out: I am thy prey
> And thou shalt have me; but I dare defend
> That I can stave thee off; and I dare say,
> What with the life I lead, the force I spend,
> I'll be but bones and jewels on that day,
> And leave thee hungry even in the end.

The poet "staves off" death by the achieved design of her stanzas. The sonnet's neat ending—fulfilling its metrical and rhyming requirements, leaving nothing formally unsatisfied—suggests the way the poet vows to use up her force completely and leave nothing behind. Not a matter of wanton wastefulness but of almost methodical, tasking exhaustiveness, Millayan freedom is thus aptly emblematized by the seemingly opposite, binding contract any sonnet must be. The sonnet's form provides the formula whereby Millay makes sure that her impulses play themselves out to the full.

One of Millay's best recent commentators, Jan Montefiore, notes that Millay's "themes are smoothed with poetic handling" and tend to be "written in a style which assumes that poetry is timeless" (p. 116). Millay's work, Montefiore plausibly implies, validates a stubborn conservatism while masquerading as daring, sallies against the way things are. Does Millay ever take a radical stance? Should we expect her to? Harold Lewis Cook's laudatory "Essay in Appreciation," prefacing Karl Yost's 1937 bibliography, claims that "American literature owes to [her] what amounts to a whole new field of expression for its women writers, the field of unrestricted, unprejudiced discussion of personal relationships, giving to woman a position in literature on a par with that of any man" (p. 54). When in 1927 the League of American Penwomen insulted Elinor Wylie with a rap on the knuckles for her scandalous personal life, Millay wrote a scathing defense, gladly joining Wylie in banishment from the League's "fusty province."

The highly emotional tone of many of Millay's poems tended to make critics see the poems as symptoms rather than as creations. But a critical protocol of the literary world included the need to uphold the belief that emotion is no subsitute for the true stuff of high poetry, ideas. When the feelings take over the ideas, it's time to call in the doctor. In 1934 Horace Gregory diagnosed Millay as infected with "elephantiasis of idea and emotion in poetry." A critical commonplace about her is that although she is technically proficient, less than proficient poems result when she allows her feelings to get the better of her. A reviewer of the 1943 *Collected Lyrics* summed up a prevailing estimate that Millay "has mistaken attitudes for convictions or mere moods for profound truths." But from our perspective today Millay's work can also be read as a constant scrutiny of the ideas and truths that "moods" can reveal.

Millay's play with names persisted to the end, when she was living alone at Steepletop in failing health. In one of her last letters she responds to her friends' protests against her isolation: "They all said, 'But you *must* have *somebody* with you! You simply *can't* be there without anybody!' " She continued to live alone, writing poems (they would be collected in the posthumous *Mine the Harvest*), but to please her anxious friends she "named my nurse Mrs. Somebody-Anybody." This late, playful rechristening was an appropriate one: "In order to help me feed myself properly and take my nasty medicines, I have artfully developed a beautiful case of schizophrenia: The strange case of Miss M. and Mrs. Somebody-Anybody." Millay's life and work pointedly illustrate how, even into this century, the strange case of the woman poet always involves an artful split of personalities. If Millay's life, more flaunted than flamboyant, prevented her from ever being nobody, we are increasingly learning how accurate an account her poems give of the lives of the many women who might be called "Mrs. Somebody-Anybody."

Selected Bibliography

PRIMARY WORKS

POETRY

Renascence and Other Poems, (New York: Mitchell Kennerley, 1917).

A Few Figs from Thistles, (New York: Mitchell Kennerley, 1920).

Second April, (New York: Mitchell Kennerley, 1921). Like its predecessors, this book was published by Harper from 1923 onward.

The Harp-Weaver and Other Poems, (New York: Harper & Brothers, 1923).

The Buck in the Snow and Other Poems, (New York: Harper & Brothers, 1928).

Edna St. Vincent Millay's Poems Selected for Young People, (New York: Harper & Brothers, 1929).

Fatal Interview, (New York: Harper & Brothers, 1931).

Wine from These Grapes, (New York: Harper & Brothers, 1934).

Conversation at Midnight, (New York: Harper & Brothers, 1937).

Huntsman, What Quarry?, (New York: Harper & Brothers, 1939).

Make Bright the Arrows: 1940 Notebook, (New York: Harper & Brothers, 1940).

Collected Sonnets, (New York: Harper and Brothers, 1941). The revised edition (1988) has twenty additional sonnets.

The Murder of Lidice, (New York: Harper & Brothers, 1942).

Collected Lyrics, (New York: Harper & Brothers, 1943).

Mine the Harvest, (New York: Harper & Brothers, 1954).

Collected Poems, (New York: Harper & Brothers, 1956).

DRAMA

Aria da Capo, First published in *Reedy's Mirror,* March 18, 1920. (New York: Mitchell Kennerley, 1921).

The Lamp and the Bell: A Drama in Five Acts, (New York: Frank Shay, 1921).

The King's Henchman, (New York: Harper & Brothers, 1927).

The Princess Marries the Page, (New York: Harper & Brothers, 1932).

PROSE

[Pseudonym Nancy Boyd] *Distressing Dialogues,* (New York: Harper & Brothers, 1924).

Letters of Edna St. Vincent Millay, Edited by Allan Ross Macdougall (New York: Harper & Brothers, 1952).

TRANSLATIONS

[With George Dillon] Baudelaire, Charles, *Flowers of Evil,* (New York: Harper & Brothers, 1936).

Prados, Emilio, "Llegada (Journey)," In Rolfe Humphries, ed. *And Spain Sings,* (New York: Vanguard Press, 1937).

SECONDARY WORKS

BIOGRAPHICAL STUDIES

Dash, Joan, "Edna St. Vincent Millay," In her *A Life of One's Own: Three Gifted Women and the Men They Married,* (New York: Harper & Row, 1973).

Drake, William, *The First Wave: Women Poets in America, 1915–1945,* (New York: Macmillan, 1987). Ch. 2, 4, 7.

Gurko, Miriam, *Restless Spirit: The Lifeof Edna St. Vincent Millay,* (New York: Thomas Y. Crowell, 1962). Includes bibliography.

Gould, Jean, *The Poet and Her Book: A Biography of Edna St. Vincent Millay,* (New York: Dodd, Mead, 1969).

Hahn, Emily, "Mostly About Vincent," *Romantic Rebels: An Informal History of Bohemianism in America,* (Boston: Houghton Mifflin, 1967).

Millay, Norma, "*The Saga of Conversation at Midnight* in the Living Theatre" *Tamarack: Journal of the Edna St. Vincent Millay Society,* 3: 36–58 (Fall 1985–Winter 1986).

Schwab, Arnold T., "Jeffers and Millay: A Literary Friendship," *Robinson Jeffers Newsletter,* 59: 18–33 (September 1981).

Sheean, Vincent, *The Indigo Bunting: A Memoir of Edna St. Vincent Millay,* (New York: Harper & Brothers, 1951).

Wilson, Edmund, "Epilogue, 1952: Edna St. Vincent Millay," In his *The Shores of Light: A Literary Chronicle of the Twenties and Thirties,* (New York: Farrar, Straus & Young, 1952).

CRITICAL STUDIES

Atkins, Elizabeth, *Edna St. Vincent Millay and Her Times,* (Chicago: University of Chicago Press, 1936).

Bogan, Louise, Review of *Huntsman, What Quarry?* (*The New Yorker,* May 30 1939). pp. 80–82. Repr. as "Unofficial Feminine Laureate," in her *Selected Criticism: Poetry and Prose* (New York: Noonday Press, 1955).

Brittin, Norman A., *Edna St. Vincent Millay,* (Boston: Twayne, 1967). Rev. ed. (1982). Includes annotated bibliography.

Clark, Suzanne, "Jouissance and the Sentimental Daughter: Edna St. Vincent Millay," *North Dakota Quarterly* 54: 85–108 (Spring 1986).

Clark, Suzanne, "The Unwarranted Discourse: Sentimental Community, Modernist Women, and the Case of Millay" *Genre* 20: 133–152 (Summer 1987).

Fairley, Irene R., "Millay in Feminist Perspective: Critical Trends of the 70's," *Tamarack: Journal of the Edna St. Vincent Millay Society* 1: 28–31 (Spring 1981).

Farr, Judith, "Elinor Wylie, Edna St. Vincent Millay, and the Elizabethan Sonnet Tradition," In Maynard Mack and George de Forest Lord, eds. *Poetic Traditions of the English Renaissance,* (New Haven: Yale University Press, 1982).

Fried, Debra, "Andromeda Unbound: Gender and Genre in Millay's Sonnets," *Twentieth Century Literature,* 32: 1–22 (Spring 1986).

Gray, James, *Edna St. Vincent Millay,* University of Minnesota Pamphlets on American Writers no. 64 (St. Paul: University of Minnesota Press, 1967). Repr. in Leonard Unger, ed. *American Writers* Vol. 3 (New York: Scribners, 1974).

Gould, Jean, "Edna St. Vincent Millay: Saint of the Modern Sonnet," In *Faith of a (Woman) Writer.* Edited by Alice Kessler-Harris and William McBrien. (Westport, Conn.: Greenwood Press, 1988).

Jones, Phyllis M., "Amatory Sonnet Sequences, and the Female Perspective of Elinor Wylie and Edna St. Vincent Millay," *Women's Studies* 10: 41–61 (1983).

McKee, Mary J., "Millay's *Aria da Capo*: Form and Meaning," *Modern Drama,* 9: 165–169 (September 1966).

Montefiore, Jan, "Romantic Transcendence: Edna St. Vincent Millay," In her *Feminism and Poetry: Language, Experience, Identity in Women's Writing* (London: Pandora, 1987).

Patton, John J., "Satiric Fiction in Millay's *Distressing Dialogues,*" *Modern Language Studies,* 2: 63–67 (Summer 1972).

Patton, John J., "The Variety of Language in Millay's Verse Plays," *Tamarack: Journal of the Edna St. Vincent Millay Society* 3: 8–16 (Fall 1985–Winter 1986).

Perlmutter, Elizabeth P., "A Doll's Heart: The Girl in the Poetry of Edna St. Vincent Millay and Louise Bogan," *Twentieth Century Literature,* 23: 157–179 (1977).

Sprague, Rosemary, "Edna St. Vincent Millay." In her *Imaginary Gardens: A Study of Five American Poets,* (Philadelphia: Chilton, 1969).

Stanbrough, Jane, "Edna St. Vincent Millay and the Language of Vulnerability," In Sandra M. Gilbert and Susan Gubar, eds., *Shakespeare's Sisters: Feminist Essays on Women Poets,* (Bloomington: Indiana University Press, 1979).

BIBLIOGRAPHIES

Nierman, Judith, *Edna St. Vincent Millay: A Reference Guide,* (Boston: G. K. Hall, 1977). Includes writings on Millay (1918–1973).

Yost, Karl, *A Bibliography of the Works of Edna St. Vincent Millay,* (New York: Harper & Brothers, 1937).

JOURNAL

Tamarack: Journal of the Edna St. Vincent Millay Society, (1981–) Elizabeth Barnett and John Patton, eds. Steepletop, Austerlitz, New York 12017. Subscribers write to: 8A Chauncy Street, 5, Cambridge, MA 02138.

JOHN MILTON
(1608–1674)

E. M. W. TILLYARD

I

IN *PARADISE LOST,* Milton described his Adam as formed for "contemplation and valour." He could thereby have been describing both his own nature and his own ideals. Milton was a natural Platonist, a natural seeker after perfection by high contemplation; but he also believed, with Sidney, that the "ending end of all earthly learning" was "virtuous action." Living before Rousseau and the age when men dreamed of human perfectibility, he believed that in this world action would always fall short of the high aims to which contemplation pointed, and he would have followed Sidney in maintaining that our erected wit maketh us know what perfection is, and yet our infected will keepeth us from reaching unto it." Nevertheless, Milton's nature both craved forms of action that would not be quite unworthy of their moving principles and was sanguine enough to make him think that a great betterment of earthly conditions was possible despite the entrance of sin into the world. That he could combine and harmonize the elements of contemplation and of action in himself and in his poetry is one of his chief claims to greatness. But his high hopes of approximating action to ideals and of living to see a better England than the one into which he was born exposed him more nakedly to the cruelty of fate than someone more skeptical and pessimistic. His final greatness consists both in the primary wealth and vitality of his nature and in the way he adjusted to the worst that fate could bring him.

Gifted with that ultimate simplicity of mind that Thucydides in his history and Mencius in his aphorisms called the mark of the truly great man, desiring to see life in strong, clear outline, more attracted by the gold pieces than by the small change of thought, Milton was unlucky in the period of history that his life covered. It was an age of transition, belonging neither to the Renaissance confidence that went before nor to the Augustan confidence that came after, an age in England of political division, philosophical skepticism, and a literature ingenious, ornate, and sophisticated rather than strong and simple. Milton was very close to his age; and the more scholars discover about him, the more sensitive they find him to the currents of contemporary thought. Yet behind this sensitivity we can detect the impression of Milton's not being spiritually attuned to his setting. Fundamentally he was a Christian humanist, a kind of rear guard of the great Renaissance army, prolonging the Renaissance faith in man into a less noble age, as Thomas Hardy, though bred in an England by then predominantly industrial, succeeded in using the relics of an older rural England for the material of his novels.

But if Milton's life span proved thus unfortunate, it was long before it definitively revealed itself to be so. Looking back, we may note that he was born three years after the ominous Gunpowder Plot of 1605, that the ill-starred Charles I came to the throne at the time Milton entered college, and that Milton's early manhood coincided with the gradual split of the active elements of the nation into two hostile parties. But in thus looking back and knowing what those various happenings actually led up to, we are in a different position from Milton, who was no more aware of the approach of civil war and all its accompanying ills than an Englishman born in 1885 was aware of the coming outbreak of war in 1914. To those living in them, the years in England before 1639 and 1914 seemed good years and full of hope for better things to come. And most of Milton's poems from before the Civil War breathe not only the vitality of youth but also contentment with the England he inhabits. In no poems more than "L'Allegro" and "Il Penseroso" does this contentment show itself. He wrote them probably near the end of his college career at Cambridge, when he was an important figure there, and in them he describes the joys first of the cheerful, and then of the thoughtful, man. And the England that provides these joys is still the united England of the days of Elizabeth, the England that, in the words of Shakespeare, was "true to herself":

Sometimes with secure delight
The upland hamlets will invite,
When the merry bells ring round,
And the jocond rebecks sound
To many a youth, and many a maid,
Dancing in the chequered shade;
And young and old come forth to play
On a sunshine holy day. . . .
("L'Allegro," 91–98)

Nor does the young Anglican Puritan yet see anything wrong in the artistic and musical adornments of the church service:

But let my due feet never fail,
To walk the studious cloisters pale,
And love the high embowed roof,
With antique pillars' massy proof,
And storied windows richly dight,[1]
Casting a dim religious light.
There let the pealing organ blow,
To the full-voiced choir below,
In service high, and anthems clear,
As may with sweetness through mine ear,
Dissolve me into ecstasies,
And bring all heaven before mine eyes.
("Il Penseroso," 155–156)

A little later, in "Arcades" and *Comus,* Milton seems to have enjoyed writing the words for that costly and aristocratic entertainment of mixed poetry, music, dancing, and scenic ingenuity called the masque. This is how he turns his delicate lyric vein to compliment the countess dowager of Derby, ancestress of many grandchildren, in whose honor "Arcades" was performed:

Mark what radiant state she spreads,
In circle round her shining throne,
Shooting her beams like silver threads,
This this is she alone,
Sitting like a goddess bright,
In the center of her light.

Might she the wise Latona be,
Or the towered Cybele,
Mother of a hundred gods;
Juno dares not give her odds;
Who had thought this clime had held
A deity so unparalleled?
(14–25)

Though a strong minority of the English nobility was on the side of Parliament against the king, the masque, along with other dramatic shows, came to be countenanced by the royalists alone. Milton, the future Cromwellian, writing the words for two masques so gaily and serenely, shows that men little understood the storm that threatened.

Comus, by far the longer of the two masques and the longest of Milton's early poems, reveals not only the still-persisting harmony of contemporary England but also the two poles of Milton's own nature, the contemplative and the active. The Attendant Spirit first pictures the earth from without, from the point of view to be reached only through meditation, talking of

1. Adorned.

> . . . the smoke and stir of this dim spot,
> Which men call earth, and, with low-thoughted care
> Confined, and pestered in this pinfold here,
> Strive to keep up a frail, and feverish being
> Unmindful of the crown that virtue gives
> After this mortal change, to her true servants
> Amongst the enthroned gods on sainted seats
> (5–11)

But he turns into an active character and rescues the benighted children from their danger. The Lady, at her first entrance, varies her speech from pure, active drama:

> This way the noise was, if mine ear be true,
> My best guide now, methought it was the sound
> Of riot, and ill-managed merriment,
> (170–172)

through the shudders of romantic superstitions

> What might this be? A thousand fantasies
> Begin to throng into my memory
> Of calling shapes, and beckoning shadows dire,
> And airy tongues, that syllable men's names
> On sands, and shores, and desert wildernesses
> (205–209)

to the contemplative rapture of

> O welcome, pure-eyed Faith, white-handed Hope,
> Thou hovering angel girt with golden wings,
> And thou unblemished form of Chastity,
> I see ye visibly. . . .
> (213–216)

Comus may not succeed completely as a whole, but it shows Milton free to indulge the wealth of his nature and full of the promise of great things. Indeed, in many details he has attained greatness. The second passage quoted from the Lady's speech is a poem in its own right, legitimately anthologized by Robert Bridges in *The Spirit of Man.* Only a major poet could have thought of using "syllable" as a verb in this context. "Syllable" is very effective onomatopoeia, but, through its uniqueness in verbal use, it also startles and makes a climax that gives the whole passage a convincing shape.

"Lycidas," published in 1637, is a rhymed poem lamenting the death of a college friend by drowning, in the strict tradition of the pastoral elegy of Greece and Rome. In it Milton at once achieves poetry of the highest order and expresses an incidental foreboding of the bitter times that are to come. There are the same large elements as in *Comus.* The element of rapturous contemplation, expressed in Lycidas' apotheosis, is there just as surely and more intensely:

> So Lycidas sunk low, but mounted high,
> Through the dear might of him that walked the waves;
> Where other groves, and other streams along,
> With nectar pure his oozy locks he laves,
> And hears the unexpressive nuptial Song,
> In the blest kingdoms meek of joy and love.
> (172–177)

Milton indulges his vein of romantic description with the utmost brilliance in imagining where the body of his drowned friend may have drifted:

> . . . Whilst thee the shores, and sounding seas
> Wash far away, where 'er thy bones are hurled,
> Whether beyond the stormy Hebrides
> Where thou perhaps under the whelming tide
> Visit'st the bottom of the monstrous world;
> Or whether thou to our moist vows denied,
> Sleep'st by the fable of Bellerus old,
> Where the great vision of the guarded Mount
> Looks toward Namancos and Bayona's hold. . . .
> (154–162)

And the urge to action, the will to match ideals with deeds, comes out with all the force of Milton s now mature power in the description of fame and its precariousness in this world:

Fame is the spur that the clear spirit doth raise
(That last infirmity of noble mind)
To scorn delights, and live laborious days;
But the fair guerdon[2] when we hope to find,
And think to burst out into sudden blaze,
Comes the blind Fury with th' abhorred shears,
And slits the thin-spun life.
(70–76)

But there is another side to "Lycidas," not found in *Comus*: the political. And this side is the more important because it comes out not only in a direct manner through St. Peter's attack on the degenerate clergy of the day and his grim reference to the inroads of the Roman church:

Besides what the grim wolf with privy paw
Daily devours apace, and nothing said,
(128–129)

but also through a mere hint in another context: proof that Milton's mind was running on politics at this time. The two resounding lines from the end of the passage quoted about the drifting of Lycidas' body, sometimes cited to prove Milton's love of the mere sound of grandiose names, are actually packed with meaning, political included. The "guarded Mount" is the rock fortress of St. Michael's Mount in Cornwall and the "great vision" is the archangel himself, so called because he appeared in a vision to some fishermen at this site. Namancos and Bayona, unidentified for many years after Milton's death, are in Galicia, the Spanish Land's End. Michael, the chief warrior-angel in heaven, is on duty on his own mount near the English Land's End, fixing his defensive gaze on the Spanish Land's End to prevent both a recurrence of the Spanish Armada and the spread through Continental influence of popery in England, of which the Puritan wing of the English church thought there was danger through the High Church doctrines of William Laud, then at the height of his power as archbishop of Canterbury.

In "Lycidas," then, Milton hints at the troubles to come but is far from believing them inevitable. These enrich rather than overshadow the poem. The troubles are, indeed, an important item in the matters that burdened Milton's mind at that time and made him wonder whether his hopes for the future were justified. But they are subordinate to the great theme of the poem, the theme that coexists with the elegiac theme and of which the elegiac theme is the symbol. Milton saw that action in this world is precarious, that the good die young, that great preparations for high and virtuous deeds often miscarry, that the wicked often prosper. It was a painful vision, but he faced it and overcame it by the hard-won admission that results in this world do not matter and that what does matter is the state of mind behind the attempt, whether successful or not, to achieve results. Lycidas died young and achieved little; yet his state of mind was one of integrity, and his "mounting high" into heaven symbolizes the ultimate victory of that state over what he failed to achieve by earthly action. Such were the mental conflict and the victory Milton achieved in "Lycidas." He was destined to fight the same fight more than once in his life—and it is a fight that cannot be avoided by anyone who believes in the necessity at once of contemplation and of action—but having won it on the first occasion, he was not likely to be defeated thereafter.

II

Shortly after writing "Lycidas" (and the last line of the poem, "To-morrow to fresh woods, and pastures new, may refer to it), Milton set

2. Reward.

out to complete his education in the Renaissance manner through the grand tour. His journey was a happy interlude between the anxieties revealed in "Lycidas" and the imminent Civil War, and its circumstances help us to understand Milton himself. He had no liking for France and did not linger there, and his anxiety about political events at home prevented him from carrying out his plan to visit Greece. Thus his grand tour pretty well resolved itself into a long residence in different parts of Italy. There is every indication that Milton adored Italy and that he was a great success there. Certainly the actual country left its mark on his later poetry. Here, for instance, is a reference to a scene in Tuscany: in the first book of *Paradise Lost,* Satan, having painfully reached the beach of the fiery lake where he had lain prone:

> . . . stood and called
> His legions, angel forms, who lay entranced
> Thick as autumnal leaves that strew the brooks
> In Vallombrosa, where the Etrurian shades
> High overarched imbower. . . .
> (300–304)

It has been argued very plausibly that the landscape of Milton's Hell derives its details from the volcanic region near Naples known as the Phlegraean Fields; and I have little doubt, though I have not met the notion elsewhere, that the garden of the Villa d'Este at Tivoli, with its abundance of water drawn from the Anio, its slopes and terraces, and its luxuriance, was at the back of Milton's mind when he created his Paradise. But there were more things than the landscape to attract Milton to Italy. By 1638, when Milton reached Italy, the cultural center of Europe had shifted to France; and Italy was living on its past rather than facing the future. The spirit of the Renaissance, prevalent so much earlier in Italy than in the rest of western Europe, lingered there the longest; and it was here above all that Milton could find an intellectual temper really to his taste. Not that we should make Milton's success in Italy a small matter or underestimate his remarkable powers of adaptation to a foreign setting. It speaks very highly indeed for the flexibility and richness of his temperament that he, bred in a Puritan family and in the more Puritan of the two English universities, strongly opposed politically to the Roman church and to any romanizing tendencies in his own, and professing an austere morality, should have grown so much at home in the center of Catholicism and in a land where morals were far from austere. And he did so at no sacrifice whatever of his own private standards.

Upon returning to England in 1639, Milton was caught in the uprush of enthusiasm that carried away the Parliamentary party and the reforming wing of the English church. There was the chance, he believed, that food might after all be provided for the "hungry sheep" of England, who, he had complained in "Lycidas," "look up" and are "not fed." So believing, he could not hold back. "Virtuous action" for him now lay in the region of politics, and not of poetry, where he had wanted it to be. When Milton committed himself, he did so with all his heart, and he devoted himself to politics instead of poetry for many years to come. And his return to poetry was along the sad road of political disillusionment.

But at first his hopes ran high. He believed, with other sincere and ardent men, that if the English church could be further reformed—if, in particular, the episcopacy could be abolished—a new golden age would be established in England; and he pictured himself as the poet chosen to celebrate the new order:

> Then, amidst the hymns and hallelujahs of saints, some one may perhaps be heard offering at high strains in new and lofty measures to sing and celebrate thy divine mercies and marvellous judgments in this land throughout all ages; whereby this great and warlike nation, instructed and inured to the fervent and continual practice of truth and righteousness, and casting far from her the rags of her old vices, may press on hard to that high and happy emulation to be found the soberest, wisest, and most Christian people. . . . ("Of Reformation")

This is superbly said, but it shows the weakness of Milton as politician. Such fervor befits ideals, but not acts of Parliament. And when the Presbyterian superseded the Episcopal form of church government in England, Milton was forced to admit that the change did not bring in the millennium and that "new Presbyter was but old Priest writ large." Under the Commonwealth, Milton worked for what we now call the Foreign Office and, after the precedent of Chaucer and Spenser, was an efficient government servant; but he was too much of an idealist to be able to hedge and compromise over the large issues that concern the high politician and that have to be reduced from their utopian potentialities to the scanty proportions of what will work in the shabby, mean-principled world of every day. Milton's pamphlets, his major expression of high political opinion, are not successful as practical tracts for the times. When he is exalted, he is too remote from the real world; when he forces himself to be controversial and lowers his tone, he carries abuse too far to be effective. Nevertheless, considered not as effective political writing but as independent prose works, Milton's pamphlets, uneven as they are, form a wonderful body of vivid and varied and powerful prose, illustrating, like his earlier poetry, his belief in both contemplation and action, and presenting certain sides of his character that might not, though surely there, have been detected in his verse.

I need not dwell on the theme of action in Milton's prose, for most of it is in itself a form of action, and efforts to persuade men to follow this or that course. What is to the point is to show how Milton's belief in contemplation keeps breaking out in contexts that should be severely practical. Thus, in one of his pamphlets against the bishops, *The Reason of Church Government Urg'd Against Prelaty* (1641–1642), he inserts a long personal passage in which he talks of his poetic plans and of his conception of the poet's high office. A true poem, he holds, is

> . . . not to be raised from the heat of youth, or the vapours of wine, like that which flows at waste from the pen of some vulgar amorist or the trencher fury of a rhyming parasite; nor to be obtained by the invocation of Dame Memory and her siren daughters, but by devout prayer to that eternal Spirit, who can enrich with all utterance and knowledge and sends out his Seraphim with the hallowed fire of his altar to touch and purify the lips of whom he pleases. . . .

And if the "eternal Spirit" is ready to inspire, he will inspire the man who has, by the act of contemplation, prepared his heart for the inspiration, for Milton goes on to talk of "beholding the bright countenance of truth in the quiet and still air of delightful studies." Milton is here remote indeed from the grasping and opportunist world of political action.

What are the sides of Milton's nature that his prose makes especially clear, and that readers might overlook in his verse?

First, the man's uncommon exuberance. Milton's total poetic output is not large, and we might be tempted to think that he wrote slowly and painfully. If we heed the torrent of his prose, with its immensely wealthy vocabulary, we can be sure that Milton wrote comparatively little poetry only because he rejected so much and selected so fastidiously. By nature he had the exuberance of a Rubens, but it was checked and compressed by the severity and the scrupulousness of a Racine. In prose, however, Milton felt no obligation to curb his magnanimity or to comb out his vocabulary. He bursts out into, vivid metaphors and allows his sentences to grow to great lengths through sheer sustention of vitality. Here, for instance, is his invective, from his tract *Of Education* (1644), against the system of studies still prevalent at the universities with its disastrous effect on the undergraduates' future careers:

> And for the usual method of teaching arts, I deem it to be an old error of universities, not yet well recovered from the scholastic grossness of barbarous ages, that instead of beginning with arts most easy (and those be such as are most obvious to the sense) they present their young unmatriculated novices at first coming with the most intellective abstrac-

tions of logic and metaphysics, so that they having but newly left those grammatic flats and shallows, where they stuck unreasonably to learn a few words with lamentable construction, and now on a sudden transported under another climate to be tossed and turmoiled with their unballasted wits in fathomless and unquiet deeps of controversy, do for the most part grow into hatred and contempt of learning, mocked and deluded all this while with ragged notions and babblements while they expected worthy and delightful knowledge, till poverty or youthful years call them importunately their several ways and hasten them with the sway of friends either to an ambitious and mercenary or ignorantly zealous divinity: some allured to the trade of law, grounding their purposes not on the prudent and heavenly contemplation of justice and equity, which was never taught them, but on the promising and pleasing thoughts of litigious terms, fat contentions, and flowing fees; others betake them to state affairs with souls so unprincipled in virtue and true generous breeding that flattery and courtshifts and tyrannous aphorisms appear to them the highest points of wisdom instilling their barren hearts with a conscientious slavery, if, as I rather think, it be not feigned; others, lastly, of a more delicious and airy spirit retire themselves, knowing no better, to the enjoyments of ease and luxury, living out their days in feast and jollity, which indeed is the wisest and safest course of all these unless they were with more integrity undertaken—and these are the errors, these are the fruits of misspending our prime youth at the schools and universities as we do, either in learning mere words or such things chiefly as were better unlearned.

This is at once a single sentence and a whole paragraph. Milton's ardor presses on, unremitting to the end.

Second, there appears in Milton's prose—fitfully, it is true—a sense of humor. This comes out at odd moments and in chance phrases, at times when his feelings have cooled and he is not concerned with a main argument. At the end of *Colasterion* (1645), a hot piece of controversy on the subject of divorce, Milton says how glad he is to have done with his adversary:

At any hand I would be rid of him; for I had rather, since the life of man is likened to a scene, that all my entrances and exits might mix with such persons only whose worth erects them and their actions to a grave and tragic deportment and not to have to do with clowns and vices. But if a man cannot peaceably walk into the world but must be infested, sometimes at his face with dorrs and horseflies, sometimes beneath with bawling whippets and shinbarkers . . . have I not cause to be in such a manner defensive as may procure me freedom to pass unmolested hereafter . . . ?

The general tone is scornful, but no man without a sense of humor could have coined the phrase "bawling whippets and shinbarkers." In *Areopagitica* (1644), the most lively and varied and readable of all the pamphlets, there occurs a delightfully humorous description of the wealthy merchant who finds "religion to be a traffic so entangled . . . that . . . he cannot skill to keep a stock going upon that trade" and who solves his problem by hiring a tame clergyman to deputize, resigning "the whole warehouse of his religion, with all the locks and keys, into his custody. . . ."

If the prose tells us certain things about Milton, so do his sonnets, written, like the prose, mostly between "Lycidas" and *Paradise Lost.* Like some of Horace's *Odes* (on which they are partly modeled) and many of Thomas Hardy's lyrics, they are occasional poems dealing with people or contemporary events. That Milton should write sonnets to Thomas Fairfax, Cromwell, and other Parliamentary leaders is not surprising, and accords with his prose. What most adds to our knowledge of the man are the feelings he displays in the personal sonnets: his tenderness toward his second wife, now dead; his uncomplaining humility in the sonnet on his blindness; the urbanity with which, in the following, he invites his friend Lawrence to dinner:

Lawrence, of virtuous father virtuous son,
Now that the fields are dank, and ways are mire,

Where shall we sometimes meet, and by
the fire
Help waste a sullen day; what may be won
From the hard Season gaining: time will run
On smoother, till Favonius reinspire
The frozen earth; and clothe in fresh
attire
The lily and rose, that neither sowed nor
spun.
What neat repast shall feast us, light and
choice,
Of Attic taste, with wine, whence we
may rise
To hear the lute well touched or artful
voice
Warble immortal notes and Tuscan air?
He who of those delights can judge, and
spare
To interpose them oft, is not unwise.
(Sonnet 17)

I have written thus far of the pamphlets and the sonnets as isolated works possessing certain literary qualities and telling us things about Milton's nature. They also, when taken in sequence, tell the story of how his hopes of national betterment through high action came to grief, and of his personal disasters or disappointments. Milton did not abandon his hopes lightly. It is true that the defeat of the episcopacy and the victory of Presbyterianism did not produce the wonderful betterment he expected. But Presbyterianism had not come to stay, and better things might issue from the professions of greater religious toleration put out by the Independents. Moreover, the richness and fervor of religious controversy gave Milton grounds for hope. *Areopagitica,* written after the first decisive victory of the Parliamentarians at Marston Moor and when there was the promise of opposition to the now-established Presbyterians, utters this hope. This pamphlet, the classic plea in literature for liberty of the press, is also an utterance of hope that England is about to enter a new era of free vitality when, unrestricted by the harsh decrees of ecclesiastical orthodoxy, she may both face the full truth of God's word and be strong and virtuous enough to draw sustenance and life from it:

> Methinks I see in my mind a noble and puissant nation rousing herself like a strong man after sleep and shaking her invincible locks: methinks I see her as an eagle mewing her mighty youth and kindling her undazzled eyes at the full midday beam, purging and unscaling her long-abused sight at the fountain itself of heavenly radiance. . . .

Note once again in this passage the union of action and contemplation: the references first to Samson with his uncut hair, the man of great deeds, and then to the eagle, symbolizing, in its supposed power to envisage the sun, the mind that has the strength to contemplate the Platonic ideas or God himself.

The story of Milton's disillusion is the story of England between *Areopagitica,* written in 1644, and the Restoration in 1660. Parliament won the war but failed to win the hearts of the English people. Representing at first a majority of the population, the Parliamentary rulers became fewer and represented an ever-dwindling minority. Of that minority Milton was an absolutely loyal member, his high idealism drawing him to those who, for whatever reason, were willing to go to extremes. Here, he felt, were real men and not time-servers or Laodiceans; and in some of his sonnets and in his great Latin prose work, *The Second Defence of the People of England,* he celebrated their virtues and gave them high advice. But all the time Milton knew that these heroic men did not have the country behind them, and he experienced a great revulsion from the sentiments expressed in the passage quoted from *Areopagitica.* He believed that lethargy was the besetting vice of most of his countrymen. It was lethargy, he thought, that caused them to sympathize with Charles for all his misdeeds and to withdraw their support from the men who had dared to put him to death; for lethargy cannot bear change, however called for, and the desire for a king was of long and rooted growth. Not that Milton despaired when men regretted Charles; on the contrary, he vented his hopes and his energies in writing in support of the regicides. His vehement efforts were the final reason for his loss of sight. But he never regretted the sacrifice, as he told Cyriack Skinner in a sonnet; nor did he argue

> Against heaven's hand or will, not bate a jot
> Of heart or hope; but still bear up and steer
> Right onward. . . .
> (Sonnet to Mr Cyriack Skinner Upon His Blindness)

This is indeed to apply the lesson of "Lycidas," the lesson that the motive of the deed, not its result, matters.

III

Milton's blindness had the effect of detaching him gradually from his position as government servant. Through his Latin defenses of the regicides he earned the gratitude of the government at home and fame abroad; but as a blind man he could no longer be of the same use. Released from regular employment, though still good for an occasional pamphlet, he returned to his plans for a great poem some four years before the Restoration.

His other personal trouble was the unhappy beginning of his first marriage. His wife returned to her parents probably a little more than a year after the wedding. But we must remember that she returned to him and bore him children, and that his two other marriages were happy. With little knowledge of the feminine heart before marriage, he acquired a sufficiency by the time he came to write *Paradise Lost.*

With Cromwell's death and the plain imminence of the restoration of the Stuarts, Milton still refused to give up hope, and risked his life by writing last-minute appeals to the English people not to submit their necks to a tyrant. The actual shock of the Restoration must have been terrible. There is no record of his feelings unless, as has been conjectured, he composed *Samson Agonistes*[3] while in hiding and in danger of execution. But if Samson's dejection reflects, as it may well do, feelings that Milton at one time experienced, it may plausibly concern the loss of sight that was common to them both. We shall be safer if we reconstruct Milton's feelings at the time of the Restoration from his more firmly dated works. However great the shock of the Restoration (and its magnitude must have corresponded roughly with the vehemence of Milton's pamphleteering immediately before it), I believe he must have faced beforehand the failure of his hopes, just as a good commander will have faced the problem of extricating his troops, should the victory he so passionately desires be denied him.

The evidence is the general scheme of *Paradise Lost,* begun, and hence, we may be certain, in the case of so rigorously architectonic a poet as Milton, already planned, some four years before the Restoration. The general scheme of *Paradise Lost* embodies the moral of "Lycidas": that results matter less than states of minds. Satan's apparently decisive act in causing man's fall, an act based on an envious and cruel state of mind, ends by being less strong than the small, sound human acts of mutual generosity and of repentance performed by Adam and Eve after they have fallen. If Milton had staked everything on the results of his political hopes, he could never have framed his poem in this way. That he cared greatly about the Restoration is proved by his pamphlets; that he had also learned not to care is proved by the scheme of *Paradise Lost.* That it cost him dear to learn not to care, and that he did suffer mental torment when his hopes failed, we cannot doubt.

Milton planned to make a single great poem the crown of his life, to do for his own country what Homer, Virgil, Luís de Camões, and Torquato Tasso had done for theirs. I believe that in *Paradise Lost* he succeeded, and hence I have intended my remarks so far to lead up to this poem. All the qualities so far

3. The date of composition of *Samson Agonistes* has been much disputed among modern scholars. The case for an early dating (1647–1653?) is set out by W. R. Parker, *Philological Quarterly,* 23 (1949) and *Notes and Queries,* 5 (1958).

enumerated find a place there. As I shall point out in detail, it largely concerns action and the proper grounds for it. The side of contemplation is included partly through the many shifts of distance from which action is viewed, partly through descriptions that suggest a static condition of eternity rather than the shifting phenomena of this world. The pageants of earthly history that Michael shows to Adam are seen as if from a distance, and Adam's comment on them at the end fixes this impression:

> "How soon hath thy prediction, seer blest,
> Measured this transient world, the race of
> time,
> Till time stand fixed: beyond is all abyss,
> Eternity, whose end no eye can reach. . . .
> (XII. 553–556)

The account of Paradise, though in the first instance borrowed from an actual garden, ends by speaking of an imagined world of incredible static beauty and felicity. Politics, though subordinated to a moral theme that goes far beyond it, is included through the infernal debates in the second book and through the characters of the different speakers. I shall refer later to instances of humor and generally to the diversity of the poem, to Milton's success in including in its compass all experience as he knew it.

Up to *Paradise Lost* the facts of Milton's life sometimes help us to understand his writing; and *Paradise Lost* itself is clearer if we know the conditions that led up to it. But after 1660, Milton lived anything but a public life, and there is little profit in connecting poetry and biography. Thus, from now on, I am concerned with his poetry alone.

The fall of man was not Milton's first choice for the subject of his great poem. At the time of his Italian journey he intended to write on King Arthur, and there are passages in his earliest pamphlets that show the kind of poem it would have been. It would have been partly religious and moral, partly patriotic. Arthur would have borne something of the character of Spenser's Prince Arthur in the *Fairie Queene,* uniting the contemplative and active virtues; but unlike Spenser's prince, he would have been the center of action in defeating the heathen Saxon invaders. British history, again as in Spenser, would have been narrated in prophecy, culminating in the defeat of the Spanish Armada. The main emphasis would have been on heroic action. If there had been no civil war and Milton had been free to write his Arthuriad around the time of *Areopagitica,* he would have given us a divinely energetic poem, but one less varied and less mature than *Paradise Lost.* He might have gone on to a second, more mature poem; and the two together might have had an even wider scope than *Paradise Lost.* But if the choice were between an Arthuriad and *Paradise Lost,* we should be content with what we have.

Milton's very earliest critics served him well. Sir Henry Wotton, commenting on *Comus* in 1638, spoke of "a certain Dorique delicacy in your Songs and Odes, whereunto I must plainly confess to have seen yet nothing parallel in our Language." Wotton was thinking of all the parts of *Comus* not in dramatic blank verse, but "Dorique delicacy" describes, like no other phrase, the mixture of austerity and sensuous sweetness that generally marks Milton's early poetry. Andrew Marvell supplied a set of commendatory verses to the second edition of *Paradise Lost* that show a just appreciation of its scope and versification. He described the scope of Milton's subject thus:

> Messiah crowned, *Gods* reconciled decree,
> Rebelling angels, the forbidden tree,
> Heav'n, hell, earth, chaos, all: . . .

This shows that Marvell saw that the actual loss of Paradise was but a fraction of the whole. His account of Milton's style follows:

> At once delight and horror on us seize,
> Thou singst with so much gravity and ease;
> And above human flight dost soar aloft
> With plume so strong, so equal, and so soft.

Softness and ease: these are the qualities of style in *Paradise Lost* often unrecognized by those who are too intent on Milton's gravity and sublimity. Dryden, who praised *Paradise Lost* unstintingly, was also the first critic to interpret it wrongly. He said in 1697 that Milton would have a better claim to have written a genuine epic "if the Devil had not been his hero instead of Adam, if the giant had not foiled the knight and driven him out of his stronghold to wander through the world with his lady errant." There you have that undue narrowing of the poem's scope to the episode of the Fall and the triumph of Satan: a narrowing that has become traditional and still continues to close the eyes of many readers and critics to the full significance of the poem. It is true that Milton himself gave countenance to this narrowing by the title he gave his epic, though I sometimes think that he was being ironical and meant us to think of *Lost* as in quotation marks. But Dryden's witty contention that the giant foiled the knight is quite at odds with the poem itself.

Paradise Lost in its grand outlines is founded on a simple irony. And we need not be surprised, for irony is one of the qualities Milton gives to God the Father. When, near the beginning of the third book, the Father looks down and sees Satan "coasting the wall of Heav'n" and about to penetrate the universe, he addresses the Son as follows:

> "Only begotten Son, seest thou what rage
> Transports our adversary, whom no bounds
> Prescribed, no bars of hell, nor all the chains
> Heaped on him there, nor yet the main
> abyss
> Wide interrupt can hold? . . .
> (III. 80–84)

One critic accused Milton of inconsistency here because when, in the first book, Satan raised himself from the burning lake, Milton tells us he did so only through the "will and high permission of all-ruling Heaven." Of course there is no inconsistency, for in the passage quoted the Father speaks ironically, adopting Satan's foolish assumption that he raised himself from the lake and set out to ruin mankind on his own initiative and responsibility alone. If we grasp God's ironical words at Satan's expense, we may be the readier to believe that irony is central to the whole plot. The irony is as follows. Satan succeeds in tempting mankind to transgress God's commandment, and he believes that his success can have only one result: as Satan and his fellows have brought complete ruin on themselves by disobedience, so must Adam and Eve by theirs. But he has made a false comparison. Satan's sin was self-motivated; that of Adam and Eve was partly motivated from without. For Satan there is no hope, for he is corrupt throughout his whole being; for Adam and Eve there is hope, because theirs was not the whole responsibility. And in the end humanity finds itself able to attain an inner paradise better than the paradise it must give up; Dryden's knight and lady errant have in fact the key to a better stronghold than the one from which the giant has driven them. Such is the irony at Satan's expense. There is the further irony that Adam and Eve are as mistaken as Satan about their ultimate fate. When, exhausted by their quarrels and bereft of their pride, they become reconciled in very simple human companionship and fellow feeling, they are quite unaware that they are following the promptings both of heaven and of the residue of good thoughts that have survived the Fall, and that, by so following, they have attained salvation: just as the Ancient Mariner blessed the watersnakes unaware, not knowing that thereby he had broken the evil spell.

There are important consequences of this fundamental irony. First, the weight of the plot is put not on the mere episode of Eve eating the apple in the ninth book but on the whole process of temptation, Fall, the judgment by the Son of the Serpent, Adam, and Eve; on the corruption of the world through the entry of Sin and the consequent despair of Adam and Eve; and then, unexpectedly evolved out of all these varied and vast happenings, their mutual reconciliation, their penitence before God, and their salvation.

These happenings occupy the whole of books IX and X. Such a weighting of the plot is of the first moment. The fall of Eve, adequate enough in a larger ironic context, is nowhere near weighty enough, as described by Milton, to be the center of the poem, the point to which all earlier happenings lead and from which all subsequent happenings derive.

But read books IX and X as a unit, treat the events after the Fall not as appendixes to a completed climax but as a sequence leading up to the real climax in man's regeneration, and you find them a brilliantly diversified and massive area of high poetry, a principal glory of the English tongue. It may be asked whether the climax as thus described will really bear the weight put on it any more than will the traditionally assumed climax, the eating of the apple. Can this purely human scene of man and wife forgetting their quarrels, coming together again, and confessing their sin to God stand the tremendous test? First, it can be retorted that Milton undoubtedly intended it to do so. Near the end of the poem there is a conversation between Adam and Michael that follows the vision of future world history Michael has given to Adam for his instruction. From its all-important position and its intensely concentrated and earnest tone, it is clearly crucial to the meaning of the poem. Adam has at last learned wisdom, and this is his statement of some of the things hard experience has taught him:

> "Henceforth I learn, that to obey is best,
> And love with fear the only God, to walk
> As in his presence, ever to observe
> His providence, and on him sole depend,
> Merciful over all his works, with good
> Still overcoming evil, and by small
> Accomplishing great things, by things
> deemed weak
> Subverting worldly strong, and worldly wise
> By simply meek. . . ."
> (XII. 561–569)

This is high moralizing verse that would be irrelevant in a narrative poem if it did not repeat in its own abstract form what had already been transacted in concrete, dramatic action; and it points precisely to the true climax of the poem, where by their "small" decent action Adam and Eve accomplish great things and in their apparent weakness subvert the apparently "strong" machinations of the prince of this world. Whether Milton not only intended to make this part of the poem his climax but also succeeded in making it a worthy one can be decided only by the verdict of competent readers. But to me, at least, the account of Adam's black despair, his ferocious and cruel repulse of Eve, her persistence, Adam's softening toward her, their coming together, Eve's still distraught state of mind and inclination to suicide, Adam's strong and comforting words, and their final resolution to confess their sins to God is true to the fundamental simplicities of human nature and composes one of the most moving dramatic episodes in literature; it can bear a very heavy weight.

The second consequence of recognizing the fundamental irony of the poem is that it puts Satan in his proper place. Dryden has had many distinguished successors in his heresy that Satan is the hero; and as long as Adam and Eve were denied heroic action in their recovery after the Fall, it was natural to fill the resulting vacuum with any other action that had heroic pretensions. And that action was the escape of Satan from the fiery lake in Hell, and his courage in undertaking alone the journey to Earth for the ruin of mankind. But Milton's Satan is never a hero; he is an archangel ruined: that terrible thing—a being with great potentialities of good corrupted; graced, indeed, to heighten the drama, with some relics of good feelings but doomed to turn those relics to even greater evil. Those who have sentimentalized Satan have failed to see the coarseness and the vulgarity that accompany and darken these lingering relics of good feelings. Here is Milton's description of Satan reviewing the army of devils now mustered in Hell:

> . . . he through the armed files
> Darts his experienced eye, and soon traverse
> The whole battalion views, their order due,

Their visages and stature as of gods;
Their number last he sums. And now his heart
Distends with pride, and hardening in his strength
Glories. . . .
(I. 567–573)

It is a most damning description. How significant the juxtaposition of number and pride. Satan is revealed as the vulgarian who is thrilled by mere quantity. No wonder he commits a fundamental error in his estimate of what fate awaits disobedient man. All this is not to deny Satan's grandeur. It is just because he combines grandeur with vulgarity, a commanding intellect with a fundamental stupidity, not to speak of other discrepant qualities, that he is so true to life and so eternally fascinating a figure.

The fundamental irony at Satan's expense and at the apparent expense—but to the ultimate profit—of Adam and Eve is surpassingly powerful because it grew out of Milton's life experience and provided the most authentic material for his supreme poetic gift, a gift both congenital and improved by intense study. Milton condemns pride with such authority because he was himself strongly tempted to it. Compare him in this matter with Shakespeare. There is in literature no finer indictment of pride than Isabella's speech to Angelo in *Measure for Measure*:

Could great men thunder
As Jove himself does, Jove would ne'er be quiet,
For every pelting, petty officer
Would use his heaven for thunder;
Nothing but thunder . . . Merciful heaven,
Thou rather with thy sharp and sulphurous bolt
Split'st the unwedgeable and gnarled oak
Than the soft myrtle; but man, proud man,
Drest in a little brief authority,
Most ignorant of what he's most assured—
His glassy essence—like an angry ape,
Plays such fantastic tricks before high heaven
As make the angels weep. . . .
(II.ii. 111–122)

In his history plays, too, Shakespeare gives convincing pictures of proud and ambitious and unscrupulous men. But Isabella's speech and Shakespeare's quarreling nobles are passionately observed, not created out of the personal stuff of Shakespeare's mind. He could objectify them from the beginning, unhampered by any unusual personal involvement. But, as his pamphlets clearly show, Milton did suffer from that impatient pride that revolts against the nature of things and demands quick results; he had an element of Satan in him, and he experienced the despairing bafflement in which such pride is bound to end. But, as "Lycidas" showed, he was also aware of this side of his nature and hated it, believing even more passionately in the need for humility. And always the victory of humility was complete. It is because of this personal conflict, absent from Shakespeare in this acute form, that the basic irony of *Paradise Lost* has its peculiar power. Milton did objectify his material: we do not, in reading *Paradise Lost,* think of Milton the man. But he objectified with greater difficulty and at a later stage of the poetic process than Shakespeare did; and his poetry makes a different impression. Shakespeare was very close to life; Milton, to his own life. And the Miltonic closeness has its own superb authenticity.

I have asserted that the basis of *Paradise Lost* is a great irony expressive of a great piece of simple morality and that Milton's own total experience of this morality makes his poem authentic. We are reluctant, however, to accept a piece of simple morality as authentic unless it is supported by a great mass of detail. We require a poet to talk about many things before we are ready to accept what he most has to say. So I come now by a quite natural sequence to the various parts of *Paradise Lost.* These are so many that I will have to select; and I will do so by dealing only with those things that have either been denied to Milton or, if granted to him, ignored or slurred over or deprecated.

First, there is the theology. While the eighteenth century was too prone to see in *Paradise Lost* a simple orthodoxy, the late nineteenth and early twentieth centuries were too prone to cut out the theology altogether as an unfortunate accretion dictated by the conditions of seventeenth-century England. The truth is that Milton's theology is not entirely orthodox and that it is inseparable from the poem. If, as I assert, the main theme of the poem has to do with pride and humility, these qualities are not independent and uncircumstantiated, but bear the form, inescapable in the postclassical tradition in Europe, given them by Christianity. However much Milton had tried to free himself from theological ties, Pride, as he presented it, would in some sort have remained the chief of the Seven Deadly Sins, and humility a quality exemplified in the story of Christ as told in the New Testament. When Milton implies the doctrine of disinterestedness in "Lycidas," he gives us neither the abstracted doctrine nor the form of it found in the *Bhagavad-Gita.* However universal the doctrine, Christian and Indian writers had to present it in the ways they had inherited. Readers today are better placed to accept Milton's theology because recent scholarship has been teaching them a great deal about the theological tradition Milton inherited. So long as readers conceived it as a narrow fundamentalism of the kind described in the Mark Rutherford novels, they had to free Milton the poet from it. But if they realize that for Milton, as for his predecessors, theology included all philosophy and a great deal of natural science, they will see that such severance is not only unnecessary but also disastrously weakening to the range of Milton's interests.

One of the great theological doctrines was that a main way to approach God was through studying the beautiful variety of his creation. I have already mentioned the exuberance of Milton's nature as something fundamental. Possessing it, he was bound to find the bounty of nature both exciting and satisfying. Living when he did and brought up as he was, he could conceive of this bounty in other than theological terms. He must see it in terms of the great orderly arrangement of the total creation pictured as a great hierarchical chain stretching from the seraph nearest the throne of God to the meanest speck of inanimate matter. Even when Comus, the champion of disorder, speaks of the bounty of God's creation, that he may tempt the Lady to license, he does so with an enthusiasm that can best be matched in the panegyrics of orthodox divinity:

> Wherefore did Nature pour her bounties forth,
> With such a full and unwithdrawing hand,
> Covering the earth with odors, fruits, and flocks,
> Thronging the seas with spawn innumerable. . . .
> (710–713)

And when, in *Paradise Lost,* Milton writes of free will, he colors a doctrine that was essential to his own nature with traditional disputes over predestination and with the special Protestant doctrine of Christian liberty based on the writings of St. Paul. Milton's theology, far from being a tie, an alien thing, was a great world of thought where an immensely wide range of passions could find their natural embodiments.

Great poets are often the subject of large popular misconceptions. Chaucer has been thought of as hearty, Shakespeare as uneducated and unacademic, Shelley as weakly neurotic, Milton as inhuman and humorless. And these misconceptions die hard. It may be difficult, therefore, to gain the reader's ear if one points to humor and a delicate human perception in *Paradise Lost.* Humor, indeed, is not what one is led to expect in the straight epic from Virgil onward; nor could humor be advertised in the uniform meter of the epic with the clarity possible in a play using both verse and prose like Shakespeare's *Henry IV.* But Milton expects his readers to be fit as well as few; and fitness indicates close reading, which in its turn reveals, perhaps as a great surprise, these qualities of humor and delicate human perception. I mentioned earlier as a humorous figure the wealthy city merchant in *Areopagitica,* who hired a divine to manage his religion for him; and I fancy he reappears in a passage of *Paradise Lost* that has been cited as an example of Milton's seeking to be funny with disastrous results. It occurs just before the great description of Paradise and is a comparison with the way Satan overleaped the leafy barriers of that place, scorning entry by the proper way:

> Or as a thief bent to unhoard the cash
> Of some rich burgher, whose substantial
> doors,
> Cross-barred and bolted fast, fear no assault,
> In at the window climbs, or o'er the tiles. . . .
> (IV. 188–191)

The point of the passage is to lower the dignity of Satan, who a little earlier has struck a highly dramatic attitude, by homely comparisons, so that the reader may have his mind cleared for the coming description of Paradise; but the actual lines are a piece of satirical humor at the expense of the rich merchant who is imaginative enough to guard against direct assault but not imaginative enough to forestall a cat burglar.

I remarked earlier that Milton acquired a knowledge of women during the years of the Commonwealth, and in *Paradise Lost* this knowledge comes, as we might expect, in the later books, where the action has converged from Hell and Heaven to the universe and finally to the narrow human stage of the mount of Paradise. It is in the long scene near the beginning of book IX, when Adam and Eve discuss whether they shall garden separately or jointly, that the human comedy is most evident. That Milton dared to introduce comedy immediately before the great disaster in human history is quite amazing; and, if that disaster had been irreparable, comedy would have been out of the question. But I do not see how any careful and honest reader can miss the comedy; and I fancy Milton introduced it because he wished to relieve the disaster of the Fall itself of too stark an emphasis and to prepare for the basic irony of the poem.

The dispute between Adam and Eve is as delicate a piece of domestic comedy as you could find. Eve proposes separate gardening on this particular morning, not because she really wants that but because she wants Adam to say that he loves her too much to bear separation from her. Adam falls into the trap and replies with a heavy piece of moralizing. Eve gets her own back by saying that Adam does not trust her. Adam grows seriously concerned and argues earnestly, even impressively; and, if only he could see it, Eve is by now quite satisfied with the effect that her stratagem has produced. But Adam does not see, and refuses the responsibility of keeping Eve at his side. Finally Eve feels that after all this she cannot refuse the offer of a freedom she did not really want at any time, and now less than ever. And so they part, and Eve is exposed alone to the wiles of Satan. It is a perfect picture of the sort of misunderstanding that can afflict any ordinary, well-intentioned married couple; and it is proof that Milton had an eye for ordinary human traffic as well as for God's empyrean. Most remarkable is the stylistic skill by which he keeps the comedy from being cheap, so that it can slide into the tragic; for Adam's failure to assert himself at the right moment is not only comedy but also a tragic moral lapse.

But Milton's success in passing from comedy to tragedy is possible only within a restricted area of contrast. Obliged by writing in the epic form to observe a certain kind of uniformity, he has to pitch his comedy in a higher style than is required for the drama; his conversational cadences have to blend with a modicum of pomp. The conversational cadence of Eve's reprimand to Adam:

> But that thou shouldst my firmness
> therefore doubt
> To God or thee, because we have a foe
> May tempt it, I expected not to hear.
> (IX. 279–281)

with its stresses on "thou" and "my" is perfect, but it is delicately, not blatantly, conveyed; and the dignity of the passage does not fall below the standard expected from epic writing in the seventeenth century. It is this delicacy and lack of blatancy that both separates Milton's art from that of the metaphysical poets and exaggerates that separation. The metaphysicals founded their art on surprise and advertised what they were doing with much emphasis. Milton resembled them in being full of surprises, but he was extremely discreet about them. Had he not been full of surprises, he would have been untrue to the age in which he lived; had he paraded the fact, he would have been intolerable as an epic poet.

The matter of surprise is connected with another: that of realism. Milton's epic has the remotest possible setting, yet he wished its application to be entirely modern. To achieve his end he constantly refers in passing to contemporary events or interests, and slips the homely and the sensuous into contexts that are grandiose and remote. In the high description of Satan's lieutenants in book I, Milton suddenly inserts his reference to the riotous young men who made the streets of London dangerous in the later years of his life:

> . . . and when night
> Darkens the streets, then wander forth the sons
> Of Belial, flown with insolence and wine.
> (I. 500–502)

It is a startling piece of realism, but slipped in so coolly and quietly that it does not impair the epic texture. In the last lines of the poem, which give the vast picture of the angels thrusting Adam and Eve out of the gates of Paradise, occurs a reference of the greatest possible homeliness: to an ordinary peasant returning home to supper on a misty evening. I give it in its setting.

> So spake our mother Eve, and Adam heard
> Well pleased, but answered not; for now too nigh
> The archangel stood, and from the other hill
> To their fixed station, all in bright array
> The cherubim descended; on the ground
> Gliding meteorous, as evening mist
> Risen from a river o'er the marish glides,
> And gathers ground fast at the laborer's heel
> Homeward returning. High in front advanced,
> The brandished sword of God before them blazed
> Fierce as a comet; which with torrid heat,
> And vapor as the Lybian air adust,
> Began to parch that temperate clime; whereat
> In either hand the hastening angel caught
> Our lingering parents, and to the eastern gate
> Led them direct, and down the cliff as fast
> To the subjected plaine; then disappeared.
> They looking back, all the eastern side beheld
> Of paradise, so late their happy seat,
> Wav'd over by that flaming brand, the gate
> With dreadful faces thronged and fiery arms. . . .
> (XII. 624–644)

I quote this passage to illustrate how successfully Milton could insinuate the homely and the realistic into the grandiose, but it will serve also to prompt a final general comment on *Paradise Lost.* It is one of the great passages, and it is typical of the poem generally in uniting so many strands and grades of feeling: the huge, almost monstrous picture of the thronged gate and the miniature picture of the two human beings; the archangel matched by the peasant; the particularity of description of the "eastern gate set against the symbolic significance of the "subjected plaine." And these many strands are made to cooperate through their common subordination to a unifying though never monotonous type of verse. Such is the general nature of *Paradise Lost,* and it corresponds to the primary wealth and vitality of Milton's own nature, as well as to the mental discipline through which he accepted and held together the good and the ill that life brought him.

Paradise Lost is exacting because it is a long, highly concentrated poem, but not so exacting as to be beyond the reach of a wide public. In the eighteenth century it was extremely popular, partly because, along with the Bible and *The Pilgrim's Progress,* it was legitimate Sunday reading for Puritans, but also partly because readers of that time were willing to give steady attention to a few great works. And it could regain such a vogue whenever a wide public cared to give it similar attention; the potential attraction, the perennial human appeal, are there all the time. *Paradise Regained* is a different case; it has always been a poem for the few. But those few have found it, in some strange way, immensely attractive. Why Milton wrote it we do not know. The old idea that it is a sequel to *Paradise Lost* does not work, because the earlier poem had included the recovery of Paradise through Christ in its scope and had taken world history far beyond the period of time to which *Paradise Regained* is confined. What is certain is that *Paradise Regained* deals once again with the dominant Miltonic theme of the prime importance of the state of mind and the dependence of action on that state.

Paradise Regained is a narrative version of Christ's temptation by the Devil in the wilderness; and in choosing this episode as the chief one in the gospels, Milton was following an earlier tradition particularly dear to Puritan thought. Puritanism loved to picture the Christian life and the chief events leading up to it as a battle. The Christian was a warrior, clad in the spiritual armor listed by St. Paul; and there had been two principal battles that had decided his fate. First, the Devil had fought with and defeated Adam, the Old Man, in the Garden of Eden; and second, Christ, the New Man, had fought with and defeated the Devil in the wilderness. And the wilderness was necessary for the proper correspondence. As Adam had lost a garden for a wilderness, so must Christ conduct his battle in a wilderness to win back the paradisiac garden. Milton accepted this rather surprising preference of the Temptation to the Crucifixion partly because he liked to work in the tradition of the religious party to which, generally, he belonged and partly because the Temptation was, in his view, the episode that marked the formation of the state of mind that governed all Christ's subsequent action, the acceptance of crucifixion included. Once Christ had acquired that state of mind, he had only to act in accordance with it, and action would take care of itself—or, rather, God in heaven would take care of it. Christ's victory in the wilderness symbolized the general moral truth that the state of mind comes first and results are subordinate.

Milton's heart was therefore thoroughly in his theme, and in his treatment of it he seems to have consulted his own inclination rather than his readers' applause, in a way different from *Paradise Lost.* There are long speeches and few deeds. The poem is more of a debate than a narrative; and it is likely that the Book of Job was Milton's model here. The language is less ornate and more restricted to simple words than that of *Paradise Lost,* and the rhythm more subdued and closer to quiet conversation. This is the cool, quiet, and yet passionately concentrated way in which Milton ends the first book. Satan has just asked, with assumed humility, permission to come and talk with Christ in the wilderness:

> To whom our Saviour with unaltered brow.
> Thy coming hither, though I know thy scope,
> I bid not or forbid; do as thou find'st
> Permission from above; thou canst not more.
> He added not; and Satan bowing low
> His gray dissimulation, disappeared
> Into thin air diffused: for now began
> Night with her sullen wing to double-shade
> The desert, fowls in their clay nests were couched;
> And now wild beasts came forth the woods to roam.
> (I. 493–502)

It is those already familiar with Milton who will appreciate this kind of writing. For them the leanness of Christ's speech will not indicate starvation or poverty, but the leanness of the perfectly trained athlete whose body is free from every trace of superfluous fat and consists of operant bone and muscle. It will further resemble the athlete's body when in gentle, not violent, motion—gentle, but containing the promise of the fiercest violence, should violence be required. It is also those already familiar with Milton who will appreciate the delicate conversational cadence of many of the speeches. This is Christ speaking of worldly glory:

> But why should man seek glory? who of his own
> Hath nothing, and to whom nothing belongs
> But condemnation, ignominy, and shame?
> Who for so many benefits received
> Turned recreant to God, ingrate and false,
> And so of all true good himself despoiled,
> Yet, sacrilegious, to himself would take
> That which to God alone of right belongs;
> Yet so much bounty is in God, such grace,
> That who advance his glory, not their own,
> Then he himself to glory will advance.
> (III. 134–144)

There is no unusual word here, no simile, scarcely a metaphor. The effect depends on the verse, the rise and fall of emphasis within narrow limits, the occasional flicker of feeling as in the word "sacrilegious," as if the poet were addressing an intimate reader, one who could catch much meaning from mere hints, one who could take so very much for granted.

If the conversations are quiet and delicately cadenced, the landscape is of twilight and suggests less a real scene than a symbol of the working of the mind. But into this dimness Milton projects brilliant visions that, whether by accident or by design, resemble the infernal creations that in medieval romance tempted Sir Galahad in his quest for the Holy Grail. Here is the description of the phantoms that attended the banquet Satan raised in the wilderness.

> And at a stately sideboard by the wine
> That fragrant smell diffused, in order stood
> Tall stripling youths rich-clad, of fairer hue
> Then Ganymede or Hylas; distant more
> Under the trees now tripped, now solemn stood
> Nymphs of Diana's train, and Naiades
> With fruits and flowers from Amalthea's horn,
> And ladies of the Hesperides, that seemed
> Fairer then feigned of old, or fabled since
> Of fairy damsels met in forest wide
> By Knights of Logres, or of Lyonesse,
> Lancelot or Pelleas, or Pellenore,
> And all the while harmonious airs were heard
> Of chiming strings, or charming pipes and winds
> Of gentlest gale Arabian odors fanned
> From their soft wings, and Flora's earliest smells.
> (II. 350–365)

Paradise Regained is unusually compounded of twilight, trancelike descriptions, conversations remote from the marketplace or senate house or inn, yet delicately suggesting the cadences of real talk, and brilliant visions. It is a varied and startling composition, but it is strange too; and it is not surprising that in general readers have not been able to take *Paradise Regained* to their hearts.

The case is very different with the other poem published along with *Paradise Regained* in 1671, *Samson Agonistes.* Milton's Samson, blind and in Philistine captivity, is, like Chaucer's *Wife of Bath* or Shakespeare's *Macbeth* or Dickens' *Mrs. Gamp*, one of those figures that helps to compose what can be called a nation's literary mythology. Anthony Trollope, in *The Last Chronicle of Barset,* makes Mr. Crawley, himself a tragic figure, talk of Milton's Samson as if he were an accepted national inheritance, the common property of all intelligent readers. Mr. Crawley has been making his daughter read about the blinded Polyphemus in the *Odyssey,* and he stops her and comments:

> The same story is always coming up; we have it in various versions, because it is so true to life.
>
> Ask for this great deliverer now, and find him
> Eyeless in Gaza, at the mill with slaves.
>
> It is the same story. Great power reduced to impotence, great glory to misery, by the hand

> of Fate. At the mill with slaves! Can any picture be more dreadful than that? The mind of the strong blind creature must be so sensible of the injury that has been done to him! The impotency, combined with his strength, or rather the impotency with the memory of former strength and former aspirations, is so essentially tragic.

Aldous Huxley chose *Eyeless in Gaza* for the title of one of his novels. And T. S. Eliot assumed a response he could not assume if he had referred to *Paradise Regained* when he wove references to *Samson Agonistes* into the texture of "East Coker":

> O dark dark dark. They all go into the dark,
> The vacant interstellar spaces, the vacant
> into the vacant. . . .

Trollope's Mr. Crawley was right. Milton's Samson is a terrible yet compelling figure of human suffering, reminding one of Sophocles' Philoctetes, Shakespeare's Lear, and one or two of Hopkins' most poignant sonnets. Milton is surely thinking of the physical pangs of Philoctetes when he makes his Samson burst into this lyrical complaint:

> O that torment should not be confined
> To the body's wounds and sores
> With maladies innumerable
> In heart, head, breast, and reins;
> But must secret passage find
> To the inmost mind,
> There exercise all his fierce accidents,
> And on her purest spirits prey,
> As on entrails, joints, and limbs,
> With answerable pains, but more intense,
> Though void of corporal sense.
> My griefs not only pain me
> As a lingering disease,
> But finding no redress, ferment and rage,
> Nor less then wounds immedicable
> Rankle, and fester, and gangrene,
> To black mortification.
> Thoughts my tormentors armed with deadly stings
> Mangle my apprehensive tenderest parts,
> Exasperate, exulcerate, and raise
> Dire inflammation which no cooling herb
> Or med'cinal liquor can assuage,
> Nor breath of vernal air from snowy alp.
> Sleep hath forsook and given me o'er
> To death's benumbing opium as my only cure.
> Thence faintings, swoonings of despair,
> And sense of heaven's desertion.
> (606–632)

But if Samson the sufferer is part of English literary mythology, what of the whole play? Here the answer is in some doubt. Milton cannot have written the play to be acted; Samuel Johnson accused it of defective action, and a general notion has prevailed that as a whole it is insufficiently dramatic. And yet *Samson Agonistes* has been played in amateur performances with great success. The general notion and the specific event do not concur. The truth is that Samson is indeed dramatic, but in a way unusual in English drama. There is little action on the stage, the most important being reported. But there is sufficient action in Samson's mind. Even so, that action is unusual. Motives on the stage are usually more obvious than they would be in life. However, mental action in Samson does not consist in obvious changes and transitions, but in the spread of an unconscious temper into consciousness. At the beginning of the play Samson is in the same case as Adam is in book X of *Paradise Lost,* when he is in despair and thinks God has quite cast him off. Actually, both Adam and Samson have accepted complete responsibility for what they have done, and thereby have touched the humility that means salvation. *Samson Agonistes* reveals the mind of its protagonist in its various stages of testing, awakening, comprehension, and finds its end in the death of a forgiven and redeemed hero. As a psychological drama it is a wonderful and satisfying piece of work. And now that the technique of choric speech has been improved (mainly through productions of T. S. Eliot's verse drama), there is no reason why *Samson Agonistes* should not take its place as one of the great acted English classics.

I have written of *Samson Agonistes* after *Paradise Regained* as if the facts of simultaneous publication and the sequence within that publication indicated the same order of composition. But, as already stated, there is no certain proof of when *Samson* was written. Nevertheless, it does supplement *Paradise Regained* very remarkably; and even if Milton wrote *Samson* earlier, he may have recast it for publication. In any case, if he chose to publish the two poems together, we are safer in considering them together than in plumping for earlier dates of composition for which there is no scrap of firm evidence. Like *Paradise Regained, Samson Agonistes* deals with the regions of reflection and action. Christ rejected all temptations to achieve quick results. He knew his own powers and wondered whether he should lead Israel to revolt against Rome. But he knew too that such was not his true fate. And he waited until, in the fullness of time, he achieved a state of mind that insured that all his actions would be soundly based. Samson, on the other hand, chose a life of physical action; and up to a point he was right, because he had been gifted with unusual strength. But success corrupted him and made him overvalue his gift. Through this pride he fell into misfortune, but he recognized his error and fell into the extremes of despair and humility:

> O impotence of mind, in body strong!
> But what is strength without a double share
> Of wisdom, vast, unwieldy, burdensome,
> Proudly secure, yet liable to fall
> By weakest subtleties, not made to rule,
> But to subserve where wisdom bears
> command.
> (52–57)

Once Samson has realized that the state of mind comes first, once his own state of mind is sound, God allows him yet again to put his gift of unusual physical strength into action. The idea of the two poems is the same; but in the first the climax is the achievement of a state of mind implying perfect actions to come, while in the second it is a piece of action based on a sound state of mind already achieved.

I think that *Paradise Lost* is worth more than all the rest of Milton's works put together, but fewer readers than in former times have the patience to master a long poem. The almost superstitious reverence for the successful epic has disappeared. It may be that for some years to come the early poems, fragments of *Paradise Lost, Samson Agonistes,* and perhaps *Areopagitica* will be the operant portions of his works. It is to be regretted if this should be so; but even if thus truncated, Milton survives as a major poet of surpassing power and variety.

Selected Bibliography

BIBLIOGRAPHY

J. Bradshaw, ed., *A Concordance to the Poetical Works of John Milton,* (London, 1894; repr. 1965); W. A. Wright, pub., *Facsimile of the Manuscript of Milton's Minor Poems Preserved in the Library of Trinity College, Cambridge,* (Cambridge, 1899) partly reproduced by F. A. Patterson (New York, 1933) (Menton, 1970); Lockwood, L. E., *Lexicon to the English Poetical Works of John Milton,* (New York, 1907); *Milton, 1608–1674: Facsimile of the Autographs and Documents in the British Museum,* London (1908); Thompson, E. N. S., *John Milton: A Topical Bibliography,* (New Haven, 1916); Gilbert, A. H., *A Geographical Dictionary of Milton,* (New Haven, 1919); L. Cooper, ed., *A Concordance of the Latin, Greek and Italian Poems of John Milton,* (Halle, 1923); Hanford, J. H., *A Milton Handbook,* (New York, 1926; 5th rev. ed. 1970); Stevens, D. H., *Reference Guide to Milton from 1800 to the Present Day,* (Chicago, 1930); H. F. Fletcher, ed., *Contributions to a Milton Bibliography, 1800–1930: Being a List of Addenda to Stevens's Reference Guide,* (Urbana, Ill., 1931); V., de S. Pinto, *The English Renaissance 1510–1688,* (London, 1938; 3rd rev. ed. 1966) contains a bibliography; Huckabay, C., *John Milton: A Bibliographical Supplement, 1929–1957,* (Pittsburgh-Louvain, 1960) also in rev. ed., *John Milton: An Annotated Bibliography, 1929–1968* (1969); E. S., Le Comte, *A Milton Dictionary,* (New York, 1960; English ed. 1961); *A Concordance to Milton's English Poetry,* William Ingram and Kathleen Swain, eds. (Oxford, 1972).

COLLECTED WORKS

J. Tolland, ed., *A Complete Collection of the Historical, Political, and Miscellaneous Works of Milton,* 3 vols. (London, 1694–1698); P[atrick] H[ume], ed., *Poetical Works, Together with Explanatory Notes on Each*

Book of the Paradise Lost, and a Table Never Before Printed, 5 pts. (London, 1695), the first collected ed. of the poetry; H. J. Todd, ed., *Poetical Works. With the Principal Notes of Various Commentators,* 6 vols. (London, 1801; 7 vols. 1809) with additions and a verbal index), a variorum ed. using the work of some of the best-known eighteenth-century editors of Milton, including R. Bentley, T. Newton, and Thomas Warton, and critical appreciations of Milton by Andrew Marvell, John Dryden, Joseph Addison, James Thomson, Samuel Johnson, Thomas Gray, William Cowper, and others; W. Hayley, ed., *Cowper's Milton, with Notes by William Cowper,* 4 vols. (Chichester, 1810); J. A. St. John, ed., *Prose Works,* 5 vols. (London, 1848–1853); J. Mitford, ed., *Works, in Verse and Prose,* 8 vols. (London, 1851) complete except for *Of Christian Doctrine* and minor items; R. C. Browne, ed., *English Poems,* (London, 1866) also with notes by H. Bradley (London, 1894); D. Masson, ed., *Poetical Works,* 3 vols. (London, 1874; rev. ed. 1890) the Globe one-volume ed. has an intro. by Masson (London, 1877); A. W. Verity, ed., *The Cambridge Milton for Schools,* 11 vols. London (1891–1899); H. C. Beeching, ed., *The Poetical Works of John Milton,* (Oxford, 1900; rev. ed., 1938); W. Aldis Wright, ed., *Poetical Works,* (London, 1903); H. J. C. Grierson, ed., *The Poems of John Milton, Arranged in Chronological Order,* 2 vols. (London, 1925); *Milton's Prose,* M. W. Wallace, ed. (London-New York, 1925); F. A. Patterson, ed., *The Student's Milton,* (New York, 1930) contains the complete poetry and most of the prose, plus early biographies of Milton-the revised edition (1933) contains annotations to the poetry and prose; F. A., Patterson, gen. ed. *Works,* 18 vols. (New York, 1931–1938) issued by Columbia University, is the only complete edition of Milton's works, the last vol. contains previously uncollected writings and marginalia, and there is a two-vol. index, F. A. Patterson and F. R. Fogle, eds. (New York, 1940) that forms an invaluable work of reference; *Private Correspondence and Academic Exercises* P. B. Tillyard, trans. (Cambridge, 1932) with intro. and commentary by E. M. W. Tillyard; J. H. Hanford., ed. *The Poems of John Milton* (New York, 1936); E. H. Visiak, ed., *Complete Poetry and Selected Prose,* (London, 1938); H. F. Fletcher, ed., *Complete Poetical Works,* (Boston, 1941) a new text ed., with intro. and notes, of the Cambridge ed., W. V. Moody, ed.; H. F. Fletcher, ed. *Complete Poetical Works* 4 vols. (Urbana, Ill., 1943–1948) reproduced in photographic facs. Hughes, M. Y., *John Milton, Complete Poems and Major Prose* (New York, 1957) with notes by Hughes; K. M. Burton, ed. *Milton's Prose Writings* (London—New York, 1958); Helen Darbishire, ed., *Poetical Works,* (London, 1958) in the Oxford Standard Authors ed.; J. T. Shawcross, ed. *The Complete English Poetry of John Milton* (London, 1963); D. M. Wolfe et al., eds., *The Complete Prose Works,* 5 vols. (New Haven, 1953–1970); D. Bush, ed., *Complete Poetical Works,* (Boston, 1965; English ed., 1966); J. Carey and A. Fowler, eds., *The Poems of John Milton,* (London, 1968).

SELECTED WORKS

Poems of Mr. John Milton. Both English and Latin. . . . Printed . . . for H. Moseley (London, 1645) facs. repr. of English poems (1968) the minor poems: "On the Morning of Christ's Nativity," "L'Allegro," and "Il Penseroso" sonnets, and others; *Poems, Etc. upon Several Occasions. By Mr. John Milton: . . . With a Small Tractate of Education to Mr. Hartlib* (London, 1673); W. Hayley, ed., *Latin and Italian Poems of Milton,* William Cowper, trans. (Chichester, 1808) also W. MacKellar, ed. *Latin Poems* MacKellar, trans. (New Haven, 1930); O. Elton, ed., *Minor Poems,* 5 vols. (Oxford, 1893–1900); J. S. Smart, ed., *Sonnets,* (Glasgow, 1921; repr., 1966) with original notes and new biographical matter; M. Y. Hughes, ed., *Paradise Regained, the Minor Poems and Samson Agonistes* (New York, 1937); D. Bush, ed., *The Portable Milton,* (New York, 1949) with intro. by Bush; *Poems of Mr John Milton,* (New York, 1951; reiss., London 1957) the 1645 ed., with analytical essays by Cleanth Brooks and J. E. Hardy; N. Frye, ed., *John Milton: Paradise Lost and Selected Poems* (London-New York, 1951); E. Le Comte, ed., *"Paradise Lost" and Other Poems,* (New York, 1961); M. Y. Hughes, ed., *Paradise Lost,* (New York, 1962); I. G. MacCaffrey, ed., *John Milton: Samson Agonistes and the Shorter Poems,* (New York-London, 1966); C. Ricks, ed., *John Milton: Paradise Lost and Paradise Regained,* (New York-London, 1968).

SEPARATE WORKS

"An Epitaph on the Admirable Dramaticke Poet, W. Shakespeare," first published in the Second Folio of Shakespeare's *Plays* (London, 1632) "A Maske Presented at Ludlow Castle, 1634 . . . ," (London, 1637) the title *Comus* was first used in the stage version of 1738 "Lycidas," *Obsequies to the Memory of Mr. Edward King* (London, 1638) a collection of memorial verses in Latin, Greek, and English; *Epitaphium Damonis,* (London: *ca.,* 1640) unique copy in British Museum; *Of Reformation Touching Church-Discipline in England: . . .* (London, 1641); *Of Prelatical Episcopacy . . .* (London, 1641); *Animadversions upon the Remonstrants Defence Against Smectymnuus,* (London, 1641); *The Reason of Church-Government Urg'd Against Prelaty,* (London, 1641); *An Apology Against a Pamphlet Call'd A Modest Confutation of the Animadversions upon the Remonstrant Against Smectymnuus,* (London, 1642); *The Doctrine and Discipline of Divorce . . .* (London, 1643; 2nd ed., rev. and enl., 1644); *Of Education. To Master Samuel Hartlib,* (London: *ca.,* 1644); *The Judgement of Martin Bucer . . .* (London, 1644); *Areopagitica . . .* (London, 1644); *Colasterion: A Reply to a Nameles Answer Against the Doctrine and Discipline of Divorce,* (London, 1645); *Tetrachordon: Expositions upon the Foure Chief Places in Scripture Which Treat of Mariage, or Nullities in Mariage,* (London, 1645) "Sonnet to Henry Lawes," Henry and William Lawes *Choice Psalmes, Put into Musick for Three Voices* (London, 1648) EIKONOKLASTHS: In Answer to a Book Intitl'd Eikwn Basilikh, the Portrature of His Sacred Majesty in His Solitudes and Sufferings (London, 1649; 2nd ed., enl., 1650); *Observations upon the Articles of Peace with the Irish Rebels* . . . (London, 1649); *The Tenure of Kings and Magistrates,* (London, 1649); *Pro Populo anglicano defensio* . . . (London, 1651) translated by J. Washington (London, 1692); *A Letter Written to a Gentleman in the Country, Touching the Dissolution of the Late Parliament and the Reasons Thereof,* (London, 1653); *Pro populo anglicano defensio secunda,* (London, 1654) translated by F. Wrangham (London, 1816); *Joannis Miltonii pro se defensio* . . . (London, 1655); *Considerations Touching the Likeliest Means to Remove Hirelings out of the Church,* (London, 1659); *A Treatise of Civil Power in Ecclesiastical Causes* . . . (London, 1659); *Brief Notes upon a Late Sermon, Titl'd, The Fear of God and the King* . . . (London, 1660); *The Readie & Easie Way to Establish a Free Commonwealth* . . . (London, 1660); *Paradise Lost,* (London, 1667; 2nd ed., 12 bks., rev. and enl., 1674) facs. of 1st ed. with intro. by D. Masson (London, 1877) also in A. Fowler, ed. (London, 1971) MS of bk. I edited by H. Darbishire (Oxford, 1931); *The History of Britain* . . . (London, 1670); *Paradise Regained,* (London, 1671) to which is added "Samson Agonistes,"; *Of True Religion, Haeresie, Schism, Toleration, and What Best Means May Be Us'd Against the Growth of Popery,* (London, 1673); *Mr. John Milton's Character of the Long Parliament and Assembly of Divines* . . . (London, 1681) originally part of bk. III of *The History of Britain; A Brief History of Moscovia* . . . (London, 1682); *Letters of State, Written by Mr. John Milton . . . from the Year 1649 till 1659* . . . (London, 1694) includes a biography by E. Phillips, several poems, and a catalog of the works; C. R. Sumner, ed. *De doctrina christiana* (Cambridge, 1825) also translated by Sumner (Cambridge, 1825).

BIOGRAPHICAL AND CRITICAL STUDIES

Early biographies of Milton by John Aubrey, Anthony Wood, Edward Phillips, John Toland, Jonathan Richardson, and Thomas Ellwood are collected in *The Student's Milton,* (1930) See also Helen Darbishire, *Early Lives of Milton* (London, 1932).

Works of the seventeenth and eighteenth centuries are Andrew Marvell *On Paradise Lost* a poem in praise of Milton prefixed to the 1674 ed. of *Paradise Lost;* Dryden, John, "Apology for Heroic Poetry," (1677) in W. P. Ker, ed. *Essays* (Oxford, 1900); Addison, Joseph, papers on *Paradise Lost* in *Spectator* from December 31, 1711 to May 3, 1712 (no. 267 and on Saturdays until no. 369), twelve papers discuss the beauties of each of the twelve books, and six discuss *Paradise Lost* as a whole; Richardson, Jonathan, *Explanatory Notes and Remarks on Milton's Paradise Lost* (London, 1734); Warton, J., *An Essay on the Genius and Writings of Pope,* (London, 1756) an interesting estimate of Milton in relation to Pope; Johnson, Samuel, "Life of Milton," in his *Lives of the Poets* (London, 1779).

Nineteenth-century writings include Lander, W. S., *Imaginary Conversations,* (London, 1824–1829) contains two "conversations" between Milton and Marvell, which were edited by C. G. Crump (London, 1891); Coleridge, S. T., *Literary Remains,* H. N. Coleridge, ed. (London, 1836–1839) contains a lecture on Milton delivered in 1818, also see Coleridge's comparison of Milton and Shakespeare in his *Biographia literaria* (London, 1817) ch. XV; Masson, D., *The Life of John Milton,* 7 vols. (London, 1858–1881) with index, 1894; Macaulay, T. B., *Critical and Historical Essays, Contributed to the Edinburgh Review,* 3 vols. (London, 1843) contains the famous essay on Milton published in August (1825) also see his *Miscellaneous Writings* (London, 1860); Arnold, M., *Mixed Essays,* (London, 1879) see also his *Essays in Criticism, Second Series* (London, 1888); Bagehot, W., *Literary Studies,* R. H. Hutton, ed. (London, 1879) contains a study of Milton; Pattison, M., *Milton,* (London, 1879) in the English Men of Letters series; Garnett, R., *Life of John Milton,* (London, 1890); Bridges, R., *Milton's Prosody,* (Oxford, 1893; rev. ed., 1901) a revised version of two essays (1887 and 1889), also another ed. with a chapter on accentual verse, and notes (1921).

During the first three decades of the twentieth century appeared Sir W. A. Raleigh *Milton* (London, 1900); Osgood, C. G., *The Classical Mythology of Milton's English Poems,* Yale Studies in English no. 8 (New Haven, 1900; repr. Oxford, 1925); Abercrombie, Lascelles, *The Epic,* (London, 1914) contains important criticism of Milton's epics; Havens, R. D., *The Influence of Milton on English Poetry,* (Cambridge, Mass., 1922); Saurat, Denis, *Milton: Man and Thinker,* (New York, 1925) a translation and adaptation of essays earlier published in French that contains a bibliography of criticism of Milton; Hanford, J. H., *A Milton Handbook,* (New York, 1926; 5th rev, ed., 1970), see also Hanford's *The Youth of Milton* in the series University of Michigan Studies of Shakespeare, Milton, and Donne (New York, 1925); Grierson, H. J. C., *Cross Currents in English Literature of the XVIIth Century,* (London, 1929) the Messenger lectures, delivered at Cornell University, 1926–1927.

Works of the 1930's are Stoll, E. E., *Poets and Playwrights: Shakespeare, Jonson, Spenser, Milton,* (Minneapolis, 1930); Tillyard, E. M. W., *Milton,* (London,

1930; rev. ed., 1966), a full treatment of Milton's literary and mental development; Eliot, T. S., *Selected Essays, 1917–1932,* (London, 1932) contains observations on Milton that were later amplified in the British Academy's "Annual Lecture on a Master Mind," (1947); Macaulay, Rose, *Milton,* (London, 1934; rev. ed., 1957); Willey, B., *The Seventeenth Century Background: Studies in the Thought of the Age in Relation to Poetry and Religion,* (London, 1934); Leavis, F. R., *Revaluation,* London (1936) contains an important essay on Milton, see also his *The Common Pursuit* (London, 1952); Grierson, H. J. C., *Milton and Wordsworth, Poets and Prophets: A Study of Their Reactions to Political Events,* (Cambridge, 1937); Finley, J. H., *Milton and Horace: A Study of Milton's Sonnets,* Harvard Studies in Classical Philology, XLVIII (1937); Tillyard, E. M. W., *The Miltonic Setting, Past and Present,* (Cambridge, 1938) a study of Milton's seventeenth-century setting and his present poetic status; *Milton on Himself,* J. S. Diekhoff, ed. (London, 1939; new ed., 1965).

During the 1940's there appeared Parker, W. R., *Milton's Contemporary Reputation,* (Columbus, Ohio, 1940); McColley, G., *Paradise Lost: An Account of Its Growth and Major Origins,* (Chicago, 1940); Kelley, M., *This Great Argument: A Study of Milton's De doctrina christiana as a Gloss upon Paradise Lost,* (Princeton, 1941); Wolfe, D., *Milton in the Puritan Revolution,* (New York, 1941) a study of the political significance of Milton's work; Barker, A. E., *Milton and the Puritan Dilemma 1641–1660,* (Toronto, 1942; repr. 1956); Lewis, C. S., *A Preface to Paradise Lost,* (London, 1942) a study of the Christian background of the poem; Bowra, C. M., *From Virgil to Milton,* (London, 1945) (New York, 1946); Bush, D., *Paradise Lost in Our Time: Some Comments,* (Ithaca, N.Y., 1945) a defense of Milton against his modern detractors; Buxton, C. R., *Prophets of Heaven and Hell: Virgil, Dante, Milton, Goethe: An Introductory Essay,* (Cambridge, 1945); Diekhoff, J. S., *Milton's Paradise Lost: A Commentary on the Argument,* (New York, 1946); Rajan, B., *Paradise Lost and the Seventeenth Century Reader,* (London, 1947); Samuel, I., *Plato and Milton,* (Ithaca, N.Y., 1947); Waldock, A. J. A., *Paradise Lost and Its Critics,* (Cambridge, 1947) an able and coolly provocative statement of doubt whether the poem is a consistent whole; Warner, R., *John Milton,* (London, 1949); J. M. French, ed., *The Life Records of John Milton,* 4 vols. (New Brunswick, N.J., 1949–1958); Hanford, J. H., *John Milton, Englishman,* (New York, 1949; London, 1950).

Works of the 1950's include: Mahood, M. M., *Poetry and Humanism,* (London, 1950); J. Thorpe, ed., *Milton Criticism: Selections from Four Centuries,* (New York, 1950; London, (1951); Rajan, B., *The Lofty Rhyme: A Study of Milton's Major Poetry,* (London-Coral Gables, Fla., 1970); Tillyard, E. M. W., *Studies in Milton,* (London, 1951) aims largely at supplementing and correcting some matters in Tillyard's *Milton* while a study on the crisis of *Paradise Lost* corrects a common assumption and advances a general interpretation of books IX and X; Sprott, S. E., *Milton's Art of Prosody,* (Oxford, 1953); Stein, A., *Answerable Style: Essays on Paradise Lost,* (Minneapolis-London, 1953); Allen, D. C., *The Harmonious Vision: Studies in Milton's Poetry,* (Baltimore-London, 1954; enl. ed., 1970); Arthos, J., *On a Mask Presented at Ludlow Castle,* (Ann Arbor, Mich., 1954); Prince, F. T., *The Italian Element in Milton's Verse,* (Oxford, 1954), an original study, embodying new discoveries; Adams, R. M., *Ikon: Milton and the Modern Critics,* (Ithaca, N.Y.-London, 1955); Dyson, A. E., "The Interpretation of Comus," in *Essays and Studies* 21 (London, 1955); Haller, W., *Liberty and Reformation in the Puritan Revolution,* (New York-London, 1955); Muir, K., *John Milton,* (London-New York, 1955; rev., 1960); Watkins, W. B., *An Anatomy of Milton's Verse,* (Baton Rouge, La., 1955); Cormican, L. A., *Milton's Religious Verse,* in B. Ford, ed. *From Donne to Marvell* (New York-Harmondsworth, England, 1956); Fletcher, H. F., *The Intellectual Development of John Milton,* 2 vols. (Urbana, Ill., 1956–1961); Tillyard, E. M. W., *The Methaphysicals and Milton,* (London, 1956); Daiches, D., *Milton,* (London-New York, 1957); Kermode, J. F., *Romantic Image,* (London, 1957); Tuve, R., *Images and Themes in Five Poems by Milton,* (Cambridge, Mass., 1957); Stein, A., *Heroic Knowledge: An Interpretation of Paradise Regained and Samson Agonistes,* (Minneapolis-London, 1957); MacCaffrey, I., *Paradise Lost as Myth,* (Cambridge, Mass.-London, 1959).

During the 1960's there appeared Broadbent, J. B., *Some Graver Subject: An Essay on Paradise Lost,* (London, 1960) a penetrating analysis of the way *Paradise Lost* evolves; J. F. Kermode, ed., *The Living Milton: Essays by Various Hands* (London, 1960), an honest and erudite attempt to define what is left of *Paradise Lost* when its many defects are taken into account; Empson, W., *Milton's God,* (London, 1961; rev. ed., with new appendix, 1965); Broadbent, J. B., *Milton, Comus and Samson Agonistes,* (London, 1961); Le Comte, E. S., *A Milton Dictionary,* (New York, 1961); Hollander, J., *The Untuning of the Sky: Ideas of Music in English Poetry, 1500–1700,* (Princeton, N.J., 1961); Williamson, G., *Seventeenth Century Contexts,* (Chicago-London, 1961); Wilkes, G. A., *The Thesis of Paradise Lost,* (Melbourne, 1961); Bush, D., *English Literature in the Earlier Seventeenth Century, 1600–1660,* vol. 5 of *The Oxford History of English Literature* (New York-Oxford, 1962); Summers, J. H., *The Muse's Method; An Introduction to Paradise Lost,* (London, 1962); Sims, J. H., *The Bible in Milton's Epics,* (Gainesville, Fla., 1962); Wright, B. A., *Milton's Paradise Lost,* (London, 1962); Ferry, D. A., *Milton's Epic Voice: The Narrator in Paradise Lost,* (Cambridge, Mass., 1963); Arthos, J., *Dante, Michelangelo and Milton,* (London, 1963); Ricks, C., *Milton's Grand Style,* (Oxford, 1963); Daniells, R., *Milton, Mannerism and Baroque,* (Toronto, 1963); Nicolson, M. H., *John Milton: A Reader's Guide to His Poetry,* (New York, 1963); Blondel, J., *Le Comus de John Milton: Masque Neptunien,* (New York-London, 1964); Bush, D., *John Milton: A Sketch of His Life and Writings,* (New York, 1964); Emma, R. D., *Milton & Grammar,* "The Hague," (1964); Hagin, P., *The Epic Hero and the Decline of Epic Poetry,* (Berne, 1964); A. E. Barker ed., *Milton: Modern Essays in Criticism,* (New York-London, 1965); M. Y. Hughes, ed., *Ten Perspectives on Milton,* (New Haven, 1965); J. Thorpe, ed., *Milton Criticism: Selections from Four Centuries,* (London, 1965); Frye, N., *The Return of Eden: Five Essays on Milton's Epics,* (Toronto-London, 1965); Williamson, I., *Milton and Others,* (Chicago-London, 1965); J. H. Summers ed., *The Lyric and Dramatic Milton,* (New York-London, 1965); Gardner, H., *A Reading of Paradise Lost,* (Oxford, 1966) the Alexander lectures, delivered at the University of (Toronto, 1962); L. L. Marle, ed., *Milton: A Collection of Critical Essays,* (Englewood Cliffs, N.J., 1966); Lewalski, B. K., *Milton's Brief Epic: The Genre, Meaning and Art of Paradise Regained,* (Providence, R.I.-London, 1966); Rudrum, A., *Milton: Paradise Lost,* (London, 1966); Gransden, K. W., *Paradise Lost and the Aeneid,* in *Essays in Criticism* 17 1967; Murray, P., *Milton: The Modern Phase. A Study of Twentieth-Century Criticism,* (London, 1967); Patrides, C. A., *Milton and the Christian Tradition,* (Oxford, 1967); C. A. Patrides, ed., *Milton's Epic Poetry: Essays on Paradise Lost and Paradise Regained,* (Harmondsworth, 1967) contains a useful bibliography; Rudrum, A., *Comus, and Shorter Poems,* (London, 1967); Samuel, I., *Dante and Milton: The Commedia and Paradise Lost,* (London, 1967); Steadman, J. M., *Milton and the Renaissance Hero,* (London, 1967); Fish, S. E., *Surprised by Sin: The Reader in Paradise Lost,* (London-New York, 1967); Arthos, J., *Milton and the Italian Cities,* (London, 1968); Demaray, J. G., *Milton and the Masque Tradition . . . ,* (Cambridge, Mass.-London, 1968); Madsen, W. G., *From Shadowy Types to Truth: Studies in Milton's Symbolism,* (New Haven-London, 1968); Reesing, H., *Milton's Poetic Art: A Mask, Lycidas and Paradise Lost,* (Cambridge Mass.-London, 1968); Rudrum, A., *Milton, Modern Judgments,* (London, 1968); Marilla, E. L., *Milton and Modern Man,* (University, Ala., 1968); C. A. Patrides, ed., *Approaches to Paradise Lost,* (London, 1968); Carey, John, *Milton,* (London, 1969); Leishman, J. B., *Critical Essays from E. L. H.,* (Baltimore, 1969) reprints articles from *Journal of English Literary History; Milton's Minor Poems,* G. Tillotson, ed. (London, 1969); B. Rajan, ed., *Paradise Lost: A Tercentenary Tribute,* (Toronto-Buffalo-London, 1969); Simmonds, J. D., *Milton Studies,* vol. 1 (Pittsburgh, 1969) vol. II (Pittsburgh, 1970); Wedgwood, C. V., *Milton and His World,* (London, 1969).

Works of the 1970's include Halkett, J., *Milton and the Idea of Matrimony,* (New Haven, 1970); Hanford, J. H., *A Milton Handbook,* 5th ed. rev. by J. H. Hanford and J. G. Taaffe (New York, 1970); J. T. Shawcross, ed., *Milton: The Critical Heritage,* (London, 1970); *A Variorum Commentary on the Poems of John Milton,* (London, 1970–) vol. I "The Latin and Greek Poems," Bush, E., "The Italian Poems," Shaw, J. E., and Bartlett Giamatti; Ryken, L., *The Apocalyptic Vision in Paradise Lost,* (Ithaca, N.Y.-London, 1970); Blamires, H., *Milton's Creation: A Guide Through Paradise Lost,* (London, 1971); Hardy, J. P., *Reinterpretations: Essays on Poems by Milton, Pope and Johnson,* (London, 1971); Potter, L., *A Preface to Milton,* (London, 1971); J. A. Wittreich, ed., *The Romantics on Milton,* (Cleveland, 1971); Rees, B. R., *Aristotle's Theory and Milton's Practice: Samson Agonistes,* (Birmingham, 1972); Brisman, L., *Milton's Poetry of Choice and His Romantic Heirs,* (Ithaca, N.Y., 1973); Grose, C., *Milton's Epic Process: Paradise Lost and Its Miltonic Background,* (New Haven, 1973); Bouchard, G., *Milton: A Structural Reading,* (London, 1974); J. D. Simmons, ed., *Milton Studies,* (London-Pittsburgh, 1975); Crump, G. M., *The Mystical Design of Paradise Lost,* (Lewisburg, Pa., 1975); Steadman, J. H., *Epic and Tragic Structure in Paradise Lost,* (London-Chicago, 1977); Stein, A., *The Art of Presence: The Poet and Paradise Lost,* (London-Berkeley, 1977).

MISCELLANEOUS

Milton's Illustrators, William Blake made 53 illustrations for Milton's poetry, including 2 sets of watercolor drawings for *Comus,* (1801), 12 watercolor drawings for *Paradise Lost* (1807) and a second set of 9 drawings, (1808), 6 watercolor drawings for the "Nativity Ode," (1809), 12 designs illustrating "L'Allegro," and "Il Penseroso," (*ca.* 1816) and 12 watercolor drawings for *Paradise Regained* (*ca.* 1816). See Geoffrey Keynes, ed. *John Milton, Poems in English with Illustrations by William Blake* (London, 1926). Other major illustrators of Milton were Jean-Henri Füssli (1802) and John Martin, (1824–1826).

Milton's Poetry Set to Music: Henry Lawes composed the music for (*Comus,* 1634) Milton's "Sonnet to Henry Lawes," was set to music by Henry and William Lawes and appeared in their *Choice Psalmes, Put into Musick for Three Voices* (London, 1648). In 1677 Dryden wrote a rhymed opera, *The State of Innocence,* based on *Paradise Lost.*

Portraits of Milton, Williamson, G. C., *Milton Tercentenary: The Portraits, Prints and Writings of John Milton, Exhibited at Christ's College, Cambridge, 1908* (Cambridge, 1908); Granniss, R. S., *The Beverley Chew Collection of Milton Portraits,* (New York, 1926).

~

Marianne Moore
(1887–1972)

CELESTE GOODRIDGE

By the time Marianne Moore died in 1972, she had become a celebrity—America's beloved poet in the tricorne hat and black cape who was probably better known for some of her interests and public appearances than for her artistic endeavors. For many people, Moore was the famous poet who loved sports, particularly baseball. In her foreword to *A Marianne Moore Reader* she commented on her by then well-established "inordinate interest in animals and athletes":

> They are subjects for art and exemplars of it, are they not? minding their own business. Pangolins, hornbills, pitchers, catchers, do not pry or prey-or prolong the conversation; . . . I don't know how to account for a person who could be indifferent to miracles of dexterity, a certain feat by Don Zimmer—a Dodger at the time—making a backhand catch, of a ball coming hard from behind on the left, fast enough to take his hand off. (p. xvi)

In a 1964 interview with George Plimpton, we find her comparing "two such battling fielders as Roger Maris and Mickey Mantle [who] have at no time been diminished by internecine jealousies." In 1968 she threw out the first baseball of the season at Yankee Stadium. Later that year she predicted for the *New York Times* that the St. Louis Cardinals would win the World Series. (They did not.)

Even those who had not read with care her "animal" poems—"The Jerboa," "The Plumet Basilisk," "The Frigate Pelican," "The Buffalo," "The Pangolin," "The Paper Nautilus," and "The Wood-Weasel"—may have remembered that she made frequent trips to the circus and the zoo. Four years after Moore died, a photograph of her taken at the Bronx Zoo in 1953 was included in a *Life* magazine special report entitled "Remarkable American Women: 1776–1976." The caption is typical of how Moore was perceived by the end of her life:

> Poet Marianne Moore was skimming nimbly from her thoughts on wine labels to grocery stores to gardening to Goethe to the pyramids, when somebody begged, "Don't jump around so." Moore merely paused: "It isn't jumping around. It's all connected." So it was, by her spanning genius that incorporated steeplejacks, swans, baseball, buffalo, granite and steel, silence and years, everything she encountered—even the Bronx Zoo, below—into poetry that won almost every prize there was to win. Nor was her research limited to places she could reach by subway, her favorite transportation; she espied things in hard-to-get-to places, too, bringing back visions of "imaginary gardens with real toads in them."

Those who applauded Moore in this context may have forgotten, if they ever knew, that her *Collected Poems,* published in 1951, won the Pulitzer Prize, the National Book Award, and, in 1953, the Bollingen Award. It is even less likely that those who read *Life* also read Moore's brilliant, difficult, and two longest high modernist poems: "Marriage" (1923) and "An Octopus" (1924). Moore's public persona suggested an accessibility that was at odds with the intricate demands of her syllabic poetry and exacting prose.

Recognizing the extent to which Moore increasingly courted her visibility in the limelight, we can begin to approach the implications of this persona by considering the celebrated photograph of her, taken by George Platt Lynes, that appeared on the cover of *A Marianne Moore Reader* in 1961. (Moore had her portrait taken many times, often by the most famous photographers of her day: Lynes, Cecil Beaton, Marion Morehouse, Henri Cartier-Bresson, Diane Arbus, and Richard Avedon.) Donning her black cape and tricorne hat and holding her white gloves conspicuously in her lap, Moore embodies decorum, distance, formality, privacy, dignity, and above all a studied self-control. As several of her best critics have pointed out, her willingness to portray herself as a nonthreatening spinster poetess has had deleterious effects on her critical reception. Moore, Taffy Martin maintains, has been treated "as a decorative oddity rather than as an active and perhaps even dangerous force." Charles Tomlinson also notes that some of Moore's critics have reduced her "to the status of a kind of national pet." He also wonders "whether Marianne Moore has not suffered more from lax adulation than almost any other significant poet of our century."

Until recently many of Moore's critics have focused on her tendency to "armor" herself in her work and life. Both the subjects of her poems and her method of composing them have received scrutiny in this light. Many of her poems make extensive use of quotations from overheard conversations, travel brochures, newspapers, and her eclectic reading. Some of her readers have suggested that she hides behind her elaborate compositions. Randall Jarrell, for example, sees her poetic preoccupation with quotations and armored animals as indicative of her own need to be shielded.

Feminist critics such as Suzanne Juhasz and Alicia Ostriker also perceive Moore as armored; Juhasz maintains that Moore "was so successful in the literary world because she could at once capitalize on and repress different aspects of her femininity." Ostriker reads Moore's work and position in the modernist community primarily in terms of the self-image Moore constructed later in her life: "Yet would a sexual and powerful Marianne Moore have met with the respect accorded the chaste and ladylike, self-effacing spinster in the tricorne? There is no reason to think so."

By examining the archive Moore left, as well as the responses her contemporaries had to her work, critics have begun to reassess Moore's aesthetic in terms other than those provided by her public persona. The record does reveal that Moore was shy, reticent, and reserved; but in her letters she also emerges as deeply ambitious, confident, and outspoken, though (as several critics have recently pointed out) she was equally capable of denying her ambition. These contradictory postures, like her gestures of revealing and concealing herself in her poetry and prose, must be seen as integral to her aesthetic.

Moore's archive, housed at the Rosenbach Museum and Library in Philadelphia, is readily available to scholars. As if certain of her place in literary history, Moore maintained fastidious records of her activities, reading, conversations, and correspondence. In addition to the letters she received, she kept carbon copies of the letters she wrote. These documents, as well as her manuscripts, library, and reading and conversation notebooks, are invaluable for readers who wish to trace Moore's development as a poet and prose stylist.

Born on 15 November 1887 in Kirkwood, a suburb of St. Louis, Missouri, Marianne Craig Moore spent her formative years in her maternal grandfather's home. Her father, John Milton Moore, suffered a nervous breakdown and was institutionalized before Moore was born; she never saw him. Mary Warner Moore took Marianne and her brother, John Warner, to live with her father, the Reverend John Riddle Warner, who was the pastor of Kirkwood Presbyterian Church. When he died in 1894, the family moved to Carlisle, Pennsylvania, where Mrs. Moore taught English at the Metzger Institute.

Moore entered the class of 1909 at Bryn Mawr College; Hilda Doolittle (H. D.) was in her class, though they were not friends at the time. By 1915, however, they were corresponding; an early champion of Moore's, H. D. wrote the first review of Moore's poetry, a short, incisive essay that appeared in the *Egoist* in 1916. In the 1920s Moore reviewed H. D.'s poetry for the *Broom* and the *Dial.*

Moore was told at Bryn Mawr that she could not major in English because her writing was neither clear nor accessible; she majored instead in "history-politics-economics" and minored in biology. Her biology courses undoubtedly enhanced her ability to see her natural surroundings with a microscopic precision. Her poetry abounds with precise observations: "The diffident / little newt / with white pin-dots on black horizontal spaced- / out bands" in "The Steeple-Jack," the cat in "Peter" whose markings resemble "shad-bones regularly set about the mouth / to droop or rise in unison like porcupine-quills," "'the nine-striped chipmunk / running with unmammal-like agility along a log'" in "An Octopus," the pangolin, "Another armored animal-scale / lapping scale with spruce-cone regularity until they / form the uninterrupted central / tail-row!"

The high point of Moore's college studies seems to have been the course she took with Georgiana Goddard King entitled "Imitative Writing," in which the focus was on seventeenth-century prose writers: Francis Bacon, Thomas Browne, Lancelot Andrewes, Thomas Traherne, Richard Hooker, and Richard Burton. Specific references to these writers abound in Moore's prose; for example, in a 1926 *Dial* "Comment" she meditates on their succinctness, a quality not often remarked upon in writers such as Bacon, Donne, or Browne:

> We attribute to let us say Machiavelli, Sir Francis Bacon, John Donne, Sir Thomas Browne, Doctor Samuel Johnson, a particular kind of verbal effectiveness—a nicety and point, a pride and pith of utterance, which is in a special way different from the admirableness of Wordsworth or of Hawthorne. Suggesting conversation and strengthened by etymology there is a kind of effortless compactness which precludes ornateness, a "fearful felicity," in which, like the pig in the churn, imagination seems to provide its own propulsiveness. (*Dial* 80:444 [May 1926])

Moore imitates in her own style the qualities she admires in these writers: Johnson's balances are captured in her own—"a nicety and point, a pride and pith of utterance"—and Browne's bravura comes alive in Moore's final metaphor in the passage.

The influence of these seventeenth-century prose writers can also be seen in the notes Moore provided for her poems. When asked by Donald Hall in a 1960 interview if any prose stylists had helped her find her poetic style, Moore replied in the affirmative, and proceeded to quote from two seventeenth-century writers—Browne and Bacon—as well as from Johnson, Edmund Burke, Henry James, and Ezra Pound.

Although Moore wrote both poetry and fiction while in college, in her letters home she sought her family's approval for the poems. She published eight poems and eight short stories in the Bryn Mawr magazine, *Tipyn o'Bob,* between 1907 and 1909 but did not attempt to write fiction again until 1929. In 1933 she wrote to H. S. Latham of the Macmillan Publishing Company that she had been working on a piece of fiction since 1929 but was not sure she would ever finish it. Indeed, Moore never published the work.

During the summer of 1911, Moore and her mother traveled extensively in England and crossed the Channel to Paris. For Moore, the trip was enormously stimulating. Letters home to John Warner refer to a lock of Shelley's hair housed in the Bodleian Library at Oxford, the armor they saw in England, a Whistler exhibition at the Tate Gallery, Assyrian art at the British Museum and the Louvre, and Moore's desire to buy a Japanese print in Paris. Her letters, particularly those to her family, provide an invaluable record of the material Moore would later include in her poetry. Typically she would see something, take heed of it, and return to it later to use in one of her poems. For example, a swan she had seen at Oxford probably inspired the one she wrote about in "Critics and Connoisseurs" (1916).

Moore's reading and conversation notebooks, which she began keeping in 1916, also functioned as repositories where she could hoard material that might later appear in her poetry and prose. For example, quotations from Henry James's fiction, letters, and memoirs, as well as things said about him, find their way into "Picking and Choosing" (1920), "New York" (1921), "An Octopus" (1924), "Sea Unicorns and Land Unicorns" (1924), and her prose tribute to James, "Henry James as a Characteristic American" (1934). Her manuscript notes for a poem or essay may send a reader back to dozens of her reading notebooks for sources. Her library is also invaluable for reconstructing her trajectory toward a poem or review-essay.

The year 1915 was Moore's last in Carlisle, where she had been living with her mother since graduating from Bryn Mawr in 1909. It proved to be a productive year for her. She saw her poems in print for the first time that spring—two poems appeared in the *Egoist* (April) and five in *Poetry* (May). "To the Soul of 'Progress' "—retitled "To Military Progress" in *Observations* (1924), Moore's second volume of poetry—typifies her best early efforts. Addressing a "you," as she did in other early poems such as "To a Steam Roller" and "To Statecraft Embalmed," Moore indicts military activity by setting up an equivalence between that enterprise and a torso without a head. The crows, who presumably feast on that severed head, become "black minutemen / to revive again, / war / at little cost." They are left ominously at the end of the poem:

> They cry for the lost
> head
> and seek their prize
> till the evening's sky's
> red.

In the same year in which Moore first published individual poems, she also sent a manuscript of sixty-four poems to Erskine MacDonald of Malory House, which published a series of modern poets. They were not accepted; but by 1916 we find Moore corresponding with H. D. about placing a volume for her. Some years later this became her first collection of verse, *Poems* (1921); with H. D.'s support on Moore's behalf, it was published by the Egoist Press and paid for by Bryher (Winifred Ellerman). Moore's book was in good company; under Harriet Shaw Weaver's direction, the Egoist Press published work by H. D., T. S. Eliot, Ezra Pound, Robert McAlmon, and James Joyce.

In a 1960 interview conducted by Donald Hall, Moore was asked what her reaction had been to H. D. and Bryher's having published *Poems* without her knowledge and why she had not pursued the task herself. Moore replied:

> To issue my slight product—conspicuously tentative—seemed to me premature. . . . For the chivalry of the undertaking—issuing my verse for me in 1921, certainly in format choicer than in content—I am intensely grateful. . . . Desultory occasional magazine publications seemed to me sufficient and plenty conspicuous. ("The Art of Poetry IV: Marianne Moore," *Paris Review* 7, no. 26:48 [Winter 1961])

Moore's self-effacing statements to Hall clearly conflict with her earlier inquiries about placing the manuscript and the eager and persistent ambition she displayed in her letters. There is often a dissonance between what Moore revealed privately and what she publicly chose to say on the subject many years later.

In 1915 she also spent a week in New York City; studies of Moore's development and movement toward high modernism frequently highlight this event. Moore was catapulted out of her isolation by this week-long exposure to prominent artists, photographers, and writers and their work. Several letters to her brother provide the record of her encounters and the effect they had on her. Alfred Kreymborg, who had accepted some of Moore's poems for *Others,* invited her to dine with him and his wife; while there she saw photographs by Alfred Stieglitz and Edward Steichen. Later in the week she visited Stieglitz at his 291 Gallery; Moore was delighted to see more of his own photographs, issues of *Camera Work,* and the paintings he had collected by Marsden Hartley and Picasso. Stieglitz also arranged for her to meet J. B. Kerfoot, a drama critic for *Life,* whose work she had admired for some time.

Another high point of the week included a meeting with Guido Bruno, the publisher of *Bruno's Weekly* and *Bruno's Chap Books;* in 1916 he published four of Moore's poems: "Apropos of Mice," "Holes Bored in a Workbag by the Scissors," "In 'Designing a Cloak to Cloak his Designs,' you Wrested From Oblivion, a Coat of Immortality for your own Use," and "The Just Man And." These, like many of Moore's early poems published before 1924, were omitted from her *Complete Poems* (1967; rev. ed. 1981).

Complete Poems, in other words, is not complete. As Moore reminds us in her epigraph to the book, "omissions are not accidents." Therefore, a reader who wishes to study her development will need to recover those poems not included in *Complete Poems.* Also, since Moore revised many of the poems she did include, one is advised to seek out the earlier versions. "Poetry," for example, which was originally twenty-nine lines, became three lines in *Complete Poems,* though Moore preserved the earlier version in the notes to *Complete Poems.* The truncated version of the poem, as Margaret Phelan observes, "reads more like a Girl Scout Oath than a wry comment on the seductions of nongenuine rhymes."

In 1918, after spending two years in Chatham, New Jersey (where John Warner had been pastor of Ogden Memorial Church since 1916), Moore and her mother moved to Greenwich Village. The move was not surprising, given Moore's attachment to the literary and artistic circles of New York City. Around this time, in poems such as "Critics and Connoisseurs" (1916), "Picking and Choosing" (1920), and "Poetry" (1919), Moore began to carve out her complicated responses to writing. The original version of "Poetry" is one of her early attempts to map out her own "place for the genuine." Using long lines, and embedding quotations within her conversational lines, Moore makes a plea for language and speech rhythms not usually found in poetry: "nor is it valid / to discriminate against documents and / school-books'; all these phenomena are important."

T. S. Eliot might have been describing this poem when he wrote in 1923 that Moore's poetry contains "at least three elements: a quite new rhythm, . . . a peculiar and brilliant and rather satirical use of what is not, as material, an 'aristocratic' language at all, but simply the curious jargon produced in America by universal university education, . . . and finally an almost primitive simplicity of phrase."

Complementing Eliot's earlier assessment, Louise Bogan in 1947 commented preceptively on Moore's poetry:

> She is never . . . indifferent to what might strike her contemporaries as either precious or rubbish. Advertisements, travel folders, yesterday's newspaper, the corner movie, the daily shop and street, the fashion magazine, the photograph and the map—these phenomena are gathered into her art with the same care with which she "observes" small mammals, birds, reptiles; or with which she microscopically examines details of human artifacts: "sharkskin, camellia-leaf, orange-peel, semi-eggshell or *sang-de-boeuf* glaze" in Chinese porcelain, for example. Unlike a magpie, she is not attracted by any kind of glittering swag . . . She is occupied with the set task of imaginatively correlating the world's goods, natural and artificial, as a physician correlates "cases," or a naturalist, specimens. ("American to Her Backbone," in Bogan's *A Poet's Alphabet,* ed. Robert Phelps and Ruth Limmer [New York: McGraw-Hill, 1970], p. 307)

But these commentaries came later. In the late 1910s Moore, like so many other Americans, was preoccupied with World War I. Her brother had joined the Navy Chaplains' Corps in 1918; perhaps, as some have speculated, Moore had Warner on her mind when she composed several of her "war poems." "Reinforcements" (1918), which was included in *Poems* (1921) and *Observations* (1924), but deleted from subsequent collections, contains a direct reference to "military progress:"

> The vestibule to experience is not to
> be exalted into epic grandeur. These men
> are going
> to their work with this idea, advancing like
> a school of fish
> through
> still water—waiting to change the course or
> dismiss
> the idea of movement, till forced to. . . .

John Slatin points out that if we read "The Fish" in conjunction with "Reinforcements," as Moore invites us to do by placing them on opposite pages in *Observations,* we will see this poem as a commentary on World War I as well. The men who are "advancing like a school of fish" in "Reinforcements" become the fish who "Wade / through black jade" in "The Fish." We are in wasteland uninhabited by a human presence, yet saturated with human destruction:

> . . . one
> keeps
> adjusting the ash heaps;
> opening and shutting itself like
>
> an
> injured fan.
> The barnacles which encrust the
> side
> of the wave, cannot hide

The swimming fish become "a turquoise sea / of bodies"; this ominous image announces a destruction that is barely contained by the form of the poem. Finally, however, Moore's patterned syllabic lines and rhymes provide an order against which the desolation and impending wreckage of this world can be controlled.

Not long after her move to New York, in 1920, Moore had her first poems accepted by Scofield Thayer at the *Dial.* In his memoir, *Troubadour,* Alfred Kreymborg claims to have been present on this momentous occasion:

> About two in the morning, she read something one could barely hear about "England with its baby rivers and little towns," "Italy with its equal shores." . . .A beautiful poem few of the guests could hear distinctly, but which the mystery man from *The Dial* heard so well, he stole over to her and, after a whispered consultation, induced her to part with it. Marianne was the first of "the old guard" to be accepted by the new magazine. (1957 ed., p. 260).

A footnote to Kreymborg's anecdote of Moore's work being solicited by the *Dial* might include the fact that Moore had sent the poem to the *Dial* some time before, but had had it rejected.

"England" appeared, along with "Picking and Choosing," in the April issue of the *Dial.* The celebration of America, and things American, in "England" would not have been wasted on those who had seen "Poetry" in 1919:

> . . . and America where there
> is the little old ramshackle victoria in the
> south,
> where cigars are smoked on the street in the
> north;
> where there are no proof-readers, no
> silkworms, no digressions;
>
> the wild man's land; grassless, linksless,
> languageless country in
> which letters are written
> not in Spanish, not in Greek, not in Latin,
> not in shorthand,
> but in plain American which cats and dogs
> can read!

In 1921, Moore took a part-time job at the Hudson Park branch of the New York Public

Library. She worked there until she became editor of the *Dial* in 1925. Louise Bogan, who worked at the same branch in the early 1920s, remembers Moore fondly:

> . . . I remember very well, working with her in the winter afternoons, upstairs in that library with its general atmosphere of staleness and city dinginess.—Her hair was then a beautiful shade of red; she wore it in a thick braid. She was continually comparing the small objects with which we worked—mucilage brushes and ink and stamping rubbers—to oddly analogous objects; and she smiled often and seemed happy. . . . (*What the Woman Lived: Selected Letters of Louise Bogan,* ed. Ruth Limmer [New York: Harcourt Brace Jovanovich, 1973], pp. 238–239)

In 1921 Moore published "New York," a poem that exemplifies her readiness to respond to the economic and historical conditions of her environment. In that year, as her note reminds us, "New York succeeded St. Louis as the center of the wholesale fur trade." The first part of the poem comically calls attention to the gap between "the scholastic philosophy of the wilderness" and the economy of "the beau with the muff":

> It is a far cry from the "queen full of jewels"
> and the beau with the muff,
> from the gilt coach shaped like a perfume-
> bottle,
> to the conjunction of the Monongahela and
> the Allegheny,
> and the scholastic philosophy of the
> widerness.

This comic dissonance, and the distance it affords Moore, allows her in the remainder of the poem to offer an extended critique of the opposition between the "plunder" that "the wholesale fur trade" of New York promotes and the " 'accessibility to experience' " the city affords:

> It is not the dime-novel exterior,
> Niagara Falls, the calico horses and the war-
> canoe;
> it is not that "if the fur is finer than such as
> one sees others wear,
> one would rather be without it"—
> that estimated in raw meat and berries, we
> could feed the universe;
> it is not the atmosphere of ingenuity,
> the other, the beaver, the puma skins
> without shooting-irons or dogs;
> it is not the plunder,
> but "accessibility to experience."

"Marriage" (1923) was critical of another economy—the institution of marriage. Perhaps prompted by Bryher and McAlmon's sudden elopement in 1921, the poem moves beyond this occasion:

> I wonder what Adam and Eve
> think of it by this time,
> this fire-gilt steel
> alive with goldenness;
> how bright it shows—
> "of circular traditions and impostures,
> committing many spoils,"
> requiring all one's criminal ingenuity
> to avoid!

Soon after the poem begins, Moore constructs a dialogue between Adam and Eve in which they agree, at Adam's urging, to be "alone together. Later a more contemporary couple takes over. Quotations from Sir Francis Bacon, Richard Baxter, *Scientific American,* the *New Republic,* Anthony Trollope, William Hazlitt, Shakespeare's *The Tempest,* Daniel Webster, and Ezra Pound enable Moore to orchestrate her critique of "eternal union" from a calculated and wry distance.

William Carlos Williams' reading of "Marriage" in 1925 serves to illuminate much of Moore's poetry up to this time, particularly the effect her mosaic of quotations can have. "A poem such as 'Marriage,' " he maintains, "is an anthology of transit. It is a pleasure that can be held firm only by moving rapidly from one thing to the next. It gives the impression of a passage through." Williams might have been describing "An Octopus" as well. In this poem, Moore's rapid eye takes us at a dizzying pace through a landscape where things are known through partial disclosures. Her celebration of epistemological uncertainty masterfully affirms the power of the glimpse, the half-seen, and the fragment as a structure of knowledge.

The very subject of the poem demands that Moore keep moving her own perspective; the glacier appears to be stationary—"it lies 'in grandeur and in mass' "—and yet is surrounded by the motion of "a sea of shifting snow-dunes." Far from being stationary and predictable, this glacier of "unimagined delicacy" can kill "with the concentric crushing rigor of the python." Even the mountain's seemingly accessible facade becomes inseparable from the forces "which prove it a volcano. Mount Rainier, despite the presence of "Paradise Park," becomes a land mine in its potential for danger. Only an attentive eye can negotiate the dangers while embracing the pleasures of "the passage through."

During the early 1920s Moore also emerged as a perceptive critic of her contemporaries. Her first published essay, "Samuel Butler," appeared in 1916 in William Rose Benét's short-lived magazine the *Chimaera,* and she continued to publish prose up until the last few years before her death. Her subjects were varied, but as with her poetry, her best efforts came early—in the 1920s and 1930s—and usually in the form of reviews of her contemporaries. Her prose contributions to the *Dial*—the reviews, essays, "Briefer Mentions," and "Comments" that she wrote between 1921 and 1929—form a separate chapter in the history of modernism; her reviews of the most difficult writers of her time—Stevens, Eliot, Pound, Williams, Stein, H. D., Auden, Bishop, and Kenneth Burke—give us new insights into her own aesthetic.

In 1918, Moore published reviews of T. S. Eliot's *Prufrock and Other Observations,* Jean de Bosschères *The Closed Door,* and W. B. Yeats's *The Wild Swans at Coole, Other Verses, and a Play in Verse.* While these do not begin to define her critical practice of imitating in her own prose style some quality of the writer under review, they do suggest that Moore's desire to be a poet was linked from the start with her commitment to the writing of prose.

In 1921 Moore reviewed Eliot's *The Sacred Wood* for the *Dial* and Williams's *Kora in Hell* for *Contact.* Praising Williams's "compression, color, speed, accuracy, and that restraint of instinctive craftsmanship which precludes anything dowdy or labored," Moore concludes:

> But one who sets out to appraise him has temerity, since he speaks derisively of the wish of certain of his best friends to improve his work and,aafter all, the conflict between the tendency to aesthetic anarchy and the necessity for self imposed discipline must take care of itself. (*Contact* 4:7 [January–March 1921])

In her review of *The Sacred Wood* Moore also openly challenges Eliot when she defends Swinburne as a critic and as a poet. She then silences, or disguises, this difference at the end of the review, when she uses a quotation from Swinburne to shed light on Eliot's criticism:

> In his opening a door upon the past and indicating what is there, he recalls the comment made by Swinburne upon Hugo:
>
> "Art knows nothing of death; . . . all that ever had life in it, has life in it for ever; those themes only are dead which never were other than dead. No form is obsolete, no subject out of date, if the right man be there to rehandle it." (*Dial* 70:339 [March 1921])

This particular use of quotation—quoting one person on someone else to reveal something about a third person—became a distinctive characteristic of Moore's critical method of approaching her contemporaries. As she quotes Swinburne on Hugo, Moore momentarily drops out of sight, fusing her own judgment implicitly with Swinburne's and avoiding an overt disagreement with Eliot concerning the value of Swinburne's criticism.

In 1924 Moore reviewed Wallace Stevens's *Harmonium.* "Well Moused, Lion," which appeared in the *Dial,* was one of the most positive reviews that Stevens received. Applauding Stevens's "appetite for color," his "precise diction and verve," and his "positiveness, aplomb, and verbal security," Moore also confronts his "deliberate bearishness."

> One resents the temper of certain of these poems. Mr. Stevens is never inadvertently crude; one is conscious, however, of a deliberate bearishness—a shadow of acrimonious, unprovoked contumely. Despite the sweet-Clementine-will-you-be-mine nonchalance of the Apostrophe to Vincentine, one feels oneself to be in danger of unearthing the ogre and in Last Looks at the Lilacs, a pride in unserviceableness is suggested which makes it a microcosm of cannibalism. (*Dial* 76:86 [January 1924])

Moore's willingness to censure her contemporaries has received little attention. Most considerations of her criticism stress the extent to which she always praised her subjects. Moore's public persona undoubtedly fueled this perception. A case in point is her self-effacing foreword to *Predilections* (1955)—the only collection of her prose published during her lifetime—in which she implies that she translated only those whose projects she unconditionally admired. A close look at her correspondence and *The Complete Prose* documents that Moore was quite capable—particularly in her early reviews—of expressing her distaste for a writer under review.

In 1924 Moore received the *Dial* Award for her second volume of poetry, *Observations.* This prestigious award, which included a generous stipend of two thousand dollars, had been given to T. S. Eliot in 1922 for "The Waste Land." Before the decade was over, Cummings (1925), Williams (1926), and Pound (1927) would receive the award.

Although Moore claimed that *Observations* was a reprint of *Poems* (1921) with some new poems, it constituted a major addition to her canon. She deleted four of the poems from her earlier volume, revised many of the poems she did include, and added thirty-three new poems. *Observations* also included fifteen pages of notes directing readers to some of Moore's obscure and unlikely sources for her many quotations, and a long, detailed index.

When Moore became acting editor of the *Dial* in 1925, that magazine was well established. In an essay for *Life and Letters To-day* (December 1940), she recalled some of the writers she had encountered as a subscriber: Yeats, Paul Valéry, D. H. Lawrence, Ford Madox Ford, Cummings, Williams, Stevens, Thomas Mann, Pound, and H. D. She also provided a catalog of some of the artwork that appeared in its pages:

> Among the pictures, as intensives on the text, were three verdure-tapestry-like wood-cuts by Galanis; Rousseau's lion among lotuses; "The Philosophers" by Stuart Davis; Adolph Dehn's "Viennese Coffee House"; and Kuniyoshi's curious "Heifer"—the forehead with a star on it of separate whorled strokes like propeller-fins . . . John Marin, Georgia O'Keeffe, . . . Brancusi, Lachaise, . . . Picasso . . . Cocteau line drawings, and Seurat's Circus. (*Life and Letters To-day* 27:177 [December 1940])

A close look at the *Dial* as it appeared when Moore was editor shows that she did not alter the character or appearance of the magazine. In fact, Moore will probably be remembered more for the prose she wrote during the years she worked there than for her editorial decisions.

When the *Dial* folded in 1929, Moore and her mother moved from Greenwich Village to Brooklyn. They sought quieter lodgings and wanted to be near John Warner, who was assigned to the Brooklyn Navy Yard. Although Moore did not publish any poems between 1925 and 1932, we do well to remember that by 1925 she had published some of her finest poems, perfected her use of syllabic and free verse, changed the shape of the poetic line, called for a new range of subject matter, and altered the way allusions and quotations had been used in poetry. Her duties at the *Dial* undoubtedly contributed to her silence during this period. Another factor may have been that when the *Dial* folded, she began working on a piece of fiction that we know from her correspondence with Macmillan she did not abandon until sometime after 1933.

By the 1930s Moore enjoyed a unique place among her contemporaries: She was a major poetic voice, an often brilliant champion of her peers' work, and she had been the editor of one of the leading journals of her time. She matched Eliot and Pound in her commitment to arts and letters. Her immersion in modernism and her astute promotion of some of the best work being produced were immediately visible. In October of 1931 Pound wrote to Harriet Monroe at *Poetry*, wondering if Moore might be persuaded to take over as editor:

> It shd. also be possible to get a certain amount of backing for Marianne that wd. *not* be available for the wild and boisterous or cerebral younger males. . . . I don't know how much she makes at whatever she is doing; someday or other she will presumably need less and have less weight to carry . . . etc. . . . Idunno 'bout the Chicago pt. of view. Nothing but a definite position wd. I suppose take M. M. to Chicago or move her from one side of 4th Ave. to the other. But Chicago might be inspirationated to BRING one of the best contemporary Amurkun minds into Chicago. After all Marianne wuz born in St. Louis and can be claimed by the West in general. (*The Selected Letters of Ezra Pound*, 1907–1941, ed. D. D. Paige [New York: New Directions, 1971], pp. 235–236)

Given Moore's position in the literary community, Pound's request was a logical one. The following month, he sent a similar letter to Moore, only to discover that she was not interested in making the move.

Also in 1931 Moore published her first review of Pound's *Cantos* in *Poetry*; it was the longest review *Poetry* had ever printed. Praising *A Draft of XXX Cantos* as "the epic of the farings of a literary mind," she did not hesitate to add her criticism to Eliot's and Williams's:

> T. S. Eliot suspects Mr. Pound's philosophy of being antiquated. W. C. Williams finds his "versification *still* patterned after classic metres"; and, apropos of "feminolatry," is not the view of woman expressed by the Cantos older-fashioned than that of Siam and Abyssinia? (*Poets* 39:4344 [October 1931])

In 1934, Moore met Elizabeth Bishop; they corresponded regularly for the next thirty-six years. Moore initially helped to promote Bishop's early poetry, but frequently asked her to consider making certain revisions. Some of Moore's suggestions were heeded. Many were not.

In 1940, for example, they had a spirited exchange about Bishop's poem "Roosters." Moore objected to the use of the phrase "water closet" and wanted Bishop to change the title from "Roosters" to "Cocks." Bishop remembers this incident in her memoir "Efforts of Affection":

> One long poem, the most ambitious I had up to then attempted, apparently stirred both her and her mother to an immediate flurry of criticism. She telephoned the day after I had mailed it to her, and said that she and her mother had sat up late rewriting it for me. . . . Their version of it arrived in the next mail. . . . My version had rhymed throughout, in rather strict stanzas, but Marianne and her mother's version broke up the stanzas irregularly. Some lines rhymed and some didn't; a few other colloquialisms besides "water closet" had been removed and a Bible reference or two corrected. I obstinately held on to my stanzas and rhymes, but I did make use of a few of the proffered new words. (Bishop, pp. 55–58)

It may strike some as odd that Mrs. Moore figured so prominently in Moore's correspondence with Bishop. It should be remembered, however, that Marianne consulted family members, particularly her mother, on many literary matters. Bishop recalls that Mrs. Moore's "manner toward Marianne was that of a kindly, self-controlled parent who felt that she had to take a firm line, that her daughter might be given to flightiness or—an equal sin, in her eyes—mistakes in grammar."

Moore frequently talked with her mother about her own poems and those she was reading or reviewing; Mrs. Moore, who was a good match for her daughter, could be quite outspoken in her criticism and assessments. Moore also incorporated her mother's phrases into her poems and reviews; she was even known to quote her mother in letters to her contemporaries: Eliot, H. D., Williams, Pound, and Stevens. And, as Laurence Stapleton points out, "In Distrust of Merits" (1943)—Moore's well-known poem about World War II—draws substantively on her mother's responses to the war.

In 1935 Faber and Faber, at Eliot's suggestion, published Moore's *Selected Poems* with an introduction by Eliot. He asserted, "Miss Moore is . . . one of those few who have done the language some service in my lifetime." And he concluded that "Moore's poems form part of the small body of durable poetry written in our time. . . ."

Between 1932 and 1935 Moore had published over a dozen new poems. Eliot placed ten of these at the beginning of *Selected Poems.* Some of these poems from the 1930s appeared initially, though not in subsequent collections of Moore's work, under a common heading: "The Steeple-Jack," "The Student," and "The Hero," were published in *Poetry* in June 1932 under the title "Part of a Novel, Part of a Poem, Part of a Play"; "The Buffalo" and "Nine Nectarines and Other Porcelain" appeared in *Poetry* in November 1934 under the title "Imperious Ox, Imperial Dish"; and "Virginia Britannia," "Smooth Gnarled Crape Myrtle," "Bird-Witted," and "Half Deity" were published in *The Pangolin and Other Verse* (1936) under the title "The Old Dominion."

Moore's poems from this period represent a notable departure from her poems of the 1920s. She abandoned her previous use of free verse and adopted stanzas with rhyme patterns. We no longer race to keep up with her eye; the aesthetic of the glimpse or partial disclosure is replaced by a more controlled marshaling of quotations, facts, and assertions; all are offered with a certain dogged conviction of incontrovertibility. We also notice that Moore minimizes her own presence in these poems: She seldom uses "I" to frame her remarks.

Moore's relationship to her "American" landscape has changed as well: she moves from an affirmation of epistemological uncertainty in "An Octopus" to the certainty of elegiac mourning in "Virginia Britannia":

> The live oak's darkening filigree
> of undulating boughs, the etched
> solidity of a cypress indivisible
> from the now agèd English hackberry,
> become with lost identity,
> part of the ground, as sunset flames
> increasingly
> against the leaf-chiseled
> blackening ridge of green. . . .

Many of these poems, particularly the ones that take as their ostensible subject certain animals, have led critics to see Moore as someone whose aesthetic required that she conceal herself. For such readers, Moore becomes "the frigate pelican" who "hides / in the height and in the majestic / display of his art," "the jerboa" who "honors the sand by assuming its color," or "the plumet basilisk . . . alive there / in his basilisk cocoon beneath / the one of living green.

Critics have been divided about the quality of Moore's poetry in the 1940s, 1950s, and 1960s. Bonnie Costello, for example, sees a decline in Moore's poetry after the 1930s, while Laurence Stapleton argues that Moore's later poetry represents an advance. While poems like "Rigorists" (1940) and "Light Is Speech" (1941) suffer from a lack of intensity of purpose, poems like "What Are Years?" (1940) and "In Distrust of Merits" (1943) are as fine as any poems Moore ever wrote. These poems are assertively confrontational in their questions and conclusions: "What is our innocence, / what is our guilt? All are / naked, none is safe." By the 1960s, however, in poems like "Baseball and Writing" and "To Victor Hugo of My Crow Pluto," Moore strives for an unnatural lightness of tone that lends her vision a certain hollowness.

In 1945, at Auden's request, Moore began her translation of La Fontaine's *Fables;* nine years later—after seven revisions—she published *The Fables of La Fontaine* with Viking Press. During the early 1940s she tended her mother, who by 1946 was bedridden; Mrs. Moore died in 1947, leaving Marianne with a deep grief and an uncertain freedom. They had been living together since 1909, when Moore returned from Bryn Mawr.

Moore produced several additional translations in the 1950s. In 1954, the same year her translation of La Fontaine appeared, she wrote a play entitled *The Absentee,* based on Maria Edgeworth's novel of the same title. It was published in 1962. In 1963 she published a translation of three Perrault fairy tales, *Puss in Boots, The Sleeping Beauty,* and *Cinderella.*

By the time her *Collected Poems* appeared in 1951, Moore had received the Helen Haire Levinson Prize from *Poetry* (1932), the Ernest Hartsock Memorial Prize (1935), the Shelley Memorial Award (1940), and a Guggenheim Fellowship (1945), and had been elected to membership in the National Institute of Arts and Letters. She had also adopted the tricorne hat and black cape. One story has it that she purchased the hat in the late 1940s with the request that she be attired so as to look like Washington crossing the Delaware; another story states that she purchased the hat for the National Book Award dinner (1951). What is clear is that Moore carved out an image of herself as an American public poet. And she offered this persona to her audience as she once had offered her poems and essays.

This persona increasingly dominated her public's perception of her. When Moore threw out the first baseball of the season at Yankee Stadium in 1968, it is unlikely that her fans knew that she had been awarded the National Medal for Literature that year. Nor was it probably known, when she died in New York City on 5 February 1972, that she had been awarded sixteen honorary degrees.

Today Marianne Moore's place in the canon of modern American poetry is secure. Lauded and taught with the same frequency that Emily Dickinson is, she is once again the poet's poet who enjoys the same visibility as her contemporaries—H. D., Eliot, Williams, Pound and Stevens.

Selected Bibliography

PRIMARY WORKS

POETRY

Poems, (London: Egoist Press, 1921).
Observations, (New York: Dial Press, 1924).
Selected Poems, (New York: Macmillan; London: Faber and Faber, 1935).
The Pangolin and Other Verse, (London: Brendin, 1936).
What Are Years, (New York: Macmillan, 1941).
Nevertheless, (New York: Macmillan, 1944).
Like a Bulwark, (New York: Viking Press, 1956).
O to Be a Dragon, (New York: Viking Press, 1959).
Tell Me, Tell Me: Granite, Steel and Other Topics, (New York: Viking Press, 1966).

TRANSLATION

The Fables of La Fontaine, (New York: Viking Press, 1954).

PROSE

Predilections, (New York: Viking Press, 1955).

COLLECTIONS

Collected Poems, (New York: Macmillan, 1951).
A Marianne Moore Reader, (New York: Viking Press, 1961).
The Complete Poems of Marianne Moore, (New York: Macmillan and Viking Press, 1967). Rev. ed. (New York: Viking Press, 1981).
The Complete Prose of Marianne Moore, edited by Patricia C. Willis (New York: Viking Press, 1986.

MANUSCRIPTS AND PAPERS

The Rosenbach Museum and Library, Philadelphia. Houses Moore's correspondence, manuscripts, notebooks, and library.

The Collection of American Literature, Beinecke Rare Book and Manuscript Library, Yale University. Houses correspondence and papers associated with Moore's tenure at the *Dial.*

The Henry W. and Albert A. Berg Collection, New York Public Library. Houses additional *Dial* correspondence: Moore's letters to and from James Sibley Watson, Jr.

MARIANNE MOORE

SECONDARY WORKS

Bishop, Elizabeth, "Efforts of Affection: A Memoir of Marianne Moore," *Vanity Fair,* 46 4:44–61 (June 1983).

Blackmur, R.P., "The Method of Marianne Moore," *The Double-Agent: Essay on Craft and Elucidation,* (New York: Arrow, 1935) 141–171.

Costello, Bonnie, *Marianne Moore: Imaginary Possessions,* (Cambridge, Mass: Harvard University Press, 1981).

Engel, Bernard F., *Marianne Moore,* (New York: Twayne, 1964); rev. ed. (1989).

Goodridge, Celeste, *Hints and Disguises: Marianne Moore and Her Contemporaries,* (Iowa City: University of Iowa Press, 1989).

Hadas, Pamela White, *Marianne Moore: Poet of Affection,* (Syracuse, N.Y.: Syracuse University Press, 1977).

Hall, Donald, *Marianne Moore: The Cage and the Animal,* (New York: Western, 1970).

Holley, Margaret, *The Poetry of Marianne Moore: A Study in Voice and Value,* (Cambridge and New York: Cambridge University Press, 1987).

Jarrell, Randall, "Her Shield," *In His Poetry and the Age,* (New York: Alfred A. Knopf, 1953; New York: Ecco Press, 1980).

Juhasz, Suzanne, *Naked and Fiery Forms: Modern American Poetry by Women-a New Tradition,* (New York: Harper Colophon, 1976).

Kalstone, David, "Trial Balances: Elizabeth Bishop and Marianne Moore," *Grand Street,* 3:115–135 (Autumn 1983).

Kalstone, David, *Becoming a Poet: Elizabeth Bishop with Marianne Moore and Robert Lowell,* edited by Robert Hemenway (New York: Farrar, Straus & Giroux, 1989).

Keller, Lynn, "Words Worth a Thousand Postcards: The Bishop-Moore Correspondence," *American Literature,* 55: 405–429 (October 1983).

Marianne Moore Newsletter, Philadelphia (1977–).

Martin, Taffy, *Marianne Moore: Subversive Modernist,* (Austin: University of Texas Press, 1986).

Molesworth, Charles, *Marianne Moore: A Literary Life,* (New York: Atheneum, 1990).

Monroe, Harriet, "A Symposium on Marianne Moore," *Poetry,* 19: 208–216 (January 1922).

Nitchie, George, *Marianne Moore: An Introduction to Poetry,* (New York: Columbia University Press, 1969).

Ostriker, Alicia S., *Stealing the Language: The Emergence of Women's Poetry in America,* (Boston: Beacon Press, 1986).

Phelan, Margaret M., "H. D. and Marianne Moore: Correspondences and Contradictions," Ph.D. diss., Rutgers University (1987).

Phillips, Elizabeth, *Marianne Moore,* (New York: Frederick Ungar, 1982).

Poesis: A Journal of Criticism 6, nos. 3/4 (1985). Special Moore/H. D. issue.

Quarterly Review of Literature 4, no. 2 (1948). Special Marianne Moore issue;

Sagetrieb 6, no. 3 (Winter 1987). Special Marianne Moore issue.

Schweik, Susan, *Critical Inquiry,* "Writing War Poetry Like a Woman," 13: 532–556 (Spring 1987).

Schulman, Grace, *Marianne Moore: The Poetry of Engagement,* (Urbana and Chicago: University of Illinois Press, 1986).

Slatin, John, *The Savage's Romance: The Poetry of Marianne Moore,* (University Park: Pennsylvania State University Press, 1986).

Stapleton, Laurence, *Marianne Moore: The Poet's Advance,* (Princeton: Princeton University Press, 1978).

Steinman, Lisa M., *Made in America: Science, Technology, and American Modernist Poets,* (New Haven: Yale University Press, 1987).

Tomlinson, Charles ed. *Marianne Moore: A Collection of Critical Essays,* (Englewood Cliffs, N.J.: Prentice-Hall, 1969).

Twentieth Century Literature 30, nos. 2/3 (1984). Special Marianne Moore issue.

Weatherhead, A. Kingsley, *The Edge of the Image: Marianne Moore, William Carlos Williams and Some Other Poets,* (Seattle: University of Washington Press, 1967).

Willis, Patricia, C. *Marianne Moore: Vision into Verse,* (Philadelphia: The Rosenbach Museum and Library, 1987).

BIBLIOGRAPHIES

Abbott, Craig S., *Marianne Moore: A Descriptive Bibliography,* (Pittsburgh: University of Pittsburgh Press, 1977).

Abbott, Craig S., *Marianne Moore: A Reference Guide,* (Boston: G. K. Hall, 1978).

SYLVIA PLATH
(1932–1963)

DAVID CRAIG AUSTIN

SYLVIA PLATH'S IS a poetry of extremes, not so much the extremes of light and dark as of darkness itself: "This is the light of the mind, cold and planetary," begins "The Moon and the Yew Tree," a poem from late 1961. "The trees of the mind are black. The light is blue." The extremes of darkness—black, blacker, blackest—also serve as biography, reductive though not far from truth. For Sylvia Plath was constantly making and unmaking both her life—she once attempted, and later committed, suicide—and her work.

Few recent poets have undergone as many literary and biographical postmortems as has Plath. The cult of her personality, and of her poems and prose, has seemed at times to be an industry. The body of work she herself saw into print—*The Colossus* (1962), a volume of poems, and *The Bell Jar* (1971), a pseudonymous novel—is far outweighed by work published posthumously. This imbalance has confused the issue of how Plath wished to present herself to the world: as tragic heroine; as accomplished poet; as author of slick magazine fiction; as dutiful if troubled daughter? She was all of these. What she was not, what she never lived to be, was a writer who matured enough, in both age and achievement, to be merely herself.

Born on 27 October 1932 in the Jamaica Plain district of Boston, Sylvia Plath was the only daughter of Otto Plath, a German immigrant, university professor, and published scientist whose book *Bumblebees and Their Ways* appeared in 1934. Aurelia Schober Plath, Sylvia's mother, was twenty-one years her husband's junior and had been one of his students; after their marriage she was her husband's assistant and typist. Thus theirs was a working home. The late 1920s and the 1930s saw the collapse of the American economy, the Great Depression, and the subsequent hardships suffered by many families. With the influx of Europeans during these difficult years, many Americans looked askance on such immigrants, particularly Germans, many of them holding Germany responsible for World War I.

The family lived under Mr. Plath's domination until he fell ill with what he feared was cancer (then perceived as a disease of the weak) but was in fact diabetes. Chiefly from a refusal to seek treatment until permanent damage had been done, Mr. Plath died shortly after Sylvia's eighth birthday. In spite of her father's death, Plath's childhood seems to have been relatively uncomplicated. "[I was] brought up . . . in the fairy-tale world of Mary Poppins and Winnie-the-Pooh," she once wrote sardonically. Being raised by a single working mother (Mrs. Plath taught German and Spanish at the high school level and then a course for medical secretaries at Boston University) was a situation in which many American children found themselves in the 1940s. Husbands and fathers went off to war, many not to return. Although Otto Plath was neither war hero nor casualty, the coincidence of his Germanic heritage, his death, and World War II contributed to his metamorphosis in "Daddy" (1962), Plath's most famous poem, into "a man in black with a Meinkampf look." The metamorphosis lay years in the future, though its seeds were almost certainly planted with his death.

Preoccupied with Plath's younger brother and the demands of running a household that now included her own parents, Mrs. Plath must have appeared to her daughter as a distant if sometimes beneficent figure. A paradigm of the bright, well-behaved young lady, Plath began at an early age to court her mother's approval and affection, often with small poems and handmade greeting cards. The work of a talented, precocious apprentice, Plath's first poems were published in the *Christian Science Monitor* and her first fiction in *Seventeen,* a magazine for young women. On the strength of these and other accomplishments, she entered Smith College in the fall of 1950.

Plath was one of a generation of women encouraged to move beyond secondary education, though college was rarely considered an end in itself. Most often, college was the means to marriage or to a brief career followed by marriage. An educated woman with no husband seemed suspect, an oddity. Plath's Smith journals are filled with such arguments, and with heated refutations. She wanted desperately to be a writer and less to marry, to lose herself in societal definitions of male-female relationships, afraid that her talents would be dismissed by a husband and thus disappear.

Plath's early poems reflect these concerns. "Female Author," an early sonnet reprinted in an appendix of juvenilia to *The Complete Poems,* is a marriage daydream cynically rendered: "All day she plays at chess with the bones of the world: / Favored . . . she lies on cushions curled / And nibbles an occasional bonbon of sin." Another recounts the tale of Cinderella, the fatherless girl whose one chance for love is spoiled (and not, in the poem, regained) by time. The quantity of Plath's juvenilia is astounding. She once hoped to write a thousand words a day and reportedly relied heavily on a thesaurus for inspiration and guidance. The poems, with their insistence on form and technique, on language as a timepiece that works best when wound to a point shy of breaking, seem almost to belong to another time.

Returning from a month-long student editorship at *Mademoiselle* magazine in the summer of 1953, Plath suffered a nervous breakdown and later attempted suicide. The ambitious, successful young student became that summer a woman whose sense of self failed. "I will have to be cheerful and constructive," she writes in her journal, a sort of pep talk. "I will learn about shopping and cooking, and try to make Mother's vacation happy and good. That in itself would be worthwhile." *I will, I will,* the litany continues. From learning shorthand to writing daily for hours, to reading James Joyce, Plath set goals for herself that she could not meet. The suicide attempt unsuccessful, Plath was hospitalized for psychiatric treatment. A journal entry from February 1956 describes one "shock treatment that went wrong" as "waking to a new world, with no name, being born again, and not a woman." (Plath's experience of electroshock therapy is memorialized in a 1960 poem, "The Hanging Man," and echoed in the fascination of *The Bell Jar's* heroine with the execution by electrocution of Julius and Ethel Rosenberg, who had been convicted of providing the Soviets with atomic secrets.)

Few writings survive from that summer, if they ever existed. What some readers take for the truth of that time is *The Bell Jar,* a somewhat fictionalized account of this period in Plath's life. But even the "truth" of *The Bell Jar* has been called into question, and a lawsuit in the late 1980s contested the portrayal of one character as a lesbian. Plath herself called the novel a "potboiler," and while the "events" may be autobiographical, they are distorted, much as they are later in the poetry. Never "confessional" in the given sense of the word, Plath's poems are her life transformed into a sort of pagan fable. That Plath has been called a confessional poet stems in part from gossip about her life and in part from Robert Lowell's introduction to *Ariel*: "Everything in these poems is personal, confessional, felt." Although Lowell tempers the claim by writing that "the manner of [Plath's] feeling is controlled hallucination, the autobiography of a fever," the temperance all but vanishes when he states that "her art's immortality is life's disintegration."

In the spring term of 1954, Plath returned to Smith, and graduated in May of the following year. She had long hoped to pursue graduate work abroad, and was awarded a Fulbright Scholarship to study at Newnham College, Cambridge University. At Cambridge her work began to throw off its undergraduate enthusiasms. "Winter Landscape, with Rooks," written in 1956, is described in her journals as "athletic," by which we can presume she meant the poem's construction, its form: three five-line stanzas, rhymes more slant than not ("ice" and "solace," "frost" and "waste"). The poem is also described as "a psychic landscape"—an example of the pathetic fallacy, which John Ruskin described as a morbid "falseness in all our impressions of external things," most importantly in nature. The pathetic fallacy was a device Plath used in nearly all of her landscape poems, sometimes to great effect. "I am at my best in illogical, sensuous description," she once wrote. The second stanza of "Winter Landscape" begins thus:

> The austere sun descends above the fen,
> an orange cyclops-eye, scorning to look
> longer on this landscape of chagrin.

These lines are characteristic of Plath's poems from the early 1950s. Not only do we find the pathetic fallacy ("this landscape of chagrin") but also the heavens as a demonic timepiece, a device that moves the poem from day to night, from remembered summer to present winter.

Plath's Cambridge studies included continued attempts to publish her work. It had already appeared in *Harper's* and in British magazines and periodicals, but she aimed for the *Atlantic Monthly* and the *New Yorker.* One submission to the latter "was rejected . . . this morning with not so much as a pencil scratch on the black-and-white doom of the printed rejection. . . . Still, the accommodating mind imagines that the poems, sent a week before, must be undergoing detailed scrutiny. I shall no doubt get them back tomorrow. Maybe even with a note."

It was at Cambridge, in the winter of 1956, that Plath met Ted Hughes, the young British poet she would marry that summer. The gossip surrounding the meeting and marriage of Plath and Hughes has often seemed the stuff of supermarket tabloids (and is best left to the gossip mongers). Plath, in her letters and journals, and particularly in her late poems, presents one image of Hughes, the brute with "a black grinning look," an image similar to those she drew of her father, and of most of the men in her life.

The day before meeting Hughes, she wrote, "I'd love to cook and make a house, and surge force into a man's dreams, and write, if he could talk and walk and work and passionately want do his career." Marriage and writing, the delicate balance she had once thought impossible, now seemed more likely. Still, the entry continues, "What I fear most, I think, is the death of the imagination." The day after their meeting, Plath began writing "Pursuit," "a poem . . . about the dark forces of lust . . . dedicated to Ted Hughes." The poem's epigraph, *"Dans le fond des forêts votre image me suit"* (In the depths of the forest, your image follows me), is from Racine, on whom Plath was then writing an academic essay, the theme of which was "passion as destiny." "Pursuit" is unrelenting in its central metaphor: man as beast ("There is a panther stalks me down") and woman as prey, albeit prey whose own hungers rage insatiate ("I hurl my heart to halt his pace, / To quench his thirst I squander blood"). The poem's language is that of the sexual hunt, and closes with a note of expectation and dread: "The panther's tread is on the stairs, / Coming up and up the stairs."

Hughes has remained largely silent on the subject of their life together. Whatever the conceptions and misconceptions about their marriage, he did provide Plath with motivation and discipline. He assigned exercises to be written on a given image or theme, and that is what she began to call many of the poems: exercises. Her poems of this period echo Dylan Thomas, Theodore Roethke, and W. H. Auden. (Plath met Auden while at Smith and "approach[ed] him with a sheaf of . . . poems." His reactions, if he did react, are not in the published journals.) She considered few women poets worthy of emulation, and she viewed her contemporaries, particularly Adrienne Rich, as rivals, and all but dismissed them. Rich was thought "dull"; Isabella Gardner, "facile"; and Elizabeth Bishop, "lesbian and fanciful."

The beginnings of Plath's own lyric strangeness, reminiscent of Emily Dickinson, Edgar Allan Poe, and Christopher Smart, appear in two poems from 1957: "The Thin People" and "All the Dead Dears." They forsake the strangeness of landscape for that of men and women. "The Thin People" seem strangers, unfathomable men and women, "empty of complaint, forever / drinking vinegar from tin cups." They are the Other:

> They are always with us, the thin people
> Meager of dimension as the gray people
>
> On a movie-screen. They
> Are unreal, we say:
>
> It was only in a movie, it was only
> In a war making evil headlines when we
>
> Were small that they famished . . .

These lines invoke newsreels, which Plath might have seen, of the prisoners' release from Nazi concentration camps, the utterly wasted bodies that so haunted the postwar years. If Plath could not yet write of oppressors, the oppressed (and, in some ways, she always counted herself among their number) would have to do.

In "All the Dead Dears," Plath considers the contents of a "fourth-century-A.D." sarcophagus: "the skeletons of a woman, a mouse and a shrew." "How they grip us through thin and thick," she writes, "These barnacle dead." Here the skeletons take on an oceanic significance. The female skeleton is "no kin / Of mine, yet kin she is." In rapt succession, the speaker reels off her own kin: "mother grandmother, greatgrandmother" and "daft father":

> From the mercury-backed glass,
> Mother, Grandmother, greatgrandmother,
> Reach hag hands to haul me in,
> And an image looms under the fishpond
>   surface
> Where the daft father went down . . .

The dead, the ocean, mother and father: she made continued use of these images until they became less image than symbol, each with its own definite sense and spirit.

In June 1957, Plath and Hughes left England for the United States, where she was to teach at Smith College that fall. Before beginning the semester, they took a cottage on Cape Cod, hoping for the time and leisure to write without distraction. Her first manuscript of poems began to take shape. (Constantly revising, Plath titled the manuscript at various times "The Earthenware Head," "Full Fathom Five" and "The Devil of the Stairs" among others—a not uncommon practice for poets with their first books.) Plath was determined to write fiction as well, and her journals are filled with fragments of plot and thumbnail character sketches for the novel that, some years later, would become *The Bell Jar.* Poetry or fiction, Plath believed that her well-being lay in "making stories, poems, novels, of experience that is why . . . it is good that I have suffered & been to hell, although not to all the hells. I cannot live for life itself: but for the words which stay the flux." (This entry echoes another, more sardonic entry from Plath's 1953 journal: "I can't be satisfied with the colossal job of merely living. Oh, no, I must order life in sonnets and sestinas and provide a verbal reflector for my 60-watt lighted head.") The journals also reveal that Plath continued to battle serious depression.

Teaching left Plath little time to write. She and Hughes decided that, the school year finished, they would move to Boston and try to survive on their writing alone. But there were months still before they could leave the academic life behind, months of hard work and continued self-doubt. Then, a letter from *ART news* "asking for a poem on art and speaking of an 'honorarium' " prompted Plath to begin a series of poems based on paintings. "The Disquieting Muses" (1957), after Giorgio di Chirico's painting of the same name, is the most successful of the series. Unencumbered by what she would later see as a characteristic "machinelike syllabic death-blow," the poem's narrative flows easily. The muses are "the three terrible faceless dressmaker's dummies in classical gowns" of di Chirico's painting; they are also "a twentieth-century version of other sinister trios of women—the Three Fates, the witches in *Macbeth,* de Quincy's sisters of madness": so Plath introduced the poem for a radio broadcast. All three evil, they are also Sleeping Beauty's fairy godmothers:

> Mother, mother, what illbred aunt
> Or what disfigured and unsightly
> Cousin did you so unwisely keep
> Unasked to my christening, that she
> Sent these ladies in her stead
> With heads like darning-eggs to nod
> And nod and nod at foot and head
> And at the left side of my crib?

"Unsightly, unwisely," "unasked": Plath's explicit negatives prefigure the hammering, implied negatives of "nod / And nod and nod" (not and not and not). Other trios inhabit the poem—the speaker, her mother, and the speaker's brother resemble Plath's own family—and words and phrases are repeated: "Thor is angry: boom boom boom!" and the chantlike "I learned, I learned, I learned elsewhere." Though controlled, the poem seems uncalculated, its final lines oddly opaque: "And this is the kingdom you bore me to, / Mother, mother. But no frown of mine / Will betray the company I keep."

The company Plath kept, her own disquieting muses, was that spring to visit her more often. Reading Robert Graves's *The White Goddess: A Historical Grammar of Poetic Myth,* in which the feminine, matriarchal moon is the poet's true muse, was a watershed. Graves's mythologies led her to studies of African folklore and "a book on demonic possession" over the next year.

"On the Decline of Oracles" (1957), another poem after di Chirico, led to "Full Fathom Five" (1958). Both poems concern a father figure, suggestively Plath's own. But while "On the Decline of Oracles" seems all checks and balances, the range of "Full Fathom Five" seems barely contained:

> All obscurity
> Starts with a danger:
>
> Your dangers are many. I
> Cannot look much but your form suffers
> Some strange injury
>
> And seems to die . . .

The poem concludes: "Father, this thick air is murderous. / I would breathe water." The poem's preoccupations unleashed a set of images that would serve as the origin for other, later poems: The sea, she wrote in her journals, "is a central metaphor for my childhood, my poems and the artist's subconscious, of the father image—relating to my own father, the buried male muse and god-creator risen to be my mate in Ted, to the sea-father Neptune." Plath's muse would always be violently androgynous, asserting in fits and starts now its masculine, now its feminine, aspects.

The "sea change" presaged in "Full Fathom Five" continued with "Lorelei" (1958). If the masculine (father, but also lover) "seems to die" in the sea, it is the feminine (Self, but also mother) that leads it there. The Lorelei are Germanic sirens luring sailors to shipwreck: "They sing / Of a world more full and clear / / Than can be." While the moon and the sea are malevolent if dormant, the Lorelei present night's greatest danger. "It is no night to drown in," the poem begins. They offer not solace, "those great goddesses of peace," but the chance for masculine and feminine to become one, for the Self to rejoin its father: "Stone, stone, ferry me down there." The stones suggest a suicide: stones in the pockets of a greatcoat, weights to keep the speaker from rising again to the ocean's surface. The dangers of drowning and "the death-wish involved in the song's beauty," as Plath notes in her journal, are fear and attraction, warning and pull—a battle waged over and again in her work. The repetition of "stone, stone" also suggests, and invokes, the repetition of "Mother, mother" in "The Disquieting Muses" and, in time, the famous repetitions in "Daddy" and "Lady Lazarus" (1962).

In Boston, to make ends meet, Plath worked briefly as a receptionist/clerk at Massachusetts General Hospital, an interlude that figures in the short story "Johnny Panic and the Bible of Dreams." She began as well a course of psychotherapy that helped break the silence she had kept since her suicide attempt five years before. Her journal from this period is largely a record of what she learned about herself in those sessions, many of which seemed to have focused on Plath's ability to write—as "an ordering, a reforming, a relearning and reloving of people and the world as they are, and as they might be." Whatever the benefits of this analysis, it forced Plath to confront a number of hardwon truths about her work. The poems of early 1959 are by and large landscapes or reformations of earlier material: "A fury of frustration, some inhibition [is] keeping me from writing what I really feel." It was also during this time that she began to attend Robert Lowell's poetry workshop at Boston University. Plath's fellow students included George Starbuck and Anne Sexton, who recalls the class in her memoir "The Barfly Ought to Sing." Both Sexton and Starbuck published their first books before Plath had published hers, and Plath's frustrations increased. Attempts at writing and publishing prose were equally daunting. For some time Plath had been at work on a novel, tentatively titled *Falcon Yard,* of which she was greatly uncertain. Its tone, its characters, and even its plot seemed to elude her. A children's book came easier ("I wrote a book yesterday!"), though it, too, met with rejection.

A visit in early March to her father's grave helped to change all this. Some days later she noted: "What good does talking about my father do? It may be a minor catharsis that lasts a day or two, but I don't get insight talking to myself." Still, the visit produced "Electra of Azalea Path" (1959), a poem that seems nothing if not filled with insight: "Small as a doll in my dress of innocence / I lay dreaming your epic, image by image." The poem recounts Plath's visit to the graveyard, with its plastic flowers that bleed in the rain but do not die. Though eventually dropped from the manuscript of *Colossus* (she dismissed it as "too forced and rhetorical"), "Electra on Azalea Path" made possible two other poems: "The Beekeeper's Daughter" and "Man in Black" (both 1959).

Plath saw "Man in Black" as a love poem for Hughes, but also recognized how its images ("the gray sea," "those white stones," "your dead black coat") were similar to those she used in poems for and about her father. "The 'dead black,' she wrote, "may be a transference from the visit to my father's grave." The striking difference in "Man in Black" between lover and father is that the lover unites the elements ("riveting stones, air / All of it, together"). In "The Beekeeper's Daughter," the father has no such power. The redolence of flowers, "peeling back their silks" to entice the bees, becomes "a well of scents almost too dense to breathe in." The similarity between this last line and the closing lines of "Full Fathom Five" is striking: "Father, this thick air is murderous. / I would breathe water.") The lover mends elements, while in the father's world the elements kill.

"The Beekeeper's Daughter" is another poem in which masculine and feminine contest one another. It is the (male) beekeeper who controls the swarm; he is "the maestro of the bees." The bees (the drones, the males) are drawn to the (feminine) flowers, "a garden of mouthings." And yet, the poem's real contest is not masculine-feminine but feminine-feminine, the battle Electra waged for her father's love: "Here is a queenship no mother can contest—/ A fruit that's death to the taste: dark flesh, dark parings." The bee-mother is overcome by the beedaughter:

> Father, bridegroom, in this Easter egg
> Under the coronal of sugar roses
>
> The queen bee marries the winter of your
> year.

The marriage proves to be uneasy. A bee's season is not winter but spring and summer. The "Easter egg," despite its intimations of resurrection and rebirth, would seem poisonous, a hibernation ending not in marriage or in waking from sleep, but in waking to death.

In the early summer of 1959, Plath and Hughes traveled cross-country. Returning to Boston in August, the two discovered they had been invited for a stay at Yaddo, an artists' colony in Saratoga Springs, New York. It was there that Hughes suggested Plath begin work on a second book of poems and not worry over publication of the first, which had already undergone several incarnations. The idea of a second book seemed to liberate her: "I . . . wrote two poems that pleased me. One a poem to Nicholas, and one the old father-worship subject. But different. Weirder. I see a picture, a weather, in these poems. . . ." Plath, who was then pregnant, believed that her first child would be a boy. Her daughter, Frieda, was born in April 1960.

"The Colossus" (1959), Plath's poem on "the old father-worship subject," is addressed to her father but is less an elegy than an admission that he eludes her still. "I shall never get you put together entirely," the poem begins, "Pieced, glued and properly jointed." It was also an important acknowledgment for Plath that death and its mythologies leave us "none the wiser" for our losses:

> Perhaps you consider yourself an oracle,
> Mouthpiece of the dead, or of some god or
> other.
> Thirty years now I have labored
> To dredge the silt from your throat.
> I am none the wiser.

Like most of Plath's poems, "The Colossus" contains echoes of her earlier work. Here is the animal farm of "Sow" (1957)—"Mule-bray, pig-grunt and bawdy cackles / Proceed from your great lips. / It's worse than a barnyard"—and the classical mythology of "Electra on Azalea Path" ("A blue sky out of the Oresteia / Arches above us"), among others. And yet "The Colossus" is more than the sum of its precedents. What this poem, and others from Yaddo, taught Plath was "not to manipulate the experience but to let it unfold and recreate itself with all the tenuous, peculiar associations the logical mind would short-circuit."

"The Colossus" was followed by "Poem for a Birthday," a long poem in seven sections, only two of which were published in the U.S. edition of *The Colossus*: "Flute Notes from a Reedy Pond" and "The Stones"; the sequence is reprinted whole in *The Complete Poems.* "Poem for a Birthday" allowed Plath to continue writing in the new voice she had found: "different" and "weirder," yes, but also detached and incantatory: "Love is the uniform of my bald nurse. / Love is the bone and sinew of my curse." One critic has suggested that "Poem for a Birthday" is an intricate retelling of Plath's suicide attempt and hospitalization; certainly, it is a poem of death and rebirth. "My heart is a stopped geranium," she writes in the first section; "This is not death, it is something safer," in the fifth. The final section, "The Stones," describes the rebirth, "the city where men are mended." (A clever if malicious pun: Plath's speaker inhabits the city where men not only are healed, made new, but are also men dead, or dead men.) The speaker is a creature of stone; her eye is pried open. Her senses return:

> This is the after-hell: I see the light.
> A wind unstoppers the chamber
> Of the ear, old worrier.
>
> Water mollifies the flint lip.

The poem includes another, implied pun—"old worrier" is very possibly a pun for "old warrior"—and another allusion to her own work—the speaker of "The Colossus" "squat[s] in the cornucopia" of the statue's left ear, "out of the wind." "The city where men are mended," "the city of spare parts," is the hospital (metaphorical or actual) where Plath is reborn, where she "shall be good as new." Or so the last, ironic line promises. Love is the "uniform" of health ("my bald nurse"), but is also "the bone and sinew of my curse." Love has the capacity to heal, though never fully:

> The vase, reconstructed, houses
> The elusive rose.
>
> Ten fingers shape a bowl for shadows.
> My mendings itch.

The alliteration of "vase," "houses," "elusive" and "rose" forces "reconstructed" into particular emphasis; and that emphasis will not let us forget that the vase was once broken. The wound, closed by stitches, by "mendings," reminds its victims of her frailty. It threatens to reopen.

In December 1959, after leaving Yaddo, Plath and Hughes returned to England, where they settled in London. In February 1960, Plath signed a contract with the English publisher Heinemann for a volume of poems, *The Colossus.* The majority of its contents are those poems which Plath had consigned to her first manuscript, "that soggy book," while the remainder were poems written at Yaddo. (U.S. publication of *The Colossus* occurred 1962.) Except for working notes and an occasional extant entry, Plath's post-Yaddo journal either has disappeared or has been destroyed. ("I destroyed it," writes Hughes in the foreword to *The Journals of Sylvia Plath,* "because I did not want her children to read it." A parenthetical aside continues, "In those days I regarded forgetfulness as an essential part of survival.") Other than *The Bell Jar,* which she would presently begin writing in earnest, and a volume of letters written to her mother, comparatively little prose survives from this period until her suicide three years later. What survive are the poems. "You're," a pregnancy poem, and "The Hanging Man," a terse six-line poem about her shock treatments, are the only poems of merit from 1960.

In the fall of 1960, *The Colossus* was published and Plath was once again pregnant. In early February 1961 she miscarried, and she underwent an appendectomy at the end of that month. Between worries about her health and the financial well-being of her marriage, Plath's depression returned. But so did her desire to write. A few days after her miscarriage, she wrote "Morning Song," an evocation of motherhood: "I stumble from bed, cow-heavy and floral / In my Victorian nightgown." The poem seems dedicated to her daughter, not yet one year old, but is also heavy with the pain of recent loss: "The window square / Whitens and swallows its dull stars." The "new statue" of "Morning Song" would, two days later, become a "museum without statues" in "Barren Woman." More and more, Plath was able to shape experience directly into poetry.

The poems Plath wrote from March until October 1961 are important for reasons at once thematic and technical, though only three appear in the *Ariel* that Ted Hughes arranged for publication after her death. They are also literally and figuratively fatter: a great number of the poems are composed of seven-, eight-, or nine-line stanzas of semi-regular line length (usually iambic pentameter). But while the poems grew fat with form, the control Plath exercised over image and voice grew lean—or, rather, precise. Nothing is wasted; nothing is extraneous. Plath's hospitalization for appendicitis provided material for two poems, "In Plaster" and "Tulips," the notes for which have survived as part of "The Inmate" in the published journals. These notes provide one of the clearest examples of how she transformed life into poetry. Significantly different in tone from previous entries, they are more novelistic and less self-absorbed, a sort of warm-up for *The Bell Jar.* A "lady with [a] sour face, chest and arm in plaster," who shared Plath's ward, provided the occasion for "In Plaster." It is unclear (and unimportant, perhaps) if Plath intended herself or the "lady with [a] sour face" for the speaker. What is clear is her fascination with the idea of the double (a thread in her work that dates back to her Smith senior thesis on Dostoevsky), and also with the idea of the fragmented self: "There are two of me now: / This new absolutely white person and the old yellow one." "One of the real saints," this figure in white seems engaged in a battle of wills that the weaker, yellow self fully expects to win. "I'm collecting my strength; one day I shall manage without her." It is not now "thick air" or a garden with its "well of scents" that is murderous, but the Self.

"Tulips," dated the same day as "In Plaster" (March 18), is the stronger poem, if only because it resists easy explications in favor of image (they are all here: stone, sea, the trappings of religion, and the colors white, red, and black) and tone. While both poems are narrative, "Tulips" is an interior monologue. There are not "two of me" but one, and this concentration drives the "I" from one stanza to the next. If there is a division between Self and Other in "Tulips," it lies between the speaker (Self, but also sickness) and the tulips (Other, but also health). "The tulips are too excitable, it is winter here," the poem begins, drawing a line between hospital winter and greenhouse spring. The next three stanzas detail a private history; the speaker's "baggage" is cast off: "I watched my teaset, my bureaus of linens, my books / Sink out of sight, and the water went over my head." And then comes a curious but important line: "I am a nun now, I have never been so pure." Common public and critical perception has centered on Plath's fascination with Judaism. "I think I may well be a Jew," she writes in "Daddy." Otto Plath was neither a Catholic nor a Jew, but a lapsed Lutheran; and neither of Plath's parents seemed overly inclined to impress a religious education upon the children. Whatever the creed, religion was for Plath much like folklore and mythology: a system of symbols and gods. In "Tulips" and other poems, religion (more specifically, Judeo-Christian religion) stands for passive acceptance of fate:

> I didn't want any flowers, I only wanted
> To lie with my hands turned up and be
>   utterly empty.
> How free it is, you have no idea how free—
> The peacefulness so big it dazes you,
> And it asks nothing, a name tag, a few
>   trinkets.
> It is what the dead close on, finally; I
>   imagine them
> Shutting their mouths on it, like a
>   Communion tablet.

The "peacefulness" is overcome by the tulips. They are "too red in the first place, they hurt me." Again, the absence of air, the inability to breath, becomes crucial. "The vivid tulips eat my oxygen," their overpowering presence emphasized by Plath's choice of the adjective "vivid" (which, from the Latin, means "full of life"). The flowers next become "dangerous animals . . . opening like the mouth of some great African cat" in a roar of warning. Yet the speaker's response (the poem's final lines) is oddly calm and laced with assent:

> And I am aware of my heart: it opens and
>   closes
> Its bowl of red blooms out of sheer love of me
> The water I taste is warm and salt, like the
>   sea,
> And comes from a country far away as health.

The heart is housed in a vase enclosing a liquid that, "like the sea," is "warm and salt." It is not water she tastes but blood, her own unimaginable health.

In the summer of 1961, Plath and Hughes left London for a cottage in Devon. "Blackberrying," a poem from September, is in many ways similar to "Tulips," both formally (its dense stanza structure, its assonance and alliteration) and thematically. Like the tulips, the berries, a "blood sisterhood," mock the speaker: "Theirs is the only voice, protesting, protesting." Certainly, the berries are as carnival and grotesque as were the tulips: "I come to one bush of berries so ripe it is a bush of flies" with "bluegreen bellies." The flies "believe in heaven," but the lane of "berries and bushes" ends at the sea. Although the poem evokes a landscape from Plath's childhood summers on Cape Cod, with its berry bushes, its ocean, what is revealed is not the sea "but a great space / Of white and pewter lights, and a din like silversmiths / Beating and beating an intractable metal." The lights might be sunlight on water; the "beating and beating," the crash of waves. But they are so transformed as to make us forget water and sun, and hear only the jarring cacophony of sound Plath wants us to hear: the *i* of "white," "lights," "din," "silversmiths"; the *b* of "beating and beating" and "intractable" (and also of "blackberries," "bushes," and "blue-green bellies"); the slant, insistent rhyme of "intractable" with "metal."

"The Moon and the Yew Tree," written the following month at the suggestion of Hughes, is, like the earlier "Winter Landscape, with Rooks," a "psychic landscape." The first two lines would make us believe the poem is set in the mind alone, that this pastoral is no more than interior: "This is the light of the mind, cold and planetary. / The trees of the mind are black. The light is blue." Thereafter, we discover that mind and landscape have fused, that everything interior (or psychic) has as its double, its twin, an exterior figure: "The grasses unload their griefs on my feet as if I were God, / Prickling my ankles and murmuring of their humility." The speaker stands just outside her house, "a row of headstones" separating her from "fumy, spiritous mists," from the moon and the yew tree in the distance. This path (house, headstones, mists, tree, moon) seems to paralyze the speaker: "I simply cannot see where there is to get to." She cannot leave the house behind, walk past the headstones and the mist, past the yew (associated with the cross of the Crucifixion and referred to by Robert Graves as the "death-tree") to rejoin the moon. "The moon is no door," writes Plath. "It is a face in its own right, / White as a knuckle and terribly upset." The tone of the poem is "complete despair"—in Christian lore the greatest sin, the belief that God is powerless to redeem. God is powerless, and so is the speaker; thus, the identification of one with the other.

The speaker's stasis is made all the more terrible by her realization that "the moon is my mother." The image should be beneficent, but this mother is "not sweet like Mary. / Her blue garments unloose small bats and owls," themselves messengers of death. "How I would like to believe in tenderness," Plath writes, a tenderness as impossible (though not unimaginable) as redemption:

> How I would like to believe in tenderness—
> The face of the effigy, gentled by candies,
> Bending, on me in particular, its mild eyes.
>
> I have fallen a long way. Clouds are flowering
> Blue and mystical over the face of the stars.
> Inside the church, the saints will be all blue,
> Floating on their delicate feet over the cold pews,
> Their hands and faces stiff with holiness.

The vision of tenderness would make forgiveness, redemption, resurrection all possible; but "the moon sees nothing of this" (it sees the vision as "nothing"), and so it ceases to exist.

In a radio broadcast Plath described the yew tree of this poem as "manipulating. . . . I couldn't subdue it." It is true that the image stands "squarely in the middle of [the] poem," and the final line would seem to grant the tree omnipotence: "And the message of the yew tree is blackness—blackness and silence." But the poem is not, as she coyly described it, "a poem about a yew tree." Like "The Beekeeper's Daughter," "The Moon and the Yew Tree" is a poem about the dual contests between masculine (tree) and feminine (moon), and between feminine (moon) and feminine (Self). The latter battle seems the more significant; it is an annihilation of the Self. The battle between masculine and feminine seems more symbolic. The yew stands mute, stonelike, impassive. "Bald and wild," the moon emerges triumphant.

In October 1961, Plath signed a contract for publication of *The Bell Jar,* the novel that fictionalized the events of her *Mademoiselle* internship, her suicide attempt, and her subsequent recovery. Although the novel received mixed reviews when it was published in 1971, its increasing popularity in the years following Plath's death is somewhat problematic. Because of *The Bell Jar's* status as an "autobiography," its importance as a secondary, albeit unreliable, source for the life has superseded attention to its actual effectiveness as a novel—critical examination, for example, of a protagonist who is a distant, unknowable character whose motivations remain elusive to the reader. There is the very real possibility that had Plath's emotional health not received such notoriety, *The Bell Jar* would have gone the way of most poets' novels: consigned, as a curiosity, to footnotes and to bibliographies.

Plath's son, Nicholas, was born in January, and 1962—unlike the year following Frieda's birth—was productive. Words such as "frenzy" and "fury" have often been applied to the energies with which Plath now devoted herself to poetry. Such words are misleading. Plath was a careful, highly disciplined writer. In his introduction to *The Complete Poems,* Ted Hughes writes, "Her attitude to her verse was artisanlike: if she couldn't get a table out of the material, she was quite happy to get a chair, or even a toy." The poems of 1962 contain an equal number of each: tables, chairs, toys. While the number of poems makes a critical appreciation of each prohibitive here, they can be divided into three major groups: the beekeeping poems; "Daddy," "Lady Lazarus," and their attendant poems; and those written after October, when Plath had separated from Hughes and had begun to make plans for a return to London. (The two notable exceptions to these technically unified and clearly defined groupings are a verse play for radio, "Three Women," and "Berck-Plage," an degy in seven sections for a Devon neighbor, both of which date from earlier in 1962.)

In June 1962 Plath and Hughes became, like many of the villagers, beekeeepers. However, the beekeeping sequence ("The Bee Meeting," "The Arrival of the Bee Box," "Stings," "The Swarm," and "Wintering") can be traced back to "The Beekeeper's Daughter." Broader and yet more concentrated, the five distinct poems form a single narrative that works on several levels: as a story in itself, as an account of the growing dissolution of the marriage, and as a series of reports from the battle between Self and Other. "The Bee Meeting" continues the black (male) and blue (female) imagery of "The Moon and the Yew Tree" and other poems: "Which is the rector now, is it that man in black? / Which is the midwife, is that her blue coat?" The villagers in their protective garments become indistinct; in their black veils, it is difficult to tell one from another, man from woman. The poem carries intimations of a sacrifice of rite of assimilation: the speaker herself is made to don a black veil. "They are making me one of them," she fears, watching as the villagers go "hunting the queen." It is the dream of a duel between the queen and her "new virgins" that exhausts Plath, leaving her cold; the dream of flee bee box, "the long white box in the grove," as something resembling a coffin.

The rite of separating virgin from queen, of preventing "a duel [the virgins] will win inevitably," is taken up in the next poem, "The Arrival of the Bee Box." The speaker's way of averting the duel is to imagine the bees, her "box of maniacs," dead. "I need feed them nothing, I am the owner," she boasts. "Stings" informs us that the bees have not died, that the queen is "old . . . and unqueenly and even shameful," and that the speaker is "in control." She begins to see herself as the queen and unleashes the swarm. The theme of these poems is a coming to power, of the feminine Self asserting its prominence over both masculine and feminine others. "The Swarm" is an extended metaphor: the bees are at war. "The white busts of marshals, admirals, generals / [Worm] themselves into niches." If "The Swarm" is indeed a "war poem," then "Wintering," the final poem, is one of women alone, making do without husbands and fathers (as Plath did as a child), without all the expendable soldiers:

> The bees are all women,
> Maids and the long royal lady.
> They have got rid of the men,
>
> The blunt, clumsy stumblers, the boors.
> Winter is for women—

In the end, the beekeeping sequence earns a hard-won peace. "The bees are flying," Plath writes. "They taste the spring." But the victory proved a burden. A draft of "Elm," a poem from earlier in 1962, includes the memo "stigma (of selfhood)"—and the Self that Plath created (or discovered) in these poems would, over the next months, indeed become a stigma, a burden.

In the poems that followed the bee sequence ("A Secret" and "The Applicant") Plath left peace for black comedy, for the acerbic wit that informs and propels the second group: "Daddy," "Medusa," "Cut," "Ariel," "Nick and the Candlestick," and "Lady Lazarus" among them. With "Daddy" and "Medusa," written back-to-back in a sort of dual exorcism, the Self is once again at war.

From its opening line, "Daddy," establishes a nearly metronomic rhythm both dire and merciless. With the simplicity of counting verse ("One, two, buckle my shoe," and so forth), Plath turns the stuff of her childhood, real and imagined, into a burlesque of revenge:

> You do not do, you do not do
> Any more, black shoe
> In which I have lived like a foot
>
> For thirty years, poor and white:
> Barely daring to breathe or Achoo.

Almost lost in the singsong and deadpan silliness of many of these rhymes is the familiar image from other "father-worship" poems ("Full Fathom Five" and "The Beekeeper's Daughter") that "air is murderous" and breathing often next to impossible. Here, the speaker confesses that she has been too frightened to breathe. And if speech is a kind of breath, she also confesses that "I could hardly speak." The punishment might well have been asphyxiation.

One of the technical qualities that make "Daddy" so visceral is Plath's use of assonance and alliteration, the fierce attention she paid to each sound. Note how the insistent repetition of "Jew" subtly mimics the sound of "an engine, an engine," its insistent whistle:

> I thought every German was you.
> And the language obscene
>
> An engine, an engine
> Chuffing me off like a Jew.
> A Jew to Dachau, Auschwitz, Belsen,
> I began to talk like a Jew.
> I think I may well be a Jew.

Note, too, the subtle rhymes of "obscene" and "engine" and "Belsen."

Plath's radio introduction to "Daddy" is artfully evasive. "Here is a poem spoken by a girl with an Electra complex," she begins. "Her father died while she thought he was God. Her case is complicated by the fact that her father was a Nazi and her mother very possibly part Jewish. In the daughter the two strains marry and paralyse each other—she has to act out the awful little allegory once over before she is free of it." Plath's "awful little allegory" is off base: the father's love is not won. The father is instead killed:

> There's a stake in your fat black heart
> And the villagers never liked you.
> They are dancing and stamping on you.
> They always *knew* it was you.
> Daddy, daddy, you bastard, I'm through.

Plath was anything but through. The poems of October, written at a rate of almost one per day, both shattered and explored her "stasis in darkness." "Ariel," which describes a horse ride in violent imagery, might be seen as a metaphor for the October poems. They act like an "arrow // . . . that flies / Suicidal, at one with the drive / Into the red // Eye, the cauldron of mourning." They range from the tender ("Nick and the Candlestick") to the acidly humorous ("Lady Lazarus").

The blue light of "Nick and the Candlestick," reminiscent of the blue light in "The Moon and the Yew Tree," is the flame in darkness that counters "the cauldron of morning." "I am a miner," Plath writes. "The light burns blue." The flame cools from blue to yellow.

The candle
Gulps and recovers its small altitude,

Its yellows hearten.
O love, how did you get here?

Metaphors of suffocation and drowning are here rendered harmless. The flame that uses oxygen is not a death image but an affirmation of the child (her son, Nicholas):

You are the one
Solid the spaces lean on, envious.
You are the baby in the barn.

The Christlike "baby in the barn" might be said to have raised the spirit of Lazarus, the man Jesus raised from death (John 11), in "Lady Lazarus." Plath's speaker has no need of divine intervention, however. Unlike the broken statue in "The Colossus," but not unlike the "reconstructed" vase in "The Stones," the character of Lady Lazarus is newly fashioned of "spare parts." More important, she is self-made, her flesh and bones the leftovers of atrocities perpetrated by "Daddy": "A sort of walking miracle, my skin / Bright as a Nazi lampshade, / My right foot / A paperweight, / My face a featureless, fine / Jew linen." The life-in-death that is Plath's speaker is also "a smiling woman," a suicidal penitent, a garish chorine.

The peanut crunching crowd
Shoves in to see

Them unwrap me hand and foot—
The big strip tease.
Gentlemen, ladies

These are my hands,
My knees.

"Dying," Plath writes, "is an art"—a painful boast. The entire poem is a swagger of pain of sarcasm: "I turn and burn / Do not think I underestimate your great concern. All is destruction. Fire is not here the sweet glow of "Nick and the Candlestick," but that element which reduces everything to "ash, ash." But, like the phoenix, Lady Lazarus promises to rise once more and exact her vengeance:

Herr God, Herr Lucifer
Beware
Beware.

Out of the ash
I rise with my red hair,
And I eat men like air.

The story of Sylvia Plath's last months has been told often: her separation from Hughes, the move to London (where the winter was bitterly cold), the illnesses she and her children suffered, her sense of helplessness and isolation (made worse by her lack of a telephone), her suicide (on 11 February). And her last poems, written in January and February 1963, have been taken apart stanza and verse as if they formed an extended suicide note. "The blood jet is poetry," she wrote in "Kindness." "There is no stopping it." These lines alone have fostered the misguided equation of poetry with self-destruction, an equation supported by little though taken as gospel by many. Plath's legacy was for many years the idea that self-destruction is "a Greek necessity." Her poems were mere evidence.

Like T. S. Eliot, Sylvia Plath has gone in and out of fashion. But her more lasting legacy will be the poems, not as evidence of a life but as the visceral, technical marvels they are.

Selected Bibliography

PRIMARY WORKS

POETRY

The Colossus, (New York: Alfred A. Knopf, 1962).
Ariel, (New York: Harper & Row, 1966).

Crossing the Water, (New York: Harper & Row, 1971).
Winter Trees, (New York: Harper & Row, 1972).
The Collected Poems, Edited by Ted Hughes. (New York: Harper & Row, 1981).

FICTION, SHORT PROSE, LETTERS

The Bell Jar, (New York: Harper & Row, 1971).
Letters Home by Sylvia Plath: Correspondence, 1950–1963, Edited by Aurelia S. Plath. (New York: Harper & Row, 1975).
Johnny Panic and the Bible of Dreams: Short Stories, Prose, and Diary Excerpts, (New York: Harper & Row, 1980).
The Journals of Sylvia Plath, Edited by Frances McCullough and Ted Hughes. (New York: Dial Press, 1982).

CHILDREN'S LITERATURE

The Bed Book, (New York: Harper & Row, 1976).

PAPERS AND MANUSCRIPTS

Plath's unpublished materials are at the Neilsen Library, Smith College, and at the Lilly Library, Indiana University.

SECONDARY WORKS

BIOGRAPHY

Stevenson, Anne, *Bitter Fame: A Life of Sylvia Plath,* (Boston: Houghton Mifflin, 1989).
Wagner-Martin, Linda, *Sylvia Plath: A Biography,* (New York: Simon & Schuster, 1987).

CRITICISM

Ariel Ascending: Writings About Sylvia Plath, Paul Alexander, ed. (New York: Harpor & Row, 1985). See especially Hardwick, Elizabeth, "On Sylvia Plath,"; Hughes, Ted, "Sylvia Plath and Her Journals," (different from his introduction to the *Journals);* Plumley, Stanley, "What Ceremony of Words,"0 Pollitt, Katha, "A Note of Triumph."
Bassett, Susan, *Sylvia Plath,* (London: Macmillan, 1987).
Harold Bloom, ed., *Sylvia Plath,* (New York: Chelsea House, 1989).
Broe, Mary Lynn, *Protean Poetic: The Poetry of Sylvia Plath,* (Columbia: University of Missouri Press, 1980).
Brundtzen, Lynda K., *Plath's Incarnations: Woman and the Creative Process,* (Ann Arbor: University of Michigan Press, 1983).
Hardwick, Elizabeth, "On Sylvia Plath," *Seduction and Betrayal: Women and Literature* (New York: Random House, 1974).
Heaney, Seamus, "The Indefatigable Hoof-taps: Sylvia Plath," In his *The Government of the Tongue* (New York: Farrar, Straus & Giroux, 1989).
Holbrook, David, *Sylvia Plath: Poetry and Existence,* (London: Athlone, 1976).
Kroll, Judith, *Chapters in a Mythology: The Poetry of Sylvia Plath,* (New York: Harper & Row, 1976).
Gary Lane, ed., *Sylvia Plath: New Views on the Poetry,* (Baltimore: Johns Hopkins University Press, 1979).
Matovich, Richard M., *A Concordance to the Collected Poems of Sylvia Plath,* (New York: Garland, 1986).
Newman, Charles, *The Art of Sylvia Plath: A Symposium,* (Bloomington: Indiana University Press, 1970).

BIBLIOGRAPHY

Lane, Gary, and Maria Stevens, *Sylvia Plath: A Bibliography,* (Metuchen, N.J.: Scarecrow Press, 1978).
Stephen Tabor, comp., *Sylvia Plath: An Analytical Bibliography,* (Westport, Conn.: Meckler, 1987).

Edgar Allan Poe

(1809–1849)

ROGER ASSELINEAU

The most contradictory judgments have been passed on Edgar Allan Poe's character and works. The Reverend Rufus Griswold, whom he had the unfortunate idea of appointing his literary executor, branded him a perverse neurotic, a drunkard and drug addict "who walked the streets, in madness or melancholy, with lips moving in indistinct curses." For Baudelaire, on the contrary, he was a "fallen angel who remembered heaven," a "Byron gone astray in a bad world." Whereas Emerson looked down upon that "jingle man" who shook his bells and called their sound poetry, Tennyson admired him as an equal and Yeats (on an official occasion, it is true) proclaimed that he was "so certainly the greatest of American poets, and always, and for all lands, a great lyric poet." For James Russell Lowell, he was "three-fifths . . . genius and two-fifths fudge," while Mallarmé piously raised the monument of a sonnet over his grave and Paul Valéry acclaimed the author of *Eureka* as one of the greatest thinkers who ever lived. Writers as dissimilar as Mark Twain and Henry James rejected him, the former because he found him "unreadable" and the latter because it seemed to him that "an enthusiasm for Poe [was] the mark of a decidedly primitive stage of reflection." But William Carlos Williams, for his part, praised him for giving "the sense for the first time in America that literature is serious, not a matter of courtesy but of truth." Who was right? Whom are we to believe? T. S. Eliot, who denounced his "slipshod writing," or George Bernard Shaw, who found him "exquisitely refined"?

These divergences are indeed perfectly justified and stem to a large extent from the constant contrast between the real and the Ideal (the capital was his) in Poe's own life and from the consequent duplicity (in the etymological meaning of the word) of his personality. Thus, though he would have liked to be of aristocratic southern lineage, he was born in Boston, on January 19, 1809, of poor actor parents who happened to be playing there at the time. His father, David Poe, who came from a good Baltimore family, was a mediocre actor and a heavy drinker who was soon to desert his wife and vanish forever. On the contrary, his mother, Elizabeth Arnold Poe, seems to have been a charming and talented actress, but she died of tuberculosis in Richmond, Virginia, in December 1811 at the age of twenty-four. This sudden death probably warped Poe for the rest of his life. He was not quite three, but he always remembered—more or less unconsciously—his mother vomiting blood and being carried away from him forever by sinister men dressed in black. He was then taken into the home of John and Frances Allan—hence his middle name. John Allan was a successful and ambitious Richmond merchant. The couple were childless, so they reared the boy as if he were their only son, but they never formally adopted him. In 1815 they took him to England and sent him to private schools there, notably to Manor House School at Stoke Newington which Poe later used as a setting for the childhood of his hero in "William Wilson." The boy was athletic and brilliant. His foster parents, especially Mrs. Allan, doted on him, but as he moved through adolescence this apparently fortunate situation quickly deteriorated; he felt more and more insecure and estranged from his schoolmates because of his lowly origin and more and more antagonistic to Mr. Allan out of love for his valetudinarian foster mother—a standard Oedipal relationship. Being a precocious and passionate boy, while still at school he fell in love with the beautiful young mother of one of his friends, Mrs. Jane Stanard, whose memory inspired the first of his poems, "To Helen," and with a young neighbor, Sarah Elmira Royster, but her parents disapproved of him since he was penniless, and the courtship was soon broken off.

Although his practical-minded foster father wanted him to work as a clerk in his business, Poe managed to be sent to the University of Virginia in 1826. There he studied French, Spanish, Italian, and Latin, read Byron and Campbell, and had an excellent scholastic record. But the University of Virginia in those days was a wild, dissolute place (like Oxford in "William Wilson"). Poe got into difficulties almost at once because Mr. Allan had parsimoniously not provided him with enough money to pay for his fees and other necessities; then he took to drinking and gambling, accumulating debts in excess of $2000. His foster father refused to pay his "debts of honor," so Poe could not remain at Charlottesville. It was the end of his dream of a university education and he decided to break with Mr. Allan. He left Richmond in March 1827 for Boston, his birthplace, and enlisted in the army as a common soldier under the name of Edgar A. Perry. He was stationed for over a year on Sullivan's Island in Charleston Harbor, which he would describe in "The Gold Bug." Surprisingly enough, he adapted very well to military discipline and quickly rose to the rank of regimental sergeant major, the highest noncommissioned grade in the army. Yet he soon became tired of the routine of military life in peacetime and fretted at the thought of serving out his full five-year term of enlistment—or, rather, he now dreamed of becoming an officer like his colonel, whom he admired. He wrote repentingly to Mr. Allan and reconciled with him after the death of Mrs. Allan in February 1829. With Allan's support he got his discharge and an appointment to West Point, which he entered on July 1, 1830.

During this period of nearly perfect social adaptation he must have cherished dreams of an entirely different kind, though, for in the summer of 1827, while still at Boston he published at his own expense a thin volume, *Tamerlane and Other Poems,* "by a Bostonian," which passed unnoticed. That he did so at such an early date (he was only eighteen) in spite of his reduced circumstances shows his faith in himself and his belief that he had something original to say. Undiscouraged by the failure of this first volume, he published a second one at Baltimore in December 1829: *Al Aaraaf, Tamerlane, and Minor Poems.* As the title shows, it was a revised and enlarged edition of his first book. It received hardly more critical attention than its predecessor.

At West Point, the same thing happened as at the University of Virginia. Mr. Allan, who had remarried in the meantime, did not provide Poe with adequate funds. In January 1831 Poe wrote to him: "You sent me to W. Point like a beggar. The same difficulties are threatening me as before at Charlottesville—and I must resign." He kept his word. Though he had been a very good student until then, he decided to have himself expelled by deliberately cutting classes and disregarding orders. He was therefore court-martialed for "gross neglect of duties" in January 1831 and left West Point the following month.

Once again, though more destitute than ever, he succeeded in 1831 in publishing a new edition of his poems, simply entitled *Poems,* Second Edition. The appearance of this new book at such a time proves his extraordinary perseverance, but he was again ignored by critics. Yet the book included "To Helen," "Israfel," "The City in the Sea," "The Sleeper," "Lenore," "The Valley of Unrest," and an interesting introductory statement of poetic principle, "Letter to Mr. ________."

By now Poe was in the greatest difficulties. He had settled in New York, but could find no job there. His pathetic calls for help to Mr. Allan remained unanswered. He devised all sorts of wild schemes—he thought for a time of joining the Polish army—which came to nothing. He was eventually obliged to take refuge with his aunt, Mrs. Clemm, in Baltimore. Baltimore was then an active publishing center and it was natural for him to seek employment there now that he had made up his mind to live by his pen.

Having failed to attract attention as a poet, he turned to story writing and worked frantically. In 1831 he competed for the prize offered for the best short story by the *Philadelphia Saturday Courier.* He submitted five: "Metzengerstein," "The Duke de l'Omelette," "A Tale of Jerusalem," "A Decided Loss," and "The Bargain Lost." He did not win the prize, which was given to a mawkish tale, but all five of his stories were later published in the *Courier* (in 1832). It must be admitted that only one of them was first-rate: "Metzengerstein." Poe had by then embarked on an ambitious project: he had planned a series of tales supposedly told by members of a rather farcical literary group, the Folio Club, in imitation of Boccaccio's *Decameron* and Chaucer's *Canterbury Tales,* a prefiguration in a way of Dickens' famous Pickwick Club. But he could find no publisher for his stories, and in an attempt to make a breakthrough he once more entered a contest in June 1833. The competition was organized by the *Baltimore Saturday Visitor* and Poe sent one poem, "The Coliseum," and six stories: "Epimanes," "MS. Found in a Bottle," "Lionizing," "The Visionary," "Siope," and "A Descent into the Maelström." This time he won the short-story award with "MS. Found in a Bottle" and his troubles were temporarily brought to an end, for one of the judges of the contest, a wealthy lawyer and amateur novelist, John P. Kennedy, befriended him.

On Kennedy's recommendation Poe became assistant editor of the *Southern Literary Messenger,* published at Richmond by T. W. White. Poe now went through a period of emotional instability during which he apparently resorted to the bottle to steady his nerves. He was no habitual drunkard and never wrote under the influence of drink, for he was very frugal and of a sober inclination, but he was extremely sensitive and given to excruciating fits of depression, so that he could not at times resist the temptation of using alcohol as a sort of moral anesthetic. Unfortunately he was inordinately affected by even one glass and then lost all sense of dignity and decency. As he put it himself: "My sensitive temperament could not stand an excitement which was an every-day matter to my companions." In any event, after a month, White discharged him but relented when Poe pleaded to be reinstated.

Poe brought Mrs. Clemm and her daughter Virginia to live with him in Richmond and in May 1836 he married his young cousin, who was boldly declared to be "of the full age of twenty-one years," while actually she was not quite fourteen and looked very immature. In all likelihood the marriage was never consummated, but Poe felt very happy with his child-wife ("Sis") and with Mrs. Clemm ("dear Muddy") as mother-in-law and devoted housekeeper.

This was a period of intense production for Poe. He wrote stories, many forceful and slashing reviews in the manner of the Edinburgh reviewers, waging war on mediocrity, trying to enforce high literary standards, attacking "the heresy of the didactic," and denouncing plagiarism even where there was none. Unfortunately his efforts were often wasted on rather trivial works. He also composed a drama in verse, *Politian,* set in Renaissance Italy in the manner of Byron and Shelley, and *The Narrative of Arthur Gordon Pym,* two installments of which appeared in the Messenger, and which was published in book form in 1838. This was his only attempt at a long story, but it is in fact a series of separate short stories strung together. Under his dynamic editorship, the *Southern Literary Messenger* became the leading review of the South and its subscription list rose, in a year's time, from five hundred to nearly thirty-five hundred. But White objected to Poe's continued intemperance and resented his editorial authority and even his success. He dismissed him in January 1837. Poe then went to New York in the hope of finding another editorial position there. He was unsuccessful and in the summer of 1838 moved to Philadelphia, where he lived for the next five years and became in July 1839 the editor of *Burton's Gentleman's Magazine.* Under the pressure of financial need he wrote unceasingly—in particular a piece of hackwork, *The Conchologist's First Book,* for which he was (justly) accused of plagiarism in his turn, but also "Ligeia" (for the *American Museum*), "The Man That Was Used Up," "The Fall of the House of Usher," "William Wilson," "The Conversation of Eiros and Charmion," and "Morella" (for the *Gentleman's Magazine*). Soon, however, the story of his editorship of the *Southern Literary Messenger* repeated itself. Burton and Poe quarreled over editorial policies and Poe was fired in the summer of 1840.

In that year he at last found a publisher for a collection of his stories, which appeared in two volumes in Philadelphia under the title *Tales of the Grotesque and Arabesque.* They were well received by critics, but sold rather slowly. So Poe's financial problem remained unsolved and, after he had failed to find backers for a literary journal called *The Penn Magazine,* of which only the prospectus was ever printed, he joined the staff of *Graham's Magazine* and became its editor in April 1841. This was another very productive period. It was then that he published his reviews of Longfellow's *Ballads* and Hawthorne's *Twice-Told Tales* in which he defined his conception of poetry and fiction, and such stories as "The Man of the Crowd," "The Murders in the Rue Morgue," "The Island of the Fay," "The Colloquy of Monos and Una," "Eleonora," "The Oval Portrait," and "The Masque of the Red Death." Yet for all his success and brilliance he once more lost his job, in May 1842, after only thirteen months, for the same reasons as before.

His dismissal from *Graham's Magazine* did not interrupt his creation of fiction, but he found it very difficult sometimes to place his stories. He sold "The Mystery of Marie Rogêt," "The Pit and the Pendulum," "The Tell-Tale Heart," and "The Black Cat" for paltry sums to second-rate magazines. In April 1844, realizing that he could not make a living in Philadelphia as a free-lance writer, though he had won a $100 prize for "The Gold Bug" in 1843, he moved to New York, which was to remain his home until his death five years later. But he encountered the same difficulties in earning a living as in Philadelphia, though at first he scored a few resounding successes. Thus he had hardly settled there when, on April 13, 1844, he published in the *New York Sun* what is now known as "The Balloon Hoax," a tale in the form of a news item. It appeared under the caption "Astounding News by Electric Express via Norfolk! The Atlantic Crossed in Three Days—Signal Triumph of Mr. Monck's Flying-Machine . . ." The description was so graphic that everyone was taken in. But Poe was none the richer for it and the only job he found was that of assistant editor of the *Evening Mirror.* It was in this periodical that "The Raven" first appeared on January 29, 1845. The poem immediately caught the imagination of the public and was reprinted all over the country and even abroad in all kinds of newspapers and magazines, but Poe pocketed only a few dollars for his pains. However, 1845 was on the whole a lucky year for him. In July there appeared another collection of his *Tales* (only twelve of them, though) and in November another edition of his poems under the title *The Raven and Other Poems.* Besides, he was offered a better position as assistant editor of the weekly *Broadway Journal,* of which he soon became the editor. He even obtained control of the paper and thus very nearly realized his ambition of becoming the sole proprietor of a periodical, but the *Broadway Journal* died on his hands during the first weeks of 1846. Despite all his feverish exertions—and though he then wrote such a fine story as "The Cask of Amontillado" and such a brilliant essay as "The Philosophy of Composition"—he had been growing poorer and poorer all the time and was in such distress at the end of 1846 that the *New York Express* and the Philadelphia *Saturday Evening Post* asked his friends and admirers to come to his aid. He was then living with Virginia and Mrs. Clemm in a diminutive wooden cottage at Fordham, and Virginia, though dying of consumption, had to sleep in an unheated room. After six years of marriage she had become fatally ill, and her slowly progressing illness between 1842 and 1847 had driven Poe to distraction.

Virginia eventually died on January 30, 1847, and Poe broke down, though he felt relieved in a way from "the horrible neverending oscillation between hope and despair." Thus, like the hero of one of his own tales, he was constantly threatened and tortured by the pendulum of fate swinging between the extremes of the human condition. All his life he craved love and tenderness, but was doomed to lose in turn all the women he loved: his mother, Mrs. Stanard, Mrs. Allan, and Virginia. He longed for wealth and luxury, and yet, for all his talent and frenzied efforts, was condemned to destitution. He dreamed of fame and never succeeded in publishing a complete edition of his works or founding a review of his own. When he reached manhood after a sheltered childhood and adolescence he encountered nothing but failures and denials. So, instead of really living, he took refuge from the physical world in the private world of his dreams—in other words, in the world of his tales—and gradually identified himself with those phantoms of himself who haunt his stories. As is frequent with artists, nature in his case imitated art. He became the spiritual brother of his doomed heroes. His life was quite literally "a descent into the Maelström," a slow, inexorable descent into the abyss which attracted him irresistibly and was to claim him at forty years of age. He remained perfectly lucid to the end, but, unlike the hero of "A Descent into the Maelström," he lost the will to extricate himself from the whirlpool which was sucking him down. His art failed to save him. His works reflect this double aspect of his personality: the abandonment of the self-destructive romantic artist and the self-control of the conscious and conscientious craftsman, the passivity of the dreamer indifferent to all that exists outside his dream world and the restless activity of a keen mind always on the alert.

Portraits of Poe always show him fullface, but the only really revelatory portrait of him would be a head with a double profile, like that of the Roman god Janus, one side turned toward reality, the other toward dreams. Poe was himself perfectly aware of this duality. When describing the detective who appears in several of his tales, C. Auguste Dupin, he pointed out: "I often dwelt meditatively upon the old philosophy of the Bi-Part Soul, and amused myself with the fancy of a double Dupin—the creative and the resolvent." He divided his tales into tales of imagination and tales of ratiocination. The former were written by a Dionysiac and inspired creator, the latter by a lucid and impassive analyst.

The tales of imagination are the undisputed domain of fear. Poe again and again tries to make us experience the same feelings as the narrator of "The Fall of the House of Usher": "a sense of insufferable gloom pervaded my spirit. . . . There was an iciness, a sinking, a sickening of the heart. . . . There can be no doubt that the consciousness of the rapid increase of my superstition . . . served mainly to accelerate the increase itself. Such, I have long known is the paradoxical law of all sentiments having terror as a basis. . . . An irrepressible tremor gradually pervaded my frame; and, at length, there sat upon my very heart an incubus of utterly causeless alarm." This irrational fear, which rises gradually and eventually invades the whole being, soon leads Poe's heroes to insanity and death.

The world of Poe's tales is a nightmarish universe. You cross wasted lands, silent, forsaken landscapes where both life and waters stagnate. Here and there you catch sight of lugubrious feudal buildings suggestive of horrible and mysterious happenings, like the gloomy abbey in which the hero of "Ligeia" takes refuge "in one of the wildest and least frequented portions of fair England." The inside of these sinister buildings is just as disquieting as the outside. Everything is dark there, from the ebony furniture to the oaken ceiling. The walls are hung with heavy tapestries to which mysterious drafts constantly give "a hideous and uneasy animation." Even the windows are "of a leaden hue," so that the rays of either the sun or moon passing through fall "with a ghastly lustre on the objects within." To make things worse, it is usually at night in the ghastly (one of his favorite adjectives) or red-blood light of the moon that Poe's tales take place—or in the middle of terrific storms lit up by lurid flashes of lightning. In this strange world even the baptism of Morella's daughter takes place at night! His heroes are tortured solitaries, with a tainted heredity, addicted to drink or drugs. They know that they are condemned sooner or later to lose their minds or their lives and presently indeed they die or kill before our eyes under horrifying circumstances. Metzengerstein is a victim of "morbid melancholy" and "hereditary ill-health." The nervous illness of Roderick Usher passes from hypochondriacal hyperesthesia to delirious telepathy. The odious protagonists of "The Tell-Tale Heart," "The Imp of the Perverse," and "The Black Cat" suffer from irresistible homicidal manias, and in "Berenice" Egaeus is impelled by a furious "monomania" to finish off the girl he loves in order to possess himself of her teeth. In this ghoulish universe love turns to vampirism and sadistic necrophilia.

Such an accumulation of horrible details inevitably leads the reader to ask himself whether Poe was sincere when he wrote these tales, whether they were the gratuitous play of his imagination or the true expression of a terror which he really felt in his inmost heart. There is room for hesitation, for there was in Poe's time a strong taste for Gothic romances and fantastic tales which he seems to have shared and at any rate deliberately exploited. He mentions Mrs. Radcliffe at the beginning of "The Oval Portrait" and on several occasions praises William Godwin's *Caleb Williams.* Moreover he must have read the works of Charles Brockden Brown and we know that he admired Hawthorne's tales. He must also have been acquainted with E. T. A. Hoffmann's tales—with "Das Majorat" in particular, at least in the summary which Walter Scott gave in his essay on Hoffman, for there exist some striking similarities between this tale and "The Fall of the House of Usher."

Some critics have therefore claimed that Poe was a mere mystifier who wrote his stories only to please the public and follow the current fashion. Indeed, more than once he himself pretends to be joking and describes horrible events with apparent unconcern. At the beginning of his career, in 1835, he wrote to White: "The subject [of "Berenice"] is by far too horrible, and I confess that I hesitated in sending it to you especially as a specimen of my capabilities. The Tale originated in a bet that I could produce nothing effective on a subject so singular, provided I treated it seriously." The next year, referring to his early tales, he wrote to Kennedy: "Most of them were *intended* for half banter, half satire—although I might not have fully acknowledged this to be their aim even to myself." And finally, eight years later, in "The Premature Burial," he spoke of tales of horror with surprising skepticism. After a misadventure which was in itself a parody of the tale of horror, since he merely dreamed his premature burial, the supposed narrator declares that from then on he completely changed his way of life and got rid of his morbid obsessions by ceasing to read Edward Young's *Night Thoughts.*

Thus Poe's attitude toward his own tales is much more complex than is commonly realized. He is never completely taken in by his own imagination. His apparent frenzy is always accompanied by lucidity. His fear is often tinged with skepticism—but conversely his skepticism with fear, as is shown by the concluding lines of "The Premature Burial": "Alas! the grim legion of sepulchral terrors cannot be regarded as altogether fanciful—but, like the Demons in whose company Afrasiab made his voyage down the Oxus, they must sleep, or they will devour us—they must be suffered to slumber, or we perish."

So, for all his gibes and feigned detachment, fear finally prevails, and there is no denying that his "tales of imagination" were not mere literary exercises or hoaxes. They wholly committed him. His own tragic life is the best proof of it. He has sometimes been accused of being a histrion, but if it is true that he sometimes behaved like one, he forgot he was playing a part and killed himself in the last act with a real dagger (figuratively speaking). He declared himself in 1840 in the preface to his *Tales of the Grotesque and Arabesque*: "If in many of my productions terror has been the thesis, I maintain that terror is not of Germany but of the soul."

This terror which haunted his soul, like any form of fear, whatever its occasion or immediate cause may be, was in the last analysis a panic fear of death, as appears in particular in the vivid descriptions of the deaths of his characters—of Ligeia especially. Sometimes it takes the form of a fear of the void, an insufferable vertigo and an unspeakable horror which overwhelms the hero's soul just as he is going to be swallowed by a bottomless pit, as in "MS. Found in a Bottle." Arthur Gordon Pym disappears in the same way in an awful white chasm at the end of the narrative that recounts his adventures. Only the hero of "A Descent into the Maelström" escapes a similar fate thanks to his Dupin-like coolness and power of observation. At other times Poe imagines final annihilation in the form of an absolute silence suddenly spreading over the whole world and filling all creatures with terror, as in "Silence—A Fable" and the sonnet also entitled "Silence."

This fear of death and engulfment by nothingness (or God?) which constitutes the very matter of most of Poe's tales is not exceptional per se. All men experience it, but it reaches a rare degree of intensity in his works and often takes the form of phobias and manias of a decidedly abnormal character. He thus describes with a curious complacency, as if they were his own, cases of morbid claustrophobia in "The Premature Burial," at the beginning of "The Pit and the Pendulum," and in the first episode of "The Narrative of Arthur Gordon Pym." On other occasions Poe visibly takes pleasure in accumulating macabre and loathsome details. He seems to have a partiality for corpses in a state of advanced decay and never fails to emphasize the nauseating smell which they exhale—as in "The Facts in the Case of M. Valdemar," for instance, when M. Valdemar's body, which had been kept for seven moths in a cataleptic state, suddenly disintegrates. There are even times when this fascination with corpses takes the form of true necrophilia, as in "The Oblong Box;" and the case of Egaeus in "Berenice" is still clearer since he goes as far as digging up the body of his beloved.

Some of Poe's tales also contain undeniable traces of sadism. His half-mad murderers delight in torturing their victims and eventually killing them with devilish savagery. "The old man's terror *must* have been extreme," jubilantly exclaims the murderer of "The Tell-Tale Heart." We are frequently made to witness the dismemberment of corpses, horrible mutilations, or scenes of cannibalism, as in "The Narrative of Arthur Gordon Pym." Even in such a sober tale as "The Murders in the Rue Morgue," Poe cannot resist the temptation of giving all kinds of precise details about the horrible condition of the victims' corpses. In "The Pit and the Pendulum," in spite of all the pity that Poe seems to feel for the unfortunate hero, we may wonder if in his inmost heart he does not secretly admire the Inquisitors' demoniac ingenuity.

Side by side with these signs of sadism, there are also unmistakable indications of masochism, which Poe in "The Philosophy of Composition" sympathetically calls "the human thirst for self-torture." Most of his sick heroes are afflicted with it. It is this perverse instinct which impels them to sink deeper into their nightmares and eventually surrender to madness and confess their crimes publicly at the end in order to be punished and thus suffer still more. In its extreme form this neurosis completely neutralizes the instinct of self-preservation and turns into a passionate desire for self-destruction. This is precisely what happens to Metzengerstein, Roderick Usher, and all the murderers who people Poe's tales. They are all irresistibly attracted and fascinated by death.

Thus Poe constantly allows unavowable thoughts and feelings to rise from the inmost recesses of his soul and give shape in his tales to horrible imaginings. He dreams aloud, and we witness the extraordinary adventures which he took pleasure in inventing because he was not allowed to live them. His heroes are projections of his real and secret self, which, for fear of being condemned and suppressed, his social self was obliged to keep hidden. At the beginning of "The Man of the Crowd" he declares: "It was well said of a certain German book that 'er lässt sich nicht lesen'—it does not permit itself to be read. There are some secrets which do not permit themselves to be told." He was unable completely to hide his own thoughts, though. Impelled by the same desire to confess as so many of his characters, he gave free play to the obsessions which tortured him and lent them to his heroes in order to revel in them by proxy. His tales—especially those which he called "tales of imagination"—were not the result of a conscious effort, but were to a large extent dictated to him by his subconscious cravings, as Gaston Bachelard has shown in his books on the four elements. They are not gratuitous inventions or intellectual fabrications, but veiled confessions. Besides, the return of the same themes and the permanence of certain phobias or manias show that Poe was a prey to well-defined obsessions and obeyed irresistible motivations.

Hence the special quality of the fantastic element in his tales. For we must here use the word "fantastic" rather than "supernatural." Poe himself used it in "The Island of the Fay": "These fancies, and such as these, have always given to my meditations . . . a tinge of what the every-day world would not fail to term fantastic." By this word he probably meant the intrusion of mysterious elements upon the world of the senses, but this intrusion in his case always took place without the exterior intervention of specters, monsters, devils, or miracles. In his tales terror intrudes into the everyday world in a more subtle way. It is aroused by the visions and hallucinations of his characters. The fantastic element is thus here of a subjective, or more precisely, oneiric, origin. No ghosts or supernatural happenings are needed. We deal only with nightmares described as such—though sometimes an objective element is slyly added, as in "Metzengerstein" when the portion of the tapestry representing the horse of one of the Berlifitzings suddenly vanishes at the very moment when the selfsame horse appears alive in the yard of the castle. We might think that Metzengerstein is the victim of an illusion if he were the only witness to this disappearance, but since it is also observed by one of his pages, we must admit that it is an objective phenomenon and not a mere hallucination. Exceptionally in this particular example, fantasy yields to the supernatural, but everywhere else it is linked up with morbid states which become the source of frightening and phantasmagoric visions. As Baudelaire noted, the fantastic element in Poe's tales is grounded in "*exceptions* in human life and in nature . . . hallucinations . . . hysteria usurping the place of the will, contradiction set up between the nerves and the mind, and personality so out of joint that it expresses grief with a laugh. He . . . describes . . . all that imaginary world which floats around a high-strung man acid leads him into evil." "Poe is a writer who is all nerves," he concluded. Indeed, in "Shadow—A Parable," Poe makes this statement which is tantamount to a confession: "There were things around us and about of which I can render no distinct account—things material and spiritual—heaviness in the atmosphere—a sense of suffocation—anxiety—and, above all, that terrible state of existence which the nervous experience when the senses are keenly living and awake, and meanwhile the powers of thought lie dormant."

If Baudelaire had written in our time, he would have spoken of neuroses rather than nerves. Poe is the writer of neuroses. "The

Premature Burial" shows he was fully aware that the epileptic and cataleptic states of his heroes were the consequence rather than the cause of their morbid thoughts; he discovered before Freud that the health of the body depends on the health of the mind.

The hidden cause of his own neurotic condition—which he desperately tried to escape by drinking and even perhaps by taking drugs—has been diagnosed by one of Freud's friends and disciples, Marie Bonaparte. She has set forth her thesis in a bulky book full of insight and ingenuity whose general conclusions are irrefutable even if some of her interpretations seem too systematic. According to her, all the disorders from which Poe suffered can be explained by the Oedipus complex and the incurable trauma caused by the tragic disappearance of his mother when he was only three years old. The image of his beautiful and frail young mother sapped by consumption seems indeed to have dominated his whole life and probably explains why he could marry only a child-wife in the person of his cousin Virginia. It is obvious too that all his "ethereal" heroines (the adjective is his), Berenice, Morella, Madeline Usher, Eleonora, Ligeia, are mere reflections of that beloved mother too soon taken from him. Most of them, besides, are introduced to us as cousins of the narrator and close kin to his mother. These lucid and translucid women, lucid like himself and translucid like his mother, inspire his heroes with intellectual rather than sensual passions, with passionate friendship rather than desire. Everything happens as if Poe had forever exhausted all the possibilities of love in his relation with his mother and he or his heroes could only love sick or dying women like his own mother. Love and death are indissolubly merged both in his works and in his life.

Thus Poe's fantastic tales, which on account of their very nature should be quite impersonal, in fact plunge their roots to the inmost recesses of his being. Each of them in a way masks the mouth of a cave in the darkness of which creep monstrous creatures, the author's obsessions and phobias. Or, to use another image, each of his tales is palimpsest, and we must try to read under the legible text the almost completely faded scrawl which it hides and which will clarify everything if we succeed in deciphering it. "The supposition that the book of an author is a thing apart from the author's *Self* is, I think, ill-founded," he once declared.

Like Baudelaire, his French translator and counterpart, Poe could have addressed his reader as "hypocritical reader, my brother!" Whether we like it or not, we feel secret bonds with him and his heroes—who at times look strangely Kafkaesque or Faulknerian. Indeed, they are both romantic figures and prefigurations of the twentieth-century existentialist hero. They live in an empty, dehumanized, and dechristianized world, plunged in deep melancholy, trailing clouds of glory (and European romanticism), absolutely pure and sexless, refusing to notice the turbid waters into which their dreams sink their snakelike roots. They are often shut up in a secluded place of no exit. They are dark Narcissuses involved in a desperate search for their identity and haunted by an obscure sense of guilt; they feel alienated from the world that surrounds them. They spend their time talking with their double (the narrator) or trying to guess his thoughts (Dupin whose intellect tries to identify itself with that of his opponent); or they struggle with him and finally kill him like William Wilson and, in a way, Prospero in "The Masque of the Red Death." Whether they kill their double (and consequently themselves) or some apparently alien victim, they do so in order to find and define themselves. "I kill, therefore I am." But self-knowledge thus leads to nothing but self-destruction. The application of Socrates' advice "Know thyself" here only results in the realization that the self is bound to die, will sooner or later be sucked in by nothingness. A rather despairing conclusion.

Though he was always unconsciously guided by the secret obsessions of his imagination, Poe did not follow his inspiration blindly. Another faculty constantly interfered. Even in his fantastic tales he never lets himself go. There is method in his madness. Madness, moreover, is not incompatible with reason, as he himself observed on several occasions, notably in "The System of Doctor Tarr and Professor Fether." It sometimes consists in stubbornly making right deductions from wrong premises. Poe, at any rate, knew how to impose a strict discipline on his nightmares. The data of his morbid and undoubtedly disordered imagination are always controlled by a severe method and presented in the form of a clear and logical train of events bound together by connections between causes and effects. In other words, his reason always rules his creative activity. He wanted it so.

According to him, inspiration and reason are compatible; they even combine harmoniously with each other. In his fantastic tales he has succeeded in balancing the two opposite faculties, but so great was the power of reason over him that he composed under its exclusive guidance a series of tales which he rather pedantically called "tales of ratiocination": "The Murders in the Rue Morgue," "The Purloined Letter," "The Gold Bug," "The Mystery of Marie Rogêt," and "Maelzel's Chess-Player." In these tales he behaves as a perfect rationalist and even goes so far as to deny the existence of the supernatural. "In my own heart," he makes the narrator of "The Mystery of Marie Rogêt" declare, "there dwells no faith in praeternature. That Nature and its God are two, no man who thinks will deny. That the latter, creating the former, can, at will, control or modify it, is also unquestionable. I say 'at will'; for the question is of will, and not, as the insanity of logic has assumed, of power. It is not that the Deity *cannot* modify his laws, but that we insult him in imagining a possible necessity for modification." Poe thus fully shares the views of the scientists for whom the only existing phenomena are those of the physical world obeying a set of immutable laws which can be rationally accounted for and expressed in mathematical formulas. We are a long way from the state of mind of the narrator of "The Fall of the House of Usher," whose intelligence on the contrary capitulates before a number of strange happenings which he considers inexplicable: "I was forced to fall back upon the unsatisfactory conclusion, that while, beyond doubt, there *are* combinations of very simple natural objects which have the power of thus affecting us, still the analysis of this power lies among considerations beyond our depth."

Thus reason triumphs in the tales of ratiocination and Poe again and again sings its praises: "As the strong man exults in his physical ability," he exclaims at the beginning of "The Murders in the Rue Morgue," "delighting in such exercises as call his muscles into action, so glories the analyst in that moral activity which *disentangles.* He derives pleasure from even the most trivial occupations bringing his talent into play. He is fond of enigmas, of conundrums, hieroglyphics; exhibiting in his solutions of each a degree of *acumen* which appears to the ordinary apprehension praeternatural."

Poe here describes his own tastes and activities. He was passionately fond of riddles and puzzles. When he was editor of *Graham's Magazine* he wrote a series of articles on cryptography and claimed in one that he had defied the readers of the *Alexander's Weekly Messenger* to send him a cryptogram which he could not decipher. He had received, he said, about one hundred coded messages, all of which he had succeeded in decoding, except one which he had proved to be indecipherable. He was very proud of his ability—though professionals nowadays look down upon him as a mere amateur—and he paraded it in particular in "The Gold Bug."

He applied his ingenuity to all kinds of other problems. In "Maelzel's Chess-Player," for instance, he proved that this famous automaton, which had just been exhibited in a number of American cities, could be nothing but a machine with a man hidden inside. His demonstration in seventeen points is conducted with impeccable logic and his conclusions are incontrovertible. Poe, besides, exhibits a truly scientific spirit by fastening on a seemingly trivial detail—the fact that the automaton always used its left hand—and by basing all his reasoning upon it. For as he points out in "The Murders in the Rue Morgue," "it is by these deviations from the plane of the ordinary, that reason feels its way, if at all, in its search for the true."

Poe could take to pieces with the greatest skill any intellectual mechanism or solve any kind of problem, but he could also do the reverse and build up piece by piece the most plausible and convincing hoax in the world, as he did when he published "The Balloon Hoax" in the *New York Sun* in 1844. "The Murders in the Rue Morgue" is a feat of the same kind, since Poe had to organize and combine the details of the murders with the same regard for logic and consistency as if he were reporting them for a newspaper. It only remained for him then to tell the events in the reverse order, beginning with the still-warm bodies of the victims and working his way back from there to the murderer. Contrary to what the reader may think, the author's ingenuity here does not consist in unraveling the threads of a complex plot, but in weaving a strong web, as Poe himself pointed out in a letter to the poet and critic Philip Pendleton Cooke: "Where is the ingenuity of unravelling a web which you yourself (the author) have woven for the express purpose of unravelling? The reader is made to confound the ingenuity of the suppositious Dupin with that of the writer of the story." At any rate, whether the creative process works backwards or forwards, the interest of this kind of tale is essentially of an intellectual order. The author poses such a complex problem that the reader is unable to solve it, but the author helps him, proves in turn the absurdity of a number of hypotheses, and eventually reaches the only possible solution. What matters is the discovery of the culprit and not the analysis of his or her motives. The human or psychological interest is therefore completely lacking—especially in "The Murders in the Rue Morgue," in which the murderer is not even a man but an orangutang.

So, by applying the most rigorous logic to the writing of fiction, Poe discovered the detective story. Voltaire, it is true, had already created Zadig, but Dupin and his companion were the immediate predecessors of Sherlock Holmes and Dr. Watson and through these had a numberless posterity. However, Poe only exceptionally gave free play to his faculties of analysis and deduction. Most of the time, he preferred to combine them with his imagination and the dark forces of his subconscious. He succeeded in effecting the difficult synthesis of these antagonistic elements thanks to a deliberate strategy of applying to the data provided by his imagination a number of well-defined aesthetic principles.

It is remarkable that even in his very first tales, though he wrote them when he was hardly over twenty, Poe reached mastery of his art. He owed it not only to his full knowledge of the requirements of this difficult genre which demands both conciseness and concentration, but also to the conscious and deliberate fusion of his visionary faculties and his analytical intelligence. In "Magazine-Writing—Peter Snook," he lays it down as a principle that "There is no greater mistake than the supposition that a true originality is a mere matter of impulse or inspiration. To originate is carefully, patiently, and understandingly to combine."

Thus, for Poe—whether he wrote in prose or verse—inspiration was necessary, but not sufficient. He reached at a very early date a voluntarist conception of literary creation which he set forth in several critical essays, "The Philosophy of Composition," "The Poetic Principle," "Fancy and Imagination," and in reviews of Longfellow's poems, Dickens' *Barnaby Rudge,* and above all Hawthorne's *Twice-Told Tales.* All these essays overlap and repeat each other, which proves Poe's belief in the importance of his thesis. And that he should have felt it necessary to write all this dogmatic criticism shows how deeply convinced he was of the power of reason in this field.

To begin with, Poe asserts that inspiration is a legend and a myth and those who claim to have written under its influence are only imposters. According to him *poeta fit, non nascitur*: you are not born a man of genius, you become one, provided you are sufficiently diligent—and intelligent, for everything depends on the will and a judicious application of the intellect. To prove the truth of this paradox, Poe gives as an example his one work that had met with the greatest and most immediate success: "The Raven." He takes it to pieces in "The Philosophy of Composition" in order to show "that no one point in its composition is referable either to accident or intuition—that the work proceeded, step by step, to its completion with the precision and rigid consequence of a mathematical problem."

Yet we cannot take Poe's word for it and blindly accept his thesis that a poet is not an inspired artist but a clever technician knowing how to obtain a deliberately chosen effect by appropriate means. Baudelaire, for all his sympathy with such an aesthetics, could not help voicing some doubts when he commented on "The Philosophy of Composition": "Did he make himself, by a strange and amusing vanity, much less inspired than he naturally was? . . . I should be rather inclined to think so." Indeed, how can we put stock in Poe's so-called confession and believe that "The Raven" was the work of Poe-Dupin alone without the help of the other Poe, the inspired neurotic? It is impossible in particular to believe that his famous refrain was not given to him after long gropings (he had already used "no more" in the "Sonnet—To Zante" and "The Haunted Palace"). Besides, we do know that "The Raven" was not the result of a few hours' lucid work. Its composition was spread over several months. He let it grow organically as it were (conformably with the precepts of romantic aesthetics), and this at a time when Virginia was dying and he was reduced to nearly complete destitution. It is not surprising under such circumstances that "The Raven" should have spontaneously expressed his agony, his haunting fear of the future, his terror at the thought that his beloved wife was soon to disappear forever. It is not a feat of virtuosity, but a cry of pain—even if its form has been cleverly wrought. Poe's account of the genesis of this poem is nothing but an a posteriori analysis. In fact, "The Raven" was to a large extent the result of inspiration, imposed on the poet before being perfected by the craftsman. In a way he confessed this semi-mystification in one of his "Marginalia": "It is the curse of a certain order of mind, that it can never rest satisfied with the consciousness of its ability to do a thing. Not even is it content with doing it. It must both know and show how it is done."

Poe, however, did not underestimate the importance of intuition, as this note shows: "That the imagination has not been unjustly ranked as supreme among the mental faculties, appears from the intense consciousness, on the part of the imaginative man, that the faculty in question brings his soul often to a glimpse of things supernal and eternal—to the very verge of the great secrets. . . . Some of the most profound knowledge—perhaps all *very* profound knowledge—has originated from a highly stimulated imagination. Great intellects *guess* well." But for all the intense awareness of what he owed to inspiration, Poe nevertheless preferred to lay emphasis on analysis and conscious arrangement, all those aspects of the creative activity which can be clearly defined and, to some extent, codified, with regard to the tale as well as poetry.

Poe considered the tale a superior form of art. It is superior to the novel, according to him, and even, to some extent, to poetry: "the tale has a point of superiority even over the poem. In fact, while the *rhythm* of this latter is an essential aid in the development of the poem's highest idea—the idea of the Beautiful—the artificialities of this rhythm are an inseparable bar to the development of all points of thought or expression which have their basis in *Truth*. But Truth is often, and in very great degree, the aim of the tale."

But in order to deserve this eminent status in literature the tale must meet well-defined requirements. And at this point Poe—like Aristotle in his *Poetics*—formulates a number of rules, the first of which bears the name of "unity or totality of interest." It could more simply be called the rule of "unity of effect or impression"—and it is meant to apply to poems as well as tales. Poe defines it in his review of Longfellow's *Ballads*: "in pieces of less extent, the pleasure is *unique*, in the proper acceptation of this term—the understanding is employed, without difficulty, in the contemplation of the picture *as a whole*; and thus its effect will depend, in great measure, upon the perfection of its finish, upon the nice adaptation of its constituent parts, and, especially, upon what is rightly termed by Schlegel *the unity or totality of interest*."

Granting the principle of unity of impression, there remains the problem of determining how it can best be obtained. According to Poe, the first requirement is brevity. One can create an effect of totality or unity only in a sufficiently brief piece. And this is the reason why he thought a poem must not exceed "what can comfortably be read at one sitting, that is to say about a hundred lines, for, if two sittings be required, the affairs of the world interfere, and every thing like totality of effect is at once destroyed." As regards prose, conditions are different. The reader can endure more without having to stretch out his legs. It seemed to him therefore that the ideal length of a short prose narrative was that of a text requiring "from a half-hour to one or two hours in its perusal." In his opinion, such a narrative is superior to a novel, which "deprives itself, of course, of the immense force derivable from *totality*" simply because it cannot be read at one sitting.

The second requirement to be met in order to obtain unity of effect is of the same kind as the first one and directly derives from it. A narrative can be brief only if the action which it recounts takes place in a fairly restricted space. Poe gives this rule a rather barbarous name. He calls it "close circumscription of space." It is much the same thing as the rule of unity of place prescribed by Aristotle, but it is less rigid. The author is not required to keep the actors in one room; he is merely advised not to let them stray away too far from a central point.

As to the third requirement, it is reminiscent of Aristotle's rule of unity of action. Poe does not give it any name, but it concerns the plot and consists in asserting that all the details of a narrative must be closely subordinated to the whole. A tale must be self-sufficient and "should contain within itself all that is requisite for its own comprehension" and nothing else, a prescription which is curiously consonant with the principles of New Criticism.

In practice Poe used two main methods to obtain that impression of unity and homogeneity which he valued so much: subjective narratives and what he called "concatenation." Indeed, all his tales are told in the first person singular, the narrative being placed either in the mouth of the hero or in that of his confidant. This device enabled Poe to link up the incidents with one another by placing them inside one consciousness, and at the same time to fuse them into one by means of comments whose presence under such circumstances seems quite natural. He was aware of the advantages of this method, for in reviewing one of Captain Marryat's books he wrote: "The commenting force can never be safely disregarded. It is far better to have a dearth of incident, with skilful observations upon it, than the utmost variety of event, without." Authorial comment, he affirmed in the review of a novel by William Ainsworth, has "a binding power" which gives unity to the most desultory narratives. On the other hand, he always strove to relate closely to one another the various incidents of a tale by very carefully establishing connections between cause and effect—which made D. H. Lawrence protest that Poe was "rather a scientist than an artist."

Another of Poe's preoccupations was the creation of verisimilitude. In his critical essays, however, he hardly touches upon it because, in his opinion, it was the natural result of that concatenation at which he aimed all the time. Yet in one of his reviews he incidentally reveals one of the devices he used to convince the reader of the authenticity of the extraordinary episodes he related, namely the extreme precision of some details. He was not the inventor of this technique; he acknowledged it implicitly when he praised Defoe. His method, however, was somewhat different from that of Defoe in *Robinson Crusoe* or *A Journal of the Plague Year* since he had to adapt it to his own purpose. "It consists principally," he said, "in avoiding, as may easily be done, that *directness* of expression which we have noted in *Sheppard Lee* [by Robert M. Bird] and thus leaving much to the imagination—in writing as if the author were firmly impressed with the truth, yet astonished at the immensity of the wonders he relates, and for which, professedly, he neither claims nor anticipates credence—in minuteness of detail, especially upon points which have no immediate bearing upon the general story [for example, the description of the House of Usher and the apparently incidental mention of the fissure in the façade]—this minuteness not being at variance with indirectness of expression—in short, by making use of the infinity of arts which give verisimilitude to a narration."

It is thus clear that Poe deliberately applied to the fantastic tale some of the devices of the realistic novel. He loved small details and, like Dupin, had a keen sense of observation. Hence his precise descriptions of the setting in some of his tales: the old abbey bought in England by Ligeia's husband, the castle where Prospero and his court take refuge in "The Masque of the Red Death," the school attended by William Wilson in his childhood—hence also the pseudo-scientific substructure of "The Unparalleled Adventure of One Hans Pfaall." It was his way of rooting fantasy in reality, but conversely he also had to avoid precision as soon as he touched on fantasy; he then had to suggest and use, as he said, "indirect" means of expression. Passages of realistic description appear in his tales only as isles of light in a dark landscape. He recommended against accumulating details: "An outline frequently stirs the spirit more pleasantly than the most elaborate picture." Generally speaking, he had only contempt for pure realism: "That the chief merit of a picture is its *truth,* is an assertion deplorably erroneous. Even in Painting, which is, more essentially than Poesy, a mimetic art, the proposition cannot be sustained."

Poe's aim was not exclusively truth, but also what he called "passion, or the excitement of the heart," which "although attainable, to a certain extent, in poetry [is] far more readily attainable in prose." Hence his emphasis on the "tone" of the tale aside from the contents, on the impression to be produced rather than on the purely narrative element. Besides, he thought that a tale must not be a mere narrative, for then its "hardness" and "nakedness" would "repel the artistical eye." "Two things are invariably required," he claimed: "first some amount of complexity, or more properly adaptation; and secondly, some amount of suggestiveness—some undercurrent, however indefinite, of meaning. . . . It is this latter, in especial, which imparts to a work of art so much of that *richness* (to borrow from colloquy a forcible term). . . ."

In other words, the reader must feel beyond the letter of the narrative the presence of a spirit which confers on all the details and incidents a precious but inexpressible meaning. Here Poe joins hands with Coleridge and the German romantics. He wants his tales to bring the reader into contact with what he called "the Ideal" or, as he also said, borrowing the word from Augustus Wilhelm Schlegel, he wants them to be "mystic."

Such was his ultimate aim. His tales were not ends in themselves, but a means to make us feel the mystery and horror of our condition. We must go beyond the surface of his narratives. Most of his texts are only pretexts which he uses to take us beyond appearances. His purpose was not simply to build perfect plots, but to make us share his dreams, and through the rational to reveal the irrational to us.

All these aesthetic principles often seem to verge on transcendentalism. But Poe, who felt only contempt for Emerson and his disciples, would have indignantly rejected such an insinuation. He equated transcendentalism with the surrender of intelligence and the failure of reason. For his part he was ready to accept the existence of a mystery at the center of the universe, but his intelligence, as *Eureka* shows, strove to pierce it and eventually reached, instead of Emerson's vague pantheism, what Allen Tate has called a form of panlogism. Poe's rationalism, like the hero of "A Descent into the Maelström," resisted the fascination of the abyss and refused to be engulfed by a hazy spiritualism.

However, though Poe tried hard to maintain equipoise on all levels between his reason and his imagination, it is obvious that Roderick Usher repeatedly got the better of the Dupin within him. He was closer at heart to his haunted criminals than to his impassive detective. In the last analysis, therefore, for all their rational construction and cleverly organized narrative contents, his tales are lyric outbursts in disguise, in which the "I" of the speaker corresponds less to fictitious characters than to Poe himself, had he let himself go. And this is one of the reasons why he never succeeded in creating any lifelike characters in his tales (his personal experience of life was much too limited). He gave as an excuse that the extreme brevity of the tale does not lend itself to the study in depth of characters, but the true reason was that he was himself the hero of all his tales. If Roderick Usher, Egaeus, Metzengerstein, and even Dupin are all alike, if Ligeia, Morella, and Eleonora look like sisters, it is because, whether he consciously wanted to or not, he always takes the story of his own life as a starting point, a rather empty story on the whole since he had mostly lived in his dreams, imprisoned by his neuroses and obsessed by the image of his dead mother. What he makes the narrator of "Berenice" confess is probably partly true of himself: "The realities of the world affected me as visions, and as visions only, while the wild ideas of the land of dreams became, in turn,—not the material of my every-day existence—but in very deed that existence utterly and solely in itself."

This further explains why he rebelled against the moralizing literature of the America of his time, why he protested against what he called "didacticism." His only care and preoccupation was to take himself, that is to say his dreams, as the subject of his tales under the pretext of entertaining the reader.

What Joseph Wood Krutch has said of Poe's detective stories, that he invented the genre in order not to go mad, applies to all his tales. Describing the arabesques of his reveries in fictional narratives helped him to exorcise his inner demons. But he had still another derivative: humor. Besides his tales of imagination and ratiocination, he also wrote what he called grotesque tales: "The Devil in the Belfrey," "Lionizing," "Four Beasts in One; the Homo-Cameleopard," "Some Words with a Mummy," "The Angel of the Odd," "The System of Doctor Tarr and Professor Fether," "The Duke de l'Omelette," "Loss of Breath," "Bon-Bon," "How to Write a Blackwood Article," "Peter Pendulum," "The Spectacles," "Mystification," "Why the Little Frenchman Wears His Hand in a Sling," "Never Bet the Devil Your Head," "The Man That Was Used Up" (which was taken up by Nathanael West in *A Cool Million*), etc. All these tales, which have often been neglected by critics, are above all parodies now of himself, now of others, or, rather, of himself as well as others, since he had such deep affinities with the fantastic tales which were then so popular. The lucid reasoner in him could not but make fun of the ghosts conjured up by his neurotic self. Torn by his neuroses, tormented in all likelihood by his sexual impotence, baffled by life, Poe nevertheless refused to acknowledge his defeat and preferred to laugh at his misfortune rather than lament over it. The black humor of his tales expresses this courageously concealed despair; it is a desperate challenge to the blind forces which overcome the defenseless individual. As André Breton put it, it is "a higher revolt of the mind."

"Loss of Breath" is quite characteristic in this respect. Its subtitle, "A Tale neither in nor out of 'Blackwood,' " immediately stamps it as a parody. It is a warning that we must not take it seriously. There is little danger that we should, for the very first lines are made comic by the incongruous contrast between the epic bombast of the tone and the triviality of the subject. Poe's humor here as elsewhere is based on exaggeration and overstatement—as in Dickens. The reader suddenly finds himself in a world of hyperboles in which there is no happy mean between obesity and extreme leanness, between a vociferating voice and a whisper. These absurd contrasts are irresistibly ludicrous and one cannot help laughing, either, at the cascade of misfortunes which happen to the hero with quasi-mechanical regularity. "Mechanics stuck on life is always laughable," as Bergson noted. The reader indulges in all this merriment without any qualms, for though his tormentors break Mr. Lacko'breath's head and arms, cut his ears, disembowel him, and finally hang him, he remains as insensitive to pain as Donald Duck in a Walt Disney cartoon. He is—and so are we—anesthetized by humor. We live with him in a nonsensical world in which man is nothing but a wooden puppet and life and death have no meaning. Everything becomes relative and extremes meet and merge. It is the realm of paradox. The most commonly accepted notions are denied or reversed in the most unexpected manner and with a great show of seriousness. The logic of the tale is impeccable, but all the incidents derive from a deliberately absurd premise, namely that you can lose and find your breath, just as you can lose and find your purse—or a character in a tale of imagination can lose and find his shadow. The starting point is the literal interpretation of a common phrase, "to lose one's breath"—humorists often use this trick—and this provides the first link in a chain of irresistibly comic episodes. The underlying subject, however, is tragic despite the apparently happy ending. It is the story of a newly married man suddenly stricken with sexual impotence and excluded from life. It reveals under the disguise of a farce the secret wound from which Poe suffered all his life, the source of all his torments and terrors.

Except for a half-dozen very popular poems, Poe is chiefly known nowadays as a teller of tales. The corpus of his poems, besides, is extremely small. Yet his supreme ambition was to be a poet: "Events not to be controlled have prevented me from making, at any time, any serious effort in what, under happier circumstances, would have been the field of my choice." He ranked poetry higher than prose (when he was not pleading the cause of the tale), because it is "the desire of the moth for the star," "the rhythmical creation of Beauty," and "Beauty is the sole legitimate province of the poem"—whereas the domain of prose is merely Truth. In other words, the writing of prose is a human occupation—whereas, when a poet writes verse, he creates something in the full sense of the word; he rivals God. Before Whitman, Poe stripped poetry of all the adventitious elements which tended to hide it, whether epic, descriptive, or didactic. His aim was pure poetry, his ideal a sheer lyric outburst. Consequently, he denounced prolixity and, as we have afready seen, insisted that a poem must be short: "a long poem does not exist . . . the phrase, 'a long poem,' is simply a flat contradiction in terms."

Such were the principles he laid down in "The Poetic Principle" (1850). In practice he succeeded only gradually in purging his own poems of heterogeneous elements. "Tamerlane" (1827) and "Al Aaraaf" (1829) are long poems somewhat in Shelley's manner and to some extent tell a story. Even "The Raven" (1845) is in a way a tale in verse rather than a pure poem. But his ultimate object was a self-sufficient and self-contained poem similar to the long, smooth, white vault painted by Usher, completely cut off from the everyday world of common sense and hard material objects, containing nothing but evanescent and ethereal dreaming visions. "Oh! nothing earthly save the ray / (Thrown back from flowers) of Beauty's eye . . ." he exclaimed at the very beginning of "Al Aaraaf." He aspired after what he called "supernal Beauty" rather than plastic Beauty, "the Beauty above" rather than "the Beauty before us." The poet according to him must be "inspired by an ecstatic prescience of the glories beyond the grave." It seemed to him that such a form of poetry produced "an elevating excitement of the Soul" independent of both the "Heart" (matter, the body) and the "Intellect" (reason).

He wanted the poet's imagination to reach beyond itself, so to speak, and his ideal was Israfel, the angel "whose heartstrings are a lute," singing "an unimpassioned song" to spiritual love ("the true, the divine Eros—the Uranian, as distinguished from the Dionaean Venus").

It is out of this rarefied matter that Poe wrote most of his shorter poems on the twin themes of Eros and Thanatos, love and death—"To Helen" (1831) for instance, which is addressed to an ideal rather than to any real woman, to a goddess from another world whom the poet worships for her holiness rather than her beauty. The last stanza is an apotheosis: Helen is suddenly metamorphosed into Psyche (the soul). The communion of souls replaces the union of bodies. Indefiniteness displaces sensuousness ("The naked senses sometime see too little—but then *always* they see too much") and the poem becomes something out of space and out of time, a rare aerial orchid without any roots. "For Annie" (1849) in the same way sings the Lethean peace of death:

> Thank Heaven! the crisis—
> The danger is past . . .
> And the fever called "Living"
> Is conquered at last.

"Ulalume" (1847) in the form of strange and infinitely sad images expresses indirectly all the mystery and terror of death—in application of the principle that "the death of a beautiful woman is, unquestionably, the most poetical topic in the world—and equally is it beyond doubt that the lips best suited for such a topic are those of a bereaved lover."

So, in his poetry as in his tales, Poe turns his back on the world of the senses and a poem in his hands becomes an end in itself. He believed in what he called the "poem *per se*—this poem which is a poem and nothing more—this poem written solely for the poem's sake." He would undoubtedly have subscribed to Archibald MacLeish's prescription that "A poem should not mean / But be." He was already preparing the way for some of the most extreme experiments of the French Symbolists.

He believed in the power of images (or more specifically of sad and dreamy evocations), and also, like the French Symbolists, in music. He wanted the reader "to see with his ear." He was an extraordinarily skillful metrist, passionately interested in prosody, as his essay on "The Rationale of Verse" (1848) testifies. He was not satisfied with mere harmony, which, according to him, consists of "the regular alternation of syllables differing in quantity" and is a matter of rhythm. He insisted that over and above harmony there must be "melody," which is a matter of sounds. Hence his emphasis on rhymes and refrains and his frequent use of alliterations. "The perception of pleasure in the equality of sounds is the principle of music," he maintained. In the name of this principle he multiplied rich and even opulent rhymes and combined them in ingenious stanzaic patterns in order to obtain, as he said, both "equality and unexpectedness," both anticipation and surprise. His supreme aim was incantation, what he called "the magic power of verse." All the clever prosodical devices he used and sometimes invented were intended to hypnotize the reader by appealing almost exclusively to his ear (which is the most passive of senses) and thus stir emotions and passions at a deep and almost elemental level.

Unfortunately, however, he had a tendency to overdo it. He too often and too deliberately strained after effect. At such times his poems develop mechanically instead of organically. They are the fruit of artifice rather than art. The excessive accumulation of alliterations and rich rhymes again and again betrays his desire to show off his technical virtuosity. Though he praises "the concord of sound and sense principle," he then completely sacrifices sense to sound and truly deserves the epithet of "jingle man" which Emerson applied to him. Aldous Huxley has devastatingly criticized his oversonorous rhymes: "Poe's rich rhymes . . . are seldom above suspicion. That dank tarn of Auber is only very dubiously a fit poetical companion for the tenth month. . . . On other occasions Poe's proper names rhyme not only well enough, but actually, in the particular context, much too well. Dead D'Elormie [in "The Bridal Ballad"] is first cousin to Edward Lear's aged Uncle Arly sitting on a heap of barley—ludicrous, but also (unlike dear Uncle Arly) horribly vulgar, because of the too musical lusciousness of his invented name and his display . . . of an obviously faked Norman pedigree. Dead D'Elormie is a poetical disaster." Allen Tate, for his part, objects to the insistence and monotony of Poe's rhythms, which, he says, are for the metronome, not the human ear. T. S. Eliot summed up the case by concluding that "his versification is not, like that of the greatest masters of prosody, of the kind which yields a richer melody, through study and long habituation, to the maturing sensibility of the reader returning to it at times throughout his life. Its effect is immediate and undeveloping; it is probably much the same for the sensitive schoolboy and for the ripe mind and cultivated ear."

There is thus a general agreement among writers of the English-speaking world that Poe as a poet has a very limited range and suffers from exasperating defects. Yet he has been praised to the skies by such French poets as Baudelaire, Mallarmé, and Paul Valéry. The reason for this discrepancy is that these poets because of linguistic differences have not felt the vulgarities of Poe's manner. They have been sensitive only to the high seriousness of his poetic quest and been filled with admiration for the boldness of his attempt to express the inexpressible by means of words.

Such was his ambition—or, according to some, his megalomania—that he considered no undertaking too difficult for his genius and he even attempted to solve the riddle of the universe in the middle of his distress after the death of Virginia. The result was a supreme "prose-poem," *Eureka.* The title itself is a shout of triumph: "I have found! I have found the answer!" Poe-Dupin had decoded the secret message of God thanks to his usual combination of intuition and deduction. In this brilliant essay written in lucid, unpretentious prose, Poe expounds a cosmogony, "a survey of the universe" contemplated in its oneness and diversity. It is a grandiose vision based on the findings of Newton, Laplace, Leibnitz, Alexander von Humboldt, and other cosmologists, and Poe's conclusions are quite consonant with the conclusions of contemporary physicists. He makes a distinction between the universe of stars studied by astronomers, which is limited, and the universe of space, which contains it and is infinite, its center, in Pascal's phrase, being everywhere and its circumference nowhere. An irresistible intuition, which is the sum of shadowy and elusive inductions and deductions in his inmost mind, makes him posit a God in the middle of this infinite void space, a God that is "not-Matter," therefore Spirit, who originally created matter by dint of volition out of his Spirit or from Nihility—pure matter in a state of absolute "simplicity," i.e., of oneness, which then exploded into apparently infinite multiplicity and diversity. Thus the physical world in Poe's hands becomes essentially energy, perpetual motion, permanent tension between centrifugal and centripetal forces, between attraction which is of the body and repulsion which is of the soul, or between gravity and electricity. Because "the atoms were, at some remote epoch of time, even *more than together* . . . because originally and therefore normally they were *One* . . . now, in all circumstances, they struggle *back* to this absolutely, this irrelatively, this unconditionally *one,*" as the law of gravity shows. This "awful Present" leads to a "still more awful Future," for all will eventually coalesce and return to Unity and therefore to that Nothingness which both fascinates and frightens so many of Poe's heroes: "The final globe of globes will instantaneously disappear, and . . . God will remain all in all." A tragic denouement to a perfect plot. *Eureka* in a way enlarges the dimensions of the cosmos of Poe's fantastic tales. It celebrates in metaphysical terms both the irresistible dynamism of life and the terror of death. It posits the essential unity of the cosmos toward which all his characters irresistibly gravitate.

The story of the cosmos does not stop there, however; there is a postscript to it, for Poe imagines the processes of diffusion and concentration may be reversed forever and forever, "a novel universe swelling into existence, and then subsiding into nothingness, at every throb of the Heart Divine," that is to say of his own heart, since we are part and parcel of the spiritual ether which pervades all matter, of "this Divine Being, who thus passes his Eternity in perpetual variation of Concentrated Self and almost Infinite Self-Diffusion." At the end of *Eureka,* the poet becomes God or God becomes the supreme poet.

Actually this apotheosis never took place—in this world at least. After he had written Eureka, Poe was torn by the two opposite forces of attraction and repulsion which he had described. He craved for death and wrote to his aunt and mother-in-law, Mrs. Clemm: "I must die. I have no desire to live since I have done 'Eureka.' " And at the same time he was frantically looking for a substitute for Virginia (and his mother) among a group of widows whom he courted all at once, rushing from one to the other, trying to make them promise to marry him. He thus went to Richmond in July 1849 to call on his former childhood sweetheart, Mrs. Sarah Elmira Royster Shelton. On the way back he stopped at Baltimore and no one knows what happened to him there. A few days later he was found unconscious in a gutter and taken to a hospital. He died there without regaining consciousness on October 7, 1849, at the age of forty.

Two days later, the Reverend Rufus Griswold, his treacherous literary executor, launched him on his checkered posthumous career by declaring that in Poe "literary art had lost one of its most brilliant but erratic stars." From then on Poe was to be reviled by some and extravagantly lauded by others. His main weakness, besides the ethereality of his matter, is indisputably his style. Although Walter de la Mare thought that his "heightened language" captures the fancy, most readers find it on the contrary irritating, pretentious, verbose, needlessly mannered and stilted. D. H. Lawrence in particular writes: "Poe has been so praised for his style. But it seems to me a meretricious affair. 'Her marble hand' [Ligeia's] and 'the elasticity of her footfall' seem more like chair-springs and mantelpieces than a human creature." But the most savage criticism came from Aldous Huxley in "Vulgarity in Literature." According to him Poe "is, as it were, one of Nature's Gentlemen, unhappily cursed with incorrigible bad taste." He cannot resist the lure of paste jewels. He loves superlatives and, contrary to what Pudd'nhead Wilson and Ezra Pound were later to recommend, he never uses a noun without coupling it with an adjective, preferably vague and suggestive of gloom, horror, vastness, strangeness, or indefiniteness.

Despite this proliferation of adjectives, Poe's language gives an impression of poverty and monotony, at least as far as the vocabulary of sensations is concerned. His is an intellectual style. He is not really interested in the physical world. The only precise sensuous details that he mentions are visual (sight being the most intellectual of our senses) and refer to colors—especially black, gray, and white (a sinister color with him), followed far behind by red and brown, the colors of blood, but even then he will be more interested in displaying his verbal virtuosity by playing with such words as "ebony," "sable," "swarthy," "dusky," "inky" for "black" than in defining a sensuous quality.

Thus lack of sensuousness, however, was to some extent deliberate and consistent with that "ideality," as he called it, with which he wanted his tales to be permeated. "The indefinite," he claimed, "is an element in the true poíhsis (poiesis.)" He had therefore to wrench the reader from his usual surroundings by using "rare and radiant" words, and that is why to common words of Anglo-Saxon origin he systematically preferred Latin terms. In the fantastic world of his tales, grass is never green but "verdant," an illness becomes a "malady," an outline a "contour." His characters do not see the sky but "heaven" or "the firmament," and they speak an outlandish language: "The days have never been when thou couldst love me—but her whom in life thou didst abhor, in death thou shalt adore."

The reason for Poe's relative failure is the discrepancy between the irrational nature of what he wanted to convey and the imperturbably intellectual character of his means of expression. In his writings, as in life, even when raving mad, he always behaved and expressed himself like an eighteenth-century gentleman. He felt like a romantic and even like a twentieth-century neurotic, but described his disintegrating personality in the prim and elegant language of an English essayist of the age of Steele and Addison, or of a romancer of the Gothic school. Whitman realized this and appraised him with his usual uncanny insight: "I was not an admirer [of Poe's poems], tho' I always saw that beyond their limited range of melody (like perpetual chimes of music bells, ringing from lower b flat up to g) they were melodious expressions, and perhaps never excell'd ones, of certain pronounc'd phases of human morbidity."

And yet it works. The charm operates. We cannot read or reread his best tales and poems without a thrill. Though his heroes behave in a Grand Guignol manner in rather inauthentic settings and speak an unreal language, we feel a secret kinship with them. The same nightmarish monsters which haunt them roam the deeper layers of our minds. Their fears and obsessions are ours too—at least potentially. They echo in our souls and make us aware of unplumbed depths in our inmost hearts.

Selected Bibliography

WORKS OF EDGAR ALLAN POE

PRINCIPAL SEPARATE WORKS

Tamerlane and Other Poems, "by a Bostonian" (Boston: Calvin F. S. Thomas, Printer, 1827).

Al Aaraaf, Tamerlane, and Minor Poems, (Baltimore: Hatch and Dunning, 1829).

Poems, Second Edition (New York: Elam Bliss, 1831).

The Narrative of Arthur Gordon Pym, (New York: Harper and Brother, 1838).

Tales of the Grotesque and Arabesque, 2 vols. (Philadelphia: Lea and Blanchard, 1840).

Tales, (New York: Wiley and Putnam, 1845).

The Raven and Other Poems, (New York: Wiley and Putnam, 1845).

Eureka: A Prose Poem, (New York: Geo. P. Putnam, 1848).

COLLECTED AND SELECTED EDITIONS

The Works of the Late Edgar Allan Poe, with a memoir by Rufus Wilmot Griswold and "Notices of His Life and Genius" by Willis, N. P. and Lowell, J. R., 4 vols. (New York: J. S. Redfield, 1850–56).

The Works of E. A. Poe, edited by John H. Ingram, 4 vols. (New York: W. J. Widdleton, 1876).

The Works of Edgar Allan Poe, edited by Richard H. Stoddard., 6 vols. (New York: A. C. Armstrong, 1884).

The Works of Edgar Allan Poe, edited by Edmund C. Stedman and George E. Woodberry, 10 vols. (Chicago: Stone and Kimball, 1894–95).

The Complete Works of Edgar Allan Poe, (Virginia Edition), edited by James A. Harrison, 17 vols. (New York: George D. Sproul, 1902) Also printed as the Monticello Edition in the same year.

The Complete Works of E. A. Poe, with Biography and Introduction by Nathan H. Dole, 10 vols. (Akron, Ohio: Werner Co., 1908).

The Complete Poems of E. A. Poe, edited by J. H. Whitty, (Boston: Houghton Mifflin, 1911).

The Poems of Edgar Allan Poe, edited by Killis Campbell, (Boston: Ginn, 1917).

The Works of Edgar Allan Poe, with Biographical Introduction by Hervey Allen (New York: W. J. Black, 1927).

Selected Poems of E. A. Poe, edited by Thomas O. Mabbott (New York: Macmillan, 1928).

The Complete Poems and Stories of E. A. Poe, with Selections from His Critical Writings, edited by Arthur H. Quinn, 2 vols. (New York: Knopf, 1946).

The Letters of Edgar Allan Poe, edited by John W. Ostrom (Cambridge, Mass.: Harvard University Press, 1948) Reprinted with Supplement (New York: Gordian Press, 1966).

Collected Works of Edgar Allan Poe, edited by Thomas Ollive Mabbott, Vol. I, *Poems* (Cambridge, Mass.: Harvard University Press, 1969).

BIBLIOGRAPHIES

Dameron, J. Lesley, *Edgar Allan Poe: A Checklist of Criticism, 1942–1960,* (Charlottesville: Bibliographical Society of the University of Virginia, 1966).

Heartman, Charles F., and Canny, James R., *A Bibliography of First Printings of the Writings of Edgar Allan Poe,* (Hattiesburg, Miss.: The Book Farm, 1943).

Hubbell, Jay B. "Poe," *Eight American Authors: A Review of Research and Criticism,* edited by James

Woodress. Revised edition (New York: Norton, 1971), paperback (1972).

Robbins, J. Albert, *Checklist of E. A. Poe,* (Columbus, Ohio: Merrill, 1969).

Robertson, John W., *Bibliography of the Writings of Edgar Allan Poe,* 2 vols. (San Francisco, 1934).

Poe Studies, a periodical (formerly *Poe Newsletter,* 1968–), publishes at least twice yearly articles, notes, and exhaustive bibliographies on Poe.

CONCORDANCE

Booth, Bradford, and Jones, Claude E., *A Concordance of the Poetical Works of Edgar Allan,* (Baltimore: Johns Hopkins Press, 1941).

CRITICAL AND BIOGRAPHICAL STUDIES

Alexander, Jean, *Affidavits of Genius: E. A. Poe and the French Critics, 1874–1924,* (Port Washington, N.Y.: Kennicat Press, 1971).

Allen, Hervey, *Israfel: The Life and Times of Edgar Allan Poe,* 2 vols. (New York: Doran, 1926).

Allen, Michael, *Poe and the British Magazine Tradition,* (Cambridge, Mass.: Harvard University Press, 1969).

Bachelard, Gaston, *L'Eau et les rêves,* (Paris: Corti, 1942).

———, *L'Air et les songes,* (Paris: Corti, 1943).

Baudelaire, Charles, *Baudelaire on Poe: Critical Papers,* translated by Lois and Francis E. Hyslop, Jr. (State College, Pa.: Bald College Press, 1952).

Benton, Richard P., *New Approaches to Poe: A Symposium,* (Hartford, Conn.: Transcendental Books, 1971).

Bittner, William, *Poe, A Biography,* (Boston: Little, Brown, 1962).

Bonaparte, Marie, *The Life and Works of Edgar Allan Poe,* translated by John Rodker (London: Imago, 1949).

Broussard, Louis, *The Measure of Poe,* (Norman: University of Oklahoma Press, 1969).

———, *Poe's Vision of Man,* (Storrs: University of Connecticut Press, 1972).

Buranelli, Vincent, *Edgar Allan Poe,* (New York: Twayne, 1961).

Campbell, Killis, *The Mind of Poe and Other Studies,* (Cambridge, Mass.: Harvard University Press, 1933).

Carlson, Eric W., ed., *The Recognition of Edgar Allan Poe,* (Ann Arbor: University of Michigan Press, 1966) An anthology of Poe criticism.

Cobb, Palmer, *The Influence of E. T. A. Hoffman on the Tales of E. A. Poe,* (Chapel Hill: North Carolina University Press, 1908).

Davidson, Edward H., *Poe: A Critical Study,* (Cambridge, Mass.: Harvard University Press, 1957).

Eliot, T. S., "From Poe to Valéry," *Hudson Review* 2: 327–43 (August 1949).

Fagin, N. Bryllion, *The Histrionic Mr. Poe,* (Baltimore: Johns Hopkins Press, 1949).

Fiedler, Leslie A., *Love and Death in the American Novel,* (New York: Criterion Books, 1960).

Foerster, Norman, *American Criticism: A Study in Literary Theory from Poe to the Present Day,* (New York: Houghton Mifflin, 1928).

Hoffman, Daniel, *Poe Poe Poe Poe Poe Poe Poe,* (Garden City, N.Y.: Doubleday, 1972).

Huxley, Aldous, "Vulgarity in Literature," *Music at Night* (London: Chatto and Windus, 1930).

Krutch, Joseph Wood, *Edgar Allan Poe: A Study in Genius,* (New York: Knopf, 1926).

Lawrence, D. H., *Studies in Classic American Literature,* (London: Thomas Seltzer, 1923).

———, *Poe and France: The Last Twenty Years,* (Baltimore: E. A. Poe Society, 1970).

Moss, Sidney, *Discoveries in Poe,* (Notre Dame, Ind.: University of Notre Dame Press, 1970).

———, *Poe's Major Crisis: His Libel Suit and New York's Literary World,* (Durham, N.C.: Duke University Press, 1970).

Parks, Edw., *Edgar Allan Poe as Literary Critic,* (Athens: University of Georgia Press, 1964).

Pollin, Burton R., *Dictionary of Names and Titles in Poe's Collected Works,* (New York: Da Capo, 1968).

Quinn, Arthur Hobson, *Edgar Allan Poe: A Critical Biography,* (New York: Appleton-Century, 1941).

Quinn, Patrick F., *The French Face of Edgar Poe,* (Carbondale: Southern Illinois University Press, 1957).

Rans, Geoffrey, *EdgarAllan Poe,* (Edinburgh and London: Oliver and Boyd, 1965).

Regan, Robert, ed., *Poe—A Collection of Critical Essays,* (Englewood Cliffs, N.J.: Prentice-Hall, 1967).

Shanks, Edward, *Edgar Allan Poe,* (London: Macmillan, 1937).

Stovall, Floyd, *Edgar Poe the Poet: Essays New and Old on the Man and His Work,* (Charlottesville: University of Virginia Press, 1969).

Tate, Allen, "The Angelic Imagination: Poe and the Power of Words," *Kenyon Review* 14: 455–75 (Summer 1952).

———, "Our Cousin, Mr. Poe," *Collected Essays* (Denver: Swallow, 1959).

Wagenknecht, Edward, *Edgar Allan Poe—The Man Behind the Legend,* (New York: Oxford University Press, 1963).

Winters, Yvor, "Edgar Allan Poe: A Crisis in the History of American Obscurantism," *Maule's Curse* (New York: New Directions, 1938).

Woodberry, George E., *Edgar Allan Poe,* Boston (1885).

———, *The Life of Edgar Allan Poe, Personal and Literary, with His Chief Correspondence with Men of Letters,* 2 vols. (Boston, 1909).

Woodson, Thomas, ed., *Twentieth Century Interpretations of "The Fall of the House of Usher,"* (Englewood Cliffs, N.J.: Prentice-Hall, 1969).

POETS OF WORLD WAR I

JOHN PRESS

INTRODUCTION

WHEN EUROPE WENT to war in August 1914 it had not witnessed a major conflict since the defeat of Napoleon at Waterloo in 1815, although the war for the liberation of Italy and Bismarck's wars against Denmark, Austria, and France had reminded politicians that violence might be an effective instrument of policy. Britain's only adventure on the continent, the Crimean War, had revealed the criminal incompetence of the army command, the scandalous state of the hospital services as exposed by Florence Nightingale, and the blundering stupidity of military tactics, seen at its most notorious in the charge of the Light Brigade. But all that was over fifty years before. A study of the American Civil War might have prepared the men of 1914 for what lay before them: the employment of artillery on a very large scale; the devastation of the countryside; the destruction of towns and the wandering of refugees from homes they had been forced to abandon. Yet nobody would have believed that the particular kind of savagery endured in the United States in the 1860's would have marked a conflict between the chivalrous professional armies of Europe fifty years later.

Leonard Woolf describes how he walked over the Sussex Downs in the summer of 1914 and how they looked almost as if unchanged since Domesday. World War I was to transform far more than the landscape of Sussex and of the other English counties. The face of the world was changed and, together with the millions who perished on the battlefields or in the influenza epidemic after the war, the civilization of Europe died. The pages that follow record how some English poets fought in the trenches and wrote poems by which they are remembered.

SOME ESTABLISHED POETS

Many of the older poets, who were well over military age, felt the impulse to write patriotic verse about the war. It is better not to quote Sir William Watson's lines about Germany or his address to the Kaiser, but to remark only that he sank to depths of vulgarity and hysteria unplumbed by any other poet in both world wars. Thomas Hardy's "Men Who March Away" is on a different level of achievement, but it moves with an uncharacteristic jaunty religious fervor that has not worn well. Charles Sorley, a great admirer of Hardy, believed that one line of the poem, "Victory crowns the just," was the worst Hardy had ever written.

Rudyard Kipling (1865–1936) summoned his fellow countrymen to brace themselves for the coming struggle and to gird themselves for sacrifice, "For All We Have and Are" is an accomplished call to arms, an attempt to stiffen the sinews and to strengthen the will. Kipling warns all patriots that "The Hun is at the gate," adroitly seizing on the Kaiser's admonition to his troops at the time of the Boxer rebellion that they should behave like the ancient Huns. Kipling's poems on the war are varied in mood and theme; some are diatribes against politicians who hid the truth before the war and sent men ill-equipped into battle after war had come. He also wrote some memorable epigrams, including one on a soldier executed for cowardice, toward whom he shows an unexpected compassion. Under most of his wartime poems one can detect anger and grief at the death in action of his beloved son.

Unlike Kipling, who was well attuned to the mood of the public, A. E. Housman (1859–1936) caused some offense by his tribute to the regular army, which fought with such courage in the early days of the war and saved the Allies from defeat. People objected to the title of his poem "Epitaph on an Army of Mercenaries," on the grounds that it was an insult to a heroic body of men, even though the word "mercenaries" was an accurate description of their calling. Nor did the pious relish the poem's last two lines:

What God abandoned, these defended,
And saved the sum of things for pay.

Today one admires the laconic precision of the phrasing, the lapidary force of the encomium bestowed by Housman on men who practiced two of the virtues he most cherished: stoical courage and devotion to duty.

One should pay a brief tribute to Ford Madox Ford (1873–1939), who insisted on joining the army and who fought in the trenches, even though overage. It is true that he was probably more of a menace to his military superiors than to the Germans, and that he had enlisted partly to get away from his mistress, Violet Hunt, who was proving even more tiresome than his wife. Nevertheless, it was a gallant gesture, and although Ford was not a very good poet, his "Antwerp" is an interesting example of an attempt to adapt and to enlarge imagistic technique for the purpose of describing war without emotion. The Belgian, with a smoking gun, is an uncomely man in an ugly tunic, and when he is killed he "lies, an unsightly lump on the sodden grass." As late as November 1917, T. S. Eliot described "Antwerp" as "the only good poem I have met with on the subject of the war," which makes one wonder what poems about the war Eliot had read.

"For the Fallen" by Laurence Binyon (1869–1943) is probably familiar to more people than any other poem of World War I. It is so widely known because it is frequently declaimed at memorial services, including services in memory of those who died in the Falkland Islands in 1982. The poem has a solemn, liturgical quality that commends it to those mourning their dead, and since it is free of any tincture of Christian devotion, it appeals to those who want religious dignity without Christian dogma:

They shall grow not old, as we that are left
 grow old:
Age shall not weary them, nor the years
 condemn.
At the going down of the sun and in the
 morning
We will remember them.
(st.4)

Although there is no warrant in the text, congregations habitually supplement the words of the officiating clergyman by intoning a repetition of the last line: "We will remember them." The poem of an individual poet is transformed into a communal liturgical rite. None of Binyon's subsequent poems attained anything like the popularity of "For the Fallen." Halfway through World War II Binyon wrote a poem called "The Burning of the Leaves," which is concerned with the necessity of laying aside all that is ended and done. It may not be fanciful to suppose that he was looking back to the previous war and drawing courage from the experience of 1914–1918 when he achieved the mingled doubt and affirmation of the poem's final line: "Nothing is certain, only the certain spring."

Most of the younger poets who had begun to make a reputation by 1914 were associated, at least in the minds of poetry readers, with the Georgians or the imagists, although these were rough and often misleading classifications. D. H. Lawrence, for example, wandered cheerfully between the two camps, glad to win whatever sustenance he could from either group.

There were obvious links between the

Georgians and the war poets, mainly because Edward Marsh printed their work in the anthologies with which he followed up his initial *Georgian Poetry 1911–1912*. His editorial labors did much to spread the fame of Rupert Brooke and to make more widely known the work of Siegfried Sassoon and of the largely forgotten but by no means untalented W. W. Gibson. Edmund Blunden and Ivor Gurney had strong affinities with Georgianism; and even Wilfred Owen was proud to be held peer by the Georgians, greatly though he surpassed them in technical mastery and imaginative force.

Imagism, on the other hand, had little influence on the war poetry written between 1914 and 1918. The younger imagist poets who served in the trenches included Richard Aldington (later famous as a novelist of the war), Herbert Read, and T. E. Hulme, who was killed in 1915, leaving no war poems. Long after the war Herbert Read sought to explain in *The Contrary Experience* (1963) why the aesthetic theories of imagism were inadequate to explain the "terrorful and inhuman events" of the conflict. Certainly Aldington's war poems, though well constructed, are too decorative and remote to move us greatly. Perhaps his best war poem is "Sunsets," the first stanza of which can be read simply as an impressionistic evocation of the sky at evening:

> The white body of evening
> Is torn into scarlet
> Slashed and gouged and seared
> Into crimson,
> And hung ironically
> With garlands of mist.
> (1–6)

It is only after reading the second stanza that one understands the sinister import of the first, in which the bloody violence of war is mirrored upon the canvas of the natural world:

> And the wind
> Blowing over London from Flanders
> Has a bitter taste.
> (7–9)

Ezra Pound alone among the imagists found adequate expression for the inner meaning of the war, in *Hugh Selwyn Mauberley*; but that poem lies outside the scope of this essay, since it was written by a man who, though living in England, was a civilian and an American.

Just as the avant-garde poetry of the immediate prewar years exerted only a marginal influence on the war poets, so the poetry of 1914–1918 barely affected the modernist movement of the 1920's. Eliot, Pound, and William Butler Yeats seem to have learned nothing even from Owen and Isaac Rosenberg; and although W. H. Auden and the poets of the 1930's professed a deep reverence for Owen, they assimilated little of his achievement except a few technical devices and a tendency to invoke pity as an emotional gesture. It was left to the poets of World War II to discover that certain poems written between 1914 and 1918 gave imaginative shape to unchanging truths about the nature of war and of human life.

MORNING HEROES

Whatever might be said against the landed aristocracy and other members of the British ruling classes in 1914, nobody could gainsay their physical courage. The main fear of the young men among them was that the war might be over by Christmas, thus preventing them from killing Germans. Almost all of them had been educated at public schools, where they had absorbed the codes of honor and duty that governed all who grew up there. The poems of Henry Newbolt (1862–1938), though written mainly during the 1880's and 1890's, still expressed the ethics of the public schools. Indeed, Newbolt in 1914 had not felt it necessary to write any new poems: he merely published a collection of his earlier work, of which 70,000 copies were sold. Poems such as "Vitai Lampada" may nowadays seem ludicrous, but young officers in 1914 accepted the injunction, "Play up! play up! and play the game!" Many of these young officers, most of whom were in no sense professional poets, wrote poems that recorded their experience of combat during the period of the war that ran from August 1914 to the end of June 1916, the eve of the Battle of the Somme. After that the world became darker: the experiences, terrifying but sometimes joyful, of Julian Grenfell and Charles Sorley were replaced by the purgatorial twilight in which Sassoon, Owen, and Rosenberg found themselves.

Raymond Asquith (1878–1916), eldest son of the prime minister, practiced at the bar after a career of exceptional brilliance at Oxford. He left no war poems and indeed was not a poet, although he wrote extremely skillful parodies and pastiches. He deserves to be remembered for his parody of Kipling's jingoistic "Soldiers of the Queen," which begins:

> The sun like a Bishop's bottom
> Rosy and round and hot. . . .

He was typical of his class and his generation in that he volunteered for military service when there was no pressure on him to do so; rejected a safe job as a staff officer for the danger and discomfort of the trenches; and died with courage and composure on the Somme in September 1916, during what the divisional commander called "the greatest of all the war achievements of the Brigade of Guards."

Herbert Asquith (1881–1947), Raymond's younger brother, managed to go through the war from beginning to end unscathed. He is remembered chiefly for a competent though old-fashioned and conventional sonnet, "The Volunteer," about a city clerk who is afraid that he will never break a lance in life's tournament. He volunteers, is killed, and lies content. This poem, with its imagery drawn from medieval knight errantry, is typical in its loftiness and total divorce from reality, the mood in which many young men went to war in 1914. This is not invalidated by the fact that Herbert Asquith wrote "The Volunteer" in 1912.

One of the closest friends of the Asquiths was Julian Grenfell (1888–1915). His father, William Grenfell, a remarkable athlete, was created Lord Desborough in 1905; his mother, "Etty," was probably the most celebrated hostess of her day. Before he was two he had displayed his vigorous enjoyment of killing: "Determined to kill a mouse. Hammer it with a hammer" (Mosley, *Julian Grenfell,* p. 13). He was a man of considerable intelligence, educated at Eton and Balliol, who in 1909 collected but did not publish a book of essays on social and political themes that his strong-minded mother and her friends heartily disliked. He received a commission in the Royal Dragoons in 1910, having passed first among all university graduate entrants to the army. After service in India and then in South Africa, Grenfell planned to give up his army career so that he might devote himself to painting. Etty, with whom his relations were always complex, mocked him and incited her circle of friends to join in the mockery. He capitulated.

On October 1914 Grenfell sailed for France. Although he had never enjoyed the mass slaughter that had characterized Edwardian and Georgian shooting parties, Grenfell had always loved solitary killing, because it represented a link with the earth and furthered his pursuit of primitive things. He perfected a technique that enabled him to stalk Germans after dark, to creep close to them and then shoot them. In mid-November he shot a German on each of two successive evenings, for which he was awarded the Distinguished Service Order. When he went home on leave he made an entry in his game book to the effect that on 16 and 17 November 1914 he had bagged a Pomeranian.

Grenfell's attitude to the war was unambiguous: it is to his credit that he did not drape his naked ferocity in sanctimonious moralizing. He was a killer from the egg, describing war as all the most wonderful *fun.* More sinister is his verdict on the life that he was leading:

> I have never, never felt so well, or so happy, or enjoyed anything so much. It just suits my stolid health, and stolid nerves, and barbaric disposition. The fighting—excitement vital-

> ises everything, every sight and word and action. One loves one's fellow-man so much more when one is bent on killing him. (*Julian Grenfell*, p. 241)

Yet he was not devoid of human feelings. After a passage in a letter from Flanders written in October 1914: "I *adore* war. It is like a big picnic without the objectlessness of a picnic" (p. 239)—Grenfell goes on to express his sense of pity at the wretchedness of the inhabitants who had been forced to leave their homes.

At the end of January 1915 Grenfell returned to France, taking with him three greyhounds—he had always loved the breed and before the war had written a poem entitled "To a Black Greyhound." On 29 April he wrote "Into Battle," the poem that is his surest title to immortality. At 4:00 A.M. on 13 May he was grievously wounded, and although his friends believed that his toughness would pull him through, his wounds proved fatal. On his deathbed, presided over by the indomitable Etty, he quoted Phaedra's song from the *Hippolytus* of Euripides, a play that he had admired since his boyhood. When on 25 May a shaft of sunlight fell across his feet, Grenfell said, "Phoebus Apollo," and did not speak again except once to say his father's name. He died on 26 May with a radiant smile on his face.

"Into Battle" is one of those poems by gifted amateurs that have taken their place in the corpus of English poetry. It brings together many of the strands woven into Grenfell's nature: his love of killing that brought him closer to the earth; the sheer exhilaration of battle; a strain of mysticism. (At the age of thirteen, during a thunderstorm, he suddenly seemed to realize God, and he became devoted to Saint Thomas à Kempis.)

The poem opens with a celebration of the spring, which will enrich the fighting man. Then follows a section in which Grenfell affirms the kinship between the fighting man and the forces of the universe: "the bright company of Heaven"; the woodland trees; the kestrel and the little owls:

> The blackbird sings to him, "Brother,
> brother,
> If this be the last song you shall sing,
> Sing well, for you may not sing another;
> Brother sing."
> (st.6)

Grenfell ends by envisaging the joy of battle, expressing his trust in the Destined Will, and committing himself to the powers of Day and Night.

Another intimate of the Asquith circle was Patrick Shaw-Stewart (1888–1917), whose career at Oxford was only slightly less brilliant than Raymond Asquith's. After leaving Oxford, he joined Baring's Bank, where he rapidly attained a senior position. Soon after the outbreak of war he became a lieutenant-commander in the Royal Naval Division and fought at Gallipoli. He was killed in action in France late in 1917, having refused to quit the field after his ear had been torn off by shrapnel. An untitled poem was found in Shaw-Stewart's copy of Housman's *A Shropshire Lad*, a book whose influence on him it is difficult to overemphasize. The poem begins:

> I saw a man this morning
> Who did not wish to die.

It then considers the fighting in the Dardanelles, reflecting for a moment on Helen of Troy and incorporating into the poem a pun on her name that derives from Euripides. Shaw-Stewart's attainments as a classical scholar rivaled those of Raymond Asquith, and, like Julian Grenfell, he turned quite naturally in moments of crisis and fear to the world of classical Greece. He communes with Achilles, asking him if it was very hard to die, and the poem concludes on a note of affirmation, in which the figure of Achilles is invoked:

> I will go back this morning
> From Imbros over the sea;
> Stand in the trench, Achilles,
> Flame-capped, and shout for me.
> (25–26)

Robert Nichols (1893–1944), although now largely forgotten, was once a name to conjure with, cherished by the reading public as all that a young heroic poet should be, and admired by Edward Marsh as one of his favorite Georgian poets. Marsh was an influential figure, a cultivated member of the English upper classes, private secretary to Winston Churchill, a patron of the arts and editor of the widely read anthology *Georgian Poetry 1911–1912,* the first of five such collections, Although Nichols' army career was in no way discreditable, he was invalided home suffering from shell shock and after five months' treatment in military hospitals received his discharge. Robert Graves, who did not like Nichols, thought him almost a phony, perhaps because after leaving the army he scored a great success with his lectures in the United States on the war, in spite of having experienced active service only for what Graves would have regarded as a ridiculously brief period.

Nichols' wartime poetry, with its mixture of homosexual eroticism and religiosity, has not worn well. Even among his contemporaries there were those who found his work distasteful. Douglas Goldring savagely but justly called "The Assault" "a masterpiece of drivel"; and Wilfred Owen regarded him as "self-concerned and *vaniteux* in his verse" (*Wilfred Owen: Collected Letters,* p. 511). Yet something survives of the romantic vitality and élan that awoke a response in Nichols' first readers. His description of "Dawn on the Somme" was written during the Battle of the Somme while he was being treated for neurasthenia in a hospital:

> Oh, is it mist, or are these companies
> Of morning heroes who arise, arise
> With thrusting arms, with limbs and hair
>   aglow,
> Towards the risen gold, upon whose brow
> Burns the gold laurel of all victories,
> Hero and heroes' gold, th'invincible Sun?
>   (7–12)

After the war his reputation faded, although a selection of his poems, *Such Was My Singing,* appeared in 1942, and he edited *An Anthology of War Poetry* in 1943. Some of his lyrical pieces deserve to be remembered, while "The Sprig of Lime," a poem of about ninety lines, surpasses in gravity and tenderness everything else that Nichols wrote. It remains one of the neglected masterpieces of our time.

A far more formidable figure than Nichols was Rupert Brooke (1887–1915), for whom Edward Marsh felt a deeper affection than for any other Georgian poet. His legendary fame persists to the present day for a variety of reasons. He had many friends of widely different callings, ranging from Virginia Woolf to Geoffrey Keynes, the distinguished surgeon and literary scholar, and Hugh Dalton, chancellor of the exchequer in the Labour government of 1945. In conversations, diaries, memoirs, and letters they united to celebrate Brooke's physical splendor, intellectual power, and literary gifts. The cult of Rupert Brooke still flourishes, given fresh impetus by the revelation that he and Virginia Woolf once bathed naked; and it is possible even now to wax sentimental over the Old Vicarage, at Grantchester, and to get honey for tea in a tea shop in the village.

The building of Rupert Brooke into a legend began almost as soon as he was dead, and it is clear that, in part at least, those who fabricated the edifice did so in order to encourage young men to volunteer for the armed forces. Winston Churchill eulogized him as joyous, fearless, and ruled by high, undoubting purpose. Brooke confessed soon after the outbreak of war that the perils of the time and the darkness of the world made him uneasy and vaguely frightened. Nor was he joyous: he was deeply neurotic, especially in his dealings with women. In a letter of August 1912 to Ka Cox, with whom he had a long affair, Brooke confessed his fear that he was incapable of any fruitful sexual relationship, and testified to his self-disgust. He probably never recovered from the nervous breakdown that ended the affair. After he left Tahiti, where he had found brief happiness with a girl called Taatamata, Brooke received a letter from her full of misspellings in French and English, and he "gulped a good deal."

Brooke had achieved a reputation as a poet before 1914. He was one of the six people who met for luncheon in Edward Marsh's rooms on 20 September 1912 and planned the genesis of *Georgian Poetry.* He was probably the most valued contributor to the first anthology, *Georgian Poetry 1911–1912,* which appeared before the end of 1912.

Brooke's response to the war, a group of war sonnets, appeared in *New Numbers,* December 1914, without attracting much attention. In September, Brooke had received a commission in the Royal Naval Division, which early in 1915 sailed for the Dardanelles in the hope of striking a decisive blow against the Turks. Before he was able to accomplish anything of note, Brooke contracted blood poisoning caused by a bite from a mosquito or a scorpion. He died in a French military hospital on the Greek island of Scyros on Saint George's Day, 23 April. The firing party at his grave on the island, traditionally associated with Achilles, was commanded by Patrick Shaw-Stewart.

Even before Rupert Brooke's death one of his five war sonnets had begun to reach a wide audience. On 5 April 1915, Easter Day, the dean of Saint Paul's, W. R. Inge, had taken as the text for his sermon Isaiah 26:19—"The dead shall live, my dead bodies shall arise. Awake and sing, ye that dwell in the dust." Inge went on to quote one of Brooke's sonnets, "The Soldier," remarking that "the enthusiasm of a pure and elevated patriotism had never found a nobler expression." Three days after Brooke's death Winston Churchill praised the war sonnets in the *Times.* On 16 June 1915 the sonnets were gathered into *1914 and Other Poems,* edited by Edward Marsh. A few months later they were given a separate edition under the title *1914. Five Sonnets.*

Brooke had a gift for the striking phrase and the rhetorical assertion, as the opening lines of three of his sonnets demonstrate:

If I should die, think only this of me:
That there's some corner of a foreign field
That is for ever England.
("The Soldier")

Blow out, you bugles, over the rich Dead!
There's none of these so lonely and poor of old,
But, dying, has made us rarer gifts than gold.
("The Dead")

Now, God be thanked who has matched us with His hour,
And caught our youth, and wakened us from sleeping,
With hand made sure, clear eye, and sharpened power,
To turn, as swimmers into cleanness leaping,
Glad from a world grown old and cold and weary,
Leave the sick hearts that honour could not move,
And half-men, and their dirty songs and dreary,
And all the little emptiness of love!
("Peace")

Yet the sonnets are inadequate, poetically and morally. Even Julian Grenfell had been content to proclaim his love of killing without prating about the cleansing power of war. Nobody since the emotionally disturbed hero of Tennyson's *Maud* (1855), who resolved to plunge into the slaughter of the Crimea, had supposed that war was likely to offer a regenerative experience. Read in the light of what we know about Brooke's psychological difficulties, these sonnets represent the struggle of a highly strung, desperate man to escape from the emotional problems in which he lay trapped. There was a conscious drive toward simplification and self-sacrifice, a barely conscious drifting toward death.

It is significant that three of his contemporaries, all poets who died in battle, were unimpressed by Brooke's sonnets. In a letter to his mother dated 28 November 1914, Charles Sorley remarks that Brooke "is far too obsessed with his own sacrifice, regarding the going to war of himself (and others) as a highly intense, remarkable and sacrificial exploit. . . . He has clothed his attitude in fine words; but he has taken the sentimental attitude" (*Letters,* p. 263). Isaac Rosenberg, who was admittedly jealous of Edward Marsh's devotion to Brooke and to his memory, refers in a letter to

Mrs. Cohen, probably written at midsummer 1915, to the commonplace phrases in Brooke's "begloried sonnets" (*Collected Works,* p. 237). Rosenberg thought that his "Clouds" was a magnificent poem, and, in a letter to Sydney Schiff dating from about August 1916, he singles out for praise Brooke's "Town and Country," but remarks of his other poems that "they remind me too much of flag days" (*Isaac Rosenberg1890–1918: Catalogue with Letters,* p. 16). Edward Thomas, in a letter to Robert Frost of 19 October 1916, while acknowledging that Brooke had "succeeded in being youthful and yet intelligible and interesting (not only pathologically) more than most poets since Shelley," passes a severe judgment on him: "He was a rhetorician, dressing things up better than needed. And I suspect he knew only too well both what he was after and what he achieved" (*Rupert Brooke: A Biography,* p. 502).

It would be ungenerous to conclude on a sour note. When Brooke encountered the reality of war in the retreat from Antwerp in late 1914 he was moved to pity by the spectacle of refugees. In the "Fragment" written on his troopship in April 1915 he describes how, after dark, he remains on deck, watching his friends, unobserved by them. The poem is infused with a profound sadness, an awareness of human fragility. It is worlds away from the mood of the sonnets. Brooke's reaction to Dean Inge's sermon evinces something of his old irony and good sense. When he lay dying, his friend Denis Browne came to his cabin to talk about the dean's sermon, of which Brooke already knew, having received a newspaper clipping from Marsh. The clipping contained Inge's reservation about "The Soldier": "And yet it fell somewhat short of Isaiah's vision and still more of the Christian hope." Brooke murmured his regret that the dean didn't think him quite so good as Isaiah. They were his last coherent words.

Charles Hamilton Sorley (1895–1915) had an intense passion for truth:

> The voice of our poets and men of letters is finely trained and sweet to hear; it teems with sharp saws and rich sentiments: it is a marvel of delicate technique: it pleases, it flatters, it charms, it soothes: it is a living lie. (*The Letters with a Chapter of Biography,* pp. 37–38)

This passage has sometimes been quoted as Sorley's response to the jingoistic poetry of 1914: in fact, it comes from a paper on John Masefield read to the Literary Society of Marlborough College on 3 November 1912.

Sorley, who went to school at Marlborough, was planning to enter Oxford in September 1914, but, after leaving school at the end of 1913, he went to live in Germany in January 1914. He loved Germany, despite his loathing for such evil manifestations as the student corps, with their drunkenness, aggressiveness, and hatred of Jews. Nor did he care for Germany's bigotry and conviction of spiritual superiority. When war broke out he was on a walking tour; he was briefly imprisoned, released, and expelled. As soon as he reached England he applied for a commission.

Sorley was unique among English poets who fought in the war in having an intimate knowledge of Germany. He was in a very small minority of people who detested the tawdry elements in official propaganda, the nauseating humbug preached by journalists and churchmen, whom he stigmatized collectively as Annas and Caiaphas. Even his beloved Hardy's "Men Who March Away" incurred his displeasure. It is, he says, in a letter of 30 November 1914, "the most arid poem in *Satires of Circumstance,* besides being untrue of the sentiments of the ranksman going to war: 'Victory crowns the just' is the worst line he ever wrote—filched from a leading article in *The Morning Post*" (*Letters,* p. 246).

As early as August 1914 Sorley had grasped the truth that Britain and Germany were engaged in a fratricidal conflict. His sonnet "To Germany" opens:

> You are blind like us. Your hurt no man designed,
> And no man claimed the conquest of your land.

The theme of mutual blindness sounds at the end of the octet:

And in each other's dearest ways we stand,
And hiss and hate. And the blind fight the
  blind.

None of Sorley's poems compares in quality with the finest poetry written during the war: his command of poetic technique was inadequate to bear the charge of his imaginative vision. It is in his superb *Letters*, still available in the original edition of 1919, that one finds the best evidence of his intellectual keenness and searing honesty. Nowhere are these qualities more vigorously exhibited than in Sorley's letter to Arthur Watts of August 1915, describing the excitement of the encounter with the enemy:

> . . . the wail of the exploded bomb and the animal cries of the wounded men. Then death and the horrible thankfulness when one sees that the next man is dead: "We won't have to *carry* him in under fire, thank God; dragging will do": hauling in of the great resistless body in the dark, the smashed head rattling: the relief, the relief that the thing has ceased to groan: that the bullet or bomb that made the man an animal has now made the animal a corpse. One is hardened by now: purged of all false pity: perhaps more selfish than before. The spiritual and the animal get so much more sharply divided in hours of encounter, taking possession of the body by swift turns. (pp. 305–306)

One of Sorley's best poems is the untitled "All the hills and vales along," which owes something in mood to Housman. Written before Sorley had seen active service, it ironically celebrates the fact that the marching men are going to their death, urges them to be joyful, and reminds them that Nature will rejoice at their death as it rejoiced at the death of Socrates and of Christ:

Earth that never doubts nor fears
Earth that knows of death, not tears,
Earth that bore with joyful ease
Hemlock for Socrates,
Earth that blossomed and was glad
'Neath the cross that Christ had,
Shall rejoice and blossom too
When the bullet reaches you.
  (st. 3)

Sorley's awareness of mortality and his sense of communion with the dead, which go back to his school days, find expression in two sonnets on death dated 12 June 1915 and in the sonnet "When you see millions of the mouthless dead," found among his possessions after his death in action on 13 October 1915. In that final sonnet, as in the June sonnets, one can detect an attempt to resolve a deep ambiguity in his attitude to death. Perhaps it would be truer to say that there coexisted in Sorley a devout belief in the Christian doctrine of the resurrection and a deep subconscious acceptance of the knowledge that death is final.

The final sonnet prefigures in certain ways Owen's apprehension of war as a tragedy in which numberless men meet their deaths:

When you see millions of the mouthless
  dead
Across your dreams in pale battalions go. . . .
  (1–2)

The sonnet emphasizes the deadness of the dead, the futility of praise or tears, the remoteness of the dead from the living. It might almost be a rejoinder to Rupert Brooke, whose war sonnets had not commended themselves to Sorley. The final line of the sonnet is difficult to read as other than a denial of immortality: "Great death has made all his for evermore.

During the last five months of his life Sorley wrote one or two poems that are no better than the average run of verse in a hymnal or the memorial tributes in a public school magazine. It is not easy to account for this descent into banality of thought and diction; but despite his rebellion against certain aspects of the ethos inculcated at Marlborough, Sorley remained deeply attached to the school and to the downs nearby, where he loved to take his long solitary runs. Perhaps, in the physical and emotional turmoil of the trenches, he at times found solace in reverting to the idiom and the values of his adolescence.

Sorley died so young that his potential as a poet had scarcely begun to develop. He had probably the keenest intelligence and the most admirable nature of all the poets of World War I. The visitor who wishes to enter the chapel at Marlborough, a splendid example of Victorian Gothic, must first pass through the antechapel. He will see, affixed to the walls, a number of memorial tablets that honor distinguished sons of the school. Most of them commemorate Victorian admirals, generals, and governors of remote colonies. One is in memory of Charles Hamilton Sorley: it is fitting that it should be there.

Sorley's view of the war was shared by few of those fighting in the trenches. When Siegfried Sassoon and Vivian de Sola Pinto, his platoon commander, first read Sorley's poems in 1916 they could scarcely believe that anybody who had died in action in October 1915 could have taken such an attitude to the war. Young poets continued to write under the influence of Rupert Brooke as late as mid-1916. One such was W. N. Hodgson (1893–1916), an athlete and an exhibitioner[1] of Christ Church, Oxford, who enlisted at the outbreak of the war and won the Military Cross in 1915. His poems, couched as they are in the deplorable idiom of late-nineteenth-century romanticism, display barely a vestige of talent. However, one poem, "Before Action," can still move the reader with its poignant intensity, partly because one knows that it was written by a brave man on 29 June 1916, two days before he died on the first day of the Battle of the Somme. The poet moves from a Ruskinian adoration of natural beauty in the opening stanza to a recognition that he has watched

> . . . with uncomprehending eyes
> A hundred of Thy sunsets spill
> Their fresh and sanguine sacrifice.
> (18–20)

Finally the poet faces the knowledge that he

> Ere the sun swings his noonday sword
> Must say goodbye to all of this;—
> By all delights that I shall miss,
> Help me to die, O Lord.
> (21–24)

The Battle of the Somme ushered in a new and even darker phase of the war. Hitherto it had been just possible to keep up the pretense that there were elements of chivalry in the conflict. At Christmas 1914 in certain parts of the line British and German troops had fraternized, exchanging gifts, singing carols, playing football. The authorities had sternly forbidden the repetition of such gestures and court-martialed Sir Iain Colquhoun and another captain of the Scots Guards for permitting their men to fraternize with the Germans on Christmas Day 1915. A new era of mass slaughter was about to begin. Before the attack on 1 July 1916, Field Marshal Douglas Haig had bombarded the German trenches for a week. Unfortunately, the German dugouts were so deep and well constructed that their machine gunners were able to scramble into position unharmed and mow down the British soldiers as they mounted their assault. The British army lost 60,000 killed and wounded on 1 July, the heaviest casualties it had ever sustained on any one day in its annals. The pattern established on the Somme repeated itself from then on: artillery bombardment, waves of infantrymen assaulting positions defended by heavy concentrations of machine guns, and an advance of a few hundred yards. At Passschendaele the following summer, a new element of horror pervaded the fighting: the sea of mud where rain fell on ground churned up by the British artillery. Not until March 1918 was the stalemate broken, when a German offensive appeared to have won the war. Yet the impetus petered out; on 8 August

1. A student who attends school by benefit of a scholarship.

an Allied counteroffensive broke through the German positions and on 11 November the war was over.

One needs to bear this background in mind when considering the work of Sassoon, Owen, and Rosenberg, all of whose best poems were written after the summer of 1916. The public at home still preferred the romantic falsities of Robert Nichols to the savage truths of Siegfried Sassoon. Nichols' *Ardours and Endurances,* published in May 1917, sold more copies than Sassoon's *The Old Huntsman,* which appeared at the same time. But no serious poet could write about the war with the devotional highmindedness that one finds in W. N. Hodgson. He was the last of the morning heroes.

Even before the Somme one or two poets were beginning to make some adequate response to the ghastly realities of the war. Sassoon was writing the first of his trench poems that aimed at presenting an objective picture of life at the front. There was also Arthur Graeme West (1891–1917), who suffered a total revulsion from the war in August 1916, returned to France, and was killed by a bullet in April 1917. His *Diary of a Dead Officer* (1919) records his growing disillusionment. It is mainly prose, with a few poems added, of which the finest is "Night Patrol," dated March 1916. West anticipates Sassoon in his determination to record the true visage of war:

> . . . and everywhere the dead.
> Only the dead were always present—present
> As a vile sickly smell of rottenness.
> The rustling stubble and the early grass,
> The slimy pools—the dead men stank
> through all,
> Pungent and sharp. . . .
> (19–24)

His polemic in "God! How I Hate You, You Young Cheerful Men," against those who wrote lyrical poetry in the manner of Rupert Brooke, forms part of his desire to clarify in his own mind the nature of the struggle in which he was enmeshed. In that same poem he makes a more subdued but perhaps more heartfelt protest against the popular concept of God, foreshadowing Wilfred Owen in his speculations about the love of God and the suffering on the battlefield:

> Ah how good God is
> To suffer us be born just now, when youth
> That else would rust, can slake his blade in
> gore
> Where very God Himself does seem to walk
> The bloody fields of Flanders He so loves.
> (34–38)

Even from these brief quotations one observes how far West had traveled from the landscape of the mind portrayed by Grenfell, Brooke, and Shaw-Stewart; how near he was to the no-man's land delineated by Sassoon, Owen, and Rosenberg. Before considering that somber region, one must turn to the achievement of three men who, belonging to no school, made highly distinctive contributions to the poetry of war.

EDWARD THOMAS, IVOR GURNEY, EDMUND BLUNDEN

In one sense Edward Thomas (1878–1917) can scarcely be called a war poet: he wrote no poems about fighting or about life in the trenches; almost all his poems that refer to the war do so glancingly; and he probably wrote no poems after he had landed in France. Yet in one way Thomas was essentially a war poet: he owed his existence as a poet to the war. He had married very young, and his struggle to support his wife and three children condemned him to a round of ceaseless publishing on a wide variety of subjects—the countryside, queens of England, English men of letters. Although some of his literary criticism, notably *Algernon Charles Swinburne* (1912) and *Walter Pater* (1913), contains perceptive insights and there are passages worth reading in most of his books, this merely proves his extraordinary stamina and his determination to do honest work for his meager pay. Being commissioned in the army meant that the worst of his financial worries were over and that he was free of the literary treadmill. Between 3 December 1914 and 24 December 1916, Edward Thomas wrote the body of verse by which he is primarily remembered.

It is not necessary to consider in any detail the debt owed by Thomas to Robert Frost. The strong-minded widows of the two poets turned into a matter of dispute something that Frost and Thomas would have discussed amicably. Frost certainly told Edward Thomas that he should write certain paragraphs of his prose in verse form and keep exactly the same cadence. This may account for the fact that although Thomas' poems are unmistakably poetry they never, even at their most formal, lose touch with the movement of prose.

Thomas' most overt declaration about the war occurs in "This Is No Case of Petty Right or Wrong," in which he disclaims all conventional patriotism. When Eleanor Farjeon asked him if he knew what he was fighting for, he picked up a pinch of the earth and said, "Literally, for this." So, in the poem, Thomas affirms his irrational love for his country:

> I am one in crying, God save England, lest
> We lose what never slaves and cattle
> blessed.
> The ages made her that made us from dust.
> (21–23)

A subtler, finer poem, "Tears," explores Thomas' feeling for his country and tells us even more about his own nature. Although not directly relevant to the war, it gives us more than a hint about his attitude toward the soldiers in the trenches and toward his native land. One April morning he stepped out of "the double-shadowed Tower" into a courtyard:

> They were changing guard,
> Soldiers in line, young English countrymen,
> Fair-haired and ruddy, in white tunics.
> Drums
> And fifes were playing "The British
> Grenadiers."
> The men, the music piercing that solitude
> And silence, told me truths I had not
> dreamed,
> And have forgotten since their beauty
> passed.
> (12–18)

There are poems by Thomas that seem to have no connection with the war until a phrase arrests one's attention, compelling one to read the poem in a new light. In "Rain," one of his most characteristic poems, one encounters a reference to those whose sympathy cannot relieve human suffering, but who lie awake,

> Helpless among the living and the dead,
> Like a cold water among the broken reeds,
> Myriads of broken reeds all still and stiff.
> (12–14)

The image of the last line is almost certainly suggested by the victims of slaughter on the battlefields of France and of Flanders.

The war is present even more explicitly in "The Owl." As in so many of his poems, Thomas writes here in the first person, describing how hungry, cold, and tired he was, until he had satisfied his needs at an inn. An owl's "most melancholy cry" leads him away from a preoccupation with his solitary pains into an imaginative sympathy with others:

> And salted was my food, and my repose,
> Salted and sobered, too, by the bird's voice
> Speaking for all who lay under the stars,
> Soldiers and poor, unable to rejoice.
> (st. 4)

The conjunction of soldiers and poor recalls Isaac Rosenberg's observation that privates in the army are akin to slaves. For Thomas, soldiers are not heroes or our gallant boys in the trenches, but rather men low on the social scale, on a level with the poor. They suffer passively, unable to rejoice.

The four-line poem "In Memoriam (Easter, 1915)" is both a beautiful elegy and a powerful comment on the war:

The flowers left thick at nightfall in the
wood
This Eastertide call into mind the men,
Now far from home, who, with their
sweethearts, should
Have gathered them and will do never
again.

The emphasis falling on "should" makes us aware that it may be read in two ways: the simple observation that the soldiers would have gathered the flowers had they been home; and the implication that the war, by destroying the dead men, has broken the ritual of courtship, the gathering of flowers that the dead men ought to have performed. Once again Thomas is showing how a tiny incident in a peaceful countryside may help us to grasp the significance of war.

One observes the same kind of strategy in "As the Team's Head-Brass." A soldier who has not yet been out to the war is watching a man plowing a field. Lovers disappear into the wood, and the plowman stops from time to time to have a word with the soldier. Their conversation veers toward the war: the fallen elm on which the soldier is seated won't be taken away until the war is over; the soldier could spare an arm but would be reluctant to lose a leg; one of the plowman's mates died on his second day in France. The talk is inconsequential and casual, yet the poem gradually pieces together a picture of the way in which the war demands and deprives. The poem ends with what is almost certainly something more than a straightforward description of the landscape:

The lovers came out of the wood again:
The horses started and for the last time
I watched the clods crumble and topple over
After the ploughshare and the stumbling
team.
(34–37)

The menace hidden in the phrase "for the last time" may remind the reader that the soldier, like the men who will never again gather the flowers, will perhaps, as he fears, lose not just an arm or a leg in battle, but his head as well. There is even a hint that the lovers and the age-old relationship between man and the soil are under threat from the destructiveness of war.

Edward Thomas is the quietest, most introspective of all the war poets, but the keenness of his observation and the probing quality of his imagination enable him to penetrate beyond the outer semblance of things into the heart of sadness.

Ivor Gurney (1890–1937) was that rare creature, a poet who was also a composer, equally gifted in the two arts. The son of a Gloucester tailor, he grew up and was educated in the cathedral city that he never ceased to love. His intelligence and his musical gifts augured well for his future, and nobody found it ominous that his fellow schoolboys gave him the nickname of "Batty Gurney."

In the autumn of 1911 Gurney won a scholarship to the Royal College of Music, where he showed his precocious skill in 1912 by his setting of five Elizabethan lyrics, a composition that he called "The Elizas." In 1912–1913 he began to write poetry, an activity that was not only of value in itself, but also an influence on his music; for Gurney was to set poems by most English poets of merit who flourished during the first two decades of the twentieth century. His joining the army did not put an end to his composition of music or of poetry: in 1916–1917 he achieved what may well be the unique feat of writing five songs while undergoing a spell of duty in the trenches. He sent home to a friend the poems that he had been writing, and in 1917 they appeared under the title *Severn and Somme,* names of the river that he had loved in childhood and the river associated with the terrible fighting that Gurney had known, and in which on 7 April 1917 he was wounded. In September 1917 he was gassed and sent home, then transferred to a mental hospital at Warrington and later to a similar hospital at St. Albans. His military career was over, formally terminating with his discharge in October 1918. There seems to be something mysterious about Gurney's last thirteen months in the army, since little is known about the circumstances of his gassing or of his confinement to the two mental hospitals. By 1919 he had apparently recovered.

From 1919 to 1921 he cut something of a figure at the Royal College of Music and in the literary world of London, a second book of poems, *War's Embers,* having appeared in 1919. Even so, he depended for his survival on a weekly allowance from a fund raised by his teacher Vaughan Williams and by friends. Back in Gloucester, he talked brilliantly and tumultuously, received financial help from Edward Marsh, and grew ever wilder. He was incarcerated in September 1922 at Barnwood House, Gloucester, and in December at the City of London Mental Hospital, Dartford, Kent. There he remained until his death on 26 December 1937, St. Stephen's Day, at a time of year that meant much to him.

Although Gurney's friends never deserted him, the story of his life at Dartford is heartrending. Apart from his bitter resentment at what he believed to be his betrayal by his country, Gurney was tormented by delusions that he was suffering from tortures inflicted from a distance by electricity. He claimed to have composed the works of Shakespeare, Beethoven, and Haydn. It is likely that he enjoyed (if that be the word) periods of lucidity. When in 1937 a friend told him that Oxford University Press was about to publish a collection of his songs, he merely said, "It is too late."

The poems written before he finally went mad are mostly acceptable exercises in the pastoral mode and reflections on various aspects of beauty. Two war poems stand out from the rest of those early poems. "To His Love," written when Gurney received a false report that his friend F. W. Harvey had died in battle, deploys in the first three stanzas the conventional properties of pastoral elegy—grazing sheep, the small boat on the Severn, the violets from the riverside. The final stanza opens decorously, but suddenly administers a shock:

Cover him, cover him soon!
And with thick-set
Masses of memorial flowers
Hide that red wet
Thing I must somehow forget.
(st. 4)

Calling a dead man a "red wet / Thing" strikes one with a raw violence, and it is almost as brutal to suggest that one should cover the corpse with masses of flowers partly in tribute and partly to blot it from sight.

Even finer is Gurney's "Ballad of the Three Spectres," a poem that somehow captures the spirit of the Border Ballads without lapsing into archaism or pastiche. The first two stanzas may yield some idea of the poem's merit:

As I went up by Ovillers
In mud and water cold to the knee,
There went three jeering, fleering spectres,
That walked abreast and talked of me.

The first said, "Here's a right brave soldier
That walks the dark unfearingly;
Soon he'll come back on a fine stretcher,
And laughing for a nice Blighty.

The curt off-rhymes in both stanzas enhance the atmosphere of menace and strangeness, just as it is sinister that one of the apparitions should speak the slang of the trenches, prophesying that the soldier will get a "nice Blighty"—a wound bad enough to ensure his return to England.

Yet the best of the poems that he wrote during his madness surpass even the most accomplished examples of his early work. One has to face the question of his insanity before turning to consider the poems composed in the asylums, and the evidence is probably inadequate for anybody to reach a verdict. The latest opinion is that he, like his mother, suffered from paranoid schizophrenia. Should this be so, one cannot lay the blame on the war for driving him mad, though the war almost certainly intensified his madness and determined the pattern that it took. Although the power to compose music left him after 1926, he was able to produce a mass of poetry throughout his confinement at Barnwood and at Dartford from 1922 to 1937.

Some of his poems are painful to read. Two long letters in verse to the metropolitan police ramble on about his war service and the pain that he is wrongfully enduring. All the sentences taken separately are logical, but something has gone wrong with the links between them, and gradually one realizes that the writer has lost his reason. A poem written at Barnwood House in December 1922 is far more controlled, despite the anguish that racks the poet as he draws up his indictment. The opening lines of "To God" are both tragic and comic in a pathetic way. Gurney's first example of God's cruelty toward him is that there are prayers with meals:

> Why have You made life so intolerable
> And set me between four walls, where I am able
> Not to escape meals without prayer, for that is possible
> Only by annoying an attendant.

What is so unnerving in the poem is the mixture of factual observation about forced meals, mere delusion about torture by electricity, and the prayer for death:

> Forced meals there have been and electricity
> And weakening of sanity by influence
> That's dreadful to endure. And there are others
> And I am praying for death, death, death.
> (9–12)

Gurney's bitter sense of having been betrayed by his country is certainly linked with his insanity, although nobody has explained precisely how. He seems to have felt outraged in that his sufferings during the war had not brought him merited fame. He may also have experienced anger and pity at the recollection of the suffering endured by others who fought. The prime emotion of "There Is Nothing" is certainly pain at his own betrayal. The poem, dated February 1925, bears the note "in torture":

> Soldier's praise I had earned having suffered soldier's pain,
> And the great honour of song in the battle's first gray show—
> Honour was bound to me save—mine most dreadfully slain.
> (12–14)

During the years at Dartford, Gurney continually reverts to his memories of the war. Some of the poems he wrote on that theme are so lucid that it is hard to believe he was other than sane when he was composing them. They display an unwavering control of mood and of tone as he remembers the killing of comrades or calls to mind with stoical irony those who for a while, until death took them, contrived to beat the system. These poems have no parallel in the work of any other war poet: the voice is Gurney's alone, speaking clearly and with authority from the depths of a mental hospital.

Two poems in particular yield a taste of Gurney's quality. "The Silent One" begins curtly in the middle of the story:

> Who died on the wires, and hung there, one of two—
> Who for his hours of life had chattered through
> Infinite lovely chatter of Bucks accent:
> Yet faced unbroken wires; stepped over, and went
> A noble fool, faithful to his stripes—and ended.

It is all there in five lines: the tale of an honest countryman, a loyal NCO, obedient to his orders, who ended up hanging on the barbed wire. Then an officer, with "a finicking accent," unlike the Bucks accent of the dead man, politely asks the narrator of the poem if he'd mind crawling through a hole in the wire. The courteous exchange between the officer and the narrator derives its savor from the fact that it is taking place in the middle of the battlefield, where one might expect orders to be rapped out. There is a measure of anger smoldering away in the poem, whose irony points at the upper-class voice of the officer, at God, and at the narrator himself. The apparent casualness hides a cool artistry. The narrator lay down under unbroken wires,

Till the politest voice—a finicking accent, said:
"Do you think you might crawl through there: there's a hole"
Darkness, shot at: I smiled, as politely replied—
"I'm afraid not, Sir." There was no hole no way to be seen,
Nothing but chance of death, after tearing of clothes
Kept flat, and watched the darkness, hearing bullets whizzing—
And thought of music—and swore deep heart's deep oaths
(Polite to God). . . .
(9–16)

Equally fine is "The Bohemians," a portrait of Gurney and his friends, who found army regulations irksome, who wanted to be left alone:

Certain people would not clean their buttons,
Nor polish buckles after latest fashions,
Preferred their hair long, puttees comfortable.
(1–3)

He describes how they never adapted themselves to military ways,

Surprised as ever to find the army capable
Of sounding "Lights Out" to break a game of Bridge,
As to fear candles would set a barn alight.
(14–16)

Only in the last line of the poem does Gurney move almost imperceptibly from gentle irony into the starkness of an epitaph:

In Artois or Picardy they lie—free of useless fashions.

It is impossible to say just how good a poet Gurney was, because most of his work remains unpublished. Michael Hurd, who has labored so long and so effectively on the texts of Gurney's poems, reckons that 600 out of his 900 poems have not been published. About 300 are viable, many of them of the highest quality. It is sad to think that such richness lies neglected in the Gurney archive of the Gloucester public library. The cruel mischance that confined him to mental hospitals for the last fifteen years of his life still has the power to obscure his fame.

Edmund Blunden (1896–1974) remains an undervalued poet, partly because even his war poems are often held to be academic and pastoral, especially by those who have not read them. Joining the army early in 1915, he had already published two small collections and was to bring out a third in 1916, *Pastorals,* which was, like the two earlier volumes, devoted to the countryside in time of peace. Yet he was rapidly changing, as he tells us in *War Poets: 1914–1918:*

> In May and June 1916, in my notebooks, the grimness of war began to compete as a subject with the pastorals of peace. By the end of the year, when madness seemed totally to rule the hour, I was almost a poet of the shell-holes, of ruin and of mortification. (p. 24)

Blunden was awarded the Military Cross and saw as much hard fighting as any other war poet. In Raymond Asquith's letters home, printed in John Jolliffe's *Raymond Asquith: Life and Letters,* one learns that, despite the killing, the pain, the fear, the acute discomfort, and the boredom, there were moments of exaltation and pleasure during the war: the singing of nightingales or the enjoyment of splendid food and drink. Such moments seldom find their way into the poems of the most powerful war poets, such as Sassoon, Owen, or Rosenberg. It is a mark of Blunden's rare honesty and range of sympathies that he can reveal the less dark sides of war:

O how comely it was and how reviving,
When with clay and with death no longer striving
Down firm roads we came to houses
With women chattering and green grass thriving.
. . .

Gazed on the mill-sails, heard the church-
bell,
Found an honest glass all manner of riches.
("At Senlis Once," 1–4; 11–12)

It is typical of Blunden that the first, Miltonic line should lead us not into deep metaphysical speculation but into a remembrance of lesser mercies.

Blunden knows that, in war, innocent relaxation may for an hour or so charm away the ferocity of killing. Both are aspects of war. In "Concert Party: Busseboom," the audience, delighted by the entertainment, reluctantly leaves the world of illusion:

We heard another matinée,
We heard the maniac blast

Of barrage south by Saint Eloi,
And the red lights flaming there
Called madness: Come, my bonny boy,
And dance to the latest air.

To this new concert, white we stood;
Cold certainty held our breath;
While men in the tunnels below Larch Wood
Were kicking men to death.
(15–24)

Blunden grew up in a Kent village where, as in Leonard Woolf's Sussex, life still went on much as in the days of the Domesday Book. Even at school he was a scholar and a poet, deeply versed in the pastoral tradition of English poetry. But his own poetry is pastoral not only because of his literary learning but because he was genuinely a countryman. The weakness of his verse over the years is that he tends to retreat into archaism and whimsy, but his love for the fields and woods that he discovered in France lends an element of strength and perceptiveness to his war poetry. He loathes the war because it violates the pieties of nature no less than the sanctity of man. As early as May 1916 he linked the two in "Festubert: The Old German Line":

Sparse mists of moonlight hurt our eyes
With gouged and scourged uncertainties
Of soul and soil in agonies.
(1–3)

One of his most moving poems, "Report on Experience," published in the collection *Near and Far* (1929), takes up the earlier theme. The good man and the enchanting Seraphina, "like one from Eden," are victims of the war, which has also devastated a landscape:

I have seen a green country, useful to the
race,
Knocked silly with guns and mines, its
villages vanished,
Even the last rat and the last kestrel
banished—
God bless us all, this was peculiar grace.
(st. 2)

The poem ends with an affirmation, not of faith as a Christian would understand it, but of a belief that we live in an ambiguous universe presided over by a distant God:

Say what you will, our God sees how they
run.
These disillusions are His curious proving
That He loves humanity and will go on
loving;
Over there are faith, life, virtue in the sun.
(st. 4)

The war continued to haunt Blunden's imagination. He collected many of his best war poems as a supplement to the prose narrative of *Undertones of War* (1928). One of the finest is a singularly beautiful elegy, "Their Very Memory," that reveals Blunden as a master of rhythmical subtlety. The imagery of the poem evokes running water, green valleys, a spring, a fountain, a greenwood, music. Although Blunden's memory of his comrades is fading, it has not wholly vanished:

When they smiled,
Earth's inferno changed and melted
Greenwood mild;
Every village where they halted
Shone with them through square and alley.
(st. 3)

Even when Blunden is not ostensibly writing about the war, it presides over his meditations. His justly admired poem "The Midnight Skaters," from *English Poems* (1925), evokes death at watch within the pond's black bed:

> What wants he but to catch
> Earth's heedless sons and daughters?
> With but a crystal parapet
> Between, he has his engines set.
> (9–12)

The word "parapet" intrudes into a tranquil, Wordsworthian scene like an icy wind blowing from no-man's-land.

Even after World War II, the memory of World War I steals into poems far distant in time and place. When Blunden was working in Hong Kong, the Communists allowed him to visit the Great Wall of China, because he was a poet and because they rightly believed that he would make no political use of his visit. His sonnet "At the Great Wall of China" is, sadly, one of the few poems of his later years fit to rank with the best of his work. The parapet reappears in the sonnet's octet, more appropriately perhaps than in "The Midnight Skaters." We look from a tower and imagine

> Where these few miles to thousands grow, and yet
> Ever the one command and genius haunt
> Each stairway, sally-port, loop, parapet,
> In mute last answer to the invader's vaunt.
> (5–8)

It is in the sextet that the memories of Blunden's war loom unmistakably clear:

> But I half know at this bleak turret here,
> In snow-dimmed moonlight where sure answers quail,
> This new-set sentry of a long dead year.
> (9–11)

For there are two ghosts at the bleak turret: that of a young Chinese soldier and that of a British sentry on the Ancre or the Somme. They merge insensibly in the mind of an English poet.

Blunden's war poetry is tougher than commonly supposed. Even though he wrote pastoral verse and, at the end of *Undertones of War* (p. 314), called himself "a harmless young shepherd in a soldier's coat," he was adopting a strategy that enabled him to confront the war and record what he observed. In old age he went to live in Suffolk at the village of Long Melford with his wife and daughters, wrote a guide to the magnificent church, and composed an obituary for his old friend Siegfried Sassoon, who was, like Blunden, a survivor of the trenches, a holder of the Military Cross, and an honored poet.

It is time now to consider the work of two men whose view of the war is darker and more tragic than that of the poets so far discussed.

SIEGFRIED SASSOON

Siegfried Sassoon (1886–1967), who was born into a rich Jewish family, left Cambridge without taking a degree and in the years before 1914 devoted himself to hunting, cricket, golf, ballet, opera, and evenings at his London club. He also began to develop a taste for literature, bringing out his privately printed collection *Poems* in 1906 and *The Daffodil Murderer* in 1913. This poem, which appeared under the pseudonym Saul Kain, was a parody of John Masefield but also a serious attempt to portray the feelings of the poor and the degraded.

Sassoon, who had joined the army on the first day of the war, rapidly acquired a reputation for courage that bordered on the insane. He stood several inches over six feet, and was lean, athletic, and reckless: it is not surprising that this formidable killer acquired the nickname "Mad Jack." His poem "The Kiss," whatever he may have thought of it later, is written in praise of "Brother Lead and Sister Steel." In the Somme offensive of July 1916 he fought with such gallantry that he was awarded the Military Cross. But his attitude toward the war had already begun to change.

It is not easy to chart the logical progress of that change, if only because Sassoon lived by generous passion rather than by calm reason. He may have reacted strongly against lectures on "the spirit of the bayonet," given at the Fourth Army School at Flixécourt in the spring of 1916, lectures that aroused the disgust of poets as various as Edmund Blunden, Robert Graves, and David Jones.[2] He had begun writing early in 1916 what he himself called genuine trench poems that were the first things of their kind. Further stages in his pilgrimage include meetings at Garsington Manor, Oxfordshire, the home of Philip Morrell, MP, and Lady Ottoline Morrell, with a number of prominent pacifists, including Bertrand Russell; and a spell in a hospital after being invalided home with a bullet wound in his lung, sustained at the battle of Arras in April 1917, the engagement in which Edward Thomas was killed.

By February 1917 Sassoon was already losing his belief in the war, and in July he made a protest against its needless prolongation. This "act of wilful defiance of military authority," as Sassoon described it, rendered him liable to court-martial and imprisonment. Thanks largely to the intervention of Robert Graves, an alternative procedure was followed, and Sassoon, who had meanwhile thrown his Military Cross into the Mersey, agreed to appear before a medical board. Graves testified that Sassoon suffered from hallucinations typical of shell shock, and himself burst into tears three times while making his statement. The board dispatched Sassoon to Craiglockhart War Hospital, appointing as his escort Robert Graves, who missed the train that was carrying Sassoon to his destination.

At Craiglockhart the doctors cured Sassoon of whatever illness had prompted him to issue his act of defiance, and he asked for a posting abroad. He arrived in Egypt at the end of February 1918, then moved to France in May. His fighting days came to an end on 13 July 1918, when, on a daylight patrol, he was accidentally shot through the head by a British sentry and sent home to pass the rest of the war in a hospital.

Two volumes of poetry, *The Old Huntsman* (1917) and *Counter-Attack* (1918), contain almost all the enduring poems that Sassoon wrote about the war. The judgment that he is primarily a satirist is questionable, but his satirical poems retain to this day their incisiveness and power. In "They," Sassoon launches an attack not only on a complacent, stupid bishop but on the apparent subservience of the Anglican church to the state, and on the windy rhetoric that was one of the main civilian contributions to the war:

> The Bishop tells us: "When the boys come
> back
> They will not be the same; for they'll have
> fought
> In a just cause; they lead the last attack
> On Anti-Christ."
> (st. 1)

The next stanza contrasts the stale abstractions by which the bishop lives with the raw truths that are the products of war:

> "We're none of us the same!" the boys reply.
> "For George lost both his legs; and Bill's
> stone blind;
> "Poor Jim's shot through the lungs and like
> to die;
> "And Bert's gone syphilitic; you'll not find
> "A chap who's served that hasn't found
> *some* change."
> And the Bishop said: "The ways of God are
> strange."
> (st. 2)

In view of his official and social position, Edward Marsh showed courage when he published the poem: the mention of syphilis was

2. Robert Graves is the subject of a separate essay in this series. Therefore, there is no discussion of his poetry here. His war poems form only a minor part of his work.

an offense against decorum and an affront to patriotic feeling.

There are moments when Sassoon's rage may seem to be in excess of its object. In January 1917, just before returning to France, Sassoon went to a revue at the Hippodrome in Liverpool and wrote a poem designed to be his farewell to England:

> . . . prancing ranks
> Of harlots shrill the chorus, drunk with din;
> "We're sure the Kaiser loves our dear old Tanks!"
>
> I'd like to see a Tank come down the stalls,
> Lurching to rag-time tunes, or "Home, sweet Home."
> And there'd be no more jokes in Music-halls
> To mock the riddled corpses round Bapaume.
> ("Blighters," 2–8)

It is a little hard on the inoffensive chorus girls to stigmatize them as harlots, and the audience hardly deserves to be massacred. But Sassoon believed that the ignorance of civilians about what was happening, on the battlefield was criminal. Songs in music halls about tanks were blasphemous insults to the troops and to their dead comrades. Viewed in this light, "Blighters" is a valid testament of justified indignation. Its final line, particularly when spoken aloud, delivers a searing curse on those who thoughtlessly mock the agony of their fellow men.

Some of Sassoon's other satirical poems have become anthology pieces, such as "Base Details," "Glory of Women," "Does It Matter?" "The General," and "Fight to a Finish," a savage attack on civilians, especially journalists and members of Parliament.

Most of his poems have scarcely any satirical element, but take as their theme trench warfare, presented with an almost brutal realism, although the underlying tenderness aroused by the spectacle of the wounded and the dead redeems what would otherwise be almost intolerable. In "Attack," Sassoon, while playing down the worst of the horror, describes what it was like to go over the top:

> Lines of grey, muttering faces, masked with fear,
> They leave their trenches, going over the top,
> While time ticks blank and busy on their wrists,
> And hope, with furtive eyes and grappling fists,
> Flounders in mud. O Jesus, make it stop!
> (9–13)

Some reviewers of *Counter-Attack* condemned Sassoon for his insistence on the ugly aspects of war. In the title poem he portrays as faithfully as a Dutch seventeenth-century painter the contents of a captured trench:

> The place was rotten with dead; green clumsy legs
> High-booted, sprawled and grovelled along the saps
> And trunks, face downward, in the sucking mud,
> Wallowed like trodden sandbags, loosely filled;
> And naked sodden buttocks, mats of hair,
> Bulged, clotted heads slept in the plastering slime.
> And then the rain began,—the jolly old rain.
> (st. 1)

This is no mere catalog of horrifying items: the dense particularity of the description achieves a sensuous richness. The green legs are ghastly because the adjective suggests both the fertility of spring and the gangrenous texture of the rotting corpses. In a similar way the word "slept" has associations of repose that are mocked by the way in which the clotted heads sink into the slime. The stanza's last line, with its casual irony, provides a moment's relief from one's scrutiny of the dismembered bodies.

Although Sassoon wrote nothing else so richly complex as "Counter-Attack," he produced a number of memorable poems about various aspects of trench warfare. One of the most effective is "The Rear-Guard," set in a tunnel under the Hindenburg Line in April 1917 and based on an experience of his own.

The narrator, who has not slept for days, is furious when a sleeping figure over whom he stumbles fails to wake up and answer his questions:

> Savage, he kicked a soft, unanswering heap,
> And flashed his beam across the livid face
> Terribly glaring up, whose eyes yet wore
> Agony dying hard ten days before;
> And fists of fingers clutched a blackening
> wound.
> (st. 3)

Two of Sassoon's poems are unusual in that they are explicitly elegiac. "To Any Dead Officer" mingles anger, mockery, and compassion, passing from a lament for one particular officer to a fine passage in which Sassoon mourns all who were reported "wounded and missing":

> Next week the bloody Roll of Honour said
> "Wounded and missing"—(That's the thing
> to do
> When lads are left in shell-holes dying slow,
> With nothing but blank sky and wounds
> that ache,
> Moaning for water till they know
> It's night, and then it's not worth while to
> wake!)
> (st. 4)

"To One Who Was with Me in the War," written in 1926, is not so much a formal elegy as a "game of ghosts," in which the poet imagines going back with a fellow officer after the war to "some redoubt of Time," where they may relive their experience of the trenches. It is a less urgent, mellower poem than those Sassoon wrote during the war, yet it conveys something of his complex emotions toward that war:

> Round the next bay you'll meet
> A drenched platoon-commander; chilled, he
> drums his feet
> On squelching duck-boards; winds his wrist-
> watch; turns his head,
> And shows you how you looked,—your ten-
> years-vanished face,
> Hoping the War will end next week . . .
> What's that you said?
> (32–37)

After the war was over Sassoon returned to his old life, combining his sporting interests with literary activity. He became widely known for a series of prose autobiographies that cover his life from the closing years of the nineteenth century to the end of the war. He continued to write poetry during the rest of a long life, happy to employ the diction and the meters of his youth, unswayed by the innovatory techniques of Pound, Eliot, and the imagists. His poems include gentle satires on, for example, the first performance of Stravinsky's *Rite of Spring* and the destruction of Devonshire House; reminiscences of the war; and explorations of religious and mystical themes. But it is by virtue of thirty or forty poems that delineate the agony of the fighting in the trenches that he holds an honored place among English poets.

ISAAC ROSENBERG

Isaac Rosenberg (1890–1918) is one of the few Englishmen to have achieved distinction as a poet and a painter. He was born in the East End of London and was the son of Lithuanian Jews who had emigrated to Britain in the 1880's. After leaving school in 1904 he was apprenticed to a firm of art publishers, but chafed at the narrowness of his life. Thanks to the generosity of some Jewish ladies, he was able in October 1911 to enroll at the Slade School, where he met gifted fellow students such as David Bomberg, Mark Gertler, Dora Carrington, Edward Wadsworth, Paul Nash, and Stanley Spencer. He published at his own expense in 1912 a booklet of poems, *Night and Day,* in which he was already expressing his perplexities about the significance of suffering and the nature of God.

On 10 November 1913 Gertler introduced Rosenberg to Edward Marsh at the Café Royal. For the rest of Rosenberg's life Marsh gave him all manner of help, buying his paintings, paying for the publication of his second book of poems, *Youth* (1915), and doing what he could to relieve Rosenberg's difficulties after he had joined the army.

The relationship between a man and his patron is always subject to strains of various kinds, and it must be admitted that Rosenberg and Marsh were seldom in perfect accord. Marsh was a cultivated member of the English upper classes, private secretary to Winston Churchill, a man of conservative tastes, editor of the Georgian anthologies, a passionate admirer of Rupert Brooke. It is easy to draw up an indictment of Marsh, pointing at his failure to recognize the genius of Rosenberg; at his exclusion of him from his anthologies, except for a speech from *Moses*; at his inability to admire "Dead Man's Dump." It is even held against Marsh that, years after the end of the war, he could still talk of "poor little Rosenberg."

Yet Marsh proved a true friend to Rosenberg. It was Marsh who ensured that Rosenberg's mother received from the army the allowance due her, just as it was Marsh who did all in his power to have Rosenberg moved to safer and less exacting military duties. Despite his failure to respond to "Dead Man's Dump," he took the trouble, before returning the manuscript to Rosenberg, to copy out the poem for fear that it might be lost. Nor did Marsh call him "poor little Rosenberg" in a spirit of upper-class condescension. Mark Gertler, a poor, working-class, East End, Jewish painter, described Rosenberg affectionately as a "funny little man." It is possible to be a poet of the first order and also a poor, funny little man.

In June 1914 Rosenberg visited Cape Town, where he stayed with his married sister, Minnie. He wrote there "On Receiving News of the War," a poem that anticipates the end of the old order, a poem of foreboding deeper than any experienced by his compatriots at home. For over a year before the outbreak of war he had been concerned with the need to reject the orthodox male God, and at about the same time he was working on a poem on the outbreak of the war, he was composing a strange poem entitled "The Female God," an exploration of the sexual and the sacred.

Rosenberg went back to England in February 1915, although he could have stayed on in Cape Town indefinitely, especially as he was much in demand as a portrait painter. Apparently he felt that he had reached an emotional and spiritual dead end. But in London things were little better, and in the autumn of 1915 he enlisted in the army, partly to obtain an allowance for his mother and partly, it has been surmised, to fulfill a long-suppressed death wish. He wrote to Marsh that he had not joined the army for patriotic reasons.

Rosenberg's life in the army was unutterably wretched. He wrote to Lascelles Abercrombie on 11 March 1916: "the army is the most detestable invention on this earth and nobody but a private in the army knows what it is to be a slave" (*Collected Works*, p. 230). On 26 January 1918, in a passage canceled by the censor, he wrote to Edward Marsh: "what is happening to me now is more tragic than the 'passion play.' Christ never endured what I endure. It is breaking me completely."[3] Everything conspired to make Rosenberg's army life a long nightmare. He detested the coarseness of his fellow soldiers' behavior and the crudity of their minds. His lot was worsened by the anti-Jewish prejudice that he encountered among officers and private soldiers alike. Because the boots issued by the army did not fit him, he suffered the agony of sore heels, not nearly as trivial a matter as civilians at home might reckon. His awkwardness, stubbornness, and forgetfulness must have made matters worse: he was punished for leaving behind his gas helmet, and the injustice of army discipline rankled with him. The continual labor that was his lot imposed severe strains on his physique. Dragging heavy coils of barbed wire into no-man's-land and setting them up, or digging latrines in the hard earth or in the excremental mud, weighed upon his body and his spirit. He refers several

3. From an unpublished letter quoted in J. Cohen, *Journey to the Trench's* (London, 1975), p. 3.

times to the difficulty of writing and of perfecting his poems in such conditions. The lives of officers were at least as dangerous as those of their men, but they enjoyed some compensations. They had the services of a batman, who would keep their uniform clean; their food and sleeping quarters were better; they were exempt from physical labor and from punishments such as pack drill for trivial breaches of discipline; they could afford to relax in decent hotels and restaurants on short leaves instead of in the bistros where private soldiers congregated; they might even make the acquaintance of cultivated Belgian or French civilians; and with luck they would find one or two congenial fellow officers in their regiment or company.

It is probably true that Rosenberg never met in the army a single person who cared for any of the arts or with whom he could have the kind of talk that meant so much to him. One of his officers, Frank Waley, asked Rosenberg for copies of some of his poems. Rosenberg was always short of paper, being obliged to write some poems on the backs of envelopes; nevertheless he gave Waley a few poems that baffled him so completely that he chucked them away. The only one Waley could remember was "Break of Day in the Trenches," and since he didn't think it was poetry he threw it out with the rest.

In 1916, at his own expense, Rosenberg published in a volume entitled *Roses* an unfinished play of that name, together with some shorter poems. It is convenient to group it with another play, *The Unicorn,* a work of only a few pages, completed in the summer of 1917, although in March 1918 he was planning to write a fuller treatment of the play, which he had always regarded as a sketch for a larger version.

Although only 470 lines long, *Moses* is an extremely complex work about whose significance there is still no general agreement. Rosenberg wrote to the poet R. C. Trevelyan in a letter postmarked 15 June 1916: "Moses symbolizes the fierce desire for virility, and original action in contrast to slavery of the most abject kind" (*Collected Works,* p. 235). Knowing Rosenberg's views about the slavery of private soldiers, one is entitled to say that *Moses* presents Rosenberg's situation in 1915–1916. It also marks the culminating stage in his rejection of the divinity whom he had scrutinized in a number of poems and stigmatized in "God" as "this miasma of a rotting God." ("This miasma of a rotting god" also occurs as line 144 of *Moses.*) One may also read the play as Rosenberg's attempt to define the historical destiny of the Jews and of the proletariat. It expresses his preoccupation with violence as a force that may possibly regenerate a crumbling, sick society, a notion that he had played with even before the outbreak of war. The only overt act of violence occurs at the end of the play, when Moses strangles the brutal Egyptian overseer, Abinoah, father of his mistress, Koelue. She may also stand for the incarnate sexuality of the earth goddess whom Rosenberg had long envisaged as the supplanter of the orthodox male God.

The Unicorn is even shorter and stranger than *Moses.* It is about a decaying race who have never seen a woman, and whose chief, named Tel, is mounted on a unicorn. The two other main characters, Saul and his wife, Lilith, belong to another tribe, as does Enoch, the only other character. The climax of the play is best described in the final stage direction:

> Through the casement they see riding under the rainbow a black naked host on various animals, the Unicorn leading. A woman is clasped on every one, some are frantic, others white or unconscious, some nestle laughing. ENOCH with madness in his eyes leaps through the casement and disappears with a splash in the well. SAUL leaps after him shouting "The Unicorn." TEL places the unconscious LILITH on the Unicorn and they all ride away. (*Collected Works,* p. 173)

In a letter to Winifreda Seaton dated 8 March 1918 Rosenberg wrote of his ambitions for an expanded version of *The Unicorn*: "I mean to put all my innermost experiences into the 'Unicorn.' I want it to symbolize the war and all the devastating forces, let loose by an ambitious and unscrupulous will" (*Collected Works,* p. 270).

Some of the themes of *Moses* reappear in *The Unicorn,* notably those of sexuality and violence as the instruments of liberation and change. Before starting work on the fragments that became *The Unicorn* Rosenberg had contemplated writing a play about Judas Maccabeus, who reconquered Jerusalem from the Romans in 165 B.C. He may also have had in mind a quotation from the Book of Numbers: "God brought them out of Egypt; he hath as it were the strength of a unicorn."

It is the richness and complexity of the themes and the way in which they mirror Rosenberg's psychological turmoil that constitute the fascination of these plays, whether one ranks them among his greatest achievements or regards them as only partially successful despite their imaginative force and the magnificent passages of verse found in them.

Although Rosenberg was a mature artist by the outbreak of war and had written some hauntingly original poems by the spring of 1916, it is on a handful of poems written between midsummer 1916 and his death on 1 April 1918 that his reputation securely rests. He wrote to Edward Marsh on 4 August 1916, enclosing "A Worm Fed on the Heart of Corinth" and "Break of Day in the Trenches." The former prophesies, in ten astonishing lines, the destruction of England by a creature akin to the invisible worm of William Blake's "The Sick Rose." With this poem Rosenberg takes his place among the Hebrew prophets and the English poets. "Break of Day in the Trenches," actually written in the trenches, is a flawless, ironical meditation, that opens with an ominous strangeness:

The darkness crumbles away.
It is the same old druid Time as ever.

In his letter to Marsh, Rosenberg observes: "I am enclosing a poem I wrote in the trenches, which is surely as simple as ordinary talk. You might object to the second line as vague, but that was the best way I could express the sense of dawn" (*Collected Works,* p. 239). The sight of a rat that leaps over the poet's hand as he plucks a poppy to stick behind his ear moves him to meditate sardonically on the rat's cosmopolitan sympathies, which lead him to touch first an English, next a German, hand. He then imagines the rat's grin as he watches men in all their bodily pride reduced to short-lived creatures with terror in their eyes. At the very end of the poem the image of the poppy returns.

The poppy held great emotional potency for the soldiers in France and Flanders: indeed Englishmen still wear paper poppies in their buttonholes on Armistice Day. John McCrae, a Canadian, wrote the most popular poem of the war, "In Flanders Fields," which begins:

In Flanders fields the poppies blow
Between the crosses, row on row.

The first half of McRae's poem is reasonably competent versifying, although the second half represents a sad decline. But Rosenberg has made the symbol of the plucked poppy ironically resonant with our sense of life's brevity and of the mortality that is the lot of rat and poppy and men:

Poppies whose roots are in man's veins
Drop, and are ever dropping;
But mine in my ear is safe—
Just a little white with the dust.
("Break of Day in the Trenches," 23–26)

In May 1917, Rosenberg sent Marsh a seventy-nine-line poem, "Dead Man's Dump," based on his own experience of carrying wire up to the line on limbers and running over dead bodies. It contains Rosenberg's only realistic descriptions of the battlefield, yet his main concern is still his search for the meaning of human existence, his desire to discover the metaphysical significance of war. He is capable of writing lines that convey with horrifying exactness the sensation of driving a cart over dead bodies:

The wheels lurched over sprawled dead
But pained them not, though their bones
crunched.
(7–8)

The poem ends in a similar vein, but at the middle of it the sight of the dead moves Rosenberg to compose a passage unrivaled in any other poem of war except in Wilfred Owen's finest work:

None saw their spirits' shadow shake the
grass,
Or stood aside for the half used life to pass
Out of those doomed nostrils and the
doomed mouth,
When the swift iron burning bee
Drained the wild honey of their youth.
(27–31)

The imagery here of honey and iron occurs also in "August 1914," a beautiful short lyric written in the summer of 1916.

Two further poems of 1917 show Rosenberg's imagination at its strangest and most potent. "Daughters of War" evokes mysterious Amazons whose lovers are soldiers killed in battle and washed clean of mortal dust. He believed it to be his best poem, and during the year that he spent on it he had "striven to get that sense of inexorableness the human (or inhuman) side of this war has" (*Collected Works*, p. 260).

Again, in "Returning, We Hear the Larks," Rosenberg explores in this brief lyric themes to which he continually recurs: war, beauty, sexuality, the menacing power of women. The lark song that at first brings only joy carries a somber reminder:

Death could drop from the dark
As easily as song—
But song only dropped,
Like a blind man's dreams on the sand
By dangerous tides,
Like a girl's dark hair for she dreams no
ruins lie there,
Or her kisses where a serpent hides.
(10–16)

Rosenberg continued to write poems of high quality until a few days before his death. In a letter to Marsh dated 28 March 1918 he enclosed his last poem, "Through These Pale Cold Days," the third of three meditations on Jewish history and Jewish destiny. On 30 and 31 March Rosenberg's regiment suffered heavy casualties while resisting the German advance, and in the early hours of the morning on 1 April his company was making its way back in order to gain a brief respite from the fighting. Rosenberg volunteered to return to the battle and within an hour was killed in close combat near the French village of Fampoux.

WHAT THE SOLDIERS SANG

The British army sang on the march, in trenches, in billets, in bistros, and in concert halls. The songs that gave strength and comfort to the troops are often ignored by literary critics, who have failed to recognize in them the most considerable body of poetry in English composed and sung by the common man.

Not all the songs were anonymous products of the trenches. "Tipperary," arguably the most famous of marching songs, although the troops came to loathe it, was written in 1912 by a professional composer. "Keep the Home Fires Burning," which belongs to 1915–1916 and the march to the Somme, brought fame and money to the youthful Ivor Novello, who after 1918 wrote, acted in, and directed a long series of spectacular musical comedies at Drury Lane.

Yet the overwhelming majority of trench songs were by anonymous soldiers. Some of them may have been written by one man for performance at a concert, before being adopted, embroidered, or parodied by troops in different parts of the line. Others may have been the work of soldiers, put together during a rest period and then transmitted by word of mouth to men of other regiments. A few songs, some of which went back to the eighteenth and nineteenth centuries, were inherited from the pre-1914 regular army.

The words sung with such gusto were often parodies of well-known hymns, ballads, and musical comedy and music-hall songs: they were usually fitted to existing tunes, sacred and profane. The authors of these songs, whoever they may have been, portrayed themselves as cowardly, lecherous, skeptical of victory, disrespectful toward their military superiors, unappreciative of the charms or the morals of French women such as "Mademoiselle from Armenteers," longing only to get back to England. "I Don't Want to Die" begins:

I want to go home,
I want to go home,
I don't want to go to the trenches no more,
Where whizz-bangs and shrapnel they
whistle and roar.

That inglorious declaration finds a parallel in "I Don't Want to Be a Soldier," a parody of "On Sunday I Walk Out with a Soldier," a song of the kind loathed by Sassoon, which was sung in a revue, *The Passing Show of 1914,* produced at the London Hippodrome:

I don't want to be a soldier,
I don't want to go to war.
I'd rather stay at home,
Around the streets to roam,
And live on the earnings of a well-paid whore.

Not all the songs referred to the war. "Wash Me in the Water," widely sung throughout the war, seems to bear no relevance to the fighting, probably because it is said to have been sung by the regular army before 1914. It was set to a Salvation Army hymn tune:

Wash me in the water
That you washed your dirty daughter
And I shall be whiter
Than the whitewash on the wall.

When no officers were present, "your dirty daughter" might become "the colonel's daughter."

But almost all the finest songs have deep roots in the daily lives of those who composed and sang them. "The Old Barbed Wire" provides a superb example of the way in which contemptuous humor, apparent callousness, and deadly accuracy combine to make an unforgettable song:

If you want to find the sergeant,
I know where he is, I know where he is.
If you want to find the sergeant,
I know where he is,
He's lying on the canteen floor.

The quarter-bloke (the quartermaster sergeant) is miles behind the line; the sergeant-major is boozing up with the private's rum; the CO is down in the deep dugouts. Then comes the final dramatic twist:

If you want to find the old battalion,
I know where they are, I know where they
are.
If you want to find the old battalion,
I know where they are,
They're hanging on the old barbed wire.

In 1963 Joan Littlewood's musical extravaganza *Oh What a Lovely War* made brilliant use of these songs; yet it would be wrong to think of them merely as part of a theatrical entertainment. They commemorate, more fittingly than the headstones of the Imperial War Graves Commission, the lives and deaths of those gallant though unheroic common soldiers who, when the noise of the guns had died down, were found lying in the mud or hanging on the old barbed wire.

THE AFTERMATH: HERBERT READ AND DAVID JONES

In the early 1920's and during the rest of the decade, English novelists tried to give order and coherence to their experience and memories of the war by writing prose fiction. No poet of any merit essayed this task by means of his art until the next decade. There then appeared two poems of some length, *The End of a War* (1933) by Herbert Read and *In Parenthesis* (1937) by David Jones. Neither can be described as a novel in verse or even as an orthodox narrative poem, yet both attempt to assimilate certain qualities of modern prose fiction and to build something less impressionistic and lyrical than the war poems that we have considered in this essay.

Herbert Read (1893–1968) fought with distinction in the war, earning the Distinguished Service Order and the Military Cross. His book of poems *Songs of Chaos* (1915) was followed by a second, *Naked Warriors* (1919). Although Read was to enjoy a long career as a literary critic and aesthetician, he had not in 1919 seen any of those works by Antonio Pollaiuolo or other Florentine painters conjured up by the book's title, whose progenitor is almost certainly Wordsworth's "Character of a Happy Warrior," a poem that is a happy source book of high-minded schoolmasters and of politicians eager to sanctify their wartime speeches with an edifying quotation from a great poet:

> Who is the happy Warrior? Who is he
> That every man in arms should wish to be?

Read gives his answer to Wordsworth's query of 1805:

> Bloody saliva
> Dribbles down his shapeless jacket.
>
> I saw him stab
> And stab again
> A well-killed Boche.
>
> This is the happy warrior,
> This is he. . . .
> (6–12)

"The Execution of Cornelius Vane" anatomizes the life and death of a soldier who shoots away his right index finger and works thereafter in a cookhouse. Required to fight in an emergency, he points to his mutilated hand that cannot fire a rifle, only to be told by a sergeant, "But you can stab." Vane deserts, is tried by court-martial, and is sentenced to death. His executioners, men of his own regiment looking very sad, blindfold him, and just before he is shot he says to the assembly:

> "What wrong have I done that I should
> leave these:
> The bright sun rising
> And the birds that sing?"
> (130–132)

"Kneeshaw Goes to War" analyzes a soldier whose passivity and failure to respond to the world of experience are perhaps more ignoble than Vane's cowardice. He loses a leg in battle and, after returning to England, accepts after long meditation the need to live by the truth and to discipline oneself. The poem anticipates, in its probing of a man's inner life, the intricate analysis of character found in Read's *The End of a War.*

Read's poetry is almost invariably marked by cool intelligence and firm restraint. Very occasionally he permits his emotion to speak nakedly and movingly; such a moment occurs in "My Company":

> But, God! I know that I'll stand
> Someday in the loneliest wilderness,
> . . .
> I know that I'll wander with a cry:
> "O beautiful men, O men I loved,
> O whither are you gone, my company?"
> (26–27; 32–34)

It is this kind of passion, this kind of rhythmical vitality, that one finds wanting in Read's most ambitious poem, *The End of a War.*

The poem comprises three interwoven monologues: "Meditation of the Dying German Officer," "Dialogue Between Body and Soul," and "Meditation of the Waking English Officer." The prose Argument summarizes the main incident of the poem (it can hardly be called the main action, for it is an almost wholly static poem). Briefly, on 10 November 1918 a wounded German officer tells a British officer that a village nearby is undefended. German machine-gunners hidden in the church tower fire on the British battalion resting in the village square, killing or wounding a hundred men. The survivors bayonet the hidden machine-gunners and a corporal dispatches the German officer, who dies impassively. Later, the British find the dismembered body of a French girl who had been raped and tortured by the Germans. The English officer falls asleep, exhausted and nauseated. When he wakes in the morning the church bells are ringing in the armistice.

Despite the grandeur of his theme, Read fails to give his poem life, and the characters are only mouthpieces through whom the poet utters his leaden, monochrome soliloquies. The language remains so inert that even the armistice bells cannot stir it into activity. Extensive quotation would not substantiate that judgment, because the reader might suspect that the hostile critic had picked out the worst passages to prove his case. Here is a short extract, which shows Read in a comparatively sprightly mood, taken from the English officer's meditation:

> . . . First there are the dead to bury
> O God, the dead. How can God's bell
> ring out from that unholy ambush?
> That tower of death! In excess of horror
> war died.
> (26–30)

The reader must discover for himself whether that extract is representative of Read's poem.

The End of a War is a praiseworthy attempt to confront some philosophical questions that have preoccupied thoughtful men and women for centuries: the existence of God, the significance of war and violence in society, the limits of political obligation. Yet although the poem has won critical acclaim during the past half-century, it can rank only as an honorable failure. One suspects that *The End of a War* has been more often referred to than read, and more frequently read than enjoyed.

David Jones (1895–1974) was, like Isaac Rosenberg, both poet and painter. He was educated at Camberwell Art School from 1909 to 1914 and enlisted in the Royal Welsh Fusiliers, serving at the front as a private soldier from December 1915 to March 1918. He became a convert to Roman Catholicism in 1921 and lived by his painting until the mid-1930's, thereafter dividing his time between his work as painter, engraver, and typographer, and his work as a writer.

In Parenthesis, begun in 1928 and published in 1937, could be described as an epic in verse about World War I, although it is unlike traditional epic, contains long passages of prose, and celebrates wars much older than the conflict of 1914–1918. It is an extremely difficult, highly allusive poem, although Jones provides thirty-five pages of notes designed, unlike those of *The Waste Land,* to elucidate rather than to tantalize. Yet even the notes offer a formidable array of theological speculation, assorted myth, army jargon, and references to historical events.

Jones sets his poem between early December 1915 and early July 1916, telling us in the preface that after the Somme battle everything became more impersonal, mechanical, and relentless. He could not have written *In Parenthesis* about the mass slaughter that characterized the war after the midsummer of 1916.

The story concerns a battalion in an infantry camp in England preparing to embark for France. It lands in France and makes its way by stages to the trenches, these preliminary movements being completed on Christmas Day 1915. The opening three sections of the poem are followed by three sections that describe a typical day in the trenches and the southward marches toward the Somme. The final section concentrates on the part played in the disastrous Somme offensive in July 1916 by number 7 platoon, under the command of Lieutenant Jenkins. We follow in particular one of its members, Private Ball, who is indeed the sole survivor of the attack. The poem ends, after the nightmare of battle, with the garlanding of the dead by a figure from Jones's private mythology, the Queen of the Woods, who is in part the goddess Diana and in part the dryad of folklore.

The poem is difficult for a variety of reasons: Jones has at his fingertips and within his imagination a wealth of allusions drawn from heterogeneous and complex sources, of which the principal are Roman history, the Gospels, the so-called Matter of Britain (the Arthurian legends), the whole Romano-Celtic tradition, early English and medieval literature, and the rites of the Roman Catholic Church, especially the Mass. Jones attempts to fuse the raw material of the epic with the technique employed in a modernist poem such as *The Waste Land,* wherein the impressionistic use of imagery and evocative incantation of rhythm largely supersede the formal logic of argument and the orderly unfolding of narrative.

Yet behind these highly elaborate literary devices one senses the presence of the private soldiers with their routine blasphemies, their cockney speech, and their daily suffering. Nor must one forget Jones's constant sardonic humour. Even private John Ball, hero of the epic tale (insofar as there is one), is so called not only because his namesake was the priest who led the Peasants' Revolt in 1381. As Jon Stallworthy observes in his *Survivors' Songs in Welsh Poetry* (1982), Ball's name has a further significance: coming after that of Private Leg in the sergeant's roster, and following the last two digits, 01, in his army number, it is both ballistic and anatomical.

When Private Ball lies wounded he finally abandons his rifle, even though he remembers the admonitions of the instructors in musketry:

> Marry it man! Marry it!
> Cherish her, she's your very own.
> Coax it man coax it—it's delicately andingeniously made
> —it's an instrument of precision—it costs us tax-payers money—I want you men to remember that.
> (pp. 183–184)

That might well come from a work of naturalistic fiction, yet it coexists with the boast of Dai-Great-Coat, uttered after the men of number 1 section have shared a meager benefit of bread and rum. In his lengthy boast Dai, a character in Thomas Malory's *Morte Darthur,* who stands here for the private soldier throughout the ages, claims to have participated in all kinds of historical and mythical events involving the use of hand weapons from the war in Heaven onward:

> I served Longinus that Dux bat-blind and bent;
> the dandy Xth are my regiment;
> who diced
> Crown and Mud-hook
> under the Tree, . . .
> (p. 83)

This is a fairly simple example of Jones's elaborate allusiveness. The Xth Fretensis is reputed to have furnished the escort party at Jesus' crucifixion, and the dicing under the Cross is equated with the gambling game Crown and Mud-hook, or Crown and Anchor, that was popular among the troops in World War I. Jones's repeated collocation of exalted moments from the past with the brutal or trivial events of the war is not designed to glorify the war or, indeed, to diminish the splendor of history and legend. He wants us to apprehend the timelessness of human action. In a later poem, "The Fatigue," he imagines that the execution of Christ is carried out not by the Xth Fretensis but by a party of British soldiers of World War I.

The prose of *In Parenthesis* ranges from the demotic to the hieratic, the brutally simple to the densely allusive. The verse covers an equally wide gamut of form and of emotional resonance. The closing pages of the poem attain a climax of rare poetic intensity, when the Queen of the Woods comes to deck with garlands all who have died in the battle, officers and other ranks, the loved and the detested, German and British alike. Nothing in the poetry of the war excels this luminous requiem:

> For Balder she reaches high to fetch his.
> Ulrich smiles for his myrtle wand.

That swine Lillywhite has daisies to his
  chain—you'd hardly credit it.
She plaits torques of equal splendour for
  Mr. Jenkins and Billy Crower.
Hansel with Gronwy share dog-violets for a
  palm, where they lie in serious embrace
  beneath the twisted tripod.
  (p. 185)

Jones ends *In Parenthesis* with René Hague's translation of lines from the *Chanson de Roland*:

> The geste says this and the man who was on the field . . . and who wrote the book . . . the man who does not know this has not understood anything. (p. 187)

Those words may serve as an epitaph for the poets of 1914–1918, whether they appear in the pages of this essay or not, and as a commemoration of all who suffered and bore witness on the battlefields of World War I.

Selected Bibliography

LAWRENCE BINYON

COLLECTED WORKS

The Four Years: War Poems (London, 1919); *Collected Poems,* 2 vols., (London, 1931).

SEPARATE WORKS

The Anvil (London, 1916); *The Cause: Poems of the War* (Boston, 1917); *For the Fallen* (London, 1917).

EDMUND BLUNDEN

BIBLIOGRAPHY

Kirkpatrick, B. J., *A Bibliography of Edmund Blunden* (Oxford, 1979).

COLLECTED WORKS

K. Hopkins, ed., *Edmund Blunden: A Selection of Poetry and Prose* L(ondon, 1950; New York, 1961); *Poems of Many Years,* (London, 1957); R. Marsack, ed., *Selected Poems,* (Manchester, 1982).

SEPARATE WORKS

Undertones of War (London, 1928), verse and prose, with new preface by author (New York, 1956); *War Poets 1914–1918,* (London, 1958), criticism.

CRITICAL STUDIES

Hardie, A. M., *Edmund Blunden,* (London, 1958; rev. ed. 1971); Thorpe, M., *The Poetry of Edmund Blunden* (Wateringbury, 1971).

RUPERT BROOKE

BIBLIOGRAPHY

Keynes, G., *A Bibliography* (London, 1954; 2nd ed., rev. 1959).

COLLECTED WORKS

Collected Poems: With a Memoir by E[dward]. M[arsh] (London, 1918); G. Keynes, ed., *The Poetical Works,* (London, 1947), paperback ed. London (1960); Hassall, C., *The Prose* (London, 1956); G. Keynes, ed., *Letters* (London, 1968).

SEPARATE WORKS

Poems (London, 1911); *1914 and Other Poems* (London, 1915); *John Webster and the Elizabethan Drama* (London, 1916); *Letters from America* (London, 1916), preface by Henry James.

CRITICAL STUDIES

de la Mare, W., *Rupert Brooke and the Intellectual Imagination* (London, 1919); Browne, M., *Recollections of Rupert Brooke* (London, 1927); Stringer, A. J. A., *Red Wine of Youth: A Life of R. Brooke* (Indianapolis, 1948); Hassall, C., *Rupert Brooke: A Biograph,* (New York, 1964); Hastings, M., *The Handsomest Young Man in England: Rupert Brooke* (London, 1967), lavishly illus.; Keynes, G., *Rupert Brooke: Drafts and Fair Copies in the Author's Hand* (London, 1974).

FORD MADOX FORD

COLLECTED WORKS

Collected Poems (New York, 1936), intro. by W. R. Benét.

JULIAN GRENFELL

SEPARATE WORKS

Battle: Flanders (London, 1915).

CRITICAL STUDIES

Meynell, V., *Julian Grenfell* (London, 1917), memoir with poems; Mosley, M., *Julian Grenfell* (London, 1976), based on Grenfell family papers.

IVOR GURNEY

COLLECTED WORKS

Poems by Ivor Gurney (London, 1954), with memoir by E. Blunden; *Poems of Ivor Gurney, 1890–1937* (London, 1973), intro. by E. Blunden and bibliographical note by L. Clark; *Collected Poems of Ivor Gurney* P. J. Kavanagh, ed., (London, 1982), first major collection of Gurney's work, includes over 300 poems, 100 not previously collected; R. K. R. Thornton, ed., *War Letters of Ivor Gurney* (Manchester, 1983).

SEPERATE WORKS

Severn and Somme, (London, 1917); *War's Embers, and Other Verses* (London, 1919).

CRITICAL STUDIES

Hurd, M., *The Ordeal of Ivor Gurney* (London, 1978).

W. N. HODGSON

COLLECTED WORKS

Verse and Prose in Peace and War (London, 1916; 2nd ed. 1917).

A. E. HOUSMAN

COLLECTED WORKS

Collected Poems (London, 1939; New York, 1940, 1959).

DAVID JONES

COLLECTED WORKS

H. Grisewood, ed., *Epoch and Artist: Selected Writings* (London, 1959), prose; R. Pryor, ed., *David Jones: Letters to Vernon Watkins* (Cardiff, 1976), foreword by G. Watkins, notes by ed.; R. Hague, ed., *Dai Greatcoat: A Self-Portrait of David Jones in His Letters* (Boston, 1980); J. Matthias, ed., *Introducing David Jones: A Selection of His Writings* (Boston, 1980).

SEPARATE WORKS

In Parenthesis (London, 1937), verse and prose; *The Anathemata: Fragments of an Attempted Writing* (London, 1952; 2nd ed. 1955), verse and prose; *The Sleeping Lord and Other Fragments* (London, 1974), verse and prose; although these later writings do not have World War I as their theme, they all throw light on *In Parenthesis.*

CRITICAL STUDIES

Blamires, D., *David Jones: Artist and Writer* (Manchester, 1971; Toronto, 1972); Hague, R., *David Jones* (Cardiff, 1975); Hooker, J., *David Jones: An Exploratory Study of the Writings* (London, 1975); *David Jones:* R. Mathias, ed., *Eight Essays on His Work as Writer and Artist* (Llandysul, 1976); Rees, S., *David Jones* (New York, 1977), includes bibliography; Blissett, W., *The Long Conversation: A Memoir of David Jones* (London, 1981).

ROBERT NICHOLS

COLLECTED WORKS

Such Was My Singing: A Selection from Poems 1915–1940 (London, 1942).

SEPARATE WORKS

Invocation: War Poems and Others (London, 1915); *Ardours and Endurances* (London, 1917).

HERBERT READ

COLLECTED WORKS

Collected Poems (London, 1966).

SEPARATE WORKS

Songs of Chaos (London, 1915), verse; *Naked Warriors* (London, 1919), verse; *In Retreat* (London, 1925), prose narrative; *Ambush* (London, 1930), prose narrative; *The End of a War* (London, 1933), verse.

CRITICAL STUDIES

Berry, F., *Herbert Read* (London, 1961).

ISAAC ROSENBERG

COLLECTED WORKS

G. Bottomley, ed., *Poems* (London, 1922), with memoir by L. Binyon; G. Bottomley and D. Harding, eds., *Collected Poems* (London-New York, 1949); I. Parsons, ed., *Collected Works* (London, 1979; rev. and enl. from 1937 ed.), intro. by ed., foreword by S. Sassoon.

SEPARATE WORKS

Night and Day (London, 1912); *Youth* (London, 1915), poems; *Moses* (London, 1916), drama.

CRITICAL STUDIES

Cohen, J., *Journey to the Trenches: The Life of Isaac Rosenberg, 1890–1918* (London, 1975); Liddiard, J., *Isaac Rosenberg: The Half-Used Life* (London, 1975); Wilson, J. M., *Isaac Rosenberg, Poet and Painter* (London, 1975). Note: Catalogs of two exhibitions contain valuable material on Rosenberg: *Isaac Rosenberg 1890–1917: Catalogue with Letters,* ed. by M. de Sausmarez and J. Silkin, (Leeds University Exhibition Catalog, Leeds, 1959) and the National Book League Exhibition Catalogue, ed. by J. Liddiard and C. Simmons (London, 1975).

SIEGFRIED SASSOON

BIBLIOGRAPHY

Keynes, G., *A Bibliography* (London, 1962).

COLLECTED WORKS

The War Poems (London, 1919); *The Complete Memoirs of George Sherston* (London, 1937), prose; *Collected Poems* (London, 1947); *Collected Poems 1908–1956* (London, 1961); *Selected Poems* (London, 1968), paperback ed.

SEPARATE WORKS

The Old Huntsman and Other Poems (London, 1917); *Counter-Attack and Other Poems* (London, 1918), intro. by R. Nichols; *Picture Show* (Cambridge, 1919), verse; *Satirical Poems* (London, 1926; enl. ed. 1933); *The Heart's Journey* (London, 1927), verse; *Memoirs of a Fox-Hunting Man* (London, 1928), memoirs; *Memoirs of an Infantry Officer* (New York-London, 1930), memoirs; *Sherston's Progress* (London, 1936), memoirs; *The Old Century and Seven More Years* (London, 1938), memoirs, paperback ed. with intro. by M. Thorpe (London, 1968); *The Weald of Youth* (London, 1942), memoirs; *Siegfried's Journey, 1916–1920* (London, 1945), memoirs; D. R. Hart, ed., *Diaries 1920–1922* (London, 1982), intro. by ed..

CRITICAL STUDIES

Thorpe, M., *Siegfried Sassoon: A Critical Study* (London, 1966).

CHARLES HAMILTON SORLEY

COLLECTED WORKS

Marlborough, and Other Poems (London, 1916; 5th ed., rev. and enl. 1922); *Letters from Germany* (Cambridge, 1916); *The Letters with a Chapter of Biography* (Cambridge, 1919).

CRITICAL STUDIES

Swann, T. B., *The Ungirt Runner: Charles Hamilton Sorley, Poet of World War I* (Hamden, Conn., 1965).

EDWARD THOMAS

COLLECTED WORKS

Collected Poems (London, 1920), foreword by W. de la Mare; R. G. Thomas, ed., *Letters from Edward Thomas to Gordon Bottomley* London, 1958); R. G. Thomas, ed., *Collected Poems* (New York-Oxford, 1978).

CRITICAL STUDIES

Moore, J., *The Life and Letters of Edward Thomas* (London-Toronto, 1939); Coombes, H., *Edward Thomas* (London, 1956); Farjeon, E., *Edward Thomas: The Last Four Years* (London, 1958); Scannell, V., *Edward Thomas* (London, 1965); Cooke, W., *Edward Thomas: A Critical Biography 1878–1917* (London, 1970); Thomas, H., *Edward Thomas* (Edinburgh, 1974), contains *As It Was* (New York-London, 1927) and *World Without End* (London, 1931), his widow's 2-vol. account of her life with him; Motion, A., *Edward Thomas* (London, 1980).

ARTHUR GRAEME WEST

SEPARATE WORKS

Diary of a Dead Officer (London, 1919).

ANTHOLOGIES

E. H. Marsh, ed., *Georgian Poetry* (London, 1914, 1916, 1918, 1919, 1922; eds. for 1911–1912, 1913–1915, 1916–1917, 1918–1919, 1920–1922); E. H. Marsh, ed., *1914 and Other Poems* (London, 1915); F. Brereton [Frederick T. Smith], ed., *Anthology of War Poems* (London, 1930), intro. by E. Blunden; R. M. B. Nichols, ed., *An Anthology of War Poetry* (London, 1943), with long intro. in form of dialogue between Nichols and J. Tennyson; J. Brophy and E. Partridge, eds., *The Long Trail: What the British Soldier Sang and Said in the Great War of 1914–1918* (London, 1965), rev. ed. of *Songs and Slang of the British Soldier 1914–1918* (London, 1938); B. Gardner, ed., *Up the Line to Death: The War Poets 1914–1918* (London, 1965), intro. by E. Blunden; I. M. Parsons, ed., *Men Who March Away: Poems of the First World War* (New York-London, 1965); M. Hussey, ed., *Poetry of the First World War* (London, 1967).

GENERAL CRITICISM

Johnston, J. M., *English Poetry of the First World War* (London, 1964), detailed study of the leading poets of the war; Bergonzi, B., *Heroes' Twilight: A Study of the Literature of the Great War* (London, 1965); Silkin, J., *Out of Battle: The Poetry of the Great War* (London, 1972); Stallworthy, J., *Poets of the First World War* (London, 1974); Fussell, P., *The Great War and Modern Memory* (New York, 1975).

Poets of World War II

JOHN PRESS

INTRODUCTION

Countless books, poems, photographs, and films have imprinted on our memories ineffaceable images of World War I: rat-infested dugouts; fields torn by shells; barbed wire festooned with corpses; men cut down by machine guns as they charged with fixed bayonets; lakes of mud that sucked men under; and brief moments of rest behind the front line in the villages of Flanders or France. World War II presents a different pattern of warfare; one in which mobility largely supersedes the front line and the system of trenches, and tanks and planes become dominant weapons, reinforced by the power of artillery and the courage of trained infantrymen.

C. E. Montague's important work *Disenchantment* (1922) records the process whereby the soldiers who with the noblest ideals and hopes volunteered in 1914 soon became embittered and disillusioned. This did not happen in World War II mainly because only the most naive recruits harbored any illusions that might wither. When Evelyn Waugh's *Put Out More Flags* appeared in 1942, nobody supposed that it would be an undiluted panegyric to the war effort.

During the last two years of World War I many soldiers who were at the end of their tether in the trenches hated their civilian fellow countrymen more than their German fellow sufferers. Siegfried Sassoon's "I'd like to see a Tank come down the stalls," written after a visit to a variety theater in Liverpool in January 1917, anticipates Wilfred Owen's letter of 10 August 1918 to his mother, in which he desires that "the Boche would have the pluck to come right in and make a clean sweep of the pleasure boats, and the promenaders on the Spa, and all the stinking Leeds and Bradford war profiteers now reading *John Bull* on Scarborough Sands."

No member of the armed services would have expressed those sentiments in World War II. Air raids, rationing, shortages, the blackout, conscription of labor, and the absence of husbands and fathers on active service imposed heavy physical and emotional strains on civilians in Britain. Many servicemen enjoying, albeit with a twinge of guilt, the green pastures of Kenya, the pleasures of Egypt, or the imperial grandeur of India might reflect that they were a great deal safer and more comfortable than people in the cities and towns of Britain.

It is significant that whereas some of the best poets of World War I—Julian Grenfell, Edmund Blunden, Siegfried Sassoon, Wilfred Owen, and Herbert Read—were decorated for gallantry, none of the poets discussed in the present essay received a decoration except Norman Cameron, who was made a Member of the Order of the British Empire for work in political intelligence and propaganda. Moreover, barely half these poets were ever in action: this reflects not on their courage but on the way in which the conduct of war had changed since 1918 and on the army's use of manpower.

There is no equivalent in World War II of the trench songs that were composed by anonymous soldiers in World War I. Instead, the ubiquitous radio poured out its message of synthetic good cheer and saccharine comfort. Vera Lynn, the Forces' Sweetheart, assured all servicemen that "There'll be blue birds over / The white cliffs of Dover," and that "We'll meet again." In the Western Desert, however, the Forces' Sweetheart was the Scandinavian Lala Andersen, who sang on the German radio "Lili Marleen," a song admired equally in its German and English versions by the opposing armies. Such musical internationalism, alas, had its limits, as British troops found when they made contact with Yugoslav partisans: to them "Lili Marleen" was taboo because the Germans had sung it when they marched partisans away to execution.

A High Court judge is said once to have advised an incompetent counsel that if he could not present his case logically or chronologically, he might present it alphabetically. It may be expedient to group the poets in this essay geographically, partly because this method enables one to make comparisons between their responses to the same environment. But there is a more cogent reason, which stems from the wartime experiences of many poets. They were moved less by the terror and brutality of war than by the impact on their imaginations of distant lands and unfamiliar civilizations. The main themes of their poems are the physical features, social conditions, and historical backgrounds of the countries where they were stationed.

This essay will first consider the poetry of those whom the fortunes of war dispatched to widely scattered theaters of either battle or comparative peace: Britain, continental Europe, the Middle East, North Africa, East Africa, India, and Burma. It will then look at the work of Alan Ross and Charles Causley, two men who served in the Royal Navy; and finish by surveying the poetry of Sidney Keyes, Keith Douglas, and Alun Lewis, three highly gifted poets who, unlike the others to be discussed, died in active service in North Africa, France, and Burma.

BRITAIN AND EUROPE

During the war hundreds of thousands of servicemen spent the years in Britain in barracks, billets, or camps, undergoing training, doing fatigues (labor), polishing boots until they could see their faces reflected in them, polishing the brass collars of antiaircraft guns until they shone so brightly that German planes could see them miles away, being inspected to check that they had not lost their blankets or acquired venereal diseases—all the traditional means of cultivating the military virtues and enforcing military discipline. It is a melancholy fact that only a handful of good poems came out of the armed forces stationed in Britain. There is no satisfactory explanation for this, unless it is that the perils of battle, the extreme loneliness, the posts in distant countries, and the shock of living in an alien civilization may inspire poetry; whereas boredom, discomfort, and a sense of aimlessness produce a dampening effect on the imagination.

Henry Reed (born 22 February 1914), joined the army in 1941 and transferred to the Foreign Office the next year. His few months in the army gave him the material for *Lessons of the War,* his sequence of three poems—"Naming of Parts," "Judging Distances," and "Unarmed Combat"—that won instant recognition as the definitive comment on one aspect of military life.

All three poems are divided between two voices: that of the noncommissioned officer who is instructing the squad and that of the recruit. The difference in idiom and in sensibility between the two voices appears less and less perceptible as the trilogy unfolds, maybe in order to suggest that the recruit is becoming assimilated to the army and learning the martial virtues. But these nuances are of secondary importance, compared with the central fact that the two voices represent two diametrically opposed principles and responses to the world: the ethos of unquestioning obedience, submission to duty, subordination of the individualistic self to the common purpose imposed from above; and the attitude that values skepticism, irony, the right to judge moral behavior for oneself.

"Naming of Parts" is the richest of the poems, because it moves with a sensuous grace not found in the other two and because Reed sustains throughout its five stanzas a series of witty puns that contrast the different parts of the rifle with the vibrant world of japonica, almond blossom, bees, and branches observed by the recruit as the instructor drones on:

> And this you can see is the bolt. The purpose of this
> Is to open the breech, as you see. We can slide it
> Rapidly backwards and forwards: we call this
> Easing the spring. And rapidly backwards and forwards
> The early bees are assaulting and fumbling the flowers:
> They call it easing the Spring.
> (19–24)

The fusion of the instructor's demotic syntax and speech rhythm with the recruit's gentle, meditative reflections is a triumph of poetic skill; and the delicate sexuality that pervades "Naming of Parts" lends it a further layer of richness.

A full analysis of the poem and of its companion pieces would reveal how wittily and movingly Reed has demonstrated, without self-pity or even protest, the struggle of the individual to keep alive his humanity, despite the attempt by the army to make him part of an impersonal machine. The final lines of "Unarmed Combat," which can be read as a straightforward acknowledgment that the individual must submit to authority, undermine by their tone and inflection the message they purport to give:

> . . . and we must fight
> Not in the hope of winning but rather of keeping
> Something alive: so that when we meet our end,
> It may be said that we tackled wherever we could,
> That battle-fit we lived, and though defeated,
> Not without glory fought.

Reed, unfortunately, has not published a book of poems since *A Map of Verona* (1946). Gavin Ewart (born 4 February 1916), on the other hand, is a prolific poet, although it is only since 1964 that he has been in full spate. In the war poems section of *The Collected Ewart 1933–1980* (1980) there are only nine works, all displaying various facets of his talent but none so distinctive as the best of his postwar verse, which is often extremely funny and outrageously bawdy, and sometimes genuinely moving.

"Officers' Mess" explores the vein of riproaring verse opened up with precocious skill by the schoolboy and undergraduate Ewart between 1933 and 1939:

> And then that new MO came in, the Jewish one, awful fellow,
> And his wife, a nice little bit of stuff, dressed in a flaming yellow.
> (5–6)

That is one reaction to the war. Another, more tender and troubled, derives its pathos from the fragility of love menaced by the shadow of separation and of approaching battle, as in the sextet of "Sonnet, 1940":

> And I, before the happy tough battalions
> Engulf me or the frozen seas of Norway,
> Have still my dreams of cities and of dalliance,
> But most of you as standing in a doorway,
> Who might, though I so dissipate my life,
> Be mistress or, fear of the young, a wife.
> (9–14)

Ewart wrote another good sonnet, "War Dead," at La Spezia in April 1945, but his most harsh and somber war poem is "When a Beau Goes In," a Beau being the shortened form of Beaufighter, one of the best-known British fighter aircraft. The long, languorous line in stanza 2, with its echoes of Gerard

Manley Hopkins and Alfred Tennyson, works against the jerky, jokey short lines and accentuates Ewart's bitterness at the cult of the stiff upper lip in the face of other people's deaths:

Although its perfectly certain
The pilot's gone for a Burton[1]
And the observer too
It s nothing to do with you
And if they both should go
To a land where falls no rain nor hail nor
driven snow—
Here, there or anywhere,
Do you suppose *they* care?
(9–16)

Behind the exuberant, baroque facade of the riotously lewd jokes that Ewart revels in, there lurk always fury and grief at the raw facts of pain and death.

Ewart is a tough-minded poet, as is Vernon Scannell (born 23 January 1922), who saw hard fighting from El Alamein to Tunis as well as in the invasions of Sicily and Normandy. His war poems are unusual in that they appear in seven collections published between 1957 and 1975 and are as much concerned with World War I as with World War II. Almost all of them dwell on the terror of battle recalled in memory or dream and on those who died in action. Scannell portrays his fellow soldiers as he knew them in all their strong and sometimes coarse physicality. These vigorous poems offer a view of war that is not to be found elsewhere, and they deserve to be more widely known. "Walking Wounded," which has, in addition to the qualities of Scannell's other poems, an extra dimension of visionary strangeness, depicts with almost photographic realism how first

the ambulances came,
Stumbling and churning past the broken
farm,
The amputated sign-post and smashed trees,
Slow wagonloads of bandaged cries. . . .
(12–15)

1. Meaning in Royal Air Force slang, "to be shot down."

Then, after a pause, the walking wounded go by, "a humble brotherhood," without splendor. And yet, says Scannell, in lines that confer mythical status on a procession remembered after eighteen years:

Imagination pauses and returns
To see them walking still, but multiplied
In thousands now. And when heroic corpses
Turn slowly in their decorated sleep
And every ambulance has disappeared
The walking wounded still trudge down
that lane,
And when recalled they must bear arms
again.
(42–48)

It may appear strange that almost all the poetry written by Royal Air Force pilots and air crew, whose courage and skill were of the highest quality, should be little more than apprentice work: often conventionally romantic, sometimes displaying seeds of promise blighted by early death in action. Scannell in *Not Without Glory* (1976) argues that most pilots and air crew lacked the temperament to devote much time to the kind of solitary meditation that gives birth to poetry. They were, moreover, constantly in action or standing by for action; and for many of them, flying and aerial combat were quasi-mystical experiences that lay beyond the reach of words. He justly singles out for praise a sonnet by John Bayliss (born 4 October 1919) that may serve as an epitaph for all the members of the RAF who died in action. "Reported Missing" tells how two men in a plane with a broken wing, and with their gunner dead, knowing that all is finished, looking at the sea,

sat in this tattered scarecrow of the sky
hearing it cough, the great plane catching
now the first dark clouds upon her wing-
base,—
patching the great tear in evening mockery.

So two men waited, saw the third dead face,
and wondered when the wind would let
them die.
(9–14)

Tens of thousands of men spent years as prisoners of war. The overcrowding, the sense of anxiety, and the complex of emotions aroused by captivity in a foreign land tended to stifle the poetic impulse. One poet, despite such discouragement, wrote a sonnet of high quality. Having taken part in the defense of Crete in 1941 and having been mentioned in dispatches, Michael Riviere (born 5 January 1919) was captured and sent to Germany. After twice escaping from other camps, he was incarcerated in Colditz (whose epigraph is a line from Sir Philip Sidney: "The poor man's wealth, the prisoner's release") in the summer of 1943; while imprisoned in that fortress, which was especially designed to make escape impossible, he wrote "Oflag Night Piece: Colditz":

There, where the swifts flicker along the
  wall
And the last light catches, there in the high
  schloss
(How the town grows dark) all's made
  impregnable
They bless each window with a double cross
Of iron; weave close banks of wire and train
Machine guns down on them; and look—at
  the first star
Floodlight the startled darkness back
  again . . .
All for three hundred prisoners of war:
Yet now past them and the watch they keep,
Unheard, invisible, in ones and pairs,
In groups, in companies—alarms are dumb,
A sentry loiters, a blind searchlight stares—
Unchallenged as their memories of home
The vanishing prisoners escape to sleep.

The level of the sonnet; the gentle irony ("They bless each window with a double cross / Of iron"); the amused reminder that the elaborate precautions are "All for three hundred prisoners of war" may give the poem its distinctive quality, but they do not account for its power to touch the reader's heart. It derives some of its potency from its affinities with two themes in English poetry that have a long history. The first is that of prison literature, beginning with the poetry written by state prisoners of the early Tudors, notably Sir Thomas Wyatt; and continuing with the poetry of Roman Catholics awaiting trial or execution under Elizabeth I. The second is that of invocations to sleep: one thinks particularly of songs and sonnets by Sidney, Samuel Daniel, John Fletcher, John Keats, and Hopkins. Although Riviere's sonnet is in no way an imitation or pastiche and contains no allusion to earlier poems, it quietly takes its place among its ancestors.

THE MIDDLE EAST AND NORTH AFRICA

In the Western Desert and in North Africa, where the British fought the Germans and the Italians, the character of the fighting had no parallel anywhere in either of the two world wars. There was no system of trenches or of other elaborate defensive measures, for this was largely a conflict of tanks that moved rapidly on the offensive over huge tracts of desert, until they were halted and harassed by a counter-offensive. Insofar as war can ever be anything but a loathsome butchery, it was a chivalrous war, fought without rancor by soldiers who respected one another's courage, dash, and tactical skill. Neither side obliterated towns, massacred civilians, or murdered prisoners. In this old-fashioned combat, individual enterprise, unorthodoxy carried to the point of eccentricity, and a cavalier disregard for the niceties of military etiquette flourished exceedingly. The Eighth Army, a gallant fighting force, chased the Germans out of Africa. Lawrence Durrell, not renowned for his conventionality, describes in his introduction to the anthology *Return to Oasis* (1980) the apparition of the poet and critic George Fraser (8 November 1915–3 January 1980):

> I recall George Fraser visiting me in the press department of the Embassy to deliver some poems of his for Personal Landscape. I was

> horrified to see that, though in uniform, he was wearing tennis shoes and a dirty scarf, while his trousers were fastened with string. I asked with concern whether he wasn't reprimanded for such wear and he said that he never had been, probably because his boss was a writer too.

Old soldiers and connoisseurs of military life will be interested to learn that Fraser eventually became a sergeant major.

During the war Alexandria and Cairo housed not only large military forces but a civilian population swollen by refugees from Europe who had sought the comparative safety of Egypt. They were highly sophisticated cities, where every pleasure could be bought and where in 1942 the prevailing frenetic gaiety was tinged with fear, as Rommel's armies marched on victoriously across the Western Desert. Durrell's *Alexandria Quartet* and Olivia Manning's Levant trilogy (*The Danger Tree, The Battle Lost and Won,* and *The Sum of Things*) have portrayed indelibly the world of the expatriates and their circle in wartime Egypt. Less melodramatic than Durrell and more kindly than Manning, Fraser in "Egypt" evokes the sultry romanticism of the land:

> The desert slays. But safe from Allah's
>   justice
> Where the broad river of His Mercy lies,
> Where ground for labour, or where scope for
>   lust is,
> The crooked and tall and cunning cities rise.
> The green Nile irrigates a barren region,
> All the coarse palms are ankle-deep in sand;
> No love roots deep, though easy loves are
>   legion:
> The heart's as hot and hungry as the hand.
> (13–20)

Those who found themselves in Cairo or Alexandria included a number of English poets: some were civilians, others were members of the forces. Three of the civilians, Durrell, Bernard Spencer, and Robin Fedden, started the poetry magazine *Personal Landscape* in the late autumn of 1941. In the course of its existence it printed work by almost every good poet in the region. The best of the civilian poets, apart from the editors, were Terence Tiller and Ruth Speirs; while the most gifted of the servicemen were Norman Cameron, Fraser, Hamish Henderson, and F. T. Prince, as well as Keith Douglas and Sidney Keyes, to whom later sections of this essay are devoted.

Hamish Henderson (born 11 November 1919) is best known for his sequence of poems *Elegies for the Dead in Cyrenaica* (1948), an ambitious attempt to portray the war in the desert. Its dedication, "For our own and the others," typifies the spirit in which it was written, one of compassion and guilt toward what Henderson calls in his foreword "that eternally wronged proletariat of levelling death in which all the fallen are comrades." He does not confine himself to a realistic description of the battles, but places them in the perspective of medieval Scottish history—the depopulated Highlands—and Karnak, the subject of the Eighth Elegy. The latter is an impressionistic evocation of a vanished way of life or, rather, of death, for Henderson condemns all that Karnak stood for because it devoted its power and resources to death.

Unfortunately, the scope and high intentions of the poems outrun their linguistic vitality. Occasionally Henderson deploys a vivid image:

>   Herons stalk
> over the blood-stained flats. Burning byres
> come to my mind.
> (Fifth Elegy, 18–20)

But all too often the elegies degenerate into sequences of ponderous rhetoric that lie inertly on the page; at its worst, as in Interlude ("Opening of an Offensive"), the rhetoric deteriorates into rodomontade garnished with echoes of Hopkins:

>   Slake
> the crashing breakers-húrled rúbble of the
>   guns.
> Dithering darkness, we'll wake you!
> Hélls bélls blind you.
> (20–23)

The description of the shrill war song is even more flatulent:

> It mounts. Its scream
> tops the valkyrie, tops the colossal
> artillery.
>
> Meaning that many
> German Fascists will not be going home.
> (41–44)

The Seventh Elegy, entitled "Seven Good Germans," an allusion to the saying that "the only good German is a dead one," offers succinct biographies of seven who died at El Eleba. It is in many ways the most humane of the elegies, sardonic and unpretentious, shedding more light on the desert war than the booming disquisitions that reverberate through the others. The poem ends with an epitaph on the good Germans, who are linked in the comradeship of the fallen; their requiem is the favorite song of the contending armies in Cyrenaica:

> Seven poor bastards
> dead in African deadland
> (tawny tousled hair under the issue blanket)
> *wie einst Lili*
> dead in African deadland
>
> *einst Lili Marleen.*
> (55–60)

Norman Cameron (1905–1953) served in British political intelligence and propaganda. He was a friend of Robert Graves, who greatly admired his poems. Cameron's work sometimes recalls the flavor of Graves's poetry, although he was far from being a slavish imitator. He is an accomplished poet, capable of writing fine lyrics, beautifully conceived and executed; but the mode he favors is one of formal irony laced with gaiety.

"Green, Green is El Aghir" is not so much a war poem as a celebration of an escape from war into a world of abundance and joy, symbolized by the waters splashing from a fountain with two full-throated faucets at El Aghir. The irregularity of the meter, compounded by the off-rhymes, emphasizes the sense of freedom from constraint felt by all, even by the Arabs who go off with the rest to drink wine:

> And we yelped and leapt from the truck and
> went at the double
> To fill our bidons and bottles and drink and
> dabble.
> Then, swollen with water, we went to an
> inn for wine.
> The Arabs came, too, though their faith
> might have stood between:
> "After all," they said, "it's a boisson,"
> without contrition.
> (13–17)

"Black Takes White" springs from a later campaign in the Apennines. A party of American blacks, attempting to desert, encounters a party of like-minded Italians. Both groups want to surrender, the impasse being surmounted only because the Italians, being led by an officer, have the whip hand. The reluctant blacks march back with their unsought booty to a heroes' welcome:

> Nobody paused to bother with such trifles
> As where the captors had mislaid their
> rifles.
> Quickly those fed-up and embarrassed
> Negroes
> Were praised, promoted, given gongs as
> heroes,
> And photographs of their victorious battle
> Were published from Long Island to Seattle.

The subtly varied rhythm and the faintly insolent rhymes point the subversive moral of the tale, in which cowardice and mendacity shamelessly mock the pomposity of government propaganda.

John Manifold (born 21 April 1916), an Australian who completed his education at Jesus College, Cambridge, saw military service in the Middle East, West Africa, and France. A convinced Marxist, he writes polemical verse that emphasizes the usefulness of poetry and the need for all to fight unquestioningly for the victory that will bring the triumph of the proletariat one stage nearer. Scannell suggests in *Not Without Glory* that there is much in common between Manifold and Campbell, though neither would greatly relish the comparison. The verse of both men has strong elements of swagger and tough talking; both despise the coward and the sensitive soul who will not fight; Campbell sings the flowering rifle and Manifold the tommy gun, "the clean functional thing." But Campbell, with his cult of the lone wolf, does not share Manifold's admiration for those who find their self-respect only when they surrender their individuality. That is the point of the latter's well-argued sonnet "Recruit"; and in "Ration Party" he again urges the need for sacrifice, exemplified by a fatigue party that bears huge loads up a hill, day after day, a menial, dispiriting task:

> Absurd to think that Liberty, the splendid
> Nude of our dreams, the intercessory saint
> For us to judgement, needs to be defended
>
> By sick fatigue-men brimming with complaint
> And misery, who bear till all is ended
> Every imaginable pattern of constraint.
> (9–14)

In "The Sirens," perhaps the wittiest and most effective of all Manifold's sonnets, the moral of the story is very largely what the reader chooses to make it. Even those who are unsympathetic to the poet's political beliefs, and to the didacticism that marks so much of his verse, can savor the freshness of the language, the ingenious refurbishing of an old legend, the relaxed wit and the stylish versification of the poem:

> Odysseus heard the sirens; they were singing
> Music by Wolf and Weinberger and Morley
> About a region where the swans go winging,
> Vines are in colour, girls are growing surely
>
> Into nubility, and pylons bringing
> Leisure and power to farms that live securely
> Without a landlord. Still, his eyes were stinging
> With salt and sea blink, and the ropes hurt sorely.
>
> Odysseus saw the sirens; they were charming,
> Blonde, with snub breasts and little neat posteriors,
> But could not take his mind off the alarming
>
> Weather report, his mutineers in irons,
> The radio failing; it was bloody serious.
> In twenty minutes he forgot the sirens.

F. T. Prince (born 13 September 1912), a South African who had attended the universities of Oxford and Princeton, had published before the war a volume of poems notable for their technical skill and meditative subtlety. Unlike the works of Henderson and Manifold, "Soldiers Bathing," Prince's best-known poem, does not primarily concern itself with the details of war in the Middle East or with the war's political and social implications. Even in 1941, when the poem first appeared, Prince, a Roman Catholic preoccupied with evil and with the Crucifixion, was already a scholar and a lover of Italian art. The scene is a beach in the Middle East, where Prince was serving in the Intelligence Corps, but the setting could just as well be an imaginary stretch of coast. The poem opens quietly:

> The sea at evening moves across the sand.
> Under a reddening sky I watch the freedom of a band
> Of soldiers who belong to me. Stripped bare
> For bathing in the sea, they shout and run in the warm air. . . .

Then follows a disquisition on the body and the sweetness of its nakedness when the sea has washed it free of fever, filth, and sweat. Every one of the soldiers

> forgets
> His hatred of the war, its terrible pressure that begets

A machinery of death and slavery,
Each being a slave and making slaves of
others. . . .
(15–18)

Contemplation of the naked soldiers awakens in Prince a memory of a Michelangelo cartoon in which bathing soldiers clamber from the water at the sudden incursion of the enemy, and fight, naked as they are:

—And I think too of the theme another
found
When, shadowing men's bodies on a sinister
red ground,
Another Florentine, Pollaiuolo,
Painted a naked battle warriors, straddled,
hacked the foe,
Dug their bare toes into the ground and slew
The brother-naked man who lay between
their feet and drew
His lips back from his teeth in a grimace.

They were Italians who knew wars sorrow
and disgrace
And showed the thing suspended, stripped: a
theme
Born out of the experience of war's horrible
extreme
Beneath a sky where even the air flows
With lacrimae Christi. . . .
(31–42)

There follows a meditation on the relation between Pollaiuollo's painting and the Crucifixion, and on the terror of the great love that is over all we do. It may be that readers must either be attuned to Prince's Christian mysticism or suspend their disbelief, if this section of the poem is not to constitute a stumbling block. No such difficulty arises in the final section: Prince recapitulates all the main themes of the poem, and as he drinks the dusky air—perhaps the sky of Egypt flows with "lacrimae Christi" (tears of Christ)—the reddening sky of the first section is linked with the Crucifixion:

These dry themselves and dress,
Combing their hair, forget the fear and the
shame of nakedness.
Because to love is frightening we prefer
The freedom of our crimes. Yet, as I drink
the dusky air,
I feel a strange delight that fills me full,
Strange gratitude, as if evil itself were
beautiful,
And kiss the wound in thought, while in
the west
I watch a streak of red that might have
issued from Christ's breast.
(59–66)

EAST AFRICA

During World War I East Africa was the scene of heavy fighting between the British and the Germans who, based in German East Africa (now Tanzania), remained undefeated at the armistice. In World War II, although no battles took place in the East African territories, the country was a training ground for the Africanized units of the British army, which were preparing to recover Burma from the Japanese; it was also a naval base for the Eastern Fleet, which sought the safety of Kilindini Harbour, Mombasa, after the Japanese had bombed it out of Singapore, Colombo, and Trincomalee. The East Africa Command was, geographically speaking, the largest in the British army, stretching from Somaliland to Southern Rhodesia (now Zimbabwe) and embracing such widely scattered islands as Madagascar, Mauritius, and the Seychelles.

Most travelers find East Africa overwhelming in its magnificence, whether they first encounter the coast, or the mountains, hills, and valleys up-country. Roy Campbell (2 October 1901–23 April 1957), being a native of South Africa and thus accustomed to something of the same natural splendor, was not bowled over by East Africa when he was posted there after having volunteered for military service when in his late thirties. He had migrated as a young man to England, where he had soon acquired a reputation as a rambunctious satirist, equally happy to castigate the narrow hypocrisy of Afrikaaners or the epicene aesthetes of Bloomsbury. In the late 1920's and early 1930's he wrote some fine lyrics. Unhappily, his loathing of leftist intellectuals and his devotion to an aggressive variant of Roman Catholicism led him to espouse the cause of General Franco and to write *Flowering Rifle* (1939), a long poem whose crude abusiveness and pretentious anthems to the glory of the Roman Catholic Church make distasteful reading.

Having arrived in Nairobi wearing his sergeant's stripes, Campbell looked at the commissioned officers with a somewhat jaundiced eye, as he records in his brief "Snapshot of Nairobi":

> With orange-peel the streets are strewn
> And pips, beyond computing,
> On every shoulder save my own
> That's fractured with saluting.

"Heartbreak Camp," a mordant extravaganza, contains two good stanzas:

> Sir Dysentery Malaria,
> A famous brigadier,
> Commands the whole sub-area,
> And stalking in his rear,
>
> A more ferocious colonel
> Lord Tremens (of the Drunks)
> To whose commands infernal
> We tremble in our bunks.
> (21–28)

Yet the poem is spoiled by feeble inversions, forced rhymes, and a slackness that Campbell would not have tolerated at his best.

The collection in which these poems appear, *Talking Bronco* (1946), is something of a ragbag. One can at least be thankful that it marks a return to sanity and decency (with a few lapses) after *Flowering Rifle.* But among pages of wearisome braggadoccio and dreary attacks on left-wing poets and all who fly to the safe retreat of the BBC, there are too few poems of high quality. Among them are the translation from St. John of the Cross, "En Una Noche Oscura," and the "Imitation (and Endorsement) of the Famous Sonnet of Bocage," that homage of one poet to a greater, Luís Vaz de Camoëns. Campbell's own tribute to the author of *The Lusiads* shows that he can still command a sinewy force and gravity infused with lyrical grace. In his sonnet "Luis de Camões," Campbell recognizes his kinship with the Portuguese poet, like himself a common soldier and a Catholic, who had served the cause of Spain; sailed to Mombasa and watched the gaunt mass of Fort Jesus rising above the harbor; followed where duty beckoned; and, bearing his cross, made poetry from his sufferings:

> Camões, alone, of all the lyric race,
> Born in the black aurora of disaster,
> Can look a common soldier in the face:
> I find a comrade where I sought a master;
> For daily, while the stinking crocodiles
> Glide from the mangoes on the swampy shore,
> He shares my awning on the dhow, he smiles,
> And tells me that he lived it all before.
> Through fire and shipwreck, pestilence and loss,
> Led by the ignis fatuus of duty
> To a dog's death—yet of his sorrows king—
> He shouldered high his voluntary Cross,
> Wrestled his hardship into forms of beauty,
> And taught his gorgon destinies to sing.

Roy Fuller (born 11 February 1912) was, like Manifold, a Marxist, but of a very different stamp. Where Manifold is optimistic, confident of victory, enthusiastic about the individual's sacrifice of himself for the common good, a believer in the virtues of the proletariat, Fuller is gloomy, perplexed, doubtful whether the subordination of the individual will advance the coming of the just society, and not particularly enamored of the working classes in the forces or in civilian life. After training as an ordinary seaman in Britain, Fuller was posted to East Africa in mid-1942 as a radar maintenance engineer; he attained the rank of petty officer and in November 1943 returned to Britain, where he worked in the admiralty after getting a commission.

He wrote about thirty poems in East Africa, a slightly larger output than between the outbreak of war in September 1939 and his sailing from Britain in the summer of 1942. The period November 1943 to the end of the war in May 1945 seems to have been comparatively barren, yielding only a half-dozen poems and a sequence of nine sonnets.

The early war poems reflect the hopes and fears of a humane, intelligent man, recently married and the father of a son, caught in the impersonal war machine and the no less impersonal historical process. Most of the poems are worth reading but few rank among his best. "The Middle of a War" deals with a theme that Fuller was to explore more deeply in his postwar verse: the poet gazing at himself, reflecting on what he sees, and making a wry observation:

> My photograph already looks historic.
> The promising youthful face, the matelot's
> collar. . . .
> (1–2)

One phrase, "The ridiculous empires break like biscuits," reminds us, like so many of Fuller's lines, of W. H. Auden, the Auden who wrote "Desire like a police-dog is unfastened." But Fuller's images have a quality of their own, less devastatingly startling and brilliant than Auden's but more in accord with common sense and common usage.

Another good early poem, "Spring 1942," records an incident when a naval chaplain joins a group of enlisted men and sits down among them:

> And under the tobacco smoke:
> "Freedom," he said, and "Good" and "Duty."
> We stared as though a savage spoke.
> The scene took on a singular beauty.
> (5–8)

Blank and uncomprehending, dumbfounded by this talk of the great abstractions, the enlisted men make no reply

> And thought: O sick, insatiable
> And constant lust, O death, our future;
> O revolution in the whole
> Of human use of man and nature!
> (13–16)

Fuller's posting to East Africa seems to have liberated him from the glum, debilitating atmosphere of wartime Britain. The splendor of the hills and plains, the superb variety of the animals and birds, and the life of the tribesmen seem to have enriched his imagination and bestowed a rhythmical sensuousness on his verse. Not that he succumbed to the picturesque enchantment of the scene: what he found there was a world in which the lions, giraffes, wildebeests, the whole panoply of birds and beasts, live their own lives, unalterably alien to our own and yet symbols of that natural world to which we also belong. The tribesmen are not romantic figures uncorrupted by civilization, but men and women whom the forces of capitalism are wrenching from their homelands, crowding into shantytowns, and offering a pittance to join the armed forces. Even their villages are in pawn to the owner of the *duka* (general store), who is usually descended from one of those Indians shipped over from Bombay forty years earlier to build the railway from Mombasa to Kampala. Fuller can see before his eyes in dramatic form the working out of capitalism and colonialism in their dying phase.

This sense of the historical process, combined with a powerful and discriminating response to the particularities of the scene, enabled Fuller to write one of the finest series of poems to have come out of World War II. Some of the poems spring directly from Fuller's observation of the landscape upcountry. In "The Green Hills of Africa" (how unlike Ernest Hemingway's green hills) the evocation of the village and its inhabitants is exact:

> The girls run up the slope,
> Their oiled and shaven heads like caramels.
> Behind, the village, with its corrugated
> Iron, the wicked habit of the store.
> The villagers cough, the sacking blows from
> the naked
> Skin of a child, a white scum on his lips.
> (11–16)

Having presented the village precisely as it is, Fuller asks us whether we expect to find here gods with healing powers, or subtle ways of life:

> No, there is nothing but the forms and
> colours,
> And the emotion brought from a world
> already
> Dying of what starts to infect the hills.
> (25–27)

It is instructive to compare Fuller's "The Giraffes" with a poem on a similar theme by Campbell, "Dreaming Spires"—his name for giraffes. Campbell's poem is a sequence of witty fancies about the extravagant absurdities of those animals. Sometimes the fancies move with a lyrical grace:

> The City of Giraffes—a People
> Who live between the earth and skies,
> Each in his lone religious steeple
> Keeping a light-house with his eyes.
> (48–51)

Sometimes they are merely ingenious, as though designed to show how clever the poet can be when he sets his mind to it:

> Some animals have all the luck,
> Who hurl their breed in nature s throat—
> Out of a gumtree by a buck,
> Or escalator—by a goat!
> (85–88)

Fuller wants to convey the essence of these strange animals who, as he drew nearer, turned,

> An undulation of dappled grey and brown,
> And stood in profile with those curious
> planes
> Of neck and sloping haunches.
> (19–21)

Although Fuller acknowledges that their height is grotesque he does not see them primarily as ludicrous creatures, but rather as animals with whom no communication is possible. The poem's closing lines evoke with controlled tenderness and reverence the otherness of the giraffes:

> So as they put more ground between us I
> Saw evidence that these were animals
> With no desire for intercourse, or no
> Capacity.
> Above the falling sun,
> Like visible winds the clouds are streaked
> and spun,
> And cold and dark now bring the image of
> Those creatures walking without pain or
> love.
> (24–30)

Another poem, "The Plains," presents in a series of snapshots the array of wildlife before the rains: zebras, gazelles, hyenas, jackals, and, caught in the headlights, a lion:

> Slowly it swung its great
> Maned head, then—loose, suède, yellow—
> loped away.
> (24–25)

As always, contemplation of the natural world leads Fuller to meditate on metaphysical themes. After observing the lion, which is followed by a pair of squint hyenas, Fuller revolves in his mind the course of human history, and archetypal myths; and when four pecking vultures fly away at his approach, he asks himself a fundamental question:

> They left a purple scrap of skin.
> Have I discovered all the plains can show?
> The animals gallop, spring, are beautiful,
> And at the end of every day is night.
> (39–42)

Fuller also wrote a small group of poems that touch on the political life of East Africa in the widest sense of the word—the way in which the coming of a war fought for the benefit of white colonial rulers has finally shattered the tribal life of the Africans. In a four-line poem, "Natives Working on the Aerodrome," Fuller gives imaginative form to some ironies of the process whereby the British impose a punishment for the transgression of their law designed to assist the war effort:

Curls powdered with chalk like a black
Roman bust,
This prisoner, convicted of a lust
For maize, is whipped to building a great
shed
For bombers; and bears the earth upon his
head.

There are a number of poems about the war and the human condition that owe little to the places where they were written. Others derive their imagery from the local scene before moving into the realm of metaphysical speculation. Thus "Autumn 1942" switches from the animals of the plains to

. . . the news at which I hesitate,
That glares authentically between the bars
Of style and lies. . . .
(29–31)

The poem ends with a nightmarish vision of humanity, the kind of vision to which Fuller became increasingly prey as the war dragged on and the news confirmed all his forebodings:

It half convinces me that some great faculty,
Like hands, has been eternally lost and all
Our virtues now are high and horrible
Ones of a streaming wound which heals in
evil.
(37–40)

Fuller wrote a handful of poems about the coastal region, one of which, "The Coast," manages to convey, in thirty-five lines, the ecology, human and natural, of the area. "Crustaceans" might be a commentary on a television nature film, so clearly and specifically does it describe the mass of crabs on the beach. The poem hints at certain affinities between the crabs and human beings; in "The Divided Life Re-Lived," an image from "Crustaceans" reappears as a simile:

While outside the demon scientists and
rulers of the land
Pile the bomb like busy crabs pile balls of
sand.
(23–24)

Perhaps the most poignant of all his wartime poems, "The Petty Officers' Mess," which is also set on the coast, develops Fuller's meditations on history before returning to the opening visit to some captive monkeys:

The monkeys near the mess (where we all
eat
And dream) I saw tonight select with neat
And brittle fingers dirty scraps, and fight,
And then look pensive in the fading light,
And after pick their feet.

They were secured by straps about their
slender
Waists, and the straps to chains. Most sad
and tender,
They clasp each other and look round with
eyes
Like ours at what their strange captivities
Invisibly engender.
(46–55)

The wartime poems written after Fuller's return home do not compare in originality and force with the best of his East African poems; this is true even of "Winter in Camp," an ambitious and accomplished sequence of nine sonnets about the slaughterous immensity of the war, the coarseness of the common man, the political inactivity of artists (including Fuller himself), and the contrast between the crude but authentic emotions stirred by the cinema and the illusory world of art.

During the past forty years Fuller has continued to write a large, varied body of verse, much of it concerned with the nature of human society and with metaphysical problems. His poems have evaded the perils of aridity and emotional anemia because he has never ceased to respond with curiosity and zest to the quirks and richness of things animate and inanimate. If he is a man for whom the visible world exists, he owes this partly to the fortunes of war that sent him to Kenya, where he could observe the crustaceans, the dhows, the animals on the plains, and the life that moves to rhythms so different from our own in the green hills of Africa.

Edward Lowbury (born 6 December 1913), who had won the Newdigate prize for poetry when he was an undergraduate at University College, Oxford, was a qualified doctor when he was called up into the Royal Army Medical Corps. During his period of service in East Africa he became acquainted with certain aspects of life that remained a closed book to most of his compatriots: African medicine, the nature of witchcraft, Swahili tales and legends. One of those tales, which an *askari* (African soldier) told him, grew into the poem "The Huntsman." It preserves the laconic simplicity and force of the original, and the short phrases of which the poem is composed heighten the tension, the dramatic plot, and the anxiety that pervade the story.

One is plunged into the action with no preliminary flourishes:

> Kagwa hunted the lion,
> Through bush and forest went his spear.
> One day he found the skull of a man
> And said to it, "How did you come here?"
> The skull opened its mouth and said
> "Talking brought me here."

Lowbury unfolds the tale, departing just enough from the flow of normal English speech to remind the reader that this is a Swahili tale. Kagwa tells his story of the talking skull to the king, who orders two guards to search for the skull, taking with them Kagwa, who is to die if his tale is proved untrue. Eventually they find the skull; despite Kagwa's pleas it says nothing. The poem comes full circle, and it is Kagwa's turn to die:

> The guards said, "Kneel down."
> They killed him with sword and spear.
> Then the skull opened its mouth;
> "Huntsman, how did you come here?"
> And the dead man answered
> "Talking brought me here."
> (25–30)

Unlike Fuller, who continually reverts to the impact of Europe on the life of East Africa, Lowbury observes that life in all its strangeness, more concerned with what is and has been than with the influence that modern Europe may have on the tribesmen and the coastal inhabitants. If anything, his curiosity is aroused by what Europeans may have to learn from East Africa. Thus, in "Miracle Cure," he restores sight to a twelve-year-old Bantu boy, who cries out:

> I see! I see!"
> And as I touched his brow
> it seemed an unsuspected power
> had passed through my bones
> to him—in a blinding
> but sight-restoring spark, that gave
> new sight also to me.
> (38–44)

Something of the same attitude informs "Total Eclipse," about a total eclipse of the sun that Lowbury witnessed in Mombasa. He asks some Africans what has come over the sun and is told:

> The Sun goes out because some blow must
> fall.
> (25)

He tries again and gets the same answer:

> "Some blow will fall."
> But a hint, this time, of a Dragon which
> devours
> The Sun. . . .
> (28–30)

Their explanations, ridiculous and superstitious though they may be, awaken

> A twilight consciousness of lost powers,
> Forgotten magic, presences
> That gave no peace, haunted our sleep and
> drove us,
> When Europe was a child, to acts of frenzy;
> And still, for all our cool endeavours, haunt.
> (33–37)

When the light returns, the scientific certainty of the astronomers seems irrelevant, because the eclipse has carried a warning of which they are unaware:

It seems we heard pre-echoes, saw
A warning vision of the great Eclipse
In store for the white Sun
In this black continent,
When the Dragon's turn comes, and with a
  shout
He snatches back the light;
His reason—simply that it's time for one,
Who shone so long unchecked, to be put
  out.
  (42–49)

In "Mua Hills," among Lowbury's strongest and most finely wrought poems, one discovers a total contrast to Fuller's "The Green Hills of Africa." Whereas Fuller anatomizes the decay of tribal life beneath the assault of colonialism and capitalism, Lowbury, while acknowledging the decadence of the tribes—

  Black eyes, black heads—Kamba,
 Kikuyu, Nandi
Sprout like grapes, expert at hanging round
And doing nothing; were they warriors once,
  Now gone to seed?
 (8–11)

—lays stress on the unbroken continuity of their traditions symbolized by the dance. In the final stanza he looks back to the middle of the nineteenth century, when explorers from Europe observed the fury of the dance and were mocked when they went home with travelers' tales of great lakes and snowcapped mountains in the heart of Africa:

I catch a glimpse of beaten shield and spear
  Of the ngoma beaten all night long;
Feel something of the astonishment and fear
Of those first hunters from the North who
  hawked
  Spirit and book, and in exchange took
  home
Stories which marked them liar if they
  talked.
  (31–36)

As a tailpiece to this section one should recall the brief campaign that wrested control of Madagascar from the Vichy French. Bernard Gutteridge (born 13 March 1916) composed some poems about the episode, one of which, "Patrol: Buonomary," was written on the spot. Like all his work, it is readable and acutely observed; the tone is detached and slightly amused; the versification is elegant. This, one feels, is exactly how it was, with ten small figures "running stumbling over the hill," pursued by British bullets:

And that was all the enemy's resistance.
The pot-bellied children fondled
Tommy-guns and Brens; brought bananas;
  stared.
The chalk road gashed into the distance,
The sea glared.
  (6–10)

Gutteridge moved on to Burma, where he fought in the ruthless campaign against the Japanese. Although he planned nothing as ambitious or systematic as Henderson's sequence about the war in Cyrenaica, he executes from time to time an incisive vignette, notable for accuracy and restraint, in a style that springs from a resolution not to overdramatize or lay too blatant an emphasis on the hideous nature of the fighting. Even so, Gutteridge does not flinch from recording the kind of physical detail that had shocked many of those who read the poems of Sassoon in World War I. In its offhand way Gutteridge's "The Enemy Dead" reveals a great deal about the stark realities of jungle warfare and the frame of mind it engenders in the combatants:

The dead are always searched.
It's not a man, the blood-soaked
Mess of rice and flesh and bones
Whose pockets you flip open.
  (1–4)

"Sniper" recounts how ten British soldiers trap one Japanese sniper:

He had killed neatly but we had set
Ten men about him to write death in jags
Cutting and spoiling on his face and broken
  body.
  (12–14)

Gutteridge's work is unusual in that it combines the lucidity of a good military dispatch with the emotional resonance of poetry. Perhaps because of its reticence it has failed to win due recognition, but no other English poet has conveyed so truthfully and concisely the nature of the war in Burma against the Japanese.

THE WAR AT SEA

Alan Ross (born 6 May 1922) wrote a sequence of poems between 1942 and 1945 about naval warfare in the Arctic. Having served as an ordinary seaman and as an officer, he knew at first hand the life of the messdeck and of the wardroom as well as the roles played in combat by all ranks. His are the only poems of either world war that portray the realities of life in a warship on patrol, the rescue of men after a shipwreck, the technical and moral implications of radar, the nature of an engagement at sea. Ross emulates the accuracy of a good prose reporter without getting bogged down in the prosaic. Instead, most of his poems employ traditional devices such as rhyme, meter, and stanzaic pattern, although he permits himself the freedom to depart from strict forms when he feels the need to do so.

"Messdeck" conveys with overpowering force the claustrophobia and stench in which sailors live:

> Bare shoulders
> Glisten with oil, tattoo-marks rippling their
> scales on
> Mermaids or girls' thighs as dice are shaken,
> cards played.
> We reach for sleep like a gas, randy for
> oblivion.
> (5–8)

"Destroyers in the Arctic" is a study in grayness, monotony, unreality:

> Landfall. Murmansk; but starboard now a
> lead-coloured
> Island, Jan Mayen. Days identical, hoisted
> like sails, blurred.
> (19–20)

The earlier poems in the sequence are impressionistic, concerned with the outer world and with the trappings of war rather than with the inner reality. "Survivors" depicts the rescue of men from a burning ship and an icy sea. The poem does not merely describe the mechanics of the operation but evokes the exhaustion, the shock to mind and spirit, endured by the victims:

> Taken on board as many as lived, who
> Had a mind left for living and the ocean,
> They open eyes running with surf,
> Heavy with grey ghosts of explosion.
>
> The meaning is not yet clear,
> Where daybreak died in the smile—
> And the mouth remained stiff
> And grinning, stupid for a while.
> (9–16)

It is not only the guns of the enemy ships that send men to flounder in the icy sea: the guns obey equipment of a subtlety and accuracy hitherto unknown in warfare. "Radar" makes the point that remote control divides the responsibility for killing between those who man the guns, release the depth charges, or fire the torpedoes and those who operate the radar, so all can shrug aside their guilt:

> And destroying the enemy by radar
> We never see what we do.
> (11–12)

"J. W. 51B A Convoy," a narrative poem over five hundred lines long, describes how a British force protecting a convoy in the Arctic engaged and drove off a superior German force and brought the convoy safely into port. Ross handles with remarkable skill the various elements of which his poem is made up: the technical details of seamanship and naval warfare that give the poem the authenticity of a documentary film; the life of the lower deck; the horror of a naval battle fought by men trapped within a confined space; the courage and coolness and devotion to duty shown by all ranks during the engagement.

Throughout the poem Ross employs lines of varying length, mainly short, not conforming to any strict metrical pattern; he diversifies the sound of the verse with a scattering of full and half rhyme. This eclectic procedure gives him the flexibility he needs, enabling him to incorporate within the structure of his narrative the stark details of the combat and the familiar trivialities of the daily round.

It is impossible to convey in a brief space the quality of a longish narrative poem whose impact depends in part on the way the story is unfolded while its disparate elements are welded into a unity. Three extracts, however, may indicate Ross's power to handle widely dissimilar aspects of a naval engagement and to find the emotional tone appropriate to the occasion.

There is the dramatic moment when the captain of the *Onslow* signals his destroyers to join him:

> And the destroyers, breaking
> Out of line, heeled over,
> Increasing revolutions, like the spokes
> Of an umbrella being opened,
> Spray icing the look-outs,
> Forming up in line ahead.
> (207–212)

The *Onslow* is hit and obliged to retire. Ross gives us a picture of what this means in human terms:

> "A" and "B" Guns unable to fire,
> Radar destroyed, aerials ripped,
> And, forward, the sea stripping
> The Mess decks, spilling over tables,
> Fire and water clinching like boxers
> As the ship listed, sprawling them.
> Tamblin, his earphones awry, like a laurel
> wreath
> Slipped on a drunken god, gargled to death
> In water with a noise of snoring.
> (307–315)

Finally, we turn to the burial at sea, in which Ross employs rhyme and meter with more formal regularity than at any other juncture in the poem:

> Beneath the ice-floes sleeping,
> Embalmed in salt
> The sewn-up bodies slipping
> Into silent vaults.
> The sea of Barents received them,
> Men with no faults
> Of courage, for the weeping
> Would be elsewhere,
> Far from its keeping.
> (418–426)

Ross's poems about the war at sea are an impressive achievement. He has gone on to write verse about people, places, and erotic love that is more subtle and sensuous then the poems of his early youth, but he has never surpassed in force and immediacy the poetic testament that he has left of life and death in the waste of Arctic waters.

We move worlds away when we turn from Ross to Charles Causley (born 24 August 1917), who served on the lower deck from 1939 to 1946. Instead of the terse, restrained emotion of Ross's poems we have a warmer, less muted lyricism, a canvas on which brighter colors are more thickly spread. "Chief Petty Officer" shows that Causley can portray things and people as realistically as Ross:

> He is older than the naval side of British
> history,
> And sits
> More permanent than the spider in the
> enormous wall.
> . . .
> He has the face of the dinosaur
> That sometimes stares from old Victorian
> naval photographs:
> That of some elderly lieutenant
> With boots and a celluloid Crippen collar,
> Brass buttons and cruel ambitious eyes of
> almond.
> (1–3; 12–16)

Yet it becomes clear as one reads on that Causley's main concern is not to present a realistic or even satirical portrait of the old monster: what comes over is the warm affection that Causley feels for a dinosaur that has survived.

Causley, though not an overtly learned poet, likes to lace his verse with literary and cultural allusions. The first two lines of "Chief Petty Officer" derive part of their effect from the incongruous comparison between the gross and sinister vulgarian as he squats in the Royal Naval Barracks at Devonport and Leonardo da Vinci's Mona Lisa, who, in Walter Pater's exquisite imagination, is "older than the rocks among which she sits"; while the joke about the CPO's remote origins is sharpened by the sidelong glance at Sir Geoffrey Callender's *The Naval Side of British History* (1924). The phrase in line 15, "a celluloid Crippen collar," with its reference to the famous Edwardian murderer, gives the portrait the kind of period touch so often found in the verse of John Betjeman, a poet whom Causley much admires.

It may be thought regrettable that Causley did not draw a whole gallery of such portraits and that he failed to present a realistic picture of war. His only description of death at sea is coached in highly romantic imagery. "Song of the Dying Gunner A.A.1" begins:

> Oh mother my mouth is full of stars
> As cartridges in the tray
> My blood is a twin-branched scarlet tree
> And it runs all runs away.

It is true that by the end of the poem the dying man has lapsed into the vernacular, but the shift from one poetic convention to another does not come off and the poem is flawed:

> Farewell, Aggie Weston, the Barracks at
>   Guz,
> Hang my tiddley suit on the door
> I'm sewn up neat in a canvas sheet
> And I shan't be home no more.
>   (13–16)

A note addressed to landlubbers explains that "Guz" naval slang for Devonport and "Aggie Weston's" is "the familiar term used by sailors to describe the hostels founded in many seaports by Dame Agnes Weston."

One of Causley's favorite modes is the ballad filled with glittering images, owing more to Auden, Betjeman, and A. E. Housman than to the traditional border ballads, and sparkling with gaiety even though the subject is war. It may be objected that his presentation of war does not convince, because it is overstylized and totally disinfected of horror, pain, filth, boredom, and discomfort. Even so, his best poems have such fizz and fire that they stay in the memory much longer than the verse of drabber poets who point out what a wretched business war is. And Causley, though he never sermonizes, reminds us constantly that war is a tragic waste of human life. In "A Ballad for Katharine of Aragon" the death of Causley's childhood friend Jumper Cross, who perished in the Italian snow, has the lyrical force of an aria of Verdi's:

> The olive tree in winter
> Casts her banner down
> And the priest in white and scarlet
> Comes up from the muddy town.
> O never more will Jumper
> Watch the Flying Scot go by
> His funeral knell was a six-inch shell
> Singing across the sky.
>   (17–24)

"Recruiting Drive" rehearses the story of a young soldier (a cousin of Housman's doomed lads) lured by the butcher-bird's song into joining up and finding death down in the enemy country. The imagery is almost surrealistic, and even at its most restrained it arouses an authentic shiver of terror:

> You must take off your clothes for the
>   doctor
>   And stand as straight as a pin,
> His hand of stone on your white breast-bone
>   Where the bullets all go in.
>   (17–20)

Causley wrote a number of poems about his wartime recollections of Freetown, Gibraltar,

Sydney, Trincomalee, Kandy, and Colombo. They are skillful evocations, shining with local color, soaked in nostalgic memories, at times degenerating into ecstatic, naive catalogs of remembered places and people. But Causley is not a naive poet, and it is by the poems glanced at above that he claims the admiration of those whose concern is with the truthfully observed and keenly felt poetry of war.

SIDNEY KEYES

Sidney Keyes was born on 27 May 1922; six weeks after his birth his mother died of peritonitis. His father, Captain Reginald Keyes, went to live with his own father, another Sidney Keyes, and the child grew up in his paternal grandfather's house. He was educated at Tonbridge, a well-known public school, where the form master of the History Sixth, Tom Staveley, was a poet who recognized Keyes's poetic gifts and encouraged him to develop them.

An example of his precocious talent is the elegy that Keyes composed for his grandfather in July 1938, the middle stanza of which runs:

> It is a year again since they poured
> The dumb ground into your mouth
> And yet we know, by some recurring word
> Or look caught unawares, that you still
> drive
> Our thoughts like the smart cobs of your
> youth—
> When you and the world were alive.

This is not so much the work of a promising poet as of one who, at sixteen, is already a poet, able to handle with easy mastery the elements of his craft and to deploy in the service of his imagination a command of rhyme, meter, imagery, and rhythm that never failed him.

Keyes was an unusually learned and literary poet. In his introductory memoir to *The Collected Poems of Sidney Keyes* (1945), one of his closest friends at Oxford, Michael Meyer, gives a list of those who most influenced Keyes:

> For direction and inspiration, he turned to such visionaries as El Greco, Blake, Holderlin, Schiller, Rilke, Yeats and Sibelius. At the same time, he found his emotional problems most completely resolved in the writings of the nineteenth-century school of haunted countrymen: Wordsworth, Clare, Van Gogh, Hardy and, later, Housman and Edward Thomas. (p. xiii)

Meyer goes on to note Keyes's love of the macabre: "Donne, Webster, Goya, Beddoes, Dickens, Picasso, Klee, Rouault, Graham Greene; and such as came his way of the early German and Russian films."

Much has been made of Keyes's admiration for Rainer Maria Rilke, whom indeed he praises unreservedly. Writing in January 1943 to Richard Church, he declares his belief that the greatest and most influential poets in the last hundred years are Rilke and William Butler Yeats. In a diary entry of March 1943, after tracing the burgeoning of the death wish implicit in romanticism, he continues: "That's why there had to be a 'Poet of Death' in C.20 [the twentieth century]; and why Rilke is the most important European poet since Goethe and Wordsworth." He was undoubtedly influenced by Rilke, especially by that poet's conception of death as something that we bear within us like a child awaiting birth. In the summer of 1942 he worked on a translation of passages of Rilke's prose and in the autumn of that year he translated an eight-line poem entitled "The Poet."

Yet it is important not to exaggerate the part played by Rilke in the life and the poetry of Sidney Keyes. The overwhelming influence on his early poems is not Rilke but Yeats, and it is likely that Rilke's metaphysical speculations about death merely intensified and deepened the intuitions and discoveries of which Keyes was himself aware. Moreover, Keyes knew that charnel romanticism and the German obsession with the death wish were dangerous models. He referred to "a vaguely bogus atmosphere" in his poems; and in a letter written nine weeks before he was killed he regretted that he had not been born in nineteenth-century Oxfordshire or Wiltshire, "because then I might have been a good pastoral poet, instead of an uncomfortable metaphysical without roots" (Meyer, p. xiii).

It is probable that the decisive influence on his poetry was not Yeats or Rilke" or any visionary artist" but his love for a girl whom he met at Oxford in May 1941. It is also arguable that his finest achievements are not his symbolist poems, of which the two most ambitious are "The Foreign Gate" and "The Wilderness," but the short lyrics on a wide variety of themes, particularly those written from March 1942 onward.

As we have seen, he was already a poet at the age of sixteen, and the first nine poems in his *Collected Poems* were written before he went up to Queen's College, Oxford, in October 1940. He composed the first of his Oxford poems in an examination room, having finished the paper early. "Remember Your Lovers," on the theme of women bereaved in wartime, was a poem that Keyes came to dislike for its "lush sensuality." Even so, it is an effective piece of plangent rhetoric that rises to a resounding climax:

> Young men drunk with death's unquenchable wisdom,
> Remember your lovers who gave you more than love.
> (29–30)

Between November 1940 and the end of April 1941 Keyes wrote only seven poems, the most accomplished being a skillful pastiche of Yeats, "William Yeats in Limbo," and "Advice for a Journey," which begins "The drums mutter for war." This was a barren period for a poet as prolific as Keyes.

During the following six months he wrote over twenty poems, including two that bring out very clearly his preoccupation with pain, "Gilles de Retz" and "Europe's Prisoners," written on 16 and 21 May, respectively. The latter is of interest mainly because it employs Dachau as a symbol of human suffering at a time when even the name was unknown in Britain to all but a handful of people. In "Gilles de Retz," which one may call variations on a theme of pain, there occurs the half-line "Pain is never personal." Events were soon to disprove that philosophical reflection.

Early in May 1941 Keyes met a girl called Milein Cosmann, who had come over to England as a refugee from Nazi Germany. Both she and Renée-Jane Scott, with whom she shared a studio in Oxford, were art students who had been evacuated from London. This is not the place to analyze the tortuous and tortured relationship between Keyes and Milein. It is enough to note that, at first sight, he fell passionately in love with her, and that although she told him she did not reciprocate his feelings he persisted in trying to keep alive a relationship with her until July 1942. He then found some kind of consolation with Renée, while acknowledging that Milein remained the most attractive person he had ever known. He wrote in his diary on 28 July: "I am a damnably self-centered, irresponsible, and often cruel man. But Renée can cure me, if she will."

Within a few days of their first meeting Keyes began to write poems to and about Milein. He continued to find themes and inspiration in literature, notably in Yeats and Rilke, but his own experience of grief now became an element in his poetry. The epitaph on the whole unhappy story is to be found in "North Sea," written in October 1942, one of his most poignant compositions:

> And eastward looking, eastward wondering
> I meet the eyes of Heine's ghost, who saw
> His failure in the grey forsaken waves
> At Rulenstein one autumn. And between
> Rises the shape in more than memory
> Of Düsseldorf, the ringing, river-enfolding
> City that brought such sorrow on us both.
> (5–11)

Düsseldorf brought Milein sorrow in that it was the place from which she was exiled; it brought sorrow to Keyes by sending her to England, where he fell in love with her.

During the long vacation of 1941 Keyes wrote a foreword to the anthology *Eight Oxford Poets,* which included poems by himself and by two other poets who were killed in the war, Drummond Allison and Keith Douglas; among the other contributors were Michael Meyer, who later became well known as a translator of Ibsen, and John Heath-Stubbs, one of the best English poets in the twentieth century. In his foreword Keyes announced on behalf of the contributors that "we have little sympathy with the Audenian school of poetry," which was, in his view, too closely concerned with political comment, social observation, modern intellectual concepts, and the employment of colloquial language.

Between September 1941 and the end of the year Keyes wrote over twenty poems, beginning with the much-anthologized "William Wordsworth," partly inspired by Herbert Read's study of the poet. It contains a tribute to Wordsworth's elemental power:

> He was a stormy day, a granite peak
> Spearing the sky; and look, about its base
> Words flower like crocuses in the hanging
> woods,
> Blank though the dalehead and the bony
> face.
> (11–14)

Of the remainder, the most accomplished are a sonnet, "Pheasant"; a lament and celebration for Glaucus, who was both drowned and glorified: "And cold Aegean voices speak his fame"; and "The Cruel Solstice," the title poem of his posthumous volume, published in 1943. In it he foresees

> A cruel solstice, coming ice and cold
> Thoughts and the darkening of the heart's
> flame.
> (3–4)

In February and March 1942 he worked on an ambitious poem of almost four hundred lines, entitled "The Foreign Gate." Its epigraph comes from Rilke's Sixth Duino Elegy and the whole poem owes much to Rilke, "a pale unlearned poet," while two lines are a direct translation of the first line and a half of the *Duino Elegies:*

> Were I to cry, who in that proud hierarchy
> Of the illustrious would pity me?
> (5.12–13)

Although the final section of the poem contains echoes of T. S. Eliot, the predominant influence, according to Meyer, is a poem by Heath-Stubbs, an Oxford contemporary and a great friend whose poetry Keyes passionately admired. Meyer admits that "few of the many literary references have been traced to their ultimate source."

The poem celebrates warrior heroes who have conquered death by sacrificing their lives and thus passing through the foreign gate of death to eternity. Keyes ransacks many lands and epochs for examples of heroes who thus attained peace. Men who died at Dunkirk and Tannenberg blend their voices with those of soldiers who perished at Naseby or in the wars of Rome against Carthage. "Gored Adonis in the myrtle thicket" and Danae make fleeting appearances in section III, which is devoted to the theme of sexual love. Despite some fine resonant passages the poem must be accounted a failure, its diffuse, cloudy symbolism failing to give the reader any sense of poetic coherence. Keyes, however, valued it highly, getting his publisher to delay sending his first volume, *The Iron Laurel,* to the printer until "The Foreign Gate" was completed.

Even as an adolescent Keyes had been aware of the conflict between the forces of death and negation and the power of love. This awareness was proved upon his pulse ever more strongly as the war increased in scale and ferocity, his call-up came ever nearer, and the painful complexity of his feelings for Milein grew more intense. In March 1942 he wrote "War Poet," the theme of which is poets trapped by war:

> I am the man who looked for peace and
> found
> My own eyes barbed.

I am the man who groped for words and
   found
An arrow in my hand.
   (1–4)

More than one commentator has found fault with Keyes for employing the image of an arrow rather than a Bren gun. One might as well censure William Blake for summoning a bow of burning gold, arrows of desire, a spear, chariots of fire, and a sword, on the grounds that, in Blake's day, those weapons of war were obsolete. A poet works through images that kindle his imagination, whether they are contemporary or archaic.

Keyes left Oxford on 8 April, in the middle of term, for Omagh in Northern Ireland, where he reported to the Infantry Training Centre. While stationed there he wrote two fine poems, "Ulster Soldier," in which he expresses his apprehension of "perplexities and terrors," and "The True Heart," a lyrical meditation on sorrow and the end of sorrow:

Guarded from love and wreck and
   turbulence
The sad explorer finds security
From all distraction but the thin lament
Of broken shells remembering the sea.
   (9–12)

On 8 May he joined the Officer Cadet Training Unit at Dunbar, Scotland. The poet Edmund Blunden, who met him at that period, remarked on his alertness and vigor; and his imaginative energy matched the force with which he mastered his military training. His first poem from Dunbar, called "Dunbar, 1650," unlike most of his work, evokes a particular historical moment in a particular place, and displays some of the characteristics of the Auden school, held in such disfavor by Keyes and his fellow poets at Oxford. Other good poems followed rapidly, displaying an assurance and a disciplined passion that he had hitherto seldom commanded. Two linked poems belong to August, "Dido's Lament for Aeneas" and "Rome Remember." Keyes wrote a number of dramatic monologues, none more rhythmically delicate and emotionally convincing than Dido's speech before her death:

The smoke blows over the breakers, the
   high pyre waits.
His mind was a blank wall throwing echoes,
Not half so subtle as the coiling flames.
   (7–9)

"Rome Remember," whose title comes from the burden of a poem by John Lydgate, is even more impressive, a lament for Carthage and for the city that destroyed her and will in its turn be destroyed by the barbarians from the north:

O Rome, you city of soldiers, remember the
   singers
That cry with dead voices along the African
   shore.
   (8–9)

The blank verse is both firm and flexible, an instrument designed to encompass the entire range of emotions awakened by the theme of imperial triumph and decay.

In late July Keyes had sent a copy of *The Iron Laurel* to Drummond Allison, inscribing on the flyleaf a couplet from George Crabbe:

Love is like gout; for both diseases spread
A kind of gloomy pomp about the bed.

He was still enthralled by his infatuation for Milein, and although his growing affection for Renée assuaged the old torment, the few poems he wrote on the theme of love are either nostalgic or uneasy. He contemplated resignation and death more steadily than love.

The finest poems that he wrote between October 1942 and the end of the year explicitly or implicitly weave variations on those twin themes. "Four Postures of Death" confronts them directly; "Moonlight Night on the Port" both mourns those drowned at sea and accepts the likelihood that the poet and his comrades will also drown. "Actaeon's Lament" meditates on a death enshrined in classical legend, while "An Early Death" contemplates the grief of a mother for a son who has died (presumably in war) and the grief of Mary over the crucified Christ. "Poem from the North" opens with three lines that are, for Keyes, unusually firmly rooted in prosaic reality:

> As I passed under the statue of Mr.
> Gladstone
> The snow came back, dancing down
> slantwise, whipping
> That righteous face with all the old sky's
> scorn.

It ends with a menacing vision of a world at war, of a city whose inhabitants are doomed:

> Winter, the hunter's season, will not pity
> The people afraid to be born who crowd the
> streets
> Or those afraid of death who crouch in bed
> Behind the darkened windows of this city.
> I hear the hunter's horn, the long halloo,
> The cold wind beating at a stone-dead
> statue.
> (17–22)

"William Byrd" is a poem of serenity and hope, qualities not often found in the body of Keyes's work. Byrd was an Elizabethan composer who refused to renounce Roman Catholicism and whose music could not be sung in Anglican cathedrals. It is one of Keyes's most assured dramatic monologues, with a rhythmical delicacy and a verbal poise that lend the poem a rare distinction.

"The Wilderness," Keyes's latest surviving poem except "The Grail," was written between December 1942 and January 1943. He regarded it as one of his "nearest misses." An ambitious poem of 150 lines, it reverts to a theme that had preoccupied him throughout his career as a poet: the journey to the desolate place. He had originally dedicated the poem to "Geoffrey Chaucer, George Darley, T. S. Eliot, the other explorers." Keyes himself believed that he had approached the style of Eliot's *Little Gidding*; and it may well be that this is precisely what is wrong with the poem. It lacks the strong individuality, the lyrical intensity, the poetic coherence that characterize the strongest and most original of his shorter poems.

Keyes embarked for Algiers with his battalion on 13 March 1943. In a letter to Heath-Stubbs dated 6 March he had reviewed his past life and found that "it was all quite worthwhile except for the sex part." But it is reassuring to know that on the voyage out he kept photographs of Milein and of Renée above his bed, "because they are both so beautiful." Although he added in his diary that he never dreamed of them, he wrote to Renée on 27 March describing what he called "a most strange and unlikely dream. I dreamt that *we* were being married and saw the actual ceremony."

Keyes enjoyed his brief stay in Algiers enormously; but all too soon his battalion moved into battle positions in Tunisia, going into action in mid-April. On 29 April Keyes led a patrol into the hills near Sidi Abdallah and, together with his orderly, Harold Smith, lost contact with the rest of the patrol. It was thought that they had been taken prisoner, but on 21 June a unit of the Army Graves Service came upon four graves, two of which bore crosses marked with the names of Sidney Keyes and Harold Smith. The bodies could not be identified, nor has the mystery of Keyes's death ever been solved. Even his personal possessions, which he had left in his billet, disappeared completely in the confusion of the war. It is highly probable that they included the manuscripts of poems.

Keyes saluted Rilke as a "Poet of Death," but he was not a decadent romantic dominated by the death wish. In a letter to Church in January 1943 he remarked that he didn't "even (consciously) follow the present trend towards a new and over-wrought Romanticism" (Meyer, p. xvii). Deeply aware as he was of the significance of death in romantic and postromantic poetry, he viewed with some disdain the persistent presence of the death wish in German poetry, and the predisposition of Germans to make an art of death: "It remains for someone to make an art of love, a much harder task . . ." (Meyer, p. xx). He passionately wanted to live, even into old age, and in a letter to Renée written just before he was killed he announced his determination to "get back *sometime* if it's humanly possible" (Meyer, p. xx).

Very few of Keyes's poems touch directly on the war. Even "Timoshenko," written in September 1942, is a portrait of a remote, historical, almost mythological, figure, only slightly more contemporary than Dido and barely more human than Adonis. Blunden put his finger on an important truth when he wrote of Keyes that "the cruel solstice was to him not war, so much as the larger commotion and dissonance of which war is a partial embodiment." Bearing in mind that qualification, we may recognize in Keyes a war poet of prodigious gifts and lasting achievement, who died in battle a month before his twenty-first birthday.

KEITH DOUGLAS

Keith Douglas was born on 24 January 1920; when he was eight years old his parents were separated. He remained with his mother, who secured a place for him when he was eleven at Christ's Hospital, a school reserved for poor boys of high academic intelligence. In October 1938 he went up to Merton College, Oxford, where his tutor was Blunden, himself a former pupil at Christ's Hospital.

Douglas had always been a difficult character, and even the kindly Blunden spoke of "an impulsive and obstinate streak which was sometimes the despair of his friends." Less charitable acquaintances found him aggressive and ruthless, unimpeded by conventional good manners or consideration for the susceptibilities of others. His biographer recounts an anecdote of April 1944, when Douglas informed

> a "truculent civilian" that if his four-year-old daughter's drawings really were as good as Graham Sutherland's, he should try and retard the child's growth, "she was obviously at her best age and might grow like Daddy." (D. Graham, *Keith Douglas,* p. 248)

Those unlikeable qualities were the obverse of his characteristic virtues: a directness of approach, a dislike of humbug, a determination to perform the task in hand, and a zest for every kind of adventure. Allied with a determined courage, they fitted him to be a good, pugnacious soldier.

Douglas was fond of women, and his tastes both in Oxford and later in Egypt were catholic and cosmopolitan. Yet although he was neither fickle nor shallow he found it hard to maintain a stable or lasting relationship with women, mainly because they could not meet the exacting emotional demands that he made upon them. He was continually shipwrecked on the wilder shores of love.

The earliest of his poems printed in *Complete Poems,* and entitled "Mummers," bears the date 1934. Like Keyes, Douglas was a precocious poet, writing verse of remarkable maturity even as a schoolboy. His style is more curt than that of Keyes, harder and more aggressive. Perhaps the finest of his early poems is "The Deceased," printed in the Oxford undergraduate periodical *Cherwell* on 15 June 1940:

> He was a reprobate I grant
> and always liquored till his money went.
>
> His hair depended in a noose from
> his pale brow. His eyes were dumb
>
> . . .
>
> You who God bless you never sunk so low
> censure and pray for him that he was so.
> (1–4; 7–8)

This slightly mannered, ironical tone recurs throughout Douglas' later poems, although it became less playful and considerably harsher.

Between July 1940 and June 1941, when he was serving in the army in England, Douglas wrote ten poems, most of which confirm his growing maturity. One in particular, "Simplify me when I'm dead," marks his farewell to England. It is an astonishing poem, especially for a man of twenty-one, a poem that contemplates with ironical detachment the poet's imminent mortality. The language is bare and intense, infusing the poem with an energy that is all the more terrifying for being so completely under control:

> Remember me when I am dead
> and simplify me when I'm dead.
>
> As the processes of earth
> strip off the colour and the skin
> take the brown hair and blue eye
>
> and leave me simpler than at birth,
> when hairless I came howling in
> as the moon entered the cold sky.
> (1–8)

The technical brilliance of the versification and the unobtrusive cunning that links the stanzas with rhymes serve to reinforce the poem's emotional balance and power.

By 25 June 1941 Douglas was on board the ship that was to land him at Suez two months later. After a few weeks in Cairo and a spell in the hospital in Palestine, he joined his regiment, the Rangers. This former cavalry regiment was not likely to be congenial to a young man of Douglas' temperament. Their senior officers were mostly rich members of the landed gentry who tended to look down on cocksure young officers like Douglas who had not hunted in prewar England. Indeed, his relations with the commanding officer and other superiors remained at best uneasy and at worst mutually hostile.

This is not the place to describe Douglas' visits to Palestine, Syria, Alexandria, and Cairo, or to follow the intricacies of his relationships with Olga, Renée, Milena, Fortunée, Reman, Marcelle, Pilar, and the girl whom he called the Turkish Delight. It is enough to observe that although some of these were passing fancies, Douglas felt genuine affection for Olga and Milena. His dealings with women, like his widening acquaintance with the life of the Middle East, gave him a greater understanding of the world and of human nature.

Like every British soldier, Douglas observed the contrast between the wretchedness of the poor and the ostentatious wealth of the great landowners. "Egypt," probably written in September 1942, describes a girl "diseased and blind of an eye":

> her beauty, succumbing in a cloud
> of disease, disease, apathy. My God,
> the king of this country must be proud.
> (18–20)

Douglas loathed King Farouk, about whom British troops sang ribald songs, and a year later, in a letter to his mother, referred to him in scatological terms, accusing him of exploiting more *fellahin* (peasants or agricultural laborers) than any of his "great fat oily subjects."

There was, however, an even more dramatic contrast that fascinated Keith Douglas: the one between the glittering, tawdry, pleasure-seeking world of Cairo and the austerity of the desert, where men were locked in mortal combat. Until October 1942 he know the desert only by repute. When his regiment moved forward in preparation for what was rumored to be a major battle, Douglas was left behind at divisional headquarters in charge of a two-ton Ford truck.

Greedily as he had enjoyed the sensual pleasures of Cairo, Douglas was not the man to skulk in safety while his regiment went into battle. On 23 October he heard the artillery barrage that preceded the El Alamein offensive; four days later he committed a serious breach of military discipline by driving his truck into the battle zone, discovering the whereabouts of the Sherwood Rangers, and presenting himself to Colonel Kellett. The officer greeted his unexpected arrival with admirable suavity: "We're *most* glad to see you—er—as always." Kellett had lost so many officers that his words of welcome were not wholly ironical.

In the days ahead Douglas proved his bravery. Kellett may have disliked him, but he admired Douglas' toughness and courage; he arranged for his unauthorized departure from headquarters to be overlooked and for him to stay with the regiment as it advanced toward North Africa. Douglas fought with such gallantry that he was recommended for a Military Cross, though he did not get one; and on 15 January 1943 he was wounded in action at Zem Zem.

On 25 January he reached No. 1 General Hospital, El Ballah, Palestine, where he spent six fruitful weeks. It was probably there that he began his narrative of the desert fighting published in 1946 under the title *Alamein to Zem Zem,* a vigorous and at times extremely vivid account of the campaign, which contains the germ of some of his war poems. He also wrote a few of his most powerful and accomplished poems at El Ballah.

In February 1943 *Selected Poems of Keith Douglas, J. C. Hall and Norman Nicholson* appeared. Douglas and Hall, who was in England, corresponded between June and August, mainly about Douglas' recent poems, which Hall found unsatisfying compared with his earlier work. Douglas replied in a letter of 10 August, which serves as the best introduction to his war poems that we can hope to have:

> . . . my object (and I don't give a damn about my duty as a poet) is to write true things, significant things in words each of which works for its place in a line. My rhythms, which you find enervated, are carefully chosen to enable the poems to be *read* as significant speech: I see no reason to be either musical or sonorous about things at present. . . . To trust anyone or to admit any hope of a better world is criminally foolish, as foolish as it is to stop working for it. It sounds silly to say work without hope, but it can be done; it's only a form of insurance; it doesn't mean work hopelessly. (Complete Poems, p. 124)

The first-fruit of Douglas' experience of battle was "Dead Men," which appeared in the March 1943 issue of *Citadel,* a periodical printed in Cairo:

> Tonight the moon inveigles them
> to love: they infer from her gaze
> her tacit encouragement.
> Tonight the white dresses and the jasmine scent
> in the streets. I in another place
> see the white dresses glimmer like moths. Come
>
> to the west, out of that trance, my heart—
> (1–7)

It is just possible to read those lines as a romantic invocation of women known and loved in Cairo or in Alexandria, inhabiting the world of Durrell's *Alexandria Quartet;* but the dry vocabulary—"inveigles," "infer," "tacit encouragement"—and the curt rhythm suggest that Douglas is deliberately eschewing romantic lyricism because, as he put it in his letter to Hall, "to write on the themes which have been concerning me lately in lyrical and abstract forms, would be immense bullshitting." And it is difficult to take the operatic invocation, "Come/to the west," as anything but a sardonic gesture, an invitation to a hideous rendezvous, where we shall find

> the dead men, whom the wind
> powders till they are like dolls.
> (11–12)

Their bodies may rest undiscovered or a wild dog may have eaten them:

> Then leave the dead in the earth, an organism
> not capable of resurrection, like mines,
> less durable than the metal of a gun,
> a casual meal for a dog, nothing but the bone
> so soon, But tonight no lovers see the lines
> of the moon's face as the lines of cynicism.
> (25–30)

"Cairo Jag," like "Dead Men" probably written at El Ballah in February 1943, resumes the themes of that poem more savagely. It opens with a satirical glance at some of the women in Cairo who were the companions of

British officers. Douglas appears to despise himself as well as the women in question:

> Shall I get drunk or cut myself a piece of
> cake,
> a pasty Syrian with a few words of English
> or the Turk who says she is a princess—she
> dances
> apparently by levitation?

The second stanza modulates from that garish world into the wretched quarters of the Egyptian poor, with the "stenches and the sour smells," which may well be the true habitat of the women of the first stanza, beneath their stink of jasmine. The poem ends with a grim description of the battlefield:

> But by a day's travelling you reach a new
> world
> the vegetation is of iron
> dead tanks, gun barrels split like celery
> the metal brambles have no flowers or
> berries
> and there are all sorts of manure, you can
> imagine
> the dead themselves, their boots, and
> possessions
> clinging to the ground, a man with no head
> has a packet of chocolate and a souvenir of
> Tripoli.
> (23–30)

Although Douglas wrote other poems at El Ballah in February and March, none has the weight of "Dead Men" and "Cairo Jag"; and the same is true of poems on which he worked during his leave in Tel Aviv after his discharge from the hospital at the end of March. In May and June, after he had rejoined his regiment in Tunisia, he completed two poems, "Aristocrats"[2] and "Vergissmeinnicht" and began work on "How to Kill," which he completed two or three months later.

"Aristocrats" bears as an epigraph the saying attributed by Suetonius to the emperor Vespasian on his deathbed: "I think I am becoming a God." The epigraph sets the tone of the whole poem, helping us to fathom the complex, even contradictory, emotions that were fluctuating in Douglas' imagination as he worked on the poem. During his absence from the regiment, three of its senior officers had fallen in action. Although Douglas had felt no liking for the men and had despised their limitations, their deaths moved him more deeply than he would have thought possible. Mingled with irritation at their stupidity, other emotions contended for mastery: a sense of comradeship in battle, admiration for their courage and unconcern, amusement at their foibles, compassion at their deaths. "Aristocrats," like all good poems, is more than an expression of emotions, and it has a wider application than any lament for fellow officers. It contains an impersonal recognition that a social order is passing away, the death of three officers of the Sherwood Rangers being a symbol that the old regime was vanishing. Out of these disparate elements Douglas made a poem:

> Peter was unfortunately killed by an 88:
> it took his leg away, he died in the
> ambulance.
> I saw him crawling on the sand; he said
> It's most unfair, they've shot my foot off.
>
> How can I live among this gentle
> obsolescent breed of heroes, and not weep?
> (1–6)

The Sherwood Rangers employed in their radio code a set of sporting terms; the practice exasperated Douglas so much that on one occasion, in the middle of a battle, he communicated a message in a parody of the code and consequently incurred a reprimand for his mild insolence. Now, in the poem's last stanza, Douglas incorporates even this private terminology into the structure of myth and enlists the dead officers of his regiment, with their anachronistic gallantry, into the company of those who fell at Roncesvalles:

2. Complete Poems (London, 1978) prints what seems to be a later version of this poem entitled sportsmen. The text of "Aristocrats" quoted here is from D. Graham, Keith Douglas 1920–1944: A Biography (London, 1974).

The plains were their cricket pitch
and in the mountains the tremendous drop
fences
brought down some of the runners. Here
then
under the stones and earth they dispose
themselves,
I think with their famous unconcern.
It is not gunfire I hear but a hunting horn.
(15–20)

"Vergissmeinnicht," perhaps the most famous of his poems, demonstrates Douglas' mastery of his art: the hard, clear narrative line of the poem, the accuracy of the epithets he uses to describe the German soldier's corpse, the skill of the versification, shifts in the rhyme scheme, and his control of what might have been a welter of disruptive emotions are factors that ensure the poem's success. Douglas comes upon the body of a German in a gunpit; among the dead man's rubbish lies a photograph of his girl on which she has written "*Vergissmeinnicht*"—forget me not. Douglas and his companions "see him almost with content," but without denying his satisfaction at the destruction of an enemy, the poet imagines how the girl will weep at the sight of her lover and observes with a measure of compassion how love and death are commingled:

For here the lover and killer are mingled
who had one body and one heart.
And death who had the soldier singled
has done the lover mortal hurt.

"How to Kill" may owe something to an early poem, "·303," probably written when he was fifteen. He looks through a machine gun's sights and sees men "weep, cough, sprawl in their entrails." Eight years later, in the most subtle and introspective of his poems, Douglas imagines the appearance of a soldier in the crosswires of his dial of glass:

I cry
NOW. Death, like a familiar, hears

and look, has made a man of dust
of a man of flesh. This sorcery
I do. Being damned, I am amused
to see the centre of love diffused
and the waves of love travel into vacancy.
How easy it is to make a ghost.

The weightless mosquito touches
her tiny shadow on the stone,
and with how like, how infinite
a lightness, man and shadow meet.
They fuse. A shadow is a man
when the mosquito death approaches.
(12–25)

No poem of Douglas' is more disquieting and chill in its apprehension of death and in its metaphysical awareness of damnation.

In September 1943 Douglas was back in Cairo, where he was overcome by various kinds of frustration. In one incident his frustration may have been partially relieved by an altercation with a taxi driver who demanded an exorbitant fare, Douglas broke the taxi's distributor. He enjoyed meeting some of the leading contributors to *Personal Landscape,* Bernard Spencer, Terence Tiller, Lawrence Durrell, and G. S. Fraser, regaling them with tales of burning tanks and roasting bodies. But Douglas was soon to bid farewell to Egypt and to his friends: his regiment embarked for Britain on 17 November. He left copies of most of his war poems with the editors of *Personal Landscape,* among them his last poem on Cairo life, "Behaviour of Fish in an Egyptian Tea Garden." The fish are men with predatory intent toward the white stone who, with red lips and carmine fingernails, sits in the sea floor of the afternoon, slyly eating ice cream. Douglas sustains the underwater image and its attendant metaphors throughout all seven stanzas of his gently satirical and relaxed poem.

The Sherwood Rangers discovered on their return home that they were to train for the invasion of Europe. During his six months in England Douglas met his last love, Betty Jesse, an intelligent, attractive young woman who worked for Nicholson and Watson, the firm that had agreed to publish a collection of Douglas' poems. Piqued by his arrogance and cynicism, she told him, half-seriously, that he was her "bête noire." This prompted him to begin a poem entitled "Bête Noire," of which we have fragments; and to write a note on a drawing for the jacket of "Bête Noire," the title for his projected volume of poems. The "Bête Noire" fragments resume the themes of certain earlier poems and, had Douglas been able to complete it, he might have achieved a masterly summing up of his life and art. But he knew it was a poem he couldn't realize.

What he could write was "To Kristin Yingcheng Olga Milena," a masterly valediction to those "Women of four countries" whom he had loved, even though he labels them "four poisons for the subtle senses." His last poem, "On a Return from Egypt," regrets that he has had to leave unpicked the lilies of ambition:

> but time, time is all I lacked
> to find them, as the great collectors before
> me.
> (17–18)

Envisaging what awaited him in Europe, Douglas ends his poem with a confession:

> I fear what I shall find.

Like Keyes fifteen months before, Douglas was about to embark on a journey from which he was certain he would not return. There are other parallels between the two poets: both accepted Rilke's notion that a man carries his death within him; and although Keyes was more completely under the influence of Rilke than was Douglas, the latter had read a number of Rilke's poems in German as well as in an English translation by Ruth Speirs. Dissimilar as they were in their approach to women, Douglas and Keyes had both endured the stresses of love and exploited the conflict of love and death.

At the end of May 1944 Douglas took communion at an altar set up beside his tank by Leslie Skinner, the regimental padre, and attended evensong in the small village church at Sway in the New Forest. The regiment sailed for France on 5 June at midnight; on 6 June Douglas commanded a tank troop in the assault on the Normandy beaches, and on 8 June he was with his regiment when it entered Bayeux. The next day, in a skirmish near the village of St. Pierre, he was killed by mortar fire.

ALUN LEWIS

Alun Lewis, who was born on 1 July 1915 at Aberdare in Glamorgan, Wales, differed sharply from Keyes and Douglas in his upbringing, education, and emotional life. The members of his family had followed a variety of callings: his grandfather worked as a miner for fifty years; his father, at one time a schoolmaster, became the director of education for Aberdare; one uncle was professor of Celtic studies at Aberystwyth and another was a Congregational minister. Although Lewis committed himself to no political or social cause, he was aware of belonging to a community, and his sense of detachment as a poet was always balanced by a feeling of sympathy with his fellowmen, whether they were British private soldiers or Indian peasants.

Whereas Douglas and Keyes moved on from English public schools to Oxford, Lewis, after winning a scholarship locally at Cowbridge Grammar School, became a student at the University College of Wales at Aberystwyth where he gained first-class honors in history before obtaining an M.A. at Manchester.

In 1941 he married Gweno Ellis, a teacher of German, thus securing the kind of loving and stable relationship denied to Douglas and to Keyes; but his constant postings in Britain and his embarkation for India made any settled life together impossible. He celebrated their love in "Postscript: for Gweno":

> If I should go away,
> Beloved, do not say
> "He has forgotten me."
> For you abide,
> A singing rib within my dreaming side;

You always stay,
And in the mad tormented valley
Where blood and hunger rally
and Death the wild beast is uncaught,
untamed,
Our soul withstands the terror
And has its quiet honour
Among the glittering stars your voices
named.

There is nothing so directly passionate as this lyric in the poetry of Douglas or of Keyes or, indeed, in the poetry of any other war poet.

Despite his early pacifism Lewis volunteered for military service in 1940, becoming a postal clerk with the Royal Engineers and gaining a commission as an infantry officer the following year. In 1942 his regiment was converted to tanks, and in 1943 Lewis embarked for India. His early poems appeared in March 1942 under the title *Raiders' Dawn,* and included work that went back to his days as a private. Some of his poems convey with remarkable fidelity the mood of the British army after all British forces had been driven out of Europe in June 1940, not to return until June 1944. Several hundred thousand troops stationed in camps or in barracks underwent training designed to make them ready to resist a German invasion and, eventually, to land in Europe as a liberating army. Units moved from place to place within Britain for no apparent reason, enduring the wretchedness that is always the lot of those serving in the ranks: boredom, discomfort, petty restrictions, the crushing weight of the military machine that is indifferent or hostile to individuality. Many soldiers knew that their wives and children were exposed to the dangers of air raids and to the wearisome routine of blackouts and rationing.

Lewis found in those conditions material for poetry that was both honest and imaginative. His best-known poem of army life, "All Day It Has Rained," presents with rare sympathy the sense of weariness and resignation, tinged with nostalgic longing, that afflicts men under canvas on a Sunday in England. The varying lengths of the lines, combined with the unemphatic rhymes, give the poem an air of relaxed formality, just as the monotony of the rain combines with the twilight to anesthetize any bitterness or pain that might arouse the soldiers from their lassitude:

And we stretched out, unbuttoning our
braces,
Smoking a Woodbine, darning dirty socks,
Reading the Sunday papers—I saw a fox
And mentioned it in the note I scribbled
home;—
And we talked of girls, and dropping bombs
on Rome,
And thought of the quiet dead and the loud
celebrities
Exhorting us to slaughter, and the herded
refugees;
—Yet thought softly, morosely of them, and
as indifferently
As of ourselves or those whom we
For years loved, and will again
Tomorrow maybe love; but now it is the
rain
Possesses us entirely, the twilight and the
rain.
(13–24)

The poem veers away from its theme when Lewis reflects on Edward Thomas, a poet whom he greatly admired, and who fell in action in 1917 at Arras. The trite observation that Thomas brooded on death and poetry does nothing for the poem or for our understanding of Thomas.

On the other hand, "To Edward Thomas" is a finely conceived and executed tribute to the poet of World War I. It contains a rich and expertly controlled passage about the view that greeted Lewis when he visited the Edward Thomas memorial stone above Steep in Hampshire:

I sat and watched the dusky berried ridge
Of yew-trees, deepened by oblique dark
shafts,
Throw back the flame of red and gold and
russet
That leapt from beech and ash to birch and
chestnut

Along the downward arc of the hill's
shoulder. . . .
(17–21)

In the last section of the poem, Lewis meditates on Thomas and on the voice, "soft and neutral as the sky," and growing ever clearer

Till suddenly, at Arras, you possessed that
hinted land.
(54)

Lewis portrays the realities of army life without hysteria or evasion in "After Dunkirk":

. . . the rough immediate life of camp
And barracks where the phallic bugle rules
The regimented orchestra of love;
The subterfuges of democracy, the stench
Of breath in crowded tents, the grousing
queues,
And bawdy songs incessantly resung
And dull relaxing in the dirty bar.
(30–36)

He was aware that he could not passively accept the dehumanizing effect of such an existence; nor could he accustom himself to the debased standards of his fellows, as he declares in "The Soldier":

But leisurely my fellow soldiers stroll
among the trees.
The cheapest dance-song utters all they feel.
(13–14)

Lewis is not preening himself on his superiority, but expressing his sadness at the emotional poverty of so many lives.

When Lewis was posted to India he was both unhappy at the prospect of leaving his wife and their unborn child and resolved to come to grips with whatever he found overseas. His approaching departure, embarkation, and voyage form the subject of various poems. "Goodbye" is a sadder, less ecstatic poem than "Postscript: for Gweno," but it is more complex and mature in that it faces the cares of everyday life and the fears that are inseparable from it. It is a poem capable of dealing with both the emerald that the soldier gives his wife and the patches she has sewn on his battle dress:

Yet when all's done you'll keep the emerald
I placed upon your finger in the street;
And I will keep the patches that you sewed
On my old battledress tonight, my sweet.
(29–32)

The voyage to India moved Lewis to write several good poems: "The Departure"; "On Embarkation"; "A Troopship in the Tropics"; "Port of Call: Brazil"; "Song." "A Troopship in the Tropics" gives a vivid picture of life aboard the ship where five thousand people are crammed into squalid quarters:

The smell of oranges and excrement
Moves among those who write uneasy
letters. . . .
(13–14)

The sharp precision of those two lines may serve as a reminder that Lewis was a short-story writer as well as a poet. His first collection of short stories appeared in 1943, and more stories were published after his death. Indeed some critics have maintained that he was basically a prose writer rather than a poet, and it is true that certain of his poems read like rather heavy descriptions in prose tricked out with conventional poeticisms. But it is more convincing to argue that he was essentially a poet who was strengthened by certain valuable prosaic elements in his writing. Lewis, besetting temptation as a poet was an over-fluent lyricism decked with hand-me-down romantic properties, and he needed sobriety of language, unsentimental observation, and the steady rhythm of prosaic speech as a corrective. His poems required the patches on the battle dress as well as the emerald and the mad tormented valley.

Occasionally he wrote hauntingly intense lyrics, such as "Song," subtitled "On seeing dead bodies floating off the Cape":

The flying fish like kingfishers
Skim the sea s bewildered crests,
The whales blow steaming fountains,
The seagulls have no nests
Where my lover sways and rests.
(21–25)

He began "To Rilke" on the troopship just before it reached Bombay; he was ill with food poisoning and had dreamed about returning home to find that he had died and his wife had been transformed into a be-jeweled blonde. The poem is not one of his best, but it is of considerable psychological interest, since it records Lewis' recognition of India's darkness, his envy for Rilke, who had been granted the gift of silence, and his own need for the simplicity that he had once discovered with his wife in distant Wales.

Lewis was overwhelmed by the immensity of India, by the grinding poverty of its people, and by the way in which patches of brilliant vegetation and the colorful Hindu festivals lend a garish contrast to the monotony of daily existence. He wrote a number of poems that evoke the landscapes he traversed in India and, later, in Burma; in these poems he is seldom content to describe the physical properties of what he saw, but relates the landscapes to the inhabitants or finds in them symbols of the spiritual life that had evolved there. Thus "The Mahratta Ghats" opens with a fierce portrayal of the land burned by drought, where a god has granted the peasants an exiguous dole:

High on the ghat the new turned soil is red,
The sun has ground it to the finest red,
It lies like gold within each horny hand.
Siva has spilt his seed upon this land.

But before the end of the poem it is the figures in the landscape that have come to occupy the center of the stage; the beggar and the soldier, each of them oppressed and economically enslaved, move hopelessly across the ghat:

Who is it climbs the summit of the road?
Only the beggar bumming his dark load.
Who was it cried to see the falling star?
Only the landless soldier lost in war.
(22–25)

Lewis is a skillful reporter of the Indian scene, of a village or a Hindu festival, or a funeral, but in spite of his sympathy for the peasants in their wretchedness and squalor he remained a detached observer. He could even view the sufferings of the people in a long perspective, wherein the war is merely a shadow that will pass, while the peasants, exploited by the economic system and at the mercy of nature, represent man's instinct to survive. Such is the moral of "The Peasants":

Across scorched hills and trampled crops
The soldiers straggle by.
History staggers in their wake.
The peasants watch them die.
(9–12)

In the closing months of his life, Lewis' thoughts turned continually toward death. This may well have been because he broke his jaw playing football and spent some time in the hospital at Poona; there he wrote two poems, about his separation from his wife and about the somber reflections engendered by a spell in hospital. "Burma Casualty," a darker poem, concerns a soldier who, after being wounded in action, has to have his leg amputated and learns to comprehend the realm of darkness.

Yet it would be false to suppose that Lewis was deliberately surrendering himself to death. He believed that his most serious work would be done after he had returned home and that he must come to grips with the details of Welsh life and Welsh thought. His preoccupation with death is understandable: he was tired; he hated the process of war and the separation it brought from everything he loved; like most Europeans he was weighed down by the oppressiveness of India, the passive suffering of its people, the omnipresent stench and panoply of death. It is not surprising that he had a presentiment of his own death, nor that it may sometimes have offered a welcome escape from a world of unease.

In the poems written toward the end of his life Lewis explored one of the themes that run through the work of Keyes and of Douglas: the conflict between life and death, negation and love. He is explicit about this in a letter to his wife:

> And although I am more and more engrossed with the single poetic theme of Life and Death, for there doesn't seem to be any question more directly relevant than this one of what survives of all the beloved, I find myself quite unable to express at once the passion of Love, the coldness of Death (Death is cold) and the fire that beats against resignation, acceptance. Acceptance seems so spiritless, protest so vain. In between the two I live. (*In the Green Tree*, p. 16)

The most richly imagined poem to spring from that conflict is "The Jungle." He wrote about it to Robert Graves, who was helping him to prepare a second collection of poems, which was published in 1945 under the title *Ha! Ha! Among the Trumpets.* Part of Lewis' letter is printed in Graves's foreword:

> I've felt a number of things deeply out here; perhaps the jungle has moved me more deeply than anything else. . . . but when I wrote a poem about the jungle I found it had become a criticism of the Western world which in a measure I understand, but of the jungle I had said nothing.

It is true that Lewis criticizes the Western world both directly and by stressing the idyllic beauty of the jungle, beside which our urban civilization is mean and drab:

> The patient queues, headlines and slogans flung
> Across a frightened continent, the town
> Sullen and out of work, the little home
> Semi-detached, suburban. . . .
> (31–34)

Yet he has said a great deal about the jungle in passages that are among the most vivid and evocative he ever wrote:

> The crocodile slides from the ochre sand
> And drives the great translucent fish
> Under the boughs across the running gravel.
> . . .
> But we who dream beside this jungle pool
> Prefer the instinctive rightness of the poised
> Pied kingfisher deep darting for a fish
> To all the banal rectitudes of states,
> The dew-bright diamonds on a viper's back
> To the slow poison of a meaning lost
> And the vituperations of the just.
> . . .
> The banyan's branching clerestories close
> The noon's harsh splendour to a head of light.
> (5–7; 37–43; 44–45)

The two final sections of the poem move between meditations on love, death, human responsibility, and the immediacy of the jungle. There is a superb moment when the poet moves away from his concern with elemental love and celebrates the individual's need for human love:

> Oh you who want us for ourselves,
> Whose love can start the snow-rush in the woods
> And melt the glacier in the dark coulisse,
> Forgive this strange inconstancy of soul,
> The face distorted in a jungle pool
> That drowns its image in a mort of leaves.
> (64–69)

Lewis seldom uses language so daringly and unerringly. The initial shock of encountering in a poem about the jungle images derived from snowfall and glaciers gives way to a recognition of their rightness. Moreover the employment of uncommon words seems equally well justified. The word "coulisse," besides being the precise geological term required by the context, echoes the sound of "snow" and "glacier" and anticipates the sibilants of the next line. And the phrase "mort of leaves" is an even greater triumph of poetic suggestiveness, for the very rare word "mort," which means a large number, carries with it associations belonging to the French word for death. Lewis seldom equaled the strength and lyrical flow of those few lines.

His own death remains as blurred as the image in the jungle pool. On 5 March 1944 at Goppe Pass in Arakan, Burma, where his regiment had advanced to face the Japanese, Lewis was wounded by a pistol shot and died in the Casualty Clearing Station at Bawli. The vagueness of that account in the official regimental history has led to rumors that he killed himself or was murdered for political reasons (he was the battalion intelligence officer). Nobody has brought forward any evidence to support either of those theories.

Lewis' poetry seldom displays the intellectual force or the hard pulsating clarity that mark the best work of Douglas; and it seldom moves with the lyrical grace and assurance that so often give distinction to Keyes's poems. But his concern for mankind, especially the poor of Wales and of India, his patient exploration of love and death, and his ability, in a handful of poems, to shape his feelings of loneliness and fear into the formal pattern of verse are likely to ensure the survival of the best work that he left behind in *Raiders' Dawn* and *Ha! Ha! Among the Trumpets.*

EPILOGUE

Some ten years after the war was over Charles Causley wrote "At the British War Cemetery, Bayeux." It is a less solemn, liturgical poem than Laurence Binyon's "For the Fallen," which ever since its publication in September 1914 has been an almost official requiem for those who die in battle. Causley's poem is more lyrical, at times even a refusal to mourn:

> On your geometry of sleep
> The chestnut and the fir-tree fly,
> And lavender and marguerite
> Forge with their flowers an English sky.
> (9–12)

Yet one notes, in this idyllic stanza, the harsh double meaning of "forge," and in the poem's last two stanzas, Causley's brief dialogue with the dead, he acknowledges the pity of war and the sacrifice of those who died so that the living might be free:

> About your easy head my prayers
> I said with syllables of clay.
> What gift, I asked, shall I bring now
> Before I weep and walk away?
>
> Take, they replied, the oak and laurel.
> Take our fortune of tears and live
> Like a spendthrift lover. All we ask
> Is the one gift you cannot give.
> (17–24)

Selected Bibliography

JOHN BAYLISS

SEPARATE WORKS

The White Knight, (London, 1945).

NORMAN CAMERON

COLLECTED WORKS

Collected Poems, (London, 1957).

ROY CAMPBELL

SEPARATE WORKS

Talking Bronco, (London, 1946).

COLLECTED WORKS

Collected Poems, 3 vols. (London, 1949, 1957, 1960).

BIOGRAPHICAL AND CRITICAL STUDIES

Alexander, P., *Roy Campbell: A Critical Biography,* (London, 1982).

CHARLES CAUSLEY

SEPARATE WORKS

Farewell, Aggie Weston, (London, 1951); *Survivor's Leave,* (London, 1953); *Union Street,* (London, 1957).

KEITH DOUGLAS

SEPARATE WORKS

Alamein to Zem Zem, (London, 1946) prose narrative with app. of poems and author's line drawings, repr. without poems and with intro. by Lawrence Durrell, (London, 1966).

SELECTED WORKS

Selected Poems of Keith Douglas, J. C. Hall and Norman Nicholson, (London, 1943); *Selected Poems,* T. Hughes, ed., (London, 1964).

COLLECTED WORKS

Collected Poems, J. Waller and G. S. Fraser, eds., (London, 1951); *Collected Poems,* J. Waller, G. S. Fraser, and J. C. Hall, eds., (London, 1966) a revision of the 1951 ed.; *Complete Poems,* D. Graham, ed. (London, 1978) variant texts for certain poems from 1951 and 1966 eds.

BIOGRAPHICAL AND CRITICAL STUDIES

Graham, D., *Keith Douglas 1920–1944: A Biography,* (London, 1974); Stratford, J., *The Arts Council Collection of Modern Literary Manuscripts 1963–1972,* (London, 1974) contains a description and discussion of the Douglas papers in the British Library.

GAVIN EWART

COLLECTED WORKS

The Collected Ewart 1933–1980, (London, 1980).

G. S. FRASER

SEPARATE WORKS

Poems, (Leicester, 1981).

ROY FULLER

SEPARATE WORKS

The Middle of a War, (London, 1942); *A Lost Season,* (London, 1944); *Souvenirs,* (London, 1980) autobiography.

COLLECTED WORKS

Collected Poems, (London, 1962).

BERNARD GUTTERIDGE

SEPARATE WORKS

The Traveller's Eye, (London, 1948).

HAMISH HENDERSON

SEPARATE WORKS

Elegies for the Dead in Cyrenaica, (London, 1948).

SIDNEY KEYES

SEPARATE WORKS

The Iron Laurel, (London, 1942); *The Cruel Solstice,* (London, 1943).

COLLECTED WORKS

Collected Poems, M. Meyer, ed., (London, 1945) with a memoir and notes by Meyer.

BIOGRAPHICAL STUDIES

J. Guenther, *Sidney Keyes: A Biographical Enquiry,* (London, 1965).

ALUN LEWIS

SEPARATE WORKS

Raiders Dawn, (London, 1942); *The Last Inspection,* (London, 1943) short stories; *Ha! Ha! Among the Trumpets,* (London, 1945) with foreword by R. Graves; *Letters from India,* (Cardiff, 1946); *In the Green Tree,* (London, 1948) with preface by A. L. Rowse, six unpublished stories and a selection of letters mainly from India.

SELECTED WORKS

Selected Poetry and Prose, I. Hamilton, ed., (London, 1966); *Selected Poems,* G. Lewis and J. Hooker, eds., (London, 1981) with afterword by J. Hooker; *A Miscellany,* J. Pikoulis, ed., (Cardiff, 1982).

EDWARD LOWBURY

SEPARATE WORKS

Time for Sale, (London, 1961).

SELECTED WORKS

Selected Poems, (Aberystwyth, 1978).

JOHN MANIFOLD

SELECTED WORKS

Selected Verse, (New York-Toronto, 1946); *Selected Poems,* (London, 1948).

F. T. PRINCE

COLLECTED WORKS

Collected Poems, (London, 1979) Anvil Press ed.; *Collected Poems,* (London, 1979) Menard Press ed.

HENRY REED

SEPARATE WORKS

A Map of Verona, (London, 1946); *Lessons of the War,* (New York-London, 1970).

MICHAEL RIVIERE

SELECTED WORKS

Selected Poems, (Nitchin, 1983).

ALAN ROSS

SEPARATE WORKS

Poems 1942–67, (London, 1967); *Open Sea,* (London, 1975).

VERNON SCANNELL

COLLECTED WORKS

New and Collected Poems 1950–1980, (London, 1980).

ANTHOLOGIES

Poems from "New Writing 1936–1946," J. Lehmann, ed., (London, 1946); *The Poetry of War 1939–1945,* I. Hamilton, ed., (London, 1965); *Components of the Scene,* R. Blythe, ed., (London, 1966); *The Terrible Rain: The War Poets of 1939–1945,* B. Gardner, ed., London (1966); Skelton, R., *Poetry of the Forties,* (Harmondsworth, 1968); *Return to Oasis: War Poems and Recollections from the Middle East 1940–1946,* V. Selwyn, E. de Mauny, I. Fletcher, G. S. Fraser, J. Waller, eds., (London, 1980) with intro. by L. Durrell.

GENERAL CRITICISM

Spender, S., *Poetry Since 1939,* (London, 1946); Ross, A., *Poetry 1945–50,* (London, 1951); Currey, R. N., *Poets of the 1939–1945 War,* (London, 1960) rev. ed., 1967; Davidson, N., *The Poetry Is in the Pity,* (London, 1972); Banerjee, A., *Spirit Above Wars: A Study of the English Poetry of the Two World Wars,* (London, 1976); Scannell, V., *Not Without Glory: The Poets of the Second World War,* (London, 1976) includes the long ch. "American Poets of the Second World War."

Alexander Pope

(1688–1744)

IAN JACK

When William Hazlitt began his fourth lecture on the English poets by saying that John Dryden and Alexander Pope were the great masters of the artificial style of poetry in English, as Geoffrey Chaucer, Edmund Spenser, William Shakespeare, and John Milton were of the natural, he lent his authority to a false distinction that survived in literary histories until the other day. The legend has grown up—and few territories of human thought are as fertile in legends as literary criticism—that between the Restoration and the late eighteenth century English poetry was diverted from its main channel. Matthew Arnold went so far as to rule that Dryden and Pope, "though they may write in verse, though they may in a certain sense be masters of the art of versification . . . are not classics of our poetry, they are classics of our prose. As late as 1933, A. E. Housman asserted that "there was a whole age of English in which the place of poetry was usurped by something very different which possessed the proper and specific name of wit." In making this statement he was not only taking his cue from Arnold; he was also (whether consciously or not) harking back to Hazlitt's unsatisfactory distinction between poetry that is "natural" and poetry that is "artificial."

The change that has come over English poetry in the last fifty years has brought with it a revolution in critical perspective. In reaction against what they feel to have been the excessive respect of the later nineteenth century for the work of the romantics, modern poets have turned to the age of John Donne for their inspiration. As a result, such features of decadent romantic theory as the exaggerated insistence on inspiration and on the difference between the genius and the ordinary man, the distrust of imitation in poetry, the preference of emotion to thought, of spontaneity to controlled form—all these have begun to be cleared away into the lumber-room of discarded ideas. This explains the fact that the new enthusiasm for the poetry of the metaphysicals has brought in its wake a new and vital interest in the poetry of the Augustans.

Attempts have even been made to trace a close affinity between the poetry of Pope and that of Donne. In an influential essay on William Collins, Middleton Murry claimed that Pope was not only a master of wit "in the Augustan sense, the verbal epigram of an extraordinarily alert mind," but also of "Wit in the best Metaphysical sense—namely, the striking expression of deep psychological perceptions." And in the chapter on "The Line of Wit" in F. R. Leavis' *Revaluation,* Pope occupies an honorable place beside Ben Jonson, Donne, and Andrew Marvell. Yet a moment's reflection will show that Murry's definitions of "wit" are inadequate, and that such resemblances as exist between Pope and Donne are greatly outweighed by the differences. I suggest that it may be more profitable to reverse the position of Hazlitt and to consider Pope as belonging to the same great tradition of English poetry as Spenser and Milton: what may be termed, in the widest sense, the Renaissance tradition. The true contrast, as it seems to me, is not between Pope and the poets who preceded him, but between Pope and his successors of the romantic age. That English poetry will never return to the romantic tradition it is perhaps too early to be certain; but at the moment all the omens are against it, and the modern reader can approach the poetry of Pope unhindered by the preconceptions that misled the readers of the nineteenth century.

In nothing is the contrast between Pope and the greatest of the romantic poets more evident than in their attitudes to earlier poetry. William Wordsworth despised most of the poetry written in the century before his own, and came to regard it as his mission to lead English poets back to the forceful simplicity of an earlier age. If Pope had written an essay on poetry as a preface to a volume of his own work, it would have been very different in tone from the celebrated preface to the second edition of *Lyrical Ballads.* As the *Essay on Criticism,* his letters, and the records of his conversation make abundantly clear, Pope considered the development of poetry in the age before his own as a matter for rejoicing. He shared the view of his contemporaries that Dryden had evolved a poetic idiom superior to that of any earlier poet, and proclaimed that he had learned the art of versification wholly from him. This does not mean that he was ignorant of the poetry written before the Restoration, or contemptuous of it (as Nicolas Boileau-Despréaux was of most of the poetry written before his own time). On the contrary, it would hardly be an exaggeration to say that Pope had read everything of value in earlier English poetry, so far as it was available in his day. Spenser was one of his earliest favorites; with Milton he was intimately conversant; Shakespeare he came to know with the familiarity of an editor. He was something of a collector of old books, numbered among his friends several of the scholars who were beginning to chart the course of English literary development, and himself made notes toward what would have been the first history of English poetry.[1] But it did not occur to him to turn back from the road along which Dryden had traveled with such acclamation; he rather felt that it was his task to use Dryden's discoveries as a basis for further exploration.

As we read Pope's early poems, in which we are watching one of the readiest learners English poetry has ever known serving his apprenticeship, we are fortunate in being able to turn (for a background) to the *Anecdotes* collected by his friend Joseph Spence. This has proved a disappointing book to those who have looked in it for something comparable to the indiscretions of Samuel Pepys or the rounded humanity of James Boswell's portrait of Samuel Johnson; yet to the student of poetics it is an invaluable document, for it gives us, in Pope's own words, an account of his early education, his reading, and his opinions. It is largely due to Spence that Pope is the first English poet of whose methods of composition we have reliable information.

If it were not for Spence, the fact that Pope's first considerable publication was his *Pastorals* might suggest that his career as a writer opened almost too discreetly. But the *Anecdotes* make it clear that Pope was as ambitious as any poet could be in his boyish experiments. When he was about twelve, he told Spence, he "wrote a kind of play, which I got to be acted by my schoolfellows. It was a number of speeches from the *Iliad;* tacked together with verses of my own" (*Anecdotes,* ed. Singer, p. 276). Soon afterward he began an epic poem that was yet more ambitious, including as it did "an under-water scene in the first book." In this poem, of which some 4,000 lines were written, Pope "endeavoured to collect all the beauties of the great epic writers into one piece: there was Milton's style in one part, and Cowley's in another; here the style of Spenser imitated, and there of Statius; here Homer and Vergil, and there Ovid and Claudian." Imitation was of the essence of these early attempts, and when Pope wrote his *Pastorals* imitation remained his lodestar. These

1. Printed in Ruffhead's *Life of Alexander Pope* (London, 1769), pp. 424–425.

four poems mark his arrival at years of poetic discretion. It had become clear to him by now, one may suppose, that his boyish rage for rhyming was to lead to his lifetime's vocation; it was time for him to lay aside the grandiose imaginings of boyhood and settle down to study his art in earnest. Precisely when the *Pastorals* were written, we do not know: they were published in Jacob Tonson's *Miscellany* in 1709, but they were written at least in part three years earlier, when Pope was seventeen or eighteen. Early work as they are, these poems in watercolor reveal a poet who has already made himself master of one sort of versification, and whose descriptive powers—as in this passage from "Autumn"—are astonishingly mature:

> Here where the *Mountains* less'ning as they rise,
> Lose the low Vales, and steal into the Skies;
> while lab'ring Oxen, spent with Toil and Heat,
> In their loose Traces from the Field retreat;
> while curling Smokes from Village-Tops are seen,
> And the fleet Shades glide o'er the dusky Green.
> (59–64)

Pope's descriptive power is one of the striking features of his early poems, and it is interesting to notice that he was not only a good judge of painting but was actually a painter himself. In his middle twenties—a fact emphasized by the late Norman Ault—he spent some eighteen months studying in the studio of his friend Charles Jervas, who was a fashionable portrait painter. The letters he wrote at this time contain some amusing references to his own apprenticeship to the art. "They tell us," he wrote to one friend, "when St. Luke painted, an Angel came & finish'd the work; and it will be thought here after, that when I painted, the devil put the last hand to my pieces, they are so begrimed and smutted. Tis however some mercy that I see my faults . . ."

While it is interesting to speculate about Pope's attainments as a painter, what is permanently significant is the value to his poetry of this apprenticeship to paint. "I begin to discover Beauties that were till now imperceptible to me," he wrote in another letter. "Every Corner of an Eye, or Turn of a Nose or Ear . . . have charms to distract me." In *Windsor Forest* it is his interest in landscape painting that is most evident:

> There, interspers'd in lawns and op'ning Glades,
> Thin trees arise that shun each others Shades.
> Here in full Light the russet Plains extend;
> There wrapt in Clouds the blueish Hills ascend;
> Ev'n the wild Heath displays her Purple Dies,
> And 'midst the Desart fruitful Fields arise.
> (21–26)

The same interest in colors and effects of light and shade is one of the features of *The Temple of Fame*:

> Of bright, transparent Beryl were the Walls,
> The Friezes Gold, and Gold the Capitals:
> As Heaven with Stars, the Roof with Jewels glows,
> And ever-living Lamps depend in Rows.
> (141–144)

Throughout Pope's work one finds passages that betray the painter's eye, and his references to the technique of painting are numerous and exact.

When the first collection of his poems appeared, in 1717, Pope's love of luxury and color could not have been overlooked, nor his growing mastery of the heroic couplet. A number of the poems included, however, went far beyond exhibiting his mastery of technique. The epistle "Eloisa to Abelard," to which both Joseph Warton and Johnson assigned a very high place among Pope's poems, is interesting because it deals with a subject with which he was not often to deal, passionate sexual love: the whole poem has a hectic quality that is dramatically appropriate. Even finer is the "Elegy to the Memory of an Unfortunate Lady"; whoever the lady may have been, if she existed at all, this is one of the greatest elegiac poems in the language. As she has died at her own hand, the lady may not be buried in consecrated ground; but what of this? asks the poet:

> What tho' no sacred earth allow thee room,
> Nor hallow'd dirge be mutter'd o'er thy tomb?
> Yet shall thy grave with rising flow'rs be drest,
> And the green turf lie lightly on thy breast:
> There shall the morn her earliest tears bestow,
> There the first roses of the year shall blow;
> While Angels with their silver wings o'ershade
> The ground, now sacred by thy religues made.
> (61–68)

Pope never wrote more tenderly than in this poem, or with a surer control of tone.

Yet the gem of the 1717 edition remains to be mentioned, *The Rape of the Lock*, of which the original version had been published in 1712, and the much expanded version (which we read now) two years later. This is the poem that Hazlitt described as "the most exquisite specimen of *fillagree* work ever invented" and that even Housman thought possibly the most perfect long poem in the language. The description on the title page, "An Heroi-Comical Poem," has misled some readers into imagining that the comic assault is leveled against heroic poetry; but in fact a mock heroic poem is no more a satire on heroic poetry than mock turtle soup is a satire on real turtle soup. The suggestion for the poem came from a quarrel that had arisen between two wealthy Catholic families in consequence of a stolen curl. When Pope was asked to write something that would restore everyone to good humor, it occurred to him to emphasize the triviality of the whole affair by describing it in the full pomp and splendor of epic verse. No poet has ever succeeded so well in "using a vast force to lift a feather" (as Pope himself described it in the postscript to his translation of the *Odyssey*). The style of the closing lines of canto II, for example,

> With beating Hearts the dire Event they wait,
> Anxious, and trembling for the Birth of Fate,

would be splendidly appropriate at a crucial moment in an epic poem; when we realize that "the Birth of Fate" is to be no more than the snipping off of a lock of hair, the result is high comedy. And yet something of the mastery of the poem is due to the fact that it is not simply and wholly ironical. When Pope wrote the line,

> *Belinda* smil'd, and all the World was gay,
> (II.52)

he was not being as directly ironical as Dryden had been when he described the "goodly Fabrick" of Thomas Shadwell. The effect of comparing a fat poetaster to Hannibal and Augustus is bluntly sarcastic: that of comparing a beautiful girl to the sun is (in this instance) satirical, yet the comparison has its own imaginative truth. In *The Rape of the Lock* Pope plays with the traditional imagery of lovesick poets, and while his treatment hints at the absurdity of their conventions it is clear that he is enjoying the license this gives his imagination. He demonstrates the superficiality of Belinda's world of fashion and scandal, of petty vanities and trivial, mean absurdities; but he does not deny its transitory beauty—the beauty of which the sylphs, the inspired addition to the later version, are in some sort the symbol. Satire is absent from some of the descriptive passages of the poem, for, as Pope pointed out, "since inanimate and irrational beings are not objects of censure . . . these may be elevated as much as you please, and no ridicule follows." This is true of the description of the coffee-equipage in canto III, which is reminiscent rather of Vergil's use of epic style in the *Georgics* to describe the lives of bees than of the directly satiric method of *MacFlecknoe*:

> For lo! the Board with Cups and Spoons is crown'd,

> The Berries crackle, and the Mill turns round.
> On Shining Altars of *Japan* they raise
> The silver Lamp . . .
> (105–108)

Any satirical intention that there may be here is unimportant: the reader enjoys the game by which the things of everyday become transformed into objects of an unfamiliar beauty.

It would be a great mistake to ignore the moral of the poem, which is explicitly stated in Clarissa's speech in the last canto, and which holds the component parts in a close-knit unity; yet seldom has a moral been enforced with more delicacy and tact. Lytton Strachey wrote of Pope as if he were above all things the poet of hatred; but it is partly because there is no hatred in this poem that it is so assured a masterpiece.

In the *Epistle to Dr. Arbuthnot* Pope looks back at his own career and claims in his defense:

> That not in Fancy's Maze he wander'd long,
> But stoop'd to Truth, and moraliz'd his song,
> (340–341)

and earlier in the same poem he contrasts the "pure Description" of his early work with the "Sense" that is now his aim. The contrast between the two halves of his career would be more complete were it not for the perfect union of Fancy and Truth, Description and Sense, in *The Rape of the Lock,* which forms a sort of bridge between his early work and his late, but there is no gainsaying the fact that in the later years of his life he held his Fancy in strict subordination to the claims of Truth. Although many critics have regretted this, it was inevitable that Pope should have "moraliz'd his song." No poet has taken his art more seriously: it would not have occurred to him to be merely "the idle singer of an empty day": his was the dedicated life of Spenser, of Milton, and of Wordsworth, who told Lady Beaumont that he desired to be regarded as a teacher or as nothing.

It was fated to be principally in satire that Pope fulfilled his moral function, but this was not his original intention. The clue to much that is puzzling in his poetic career lies in a poem that was never completed—his epic, *Brutus.* The plan of this poem is printed in Ruffhead's *Life of Pope,* and it is there stated that the author has part of the manuscript, in blank verse, lying before him. Although it is difficult to believe that Brutus would have been a great poem—it seems unlikely that anyone could have written a successful epic at the middle of the eighteenth century—it is essential to an understanding of Pope to remember that he, like Dryden before him, shared the Renaissance ambition of writing a great heroic poem. The notion that the Augustans were content to disport themselves on the lower slopes of poetry, ridiculing the soaring ambitions of the more vigorous race of writers who had preceded them, is a travesty of literary history. It was because Pope had thought so much about heroic poetry that he was able, in a *pièce d'occasion* that chanced to become his masterpiece, to write the greatest of all mock heroic poems. From the age of twelve onward his object was to write an epic poem, and the great epics of the world, with the yet more intoxicating Idea of the Epic, were the constant subjects of his meditation. He knew Vergil and Milton almost by heart, and spent more than a decade producing his triumphant translations of Homer. This continual devotion to the greatest of all poetic forms confirmed him in his exacting estimate of the moral function of the poet.

There was one poetic kind that was felt to share something of the dignity of the epic while sparing the poet the difficulty of finding an acceptable myth: didactic poetry. The suggestion that Pope should write a poem in this kind, justifying the ways of God to man, may have come from his friend Henry St. John, Viscount Bolingbroke: much of the philosophy in it certainly did. But the evidence of the poem itself suggests either that there was some conflict between the philosophy that Bolingbroke expounded to Pope and that which took form in the poet's own mind, or that Pope's understanding of his friend's philosophy was incomplete. It was the somber implications of Bolingbroke's philosophy that touched Pope's mind and heart most deeply. Like Jonathan Swift's, Pope's spiritual roots lay deep in the seventeenth century: he was accessible, to a degree in which Joseph Addison (for example) was not, to the terror and despair that lie beneath the surface of human life. In this Lucretian poem it is not when he is celebrating the power of man that he is at his greatest, but when he is emphasizing the paradoxes and perils of the human situation:

> Plac'd on this isthmus of a middle state,
> A being darkly wise, and rudely great:
> With too much knowledge for the Sceptic side,
> With too much weakness for the Stoic's pride,
> [Man] hangs between; in doubt to act, or rest,
> In doubt to deem himself a God, or Beast;
> In doubt his Mind or Body to prefer,
> Born but to die, and reas'ning but to err.
> (II.3–10)

It is, indeed, as Paul Hazard has said, "déisme impur" that we find in the *Essay on Man,* "déisme où persistaient quelques-unes des données psychologiques que, précisément, on voulait proscrire: un effort de volonté, plus qu'une évidence rationelle; et une acceptation du mystère."[2]

The *Essay on Man* attracted a great deal of attention, becoming a center of religious controversy and making Pope a European celebrity. Yet, though the poem contains many brilliant passages, it might have been as well for his reputation if it had never been written. For no other of his poems—unless it be the *Essay on Criticism,* an early and successful attempt at a humbler sort of didactic poetry—has done so much to lend credence to the notion that Pope was a gnomic versifier of genius, and that his work is "poetry of the surface" characterized by the directness of prose rather than the complex suggestiveness of great poetry. For all its brilliance, the *Essay* should not be taken as an example of his greatest work.

Heroic and didactic poetry are two of the forms in which a poet may embody his teaching: there remains the reverse of the medal, satire, in which he sets out to teach us what is good by painting evil in its true colors. To this form of writing, in which he had already shown himself a master, Pope devoted the best of his remaining energies.

One has only to remember Aristophanes, Miguel de Cervantes, Swift, and Jane Austen to acknowledge that the satiric impulse has been the inspiration of much of the world's greatest literature. Yet it remains true, perhaps because we are still in some respects the heirs of the romantics, that critics are apt to let intrusive biographical and ethical considerations confuse them in their attempt at assessing satiric writings. In its most naive form the objection to satire seems to be an objection to grumbling, and the only answer to it is that man has a great deal to grumble about. Before the Fall there was no satire, because there was no need of it; anyone who still feels that there is nothing to cry out against in life will find satire little to his taste. Satire is born of the impulse to protest: it is protest become art. If Voltaire and Swift had never lost their tempers, the world would be an immeasurably poorer place.

While the work of every satirist is liable to be misunderstood by those who dislike satire, even among satirists Pope has been particularly unfortunate. That critics during his lifetime should too often have discussed his character instead of his poetry is at least understandable; that this tendency should have continued for almost two centuries after his death is striking evidence of the difficulty, in literary criticism, of keeping to the point. The common reader of the late nineteenth century was too often content to read the hysterical condemnation of Pope's character in Thomas Macaulay's mendacious essay on Addison, and to reflect that only a very limited satisfaction could be derived from the work of

2. A modified deism in which there persisted some of the very psychological data which the deists wished to proscribe: an effort of the will rather than a rational demonstration; and an acceptance of mystery."

a man as deformed in mind and body as Alexander Pope.

In the last thirty years various factors—including, no doubt, the increased sympathy for the unfortunate that psychology has brought with it, as well as a growing body of accurate information about his life and times—have combined to lead critics toward a more favorable estimate of Pope's personality. Edith Sitwell's enthusiastic biography was followed by George Sherburn's scholarly account of Pope's early life, and the researches of a number of scholars have now obscured the bogeyman of the Victorians, putting in his place a human being who is often attractive and always comprehensible. Pope had a great deal to contend with. As a Roman Catholic, he was debarred from the principal careers, as well as being liable to double taxation and other species of legal persecution; while his poor health and wretched physique—he was only four feet six inches tall and suffered from severe curvature of the spine, apparently due to a tubercular infection—made of his whole life one long disease. It is hardly surprising that he was touchy and liable to fits of moroseness and to unfounded suspicions. What is astonishing is that he was able to rise above his disabilities, to support his parents and himself by being a pioneer in the independent profession of a man of letters, and to behave (on occasion) with great forbearance and generosity, as well as becoming the greatest poet of his century.

The ultimate justification of Pope's satire lies in the sincerity of his purpose and the soundness of his code of values. He is a moral satirist in a sense in which Dryden is not. (Of Dryden's three main satires, two are essentially political pamphlets, while the third is an attack on a personal enemy.) But this central fact about Pope's satire has frequently been obscured by two things: his habit of centering much of his satire in attacks on individuals, often individuals who had given him personal offense (a method traditional to satirists, and wholly justifiable); and the fact that his longest satire, *The Dunciad,* is less securely based on moral premises than most of his work. In its original form, as a poem in three books, *The Dunciad* is essentially a satire on bad writing. Pope would have agreed with the later critic who said that "the number of books has increased—is increasing—and ought to be diminished." The poem is many times the length of its model, *MacFlecknoe,* and all the brilliance of individual passages cannot prevent the feeling that it is too long. No doubt it was because he felt this that Pope's friend William Warburton suggested he should widen the scope of the poem. The result was a new book, *The New Dunciad,* written more than a decade later, in which the satire is of the widest possible sort—moral and political as well as literary. From the opening lines:

> Yet, yet a moment, one dim Ray of Light
> Indulge, dread Chaos, and eternal Night!
> Of darkness visible so much be lent,
> As half to shew, half veil the deep Intent

to the sublime conclusion:

> Lo! thy dread Empire, CHAOS! is restor'd;
> Light dies before thy uncreating word;
> Thy hand, great Anarch! lets the curtain fall;
> And Universal Darkness buries All

this continuation far transcends the first three books, and it is not surprising that Pope himself considered it his masterpiece. Unfortunately, however, he was not content to leave *The New Dunciad* to stand by itself, but made an attempt to weld the four books into one poem. He substituted Colley Cibber for Lewis Theobald as his hero, introduced strokes of moral and political satire into the first three books, and endeavored to give Dullness a much wider connotation than it had had before, until (as Warburton explained) it did not stand for "mere Stupidity" but for "all Slowness of Apprehension, Shortness of Sight, or imperfect Sense of things." But a much more comprehensive revision would have been necessary to make a perfect unity of the four books (if indeed the feat was possible), and *The Dunciad* as it now stands is flawed by this uncertain direction.

It is fortunate for us that Pope completed the original *Dunciad* in 1728 and laid it aside, for it was in the years immediately following this that he wrote most of the poems that, with *The Rape of the Lock* and *The New Dunciad,* constitute the summit of his achievement. In these he left mock heroic poetry for satire in the Latin sense of the word. Instead of embodying his criticism of life in narrative form, he turned to the form of satura used by Horace and Juvenal, and in modern times by Boileau and Edward Young. In this he was doing something that Dryden had never done, although (characteristically) he is hardly less clearly Dryden's pupil in these poems than elsewhere. Perhaps because it was too personal a form for him, Dryden never made use of the classical form of satire on his own account, although he translated part of Juvenal and the whole of Persius.

Everything about this epistolary form of satire suited Pope. There was no need to find a plot: the poem could be long or short: the poet was free to move from one subject to another, as in conversation, so long as an underlying continuity was preserved: swift changes of tone and temper were expected: while the accommodating freedom of the form made it possible for him to find a home in these discursive poems for. the detached passages that he was forever writing. In particular this sort of poem provided a perfect setting for the satiric "character." The creation of these was an art that Pope learned from Dryden, and if anyone has excelled the creator of Achitophel and Zimri it is he. He is extraordinarily skillful in adapting the scope and tone of his "character" to the nature and vulnerability of the person attacked. It is instructive, for example, to compare the direct loathing of the assault on Lord Hervey,

> This painted Child of Dirt that stinks and
> stings,
> (*An Epistle to Dr. Arbuthnot,* 310)

with the covert malice of the lines on Addison in the same poem. Remembering, perhaps, the touch of genius with which Dryden had rendered his attack on the earl of Shaftesbury yet more lethal by inserting a passage praising his integrity as a judge, and so giving the illusion of impartiality, Pope moves to the attack with a well-turned compliment to a man,

> Blest with each Talent and each Art to please,
> And born to write, converse, and live with
> ease,
> (195–196)

before he brings the charge that Addison will

> Damn with faint praise, assent with civil leer,
> And without sneering, teach the rest to sneer;
> Willing to wound, and yet afraid to strike,
> Just hint a fault, and hesitate dislike.
> (201–204)

From the narrow prison of such interlocking antitheses a man's reputation can hardly escape. It should be noted that when Pope revised these "characters" he often eliminated the merely particular in favor of the universal: Addison becomes Atticus, and what began as an attack on a personal enemy is transformed into an eternal type of the petty jealousy of a man of letters. When Pope satirizes an individual it is as if he set fire to an effigy: the effigy crackles, blazes, and is burned up; but in the process it ignites a wider conflagration, and in the flames we see, brightly illumined, the hateful figure of Folly or Vice itself. Personal hatred often provides Pope's impetus, but it is the sanity of the position from which the attack is launched that gives his satire its penetration and permanence. We will not do justice to his fierce sincerity unless we understand that his feeling for order, "Nature," the sane norm of the good life, was as passionate and as personal as John Keats's love of Beauty or Wordsworth's love of a Nature very differently defined.

Satire in the modern sense of the word was not the only ingredient of the Latin *satura,* nor is it of Pope's satiric epistles. There are also eloquent passages in praise of his friends, such as the lines on John Gay:

> Blest be the *Great*! for those they take away,
> And those they left me—For they left me
> GAY,

Left me to see neglected Genius bloom,
Neglected die! and tell it on his Tomb;
Of all thy blameless Life the sole Return
My Verse, and QUEENSB'RY weeping o'er thy Urn!
(*Arbuthnot*, 255–260)

and the moving description of his father:

Unlearn'd, he knew no Schoolman's subtle Art,
No Language, but the Language of the Heart.
(*Arbuthnot*, 398–399)

Literary criticism is ubiquitous, as is an element of autobiography and self-justification:

Ask you what Provocation I have had?
The strong Antipathy of Good to Bad.
When Truth or Virtue an Affront endures,
Th' Affront is mine, my Friend, and should be yours.
Mine, as a Foe profess'd to false Pretence,
Who think a Coxcomb's Honour like his Sense;
Mine, as a Friend to ev'ry worthy Mind;
And mine as Man, who feels for all mankind.
(*Epilogue to the Satires*, dial. II, 197–204)

Whether one turns to the *Moral Essays*, which bear a close relation to the *Essay on Man* and are constructed comparatively systematically, or to the more loosely organized *Imitations of Horace*, one finds Pope in these epistolary poems writing at the top of his bent. Never did he handle words more surely, or with more extraordinary economy. Words are like people: you can get them to do almost anything, if only you understand them well enough. You get your way with them not by bullying but by studying their natures. This Pope did, and made words his slaves. He could take two sets of familiar substantives and arrange them in a couplet that says all about pedants that there is to say:

Pains, reading, study, are their just pretence,
And all they want is spirit, taste, and sense.
(*Arbuthnot*, 159–160)

With five of the commonest words in the language he could conclude the most terrible of all epitaphs:

See how the World its Veterans rewards!
A Youth of frolicks, an old Age of Cards,
Fair to no purpose, artful to no end,
Young without Lovers, old without a Friend,
A Fop their Passion, but their Prize a Sot,
Alive, ridiculous, and dead, forgot!
(*Moral Essays*, II, 243–248)

In considering Pope's poetry as a whole, one is struck by the fact that a remarkably high proportion of it is written in one meter—the heroic couplet. This was not a premeditated self-denial on his part, and he did not consider this meter the only satisfactory one for English verse. His epic was to be written in blank verse, he wrote a number of poems in stanzas of various sorts, while the squibs and occasional poems that he was forever throwing off were most often in ballad meter or tetrameters. Yet it remains true that no English poet of comparable stature is to the same degree a poet of one meter. Why is this?

To answer the question one must remember the revolution in English poetry that followed the Restoration. It is the function of poetic idiom to enable poets to express their own sensibility and that of their age with the greatest possible accuracy. As sensibility changes from one age to another, it follows that the need arises, from time to time, for a revolution in the idiom of poetry. When this takes place one usually finds that each of the main constituents of the new idiom—diction, imagery, syntax perhaps, rhythm and meter almost always—has undergone some alteration; but in any particular revolution the change in one of these constituents is often found to be of primary importance, to be in a sense the root from which the other changes are derived. In the Wordsworthian revolution a change in diction was the heart of the process; in the Augustan revolution it was the discovery of a new rhythm that was vital. The discovery of the rhythmical possibilities of the heroic couplet had an effect as electrical as the discovery of "sprung rhythm" by Gerard Manley Hopkins when his poems were published in 1918. When Pope began to write, the heroic couplet (as developed by Dryden) was still a recent discovery, and he was intoxicated by it.

One of the attractions of the new meter for Pope was its almost endless adaptability. When he aspired to rhythmical or syntactical effects that could better be achieved in some other measure, he was prepared to use another measure; but he found that he had so mastered the heroic couplet that he could compass in it an extraordinary variety of effect. Compare the description of the foolish man-about-town in *The Rape of the Lock*:

> With earnest Eyes, and round unthinking Face,
> He first the Snuff-box open'd, then the Case,
> And thus broke out—"My Lord, why, what the devil?
> Z—ds! Damn the Lock! 'fore Gad, you must be civil!
> Plague on't! 'tis past a Jest—nay prithee, Pox!
> Give her the Hair".—he spoke, and rapp'd his Box.
> (IV. 125–130)

with the translucent beauty of the lines that describe the sylphs:

> Soft o'er the Shrouds Aerial whispers breathe,
> That seem'd but *Zephyrs* to the Train beneath,
> Some to the Sun their Insect-Wings unfold,
> Waft on the Breeze, or sink in Clouds of Gold.
> Transparent Forms, too fine for mortal Sight,
> Their fluid Bodies half dissolv'd in Light.
> Loose to the Wind their airy Garments flew,
> Thin glitt'ring Textures of the filmy Dew.
> (II. 57–64)

Compare the romantic melancholy of this passage from "Eloisa to Abelard":

> But o'er the twilight groves and dusky caves,
> Long-sounding aisles, and intermingled graves,
> Black Melancholy sits, and round her throws
> A death-like silence, and a dread repose:
> Her gloomy presence saddens all the scene,
> Shades ev'ry flower, and darkens ev'ry green,
> Deepens the murmur of the falling floods,
> And breathes a browner horror on the woods
> (163–170)

with the precise satiric observation of the Epistle to Miss Blount, "On Her Leaving Town after the Coronation":

> To part her time 'twixt reading and bohea,
> To muse, and spill her solitary tea,
> Or o'er cold coffee trifle with the spoon,
> Count the slow clock, and dine exact at noon.
> (15–18)

If one sets these passages beside the quotations already given from *The New Dunciad* and the *Epistle to Dr. Arbuthnot,* the absurdity of the notion that all poems in heroic couplets are monotonously similar becomes very evident. All that is necessary is to read Pope's verse aloud, taking care to find the correct tempo for each passage.

Great as is the variety of Pope's work in tone and style, there is one quality that may be found almost everywhere, and that is a remarkable conciseness. Another master of condensed expression, Swift, paid Pope the compliment of saying that he could

> . . . in one couplet fix
> As much sense as I can in six.

A Mr. Dobson who won a brief fame by translating Matthew Prior's *Solomon* into Latin verse was asked by Pope himself or by Lord Oxford to do the same for the *Essay on Man,* but he abandoned his attempt "on account of the impossibility of imitating its brevity in another language"—a remarkable testimony, in view of the habitual brevity of Latin. It is clear that this conciseness was the result of deliberate effort on Pope's part, and that he took pride in it. In the design prefixed to the *Essay on Man* he says that he chose to write this poem in verse instead of prose partly because "I found I could express them [his principles] more *shortly* this way than in prose." Reading his letters and other prose writings, we often come on confirmation of this claim; for we find numerous reflections and images that were later incorporated in a poem, and comparison of the prose and the verse always reveals the superior brevity of the latter—a brevity that is often accompanied by an increase in point and wit. This conciseness provides a reason why Pope's poetry should usually be read slowly, and read more than once; only so will the full meaning (in his favorite phrase) "open" itself to the reader's mind.

And what of the end to which all this skill in words and rhythms was employed? If Pope was a serious poet as well as a poet of extraordinary technical accomplishment, what was his "message"? Of course a great writer does not offer us a message that can be detached from his work; the greater he is, perhaps, the less does he do so. It is for us to read what he has written, and so to see life as he sees it. But two generalizations may be made about Pope's vision of life. The first is that it is less personal and private than that (for example) of Wordsworth. Just as it would not have occurred to him to write a poem of epic length and seriousness about the development of his own mind, as Wordsworth did in *The Prelude,* so it would have seemed to him ridiculous to offer his readers a reading of life as idiosyncratic as that of the "Immortality Ode." The values on which his work is based, and that he regarded it as his poetic duty to promulgate, are values that have a longer history than those of Wordsworth: they would have been understood and accepted, in general terms, by Socrates, by Cicero, and by Jean Racine, as well as by civilized people in his own day and in ours. Secondly, the fallacy that Pope was a shallow optimist should be allowed to go into honorable retirement. Even in the *Essay on Man* he is an optimist only in a specialized and technical sense that makes the word highly misleading, while the greatest passage of the poem is a somber "diminishing" of man's estate reminiscent rather of a medieval *contemptus mundi* than of the thought of the more shallow among the thinkers of the Enlightenment. Hazlitt was right when on reading *The Rape of the Lock* he did not know whether to laugh or to cry. Pope often reminds one of Mozart: there is in his work the same depth of emotion, perfectly restrained by the strict patterning of art

> . . . since Life can little more supply
> Than just to look about us and to die.

Charles Augustin Sainte-Beuve said of Molière, "Il a au coeur la tristesse": the same words might form the epitaph of Pope.

Selected Bibliography

BIBLIOGRAPHY

Detailed bibliographical information can also be found in the *New Cambridge Bibliography of English Literature,* vol. II. Griffith, R. H., *Alexander Pope: A Bibliography* (Austin, Tex., 1922; repr. London, 1962) vol. I, part i, *Pope's Own Writings,* 1709–1734; vol.I, part ii, *Pope's Own Writings, 1735–1751;* vol. II, intended to be "a record of books about Pope," has not appeared; additional bibliographical information may be found in the standard modern eds. of Pope's writings, notably in the Twickenham ed.; Abbott, E. A., *A Concordance to the Works of Alexander Pope,* (London, 1875; facs. repr. New York, 1965).

COLLECTED EDITIONS

The Works of Alexander Pope . . . with His Last Corrections, W. Warburton, ed., 9 vols. (London, 1751); J. Warton, ed., *The Works of Alexander Pope with Notes and Illustrations,* 9 vols. (London, 1797); W. Elwin and W. J. Courthope, eds., *The Works of Alexander Pope, Including Several Hundred Unpublished Letters and Other New Materials,* 10 vols. (London, 1871–1889); J. Butt, gen. ed., *The Twickenham Edition of the Poems of Alexander Pope,* (London, 1939–1969), an admirable ed. that is unlikely to be superseded for a long time; a less elaborate ed., based on the text of the Twickenham ed. and also edited by J. Butt, appeared in 1963 (paperback ed. 1965); vol. IV: J. Butt, ed. *Imitations of Horace, with an Epistle to Dr. Arbuthnot and the Epilogue to the Satires,* (1939) 2nd ed. (1953) also includes the two adaptations from Donne and *One Thousand Seven Hundred and Thirty Eight;* vol. II: G. Tillotson, ed., *The Rape of the Lock and Other Poems,* (1940; 2nd ed., 1954) 3rd ed. (1962) includes both texts of *The Rape of the Lock* as well as translations *The Temple of Fame* "Eloisa to Abelard," and "An Elegy to the Memory of an Unfortunate Lady"; vol. V: J. Sutherland, ed., *The Dunciad* (1943), rev. ed. (1953) gives the text of *The Dunciad Variorum* and *The Dunciad Fourt Books;* vol. III, pt. i: M. Mack, ed., *An Essay on Man* (1950); vol. III, pt. ii: F. W. Bateson, ed., *Epistles to Several Persons (Moral Essays)* (1951) 2nd ed., with new material

(1961); vol. VI: N. Ault, ed., *Minor Poems* (1954) completed by J. Butt; vol. I: E. Audra and A. L. Williams, eds., *Pastoral Poetry and the Essay on Criticism* (1961) also includes "The Messiah," *Windsor Forest* and Pope's translations from Ovid and Statius; vols. VII-X: M. Mack et al., eds., *Homer's Iliad and Odyssey* (1967); vol. XI: M. Mack, ed., *Index* (1969); H. Davis, ed., *Pope: Poetical Works* (London, 1969) and admirable ed. in the Oxford Standard Authors series, includes everything except the Homer translations, with a new intro. by P. Rogers paperbacked ed. (1978).

SELECTED WORKS

G. Sherburn, ed., *Selections . . .* (New York, 1929), reissued as *The Best of Pope* (1931); H. V. D. Dyson, ed., *Poetry and Prose* (Oxford, 1933), brief selections; W. K. Wimsatt, ed., *Alexander Pope: Selected Poetry and Prose,* (New York, 1951); R. P. C. Mutter and M. Kinkead-Weekes, *Selected Poems and Letters of Alexander Pope* (London, 1962), a well-annotated volume that makes and excellent intro. to Pope.

PROSE AND LETTERS

Various writings in prose, including prefaces to Shakespeare and Homer as well as numerous letters, appeared during Pope's lifetime. They are listed in the *New Cambridge Bibliography,* only a selection is listed here. N. Ault, ed., *Prose Works,* (London, 1936), vol. I of an uncompleted ed., covering the years 1711–1720 C. Kerby-Miller, ed., *Memoirs of . . . Martinus Scriblerus* written by Dr. Arbuthnot, Pope, Swift, Gay, Parnell, and Robert Harley (earl of Oxford) (New Haven, 1950); E. L. Steeves, ed., *The Art of Sinking in Poetry: Martinus Scriblerus'* PEPI BAqOUS (New York, 1952); G. Sherburn, ed., *The Correspondence of Alexander Pope,* 5 vols. (London, 1956) an admirable ed. that throws a good deal of new light on Pope's career; J. Butt, ed., *Letters of Alexander Pope* (London, 1960).

PRINCIPAL POEMS AND TRANSLATIONS

A much fuller and more detailed list may be found in Griffith and in the *New Cambridge Bibliography. Poetical Miscellanies, the Sixth Part,* (London, 1709), vol. VI of Dryden's collection *Miscellany Poems,* published by Tonson, which contains pastorals and other poems by Pope; *An Essay on Criticism,* (London, 1711); *The Rape of the Lock and Other Poems,* in Lintott's *Miscellaneous Poems and Translations,* (London, 1712) two cantos, 334 lines; see 1714 below; *Windsor Forest,* (London, 1713); *The Rape of the Lock, in Five Cantos,* (London, 1714), 794 lines. The sylphs, and much else, have now been added; this is the text usually reprinted; *The Temple of Fame: a Vision,* (London, 1715); *The Works of Mr. Alexander Pope;* (London, 1717–1735), contains "Verses to the Memory of an Unfortunate Lady," "Eloisa to Abelard," and other poems; *The Iliad of Homes,* vols. I–VI London (1715–1720); *The Odyssey of Homer* vols. I–V London (1725–1726) books II, VI, VII, VIII, XI, XII, XVI, XVIII, and XXIII were in fact by William Broome, and books I, IV, XIX, and XXII by Elijah Fenton; most reprints of these translations omit the footnotes and other interesting material; *The Dunciad,* (London, 1728) in three books, with Theobald as hero, see 1729, 1742, and 1743; *The Dunciad VarioURUM,* (London, 1729) an expanded text, with elaborate satirical prolegomena, footnotes, and other "scholarly" apparatus; *An Epistle to the . . . Earl of Burlington,* (London, 1731) often called *Moral Essays, IV; Of the Use of Riches, and Epistle to . . . Bathurst,* (London, 1732) often called *Moral Essays, III; The First Satire of the Second Book of Horace, Imitated,* (London, 1733) other *Imitations of Horace* appeared between 1743 and 1738, but not separately listed here; *An Essay on Man* (London, 1733–1734). Epistles I-III appeared separately in 1733, Epistle IV appeared in 1743, followed by a collection of the four in the same year; *An Epistle to Cobham* (London, 1733), often called *Moral Essays, I; An Epistle . . . to Dr. Arbuthnot* (London, 1735), later called *Prologue to the Satires; Of the Characters of Women: An Epistle to a Lady* (London, 1735), often called *Moral Essays, II; Epilogue to the Satires, in Two Dialogues* (London, 1738), published separately in the same year, the first under the title *One Thousand Seven Hundred and Thirty Eight; The New Dunciad* (London, 1742); *The Dunciad in Four Books* (London, 1743).

BIOGRAPHY

Throughout his life Pope was involved in controversy. The resultant "Popiana" have often little relevance to his poetry, and they are not listed here. J. V. Guerinot's *Pamphlet Attacks on Alexander Pope, 1711–1744: A Descriptive Bibliography* (London, 1969) gives an admirable account of them. Ayre, W., *Memoirs of the Life and Writings of Alexander Pope, Esq,* 2 vols. (London, 1745; repr. Hildesheim, 1968) the value of these and other early biographies is discussed by Sherburn in the preface to his *Early Career of Alexander Pope,* (London, 1934); Johnson, S., *Prefaces, Biographical and Critical, to the Works of the English Poet,* 10 vols. (London, 1779–1781), often reprinted as *Lives of the English Poets;* the best ed. is that of G. Birbeck Hill, 3 vols (London, 1905), vol. III: "The Life of Pope"; the biographical part of the Life is sometimes inaccurate and inevitably out of date; but the assessment of Pope's character is shrewd and refreshingly free from the tendency to confuse a man's personality with his merit as a poet; the critical part is of the greatest interest to anyone who reads Pope's poetry; S. W. Singer, ed., *Anecdotes, Observations, and Characters of Books and Men Collected from the Conversation of Mr. Pope and Other Eminent Persons of His Time by the Rev. Joseph Spence,* (London, 1820), indispensable; an admirable ed. in 2 vols. by J. M. Osborn, with full annotation, was published in 1966; Dilke, C. W., *The Papers of a Critic,* 2 vols. (London, 1875), most of vol. I consists of a series of scholarly investigations of Pope's writings; Stephen, L., *Alexander Pope* (London, 1880) in the English Men of Letters series Courthope, W. J., *The Life of Alexander Pope* (London, 1889), in vol. V of the Elwin-Courthope ed.

Sitwell, E., *Alexander Pope,* (London, 1930) unusual in its day for its sympathetic approach; Sherburn, G., *The Early Career of Alexander Pope* (Oxford, 1834), the standard biography "to about 1726 or 1727"; Ault, N., *New Light on Pope with Some Additions to His Poetry Hither-to Unknown* (London, 1949), a series of studies Pope's life and the canon of his poems; some of the attributions are very uncertain; the chapter on Pope as a painter throws interesting light on the poems; Wimsatt, W. K., *The Portraits of Alexander Pope* (New Haven-London, 1965), a beautifully produced book that throws a great deal of light on Pope and his background; Guerinot, J. V., *Pamphlet Attacks on Alexander Pope 1711–1744: A Descriptive Bibliography* (London-New York, 1969).

CRITICISM

Spence, J., *An Essay on Pope's Odyssey,* 2 parts (London, 1726; repr. Hildesheim, 1968) in the "Anglistica and Americana," series; Warton, J., *An Essay on the Writings and Genius of Pope,* vol I (London, 1756), vol. II (London, 1782), this digressive study, in which each of Pope's principal poems is considered in turn, is still illuminating. Warton is often called a "pre-romantic," and his admiration of Pope was less whole-hearted than Johnson's, but the extent of his reservations is often exaggerated; Johnson, S., *Prefaces . . . to . . . the English Poets* (London, 1779–1782), see "Biography" above; Stockdale, P., *An Inquiry into the Nature and Genuine Laws of Poetry, Including a Particular Defence of the Writings and Genius of Mr. Pope* (London, 1778); Hazlitt, W. C., *Lectures on the English Poets* (London, 1818); D. Masson, ed., *The Collected Writings of Thomas De Quincey* (London, 1889–1890), vols. IV and XI contain interesting criticism of Pope; much of this is reprinted in H. Darbishire, ed., *De Quincey's Literary Criticism* (London, 1900); Stephen, L., *Hours in a Library,* vol. I (London, 1874), contains the essay "Pope as a Moralist"; Stephen, L., *History of English Thought in the Eighteenth Century,* 2 vols. (London, 1876), pioneering study that is still of great interest, see particularly vol. II, 348–365; Beljame, A., *Le Public et les hommes de lettres en Angleterre au dixhuitième siècle, 1660–1744: Dryden, Addison, Pope* (Paris, 1881), translated by E. O. Lorimer as *Men of Letters and the English Public in the Eighteenth Century, 1660–1744: Dryden, Addison, Pope* (London, 1948), edited with an intro. and notes by B. Dobrée; Stephen, L., *English Literature and Society in the Eighteenth Century* (London, 1904), the Ford lectures, 1903; Strachey, L., *Pope* (Cambridge, 1925), the Leslie Stephen lecture, 1925 repr. in *Characters and Commentaries* (London, 1933), in *Literary Essays* (London, 1948), and in A. S. Cairncross, ed., *Modern Essays in Criticism* (London, 1938), an entertaining and stimulating lecture based on an imperfect understanding of Pope's character; Warren, A., *Alexander Pope as Critic and Humanist,* Princeton Studies in English no. 1 (Princeton, N.J., 1929), a pioneering study, now inevitably out of date; Audra, E., *L'Influence française dans l'oeuvre de Pope* (Paris, 1931); Leavis, F. R., *Revaluation: Tradition and Development in English Poetry* (London, 1936), still of interest; Lovejoy, A. O., *The Great Chain of Being: A Study of the History of an Idea* (Cambridge, Mass., 1936), see particularly chap. 6; Tillotson, G., *On the Poetry of Pope* (Oxford, 1938), an enthusiastic and stimulating introduction; Root, R. K., *The Poetical Career of Alexander Pope* (Princeton, N.J., 1938); Knight, G. Wilson, *The Burning Oracle: Studies in the Poetry of Action* (London, 1939), unusual and often suggestive, see chap. 5; Davies, H. Sykes, *The Poets and Their Critics: Chaucer to Collins* (London, 1943; rev. ed. 1960), brief passages of criticism on Pope's poetry by critics from Pope's own time onward; *Essays on the Eighteenth Century Presented to David Nichol Smith* (Oxford, 1945), see particularly Sherburn, G., "Pope at Work"; Brooks, C., *The Well Wrought Urn: Studies in the Structure of Poetry* (New York, 1947), chap.5 is an interesting study of *The Rape of the Lock*; Sutherland, J., *A Preface to Eighteenth Century Poetry* (Oxford, 1948), an excellent introduction to the period of Pope and that which followed it; Clifford, J. L., and Landa, L. A., *Pope and His Contemporaries: Essays Presented to George Sherburn* (Oxford, 1949), see particularly Mack's, M., "Wit and Poetry and Pope: Some Observations on His Imagery"; Butt, J., *The Augustan Age* (London, 1950), contains admirable brief introductions to Dryden, Addison, Swift, Pope, Johnson, and others; Knight, D. M., *Pope and the Heroic Tradition: A Critical Study of the Iliad* (New Haven, Conn., 1951); Jack, I., *Augustan Satire: Intention and Idiom in English Poetry; 1660–1750* (Oxford, 1952), chaps. 5–7 deal with Pope; Rogers, R. W., *The Major Satires of Alexander Pope,* Illinois Studies in Language and Literature: vol XL (Urbana, Ill, 1955), makes some use of MS material; Williams, A. L. *Pope's "Duncaid": A Study of Its Meaning* (London, 1955); Tillotson, G., *Pope and Human Nature* (Oxford, 1958), deals with "the material Pope expresses" rather than with his manner of expressing it, the subject of Tillotson's earlier study; Hagstrum, J. H., *The Sister Arts: The Tradition of Literary Pictorialism and English Poetry from Dryden to Gray* (Chicago, 1958), a general study of great interest; Sühnel, R., *Homer und Die Englische Humanität: Chapmans und Popes Ubersetzungkunst im Rahmen der humanistischen Tradition* (Tübingen, 1958), R. A. Brower, *Alexander Pope: The Poetry of Allusion* (Oxford, 1959), illustrates the fact that an awareness of the allusions throughout Pope's poetry enriches our experience as we read it; J. L. Clifford, ed. *Eighteenth-Century English Literature: Modern Essays in Criticism* (New York, 1959), reprints three important articles in convenient form: Mack, M., "Wit and Poetry and Pope," Hooker, E. Niles, "Pope on Wit: The Essays," and Butt, J., "Pope Seen Through His Letters"; Dobre, B., *English Literature in the Early Eighteenth Century, 1700–1740,* vol. VII: *Oxford History of English Literature* (Oxford, 1959), two long chaps. contain a full account of Pope's poetry; Amarasinghe, U., *Dryden and Pope in the Early Nineteenth Century* (Cambridge, 1962), the reputation of these two poets in the romantic period; Edwards, T. R., *This Dark Estate: A Reading of Pope* Berkeley-(Los Angeles, 1963); M. Mack, ed., *Essential Articles for the Study of Alexander Pope* (London, 1964), essential for the advanced student; Price, M., *To the Palace of Wisdom: Studies in Order and Energy from Dryden to Blake* (New York, 1964); Trickett, R., *The Honest Muse: A Study in Augustan Verse* (Oxford, 1967), an interesting account of "the underlying ethos of Augustan poetry" that has a long chapter on Pope; Jones, E., "Pope and Dulness," *Proceedings of the British Academy* vol. LIV (1968), the Chatterton lecture delivered 13 November 1968, reprinted as an offprint (1970); Dixon, P., *The World of Pope's Satires* (London, 1968); Nicholson, M. H., and Rousseau, G. S., *"This Long Disease, My Life": Alexander Pope and the Sciences,* (Princeton, N.J., 1968); G. S Rousseau, ed., *Twentieth Century Interpretations of "The Rape of the Lock": A Collection of Critical Essays* (Englewood Cliffs, N.J., 1969); Jones, J. A., *Pope's Couplet Art* (Athens, Ohio, 1969); Mack, M., *The Garden and the City: Retirement and Politics in the Later Poetry of Pope, 1731–1743* (Toronto-London, 1969), the most important and interesting of recent books on Pope; White, D. H., *Pope and the Context of Controversy: The Manipulation of Ideas in "An Essay on Man"* (London, 1971); J. Barnard, ed., *Pope: The Critical Heritage* (London, 1973); Rogers, P., *An Introduction to Pope* (London, 1975). Erskine-Hill, H., *The Social Milieu of Alexander Pope* (New Haven, Conn., 1975); Leranbaum, M., *Alexander Pope's "Opus Magnum,"* 1729–1744 (London, 1977); Brownell, M. R., *Alexander Pope and the Arts of Georgian England* (London, 1978).

Ezra Pound
(1885–1972)

WILLIAM VAN O'CONNOR

On the afternoon of December 7, 1941, Ezra Pound, a famous American literary expatriate, left his home in Rapallo, Italy, took a train for Rome, and over the state radio read the following:

"Europe calling. Pound speaking. Ezra Pound speaking, and I think I am perhaps speaking a bit more to England than to the United States, but you folks may as well hear it. They say an Englishman's head is made of wood and the American head made of watermelon. Easier to get something into the American head but nigh impossible to make it stick there for ten minutes. Of course, I don't know what good I am doing. I mean what immediate good, but some things you folks on both sides of the wretched ocean will have to learn, war or no war, sooner or later. Now, what I had to say about the state of mind in England in 1919, I said in Cantos 14 and 15. Some of your philosophists and fancy thinkers would have called it the spiritual side of England. I undertook to say state of mind.

"I can't say my remarks were heeded. I thought I got 'em simple enough. In fact, some people complained that several of the words contained no more than four or five letters, some six. Now I hold that no Catholic has ever been or ever will be puzzled by what I said in those Cantos. I have, however, never asked for any sympathy when misunderstood. I go on, try to make my meaning clear and then clearer, and in the long run, people who listen to me, very few of 'em do, but the members of that small and select minority do know more in the long run than those who listen to say H. G. (Chubby) Wells and the liberal stooges. What I am getting at is, a friend said to me the other day that he was glad I had the politics I have got but that he didn't understand how I, as a North American United Stateser, could have it. Well, that looks simple to me. On the Confucian system, very few start right and then go on, start at the roots and move upwards. The pattern often is simple. Whereas, if you start constructing from the twig downwards, you get into a muddle. My politics seem to me simple. My idea of a state or empire is more like a hedgehog or porcupine—chunky and well-defended. I don't cotton to the idea o' my country bein' an octopus, weak in the tentacles and suffering from stomach ulcers and colic gastritis."

For this, one of a hundred broadcasts, he was paid about ten dollars.

Pound's sentences and paragraphs suggest the disordered mind of a cracker-barrel sage. They do not sound like the work of a man who had made a career out of refining and purifying the English language, improving it as a vehicle for civilized discourse, or of the poet whom T. S. Eliot had called *il miglior fabbro,* the better craftsman. In fact, the broadcasts were so incomprehensible that the Italian government once took Pound off the air, suspecting him of sending code messages to the United States.

Pound (born in 1885) entered the University of Pennsylvania in 1901, but took his degree at Hamilton College. He returned to Pennsylvania for an M.A. At Pennsylvania he was friendly with William Carlos Williams and Hilda Doolittle. He spent a year in Europe before doing a teaching stint at Wabash College, in Indiana. The young Pound was a curious combination of bohemian, scholar, and poet. He also saw himself as a very important teacher. In the early years of his career there were those who accepted Pound not merely as a poetic genius but as a writer who was revolutionizing English and American poetry. There is some justification for both of the latter claims.

There is also, however, a great deal of misunderstanding about Pound, and perhaps even misrepresentation. The fact is that in December 1945 Ezra Pound was declared insane. There can be no doubt that his rantings over the radio are mad. In this respect, they are not very different from some of the later *Cantos* and the later essays. The earliest prose—for example, the fine study of Henry James—is perceptive and cogent, and the poetry written during the same period, mostly before World War I, is often carefully wrought and subtle. But even then, in the poetry, one is never wholly certain which of the Pound voices is the real Pound.

Pound the lyricist is most frequently in view, and it is in his lyricism that he has had his greatest success. This is best exhibited, perhaps, in the early *Cantos.* It appears intermittently, sometimes in explosive flashes, in the later *Cantos,* but usually the lyricism is not sustained; in its place one finds anecdotes, cryptic and gnomic utterances, dirty jokes, obscenities of various sorts, and a harsh insistence on the importance to culture of certain political leaders and economists.

The majority of Pound's critics find the *Cantos* his most important literary contribution. Various efforts have been made to say what they are about. Perhaps the easiest way of getting at their subject matter is to say they are about Pound's reactions to his own reading, of Homer, Ovid, or Remy de Gourmont, of various economists and political leaders, and Pound's own literary recollections, usually memories of London or Paris. As the years went by Pound became less interested in literature than in economics, although he continued to express literary interests in the *Cantos,* and his interest in translating from Greek and Latin remained fairly constant.

After leaving London, in 1920, Pound became less and less a discoverer of true talents, and more and more the angry and, as he saw it, rejected prophet. Occasional successes in his poems and translations are reminiscent of the early genius and promise of Pound, but for the most part Pound's literary career was all downhill.

The young Pound had long wanted to meet William Butler Yeats, whom he believed to be the greatest poet of the previous one hundred years. In 1908, during his second trip abroad, they did meet. In London, Pound set up a lecture course at the Regent Street Polytechnic, and here during the winter of 1908–09, he met Dorothy Shakespear and her mother, Olivia Shakespear, friend of many literary men and in particular of Yeats. Pound and Yeats were to see a great deal of each other, drawn together by common interests and perhaps later by Pound's marriage to Dorothy Shakespear and Yeats's marriage to the daughter of Mrs. Shakespear's sister-in-law.

Personoe of Ezra Pound was published in 1909, and at least one reviewer found in it echoes of Yeats. The same year, Pound was advising Williams to read Yeats's essays, and Yeats was writing to his friend Lady Gregory that Pound's poetry is "definitely music, with strong marked time and yet it is effective speech." Sometimes their egos contended, as on the evening, according to fellow poet Ernest Rhys, a group went to the Old Cheshire Cheese, where Yeats held forth at length on the ways of bringing music and poetry together. Pound sought attention by eating two red tulips. When Yeats finished his monologue, Pound recited "Ballad of the Goodly Fere."

Pound was soon recognized as a literary figure of some eminence. In 1909 he became friendly with Ford Madox Hueffer (later Ford Madox Ford) and at one of the latter's parties met the young D. H. Lawrence. In 1910 he returned to the United States. After several months spent with his parents, Pound lived for a short time in New York. He saw quite a bit of Yeats's father, John Butler Yeats, who was living and painting in New York, and Dr. Williams. He also strengthened his position as literary foreign correspondent, and when he returned to London he was busily officious, writing advice to Harriet Monroe, editor of *Poetry,* and pontificating in literary groups. Pound's *Ripostes* was published in 1912. The widow of Ernest Fenollosa, having seen Pound's work in *Poetry,* brought him her husband's manuscripts. Fenollosa, a Bostonian, was the first Westerner to open up classical Japanese drama. Pound spent several years working on the plays. *Certain Noble Plays* of Japan was published, in 1916, by the Cuala Press, run by Yeats's sister, and Yeats wrote the introduction.

Reminiscences of the period, including those by Douglas Goldring, Richard Aldington, J. G. Fletcher, Conrad Aiken, Ernest Rhys, Wyndham Lewis, Ford Madox Ford, and many others, have amply testified to Pound's literary activities in London in the years before World War I.

William Carlos Williams, who visited London in 1910, recalled that Pound "lived the poet as few of us had the nerve to live that exalted role in our time." Having little money, he wore a fur-lined overcoat indoors and out during cold weather, and a broad-brimmed hat. Williams observed that Pound kept a candle lit before the picture of Dorothy Shakespear on his dresser. Pound as a dandified bohemian was never offstage.

In May 1911 Pound wrote his father: "Yeats I like very much. I've seen him a great deal, almost daily. . . . He is, as I have said, a very great man, and he improves on acquaintance." In London, Yeats lived at Woburn Place, off the Euston Road. Yeats believed his reputation was declining; he had digestive trouble and difficulties with his eyes. Pound attended to the older poet's needs, reading to him and instructing him in ways of being more "definite and concrete" in his poetry. Pound sometimes organized dinners for literary people, then took them to Woburn Place, where Yeats held forth.

In 1912, Pound altered, without permission, some poems Yeats had given him to send to *Poetry.* Yeats was infuriated, but then forgave the bumptious and arrogant young Pound. Pound had set out to make Yeats more modern. During the winters of 1913–14, 1914–15, and 1915–16 he acted as "Uncle William's secretary" at a small house, Stone Cottage, in Sussex. Pound wrote his mother that he regarded the job "as a duty to posterity." When Pound married, he brought his wife to live at Stone Cottage. Yeats enjoyed hearing the young couple discuss modern critical doctrines. He was not enthusiastic about *des imagistes* with whom Pound was closely associated, but admitted their "satiric intensity." In 1916 Yeats handed over his father's letters for Pound to edit for the Cuala Press, saying he represented "the most aggressive contemporary school of the young."

Pound's revisions of Yeats's poetry were in the direction of conciseness and clarity. A revision from the later years perhaps illustrates the nature of the changes. This is from a draft of "From the Antigone":

Overcome, O bitter sweetness,
The rich man and his affairs,
The fat flocks and the field's fatness,
Mariners, wild harvesters;
Overcome Gods upon Parnassus;
Overcome the Empyrean; hurl
Heaven and Earth out of their places—
Inhabitant of the soft cheek of a girl
And into the same calamity
That brother and brother, friend and friend,
Family and family,
City and city may contend
By that great glory driven wild—
Pray I will and sing I must
And yet I weep—Oedipus' child
Descends into the loveless dust.

Pound made the eighth line follow the first, substituted "That in" for "And into" in the ninth line, and dropped "that" from the tenth line. Thus the poem was made to read:

Overcome—O bitter sweetness,
Inhabitant of the soft cheek of a girl—
The fat flocks and the field's fatness . . .
hurl
Heaven and Earth out of their places,
That in the same calamity
Brother and brother, friend and friend,
Family and family,
City and city many contend . . .

Without question, Pound's changes greatly improve the poem.

On one occasion, in the winter of 1914, Pound organized a small group of poets to honor Wilfrid Scawen Blunt, then seventy-four. The poets were Sturge Moore, Victor Plarr, Frederic Manning, F. S. Flint, Richard Aldington, and Yeats. A dinner was held at Blunt's estate. Pound presented Blunt a marble box carved by Gaudier-Brzeska, containing poems by all the poets. Pound also read an address honoring Blunt. The latter replied; then Yeats talked about the state of poetry, saying those who came to honor Blunt represented different schools. "To Sturge Moore, for instance, the world is impersonal. . . . Pound has a desire personally to insult the world. He has a volume of manuscript at present in which his insults to the world are so deadly that it is a rather complicated publishing problem." Writing Canto LXXXI, years later, Pound recalled the occasion, saying it was not vanity to have taken the pains to honor Blunt—

To have gathered from the air a live tradition
or from a fine old eye the unconquered flame.

One may say the same for Pound's relationship with Yeats. Pound took from the air a live tradition. And Yeats sloughed off more and more of the 1890's. Perhaps it was Pound's work on the Japanese Noh plays, as much as anything, that helped Yeats discover a new direction, at least gave him a new kind of symbolic action. His *The Hawk's Well,* founded on the Noh, was performed at Lady Cunard's house in Cavendish Square, April 2, 1916. Seeing the play changed Eliot's view of Yeats: "Yeats was well-known, of course; but to me, at least, Yeats did not appear, until after 1917 [he should say, 1916], to be anything but a minor survivor of the 90's. After that date, I saw him very differently. I remember clearly my impression of the first performance of *The Hawk's Well,* in a London drawing room, with a celebrated Japanese-dancer in the role of the hawk, to which Pound took me. And thereafter one saw Yeats rather as a more eminent contemporary than an elder from whom one could learn."

Conrad Aiken had introduced Eliot to Pound in 1915. Eliot was unable to find an editor willing to accept any of his poems. Pound admired Eliot's work, and sent "Prufrock" to *Poetry.* It caused at least a mild sensation, helped to get the modernist movement under way, and launched Eliot's career. Pound edited *Catholic Anthology* (1915) for the purpose, he said, of getting sixteen pages of Eliot into print at once. Also through Pound's efforts Eliot's first volume of poems was published in 1917 by the Egoist Press.

Eliot remembers Pound's quarters at 5 Holland Place, "a small dark flat in Kensington." Because of his restless energy and fidgety manner, Pound struck Eliot as ready for some new move or involvement. "In America, he would no doubt have seemed on the point of going abroad; in London, he always seemed on the point of crossing the Channel."

Pound's attitude toward the United States and, by implication, his hopes and ambitions for himself can be seen in *Patria Mia,* written in 1912 but unpublished until 1950. A publisher in Chicago, to whom it had been sent, lost the manuscript, and it was recovered, more than a generation later, when the firm moved to new quarters. Between 1913 and 1950 Pound had lived in Paris and Rapallo, witnessed two wars, published innumerable articles and books, been indicted for treason and imprisoned in an institution for the insane for several years. *Patria Mia* sheds light on Pound's career in the years following its composition. It is not as incoherent as his later books and pamphlets on politics and economics, but it rambles and is certainly not the tightly organized argument Pound believed he was writing. It also suggests the disappointment he would suffer.

Pound, in *Patria Mia,* is giving advice to America. He says, for example, what changes should be made in American colleges and graduate schools, and how magazine editorial policies should be altered. The underlying theme of each of his suggestions is that a genuine poet—and he would not have had to go far to find one—should be hired to stimulate academic life or give the right sort of advice to editors.

Pound's essential criticism of America repeats what Henry James said in *The American Scene* (1907), that Americans were obsessed by money and material acquisitions. Pound wrote: "It is not strange, for every man, or practically every man, with enough mental energy to make him interesting to be engaged in either business or politics. And our politics are by now no more than a branch of business." A detailed comparison of *Patria Mia* and *The American Scene* might prove useful. Probably it would show that James's perceptiveness as well as his capacity for coherently ordering his impressions and arguments greatly transcended Pound's.

Curiously, Pound's affection for America comes through strongly. After his visit, James had to return to Rye in England to compose himself. Something in Pound responds to the vigor and rawness of America. One finds him, for example, saying New York City is probably the most beautiful city in the world:

"And New York is the most beautiful city in the world?

"It is not far from it. No urban nights are like the nights there. I have looked down across the city from high windows. It is then that the great buildings lose reality and take on their magical powers. They are immaterial; that is to say one sees but the lighted windows.

"Squares after squares of flame, set and cut into the aether. Here is our poetry, for we have pulled down the stars to our will.

"As for the harbour, and the city from the harbour. A huge Irishman stood beside me the last time I went back there and he tried vainly to express himself by repeating:—

"'It uccedes Lundun.'

"'It uccedes Lundun.'

"I have seen Cadiz from the water. The thin, white lotus beyond a dazzle of blue. I know somewhat of cities. The Irishman thought of size alone. I thought of the beauty, and beside it Venice seems like a tawdry scene in a playhouse. New York is out of doors.

"And as for Venice; when Mr. Marinetti and his friends [a "modernist" group] shall have succeeded in destroying that ancient city, we will rebuild Venice on the Jersey mud flats and use the same for a tea-shop."

Pound has great hopes for America. The millionaires and industrialists will be obliged to subsidize the arts, just as wealthy merchants and princes had during the Renaissance. He believes they will do this. Pound also says that when an American investigating "in any art or *metier* has learned what is the best, he will never after be content with the second-rate. It is by this trait that we are a young nation and a strong one. An old nation weighs the cost of the best, and asks if the best is worth while."

Pound tries to isolate American qualities. He cites "a certain generosity, a certain carelessness, or looseness," "a hatred of the sordid," a "desire for largeness," and "a willingness to stand exposed." He feels these qualities in Whitman—

Camerado, this is no book,
Who touches this touches a man.

Pound dismisses Whitman because he is not a craftsman, not an artist, but at the same time makes him an American symbol: "Whitman established the national *timbre.* One may not need him at home. It is in the air, this tonic of his. But if one is abroad; if one is ever likely to forget one's birth-right, to lose faith, being surrounded by disparagers, one can find, in Whitman, the reassurance. Whitman goes bail for the nation."

Pound deplores the genteel tradition, although he does not refer to it as such. He deplores the practice of editors of the *Atlantic* and other magazines (he cites Howells by name) of running imitations from the Greek Anthology, regular in meters and optimistic in attitude. They do not ask, he says, whether a poem is the work of a serious artist, whether the form is in accordance with the subject and the author's intention, or whether the idiom is the inevitable expression of a generation's collective view. At one point he refers to Coleridge's doctrine of organic form.

America can, he adds, produce genuine art. He says James was a true novelist, in the school of Flaubert and Turgenev, and a diagnostician "of all that is fine in American life." His second example is the painter Whistler, who "proved once and for all . . . that being born an American does not eternally damn a man or prevent him from the ultimate and highest achievement in the arts."

Considering Pound's long years in Europe, and his later attacks on American society and culture, *Patria Mia* is a strange book. In one place Pound wrote: "If a man's work require him to live in exile, let him suffer, or enjoy, his exile gladly. But it would be about as easy for an American to become a Chinaman or a Hindoo as for him to acquire an Englishness, or a Frenchness, or a European-ness that is more than half a skin deep."

Eliot observed Pound's passion to teach, saying he was reminded of Irving Babbitt, who also had a passion for giving people the right doctrines to believe. Eliot adds that the two men might have appeared even more alike if Pound had stayed at home and become a professor. And since he wrote this in 1946, Eliot might be implying that if Pound had been connected with an American university his mental health might have been better and he would not have managed to get into so much trouble.

Pound, however, had an enormous talent for getting into trouble. Wyndham Lewis' theory about Pound and England is fairly simple, and may well be true. English literary life, he said, was filled with well-educated amateurs. They resisted Pound's "fierce quest for perfection," and besides they disliked Americans. By 1918 Pound had grown into a "prickly, aloof, rebel mandarin." Pound, he says, "knew his England very well," but refused to "come to terms with it." He did what he had to do—he moved across the Channel to Paris.

But first a look at some of Pound's many concerns during his English period.

Between 1908 and 1920, Pound edited anthologies and contributed to them translations from various languages, and wrote his own poetry. During this period, which probably was the high point of his career as a poet and of his influence on other poets, he published at least fourteen volumes of poetry. What sort of poet was he in those years? As usual in discussing Pound, there can be no simple answer. Wyndham Lewis tries to say why: "Ezra Pound, I feel, is probably a poet of a higher and rarer order than it is easy at all times to realise, because of much irrelevant dust picked up by his personality as it rushes, strides, or charges across the temporal scene." Also, the poetry is very uneven, and Pound writes in different voices.

Pound could be a sort of Sinclair Lewis, blasting the amenities of the genteel tradition. In "L'Homme Moyen Sensuel," for example, he wrote:

> Still I'd respect you more if you could bury
> Mabie, and Lyman Abbot and George
> Woodberry,
> For minds so wholly founded upon
> quotations
> Are not the best of pulse for infant nations.
> . . .

While he was in England, he would take similar swipes at anyone or any expression that threatened his notions of perfection in verse or any of various critical theories. In these years Pound's blasts sometimes had verve and resonance; in later years they would often be harsh and vituperative.

R. P. Blackmur has made a good point about Pound as poet. He compares "Hugh Selwyn Mauberley" with "Homage to Sextus Propertius." The former—a series of related poems about a figure much like Pound himself who is critical of his milieu and is offering advice on how poetry should be written—he finds clever, the work of an excellent craftsman. The things the poem "says" are not very original or they are the usual complaints of the exiled poet, looking out from his *tour d'ivoire.* Oddly, it is as "translator" that Pound is original. Blackmur points out that Pound does not translate Propertius; he presents an English equivalent. For example, when Propertius writes, "Let verse run smoothly, polished with fine pumice," Pound writes, "We have to keep our erasers in order." Propertius writes, "Narrow is the path that leads to the Muses"; Pound writes, "And there is no highroad to the Muses."

Pound is not especially imaginative in creating the substance of his own poems. His gift is verbal, and he is at his best when using another poet's substance for his own purposes. In the *Cantos,* as we shall see, he is not quite a translator, but he does rely on the substance of earlier poems.

F. R. Leavis has emphasized Pound's wit, especially in "Hugh Selwyn Mauberley." He finds the "verse is extraordinarily subtle," says that "critical activity accompanies feeling," and finds the poem "serious and light at the same time, sardonic and poignant, flippant and intense;" "Mauberley," he concludes, is a "great poem." John Espey in *Ezra Pound's Mauberley* has studied the poem brilliantly and with a detailed attention, especially to sources, probably never before given a poem. One's response to this sort of exegesis could be, *Now, really, ought not a poem so obviously witty, poised, critical, etc., give up its secrets more easily?* Perhaps the answer would be that the odd bits of arcana in Pound's mind are of such a nature that one must studiously search them out before being able to respond fully to his wit, grace, and critical poise. In other words, one has to decide whether the finished poem justifies a special course of study in preparation for reading it.

There is, as indicated earlier, yet another side to Pound's poetry—its lyricism. This will probably prove to be his greatest strength. In *The Translations of Ezra Pound* there are about seventy pages of poems translated from Provençal and Italian poets. All of these translations are lyrics.

During the years when Pound was leading the modernist revolt he was also writing poems from older literary conventions. A few lines from "'Blandula, Tenulla, Vagula'" will serve as an example:

> What has thou, O my soul, with paradise?
> Will we not rather, when our freedom's
>   won,
> Get us to some clear place wherein the sun
> Lets drift in on us through the olive leaves

This has the lyric force, though not the meditative quality and natural colors, of Wallace Stevens' "Sunday Morning," one of the great poems of our age, and a sustained performance probably beyond Pound at any stage of his career.

Another characteristic early lyric is "Erat Hora." It exhibits Pound's preoccupation with light as a symbol of love, beauty, and mutability.

>   Nay, whatever comes
> One hour was sunlit and the most high gods
> May not make boast of any better thing
> Than to have watched that hour as it
>   passed.

Pound is commonly seen as one who explained, justified, and rationalized the modernist idiom in poetry. All this is true. He has also written in that idiom. But at his best, as in occasional passages in the *Cantos,* he is a lyricist in the company of Herrick, Waller, or Ben Jonson, though certainly of a lesser order. His "translations" from Chinese poetry have a similar lyric quality. "The River Merchant's Wife: A Letter," written in a subdued tone, is as beautiful as any poem in the Pound canon.

In literary histories, however, Pound is usually treated as an Imagist or Vorticist. He was involved with both Imagism and Vorticism, but the nature of his involvement is a somewhat complicated story. In 1909, Pound had been introduced to a group led by T. E. Hulme that met regularly in a Soho restaurant to talk about poetry. He read "Sestina Altaforte" in tones that brought all eyes in the room to astonished attention. It was this group that began the Imagist movement, but within a year it broke up. There was a second group, in 1910, which also lasted about a year.

T. E. Hulme, a Cambridge man, a poet of sorts and a philosopher, was the dominating figure. He was a hard-living man, given to violence. He was killed later in the war. Hulme was skeptical, but willing to analyze as well as scoff. At the Soho meetings, on Thursdays. over spaghetti and wine, Hulme expounded his ideas. Poetry, he said, was lost in romantic smoothness, vagueness, fatuousness, and general insipidity. He wanted a period of dry, hard verse. Poetry needed a new convention. Man, he also said, was a limited creature. One need not descend a deep well to plumb his depths; a bucket would do!

In *Ripostes* Pound printed five of Hulme's poems. "In publishing his *Complete Poetical Works* at thirty," Pound wrote, "Mr. Hulme has set an enviable example to many of his contemporaries who have had less to say. They are reprinted here for good fellowship; for good custom, a custom out of Tuscany and of Provence; and thirdly, for convenience, seeing their smallness of bulk; and for good memory, seeing that they recall certain evenings and meetings of two years gone, dull enough at the time, but rather pleasant to look back upon."

F. S. Flint and others have said that Pound did not establish the Imagist movement—he promoted it. Flint said the Hulme group assumed the need for experiment and studied Japanese, Hebrew, and French Symbolists, always giving close attention to imagery. Pound, according to Flint, was studying troubadour poetry and the discussions interested him only when he could relate them to troubadour poetry. In one of his essays Pound wrote: "I think the artist should master all known forms and systems of metric, and I have with some persistence set about doing this, searching particularly into those periods wherein the systems came to birth or attained their maturity." It is true that Pound was studying troubadour poetry but he was also studying music, art (he especially promoted the sculptor Gaudier-Brzeska), the relationship of prose to poetry, and Oriental drama and poetry, among other things.

Rhythms in music and poetry were a fairly constant preoccupation with Pound. Rhythm, he said, determines pitch and melody; pitch depends on the frequency with which sounds strike the ear; variations in pitch control melody. In poetry, he continued, the frequency of vowel or consonant sounds produces a pitch; a changed frequency makes for higher or lower sound, and variation produces the melody of a line. Pound wrote articles and talked volubly about this and related observations, after he had met Arnold Dolmetsch and read his book, *The Interpretation of Music of the XVIIth and XVIIIth Centuries.* In one article he quotes from one of Dolmetsch's eighteenth-century sources, François Couperin, *L'Art de toucher le Clavecin* (1717): "I find that we confuse Time, or Measure, with what is called Cadence or Movement. Measure defines the quantity and equality of the beats; Cadence is properly the spirit, the soul that must be added." There seems to be nothing revolutionary in this, but Pound uses it to whip the vers libre movement. "It is too late to prevent *vers libre.* But, conceivably, one might improve it, and one might stop at least a little of the idiotic and narrow discussion based on an ignorance of music." He sees Couperin as justification for saying true vers libre ("You must bind perfectly what you play") was in the old music. Pound also quoted Eliot: "*Vers libre* does not exist. . . . There is no escape from metre; there is oniy mastery of it."

Another considerable influence on Pound was Ford Madox Ford (he was Ford Madox Hueffer until World War I), who had been a close associate of Conrad and James. In 1935, Pound wrote Dr. Williams: "I did Fordie as much justice as anyone (or almost anyone) did—but still not enough! Fordie knew more about writing than any of 'them' or 'us.'"

Ford belonged to what he called the Impressionist tradition. A scene is described and reacted to—it exists in the descriptions and in the vividness of the reaction. But the reaction is aesthetic, not didactic. He avoided a poetic stance, or being "literary." He used the "language of my own day," frequently a kind of prose, "to register my own times in terms of my own times." Especially, he said, poetry should be a response to life, not to books. (It is odd that Pound should single this out, since his own response is largely to books.)

Pound contributed a fairly long article to *Poetry,* entitled "Mr. Hueffer and the Prose Tradition," during the same year he issued *Des Imagistes,* a collection of poems by the Imagists. Pound refers to Stendhal's remark that prose was a higher form than poetry, and says Mr. Hueffer is a distinguished prose writer. He finds Hueffer a fine poet, saying "On Heaven" is "the best poem yet written in the 'twentieth-century fashion.'" Hueffer believed "poetry should be written at least as well as prose." Pound says Hueffer's poetry is "revolutionary," because of an "insistence upon clarity and precision, upon the prose tradition." The prose influence on modern poetry has been considerable, and one might reasonably infer that Pound's comments as well as his own practice were a considerable influence on other poets.

Before 1912, Pound had little to say about images, but thereafter he had much to say. Among Pound's "discoveries" were Hilda Doolittle ("H.D.") and Richard Aldington. In talking to them about their poetry he called them *imagistes.* In *Ripostes* he connected *des imagistes* and the "group of 1909." (Later, in 1939, Pound minimized the Hulme influence, and emphasized Ford's.) In 1913, in *Poetry,* Pound published "A Few Don'ts" and defined the Image: "An 'Image' is that which presents an intellectual and emotional complex in an instant of time. I use the word 'complex' rather in the technical sense employed by the newer psychologists. . . . It is the presentation of such a 'complex' instantaneously which gives that sense of sudden liberation; that sense of freedom from time limits and space limits; that sense of sudden growth, which we experience in the presence of the greatest works of art."

Other magazines followed *Poetry* in promoting Imagism. Alfred Kreymborg had asked for contributions to his magazine, the *Glebe,* and Pound sent him poems by Aldington, H.D., Flint, Hueffer, Williams, Connell, Lowell, Upward, Cournos, and James Joyce. *Des Imagistes* received a lot of attention in the United States, but in England, published by Harold Monro, it was a bust. Amy Lowell, in London, wanted to do a new anthology of Imagist poetry. Pound insisted on being editor, but she fought him and won. Thereafter the movement became what he called "Amygism."

Besides, Pound was in a new movement and associating with painters and sculptors. It was called Vorticism. Wyndham Lewis, Gaudier-Brzeska, and Pound were the guiding spirits. *Blast,* edited by Lewis, appeared in 1914. Two of the principles governing its policy were developed from earlier Pound statements: one, the necessity for a vigorous impact ("The vortex is the point of maximum energy"), and, two, recognition of the image as "the primary pigment of poetry." A long Imagist poem is not possible because the image is a vortex "from which, through which, and into which, ideas are constantly rushing." A poem has a visual basis, and makes the intangible concrete. The doctrine seems remarkably close to the one he had stated in *Poetry.*

Pound's interest in the image also derived from his deep involvement with Fenollosa's manuscripts, on Chinese as well as Japanese literature. As "Hugh Selwyn Mauberly" suggests, Pound felt a kinship with the poets of the 1890's. He was also very taken with Whistler; in fact, the first poem Pound published in *Poetry* (October 1912) was "To Whistler, American." From Whistler he took the idea of "poetry as picture." In "Au Jardin" there are lines such as these: "she danced like a pink moth in the shrubbery" and "From amber lattices upon the cobalt night."

In his September 1914 article in the *Fortnightly Review* on Vorticism he says he wrote a haiku-like sentence:

> 'The apparition of these faces in a crowd;
> Petals on a wet, black bough.'

He quotes a well-known haiku—

> The fallen blossom flies back to its branch:
> A butterfly.

Pound recognized in studying this that a descriptive or sometimes lyrical passage was followed by a vivid image. Earl Miner, the closest student of Japanese influences on Pound, calls this the "super pository method." Pound was to employ this technique frequently; for example, in these lines from the lovely "Liu Ch'e":

> There is no sound of foot-fall, and the leaves
> Scurry into heaps and lie still,
> And she the rejoicer of the heart is beneath
> them:
>
> A wet leaf that clings to the threshold.

Other notable examples are "A Song of the Degrees," "Ts'ai Chih," "Coitus," "The Encounter," "Fish and Shadow," and "Cantus Planis." One also finds the super pository method employed in the *Cantos.* In using the Chinese written characters, or ideograms, which he does in certain *Cantos,* Pound believed his method was similar to the super pository—use of a vivid image causing many of the preceding elements to cohere. However, since few of his readers understand the ideograms it is difficult to accept Pound's insistence on using them.

Miner says that Arthur Waley's *The No Plays of Japan* is the authoritative scholarly translation; the Pound-Fenollosa version is often unscholarly and based on misunderstanding of the historical contexts. Occasional passages, he adds, are beautifully executed. Although Pound's efforts with the Noh were not generally successful, he did learn things that contributed to his theory of the image.

In a note at the end of *Suma Genji,* Pound said the Noh has "what we may call Unity of Image . . . the red maple leaves and the snow flurry in *Nishikigi,* the pines in *Takasago,* the blue-grey waves and wave pattern in *Suma Genji,* the mantle of feathers in the play of that name, *Hagoromo.*" The Noh gave Pound suggestions for organizing poems longer than the haiku, or concise imagistic poems. Frequently in the *Cantos* Pound juxtaposes legends from Greek and Japanese sources, scenes from different cultures, and various heroes or villains, all in a seemingly haphazard way. Then he employs an image, or metaphor (a term he apparently chose not to use), that discovers a theme or essence common to the hitherto disparate elements.

Thus Pound's involvement with the image is not a simple matter.

Especially through Whistler and Théophile Gautier he felt the pull of the "Art for Art's Sake" movement. Pound was an aesthete. His commitment to Imagism and Vorticism was complicated by his interest in Chinese poetry and the Japanese Noh. Pound also theorized about the relationship between music (in the British *Who's Who* he identified himself as "poet and composer") and the conversational or prose line. On one occasion he had provided his contemporaries with a little anthology of nineteenth-century French poets, Baudelaire, Verlaine, Laforgue, the Symbolists. Their influence on Eliot, however, was greater than it was on Pound. The city, the automobile, and social life did not deeply engage him. There is a sense, then, in which Pound is not a modernist poet. Or perhaps one should say he was a modernist only briefly. Pound has a pantheon of writers who helped sustain his vision of the world as it ought to be, and more and more he turned to them.

During the English period, Pound studied Propertius, Arnaut Daniel, Dante, Cavalcanti, Stendhal, Flaubert, Gautier, James, and many others. The writers who did not interest Pound reveal strange deficiencies in his views of human conduct and in his own sensibilities. Joseph Conrad does not loom very large, and "them Rooshans," as he called them, go almost unmentioned. Tolstoi, Dostoevski, and Chekhov were uninteresting to Pound.

Three writers, Rémy de Gourmont, Ovid, especially in Golding's translation of the *Metamorphoses,* and Robert Browning seem to have held pre-eminence in his pantheon. One might guess that Gourmont and Ovid, more than any other writers, satisfy Pound's dream of the world, and help him create his imaginary Great Good Place. Browning he likes for other reasons: for his craftsmanship, and apparently for writing poetry so much like Pound's own. He especially likes Browning for having written *Sordello,* the poem that made possible the *Cantos,* in which one finds exquisitely beautiful lyric passages, vivid imagistic scenes, tags from many languages, and Pound's racist and economic theories.

Pound several times links the names of Ovid, Propertius, and Remy de Gourmont. He quotes Propertius as saying: *Ingenium nobis ipsa puella facit.* In "Rémy de Gourmont, A Distinction," he says: "Gourmont's wisdom is not wholly unlike the wisdom which those ignorant of Latin may, if the gods favor their understanding, derive from Golding's *Metamorphoses.*"

Gourmont (1858–1915) profoundly impressed Pound. In the months before Gourmont's death, Pound was in correspondence with him about contributing to an international journal. Gourmont replied that he was exhausted, sick, and probably would not be of any great help in Pound's enterprise; he also doubted that Americans were "capable of enough mental liberty to read my books." However, he was willing to let Pound help them try to "respect French individualism," and "the sense of liberty which some of us have in so great degree."

In the essay cited above, Pound says, "Gourmont prepared our era." As in most of his other essays, Pound generalizes for a page or two, sets up a thesis, points out the writer's special contributions to civilized understanding, quotes copiously, lists bibliography, then clouts the reader on the back of the head, telling him to pay closer attention.

Gourmont does not, Pound says, "grant the duality of body and soul, or at least suggests that this medieval duality is unsatisfactory." James, whom Pound contrasts with Gourmont, intellectualized passion; emotions to him "were more or less things other people had and that one didn't go into." Sex in Gourmont's works is pervasive, like a drop of dye in a clear jar of water. Sex is related to sensibilities, and therefore to "the domain of aesthetics." This belief was back of Gourmont's concern with resonance in expressing emotion; knowing that ideas have little value apart from the modality of the mind receiving them, he differentiated characters by the modes of their sensibilities.

Gourmont's thesis is that man is a sensual creature, and should not be intimidated by the Christian teachings about modesty, chastity, and so on. Voluptuousness and sensual pleasure are their own excuse for being.

Gourmont's *Physique de l'Amour,* which Pound translated, is filled with such remarks as this: "Il y aurait peut-être une certaine corrélation entre la copulation complète et profonde et le développement cérébral." A great deal of biological lore is exhibited, all of it focused on the sex habits of insects, fish, birds, and animals.

Probably Gourmont felt he was writing an amusing and mildly titillating essay on man in nature. Pound, in a postscript, is less playful, and develops a thesis that "the brain itself is, in origin and development, only a sort of great clot of genital fluid held in suspense or reserve. . . ." Pound offers no scientific information to justify his theory. He is creating a little myth. There need be no quarrel between "cerebralist and viveur," he says, "if the brain is thus conceived not as a separate and desiccated organ, but as the very fluid of life itself."

Gourmont and Pound were both interested in Provençal poetry, in late Latin poets, and in literary eroticism. John Espey says that many sections and stanzas of "Hugh Selwyn Mauberley" bear witness to Pound's reading of Gourmont. Pound's earliest pieces on Gourmont appeared in 1913. Evidences of Gourmont's influence appear, for example, in the unabashed sexuality of Canto XXXIX. Pound's admiration for Gourmont never changed. He refers admiringly to him in *Jefferson and/or Mussolini* (1935) and elsewhere. When Gourmont died, Pound wrote: "his thoughts had the property of life. They, the thoughts, were all related to life, they were immersed in the manifest universe while he thought them, they were not cut out, put on shelves and in bottles." Over the years in one form or another, Pound continued to repeat this; it is an expression of his doctrine, *make it new.*

Early and late in his career, Pound praises Ovid—"there is great wisdom in Ovid." In 1934, from Rapallo, in making up a reading list for a correspondent, he wrote: "There are a few things out of print. Golding's translation of Ovid's *Metamorphoses,* CERTAINLY . . . and being an institution of learning yr. Eng. prof. will never have heard of it; though it was good enough for Wm. Shakespear. *And* any dept. of English is a farce without it." Elsewhere he uses Golding's translation to berate Milton's Latinity, contrasting the former's natural "contemporary speech" with Milton's "vague pompous words." The quality of translations, he says, decreased as "translators ceased being interested in the subject matter of their original."

Golding's Ovid has some charm, if only because of its studied innocence and naïveté. If Golding falls short of greatness, as he does, he manages a difficult meter about as well as could be expected. For example,

> The Damsels at the sight of man quite out
> of countnance dasht,
> (Bicause they everichone were bare and
> naked to the quicke)
> Did beate their hands against their brests,
> and cast out such a shricke,
> That all the wood did ring thereof: and
> clinging to their dame
> Did all they could to hide both hir and eke
> themselves for shame

It seems unlikely that Pound was greatly influenced by Golding's language, or his ingenuous playfulness. Pound's *Metamorphoses* is more "distanced," calmer, and seen in lights and shadows. There can be no doubt that he responds at some very deep level to the *Metamorphoses.* Gilbert Murray's account of Ovid's vision is a prose equivalent to what Pound tries to catch in his poetry. "What a world it is that he has created in the *Metamorphoses*! It draws its denizens from all the boundless resources of Greek mythology, a world of live forests and mountains and rivers, in which every plant and flower has a story and nearly always a love story; where the moon is indeed not a moon but an orbè d maiden, and the Sunrise weeps because she is still young and her belovèd is old; and the stars are human souls; and the Sun sees human virgins in the depths of forests and almost swoons at their beauty and pursues them; and other virgins, who feel the same way about him, commit great sins from jealousy . . . and turn into flowers; and all the youths and maidens are indescribably beautiful and adventurous and passionate. . . . A world of wonderful children where nobody is really cross or wicked except the grown-ups; Juno, for instance . . . His criticism of life is very slight."

Robert Browning, as was observed earlier, was another of Pound's culture heroes. In his usual fashion of reordering literary history in a sentence or two, Pound has said the decline of England began on the day Landor packed his bags and moved to Tuscany. Thereafter Shelley, Keats, Byron, Beddoes lived on the Continent. Later there was "the edifying spectacle of Browning in Italy and Tennyson in Buckingham Palace." Pound admired in Browning many of the virtues he saw in Crabbe—realism, precision, terseness, the charged line, objectivity. And perhaps Pound's affection for Italy is involved with Browning's love for that country. On a number of occasions Pound had advised perplexed readers of the *Cantos* to take a good look at *Sordello.*

A passage in Book Two of *Sordello* seems to have suggested the method of the *Cantos.*

The troubador Sordello is musing on the delights of reading:

> —had he ever turned, in fact
> From Elys, to sing Elys?—from each fit
> Of rapture to contrive a song of it?
> True, this snatch or the other seemed to
> wind
> Into a treasure, helped himself to find
> A beauty in himself; for, see, he soared
> By means of that mere snatch, to many a
> hoard
> Of fancies; as some falling cone bears soft
> The eye along the fir-tree spire, aloft
> To a dove's nest. . . .
> Have they [men] fancies—
> slow, perchance,
> Not at their beck, which indistinctly glance
> Until, by song, each floating part be linked
> To each, and all grow palpable, distinct!
> He pondered this.

Pound found in *Sordello* a method that would allow him to muse upon and re-create his readings.

The first three Cantos appeared in *Poetry,* June, July, August 1917. In the June 1917 Canto i, subsequently dropped, Pound addresses Browning affectionately as "Bob Browning," telling him *Sordello* is an "art-form" and adding the modern world needs such a "ragbag" in which to toss "all its thought." It does not matter, he says, that the anachronisms in *Sordello* are egregious—a poem should create a sense of life. He proposes to give up the "intaglio method," presumably the images associated with *des imagistes* and haiku, and enter a timeless fictional world—"you mix your eras," peopled by soldiers with robes "half Roman, half like the Knave of Hearts." Pound also proposes to use the "meditative, semidramatic, semi-epic" form of *Sordello.*

In *Sordello,* Browning had one man, Sordello, against whom to focus his "catch," and the Vitorians had a set of beliefs. In Pound's "beastly and cantankerous age" doctrine is elusive and contradictory. Who ought to be Pound's Sordello? He cannot be sure. Pound evokes earlier worlds—Tuscany, China, Egypt He does not believe that re-created history is true—"take it all for lies." Nor are his own imaginings "reality." There is a plurality of worlds. What the artist creates are "worlds enough." Artists discover new ways of seeing as in Pound's own time. There are, for example, the paintings of Lewis and Picasso, reflecting "the new world about us." Pound later said there are three planes in the *Cantos,* the "permanent" represented by characteristics of the gods; the "recurrent" archetypal fictional characters like Odysseus, or real, like Sir Philip Sidney; and "casual," the trivial, accidental events that form no pattern or design.

Canto I ends with "So that:" and Canto II begins with "Hang it all, there can be but one *Sordello*!" Browning takes his place with the many authors and texts Pound will cite.

Pound and Browning continue the descent into Hades introduced by Odysseus in Canto I. In *The Spirit of Romance,* Pound wrote, "Ovid, before Browning, raises the dead and dissects their mental processes; he walks with the people of myth." In *Make It New* Pound described Canto I as a close translation from the *Odyssey.*

Pound has also pointed out that the language of Canto II is, like the language of *Sordello,* highly charged. "The artist seeks out the luminous detail and presents it. He does not comment."

In the new Canto I, Odysseus symbolizes the male, active, and intelligent, and Aphrodite the female, stimulant to creative action. Canto II develops these themes. Sordello is looked upon in different ways, in Browning's mind, in Pound's, and in the finished work *Sordello.* The focus shifts to So-shu, a demiurge in Chinese mythology. The scene fades into yet another, and a seal appears: the seal is feminine, it suggests the human; and, strangely, its eyes are the eyes of Picasso. Patterns recur. Eleanor of Aquitaine is like Helen of Troy, who is like Aphrodite, who is like Atalanta. The waves cover a new scene—and other metamorphoses take place. These changes come about as Pound thinks of a passage in the *Iliad* or *Odyssey,* or a Noh drama.

A new image lights up, frequently emerging from the shadows of an ancient book. One character suggests another. A Greek waterscape suggests an Irish waterscape. A tree suggests Daphne. Always there is flow. New identities emerge and fade. Pound loves to work variations on the old myths. His imagination responds to them, as it almost never does—except in anger or contempt—to the civilization around him.

In Canto III, Pound remembers his stay in Venice in 1908, in his self-imposed exile. It was there he paid to have A Lume Spento printed. Pound recalls (this first appeared in the June 1917 Canto I) his own visit to Venice, eyeing young Italian girls, as Browning had, and eating hard rolls for breakfast—

So, for what it's worth,
I have my background;
  And you had your background . . .

The Fourth Canto was published in forty copies on Japanese vellum by John Rodker in October 1919. In America it appeared in the *Dial* for June 1920. Canto IV is interesting if oniy because the literary allusions show how profoundly Pound's culture is the culture of books. In this Canto there is an illusion to Pindar, another to Catullus, yet another to the swallow Itys, and this suggests a similar tale by one of the troubadors, and so on.

Culture, for Pound, is the Mediterranean basin, especially in antiquity, with brief visits to the Renaissance or times long ago in Japan or China. The scenes evoked are like the winter dreams of a literary man with special interests in the classics, Provençal poetry, the Japanese Noh, and Chinese poetry. And the metamorphoses provide a constant discovery of the vitality in the old tales and a temporary stasis in a world of flux. They also provide escape from the dismal realities of the twentieth century.

In *It Was the Nightingale,* Ford Madox Ford said Pound's move to Paris was caused by Pound's challenging Lascelles Abercrombie to a duel. Abercrombie had written a piece for the *Times Literary Supplement,* favoring Milton. Prior to this he had enraged Pound by successfully running a magazine, *New Numbers,* in which he printed Georgian poetry. After his challenge, according to Ford, Pound was visited by the police. Another version of the story is that Abercrombie suggested they bombard each other with unsold copies of their books. In either case, Pound's ire would not be easily soothed. Shortly thereafter Pound took up residence in Paris.

Paris was soon to have a great deal of literary excitement, because of the presence of Joyce, Gertrude Stein, Ford, Hemingway, F. Scott Fitzgerald, Proust, Aragon, Cocteau, and many others. Pound was involved with some of these writers. He also continued to contribute to various magazines, and did a Paris letter for the *Dial.* And in Paris he could more easily live his role as aesthete. Margaret Anderson, for whose *Little Review* Pound was foreign editor, recalls his wearing a velvet beret, a flowing tie, and an emerald on his earlobe! He seemed more at home in Paris, but he did not give up all the relationships he had established in London. For example, his relationship with Joyce entered a new and, for Joyce, a very significant phase.

Pound's "discovery" of Joyce had come about as a result of his asking Joyce—who was struggling against poverty and suffering the refusal of printers to handle *Dubliners*—for permission to reprint "I hear an army charging upon the land" in *Des Imagistes.* As advisory editor for the *Egoist,* edited by Dora Marsden and later Harriet Weaver, he had asked for work in prose. Joyce sent the opening of *A Portrait of the Artist as a Young Man.* It was accepted, and, following a generous advance to Joyce, the novel ran serially in the *Egoist.* At the end of 1913, thanks to Pound, Joyce found himself in the very middle of a literary revolution. While the *Portrait* was still being serialized, *Dubliners* finally appeared, and Pound reviewed it, saying Joyce had earned a place for himself "among English contemporary prose writers."

From Paris, Pound advised Joyce to join him. Joyce wrote a letter (July 1, 1920) saying, "My address in Paris will be chez M. Ezra

Pound, Hotel de l'Elysée, rue de Beaune 9." Temperamentally the two men were unlike and did not make easy companions—but they remained friendly. Joyce never forgot Pound's generosity. And when he was broadcasting over Rome radio during the war Pound devoted one talk to celebrating Joyce's career.

In Paris, Pound also continued his relationship with Eliot. On one, now famous, occasion, Pound blue-penciled the poem that would be published as *The Waste Land.* "It was in 1922 [1921]," Eliot has written, "that I placed before him in Paris the manuscript of a sprawling chaotic poem called The Waste Land, which left his hands about half its size, in the form in which it appears in print." With the publication of the earlier version in the facsimile edition readers can now judge the rightness or wrongness of his admiration for Pound's performance as editor.

In Paris, Pound also continued his relationship with Ford, who later recalled Pound's sponsoring the music of George Antheil, and taking up sculpture. "Mr. Pound fiercely struck blocks of granite with sledge hammers." Pound told Ford he had little time for literature, but he did help Ford to get John Quinn, a New York philanthropist, to subsidize the shortlived *Transatlantic Review* and also helped get contributions. Pound introduced Ford to Ernest Hemingway, who had submitted his stories to Pound's blue pencil. Pound was ballyhooing him as a magnificent new writer. As one might expect, Gertrude Stein, Hemingway's other mentor, and Pound were not ardent admirers of each other. Miss Stein called him a "village explainer" and he called her "a charming old fraud."

In 1923, Pound and Hemingway toured Italian battlefields. Hemingway explained the strategy of a Renaissance soldier of fortune, Sigismondo de Malatesta. The trip was the beginning of Pound's decision to live in Italy, and in Malatesta he found a new hero for glorification in the *Cantos.*

Sigismondo de Malatesta, warrior, schemer, passionate male, and lover of beauty, delighted Pound. Malatesta must have been full of guile and a violent man even to survive in the political struggles in which he contested, with Pius II and other feudal monarchs, but in honoring his powers as an opportunist Pound jauntily shapes fifteenth-century Italian history to suit his own purposes. His use of letters and documents gives his "history" (in Cantos VIII, IX, and X) an air of being a disinterested glimpse of a thoroughly great man, Sigismondo Malatesta.

Clearly what endeared Malatesta to Pound was that he left behind him, although unfinished, a beautiful building, the Tempio. Sword in hand, standing neck deep in a marsh, or despoiling a city, Malatesta carried a dream in his head.

Considering his earlier productivity, Pound published little during his Paris period. He had, however, discovered Malatesta. And a look at *A Draft of XVI Cantos,* published soon after he moved to Rapallo, shows that he had discovered another cultural hero, Kung, or in the Latinized version of his name, Confucius. (Pound had acquainted himself with James Legge's twenty-eight volumes of *Chinese Classics,* 1861–86.) Mostly he refers to *The Analects* and *The Unwobbling Pivot* and the *Great Digest,* later translated by him under these titles.

Confucius had gained a reputation as a philosopher prime minister of Lu, but he resigned in 495 B.C. when the monarch gave himself to pleasure, and he visited other states as a teacher. Confucius, in Pound's words, said such things as "If a man does not discipline himself he cannot bring discipline into his home," and "One courteous family can lift a whole state into courtesy."

A difficulty in reading Canto XIII and others like it is that one cannot understand the allusions—for example, the elliptical conversation Confucius has in one village or another—unless one knows the context from which Pound took them.

Occasionally there are lovely passages in the *Cantos,* but increasingly Ezra Pound becomes less and less the poet bent on creating new images and identities, and more and more the insistent teacher.

After some months of indecision, Pound and his wife settled in Rapallo, a seaside village on the Italian Riviera. It has been described by Yeats, who took up residence there in 1929: "Mountains that shelter the bay from all but the strongest wind, bare brown branches of low vines and of tall trees blurring their outline as though with a soft mist; houses mirrored in an almost motionless sea . . . The little town described in An Ode on a Grecian Urn." There Pound lived for twenty years, until his arrest by American troops, following his indictment for treason. Occasionally he visited Paris and London, but mostly he remained in Rapallo. The dramatist Gerhart Hauptmann lived there in the summer, and visitors included Aldington, Ford, Antheil, Max Beerbohm, and others. Pound occasionally had disciples living nearby. Knowing him to be a famous poet, the townspeople treated him deferentially.

One might expect the quiet town and the almost motionless sea to have helped Pound write more *Cantos* in which Ovidian nymphs were pursued by ardent young swains, and there are some such *Cantos.* But there are many more in which he quarrels with America, its culture and universities, but especially its economy and banking system.

Pound believed that a good government was possible only when the state controlled money. This was best done, for the good of all of the people, by a benevolent dictator, like Mussolini. Other ideal "dictators," as seen by Pound, are Jefferson, Adams, Jackson, Confucius, a Chinese ruler, Quang-Ngau-chè, and others. Another wise ruler, according to Pound, was Martin Van Buren, and he implies there has been a conspiracy, at least of stupidity, to keep his *Autobiography* untaught in American universities.

Pound's objections to American capitalism derive from his belief that a man should be rewarded according to the worth of his work. Under our "leisure class" society, one makes money by manipulating money, not by producing worthwhile products or beautiful artifacts. Thus the many references in the *Cantos* to usury.

In Rapallo, Pound appears to have read certain works in an obsessive way; for example, the works of John Adams. About eighty pages of the *Cantos* deal with Adams. As he had in the Malatesta *Cantos,* Pound quotes endlessly, transcribing phrases. Malatesta, however, was partially transformed and lives as a fictional creation. Adams is lost in the transcription from his own writings.

At one period, Pound seemed ready to give up literature. Salvation was to be found only in economics, in the writings of Douglas, Gesell, and Orage. In a letter written in 1934, Yeats reported that Pound "would talk nothing but politics. . . . He urged me to read the works of Captain Douglas who alone knew what caused our suffering. He took away my manuscript ["King of the Clock Tower"] and went away denouncing Dublin as 'a reactionary hole' because I had said that I was reading Shakespeare, would go on to Chaucer, and found all that I wanted of modern life in 'detection and the wild West.' Next day his judgment came and that in a single word 'Putrid.'"

In addition to his explaining the nature of economics and politics to the English-speaking world, Pound had been explaining the ABC's of reading and how to read. In the *New York Herald Tribune Books* he wrote: "The great writers need no debunking. The pap is not in them and doesn't need to be squeezed out. They do not lend themselves to imperial and sentimental exploitations. A civilization was founded on Homer, civilization not a mere bloated empire. The Macedonian domination rose and grew after the sophists. It also subsided." In such an article, Pound sometimes makes acute observations, but the sentences and paragraphs are often discrete, and the author seems distracted and unsure of the unifying idea of his discourse. There is also a disturbing immaturity and naïveté in Pound's pronouncements: "Really one DON'T need to know a language. One NEEDS, damn well needs, to know the few hundred words in the few really good poems that any language has in it." Or "It takes about 600 to make a civilization."

Pound's prose works during the late 1920's and the 1930's reveal that he repeated many things he had said earlier, and that he continued his engagement with America. His slangy wit gradually grows cruder, and his vulgarity coarser.

In 1930, the Black Sun Press of Caresse Crosby issued his *Imaginary Letters.* Some of these were written during his London period, and some of them were from later years. In one of the letters, he says he is told Russia is much like America. He infers that both are "barbarous" countries. In another, he says he hopes "to hear the last of these Russians," adding that the talk about the Russian soul bores him silly—"The Russian (large R, definite article, Artzibasheff, Bustikosseff, Slobingobski, Spititoutski and Co. Amalgamated, communatated, etc.). 'The Russian,' my dear Caroline, is nothing but the western European with his conning-tower or his top-layer . . . removed. . . . Civilized man, *any* civilized man who has a normal lining in his stomach, may become Russian for the price of a little mixed alcohol, or of, perhaps a good deal of mixed alcohol, but it is a matter of shillings, not a matter of dynamic attainment. Once, and perhaps only once, have I been drunk enough to feel like a Russian. Try it, my dearest young lady, try it. Try it and clear your mind, free your life from this obsession of Russians (if Lenin and Co. have not freed you.)"

In a letter on the language of Joyce and modern literature at its best, he says: "The author [of an article he is citing] says, and I think with reason, that wherever Joyce has made use of lice, or dung, or other disgusting unpleasantness he has done so with the intention, and with, as a considerable artist, the result of heightening some effect of beauty, or twisting tighter some intensity." He calls this Joyce's "metal finish." It is, he says, similar to his own "sterilized surgery." Shortly he adds, as an example of his own "vigour," a "fairly Baudelairian but . . . nowhere inevitable" sonnet of his, or, rather, the two stanzas he can recall:

> One night stretched out along a hebrew
>   bitch—
> Like two corpses at the undertakers—
> This carcass, sold alike to jews and quakers
> Reminded me of beauty noble and rich.

These lines are not unlike those to be found in many of the later *Cantos.* Pound is like a small boy writing dirty verses on the lavatory wall. Pound's comments indicate he knew he had not written a successful poem, but he seems not to have recognized the shocking crassness of which he was capable.

From Rapallo, Pound sent out his advice to the world, especially to his "fellow 'Muricans." One such piece of advice is called *ABC of Reading.* It was published by an American university press, Yale. "How to Study Poetry," two prefatory paragraphs, never mentions poetry—or the study of poetry. "Warning," a kind of introduction, contains seven paragraphs, each about a different subject. In Section One, Chapter One, he says our way of looking at objects should be more scientific; we should emulate the biologist who compares one specimen with another. Then he discusses Fenollosa's *Essay on the Chinese Written Character,* adding that organized university life in America and England had made it almost impossible for him to get the essay published. Next he says medieval man wasn't as victimized by terminology as we are. He then returns to Fenollosa, and presents the Chinese picture words or images for man, tree, sun, and sun in the tree's branches, meaning the East. Fenollosa, he continues, demonstrated that the Chinese "word" or "ideogram" for red "is based on something everyone KNOWS." The implication seems to be that the English word *red* is based on knowledge no one has or experience no one has had! In Section Two we are told about Laboratory Condition—that is, that experiencing art is preferable to hearing discussions of it. To make this point, Pound lists the programs played by several "serious musicians" on one occasion in Rapallo, adding that the best volume of musical criticism he has ever encountered is Boris De Schloezer's *Stravinsky.* Lastly there is "The Ideogrammic Method or the Method of Science." In these paragraphs he mentions neither ideograms nor scientific methods. He says you cannot prevent Mr. Buggins from preferring a painting by Carlo Dolci to one by Cosimo Tura, but if you have them next to each other "you can very seriously impede his setting up a false tradition. . . . Finally he says that a middle-aged man knows the *rightness* of what he knows. A young man may be right, but he doesn't know *how* right he may be.

The chapter says almost nothing, and is wildly incoherent. Certainly a writer lacking Pound's reputation, ironically a reputation as a great explicator, would not have stood a chance of having a publisher accept this book. If an academic adviser had received such a chapter as the opening of a candidate's M.A. thesis he would have been obligated to dismiss it as the gibberish it is. *ABC of Reading* reads like the comments of an ex-schoolmaster who has been bereft of his senses. One reading an occasional sentence might feel that the ex-schoolmaster was only mad north-northeast, but reading it entirely makes clear that this is the work of a deranged mind.

Another of these strange volumes was published in England as *Guide to Kulchur,* and in the United States as *Culture.* The same subjects recur. There are discussions of Confucius, Vorticism, tradition, textbooks, Provençal poets, the nature of first-rate novels, decline of the Adams family, etc., etc. Typically, "Tradition" examines several discrete subjects, none of them especially illuminating. It opens with a discussion of Frobenius, one of Pound's heroes. He quotes several tags from antiquity, refers to Confucian harmonies, Madame Tussaud's, an unnamed general, etc. Pound is telling the reader that he can understand his own culture only if he understands some other culture. *"I am not, in these slight memories, merely 'pickin' daisies.' A man does not know his own ADDRESS (in time) until he knows where his own time and milieu stand in relation to other times and conditions."* But the "slight memories" Pound recounts are mostly empty prattling. For example, he mentions a book entitled *With the Empress Dowager of China* by K. A. Carl. "This book," he says, "records a high degree of civilization." Then these sentences follow, in the same paragraph. "Fenollosa is said to have been the second European to be able to take part in a Noh performance. The whole civilization reflected in Noh is a high civilization." Individually the three sentences make a kind of sense. In sequence they make no sense. Nor do they make sense in terms of the paragraphs preceding them, or the paragraphs that follow.

It needs to be said that Pound's prose in these books, as well as in his economic and political pamphlets, is quite as disordered as the phrases and sentences in the later *Cantos.* Some critics have rationalized the fragmented passages of the *Cantos* as a new "poetic strategy." The truth would seem to be that Pound was no longer capable of the kind of coherence he had sometimes achieved as a young man.

In the *Cantos,* as the years pass, there is an increasing dependence on violence and shock, on obscenities and scatological descriptions. Worse, there is an airy indifference when Pound mentions genocide or mass suffering. F. R. Leavis, an early admirer of Pound's contributions as poet, critic, and man of letters, has said, "The spectacle of Pound's degeneration is a terrible one, and no one ought to pretend that it is anything but what it is."

Pound returned to the United States in 1939; received an honorary degree from Hamilton College; and went to Washington, where he talked with Senator Borah, Secretary of Agriculture Wallace, and others, attempting to prove to them that a change in economic policies would avert war. Back in Italy when the war began, he broadcast over Rome radio, attacking Roosevelt's policies. After Pearl Harbor, when Pound and his wife tried to leave Italy, an unidentified American official refused them permission to board a diplomatic train leaving Rome. Shortly he resumed his broadcasts. As a series they are undoubtedly the most curious efforts at propaganda ever allowed over a national radio. Pound talked about London as he had known it, E. E. Cummings, Joyce, Chinese philosophy, economics, and his own *Cantos.* No wonder the Italians suspected him of being an American agent. But the United States attorney general asked for his indictment, and when the Americans reached Genoa, in northern Italy, Pound gave himself up.

Imprisoned at Pisa in the summer of 1945, under harsh circumstances, he suffered hallucinations and a collapse. After medical care, he was treated more humanely and resumed his writing. In November he was flown to Washington. Eventually he was committed to St. Elizabeth's, a federal hospital for the insane, and remained there until the United States dropped its indictment thirteen years later, when he returned to Italy.

During this period he continued to write pamphlets, contribute *Cantos* to various magazines—and generally repeat the same opinions he had expressed in his broadcasts.

Much of the writing from this period is rant, fustion, and bombast, but there are two partial exceptions, *The Pisan Cantos,* for which he received the Bollingen Award (which fluttered literary dovecotes and caused several angry editorials), and *Women of Trachis,* a translation from Sophocles. In *The Pisan Cantos* there are occasional beautiful phrases, but there is no evidence that Pound had recovered the clarity of vision and metaphorical powers of the early *Cantos. The Pisan Cantos* are, like his radio talks, filled with discrete observations, and non sequiturs. But there is also a new dimension.

He thinks back over his life in London, France, and Rapallo, and recalls what Ford, or Yeats, or Hemingway, or whoever, had said. Pound the aesthete has disappeared and Pound the preacher appears only intermittently. There is an awareness of human anguish, of ancient folly, and of Pound's own vanity.

> If the hoar frost grip thy tent
> Thou wilt give thanks when night is spent.

The Pisan Cantos are the disordered work of a man who has been through hell.

In *Women of Trachis,* Pound achieves something like the immediacy of language that he achieved in "Propertius." Where Lewis Campbell has

> Dear child, dear boy! even from the lowliest
> head
> Wise counsel may come forth.

(he is referring to wise advice coming from a slave), Pound says:

> See here, son, this slave talks sense, more
> than some free folks.

It's the American idiom, but probably a lot closer to Sophocles' intent than is Campbell's idiom. *Women of Trachis* is a remarkable performance when set against some of Pound's ranting prose.

How should one view the life and career of Ezra Pound? Several eminent writers, including Yeats, Eliot, and Hemingway, have stated their indebtedness to him. Without doubt he was a catalytic agent in many of the movements associated with modernism. As for his place as a poet, posterity will decide. Current critical estimates are diverse and irreconcilable. What Auden had to say about Yeats applies to Pound:

> Time that is intolerant
> Of the brave and innocent,
> And indifferent in a week
> To a beautiful physique,
>
> Worships language and forgives
> Everyone by whom it lives;
> Pardons cowardice, conceit,
> Lays its honours at their feet.

Presumably Time will forgive or at least forget the offenses or errors of Ezra Pounds. If his poetry achieves a place in the permanent canon of English and American poetry, Time, as Auden says, will lay its honors at his feet.

* * * * *

Ezra Pound died in Venice, in self-imposed exile from the United States, on November 1, 1972. He was 87 years old.

Selected Bibliography

SELECTED WORKS OF EZRA POUND

Pound has published such a large number of books and contributed to so many collections, anthologies, and magazines that a full listing of his works would fill many pages. The titles listed below are intended to suggest the variety of his writing.

A Lume Spento, (Venice: A. Antonini, 1908) Limited edition.

Personœ of Ezra Pound, (London: Elkin Mathews, 1909).

Excultations of Ezra Pound, (London: Elkin Mathews, 1909).

The Spirit of Romance, (London: Dent, 1910).

Provença: Poems Selected from Personœ, Exultations, and Canzoniere of Ezra Pound, (Boston: Small, Maynard, 1910).

Canzoni of Ezra Pound, (London: Elkin Mathews, 1911).

The Ripostes of Ezra Pound Whereunto Are Appended the Complete Poetical Works of T. E. Hulme, with Prefatory Note, (London: Swift, 1912).

Des Imagistes: An Anthology of the Imagists, edited by Ezra Pound (New York: Boni, 1914); (London: Poetry Book Shop, 1914).

"Homage to Wilfrid Blunt," *Poetry* 3: 220–23 (March 1914).

"Vorticism," *Fortnightly Review* 102: 461–71 (September 1914).

"Review of *Ernest Dowson*," Plarr, Victor, *Poetry* 6: 43–45 (April 1915).

'Noh', or Accomplishment: A Study of the Classical Stage of Japan, with Ernest Fenollosa, (London: Macmillan, 1916); (New York: Knopf, 1917).

Gaudier-Brzeska: A Memoir, (London: John Lane, 1916) Reissued (New York: New Directions, 1960) Reissued again by New Directions (1970) Edition includes 30 pages of illustrations and articles about Gaudier-Brzeska since 1916.

Certain Noble Plays of Japan, from the manuscripts of Ernest Fenollosa, chosen and finished by Ezra Pound. (Churchtown, Dundrum: Cuala Press, 1916).

Lustra of Ezra Pound, (London: Elkin Mathews, 1916); (New York: Knopf, 1917).

"T. S. Eliot," *Poetry* 10: 264–71 (August 1917) Review of *Prufrock and Other Observations* by T. S. Eliot.

"Irony, Laforgue, and Some Satire," *Poetry* 11: 93–98 (November 1917).

Pavannes and Division, New York (Knopf) (1918).

"The Hard and the Soft in French Poetry," *Poetry* 11: 264–71 (February 1918).

The Natural Philosophy of Love, by Remy de Gourmont, translated by Ezra Pound, (New York: Boni and Liveright, 1922).

A Draft of XVI Cantos of Ezra Pound, (Paris: Three Mountains Press, 1924 or 1925) Limited edition.

Personœ: The Collected Poems of Ezra Pound, (New York: Boni and Liveright, 1926) Reprinted with additional poems (New York: New Directions, 1949).

Imaginary Letters, (Paris: Black Sun Press, 1930) Limited edition.

ABC of Reading, (London: Routledge, 1934); (New Haven: Yale University Press, 1934).

Jefferson and/or Mussolini, (London: Nott, 1935); (New York: Liveright, 1936).

Polite Essays, (London: Faber and Faber, 1937); (Norfolk, Conn.: New Directions, 1939).

Guide to Kulchur, (London: Faber and Faber, 1938); as *Culture* (Norfolk, Conn.: New Directions, 1938).

The Pisan Cantos, (New York: New Directions, 1948).

The Cantos of Ezra Pound, (New York: New Directions, 1948) Cantos 1–71 and 74–84.

Selected Poems, (New York: New Directions, 1949).

Section: Rock-Drill: 85–95 de los cantares, (New York: New Directions, 1949).

Money pamphlets. 6 vols. (London: Peter Russell, 1950–52) These were published earlier in Italy.

The Letters of Ezra Pound, edited by T. D. D. Paige (New York: Harcourt, Brace, 1950).

Patria Mia, (Chicago: R. F. Seymour, 1950).

The Translations of Ezra Pound, edited by Hugh Kenner, (New York: New Directions, 1954).

Literary Essays, edited by T. S. Eliot, (New York: New Directions, 1954).

The Classic Anthology Defined by Confucius, (Cambridge, Mass.: Harvard University Press, 1954).

Women of Trachis, by Sophocles, translated by Ezra Pound (London: Neville Spearman, 1956).

Thrones: 96–109 de los cantares, (New York: New Directions, 1959).

Impact, (Chicago: Regnery, 1960).

Pound/Joyce: Letters of Ezra Pound to James Joyce, edited by Forrest Read, (New York: New Directions, 1967).

Drafts and Fragments of Cantos CX–CXVII, (New York: New Directions and The Stone Wall Press, 1968).

BIBLIOGRAPHICAL AIDS

A Preliminary Checklist of the Writings of Ezra Pound, Edwards, John, comp., (New Haven: Kirgo-Books, 1953).

Annotated Index to the Cantos of Ezra Pound, Edwards, John, and W. W. Vasse, eds., (Berkeley: University of California Press, 1958).

Gallup, Donald C., *A Bibliography of Ezra Pound*, (London: Rupert Hart Davis, 1963).

CRITICAL AND BIOGRAPHICAL STUDIES

Baumann, Walter, *A Rose in the Steel Dust: An Examination of the Cantos of Ezra Pound*, (Coral Gables, Fla.: University of Miami Press, 1970).

Blackmur, R. P., *Language as Gesture*, (New York: Harcourt, Brace, 1952).

Davie, Donald, *Ezra Pound: Poet as Sculptor,* (New York: Oxford University Press, 1964).

Dembo, L. S., *The Confucian Odes of Ezra Pound: A Critical Appraisal,* (Berkeley: University of California Press, 1963).

Edwards, John, ed., *The Pound Newsletter,* (Berkeley: University of California, 1954–56).

Eliot, T. S., *The Waste Land: A Facsimile and Transcript of the Original Drafts, including the Annotations of Ezra Pound,* edited by Valerie Eliot, (New York: Harcourt Brace Jovanovich, 1971).

Elliott, George P., "On Pound—Poet of Many Voices," *Carleton Miscellany* 2: 79–103 (Summer 1961) Published at Carleton College, Northfield, Minn.

Emery, Clark, *Ideas into Action: A Study of Pound's Cantos,* (Coral Gables, Fla.: University of Miami Press, 1958).

Espey, John, *Ezra Pound's Mauberley; A Study in Composition,* (Berkeley: University of California Press, 1955).

Goodwin, K. L., *The Influence of Ezra Pound,* (New York: Oxford University Press, 1967).

Hutchins, Patricia, *Ezra Pound's Kensington: An Exploration, 1885–1913,* (London: Faber and Faber); (Chicago: Regnery, 1965).

Kenner, Hugh, *The Poetry of Ezra Pound,* (New York: New Directions, 1951).

Leary, Lewis, ed., *Motive and Method in the Cantos of Ezra Pound,* (New York: Columbia University Press, 1954).

Leavis, F. R., *New Bearings in English Poetry,* (London: Chatto and Windus, 1932).

Mayo, Robert, ed., *The Analyst,* (Evanston, Ill.: Northwestern University, Department of English, 1953-date) Various scholars annotate the *Cantos* in this publication, which appears at intervals.

Miner, Earl, *The Japanese Tradition in British and American Literature,* (Princeton, N.J.: Princeton University Press, 1958).

Mullins, Eustace, *This Difficult Individual, Ezra Pound,* (New York: Fleet, 1961).

Norman, Charles, *Ezra Pound,* (New York: Macmillan, 1960) Revised edition, (New York: Funk and Wagnalls, 1969).

O'Connor, Willian Van, and Edward Stone, eds., *A Casebook on Ezra Pound,* (New York: Crowell, 1959).

Pearlman, Daniel, *The Barb of Time,* (New York: Oxford University Press, 1969).

Putnam, Samuel, *Paris Was Our Mistress,* (New York: Viking Press, 1947).

Quarterly Review of Literature, Ezra Pound Issue, Vol. 5, No. 2 (1949) Published at Bard College, Annandale, New York.

Quinn, Sister M. Bernetta, *The Metamorphic Tradition in Modern Poetry,* (New Brunswick, N.J.: Rutgers University Press, 1955).

Rosenthal, M. L., *A Primer of Ezra Pound,* (New York: Macmillan, 1960).

Russell, Peter, ed., *An Examination of Ezra Pound,* (New York: New Directions, 1950).

Stock, Noel, *Poet in Exile: Ezra Pound,* (Manchester, England: Manchester University Press); (New York: Barnes and Noble, 1964).

Stock, Noel, *Reading the Cantos: A Study of Meaning in Ezra Pound,* (London: Routledge and K. Paul, 1967).

———, *The Life of Ezra Pound,* (London: Routledge and K. Paul, 1970).

———, ed., *Ezra Pound Perspectives: Essays in Honor of His Eightieth Birthday,* (Chicago: Regnery, 1965).

Sutton, Walter, ed., *Ezra Pound: A Collection of Critical Essays,* (Englewood Cliffs, N.J.: Prentice-Hall, 1963).

Wright, George, *The Poet in the Poem,* (Berkeley: University of California Press, 1960).

The Restoration Court Poets

VIVIAN DE SOLA PINTO

INTRODUCTION

THE LAST GROUP of English courtier poets belonged to a set of lively young people in whose company Charles II spent much of his time after the Restoration. In 1661 James Butler, duke of Ormonde, described them to the lord chancellor, Edward Hyde, earl of Clarendon, as "confident young men who abhorred all discourse that was serious, and, in the liberty they assumed in drollery and raillery, preserved no reverence towards God or man, but laughed at all sober men, and even at religion itself." The historian Gilbert Burnet gives us the names of some of these "confident young men "the three most eminent wits of that time . . . the earls of Dorset and Rochester and Sir Charles Sidley." A brilliant addition to the group was George Etherege, who became acquainted with Lord Buckhurst (later earl of Dorset) as a result of the success of his first play, *The Comical Revenge,* in March 1664. These young men, together with the slightly older and immensely rich George Villiers, duke of Buckingham, and a number of less distinguished figures, formed the circle known as the court wits, described by Andrew Marvell as "the merry gang," who led a gay, dissipated life in the 1660's and 1670's, the period called by Dryden "A very Merry Dancing, Drinking, Laughing, Quaffing, and unthinking Time." Legends clustered round the personalities of the court wits, and they were built up into figures of diabolical wickedness in the age of the new puritanism that followed the Glorious Revolution. Thomas Macaulay in the second chapter of volume I of his *History of England* speaks in horrified tones of "the open profligacy of the court and Cavaliers" after the Restoration and "the outrageous profaneness and licentiousness of the Buckinghams and the Sedleys." Unfortunately criticism of their writings was for long colored by this moralistic condemnation of their lives. Now that the great flood of English puritanism has subsided, it is possible to see the court wits and their writings in a truer perspective.

They were certainly no mere idle profligates. Their diversions included music, the theater, reading and translating the classics, and literary discussion as well as women and drinking. Both Rochester and Buckhurst fought as volunteers at sea in the second Dutch war. Rochester, surprisingly, seems to have been an affectionate, if not a faithful, husband and a good landlord. Dorset (Buckhurst) was a generous and discerning patron of poets and dramatists. Sedley, after a riotous youth, became a useful member of the House of Commons, and Etherege was a successful dramatist and later, by seventeenth-century standards, an efficient diplomat. They were men living between two worlds, on the one hand the old hierarchical universe mirrored in the traditional life of the court, and on the other, the new materialistic philosophy and science and the atomized society of free individuals. They now can be seen not, as they have been traditionally pictured, as a set of young royalists indulging in wild orgies as a reaction against the austerity of the Rule of the Saints, but as a postwar generation reacting as much against the stiff formality of the old cavaliers as against the narrow religiosity of the Puritans. They were intellectuals as well as gay young men about town. Both Rochester and Sedley received part of their education at Wadham College, Oxford, one of the cradles of the new experimental science; and they all read and admired the works of Thomas Hobbes, the first English philosopher to propound a purely materialistic and utilitarian system. Hobbes was to them something very much like what Karl Marx was to the young English poets of the 1930's, a symbol of liberation from antique inhibitions and outworn ideas. Sedley, addressing a typical court wit, wrote:

> Thou art an Atheist, *Quintus,* and a Wit,
> Thinkst all was of self-moving Attoms
> made.

If Hobbes was right and the universe consisted merely of atoms governed by mathematical laws, it surely was only sensible to enjoy the good things of this world and ignore the croakings of killjoys, whether they were Anglican parsons, Puritan preachers, or old-fashioned cavaliers. The age was one of experiment, and the court wits tried the experiment of living in a little pagan paradise of sensual, aesthetic, and intellectual pleasure. Behind the experiment lay a vision and a theory. The vision was well described by Charles Lamb as "the Utopia of gallantry, where pleasure is duty and the manners perfect freedom." The theory was what was known in seventeenth-century Europe as "libertinism,"[1] a term that implied a revolt against traditional morality and institutions, and a way of life based on the satisfaction of natural passions and appetites. Rochester, who had the most philosophical mind of the group, summed up the libertine theory in the following lines:

1. It is well described by Dale Underwood in Etherege *and the Seventeenth-Century Comedy of Manners* (1957), pp. 10–36.

> Thus, whilst 'gainst false reas'ning I
> inveigh,
> I own right *Reason,* which I wou'd obey;
> That *Reason,* which distinguishes by sense,
> And gives us *Rules* of good and ill from
> thence:
>
> Your *Reason* hinders, mine helps t' enjoy,
> Renewing Appetites, yours wou'd destroy.
> ("A Satyr Against Mankind," 98–101;
> 104–105)

The attempt to live in accordance with these principles was bound to fail in the face of the realities of the human condition; but the vision that lay behind it, as well as the contradictions that it involved, provided material for the best comedies of the period and for the poetry of the courtiers.

The court wits must not be judged as professional poets. Like their predecessors, the cavalier poets of the court of Charles I, they were gentlemen amateurs and their verses, which were mostly "occasional," were written not for publication in the modern sense of the word but for circulation in manuscript among their friends. This does not mean that they were mere *dilettanti,* for whom the writing of verse was simply an elegant game. This was, doubtless, true of the minor figures in the court circle, but for the leading wits poetry was an art and a vital expression of a truly creative culture founded on a knowledge of books and experience of life. They aimed at what they called "ease" or colloquial naturalness in poetry, and were well aware that this could be achieved only by craftsmanship, even though their practice was sometimes marred by gentlemanly carelessness. Their poetry belongs to the courtly-classical or polite tradition, which descends from Ben Jonson through the cavalier poets of the reign of Charles I. This tradition underwent a change somewhere about the middle of the century, when it began to acquire the character that is called Augustan. The change is apparent in the poetry of Edmund Waller and Abraham Cowley, two poets of the midcentury whose work was greatly admired by the wits.

Hobbes, who was influential both as a literary critic and as a philosopher, had close connections with both these poets; and in their best work they are trying to carry into effect his demand for a new "perspicuity," worldliness, and realism in poetry.[2] They saw themselves as new Augustans renovating English poetry after the English Civil War, as Virgil and Horace renovated Latin poetry after the civil wars of Rome. This new "Augustan" movement could tend either toward a greater actuality and realism, in accordance with the spirit of the new science and the new philosophy, or toward an elegant, rococo neoclassicism, not without charm but always in danger of becoming pompous and insipid. Both tendencies are apparent in the poetry of the court wits. At its worst it is not very far removed from Etherege's parody of the fashionable love lyric in *The Man of Mode* (1676):

How Charming Phillis is, how fair!
Ah that she were as willing,
To ease my wounded heart of Care
And make her Eyes less killing.

But in their best poetry they were saved from this kind of thing by their good sense, their wit, and their irony. They were helped, too, by their contact with a tradition that is commonly ignored by the literary historians. This was the tradition of the street ballad and popular song, that lusty growth of English vernacular poetry found in innumerable broadsides sold in the streets and taverns, and in the popular verse miscellanies such as the *Drolleries* and *Academies of Compliments*, which were best-sellers in the Restoration bookshops.

The two chief kinds of poetry the court wits practiced were the love lyric and the satire or "libel." They often tend to shade into each other, of which one of the distinguishing marks is the combination of the singing voice of the lyric with the critical and ironic spirit of satire. They were the last English poets successfully to use the pastoral convention as part of the courtly love game. This convention had lost the imaginative grandeur with which it was invested in the High Renaissance, but it remained a symbol for a nonmoral dream world of delicate charm and grace. At the end of the century it had become absurd when Lady Wishfort, in Congreve's *The Way of the World* (1700), proposed to "retire to deserts and solitudes, and feed harmless sheep by groves and purling streams." The court wits in their best lyrics avoid this sort of silly escapism by disinfecting the pastoral with what Ezra Pound called "a dash of bitters." With them reality, like cheerfulness in the philosophy of Dr. Johnson's friend, kept breaking in. At times, too, their realistic temper enabled them to use the convention to express a human situation when it became clear that Thirsis or Strephon was a real man feeling a genuine affection for his Celia or Phillis. The "libel," lampoon, or satire was a feature of Restoration court life as common as the love song. It could be simply a string of witty and usually bawdy insults in verse, but, in the hands of its ablest practitioners, notably Rochester, it became a vehicle for genuine social criticism based on a perception of the glaring contradictions between the smooth exterior of court life and the sordid actualities that lay behind it.

The court wits were a small, rather closely knit community. Professor J. H. Wilson has estimated that about fourteen persons can be reckoned as belonging to the inner circle. As far as is known, they never authorized the printing of any of their works; and a large quantity of their songs, "libels," and other verses have survived in manuscript miscellanies, printed broadsides, contemporary anthologies, and editions, often of doubtful authenticity, published after their deaths. The result has been that it is extremely difficult for modern editors to establish either a reliable text or an authentic canon of the writings even of the leading figures.

As with the circle of Thomas Wyatt and Henry Howard, earl of Surrey, in the early sixteenth century and that of the "Sons of Ben

2. See his "Answer to Davenant" (1650) in J. E. Spingarn, ed., *Critical Essays of the Seventeenth Century*, II, p.63

Jonson" in the early seventeenth, there is a kind of basic poetic voice common to all the Restoration wits who wrote verse. One can hear it in the opening lines of a poem ascribed rather doubtfully to Dorset:

> Though, Phillis, your prevailing charms
> Have forc'd me from my Celia's arms,
> That kind defence against all powers,
> But those resistless eyes of yours:
> Think not your conquest to maintain
> By rigour and unjust disdain;
> In vain, fair Nymph, in vain you strive,
> For love does seldom hope survive . . .

This sort of rather thin, graceful poetry of conventional gallantry, strongly influenced by Waller and the slightly earlier French poetry of writers like Voiture and Sarrazin, could be written by almost any member of the circle, including such minor poetasters as Lord Mulgrave and Wentworth Dillon, earl of Roscommon, Sir Car Scroop, or Sir Fleetwood Shepherd. The "most eminent wits," to use Gilbert Burnet's expression, all sometimes use this "basic" poetic voice, but they are distinguished from their fellow courtiers by their power of speaking (or singing) in other voices covering wider and more interesting areas of experience.

JOHN WILMOT, EARL OF ROCHESTER (1647–1680)

John Wilmot, second earl of Rochester, was the son of a cavalier general. Born in 1647, he was educated at Wadham College, Oxford, where he took the M.A. in 1660. He then traveled in France and Italy, returning to England in 1664, when he appeared at court and earned a reputation for wit and dissipation. He served at sea in the Dutch war in 1665–1666. Charles II enjoyed his company, but he was banished from court more than once for his outspoken satires on the king. His health declined in the late 1670's. In 1679 he made the acquaintance of Gilbert Burnet, later bishop of Salisbury, with whom he had a series of conversations on religion in the winter of 1679–1680. After a dramatic conversion to Christianity, he died on 26 July 1680.

Rochester had by far the most powerful and original mind of all the court wits. His distinguishing characteristics are an unusual capacity for intellectual and sensual experience, a profound skepticism, and a share in that quality of "terrifying honesty" that T. S. Eliot ascribed to William Blake. He began his career as a wholehearted disciple of Hobbes, but this was only the starting point for an intellectual voyage that ended with his deathbed conversion to Christianity and his total rejection of what he then described as "the absurd and foolish philosophy that the world so much admired, propagated by Mr. Hobbes and others." In a letter to his wife he writes of "so great a disproportion 'twixt our desires and what it has ordained to content them" and of those who are "soe intirely satisfyed with theire shares in this world, that theire wishes nor theire thoughts have not a farther prospect of felicity & glory." One of his admirers called him an "Enthusiast in Wit," and if this is interpreted as meaning that he combined intellectual toughness with a passionate aspiration to "felicity and glory," the description is apt.

In the lyric he can play the game of the courtly pastoral and can also enjoy the fun of deflating its sentiment by substituting for the languishing swain and the chaste nymph a pair of cynical sensualists:

> How perfect, Cloris, and how free
> Would these enjoyments prove,
> But you with formal jealousy
> Are still tormenting Love.
>
> Let us (since Wit instructs us how)
> Raise pleasure to the top,
> If Rival bottle you'll allow,
> Ill suffer rival fop.
>
> There's not a brisk insipid spark
> That flutters in the Town
> But with your wanton eyes you mark
> Him out to be your own. . . .
> ("To a Lady in a Letter," 1–12)

Such a poem as this is obviously a deliberate "shocker." One can hear in it the voice of the hard-boiled "confident young men" who made people like the duke of Ormonde shudder. J. M. Synge wrote in 1908 that "before verse can become human again it must learn to be brutal." These words can be applied to the age when seventeenth-century romanticism was dying, as well as to that which saw the collapse of Victorian romanticism.

Rochester is writing from a far deeper level of experience in the following poem, in which he gives a philosophic dimension to a favorite theme of the court wits, inconstancy:

All my past Life is mine no more,
    The flying hours are gone:
Like transitory Dreams giv'n o'er,
Whose Images are kept in store
    By Memory alone.

The Time that is to come is not;
    How can it then be mine?
The present Moment's all my Lot;
And that, as fast as it is got,
    Phillis, is only thine.

Then talk not of Inconstancy,
    False Hearts, and broken Vows;
If I, by Miracle, can be
This live-long Minute true to thee,
    'Tis all that Heav'n allows.
  ("Love and Life," 1–15)

This attitude is very different from that of the thoughtless pleasure-seeker. The plangent cadences of the opening lines convey a sense of the mystery of the time process, and the whole poem is suffused with melancholy for the precariousness of the artificial paradise that the lover finds in the arms of his Phillis.

Rochester's breakthrough to reality in the lyric can take the form of passionate tenderness as well as of brutality. This is found in a handful of lyrics that F. R. Leavis has well described as "peculiarly individual utterances and that were aptly compared by Sir Herbert Grierson with the songs of Robert Burns:

My dear Mistress has a Heart
    Soft as those kind looks she gave me;
When, with Love's resistless Art,
    And her Eyes, she did enslave me;
But her Constancy's so weak,
    She's so wild, and apt to wander;
That my jealous Heart wou'd break,
    Should we live one day asunder.

Melting Joys about her move,
    Killing Pleasures, wounding Blisses;
She can dress her Eyes in Love,
    And her Lips can arm with Kisses;
Angels listen when she speaks,
    She's my delight, all Mankind's wonder;
But my jealous Heart would break,
    Should we live one day asunder.
  ("A Song," 1–16)

Here the "ease" and unaffected naturalness that the court wits prized are combined with a note of rapture and a crystalline perfection of phrase and form of which Rochester alone among them knew the secret.

His satiric poems are of two kinds. Some, like his attacks on Lord Mulgrave and Sir Car Scroop, are simply "libels" in the fashion of the day, and distinguished from the numerous other contemporary squibs only by their greater pungency and literary force. His lampoons on the king deserve special mention. The character of Charles II seems to have fascinated him, perhaps because, like his own, it was full of paradoxes. The contrast between the traditional view of the monarch hedged by divinity and the actual person of the "sauntering," informal Charles Stuart was a never-failing source of ironic amusement to the poet. It is neatly embodied in his celebrated extempore epigram:

We have a pritty witty king
    And whose word no man relys on:
He never said a foolish thing,
    And never did a wise one,

Charles's good-humored reply is said to have been that what Rochester observed was easily explained. He was responsible for his words; his ministers, for his actions. This epigram, though, is mild compared with some of the longer lampoons on the king ascribed to Rochester. What seemed to him especially despicable in the king was not that he took his pleasure with his mistresses, but that he allowed himself to be governed by them:

> Restless he rolls about from Whore to
> Whore,
> A merry Monarch, scandalous and poor.

Rochester's more serious work in satire deserves to be called philosophic; it can be seen as reflecting the dialectical process that transformed the gay young spark of the 1660's into the dying penitent of 1680. One characteristic of these poems is his intense and vivid perception of the "waste land" of the world revealed by the new materialistic philosophy and the sordidness of a society vulgarized by the growth of the money power. The other is the creative use of his reading. He was the first poet to use the Augustan method of "imitation," later brilliantly exploited by John Oldham, Pope, and Johnson. Not only his fine "Allusion to the Tenth Satire of the Second Book of Horace" but also each of his major satiric works is at once a criticism of contemporary life and in some measure an "imitation" or recreation of a work of ancient or contemporary poetry, often with a touch of parody. His famous "Upon Nothing" is a kind of inversion of Cowley's "Hymn to Light," and at the same time he makes use of the conception of Nothing as an active force found in the Renaissance Latin poems quoted by Johnson in his account of Rochester in *The Lives of the Poets*; behind the poem, too, lie still more august antecedents: the book of Genesis, the first verses of the Fourth Gospel, and the Aristotelian doctrine of form and matter.

> Nothing! thou Elder Brother ev'n to Shade,
> That hadst a Being ere the World was made,
> And (well fixt) art alone, of ending not afraid.
> (1–3)

In the last stanzas the irony is transferred from metaphysics to contemporary society:

> Nothing who dwell'st with Fools in grave
> Disguise,
> For whom they rev'rend Shapes, and Forms
> devise,
> Lawn Sleeves, and Furs, and Gowns, when
> they like thee look wise.
>
> The great Man's Gratitude to his best Friend,
> King's Promises, Whore's Vows, tow'rds thee
> they bend,
> Flow swiftly into thee, and in thee ever end.
> (43–45; 49–51)

The emptiness that lies behind the facade of human institutions and social life is visualized here as a kind of evil abstract deity (Blake's "Nobodaddy"), and Swift's doctrine of man as a "micro-coat" (see *A Tale of a Tub*) is clearly foreshadowed. Pope must have studied this poem carefully, for he wrote a clever imitation of it in his youth, and the triumph of Dullness at the end of *The Dunciad* probably owes much to Rochester's triumph of Nothing.

"The Maim'd Debauchee," described by Charles Whibley as a "masterpiece of heroic irony," recalls William Davenant's epic *Gondibert* as "Upon Nothing" recalls Cowley's "Hymn to Light." The stately meter and diction of Davenant's "heroic" poem are used to exhibit the old age of a gentlemanly rake, who is ironically equated with a superannuated admiral watching a naval battle from a safe position on shore. Like all of Rochester's best satiric work, this poem is not a statement but a vision. We are made to see the absurdly ferocious old sailor:

> From his fierce Eyes flashes of Rage he
> throws
> As from black Clouds when Lightning
> breaks away,
> Transported thinks himself amidst his Foes,
> And absent, yet enjoys the bloody Day.
> (9–12)

This image is, as it were, superimposed upon that of the old roué inciting his young friends to the life of pleasure:

My pains at last some respite shall afford,
While I behold the Battels you maintain:
When Fleets of Glasses sail around the Board,
From whose Broad-Sides Volleys of Wit shall rain.
(17–20)

Is one looking at a riotous banquet or a naval battle? It is impossible to say; the two images are fused into a simple whole.

In his most powerful social satire, "A Letter from Artemiza in the Town to Chloë in the Country," Rochester shows us the obverse of the utopia of gallantry in which the court wits and ladies of Whitehall spent their time. In this poem the horror of the life of a prostitute in Restoration London is etched with the mordant realism of a Hogarth or a Goya:

That wretched thing *Corinna,* who has run
Through all the sev'ral ways of being undone:
Cozen'd at first by Love, and living then
By turning the too-dear-bought-cheat on Men:
Gay were the hours, and wing'd with joy they flew,
When first the Town her early Beauties knew:
Courted, admir'd, and lov'd, with Presents fed;
Youth in her Looks, and Pleasure in her bed:
. . .
Now scorn'd of all forsaken and opprest,
She's a *Memento Mori* to the rest:
Diseas'd, decay'd, to take up half a Crown
Must Morgage her Long Scarf, and Manto Gown;
Poor Creature, who unheard of, as a Flie,
In some dark hole must all the Winter lye:
And want, and dirt, endure a whole half year,
That, for one month, she Tawdry may appear.
(189–196; 201–208)

This is a glimpse of the hell over which the heaven of the Strephons and Chloës of Whitehall was precariously constructed.

The culmination of contemporary society is seen in Rochester's "Satyr Against Mankind," in which the revolt is extended to an attack on the human condition itself. The poem was suggested by the eighth satire of Nicolas Boileau, reinforced by hints from Montaigne and La Rochefoucauld. Nevertheless, it is a profoundly original work, for Rochester, like Pope, is never so original as when he is making full use of his reading. The poem is stamped with the peculiar strength of his personality in every line, and expresses with an almost frightening intensity his mood of indignation and disillusionment. He never created a more striking image than that at the opening of the poem, of mankind as the Lost Traveller, who, deceived by Reason, "an *Ignis fatuus* of the Mind,"

Stumbling from Thought to Thought, falls headlong down
Into Doubt's boundless Sea, where like to drown,
Books bear him up awhile, and make him try
To swim with Bladders of Philosophy,

Then old Age, and Experience, hand in hand,
Lead him to Death, and make him understand,
After a Search so painful, and so long,
That all his Life he has been in the wrong.
Hudled in dirt, the reas'ning Engine lyes,
Who was so proud, so witty, and so wise.
(18–21; 25–30)

Nowhere in the English poetry of the seventeenth century is the moral crisis of the age expressed with such force and precision; in the new mechanical-materialist universe of Descartes, Hobbes, and the scientists, man is only a "reas'ning Engine" (the phrase was probably suggested by an expression of Robert Boyle, the great contemporary chemist), yet the pitiful creature has the presumption to call himself witty and wise, and to seek an explanation of a universe in which he seems to be little better than an irrelevant accident. The central passage of the poem, containing a comparison between man and the beasts, is one of the most searching pieces of moral realism in English poetry:

Be Judge yourself, I'le bring it to the test,
Which is the basest Creature Man or Beast?
Birds feed on Birds, Beasts on each other
prey;
But Savage Man alone does Man betray:
Prest by necessity, they Kill for Food,
Man undoes Man to do himself no good.
With Teeth and Claws by Nature arm'd they
hunt,
Nature's allowances, to supply their want;
But Man with smiles, embraces,
Friendships, praise,
Unhumanely his Fellows life betrays;
With voluntary pains works his distress,
Not through necessity, but wantonness.
For hunger, or for Love, they fight or tear,
Whilst wretched Man is still in Arms for
fear;
For fear he arms, and is of Arms afraid,
By fear, to fear, successively betray'd,
Base fear, the source whence his best
passions came,
His boasted Honor, and his dear bought
Fame.
That lust of Pow'r, to which he's such a
Slave,
And for the which alone he dares be brave . . .
(127–146)

Rochester is here piercing the defenses of his aristocratic readers and showing the real passions that lay behind their high-flown talk of honor and fame. It is a passage that communicates forward to the Swift of *Gulliver's Travels*: the king of Brobdingnag's denunciation of the Europeans and the superiority of those wise and humane quadrupeds, the Houyhnhnms, to the filthy, cowardly Yahoos.

Rochester's reputation, like Byron's, has suffered from the blaze of notoriety that surrounded his life and personality. Andrew Marvell, no mean judge, declared that he was "the best English satyrist and had the right veine"; Voltaire went further and called him "a man of genius and a great poet." As a craftsman in verse, compared with his contemporary John Dryden, he is a brilliant amateur. His place is among the daring thought-adventurers of English poetry, whose work lives by the intensity of their passion, the forthrightness of their speech, and the searching clarity of their vision.

CHARLES SACKVILLE, EARL OF DORSET (1643–1706)

Charles Sackville, sixth earl of Dorset, born in 1643, became Lord Buckhurst in 1652, when his father inherited the title of earl of Dorset. After spending a year at Westminster School, he traveled on the Continent, returning to England soon after the Restoration. He collaborated with Sedley and others in a translation of a tragedy by Corneille, which was produced in 1663, and in June of that year took part with Sedley in a wild frolic at the Cock Tavern in Covent Garden. He served at sea against the Dutch in 1665, and in 1677 inherited the earldom of Dorset. In the House of Lords, in 1689 he voted in favor of offering the throne to William and Mary, and he became lord chamberlain to the new monarchs. A generous patron to many men of letters, he died in January 1706.

Dorset (known throughout the early part of his career as Lord Buckhurst) was the least productive, though by no means the least gifted, of the Restoration wits. The works that can be certainly attributed to him are a translation of one act of a tragedy by Corneille; a few lampoons, prologues, and epilogues; a ribald parody; the well-known ballad "Song Written at Sea, in the first Dutch War"; and a small sheaf of lyrics. He was rich and indolent, and delighted in the company of men of letters, to whom he was a munificent host and patron. The condition of such a wealthy and universally flattered nobleman, "fed," like Pope's Bufo, "with soft dedication all day long," was perhaps even worse for a creative artist than the poverty and obscurity of an Oldham or a Thomas Otway. When Dryden couples his name with those of Virgil, Shakespeare, and Donne, and Matthew Prior states that "There is a Lustre in his Verses, like that of a Sun in Claude Loraine's Landskips," we are listening to the courtly hyperboles of the grateful recipients of his bounty. Pope, though, who was under no obligation to him, rated his poetry very highly, and if one can trust Joseph Spence's *Anecdotes,* surprisingly preferred it even to Rochester's. His own work shows that he studied it carefully.

Dorset's celebrated ballad deserves its reputation. An excellent example of the benefit that the court wits derived from their contact with the vernacular tradition, it is a true street ballad written to be sung to the traditional tune of "Shackerley Hay." We know from the Stationer's Register and from Pepys's diary (2 Jan. 1665) that it was actually published under the title of "The Noble Seaman's Complaint" as a broadside, and was a popular hit. In this poem, as can be judged from the following quotation of the three opening stanzas, the rhythmic vitality of vernacular poetry is happily combined with the sophisticated wit and irony of the courtier, producing an effect that remains fresh and sparkling after more than three centuries:

To all you Ladies now at Land
  We Men at Sea indite;
But first wou'd have you understand
  How hard it is to write;
The Muses now, and Neptune too,
We must implore to write to you.

For tho' the Muses should prove kind,
  And fill our empty Brain;
Yet if rough Neptune rouze the Wind,
  To wave the azure Main,
Our Paper, Pen, and Ink, and we,
Roll up and down our Ships at Sea.

Then if we write not by each Post,
  Think not we are unkind;
Nor yet conclude our Ships are lost
  By Dutchmen, or by Wind:
Our Tears we'll send a speedier way,
The Tide shall bring 'em twice a day.
(1–18)

Another lyric in the ballad style and meter has a touch of the sturdy vulgarity and sensuality of popular art:

Methinks the poor Town has been troubled
  too long,
With Phillis and Chloris in every Song;
By Fools, who at once can both love and
  despair,
And will never leave calling 'em cruel and
  fair;
Which justly provokes me in Rhime to
  express
The Truth that I know of bonny black Bess.

This Bess of my Heart, this Bess of my Soul,
Has a Skin white as Milk and Hair black as
  Coal,
She's plump, yet with ease you may span
  her round Waste,
But her round swelling Thighs can scarce be
  embrac'd:
Her Belly is soft, not a word of the rest;
But I know what I think when I drink to the
  best.

The Plowman and 'Squire, the arranter
  Clown,
At home she subdu'd in her Paragon Gown;
But now she adorns the Boxes and Pit,
And the proudest Town-gallants are forc'd
  to submit;
All hearts fall a-leaping wherever she comes,
And beat Day and Night, like my Lord
  Craven's Drums.

Perhaps Dorset's most original and distinctive work is seen in the sequence of his four little poems on Katherine Sedley, the daughter of his friend Sir Charles Sedley. The character of this bold, witty young woman, who became the mistress of the duke of York, later James II, seems to have fascinated him. In these verses Dorset is creating a new kind of poem, in which lyrical movement is combined with satiric force. It was, doubtless, of them that Rochester was thinking when he called Dorset "the best good Man, with the worst natur'd Muse." The following poem has an economy of language and a classic perfection of form unrivaled in English poetry outside the works of Walter Landor:

Dorinda's sparkling Wit, and Eyes,
United, cast too fierce a Light,

Which blazes high, but quickly dies,
Pains not the Heart, but hurts the Sight.

Love is a calmer, gentler joy,
Smooth are his Looks, and soft his Pace;
Her Cupid is a black-guard Boy,
That runs his Link full in your Face.

The metaphor of a painfully dazzling fire links the two stanzas with admirable art, and the sudden transition in the last two lines from the rococo cupid to the "black-guard Boy" with his flaming "Link" (torch) takes one with a pleasurable shock from the dream world of the pastoral convention to the actuality of night in the murky streets of Restoration London, where there were no street lamps and the only illumination was provided by the torches of link-boys.

In another poem on Katherine Sedley, the same verbal economy and felicity of imagery give force to a penetrating piece of social satire:

Tell me, Dorinda, why so gay,
Why such embroid'ry, fringe and lace?
Can any Dresses find a way,
To stop th' approaches of decay,
And mend a ruin'd Face.

Wilt thou still sparkle in the Box,
Still ogle in the Ring?
Canst thou forget thy Age and Pox?
Can all that shines on Shells and Rocks
Make thee a fine young Thing?

So have I seen in Larder dark
Of Veal a lucid Loin
Replete with many a brilliant Spark,
As wise Philosophers remark,
At once both stink and shine.

This is not merely an attack on Katherine Sedley. It is a dramatization of a true social criticism that sees all the glittering apparatus of court life ("embroid'ry, fringe and lace" and "all that shines on Shells and Rocks") as a mockery masking the hideous realities of venereal disease and decaying flesh. There is a sharp visualization of ugly and sordid images in this poem, revealing a new kind of poetic sensibility that was to be exploited with remarkable results by Pope and Swift. A similar quality is found in one of Dorset's lampoons on the Hon. Edward Howard, a contemporary dramatist who was one of the favorite butts of the court wits:

Thou damn'd Antipodes to Common sense,
Thou Foil to Flecknoe, pry'thee tell from whence
Does all this mighty Stock of Dullness spring?
Is it thy own, or hast it from Snow-Hill,
Assisted by some Ballad-making Quill?
No, they fly higher yet, thy Plays are such
I'd swear they were translated out of Dutch,
Fain wou'd I know what Diet thou dost keep,
If thou dost always, or dost never sleep?
Sure hasty-pudding is thy chiefest Dish,
With Bullock's Liver, or some stinking Fish;
Garbage, Ox-cheeks, and Tripes, do feast thy Brain
Which nobly pays this tribute back again,
With Daisy roots thy dwarfish Muse is fed,
A Giant's body with a Pygmy's head.

. . .

Think on't a while, and thou wilt quickly find
Thy Body made for Labour, not thy Mind.
No other use of Paper thou should'st make,
Than carrying Loads and Reams upon thy Back.
Carry vast Burdens till thy Shoulders shrink,
But curst be he that gives thee Pen and Ink:
Such dang'rous Weapons shou'd be kept from Fools,
As Nurses from their children keep Edg'd-Tools:
For thy dull Fancy a Muckinder[3] is fit
To wipe the slabberings of thy snotty Wit.

Dr. Johnson rightly saw in these lines evidence of "great fertility of mind." They show a strength and a freedom of imagination that make one think of *The Dunciad* and regret that Dorset's birth and fortune prevented him from developing his considerable literary potential.

3. Handkerchief.

SIR CHARLES SEDLEY
(1639–1701)

Sir Charles Sedley (or Sidley), born in 1639, was the son of a Kentish baronet. He was educated at Wadham College, Oxford, and inherited the baronetcy on the death of his brother in 1656. After the Restoration he became a lively member of the merry gang" at court. His comedy *The Mulberry Garden* was staged in 1668, his tragedy *Antony and Cleopatra* in 1677, and a second comedy, *Bellamira,* in 1687. He was member of Parliament for New Romney, and was a frequent and vigorous speaker in the House of Commons after the Glorious Revolution. He died in August 1701.

Pope described Sedley as "a very insipid writer; except in some few of his little love-verses." This is not quite fair to Sedley, who wrote some good poetry besides his "little love-verses," but it is possible to understand what Pope meant. Sedley's poetry has neither Rochester's passionate intensity and intellectual energy nor the satiric bite and sensuality of Dorset's best work. He uses the old stereotypes of the courtly pastoral convention with grace and wit, sometimes with tenderness, but rarely with passion. His attitude to the sexual relationship is rational and humorous:

Phillis, let's shun the common Fate
And let our Love ne'r turn to Hate.
I'll dote no longer than I can
Without being call'd a faithless Man.
When we begin to want Discourse
And Kindness seems to taste of Force,
As freely as we met we'll part
Each one possest of his own Heart.

In two poems he uses the theme of the address to a very young girl, already treated with imaginative richness by Marvell and with courtly grace by Waller. The following are the opening stanzas of the song to Cloris in Sedley's comedy *The Mulberry Garden*:

Ah Cloris! that I now could sit
As unconcern'd, as when
Your Infant Beauty cou'd beget
No pleasure, nor no pain.

When I the Dawn us'd to admire,
And prais'd the coming Day;
I little thought the growing fire
Must take my Rest away.

Your Charms in harmless Childhood lay,
Like metals in the mine,
Age from no face took more away,
Than Youth conceal'd in thine.

But as your Charms insensibly
To their perfection prest,
Fond Love as unperceiv'd did flye,
And in my Bosom rest.

My Passion with your Beauty grew,
And Cupid at my heart,
Still as his mother favour'd you,
Threw a new flaming Dart.

This is, perhaps, a little too pretty. It might be described as boudoir poetry, recalling some erotic French eighteenth-century painting of the school of Boucher. More astringent and satisfying to a modern taste in its delicate, playful humor is the poem addressed "To a Devout Young Gentlewoman":

Phillis, this early Zeal asswage,
You over-act your part;
The Martyrs, at your tender Age,
Gave Heaven but half their Heart.

Old Men (till past the Pleasure) ne're
Declaim against the Sin;
Tis early to begin to fear
The Devil at Fifteen.

The World to Youth is too severe,
And, like a treacherous Light,
Beauty, the Actions of the Fair,
Exposes to their sight.

And yet the World, as old as 'tis,
Is oft deceiv'd by't too;
Kind Combinations seldom miss,
Let's try what we can do.

The first two stanzas of this poem are nearly flawless, but the last two are marred by both banality of thought and verbal clumsiness, seen in the awkward inversions and the slipshod grammar of the penultimate stanza. A similar failure of inspiration mars the lyric beginning with the following often-praised and beautiful lines:

Love still has something of the Sea,
From whence his Mother rose . . .

The expectation aroused by this rich opening is immediately damped by the next two lines, with their hackneyed imagery and inversion for the sake of the rhyme:

No time his Slaves from Doubt can free,
Nor give their Thoughts repose: . . .

After a series of stanzas filled with frigid allegory, the poem ends with lines almost worthy of its superb opening:

And if I gaz'd a thousand Years
I could no deeper love.

None of the weaknesses noted in these poems is found in two of Sedley's songs that long retained their popularity through the contemporary musical settings. In the following poem the courtly convention is most happily wedded to the appreciation of an exquisite moment of actual experience:

Hears not my Phillis, how the Birds
Their feather'd Mates salute?
They tell their Passion in their Words;
Must I alone be mute?
Phillis, without Frown or Smile,
Sat and knotted all the while.

The God of Love in thy bright Eyes
Does like a Tyrant reign;
But in thy Heart a Child he lyes,
Without his Dart or Flame.
Phillis, without Frown or Smile,
Sat and knotted all the while.

So many Months in Silence past,
And yet in raging Love,
Might well deserve one Word at last
My Passion shou'd approve.
Phillis, without Frown or Smile,
Sat and knotted all the while.

Must then your faithful Swain expire,
And not one look obtain,
Which he to sooth his fond Desire,
Might pleasingly explain?
Phillis, without Frown or Smile,
Sat and knotted all the while.

This lyric must be heard sung to Henry Purcell's exquisite setting if its full effect is to be realized, but even on the printed page it succeeds in conveying the poet's delight in the balletlike situation, in the movement of the verse and the conventional images, which his emotion endows with a surprising freshness and vitality. Equally successful is an even more famous song that shows an originality of metrical invention unusual in Sedley's work and is due, doubtless, in some measure to the music:

Phillis is my only Joy,
Faithless as the Winds or Seas;
Sometimes coming, sometimes coy,
Yet she never fails to please;
If with a Frown
I am cast down,
Phillis smiling,
And beguiling,
Makes me happier than before.

Tho', alas, too late I find,
Nothing can her Fancy fix;
Yet the Moment she is kind,
I forgive her all her Tricks;
Which, tho' I see,
I can't get free;
She deceiving,
I believing;
What need Lovers wish for more?

In one lyric Sedley achieves the expression of tender feeling in language of diaphanous simplicity that almost equals that of Rochester's best songs, though, as so often in his poetry, the magnificent promise of the opening lines is hardly sustained:

Not Celia, that I juster am
Or better than the rest,
For I would change each Hour like them,
Were not my Heart at rest.

But I am ty'd to very thee,
By every Thought I have,
Thy Face I only care to see,
Thy Heart I only crave.

All that in Woman is ador'd,
In thy dear self I find,
For the whole Sex can but afford,
The Handsome and the Kind.

Why then should I seek farther Store,
And still make Love anew;
When Change itself can give no more,
'Tis easie to be true.

Sedley is not exclusively what Ben Jonson calls "a woman's poet." There is a more masculine quality in some of the poems probably written in the later part of his life. This quality is found especially in his translations and imitations of Latin poetry. Matthew Prior, with true critical insight, described him as "Sir Charles that can write and better Translate." His version of the eighth ode of the Second Book of Horace is one of the finest verse translations of the seventeenth century. It is one of those rare translations that reads like an original poem. Horace's dangerous old harlot is transmuted into one of the glittering, rapacious courtesans of the court of Charles II, and the poem is as vivid, incisive, and carefully controlled as the Latin original:

Did any Punishment attend
Thy former Perjuries
I should believe a second time
Thy charming Flatteries:
Did but one Wrinkle mark this Face,
Or hadst thou lost one single Grace.

No sooner hast thou, with false Vows,
Provok'd the Powers above;
But thou art fairer than before
And we are more in love,
Thus Heaven and Earth seem to declare,
They pardon Falshood in the Fair.

Sure 'tis no Crime vainly to swear,
By ev'ry Power on high,
And call our bury'd Mother's Ghost
A witness to the Lye:
Heaven at such Perjuries connives,
And *Venus* with a Smile forgives.

The Nymphs and cruel *Cupid* too,
Sharp'ning his pointed Dart
On an old hone besmear'd with Blood,
Forbear thy perjur'd Heart.
Fresh Youth grows up, to wear thy Chains,
And the Old Slave no Freedom gains.

Thee, Mothers for their eldest Sons,
Thee, wretched Misers fear,
Lest thy prevailing Beauty should
Seduce the hopeful Heir.
New-marry'd Virgins fear thy Charms
Should keep their Bridegroom from their
Arms.

A similar strength is found in a series of adaptations of epigrams by Martial, one of the best of which is cast in the form of a Shakespearian sonnet and must be one of the very few poems in this form written between the early seventeenth and early nineteenth centuries:

Thou art an Atheist, *Quintus,* and a Wit,
Thinkst all was of self-moving Attoms
made,
Religion only for the Vulgar fit,
Priests Rogues, and Preaching their
deceitful Trade;
Wilt drink, whore, fight, blaspheme, damn,
curse and swear:
Why wilt thou swear by God, if there be
none?
And if there be, thou shouldst his
Vengeance fear:
Methinks this Huffing might be let alone;
'Tis thou art free, Mankind besides a Slave,
And yet a Whore can lead thee by the
Nose,
A drunken Bottle, and a flatt'ring Knave,
A mighty Prince, Slave to thy dear Soul's
Foes,
Thy Lust, thy Rage, Ambition and thy Pride;
He that serves God, need nothing serve
beside.

This poem shows that Sedley was capable not only of living in the libertine "Utopia of Gallantry" but also of outgrowing it and criticizing it, though his criticism lacks the philosophic depth and fierce irony of Rochester's.

At the end of his life he wrote a long poem on marriage called *The Happy Pair.* In spite of some rather banal theorizing, the passages denouncing mercenary and loveless marriages have a note of actuality due, no doubt, to the poet's own bitter experience; he was married at the age of seventeen to a woman who became a paranoiac. The conclusion of the poem, with its praise of quiet domesticity, shows that the wild gallant of the 1660's had by the end of the century developed into an Augustan man of feeling." In the following lines there is a sensuous perception of "images of external nature that foreshadows the rural-sentimental poetry of the eighteenth century:

Love, like a cautious fearful Bird ne'er builds,
But where the Place Silence and Calmness yields:
He slily flies to Copses, where he finds
The snugging Woods secure from Blasts and Winds,
Shuns the huge Boughs of a more Stately Form,
And laughs at Trees torn up with ev'ry Storm.

SIR GEORGE ETHEREGE (1635–1692)

Sir George Etherege, born in 1635, probably spent part of his early life in France, where his father died in 1649. He was apprenticed to a London attorney in 1653, and made the acquaintance of Buckhurst (Dorset) through the success of his play *The Comical Revenge* in March 1664. His second comedy, *She Wou'd if She Cou'd,* was staged in February 1668, and in August 1668 he went to Constantinople as secretary to the British ambassador. He was in London in 1671, and his best comedy, *The Man of Mode,* was produced with great success in 1676. In 1679 he was knighted, and in 1685 he went to Ratisbon (Regensburg) as British envoy to the Diet of the Empire. At the Glorious Revolution he relinquished his post at Ratisbon and went to Paris, where he died in May 1692.

Unlike the other members of the court circle, Etherege did not come from a wealthy, aristocratic background. His grandfather was a "vintner," or publican, at Maidenhead; his father, after spending some time in Bermuda, held a small appointment at the court of Charles I and died in exile in France after the royalist defeat. The only certain fact about the young George Etherege is that he was apprenticed by his grandfather to a London attorney at the age of eighteen. Eleven years later his first play was produced with great success at the Duke's Theatre; he dedicated it to Lord Buckhurst (Dorset), and there is no doubt that it was through his friendship with that nobleman that he was accepted as a member of the "merry gang." This experience was the central fact of his life. Like Oscar Wilde two centuries later, he was a wit and an artist in comedy who was admitted into aristocratic circles, and was enchanted by the ideal of the man of fashion and leisure who was master of the art of living. In each of his three comedies one finds this figure, beginning with the sketch of the gay and charming Sir Frederick Frollick in *The Comical Revenge,* proceeding to the two attractive young sparks, Courtall and Freeman in *She Wou'd if She Cou'd,* and culminating in the finished portrait of Dorimant in *The Man of Mode,* said to be based on the character of Rochester. Contrasted with Dorimant in this play is Sir Fopling Flutter, that "eminent Coxcomb," who embodies all that is absurd in the fashionable ideal.

Etherege himself was probably something halfway between Dorimant and Sir Fopling. Just as Wilde called himself a poseur, so Etherege called himself a fop. In one of his letters he writes, "I confess I am a fop in my heart; ill customs influence my senses, and I have been so used to affection [affectation] that without the air of the Court nothing can touch me." Unlike the other members of the "merry gang," he never outgrew the courtly-libertine ideal of the 1660's. Like Wilde he was never so much himself as when he was acting a part, and the part of the fop or perfect aesthetic hero became second nature to him. It might be imagined that such a man, when he wrote verse, would speak only in the "basic voice" of the court poet. Actually, in Etherege's poetry, slight as it is in quantity, one can hear other and more individual voices. John Palmer acutely ascribed to him "a worldly simplicity captivating from its entire lack of self-consciousness," and this describes very well the quality of his best lyrics. His poem addressed "To a Very Young Lady" has none of the playfulness and boudoir eroticism of Sedley's "Song to Cloris," but a kind of innocent freshness that brings him nearer to Marvell or even Henry Vaughan than to Waller or Sedley:

Sweetest bud of beauty, may
No untimely frost decay
The early glories that we trace,
Blooming in thy matchless face;
But kindly opening, like the rose,
Fresh beauties every day disclose,
Such as by nature are not shown
In all the blossoms she has blown—
And then what conquest shall you make
Who hearts already daily take?
Scorched in the morning with thy beams,
How shall we bear those sad extremes
Which must attend thy threatening eyes
When thou shalt to thy noon arise.

The following lyric is more characteristic. Here the voice is that of a persona, the "shepherd" or ideal poet of the court pastoral, a fairy-tale or tapestry world. The attitude of the "shepherd," one may notice, is highly ambiguous. Ostensibly he is issuing a warning against the love of women, but the reader is told that love's "chain" is "imperial" and its pain enchanting." It seems obvious that the loss of "quiet" by those who gaze on "beauteous eyes is a not unenviable condition:

Ye happy youths, whose hearts are free
From Love's imperial chain,
Henceforth be warned and taught by me
T'avoid the enchanting pain.
Fatal the wolves to trembling flocks,
Sharp winds to blossoms prove,
To careless seamen hidden rocks,
To human quiet Love.

Fly the fair sex if bliss you prize,
The snake's beneath the flower;
Whoever gazed on beauteous eyes
That tasted quiet more?

How faithless is the lover's joy!
How constant is his care!
The kind with falsehood do destroy,
The cruel with despair.

The craftsmanship of this poem is remarkable. The common ballad quatrain is enlivened by a subtle pattern of alliteration and assonance, and the cadences ("human quiet Love," "gazed on beauteous eyes," "tasted quiet more") are the work of a fine artist in verbal music. He is equally successful with flowing anapaests in the song called "Silvia." Here the feeling is genuine, but it is of the kind that can be called operatic, like that of Tom Moore's best songs, the manner of which is remarkably foreshadowed in this poem. It is interesting to find that it was immensely popular as "words for music," and was set by no fewer than four different contemporary composers:

The Nymph that undoes me is fair and unkind,
No less than a wonder by Nature design'd;
She's the grief of my heart, the joy of my eye,
And the cause of a flame that never can die.

Her mouth, from whence wit still obligingly flows
Has the beautiful blush and the smell of the rose;
Love and destiny both attend on her will,
She wounds with a look, with a frown she can kill.

The desperate Lover can hope no redress
Where beauty and rigour are both in excess:
In *Silvia* they meet, so unhappy am I,
Who sees her must love and who loves her
  must die.

Etherege can speak in other voices besides that of the courtly gallant. In some of the lyrics in his plays, one can hear the voice of the man of the street, the tavern, and the coffeehouse, using the idiom of the popular song, catch, and street ballad. The following lines, trolled by the sharper Palmer in the tavern scene in *The Comical Revenge* (II. 2), have the salty tang of vernacular speech and the hearty sensuality of popular poetry:

If she be not kind as fair
  But peevish and unhandy,
Leave her—she's only worth the care
  Of some spruce Jack-a-dandy.

I would not have thee such an ass,
  Hadst thou ne'er so much leisure
To sigh and whine for such a lass
  Whose pride's above her pleasure.

Make much of every buxom girl
  Which needs but little courting;
Her value is above the pearl,
  That takes delight in sporting.

The song sung by the "wanton" Gatty in the first scene of the fifth act of *She Wou'd if She Cou'd* is a genuine street ballad that was reprinted in two broadsides. It is poetry that springs as directly from the life of Restoration London as an entry in Pepys's diary:

To little or no purpose I spent many days,
In ranging the Park, the Exchange, and the
  Plays;
For ne'er in my rambles till now did I prove
So lucky to meet with the man I could love.
Oh! how I am pleased when I think on this
  man,
That I find I must love, let me do what I
  can!

How long I shall love him, I can no more
  tell
Than had I a fever when I should be well.
My passion shall kill me before I will
  show it,
And yet I would give all the world he did
  know it;
But oh how I sigh when I think he would
  woo me,
I cannot deny what I know would undo me.

As a poet Etherege is seen at his best in his lyrics; his few complimentary and erotic poems in the heroic couplet are polished but undistinguished. His lines to the marchioness of Newcastle "After the Reading of Her Incomparable Poems" might have been written by any competent imitator of Waller:

Those graces nature did till now divide
(Your sex's glory and our sex's pride)
Are joined in you, and all to you submit,
The brightest beauty and the sharpest wit.
No faction here or fiercer envy sways,
They give you myrtle, while we offer bays.
What mortal dares dispute this wreath with
  you,
Armed thus with lightning and with
  thunder too.

He is said to have written lampoons railing at women, but no "libel" can be certainly ascribed to him. If he is the author of "Mrs. Nelly's Complaint," a satire on Nell Gwynn attributed to him in *The Miscellaneous Works of the Duke of Buckingham,* he cannot be credited with a satiric talent beyond that of those whom Dryden calls "our common libellers." The best passage in the poem gives an amusing glimpse of the strangely variegated company that was to be found in the royal presence at Whitehall in the reign of Charles II:

Let mountebanks make market houses ring
Of what great feats they've done before the
  King,
Let learned Sir *Sam* his
Windsor Engine try,
Before great Charles let guacks and seamen
  lie.
He ne'er heard swearers till *Moll Knight*
  and I,

Never heard oaths less valued, or less true
(And yet 'tis said, he has paid for swearing
 too)
Loudlier we swore than plundering
 dragoons,
'Sblood followed 'Sblood, and Zoons
 succeeded Zoons.

A more individual note is heard in a series of verse epistles written by Etherege to his friends in the tumbling, four-accent "Hudibrastic" meter popularized by Butler's famous poem. In this meter he conducted a witty but obscene correspondence with Buckhurst and, later, when he was British envoy at Ratisbon, wrote verse epistles to his friend and official superior Lord Middleton. One of these epistles contains a description of one of "rough Danube's beauties" that combines the picturesque with the comic in a manner that Byron would not have despised:

How would the ogling sparks despise
The darling damsel of my eyes,
Did they behold her at a play,
As she's tricked up on holiday,
When the whole family combine
For public pride to make her shine.
Her hair which long before lay matted
Are on this day combed out and platted
A diamond bodkin in each tress
The badges of her nobleness;
For every stone as well as she
Can boast an ancient pedigree

. . .

No serpent breaking in the air
Can with her starry head compare
Such ropes of pearls her hands encumber
She scarce can deal the cards at ombre;
So many rings each finger freight,
They tremble with the mighty weight:
The like in England ne'er was seen
Since Holbein drew Hal and his Queen.
But after these fantastic sights
The lustre's meaner than the lights
She that bears this glittering pomp
Is but a tawdry ill-bred ramp
Whose brawny limbs and martial face
Proclaim her of the Gothic race,
More than the painted pageantry
Of all her father's heraldry . . .

Unlike the other "eminent wits," Etherege never goes beneath the surface in his poetry. It is all light verse but, at the same time, it is the work of a true artist and succeeds in transmitting his gaiety, insouciance, and attractive mixture of innocence and sophistication.

CONCLUSION

The pattern of life and writing of the "merry gang" arose from a particular phase of society and culture, and could not be repeated. Men like George Granville, Lord Lansdowne, and William Walsh, who tried to reproduce it after the Glorious Revolution, appear now as Young Pretenders, mere pale and colorless imitations. By the end of the century the character of the libertine court wits had become the absurd anachronism that Swift caricatures in *A Tale of a Tub* when he describes the activities of the three brothers in high society: "they writ and rallied, and rhymed and sung and said, and said nothing: they drank and fought, and slept, and swore, and took snuff: they went to new plays on the first night, haunted the chocolate houses, beat the watch, lay on bulks, and got claps: they bilked hackney-coachmen, ran in debt with shopkeepers, and lay with their wives: they killed bailiffs, kicked fidlers downstairs, eat at Will's, loitered at Lockets. . . ." The men who did these things in Swift's time were, to use his own expression, mere micro-coats, imitators of the externals of what had once been a life of gaiety, poetry, and adventure. Alone among men of the post-Revolution generation William Congreve caught the authentic note of the Restoration wits in a few poems such as the following lyric, the first stanza of which, at least, Rochester would not have disowned:

False though she be to me and love,
 I'll ne'er pursue revenge;
For still the charmer I approve
 Though I deplore her change.

In hours of bliss we oft have met,
They could not always last;
For though the present I regret,
I'm grateful for the past.

The best of the poetry of the court wits lives today by virtue of its youthfulness, insouciance, direct and unaffected speech, Irreverence, and sensuality. These qualities are, perhaps, more acceptable now than at any time since the latter part of the seventeenth century. For long the aura of scandal surrounding the personalities of the wits obscured the historical significance of their writings. They rendered two great services to English poetry. One was to keep the singing voice of the lyric alive in an age of mathematics and scientific positivism. Boileau said that Descartes had cut the throat of poetry. It was to a large extent due to the "merry gang" that the positive spirit of Descartes, Hobbes, and the scientists failed to cut the throat of the English lyric. Their other memorable achievement was to diversify and invigorate the Augustan tradition by preserving the happy freedom of colloquial, informal English poetry, a heritage they handed on to the Queen Anne wits, Swift, Pope, Prior, and Gay, and through them to the Byron of *Beppo, The Vision of Judgment,* and *Don Juan.*

Selected Bibliography

JOHN WILMOT, EARL OF ROCHESTER

BIBLIOGRAPHY

Prinz, J., *John Wilmot, Earl of Rochester: His Life and Writings,* (Leipzig, 1927) contains a full descriptive bibliography of Rochester's writings; J. Thorpe, ed., *Rochester's Poems on Several Occasions,* (Princeton, 1950) deals with the complex status and order of the "Antwerp" eds. (see below)—it and Vieth (below) contain valuable bibliographical information not in Prinz; Vieth, D. M., *Attribution in Restoration Poetry: A Study of Rochester's Poems of 1680,* (London, 1963).

COLLECTED WORKS

Poems on Several Occasions, "Antwerp," (1680) includes a number of poems not by Rochester and an Antwerp imprint that is almost certainly spurious—at least ten eds. (fewer than twenty copies of which survive) were surreptitiously printed from 1680 on, dated or antedated that year, or without date (a facsimile of the Huntington Library copy, J. Thorpe, ed. (Princeton, 1950) contains a valuable intro. and notes; *Poems on Several Occasions,* (London, 1685) repr. (1701, 1712) omits nine poems that appeared in the 1680 collection but adds five others; *Poems &c. on Several Occasions, with Valentinian, a Tragedy,* (London, 1691) repr. (1696, 1705) published by Jacob Tonson, with preface by Thomas Rymer, is an expurgated text that contains additional authentic poems; *The Miscellaneous Works,* (London, 1707) printed and sold by B. Bragge, pirated by Edmund Curll (London, 1707 1709) contains poems by other authors besides Rochester (the "Life of Rochester" is not, as stated in the title, by Charles de Saint-Évremond); *The Works,* (London, 1714) a reprint of Tonson's ed. of 1705, including a number of Rochester's letters (for later eds., notably the 2-vol. collection of poems by Rochester, Roscommon, Dorset, and others (London, 1714) reprinted many times during the eighteenth century with or without "The Cabinet of Love," appendix, see Prinz's bibliography; J. Hayward, ed. *The Collected Works,* (London, 1926) a Nonesuch lim. ed., contains almost everything that has been attributed to Rochester, including a number of spurious poems; V. de S. Pinto, ed. *Poems,* (London, 1953) rev. ed. (1964) in the Muses' Library, the first attempt to establish a reliable canon (though not a definitive text) of the poems, includes an appendix of poems attributed to Rochester on doubtful authority; D. M. Vieth, ed. *The Complete Poems,* (New Haven–London, 1968).

SEPARATE WORKS

"A Satyr Against Mankind Written by a Person of Honour," (London: *ca.,* 1679) a folio poem published, according to Anthony à Wood, in June 1679; "Upon Nothing by a Person of Honour," (London: *ca,* 1679) two undated folios published about 1679 repr. by E. Curll (London, 1711) and by R. H. Griffiths (Austin, Tex., 1946); "A Letter from Artemizia in the Town of Chloë in the Country," (London: n.d., 1670) of which two eds. exist in folio; *Valentinian: A Tragedy as 'Tis Alter'd by the Late Earl of Rochester,* (London, 1685) twice issued in 1685, contains an important preface by Robert Wolseley and was repr. in J. E. Spingarn, ed. *Critical Essays of the Seventeenth Century, III* (London, 1909); *Familiar Letters,* 2 vols. (London, 1697) repr. (1699, 1705); *The Rochester-Savile Letters 1671–1680,* J. H. Wilson, ed. (Columbus, Ohio, 1941) a modern ed. of the letters to Henry Savile in *Familiar Letters* together with Savile's extant letters to Rochester; V. de S. Pinto, ed. "The Famous Pathologist or the Noble Mountebank," (Nottingham, 1961) Rochester's "Mountebank Bill," printed from the MS of his servant Thomas Alcock, with Alcock's preface telling how he masqueraded as the Italian quack doctor "Bendo" (a contemporary, possibly the original, printed edition of Alexander Bendo's advertisement—without place, printer, or date—has survived in an apparently unique copy).

BIOGRAPHICAL AND CRITICAL STUDIES

Parsons, R., *A Sermon Preached at the Funeral of the Right Honourable John Earl of Rochester,* (Oxford, 1680); Burnet, G., *Some Passages of the Life and Death of the Right Honourable John Earl of Rochester,* (London, 1680) repr. in many eighteenth-century eds. and in V. de S. Pinto, ed. *English Biography of the Seventeenth Century* (London, 1951) and the basis of many hortatory tracts and pious pamphlets issued as religious propaganda until the end of the nineteenth century; Johnson, S., *The Lives of the Most Eminent English Poets,* (London, 1781) includes Johnson's "Life of Rochester,"; Forgues, E. D., "John Wilmot comte de Rochester," (*Revue des deux mondes,* Aug.–Sept. 1857); *Rochesteriana,* J. Prinz, ed. and comp. (Leipzig, 1926); Prinz, J., *John Wilmot, Earl of Rochester: His Life and Writings,* (Leipzig, 1927); Williams, C., *Rochester,* (London, 1935); Whitfield, F., *Beast in View: A Study of the Earl of Rochester's Poetry,* (Cambridge, Mass., 1939); de, V., S.Pinto "Rochester and the Right Veine of Satire," *Essays and Studies by Members of the English Association* n.s. 5 (London, 1953); Vieth, D. M., "Rochester's 'Scepter Lampoon' on Charles II," *Philological Quarterly* 37 (1958); de, V., S. Pinto "Rochester and Dryden," *Renaissance and Modern Studies* 5 (1961); de, V., *Enthusiast in Wit: A Portrait of John Wilmot Earl of Rochester,* S. Pinto (London 1962) a rev. and enl. ed. of his *Rochester: Portrait of a Restoration Poet* (London, 1935); Berman, R., "Rochester and the Defeat of the Senses," *Kenyon Review* 26 (Spring 1964); *Renaissance and Modern Essays: Presented to V. de Sola Pinto in Celebration of His Seventieth Birthday,* G. R. Hibbard, G. A. Panichas, and A. Rodway, eds. (London, 1966) includes H. Erskine-Hill's essay "Rochester: Augustan or Explorer?".

CHARLES SACKVILLE, EARL OF DORSET

BIBLIOGRAPHY

Bagley, H. A., "A Check-List of Dorset's Poems," *Modern Language Notes* 47 (Nov. 1932) 454–461; Howarth, R. G., "Some Additions to the Poems of Lord Dorset," *Modern Language Notes* 50 (Nov. 1935) 457.

COLLECTED WORKS

The Works of the Earls of Rochester, Roscommon, Dorset &c., 2 vols. (London, 1714) vol. II of which contains the earliest known collection of "Poems by the Earl of Dorset"; *The Works of the Most Celebrated Minor Poets,* 2 vols. (London, 1749) repr. (Dublin, 1751) vol. I of which contains "Poems by the Earl of Dorset"; *A Supplement to the Works of the Minor Poets, Part I,* London n.d. contains additional poems by Dorset.

SEPARATE WORKS

Pompey the Great, (London, 1664) translation of Corneille's *La mort de Pompée* see below, under Sedley; "Hay Hay," a broadside ballad, entered in the Stationers' Register on 30 Dec. 1664 of which no copy if known to survive—usually known as "Song Written at Sea in the First Dutch War," the earliest extant printed version is in *Wit and Mirth or Pills to Purge Melancholy* V (London, 1714) 168–170 under the title "A Ballad by the Late Lord Dorset When at Sea," an early MS version of the poem is in Br. Mus. Harl. MS 3991, printed by N. Ault in his *Seventeenth Century Lyrics* (London, 1928) 333; *A Collection of Poems Written Upon Several Occasions by Several Persons,* (London, 1672) printed for Hobart Kemp, contains three poems probably by Buckhurst (Dorset), and was the predecessor of a number of other Restoration miscellanies containing a few poems by him; *Poems on Affairs of State,* (London, 1697) contains Dorset's "The Duel of the Crabs," a parody of Sir Robert Howard's "The Duel of the Stags".

BIOGRAPHICAL AND CRITICAL STUDIES

Johnson, S., *The Lives of the Most Eminent English Poets,* (London, 1781) includes his "Life of Dorset"; Harris, B., *Charles Sackville, Sixth Earl of Dorset: Patron and Poet of the Restoration,* (Urbana, Ill, 1940).

SIR CHARLES SEDLEY

BIBLIOGRAPHY

V. de S. Pinto, ed. *The Poetical and Dramatic Works,* 2 vols. (London, 1928) contains a bibliography of Sedley's writings.

COLLECTED WORKS

Capt. Ayloffe, ed. *The Miscellaneous Works,* (London, 1702) repr. with additional material, not all of which is by Sedley (London, 1707 1710); *The Works,* 2 vols (London, 1722) repr. (1776, 1778) contains an account of the life of Sedley, possibly by Defoe; V. de S. Pinto, ed.*The Poetical and Dramatic Works,* 2 vols. (London, 1928).

SEPARATE WORKS

Pompey the Great, (London, 1664) a translation of Corneille's *La mort de Pompée* by Waller, Buckhurst, Sedley, Godolphin, and Filmer (act III possibly by Sedley); *The Mulberry Garden: A Comedy,* (London, 1668) repr. (1675, 1688); *A Collection of Poems Written Upon Several Occasions by Several Persons,* (London, 1672) printed for Hobart Kemp, contains about thirty poems by Sedley—repr. with some additional matter for T. Collins and J. Ford (London, 1673) and with further additional matter and some alterations for F. Saunders (London, 1693); *Antony and Cleopatra: A Tragedy,* (London, 1677) repr. (1696); *Bellamira or the Mistress: A Comedy,* (London, 1687); *The Happy Pair, or, A Poem on Matrimony,* (London, 1702).

BIOGRAPHICAL AND CRITICAL STUDIES

de S. Pinto, V., *Sir Charles Sedley,* (London, 1927); Davies, H. N., "Dryden's *All for Love* and Sedley's *Antony and Cleopatra,*" (*Notes and Queries,* June 1967).

SIR GEORGE ETHEREGE

BIBLIOGRAPHY

H. F. B. Brett Smith, ed. *The Dramatic Works,* 2 vols. (Oxford, 1927) contains a bibliography of the plays; J. Thorpe, ed. *The Poems,* (Princeton, 1963) contains valuable bibliographical information about the poems.

COLLECTED WORKS

The Works, (London, 1704); A. W. Verity, ed. *The Works,* (London, 1888); H. F. B. Brett Smith, ed. *The Dramatic Works,* 2 vols. (Oxford, 1927) repr. (1971); J. Thorpe, ed. *The Poems,* (Princeton, 1963).

SEPARATE WORKS

The Comical Revenge, or, Love in a Tub, (London, 1664) repr. (1667, 1669, 1689, 1697); *She Wou'd if She Cou'd: A Comedy,* (London, 1668) repr. (1671, 1693, 1710) also in C. M. Taylor, ed., Regents Restoration Drama series (Lincoln, Nebr., 1972); *The Man of Mode, or, Sir Fopling Flutter,* (London, 1676) repr. (1684, 1693, 1711) also in W. B. Carnochan, ed., Regents Restoration Drama series (Lincoln, Nebr., 1972); S. Rosenfeld, ed. *The Letterbook of Sir George Etherege,* (Oxford, 1928).

BIOGRAPHICAL AND CRITICAL STUDIES

Gosse, E., *Seventeenth Century Studies,* (London, 1883); Palmer, J., *The Comedy of Manners,* (London,(1913); Dobré, B., *Essays in Biography,* (London, 1925); Dorothy Foster, contributions to *Notes and Queries* 153 (1927) 154 (1928) and to *Review of English Studies* 8 (1932); Dennis, J., "A Defense of Sir Fopling Flutter," (London, 1722) repr. in E. N. Hooker, ed. *The Critical Works of John Dennis* 2 vols. (Baltimore, 1939–1943); Underwood, D., *Etherege and the Seventeenth Century Comedy of Manners,* (New Haven, 1957) vol. 135 of Yale Studies in English; Boyette, P. E., "Songs of George Etherege," *Studies in English Literature, 1500–1900* VI (Houston, Tex., 1966).

GENERAL WORKS

BIBLIOGRAPHY

Case, A. E., *A Bibliography of English Poetical Miscellanies, 1521–1750,* (London, 1935); Day, C. L., *English Song Books, 1651–1702, a Bibliography,* Boswell, E., (London, 1940).

BIOGRAPHICAL AND CRITICAL STUDIES

Wood à, Anthony, *Athenae Oxonienses,* Wood 2 vols. (London, 1691–1692) also in P. Bliss, ed., 4 vols. (London, 1813–1820); Johnson, S., *The Lives of the Most Eminent English Poets,* 4 vols. (London, 1781) rev. ed. of 1783 by G. B. Hill, ed., 3 vols (Oxford, 1905); Spence, J., *Anecdotes, Observations and Characters of Books and Men Collected From the Conversation of Mr. Pope and Other Eminent Persons of His Time,* S. W. Singer, ed. (London, 1820) a def. ed. by J. M. Osborn, ed. (London, 1966); Aubrey, J., *Brief Lives,* A. Clark, ed., 2 vols. (Oxford, 1898) also in A. Powell, ed. (London, 1949); *Critical Essays of the Seventeenth Century,* J. E. Spingarn, ed. 3 vols. (Oxford, 1908); *Cambridge History of English Literature,* VIII (London, 1912) contains C. Whibley, "The Court Poets"; Leavis, F. R., *Revaluation,* (London, 1936); Wilson, J. H., *The Court Wits of the Restoration,* (Princeton, 1948); de, V., *Restoration Carnival,* S. Pinto (London, 1954) a Folio Society lim. ed.; Sutherland, J. R., *English Literature in the Late Seventeenth Century,* (Oxford, 1969).

HISTORICAL AND SOCIAL BACKGROUND

Hamilton, A., *Mémoires du Chevalier de Gramont,* (Cologne, 1713) also by Peter Quennell, trans. (London, 1930) and in C. Engel, ed., (Monaco, 1958); Burnet, G., *The History of My Own Time,* 2 vols. (London, 1724–1734) in O. Airy, ed., 2 vols. (Oxford, 1897–1900); *The Life of Edward Earl of Clarendon Written by Himself,* (Oxford, 1759) 2nd ed., 2 vols. (Oxford, 1857); *The Diary of Samuel Pepys,* H. B. Wheatley, ed., 10 vols. (London, 1893–1899); Bryant, A., *King Charles II,* (London, 1931); *The Diary of John Evelyn,* E. S. de Beer, ed., 6 vols. (Oxford, 1955); Ogg, D., *England in the Reign of Charles II,* 2 vols. (Oxford, 1956); Wedgwood, C. V., *Poetry and Politics Under the Stuarts,* (London, 1960); G. de F. Lord, ed., *Poems on Affairs of State,* Vol. I *1660–1678* (New Haven–London, 1863).

Adrienne Rich
(b. 1929)

HARRIET DAVIDSON

Adrienne Rich is widely recognized as the preeminent American poet-critic of the post–World War II years. Such claims about living authors are always controversial; in Rich's case her gender and her radical politics make her status even more contested. Still, her powerful and moving poetry and her often chillingly lucid essays have brought her a large popular following, as well as critical acclaim, for her dual role as poet and political spokesperson of the contemporary feminist movement. One of the most passionate and complex statements of the evolution of feminist thought in a time when feminism is challenging and changing virtually every field of endeavor, Rich's work draws on the great tradition of social and political poetry but enriches that tradition with the revolutionary feminist insight that the personal is political. In her poems and essays, her life and the lives of countless other women become the site of social and political analysis. And through this analysis, Rich's poetry breaks the mold of the modernism she was trained in, shattering the confinement of formalism, aestheticism, and universalism to achieve a distinctly postmodern engagement with history, society, and identity.

In the foreword to *The Fact of a Doorframe* (1984), Rich writes: "One task for the nineteen or twenty-year-old poet who wrote the earliest poems here was to learn that she was neither unique nor universal, but a person in history, a woman and not a man, a white and also Jewish inheritor of a particular Western consciousness, from the making of which most women have been excluded." Rich's career charts her refusal of the dual idealism of the unique, which seeks an authentic self repressed by patriarchal society, and the universal, which seeks a female essentialism.

In its progress Rich's writing and, indeed, her life seem an allegory of American feminism. She began as the privileged daughter, wife, and mother writing carefully constructed formalist poems, became radicalized by the repression of the 1950s and the politics of the 1960s, and turned to writing passionate, experimental, political poems that rage against "the oppressor's language," which will not let her speak herself. Rich emerged in the 1970s as a radical spokesperson for women's rights and lesbian feminism, writing a consciously woman-centered poetry and prose. But in the late 1970s and 1980s, under pressure from those women of color who felt excluded by the white, middle-class biases of the feminist movement, Rich was moved to examine her own complicity in oppression by virtue of her privileged background. In doing so, she had to discover the importance of differences beyond the simple binary of male/female.

In her influential essay "Notes Toward a Politics of Location" (1984), Rich emphasizes the myriad differences "among women, men, places, times, cultures, conditions, classes, movements," finding that she must first locate herself, hold herself accountable for where she is in her particular place, historical moment, and personal history: "I need to understand how a place on a map is also a place in history within which as a woman, a Jew, a lesbian, a feminist I am created and trying to create." Rich's emphasis on "location" keeps her tied to the material world and away from the temptations of philosophical idealism and transcendence that tend to obscure the material conditions of different people's lives. Instead, in her most mature poetry Rich grapples with history and difference, and the webs of knowledge and power in a poetic expression of the most sophisticated critical theory of our time.

Rich was born on 16 May 1929 in Baltimore, Maryland. Her father, Arnold Rich, was Jewish, a shopkeeper's son raised in Birmingham, Alabama, and sent in his teens to a military school in North Carolina that Rich describes in her autobiographical essay "Split at the Root: An Essay on Jewish Identity" (1982) as "a place for training white southern Christian gentlemen." Intense, brilliant, and cultured, he became a doctor at Johns Hopkins University. At Hopkins, where no Jew had ever held a chair in the medical school, his appointment to a professorship of pathology was delayed for years. Nevertheless, Arnold chose to identify himself as a scientist and a deist rather than as a Jew. It was a choice he imposed on his children as well, although, as Rich saw in retrospect, it is not something about which society gives one a choice.

Rich's gentile mother seems to have been as brilliant and independent as Rich's father. Helen Jones was a talented concert pianist and composer who won a scholarship to the Peabody Conservatory in Baltimore and later studied in New York, Paris, and Vienna. After marrying, she gave up her career to devote herself to her family, managing the household and teaching Adrienne and her younger sister, Cynthia, all of their lessons, including music, until they were in the fourth grade.

In *Of Woman Born* (1976) Rich compares her parents with Louisa May Alcott's parents, Bronson and Abigail Alcott, transcendentalists who believed they could raise their children according to "a unique moral and intellectual plan" removed from the determinants of society or history. Rich's charismatic father seized upon his precocious first child and educated her like an elder son:

> My father was an amateur musician, read poetry, adored encyclopedic knowledge. He prowled and pounced over my school papers, insisting I use "grown-up" sources; he criticized my poems for faulty technique and gave me books on rhyme and meter and form. His investment in my intellect was egotistical, tyrannical, opinionated and terribly wearing. He taught me, nevertheless, to believe in hard work, to mistrust easy inspiration, to write and rewrite; to feel that I was a person of the book, even though a woman; to take ideas seriously. He made me feel, at a very young age, the power of language and that could share in it. (*Blood, Bread, and Poetry,* p. 113)

Rich did take herself seriously as a writer from a very young age, having some of her work published when she was only ten.

Arnold Rich occupies a place of ambivalence for Rich; he is the inspired source of her art but also the cruel patriarch who would make the world, including himself, into an ideal image of intellectual perfection. She sees her first resistance to him as a bodily one, recognizing, perhaps, how impossibly her female, child's body fit into his ideal vision. Early on, she was given to "tics and tantrums" caused, she feels, by her father's perfectionist pressures on her; the crippling arthritis she developed in her early twenties also becomes for her an emblem of her body's resistance to perfection. Rich's need to assert her difference from her father's vision is one seed of her later feminism.

Her first conscious rebellion focused on her Jewishness. In "Split at the Root" Rich describes how, at age sixteen, she slipped off to a theater to watch films of the liberation of the death camps, looking at the evidence of the Holocaust with uncomprehending eyes, knowing that she "was connected to those dead by something—not just mortality but a taboo name, a hated identity." But the connection was vague and tenuous in a house where anti-Semitism had never been discussed, where the belief endured that you could choose to transcend society. Only later did Rich learn that, in spite of her father's disregard of his Jewishness, "according to Nazi logic, my two Jewish grandparents would have made me a *Mischling,* first degree—nonexempt from the Final Solution."

Rich's parents disapproved of her interest in the Holocaust. Though they felt they were encouraging intellectual objectivity, Rich later recognized that they actually encouraged conformity to the anti-Semitism of the dominant culture. Her household respected the norm of "white social christianity," and she was taught Southern manners and female passivity even while she was encouraged to be critical, assertive, and independent. No wonder this alternative world of the intellect came to be associated with the secret Jewishness. From the beginning she felt "split at the root": both Jewish and casually anti-Semitic, educated to conform to stereotypes of feminine behavior and to question, critique, and aggressively challenge the world as it is from the position of a transcendentalist's "unique moral and intellectual" perspective.

When Rich left the South—for good, it turns out—to attend Radcliffe (from which she graduated with honors in 1951), she tried to turn away from the contradictions of her home through both intellectual achievements and associating with Jewish friends. When in 1953 she married Alfred Conrad, a divorced Jew from Brooklyn, her parents refused to attend the wedding. By the time her first child was born, she says, "I was barely in communication with my parents."

But Rich had hardly left her parents behind. Alfred Conrad, seemingly so different from Rich's father in his acceptance of Jewish culture, was also similar in many ways. He, too, was a university professor, teaching economics at Harvard, he, too, had deep, though more conflicting, ambivalences about his heritage, having changed his name to assimilate into the Yankee Protestant culture more easily. Rich, like her mother, pushed aside her own rising career as a poet to be the proper academic wife and mother, having three children before she was thirty.

Even her early poetry was under the spell of her father's perfectionist eye and her family's respectability. Rich's first book, *A Change of World* (1951), was chosen by W. H. Auden for the Yale Younger Poets Award. Auden's rather indirect and patronizing foreword to this book personifies Rich's poems in saying they are "neatly and modestly dressed, speak quietly but do not mumble, respect their elders but are not cowed by them, and do not tell fibs." Indeed, these early poems are beautifully crafted, displaying a wide range of reading and the influence of the modernist masters Robert Frost, Wallace Stevens, William Butler Yeats, and Auden. What Auden misses is the repressed passion, the struggle, so evident to readers today, against the boundaries of life. In her 1971 landmark essay "When We Dead Awaken: Writing as Re-Vision," Rich writes of these poems:

> Looking back at poems I wrote before I was 21, I'm startled because beneath the conscious craft are glimpses of the split I even then experienced between the girl who wrote poems, who defined herself in writing poems, and the girl who was to define herself by her relationships with men. "Aunt Jennifer's Tigers," written while I was a student, looks with deliberate detachment at this split. . . . It was important to me that Aunt Jennifer was a person as distinct from myself as possible—distanced by the formalism of the poem, by its objective, observant tone. . . . In those years formalism was part of the strategy—like asbestos gloves, it allowed me to handle materials I couldn't pick up barehanded. (*Adrienne Rich's Poetry,* p. 93)

"Aunt Jennifer's Tigers" contrasts the creative needlework produced by Aunt Jennifer's fingers with "the massive weight of Uncle's wedding band," which "sits heavily upon Aunt Jennifer's hand." As the fingers that metonymically represent Aunt Jennifer's desires remain bounded by the wedding ring, so Rich's feminist awareness remains bounded by the formal demands of her verse:

When Aunt is dead, her terrified hands will
lie
Still ringed with ordeals she was mastered by.
The tigers in the panels that she made
Will go on prancing, proud and unafraid.

The irony of the poem seems diminished by the neat and undisturbed closure; indeed, this ending emphasizes the ability of art to transcend the terror of a woman's life.

Other poems from this volume also view life as difficult and constraining, but they ascribe problems to universal, existential causes rather than social, historical ones. In Rich's lovely "Storm Warnings," "weather abroad" is likened to "weather in the heart"; both are forces of nature that we can only shelter ourselves against, not change: "We can only close the shutters." Again, in the tradition of modernism her ending sets her art against an alien world:

I draw the curtains as the sky goes black
And set a match to candles sheathed in glass
. . .
This is our sole defense against the season;
These are the things that we have learned
to do
Who live in troubled regions.

Rich recognizes the trouble in her world, the contradictions in her life and her husband's, and yet, like her parents, tries to see herself as exceptional, and art as a sheltered world—behind the curtains, sheathed in glass—apart from the turbulence of life.

Rich's second book, *The Diamond Cutters and Other Poems,* was published in 1955, in the same month her first child, David, was born. It received wide acclaim, winning the Ridgely Torrence Memorial Award of the Poetry Society of America (1955) and leading to a National Institute of Arts and Letters Award in 1960 and a second Guggenheim Fellowship in 1961 (her first was in 1952). Still, she writes in "When We Dead Awaken," "By the time that book came out I was already dissatisfied with those poems, which seemed to me mere exercises for poems I hadn't written."

Showing the influence of Frost in masterful narrative pieces about domestic life such as "The Perennial Answer" and "Autumn Equinox," the poems in this volume speak of people torn between their desire and their social roles. The erotic passion of women is hinted at but repressed, seemingly by the demands of, art as well as of society. The title poem provides Rich's metaphor for the poet; the diamond cutter, by his careful craft, can "liberate" the light of the diamond from the stone, as poems create light from the darkness and pain of our lives. Africa is the unexamined metaphor for that darkness, as diamonds are used as universal symbols of value. When the poem was reprinted in 1984, Rich added this note:

> Thirty years later I have trouble with the informing metaphor of this poem. I was trying, in my twenties, to write about the craft of poetry. . . . The enforced and exploited labor of actual Africans in actual diamond mines was invisible to me, and therefore invisible in the poem, which does not take responsibility for its own metaphor. (*The Fact of a Doorframe,* p. 329)

For Rich the process of taking responsibility for her metaphors began with trying to understand how supposedly "natural" meanings are political and historical. Nowhere was this process more urgent for her than in her understanding of the roles of woman, mother, and wife. After the births of her second and third sons, Paul (1957) and Jacob (1959), Rich found that the exhausting task of caring for three young children led to frustration, anger, and guilt never associated with her image of mother. In 1960 she felt monstrous in her anger toward her children. She wrote in her diary:

> My children cause me the most exquisite suffering of which I have any experience. It is the suffering of ambivalence: the murderous alternation between bitter resentment and raw-edged nerves, and blissful gratification and tenderness. Sometimes I seem to myself, in my feelings toward these tiny guiltless be-

ings, a monster of selfishness and intolerance. Their voices wear away at my nerves, their constant needs, above all their need for simplicity and patience, fill me with despair at my own failures, despair too at my fate, which is to serve a function for which I was not fitted.

Later, in *Of Woman Born* (1976), Rich would write with eloquence about how the isolation of women and children in middle-class America of the 1950s put an impossible burden upon mother and child. But in 1960 Rich blamed herself for failing to meet her "fate," seeing her difference from the ideal as monstrous.

The admission of the monstrous, however it covered over the systemic causes of her problems, was the admission of difference. Rich needed to disengage herself from allegiances to poetic masters and to her father's craft, leading her to a critique of the definitions of woman in the brilliant, angry poems of *Snapshots of a Daughter-in-Law* (1963). The title poem, her first fully feminist poem, is written in ten loosely connected free-verse sections; the force of "snapshots" in the title of the poem indicates how much she was abandoning her idea of poetry as careful craft set against the storms of life. Now there is no refuge in the home, no place for transcendence and self-definition apart from the social forces. In "When We Dead Awaken Writing as Re-Vision" she writes of this poem:

> In the late fifties I was able to write, for the first time, directly about experiencing myself as a woman. The poem was jotted in fragments during children's naps, brief hours in a library, or at 3 A.M. after rising with a wakeful child. . . . Yet I began to feel that my fragments and scraps had a common consciousness and a common theme, one which I would have been very unwilling to put on paper at an earlier time because I had been taught that poetry should be "universal," which meant, of course, non-female. . . . It was an extraordinary relief to write that poem. (*Adrienne Rich's Poetry*, p. 97)

This poem teems with images of the monstrous and violent consequences of the oppression of women. The repressed mother has a mind "mouldering like wedding-cake," "crumbling to pieces under the knife-edge"; the angry daughter trapped in the kitchen lets "the tapstream scald her arm, / a match burn to her thumbnail"; the thinking woman "sleeps with monsters"; later, "she shaves her legs until they gleam / like petrified mammoth-tusk"; men label the independent Mary Wollstonecraft "harpy, shrew and whore." The poem uses literary allusion and quotation to indict literature and deny its distance from politics. If, as she says, "Time is male," then so are literature and history. Rich's violence lashes out at women as well as men, at herself as well as others: women are victims but also inevitably perpetrators of the culture that oppresses them.

The final section of the poem provides a way out of this vicious circle, but it, too, is monstrous in a way: the apocalyptic vision of a new woman who would "smash the mould straight off" can only be defined as a strange and monstrous being, part woman, part bird or avenging angel, part boy, part machine:

> Well,
> she's long about her coming, who must be
> more merciless to herself than history.
> Her mind full to the wind, I see her plunge
> breasted and glancing through the currents,
> taking the light upon her
> at least as beautiful as any boy
> or helicopter,
> poised, still coming,
> her fine blades making the air wince
> but her cargo
> no promise then:
> delivered
> palpable
> ours.

Rich's now famous image alludes to a similar one in Simone de Beauvoir's *The Second Sex* and complexly combines irony, war, and sexuality in this powerful, otherworldly vision. The vision aspires to a freedom beyond human knowledge, a vision of woman as Other, a triumph of the imagination that marks a beginning, not an ending, of work to be done. In spite of its bitterness and self-hatred, the poem begins the work of reshaping the world by recovering women's voices in Rich's allusions to de Beauvoir, Wollstonecraft, and Emily Dickinson and by rewriting the male tradition to include women (as she rewrites T. S. Eliot's allusion to Baudelaire's "mon semblable, mon frère" as "ma semblable, ma soeur").

The poems in this volume completely shake off Auden's epitaph of "modest" and instead present bold, disturbing images, particularly of women in domestic situations. Rich's need to get out of the house and, in a figurative sense, out of the house of this culture, is figured in the apocalyptic flying woman of "Snapshots." A similar image of escape informs "The Roofwalker," where she identifies with the builder, the roofwalker, standing on the roof of the unfinished house: "exposed, larger than life, / and due to break my neck." What she wants to rise above is both her own handiwork—"Was it worth while to lay— / with infinite exertion— / a roof I can't live under?"—and something she is a victim of: "A life I didn't choose / chose me." Given her complicity in the building of the unlivable house and home, she must leave behind not just the house but also her clothes and her very identity as female—wife and mother—and be "a naked man fleeing / across the roofs."

The urge to transcend the world remained strong in Rich's most visionary poems for two decades. But it was met with an equally powerfully realism that kept her struggling to find community and protesting the inadequacy of language to represent the reality of women's lives.

The title poem of *Necessities of Life* (1966) defines the poet, but this time as one who turns from all models for her existence, models that "swallowed me like Jonah," to "the bare necessities": "I learned to make myself / unappetizing. Scaly as a dry bulb / thrown into a cellar." This reduction does not lead to finding an authentic voice; instead, she rather comically wants to see herself as a cabbage or an eel, and her inspiration comes from outside:

> . . . I have invitations:
> a curl of mist steams upward
>
> from a field, visible as my breath,
> houses along a road stand waiting
>
> like old women knitting, breathless
> to tell their tales.

Rich's play on "breath" as the etymological root of inspiration, as well as a metonym for speaking, links her poetic project to telling the stories of those who are silent in this culture, the old women who, like Aunt Jennifer, have only their (much undervalued) needlework to speak for them. This feminist project would not be completely realized until 1974, when Rich returned to the house for her tales in the powerful "From an Old House in America." The poems in *Necessities of Life* still generally shun the house and female roles, often imaging the active resistance to these roles as masculine. She praises Emily Dickinson in "I Am in Danger—Sir—" as "you, woman, masculine / in single-mindedness," and her vision of herself as mother is still monstrous: In "Night-Pieces: For a Child" she sees herself as "death's head, sphinx, medusa." But she also expresses moments of great tenderness for her family and of belief in the "difficult, ordinary happiness" that "finds us" in the midst of existential and historical death and despair ("In the Woods").

In 1966 Rich moved with her family to New York City, where Alfred Conrad taught at City College of New York. With all three of her children in school, Rich was able to turn her attention more fully to her own interests. She lectured at Swarthmore College from 1966 to 1968 and was also adjunct professor of writing in the graduate school of Columbia University from 1967 to 1969. She had amassed an impressive number of awards for her work; in addition to two Guggenheim Fellowships she had won two prizes from *Poetry* magazine, and her work was generally respected and praised. She had begun to write essays and reviews and could, it seems, have settled comfortably into the role of the academic poet. Instead, her life and her writing took a radical turn toward a political engagement and profound self-questioning that still distinguish her work.

In 1968 Rich began teaching writing in City College's open admissions and SEEK programs, instituted to provide remedial instruction to freshmen entering City College from substandard ghetto high schools. In "Teaching Language in Open Admissions" (1972) she describes how the "unnerving and seductive" experience of teaching in such a program reinforced her sense of the complicity between language and power. Many of her students who were inarticulate within the bounds of white, middle-class academic work were forceful and articulate intelligences within the bounds of their own cultures. She and many of her colleagues felt neither willing nor able to reconcile these students to an academic way of speaking and writing that, far from objective, was in fact a language full of the biases of race, class, and sex that helped keep them economically disadvantaged. Still, Rich hoped to use the resources of both the language of the status quo and the language of the street, believing that "language can be used as a means of changing reality."

At this time Rich was increasingly involved in protests against the Vietnam war, and her heightened political awareness put pressure on her poetry. The poems in *Leaflets* (1969) achieve a strong, consistent voice, rich with erotic passion, rebellious energy, and political commitment. The language of war, often figured as the Holocaust or as a war between women and men, runs throughout this collection. Increasing in intensity, especially after 1967, many of the poems mirror the violence of the race riots, student demonstrations, and assassinations of 1968. Rich was working in two modes in this book. While she continued to craft images contrasting the oppression of the house to a transcendent freedom in the sky, a dualism beautifully realized in the poem "Orion," she was also working into a much more radical and experimental vision. The title poem finds yet another image for poetry:

I want to hand you this
leaflet streaming with rain or tears
but the words coming clear
something you might find crushed into your
hand
after passing a barricade
and stuff in your raincoat pocket.
I want this to reach you
who told me once that poetry is nothing
sacred
—no more sacred that is
than other things in your life—

Here, much more clearly than in the quite literary poems of *Snapshots,* Rich desires a poetry not removed from the world but, rather, engaged, active, a part of the political and emotional turmoil of the time. Using the work of Urdu poet Mirza Ghalib (1797–1869) as a model, in the summer of 1968 Rich wrote some of the most formally experimental poems of her career. Her "Ghazals: Homage to Ghalib" consists of seventeen sections, each dated and including at least five thematically unconnected couplets. This form produces cryptic and enigmatic images with almost none of the discursive clarity that marks much of Rich's other verse. Instead, the poems suggest her profound distrust of language as communication yoked to her deep belief in the expressive powers of the poet: "These words are vapor-trails of a plane that has vanished; / by the time I write them out, they are whispering something else."

In "Tear Gas," a powerful, emotionally wrought poem written in 1969 but not collected until 1975 (*Poems Selected and New*), Rich again brings the weight of political activity to bear upon her private life and her poetry. In this poem she wants "a word that will shed itself like a tear / onto the page / leaving its stain." This desire for emotional immediacy and physical presence in language indicates her frustration with the inadequacy of language, both in its publicness and in its inevitable split between word and thing. But she is also increasingly aware of the body as a political issue. She connects the demonstrators being teargassed outside Fort Dix, New Jersey, with her memory of a childhood punishment: "Locked in the closet at 4 years old I beat the wall with my body / that act is in me still." What shall be done with bodies—their killing, maiming, imprisonment, or their more subtle disciplining by a culture (as Michel Foucault so eloquently chronicles in *The History of Sexuality*)—becomes the crucial issue for Rich: "The will to change begins in the body not in the mind / My politics is in my body."

This poem foreshadows the politics of the body that would become central to feminism in the 1970s, both in the practical world of political action and in the theoretical writings of French feminists, who speak of writing the body as an alternative to the oppressor's language. But Rich has never believed it is possible to write the body, even metaphorically, given the nature of language and its tie to institutions of power. Instead, after listing a series of images of a more physical, apprehensible language, she says: "but this is not what I mean / these images are not what I mean / . . . I want you to listen / when I speak badly / not in poems but in tears / not my best but my worst." A raw, risky poem that admits the failure of poetry, it nevertheless uses rhetorical resources—short lines, repetition—to touch the reader emotionally in a shameless exposing and manipulation of emotions. This poem, as well as the longer poems in *Leaflets* and in her magnificent next volume, *The Will to Change* (1971), show Rich making the longer poem her own, using it as a vehicle for building emotional intensity and turning meditation into a form of rhetorical action. Siding with the rhetoricians against Plato, she accepts the fact that language is always interested, political. She will want nothing less from poetry than for it to become intertwined with politics and history, a move still resented by readers of poetry for whom a political poem equals propaganda.

In *The Will to Change,* Rich rewrites the figure of Orion, who symbolizes freedom and creativity, as a female, human heroine who fulfills Rich's earlier dream of "smashing the mould straight off." In "Planetarium" she writes of Caroline Herschel, the eighteenth-century astronomer who discovered eight comets but is almost unknown (unlike her famous brother, the astronomer William Herschel). The poem begins with monster images of the woman who fits no categories, "levitating into the night sky / riding the polished lenses." The images of ascension and power ("what we see, we see / and seeing is changing") are not, in this poem, allowed to become transcendent. The woman's body remains in the foreground through direct reference ("she whom the moon ruled / like us"), through the historical references in a factual headnote to the poem, and in quotations from historical documents.

Most important, the final images of the poem combine the body and outer space. The diffusing, confusing, and "untranslatable" forces entwine with a body that absorbs, resists, and translates these forces: "Heartbeat of the pulsar / heart sweating through my body / . . . I am bombarded yet I stand." The breakdown of the dualism between body and world and the many other dualisms implied in that one—self and other, inner and outer, transcendence or freedom and necessity, body and mind—is implied in the feminist principle that the personal is political. The end of the poem breaks down formally, also; the prosaic rhythm and irregular lines turn the final stanza into a paragraph rushing formlessly along. Poetic form itself is questioned, used, and undermined at the same time.

In "The Burning of Paper Instead of Children," Rich again questions the efficacy of langage and of poetry. This magnificently realized poem juxtaposes prose sections with lyrical poetry, probing the various relations between language and power, literature and life. The poem layers images of burning: Daniel Berrigan's burning of draft records in Catonsville, Maryland, to protest the Vietnam war; the use of napalm in Vietnam; Hitler's book burnings; Joan of Arc burning at the stake; sexual desire. While the title indicates her clear devaluing of literature before the demands of life, still the poem presents a great standoff: "this is the oppressor's language / yet I need it to talk to you." The ending of the poem is in prose, abandoning poetic form as it rushes toward an apocalyptic ending: "The burning of a book arouses no sensation in me. I know it hurts to burn. There are flames of napalm in Catonsville, Maryland. I know it hurts to burn. The typewriter is overheated, my mouth is burning, I cannot touch you and this is the oppressor's language." In this poem language is both the problem and the solution, as that final clause rings with despair at the enormity of the problem and her complicity in it, and with the ironic triumph of how much her poem succeeds in making language new. Over and over again, the poems in *The Will to Change* repeat these moments of despair and triumph as Rich focuses on the modes of representation—not only poems but also films, photographs, newsreels—by which we seek knowledge and change.

The year 1970 marked a point of crisis in Rich's life: her marriage broke up, and her husband committed suicide. These two events remain great silences in Rich's work. When Rich finally speaks of her husband in "Sources" (1982), she addresses her own silence and hints at the depth of his despair about life: "I've had a sense of protecting your existence, not using it merely as a theme for poetry or tragic musings; letting you dwell in the minds of those who have reason to miss you, in your way, or their way, not mine." Speaking to him now in a poem about Jewish culture and identity, she writes:

> No person, trying to take responsibility for her or his identity, should have to be so alone. There must be those among whom we can sit down and weep, and still be counted as warriors. (I make up this strange, angry packet for you, threaded with love.) I think you thought there was no such place for you, and perhaps there was none then, and perhaps there is none now; but we will have to make it, we who want an end to suffering, who want to change the laws of history, if we are not to *give ourselves away.* (xxii)

Alfred Conrad's failure to find community, and his belief that he could make himself new, as Rich's father had believed, is seen by Rich as a tragedy that the women's community will help her avoid.

That her marriage was difficult seems evident from Rich's poetry, which protests her role as wife and mother but also suggests the difficulty of male-female relationships. On the other hand, her poems addressed to her husband remain loving, pained, struggling. But around 1970, Rich's increasing involvement with the women's movement led her to a radical break with her married life: "The passion of debating ideas with women was an erotic passion for me, and the risking of self with women that was necessary in order to win some truth out of the lies of the past was also erotic. The suppressed lesbian I had been carrying in me since adolescence began to stretch her limbs. . . ." Rich's lesbian, woman-centered consciousness gives her radical politics a focus that is reflected in *Diving into the Wreck* (1973). Coinciding as it does with the acceleration of the women's movement in the United States, this book, which concentrates on male violence and on women's anger toward men, established Rich as a leading figure of feminism and won the National Book Award in 1974. Rich refused to accept the award for herself; instead, she accepted it with two other feminist nominees, Audre Lorde and Alice Walker, saying: "We symbolically join here in refusing the terms of patriarchal competition and in declaring that we will share this prize among us, to be used as best we can for women."

"Diving into the Wreck," perhaps Rich's most anthologized piece, is a well-crafted poem that symbolically delves into an androgynous unconscious, thus appealing to readers worried about her rejection of men and poetic beauty. As such, it is somewhat at odds with the scorching anger of other works in the collection, such as "Rape," a poem that in its raw indictment of the pervasiveness of male violence toward women refuses poetic subtlety or complexity. "Rape" remains a controversial poem, often criticized as a simpleminded and propagandistic condemnation of all men. But neither "Rape" nor the aesthetized vision of "Diving into the Wreck" is quite representative of Rich's poetry; the longer "Phenomenology of Anger" and "Meditations for a Savage Child," in their searching explorations of violence and victimhood, draw on Rich's work from the late 1960s to question both aesthetic form and the possibility of clear political categories.

After *Diving into the Wreck,* Rich began more and more to combine her critique of patriarchy with a positive search for women's community, a search based on both utopian visions and historical understanding of women's lives. In "From an Old House in America" (1974), the house becomes a place of female resistance to male domination, as well as a place revealing America's history of violence toward women. While Rich continues to insist on the historical and cultural forces shaping identity, she also wants to assert the positive force of what she calls "local" power: "my power is brief and local / but I know my power." This local power gives Rich a place to begin, a place of identity from which to speak. But her identity refuses "isolation, the dream / of the frontier woman" and instead reaches out to the community in a final line that echoes John Donne: "Any woman's death diminishes me."

In what may be her most widely read book, *Of Woman Born: Motherhood as Experience and Institution* (1976), Rich uses her experience of motherhood as a place from which to begin a historical critique of the seemingly natural role of mother as a cultural institution constructed to support male control of women. This scholarly work is an impressive example of cultural materialism—an analysis of how identity is shaped by institutions and practices rather than some essential femaleness or even an essential humanness. But because the book was one of the first popular critiques of patriarchal structures and coincided with a rather official declaration of her lesbianism in *Twenty-One Love Poems* (1976), Rich was widely labeled as a man hater and ideologue, an advocate of a female essentialism that defines female qualities as natural and superior to male qualities. But for a poet so suspicious of natural meanings and so aware of the shaping powers of language, society, and history, the essentialist label has never fit comfortably. Rich's clear ethical stance and willingness to speak harsh truths are always combined with a critique of the categories of her own and others' thought, a critique that undermines the idea of ideological purity or separatism.

In this book Rich's final vision of mother love as a model for a non-oppressive and nonhierarchical society is utopian rather than essentialist. Indeed, she warns that "it can be dangerously simplistic to fix upon 'nuturance' as a special strength of women, which need only be released into the larger society to create a new human order." She believes, quoting Susan Sontag, that "there are ways of thinking that we don't know about yet." Like the monstrous flying woman at the end of "Snapshots of a Daughter-in-Law," this formulation reaches out into the unknown, but now Rich keeps herself firmly planted in the historical and material world. This dual movement of being within and without the culture at once allies Rich's thought with many projects of poststructural theorists.

With the publication of Rich's essays on poetry and politics in *On Lies, Secrets, and Silence: Selected Prose, 1966–1978* (1979), the revisionary power of her woman-centered critique emerged more clearly. These essays clarify the dual vision of her poetry: the negative critique of the representations of women, including her own visionary ones, and the affirmative recovery of women's history and voices that may lead us to think in ways we do not yet know. Her perspective is simultaneously inside a history and culture and outside of it; she wants to change prevailing histories and representations while she is constantly critiquing even her language of change. Her vision is always a split one, inside and outside at once, the assimilated Jew, the Southerner/Northerner, the wife/lesbian.

Rich's lesbianism provides a particularly telling perspective on the culture. In the controversial and influential essays "The Meaning of Our Love for Women Is What We Have Constantly to Expand" (1977) and "Compulsory Heterosexuality and Lesbian Existence" (written in 1978 and published in 1980), Rich argues that sexuality, as much as motherhood, is mediated by the culture and that lesbianism is more than just "sexual preference"; it is a challenge to the institution of heterosexuality, which, in its present form, is structured to keep women under male power. Because of its potential subversiveness, lesbian existence has been erased from history, transformed into tales of witches, or simply ignored. As she says in *Twenty-One Love Poems,* "No one has imagined us." Rich's task is to imagine, to place lesbian love within a tradition. But this task faces formidable obstacles from within and from without. In *Twenty-One Love Poems* the struggle to write, especially within a heterosexual tradition of the sonnet sequence, is seen as part of the problem: "What kind of beast would turn its life into words? / . . . when away from you I try to create you in words / am I simply using you?" The relationship eventually founders on this conflict between public and private, but Rich ends the poems with an assertion of her continuing effort to "stake out" a territory in which she can live.

Critics were slow to understand the innovative critical and poetic position Rich was developing. Many mainstream critics, schooled in New Critical principles stressing craft and the autonomy of the poem, disliked political poetry and were even more offended by her critique of patriarchy; some labeled her an ideologue and stopped reading and reviewing her poetry. Many of her feminist supporters discussed her politics to the exclusion of her poetry, especially after her prose work began to appear. Only in the 1980s, when political poetry became important and feminist critiques widespread, did fine critical studies of Rich as an important political poet and feminist theorist begin to appear.

The splendid poems of *The Dream of a Common Language* (1978) and *A Wild Patience Has Taken Me This Far* (1981) continue the project of double vision: affirming and critiquing women's power and place in history. In "Power," Marie Curie's death from radiation sickness becomes a symbol of this dual vision of affirmation and negation:

> She died   a famous woman   denying
> her wounds
> denying
> her wounds   came   from the same
>   source as her power

In "Phantasia for Elvira Shatayev," the leader of a women's climbing team, all of whom died in a storm on Lenin Peak, speaks of the visionary triumph of a community of women striving to climb the mountain, an image of transcendence. But Shatayev speaks from the grave. The final triumphal vision, *"We have dreamed of this / all our lives,"* is words written in a diary "torn from my fingers" by the destroying wind. The choice of the women to strive toward community and achievement is both powerful and ineffective, an inspiration that challenges cultural presuppositions but also a doomed, quixotic mission.

This dual vision is best articulated in "Transcendental Etude" (1977), dedicated to Michelle Cliff, a writer and poet who would become Rich's long-time companion. Here, Rich once again turns to the image of the galaxies as freedom, only to end back in the kitchen she had so bitterly scorned in "Snapshots." The poet understands that "there come times" when we have to

> . . . cut the wires,
> find ourselves in free-fall, as if
> our true home were the undimensional
> solitude s, the rift
> in the Great Nebula.

But this necessary dislocation leads to "the pitch of utter loneliness / where she herself and all creation / seem equally dispersed," an image recalling the fate of the women climbers. Rich connects the need to break away with a recognition that women "were always like this, / rootless, dismembered," because of a historical situation in which women and mothers are repressed, denied, and destroyed. Thus, the breaking away, essential to Rich in so many poems, becomes complicit with a culture that wants to keep women ungrounded, without a base of power, "homesick" for a woman, the mother, her self. Rich's solution is to come back home to a dual subject: "*I am the lover and the loved, / home and wanderer, she who splits / firewood and she who knocks, a stranger.*" Rich's new home wants to tremble on the dangerous, shifting margins of representation but also remain enclosed within representations that give us a ground for identity and action. The poem ends with Rich's most extensive paean to the domestic particular:

> Vision begins to happen in such a life
> as if a woman quietly walked away
> from the argument and jargon in a room
> and sitting down in the kitchen, began
> turning in her lap
> bits of yarn, calico and velvet scraps

These lines are followed by a long catalog of particular ordinary things to be woven into the woman's "composition." She is "pulling the tenets of a life together / with no mere will to mastery, / only care for the many-lived, unending / forms in which she finds herself."

This poem may best articulate the tension in the phrase "dream of a common language." The dream of transcending the cultural determinants of language, of communicating immediately in a commonality of women, is countered by a need for the ordinary, rooted, "common" language in history from which action and change can arise. Transcendence of history, place, culture, and discourse is impossible; still, our visions must lead us into uncharted territory. The new, the unsaid, the monstrous can be thought only from within a discourse: "a whole new poetry beginning here," she says, with as much emphasis on "here" as on "new."

Rich developed this mature, complex vision in her poems and prose throughout the 1980s, as well as in the lesbian-feminist journal *Sinister Wisdom,* which she coedited with Michelle Cliff. In the poems of *A Wild Patience Has Taken Me This Far* (1981) she intensifies her use of historical material, focusing on the lives of women in the past and liberally using quotations from their writings. But these historical facts also point up the limitations of any act of revision: "history / is neither your script nor mine," Rich writes of Willa Cather. She tries to imagine Ethel Rosenberg, only to leave her "political in her ways not in mine"; she writes of her admiration for the nineteenth-century women reformers, only to criticize them, and implicitly herself, for their "class privilege" and "partial vision." In the magnificent "Turning the Wheel," Rich speaks of the Indian woman, lost in mythic history, who "stifles in unspeakable loneliness," yet she warns: "look at her closely if you dare / do not assume you know those cheekbones / or those eyesockets; or that still-bristling hair."

The ability to revise history is limited by Rich's own complicity in the culture she wishes to change; yet this awareness of limitations is joined to an imperative to know. In "The Spirit of Place" the need for lucidity, figured in a crystal-clear night (so like her earlier transcendent images), is entwined with the complex "compost" of history, the obscuring river fog and underground journey. Rich rejects amnesia or nostalgia, both forms of forgetting history, in favor of trying to understand the world "as it is not as we wish it." The struggle to recover history is part of finding a "here" to change from. As she says in "For Memory," "The past is not a husk yet change goes on." Not a husk to be shaken off, nor a permanent mold, the past becomes a key to freedom that is not transcendence of the world:

> Freedom. It isn't once, to walk out
> under the Milky Way, feeling the rivers
> of light, the fields of dark—
> freedom is daily, prose-bound, routine
> remembering. Putting together, inch by inch
> the starry worlds. From all the lost
> collections.

This assertion of individual agency remains in tension with Rich's uncomfortable sense of her limited vision, a sense that was accentuated in the late 1970s and early 1980s by the attacks on feminism by women of different color, class, and ethnicity as a white, middle-class movement. Her need to understand her own frame of reference led Rich more and more toward her own past in the poems of *Sources* (1983) and *Your Native Land, Your Life* (1986). These poems, along with the essays published in *Blood, Bread, and Poetry* (1986), fully articulate a shift in feminism away from the single difference of male and female to an understanding of the multiple differences of gender, race, class, ethnicity, and sexual preference, each of which shapes the world differently. Rich's essay "Notes Toward a Politics of Location" has been lauded by critics in many fields for its lucid and complex articulation of a clear political focus within the dispersed field of differences that feminism must acknowledge. Rich agonizes over the question "Who is we?" as she contemplates the problem: "You cannot speak for me. I cannot speak for us. Two thoughts: there is no liberation that only knows how to say 'I'; there is no collective movement that speaks for each of us all the way through." "Location" is the term she uses to acknowledge differences and identity, necessity and chance.

The poems of *Your Native Land* (which reprints the poems of *Sources*) explore Rich's location: many reflect upon her move in 1984 from the Northeast to Northern California; others probe her Jewishness, speak to her father, contemplate her racism and Southern roots, and wonder what it means to be North American. These roots can no more be escaped than her body, twisted by the pain of lifelong arthritis. But the particularity of the body is embraced, as she writes in "Contradictions: Tracking Poems":

> The best world is the body's world
> filled with creatures   filled with dread
> misshapen so   yet the best we have
> our raft among the abstract worlds

The body's world is in history, in places, in discourses, a world we cannot escape or control. In a compelling long poem from this volume, "North American Time," Rich rejects the ideal of the "politically correct" for the confusions of history: "Poetry never stood a chance / of standing outside history." Instead, "Words are found responsible." Her attempt to remain responsible to the profusion of historical fact and event leads her to despair; but the thought of North American amnesia about history (as she says in "Notes Toward a Politics of Location," "I come from a country stuck fast for forty years in the deep-freeze of history") leads her to action. The poem ends with the line "and I start to speak again."

Rich's *Time's Power* (1989) keeps its focus on memory and history in a series of meditative poems. As she says in "Living Memory," recovering the details "bunched, packed, stored / in these cellar holes of memory" is a way to gain knowledge and power, "time's / power, the only just power. . . ." Only through the past can a new future be imagined, can what we don't yet know be called upon. These poems ring with optimism in a troubled world, as she writes of Middle Eastern conflict in "Turning": "the subject is how to break a mold of discourse, / how little by little minds change / but that they do change."

Rich has remained deeply committed to a material world and to women's role in maintaining and bettering that world through the minute, daily tasks of survival. In "Divisions of Labor" she speaks of "the women whose labor remakes the world / each and every morning." The attention to the daily task becomes a remaking, a creative revisioning of the world. In this poem Rich gives us an image for herself, for the world created by her poetry:

> I have seen a woman sitting
> between the stove and the stars
> her fingers singed from snuffing out the candles
> of pure theory   Finger and thumb: both scorched:
> I have felt that sacred wax blister my hand

Between the kitchen stove and the galaxies of stars, Rich continues her feminist project of revisioning the world and embracing its contradictions through unflinching critique and passionate commitment.

Selected Bibliography

PRIMARY WORKS

PLAYS

Ariadne: A Play in Three Acts and Poems, (Baltimore: J. H. Furst, 1939).

Not I, But Death: A Play in One Act, (Baltimore: J. H. Furst, 1941).

POETRY

A Change of World, (New Haven: Yale University Press, 1951; London: Oxford University Press, 1952).

The Diamond Cutters, and Other Poems, 1954–1962, (New York: Harper & Bros., 1955).

Snapshots of a Daughter-in-Law: Poems, 1954–1962, (New York: Harper & Row, 1963; London: Chatto Windus/Hogarth Press, 1970).

Necessities of Life: Poems, 1962–1965, (New York: Norton, 1966).

Selected Poems, (London: Chatto & Windus/Hogarth Press, 1967).

Leaflets: Poems, 1965–1968, (New York: Norton, 1969; London: Chatto & Windus/Hogarth Press, 1972).

The Will to Change, (New York: Norton, 1971 & London: Chatto & Windus, 1972).

Diving into the Wreck: Poems, 1971–1972, (New York: Norton, 1973).

Poems: Selected and New, 1950–1974, (New York: Norton, 1975).

Twenty-One Love Poems, (Emeryville, Calif.: Effie's Press, 1976).

Dream of a Common Language: Poems, 1974–1977, (New York: Norton, 1978).

A Wild Patience Has Taken Me This Far: Poems, 1978–1981, (New York: Norton, 1981).

Sources, (Woodside, Calif.: Heyeck Press, 1983).

The Fact of a Doorframe: Poems Selected and New, 1950–1984, (New York: Norton, 1984).

Your Native Land, Your Life, (New York: Norton, 1986).

Time's Power: Poems, 1985–1988, (New York: Norton, 1989).

PROSE

"Teaching Language in Open Admissions," In *The Uses of Literature* Edited by Monroe Engel. (Cambridge: Harvard University Press, 1973). pp. 257–273. Reprinted in *On Lies, Secrets, and Silence.*

Of Woman Born: Motherhood as Experience and Institution, (New York: Norton, 1976; London: Virago, 1977).

"The Meaning of Our Love for Women Is What We Have Constantly to Expand," (Brooklyn, N.Y.: Out and Out Books, 1977). Pamphlet, reprinted in *On Lies, Secrets, and Silence.*

On Lies, Secrets, and Silence: Selected Prose, 1966–1978, (New York: Norton, 1979).

"Compulsory Heterosexuality and Lesbian Existence," *Signs* 5: 631–660 (Summer 1980). Reprinted in *Blood, Bread, and Poetry.*

"Split at the Root: An Essay on Jewish Identity," *Nice Jewish Girls: A Lesbian Anthology.* Edited by Evelyn Torton Beck. (Watertown, Mass.: Persephone Press, 1982). pp. 67–84. Reprinted in *Blood, Bread, and Poetry.*

Blood, Bread, and Poetry: Selected Prose, 1979–1985, (New York: Norton, 1986).

SECONDARY WORKS

CRITICAL STUDIES

Altieri, Charles, *Self and Sensibility in Contemporary American Poetry,* (Cambridge and New York: Cambridge University Press, 1984).

Bennett, Paula, *My Life, a Loaded Gun: Female Creativity and Feminist Poetics,* (Boston: Beacon Press, 1986).

Carruthers, Mary J., "The Re-vision of the Muse: Adrienne Rich, Audre Lorde, Judy Grahn, Olga Broumas," *Hudson Review* 36: 293–322 (Summer 1983).

Christ, Carol P., *Diving Deep and Surfacing: Women Writers and Spiritual Quest,* (Boston: Beacon Press, 1980).

Cooper, Jane Roberta, ed., *Reading Adrienne Rich: Reviews and Re-Visions, 1951–81,* (Ann Arbor: University of Michigan Press, 1984). Contains useful articles, reviews, and a complete primary and secondary bibliography.

Deane, Patrick, "A Line of Complicity: Baudelaire—T. S. Eliot—Adrienne Rich," *Canadian Review of American Studies* 18: 463–481 (Winter 1987).

Des Pres, Terrence, *Praises and Dispraises: Poetry and Politics—the 20th Century,* (New York: Viking, 1988).

Diaz-Diocaretz, Myriam, *The Transforming Power of Language: The Poetry of Adrienne Rich,* (Utrecht: HES Publishers, 1984).

———, *Translating Poetic Discourse: Questions on Feminist Strategies in Adrienne Rich,* (Amsterdam and Philadelphia: John Benjamins, 1985).

DuPlessis, Rachel Blau, "The Critique of Consciousness and Myth in Levertov, Rich, and Rukeyser," In *Shakespeare's Sisters: Feminist Essays on Women Poets,* edited by Sandra M. Gilbert and Susan Gubar, (Bloomington: Indiana University Press, 1979). pp. 280–300.

Erkkila, Betsy, "Dickinson and Rich: Toward a Theory of Female Poetic Influence," *American Literature* 56: 541–559 (December 1984).

Farwell, Marilyn R., "Adrienne Rich and an Organic Feminist Criticism," *College English* 39: 191–203 (October 1977).

Ferguson, Ann, "Patriarchy, Sexual Identity, and the Sexual Revolution," In "On 'Compulsory Heterosexuality and Lesbian Existence': Defining the Issues." *Signs* 7: 158–172 (Autumn 1981).

Flowers, Betty S., "The 'I' in Adrienne Rich: Individuation and the Androgyne Archetype," In *Theory and Practice of Feminist Literary Criticism.* Edited by Gabriela Mora and Karen S. Van Hooft. (Ypsilanti, Mich.: Bilingual Press, 1982). pp. 14–35.

Friedman, Susan Stanford, " 'I Go Where I Love': An Intertextual Study of H. D. and Adrienne Rich," *Signs* 9: 228–245 (Winter 1983).

Gelpi, Barbara Charlesworth, and Albert Gelpi, eds. *Adrienne Rich's Poetry: A Norton Critical Edition,* (New York: Norton, 1975) Contains selected poems, interviews, reviews, articles, and a bibliography.

Harris, Jeane, "The Emergence of a Feminizing Ethos in Adrienne Rich's Poetry," *Rhetoric Society Quarterly* 18: 133–140 (Spring 1988).

Janows, Jill, "Mind-Body Exertions: Imagery in the Poems of Adrienne Rich," *Madog* (Wales) 3: 4–18 (Winter 1979).

Juhasz, Suzanne, *Naked and Fiery Forms: Modern American Poetry by Women—a New Tradition,* (New York: Harper & Row, 1976).

Kalaidjian, Walter, *Languages of Liberation: The Social Text in Contemporary American Poetry,* (New York: Columbia University Press, 1989).

Kalstone, David, *Five Temperants: Elizabeth Bishop, Robert Lowell, James Merrill, Adrienne Rich, and John Ashbery,* (New York: Oxford University Press, 1977).

Kennard, Jean E., "Ourself Behind Ourself: A Theory for Lesbian Readers," In *Gender and Reading: Essays on Readers, Texts, and Contexts.* Edited by Elizabeth A. Flynn and Patrocinio P. Schweickart. (Baltimore: Johns Hopkins University Press, 1986).

Keyes, Claire, *The Aesthetics of Power: The Poetry of Adrienne Rich,* (Athens: University of Georgia Press, 1986).

Martin, Wendy, *An American Triptych: Anne Bradstreet, Emily Dickinson, Adrienne Rich,* (Chapel Hill: University of North Carolina Press, 1984).

Middlebrook, Diane Wood, *Worlds into Words: Understanding Modern Poems,* (Stanford, Calif.: Stanford Alumni Association, 1978).

Mohanty, Chandra Talpade, "Feminist Encounters: Locating the Politics of Experience," *Copyright* 1: 30–44 (Fall 1987).

Nelson, Cary, *Our Last First Poets: Vision and History in Contemporary American Poetry,* (Urbana: University of Illinois Press, 1981).

Ostriker, Alicia, *Writing Like a Woman,* (Ann Arbor: University of Michigan Press, 1983).

Stimpson, Catharine, "Adrienne Rich and Lesbian/Feminist Poetry," *Parnassus* 12–13: 249–268 (Spring–Winter 1985).

Strine, Mary S., "The Politics of Asking Women's Questions: Voice and Value in the Poetry of Adrienne Rich," *Text and Performance Quarterly* 9: 24–41 (January 1989).

Templeton, Alice, "The Dream and the Dialogue: Rich's Feminist Poetics and Gadamer's Hermeneutics," *Tulsa Studies in Women's Literature* 7: 283–296 (Fall 1988).

Vendler, Helen, *Part of Nature, Part of Us,* (Cambridge, Mass.: Harvard University Press, 1980).